About the Authors

Jessie Carney Smith, born in Greensboro, North Carolina, is a noted author, biographer, and black studies scholar, university librarian, and William and Camille Cosby Professor in the Humanities at Fisk University in Nashville. She was educated at North Carolina A and T State University, Michigan State University, Vanderbilt University, and the University of Illinois. Her work includes *Notable Black American Women* (books I and II), published by Gale Research, and *Black Firsts, Epic Lives,* and *Powerful Black Women,* published by Visible Ink Press. Her book *Notable Black American Men* is forthcoming. Among Dr. Smith's numerous honors are the 1992 National Women's Book Association Award, the Candace Award for excellence in education, and *Sage* magazine's Anna J. Cooper Award for her published works on African American women.

Nikki Giovanni, born in Knoxville, Tennessee, is an award-winning poet and prolific writer, once called the "Princess of Black Poetry" in the 1960s. She received her B.A. in 1967 from Fisk University and has attended Columbia University's School of Fine Arts. Giovanni has taught English and creative writing at Queens College, Rutgers University, Ohio State University, and Virginia Polytechnic. Always an outspoken and charismatic presence, Giovanni has written on various themes over the decades, evolving from militancy to introspection to a global and humanistic outlook. Her published work includes poetry anthologies (*Black Feeling, Black Talk, Gemini, Creation, My House, The Women and the Men*), prose (*Sacred Cows and Other Edibles, Racism 101*), and spoken word recordings (*Truth Is on Its Way*). Giovanni has numerous honorary degrees and keys to many cities, and was named woman of the year by both *Mademoiselle* and *Ladies Home Journal* magazines.

Also from Visible Ink Press

Black Firsts ISBN 0–8103-9490–1. 556 pages, 200 illustrations.

"A superb historical study of black achievement."—*Houston Chronicle*

Powerful Black Women ISBN 0–7876-0882–3. 423 pages, 70 photos.

"*Powerful Black Women* is dynamic, engaging and informative."—Joanne Harris, editor, *American Visions: The Magazine of Afro-American Culture*

Epic Lives ISBN 0–8103-9426-X. 632 pages, 100 photos.

"Information to heal our ignorance, about lives luminous with courage."—*Ms.* Magazine

African America: Portrait of a People ISBN 0–8103-9453–7. 811 pages, 200 photos.

"Thoughtfully addresses the challenges and triumphs of Black Americans during the last 400 years."—*Christian Science Monitor*

The Essential Black Literature Guide ISBN 0–7876- 0734–7. 446 pages, 138 illustrations and photos.

"Essential is the key word for this treasure."—*Copley News Service*

Lay Down Body: Living History in African American Cemeteries ISBN 0–7876-0651–0. 330 pages, 75 photos.

Anyone who has ever tried to trace their African American heritage understands the frustration of not knowing where to start or where to look. The unique glimpse into African American culture blends moving, personal accounts with painstaking research to describe and help locate 300 cemeteries.

Historic Black Landmarks: A Traveler's Guide ISBN 0–8103-9408–1. 408 pages, photos and maps.

"An important contribution to American society."—*Washington Post*

BLACK HEROES *of the* *20th Century*

BLACK HEROES of the 20th Century

Jessie Carney Smith
Editor

Foreword by
Nikki Giovanni

VISIBLE INK PRESS

DETROIT • NEW YORK • TOR

Black Heroes of the 20th Century

Edited by Jessie Carney Smith

Copyright © 1998 by Visible Ink Press

Published by Visible Ink Press® a division of Gale Research
835 Penobscot Building
Detroit, MI 48226–4094

Visible Ink Press is a registered trademark of Gale Research.

Most Visible Ink Press books are available at special quantity discounts when purchased in bulk by corporations, organizations, or groups. Customized printings, special imprints, messages, and excerpts can be produced to meet your needs. For more information, contact Special Markets Manager, Visible Ink Press, 835 Penobscot Bldg., Detroit, MI 48226. Or call 1–800–776–6265.

Cover photo of Maya Angelou (c) AP/World Wide.
Back Cover photo of Michael Jordan (c) Reuters/Corbis-Bettman Archive.
Art Director: Pamela A. E. Galbreath

Library of Congress Cataloging-in-Publication Data
Black heroes of the 20th century/Jessie Carney Smith, editor ;
    foreword by Nikki Giovanni
        p. cm.
    Includes bibliographical references and indexes
    ISBN 1-57859-021-3
        1. Afro-Americans—Biography. 2. Heroes—United States—
    Biography. I. Smith, Jessie Carney.
    E185.96.B5337   1997
    920'.009296073—dc21   97-37308
                                    CIP

Contents

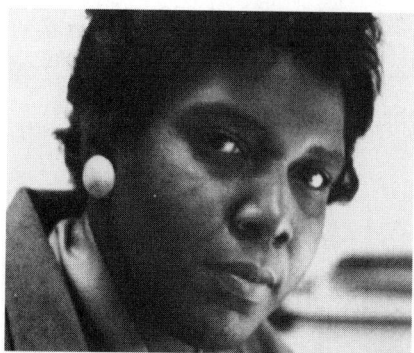

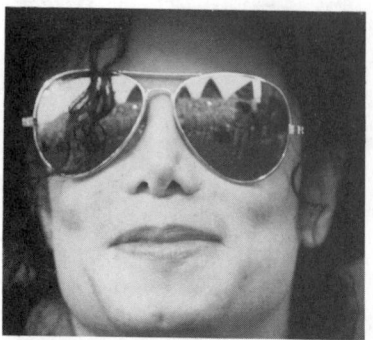

Introduction

No one needed to help the men and women whose biographies are given here to define themselves. Their work did it for them. For the purpose of introducing our selection of black heroes, we borrow from what Janet Cheatham Bell in Famous Black Quotations *(Warner Books, 1995) calls the "portable wit and wisdom of a great people."*

We quote some of the wisdom of the foremothers and fathers of twentieth-century heroes as well as our black leaders of this century. "If there is no struggle, there is no progress," wrote Fredrick Douglass: "This struggle may be a moral one; or it may be a physical one; or it may be both moral and physical; but it must be a struggle. Power concedes nothing without a demand."

The heroes represented in this book are men and women who have struggled and advanced. Writer Ralph Ellison took a look at black identity: "I am invisible, understand, simply because people refuse to see me." Some of our heroes—in particular, those of the early twentieth century—were invisible because society refused to see the work and worth of black writers, artists, actors, educators, journalists, musicians, scientists, and others.

Among our women heroes who improved black life, we have included Mary McLeod Bethune, who said, "Next to God we are indebted to women, first for life itself, and then for making it worth living."

Frederick Douglass also helped us recognize the black men included here: "I have always thanked God for making me a man." But Martin Delany always thanked God for making him a black man. While both men were abolitionists, the former slave, Douglass, looked beyond his blackness to the recognition of manhood, whereas Delany's pride was in being a black male. Although men view themselves differently, those included in this work serve to reinforce a positive black male image and represent power and strength. Sterling Brown further helps us see what has happened to black men and helps us recognize their power and strength:

One thing they cannot prohibit

The strong men . . . coming on

The strong men gittin' stronger.

Strong men. . . .

Stronger.

Not all work of African American heroes is recognized or known. Nor is the work of the silent heroes—many who are, indeed, heroes by virtue of their efforts as molders of the positive black image—necessarily unknown. Yet, *Black Heroes of the 20th Century* aims to present men and women from a variety of positions in life, and from different periods of this century—to open their lives to greater public view.

The task of screening and the desire to add just one or two more names to this list of 150 was difficult and tempting, for surely we want to satisfy you, as you search here for your own heroes. Selections can never be made without some degree of arbitrariness, for the question arises: Should we select both Nikki Giovanni and Toni Morrison, or either one or the other, since both women are writers? In the end, we included Giovanni because of her distinction as a poet, and Morrison as the first black American to win the Nobel Prize in literature. It follows as well that, although both are athletes, we would include basketball star Michael Jordan as well as golfer Tiger Woods, and that other sports such as tennis, baseball, and boxing are represented as well. There are activists, lawyers, politicians, actors, religious leaders, educators, business leaders, school founders, scientists, and union leaders to demonstrate the diversity of black achievement. We had the task of trying to assemble groups of black Americans whose lives would appeal to you, where the universe was broad but our space limited. In either case, we advise the reader that names omitted are not forgotten.

This collection adds to the body of biographical literature published on African American men and women. Its purpose is to present in a handy volume essays on the lives of black American women and men who are heroes and who will appeal to the young and the not-so-young, to students, educators, researchers, and the general public.

Black Heroes is the work of many. We acknowledge the contributions of the authors whose names are published at the end of the essays here. My faculty colleague at Fisk University, Robert L. Johns, worked diligently in editing a number of the essays, thus extending the years of assistance he has provided for my various biographical projects. As well, the staff of Visible Ink Press was much behind the creation of this book. Michelle Banks and Christa Brelin guided the preparation of this work, aided by James Craddock, Amber Foulkrod, Jeffrey Hermann, Holly Monacelli, Brad Morgan, Leslie Norback, Terri Schell, and Devra Sladics. Carol Schwartz, Noreen Frede, and Sharon Remington provided additional assistance; Anne Janette Johnson proofread the entire book and compiled the index; art director Pamela A. E. Galbreath created a lovely interior and cover design; Maria Franklin and Andrea Rigby gathered the photo permissions; and BookComp typeset the book. Finally, we acknowledge the African American men and women of this century who led fruitful lives and fought great battles, and whose myriad achievements gave us enduring chapters in black and American history.

Jessie Carney Smith
Editor, **Black Heroes of the Twentieth Century**

True Strength

In many respects, Samson was a vain, if not actually silly, man. Certainly he knew the source of his great

strength, though he mistakenly thought it was his hair and not the God who gave it to him. Achilles' strength

was thought to be the water he was dipped in, not the faith of his mother who took him to the river. Women

count on their looks; adolescents, their youth—yet we all look for a champion. We all believe in some sort

of magic.

Whether it is the state lottery or a long shot at the races, we turn to some sort of "otherness" to change our luck. Superman fell in love with Lois and was willing to give up his great powers for her. In order to marry Wallis Simpson, Edward gave up the throne of England. One wonders not if the right thing were done but if what was given was worth what was taken.

The very nature of sacrifice says there is no parity. One does what one must in order to be a whole, complete human. And then there is that cry. That cry of Samson who recognized his own foolishness; that cry of Superman who finally realized he was, indeed, more than mortal man and must face his destiny.

We don't know the last thought of Malcolm X or Martin Luther King Jr. We can't know the deeper thought of the Brown family as they sent little Linda off to school. We might guess that Emmett Till's mother wishes she could take her boy back. As we might understand Afem Shakur begging her son: Honey, wake up and let's go home.

The greatest heroes probably have no idea how heroic they are. Most people think of heroes as saving children from flaming buildings or pulling housewives from automobile wrecks. But it is, indeed, heroic to pay one's bills at the end of the month; to go to church on Sundays and sing in the choir; to referee a softball game or teach some children how to make apple cobbler. The heroes of our time do the ordinary things that must be done whether they are applauded or not.

Most of us are good people. Most of us want to do the right things. We want to be loving to our families; caring for our elderly; wise for our young. We want to be a hero in our own eyes. We celebrate these *Black Heroes of the 20th Century* because they went one step further. They willingly made a sacrifice of time, fortune, and in some cases, their lives to make life on the planet a more meaningful experience. That they are African American can come as no surprise. The African American has continually stepped up when the right, the good, the proper needed to be counted. The heroes of the twentieth century have their lives, their hopes, their best wishes on the line so that future generations will sing the praises of our people, who know where the true strength comes from.

Nikki Giovanni

BLACK HEROES

HEROES
of the
20th Century

HANK **AARON**

1934–
Athlete

Hank Aaron, known to millions of baseball fans around the world as "The Hammer," holds the game's most prestigious record of 755 home runs. He is a legendary baseball figure who is known for speaking out in protest of racial discrimination in baseball, particularly in the front office.

Henry Louis Aaron was born February 5, 1934, in Mobile, Alabama. The third child born to Herbert and Estella Aaron, he was affectionately nicknamed "Man" by family members when the future home run king entered the world weighing a whopping twelve pounds. He grew up poor in a family of eight children and attended Central High School but finished at the Josephine Allen Institute, where he was a star high school athlete. He received many scholarship offers to play football at the collegiate level after high school; however, by then he had set his goal to play major league baseball. His first swings had been at bottle caps with broomsticks, but by his junior year in high school Aaron was playing semiprofessional baseball with the Mobile Black Bears, destined for greatness as an American sports hero.

Aaron was eighteen when he signed his first professional contract with the Indianapolis Clowns of the Negro League. Until that time, 1952, he had never left the Mobile area. The next year found him coping with the trauma of integrating the Sally League with the Jacksonville Suns, where he managed to win the league's Most Valuable Player award. It was during these early days of his career, when travel was by bus, that Aaron suffered the indignities of a segregated South in eating and overnight accommodations. In many instances he was forced to make his own arrangements while white teammates were housed and fed as a group. He did the same thing during the next season with the Atlanta Crackers of the Southern League, when the Milwaukee Braves called him up to the majors in 1954.

By 1957 Aaron led the league in every batting department except batting average, where he tied for fourth. His home run off Billy Muffet of the Cards clinched the National League pennant for the Braves. He hit it in the bottom of the eleventh inning with the score tied 2–2 and was named Most Valuable Player of the playoffs. In that year's World Series, he hit three home runs as the Braves beat the Yankees and became the most revered twenty-three year old in all of baseball.

When the team moved to Atlanta in 1966, Aaron had become a baseball superstar. For more than ten years he had hit singles, doubles, triples, and home runs, stolen bases, won Gold Glove Awards, driven in runs, thrown out runners, and maintained a 300+ batting

Hank Aaron hits his 714th career home run,
tying Babe Ruth's record, April 5, 1974.

average. It was not until 1969, however, that anyone realized that he was on his way to breaking the record of all records, Babe Ruth's lifetime home run total of 714. Only when he reached 500 career homers and his 3,000th hit on May 17, 1970, against Wayne Simpson of the Cincinnati Reds, did sports writers begin to debate seriously whether or not he would pass Ruth's magical number of 714.

Ivan Allen, former mayor of Atlanta, remarked on the apprehension that greeted the South's first major league sports franchise and its black players in 1966. Aaron, he said, was key in smoothing the transition and confirming the end of segregation in the South through his thoughtful consideration and cooperative attitude.

Aaron faced few problems as a player in Atlanta until he approached Babe Ruth's home run record in 1973. The vast majority of the fans cheered him on and hoped that the record would be broken in the team's home ballpark. However, one bitter consequence was the minority of fans who greeted his accomplishments with hatred, especially through the mail. Security at the stadium was tightened after some letters suggested that he would be shot down from the stands. The FBI was brought in and he had to travel apart from the rest of the team with a bodyguard. Other letters were addressed "Dear Nigger" and worse, and one of his daughters was threatened at college.

Aaron credited his strong faith in God for his being able to withstand the negative attitudes he encountered while pursuing the home run title. Throughout his life, both in and outside of baseball, he was guided by the principles of working hard, treating other people right, keeping the rules, practicing self-discipline, always giving his best, and trusting that nothing would happen to him that God did not ordain. Strengthened by his faith, Aaron was able to excel on the baseball field during one of the most stressful periods of his life.

While Aaron always spoke out against racism and prejudice, he was not perceived as a civil rights spokesperson until he began to close in on the record. Even after he retired, he received hate mail whenever he spoke out publicly—calling for more blacks in baseball front offices, for example, or condemning racist comments made by baseball owners. Aaron kept all of the letters, good and bad, with plans to donate them to a museum one day.

It was widely assumed that most of the ugliness that Aaron experienced before and after the record came from the race-haunted South. Aaron recalled, however, that most came from the North, especially New York, and that none came from Atlanta. An indication of the nastiness he encountered from hostile fans occurred outside Chicago's Wrigley Field when a woman walked up to him and threw a glass of whiskey in his face.

In addition to the hatefulness that he experienced from racist fans, Aaron got an indication of the insensitivity of organized baseball when he hit home run number 700. Being only the second man in the history of the game to reach the milestone, he assumed that congratulations would come from then-commissioner Bowie Kuhn, but that was not to be. Aaron accepted Kuhn's explanation that he had only planned to wait until the record was broken, but he never forgot the snub.

Sets home run record A near melee erupted when Aaron hit home run number 715 on April 3, 1974, in the Braves's home ballpark against Al Downing of the Dodgers. He had achieved a "super-human accomplishment, as mysterious and remote as Stonehenge, and certain to stand forever," wrote Tom Buckley in the *New York Times*. It is remarkable that the record came not at the end, but in the middle of Aaron's extraordinary twenty-three year career as a professional baseball player, two years before he retired as an active player.

When Aaron retired from baseball in 1976, he left the game with four career batting records. In fact, he retired holding more records than any other player in the game, including those for runs batted

Hank Aaron.

in and total bases. It was, however, Aaron's career record 755 home runs in twenty-three years that placed him at the pinnacle of professional athletics.

Henry Aaron acquired a number of different nicknames throughout his professional career that characterized his extraordinary ability as a baseball player. Dubbed "Bad Henry" by Don Drysdale and Sandy Kofax, he is also known as "Hammerin' Hank" and "Hammer" to fans and admirers around the world. Aaron was elected to the Baseball Hall of Fame in 1982.

Aaron was spotted by Dewey Griggs, a scout for the Braves, while playing for the Indianapolis Clowns of the American Negro League. Griggs eventually signed Aaron for the Braves Eau Claire, Wisconsin, Farm team at $350 per month in June 1952. When Ted Turner bought the Atlanta Braves baseball team in 1976, one of his first moves was to phone Hank Aaron in Milwaukee where he was finishing his playing career with the Brewers. Turner thought that Aaron belonged with the Braves and asked him what job he wanted with the team. Aaron returned to head the minor league farm system, developing the talents of Tom Glavin, David Justice, and several other Braves star players. Not long after, Aaron was asked to manage the Braves. He wore several hats with the Braves organization throughout the early 1990s, serving as board member of both the Turner Broadcasting System and the Atlanta Braves, and as vice president for business development with the *CNN Airport Network*, the position he now holds.

Aaron made time for nonprofit work throughout his professional career. An educational scholarship program bears his name, and the Hank Aaron Rookie League establishes baseball in low-income housing projects. He supports Big Brothers/Big Sisters and is active with the Boy Scouts of America, having never forgotten how important such organizations were to him. "The Scouts put me on the right path," Aaron told the *Atlanta Journal/Constitution* in 1996. "One of my proudest memories is the day I got to blow the whistle and direct traffic in Mobile wearing my scout uniform. I still know the pledge."

Aaron's first marriage to Barbara Lucas ended in divorce in 1971. Four children, Gaile, Hank Jr., Dorinder, and Lary, were born to that union. He has been married to Billye Williams, widow of a former civil rights leader and former cohost of the *Today in Georgia* television show since 1973. He and Billye Aaron have one adopted child.

An intensely private person according to his wife, Aaron borders on reclusiveness. Nonetheless, his life outside of baseball has been as impressive as his professional athletic career. A 1976 recipient of the Spingarn Medal from the NAACP, his autobiography, *I Had a Hammer*, made the *New York Times* best sellers list in 1991, and the 1995 TBS documentary, *Hank Aaron: Chasing the Dream*, was nominated for an Academy Award. A statue of Aaron at the Atlanta-Fulton County Stadium stands as testament to the slugger's prowess and popularity and will grace the new Turner Field when renovations to the 1996 Olympic Stadium are completed. When the decision was made not to name the Braves's new home park after the legendary batter, but instead after the team's owner, Mobile officials moved quickly to name their city's new 6,000-seat stadium, home of the minor league Mobile Bay Bears, in Aaron's honor. A 1994 poll of young people ranked Henry Aaron behind only Michael Jordan as America's most admired athlete.

Aaron spends considerable time working for improvement in Atlanta neighborhoods and communities. He is a highly respected sports figure who is often called on for comments at athletic events and who continues his push for racial parity in professional baseball. —
ARTHUR C. GUNN

ROBERT SENGSTACKE **ABBOTT**

1868–1940
Newspaper publisher, editor

Robert Sengstacke Abbott founded one of the major black newspapers in the United States, the Chicago
Defender. *Helped by a massive migration to the north inspired by his own newspaper, he made a fortune.*
Although his central contribution was his newspaper, his exceptionally well-documented life throws light
on many aspects of black life in the nineteenth century and the first half of the twentieth century. Through
both the news and the editorial columns of the Chicago Defender, *Abbott must be counted one of the major*
black spokesmen of his time.

Robert Abbott was born on November 24, 1868, in Frederica, on St. Simon's Island,
Georgia, to Thomas and Flora Butler Abbott. Thomas Abbott, a man of unmixed African
heritage, had been a house servant, the butler on the Charles Stevens plantation. When the
Stevenses fled to the mainland in the face of the imminent Union occupation of the island,
Thomas Abbott successfully hid the family's property, from silver to furniture, and restored it
all after the Civil War. At his death in 1869, he was one of the few African Americans to be
buried in the Stevens family cemetery. Thus, his grave was marked, unlike those in the slave
burying ground, and his son was able to place a granite monument on the grave in 1928.

At the war's end, Thomas, then aged between forty and fifty, left the island for Savannah; there he met and married Flora Butler (1847–1932), who was working as a hairdresser in
the Savannah Theater. Flora Butler had been born in Savannah, on December 4, to African-
born parents. Shortly after the marriage, Thomas and Flora Butler moved back to St. Simons
where Thomas ran a grocery store and dissipated the meager earnings in Savannah. The
Abbott family resented Flora because of her status, and when she gave birth to Robert, she
was given no help from her in-laws.

When Thomas Abbott died of tuberculosis in 1869, Flora Abbott moved back to
Savannah with her son. The Abbott family started legal proceedings to gain custody of Robert,
but John Hermann Henry Sengstacke (1848–1904) came to her aid by hiring a white lawyer,
who secured a restraining order.

John Sengstacke, who appeared white, was born in Charleston, South Carolina to a
German grocer, who had purchased a young slave girl named Tama in Savannah and then
moved to Charleston, where they could legally marry.

John Sengstacke married Flora Butler Abbott on July 26, 1874; they eventually had
seven children: John Jr., Alexander, Mary, Rebecca, Eliza, Susan, and Johnnah. John Jr. and
Susan died young. The five-year-old Robert Abbott became known as Robert Sengstacke.
John Sengstacke's business enterprises had become entangled in debt, and he took up
schoolteaching. He also became a Congregational minister in 1876, and he held these two
positions for the rest of his life.

Eight-year-old Robert enjoyed the Woodville suburb of Savannah, where his stepfather's church and school were located. The boy was introduced early to the work ethic. An
early summer job was as errand boy in a grocery. As part of his training his mother insisted

he pay ten of the fifteen cents a week he earned at the grocery for his room and board. Later jobs included one as a printer's devil at a newspaper. His stepfather emphasized education in the home, and as Robert grew older the boy became his constant companion.

Abbott attends schools   In the fall of 1886 Robert Stengstacke Abbott entered Beach Institute, an American Missionary School in Savannah, to prepare for college. As one of the two or three dark-skinned students, he suffered deeply from the color prejudices of his light-skinned fellows. John Sengstacke, with his limited understanding of black Americans due to his upbringing in Germany, did not know what was going on, but Robert managed to persuade his stepfather to send him to Claflin University, then still a Methodist elementary school in Orangeburg, South Carolina. After six month's study there, Abbott decided to learn a trade and applied to Hampton Institute. While waiting for a place to become available, Abbott worked as an apprentice at the *Savannah Echo.* He was probably associated with his stepfather's preparations to put out a local paper, the *Woodville Times,* which began publication in November 1889, the same month the twenty-one-year-old Abbott entered Hampton Institute to learn the trade of printing.

At Hampton, Abbott still experienced difficulties due to color prejudice from both whites and blacks and also initially due to his own clumsy social behavior. The intervention of Hollis Burke Frissell, a white teacher and second head of Hampton, enabled Abbott to talk through some of his problems. As quoted by Ottley, Abbott later summarized Frissell as saying, "I should so prepare myself for the struggle ahead that in whatever field I should decide to dedicate my services, I should be able to point the light not only to my own people but to white people as well."

With his fine tenor voice, Abbott became a member of the Hampton Quartet, becoming the first first-year student ever to do so. A classmate said that Abbott's dark skin was an important factor in the choice since school officials preferred to send out dark students on fund-raising missions. He completed his printing course in 1893 and his academic work in 1896, all at Hampton.

At the age of twenty-eight, Abbott was still casting about for a career. He returned to Woodville and took part-time jobs as printer and schoolteacher, but, after a failed romance, left for Chicago. In the fall of 1897 Abbott enrolled in the Kent College of Law (later Chicago-Kent). Although he had been known as Robert Sengstacke for more than twenty years, he used the name Robert Sengstacke Abbott when he registered, to his stepfather's sorrow. On May 20, 1899, he graduated with a bachelor of law degree, the only African American in the class. Edward H. Morris, a prominent, fair-skinned black lawyer and politician, advised Abbott that his skin color would be a major impediment to law practice in Chicago, where black lawyers generally found law to be a part-time profession in the best of cases. After futile attempts to practice law in Gary, Indiana, and Topeka, Kansas, Abbott returned to Chicago, giving up all hope of practicing as an attorney. He never did pass the Illinois bar examination.

Abbott turned to printing. Earlier he had secured a card from the printers' union, but there was a tacit understanding that he would be hired for only one day. At this point, however, black politician Louis B. Anderson forced a printing house doing city work to hire Abbott. Abbott had steady work doing the tedious job of setting railroad time tables and correcting any errors on his own time. After John H. H. Sengstacke died of nephritis on June 23, 1904, Abbott and his sister Rebecca planned to open a school in the premises of his stepfather's

Pilgrim Academy, even reaching the point of advertising the school. Abbott suddenly changed his mind, however, and decided to stay in Chicago to launch a newspaper. This did not at first appear to be a likely idea since Chicago already had three black newspapers, all only marginally successful.

Chicago Defender *appears*   The first issue of the *Chicago Defender* appeared on May 5, 1905. Abbott printed, folded, and then distributed his paper himself. It was 1912 before the *Defender* acquired its first newsstand sales. Abbott canvassed every black gathering place in the community, selling his paper, soliciting advertising, and collecting news. His rounds, which he continued even after he could rely on others to distribute his papers, gave him great insight into the concerns of Chicago's black community. In spite of Abbott's hard work and personal sacrifice, the paper nearly closed down after a few months.

At this point, his landlady, Henrietta Plumer Lee, made a decisive intervention. She allowed him to use the dining room in her second-floor apartment at 3159 State Street as an office for the newspaper. The newspaper now began to prosper, eventually taking over the whole building at the address that became its headquarters for fifteen years.

In 1904 Lee nursed Abbott through an attack of double pneumonia. For four years, she accepted token payments on his rent and food. Lee was moved not only by maternal feelings; she also shared Abbott's vision of a newspaper to champion black concerns. Henrietta Lee almost certainly saved the *Defender* from closing and allowed it to become a major force in the black community. In 1918 Abbott bought her an eight-room brick house; when she moved in, he again followed as her lodger. Lee's daughter became a long-time employee, and her son became a stockholder in the Robert S. Abbott Publishing Company.

Robert Abbott's paper slowly grew until it had a press run of a thousand copies. He now discovered a cause that contributed growth. Great fires in Chicago had forced the red-light district into the unburnt black sections of town, and it stayed there. In 1909 Abbott launched a campaign against vice in black neighborhoods. This proved a way of selling papers until reformers forced prostitution underground in 1912, depriving him of his best issue.

By 1908 Abbott reduced his overhead by taking the printing to a larger, white publishing house. Weekly costs ran about $13, but the paper was still essentially a one-man operation and Abbott could not even give himself a salary. Many people made unpaid contributions; reporting, collecting out-of-town news, and even writing editorials. Pullman and railroad porters collected printed materials left on the trains, which were scanned for news of interest to blacks.

In 1910 the *Defender* experienced another lift when J. Hockley Smiley was hired as managing editor. Smiley was able to give coherence to Abbott's racial vision and to build up the paper by adopting some of the sensational tactics of yellow journalism. Under Abbott's supervision, Smiley oversaw a radical overhaul of the paper's format, which now included sensational banner headlines, often printed in red. If sensational news was lacking, Smiley was not above making up stories. He also led the way in establishing departments like theater, sports, editorial, and society, an innovation in the black press. He followed Abbott's wishes in abolishing the use of the terms *Negro, Afro-American,* and *black* in favor of *race,* with an occasional use of *colored.*

Financial irregularity would be a common event during the *Defender*'s early history. Smiley died of pneumonia in 1915, suffering from neglect by Abbott according to a rival paper.

By this point in time, Abbott was attracting able associates. While he remained the paper's leader, he was able to rely on a growing number of talented people. For example, Fay Young, long-time sports editor, began unpaid work for the paper in 1912 while he was also working as a dining-car waiter. In time, Abbott could begin paying salaries.

The* Defender *grows   In 1915 Abbott broke new ground for black newspapers by putting out an eight-column, eight-page, full-size paper. The format appeared in the first extra of the *Defender*, on November 14, announcing the death of Booker T. Washington. By this time, Abbott had begun to distance himself from Washington by urging blacks to leave the South to seek out better opportunities in the North. At the same time, however, Abbott moved no closer to the position of W. E. B. DuBois, as the newspaper editor championed the hopes of the black masses rather than those of a talented tenth.

The *Defender*'s sensational, in-depth coverage of the Brownsville incident in Texas led to a nationwide, 20,000 copy increase in circulation. The *Defender* was launched on its career as a national newspaper. By 1920 the *Defender*'s circulation was at least 230,000. More than two-thirds were sold outside of Chicago, with a tenth of the total going to New York City.

The *Defender* also drew attention from the authorities. Although Abbott was unfailingly patriotic in his editorial position, the Wilson administration was perturbed by the paper's frank reporting of the armed forces' treatment of blacks as second-class citizens. The *Defender* had launched its official campaign for blacks to move north—"The Great Northern Drive"—on May 15, 1917. In the South, the paper's support of migration and its frank reporting on racial conditions drew the hostility of state and local officials to the point that its distribution to eager black readers became clandestine in certain regions.

At the end of World War I the paper's circulation stabilized at approximately 180,000. Printing and costs were major problems, especially since, unlike most newspapers, the *Defender* made most of its money from circulation. On May 6, 1921, Flora Abbott Sengstacke pressed the button that put a high-speed rotary printing press in operation at 3435 Indiana Avenue, another first for black journalism. But, with the advanced technology of the press, there were no black printers able to run it. Abbott hired a union crew of whites. The arrangement worked with no problems until the Depression years, when the use of whites and their union wages came under attack. The *Defender* replaced its white printers with blacks. The new plant cut the printing costs by a thousand dollars a week, and Abbott became known for the frugality of his salaries and other overhead. He was also becoming a very wealthy man.

As the paper's circulation grew, Abbott began to favor a policy of gradualism in race progress. Although coverage of lynchings and racial conflict continued, the space devoted to it declined in favor of a sharp increase in stories about crime. The coverage now included such topics as fashion, sports, arts, and blacks outside the United States. Abbott continued to push for integration and the upgrading of blacks in the workforce, eventually contributing to important gains in the police and fire departments.

Abbott himself was becoming an establishment figure: he received honorary degrees from universities such as Morris Brown and Wilberforce. He became president of the Hampton alumni association and a member of the board of trustees. On September 10, 1918, he married Helen Thornton Morrison, a fair-skinned widow some thirty years younger than himself. The Abbotts became patrons of such institutions as the Chicago Opera and began to entertain widely. In 1923 the Abbotts toured Brazil, and in 1929, Europe. The marriage was not happy, however, and it seems likely that his wife never loved Abbott. Toward the end of the marriage Abbott suddenly moved out of his house, charging her with infecting him with tuberculosis and hiring people to kill him. Helen Abbott obtained a divorce decree on June 26, 1933, receiving fifty thousand dollars, the furnishings of the house, the limousine, and lawyer's fees. On August 7, 1934, Abbott married Edna Denison, who, like Helen, was a very light-complexioned woman. She too appears not to have been moved by love. Abbott himself had no children and claimed to be unable to have any.

Abbott did have family; over a hundred relatives to whom he was very generous. Included among the objects of his attention were his German cousins, offspring of his father's sister, and the white Stevenses, descendants of the family who had owned his father. The Stevenses fell on hard times during the Depression, and Abbott provided help for several years. A special focus of his attention was the son of his half-brother Alexander, John Herman Henry Sengstacke, who was educated and trained to take over the *Defender* on Abbott's death, an aim he fulfilled.

Soon after the 1923 trip to Brazil, Abbott once again faced charges of financial irregularities at the *Defender:* the problem was inadequate bookkeeping. He promptly fired Phil Jones, the managing editor, and replaced him with Nathan K. Magill, his sister-in-law's husband. Unfortunately, he lacked Abbott's almost instinctive understanding of the *Defender's* readers and supporters. Magill took an anti-union stand in the fight of railroad porters to unionize. Since the *Defender's* distribution depended on the cooperation of porters, Abbott had to intervene to change the paper's position. In spite of his limitations, Magill was tight-fisted and helped the paper continue to make money.

The **Defender** *survives the Depression*   The Great Depression and illness took their toll on Abbott. Just one month before the stock market crash of 1929, he launched the first well-financed and supported attempt to publish a black magazine, *Abbott's Monthly.* A success upon its launch, in 1933 the monthly was a victim of the massive black unemployment caused by the dire economic situation. The *Defender* itself initially ran into problems, although it was again showing a profit by the end of 1933. Again due to financial mishandling, Abbott promptly fired Magill and took over running the paper himself, bringing his nephew John H. H. Sengstacke into the organization. In rebuilding his staff, Abbott rehired a number of people Magill had fired. In the next three years, Abbott became very ill and was in the office for only twenty months. In 1933 he was found to have tuberculosis, the disease that had killed his birth father. In addition, he became so myopic that others had to read to him. At the end of his life he was almost permanently confined to bed. Abbott ultimately died of a combination of tuberculosis and Bright's disease on February 29, 1940. There was a large and elaborate funeral at Metropolitan Community Church followed by burial in Lincoln Cemetery.

Abbott was a shrewd businessman and a hard worker, but his success as a publisher is due in large part to his skill at discerning and expressing the needs and opinions of ordinary blacks. Abbott had the good fortune to have his beloved paper fall into the capable hands of his nephew, John H. H. Sengstacke, who was able to carry on Abbott's creation.
—ROBERT L. JOHNS

KAREEM **ABDUL-JABBAR**

1947–

Athlete, humanist, writer

Kareem Abdul-Jabbar played basketball on championship teams at the University of California at Los Angeles and on professional teams in Milwaukee and Los Angeles, from 1965 until he retired at the end of the 1984–85 season. He combined exceptional athletic ability with high scholastic competence, interest in his fellow man, and devotion to his Muslim religion that sustained him on and off the basketball court. He was the highest scorer of all basketball players.

Born Ferdinand Lewis Alcindor, Jr. on April 16, 1947, in Harlem, New York, an only child, he legally adopted the name Kareem Abdul-Jabbar (Generous Servant of Allah) after his conversion to Islam. His father, Ferdinand Lewis Alcindor, Sr., had a degree in classical musicology from the Julliard School of Music but was unable to find employment in that field. He worked as a prison officer and policeman for the New York Transit Authority. Kareem's mother, Cora Alcindor, was a price checker in a department store.

His parents, originally from Trinidad, were not affectionate in their relations with their son, but they wanted the best for his educational, physical, and social development. Devout Catholics, they sent him to St. Jude's Elementary School for its curriculum and discipline. He learned to use his size and dexterity on the basketball court in the fourth grade, and eventually he developed the hook shot for which he became famous. He did well in his studies, and basketball became an important part of his existence. From St. Jude's, the young man went to Power Memorial Academy, an all-boys parochial high school, in Manhattan in 1961.

Abdul-Jabbar was always an introspective person who enjoyed the company of school mates. Gradually, he became more and more suspicious that people did not like him because of his size, race, politics, or religious preference. The civil rights movement escalated during his adolescence, and Abdul-Jabbar began to read about underprivileged people, especially African Americans. When a 1963 church bombing killed four African American girls, his anger over the incident caused him to withdraw further into a shell. He thought that his father and mother did not understand his grief. Luckily, at about the same time, Abdul-Jabbar discovered the value of jazz music to help release his frustrations.

Abdul-Jabbar used music, books, and basketball to fill his hours at home and at school. He was on Power's honor roll, debating team, and basketball team. Coach Donohue took him to Madison Square Garden to see Bill Russell and Wilt Chamberlain play, and groomed him for recognition on All-American and All-City teams. In one instance, Abdul-Jabbar resented Coach Donohue's use of the word "nigger" to stimulate him to put forth his ultimate ability. It took a lot of time and willpower for Abdul-Jabbar to put aside his hurt and questions about the coach's true feelings about him.

Abdul-Jabbar worked the summer before his senior year in the journalism workshop of the Harlem Youth Action Project writing about its dance, drama, music, and community projects. He visited the Schomburg Center for Research in Black Culture and immersed himself in the works of W. C. Handy, Paul Lawrence Dunbar, Langston Hughes, Countee Cullen, Richard Wright, and Ralph Ellison. This was his first exposure to a wealth of information about

African Americans, and his first opportunity to participate in community action by writing about what the organization was doing in Harlem and about conditions of black people all over the country.

Starts collegiate basketball play   After high school, Abdul-Jabbar chose the University of California at Los Angeles (UCLA) with its advantages of an attractive campus in a sunny location and an apparent amiable association between black and white students. He liked the ample facilities and its winning basketball team, coached by legendary John Wooden.

Abdul-Jabbar made few friends at UCLA since he concentrated on basketball and study. He started as an English major but changed to history when he saw that it was impossible to produce weekly papers for English classes while preparing for basketball competition. The change helped him give equal time to academics and to athletics. History turned out to be a fine choice for pursuit of the interests of his later life.

Kareem Abdul-Jabbar.

Abdul-Jabbar had to wait until his sophomore year at UCLA to play in league games and to work directly with Coach Wooden, whom he had honored for years from a distance. Abdul-Jabbar and the coach found an immediate mutual affection from their first meeting. With his classes going well and the basketball team defeating all opponents, Abdul-Jabbar's remaining problem was dealing with the ever-present press. He resented reporters who had no concept or feeling for his views as an African American concerned not only about basketball, but also about the treatment of black people nationwide, and he disliked the inevitability of his remarks being distorted or taken out of context for sensationalism. When he learned to completely ignore obnoxious media representatives or respond in terse terms, he earned the reputation of an uncooperative, sullen, and ill-bred man.

During the summer after the 1966–67 national championship season at UCLA, Abdul-Jabbar worked for the New York City Housing Authority teaching basketball techniques to young people from housing projects all over the city. He gave the children a mixture of athletics and lessons in black pride. A year later he did the same in New York City's Bedford-Stuyvesant, Brownsville, and the East Bronx, passing on basketball skills, and instilling in young people a desire to remain in school and develop into good citizens.

Interest in the religion of Islam   With the maturity of an upper-division college man, Abdul-Jabbar started to search for a spiritual outlet. He took courses in African and black studies, read about the major religions of the world, and explored the Bible and the Qur'an. *The Autobiography of Malcolm X* prompted him to rethink his beliefs and attitudes about race, the goals of African Americans, and the role of religion in his life. Knowing that Catholicism

11

was not the solution for him convinced Abdul-Jabbar that he needed to search for his own solutions.

Abdul-Jabbar's in-depth analysis of Islam culminated with his acceptance of that religion in a mosque on 125th Street in New York City in the summer of 1968, and the taking of his new name. With the training of Haamas Abdul-Khaalis, a well-read Muslim, and a course in the Arabic language at Harvard University, Abdul-Jabbar refined his knowledge of Islam. Because of his friendship with Haamas, Abdul-Jabbar ultimately founded a center in New York for Haamas and other Muslims—a center that was shaken when a rival Muslim group took the lives of Haamas's three sons by gunfire.

Abdul-Jabbar's refusal to participate in the 1968 Olympics in Mexico City, and his support of John Carlos and Tommie Smith's clenched fist salute on the victory stand, brought mounds of hate mail to his door. However, he remained firm in his commitment.

Before Abdul-Jabbar graduated from UCLA in 1969, his team had won three consecutive championships, Abdul-Jabbar had scored 2,325 points with an average of 26.4 points each game, and he was named All-American each of his years of play. From UCLA, Abdul-Jabbar joined the Milwaukee Bucks professional team where he was named Rookie of the Year. In six seasons with the Bucks, he averaged more than thirty points a game and won three Most Valuable Player (MVP) awards.

In 1975 he went to the Los Angeles Lakers and won three MVP honors in the first five years. Playing for the Lakers, Abdul-Jabbar won six MVP awards and was chosen for nineteen All-Star games. He retired after the 1989–90 season, having scored more points than any other player in the history of basketball.

The greatest catastrophe for Abdul-Jabbar was the destruction of his home in 1983 by a fire that caused no personal injury, but consumed priceless treasures, including copies of the Qu'ran and items important to his artistic, musical, and athletic loves. He turned to his religion for consolation and accepted the outpouring of gifts and good wishes from people who loved him.

Abdul-Jabbar, who married Janice (later Habiba) Brown in 1971, is the father of two sons, Kareem and Amir, and two daughters, Habiba and Sultana. He was divorced in 1973. Now free of the game he played since he was eight years old, his days are brightened by the closer relations with his parents that emerged before he left basketball, and he is overall more comfortable with meeting people in social and business circumstances. When he was playing, he passed his knowledge of strategy to younger men on the team; in retirement, he has gone back to playgrounds in Harlem to interact with elementary and high school boys, to spur them to make the best of their mental and physical talents. In addition to his autobiography, Abdul-Jabbar has written a historical volume that was conceived during his attempt to help his son search for information to complete a black studies assignment. *Black Profiles in Courage*, stories about little-known contributors to African American history, was published in 1996 by William Morrow.

Since retiring from basketball as a professional player, Abdul-Jabbar has continued his involvement in the game by promoting an exhibition team's tour of Saudi Arabia, in 1991, and in 1992 played in a one-on-one game with another former basketball great, Julius "Dr. J." Erving. Abdul-Jabbar has also been active in the motion picture industry, appearing in several movies. He had bit parts in several television shows and movies, including one on the old black baseball leagues. Through Cranbery Records, which he heads, he promotes the work of young jazz artists. President Bill Clinton honored Abdul-Jabbar in 1994 when the first National Sports Awards program was established, naming him, along with Arnold Palmer, Muhammad Ali, Wilma Rudolph, and Ted Williams, one of "The Great Ones."

Abdul-Jabbar's reputation as a dominant player in college and professional basketball can be balanced by his lesser-known contributions. Abdul-Jabbar is known for an awareness and concern about the history and present-day status of African Americans. A scholar in world religions and the history of African Americans, he continues his relentless efforts to motivate African American boys and girls to excel and be proud of their heritage. —DONA L. IRVIN

ALVIN **AILEY**

1931–1989

Choreographer, dancer, dance company founder

A pioneer in modern dance, Alvin Ailey founded the racially integrated and popular modern dance troupe, the Alvin Ailey Dance Theatre. His was the first black dance company sent abroad under the International Exchange Program in 1962, the first American modern dance company to perform in the Soviet Union since the 1920s, the first black modern dance company to perform at the Metropolitan Opera, and the first modern dance company sponsored by the U.S. government to tour the People's Republic of China since Sino-American relations were strengthened. Revelations, his signature dance piece, drew upon African American religious music he knew in his childhood.

Ailey was born in his grandfather Henry Ailey's home in Rogersville, near Waco, Texas, on January 5, 1931, the only child of Alvin, a laborer, and Lula E. Cliff Ailey. He was the thirteenth member of an overcrowded household where he lived with his grandfather, parents, aunt, eight cousins, and other family. Alvin Sr. left the home soon after his son was born, returned briefly when his son was about four years old, then deserted the family again. Ailey admitted in his autobiography *Revelations,* in which he spoke frankly of his search for identity and his homosexuality, that growing up as a fatherless child led to an inferiority complex that he never overcame. The two had no further contact until about 1975, when Ailey located his father and they had a cold, unproductive ten-minute telephone conversation.

Lula Ailey moved from town to town working as a housekeeper to support herself and her young son. Ailey was dismayed over her frequent absences. By the time he was twelve years old, the Aileys lived in Navasota, where his mother worked in a hospital. Despite the racism and the economic conditions prevalent in Texas at the time, Ailey enjoyed the abundance of entertainment available to blacks, including Silas Green, a traveling vaudeville show from New Orleans, and such musicians as Big Boy Crudup, who often played for community gatherings. In May 1941 his mother relocated to Los Angeles and left Ailey behind to complete school. He moved to Los Angeles in 1942.

Ailey graduated from George Washington Carver Junior High School and Thomas Jefferson High School, where he was practically an "A" student. He became an avid reader

*Alvin Ailey
instructs a class.*

in high school, continuing into college. Having been introduced to Spanish when he lived in Texas, Ailey had an affinity for the language. By his high school years he was so fluent in the language that he was allowed to teach the class at times. Although Ailey danced around in the backyard of his house, sometimes imitating Gene Kelly and the Nicholas Brothers, and studied tap dancing from a private teacher, he had no intention of becoming a dancer. He watched Katherine Dunham perform Afro-Caribbean dances at the Biltmore in Los Angeles and was impressed with her performance, but still not inspired to become a dancer.

Carmen de Lavallade, a neighbor and schoolmate in Los Angeles, gave an extraordinary dance performance at a school assembly that impressed Ailey, and he fantasized about dancing with her. He dared not try, however, for fear of being labeled a "sissy." Later, after watching Ailey perform gymnastics, de Lavallade encouraged him to study under Lester Horton, who had a studio in Hollywood. After several lessons with Horton, the instructor asked Ailey to rehearse with de Lavallade, his leading dancer. Ailey recalled in his autobiography that "the combination was electric." After completing high school, Ailey studied under Horton on a regular basis, paying twelve dollars a month for classes. De Lavallade continued to encourage, inspire, and support Ailey's development from the time of his initial study throughout his life. "Dance, for me, would have been impossible without Carmen de Lavallade," he later wrote in his autobiography.

Ailey enrolled in the University of California, Los Angeles, where he was attracted to literature, especially Spanish literature, and found spiritual uplift in the works of Octavio Paz, Pablo Neruda, and other South American poets and writers. He also discovered black writers and poets John Oliver Killens, Richard Wright, Countee Cullen, and Langston Hughes. At night he continued his dance instruction at the Horton Theater with little time for study. The tug of war between Ailey's attraction to dance and his family's desire that he have a college education left him confused and prompted him to leave Los Angeles for San Francisco.

Becomes a choreographer   Once in San Francisco, Ailey borrowed fifty dollars from a friend and lived in cheap hotels and later the YMCA. Hungry and jobless, he found employment as a clerk at the tax bureau. Later he enrolled at San Francisco State College, taking a job with the Greyhound Bus Company to pay the tuition, but soon found that he missed dancing. Ailey frequently attended the Halprin Lathrope Dance Studio, where he met Marguerite Angelos, a tall, thin black girl, later known as Maya Angelou. They rehearsed routines on weekends while Ailey made his first attempts at choreography. After a successful dance performance at the Champagne Supper Club, Ailey and a group of dancers went to Los Angeles to perform a benefit. A visit to the Horton Studio and a talk with Lester Horton convinced Ailey to give up school and become a dancer rather than a language teacher.

Returning to the Horton Company in 1953, Ailey watched his friend Carmen de Lavallade become a radiant star with the Lester Horton Dance Theater. Horton created a *Bal Caribe*—a Caribbean Ball, which featured a stylized suite of five dances including *Tropic Trio and Dedication to José Clemente Orozo*. In one segment of the suite, Horton made a dance for Ailey and de Lavallade, which was an instant success. Their fame spread and they were invited to dance at Circo's, a Los Angeles nightclub where big bands performed. While Ailey and de Lavallade danced on stage, Horton died of a heart attack.

Since the company was now without a choreographer and Ailey was well prepared for the job, he was appointed to the position. He choreographed a tribute to Horton, his first ballet, called *According to St. Francis,* relating Horton to St. Francis of Assisi. For his second ballet, *Mourning Morning,* Ailey said in his autobiography that he "took everything Tennessee Williams had ever written and put it onstage."

In 1954, Ailey and the Horton Company took the two ballets to the Jacob's Pillow Dance Festival in Massachusetts. After a brief return visit to Los Angeles, in December Ailey and de Lavallade accepted an invitation to join the cast for the Broadway musical *House of Flowers.* Ailey never returned to California, and in 1958 the Horton organization closed permanently.

Now twenty-four-years-old, lively, athletic, and charismatic, Ailey felt that he needed more training. He studied the techniques of Louis Johnson, Pearl Reynolds, and Arthur Mitchell. He also enrolled in Martha Graham dance classes and studied ballet under Karel Shook. Ailey danced in several musical shows, including *The Carefree Tree* (1955) and *Show Boat* (summer

1956), and Harry Belafonte asked him to choreograph *Sing, Man Sing* (1956), in which Ailey also danced. In 1957, he appeared as lead dancer in the last musical in which he would perform—*Jamaica,* starring Lena Horne. Ailey had acting parts in several plays, including *Call Me by My Rightful Name; Talking to You;* and *Tiger, Tiger, Burning Bright.* At the direct request of Langston Hughes, in 1963 he appeared in *Jericho Jim Crow.*

Founds dance company   Although there were many skilled black dancers in New York in 1958, they had few places to perform. Ailey formed a group that grew into the Alvin Ailey Dance Theatre to show the world their talent as well as his own. It became multiethnic in appearance, with thirteen men and eleven women who were black, white, and Asian American. Ailey and Ernest Parham decided to do a concert together, and each assembled a group of extraordinary dancers, many from the cast of *Jamaica,* for Ailey's choreographed dance *Blues Suite,* based on the Dew Drop Inn from his Texas childhood. Geoffrey Holder designed the costumes. The group gave its first concert in 1958 at the Young Men's Hebrew Association (YMHA) on 92nd Street and Lexington Avenue. In his autobiography Ailey quoted *Dance* magazine, which called him "exceptional" and added that he "reminds one of a caged lion full of lashing power that he can contain or release at will."

Ailey then found a former hotel, later known as Clark Center for the Performing Arts, where his company could rehearse and where Ailey could concentrate on his work. For a second performance he made a ballet called *Arietta Oubliée,* in which he and Carmen de Lavallade appeared; prepared a new version of *Blues Suite;* offered *Cinco Latinos;* and did one performance of *Arietta Oubliée,* in which he and de Lavallade appeared as well. *Dance News* for February 1959 commented on the enthusiastic audience and called "the stage world created by Alvin Ailey an altogether stimulating, exciting, beautiful, funny and original entertainment, meticulously presented."

Ailey's masterwork, *Revelations,* was his way of expressing the faith, hope, and joy of black choirs, congregations, and preachers he had heard singing spirituals and gospel songs in Texas, particularly "Wade in the Water" and "I've Been 'Buked, I Been Scorned." *Revelations,* a gigantic suite of spirituals, was well received at its premiere at the YMHA on January 31, 1960, but did not reach its current popularity until it was edited and performed at Jacob's Pillow in 1961. From then on *Revelations* evoked a tumultuous response from audiences wherever it was performed.

After successful performances at the Clark Center, the Boston Arts Festival, and elsewhere, in February 1962 the Alvin Ailey company, with Carmen de Lavallade as codirector, began a thirteen-week tour of Australia, Southeast Asia, and Brazil sponsored by the U.S. Department of State under President John F. Kennedy's International Exchange Program. The group toured under the name de Lavallade-Ailey Dance Theater, and its tour of Southeast Asia was a first for a black company. They won universal acclaim and, according to *Current Biography,* they also "set the pattern for the extended international engagements that followed."

The group returned to the United States in the summer of 1962 and performed during the American Dance Festival in New London, Connecticut. Ailey and six other choreographers were invited to attend a workshop at the Watch Hill, Rhode Island, estate of Rebekah Harkness. Here he experimented with larger companies, trying out new ideas. Ailey taught workshops and dance techniques at Connecticut College in New London as well as at Watch Hill. His work at Watch Hill resulted in a ballet called *Feat of Ashes.*

In 1966 Ailey and his troupe returned to Europe for a two-month stay. In April that year they were the only integrated company to perform at the World Festival of the Negro Arts in Dakar, Senegal. They began a sixteen-week tour of Europe in Spring 1967, playing at the Holland Festival in Amsterdam, the Venice Biennale of Contemporary Music, and elsewhere. They visited Europe in August 1967 and that fall made a State Department–sponsored tour of nine African nations. Ailey's choreography of a work based on the Seven Deadly Sins won the Grand Prix Italia in an Italian competition. The group returned home late in 1967 and began a three-month American tour. In 1970 the dancers had a triumphant Russian tour; the audience in Leningrad gave them a twenty-three-minute standing ovation. They were the first American modern dance company to perform in the Soviet Union since the Isadora Duncan Dancers of the 1920s.

Ailey created ballets for such notable companies as the American Ballet Theatre, Royal Danish Ballet, London Festival Ballet, the Joffrey Ballet, Paris Opera Ballet, and La Scala Opera Ballet. He choreographed Samuel Barber's *Anthony and Cleopatra* for the 1966 opening of the Metropolitan Opera's inaugural season at the Lincoln Center for the Performing Arts and Leonard Berstein's *Mass* for the 1971 opening of the Kennedy Center for the Performing Arts. He also worked with other leading artists, such as Duke Ellington, as choreographer for Ellington's show *My People,* which opened in Chicago around 1963.

In 1971 he choreographed *Cry* especially for Judith Jamison, who made the fifteen-minute solo one of the troupe's most celebrated pieces, generally performing to sold-out houses. Created as a birthday present for Ailey's mother, the work was a hymn to celebrate the endurance, joys, victories, and sorrows of black women, especially mothers. In 1974 and 1976 he did a dance salute to Duke Ellington called *Ailey Celebrates Ellington.* In 1983 the Ailey troupe became the first black modern dance company to perform at the Metropolitan Opera, and in 1985 they were the first modern dance company sponsored by the U.S. government to tour the People's Republic of China since Sino-American relations were strengthened.

Sometime in 1979 Ailey began to suffer from extreme mood swings and subsequently developed a cocaine habit. The death in October 1979 of his good friend Joyce Trisler compounded his despair, and Ailey became manic-depressive. In 1980 he was arrested for assault and later burglary. In July, he was hospitalized in Westchester County's Bloomingdale Center for seven weeks; lithium was prescribed for his treatment. After his release, Ailey went back to choreography, this time with *Phases,* with music by Max Roach. It was his last work. Ailey died in New York City on December 1, 1989, of dyscrasia, a blood disorder. His memorial service was held at the Cathedral of St. John the Divine, where thousands of friends came to honor the fallen giant of the international dance scene. After his death, Jamison, his protegee, headed the Ailey dance troupe, which opened in 1991 under her direction.

Among the numerous awards Ailey received for his work were first prize at the International Dance Festival in Paris (1970), a *Dance* Magazine Award (1975), the NAACP Spingarn Medal (1976), the Capezio Award (1979), the Samuel H. Scripps American Dance Festival Award (1987), and the Kennedy Center Award (1988). He received honorary degrees from a number of institutions, including Princeton University, Bard College, Adelphia University, and Cedar Crest College.

Reflecting on his life, Ailey admitted that he had been obsessed with dancing and his dance company. He found choreography mentally and physically draining, but discovered great joy in "creating something where before there was nothing." Ailey lamented that an overlay of racism continued in American dance companies, however, and black dancers were rarely seen in classical companies. He found European companies more open to black dancers than American companies. Considering such obstacles, Ailey's achievements were extraordinary.

Ailey was a world-class choreographer who combined African American soul with dance, giving modern dance mass appeal. But perhaps more importantly, Ailey used his art form to celebrate people and humanity and to give joy. —JESSIE CARNEY SMITH

MUHAMMAD **ALI**
1942–
Boxer, civil rights activist, humanitarian

Undoubtedly one of the most internationally renowned athletes of all times, Muhammad Ali serves as a role model for youth and athletes throughout the world. Ali has won the title of World Heavyweight Boxing Champion an unprecedented three times, 1964–67, 1974–78, and 1978–79. Called "The People's Champion," he has also captured the hearts of many who have seen or heard of him through his flamboyant manner and his humanity. In 1964 when Ali boldly challenged the U.S. government by his refusal to serve in the military, he became a global hero to many who also opposed the Vietnam War.

Ali was born Cassius Marcellus Clay Jr. on January 17, 1942, in Louisville, Kentucky, to Cassius Marcellus and Odessa Grady Clay. He and his brother Rudolph Valentino (now Rahaman Ali) grew up in an impoverished family. By trade, Ali's father was a sign painter and occasionally painted murals on church walls. According to Ali, the elder Clay was also a talented dancer, actor, and singer. Ali's mother, whom he affectionately calls "Bird," worked as a domestic in the homes of wealthy whites. The family attended Mount Zion Baptist Church.

Ali's first introduction to boxing came at the age of twelve after his bicycle, a Christmas present, was stolen. Ali went to a gym to report the theft to a police officer and became overwhelmed with the sight of boxing and the smell of the gym. The police officer, Joe Martin, was also the boxing trainer at the Columbia Gym. Ali signed up for the boxing program, and Joe Martin became his first trainer. Soon Ali discovered the talents of Fred Stoner, a black man who trained young boxers at the Grace Community Center. Stoner taught Ali the fundamentals of the game, including style and how to build up stamina. Ali trained six days a week for six hours, two hours with Martin and four hours with Stoner. Rather than ride the school bus, as a teenager Ali ran to school each day to work on his wind. Ali often imagined his name being announced as the heavyweight boxing champion of the world. He graduated from DuValle Junior High School and Central High School in Louisville. Ali admitted he was more interested in boxing than school and therefore did not perform at a high level as a student.

Becomes boxing champion   In the 1950s young Ali regularly appeared on the weekly Louisville television boxing program "Tomorrow's Champions." He was paid four dollars

Three-time heavyweight champion Muhammad Ali.

for each match that appeared on the program. He won six Golden Gloves tournaments in Kentucky in three weight classes, from light welter to heavy. In 1959 and 1960 Ali won both the Light Heavyweight National Golden Gloves and the National Amateur Athletic Union (AAU) tournaments. As the National AAU boxing champion, he was invited to the Olympic trials and won the position of light heavyweight entry for the United States. In the 1960 Olympics, Ali won the gold medal by defeating "Ziggy" Pietrzykowski of Poland.

Ali predicted that he would win the heavyweight championship by the time he was twenty-one. After the Olympics, Ali signed a lucrative contract with ten Louisville millionaires, the Louisville Sponsoring Group, who backed his budding career. The Group hired Archie Moore, a retired fighter, to serve as Ali's trainer. Ali, however, hired Angelo Dundee as his trainer and manager. On October 29, 1960, in his hometown of Louisville, Ali had his first professional fight. He easily defeated Tunney Hunsaker for the two-thousand-dollar purse. Over the next four years Ali had a total of nineteen professional fights, all of which he won.

In 1964, at the age of twenty-two, Ali announced that he had become a member of the Muslim faith and changed his name from his "slave name," Cassius Clay, to the Islamic name Muhammad Ali. Muhammad means "worthy of all praises" and Ali means "most high."

During the same year, Ali became the heavyweight champion by defeating Sonny Liston in Miami. As the champion, Ali taunted his opponents by predicting the round in which he would defeat them, loud boasting, and poems about his fighting abilities. Ali coined such phrases as "float like a butterfly, sting like a bee," to describe his boxing style. He also bragged about his natural good looks and abilities with statements like "I'm pretty" and "I'm the greatest fighter of all times." Ali knew that the more publicity he achieved for each fight the higher the final count for the box office. His braggadocio and flippant style earned him the nickname "the Louisville Lip." During the next three years, Ali defended his title nine times, including a rematch with Sonny Liston.

In 1966, when his contract with the Louisville group expired, he signed with Herbert Muhammad, the son of Elijah Muhammad, who founded the Black Muslim movement. Under Muhammad's management, Ali earned more money in six fights than he had earned in six years under the Louisville Sponsoring Group.

Defies military draft In April 28, 1967, Muhammad Ali took a courageous stand against the U.S. government when he refused induction in the army on religious grounds. Ali had earlier explained his position on the Vietnam War in a 1966 poem published in *The Greatest*:

> Keep asking me, no matter how long
> On the war in Vietnam, I sing this song
> I ain't got no quarrel with those Vietcong. . . .

Ali's decision brought various responses from people all across the country. Politicians and some veterans wanted him imprisoned, and some people sent death threats. Thousands of people, however, supported his refusal to be drafted. Ali's action marked the beginning of a new era of black athletes who challenged the system. The World Boxing Association (WBA) stripped him of his boxing title, naming Joe Frazier champion instead, and the New York State Athletic Commission and every state boxing commission banned him from fighting. Ali was also forbidden to travel abroad. Ali was later convicted, sentenced to five years in prison for draft evasion, and fined ten thousand dollars.

Although for the next three and a half years Ali was prohibited from boxing, he stood steadfast for his religious beliefs. During the time he was barred from boxing, Ali earned a living by speaking on college campuses about civil rights and justice. Worldwide, Ali had a large following, including college students, peace movement activists, blacks, and the Third World.

Finally in June 1970 the U.S. Supreme Court reversed Ali's draft-dodging case on a technicality. Ali said the Supreme Court decision was the biggest victory of his life. In September of that year the NAACP also won its suit in the New York federal court against the New York State Athletic Commission, proving that denial of his boxing license violated Ali's constitutional rights.

Ali returned to the ring, and his first fight after the Supreme Court decision was against Jerry Quarry in November 1970 in Atlanta. Ali won by knocking Quarry out in the third round. After having his New York license reinstated, Ali fought Joe Frazier, reigning heavyweight champion, in New York on March 1971. Frazier retained the heavyweight title. This fight was Ali's first professional loss. By the end of his career Ali would fight Frazier three times—a series of the most widely discussed bouts in the sport because of their intensity, devastation, and duration.

Regains title   In 1974 Ali again became the undisputed heavyweight champion by defeating Joe Frazier in January and George Foreman in October. In the so-called "Rumble in the Jungle" in Kinshasa, Zaire, Ali knocked Foreman out in the eighth round. In September 1975 Ali fought the unrelenting Frazier for the third time. The fight was billed as "the Thrilla in Manila," and Ali won when Frazier was unable to answer the bell for the final round.

Ali lost the championship title early in 1978 to Leon Spinks, but later in the year defeated Spinks in a rematch to regain his title for the third time. On June 26, 1979, at the age of thirty-seven, Ali retired as champion with a professional record of fifty-nine victories and three defeats. Because of his lavish lifestyle, however, Ali found himself in need of money and in 1980 returned to boxing to fight Larry Holmes for the World Boxing Council's title. Ali was unable to answer the bell for the eleventh round, and Holmes won with a technical knockout. For this fight, regardless of the outcome, Ali was to receive eight million dollars. One year later Ali returned to the ring for the last time, when he fought Trevor Berbick. In this final boxing match, one month before his fortieth birthday, Ali was defeated for the fifth time in his professional career.

In 1975 Ali was coauthor of his autobiography, *The Greatest: My Own Story*. Playing himself,

Muhammad Ali.

Ali starred in the film autobiography, *The Greatest*, in 1976. He also appeared in the 1979 NBC television movie *Freedom Road*. Muhammad Ali's life has been the subject of countless books, including many works written specifically for children and young adults. The film *When We Were Kings* was released in 1996 and documents the 1974 heavyweight title fight "the Rumble in the Jungle." In this fight, Ali was not favored to win over the younger, stronger, and larger boxer, George Foreman. In fact, the odds were seven to one against Ali. The Academy Award-winning documentary film records Ali's "rope-a-dope defense," in which he rested on the ropes and allowed George Foreman to hit him until his opponent became exhausted. Then in the eighth round, thirty-two-year-old Ali responded with an explosion of rights to Foreman's head to win the fight and his title for an unprecedented third time.

Diagnosed with Parkinson's disease

In 1977 Ali's doctor advised him to quit boxing because Ali's reflexes were beginning to slow down. Seven years later, Ali entered the hospital to undergo tests for symptoms of neurological damage. The doctors diagnosed Ali with Parkinson's disease. In the 1991 Thomas Hauser book, *Muhammad Ali: His Life and Times*, Ali admits that boxing was the cause of his current disease, which slurs his speech and causes him to be listless and tired, often with tremors in his legs and hands. Despite his impaired vigor and speech, Ali remains involved, as much as possible, with family, religious, political, and social activities. He travels as much as nine months a year making public appearances to spread a message of love and brotherhood.

Many have not seen the various sides to Muhammad Ali. In addition to writing poetry, Ali paints. His father, a talented artist, taught Ali painting techniques as a youngster. Ali held his first one-man show in January 1979 in New York at the Roseland Ballroom. These twenty-four paintings and drawings were donated to the United Nations. A fan of horror movies, Ali lists *The Invasion of the Body Snatchers* and *The Mummy* as his favorites. He also likes to perform amateur magic tricks.

In the 1980s President Jimmy Carter sent Ali to Africa to gain support for the U.S. boycott of the 1980 Olympic games in Moscow. Ali's second diplomatic mission came in 1985 in Lebanon, where he tried to obtain the release of four kidnapped Americans. Both of these missions were unsuccessful. In November 1990 Ali went to Baghdad, Iraq, to meet with Iraqi President Sadam Hussein for several days to secure the release of American hostages. On December 4, 1990, Ali, having successfully negotiated the release of fifteen American citizens, returned to the United States.

Muhammad Ali has had four wives: Sonji Roi from 1964 to 1966; Belinda Boyd (Khalilah Tolona) from 1967 through 1976; Veronica Porche from 1977 to 1985; and Yolanda "Lonnie" Williams, whom he married in November 1986. He has seven daughters and two sons. Ali is a devoted father and husband, who maintains a friendly, respectful relationship with all his former wives.

Many honors have been bestowed on Ali. In 1970 following his fight against Jerry Quarry, Coretta Scott King and Ralph Abernathy presented the Dr. Martin Luther King Memorial Award to Ali for his contributions to equality and human rights. In November 1978 the ground was broken for the Muhammad Ali Youth Opportunities Unlimited Complex in Newark, New Jersey. Ali accepted an honorary doctorate in humane letters from Texas Southern University at its 1979 commencement. He has received numerous other honorary degrees, including one from the Ortanez University in Manila. Other honors include the naming of a street after him in his hometown, Louisville, in 1979. He was recognized for his long, meritorious service to boxing by the World Boxing Association in 1985. In 1987 Ali was honored by *The Ring Magazine*, which elected him to the Boxing Hall of Fame. Ali was inducted in the inaugural class of the International Boxing Hall of Fame in 1990.

Carries Olympic torch At the Atlanta Centennial Olympics in 1996, Ali carried the torch for the last leg of the opening ceremony and lit the Olympic caldron, marking the official beginning of the Games. Athletes and people the world over cheered, and many choked back tears at the sight of Muhammad Ali lighting the flame with his right hand as his left arm trembled from Parkinson's syndrome. After the ceremony, President Bill Clinton admitted to Ali that he had cried as Ali lit the cauldron.

In February 1997 at the fifth annual ESPY Awards, Sidney Poitier presented the Arthur Ashe Award for Courage to Ali. At the ceremony, when asked which moment in his life had most tested his courage, Ali responded, "Resisting Vietnam," which resulted in the loss of his heavyweight title.

During the tenth annual Essence Awards in May 1997, Bryant Gumbel presented Ali with the first Essence Living Legend Award. In making the presentation, Gumbel said, "More than just a great boxer, Muhammad Ali is a great human being, an icon of black pride, a global ambassador of peace, and today as he battles Parkinson's syndrome, a symbol of courage."

In the sport of boxing few champions have stood the test of time like Ali. As a fighter he brought the sport to new heights through his promotional tactics, his playful poetry, and his grandiose style. Ali displayed incredible boxing skills throughout his career, dazzling crowds with his ballet-like grace and his flashy "Ali Shuffle." He continues to stop crowds wherever he appears. Ali, the extrovert, was always accessible and open to the news media and the public. Since Ali retired, each fighter who has fought for the heavyweight championship title has invariably been compared to him, yet no one has been able to measure up to his wit, charm, personal appeal, or staying power as the champion. Muhammad Ali is truly one of the greatest boxers of all times, and for his courage and charity, a great humanitarian.—KAREN COTTON MCDANIEL

MARIAN **ANDERSON**

1897–1993

Opera singer, humanitarian

Marian Anderson rose from inauspicious beginnings to become one of the twentieth century's most celebrated singers. In 1991 Ebony *magazine called Anderson "the standard bearer for grace and elegance among Black singers, and many White singers as well." The contralto—who first sang in her church choir— astonished audiences around the world and in doing so became a symbol of the struggle to overcome discrimination in the arts. Furthermore, she never compromised her identity: she included beloved black*

spirituals among the traditional pieces of her repertoire.

Anderson, the first of three daughters of John Berkeley Anderson and Anna D. Anderson, was born in Philadelphia, Pennsylvania, on February 27, circa 1897. Anderson began singing at the Union Baptist Church, joining the senior choir by age thirteen, and she became known as the "baby contralto." Anderson further developed her voice during her high school years, when she took lessons from soprano Mary Saunders Patterson, joined the Philadelphia Choral Society, and embarked on a schedule of singing at nearby churches and schools that often meant missing classes. G. Grant Williams, editor of the *Philadelphia Tribune,* became her first manager. She continued voice study with Patterson while beginning to learn from Agnes Reifsnyder, a contralto, who helped develop Anderson's medium and low tones. Meanwhile, another well-respected instructor, Giuseppe Boghetti, also accepted her as a student. Boghetti remained her voice teacher for many years and continued as her musical advisor until his death.

Anderson graduated from South Philadelphia High School for Girls in 1921, and by 1924 she felt competent enough to make a New York concert debut. She sang to a very small audience at Town Hall in what she considered a major career fiasco. She sang lieder, and the critics' comments about her German so depressed her that she stopped studying music and put aside any hope for a musical career. Although this was not the first time her lack of extensive language study was mentioned, it was the most devastating. Anderson had studied French in high school, was tutored in French in Boghetti's studio, and was also coached in French songs by Leon Rothier in New York City. She learned Italian from Boghetti as well, and was urged by many to go to Europe to study and develop language proficiency.

Eventually Anderson returned to music, and by 1928 Anderson had saved enough money to go to England, intent on studying German lieder with Raimund von Zur Mühlen. She was also given the address of Roger Quilter, the English composer who had befriended Roland Hayes and other black musicians. She had only two lessons with the aged and ill von Zur Mühlen, but she did study with a student of his, Mark Raphael. She also sang for guests of Quilter and made her English debut at Wigmore Hall on September 16, 1930. A Rosenwald Fellowship allowed her to study in Berlin, where she lived with a German family in order to absorb and master the German language. She studied music for a short period with Sverre Joran and had more extensive coaching with Michael Raucheisen.

Berlin concert brings critical acclaim   Anderson's concert in the Bach Saal in Berlin in October of 1930 brought her critical acclaim. She embarked on an extensive European career,

Marian Anderson.

making occasional returns to the United States, and she received a second Rosenwald grant in 1933. She credits Kosti Vehanen, her new accompanist, for her extended repertoire and her career advancement. She sang more than 108 concerts in a twelve-month period in the Scandinavian countries, learning songs in Swedish, Norwegian, and Finnish. She visited the home of Sibelius and sang for him, and he dedicated his composition "Solitude" to her.

Anderson continued to study in Europe—French repertoire with Germaine de Castro and Mahler songs with Madame Charles Cahier (Sara Jane Layton-Walker), who had studied with Mahler. Her programs now showed works by the composers Handel, Scarlatti, Pergolesi, Strauss, Brahms, Schubert, Schuman, Dvorak, Rimsky-Korsakov, and Rachmaninoff. Audiences all over the world, including those in the Soviet Union, called for her to sing or repeat Schubert's "Ave Maria." Always a part of her concerts were spirituals. She usually sang those as arranged by her friend Harry Burleigh, but she also sang and recorded the spirituals of Lawrence Brown, Hall Johnson, Roland Hayes, R. Nathaniel Dett, and Florence Price.

At Salzburg in 1935, Arturo Toscanini made his often repeated remark regarding Anderson: "Arturo Toscanini told Mme Cahier, 'What I heard today one is privileged to hear only in a hundred years.' He did not say the voice he heard, but *what* he heard—not the voice alone but the whole art."

At a concert at the Salle Gaveau in Paris, the impresario Sol Hurok heard Anderson, introduced himself, and told her he wished to become her manager. On December 31, 1935, Anderson's career under Hurok Management began with a critically acclaimed concert at Town Hall in New York City, followed by a January 1936 concert at Carnegie Hall. Under Hurok, Anderson began a most intensive and extensive concert career. Vehanen retired as her accompanist in 1941; Franz Rupp became her accompanist from 1941 through her final farewell concert in 1965.

DAR actions stir controversy   Events of February 1939 catapulted this serene and dedicated artist from the music review pages of newspapers to front-page stories. The refusal of the Daughters of the American Revolution (DAR) to schedule Anderson in concert in their Constitution Hall captured the most headlines. Howard University, the original sponsor of the Anderson concert, was caught in the furor of the DAR refusal, which led to the resignation of Eleanor Roosevelt from the DAR, and the subsequent Lincoln Memorial concert on April 9, 1939. This was a free concert given through the auspices of Harold Ickes, the Secretary of the Interior. The audience, estimated at seventy-five thousand, included congressmen, Supreme Court justices, and ordinary citizens.

In July 1939 Eleanor Roosevelt was selected to present the NAACP's Spingarn Medal to Anderson. Additional recognition came to Anderson when she received the ten-thousand-dollar Bok Award in March of 1941. This award, created by Philadelphian Edward Bok in 1921, was designated for an individual making a contribution to Philadelphia and the surrounding community. Anderson used the funds to establish a scholarship award for young singers.

On July 24, 1943, at Bethel Methodist Church in Bethel, Connecticut, Anderson married Orpheus Hodge Fisher, a New York architect. Rumors of their impending marriage had surfaced over the years. "King," as she called him, was the boyfriend of her youth. She met him in Wilmington, Delaware, when they were both in high school; Anderson sang at a benefit concert and attended a reception at the Fisher home afterwards. The newlyweds purchased a farm in Danbury, Connecticut, and King designed and helped build their home. There

Anderson had her music studio and engaged in her hobbies of photography, playing jazz piano, collecting jazz recordings, sewing, and upholstery.

Anderson's extraordinarily busy concert schedule continued in the 1940s with additional concerts for servicemen and for bond drives. One such concert was given at Constitution Hall in December 1942. She requested that on this occasion the audience not be separated in the usual racial seating; the DAR would not agree to this stipulation. In the end, Anderson chose to sing in the interest of the benefit for the Army Emergency Relief Fund.

Anderson debuts at Metropolitan Opera   In September 1954 an extraordinary event occurred which, as with other events in Anderson's life, had implications in the broader musical world for other black singers. Langston Hughes wrote of this as "a precedent-shattering moment in American musical history." She was asked by Rudolph Bing, general manager of the Metropolitan Opera, to join the Metropolitan Opera in the role of Ulrica in Verdi's *Un Ballo in Maschera*. Anderson's 1955 debut at the Metropolitan Opera at the age of 58 was of such significance in the history of American race relations that it was given a front-page story the next morning in the *New York Times* with a picture of Anderson and her mother taken after the performance. Critics have often written about Anderson's age and voice at this debut; few have commented on Bing's astute casting of her in the role of Ulrica, the sorceress/fortune-teller who need not have a youthful voice.

In her only operatic run, Anderson sang with the Metropolitan Opera for seven performances, including a performance in her home city at the Philadelphia Academy of Music. After *Un Ballo in Maschera* Anderson resumed touring, embarking in September of 1957 on a ten-week tour of south Asia and the Far East sponsored by the U.S. Department of State. This tour was filmed by the television crew of the CBS television program "See It Now" as the "Lady from Philadelphia."

Anderson's farewell tour began in 1964 at Constitution Hall in Washington, D.C., and ended with a concert at Carnegie Hall on Easter Sunday in 1965. After this extensive tour, in which she revisited cities of her many recitals over the years, Anderson generally lived in retirement on Marianna Farm in Danbury.

After her retirement Anderson sang in Paris at the Sainte Chappelle and on behalf of the First World Festival of Negro Arts, which was held at Dakar, Senegal, in 1966. She also appeared as narrator on several occasions with various orchestras in Aaron Copland's *Lincoln Portrait*. In 1977 a seventy-fifth birthday gala concert was sponsored by Young Artists Presents with performers including Clamma Dale, Mignon Dunn, Shirley Verrett, James Levine, and others. In 1982 an eightieth birthday concert in Anderson's honor was given at Carnegie Hall with Verrett and Grace Bumbry.

Anderson was honored by the Danbury community and many others in a gala concert that served to establish a Marian Anderson Award, reestablishing the award she started in 1941 with the ten-thousand-dollar Bok Award. Musicians performing at this gala included Jessye Norman and Isaac Stern, with Julius Rudel conducting the Ives Symphony Orchestra.

Recordings by Anderson span four decades—from the acoustic recordings of the mid-1920s to the long-playing album of Brahms and Schubert lieder that was recorded at Webster Hall in New York City in 1966 and released by RCA in 1978. Several recent recordings are compact disc reissues of earlier works.

*Marian
Anderson.*

Anderson died in 1993 at the age of ninety-six. She won many awards and accolades, including the first Kennedy Center Honors in 1978 and the National Medal of Arts in 1986. She was also the first recipient of the Presidential Medal of Freedom. In 1997, Carnegie Hall paid tribute to Anderson with a 100th anniversary celebration to a woman who paved the way for many blacks to contribute their genius to the perfoming arts. Marian Anderson was truly an American symbol with a beautiful singing voice who prompted opera fans, black and white, to listen in awe.—PATRICIA TURNER

MAYA **ANGELOU**
1928–
Writer, poet

Any biography of Maya Angelou must necessarily rely on Angelou's own account of her colorful life. To date Angelou has written five volumes of a serial autobiography: I Know Why the Caged Bird Sings, Gather Together in My Name, Singin' and Swingin' and Gettin' Merry Like Christmas, The Heart of a Woman, *and* All God's Children Need Traveling Shoes. *She has also written several volumes of poetry, and at various times in her life she's been a dancer, actress, scriptwriter, director, producer, songwriter, and editor. She currently holds an endowed chair as Reynolds Professor of American Studies at Wake Forest University in Winston-Salem, North Carolina.*

Maya Angelou was born Marguerite Johnson on April 4, 1928, in Saint Louis, Missouri. When she was three, she and her four-year-old brother, Bailey Jr., were sent on a train by their divorced parents, Bailey and Vivian (Baxter) Johnson, to live in Stamps, Arkansas, with their paternal grandmother. "Momma" Henderson, as they called her, supported her family on meager proceeds from her general store, and she taught Angelou "common sense, practicality and the ability to control one's own destiny that comes from constant hard work and courage." Although living during the Depression years in the South was a struggle for blacks, Angelou found love and the sense of the black tradition there, primarily from her grandmother and the local church.

When Angelou was seven she spent eight months with her mother in Saint Louis. There Angelou's trust in the adult world crumbled: her mother's boyfriend, Mr. Freeman, raped her. After an initial close encounter with Freeman, she says that she thought "he held me so softly that I wished he wouldn't ever let me go. I felt at home. From the way he was holding me I knew he'd never let me go or let anything bad ever happen to me. This was probably my real father and we had found each other at last. But then he rolled over leaving me in a wet place, and stood up."

Rape prompts a vow of silence   On a subsequent encounter, when he did rape her, Angelou was confused and felt increasingly guilty, especially at Freeman's trial. When Freeman was kicked to death, Angelou, feeling responsible for his murder, entered a self-imposed world of silence that lasted five years. Annoyed by her daughter's stony silence, Vivian Baxter sent Angelou back to Stamps. However, just as an adult had forced Angelou to retreat into a world of silence, so an adult, Bertha Flowers, another role model, helped to draw Angelou out again. According to critic Dolly McPherson, "Mrs. Flowers throws Maya her 'first life line' by accepting her as an individual not in relation to another person." Angelou's grandmother remained equally supportive, but shortly after Angelou's graduation from eighth grade, at the top of her class, she and Bailey left the security of her home to live with their mother in San Francisco.

Vivian Baxter, now a professional gambler, introduced Angelou to a world vastly different from Stamps. While attending George Washington High School and taking drama and dance lessons on scholarship at the California Labor School, Angelou met a variety of people at her mother's rooming house. From her mother, stepfather, and boarders, Angelou learned everything from etiquette to card-playing. A serious and permanent testing of her emerging adulthood was her unplanned pregnancy and motherhood at age sixteen. Angelou ends *Caged Bird* with the birth of her son, Guy, because "I wanted to end it on a happy note. It was the best thing that ever happened to me."

Motherhood as well as the growing need for independence from her own mother prompted Angelou to move from her mother's home. Angelou first tried to get a job as a telephone operator, then tried to enlist in the WACS, and she finally accepted a position as a cook in a Creole restaurant even though she knew nothing about Creole cooking. A subsequent job as a nightclub waitress in San Diego inadvertently plunged Angelou briefly into the world of prostitution; for a short while, she "managed" two lesbian lovers. Angelou states:

*A young
Maya Angelou.*

> At eighteen I had managed in a few tense years to become a snob at all levels, racial, cultural and intellectual. I was a madam and thought myself morally superior to the whores. I was a waitress and believed myself cleverer than the customers I served. I was a lonely unmarried mother and held myself to be freer than the married women I met.

At age twenty-two Angelou married a white man, Tosh Angelos. The two-and-a-half-year marriage failed because of Angelou's insistent need for freedom from a constricting life, and Angelou began a career as a dancer in a bar. Soon performers from the well-known Purple Onion offered Angelou a job dancing at that establishment—a move that became a turning point in Angelou's halting career. It also modified her view of the white world: "There whites were treating me as an equal, as if I could do whatever they could do. They did not consider that race, height, gender or lack of education might have crippled me."

Angelou got more opportunities to develop as an entertainer, and in 1954–55 she toured Europe and Africa in *Porgy and Bess*. Around this time, Angelou adopted her present name, derived from her brother's nickname for her and a variation of her first husband's surname, Angelos. McPherson describes this time in Angelou's life as one of liberation, "the triumphal blooming of a talented, determined young Black woman into the adult self and into a fully liberated woman."

Angelou becomes social activist   Returning to the United States after the tour, Angelou resumed her career as a nightclub performer. During this time, she also became a social activist and with comedian Godfrey Cambridge co-wrote a revue, "Cabaret for Freedom," a benefit for Martin Luther King's Southern Christian Leadership Conference. Recognizing her commitment to the civil rights cause, King asked her to serve as northern coordinator for the SCLC from 1960 to 1961.

By this time, according to Lynn Z. Bloom, "Angelou had made a commitment to become a writer." She was introduced to the Harlem Writers Guild by social activist/author John Killens. Undoubtedly her close association with such noted authors as James Baldwin, Paule Marshall, and John Henrik Clarke inspired Angelou.

In late 1961, Angelou left the United States with her son and Vusumzi Make, a South African freedom fighter, who persuaded her to accompany him to Cairo, Egypt, saying that their union would be "the joining of Africa and Africa-America." Angelou never married Make, though they lived together for several years. Because of Make's poor financial management, Angelou did the unheard of—she sought employment as an editor of the *Arab Observer,* a move that infuriated Make. Their disagreement over her new independence as well as his adultery confirmed Angelou's decision to leave Make and move to Ghana. Although she had not planned to stay there long, her son Guy's automobile accident in Ghana changed her mind. In *All God's Children Need Traveling Shoes* Angelou connects Ghana with her past in Arkansas and California:

> Their skins were the colors of my childhood cravings: peanut butter, licorice, chocolate, caramel. There was the laughter of home, quick and without artifice. The erect and graceful walk of the women reminded me of my Arkansas Grandmother, Sunday-hatted, on her way to church. I listened to men talk, and whether or not I understood their meaning, there was a melody as familiar as sweet potato pie, reminding me of my Uncle Tommy Baxter in Santa Monica, California.

However, Angelou was never completely accepted by native Africans, who regarded her, despite her African heritage, as an outsider. While in Ghana, Angelou served as a feature editor of the *African Review* in Accra, wrote articles for the *Ghanian Times* and Accra's Ghanaian Broadcasting Corporation, and taught at the University of Ghana.

Since her return from Ghana, Angelou has demonstrated her versatile talent in several areas. In 1966 she had a part in Jean Anouilh's *Medea,* produced in Hollywood, and she wrote and acted in plays nationwide. She also was busy writing songs and a television series, and in 1972 Angelou became the first black woman to have a screenplay, *Georgia, Georgia,* produced. Five years later Angelou's performance in the television production of Alex Haley's *Roots* earned her an Emmy nomination, and in 1979 her first autobiography, *I Know Why the Caged Bird Sings,* was made into a television movie, for which Angelou wrote the script and music. In the national arena, the versatile Angelou was appointed by President Gerald Ford to the Bicentennial Commission and by President Jimmy Carter to the Commission of International Woman's Year. Since 1981, Angelou has held the lifetime appointment position as Reynolds Professor of American Studies at Wake Forest University in Winston-Salem, North Carolina.

Angelou distinguishes "truth" from "facts"   Angelou has also published several volumes of poetry about issues in the black experience and in society as a whole, including *Just Give Me a Cool Drink of Water 'fore I Diiie, And Still I Rise,* and *I Shall Not Be Moved.* Most critics agree that Angelou's outstanding works are *I Know Why the Caged Bird Sings* (nominated for the National Book Award in 1974) and *The Heart of a Woman.* Critics find

Maya Angelou reads "On the Pulse of Morning"
during Bill Clinton's presidential inauguration, 1993.

that Angelou, in her autobiographies, "mixes fact with fantasy." However, in a 1989 interview, Angelou states that in telling her life, she tells the "truth" as distinguished from "facts": "There's a world of difference between truth and facts. Facts can obscure the truth. You can tell so many facts that you fill the stage but haven't got one iota of truth."

Most critics assess Angelou's autobiographies as a significant contribution to American literature of the self and to black American literature in particular. Placing the autobiographies firmly within the tradition of such black autobiographies as those of Frederick Douglass, Anne Moody, Richard Wright, and Malcolm X, critics appreciate Angelou's growing awareness of the environment and of the self within that environment. Eugenia Collier notes another achievement of the autobiographies:

> The pervasive theme, naturally developed in all the autobiographies, is the
> strength of the Black woman, her ability to prevail despite the awful hurting

put upon her by the world, even by her own Black man, who often assuages his own hurt by further oppressing her. Yet there is no blatant preaching, no anti-male rhetoric.

Angelou's writings and speeches, which stress the hope of children, have drawn a wide range of fans. Such devoted enthusiasts include Oprah Winfrey and President Bill Clinton, who invited Angelou to deliver a poem at his inauguration in 1993. The poem was heard by millions and electrified the audiences. The poem, "On the Pulse of Morning," was published in a hardcover collection of Angelou's poetry.

Angelou, with her booming laughter and deep rythmic voice, has been a symbol of strength and leadership for the plight of women and the underprivileged. She was named keynote speaker for the Chicago Foundation for Women in 1994. In September of 1996, Angelou and Camille Cosby joined to help African American women chart new directions in their lives with a $30 million fund-raising campaign for the National Council of Negro Women.

Because of her moving literary works and devotion to the power of expression, Angelou has been awarded the NAACP's Spingarn Award and the first Medal of Distinction from the University of Hawaii Board of Regents.

Maya Angelou continues to journey through and record her life truthfully and eloquently—an accomplishment that has led to her universal appeal and admiration.— GRACE E. COLLINS

ARTHUR **ASHE**
1943–1993
Athlete, activist

The dust jacket for his memoir Days of Grace accurately portrays the man the world knew, calling Ashe the embodiment "of courage and grace in every aspect of his life, from his triumphs as a great tennis champion and his determined social activism to his ordeal in the face of death." Internationally known and respected as an athlete, Ashe was the first black man named to the American Davis Cup team, the first black on the U.S. Junior Davis Cup team, the first black man to win a major tennis title—the national men's singles in the U.S. Lawn Tennis Association—and the first black man to win singles titles at Wimbledon. He won three of the four Grand Slam tournaments, the pillars of international professional tennis—the United States Open, the Australian Open, and Wimbledon—and shared the fourth Grand Slam event, the French Open.

Born in Richmond, Virginia, on June 10, 1943, Arthur Robert Ashe, Jr. had a mixed ethnic background consisting of black American, American Indian, and Mexican ancestry. His father, Arthur Robert Ashe, Sr., was guardian and caretaker of a large, segregated city park for blacks in Richmond and owned a landscaping business as well. His mother, Mattie Cordell Cunningham Ashe, died when Ashe was nearly seven years old, then a housekeeper was hired to help raise Ashe and his only sibling, a younger brother, John. As he grew older,

Ashe had a problem understanding himself and the loss of his mother and briefly sought counseling.

As Ashe grew up in the caretaker's cottage in Brookfield Park where his father worked, he began to play tennis when he was only seven years old. Part-time playground instructor Ronald Charity observed his talent and arranged for him to meet Walter Johnson, a black physician in Lynchburg, Virginia, who for more than two decades had been a patron for talented black tennis players. He kept the players in his home, provided the equipment they needed, and trained them on the court that adjoined his house. Up to that time, Wimbledon champion Althea Gibson was Johnson's most celebrated student.

Ashe started winning tournaments in 1955 with the American Tennis Association's

Arthur Ashe at Wimbledon, 1975.

twelve-and-under singles match. He won other tournaments in 1956 and 1957. Johnson entered Ashe in the junior national tennis championship in 1958, when Ashe was fourteen, and he became a semifinalist in the under-fifteen division. In 1960 and again in 1961 he won the junior tennis indoor singles title. Then he received an offer from Richard Hudlin, a St. Louis tennis official, who offered to coach him. Ashe accepted and left Maggie Walker High School in Richmond during his junior year to move to St. Louis. He lived with Hudlin and his family while he completed secondary school training at Sumner High School with virtually a straight-A average.

In St. Louis and under Hudlin's tutelage, Ashe's tennis game continued to improve. He became the fifth-ranked junior player in the United States in 1962. After graduation, he accepted a tennis scholarship to study at the University of California at Los Angeles (UCLA), where he received a bachelor's degree in business administration in June 1966. The university's tennis coach, J. D. Morgan, and Pancho Gonzales, who lived near the campus, were his trainers. In 1963 Ashe was ranked eighteenth in the senior men's amateur division, then was named to the Davis Cup team. Over the next fifteen years he played thirty-two Davis Cup matches and won twenty-seven. He also won the Eastern Grass Court matches in August 1964 and a month later the Perth Amboy Invitational in New Jersey. He was sixth in the national rankings for amateurs.

Until 1965, Ashe had won no major titles and among amateurs was ranked third in the nation. That year, however, he played in the United States national tennis championship at Forest Hills, New York, and in four sets beat Roy Emerson, who had won the nationals in 1961 and 1964. He received a fifteen-minute standing ovation from the eleven thousand spectators in the West Side Tennis Club. He won two singles matches in the 1965 Davis Cup American Zone finals against Mexico.

In 1966 he spent six weeks with the Reserve Officers' Training Corps serving as a first lieutenant, and from 1967 to 1969 he was a lieutenant in the U.S. Army. His tennis game continued during this time, as did his winnings. In 1967 he won the Men's Clay Court championship; when he also won the United States amateur championship that year he was invited to the U.S. Open Tournament. Winning that championship as well, in 1968 he became the nation's top-ranked player.

Wins Wimbledon Singles   Ashe turned professional in 1969 and played in a number of matches. In 1975 he beat Jimmy Connors and became the first black man to win the Wimbledon Singles and the first black ranked number one internationally. That year he also won the World Championship Singles over Bjorn Borg. In 1978, his career faced a sudden change.

After suffering a heart attack in mid-summer of 1979, Ashe underwent a quadruple coronary bypass operation in St. Luke's–Roosevelt Hospital in Manhattan on December 13 of that year. He was only thirty-six. Ashe thought that he was completely recovered three months later, but on March 9, 1980, he learned that his life would never be the same. Angina struck while he was in Cairo; he had to end his career as a competitive tennis player, becoming a professional patient instead. He underwent a double bypass heart operation at St. Luke's on June 21, 1983, and, due to tough scar tissue from his first surgery, he was in worse condition this time. Feeling weak and anemic, he decided to receive two units of blood. Ashe wrote in *Days of Grace*: "This transfusion indeed picked me up and sent me on the road to recovery from surgery; it also . . . set in motion my descent into AIDS."

Ashe retired from tennis in April 1980. Although Ashe played his last Davis Cup Match in 1978, between 1980 and 1985 he was captain of the United States Davis Cup Team. This was a significant period in the Cup's history, since its national and international prestige was beginning to wane. Ashe's captaincy of the Davis Cup gave him continued public exposure in sports magazines and elsewhere. He resigned the position in October 1985 but remained loyal to the Davis Cup competition by serving as vice-chair of the cup committee.

Active in protest and politics   Since the 1970s Ashe had been adamant in his opposition to apartheid in South Africa. He remembered the segregated Richmond, Virginia, of his childhood and the civil rights protests of the 1960s. He was aware of the different world in which he played tennis. "You never forget that you are a Negro, and you certainly can't in my case," he told Frank Deford for *Sports Illustrated*, quoted in *Current Biography*. He also resented the "whites only" signs that he saw in Johannesburg, South Africa. Although he had visited the country four times between 1973, when he played in the South African Open, and 1977 and played other matches there, he insisted that there be no segregated seating at his matches. He consciously made South Africa the focal point of his political activities within and beyond the United States. He admits in his memoirs that he played a major role in having the country banned from Davis Cup Play.

Ashe wrote in his memoirs that "My Davis Cup campaigns, my protests against apartheid in South Africa, and my skirmishes over academic requirements for athletes were doubtless the most highly publicized episodes of my life in the 1980s after my retirement." In the 1980s Ashe worked quietly as a lobbyist for higher academic standards for athletes in colleges as addressed by Proposition 42 and Proposition 48, implemented in 1984 by the National Collegiate Athletic Association (NCAA). Clearly the 1980s were a period of protest and politics for Ashe. He protested apartheid by serving as cochair of the TransAfrica Forum, which raised funds for TransAfrica, a think tank and lobby for African and Caribbean affairs founded by his childhood friend Randall Robinson. He also became a founding member of Artists and Athletes Against Apartheid and cochaired the committee with Harry Belafonte. Among the group's goals were to bring pressure on South Africa and to dissuade athletes and entertainers from performing there.

On January 11, 1985, he was arrested outside the South African Embassy in Washington, D.C., for taking part in a demonstration against South Africa because of its apartheid policies and practices. He wrote in his memoirs that "the experience of being handcuffed, carted away, and booked was daunting. I also knew that, in certain circles, my arrest could cost me some influence and prestige."

Ashe lived long enough to see social and political changes in South Africa. His last trip to South Africa was in 1991 with a delegation of African Americans that Nelson Mandela, whom he admired, had invited. Mandela was also a sports enthusiast. By the time Mandela and Ashe met again, Ashe had announced to the world that he had AIDS; the two spoke openly and freely about AIDS and efforts to fight it in America and Africa.

After retiring from tennis, Ashe devoted his time to public speaking, teaching, writing, business affairs, and voluntary services. In his memoirs Ashe said that his work as board member of the Aetna Life and Casualty Company, which he had served for ten years, was his "single most fascinating and satisfying involvement outside my family." This was due largely to the company's concern for health care—in the absence of a national health care program—and its fair treatment of minorities.

He began to receive invitations to teach college courses. He turned down Yale for Florida Memorial College, a historically black college in Miami with an enrollment of twelve hundred. There he taught a seminar on "The Black Athlete in Contemporary Society." He also was inspired to do a serious study of African Americans in sports and publish the findings. As he prepared his course syllabus he found the literature of blacks in sports seriously wanting. At the same time, blacks had been leading athletes in such sports as boxing, baseball, football, basketball, and track, and he knew that their story needed to be told. Using his own funds, he hired a team of researchers and writers for a comprehensive work, eventually spending about $300,000. Few primary sources existed, yet the team consulted old issues of college yearbooks and black newspapers, interviewed parents, called for a search of medals and mementos to help reconstruct the past, and appealed to the public through the media for further information. From interviews with various historians Ashe determined that the subject of the black athlete had been neglected due to "academic snobbery and timidity." Although their interest in sports was widespread, writing about it was beneath the notice of serious historians, and publishers were unwilling to subsidize research in the field. The results of Ashe's study were published as *A Hard Road to Glory: A History of the African American Athlete*, in three volumes, covering the period from 1619 to 1985 (Warner Books, 1988).

"The Beast in the Jungle"   The last chapter of Ashe's life, when he learned that he had AIDS, is discussed candidly in his memoirs as "The Beast in the Jungle." He had encountered four operations in his lifetime: a heel surgery in 1977, a quadruple bypass in December 1979, corrective double bypass in June 1983, and brain surgery in September 1988. The brain surgery revealed that he did not have a brain tumor, but had an infection instead. The following day he and his wife Jeanne learned of his HIV infection and that he had full-blown AIDS. After searching for the roots of his infection, Ashe learned that his blood transfusion following surgery in 1983 was the cause of his problem. He wrote in his memoirs that people often committed suicide because of despair caused by HIV infection and that "the news that I had AIDS hit me hard but did not knock me down." He refused to surrender to depression or to consider suicide. "AIDS does not make me despair," he continued, "but unquestionably it often makes me somber."

The possibility of a published report in *USA Today* on his health prompted him to reveal to the world on April 8, 1992, that he had AIDS.

In time, Ashe stepped up his speaking engagements and lectured at such institutions as McGill in Canada, Duquesne, Brown, the University of Virginia, and elsewhere, answering students' questions about AIDS and his own struggle. Secretary-General Boutros Boutros-Ghali invited Ashe to address the United Nations on World AIDS Day. Quoted in his memoirs, he told the audience, "It has been the habit of humankind to wait until the eleventh hour to spiritually commit ourselves to those problems which we knew all along to be of the greatest urgency." Ashe also spoke to a wide range of professional groups, such as the National Press Club, public school teachers, employees of drug companies, business people, and journalists on issues of privacy and freedom of the press.

In the face of his illness, Ashe and his wife found solace in the teachings and writings of black theologian Howard Thurman. Thurman's teachings in particular helped Ashe to keep control despite the changes that occurred in his life. Ashe stated that he also had a steadfast faith in God.

In retirement Ashe wrote columns for the *Washington Post* and served as a commentator for tennis matches. He worked in a variety of social programs and foundations that he either started or helped to start, such as the Ashe-Bollettieri Cities program which used tennis to hold the attention of youth in inner cities and poor environments; Athletes Career Connection, which addressed the high attrition rate of black athletes in football and basketball at Division One schools; and the Safe Passage Foundation, to help poor young people, especially blacks, to make a healthy transition from youth to adulthood. After learning that he had AIDS, Ashe founded the Arthur Ashe Foundation for the Defeat of AIDS, to fight and help conquer the infection; and the African American Athletic Association to counsel and advise young black athletes, especially student athletes, and help to address their academic performance.

In summer 1985 he was inducted into the International Tennis Hall of Fame at Newport, Rhode Island, as soon as he was eligible—five years after retirement. His other writings included *Off the Court* (1981), which he dedicated to one of his ancestors who had been a slave. This was his means of expressing pride in his roots, which were deep in the black past. He also wrote *Arthur Ashe on Tennis Strokes, Strategy, Traditions, Players, Psychology, and Wisdom*, with Alexander McNab (published in 1995 after his death). His memoir *Days of Grace*, coauthored with Arnold Rampersand, was nearly completed before his death.

During his lifetime Ashe was widely recognized, with some of his honors coming from academic institutions. He received a number of honorary degrees from such institutions as Princeton, Kalamazoo College, Loyola College of Baltimore, and Virginia Commonwealth University. He was committed to education and had a high regard for historically black colleges; he demonstrated his commitment by becoming a veteran supporter of the United Negro College Fund. President Bill Clinton awarded him the Presidential Medal of Freedom posthumously in June 1993, at the first annual National Sports Award presentation held in Washington, D.C.

The six foot, one inch tall Ashe was a devoted family man; he wrote in his memoir that family was "the central social unit." His letter to daughter Camera, published in his memoir, speaks to her about family roots, race, languages, health, music, and art. Ashe died of pneumonia on Saturday afternoon, February 6, 1993, in New York Hospital–Cornell Medical Center in Manhattan, and was buried the following Wednesday in Woodland

Arthur Ashe.

Cemetery in Richmond, Virginia. He was survived by his wife, Jean Moutoussamy Ashe, whom he married on February 20, 1977, and who is a professional photographer, and their daughter, Camera. A twelve-foot bronze monument commemorating his achievements was unveiled near monuments of several Confederate leaders on Monument Avenue in his hometown, Richmond, on July 10, 1996. The monument drew bitter opposition from some whites who believed the street should be reserved for leaders of the Confederacy. Inscribed on the monument is a Biblical passage that is also quoted in Ashe's autobiography: "Since we are surrounded by so great a cloud of witnesses, let us lay aside every weight, and the sin which easily ensnares us, and let us run with endurance the race that is set before us." It is possible that the statue will be moved in front of the proposed African American Sports Hall of Fame when the building is completed. In his honor as well, the U.S. Tennis Association named its new stadium for the U.S. Open National Tennis Center at Flushing Meadows–Corona Park in Queens, New York, the Arthur Ashe Stadium.

Arthur Ashe, who won widespread admiration and who had achieved greatness as a world-class tennis player, also spent his career protesting racial injustices in sports and called for equal opportunity in all athletic activities.—JESSIE CARNEY SMITH

JOSEPHINE **BAKER**
1906–1975
Dancer, entertainer

Flamboyant and colorful on and off the stage, controversial, erratic, difficult, eccentric, and domineering, Josephine Baker was a singer, entertainer, dancer, French spy, and a woman who tried to create a utopian community in a world that doesn't allow such impracticalities. Baker was a consummate and working entertainer until the day of her death, a vigorous spokesperson for causes she believed in, and a brave woman who tried, but didn't always succeed, to make her dreams come true. An "icon of the Jazz Age," as biographer Phyllis Rose calls her, Baker was the first black woman to become an international star.

Baker was born in Saint Louis, Missouri, on June 3, 1906. Her mother, who worked as a domestic, was Carrie McDonald, and she was not married to Baker's father, Eddie Carson, a local musician who played the drums. Abandoned by her real father and living with a stepfather who was prone to violence and abuse, Baker developed a mistrust of men and a feeling that she must rely on herself. Her mother's temperament added little to the stability of the family, who lived in extreme poverty, moving often and struggling for survival. The law at that time permitted children of eight years old to perform domestic work, providing they also attended school, so Baker went to work at that age. She had the misfortune of encountering an abusive employer in her first job, which ended when the woman plunged the child's arm into a pot of boiling water.

Before she was fourteen, Baker had run away from home, found a job supporting herself by waiting on tables, and married and discarded a husband, Willie Wells. (She would marry several more times during her lifetime.) Her pregnancy by Wells ended either by early miscarriage or by abortion. Strongly attracted to show business, she then joined a street band that was eventually incorporated into the Dixie Fliers, a traveling show that featured Clara Smith. Baker worked as a dresser for Smith and developed her skills as a dancer. When the troupe reached Philadelphia, she met and married William Howard Baker in 1921, much to his family's dismay.

Baker was turned down for the original production of Sissle and Blake's *Shuffle Along* because she was not yet sixteen, the minimum age to work in New York theaters. She managed to get a job in the road company, however, and eventually found a place in Sissle and Blake's new production, *Chocolate Dandies,* in 1924. When the show closed the next year, Baker found work at the Plantation Club. Caroline Dudley, a wealthy white Chicago woman with a passion for black shows, conceived the idea of taking authentic black performers to Paris. Dudley offered Baker a position, and after hesitating, she accepted. Originally, Baker was not the most important member of the troupe, but when she reached Paris the balance began to turn quickly. Paul Colin, who soon became her lover, selected Baker for the central figure of his poster for the *Revue Nègre* rather than the nominal star, Maude de Forest.

As rehearsals progressed, the producers became worried about the success of the show, and they persuaded Baker to dance nude. The *Revue Nègre* opened on October 2, 1925, at the Théâtre des Champs-Elysées. As Baker first appeared dancing the Charleston to "Yes, Sir, That's My Baby!" there were some hostile reactions from a small part of the audience scandalized by the "vulgarity" of the dancer, but Baker's nude dance with Joe Alex overwhelmed the spectators. Quickly, Josephine Baker became the rage of Paris.

Baker makes world tour   Baker embarked on a world tour in 1928. While traveling through Europe and South America, Baker also worked on her voice and her dancing, and by the time she returned to Paris in 1930, her performances demonstrated a genuine difference. The comic elements had disappeared; she struck many people as a much-changed performer, and not all people liked the change, seeing the toning down of her "vulgarity" as a loss of vigor.

Her performance for the revue *Paris Qui Remue* in 1930 represented a step upward in show business, since the Casino de Paris was considered to be a cut above the Folies Bergère. This advancement brought Baker into conflict with the aging but still-reigning queen of Paris music halls, Mistinguett; in one public confrontation the two women spat at each other. The song that became Baker's theme, performed at every subsequent appearance, was written for this show—"J'ai Deux Amours": "I have two loves, my country and Paris." As publicity for the show, she led a baby leopard about Paris on a leash. The leopard's collar was a diamond choker that was later sold for twenty-two thousand dollars when Baker was desperate for money.

The time had come to try to return to the United States. After considerable hesitation, Baker accepted an offer to appear in the 1936 *Ziegfeld Follies*. She knew she was in her homeland when the Saint Moritz hotel in New York City gave her and her companion, Giuseppe Abatino, a suite but asked her to use the back entrance to avoid offending the sensibilities of visiting southerners. She returned to France later that year to appear in the Folies Bergère.

Baker now fell deeply in love with Jean Lion. The son of moderately prosperous Jewish parents, he had entered the stock exchange at the age of eighteen and found that he had a flair for making money. Blond, very handsome, and athletic, he was now a millionaire several times over. He taught Baker to fly and proposed one day while they were in the air. They were married in the spring of 1937, and after the shock of the wedding the family accepted her. This marriage brought Baker French citizenship. She became pregnant but had an early miscarriage, and the incompatibility of each partner's goals in the marriage soon became evident. They separated, but the divorce did not take place until 1942. Baker hoped for some time for a reconciliation, which never took place. Her grief over the breakdown of her marriage did not prevent Baker from taking new lovers, and it was while she was traveling with Claude Meunier, whose family fortune came from chocolate, that she saw and rented a chateau, Les Milandes.

Baker recruited for French Resistance   Baker's opening in the Casino de Paris revue *Paris-Londres* in September 1939 coincided with the opening of World War II. In the late spring of 1940 she was recruited as a spy by Jacques Abtey. Baker was chosen because she was a persona grata at the Italian Embassy and because of the favorable remarks she had made about Mussolini during her appearances in Italy in 1935. When the German invasion of France came, she and Abtey joined the flight from Paris. They went first to Baker's chateau Les Milandes, then to Lisbon. They returned to Marseille in late 1940 and set up operations there. Barred from performing in German-occupied France, Baker arranged a revival of *La Créole*. She cut short the run of the operetta to go to Casablanca in January 1940. As a performer she had freedom to travel from there to Portugal through Spain. During this period she continued to function as a spy; thus, she was a member of the French Resistance from the very beginning. Her conduct earned her the Medal of the Resistance with rosette at the end of the war, and later she was awarded the Legion of Honor.

In December 1941 Baker delivered a stillborn child in a Casablanca clinic; the father is unknown. There were complications, and an emergency hysterectomy seemed the only way to save her life. Until June 1942, Baker's life was in serious danger from the resulting complications; at one point United Press International carried the news that she had died. Even in the hospital, she continued to serve the Resistance, since visiting her offered a convenient pretext for Resistance workers to meet and exchange messages. When the American Army landed in Morocco on November 8, 1942, Baker had recovered. She spent the time after the landing entertaining the Allied troops in North Africa.

Baker made a successful return trip to the United States in 1951. She attracted wide attention with her statements against segregation and her refusal to perform at segregated venues. Baker was the first African American performer to appear before integrated audiences in a Miami Beach hotel and the first to house her entire troupe in a Las Vegas hotel; she canceled engagements in such places as Atlanta and Saint Louis when her conditions were not met. On May 29 Harlem turned out to honor her on Josephine Baker Day, and the NAACP honored her as the Most Outstanding Woman of the Year.

Baker adopts Rainbow Tribe   Baker continued working outside the United States and began to transform Les Milandes into a tourist center, the showpiece of the ideal community she wished to show the world. Between 1954 and 1965 she adopted twelve children from different ethnic backgrounds and nationalities—ten boys and two girls, her Rainbow Tribe. After the success of the initial years, the efforts at Les Milandes began to unravel, due in large part to Baker's long absences performing and her management by caprice. Relations with the neighbors became very strained. Unable or unwilling to pay employees, she prompted them to feel entitled to steal items from the house. Between 1953 and 1963 Baker spent more than $1.5 million and was $400,000 in debt.

In August 1963 Baker returned to the United States to appear at the March on Washington. After finding a manager, she gave a benefit in New York on October 12 for the Student Nonviolent Coordinating Committee, the Congress of Racial Equality, and the NAACP. By this time it was not easy for her to find managers, since she had become notorious for refusing to pay them. Baker returned to Europe, where she had her first heart attack while performing in Denmark in 1964. Her financial affairs were becoming increasingly disordered, and she no longer automatically commanded the highest fees. Finally in the spring of 1969

Les Milandes was seized. Baker had to be carried out. For seven hours she sat barefoot, cap on head, crying on the back-door steps until an ambulance drove her to a local clinic, where she was treated for exhaustion. The subsequent sale of the chateau and what remained of its furnishings brought in very little money.

The late Grace Kelly, Princess Grace of Monaco, came to Baker's rescue by providing the down payment on a villa at Roquebrune, near the principality. The four bedrooms provided scant room for twelve children. Baker worked when she could; when she could not, she would from time to time wander the streets begging for her children. Without her fine clothes, makeup, and wig, she now appeared to be an old woman, but she retained the ability to appear glamorous and beautiful the moment she stepped onto the stage.

In the first part of 1973, Baker returned to the United States for a successful appearance at Carnegie Hall. Encouraged by her reception, she planned a seventeen-city tour beginning in the fall. In July while performing in Denmark, she had a second heart attack and a stroke that left her face partially paralyzed. In spite of her memory lapses, the United States tour went well until her Christmas season performances at the Palace flopped.

The Société des Bains de Mer, the company that runs the Monte Carlo casino, provided the last turn in Baker's career as a performer by sponsoring a show starring Baker, called *Joséphine,* in August 1974. This revue was so successful that the company took it to Paris. A large theater would not entertain the idea out of concerns for Baker's health, but a small music hall was located and rehearsals begun. In rehearsal, Baker was still able to summon up immense energy and pay close attention to detail. She was to be on stage almost continuously, sing many songs, and dance the Charleston. *Joséphine* officially opened on April 8, 1975, after several trial runs. Performances sold out many days in advance. That evening a gala was held at the Hotel Bristol to celebrate Baker's fifty years as a performer in Paris.

The following afternoon she did not wake up from her regular nap; she had suffered a massive cerebral hemorrhage and was in a coma. She died early in the morning of April 14, 1975. Her televised state funeral the following day at the Madeleine church drew twenty thousand people, and she is the only American woman to receive an official twenty-one gun salute from the French government. A quiet, private funeral service attended by her children was held in Monaco, and Josephine Baker of Saint Louis finally found a resting place in the cemetery of Monaco.

American interest in Baker was evident in the 1991 HBO Pictures production of *The Josephine Baker Story,* in which actress Lynn Whitfield won an Emmy portraying Baker, and in the recent re-release of the movies *Zou-Zou* and *Princesse Tam-Tam,* which played to capacity crowds during a screening at Manhattan's Film Forum. The captivating presence with which Baker won her audiences also created an obsession with one of her associates, Jean Claude Baker. He met Josephine in 1958 while he was a lonely bellhop in a French hotel. Although he never officially became one of her Rainbow Tribe, it was noted that Baker treated him like a son. Their relationship was tumultuous at the time, with Baker discarding him once her career had revived, but Jean Claude remained captivated. In a cathartic move to understand this complex woman he had loved and hated, Jean Claude wrote a searing, but honest and loving biography in 1994 titled *Josephine: The Hungry Heart.* Heroine to the French Resistance and staunch supporter of American civil rights, Josephine Baker is also considered an icon in music halls, cabarets, and films worldwide.—ROBERT L. JOHNS

ERNIE **BANKS**

1931–

Athlete, coach, businessman, philanthropist

Known as "Mr. Cub," Ernie Banks is one of the best-known and best-loved athletes in Chicago sports history, having played shortstop and first base for the Chicago Cubs from 1953 to 1971. He began his professional baseball career in 1950 with the Kansas City Monarchs of the Negro Leagues, after apprenticing for a couple of high school summers on a travel team called the Colts. As a player he was one of the foremost power hitters of his era, unusual at a time when the prototypical shortstop was a light-hitting defensive specialist. He also stood out for his boundless enthusiasm and love for the game. This attitude is displayed perfectly in his famous quote, "What a beautiful day! Let's play two!"

Ernest Banks was born in Dallas, Texas on January 31, 1931, one of eleven children of Eddie and Essie Banks. Ernie's father, a former semiprofessional baseball player, picked cotton, worked for the Works Projects Administration (WPA), and did construction to support his family during the Depression. He eventually secured more permanent work as a janitor. He also encouraged his reluctant son to pursue athletics. Ernie starred in basketball, football, track, and, of course, baseball at Booker T. Washington High School. During his summer tour with the barnstorming Amarillo Stars, he was scouted and signed by Cool Papa Bell for the Kansas City Monarchs of the Negro American League, where he reported after graduation in 1950.

A contemporary of Hank Aaron, Banks was part of the wave of players who participated in the waning years of the Negro Leagues. By 1948, the Negro National League had dissolved, while the American League would hang on until 1960, providing old timers with a few more precious seasons and youngsters like Banks, Aaron, and Willie Mays a chance to impress the white scouts who funneled talent to the white teams. By the mid-1950s the Negro League teams were serving as farm teams for Major League Baseball. While with the Monarchs, Banks served a two-year hitch in the Army, starting in 1951. While in the Army, he married his high school sweetheart, Mollye Louise Ector. Upon returning to the Monarchs in 1953, Banks made quite an impression on major league scouts. The Chicago Cubs paid $15,000 to Kansas City for his rights, and on September 14th of that year, he made his Major League debut in Chicago.

Banks debuts with Cubs   Banks was the first African American to play for the Cubs. Like his predecessors and contemporaries, he had to deal with racial slurs, taunting, and death threats. And like the others, he let his play on the field be his answer. His rookie year statistics (154 games, a .275 batting average, 19 home runs, and 79 runs batted in), while solid, only hinted at the prowess that was to follow. After a switch to a lighter bat at the end of 1954, Banks's career would take off. In 1955, Banks raised the bar on hitting expectations for a shortstop by batting .295 and driving in 117 runs with 44 home runs. The latter stat set the record for home runs in a season by a shortstop, a record he would break again in 1958. He also set a record by hitting five grand-slam home runs during the season (breaking the long-standing record of four held by Babe Ruth and Lou Gehrig, among others) and played

*Banks leaps to complete a
double play for the Cubs.*

solid defense. He finished third that year in voting for the Most Valuable Player award, behind two members of the pennant-winning Brooklyn Dodgers: Roy Campanella and Duke Snider.

Having established his talent and credentials, he would no longer be able to "surprise" anyone, and his 1956 power numbers may have reflected this. He hit 28 home runs, a noticeable drop, but his batting average improved to .297 as he proved that the spectacular 1955 season was no fluke. In 1957, he regained the 40-plus homer stroke with 43. These performances were only a prelude to what he would accomplish in the next two years. In 1958, Banks led a projected eighth-place team to a tie for fifth with a .313 average, a career-high and league-leading 47 home runs, and a league-leading 129 runs batted in. He was rewarded for this spectacular season with the Most Valuable Player (MVP) award. This was only the second time in the award's history that a shortstop won, the first being Marty Marion in 1944. It was also only the second time that a player from a second-division team won. Hank Sauer, another Cub, had done it in 1952. Banks's dominance continued in 1959, as he again blistered pitchers for a .304 average, 445 home runs, and 143 runs batted in. The latter total represented a career high and another league title. He also committed a league-low 12 errors and set the single-season record for fielding percentage at shortstop. He was again named the MVP, the ninth time since 1949 that an African American won the award in the National League.

While he never again attained the all-around dominance of his twin MVP years, Banks continued to set the standard at shortstop for several seasons. He led the league in fielding in 1960 and 1961. In 1960 he won his only Gold Glove, led the league in homers with 41, and drove in 117 runs. In that year's first All-Star Game he hit a two-run homer in the National League (NL)'s 5–3 win.

By 1962, a variety of leg injuries had robbed Banks of his range at shortstop, so he moved to first base. His initial season as a first baseman was a rousing success offensively, as he knocked 37 home runs and drove in 104 runs. He soon became as fine a fielder at first base as he had been at shortstop, winning the fielding title in 1969, and leading NL first basemen in assists five times. After 1962, Banks had only two other seasons in which he drove in more than 100 runs (106 in 1965 and 1969) and only topped 30 homers once more (32 in 1968), but his numbers were generally strong, he remained an imposing presence in the Cubs lineup, and he was still the symbol of the Cubs for fans in the mid-to-late decade as the team re-tooled and rebuilt toward their ill-fated chase of the pennant in 1969. Through the mounting disappointments of mediocre Cub seasons, and the ultimate letdown of having a good team come up short in 1969, Banks never lost his enthusiasm for the game. Because of his popularity in Chicago by the end of 1959, the team wanted to honor him with his own commemorative day. He modestly

Ernie Banks

refused, citing the fact that he'd been in the league only five seasons, not long enough to merit such consideration. By 1964, he finally agreed and the day was held.

Banks enters Hall of Fame   By 1970, the leg injuries that had necessitated his move to first base, coupled with early stages of arthritis, signaled that Banks's playing days were winding down. At the time, he was approaching the rarified plateau of 500 home runs. The anticipation of the momentous event was unprecedented in Wrigley Field history. On May 7, 1970, Banks hit number 500, putting an exclamation point on a Hall-of-Fame career. Banks retired after the 1971 season, finishing with 512 home runs, a .274 lifetime batting average, 2,583 hits, 1,636 RBI, the love of an entire city, and the respect of anyone who ever played with or against him. When the Cubs retired his number, 14, at the end of that 1971 season, he became the first player in franchise history to be so honored. In 1977, he was elected to the Baseball Hall of Fame in his first year of eligibility, only the eighth player in history to make it on the first try. In his acceptance speech, he was, as always, humble and positive, thanking his parents, wife, and children.

After retirement, Banks stayed with the organization in various capacities while adjusting to civilian life. He served as a roving minor league hitting instructor, where he enjoyed passing on his wisdom and experience. He also served briefly as a manager in the minors and as a coach for the big club. He eventually moved into group sales, and also did extensive work for the promotions department, attending functions and acting as a goodwill ambassador for the team and the game. His official affiliation with the team ended in 1983, when he was unceremoniously let go by new general manager Dallas Green. He went on to pursue opportunities in banking and later insurance. Throughout his post-playing days, Banks has worked with, or founded, many charities, including the Let's Play Two Foundation for Experienced People, which works with senior citizens; the World Children's Baseball Fair; and the School for Dyslexic Children in Los Angeles.

Ernie Banks changed the way shortstops were perceived and paved the way for the new generations of power-hitting shortstops that would come later. He captivated a whole city at a time when race relations were still tenuous at best, and he provided a sense of pride to a team that, during most of his career, wasn't very good. But for all his accomplishments on the field, he is best appreciated as a man who genuinely loved to play the game, treated everyone with respect, kindness, and enthusiasm, and continues to use his popularity to reach out to help others.—JAMES CRADDOCK

COUNT **BASIE**

1904–1984

Jazz pianist, band leader, song writer

Count Basie gained international recognition in the 1930s and 1940s as he helped create, refine, and

perfect the big band and swing jazz sound of his era. As a pianist and band leader, he wrote and performed such hits of the time as "One O'clock Jump" and "Jumpin' at the Woodside." In one of the few relatively

open avenues for African Americans in the early and middle twentieth century, Basie excelled with great

talent and dedication, and with equal amounts of humility and integrity. His outer composure and subtlety

mixed well with his inner drive to leave a new and extraordinary mark on American music.

William "Count" Basie was born in Red Bank, New Jersey, on August 21, 1904, an only child. Both of his parents being amateur musicians, Basie's childhood was filled with music. While his father played the horn, his mother played and taught her son the piano. Showing talent and a real affection for the instrument that would one day make him famous, his parents hired a tutor, "a wonderful German woman named Halloway" as Basie would recall, who charged twenty-five cents for her piano lessons. As a boy, Basie actually was more interested in playing the drums, and played them in his school band until becoming discouraged by another talented drummer in his class named Sonny Greer. Greer would later become the drummer for the Duke Ellington band, a position he held for thirty-one years.

As a teenager, Basie pursued his musical ambition, setting out for New York and the very lively music scene in and around Harlem. Harlem in the 1920s was attracting musicians and other artists by the hundreds. Pianists like Basie were sharpening their skills and playing their hearts out at countless cabarets, saloons, and dance halls in the community. There he played with numerous jazz acts, and accompanied such blues singers as Clara Smith and Maggie Jones. Harlem became the training ground for dozens of future jazz and blues greats. Pianists such as Duke Ellington, Fletcher Henderson, Fats Waller, and Basie himself were listening and learning from ragtime legends like James P. Johnson and Lucky Roberts. While the young Count Basie's influences at this time were many and varied, none had a more lasting impression on him than Fats Waller. Basie would visit Waller's shows on a nightly basis, sitting as close as he could to the organist, soaking up Waller's magic moves and marvelous sound.

Another way for a young musician to make a living at that time was by playing the vaudeville circuit. Basie traveled with a number of shows that featured musical acts and entertainment, and were geared mostly toward black audiences in everything from big venues in Chicago and New Orleans to tent shows all across the rural south. Jimmy Rushing, who later became a popular Basie vocalist, also played vaudeville and remembers his first meeting with Basie in Tulsa, Oklahoma: "I was with Walter Page's Blue Devils and Basie was still in the Gonzel White show, playing piano in the four-piece band and even acting the part of a villain in one of the comedy skits. It was on a Saturday afternoon and both bands were 'bally-hooin from horse drawn wagons. The Blue Devils were trying to entice customers to the Southern Barbeque and Basie's band

Count Basie.

47

*Count Basie in
his element.*

was advertising the White show. We were playing a piece called Blue Devil Blues and up comes Basie and sits himself down at the piano. Man, but he played!"

After his traveling show disbanded, leaving him and others stranded in Kansas City (a common occurrence with vaudeville shows), Basie joined the Blue Devils, later calling it "the happiest band I've ever been in." They were having fun to be sure, and Basie was beginning to make a name for himself. He, Rushing, and fellow Blue Devil member Walter Page often visited jazz haunts while on tour, challenging all comers to piano contests. Recalls Rushing, "If Basie decided to go somewhere and break up the place, he'd just sit down and play. Then, watch out! Nobody could do anything after that."

Basie earns title of Jump King
In the mid-1930s, after numerous band formings and band breakups, Basie and a small group of others began playing regular shows at the Reno

Club in Kansas City. The scale wage for musicians there was $15 a week, and they played from 8 p.m. until 4 a.m., except on Saturdays when they played twelve hours, from 8 p.m. to 8 a.m. With Count Basie at the helm, the band quickly became a local favorite, known for their energy and rhythm, and earned Basie the title of "Jump King." Soon, their live shows were getting air play on Kansas City radio where, in December of 1935, John Hammond—a jazz writer, talent scout, and recording executive extraordinaire—heard them on his car radio. Excited by the "driving, restless rhythm" coming from this nine-piece band, Hammond began writing about Basie in *Down Beat* and *Melody Maker* magazines. He also spread the word to jazz and swing artists, most notably Benny Goodman, who was also impressed with Basie's playing and smooth leadership within the band. With Hammond's enthusiasm and industry connections, he helped secure a deal for Basie and his band with a prominent booking agency. With the addition of four more members, the Count Basie band came into existence and began touring, eventually signing with Decca Records in 1938.

From the late 1930s all the way through the 1940s, Basie's talent and popularity only increased. A slew of hits were generated by the band including *"One O'clock Jump," "Jumpin' at the Woodside," "Swingin' the Blues,"* and *"Every Tub,"* many of which are considered classics of the swing era, and are still covered by contemporary musicians. Basie was a short, stout man, who, from his off-center position at the keyboard, would direct his band with uncharacteristically subtle gestures: slight nods, stares and smiles, or just a lifted eyebrow could send his band wherever he wanted, all the while producing witty, enthusiastic sounds from his piano.

With the declining popularity of big band and swing by 1950, Basie reduced the size of his band to eight pieces and continued to tour. He formed a second big band in 1952, and despite changing fads, continued to draw huge, adoring audiences throughout the rest of his career, touring right up until the last years of his life. William "Count" Basie died at he age of seventy-nine on April 26, 1984.

Count Basie viewed his talents as his job, which he loved dearly. His assurance at the piano and his joy of playing were the elements that made his music so popular. He was a very private person, allowing his personality to be reflected through his piano: vitality, dedication, and honesty came first; showmanship was nonexistent. He is remembered as a generous man, both as a human being and as a musician.—JEFFREY HERMANN

ROMARE **BEARDEN**
1912–1988
Artist, author

Throughout his lifetime, Romare Bearden documented the rites, rituals, and ceremonies of African American culture based on the artist's memories and observations of his past. The theme of his work exceeds the category of genre pictures; Bearden created an intimate view of the African American experience, imbued with humanistic values and metaphors that connect to universal themes. Bearden is primarily known for his unique interpretation of mixed media collage and nonconventional use of artistic materials.

Bearden's groundbreaking work has garnered him the title "Dean of Black Painters."

Romare Bearden was born in Charlotte, North Carolina, on September 2, 1912, to Howard and Bessye Bearden. After his birth, the Bearden family moved to Harlem, where Romare spent his youth and adulthood. Romare Bearden's mother was employed as a New York–based editor for the *Chicago Defender* and a political organizer, and his father worked as a local sanitation inspector and steward for the Canadian railroad. The Bearden home, an apartment on West 131st Street, became a gathering place for such noteworthy Harlem Renaissance intellectuals, artists, and musicians as Langston Hughes, Paul Robeson, W. E. B. Du Bois, Aaron Douglas, Charles Alston (also the artist's cousin), Duke Ellington, Fats Waller, and Andy Razaf. Bearden summered at the home of his paternal grandparents in Charlotte, North Carolina, during his youth. Later, Bearden spent his high school years at the home of his maternal grandmother, who owned a boarding house occupied by black steelworkers in Pittsburgh, Pennsylvania. The visual memories of the times and places where Bearden grew up and lived as an adult became the repertoire of subject matter throughout the artist's career. These subjects range from images of rural black workers from Mecklenburg County, North Carolina, to newly transplanted black Southerners laboring at the steel mills in Pittsburgh, to neighborhood scenes of Harlem, to the Island of St. Martin in the Caribbean.

Bearden received very little formal training in art during his youth. His earliest interests in art were fostered by his childhood friendship with Eugene Bailey, whom Bearden met while staying with his maternal grandmother in Pittsburgh. Bearden drew actively until Bailey's death in 1925. As the result of an encounter with leading black cartoonist Elmer Simms Campbell, Bearden was inspired to market his political cartoons. His work was accepted by the *Baltimore Afro-American*. He also worked at *Colliers* and the *Saturday Evening Post*. Bearden attended Pittsburgh and Columbia universities, and in 1935 he completed a B.S. in mathematics at New York University. While at NYU, the artist contributed his original cartoons to the humorous campus publication, the *Medley*.

Many of the visual artists from Harlem were financially supported through the Federal Arts Projects of the Works Projects Administration (FAP/WPA) during the Depression. The themes and subjects of these federally supported art projects were conscientious and social by nature, underscoring the ideals of President Franklin D. Roosevelt's New Deal. Although Bearden did not participate in the WPA-sponsored projects during his adolescence, he became an active member of the Harlem artistic community. Among his achievements, Bearden helped organize the Harlem Artists Guild and wrote

Romare Bearden.

several articles about African American art and social topics for the Urban League's *Opportunity* magazine.

In the article "The Negro Artist and Modern Art," published in *Opportunity* for December 1934, Bearden openly criticized African American art and artists on several grounds: the lack of a common aesthetic ideology, an absence of art criticism representing African American artists, and the poor quality of exhibitions representing African American artists. Furthermore, the artist defined two criteria essential to all artists. First was the ability to display inner truths, and the second was to create images based on personal experience and authentic cultural traditions.

In 1935 Bearden participated in a gathering of approximately fifty WPA artists at the YMCA in Harlem, on 135th Street. Attendees at the address were commonly known as "the 306 Group," which attracted artists, musicians, poets, and writers from Harlem, New York, and Europe. Many of the group's participants were also active members of the Harlem Artists Guild and were familiar with "Professor" Charles Siefert, who possessed a vast library referencing African art, culture, and history. The contacts made at this time would prove to become invaluable in shaping Bearden's career.

In 1936 and 1937, Bearden studied with Eastman Campbell and German artist George Grosz at the Art Students League in New York City. As a result of Grosz's influence, Bearden became inspired by the sympathetic and social nature of the work of Goya, Daumier, Kollwitz, Breughel, Ingres, Durer, Holbein, Poussin, and the Dutch Masters. After finishing his studies, Bearden took a studio at 33 West 125th Street, along with Jacob Lawrence and Claude McKay, where he produced works on brown paper using gouache.

Paints African American subjects From 1940 to 1942, the artist painted genre pictures representing socio-cultural aspects of African American subjects. In 1940 Bearden exhibited twenty-four works at his first one-man show, sponsored by Addison Bates. In 1941 Bearden showed two works in "Contemporary Negro Art" and contributed one work in the 1942 exhibition "American Negro Art 19th and 20th Centuries." In 1944, the artist had a solo exhibition entitled "Ten Hierographic Paintings by Sgt. Romare Bearden," and one of his works was included in the group exhibition "New Names in American Art."

During the early phases of Bearden's career, the artist was classified as a social realist painter, along with his contemporaries Philip Evergood, Jacob Lawrence, Ben Shahn, and the noted Mexican muralists Jose Clemente Orozco, Diego Rivera, and David Siqueiros. Bearden's choice of themes at this time included the depiction of blacks living in the rural South and the great migration of blacks from the South to the North. Subjects such as the mother and child, folk musicians, a pair of women, a man serenading a woman, and women seated, seen initially in Bearden's work of this period, recur prominently in his collages from the 1960s.

At the end of the WPA and World War II, artists turned to private patronage and directed their attention away from social issues. In response to the changing aesthetics, Bearden shifted from social realism and genre subjects to flat geometric abstractions resembling stained glass windows, inspired by Cubism.

Bearden served in the army from 1942 to 1945. After the war, the artist was represented by Samuel Kootz Gallery in New York City, along with other noteworthy Abstract Expressionist painters such as Robert Motherwell, Adolph Gottlieb, William Baziotes, and Carl Holty.

Bearden's work was featured in three exhibitions at the Kootz Gallery: "The Passion of Christ," 1945; "Bearden," 1946; and "New Paintings by Bearden," 1947. Although Bearden's work was exhibited with that of the Abstract Expressionists, he never fully acquired the attributes of the movement. While the majority of Abstract Expressionist painters were producing large-scale action or color field paintings, abandoning the conventional use of stretched primed canvas and traditional methods of paint application, from 1942 to 1949 Bearden produced small-scale, Cubist-inspired transparent and opaque oil paintings based on biblical, historical, and literary themes. The artist drew inspiration from Homer, Rabelais, and Federico Garcia Lorca. Bearden gradually became opposed to the central tenants of Abstract Expressionism due to its idiosyncratic nature, and the lack of representation of social concerns. Eventually, he disassociated himself with the Abstract Expressionists and turned for advice to American artist Stuart Davis, who encouraged Bearden to incorporate musical themes and structures borrowed from jazz in his painting.

A mid-life crisis In search of new inspiration, Bearden went in 1950 and 1951 to Paris to study philosophy part time at the Sorbonne on the G.I. Bill. While in Paris, the artist made the acquaintance of Braque, Brancusi, and Leger, among others. Despite the cosmopolitan variety of art, music, and literature Bearden witnessed in Paris, he abstained from painting altogether during his stay. Bearden used the opportunity to increase his knowledge of art history and awareness of contemporary trends in the arts.

Bearden was a consummate fan of American jazz music and regularly attended night clubs, cabarets, and speakeasy performances. After his return from Paris, the artist continued to forego painting for another two-year period and turned instead to composing jazz. One of Bearden's many songs, "Sea Breeze," became a hit after it was recorded by Dizzy Gillespie, Billy Eckstein, and Oscar Pettiford. Looking back over his career, the artist reflected that he had translated sound into color by listening to the music of Earl Hines.

The 1950s was a turbulent era as well as a triumphant one. Bearden suffered a mental breakdown in the mid 1950s due to the constant pressure he placed on himself to create something artistic. In 1954 Bearden married artist and dancer Nanette Rohan. With the encouragement of his wife and friends, Bearden began to paint again. He initiated a period of self-study and rendered personal artistic interpretations of works based on paradigms of art history. Bearden was a devout scholar and life-long student of art history. He manifested his expertise in this area both as a practicing artist incorporating ideas, techniques, and styles inspired by European, Western, African, and Asian traditions of art, and as a noteworthy author. Among the artist's particular interests were Italian Renaissance painters Cimabue, Duccio, Giotto, Titian, and Veronese. Bearden looked carefully at the subject of seventeenth-century Dutch genre paintings and interior subjects in the work of DeHooch, Vermeer, Rembrandt, and Steen. Bearden studied methods of traditional Chinese and Japanese brush painting and was familiar with Japanese block prints. He also read the writings of Wang Wei and Hokusai. The artist was deeply inspired by twentieth-century Modernist painters, especially Matisse, Mondrian, and Picasso. Other influences which inspired the artist's choice of subject matter were African art, the Bible, blues and jazz music, and Homer.

During the late 1950s and early 1960s, as contemporary artists were heading into the Pop Art movement, Bearden engaged in a brief period of Abstract Expressionism. He painted large canvases with nonobjective subject matter in oils, inspired by Zen Buddhism. Bearden's interests in Zen, Asian brush painting, and calligraphy had begun in the early 1950s. In January of 1960, Bearden's work was exhibited at the Michael Warren Gallery, and in April of 1961 his work was featured at Cordier and Warren Gallery. His canvases of this period were large, unstretched and unprimed, covered with drips, splatters, and stains of oil and acrylic paints. The artist was impressed with the theories of German-American painter Hans Hofmann, who observed how composition and spatial orientation on the surface of the picture plane was achieved as the result of color harmonies. A friend of Bearden's and fellow artist Carl Holty, who had been a student at the Hofmann School in Munich, Germany, introduced Bearden to Hofmann's aesthetic theories.

Turns to collages   In the spirit of the Civil Rights Movement of the early 1960s, Bearden united with a group of African American artists known as "Spiral" to establish common concerns and pioneer African American identity through art. In 1963 Bearden suggested that the members of Spiral participate in a group collage project incorporating ripped and cut images from magazine sources. After his suggestion met opposition from the group, Bearden proceeded alone on his idea. In 1964 the artist actively began making collages, composed largely of images of African Americans gathered from issues of *Ebony, Look,* and *Life* magazines from the 1950s and 1960s. Bearden reinterpreted each of these individual periods of collage emphasizing African American events, ceremonies, rituals, culture, and history.

Acting on the advice of fellow Spiral member Reginald Gammon, Bearden enlarged one of his photomontages using a photographic method. Dissatisfied with the results, Bearden temporarily abandoned the project. Art dealer Arne Ekstrom discovered the aborted piece in Bearden's studio and organized a forthcoming show of the artist's montages reproduced photographically. Bearden learned to utilize printing as a method of regenerating his ideas to a wider audience through mass production. In October 1964 "Projections" was exhibited at Cordier & Ekstrom. The show contained twenty-seven original photomontages and corresponding photo-generated prints of the same subjects, consisting of a limited edition of six.

The following year, Bearden was given a second show also titled "Projections" at the Corcoran Gallery in Washington, D.C., which was his first exhibition at a major museum.

Through exhibitions of his collages at galleries and museums, the artist achieved enormous popularity in the early 1960s among the general public, private patrons, scholars, and the art establishment. Due to the financial success derived from his exhibitions, Bearden devoted his fullest attention to a career as an artist, author, and art historian of African American art.

The last two decades   Bearden focused on three subjects in his work of this period: the female nude, jazz, and Martinique. During the early 1970s, Bearden began a new interpretation of the female not seen previously in his oeuvre—notably that of the female temptress. Bearden's nudes of this period were characteristically staged from the vantage point of the voyeur, with erotic overtones. During the early 1970s, Bearden became interested in monoprinting and created a series of prints and paintings based on jazz themes. His use of color and tropical imagery became more vibrant than ever during the last two decades of the artist's life. This shift in the artist's palette has been attributed to his exposure to tropical color, flora, and fauna witnessed on visits with his wife to St. Martin, her native country.

Bearden died in 1988, due to complications from cancer. His ashes were spread over the island of St. Martin in a spiritual burial. Bearden was survived by his wife, who died several years later. The couple had no children.

Exhibitions and honors   Romare Bearden had numerous noteworthy shows during the last three decades of his life, and he received several honorary doctorates. The artist was voted into the American Academy of Arts and Letters and the National Institute of Arts and Letters in 1966. In 1976 Bearden was awarded the State Medal of North Carolina in Art and named Honorary Citizen of Atlanta. In 1978 Bearden was awarded the Frederick Douglass Medal by the New York Urban League and the James Weldon Johnson Award by the NAACP. He was also a member of the board of the New York Council on the Arts. In 1987, the artist was awarded the National Medal of Arts.

Bearden was a pioneer in the history and recognition of African American artists and wrote several books on the history of African American art, including *The Painter's Mind: A Study of the Relations of Structure and Space in Painting,* with Carl Holty (1969); *Six Black Masters of American Art* (1972); and *The Caribbean Poetry of Derek Walcott and the Art of Romare Bearden* (1983). Bearden also wrote numerous articles for a variety of publications.

Although Bearden assumed legendary status among his colleagues and had mass appeal for the public, his contribution to American art of this century has been largely neglected by scholars, as shown by an omission of information concerning the artist in text books on American art and Western art historical surveys. Fortunately, Bearden documented his personal manifesto of art through letters and journals.—BETTY LOU WILLIAM

HARRY **BELAFONTE**

1927–

Entertainer, civil rights activist, humanitarian

Known for his popular renditions of Calypso music, Harry Belafonte received an honorary degree from the University of the West Indies in 1996 for widening the influence of Caribbean music and for reaching the higher echelons of the performing arts. Belafonte has also hit "pay dirt" with Robert Altman's motion picture Kansas City, *a depression-era drama, receiving the 1996 Best Supporting Actor award from the New York Film Critics Circle. Even before his recent return to the silver screen, Belafonte was never inactive: his life has always consisted of more than the entertainment world of glitter and glamor. Belafonte has long devoted time, energy, and money to civil rights and other humanitarian activities that have benefited those in need at home and abroad.*

Harold George Belafonte Jr. was born on March 1, 1927, in Harlem, New York City. His mother, Melvine Love Belafonte, was a Jamaican married to Harold George Belafonte Sr., a native of the island of Martinique. Belafonte's childhood years were unstable because

Young Harry Belafonte.

his father was an alcoholic who worked sporadically as a merchant marine chef, and his mother, a domestic worker, was away from home for long periods of time. His mother took Belafonte and his brother to Jamaica to live for seven years in St. Anne's and Kingston with her relatives. In this setting, the young boy was immersed in a black dominant culture where high-ranking and highly respected professionals were of his race, although the island suffered colonialism. Sidney Poitier, a friend and fellow West Indian, spoke of their childhood years abroad in a *New Yorker* article:

> I firmly believe that we both had the opportunity to arrive at the formation of a sense of ourselves without having it [messed] with by racism as it existed in the United States.

When Belafonte returned to America at the age of thirteen, nothing had changed at home. He attended St. Thomas the Apostle School and, suffering from dyslexia, was soon a ninth-grade dropout from George Washington High School.

In 1943 Belafonte joined the navy as an alternative to the streets of New York. In a segregated southern setting, he was assigned the menial tasks delegated to blacks in the navy at the time, but his consciousness was being raised because of his fellow seamen. Many were older men more widely traveled and better educated; their rap sessions focused on the philosophical, historical, and sociological aspects of race and racism. When Belafonte was given a W. E. B. Du Bois article to read, he was motivated to overcome his reading deficiency and learn about himself as a black American. When his tour of duty was over, Belafonte returned to New York and worked in maintenance at an apartment house. He was given tickets to attend a play at Harlem's American Negro Theatre and became enamored of the acting profession. Using his G.I. Bill benefits, he enrolled in Erwin Piscator's Dramatic Workshop at the New School for Social Research and joined a class whose fledgling actors included Marlon Brando and Bea Arthur. For a class assignment, Belafonte sang an original composition and was encouraged by the positive responses. Despite signs of promise, he still had to earn a living and continued with low-paying jobs while affiliating with the American Negro Theatre, directed by Abram Hill and housed in the basement of a public library. Belafonte worked backstage as a janitor's assistant, and there he met Sidney Poitier, the man who would become his lifelong friend and chief rival. Even at this juncture in their budding friendship, they were vying for the same roles. Poitier, his understudy in *Days of Our Youth,* played the lead role on the night when prominent show backers were in the audience. This was Poitier's big break since it led to a prime role in an all-black show that led directly to Hollywood, while Belafonte was left behind in New York.

With his acting career on hold for a while, Belafonte's singing career got a boost. The owner of the Royal Roost night club remembered hearing him at the Dramatic Workshop and, after hearing him at the club's Amateur Night, hired him for what turned out to be a full-time job. As a pop singer, Belafonte was, according to his former manager in the *New Yorker,* "a vanilla imitation of Billy Eckstine," but it paid bills and led to him becoming an entrepreneur. With some friends, he opened a small eatery in 1950 that lasted less than a year. It did offer the opportunity and a place for him to experiment with folk singing, the seeds of a new singing act. After the business failed, he began to study folk music seriously and even spent some time in the Library of Congress archives listening to recordings of rare and authentic music to increase his repertoire, which included Irish, South American, African, and Hebrew songs in addition to his beloved island music.

In 1951 Belafonte, along with his friend and guitarist-accompanist Millard Thomas, opened at Max Gordon's Village Vanguard and then moved to Gordon's Blue Angel. As a folk singer, Belafonte was an unqualified success and soon had an contract with RCA as a recording artist.

Belafonte never had a spectacular voice, but he created a persona based on sheer charisma and command of the new song genre, and his physical appearance was undeniably striking. His attire captured the audience's attention: his uniform was skin-tight mohair pants and bright silk shirts opened to expose a mocha brown chest. Despite outward appearances, all was not well with Belafonte's new-found success; as in life, racial segregation was still a reality in show business. His bookings were in the swankiest and biggest venues, but like other black entertainers, he was denied the right to eat and sleep in the hotels or socialize in the night clubs where he performed. His new career continued to open doors at the best night clubs: the Cocoanut Grove in Los Angeles, the Copacabana in New York, and the Empire Room at Chicago's Palmer House, where he was the first black performer to appear.

Film career begins   In 1952 Belafonte's film career started off with a leading role in *Bright Road.* This led to a role in a Broadway revue, John Murray Anderson's *Almanac,* which earned him a Tony Award in 1954. He then appeared on the *Ed Sullivan Show* and became one of its most frequent guests. In 1954 Belafonte starred with Marge and Gower Champion in the Broadway musical *Three for the Road.* During the same year, Mike Todd's all-black version of Bizet's opera *Carmen* was adapted for film. Belafonte and Dorothy Dandridge starred in the production, which transformed the heroine from a Gypsy cigarette maker into a black parachute factory worker. Although the film received poor reviews from critics, black movie-goers were overwhelmed at the sheer physical beauty of the two black stars. Belafonte subsequently starred in *The World, the Flesh and the Devil* in 1959. He had simultaneously refined his folk-singing repertoire to concentrate on calypso songs, a genre popular in the Caribbean. Although he was severely criticized by purists and legitimate Calypsonians of Trinidad, he was crowned the "King of Calypso" and by 1957 was regarded as America's most popular performer. The album *Harry Belafonte—Calypso* sold 1.5 million copies, a record at the time for a single artist album. He outsold two legendary singers, Elvis Presley and Frank Sinatra, and the album stayed on the charts for nearly two years. With his musical triumph, Belafonte had succeeded in modifying the dialect and rhythm to make the songs more palatable to the American music-buying public. He also deleted racist and sexist connotations and emphasized positive aspects of calypso music.

Lifestyle changes   Belafonte's professional career was soaring while his personal life was steadily disintegrating. His 1948 marriage to Margurite Byrd had been seriously imperiled during the filming of *Carmen Jones.* He and Byrd had met in 1944 while he was stationed in Norfolk, Virginia, and she was a student at Hampton Institute, as it was known then. They were a study in contrasts because of their disparate backgrounds and outlooks on life. Byrd, now Margurite Mazique, spoke of their early relationship in a *New Yorker* article: "Our courtship was one long argument over racial issues. . . . He reminded me of a big kid who was about to get into trouble if somebody didn't watch and help him." They are parents of two children: Adrienne, a family counselor, and Shari, an actress.

Before the marriage ended, Belafonte had met Julie Robinson, who had once performed with the Katherine Dunham Company. In 1957, while he was filming *Island in the Sun,* Belafonte's first marriage ended and news of his subsequent marriage to Robinson became public knowledge. Perhaps fittingly, the film was about an interracial love affair. Robinson, a Russian-Jew, had an eclectic upbringing and was part of the New York Village's arty, bohemian crowd; she was also able to fit in well with Belafonte's show business lifestyle. Black and white Americans were predictably upset at this turn of events, the former because of perceptions of racial betrayal, and the latter because of perceptions of Belafonte's "uppityness." Belafonte and his current wife are parents of David, a model and head of Belafonte's production company, and of Gina, an actress.

Belafonte's remarriage and his political leanings both affected his film career, but Sidney Poitier, his old rival, continued to soar with the films *Porgy and Bess; To Sir, with Love;* and the film that netted him an Academy Award as the first nonhonorary black recipient, *Lilies of the Field.* Belafonte turned down the two latter films in disgust at the content, and has said of Poitier, in the *New Yorker:* "Sidney was always more pliable, more accommodating . . . he never disturbed the white psyche in anything he did." Television, however, continued to be a major venue for Belafonte and, in 1960, he won an Emmy for the show "Tonight with Belafonte," a Revlon Hour special. He continued to introduce African artists to American audiences. In 1964 he brought Kandia Conte Fode, a Guinean tenor, and a Gueckedour Orchestra to Lincoln Center. In 1966 he became the first black American performer to produce an hour-long CBS show. "Strolling Twenties," produced by Belafonte's Harbel Company, began in 1959. The show starred Sammy Davis Jr., Diahann Carroll, Duke Ellington, Joe Williams, and Nipsey Russell; Sidney Poitier narrated the Langston Hughes script. In 1968 *The Tonight Show with Johnny Carson* was guest-hosted for a week by Belafonte and featured more prominent blacks, including Martin Luther King Jr. In 1971 Belafonte returned to the movies as a costar with Poitier and Ruby Dee in *Buck and the Preacher,* and in 1974, in *Uptown Saturday Night.* In 1984 he was coproducer of the hip-hop film *Beat Street.*

Belafonte has a reputable catalog of recordings and songbooks. Three of his recordings of note are *Belafonte Returns to Carnegie Hall,* with Odetta, Miriam Makeba, and the Chad Mitchell Trio (1960); *My Lord What a Mornin',* with Belafonte Singers (1960); and *Paradise in Gazankulu,* an album of South African music (1988). In 1962 a collection of forty songs, *Songs Belafonte Sings,* was published; it was illustrated by Charles White, one of America's premier black artists.

Shifts to activism   Belafonte's disenchantment with Hollywood was lodged on a deeper level than personal disappointment and dissatisfaction with demeaning roles. A *New Yorker* interview describes his feelings:

> Hollywood was symptomatic, and the problem was the nation. I figured unless
> you change the national vocabulary, the national climate, the national attitude,
> you're not going to be able to change Hollywood.

When Belafonte first met Martin Luther King Jr. in 1956, he was impressed by King's humble demeanor and sincerity, and he responded immediately when King asked for help. This was not Belafonte's first civil rights venture. As a struggling twenty-four-year-old actor, he had walked a picket line for W. E. B. Du Bois. In 1950 Belafonte and Bayard Rustin led one thousand students from New York to the nation's capitol to join A. Philip Randolph's March for Integrated Schools. On King's behalf, Belafonte provided two major contributions: money and intercession. He was the catalyst in persuading many famous entertainers to headline or sponsor concerts to raise funds for civil rights. In 1963 he helped found the Southern Free

Theater in Jackson, Mississippi and he often used personal funds to provide bail money for workers of the Student Nonviolent Coordinating Committee (SNCC). He also put up seed money to support the group at its inception. The $50,000 needed to bail King out of the Birmingham jail was raised by Belafonte with the promise to secure more when needed. When that time came, he was instrumental in securing $50,000 in cash from the New York Transportation Worker's Union and then $40,000 in cash from Governor Nelson Rockefeller's assistant, Hugh Morrow. At a Cleveland, Ohio, fund raiser, Belafonte was able to net $15,000. Realizing that King's life was always in danger, Belafonte heavily insured King's life. When King was in serious trouble over income tax matters, Belafonte and Bayard Rustin devised a fund-raising appeal through the *New York Times* in an advertisement entitled "Heed Their Rising Voices." He and Reverend Gardner Taylor devised a plan to bypass foundations for a direct appeal to black church-goers while the tax case was ongoing.

Harry Belafonte.

Belafonte's other asset was his ability to intercede and mediate between people and groups that were often hostile toward one another. He forged and maintained the relationship with the Washington, D.C., establishment, one that was crucial in keeping King alive during his jail sentences. He first met Robert Kennedy in his own home when Kennedy came to solicit Belafonte as a campaigner, but Belafonte preferred Adlai Stevenson and urged Robert Kennedy to meet King and actively support civil rights causes. Surprisingly, Kennedy knew nothing of King's reputation and could not understand why he should get involved with him. After they finally met, it was Belafonte who acted as mediator and often as a bargaining agent for King. As an unofficial liaison, he was named to the advisory board of the Peace Corps in 1961.

On a personal level, Belafonte was called on to intercede between King and his father, who insisted that his son owed Robert Kennedy loyalty while Belafonte urged that the younger King support whomever he wanted. For his efforts, Belafonte and his cohorts were vilified and attacked largely on the basis of FBI wiretap reports. One of the most vicious allegations Kennedy made was that Belafonte was unstable due to his mixed-race marriage. The FBI New York field office knew of every New York meeting held or attended by Belafonte. In 1960 they had reported that King and Belafonte had met with Benjamin Davis, then America's best-known black Communist. Belafonte's relations with Stanley Levison, a wealthy friend and unpaid counsel of Martin Luther King Jr., were of particular interest to Hoover, and they were hounded to the extent that Levison was finally forced to withdraw as King's counsel. The FBI was relentless in its efforts to discredit King and reduce the attendance at SCLC fund raisers that starred Belafonte.

The negativism never slowed Belafonte's efforts toward promoting justice and dignity for all humanity. Since 1986 he has traveled the globe as a United Nations International

Children's Education Fund (UNICEF) goodwill ambassador. In 1985 Belafonte conceived the idea of the concert and recording of *We Are the World,* efforts that raised $100 million for the Ethiopian famine relief fund. In 1990 Belafonte chaired the committee that arranged the visit of the newly-freed Nelson Mandela to America, and he was also appointed by Mario Cuomo to oversee the Martin Luther King Jr. Commission to Promote Knowledge of Nonviolence.

Receives numerous honors   Belafonte has received numerous honorary doctorates, along with a Tony Award (1953); the James J. Hoey Award for Interracial Justice from the Catholic Interracial Council (1956); the ABAA Music Award for helping African famine victims through producing the album and video *We Are the World* (1985); and a Grammy Award (1985). He is again performing with a new group, an African and Third World music band, DJOLIBA.

Belafonte and his wife, Julie, continue to collect Caribbean, African, and European art and to enjoy their Manhattan apartment. Belafonte bought the building where he lives as a real estate investment, sold the apartments as cooperatives, and retained one floor as living quarters. Their accumulation of artistic treasures is displayed there and stand as a record of the past, that of heroes and heroines and of their own struggles to survive and live in a country that still values skin color over character.

Belafonte has expressed regrets over not having read and learned more. In the *New Yorker,* Belafonte's oldest daughter said of her father, "He wants to fix the world, and he's sad because he sees it slipping away. I believe he feels alone."

Belafonte's recent surgery for prostate cancer was deemed successful. Belafonte said in a *New Yorker* interview with Henry Louis Gates: "There wasn't all that much I would have done differently when I look back on it." Belafonte can live with that pronouncement as he forges ahead with creative projects in music and film that will continue to astound and even anger some, but never fail to entertain and educate all.—DOLORES NICHOLSON

LERONE **BENNETT JR.**
1928–
Editor, writer

Lerone Bennett Jr., is an editor and writer who has served for more than four decades on the staff of

Ebony and has published several volumes on black American history. His achievements have brought him

recognition as an accomplished historian whose efforts illuminate the past and inspire readers.

Bennett was born in 1928 in Clarksdale, Mississippi, to Lerone and Alma Bennett. He studied at Morehouse College, a predominantly black school in Atlanta, Georgia. After graduating from Morehouse in 1949, he studied briefly at Atlanta University, then found work as a reporter and city editor at the *Atlanta Daily World.* He left the newspaper in 1953 to become an associate editor at *Jet,* a black-oriented magazine based in Chicago. Later that year he assumed the same position at *Ebony,* another Chicago-based black periodical, which had been founded by John H. Johnson eight years earlier. In 1956 Bennett married Gloria Sylvester. They have four children: Alma Joy, Constance, Courtney, and Lerone III. Bennett assumed the position of senior editor at *Ebony* in 1958, and he remained in that post until becoming executive editor in 1987.

At *Ebony* Bennett quickly proved himself an accomplished writer and editor with a particular flair for provocative and incisive accounts. For *Ebony* he produced a series of articles detailing the history of blacks in America from pre-colonial times to the early 1960s. His subjects in this series include the development of black enslavement in America; the plight of blacks during such key periods as the American Revolution, the Civil War, and the post-Civil War Reconstruction; the enforcement of legal segregation; and the achievements of black soldiers in conflicts such as the Civil War and World War I. The book features harrowing accounts of blacks fighting in World War I and succumbing to lynch mobs.

In 1962 Bennett collected the series of historical articles and published them as *Before the Mayflower: A History of Black America, 1619–1962*, which was roundly hailed as a breakthrough study of the black experience in America. In addition to hailing the book's compelling perspective on black history, critics noted its sobering consideration of blacks as a potentially dynamic, yet inevitably disenfranchised, portion of the American population. *Before the Mayflower* was declared book of the year by the Capital Press Club in 1963.

In 1964 Bennett followed *Before the Mayflower* with *The Negro Mood, and Other Essays* an occasionally caustic examination of the black plight and white attitudes towards racial equality. Here Bennett charges white liberals with failing to effectively change a social system that they decry as biased. That same year Bennett also completed *What Manner of Man: A Biography of Martin Luther King, Jr.* This work recounts the life and achievements of the nonviolent civil-rights activist who exerted considerable influence on black rights and race relations in the United States before his assassination in 1968. *What Manner of Man* was accorded the Patron Saint Award from the Society of Midland Authors in 1965.

Bennett next produced *Confrontation: Black and White,* which recalls *The Negro Mood* in making pointed observations about black rights and race relations. In *Confrontation* Bennett analyzes various social problems plaguing blacks in America, but he also addresses problems within the black community. He criticizes some portions of black leadership for living at too great a removal—socially and financially—from the general black population. He also calls for greater unity within the substantial black community—and, particularly, black leaders—and advocates stronger ties between blacks and America's more prosperous, more powerful white population.

In 1967 Bennett produced one of his most significant historical writings, *Black Power U.S.A.: The Human Side of Reconstruction, 1867–1877*. Here Bennett documents black efforts to maintain ties with both the industrial American North and the segregationalist South. He also notes the advent of segregationist policies in the American South after the Civil War, and he charts the development of black activism as a consequence of discriminatory practices during the Reconstruction era.

In the ensuing decades Bennett has continued to produce a range of writings on various aspects of black history and contemporary issues. In 1968 he published *Pioneers in Protest,* and in 1971 he collaborated on the compilation of *Ebony Pictorial History of Black America,* a four-volume study. In 1972 he turned again to contemporary black issues and produced *The Challenge of Blackness,* and in 1975 he published *The Shaping of Black America.*

Another important work, *Wade in the Water: Great Moments in Black History,* appeared in 1979. This was followed in 1989 by *Succeeding Against the Odds,* which was followed, in turn, by *Listen to the Blood: Was Abraham Lincoln a White Supremacist?, and Other Essays and Stories.* Another volume, *Whipped into Glory: Abraham Lincoln and the White Dream,* appeared in 1996.

Although Bennett, as a writer, is probably best known for his *Ebony* articles and his many volumes on black history and African American issues, he has also produced fiction and poetry, which he has contributed to various publications. His fiction has also been featured in *Contemporary American Negro Short Stories,* and his verse was included in *New Negro Poets: U.S.A.,* a volume edited by Langston Hughes.

Bennett has also devoted himself to education and various philanthropic and executive endeavors. He taught at Northwestern University in the late 1960s, when he also served as a senior fellow at the Institute of the Black World. He has also been a fellow at the Black Academy of Arts and Letters, a member of the board of directors of the Chicago Public Library, and a trustee of the Martin Luther King Memorial Foundation.

For his varied contributions and accomplishments, Bennett has received a range of awards and honors. He has been given honorary doctorates from such institutions as Morehouse College, Wilberforce University, and—in 1980 alone—the University of Illinois, Lincoln College, and Dillard University. In addition, he received a literary award from the American Academy of Arts and Letters in 1978. At *Ebony,* he continues to serve with distinction as executive editor.—LES STONE

MARY FRANCES **BERRY**

1938–

Historian, lawyer, government official

Mary Frances Berry is internationally recognized as a historian, educator, lawyer, public servant, and civil and human rights activist. A member of the United States Commission on Civil Rights under both the Carter and Reagan administrations and an expert on U.S. constitutional history, she has written such books as Black Resistance/White Law *to call attention to government-sanctioned racism in the United States.*

The second of three children, Berry was born on February 17, 1938, to Frances Southall Berry (now Wiggins) and George Ford Berry in Nashville, Tennessee. Economic and personal hardships beset the family in Mary's earliest years; insurmountable difficulties compelled Frances Berry to place Mary and a brother in an orphanage for a time. While she was still a child, the ravages of poverty and the human capacity for cruelty, selfishness, and racial prejudice created for Mary Frances Berry a period in her life akin to a "horror story."

Neither poverty, hunger, nor inhumane treatment at the orphanage, however, prevented Berry from demonstrating at an early age exceptional determination, resilience, and intellectual ability. She obtained her first years of formal education in the segregated schools of Nashville. It was while Berry was in Pearl High School, however, with "no idea of what [she]

*Mary Frances
Berry.*

was going to do with [her] life," that a black teacher, Minerva Hawkins, saw in the teenager a "diamond in the rough" and changed Berry's life irrevocably. Berry recalls in *Ebony* that as a tenth-grade high school student she felt unchallenged:

> I would hang out of school, leave school early, leave for lunch. It wasn't that I couldn't do the work. I always finished ahead of the other students. I was just bored with school. When I got to Ms. Hawkins's class, she noticed that. She started giving me extra books and extra assignments. Then she would talk to me about it. She would even invite me over to her house after school. She then started talking to me about my life and got me interested in intellectual pursuits.

Upon graduation from high school (with honors), Berry sought and found work, and she began her college education at Hawkins's alma mater, Fisk University, and continued at Howard University. After graduating from Howard in 1961, she enrolled in its graduate school and then became a doctoral student at the University of Michigan, studying history. In addition to her Ph.D., Berry earned a J.D. in 1970.

Berry takes the helm in academe   Berry has enthusiastically and energetically developed a career in academe, which began with and continues to include teaching. Berry's teaching activities as a professor of U.S. history and legal history have included the incorporation of racially plural materials into traditional courses, the introduction of new courses, and instruction of young scholars pursuing graduate degrees in history. Berry's career as a scholar-educator has been marked by a series of noteworthy achievements beyond teaching. In 1972 she was named the first director of the Afro-American Studies Program at the University of Maryland and the interim chairperson of Maryland's Division of Behavioral and Social Sciences for the College Park campus. She was appointed provost for the same division in 1974, becoming the highest ranking black woman at College Park.

In 1976 Berry accepted the invitation of the University of Colorado to become chancellor at that institution, thereby becoming the first black woman and one of only two women to join the ranks of presidents and chancellors of major research universities. (The only other woman at the time of Berry's appointment was Lorene Rogers, president of the University of Texas.) Unquestionably, the most prominent and significant academic administrative post in which Berry has served has been the chancellorship of this 21,000-student campus (then 3 percent black, 14 percent Hispanic), with a faculty of 2,300 members and an annual budget of $113.3 million. Her concerns and her goals during the chancellorship were best described by Berry on the occasion of the university's 163rd commencement: "My task . . . will be to foster and continue the effort to attain excellence in our academic programs, despite the increasing difficulty of explaining the value and power of knowledge and its creation, to . . . many constituencies." Berry has accepted two subsequent academic appointments. In 1980 she joined the faculty of her undergraduate alma mater, Howard University, as a professor of history and law and became a senior fellow at Howard's Institute for the Study of Educational Policy. After nearly a decade, Berry resigned from the faculty of Howard University to accept a professorship at the University of Pennsylvania, where she has served as the Geraldine R. Segal Professor of Social Thought and Professor of History.

Race, gender, and law explored in publications   Berry has achieved particular distinction among scholars for her research, critical analyses, lucid writing style, coverage of timely issues from a historical perspective, and specific expertise in legal and African American history. In addition to *Black Resistance/White Law,* which analyzes the practice of Constitutional racism, Berry has written five major books: *Military Necessity and Civil Rights Policy: Black Citizenship and the Constitution, 1861–1868; Stability, Security, and Continuity: Mr. Justice Burton and Decision-Making in the Supreme Court, 1945–1958; Long Memory: The Black Experience in America; Why ERA Failed;* and *The Politics of Motherhood.* John W. Blassingame, who co-wrote *Long Memory,* has perceptively argued that Berry's "works tend to close debate. Rarely does one put down a book she has written with the feeling that the subject should be explored again. Instead her books . . . [have become] standards in the field."

Beyond *Black Resistance/White Law,* two of Berry's works have made significant contributions to the field of black American history. In *Military Necessity and Civil Rights*

Policy, Berry offers the thesis that blacks have gained the greatest benefits with respect to civil rights during times of national crises. Focusing on the Civil War period, she notes the federal government's concurrent need for black soldiers and the violation of their constitutional rights. In contrast to this monograph stands *Long Memory,* which interprets the black experience through 1980, offering "a wide historical sweep and masterful weaving of cultural, literary and social patterns," as *Library Journal* noted.

Why ERA Failed, a widely reviewed and successful book, examines the legal process, gender, race, and cultural conflict as well as external and internal factors that affect social movements designed to amend the Constitution. Berry clearly and incisively identifies the essential elements required to create the sense of need to alter the Constitution and, within a broad historical analysis, addresses specifically the problems of the movement to obtain an Equal Rights Amendment. As John Hope Franklin has commented, *Why ERA Failed* is "an excellent analysis of the historical as well as current forces that doomed this effort to extend equal rights to women by Constitutional amendment." Berry's next study, *The Politics of Motherhood,* presents a historical view of culture, gender, race, politics, and economics in an effort to facilitate understanding of the status of women as mothers, the policy and political questions germane to child care, and concepts of the good and just within society.

Mary Frances Berry.

Berry challenges Reagan   From 1977 to 1979, Berry was the first black woman to serve as chief educational officer of the United States. She is best known, however, in her public service as a commissioner of the United States Commission on Civil Rights. Berry's association with the commission preceded her appointment. In 1975 she had prepared for the commission an extensively researched and well-documented special study, *Constitutional Aspects of the Right to Limit Childbearing.* Subsequent to her service as assistant secretary for education, President Jimmy Carter appointed Berry to the United States Civil Rights Commission, which had been established in 1957 to function as an independent, bipartisan agency within the executive branch. Responsible for the investigation of discrimination, the commission had engaged in monitoring and fact-finding, but it had also been the recommending body for the Civil Rights Act of 1964 and Voting Rights Act of 1965.

However distinguished Berry's service as commissioner and vice-chairperson from 1980 to 1982, President Ronald Reagan sought to dismiss her before the 1984 election. This effort to remove Berry and two other appointees holding viewpoints opposed to Reagan's was characterized by Berry as the reduction of the commission from the "watchdog of civil rights" to "a lapdog for the administration," wrote the *Washington Post* in 1984. Berry's prestige and notoriety increased when she successfully challenged in federal court Reagan's attempt to remove her from the commission.

An outspoken critic of oppression, exploitation, and denials of human as well as civil rights, whether the victims be a race of people, a small nation, women, the poor, the marginalized, the disabled, or single mothers, Berry has a record of and reputation for articulate, historically grounded advocacy of justice. At various periods Berry has addressed the Vietnam War, women's rights, federal remedies for past institutionalized racism, black American civil rights and liberation, African liberation, or the specific recognition of black self-determination required by the principle of justice in South Africa.

Berry's leadership in the Free South Africa Movement—of which she is a founder—and her Thanksgiving 1984 arrest at the South African embassy while protesting apartheid and U.S. policy toward South Africa have catapulted Berry to greater national and international prominence. Her outspoken responses to racial injustice have even affected the Clinton adminstration's policies toward Haitian refugees. She consistently participates in protests, whether they be authorized public demonstrations or actions of civil disobedience. Her praxis has established Berry as one of the outstanding scholar-activists of the second half of the twentieth century. "When it comes to the cause of justice," she has explained, "I take no prisoners and I don't believe in compromising."—GENNA RAE McNEIL

MARY McLEOD **BETHUNE**

1875–1955
Government official, activist

A champion of humanitarian and democratic values throughout the United States for more than thirty years, Mary McLeod Bethune made essential contributions to the development of black America. Through her prominent position in the administration of President Franklin D. Roosevelt she assumed the role of race leader at large, thus becoming the most influential black woman in the annals of the country. Bethune provided the leadership to raise black women from the social and political invisibility they suffered to a sustained presence in national affairs.

Mary McLeod Bethune was born in 1875 in Sumter County near Mayesville, South Carolina. She was the fifteenth of seventeen children of Sam McLeod and Patsy (McIntosh) McLeod. Her parents and most of her brothers and sisters were slaves emancipated through the Union victory in the Civil War. One major consequence of freedom for the McLeod family was the acquisition, in the early 1870s, of a farm of about thirty-five acres.

During the post-Reconstruction era in white-controlled Sumter County, the overwhelming black majority had little access to public schooling. But Bethune was fortunate to attend the rural Trinity Presbyterian Mission School four or five miles from her home when it opened in 1885. Three years later she attended Scotia Seminary (later Barber-Scotia College) in Concord, North Carolina. Bethune spent six years at this outreach of northern

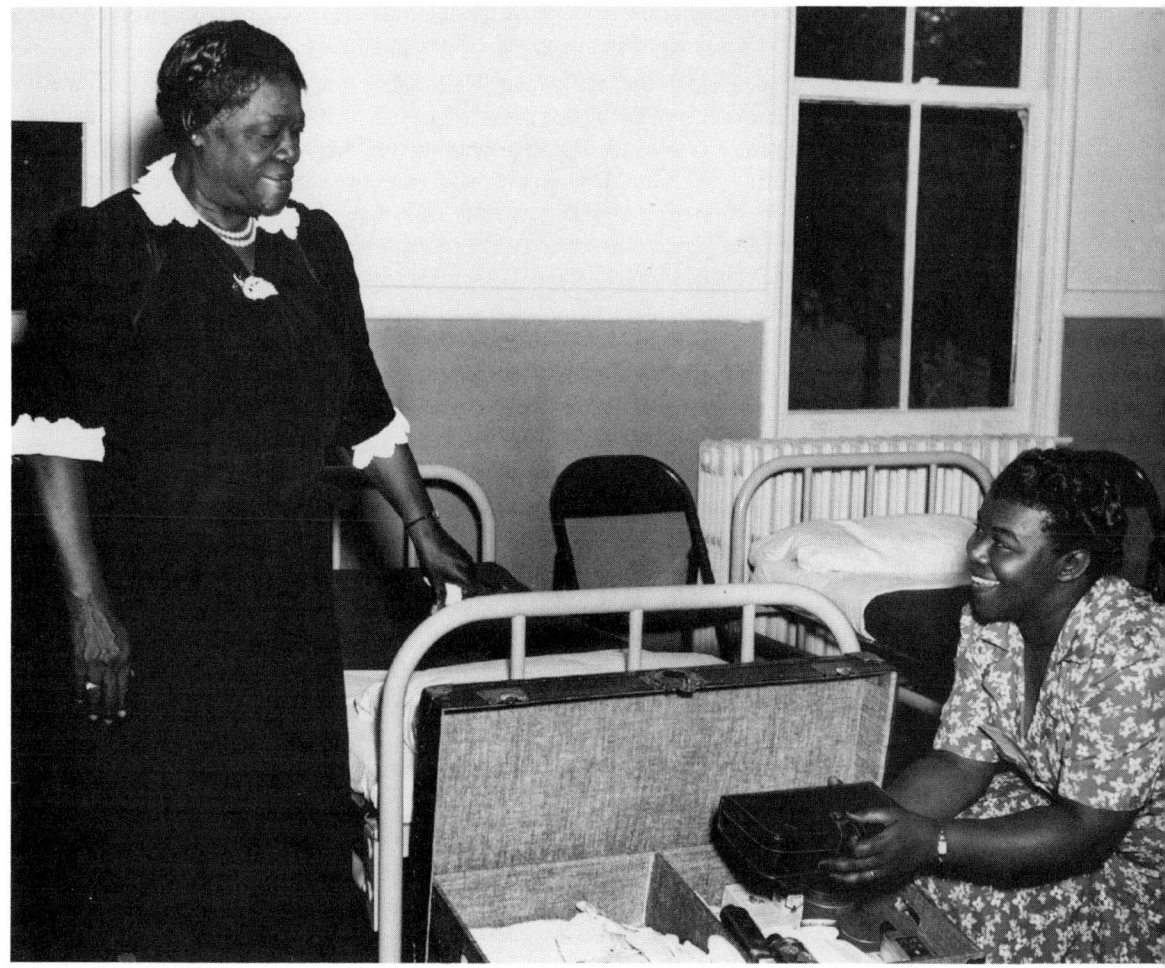

Mary McLeod Bethune, at left.

white Presbyterians. Beyond academics she was submerged in a regime emphasizing religious concerns, "culture and refinement," and "industrial education"—sewing, cooking, laundering, and cleaning.

Bethune's greatest disappointment Upon graduation, Bethune, who was preparing to be an African missionary, entered the Bible Institute for Home and Foreign Missions (later Moody Bible Institute), an interdenominational school in Chicago. Upon applying to the Presbyterian Mission Board for an assignment after a year's study, however, Bethune was greatly disappointed, learning that it did not place African Americans in such positions. Although time and again life would jolt Bethune, she later certified that this blow was the greatest disappointment of her life.

Believing that foreign missions were closed to her, Bethune entered virtually the only field open to a black woman of her inclination and training—teaching black students. For the next five years she taught in Georgia and South Carolina, during which time she met Albertus Bethune, a tall and handsome man five years her senior. In May of 1898 the couple married, and they soon made Savannah their home. Here he found work as a porter, and their only child, Albert Bethune, was born. Though the couple remained together for at least eight years and were legally married until Albertus's death in 1918, theirs was not a happy union. Perhaps because marriage and family experiences were unsatisfying for her, Bethune ultimately failed to accord these institutions priority status in advancing black Americans.

Bethune saw education as the primary route to racial uplift, and this field consumed her youthful energies. In 1900 she established a Presbyterian parochial school in Palatka, Florida. Two years later, she opened an independent school that she maintained in conjunction with rendering volunteer social services and selling life insurance. After two more years she left the declining Palatka for greener pastures on the state's east coast.

Bethune founds educational institution   In Daytona, Florida, on October 3, 1904, in a rented house sparsely furnished with dry-goods, boxes for benches, and other improvised essentials, Bethune founded the Daytona Educational and Industrial Institute, with her assets of "five little girls, a dollar and a half, and faith in God." In addition, she had her own five-year-old son and well-formed ideas of the school she wanted, a re-creation of "dear old Scotia." But she would modify the model by having her students work a large farm to put food on the institute's table and to provide cash income from the sale of produce. Bethune hoped in time to offer nurse training and advanced subjects and attain national respectability.

Fortunately, Bethune had chosen well the city in which to realize her ambition. Daytona's black leaders eagerly assisted her, particularly A. L. James, pastor of Mount Bethel Baptist Church, one of the two black houses of worship in this town of two thousand. In 1905, besides Bethune, he became the only other black member of the school's trustee board, which meant that the whites gave the institute critical assistance. Socially prominent white women frequently exerted hands-on influence in the school's regular activities and even more in special events. Beginning in 1905 the most energetic of them were organized into a Ladies' Advisory Board to the institute, consisting of both local residents and winter tourists. Though on occasion Bethune used her female supporters as a means of interesting their husbands in the Daytona Institute, her largest individual contributors were white males with whom she dealt directly, including James N. Gamble of Proctor and Gamble Manufacturing Company. By 1922, with black and white support, Bethune had developed a thriving institution that enrolled three hundred girls and had a dedicated faculty and staff of about twenty-five.

Beyond study, religion, and work, the girls at the Daytona Institute benefited from contact with an incomparable professional role model, Bethune. With her extremely dark skin, flat nose, and full lips, which clashed sharply with America's ideal of physical attractiveness and which both blacks and whites deemed liabilities to leadership in middle-class black America, Bethune transcended the restricted sphere that society usually assigned to one of her color and, for that matter, one of her gender. Her sense of an unfettered self was so great that she defied Jim Crow customs and ordinances, most notably in her insistence on desegregated seating at the Daytona Institute. And despite Ku Klux Klan threats, she and her entire faculty and staff voted in 1920 and afterwards. With a vision of better opportunities for blacks and black women in particular, Bethune extended her influence throughout black America.

Merged institutions form Bethune-Cookman College   In 1923 her school, then the Daytona Normal and Industrial Institute, merged with the coeducational Cookman Institute in Jacksonville, Florida. Though declining at the time, the latter claimed a distinguished fifty-one-year-old heritage and sponsorship of the Methodist Episcopal church. The church had arranged for the institutional marriage between Daytona and Cookman on the basis of developing the union, under Bethune's leadership, into a coeducational junior college. To reflect the collegiate direction, the institution officially changed its name to Bethune-Cookman College in 1929. By 1935, having weathered the worst of the Great Depression, the college's development garnered Bethune the NAACP's coveted Spingarn Medal.

Bethune's relationship to her beloved school took a momentous turn in 1936 when she accepted a full-time government position in Washington, D.C. Consequently, the college suffered from her divided attention until 1942. At that time, after a life-threatening illness, Bethune resigned the presidency. Yet when a great measure of her political effectiveness in Washington ended, she worked her way back into the school's presidential office. In 1947, however, she seemed to have accepted the fact that the escalating rigors of the job required a younger person and consequently vacated the position. At this time Bethune basked in a phenomenal educational record. No other woman of her generation had created an institution for disadvantaged youth and developed it into a senior college.

School hosts club activities   Establishing a school, the achievement for which Bethune has been best known, assumes greater significance when it is understood that it was the foundation of her exalted stature in the women's club movement. By hosting state and regional conclaves and channeling personnel and other resources into club work, Bethune progressively made her school a hub of clubwomen's activity. This occurred in tandem with her presidency of state, regional, and national federations, beginning with the Florida Association of Colored Women in June 1917. In keeping with self-help trends in other southern states, on September 10, 1920, Bethune led Florida's women in opening a home in Ocala for wayward and delinquent girls.

Like the best of patriotic leaders during World War I, Bethune directed her constituents into well-publicized war-support endeavors. Bethune's presidency of the Southeastern Association of Colored Women, which she established in 1920 and presided over for five years, encompassed especially a turning outward to the broader society. The striking development occurred in 1922 when the Southeastern's Interracial Committee became the black contingent of the Women's General Committee of the Atlanta-based Commission on Interracial Cooperation. Through this, the most representative female leadership corps in the South was formed.

But from 1924 to 1928, in the presidency of the ten-thousand-member National Association of Colored Women (NACW), the premier black women's secular organization, Bethune found her greatest platform for leadership in the established voluntary organization. Bethune's stature within the NACW derived in part from her brilliant vision of an activist public affairs role for black women in both national and international arenas. Like some other association leaders, particularly Margaret Murray Washington, Bethune determined to reach out to "the scattered people of African descent." She declared to her members, "We must make this national body of colored women a significant link between the peoples of color throughout the world."

To achieve her primary goal—effective representation of black women in public affairs—Bethune sought to transform the amorphous NACW into a cohesive body with a common program in all constituent regional, state, city, and individual club entities. For her this necessitated, above all, a permanent, fixed, national headquarters employing an executive secretary. Bethune crossed the country raising money for the project. On July 31, 1928, in Washington, D.C., the association proudly dedicated its newly acquired headquarters. The NACW was the first all-black group geared to operate in the nation's capital as scores of other national organizations already did.

Bethune establishes NCNW   Under the brutality of the Great Depression, Bethune's focus upon black women's energetic presence in national affairs and the mechanisms that she had vitalized to achieve this goal languished within the NACW. Increasingly reasserting its historic decentralized character, the organization retreated from her emphasis upon a cohesive body. Given these developments, coupled with Bethune's domineering personality and her belief in the necessity of linkages between the distaff leadership of black Americans and New Deal administrators, on December 5, 1935, in New York City, she established the National Council of Negro Women (NCNW). Essentially, Bethune transferred to the council the brilliant vision that she had once vested in the NACW. As council president for fourteen years, she poured into the new entity all of her fine-tuned organizational skills. By 1949, when Bethune left office, the NCNW included twenty-two national professional and occupational groups and sororities, with eighty-two metropolitan councils.

Mary McLeod Bethune.

Insider status in FDR administration

Bethune's NCNW success derived in part from her contacts and insider status in the Franklin Roosevelt administration. Her base was the National Youth Administration, an agency that race liberals in Washington shaped and administered. Established in 1935 to assist young people aged sixteen to twenty-four in the Great Depression, and continuing to exist during World War II primarily to provide youth with vocational training and placement in vital defense industries, the NYA served several million constituents for more than eight years.

Consequently, with administrative sanction, Bethune established herself as the director of the Division of Negro Affairs, an arrangement that the Civil Service Commission made official in January 1939. With this position, she occupied a slot in government higher than that of any other black woman in the history of the country up to that time. Although it was only a low-echelon berth within the broad framework of the federal bureaucracy, it was one of twenty or so of the highest appointed positions held by women in the New Deal. Regardless of Bethune's place on an organizational chart, she consistently operated on a level requiring consummate political skill in navigating through disputes in which her white colleagues and her black constituents were at odds, and both expected her loyalty. She brought tremendously impressive assets to her job: a charismatic personality, an unexcelled platform style, keen insight into race relations, superb abilities to influence people, and a well-known reputation. Her accomplishments with the Civil Service Commission included the establishment of the Special Negro Fund and the advancement of qualified blacks in state and local organizations; by 1941 Bethune's diligent work had led to the employment of black assistants to state directors in twenty-seven states, including all of the South except Mississippi, as well as in New York City and the District of Columbia.

Aware of her impeccable race leadership credentials, the Roosevelt Administration drafted Bethune to help sell its policies to black America. In both Depression and war she did so with gusto, and her efforts contributed to the improving stature of blacks at the national level in the Democratic party coalition. Holding Bethune in high esteem, President Roosevelt supported Bethune's NYA directorship, saw her when she deemed circumstances warranted it, on occasion called her in to visit, extended messages to black organizations when she requested them, and within very narrow limits beyond NYA business acquiesced to her requests as a race leader.

Eleanor Roosevelt associated with Bethune in a much closer way both politically and personally. She gained from the black leader a sensitive understanding of the country's racial problems and expert counsel on them. In addition to bringing Bethune into government, Roosevelt championed all her priority causes—her college, the NCNW, the NYA, and civil rights in general. And unlike scores of white female appointees in government who excluded Bethune from their informal support network, the First Lady consistently accorded her every consideration.

Bethune's unrestricted access to the White House, her standing in black America, and the security of her NYA bailiwick augured well for her becoming race representative-at-large in the administration. In its broader context, such a position required an individual to keep track of proliferating federal programs, to devise strategies by which black Americans could best obtain a fair share from them, and to work towards implementing them. Though Bethune enjoyed no government authorization for at-large activity, she confidently took this responsibility upon herself.

Bethune understood that at-large effectiveness necessitated competent staff. For this reason, in 1936 she helped organize the Federal Council on Negro Affairs, popularly acclaimed as the Black Cabinet. This council was made possible through the New Deal's recruitment into government of more than one hundred black advisers. These professionals embodied the regeneration of a black American political presence that had been lacking in the nation's capital since the demise of Reconstruction. According to Bethune's plan, the cabinet did, in fact, effect a loose coordination of government programs for blacks. Leaders from the National Urban League, the NAACP, the black press, and other race institutions as individuals and groups often took part in it.

The Black Cabinet's most publicly acknowledged service was as facilitator to two precedent-setting national black conferences held in Washington at the Labor Department in

1937 and 1939. Bethune not only presided over the proceedings but also the process through which the findings of the conferences were disseminated throughout official Washington, from the president on down.

The Black Cabinet's less publicized work also contributed an edge to Bethune's at-large status in government. Members of the black network notified Bethune on an ad hoc basis of any sticky situation that required action from higher-ups. Once alerted, Bethune usually contacted Eleanor Roosevelt, as she did in 1942 after influential whites had created a racial tinderbox in Detroit by attempting to transfer to whites a federally funded housing project built for blacks. Partly as a consequence of a meeting between Bethune and Roosevelt, word soon passed down to the appropriate parties that the Sojourner Truth Project would indeed house blacks. At regular cabinet meetings, Bethune's salient activity was often receiving information—frequently meticulous analyses and program proposals. Armed with them, she strode forth to interact authoritatively with white individuals and groups on particular aspects of black welfare.

Yet on occasion rejection stared her in the face. During the McCarthy hysteria, the Board of Education in Englewood, New Jersey, denied Bethune a school's platform because she had been labeled a Communist subversive. In response, Americans who knew the vision that had undergirded her life—a vision of a country eschewing segregation and discrimination in order to appreciate the value of individuals regardless of race, color, creed, or gender—rallied to her defense in a movement reversing the board's action. Honors and awards came to Bethune until her death from a heart attack on May 18, 1955. A memorial tribute to Mary McLeod Bethune stands in Lincoln Park on Capitol Hill in Washington, D.C. The bronze sculpture by Robert Berks was erected in 1974 and depicts Bethune leaning on a cane that President Roosevelt gave her, and handing her will to two children.—ELAINE M. SMITH

JULIAN **BOND**

1940–

Civil rights activist, politician, educator

A public servant and advocate for political freedom and justice, Horace Julian Bond moved from being cofounder of SNCC, the Student Nonviolent Coordinating Committee, in 1960 to serving in the Georgia State Senate from 1974 to 1987. Organizer of the Georgia Legislative Black Caucus and sponsor of more than sixty bills that became laws, Bond narrated the acclaimed Eyes on the Prize *documentary of the Civil Rights Movement. He represented the quintessential African American college student struggling for freedom and equality in the Jim Crow South.*

Bond was born in Nashville, Tennessee, on January 14, 1940, the elder son of well-known educator and scholar Horace Mann Bond, president of Fort Valley State College, a historically black institution in Georgia, and Julia Washington Bond, a librarian. Bond has an older sister, Jane, and a younger brother, James.

*Julian Bond speaks with Ku Klux Klan imperial wizard
Bill Wilkinson on Phil Donahue's television show.*

Bond spent his childhood in the North. His father, who graduated from Lincoln University in Pennsylvania, returned there as its first black president in 1943. He used his own children as plaintiffs in a case that successfully integrated the county schools of Pennsylvania. Thus, Julian Bond was no stranger to the struggle for civil rights. Yet, as he stated in *Up From Within,* "I never really lived the life of a Southern Negro kid."

At twelve, Bond enrolled in the George School in Bucks County, Pennsylvania. He was the only black in the private Quaker school. Bond excelled in everything but academics. Although expected by his parents to become a scholar, Bond was the goalie on the soccer team, a star swimmer, and a member of the wrestling team; it took him five years instead of four to graduate. At the George School, Bond encountered several racist incidents, and singlehandedly integrated the Newtown movie theater by refusing to sit in the balcony section reserved for blacks.

In 1957 Bond's father accepted a position as dean of Atlanta University's School of Education. The family moved to Atlanta, where Bond enrolled as a freshman at Morehouse College. His preparatory school background enabled him to score better than all of his classmates. Bond, however, had the classic symptoms of an underachiever. While his classmates scored lower in aptitude, they were ambitious and hard working. By midyear Bond found himself no longer at the head of the class. It was not that he disliked college; he suffered the malaise affecting many second- and third-generation children of college-educated, middle-class blacks. Never having had to struggle, he did not know how. Nor did he feel the need. Bond's attitude about college was lackadaisical. He told John Neary in *Julian Bond,* "It wasn't a question of being interested in something else and not being interested in college; it just wasn't that big a thing. I thought it would be enough to get through, to pass, to get a degree . . . and make a 'career choice.'"

Bond was thinking of becoming a writer, and poetry was the genre he selected. He published several poems while still in college.

From rebel to radical   Clearly from the black elite traditions, Bond might have rebelled—perhaps—even without a cause. Given a cause, Bond's rebellion quickly metastasized into radical political protest. The catalyst for change came in the form of Lonnie King, a Morehouse student politically more active than Bond, who enlisted Bond's assistance in organizing a meeting to discuss the black student sit-in movement. By the end of the meeting, which took place in February 1960, they had formed COAHR, Atlanta's Committee on Appeal for Human Rights. Their first agenda item was to stage a sit-in at eating establishments that refused to serve Atlanta blacks. On March 15, 1960, Bond led a group of students to the all-white cafeteria inside City Hall. This protest resulted in his first and only arrest.

On Easter weekend, April 1960, Bond, Lonnie King, and other COAHR members attended a mass meeting in Raleigh, North Carolina, called by Martin Luther King Jr. and the Southern Christian Leadership Conference (SCLC). Student leaders and groups throughout the South met at Shaw University to formulate strategies for obtaining civil rights. From this initial meeting the Student Nonviolent Coordinating Committee (SNCC; pronounced *snick*) was born. James Forman was the director.

The SNCC Atlanta chapter was the best organized and the best financed. Bond recalled in the book *Julian Bond,* "We had nearly $6,000 in the bank, and we had almost 4,000 people picketing in downtown Atlanta, a masterpiece of precision. Oh, man, we had waterproof picket signs and football parkas for the girls to wear to keep the spitballs off. Martin Luther King Jr. got arrested with us one time—and the lunch counters were integrated." It took eighteen months to integrate the lunch counter at Rich's, the largest department store in the South.

Atlanta's black newspaper, the *Daily World,* attacked Bond's Appeal for Human Rights group, calling it ill-advised. In response, students and some faculty advisors started another black paper to voice student concerns. Bond started as a reporter for the *Atlanta Inquirer* and ended up as managing editor. Soon COAHR became part of SNCC. The students of the Atlanta University Center began voter-registration campaigns led by Bond, and during the summer of 1960 they signed up close to 10,000 new black voters.

Bond's involvement in civil rights played havoc on his academic life. Basically, he was failing at Morehouse, and he was in love with a Spelman student he wanted to marry. Deciding to forego his degree, Bond married Alice Clopton on July 28, 1961. He began working full time for SNCC as its public relations spokesman and edited its newspaper, the *Student Voice.* He earned forty dollars a week. By 1964, Bond was the father of two children and he and Alice were expecting a third child. SNCC's mood was changing and Bond worried over what the change would ultimately mean for him and his growing family.

Members of SNCC disagreed about the power whites should have in the organization. As more whites entered and assumed authority, black members came to believe that the organization needed black leadership. Bond agreed. By 1964 many blacks were not only disgusted with the power struggles within SNCC but were disillusioned with the treatment of the Mississippi Freedom Democratic Party (MFDP) at the 1964 Convention. Bond recalls that when the MFDP claimed that Mississippi's regular delegation did not represent all the Democratic votes of Mississippi, especially not the black members, party leadership went to work to prevent the credentials committee from supporting the MFDP minority report. Bond stated in *Julian Bond,* "it was a sell-out, and for a lot of people that was just the last straw."

Young Julian Bond.

Entering the political ring The Georgia legislature reapportioned the state in 1964, and Bond decided to run for one of the newly created Atlanta seats. Campaigning on the issues of unemployment, minimum wages, and fair housing, Bond walked away with 82 percent of the votes. Assuming his legislative seat was a different matter, however. In 1966, when SNCC condemned the United States' involvement in Vietnam, Bond made a public statement in agreement, praising those who were brave enough to protest by burning their draft cards.

The Georgia legislature accused Bond of treason and, according to *Contemporary Black Biography,* of "giving aid and comfort to the enemies of the United States and the enemies of Georgia." Bond refused to rescind his statement, and the controversy grew. On January 10, 1966, the Georgia House voted 184 to 12 against seating Bond on the grounds of disorderly conduct. The controversy catapulted Bond to national prominence. The press and news media defended his right to take his seat. Bond took the issue to the federal district court, where the legislature's decision was upheld.

Refusing to give up, the next step, therefore, was the Supreme Court. On December 5, 1966, the U.S. Supreme Court ruled that the Georgia House had violated Bond's right to free speech under the First Amendment. The legislature, forced to seat Bond, treated him as an outcast.

In 1968 Bond was again in the national spotlight. Georgia governor Lester Maddox appointed only six blacks as delegates for the Democratic National Convention. The national party wanted the delegation to be representative of the state. Six delegates out of 107, however, was not. Bond, a member of the Georgia Democratic Party Forum, challenged the official delegation. Cochairing the rival delegation, Bond's delegation won nearly half of the delegates' votes. He became the Democratic Party's first black candidate for the U.S. vice presidency, but at twenty-eight he was too young for the job, for which minimum age was thirty-five.

During the 1970s, Bond's popularity began to wane. He appeared to have lost interest in politics, and when Jimmy Carter's administration went to Washington, although invited, he declined to go. By 1979 he could be described as a political outsider. Bond applied for the directorship of the NAACP but was considered too radical for the job.

Things fall apart   The lack of ambition that plagued Bond in his school days returned to shadow him during the 1980s. He and his wife now had a family of five—two daughters and three sons—and his wife and children were unhappy taking a backseat to politics. Trouble also loomed on the political front. Bond almost lost his senate seat and was charged with inaccessibility, excessive absenteeism, and lack of attention to local concerns. In 1986 he gave up his senate seat to run for U.S. Congress against his longtime friend and SNCC associate, John Lewis. He lost the election.

In 1987 Alice Bond accused him of using cocaine, and although she publicly rescinded her charge, Bond's alleged girlfriend received a twenty-two-year prison sentence on drug charges. His reputation suffered.

While his political and private life seemed to fall apart, Bond continued to write and lecture around the country. He narrated *Eyes on the Prize,* a PBS documentary on the Civil Rights Movement; hosted the television program *America's Black Forum;* wrote "Viewpoint," a nationally syndicated newspaper column; and was a visiting professor at Drexel University in 1968 and at Harvard University in 1989.

On March 17, 1990, Bond married Pamela S. Horowitz, an attorney. Currently Bond is a distinguished scholar in residence at American University, and has been a member of the department of history at the University of Virginia since 1990. He received his B.A. from Morehouse College in 1971. He has honorary degrees from Dalhousie, Oregon, Syracuse, Tuskegee, Howard, and Lincoln universities. His affiliations include honorary trustee of the Institute of Applied Politics, national board member of the NAACP, and member of the New Democratic Coalition, the Southern Regional Council, and the Delta Ministry Project of the National Council of Churches. Bond was president of the Atlanta NAACP from 1974 to 1989, and in 1989 was Pappas Fellow at the University of Pennsylvania. He is the author of *A Time to Speak, A Time to Act* (1972) and has contributed poems to three anthologies. Julian Bond continues to speak out for human justice, a trait he has not lost since becoming an important figure in the history of the civil rights movement.—NAGUEYALTI WARREN

ARNA **BONTEMPS**
1902–1973
Writer, librarian, teacher

Arna Bontemps was a prolific writer who emerged during the Harlem Renaissance and wrote, edited, and compiled numerous works in a variety of genres for nearly sixty years. In his life's works he championed freedom for all people. A librarian as well as a prolific reader, he ensured the preservation of the African American heritage by building at Fisk University one of the nation's most outstanding repositories.

Bontemps was born October 13, 1902, to Paul Bismark Bontemps and Maria Carolina Pembroke Bontemps in Alexandria, Louisiana. He had one younger sister, Ruby Sarah. His father, was a strong-willed, austere, dark-skinned man with straight hair, who, like his father and grandfather, was a brick mason; later he became a lay minister in the Seventh Day Adventist Church. He was also a musician. Prior to her marriage, Arna Bontemps's mother, was a public school teacher in Louisiana. When Bontemps was three and a half years old, in 1906, the family headed for San Francisco but settled in Los Angeles. According to *Black Voices,* their move was prompted by the elder Bontemps's refusal to act submissive to a group of drunken, racist, white men on an Alexandria street who threatened to "walk over the big nigger." In Los Angeles they moved into a big house in a white neighborhood. Bontemps's maternal grandmother and a host of other relatives followed. Maria Bontemps died when Bontemps was twelve years old; after that, Bontemps lived with his grandparents for a time.

The mother had stimulated in her son a love for books and reading. Bontemps and his father had a much less comforting relationship. Paul Bontemps wanted his son to continue in the brick masonry trade that was a part of family tradition, but Arna Bontemps wanted to write instead. The father also resented his son's relationship with Uncle Buddy (Joe Ward), the younger, mulatto brother of Arna Bontemps's maternal grandmother, who had a positive influence on the young man's life and writing skills. Not only was the uncle's alcoholism a problem for the father, but Buddy's circle of friends from the lower class were as well. Young Bontemps, however, was influenced by his Uncle Buddy's stories in dialect as well as his preacher and ghost tales, and slave and master stories. Later, Bontemps drew on these oral narrations in his writings.

To help support himself after his mother died, Bontemps worked as a newsboy and a gardener in Hollywood. He entered San Fernando Academy, located in San Fernando Valley, a white Seventh-Day Adventist boarding school, in 1917. Bontemps wrote in *Black Voices* that his father cautioned him, "Now don't go up there acting colored;" Bontemps continued, "I believe I carried out his wish." Reflecting on this advice, he wrote in the same source, "How dare anyone . . . tell me not to act *colored?* White people have been enjoying the privilege of acting like Negroes for more than a hundred years." By the time he was in college Bontemps felt that he had been miseducated at the school.

He finished the school in only three years, graduating in 1920 at the age of seventeen. He studied both at the University of California at Los Angeles and at Pacific Union College near St. Helena (Angwin), California. In college, he had developed skills as an imaginative writer. While in a freshman English class, Bontemps received the initial stimulus that led him to New York three years later. He wrote in *The Harlem Renaissance Remembered* that he saw his teacher smile approvingly at a paper he submitted as a part of an assignment: "I was more embarrassed than flattered by the attention it drew, but the teacher's smile lingered, and I came to regard that expression as the semaphore that flagged me toward New York City three years later." In college he sang in the glee club, known as the jubilee singers, and helped support himself by working as a postal clerk.

Before he graduated in 1923—again completing his work in three years—from Pacific Union with a bachelor of arts degree, Bontemps had considered a career either in medicine, which he soon discounted, or in music, but his inclination to pursue a career in music was more difficult to dismiss. Later, he planned to study for a doctorate in English, but pressing matters such as the hardships of the Depression years, the responsibilities of employment and family, and the demands of his promising writing career interfered.

After graduation he completed a series of postgraduate courses at UCLA, worked nights in the post office and, unable to sleep well afterward, spent his days reading literature with a "frenzy," as he said. He read novels, poems, dramas, biographies, and whatever interested him at the neighborhood library. He also began to write and send poems to several magazines hoping to be published, but was unsuccessful. After he noticed that the *Crisis* encouraged young blacks to contribute works, he sent one of his rejected poems, "Hope," to Jessie Fauset, literary agent for the magazine, who published the work in 1924, giving him literary visibility. Meanwhile, he and Wallace Thurman, who was also a post office employee and a writer, met and discussed their mutual interests. Once Bontemps received a copy of the August issue of *Crisis* that carried his poem, he resigned and headed for New York City. As Bontemps wrote in *Black Voices,* it was impossible and unthinkable to shed his past, his "Negro-ness," and he took these riches with him to New York.

*Arna
Bontemps.*

In New York, Bontemps soon met Countee Cullen, who took him to a small gathering held for Langston Hughes on Edgecombe Avenue held in Regina Anderson's and Ethel Ray Nance's apartment. This was one of the places where Harlem Renaissance artists were likely to gather; the other was the 135th Street Branch of the New York Public Library, where Bontemps also spent time. At this gathering Bontemps met Jessie Fauset, as well as Harlem Renaissance entrepreneur Charles S. Johnson, Alain Locke, Eric Walrond, and of course, the honored guest and Bontemps's look-alike at the time, Hughes. He made lasting friendships and associations with the Renaissance artists, young and old. At that time he established a relationship with Hughes. That relationship was cemented in December 1931, when according to Arnold Rampersad in *The Life of Langston Hughes,* they had "virtually a marriage of minds, that would last without the slightest friction" and included personal visits as well as the exchange of some 2,500 letters that continued until Hughes's death in 1967. Charles H. Nichols published their correspondence in 1980 as *Arna Bontemps—Langston Hughes Letters, 1925–1967,* noting that Bontemps told his own publisher in 1969: "All told I am convinced we have the fullest documentation of the Afro American experience in the new world, artistic, intellectual, covering the mid-20th century, one is likely to find anywhere."

After Charles S. Johnson promoted the awards dinners for the *Opportunity* magazine literary contests, Bontemps wrote in *The Harlem Renaissance Remembered,* he decided to enter, and his life "has never been the same since." Not only did he receive recognition, but he came in contact with other influential leaders of the time, including the benefactor of the period and unofficial record-keeper of the "New Negro" movement, Carl Van Vechten.

To broaden his knowledge and prepare himself for creative writing, Bontemps studied at Columbia University, New York University, and the City College of New York. To earn a living as his writing career developed, Bontemps was teacher and later principal at the Harlem Academy, a Seventh Day Adventist high school, from 1924 until 1931. While the school's officials tolerated Bontemps's association with the Renaissance artists, when he used "God" in the title of his novel, *God Sends Sunday*—his first book, published in 1931, for which Harlem Renaissance writer Louise Thompson was typist—they called it blasphemy and, according to some sources, shipped him off to Oakwood Junior College in Huntsville, Alabama. Kirkland Jones, however, wrote in *Renaissance Man from Louisiana* that the academy closed, leaving Bontemps unemployed. He went to the Oakwood school as English teacher and librarian. Bontemps's biographical statement in the Bontemps Collection at Fisk University indicates that the Depression, the scatting elsewhere of the Harlem Renaissance artists, and Bontemps's urge "to undertake more serious and sustained writing tasks" compelled him to leave New York.

Bontemps was not a disbeliever; neither was he a religious zealot. The Oakwood officials thought Bontemps was a Harlem radical. According to Kirkland Jones, school officials were concerned with his association with "outside agitators"; thus, when Langston Hughes visited him sometime in late 1932 or in 1933, Bontemps nearly lost his job. He created local suspicion by receiving so many books in the mail and spending so much time typing. Officials began to label writing and teaching novels sinful, and the president ordered Bontemps to burn his secular books. Rather than reform, at the end of the school year in May 1934 Bontemps resigned, perhaps with the school's encouragement; he, his wife, and three young children spent the 1934–35 year with his father and stepmother in southern California. He conducted research in the local library, studying dialect and analyzing children's books. He also talked to the children at the library story hour and invited his friend Langston Hughes, then en route from Mexico, to lecture in the library as well. Bontemps spent the summer writing what became his most renowned novel, *Black Thunder;* after receiving a publisher's advance for the book, Bontemps left for Chicago.

From 1935 to 1938 Bontemps taught in Chicago at another Seventh Day Adventist school, the Shiloh Academy. From 1938 to 1942 he worked as a technical assistant—in charge of black students—to the state director of the Illinois Writer's Project of the Works Progress Administration (WPA). He and Richard Wright, also a Seventh-Day Adventist and hired on the project as well, had mutual admiration and respect for each other. In 1936 Bontemps enrolled as a graduate student in English at the University of Chicago, where he completed residency requirements for the master's degree but did not complete the degree. Instead, he studied on a Rosenwald Fellowship for creative writing and traveled to the Caribbean. Meanwhile, James Weldon Johnson, who had been professor of creative writing at Fisk University, died in

1938, and Thomas Elsa Jones, president of Fisk, asked Bontemps to fill the post; a little later the school was without a head librarian as well. Jones asked Bontemps to fill both posts, but Bontemps wanted formal training in library science before he took the library position. In 1940 Bontemps was cultural director of the American Negro Exposition held in Chicago, worked with black materials, and was primarily responsible for *The Calvacade of the American Negro* that the WPA project issued for the celebration. During his Chicago years, Bontemps's favorite hangout was the Hall Branch of the Chicago Public library. In 1942 Bontemps received a second fellowship to study for his master's degree at the Graduate Library School, University of Chicago.

In September 1943 Bontemps became head librarian and full professor at Fisk University and six months later, in December, he received his master's degree in library science from Chicago. At Fisk he joined his Harlem Renaissance friends, artist Aaron Douglas and sociologist Charles S. Johnson. Bontemps became noted for building the special collections division of the library into a leading repository for research on African American themes. He gathered the papers of such black writers as Jean Toomer, Charles Waddell Chesnutt, and Langston Hughes and also strengthened the book collection by adding retrospective as well as contemporary works by and about African Americans. He remained at Fisk until he retired from the full-time position in 1964; then he was appointed acting librarian while he also served as director of university relations until 1965. It was at this time that he gave the advice of the sage that he was: he advised the library staff to enter the emerging reprint program so that black books, then becoming scarce, would be more easily available.

From 1966 to 1969 he was a professor of English at the University of Illinois, Chicago Circle. He said in an interview for Fisk's Black Oral History Program that "they wanted me to introduce something in literature which is one of the things that I was promoting all of the time: that the black experience is seen better through the literature than through the history. And I think that has caught on." Regarding all of the literature predominating in black studies programs, Bontemps believed that he "was the one who initiated that emphasis." Bontemps moved to Yale University in 1969 as curator of the James Weldon Johnson Memorial Collection in the Beinecke Library. Returning to Nashville in 1970, Bontemps was writer-in-residence at Fisk until 1973.

Creates literature for children   Bontemps wrote in a variety of genres and for wide audiences, publishing single works as well as scholarly anthologies. In his writings he frequently drew upon the dialect of his Creole parents and often used it in his letters to Langston Hughes as well. His fiction included his first book, *God Sends Sunday,* published in 1931, followed by *Black Thunder* (1936), *Drums at Dusk* (1939), and *The Old South: "A Summer Tragedy" and Other Stories of the Thirties* (1973). Best known as a writer of biographies, anthologies, and historical novels for young people, the works that he wrote, compiled, or edited include *Sad-Faced Boy* (1937); *Golden Slippers: An Anthology of Negro Poetry for Young People* (1941); *Story of the Negro* (1948), *Chariot in the Sky; A Story of the Jubilee Singers* (1951); *Lonesome Boy* (1955); *Frederick Douglass: Slave, Fighter, Freeman* (1958), and *Young Booker: The Story of Booker T. Washington's Early Days* (1972).

He worked with collaborators on a number of other books. In 1934 he and Countee Cullen adapted the novel *God Sends Sunday* for the stage, and again they used the novel as a base for *St. Louis Woman,* a stage play that opened on Broadway in 1946.

Metro-Goldwyn-Mayer bought the movie rights to the play in 1952. Bontemps and Jack Conroy wrote *They Seek a City* (1945), which was revised and published in 1966 as *Anyplace But Here,* and *Slappy Hooper, the Wonderful Sign Painter* (1946). Bontemps told the *Nashville Tennessean* for February 18, 1951, that "My friend, Langston Hughes, indirectly started me writing. He had just returned from the West Indies and brought back loads of snapshots and toys (for my kids) from Haiti. I got interested and he and I collaborated on a book, *Popo and Fifina,*" published in 1932. The well-known illustrator E. Simms Campbell illustrated the book. Bontemps and Hughes also collaborated on *I Too Sing America* (1964); *The Poetry of the Negro, 1746–1949,* revised and published in 1970 as *The Poetry of the Negro, 1746–1970,* and on *The Book of Negro Folklore* (1958). His other books included *We Have Tomorrow* (1945), *One Hundred Years of Negro Freedom* (1961), *Personals,* (a collection of his own poetry, 1963), and an anthology, *Hold Fast to Dreams: Poems Old and New* (1969). Among the books that Bontemps edited are *Father of the Blues: An Autobiography of W. C. Handy* (1941) and *The Harlem Renaissance Remembered: Essays with a Memoir* (1972). He also published works in a number of journals.

Highly honored for his work, among the awards and honors Bontemps received were, in addition to the *Crisis* award for poetry in 1926, the Alexander Pushkin poetry prizes in 1926 and 1927; *Opportunity* magazine's short story prize in 1932; Guggenheim Fellowships for creative writing, 1949 and 1954; Jane Addams Children's Book Award for *Story of the Negro,* 1956; and, with Jack Conroy, the James L. Dow Award from the Society of Midland Authors, for *Anyplace But Here,* 1967. He was named honorary consultant in American Cultural History at the Library of Congress in 1972. He received honorary degrees from Morgan State University in 1969 and Berea College in 1973.

Bontemps was a member of the NAACP, PEN, the American Library Association, and the Dramatists Guild. He served on the Metropolitan Nashville Board of Education, and was a member of Sigma Pi Phi (the Boulé) and Omega Psi Phi Fraternity.

Writing was always uppermost in Bontemps's mind, and he took pains to record his thoughts and ideas so that they might be used in his works. Quoted in the *Alexandria Louisiana Daily Town Talk,* Paul Bontemps said of his father, who always kept a note pad with him, "I thought this was the normal way that people lived, with a note pad beside the bed. In the morning there'd be scribbles all over it." Bontemps's writing began at five o'clock in the morning on a card table in the living room. Bontemps told the *Nashville Tennessean* for February 18, 1951, that "I've done some of my best books at home with the children playing . . . all around me. I just pull up the card table, close the door (if that's possible) and go to work." A meticulous writer, he composed on the typewriter and rarely needed to do more than one or two drafts. Paul Bontemps also saw his father as one who was just as concerned about his French heritage as his African American.

Bontemps was a lover of art and collected works by his friend, Harlem Renaissance painter Aaron Douglas, who refused to accept payment for the items that Bontemps wanted.

In his honor, the Arna Bontemps African American Museum and Cultural Center was opened in the Bontemps birthplace and childhood home in Alexandria, Louisiana, dedicated on November 12, 1992. The home, called the Arna Wendell Bontemps House, was listed on the National Register of Historic Places on September 13, 1993. Mayor Philip Bredesen of Nashville declared October 7, 1994, as Arna Bontemps Day in Nashville, in recognition of his gifts "especially to African American children's literature—paving the way for others to follow his courageous paths to success."

Stricken while attending a celebration of life for a friend, Bontemps died of a heart attack on December 4, 1973, in Nashville and was buried in Greenwood Cemetery. His closest survivors were Alberta Johnson Bontemps, who had been his student at Harlem Academy and who became his wife on August 26, 1926; and six children: Joan Marie Bontemps Williams, Paul Bismark, Poppy Alberta Bontemps Booker, Camille Ruby Bontemps Graves, Constance Rebecca Bontemps Thomas, and Arna Alexander Bontemps. He had been deeply devoted to his family throughout life.

Bontemps was a strong voice of the Harlem Renaissance and was known for his work as poet, writer, essayist, biographer, anthologist, librarian, and an advocate of libraries. Always an avid reader, he stimulated children and adults to read as well through the works that he wrote, through the numerous lectures that he gave, and through the African American collection that he built at Fisk University. The *Norton Anthology of African American Literature* called his writing "characteristically graceful, serene, and . . . intellectually challenging and independent." He had a deep sense of racial pride, intellectual and emotional integrity, and deep religious and spiritual interests and was able to balance these characteristics and reflect them in his writings with a "confidence matched by few other writers."—JESSIE CARNEY SMITH

EDWARD W. **BROOKE**

1919–

U.S. Senator, state attorney general, lawyer, military officer

Born into a world that invariably would try to view or describe him primarily by the color of his skin, Edward Brooke has obdurately insisted that society focus on his careers rather than his race. As a World War II officer, Boston attorney, Massachusetts attorney general, U.S. senator, and Washington attorney, Brooke has exerted his considerable influence in efforts to benefit all Americans.

Edward William Brooke III was born on October 26, 1919, in Washington, D.C. His father, Edward Brooke Jr., graduated from Howard University's School of Law in 1918 and for fifty years was an attorney for the Veterans Administration—a rare position for a black American at that time. His mother, Helen Seldon Brooke, would later be active in each of Brooke's campaigns; Brooke regarded his mother as an effective speaker on the campaign trail. In 1966 the National Shriners named her Mother of the Year.

Brooke lived with his parents and his older sister, Helene, in a middle-class Washington neighborhood. He attended Minor Teachers' College, a teacher-training school; William Lloyd Garrison and John F. Cooke elementary schools; Robert Gould Shaw Junior High School; and the historic Dunbar High School, considered by many the finest black high school in America. He graduated from Dunbar in 1936. Reflecting on his youth as cited in Cutler's biography, *Edward Brooke,* he remarked:

> I was a happy child. I was conscious of being a Negro, yes, but I was not conscious of being underprivileged because of that. . . . I grew up segregated, but there was not much feeling of being shut out of anything. . . . When we

couldn't buy tickets for a concert or the opera in the segregated theaters of Washington, my mother simply took us to New York to Carnegie Hall or the Metropolitan.

At the age of sixteen, Brooke entered Howard University with plans of becoming a surgeon; however, upon finding science courses boring, he changed his major to sociology. His political science course was taught by Ralph Bunche, who later earned distinction as a diplomat, statesman, and Nobel Prize winner. Brooke was elected president of Beta Chapter of the Alpha Phi Alpha fraternity in his senior year. He later became eastern national vice president of the organization. He received his B.S. from Howard in 1941.

Earns distinction in military service   After graduating from college and the Reserve Officers Training Corps, Brooke was drafted into the army. He served as a second lieutenant in the all-black 366th Combat Infantry Regiment. At Massachusetts' Fort Devens, Brooke, in charge of discipline and recreation, also had the opportunity to defend enlisted men in military court cases. The 366th's travels included North Africa and Italy. Brooke spent 195 days in combat and was promoted to captain. He received the Bronze Star for his leadership in a daylight attack on an artillery battery and observation post that was heavily fortified. In *Challenge of Change,* Brooke, who also received the Distinguished Service Award, described the ironic situation experienced by members of the 366th. He said that the men fought hard and well, and despite heavy casualties, maintained a high morale. Because the regiment was segregated, however, there was an undercurrent of resentment in the unit. They were also "treated as second-class soldiers." He said:

> Our soldiers (first-class by any definition) asked, "Why are *we* fighting this war? It's supposed to be a war against Nazism—against racism and for democracy. Well, what about *us?* Why are black men fighting a white man's war? What's all this double-talk about democracy?" They were not easy questions to answer. I tried to explain that the first task was to defeat the common enemy. And I asked them to bear with America's racial injustices until the war was won. But I knew that this was no more than a rationalization.

He continued to serve as a defense counsel in court martial cases and also assumed the identity of an Italian, Captain Carlo, in order to cross enemy lines as a liaison officer with the Italian partisans.

Before returning to the United States in 1945, Brooke met Remigia Ferrari-Scacco, the daughter of a prominent Genoan paper merchant. For two years they maintained a long-distance relationship by mail. They were married on June 7, 1947, in Roxbury, Massachusetts.

Law school and beyond   Brooke's military experiences with legal proceedings motivated him to enroll in Boston University Law School in September 1946. He served as editor of the *Boston University Law Review* and received an LL.B. in 1948 and an LL.M. in 1949. Brooke took the bar examination with 598 candidates and was among the 197 who passed.

He began practicing law in Roxbury. Brooke rejected offers to join other law firms, including a request from his father. The elder Brooke, who had never practiced private law, wanted to establish a father and son firm in Washington. When Brooke invited his father to join him in Boston, his father declined. Brooke later moved his office to downtown Boston.

Edward Brooke.

His friends encouraged him to enter politics. Having decided to seek election to the Massachusetts legislature, Brooke, a man who had previously never voted (as Washington, D.C., residents did not have the right to vote), ran in the 1950 Democratic and Republican Primaries in a practice known as cross-filing. He won the Republican nomination but lost the general election.

Brooke's political ambition caused domestic friction. Remigia Brooke was upset by the unkind comments about their interracial marriage during the 1950 campaign. Brooke reportedly considered abandoning his political aspirations.

In 1952 he sought office a second time. In the first Massachusetts primary in which candidates were not allowed to cross-file, Brooke filed as a Republican in his bid for the state legislature. His campaign was unsuccessful. During the next eight years, Brooke focused on his law practice and increased his involvement in community affairs. He was the second vice president of the Boston branch of the NAACP, a member of the board of directors of the Greater Boston Urban League, director of the Boston Council of the Boy Scouts, state commander and national judge advocate of the American Veterans of World War II, and a member of numerous civic clubs.

In 1960 Brooke entered his third political race. In his bid to capture Massachusetts' third highest office—secretary of state—he became the first black to be nominated for a statewide office in Massachusetts. Brooke boldly sought election in a state where only 93 thousand blacks resided by campaigning as an American rather than a member of a minority group. Although Brooke lost the election, he made an impressive showing with over one million votes. After the 1960 election, Brooke rejected several governmental appointments before accepting the chairmanship of the Boston Finance Commission. Until Brooke's association with the organization, it accomplished little. Under Brooke's leadership, the commission exposed corruption in the city's building, real estate, and fire departments. He benefited from the frequent publicity generated by the commission's activities; Brooke was now one of the most popular political figures in Massachusetts.

In 1962 he sought the office of attorney general of Massachusetts. Although Republican leaders had endorsed Brooke's candidacy for lesser positions in previous elections, they were reluctant to offer him their support for the second highest position in the state. Thus the GOP offered him opportunities to run for lieutenant governor or to accept a judgeship, but Brooke would not be swayed. He went on to win his party's nomination and to win the primary and general election. He was the only Republican elected statewide that year, and he was the first black American to be elected to a major state office.

In 1964 Brooke ran for re-election as attorney general, although his supporters encouraged him to run for governor. During his two terms as attorney general, he continued to battle corruption in government and elsewhere. He endorsed and proposed legislation that, among other results, protected consumers, ended housing discrimination, and reduced air pollution. Brooke endured the wrath of civil rights leaders when he labeled the 1963 black student boycott to protest segregation of Boston schools illegal. Brooke told his critics that as a lawyer and attorney general, he had to serve all the people of Massachusetts; to do any less would result in his failing to do justice to his office or to advance the cause of civil rights.

Becomes junior senator from Massachusetts   In 1965 Brooke announced his candidacy for the U.S. Senate. Some people believe that Brooke's book published in 1966, *The Challenge of Change: Crisis in Our Two-Party System,* was an important campaign asset; in it he urged the Republican party to be more responsive to social change, and he wrote, "The conquest of space, the soaring increase in our national wealth, the flowering of our arts and sciences—our finest achievements are tarnished while more than a tenth of all Americans remain second-class citizens because of the color of their skins." Brooke won the election with a plurality of more than 400 thousand votes. He became the third black American to serve in the Senate.

Upon returning to the city of his birth, Brooke received a standing ovation as he was escorted down the aisle of the Senate chamber by the senior senator from Massachusetts, Edward Kennedy, at his swearing-in ceremony. He wished his father had been in the gallery and thought about his father's frustrations about not having the opportunity to do more. His father would not have "foreseen that some day his son would sit in the U.S. Senate," Brooke wrote. He continued:

> There was one scene I shall never forget. As I left the Capitol building I noticed hundreds of high-school students crowding the steps, some from Mississippi and some from Cardozo High School in Washington. I thought of what my grandmother used to say—"Stay in your place." This advice was given to protect me from injury, because if you didn't follow this advice, you knew what would happen. But this was a statement I never could accept. Your place is anywhere you want to make it.

Brooke served two terms in Congress, where he became one of the most respected members of the Senate. During his first year, Vietnam and civil rights issues claimed much of his attention. Several months after his swearing-in ceremony, he traveled to South Vietnam and other Asian destinations on a fact-finding mission. Upon his return, Brooke demanded that the United States replace deadly napalm with tear gas, and he said that Americans continued to fundamentally support the South Vietnamese. While America, Brooke added, was ready to discuss settlement of the discord, military and economic assistance to the South Vietnamese would continue as needed.

During the summer of 1967, racial riots occurred in urban areas throughout the United States. President Johnson appointed Brooke to the President's Commission on Civil Disorders. One of the commission's recommendations was the protection of blacks and civil rights workers from harassment. Brooke and Senator Edward Mondale asked that the recommendations be broadened to include housing discrimination; it was ultimately approved by the House and Senate in the 1968 Civil Rights Act.

Brooke was also a Senate advocate of affirmative action, minority business development, school integration, improving the Social Security program, increasing the minimum wage, and increasing Medicare funds. As early as 1968, Brooke called for an end of U.S. trade with South Africa because of its oppression of blacks.

Brooke, who had endorsed President Richard M. Nixon in the 1968 and 1972 campaigns, clashed with the president on a number of issues, including Brooke's failure to vote for three Nixon nominees to the Supreme Court. Brooke became the first senator to publicly call for Nixon's resignation for his involvement in the Watergate scandal.

In 1978 Brooke was defeated in the General Election by Paul Tsongas. Brooke, the recipient of more than thirty honorary degrees and various awards, including the NAACP Spingarn Medal and the National Conference of Christians and Jews' Charles Evans Hughes Award, resumed his law practice after his senatorial career ended.

Brooke is a man who defies classification. He is a black American who demands recognition for his career accomplishments rather than his race. He is a Republican who sometimes appeared more Democratic than some of his Democratic colleagues in the Senate. Above all, Edward Brooke has endeavored to make America a better place for all Americans.— LINDA CARTER

GWENDOLYN **BROOKS**
1917–
Poet

With poetry that reflects changes in society and in her own life, Gwendolyn Elizabeth Brooks became the

first African American to receive a Pulitzer Prize. Her writing has been both celebrated and criticized by

audiences black and white, but her talent and skill with language have made her voice impossible to ignore.

Brooks was born June 7, 1917, in Topeka, Kansas, the daughter (and second child) of David Anderson Brooks and Keziah Corinne (Wims) Brooks. She graduated from Wilson Junior College in 1936, and since then she has received more than fifty honorary doctorates. Brooks's autobiography, *Report from Part One,* gives a joyful accounting of the poet's youth, which helps to explain Brooks's attitudes about family, race, friendship, teaching, learning, and all that has gone into the making of an American poet of Brooks's talent and stature. According to Brooks's mother, young Gwendolyn started writing at age seven, and Brooks writes, "I have notebooks dating from the time I was 11, when I started to keep my poems in composition books. My mother decided that I was to be the female Paul Laurence Dunbar."

Brooks's high school years were punctuated with easily remembered highs and lows, some of which were recorded in her 1971 interview with Ida Lewis: "I'd gone to several high schools. . . . I'd spent one year at Hyde Park Branch, which I hated. It was my first experience with many whites around. I wasn't much injured, just left alone. I realized that they were a society apart, and they really made you feel it."

This was the social creature speaking; meanwhile, the poet was reading and learning about newer poets such as T. S. Eliot, Ezra Pound, e. e. cummings, William Carlos Williams, and Wallace Stevens. She received enthusiastic encouragement from Langston Hughes, who read her poems upon meeting her when she was sixteen. His enthusiasm served as inspiration to the young Brooks, and years later, she and her husband gave him a party in their two-room kitchenette.

The September following her high school graduation Brooks enrolled in the newly opened Woodrow Wilson Junior College, and two years after her college graduation she met her future husband, Henry Lowington Blakely II. Both were twenty-one; Blakely, one of two blacks who worked on the student newspaper, was told by more than one person that there was "a shy brown girl who attended Junior NAACP meetings and wrote poetry." When he went to a meeting where Brooks and her friend, Margaret Taylor (later Burroughs, of the DuSable Museum), were seated, Taylor called to Blakely: "Hey Boy . . . This girl wants to meet you." Brooks later told Blakely that on seeing him she confided to Margaret, "That's the man I'm going to marry." And marry they did, sharing the good and the bad for thirty years until they separated in 1969: "We

Young Gwendolyn Brooks.

understood that our separation was best for the involved. (That won't be enough for the reader but it is enough for me.)" In 1973 the Blakelys reunited, and they celebrated their golden anniversary on September 17, 1989.

The 1940s and 1950s proved to be a stimulating time for her writing. She received her first public award in 1943 from the Midwestern Writers' Conference, and two years later Harper & Brothers published a book of her poems, called *A Street in Bronzeville.* Reviewing this book, which launched her career, a *New Yorker* critic said of Brooks: "She writes with style, sincerity, and a minimum of sentimentality." And *Poetry* magazine noted: "She shows a capacity to marry the special quality of her racial experience with the best attainments of our contemporary poetry tradition." She also received friendly and encouraging letters from Claude McKay and Countee Cullen. Indeed, Brooks had arrived in the world of poetry.

In 1945 she was one of the ten women to receive the Mademoiselle Merit Award for Distinguished Achievement. This was, indeed, a heady time, for she went to New York where she met Richard Wright and Ralph Ellison, among others. She was a strong admirer of such contemporary poets as John Crowe Ransom, Wallace Stevens, James Joyce, T. S. Eliot, Langston Hughes, and Merrill Moore, as well as older writers within the accepted canon of universal expression, such as Anton Chekov and Emily Dickinson. The concerns in the poetry of her first book, to be sure, were of the black community, but the style of her writing was considered "white." Houston Baker remarks on this when he observes that some of her writing possesses "the metaphysical complexities of Apollinaire, Eliot, and Pound."

Annie Allen appeared in 1949, a time when Brooks had been working hard on both poetry and prose. A proposed novel, *American Family Brown,* was rejected by her publisher in 1947, and thereafter she concentrated on the poetry that appeared in *Annie Allen,* including a long piece called "The Anniad." The promise of her book was fulfilled, although some critics took Brooks to task for the high tone of her language; her friend Don L. Lee (who later changed his name to Haki Madhubuti) even proclaimed the book to have been "unread by blacks."

Brooks receives Pulitzer for poetry   The more serious criticisms of *Annie Allen,* however, did nothing to deter the awarders of the Pulitzer Prize in 1950. Brooks was the first African American to receive a Pulitzer Prize for a book of poetry.

1953's *Maud Martha* is an autobiographical novel and, in the author's belief, this form "is a better testament, a better thermometer, than memory can be." The novel remains a manipulation of Brooks's experiences and the people she had known or shared deep moments with, but not a record of absolutely true happenings. In a rereading of this book, scholar Mary Helen Washington suggests feminist values and techniques that were not acknowledged when the book was first published, saying: "Current feminist theories which insist that we have to learn how to read the coded messages in women's texts—the silences, the evasions, the repression of female creativity—have helped me to reread *Maud Martha."*

Brooks's first of four books of children's poetry was published in 1956, and adult collections followed: *The Bean Eaters, Selected Poems,* and *Riot.* Ezekiel Mphahlele points out that "Brooks is essentially a dramatic poet, who is interested in setting and character and movement. . . . She is interested in bringing out in its subtlest nuances the color of life that conflict eventually creates." *The Bean Eaters* allowed Brooks the full range of her poetic involvement in the lives of blacks. She writes of the murder of Emmett Till, she cuts through the bravura of young black boys in "We Real Cool," she is biting and sardonic in "Lovers of the Poor," and she describes the visit of a black reporter to Little Rock in 1957. *The Bean Eaters,* the last book before a spectacular and surprising new direction in her work, was seen by one critic as "Brooks's ascent to the foothills of her grand heroic style."

She had reached a high point in her writing career, but she was about to change her writing to follow more closely the moods of her own people.

Black writers' conference influences Brooks   *In the Mecca* seemed to burst upon the scene after a 1967 visit Brooks made to the Second Black Writers' Conference at Fisk University, which she described in 1971 as discovering "what has stimulated my life these past few years: young people, full of a new spirit. They seemed stronger and taller, really ready to take on the challenges. . . . I was still saying 'Negro,' for instance."

In the Mecca started out as a novel, and it had various revisions before appearing as it stands now: a book of poems that presents a microcosm of black life in an all-too-crowded urban setting. The title poem is long and poignant, detailing the search for Pepita, the young daughter of Mrs. Sallie Smith, who has just come home from working in some white person's fine house. The poems introduce the reader, bit by bit, to certain types of characters who inhabit the Mecca, that teeming crowded building that houses not only poverty and failed dreams, but violence. In search of Pepita, then, black life and thought are explored in vignettes of real-life situations during the mid-1960s.

Poems in the second section of the book are short and include those dedicated to Medgar Evers and Malcolm X. Brooks was moving more deeply and inextricably into her native black world. Before the late 1960s, she told Claudia Tate, "I wasn't writing consciously

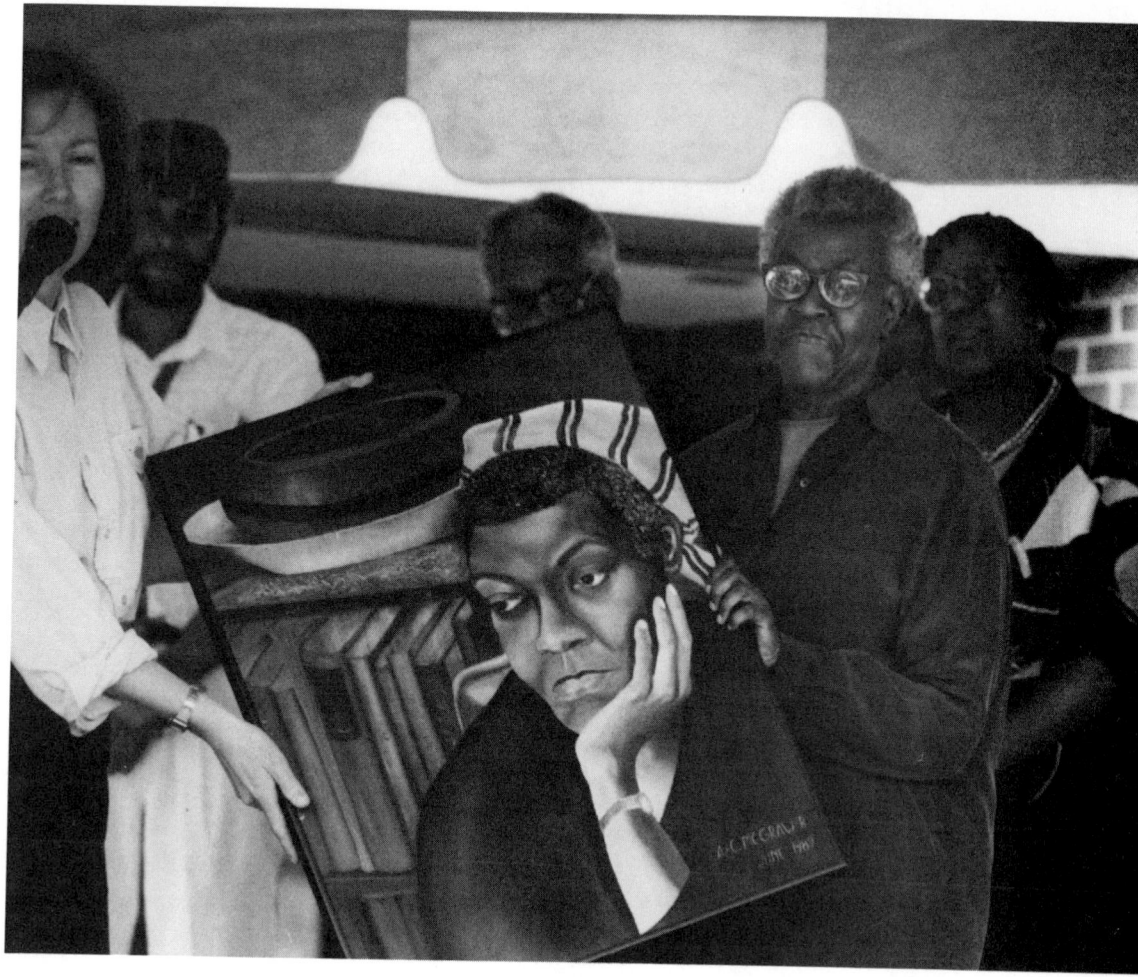

Gwendolyn Brooks, right, displays a portrait of herself painted by Anne Cressy McGraw Beauchamp, 1989.

with the idea that blacks *must address* blacks, *must write* about blacks. . . . I'm trying [now] to create new forms, trying to do something that could be presented in a tavern atmosphere." *In the Mecca,* which received a National Book Award nomination, was Brooks's declaration of independence from integration, because by 1969 she had changed her relationships with Harper and was publishing exclusively with blacks. (Her last book published by Harper came out in 1971: *The World of Gwendolyn Brooks.*) As she told one interviewer: "I have no intention of ever giving my books to another white publisher."

Riot, Aloneness, Broadside Treasury, Jump Bad, Report from Part One, and *Beckonings* were published by Broadside, the Detroit-based press started by Dudley Randall, a black librarian and Detroit's poet laureate. *Blacks,* published in 1987 by the David Company (Brooks's own company), is an anthology of her published works through 1987.

J a m e s   B r o w n

Poetry spans two distinct periods   The poetry of Brooks spans two distinct periods, pre-1967 and post-1967, or to quote Brooks: "The forties and fifties were years of high poet-incense; the language-flowers were thickly sweet. Those flowers whined and begged white folks to pick them, to find them lovable. Then—the sixties: independent fire!" Despite what seems a stated philosophical dichotomy in Brooks's work, her friend Lerone Bennett aptly points out: "She has always written about the sounds, sights and flavors of the Black community." And another close friend, Madhubuti, states: "Her greatest impact has been as key player in the literature of African-American people." What is important, then, is an understanding that Brooks's writings, whether poetry or prose, have been directly involved around the ethos of blacks. In 1985–86, Brooks was the Library of Congress's consultant on poetry.

Brooks is a generous poet who works with children and prisoners, and she uses her own money to sponsor a poetry contest. On June 11, 1989, she was feted at Navy Pier in Chicago by fifty poets reading to her in celebration of her seventieth birthday, and she was given a $48,000 lifetime achievement award that year from the National Endowment for the Arts. In 1990 she became the first scholar to hold the newly established Gwendolyn Brooks Distinguished Chair of Creative Writing at Chicago State University. Brooks has received many other honors, such as the National Book Foundation Medal for her lifetime contribution in 1994; a bronze bust of her image on display at the Harold Washington Library Center in Chicago; the National Endowment for the Humanities 1994 Jefferson Lecturer Award; and the National Medal for the Arts, bestowed by President Bill Clinton in 1995.

Brooks is highly regarded for her willingess to indulge a crowd poised to hear the words of this renowned literary pioneer. Brooks has offered poetry readings at Chicago's Three Art Club, a nonprofit organization that provides free counseling and advocacy to people who have been sexually abused, and to Atlanta's Symphony Hall as part of the National Black Arts Festival in 1996. In between poetry readings and her professorship at Chicago State University, Brooks has been gathering poems for her *Collected Poems* and writing a follow-up to her autobiography. A busy schedule for the eighty-year-old poet laureate, but work that will further immortalize a poetry giant.—MARGARET PERRY

JAMES **BROWN**
1933–
Musician, composer

James Brown is a major American musician. He first gained prominence in the field of rhythm and blues, then was instrumental in developing the fusion of R&B with gospel that became soul. In his search for new sounds he led the way from soul to funk, and his music remains an inspiration to the new generation of hip hop and rap musicians. Brown achieved immense popularity with frantic stage performances and a series of hit records, and only Elvis Presley and the Beatles have more songs on the pop charts. His driving belief in himself allowed him to overcome his apparently unpromising origins and made Brown an emblem of black pride for many people.

James Brown is known for his dynamic performances.

James Joe Brown Jr. was born on May 3, 1933, to Joe Brown and Susie Behlings Brown nine miles from Barnwell, South Carolina. James appeared stillborn, but his great-aunt Minnie Walker was able to revive him. The child was supposed to be named for his father, with James added as a middle name, but the given names were reversed on the birth registration. The "junior" was retained nonetheless, and to his family he was known as Junior or—when living with an elder cousin also called Junior—as Little Junior.

When Brown was four his mother departed, and he did not see her again for over twenty years. For the next two years James Brown was alone much of the time in a number of isolated cabins in the area. In his solitude he learned to play the harmonica. Finally Joe Brown asked Minnie Walker to join him to care for the child, and at the end of 1938 the family moved to Augusta, Georgia.

In Augusta James Brown and great-aunt Minnie Walker lived at 944 Twiggs Street with another aunt, Handsome (Honey) Washington, her brother Jack Scott, and Washington's grandson Willie Glenn Jr. (Big Junior) in a whorehouse. Both Jack Scott and Joe Brown were violent men who beat the child severely on occasion.

James Brown ran into problems in school because of his background. A neglected child, he was sent home at least twice for insufficient clothing. Still, he became popular at school because of his athletic ability and his musical talents. After school James Brown and Jack Scott made money by dancing in the streets and soliciting business for the house. Brown also learned to play more instruments: the drums, the piano, and some guitar. One of his occasional mentors on the guitar was the famous blues guitarist Tampa Red (Hudson Whittaker), although James Brown did not generally like the blues.

During World War II the federal government began a crackdown on prostitution, forcing the shutdown of redlight districts nationwide. The Twiggs Street house was closed down, and James Brown and Minnie Walker moved into a two-room shack. Joe Brown was soon taken into the navy, and the two remaining received a monthly allotment check for $37.50. This was their support, augmented by what James Brown could hustle in the streets. James continued his interest in music. In particular, he became interested in the movie shorts of Louis Jordan and his Tympany Five. Brown began to win amateur night contests with his singing, first at the Lennox Theater and later at Harlem. He also formed a group, the Cremona Trio. A staple of his early performing career was his version of Louis Jourdan's hit "Caledonia, What Makes Your Big Head So Hard?"

When he became a teenager, James Brown was good at music, but his ambition ran to sports, especially boxing and baseball, where being left-handed gave him an edge. His career aims were seriously jeopardized by another of his activities—burglary. After a first arrest for which he received a warning, he was arrested again and charged with four counts of burglary. Brown turned sixteen in jail and was tried as an adult. On June 13, 1949, he pled guilty and received two to four years for each of the four counts. The sentences were to be served consecutively. Brown was taken to the Georgia Juvenile Training Institute.

Music and sports eased Brown's adaptation to reformatory life. He formed a gospel quartet soon after his arrival, and a band using homemade instruments. Because of his music activity he was nicknamed Music Box. In 1951 the reformatory was moved from Rome, Georgia to Toccoa, Georgia. There he became a trustee as he continued his involvement in sports and music. He also met a local boy with a reputation as a musician, Bobby Byrd. On June 14, 1952, Brown was paroled on the condition that he stay out of Augusta and Richmond County.

He got a job at an automobile agency washing cars and cleaning up, and lived briefly with the Byrd family before he found his own place to live.

Brown lost his job at the car agency after taking a customer's car out for an unauthorized spin and bringing it back damaged. This action jeopardized his freedom, but the Byrd family helped him with his parole officer, and soon he found a job in a plastics factory. Meanwhile, Brown formed a gospel group, the Every Ready Gospel Singers, with three women, then joined Bobby Byrd's group, which was then comprised of seven musicians. Since their only instrument was a piano, the group used their voices to imitate other instruments. After flirting with gospel music, the group developed a repertory of ten rhythm and blues numbers. After a friend of Brown's from the reformatory, Johnny Terry, joined them, they began to pick up a few dollars performing at area juke joints, using the name The Toccoa Band. They acquired a manager, improvised drums and a cymbal, and added a man on electric guitar. Local bookings began to pick up, but Brown had a couple more close brushes with having his parole revoked.

On June 19, 1953, Brown married Velma Warren. This marriage produced three sons, Teddy, Terry, and Larry. The marriage broke up around 1957, and Brown took up housekeeping with another woman. The couple officially separated in 1964 and divorced in 1969.

Brown helps create the Flames   Just about the time of Brown's marriage, the band ran into internal problems from jealousy over the lead positions assumed by Brown and Byrd. Since the band's success was growing, the members resolved their problems and, to mark a new start, took a new name, the Flames. They were assiduous in seeing all the top professional groups they could and acquiring ideas to make their own shows exciting. Brown began to create his own material with the song "Please, Please, Please," which became the regular closing number for the group. On occasion in later years, Brown would work the audience and sing this song for as long as forty minutes until his shoulders were covered with a cape and he was helped, exhausted, from the stage.

The Flames became a well-established local group and even performed on an Atlanta radio program, but they sought a wider recognition. They took over the stage uninvited during the intermission in a show by Little Richard, who would soon cut his first major hit "Tutti Frutti." They made such an impression that Little Richard's manager, Clint Brantly, of Macon, signed them. Brown received permission of the parole board for his move to Macon. Brantly renamed the group the Famous Flames, and they began to find more lucrative gigs.

Brown received the tacit approval of his parole officer for his trips out of state, but he still continued to run into problems that threatened his freedom. Once when the police were called in to stop a fight in a club, Brown was found working in a place that sold alcohol. Later he was arrested and held in jail after a traffic accident, and a warrant for his return to prison was issued on October 28, 1955. In both cases Clint Brantly was influential enough to smooth over the difficulties.

Soon thereafter the Famous Flames cut their demonstration record of "Please, Please, Please," which became extremely popular locally when a Macon radio station aired it. The recording attracted the attention of Ralph Bass, a talent scout for Cincinnati-based King Records, a small independent label run by Syd Nathan. When the group arrived in Cincinnati to record, Syd Nathan immediately took a dislike to "Please, Please, Please," and had to be persuaded to record it during the session on February 4, 1956. Nathan took another month before issuing the record, which began the slow process of becoming a hit in different local markets. After a slow start it reached number six on the Billboard Rhythm and Blues chart, remained on the charts for nineteen weeks, and eventually sold over a million copies. As usual with new artists, the direct financial returns were meager—the money came from touring.

As the Famous Flames made more records, they began to receive better bookings and attracted the attention of Ben Bart of Universal Attractions in New York. Bart began booking the group. Eventually he became Brown's manager and business partner and one of the few persons Brown fully trusted. Even as this relationship began, King Records was beginning to lose interest in the group since the records after *Please, Please, Please* did not sell well. As part of the campaign to rebuild the group's recognition, in early 1957 Bart recommended changing the name to James Brown and the Famous Flames. The band's reaction was immediate—every one except Brown left. This would become a pattern in Brown's relations with his bands.

In late 1957 Brown recorded for King records again with little success. Then Brown made a demonstration recording of "Try Me," which Nathan refused to issue. Air play, however, built up such a demand for the song that it was re-recorded on October 18, 1958, and went immediately to number one on the rhythm and blues charts and forty-eight on the pop charts when it was issued the following month. In January 1959 Brown's first album, called *Please, Please, Please,* was released to great success. This success reinforced Brown's belief in his musical and marketing skills.

Brown also recruited and dissolved a new group of Flames in early 1959. This meant he had two weeks to recruit a third group since he was signed to appear at New York's Apollo Theater for the week beginning April 24. Bobby Byrd rejoined the group for the occasion and remained with Brown for many years. At the Apollo the group's success took it from the opening spot to the next-to-last position. The day after the engagement closed, Brown saw his mother for the first time since she'd left him over twenty years earlier.

Brown continued to argue with Syd Nathan about recordings. Using an assumed name, Brown and his band issued *Mashed Potatoes, Parts One and Two* on Dade records in February 1959. This record made the rhythm and blues chart's top ten. Brown continued to work hard, performing as many as 350 nights a year with an act noted for its high level of energy and fast dancing. These efforts earned him the title "The Hardest Working Man in Show Business," and a growing black audience. Brown also became famous for the tight discipline of his band. Fines were imposed if musicians had unshined shoes or showed up late. Later fines would be imposed for mistakes in music and in dancing.

Brown launches soul music   The sound of Brown's music was changing by 1960, the year his career really took off. Brown takes credit for inventing soul with his combination of gospel, rhythm and blues, and jazz. The first smash hit to embody his new sound was "Think," Brown's third record to sell a million copies. Nathan and the other executives of King records were still not in tune with the new direction, but Brown relied on the reactions of his audiences to the changes in his material. By the end of the year Brown and the Famous Flames were heading the bill at the Apollo Theater.

Brown's success continued to build the following year as he continued the rigorous schedule of live performances. By 1962 he wanted to record a live performance and issue it as an album. Since at this time live performance albums were still a novelty, King records would not back the project. Brown put his own money into the project and rented the Apollo Theater for a series of four performances beginning on October 19. When *Live at the Apollo* appeared in January 1963, it was an immediate success, reaching number two on the pop charts and appearing there for sixty-two weeks. It opened up a new market for Brown among white teenagers, who heard of the album by word of mouth. Today, it still ranks as one of the best live albums ever made.

In 1963 Brown moved to the borough of Queens in New York City. At the end of the year he also set up his own record label, Fair Deal, which was affiliated with Mercury records. "Out of Sight," which Brown cut for Mercury in June 1964, reached number twenty-four on the pop charts. Brown also recorded with a band called the Flames for the last time at those sessions for Mercury. "Out of Sight" also marked a new stage in Brown's music: Using all musical elements, including voice and lyrics, to establish rhythms with few chord changes, the record marked the beginning of funk. By October King records had obtained an injunction that prevented him from recording vocals for another label—although Mercury did have rights to his instrumental performances.

As 1964 ended Brown taped the "T.A.M.I. (Teen Age Music International) Show," which, along with other television appearances, began to give mainstream audiences exposure to the visual aspect of his performances. There was still the problem with King records. For a year from July 1964 to July 1965, Brown did not record. King records finally yielded and gave him complete artistic and marketing control of his records, as well as his own publishing company and a greatly increased royalty. From now on Brown took physical possession of the recording masters and returned them to King only when he thought the music should be issued.

In mid-1965 "Poppa's Got a Brand New Bag" developed the musical direction begun with "Out of Sight." At number eight, the record was Brown's first in the top ten on the pop charts. It topped the rhythm and blues charts for eight weeks and sold one million copies. It was also Brown's first big crossover hit and earned him a Grammy in 1966. The year closed with a similar success for "I Got You (I Feel Good)." To facilitate his heavy touring schedule, Brown leased a Lear jet, the first in a series of private planes.

Brown's recording success continued in 1966 with another million-selling record, "It's a Man's, Man's, Man's World," but "Soul Brother No. 1," as he was now called, was having to respond to the political pressures surrounding the civil rights movement. Inevitably he ran into the problem of not being able to satisfy everyone. On the stage of the Apollo in the spring, he took out a life membership in the NAACP. In the summer, he visited James Meredith in the hospital after Meredith had been shot during his Freedom March in Mississippi and gave a show for the persons who had gathered in

James Brown

Tupelo to continue the march. He also did a record, "Don't Be a Dropout," as part of a Stay in School campaign.

Brown was attracted more by black capitalism than by armed revolution. By the end of 1967 he had purchased the radio station WJBE of Knoxville, Tennessee. The following year he bought WEBB of Baltimore, Maryland, and WRDW of Augusta, Georgia. Brown's touring continued unabated. The record "Cold Sweat" continued Brown's movement toward funk, and it, too, sold one million.

Martin Luther King Jr. was assassinated in Memphis on April 4, 1968. With some difficulty, arrangements were made to televise Brown's Boston concert on April 5 with the aim of keeping people off the streets. Between songs, Brown talked of King and urged calm. The following day Brown repeated his performance in Washington, D.C., which had been hit by two nights of rioting.

Brown builds bridges   Brown appeared to be building bridges to the establishment. On May 8, 1968, Brown attended a dinner at the White House hosted by President Lyndon B. Johnson. The patriotic record *America Is My Home* drew much criticism, especially from the black community, as did the presence of a white bass player in his band. In June, Brown went to Vietnam to entertain the troops. In October *Say It Loud—I'm Black and I'm Proud* became another million-selling record. Brown claims that this statement of black pride alienated most of his white audience.

Brown not only was becoming visible for his politics in 1968, he was also developing his music. "I Got the Feeling" became another million-selling record after it appeared in April, and "Licking Stick, Lickin Stick," which appeared in June, was hailed as the definite presentation of funk. More ominous developments for Brown's personal life that year were the death of his longtime business manager, Ben "Pop" Bart, and shortly thereafter a claim from the Internal Revenue Service that Brown owed $1,879,000 in back taxes.

In 1969 Brown moved back to Augusta; rioting had broken out in the city, and Brown returned to use his influence to calm the situation. "Mother Popcorn (You Got to Have a Mother for Me)" launched a new dance in August and sold one million records. In that month Brown also announced his intention to stop touring after July 1970; in fact, he did not appreciably slow down until 1975.

Brown played Las Vegas for the first time in 1970 to great success. *Get Up, I Feel Like a Sex Machine* became another million-selling record. In 1971 *Hot Pants (She Got to Use What She Got to Get What She Wants)* did the same. But Brown would soon run into problems with his career.

Syd Nathan of King records died, and after long negotiations Brown signed with Polydor, a multinational recording company, in August 1972, bringing with him his entire catalog. Although Brown still had full creative control of his recording, he blames Polydor for the decline in his success in selling records in the late 1970s, overlooking the changes in the music business that affected his appeal. These changes ranged from the new play lists and formats on radio to the decline in black venues able to bear the expense of his show. In 1972 disco was just beginning in Europe, but by the end of the decade it dominated the musical landscape. In this election year Brown raised a storm of criticism by endorsing the re-election of President Richard Nixon.

Although Brown's success in music continued, 1973 marked a downturn in his fortunes. His oldest son died in June. Longtime colleague Bobby Byrd left for good. The IRS claimed that Brown owed $4.5 million in taxes and were contemplating charging him with fraud. By 1975 Brown had cut back on his touring and was faced with the new vogue for disco. In 1979 *Body Heat* was Brown's last record to make the top pop hundred for seven years, when it reached eighty-eight on the pop charts.

Personal and financial difficulties began to mount. In January 1978 Brown had to sell WJBE; by 1980 the other two stations were also gone. Other ventures did not work out. Brown sustained a syndicated television dance program, *Future Shock,* from 1974 to 1976; it didn't make money. Brown was peripherally involved in a payola trial, and he had to give up his jet. In 1978 his second marriage broke up, and he spent time in jail for contempt of court in a case involving his radio stations. One result of his difficulties was a turn to religion, which began to play an increasing part in his life.

Brown now began to work in rock and roll clubs—although he strenuously resisted the labeling, his audiences began to view him as a musician from an earlier era and his former hits as golden oldies. A boost to his career came with his cameo appearance in the film *The Blues Brothers* in 1980. His status as a pioneer was recognized when he was inducted into the Rock and Roll Hall of Fame at the first annual dinner in January 1986. Also in 1986 "Living in America," the theme from *Rocky IV,* became Brown's first million-selling record in thirteen years, reaching number four on the pop charts. For the recording, Brown received a Grammy for best male rhythm and blues singer.

In the meantime, news accounts began to depict a personal life that appeared to be in considerable disarray. No one denies Brown's considerable ego and the fact that he was a difficult—although exciting—person to work for. In addition, rumors of women-beating had circulated for years, along with rumors of drug use, in particular the use of phencyclidine, better known as PCP or angel dust. The headlines now lent plausibility to the charges as Brown and his wife accumulated eight arrests between them in the period from November 1987 to October 1988.

Brown met his third wife, Adrianne, a television hair stylist and make-up artist who used the professional name of Alfie Rodriguez, in 1982. They established a home on sixty-two acres near Beach Island, South Carolina, across the river from Augusta. Their homelife became marred by frequent run-ins with the law.

On July 21, 1988, Brown pleaded no contest to PCP possession and guilty to carrying a gun and resisting arrest. He received a two-year suspended sentence and $1,200 fine. On September 24 Brown interrupted an insurance seminar at his headquarters in Georgia by waving a rifle and demanding to know who had used his personal bathroom. The subsequent police chase involved two states. On December 15 Brown was sentenced to a six-year jail term.

Brown remained in prison until February 27, 1991. He was transferred from his initial assignment at a minimum security facility in July 1989 after more than $40,000 in checks and cash was discovered in his possession. Then in April 1990 he was transferred to an Aiken County work center, where he became a youth drug counselor in a work release program. His wife waited for him in the Beach Island home, which now belonged to Brown's lawyer.

On his release Brown began a five-year period of probation. It appears that there may still be difficulties in his personal life. Brown filed for legal separation from his wife in April 1994, and he was charged with misdemeanor wife-beating in an incident that is alleged to have occurred on December 7, 1994. The charge was dropped. The IRS also claimed an outstanding tax liability of $11 million dollars. The couple was still together when Adrienne Brown died in January 1995 due to a combination of heart disease and PCP use after elective surgery.

In his statements after his release from prison, James Brown said that he faced the future with confidence. What is sure is that his musical achievements will endure. In 1992 he was honored with the Lifetime Achievement Award from the Rhythm and Blues Foundation. Few artists have surpassed Brown's accomplishments in the field of popular music, where his records not only sold in the millions but defined soul, created funk, and influenced rap.—ROBERT L. JOHNS

RON **BROWN**
1941–1996
Politician, lawyer

The first African American in the history of the United States to head a major political party, Ron Brown demonstrated a political savvy, traditional values, and progressive vision that accounted for much of his success. As deputy chairman of the Democratic National Committee, Brown was a highly visible power broker. His appointment as Secretary of Commerce in 1993, by President Bill Clinton, placed him at the summit of a career begun just twenty-three years earlier. In this time, he redefined the role of the department and transformed it into a high-profile advocate for U.S. businesses everywhere.

Ronald Harmon Brown was born in Washington, D.C., August 1, 1941. His parents, William H. and Gloria Osborne Carter Brown, both graduates of Howard University, moved to New York following the birth of their only child and settled in Harlem. William Brown managed the Theresa Hotel on 125th Street, where the family resided next door to the legendary Apollo Theater. The theater and hotel were both famous for attracting celebrities of all races. *Current Biography* reported that eleven-year-old Brown took a campaign photograph in 1952 with Richard M. Nixon. Young Brown acquired his social grace in the company of experts.

Brown's formal education was exclusive. In 1946 he was the only African American student at Hunter College elementary school located on the city's Upper East Side. He learned early to balance the politics of two worlds—those of Harlem and the elite white world beyond. His parents' determination for him to have the best education New York had to offer led him to travel great distances across the city. He attended the Rhodes School and the Walden School, both private prep schools on New York's West Side. In 1958 Brown entered Middlebury College in Vermont.

Politics for Brown was formed not in the hotbed of civil rights activism sweeping the South at the time; rather, his isolated situation forced him to become expert at nonconfrontational negotiations. One situation in particular tested his courage but strengthened his resolve to stand for what's right even when it meant standing alone. As the only African American freshman on campus, Brown was rushed by Sigma Phi Epsilon fraternity. But the fraternity

A jubilant Ron Brown.

had a clause excluding African Americans. The national organization objected to Brown's membership, but he refused their offer of house privileges without full membership. When it was clear Brown would not back down nor ignore their bigotry, fraternity members supported him, which resulted in the chapter's expulsion from national membership. This single act of bravery by eighteen-year-old Brown caused Middlebury to prohibit from campus all organizations with exclusionary clauses. Later, Brown became a trustee at the still predominantly white school.

Brown earned a B.A. in political science in 1962. Having helped finance his education through service in the Army ROTC, upon graduation he joined the United States Army. Stationed overseas, Brown supervised a staff of sixty German civilians where, again, he was the only African American officer at the U.S. Army post in West Germany. When transferred to Korea he attained the rank of captain, training Korean soldiers. In an interview with *Time* magazine reporter Walter Isaacson, Brown revealed that in Korea he "learned to be comfortable taking charge."

Brown returned to New York in 1966 and accepted a job with the National Urban League as welfare caseworker and job training coodinator in the Bronx. He also enrolled in St. John's University School of Law, where he took evening classes. He received his law degree in 1970. Brown held various positions with the Urban League, including that of Washington lobbyist, until 1979.

Climbing the political ladder   In 1971 Brown won his first political election, becoming district leader of the Democratic party in Mount Vernon, Westchester County, New York. His popularity was based on his ability to make peace between warring factions. Brown himself credited his 1973 move from New York to Washington, D.C., for his rise to prominence. He told Thomas Edsall of the *Washington Post* for February 11, 1989, "Coming to Washington was a way for me to establish my own identity, my own base, my own group of contacts and relationships, putting me into a spokesman role . . . when the Urban League was a very important organization."

Brown's growing prominence brought him to the attention of Senator Edward Kennedy, who wanted him to become the deputy manager of his 1979 presidential campaign. Brown's acceptance thrust him onto the stage of national politics. His successful engineering of the California campaign paid off more for Brown than for Kennedy, who lost his bid for the presidency. In 1980 Brown became chief counsel to the Senate Judiciary Committee and the following year general counsel and staff director for Senator Kennedy. In 1981, he took over as chief counsel for the Democratic National Committee, the following year becoming its deputy chairman. As deputy chairman Brown enabled more low-income voters to participate in the national conventions without upsetting conservative budget watchers in the National Committee.

Brown's term as deputy chairman expired in 1985. Deciding to remain in the Washington area, he accepted a job with the prestigious law firm Patton, Boggs and Blow, where he earned a reputation as a first-rate corporate attorney.

In a 1989 *Washington Post* article, African American Harvard professor Martin Kilson dubbed Brown "the new black transethnic politician." He was referring to Brown's acceptance statement to head the Democratic National Committee. Throughout his campaign Brown had avoided the issue of race. But in his acceptance speech for the chairmanship, cited in the same article, he said: "Let me speak frankly. I did not run on the basis of race, but I will not run away from it. I am proud of who I am and I am proud of this party, for we are truly America's last best hope to bridge the divisions of race, region, religion, and ethnicity. . . . The story of my chairmanship will not be about race. It will be about the races we win in the next four years."

Despite his best intentions, Brown was not free from the race issue. His work as Jesse Jackson's top strategist in the 1988 convention made it difficult for him to raise funds for the National Committee because, in the eyes of many Jewish contributors, Brown had not sufficiently distanced himself from Jackson, whom they believed guilty of making anti-Semitic remarks. Conservative white Democrats thought that Brown's election would further tarnish the party image as being too black and too liberal, despite Brown's declaring in *Gentlemen's Quarterly,* "I embrace the traditional values of the Democratic party, but I'm progressive."

Ron Brown.

Political power broker   As the first African American chairman of the Democratic National Committee, Brown successfully raised funds, and he saw the election of a black Democrat governor in Virginia and a black mayor in New York City. Brown's skills in dealing with opponents and his ability to walk a political middle road unified the party, and his expert maneuvering behind the scenes helped Bill Clinton win the 1992 nomination and the election.

When Clinton won the presidency, he appointed Ron Brown Secretary of Commerce. This came despite objections raised by many people who thought Brown's experience as a Washington insider and political lobbyist might pose ethical questions. Brown was confirmed by the U.S. Senate on January 14, 1993, becoming the first African American Secretary of Commerce.

As Commerce secretary, *Emerge* magazine reported, "he led the way on trade and economic policy." Often controversial, his role as architect of Clinton's China policy was deemed especially controversial, and enabled China to retain its Most Favored Nation trade status.

Accused of corruption   In spite of his outstanding performance as Secretary of Commerce, Brown was attacked by Republicans who, in May of 1995, accused him of shady business dealings and influence-peddling. Brown challenged his detractors to prove their allegations. Attorney General Janet Reno in July 1995 appointed Daniel S. Pearson independent counsel to investigate Brown's business dealings with Nolanda Hill. Investigations into business activities continued. Undaunted, Ron Brown continued to perform his duties as commerce secretary with the finesse that first won him recognition.

Brown received American Jurisprudence awards for outstanding achievement in poverty law in 1975 and for outstanding achievement in jurisprudence in 1990. He received honorary doctor of law degrees in 1989 from Hunter College and Rhode Island College. In 1980 Harvard University awarded Brown a fellowship to its Institute of Politics at the John F. Kennedy School of Government. Brown served on the boards of trustees for the United Negro College Fund, the University of the District Columbia, and the Community Foundation of Greater Washington.

Brown, who was said to have a towering ego and loved the spotlight, was also deemed a sincere person who could disarm his adversaries instantly with his trademark smile and overpowering personality. He retained the respect of people from high-powered establishments to the streets of Harlem.

Ron Brown married Alma Arrington on August 11, 1962. They lived in a town house near Rock Creek Park in Washington, D.C. Tracey Lyn and Michael Arrington, their two adult children, are both attorneys.

On April 3, 1996, Brown and thirty-six federal officials on board an airplane attempting to land in bad weather at Dubrovnik off the coast of Croatia crashed into a mountain. All aboard the plane were killed. Brown and his staff had gone to the war-torn area to assist American businesses in rebuilding the region.

Services for Brown were held April 10 at Washington Cathedral. He is buried at Arlington National Cemetery. As the nation mourned his death, flags were flown at half-staff, and he was honored with a nineteen-gun salute. Called the Standard Bearer, Brown was extraordinary because he recognized and remembered the best about people, which enabled him to get along with friend or foe. He opened doors previously closed to African Americans because he was adept at building bridges between races, classes, gender, and other identities that often divide Americans. *Emerge* magazine said at his death: "When the game was lobbying, Brown was rainmaker extraordinaire, hauling in high-powered clients by the dozens; when the game was politics, he was kingmaker . . . laying the groundwork for the Clinton victory in 1992; and when the game was commerce, he was a visionary leader inventing 'commercial diplomacy.'" He was highly visible both as head of the Democratic National Committee and as U.S. Secretary of Commerce. At Brown's funeral, President Clinton said that "Ron Brown was a magnificent life force."—NAGUEYALTI WARREN

RALPH J. **BUNCHE**
1903–1971
Statesman, diplomat, scholar, United Nations official

To see the world not as it is but as it should be, to accept people with all their foibles, and to embrace goodness

characterizes the vision of Ralph J. Bunche, the first African American Nobel laureate and highest ranking

black American in the United Nations.

Ralph Johnson Bunche was born on August 7, 1903, at 434 Anthony Street, in Detroit, Michigan, to Olive Johnson and Fred Bunche, a trained banker. Ralph's early upbringing included problems. Fred was a neglectful father and Olive suffered from tuberculosis when Ralph was a young child. Ralph's mother spent two years in a sanitarium to recover.

Yet, the best times of his childhood are recorded in a letter Bunche wrote in late 1959 to William T. Nobel of the *Detroit News*. He recalled what he enjoyed was:

> hitching my sled in winter onto the tailgates of horsedrawn beer trucks; swimming on Belle Isle in the summer and in the river down by the ice-house; . . . the thrill of the circus parade, and particularly the calliope at the end of it, when Barnum and Bailey came to town—and the still bigger thrill of slipping into the big tent under the canvas sides; rooting for the Tigers and especially Ty Cobb.

Due to another illness, the Johnson family left Detroit in 1914. Charlie, Ralph's uncle, who suffered from tuberculosis like his sister Olive, was sent to Albuquerque, New Mexico, to recover. Olive followed, along with her mother and son. Lucy Johnson, Ralph's grandmother, took Ralph Bunche in October 1915 to New Mexico on the train.

In October 1916, Fred Bunche left Albuquerque to look for regular work. He promised to send for his family when he found work and could support them. In February, Olive's health was complicated by a rheumatic condition; she died in February 1917. Three months later, Ralph's Uncle Charlie committed suicide with a shotgun. Bunche was only thirteen and suffered greatly at the loss of his mother and agonized over guilt. In 1967 Bunche wrote: "I can never get out of my mind that on the night of her death in Albuquerque she had asked for milk and there was none in the house because I had drunk it up."

Bunche's father did not return for him and his sister after his mother's death. He remarried and in 1928 contacted Ralph Bunche's aunt Ethel in Los Angeles in an effort to talk to Grace, Ralph's sister. Bunche never saw his father again. As an adult he contacted his father's second wife, Helen, in an attempt to locate his father, but she did not know his whereabouts.

The Johnsons took Ralph and his sister to Los Angeles, where they settled in a house on 37th Street and Central Avenue. In 1918 the neighborhood was white and middle class. In the 1920s, however, it began a rapid decline, and today is part of the notorious South Central, Slauson and Watts Area of Los Angeles. Bunche enrolled at Jefferson High School just half a block from his new home.

Ralph's grandmother, Lucy Johnson, called Nana by Bunche, set a simple but high standard for the children to follow. Although she could have passed for white, she did not and taught her family a fierce pride in race. Recalling his grandmother's teachings, Bunche, quoted by Urquhart, said:

> In and out of school, I have always been motivated by a spirit of completion, particularly when pitted against white people. I suppose this was an inevitable response to Nannie's constant adamantine to let them, especially white folks, know that you can do anything they can do.

Ralph Bunche graduated from Jefferson High School in 1922. The school principal, a Mr. Fulton, made the mistake of saying to Bunche and his grandmother that they had never thought of Ralph as a "Negro." Lucy Johnson's reply epitomized for her grandson the dignity and self-respect she expected him to demand for himself.

*Ralph Bunche displays his
Nobel certificate, 1950.*

In high school Bunche had played basketball and also worked as a paperboy for the *Los Angeles Times*. He was the valedictorian of his class and delivered the graduation address entitled "Our New Responsibility."

The genesis and the catalyst   According to Bunche, he never would have attended college had it not been for Lucy Johnson's insistence. Bunche worked all summer laying carpet and knew that his family needed the money he earned. At summer's end, however, Lucy Johnson made him quit his job to attend college. Bunche enrolled at the University of California, Los Angeles (UCLA), on Vermont Avenue, now the site of Los Angeles City College. Speaking at the dedication of Ralph Bunche Hall at UCLA on May 23, 1969, and quoted by Urquhart, Bunch said that UCLA "was where it all began . . . where in a sense, I began; college for me was the genesis and the catalyst." At UCLA Bunche became an all-around scholar-athlete. He wrote for the *Daily Bruin,* the campus newspaper, became president of the Debating Society, and was a star basketball and football player until he injured his leg.

Bunche graduated summa cum laude from UCLA in 1927 with a B.A. in political science and a Phi Beta Kappa key. Again he was class valedictorian and delivered a commencement address. His speech attacked excessive materialism, urged international mindedness, and promoted the importance of being a socially valuable man. Bunche would become such a man.

A tuition fellowship enabled Bunche to enroll at Harvard and earn a master of arts degree in June 1928. At Harvard Bunche had supported himself by working in John Phillips's secondhand bookstore in Harvard Square for ten dollars a week. Robert Weaver, who became U.S. secretary of the Interior and later chief of Housing and Urban Development, and William Hastie, who became a U.S. Federal Appeals Court judge, were classmates and friends of Bunche. Bunche was offered the Thayer Fellowship to continue his study for a Ph.D. at Harvard but he declined. Percy Julian, a Howard University professor, had recruited Bunche to come to Howard in Washington, D.C., to organize a political science department.

Bunche came to Howard under the presidency of Mordecai Wyatt Johnson, the first African American to head the historically black university. This was an exciting time at Howard, and Bunche benefited from such colleagues as poet and critic Sterling P. Brown, philosopher and culture critic Alaine Locke, and sociologist E. Franklin Frazier. Bunche also chafed under the blatant racism and segregation in the nation's capital and felt inhibited by Mordecai Johnson's iron rule of the university. In the fall of 1929, Bunche took a leave from Howard and started course work for his doctorate at Harvard.

On June 23, 1930, Bunche married a young woman he had met at Howard University in 1928. Ruth Ethel Harris was a teacher in Washington, D.C. She attended night classes at Howard and had taken Bunche's course in political science. Ruth had been born in 1906 in Montgomery, Alabama, and had graduated from Alabama State Normal School. Their marriage lasted forty-one years and produced three children: Joan Harris Bunche was born in 1931, Jane Johnson Bunche in May 1933, and Ralph J. Bunche Jr. in 1943.

Bunche completed his dissertation in February 1934. His thesis on decolonization in Africa won the Toppan Prize for the year's best dissertation. He received his Ph.D. in government and international relations. Two years later he published his first book, *World View of Race,* which examines colonial policy throughout the world and studies the status of non-European people in South Africa. Bunche also took courses in anthropology at Northwestern

University in Chicago to prepare for his research abroad, where he studied at the London School of Economics and at the University of Cape Town.

The American dilemma   Bunche returned to Howard University after twenty months abroad. In 1938 he began working with Gunnar Myrdal, a Swedish social scientist commissioned by the Carnegie Corporation to study African Americans. This study became *An American Dilemma: The Negro Problem and Modern Democracy,* published in 1944. Bunche was one of Myrdal's six top staff and the one closet to Myrdal. Bunche wrote four monographs for this study; the last monograph consisted of nineteen chapters. It was published in 1973 as *The Political Status of the Negro in the Age of FDR.*

Conducting field work in the South—mainly North Carolina, South Carolina, Alabama, and Georgia—Bunche was away from home more than he or his wife and family wanted. In 1941 when the children were eight and ten years old, Bunche had a few months of extended time with them when the family moved into a house at 1510 Jackson Street in Washington D.C. As Bunche achieved more acclaim, there was a terrible price to pay. His wife's poignant letter, quoted by Urquhart in *Ralph Bunche,* summarizes the price of success. In 1945 she wrote:

> I know you think you are the Miracle Negro with the Whites, but I am sure you are just a novelty and whom they can get two men's work out of one from you, though it may be killing you and hurting your family. . . . Achievement is a grand thing and I am very proud of yours but we shouldn't let it blind us to the values of life. . . . I must realize that as you grow more important you will be away from us the best part of our lives and I'll always have the responsibility of rearing the three children alone.

Both valued the sanctity of marriage, and for them separation or divorce were inconceivable.

Bunche was rejected for military service in World War II because of an injury he received playing football at UCLA. This same injury to his left leg left a permanent blood clot that caused him increasing difficulty as he grew older. He was also deaf in his left ear because of a punctured eardrum. Therefore, he served his country by joining the National Defense Program Office of Information as senior analyst. He soon advanced to chief of the African section and worked at the U.S. State Department where he became part of the first conferences leading to the formation of the United Nations. Bunche wrote the charter for handling the colonies of defeated countries.

As the first African American to serve on the U.S. delegation to the first General Assembly of the United Nations, Bunche was well placed for his next promotion. In 1947 U.N. secretary general Trygve Lie appointed him director of the Trusteeship Department. He became undersecretary general of the United Nations and was now the highest U.S. official at the United Nations. Bunche became the highly respected and valued assistant of three U.N. heads, Lie, Dag Hammarskjold and U Thant.

A bias for peace   The United Nations was the perfect place for Bunche to fulfill his calling. All his years of preparation and experience equipped him with needed perseverance for his diplomatic challenges. His clearly articulated biases proved to be a winning combination.

Bunche once revealed his biases to a writer for *Ebony* in 1972, quoted in *Contemporary Black Biography:*

> I have a bias which leads me to believe in the essential goodness of my fellow man, which leads me to believe that no problem in human relations is ever insoluble. And I have a strong bias in favor of the United Nations and its ability to maintain a peaceful world.

Bunche accompanied United Nations–appointed mediator Folke Bernadotte of Sweden to the Middle East to attempt a peaceful resolution of the Arab-Israeli conflict in 1948. The Arabs and Israelis were on the verge of war following the establishment of the Jewish state. This was a perilous assignment as it involved not only land issues but religious differences. Near the end of the year, Bernadotte was assassinated by Israeli terrorists. The task for making peace thus fell to Bunche. He gained the confidence of both sides through his fairness and objectivity, and in 1949 Bunche successfully negotiated a truce.

Bunche was eating lunch in the United Nation Delegates Dining Room on September 22, 1950, when his secretary informed him he had been awarded the Nobel Peace Prize. But Bunche felt that he should not receive an award for a job he was paid to do. According to Urquhart in *Ralph Bunche,* he drafted a letter stating that "peacemaking at the United Nations was not done for prizes." But Lie was of a different opinion. He insisted that the letter not be sent. Ralph Bunche was the first black person in the history of the Nobel awards to receive the prize.

Bunche exhibited a single-minded commitment to keeping peace. In 1956 Bunche's efforts during the Suez crisis in Egypt was responsible for the creation of the six-thousand-man U.N. Emergency Forces, which supervised the Egypt-Israeli border for eleven years. The 1960 assignment to keep peace in the former Belgian Congo (Zaire) was, in Bunche's opinion, his most difficult. He did succeed, however, after two months of intense work in enabling Zaire's survival. The treacherous transition from colonialism to independence resulted in two tragic deaths. The first was that of Zaire's first prime minister, Patrice Lumumba, who was murdered in February 1961. African Americans were outraged, and some even blamed Bunche for the chaotic circumstances leading to Lumumba's death. Later that year, in September, U.N. secretary general Dag Hammarskjold was killed in the crash of a United Nation DC-6 over Zaire.

Bunche's troubles with his fellow African Americans did not end with the Congo crisis. America was facing its own revolution in the late 1950s and early 1960s, and Bunche was called upon to choose sides. Some black militants called Bunche an "Uncle Tom" for even negotiating with whites. Bunche quickly reminded the newcomers to the civil rights struggle that he had carried his first picket for civil rights in 1937, had demonstrated with Martin Luther King Jr. at the March on Washington, and had participated in the march from Selma to Montgomery.

For his work in the areas of race, international relations, and peace, in 1949 Bunche was awarded the NAACP's Spingarn Medal. In addition to the Nobel Prize, he received the Theodore Roosevelt Association Medal of Honor in 1954; the Presidential Medal of Honor, 1963; and the U.S. Medal of Freedom, 1963. In 1991 he was inducted into the African American Hall of Fame.

Bunche's role in contributing to international affairs and public life is unimpeachable, but it came at great cost and personal sacrifice. The most traumatic event of his adult life occurred October 9, 1966, following a game at Shea Stadium; when Bunche and his wife arrived home after 2 a.m., a police officer notified them of Jane's death. The thirty-three-year-old mother of three had committed suicide. The old guilt originating with the loss of his mother and abandonment by his father did not make his grief any easier to bear. It may have increased the rapid decline in his physical condition. An insulin-dependent diabetic, Bunche suffered from phlebitis and was losing his eyesight.

In 1967 Bunche tried to resign from his post at the United Nations. However, the pressure from U Thant and from President Lyndon B. Johnson was overwhelming. In the end he gave in and remained on the job. For his wife his decision was the last disappointment in a long series of disappointments. Ralph Bunche remained undersecretary general until the fall of 1971. He was then relieved of his duties because of his health. On December 9, 1971, he died in New York Hospital at 12:40 a.m. His funeral took place in New York's Riverside Church at noon on Saturday, December 11. People all over the world mourned his passing. He is buried at Woodlawn Cemetery in the Bronx.

Peace Form On, a great steel monolith, was erected in 1980 in a park on First Avenue across the street from the United Nations. This memorial was created by Daniel Johnson, a young African American sculptor whose father had known Bunche in Los Angeles. The park was renamed Ralph Bunche Park. Perhaps the most meaningful memorial took place in 1992 when Anthony Perry, a former gang member in Los Angeles, visited the University of Southern California library and researched the Rhodes Armistice of 1949 that Bunche had drafted. On the basis of that document, Perry negotiated a truce between the Bloods and the Crips, two of the largest and most violent Los Angeles street gangs. A lasting peace among young African American men would surely serve as a fitting tribute to one who gave his life in the struggle for peace.—NAGUEYALTI WARREN

NANNIE HELEN **BURROUGHS**
1879–1961
Educator, civil rights activist, feminist, religious leader

Nannie Helen Burroughs was a spellbinding, outspoken orator and a member of a network of southern black female activists who emerged as leaders of national organizations. William Pickens, a pioneer NAACP administrator and writer, commented that "no other person in America has so large a hold on the loyalty and esteem of the colored masses as Nannie H. Burroughs. She is regarded all over the broad land as a combination of brains, courage, and incorruptibleness."

Nannie Helen Burroughs was born in Orange, Virginia, on May 2, 1879, to John Burroughs and Jennie (Poindexter) Burroughs. Her parents belonged to that small and fortunate class of ex-slaves whose energy and ability enabled them to start towards prosperity almost as soon as the war that freed them was over. Young Nannie moved with her mother to Washington, D.C., in 1883. She was educated through the high school level at the M Street

High School in the nation's capital and graduated with honors in 1896. She studied business in 1902 and received an honorary A.M. from Eckstein-Norton University in Kentucky in 1907.

Burroughs was employed in Louisville, Kentucky, from 1898 to 1909 as bookkeeper and editorial secretary of the Foreign Mission Board of the National Baptist Convention. While in Louisville, she organized the Women's Industrial Club, which conducted domestic science and secretarial courses. She was also one of the founders of the Women's Convention, auxiliary to the National Baptist Convention USA, and served efficiently as its corresponding secretary for almost a half century (1900–1947). From 1948 until her death in 1961 she was president of the Women's Convention. The convention comprised the largest group of African Americans in the world, and the auxiliary was a potent force in black religious groups.

Burroughs's childhood dream of establishing an industrial school for girls led her to mobilize the Women's Convention to underwrite such a venture. On October 19, 1901, the National Training School for Women and Girls opened in Washington, D.C., with Nannie Burroughs as president. By the end of its first year the school had enrolled thirty-one students. Twenty-five years later it boasted of more than two thousand women trained at the secondary and junior college level. Taking in girls from all over the United States, Africa, and the Caribbean Basin, Burroughs placed great significance in training for spiritual values. She thus dubbed her school the "School of the 3 B's—the Bible, bath, and broom." In 1934 the school was named the National Trades and Professional School for Women, but the school was inactive for a time during the Great Depression of the 1930s. Burroughs later reopened it, and she continued to direct the school until her death. In 1964 the board of trustees abandoned the old trade school curriculum and reestablished it as the Nannie Helen Burroughs School for students at the elementary school level.

Burroughs's sensitivity for the African American working woman was expressed during her participation in the club movement during the late decades of the nineteenth century and the early decades of the twentieth century. Black women organized first on a local level and then nationally to shoulder educational, philanthropic, and welfare activities. The growing needs of the urban poor in a period of rapid industrialization, coupled with the presence of a sizeable group of educated women with leisure time, led to the emergence of a national club movement. These women's clubs proved tremendously beneficial in many communities. The dearth of social welfare institutions in many southern areas, and the recurrent exclusion of blacks from those facilities that did exist, led black women to found orphanages, day-care facilities, homes for the aged, schools, and similar services. In the case of the most prominent female founders of black educational institutions—Lucy Craft Laney, Charlotte Hawkins Brown, Mary McLeod Bethune, and Nannie Burroughs—their schools became centers for community organizations, women's activities, and a network of supporting institutions.

In the 1890s local clubs began to form federations almost simultaneously in a number of cities. In 1896 the newly formed National Association of Colored Women (NACW) united the three largest of these groups as well as more than a hundred local women's clubs. In addition to her laudable contributions to the NACW, Burroughs also founded the National Association of Wage Earners to draw public attention to the dilemmas of Negro women. Its national board included Burroughs as president, with well-known clubwoman Mary McLeod Bethune as vice president and banker Maggie Lena Walker as treasurer. The women placed more significance on educational forums of public interest than on trade union activities.

Equal rights for black women advocated Nannie Burroughs and several other clubwomen contended that black women should not take a passive or subordinate position to men. While they criticized those black males who refused to support efforts toward equal rights, these reformers differed from their white sisters in that they did not define feminism as a response to male exploitation. Burroughs, a majestic, dark-skinned woman with a commanding presence and voice, was a vocal supporter of racial and sexual consciousness. An unyielding advocate of racial pride and African American heritage, Burroughs was a longtime member of the Association for the Study of Negro Life and History. She continually urged blacks to learn and understand their history and culture.

In addition to her work for various organizations, Burroughs was a steadfast supporter of the religious and secular program advanced by Walter Henderson Brooks and the Nineteenth Street Baptist Church in the District of Columbia. Brooks was a prominent clergyman, scholar, and temperance advocate who—while capable of directing withering criticism at those who succumbed to drunkenness, gambling, fornication, and adultery—also preached and advocated the social gospel. The NACW was founded at his church in 1896. Finally, as a devout Baptist, Burroughs worked for almost fifty years with the Baptist World Alliance.

Burroughs's influence grows Throughout her life Burroughs fought hard for issues she believed in. Burroughs was active in anti-lynching campaigns and in the successful effort to memorialize the home of abolitionist Frederick Douglass. She was also a member of the Women's Division of the Commission on Interracial Cooperation (CIC), although she disagreed vehemently with the views of the CIC's Association of Southern Women for the Prevention of Lynching regarding the legitimacy of federal intervention in the matter: the association opposed the intervention, while Burroughs favored it.

Burroughs came to be regarded as one of the most stirring platform orators in the country, and her writings likewise reflected her belief in desegregation, self-help, and self-reliance. Her public pronouncements were deeply influenced by her faith in God, and she felt that racial equality was an ethical priority—a spiritual mandate from heaven. As related in *Afro-American,* April 28, 1934, she told her readers to use "ballots and dollars" to fight racism instead of "wasting time begging the white race for mercy," and hailed the great moral, spiritual, and economic assets of the black woman. On other occasions, according to the *Pittsburgh Courier,* she exhorted blacks to "chloroform your Uncle Toms," warning that "the Negro must unload the leeches and parasitic leaders who are absolutely eating the life out of the struggling, desiring mass of people."

In 1944 the Baptist Woman's Auxiliary initiated a quarterly journal, *The Worker,* under the editorship of Nannie Burroughs. She also wrote several longer works of a religious nature, including *Grow: A Handy Guide for Progressive Church Women* and *Making Your Community Christian.* For a number of years she wrote a syndicated column, "Nannie Burroughs Says," which was carried by several black newspapers in a prominent position. In a lighter vein, she authored *The Slabtown District Convention: A Comedy in One Act,* which was a popular church fundraiser.

At one point the intrepid Burroughs took W. E. B. Du Bois of the National Association for the Advancement of Colored People (NAACP) to task after Du Bois suggested to black Americans that they submit to segregation. "You would think that the world is coming to an end because one man 'does not choose to fight' segregation any longer," said Burroughs in the

Afro-American in April 1934. "Any man who is hired can quit when he pleases. A person who is getting paid to solve the Negro problem is no exception to the rule. . . . Du Bois is at least or at last honest. He could have kept his mouth shut and continued to draw his decreasing stipend from the NAACP. . . . Dr. Du Bois is tired. He has fought a good fight. It is too bad that he did not keep the faith and finish his course."

Self-help project launched   In July 1934 Nannie Burroughs launched Washington's first "Negro self-help project." A laundry, formerly owned by the training school, was turned over to the federal government by Burroughs. The Federal Emergency Relief Authority renovated the building, which included a laundry and dry cleaning plant, a barber shop, a sewing and canning center, a commissary, a garment-making and upholstery shop, and a shoe repair shop. Nationwide interest was kindled in the project, and it subsequently served as a model for other projects that were inaugurated during the Great Depression in other parts of the United States.

Nannie Helen Burroughs died of natural causes in Washington, D.C., in May 1961. Funeral rites were held in the Nineteenth Street Baptist Church with interment in Lincoln Memorial Cemetery, Suitland, Maryland. There were no immediate survivors. In 1906, Nannie Helen Burroughs brought much attention to the role black women had even in the most sexist of churches by establishing "Women's Day." Over the years, Women's Day grew into a series of events that acknowledged the important role women had in black churches. It was a day for women to be heard and one woman to be remembered.—CASPER LE ROY JORDAN

SHERIAN GRACE **CADORIA**

1940–

U.S. Army officer

The United States Army's motto "Be All That You Can Be" is a mantra for many of its enlisted men and women. This could not be truer for retired Brigadier General Sherian Cadoria, who proudly served for twenty-nine years. During her time of service, she was one of the highest-ranking black women in the U.S. Army. Her career and accomplishments are especially noteworthy since she was the first woman from the Military Police Corps/Combat Support Arms, a traditionally male unit, promoted to general.

The youngest of three children, Cadoria was born on January 26, 1940 to Bernice McGlory Cadoria and Joseph Cadoria in Marksville, Louisiana. Her parents were farmers who stressed hard work and a strong belief in God. "I was brought up believing that if you're going to do something, excel at it. Go after it and give it everything you've got," recalled Cadoria in an interview with *Ebony* magazine.

Her fierce drive and determination enabled her to succeed in the Army at a time when not a lot of women enlisted. In 1961 Cadoria joined after earning a bachelor of science degree in business education from Southern University A&M, a predominantly black university. Her decision to join the Army may have bewildered some given her sex (women were not treated equally) and her business degree (she could have chosen a business career). This was thirteen years before the expansion of women's programs by the Department of Defense in 1973. Before this, for example, women with children were not allowed in the Army. This and other inequalities contributed to the overall low percentage of enlisted women in the armed services. According to the U.S. Department of Defense, in 1973 women made up only 2.5 percent of all services. Cadoria had acknowledged to *Ebony* magazine that the strain of being the lone black female advancing through the military took its toll.

One of Cadoria's first assignments was as platoon officer for Women's Army Corps Training Battalion in Fort McClellan, Alabama, from January 1962 to May 1963, after receiving a commission by direct appointment. From June 1963 to May 1965, she served as executive officer for the Women's Army Corp Company, and as assistant adjutant for the United States Army Communication Zone, Europe.

Cadoria's hard work was soon recognized, and she was promoted to captain on May 17, 1965. Her military record goes on to list major promotions and honors—all of this achieved during a time when women were not given the same playing field as their male counterparts.

After three years, Cadoria was promoted to major. With this promotion, she served first in Vietnam and later as chief, Personnel Division/Adjutant, at the United States Army Ordinance Center and School, Aberdeen Proving Ground, Maryland.

Her promotions did not surprise her family. Her brother, Adrian Cadoria, once told *Ebony* magazine that "she's always the one who tries hardest to be the best. She just works harder than anybody else." Hard work is just a part of who Cadoria is. Her mother remembered her determination and can-do spirit even as a child. "She always wanted to help. At three years old, she was carrying fifty pound bags of cotton."

Her physical strength and her strength of character allowed Cadoria to face one of her most challenging situations in the Army. While serving in Vietnam, she was rejected for a job as a protocol officer because of a sexist colonel. She was told that women were not fit to escort VIPs because they could not carry luggage. Cadoria shared with the colonel her childhood experience of carrying fifty-pound bags of cotton. Her story did not move him to hire her. Cadoria told *Ebony* that the colonel had said that "the only reason he was talking to me was because he was forced to."

Eventually, Cadoria was assigned as a protocol officer of the Qui Nhom Support Command in Vietnam. During this violent time, she volunteered with the Dominican nuns stationed in the area. Her volunteer work entailed visiting hospitals and leper colonies. Her deep devotion to God and her faith led her to consider becoming a nun, so much so that she began counseling and preparation with a priest. After three months, she decided to continue with her military career. "[I can] still do all the volunteer work and be religious in everything I do while serving in the military. If we can have a strong defense, maybe we will never have another war," said Cadoria.

Following her term in Vietnam, she became a student at the United States Army Command and General Staff College in Fort Leavenworth, Kansas, from July 1970 to June 1971. Cadoria then returned to Alabama's Fort McClellan as an instructor at the Officer Education and Training Branch for the U.S. Army Women's Army Corps Center and School. From June 1973 to June 1975, Cadoria served as a personnel management officer; later, she became the executive officer. While serving, she received a master of arts degree in human relations from the University of Oklahoma. Her next major promotion, to lieutenant colonel, came on July 1, 1976.

Her ability to work well with people helped her to succeed. "She gets the best from her people. She's very caring and it's that quality that gets the people who work for her right in the palm of her hand," confirmed fellow officer Major General Eugene R. Cromartie. Cadoria had worked as a division chief for him in Europe in the early 1980s. As a lieutenant colonel, Cadoria was a commander at the Student Battalion, Training Brigade, United States Army Military Police School at Fort McClellan. She later attended the United States Army War College in Carlisle Barracks, Pennsylvania.

After nineteen years of service with an outstanding military record, Cadoria was promoted to colonel. For the next few years, she was the commander of the First Region, United States Army Criminal Investigation Command in Fort George G. Meade in Maryland. It was while serving in Washington, D.C., that Cadoria received her highest rank—brigadier general—on October 1, 1985. Two years later she was assigned to deputy commanding general of the Total Army Personnel Command in Alexandria, Virginia.

Her honors have not ended since retiring from the Army. She was named one of seventy-five black women who helped to change history in the *I Dream a World* traveling photographic exhibit and book that chronicles outstanding women. Brigadier General Sherian Grace Cadoria has proven that with hard work and determination anything is possible, and you can indeed be all that you can be in the United States Army.—KENNETTE CROCKETT

STOKELY **CARMICHAEL (KWAME TURE)**
1941–
Civil rights activist, organization official, Pan Africanist

Stokely Carmichael was a 1960s black radical who could raise his fist in the air, shout "Black Power!" and polarize white and black Americans in an instant. As a Freedom Rider, he went to Mississippi to get a firsthand view of the South's mistreatment of black Americans. As chairman of the Student Nonviolent Coordinating Committee (SNCC) and prime minister of the Black Panthers, he became a leading spokesperson for the black power movement, and a messianic leader to many young people.

Born on June 29, 1941, in Port-of-Spain, Trinidad and Tobago, Stokely Carmichael came to America in 1952. His parents were Adolphus Carmichael, a carpenter, and Mabel Charles Carmichael, now a retired domestic worker. She lives in Miami, Florida, as does his sister, Nagib Malik, a psychiatric nurse. The family settled in Harlem, where Carmichael graduated from the Bronx High School of Science in 1960. Then he entered Howard University in Washington, D.C., with the intention of majoring in philosophy.

On television news programs he watched the repeated showings of lunch counter incidents in the South. As he watched the young integrationists being violently manhandled while refusing to resist, he said in a *People* interview, "Something happened to me, suddenly I was burning."

In 1961 Carmichael responded to an advertisement in the new SNCC newsletter the *Student Voice* for volunteers to join the Freedom Rides. Carmichael was in the group of Freedom Riders that originated in Washington, D.C., nearly three weeks after the first one that resulted in the vicious beating of John Lewis. Carmichael was arrested. This event was a catalyst for the budding Marxist, Southern Christian Leadership Conference (SCLC) scholarship student, who was an early admirer of Martin Luther King Jr. and his nonviolent demonstrations. Carmichael became a hard-core civil rights activist credited with popularizing the slogan "Black Power!"

He was transferred to the infamous Parchman Penitentiary, where he spent seven weeks stoically awaiting news of his fate. Along with other students who had not undergone the advanced and highly sophisticated training in Mahatma Gandhi–based nonviolent techniques perfected by the Nashville, Tennessee, students, he was not overly impressed by the often fanatically religious fervor and lofty discourses on fasting. The headiness of being martyrs for the cause was tempered by the news that SNCC was planning to make the voter registration drive a top priority. Under the leadership of James Forman, this campaign spread all across Mississippi, but personal violence was soon supplanted by shotguns and bombs.

Stokely Carmichael distributes anti-war flyers.

SNCC was formalized in May 1960 with the adoption of the group's formal name and statement of purpose. This Atlanta University conference had developed from April 1960 meetings at Highlander Folk School in Tennessee and at Shaw University in North Carolina, hosted by Septima Clark and Ella Baker respectively. The SCLC emerged in 1957 from the aftermath of the Montgomery church and home bombings and as an outgrowth of the Montgomery Improvement Association (MIA), which had coordinated the Montgomery bus boycott. As it widened its focus to nonviolent mass movement and civil disobedience tactics, it also supported SNCC with financial gifts and temporary office space. By 1966 many SNCC members had become disillusioned by the political system and by black leaders they perceived as being willing to compromise the issue of full equality for black Americans. By the time Carmichael assumed leadership of SNCC, he had become disillusioned by internecine divisiveness and by the increasing retaliation by violence to voter registration projects. This was the basis for his alliance with the Black Panthers, who advocated a more militant stance and outright separatism to achieve black power.

Under Carmichael's chairmanship, SNCC became more militant and known for the "Black Power" slogan that struck terror and evoked hatred in much of white America. According to Ronald Copeland, a New Jersey community activist, the term was originally a concept focusing on three issues: 1) an economic base within the black community; 2) collective efforts to halt financial exploitation of the black community; and 3) building a political base in the black community by raising political consciousness and electing black representatives to local, state, and national offices. It was meant to help end de facto segregation in a small New Jersey township by involving working-class black families in efforts to obtain better educational conditions for all the citizenry.

To Carmichael the concept of black power was far removed from community-based efforts to rectify economic inequalities. Gordon Parks traveled with Carmichael as a photojournalist after Carmichael had outgrown SNCC and became a Black Panther leader, and thus anathema to all black civil rights groups as a die-hard critic of the white man. In his 1990 autobiography, Parks quoted his remarks made at a Berkeley, California, student gathering:

> The white man says, "work hard nigger, and you will overcome!" If that were true, the black man would be the richest man in the world! He worked like a dog, day and night! But only death came to that poor black man!—and in his early forties! My grandfather had to run, run, run. I ain't running no more.

In answer to a charge of inciting violence, Parks quotes Carmichael's answer: "I'm just telling the white man he's beat my head enough. I won't take anymore." Parks further relates how Carmichael witnessed a pregnant black woman flattened in the street by a burst of water from a fire hose, how he saw people trampled by police horses and left bleeding in the streets. It was too much and he was bodily carried to the airport in a state of shock. To Parks, he said: "From that day on, I knew if I was hit, I would hit back."

As chair of SNCC, Carmichael kept Mississippi and Alabama as operations bases through 1966. Using the symbol of a black panther as a challenge to the Alabama Democratic Party's use of a white rooster, Carmichael tried to develop black consciousness in the black county residents and in Selma as well, by stressing black power and separatism. Carmichael became the living symbol of the group that adopted a militant stance leading to its polarization from more moderate groups. With Charles V. Hamilton, he coauthored *Black Power* in 1967 before leaving his SNCC post that same year.

By summer's end, Carmichael had traveled to Hanoi to meet with leaders of the North Vietnamese National Assembly. There he said that American blacks and the Vietnamese were allies against American imperialism. On the day he pledged support of American blacks to the Vietnamese cause, Thurgood Marshall was pledging his support to the Constitution of the United States of America as the first black member of the Supreme Court.

Carmichael left SNCC and became a Black Panther in 1967, and in 1968 was the prime minister of the most militant group of young black separatists of the mid-1960s. Their symbol, as noted in *Pride and Power*, was the black panther, described as "a sleek, cunning, black, and beautiful animal . . . that attacked only when it was attacked." It was a fitting symbol. The party, organized in Oakland, California, in 1966, believed in defensive violence, as described by its founder Huey Newton and cited in *The Negro in the Making of America:* "We feel it necessary to prepare the people for the event of an actual physical rebellion." The Panthers and

Stokely Carmichael.

other groups of its ilk saw racial conflict as being parallel to international struggles, especially of the darker races across the world. While other groups espoused either integration or mere separatism, the Panthers declared that blacks would be free or America would be destroyed.

By 1969 Carmichael had become disenchanted with the Black Panthers and moved on to the Pan African movement. He became an organizer for Kwame Nkrumah's All-African People's Revolutionary Party. This change in allegiance was a natural outcome of Carmichael's adherence to cultural nationalism, with its focus on nation-building within the black community—a stance rejected by the Panthers, especially Eldridge Cleaver, minister of information, and those of a more revolutionary bent. In *Voices in a Mirror,* Parks described the enmity among the once notorious and feared Panthers:

Stokely shares no enthusiasm for Newton or Seale, nor they for him. The kinship has blown apart. The affinities that once forged them into a heroic brotherhood disintegrated with the unfolding of history. All of them have changed clothes and moved to quieter landscapes, vanished without hardly a sound.

Carmichael had not vanished. He moved to Conakry, Guinea, to escape police harassment in the United States, changed his name, and married the internationally famed South African singer Miriam Makeba. They divorced in 1978. Later he married a Guinean physician, Marlyatou Barry, with whom he had a son, Boca Biro. The couple divorced in 1992.

Since 1969 Carmichael has been involved with the Marxist political party of the late Guinean president Sekou Toure. Citing lack of organization and failure to see the need for a unifying ideology, Carmichael still believes that America will undergo a revolution because Americans, especially women, are more politicized than they were in the 1960s. The ultimate goal for black people, according to Carmichael, is a unified and socialist Africa. This is the reason Carmichael makes annual visits to America, to seek out recruits who will be mesmerized by the clipped voice, still piercing eyes, and the strident, pounding, insistent message of what *People* called "an unreconstructed rebel . . . a black separatist who proselytizes for a unified, Socialist Africa . . . [who] expects America's dispossessed to overthrow the capitalist system one day."

The increasingly strident rhetoric that acknowledged and approved the need for violence and hatred of whites alienated the black old guard of the more moderate civil rights organizations. Now a thirty-year resident of Guinea and a Pan Africanist, he is no longer Stokely Carmichael, having renamed himself Kwame Ture after two leading African Socialists—Kwame Nkrumah and Sekou Toure. As of the late 1990s, he has been suffering from the effects of prostate cancer and has undergone radiation therapy at New York's Columbia-Presbyterian

Medical Center and at a Havana, Cuba, hospital. Although gray-headed, gray-bearded, and physically weakened, he cheerfully answers the telephone with the 1960s greeting of "Ready for revolution!"

In 1994, he was awarded an LL.D. by Shaw University, recognizing his efforts to free black people.—DOLORES NICHOLSON

ELIZABETH **CATLETT**
1915–
Sculptor, painter, printmaker

Celebrated internationally for her figurative sculpture and prints, Elizabeth Catlett is one of the premier

black American artists of the twentieth century. Catlett is also known, however, as a cultural nationalist

and civil rights activist. Her left-of-center political beliefs have led her to become an expatriate, living in

Mexico as a citizen of that country since 1962.

The grandchild of slaves, Elizabeth Catlett was born in Washington, D.C., on April 15, 1915, and grew up in a middle-class home built by her father's family. Catlett's father, a mathematics professor at Tuskegee Institute, died before she was born. Encouraged by her mother and a high school teacher impressed with her skills in drawing and carving, Catlett entered Howard University in 1933. It was the first black college to establish an art department since Catlett's initial choice, Carnegie Institute, did not accept blacks. At Howard, she began to major in design under the tutelage of Lois Mailou Jones. She also studied printmaking with graphic artist James Lesene Wells and drawing with artist and art historian James A. Porter. Porter, as author of one of the first books on black American art, knew well the obstacles Catlett would face in her artistic career. He urged her to gain professional experience by working for the government-sponsored Works Progress Administration/Public Works of Art Project (called the Federal Art Project in 1934), where she worked in the mural division for two months. There she became aware of the Mexican muralists Diego Rivera and Miguel Covarrubias, whose political beliefs about the purpose of art would significantly influence her later work. Catlett's experience on the federal relief program profoundly affected both her art and her life. She declared her new major to be painting and gradually began her lifelong commitment to social change for the betterment of those less fortunate than herself.

When Catlett graduated cum laude with her bachelor's degree in art in 1936, the United States was still recovering from the Great Depression. Few jobs in the arts were available, but she secured a position teaching high school in Durham, North Carolina, at fifty-nine dollars a month. Frustrated with a year of earning a wage less than that of white instructors, Catlett joined the North Carolina Teachers Association in an effort to equalize salaries for black faculty members. She was joined in this campaign by an NAACP attorney, Thurgood Marshall. Realizing the grim situation of the segregated South, Catlett returned to Washington, D.C., to earn money for graduate school.

At the University of Iowa in 1940, she was the first student ever to earn an M.F.A. in sculpture. After graduation Catlett taught at Prairie View College in Texas during the summer of

***Elizabeth Catlett in her
Manhattan apartment, 1993.***

1940. That same year she won first prize in sculpture in the Golden Jubilee National Exposition in Chicago. She then worked as head of the art department at Dillard University in New Orleans for two years. There Catlett continued to campaign for higher wages for the faculty. Though not successful, she did win two other victories. Nude models were permitted in her life classes, and she persuaded a local museum to admit black students for the first time ever to see an exhibition of Picasso's works.

During the summer of 1941 Catlett took a ceramics class at the Art Institute of Chicago and while in Illinois met and married artist Charles White. In 1942 the couple moved to Hampton, Virginia, where Catlett taught at Hampton Institute and White executed a mural commission. The same year Catlett's work was exhibited at Atlanta University. The pair then moved to Harlem, New York.

Catlett supported herself in New York by teaching at a community institution for adult education, the George Washington Carver School. With her salary she continued her studies in several media, working privately with the French sculptor Ossip Zadkine in Greenwich Village and learning lithography at the Art Students League. She also continued to show her work around the country, at the Institute of Contemporary Art in Boston in 1943; the Baltimore Museum of Art, the University of Chicago, the Renaissance Society, and the Newark Museum in New Jersey, all in 1944; and at the Albany Institute of History and Art in 1945.

Works honor black women   In recognition of Catlett's achievements, including winning second prize in sculpture at the Atlanta University Annual in 1946, the Julius Rosenwald Foundation awarded Catlett a fellowship to do a series of works honoring black women. At that time the Whites were having marital problems but accepted an invitation to work in Mexico City. At the Taller de Grafica Popular (TGP), they worked together with other artists on a volume of prints portraying life throughout the Mexican republic. The TGP was a graphic arts and mural workshop where artists collaboratively created art to aid socio-political change. It was founded in 1937 by Leopoldo Mendez, Luis Arenal, and Pabio Higgins. Catlett recalls to art historian Samella Lewis what the institution meant to her:

> The search for learning took me to Mexico, to the Taller de Grafica Popular, where we worked collectively, where we had strong artists and weak artists, and each one learned from the other. Everybody offered something—and when you saw the product, even if you were weak, you saw a collective product that you had helped form. It makes a difference in your desire to work and your understanding of what you're doing. At the same time we did individual work. I would say it was a great social experience, because I learned how you use your art for the service of people, struggling people, to whom only realism is meaningful.

It was at the TGP with the sponsorship of the Rosenwald grant that Catlett produced a significant portfolio of linocuts depicting black laborers, artists, and farmers. "The Negro Woman" earned Catlett her first solo show; the exhibition was held at the Barnett-Aden Gallery in Washington, D.C., 1947–48.

Although the sojourn in Mexico proved artistically beneficial for both Catlett and White, their relationship floundered and upon their return to New York City, they separated. Catlett then went back to work at the TGP and continued her studies with Francisco Zuniga. She also developed her wood carving at *la Esmerelda, La Escuela de Pintura y Escultura* in Mexico in 1948.

Among the members who joined the TGP in the 1940s was Francisco Mora, Catlett's second husband. Born in Uruapan, Michoacan, Mexico, in 1922 to an urban working-class family, Mora sympathized with the lower class, especially miners who were exposed to dangerous working conditions and poor wages. In oil painting, lithographs, and murals, Mora depicted the life of the Mexican people and made a firm commitment to the practice of social art.

In 1947 when Catlett and Mora married, both of their countries were in political and social turmoil. In the United States leftist-oriented people in the arts continually battled the House of Representatives Un-American Activities Committee and Senator Joseph McCarthy. Despite the oppressive atmosphere during the following decade, the couple persevered in creating work with political content. Catlett won second prize again at the Atlanta University Annual in 1956 and received a diploma in printmaking from the First National Painting and Printmaking Exhibition in Mexico City in 1959. Mora executed three murals commissioned between 1950 and 1958: "Freedom of the Press" at the *El Sol de Toluca* newspaper office, "Folklore Map of Mexico" at the Hotel de Prado, and "Education for the People" at a primary school in Santa Maria Tarasquillo, Mexico. Because their art and their association with the TGP were deemed radical, Catlett and Mora were suspected of being Communists. The charge became explicit in 1959. Accused of belonging to the Communist party, Catlett was arrested as an undesirable alien. Three years later she left the United States to become a Mexican citizen. Like Barbara Chase-Riboud, another black American sculptor who has made her permanent home abroad (in Paris, France), Catlett insists that her decision was not a condemnation of the United States, but instead a dedication to her adopted country where she could live as a responsible, active member of society. To Stephanie Stokes Oliver in *Essence,* she explained: "I changed my citizenship because I have been living in Mexico since 1946, and I'm a political person. . . . I couldn't do anything political in Mexico unless I was a citizen." Not pleased with her political statements, the United States government banned Catlett from traveling in the United States for nine years.

Nonetheless, Catlett thrived in her new environment. She had been hired in 1959 as the first woman professor of sculpture at the National School of Fine Arts in San Carlos, Mexico. Catlett served there as chair of the department and taught classes until her retirement in 1973, and she received numerous awards from the Latin American artistic community.

While Catlett is perhaps best known as a sculptor, she is also well recognized for her prints—a medium she appreciates because many originals can be made at relatively low cost and sold to people with low incomes. In 1969 she won the first purchase prize from the National Print Salon in Mexico. The following year she received a prize to study and travel in the German Democratic Republic and showed her work at the Intergrafic Exhibition in Berlin.

Inspired by her sojourn abroad, Catlett applied for and received a grant from the British Council to visit art schools in Britain in 1970. Her travels made her more firmly committed to what she termed the "worldwide drive for national liberation." While Catlett deeply appreciated the chance to see artistic developments in other countries, she emphatically stated in *Ebony* that art must address the needs of people around the world. "I don't think we can still keep going to Paris and Rome to see what the last word is in art and come back to our desperate nations and live in intellectual isolation from what's going on in our countries and ghettos."

Great black figures portrayed　　Joining many other black American artists in the 1960s and 1970s, Catlett sought to educate the public with her portrayals of great figures in black history. Her depictions ranged from abolitionists in the nineteenth century, such as Harriet Tubman, to contemporary heroes, as evidenced in *Homage to the Panthers* and *Malcolm Speaks for Us.* The latter work won a top purchase prize, was bought by the National Institute of Fine Arts, and now belongs to the Mexican government. Catlett explained the purpose of her portraiture in 1971 when she wrote in *American Women Artists,* "I have gradually reached the conclusion that art is important only to the extent that it aids in the liberation of our people. . . . I have now rejected 'International Art' except to use those if its techniques may help me make the message clearer to my folks."

Internationally recognized for her well-researched and sensitive renderings of black heroes, Catlett was commissioned to depict two historical black Americans in the land of her birth. In 1973 she produced a life-size bronze bust of Phillis Wheatley for Jackson State College in Mississippi. Two years later she created a ten-foot-tall bronze sculpture of Louis Armstrong for the City Park of New Orleans. The work was unveiled in the Bicentennial Celebration of 1976.

In addition to portrait studies, Catlett produced more abstract works with symbolic content and titles, such as *Black Flag* and *Magic Mask*. Works in this vein are powerful acknowledgements of a history of oppression, but also expressions of black pride. *Target Practice* is the head of a black man framed by a large rifle sight and mounted trophy-like on a wooden pedestal; *Black Unity* depicts two calmly dignified heads reminiscent of certain West African masks. Seen from the other side, however, the sculpture reveals a large clenched fist, a symbol of black power. Catlett affirms her heritage artistically in formal terms as well as in content. Rather than work in the Western medium of white marble, she seeks materials that reflect the beauty and diversity of skin tones among black peoples. She sculpts wood such as walnut, Spanish cedar, and mahogany, stones such as black marble and onyx, and she shapes terra-cotta and bronze.

By far Catlett's favorite theme is motherhood. Beginning with her master's thesis depiction of a mother and child, Catlett has spent years exploring the topic. She executed many pieces with the same title in terra-cotta and wood, as well as variations on the motif in lithography (such as *Black Maternity*) and marble (*Negro Mother and Child*). *Maternity* in black marble is a strong expression of that special bond. Catlett abstracts a woman's bust into a hollow shape reminiscent of West African heddle pulleys. Although the mother's uplifted head looks to the side, her arms cradle the fetus/child in a firm but open embrace. The small figure reaches towards life-sustaining breasts. Situated in this cavity, the baby is symbolically at once in the uterus, and always in the mother's heart. Catlett finds special pleasures in portraying motherhood for personal reasons. For ten years after her marriage to Mora and the birth of their three children, Catlett had no time to sculpt. Nonetheless, she believes that being a mother gave her work "immeasurably more depth." She maintained in *Ebony* that "raising children is the most creative thing I can think of." Other women concurred with Catlett's statement and held both her parental care and artistic creativity in high esteem. Women's groups on both coasts of the United States showed their appreciation of Catlett's work by giving her awards in the early 1980s. In 1981 she received an award from the Women's Caucus for Art at the national congress in San Francisco. And in 1985 she achieved a bronze sculpture award from the National Council of Negro Women in New York.

Catlett's art continued to merit attention from other groups as well. In 1976 Howard University commissioned her to create a twenty-four-foot-high bronze relief for the Chemical Engineering Building. The following year she was given an Alumni Award by that same institution, her alma mater. The next commission came from the Secretary of Education in Mexico City; in 1981 Catlett completed two life-size bronze sculptures, *Torres Bodet* and *Vasconcelos*.

Aptly called "La Maestra" by her students, Catlett continues to enrich our vision of the world with her art. Still residing in Mexico, she and her husband now devote their time to traveling and creating "art for liberation and for life."

Enduring an artistic career that spans fifty years, Catlett's artwork is still in demand. In 1995, Chicago requested Catlett's work to grace the entrance to the Legler Public Library. The commission could only designate a small amount to Catlett, but she was more than happy to oblige. "I was very excited by the fact that the building is so beautiful," she said. "It has all this lovely wood and marble throughout. I was excited just about the prospect of people sitting in there, black people sitting in that building, reading. That's my main aim . . . to use my art to benefit black people." Catlett has benefited not just black people, but the entire world with her frank and innovative works of art.—THERESA A. LEININGER

SHIRLEY CHISHOLM
1924–
Politician, author

Shirley Chisholm was, in her own words, "the first American citizen to be elected to Congress in spite of the double drawbacks of being female and having skin darkened by melanin." Elected to the House of Representatives in 1968, she was the first black woman to be elected to the United States Congress, and in 1972 she became the first woman or black to seek a major party nomination for president.

Shirley Anita St. Hill Chisholm was born in Brooklyn on November 20, 1924, to Charles and Ruby St. Hill. At the age of three, she and her two younger sisters, Muriel and Odessa, were sent to Barbados to live with their grandmother, Emily Seale, to allow the St. Hills to save some money. Chisholm's Aunt Myrtle and Uncle Lincoln helped the grandmother care for the three girls, and the children stayed in Barbados seven years. It was here that Shirley Chisholm received the foundation for her further learning. "Years later I would know what an important gift my parents had given me by seeing to it that I had my early education in the strict, traditional, British-style schools of Barbados. If I speak and write easily now, that early education is the main reason."

Eventually the three sisters returned to Brooklyn, where the Depression had kept the St. Hills from realizing their financial goals. However, in 1934, after seven years, Ruby St. Hill had gone to Barbados to retrieve her children. Back in Brooklyn, they were introduced to their new baby sister, Selma. After years of living in warm and beautiful Barbados, the transition to New York—and an apartment with only cold water and heated by a coal stove—was difficult.

The return was made easier by caring and stimulating parents. Charles, the father, was an impressive man who, despite having finished only the equivalent of the fifth grade, read voraciously. He read several newspapers a day in addition to anything else he could get his hands on; in later years, Chisholm recalled that "if he saw a man passing out handbills, he would cross the street to get one and read it." During these early years, his daughter grew to idolize him, and his effect upon her was lifelong. Her mother also had a profound impact upon her life; she worked to make her daughters renaissance women: "We were to become young ladies—poised, modest, accomplished, educated, and graceful, prepared to take our places in the world." Although living in the Depression, her parents sought to provide the best they could for their daughters.

Chisholm's initial experience in New York schools was very different from the positive situation in Barbados. A sixth grader in Barbados, Chisholm was placed in grade Three-B with

Shirley Chisholm demonstrates with the National Black Women's Political Caucus.

children two years her junior due to a deficiency in her knowledge of American history and geography. With a tutor's help, however, she eventually caught up to her peers. During her high school years, her mother kept a tight rein on her, forcing her to develop good study habits. This allowed her to graduate with a grade point average that drew several scholarship offers, including ones from Vassar and Oberlin. Finances, however, forced her to enroll in Brooklyn College.

Brooklyn College was a period of immense growth for Chisholm. She chose to become a teacher, believing there was no other career option for a young black woman. She majored in psychology and minored in Spanish. During her sophomore year, she joined the Harriet Tubman Society, where, she says, "I first heard people other than my father talk about white oppression, black racial consciousness, and black pride." As her college career progressed, her immense abilities became evident. Chisholm later recalled, "More and more people, white and black, began to tell me things like, 'Shirley, you have potential. You should do something with your life'." Her belief that she needed to do something important strengthened her resolve to become a teacher. She believed she could better society by helping children, and she also had a growing desire to help alter the treatment of her race. It was during this period that the seed for a political career was first planted, by a blind, white political science professor, Louis Warsoff. One of Chisholm's favorite teachers, he suggested she go into politics. At the time, however, this seemed impossible for her, and she responded, "You forget two things. I'm black—and I'm a woman." But the seed, not yet ready to sprout, was planted.

Upon receiving her diploma, Chisholm began looking for a job. Despite her graduation cum laude, the search was difficult. Small and young-looking, she did not look old enough to be a teacher and was repeatedly told so. Ella Hodges of the Mount Calvary Child Care Center in Harlem hired her on probation, and she stayed there seven years. During this time, she also enrolled in Columbia University night school to seek her master's degree in early childhood education. At Columbia she met a graduate student who had recently migrated from Jamaica, Conrad Chisholm. During their early conversations, he attempted to convince her there was more to life than work—such as spending time with him. Easy-going Conrad was a perfect match for the outgoing, ambitious, driven Shirley. The year after they met, they were married.

Chisholm' became active in politics in 1960, when she helped form the Unity Democratic Club. Its plan was to defeat the Seventeenth Assembly District political machine and take over the district. While pushing for reform, the Unity Democratic Club teamed with the Nostrand Democratic Club to push for the election of two committee members. Despite good showings, both men were defeated. With long-range planning, the groups were more successful in 1962. Both their candidates were elected, and control of the Seventeenth Assembly District fell to them. This victory would be particularly important when in 1964 their candidate was appointed to the bench. A new candidate for assemblyman had to be chosen, so Chisholm immediately began campaigning for herself. The campaign was difficult; she recalls that "it was a long, hard summer and fall. I won by a satisfying margin, in a three-way contest, with 18,151 votes to 1,893 votes for the Republican, Charles Lewis, and 913 votes for the Liberal, Simon Golar." As a result of her victory, Chisholm spent the next four years in the New York State Assembly.

Baptism in public service   Chisholm began her service in the New York State Assembly with flair, quickly establishing her own independence from the state party structure. At the beginning of her first term, there was a highly contested race for party leader between Anthony Travia, the former minority leader, and Stanley Steingut. Bucking expectation, Chisholm sided with Travia, one of only two Brooklyn assemblypersons to do so. She also was an active legislator, and two of her bills are particularly noteworthy. The first created a SEEK program, which made it possible for disadvantaged young people to go to college. Her other bill created unemployment insurance for domestic and personal employees. During her tenure, she won acclaim as one of the most militant and effective black members of the Assembly. With this experience behind her, she was ready to move on to the next challenge.

The Congressional campaign was made possible by the correction of an old evil. When the Supreme Court ordered redistricting because of previous gerrymandering, a primarily black Twelfth District of New York was created. Chisholm was the choice of a citizens' committee because of her independent and indomitable spirit. She entered into a primary race with William Thompson, the party machine candidate, and Dolly Robinson. Facing odds like these, she seemed to need a miracle. She launched a campaign effort, and this rigorous schedule paid high dividends. She won by about one thousand votes following a small voter turnout. The Republican candidate was James Farmer, the former national chairman of CORE, the Congress of Racial Equality.

About the time Farmer's nomination was announced, Chisholm became seriously ill and was diagnosed as having a massive tumor. It was benign, but surgery was still necessary; this took place in late July. After a short convalescence, Chisholm began campaigning again. Many women's organizations offered assistance, particularly after Farmer began to turn the campaign into a gender issue. Despite Farmer's money and his attempt to use her gender against her, Chisholm was too powerful. In the November election, Chisholm beat him decisively. Washington was the next stop for Congresswoman Chisholm.

Chisholm quickly demonstrated that the rebelliousness she displayed in the New York State Assembly was still prevalent. "Her House tenure started in controversy in 1969," explains Alan Ehrenhalt in *Politics in America,* "when House leaders put her on the Agricultural Committee, believing they were doing her a favor because of the committee's jurisdiction over food stamps." She demanded to be taken off this committee, feeling that it was not where she could best serve her constituency. Surprisingly, she was successful in her attempt and was switched to the Veterans' Affairs Committee. She stayed on this committee for only two years, switching in 1971 to the Education and Labor Committee, which is where she wished to be. Here is an example of Chisholm learning to work within the system, for the appointment may have been part of a deal. "She was widely believed to have won that assignment by supporting Hale Boggs of Louisiana in his successful campaign for majority leader against the more liberal Morris K. Udall of Arizona," noted Ehrenhalt. On that committee she campaigned for the poor, working for minimum wage increases and federal subsidies for day care centers, a bill that President Gerald Ford vetoed. Even before this, Congresswoman Chisholm had decided it was necessary to change the power structure from the top. Thus, she campaigned for the United States Presidency in 1972.

She was the first black and the first woman to seek a major party nomination for president. She began the race as she had all her previous political ventures—as a poorly funded and hard-working underdog. This time, however, her work ethic and drive were not enough to succeed. She attempted to put together a coalition of blacks, feminists, and other minority groups, but this effort failed. She failed even to win the support of the Congressional Black Caucus, creating a rift between the two. By the time the convention rolled around, a

Shirley Chisholm, 1980.

loss was already assured. Chisholm went to the 1972 convention with 24 delegates. In the end she got 151 votes, released to her by Hubert H. Humphrey and other candidates who had given up on the "stop George McGovern" campaign. Her campaign cannot be deemed a true failure because of the groundbreaking nature of the endeavor. "In terms of black politics, I think an effect of my campaign has been to increase the independence and self-reliance of many local elected black officials and black political activists from the domination of the political 'superstars'." Never shy to suggest her own importance or the importance of her actions, Chisholm spoke on the further impact of her campaign:

> The United States was said not to be ready to elect a Catholic to the Presidency when Al Smith ran in the 1920's. But Smith's nomination may have helped pave the way for the successful campaign John F. Kennedy waged in 1960. Who can tell? What I hope most is that now there will be others who will feel themselves as capable of running for high political office as any wealthy, good-looking white male.

Chisholm remained in Congress and in 1977 moved to the powerful House Rules Committee. She also was elected secretary of the Democratic Caucus, a largely honorific post. In 1980 she went against tradition when she and two Democrats joined the committee's Republican members to force a floor vote on a bill calling for twice-yearly cost-of-living raises for federal retirees. She voted this way despite intense lobbying from Speaker Thomas "Tip" O'Neal. A more important disappointment to her party is her failure to support strict environmental laws that she feels would cost people jobs. However, as the years have passed, she has gradually become a more loyal party member. In her first two years in Congress, she only supported the party on 97 of 127 bills. In 1979 and 1980, she voted the party way on 154 of 163 bills.

The years passed and Chisholm gained more power in Congress. Her increasing length of tenure moved her up in the seniority system. Also, her position in the House of Representatives was safe. Even during the late seventies, when the conservatives were beginning to win elections, her power base in the Twelfth District remained secure. Her personal life was not as uniformly successful: she and Conrad Chisholm divorced in February, 1977. She did not remain single long, remarrying later that same year. This time she wed Arthur Hardwick, Jr., a black businessman she had met ten years earlier when both of them were in the New York State Assembly. In 1979 he was almost killed in a car accident. During his convalescence, she was regularly called away to perform her Congressional duties, and these demands began to weigh heavily upon her. "Her husband's accident and the new conservative climate in Washington prompted Shirley to think about her own goals," wrote biographer Catherine Scheader. On February 10, 1982, Chisholm announced her retirement.

She remained active on the lecture circuit and also was named the Purington Professor at Mount Holyoke College, where she taught classes in political science and women's studies. In 1985 she was visiting scholar at Spelman College. In 1986 Arthur Hardwick died of cancer, and following the 1987 spring semester, she retired from teaching.

She didn't abandon politics, though. When Jesse Jackson started his campaign for the presidency in 1984, Chisholm began working for him. With more time available, her support increased for his 1988 campaign. In the eyes of many, his campaigns were a direct result of her earlier attempt. Jackson's New Jersey chairman, Newark Mayor Sharpe James, credits Shirley with Jesse's successes. "If there had been no Shirley Chisholm," Scheader quoted him, "there would have been no 'Run, Jesse, run' in 1984 and no 'Win, Jesse, win' in 1988." Working for the Jackson campaign was not the extent of her political activities.

Chisholm leads NPCBW Following several disappointments at the 1984 Democratic Convention, Chisholm was determined to continue the struggle. She gathered nine black women together. This led to a major four-day convention of five hundred black women who created a new organization, the National Political Congress of Black Women (NPCBW), with Chisholm as its first leader. The group grew fast, with 8,500 members in thirty-six states by 1988. By this point, it was beginning to wield some real political power. According to Scheader, "The group sent a delegation of 100 women to the 1988 Democratic National Convention to present demands for promoting civil rights and social programs." Chisholm has remained a potent force in politics.

Chisholm has been active in the League of Women Voters, the Brooklyn Branch of the NAACP, the National Board of Americans for Democratic Action, and Delta Sigma Theta Sorority. She has been on the advisory council of the National Organization of Women and an honorary committee member of the United Negro College Fund. Among her many achievements, her most lasting may be her books. The first, *Unbought and Unbossed,* details her early life and her rise, culminating in her election to the House of Representatives. The second book, *The Good Fight,* details her unsuccessful run for the 1972 Democratic party nomination. Both works express her confidence in her ability and her beliefs and hopes for the future of blacks and women. For her ground-breaking political career, in 1993, President Bill Clinton announced that he would nominate Chisolm for the position of Ambassador to Jamaica. Clinton summed up his choice for the job by saying, "Shirley Chisholm is a true pioneer of American politics, whose passion for social justice is unparalleled."

Chisholm has been a maverick her entire life, refusing the role society created for her. By rebelling, she has achieved many great things. She has been elected to offices and honored with awards and degrees. But, as biographer Catherine Scheader recorded, these achievements are not what she considers important:

> I do not want to be remembered as the first black woman to be elected to the
> United States Congress, even though I am. I do not want to be remembered
> as the first woman who happened to be black to make a serious bid for the
> presidency. I'd like to be known as a catalyst for change, a woman who had
> the determination and a woman who had the perseverance to fight on behalf
> of the female population and the black population, because I'm a product of
> both, being black and a woman.—ALAN DUCKWORTH

KENNETH B. **CLARK**

1914–

Educator, psychologist, writer

Kenneth B. Clark has been at the forefront in exposing the damage that racism has caused in children. His psychological research dismantled the "separate but equal" doctrines of Plessy v. Ferguson and helped overturn that decision, which led to the historic, unanimous Supreme Court decision of Brown v. Board of Education in 1954. This landmark decision concluded that separate is unequal, and paved the way for school desegregation. Clark's work revealed the harm discrimination wrought not only on African American children, but on white children as well. The decision of the Supreme Court in 1954 helped spark the civil rights movement, and Clark has been an active participant throughout. As astute commentator and author, Clark has written many highly praised articles and texts on education, poverty, and what African Americans as a whole, want from their schools, government, and fellow man—which has always been equality.

Kenneth Bancroft Clark was born on July 24, 1914 to Arthur Bancroft Clark and Miriam Clark in the Panama Canal Zone. His sister, Beulah, was born soon after. Arthur Clark was a superintendent at the United Fruit Company and provided adequately for his family. But

living in Panama Canal did not satisfy Miriam Clark, a strong-willed Jamaican woman who foresaw great things for her son. She wanted to move the family to the United States against the wishes of her husband. The ultimatum was given, and Arthur Clark stayed behind, fearing that America would not be the land of opportunity Miriam believed. In 1919, Miriam Clark moved to Harlem and supported her children as a seamstress in one of the sweatshops in New York City. Clark's mother was an influential figure in his life. She helped organize a union with her fellow workers and was one of the first stewards for the International Ladies Garment Workers Union. It was through his mother's struggles for unity at her job that initially exposed young Clark to social issues, but it was his schooling that unmasked the evils of racism and awoke his curiosity about its roots and effects.

In his first years of schooling, Clark attended Public School 5 in Harlem, an integrated school. But as the neighborhood changed, so did Clark's schoolmates and education. By ninth grade, Public School 139, Clark's first high school, was mainly

Kenneth Clark.

made up of African American students. Instructors and counselors advised their African American pupils to learn a trade since job opportunities were limited. When Clark passed this information to his mother, Miriam Clark accosted a counselor by saying that her son was not brought to America to study a trade. While Clark attended an integrated school, he experienced positive interactions with his teachers who did not blame his difficulty in algebra on his skin color. But as a student in a new school, George Washington High School, Clark witnessed his teachers' behavior with anguish and curiosity. In high school, Clark was an exceptional student who excelled in economics. He once considered a career in the field until he was denied an economic class award by a teacher who found Clark's intelligence bewildering. Clark has reflected on this moment as being his first encounter with discrimination and his desire to study its roots.

Studies to become a psychologist

Clark entered Howard University to become a medical doctor, but his constant exposure to racial injustices and his contact with Ralph Bunche, who was teaching political science at Howard at the same time, further stirred his interest to study any and all behavior associated with racism. He obtained his B.A. in psychology from Howard in 1935 and his M.S. the following year. After five years of schooling, Clark chose a teaching position at Howard for a year. Teaching seemed limiting for Clark, whose thirst for knowledge never subsided. One of his psychology professors urged him to earn his doctorate. Without much more convincing, Clark was enrolled at Columbia University for his Ph.D. in psychology. In 1940 Clark became the first African American to obtain a Ph.D. from Columbia.

During the last phases of his doctoral years, Clark was gaining much field experience as he examined the problems and behavior of African Americans in northern cities. His studies included projects headed by Swedish economist Gunnar Myrdal and involved studying the morale of African Americans during wartime for the Office of War Information.

In 1938, he married fellow psychologist Miriam Phipps, who collaborated on many of his studies and co-authored several articles on social and psychological behavior. In between his research, Clark maintained assistant professorships at Hampton Institute and the College of the City of New York. Soon, Clark and his wife devoted much of their time researching the effects of segregation on minority children and publishing their findings. These publications led to their fame. The Clarks became pioneers in their vocation by establishing a treatment center in Manhattan for African American children with personality disorders. The center was named Northside Testing and Consultation Center in 1946. As the importance of the center grew, it was renamed Northside Center for Child Development and began to treat children of all races. In 1950 Kenneth Clark wrote an article for the Mid-century White House Conference on Children and Youth, detailing his work and that of other researchers on the effects of school segregation. It was this report that caught the eyes of a group of lawyers at the National Association for the Advancement of Colored People (NAACP), who were on a mission to prove the criminal nature of segregation.

Clark's testimony persuades Supreme Court

Thurgood Marshall led an elite group of African American lawyers determined to overturn the Supreme Court's decision of *Plessy v. Ferguson* that legalized school segregation. Marshall and his team wanted to prove that

Kenneth Clark.

segregation violated African Americans' equal protection and rights allowed by the fourteenth amendment. But Marshall was faced with the challenge of providing tangible evidence that the legacy of *Plessy v. Ferguson* caused significant damage to young school children. In 1950, Marshall relied on Clark to prove that segregation was not only morally unsound, but its purpose and adverse effects were unlawful. Clark's method of proving this included his famous use of dolls with his young test subjects in South Carolina.

The children were shown four dolls with two distinct skin tones, black and white. Clark asked the children a series of questions determining their feelings toward the dolls. When asked which dolls they thought were the bad ones, the children unanimously chose the black dolls. When asked by Clark which dolls they would most likely want to play with, without hesitation the majority of children chose the white dolls. Clark's research undeniably proved that segregation and discrimination branded minority children with the stigma of inferiority. In his court testimony in the *Brown v. Board of Education* case, he stated that this stigma therefore instilled a sense of low self-esteem, which prevented the African American child from learning effectively and becoming a productive member of society. Clark also noted in his testimony that as the United States upholds its doctrines of democracy during war and adheres to the Constitution stating that all men are created equal, but at the same time mistreats African Americans, it sends a mixed message to children of the majority. This hypocritical methodology "teaches children to gain personal status in an unrealistic and nonadaptive way and in effect, confusion, conflict, moral cynicism and disrespect for authority may arise."

In May 1954, the Supreme Court handed down its decision in *Brown v. Board of Education* and was convinced by Clark's scientific findings that segregation "deprived the children of the minority of equal educational opportunities." The high court voted unanimously to overturn the decision of *Plessy v. Ferguson.* The decision of the Supreme Court was a milestone for the civil rights movement and placed Clark on top of the list of academic scholars. He received much attention after the trial, along with awards, including the NAACP's Spingarn Award, and honorary degrees. Clark remained a proponent of integrated schools based on his positive experiences in elementary school and fought continuously to see African Americans obtain integrated and adequate schooling.

Clark attacks de facto segregation   After the *Brown v. Board of Education* case, school desegregation took a long course into fruition. In 1954, Clark realized more and more that as the population of African Americans increased in Harlem, the New York City public schools were preventing minority children from obtaining academic acceptance. He criticized the New York public school system of practicing de facto segregation and blasted the system for not preparing African American children academically for scholastic tests, which once again lead to "racial exclusion." Clark's charges were initially disregarded, but further investigation proved Clark's claims to be true, and reform was ordered within the New York City school system.

In 1956, Clark headed a study for the Board of Education's Commission on Integration in the Schools that suggested curriculum changes for African American as well as Mexican students in public schools. This study would be noted for its findings that proved academic and intellectual abilities were affected not by innate racial differences, but by environmental conditions, such as poor schooling. Clark's continued research during the 1950s led to his appointment to two significant positions in the following decade. He was offered a permanent professorship at City College in 1960. Clark accepted it, becoming the first African American in the history of New York to receive such a position.

Clark was also appointed, in 1962, head of an organization that set out to reduce the rise in school dropouts, juvenile delinquents, and unemployment in Harlem with the Harlem Youth Opportunities Unlimited (HARYOU). Over the next two years this organization, made up of social workers, psychologists, and leading citizens, produced a 620-page report recommending the "thorough reorganization of the schools" in Harlem. This would include increased integration, a massive program to improve reading skills among students, stricter review of teacher performance, and, most importantly, a high level of participation by the residents of Harlem in implementing these changes. But HARYOU's efforts and report fell on deaf ears. The organization became a victim of urban politics, and the conditions in Harlem remained unchanged. Clark commented that his work at HARYOU did nothing but produce a document. Clark's desire to reveal and elaborate on the findings of HARYOU led him to write *Dark Ghetto: Dilemmas of Social Power,* which revealed the hopelessness that children in ghettos drown in day to day. In his introduction, Clark pleads with his readers for change by describing his book as "no report at all, but rather the anguished cry of its author." *Dark Ghetto* has become a required text in many sociology classes around the country.

In 1967, Clark formed and presided over the nonprofit Metropolitan Applied Research Center, or MARC Corp., in Washington, D.C. Similar to HARYOU, the center comprised social scientists and other professionals looking for answers and solutions to the ills of the urban poor, centering on the lack of adequate education. Clark's program offered such solutions as a massive and immediate upgrading of reading skills, teacher evaluations based on student performance, and community involvement in school activities. But even when hordes of people were clamoring for change in the system, many, including teachers, were not willing to risk their jobs as a result of their pupils' performance on scholastic tests. A new superintendent was appointed and even countered Clark's findings by stating that children from the ghetto should not be expected to perform "normally" compared to children in other areas simply because they live in the ghetto. "Ghetto life," he argued, "was anything but normal, and it would be unfair to hold teachers and schools responsible for the performance of students handicapped by living in the ghetto." Once again, Clark's report, findings, and solutions, which offered harsh remedies for hard times, were thrown aside.

Continues his eye on education reform   The statement of the superintendent contradicted the verdict of *Brown v. Board of Education.* If ghetto children are not expected to perform equally to other children, then the schools they were attending were separated from—and inferior to—the mainstream, and therefore, not equal. Clark's defeat in Washington did nothing to affect his adherence in promoting integrated education in America's schools. He even opposed black nationalists who preached separatism, only to subject himself to death threats and many emotional reprisals. In 1975, Clark retired from teaching at City College. Clark, his wife, and two children, social scientist Kate Miriam and Hilton Bancroft, founded the consulting firm Clark, Phipps, Clark & Harris, Inc., which helps corporations implement programs to hire minorities. This work has kept Clark in the forefront of African American concerns in the workplace through the 1990s.

Nonetheless, Clark's previous fight in education has resurfaced in interviews. In 1982, he stated in the *New Yorker* that the outlook for education for minorities was dismal. "Things are worse. In the schools . . . more black kids are being put on the dung heap every year." In 1993 Clark wrote in *Newsweek* that educators have not fulfilled the prophecy of the *Brown v. Board of Education* decision by not fully educating students on how to adhere to and promote nonviolence, and by not teaching students "to respect the inalienable dignity of other human beings." For America to truly educate its youth, Clark stressed these three important factors:

> Children must be helped to understand the genuine meaning of democracy from the earliest grades; children must be helped to understand that one cannot keep others down without staying down with them; and children must be helped to understand the importance of empathy and respect. Those who are capable of meeting high academic standards can assist others who are not as fortunate.

Clark emphasized that there is more to education than learning how to read and write. Social sensitivity is just as important, as it promotes nonviolence.

Kenneth Clark is one of the foremost African American social scientists of the modern era. Aside from his unprecedented studies on African American children, he has been quoted by mainstream advocates on the goals of African Americans. In testimony and in print, Clark merely states that "African Americans want what other human beings want—respect, dignity, the opportunity to grow and to be evaluated in terms of their worth as individuals. The term 'equality' means to every thoughtful African American exactly what it says. Equality is not qualifiable."—MICHELLE BANKS

SEPTIMA **CLARK**
1898–1987
Educator, humanitarian, civil rights activist

Septima Poinsette Clark is known for her pioneering efforts to establish equality across all social and racial lines. Her years of dedication to the cause of black literacy, black voter registration, and women's and civil rights led others to recognize her as the "queen mother" of the civil rights movement.

Clark was born on May 3, 1898, in Charleston, South Carolina, the second of eight children of Peter Porcher Poinsette (who was a slave until the age of eighteen) and Victoria Warren (Anderson) Poinsette. Septima was a gregarious youngster. She often gathered younger children together for outings, thus earning the nickname "Little Ma" or "Le Ma." After completing her elementary education, Clark attended Avery Normal School, a private school for educating black teachers that was operated by the American Missionary Association. After graduation her teachers encouraged her to attend Fisk University, but her parents were unable to afford the tuition.

Clark begins to teach In the early twentieth century black teachers were forbidden to teach in the public schools of Charleston. Clark was free to teach in the surrounding communities, and she began her teaching career at Promise Land School on Johns Island in 1916. She soon joined the National Association for the Advancement of Colored People (NAACP). When the Charleston chapter of the NAACP fought to strike down the state law that forbade black teachers from teaching in public city schools, Clark was a leading force in the effort. The NAACP bid proved successful, and the law was changed in 1920.

Septima Clark.

On May 23, 1920, the young teacher married Nerie Clark, a sailor she met in Charleston. Clark had two children, one died after twenty-three days but another lived and was named Nerie. The marriage ended with her husband's death from kidney failure about 1924. Clark never married again. Leaving the baby with her parents-in-law in Hickory, North Carolina, Clark returned to Johns Island to teach for three more years, then moved to Columbia, South Carolina. She received her bachelor's degree from Benedict College and her master's degree from Hampton Institute (now University) in Hampton, Virginia.

Active in many clubs and civic groups, Clark learned to organize programs of all kinds in an atmosphere that was more democratic than Charleston had been. Back in Charleston, the city's rigid caste patterns did not permit Clark to associate with lighter, upper-class blacks. In Columbia she worked with the NAACP to secure equal pay for black teachers. Attorney Thurgood Marshall successfully argued the case put together by the local chapter before a federal court.

In 1947 Clark returned to Charleston to care for her mother, who had suffered a stroke. During the ensuing years she taught remedial reading and worked in several civic organizations. In 1947 Julius Waties Waring, a local white judge of the federal district court, ruled that blacks must be permitted to vote in the Democratic primary. Clark, who admired this principled stand, established a friendship with Waring and his wife. The courage of Clark and the Warings was greatly tested, though, for white society ostracized the Warings, while some blacks began to shun Clark for stirring up trouble.

Highlander Folk School provides new outlet In 1954 a coordinated legislative attack by white southerners led the South Carolina legislature to bar teachers from belonging to the NAACP. Clark refused to deny her membership and lost her job just four years short of retirement. Unable to find employment anywhere in South Carolina, in 1956 she was named director of education for the Highlander Folk School in Tennessee, a noted planning center for both black and white community activists that had been founded by Myles Horton.

In the mid-1950s Clark directed a workshop at Highlander on the United Nations that was attended by Rosa Parks. Parks later commented that "I am always very respectful and very much in awe of the presence of Septima Clark because her life story makes the effort that I have made very minute. I only hope that there is a possible chance that some of her great courage and dignity and wisdom has rubbed off on me."

Although Clark had left Johns Island, she had not forgotten the people there. In January 1957 Clark and others opened a citizenship school on the island. This school served as the prototype for similar schools all over the South. Clark coordinated the citizenship schools program from Highlander while simultaneously pushing ministers and other local leaders all over the South to establish similar programs. By the spring of 1961, eighty-two teachers who had been trained at Highlander were holding classes in Alabama, Georgia, South Carolina, and Tennessee.

A foreboding cloud descended over Clark's work, however, in the summer of 1959. Tennessee state police raided Highlander in an attempt to find evidence they could use to revoke Highlander's charter and shut it down. The state closed Highlander and in December 1961 auctioned off all its property without compensation.

Horton, however, had anticipated the closing of the school. He had negotiated with Martin Luther King Jr. to transfer the sponsorship of the citizenship program from Highlander to the Southern Christian Leadership Conference (SCLC). Undaunted by the events in Tennessee, Clark moved to Georgia and set up her training sessions at the Dorchester Cooperative Community Center. She and two other SCLC staff-members—Dorothy Cotton and Andrew Young—drove all over southern states, herding busloads of students to the center, which became an important shaper of future civil rights leaders. Clark used the practical teaching methods she had been developing for more than forty years at the center. Her great gift, however, lay in recognizing natural leaders among the poorly educated students and imparting to them her unshakable confidence and respect.

In 1962 the SCLC joined four other civil rights groups to form the Voter Education Project. In the next four years, ten thousand teachers were trained for citizenship schools and almost seventy thousand black voters were registered across the South. After the passage of the Voting Rights Act in 1965, registration increased rapidly, and at least one million more black people were registered by 1970. Two years later Barbara Jordan and Andrew Young were elected to the U.S. Congress, the first blacks to serve in that legislative body since Reconstruction.

Clark leads in the women's movement　　Clark fought discrimination of all kinds throughout her life. Known for her civil rights work, she also defended the rights of women, encouraging women's rights activists wherever she went and criticizing some ministers of the SCLC for their arrogance toward women. Clark was emphatic in her belief that the civil rights movement grew out of the women's movement, not the other way around, as is commonly interpreted:

Many people think that the women's liberation movement came out of the civil rights movement, but the women's movement started quite a number of years before the civil rights movement. In stories about the movement you hear mostly about the black ministers. But if you talk to the women who were there, you'll hear another story. I think the movement would never have taken off if some women hadn't started to speak up. . . . It took fifty years for women, black and white, to learn to speak up. I had to learn myself, so I know what a struggle it was.

When Clark retired from active SCLC work in the summer of 1970, she was presented with a flurry of awards in recognition of her accomplishments, including the Martin Luther King Jr. Award for great service to humanity and South Carolina's highest civilian award, the Order of the Palmetto, in 1982. Clark still had to fight the state for her pension and back pay, though. After her dismissal in 1956, all her retirement funds in the state pension had been canceled. By 1976, though, the National Education Association was airing her case all over the United States. Stung by the publicity, South Carolina's state legislature decided to pay her an annual pension of $3,600. In July 1981 the state, which still owed her a salary from 1956 to 1964, approved paying her back salary.

Clark celebrated her seventy-eighth birthday by winning election to the Charleston School Board; she served two terms before turning it over to younger leadership. In 1987 she received an American Book Award for her second autobiography, *Ready from Within: Septima Clark and the Civil Rights Movement.* Later that year, on December 15, 1987, Clark passed away after enduring a series of strokes.

"Queen Mother" of civil rights movement   Sometimes known as "Mother Conscience," Clark was also known and loved as the "queen mother" of the civil rights movement. At Clark's funeral many leaders testified to the enduring importance of Clark's life. Charleston Mayor Joseph P. Riley Jr. spoke for many when he remarked that "her purity is everlasting and universal; her legacy is everywhere." Reverend Joseph E. Lowery, president of the SCLC, testified: "Like Harriet Tubman, who led her people to freedom through territorial pilgrimages, Septima Clark led her people to freedom through journeys from the darkness of illiteracy to the shining light of literacy."—CYNTHIA STOKES BROWN

ELDRIDGE **CLEAVER**

1935–

Civil rights activist

Eldridge Cleaver ranks among the most important radicals of the 1960s, and his Soul on Ice, *an autobiographical volume replete with political commentary, stands as an incisive record of the issues and concerns that were prominent in those times.*

Cleaver was born in 1935 in Wabbaseka, Arkansas, but when he was still a child he moved with his family to Los Angeles, California. The family settled in the Watts district, which

*Eldridge Cleaver
at home.*

was notorious for its impoverished residents and its high crime rate. When he was still only a teenager, Cleaver was arrested for various thefts and drug deals, and he consequently spent time in juvenile reformatories. But at age nineteen he was found guity of marijuana possession and was sent to serve a term at California's Soledad penitentiary.

At Soledad, Cleaver worked to improve his education and even managed to complete his high-school studies. Furthermore, he read the political writings of such figures as Voltaire, Karl Marx, and W. E. B. Du Bois. But after leaving Soledad, Cleaver again ran afoul of the law and was charged with rape and assault. He served much of the term for these crimes at Folsom Prison, where he again devoted himself to political study. While in prison, Cleaver also joined the Black Muslims, a religious sect advocating black separatism from white society, and he became particularly inspired by Malcolm X, who was a prominent member of the

Black Muslims. When Malcolm X eventually broke from the Black Muslims, Cleaver followed his lead.

In Folsom Prison, Cleaver began writing various essays expressing his own dissatisfaction with what he viewed as racist America. He decried the relatively lesser social conditions endured by blacks in America, and he railed against a social system that afforded blacks fewer opportunities to realize the prosperity constituting the American dream. In addition, he wrote about his own life, including both his experiences in impoverished, crime-torn Watts and within the harrowing walls of both Soledad and Folsom prisons. Cleaver managed to smuggle his writings out of prison and have them delivered to editorial personnel at *Ramparts,* a leftist magazine. Around this time, the inspirational Malcolm X was shot dead by assassins believed to be affiliated with the Black Muslims.

In 1966, while Cleaver was still in prison, *Ramparts* published his essay "Notes on a Native Son," in which he attacked prominent black writer James Baldwin for his homosexuality and accused him of hating blacks. Later that year, through the efforts of *Ramparts* editors and such noted literary figures as Norman Mailer, Cleaver received his parole. He promptly joined the staff of *Ramparts* and assumed the post of information minister for the radical Black Panther Party, which advocated the violent demise of the U.S. government and the establishment of black socialist rule. Two years later he married a fellow Panther, Kathleen Neal.

Although the Black Panthers were decried by FBI head J. Edgar Hoover as a threat to national security, the party actually provided valuable social services, including free lunches, in black areas throughout the United States. But clashes occurred with police in Oakland, California, where Cleaver was living and working as *Ramparts* editor in chief. In 1968, a particularly violent conflict resulted in the death of one Black Panther and and the wounding of Cleaver and two police officers.

After the gun battle in Oakland, Cleaver was arrested and charged with assault and attempted murder. His arrest prompted widespread protests in the United States and even abroad. French filmmaker Jean-Luc Godard, for instance, called for French cinema patrons to fund Cleaver's defense. Cleaver was kept in prison for two months before a judge demanded his release, ruling that he was being held for political reasons. Shortly after his release, Cleaver accepted the Peace and Freedom Party's nomination as its candidate for the American presidency.

In late 1968, the judgment freeing Cleaver was reversed and he was ordered back to prison. He chose to flee instead, and for the next seven years he wandered the world as a fugitive from American justice. At various times he lived in Cuba, Algeria, and France, but he also visited the Soviet Union and other communist states, including China, North Korea, and North Vietnam. Cleaver's wife joined him abroad, and they eventually had two children: a son, Maceo, born in Algiers; and a daughter, Joju, born in North Korea.

In 1969, soon after leaving the United States, Cleaver published *Post-Prison Writings and Speeches* and *Eldridge Cleaver's Black Papers,* volumes in which he delineated the Black Panthers' ideology and endeavored to eradicate the group's image as a principally antagonistic body. But even as he persevered abroad on behalf of the Black Panthers, his own role within the organization had become problematic. He had earlier held misgivings about leftist rhetoric espousing the achievements of communist leaders. And after actually staying in communist countries, Cleaver came to believe that the communist system, at least as practiced, could scarcely provide freedom and equality for blacks.

After several years abroad, Cleaver experienced a religious conversion to Christianity, and in 1975, despite facing formidable charges, he returned to the United States and surrendered to federal authorities. He then brokered a deal, agreeing to plead guilty to the original assault charge in exchange for the dropping of the attempted murder charge. This pact proved fruitful for Cleaver: he eventually received a sentence of two thousand hours of community service, but he avoided a return to prison.

Cleaver undertook a range of activities after arriving back in the United States. In 1978 he opened a clothing store and introduced his own designs for men's pants. That same year he published *Soul on Ice,* an autobiographical account of his Black Panthers experiences, his years abroad, his religious conversion, and his newfound patriotism. In 1979 he established the Eldridge Cleaver Crusades for promoting Christianity, and in 1984, after completing his community-service sentence, he returned to American politics as a conservative, independent candidate for a seat representing a California district in the House of Representatives. He failed to win election.

In the ensuing years Cleaver traveled America as a lecturer. He remained involved in the democratic process, though, and in 1992 he contested a position with San Francisco's regional transit board. Two years later he suddenly returned to controversy following an altercation with police in Berkeley, California. After being arrested for intoxication and possession of cocaine, he incurred a serious head injury that ultimately necessitated brain surgery. It is, therefore, difficult to speculate on Cleaver's future activities.—LES STONE

JOHNNIE COCHRAN
1937–
Attorney

Long before serving as the lead defense attorney on the O. J. Simpson murder trial in 1995, which the media nicknamed "the trial of the century," Johnnie L. Cochran Jr. had established a reputation as one of the best defense attorneys in the United States. His first major case, in 1965, involved a young black man, Leonard Deadwyler, who was shot and killed by the Los Angeles police while driving his pregnant wife to the hospital; this trial placed the young defense lawyer instantly in the public eye. Wanting to avoid charges of racism following the city's Watts riots, Los Angeles decided to broadcast the trial on television, and Cochran became an overnight star in the legal field. With his brilliant defense technique and ability to connect with jurors, Cochran has won some of the most difficult cases in trial history. His fame has brought him some notable clients as well, including singer Michael Jackson, television actor Todd Bridges, and former football star O. J. Simpson.

Born in Shreveport, Louisiana, on October 2, 1937 to Johnnie and Hattie Cochran, the younger Cochran knew he wanted to be a lawyer after another famous African American attorney (and later Supreme Court justice), Thurgood Marshall, convinced the Supreme Court that segregation in public schools was not constitutional. In an interview with *Ebony* magazine, Cochran shared his revelation: "Thurgood Marshall and Dr. Kenneth Clark devised this strategy that convinced those old White men that school segregation was wrong. I knew from that point on that the law could be used to change society."

As a young black man coming of age in the 1950s, Cochran had to battle racism to achieve his goals. His journey was very much like his father's. Johnnie Cochran Sr. did not let society hinder him. The opportunities available to the son of a Louisiana sharecropper might seem limited, especially if the time were the 1940s. Cochran Sr. still became a successful salesman for Golden State Mutual, one of the major black owned companies in the United States, and he later became head of their training program.

Johnnie Cochran.

Career opportunities in California seemed good—good enough to move the family to the West Adams section of Los Angeles. In West Adams, unlike Shreveport, the neighborhood and the schools consisted of both blacks and whites. Los Angeles was good for the Cochrans, where hard work and a deep respect for God was deeply instilled into Johnnie Jr. and his two sisters.

Even after graduating in 1955 from Los Angeles High, Cochran still had law on the brain. So he enrolled at the University of Southern California, Los Angeles. After UCLA, Cochran attended the Loyola Law School, where he graduated in 1962. He once told *People* magazine, "I was one of those guys who prayed he'd be called on. I was that competitive." Following graduation, he landed his first job at the Los Angeles city attorney's office. In 1965 he left to start his own practice, Cochran, Atkins & Evans. Then the Deadwyler case happened and his reputation for fighting police misconduct was born. Although he lost the case, he proved himself a challenger of legal injustice.

At a time when police officers were considered above the law, many blacks who were often victims of police abuse had nowhere to turn for help. Cochran, with his street smarts and law knowledge, became a godsend to people who were voiceless within the legal system. In 1977, he was named criminal trial lawyer of the year by the Los Angeles Criminal Bar Association.

Cochran soon realized that the best way to make changes was from within the system. So he took a pay cut and returned to working for the city as the assistant district attorney. "I was able to make changes from the inside," he told *People* magazine. "I created a special 'roll-out' unit of the deputy Defense Attorney's to investigate police shootings." During this time, he was named the third ranking lawyer in the nation's largest law office.

In 1979, Cochran found out first-hand how easy it is for a black man to be victimized by the Los Angeles police. While driving one evening with his three children, Melodie, Tiffany, and Jonathan, Cochran was stopped by the police. He told *People* magazine, "I think that they couldn't believe an African American could be driving his own Rolls-Royce. They pulled out their guns and yelled, 'Get out with your hands up.' My children were terrified. Only after they allowed me to pull out my wallet and saw my badge did they apologize."

The incident left Cochran more determined than ever to bring to the public eye police misconduct. So he returned to his private practice in 1981. Cochran was blessed to live to retell his brush with the Los Angeles police; many of his clients were not so lucky. California State, Long Beach football star Ron Settles had everything to live for: his chances were excellent for being signed to a high-paying professional contract. So in 1981, when the Los Angeles police claimed that he had hung himself in his jail cell following an arrest for a speeding ticket, it did not make sense to his family, who hired Cochran. The attorney persuaded the Settles family to have his body exhumed and had another autopsy performed, which revealed that Settles had been choked to death. In a landmark case, Cochran won for the family $760,000.

Since the Settles case, Cochran's firm has won over $43 million in judgments against the police department. Misconduct is not limited to the police, so Cochran and his firm make themselves available to handle various cases. One such case involved eighteen young black girls who were allegedly sexually abused by their third grade teacher. "Nobody did anything about it because these people were poor and minority," Cochran told *Ebony* magazine in 1994. Cochran's legal expertise won the case, and in 1990 he negotiated the largest settlement in the history of the Los Angeles School District.

Other cases followed, including one for former Black Panther Geronimo Pratt, who was accused of murder. Although Cochran lost the first trial, he remained active in the appeals until the day Pratt was released in 1997. He went to battle for white truck driver Reginald Denny, who was attacked by blacks during the riots following the recent Rodney King trial. Cochran sees the police as responsible for failing to protect Denny. His work with Michael Jackson, Todd Bridges, and former football star Jim Brown made him sought-after among Los Angeles rich and famous. But it was the O. J. Simpson murder case that made him a household name around the world. To many it seemed clear that the former football star had murdered his ex-wife, Nicole Brown Simpson, and waiter Ron Goldman. Simpson, after all, did run from the police in a highly televised chase. However, when Cochran put forth the argument that Simpson, like many black male defendants, was a victim of police misconduct, the attorney convinced the jury to find O. J. Simpson not guilty. "The Simpson case was like pulling back this carpet," Cochran told the *Chicago Tribune*. "And under this carpet is all this dirt and nobody is dealing with it. It's interesting that two Americas, one black and one white, could see the same evidence and honestly read it differently because of their life experiences. The black person may say, 'I don't always trust the police. I don't think that they always tell the truth.' The white person says, 'What are you talking about?'"

By bringing to the forefront the bias against African Americans, Cochran has managed to make the law work to their advantage. This is why he has such a stellar reputation within the African American community and the legal profession at large. He has won many awards, and his achievements extend outside of the law. He and his second wife, Dale, have established the Cochran Villa, a subsidized housing complex for previously homeless people. In his autobiography, *Journey to Justice* (1996), Cochran writes: "I am an advocate. An advocate for the law as much as an advocate for the individual. For over thirty-three years I've been fighting in the trenches, defending the principles of justice outlined in the Constitution."—KENNETTE CROCKETT

NAT "KING" COLE
1919–1965
Musician, singer, composer, entertainer

Nat "King" Cole was one of this country's most successful, versatile, and beloved performers. He was the first black to have national radio and television shows. He began to win major recognition with the cafe-society crowd in the 1940s, primarily as a pianist. As such, he was an important figure in the transition from swing era styles to modern jazz. His career as a singer was launched in 1943 and his vocal contributions became "unforgettable." As Cole explained to Time *magazine, "I'm an interpreter of stories, and when I perform, it's like I'm just sitting down at my piano and telling fairy stories."*

Nathaniel, the youngest son of Reverend Edward James and Perlina Adams Coles (spelled with an "s"), was born in Montgomery, Alabama, on March 17, 1919. The family consisted of four boys and one girl. In addition to Nathaniel, brothers Isaac, Eddie, and Freddie all became professional musicians. Sister Evelyn was also a musician, though nonprofessional.

In 1924 the family moved to Chicago where Cole's father assumed the pastorate of True Light Baptist Church, and Cole was surrounded by the best of jazz during the 1920s and 30s. In addition, the family lived within four blocks of the old Grand Terrace, home of the Earl "Fatha" Hines Orchestra. Earl became Cole's idol. By age twelve Coles had become the church organist and sang in the church choir, which his mother directed. All of the Coles children's first musical instruction came from their mother.

Nat Coles attended Wendell Phillips High School, where he encountered one of Chicago's finest musical pedagogues, Walter Dyett. While at Phillips, he played in various combos and organized his first band, consisting of twelve pieces. Though the leader was only a teenager himself, according to Henry Ford as quoted in Dempsey Travis's *An Autobiography of Black Jazz:*

> He was authoritative without being dictatorial, and he was able to whip a bunch of undisciplined teenagers into a music unit in less than sixty days. His objective was to make us sound like Earl "Fatha" Hines' band.

The group's name was Royal Dukes and it collected one dollar and fifty cents for its one-night stands.

When his brother Eddie formed a band called the Rogues of Rhythm, Nat Coles became the pianist. Their pay was a substantial improvement—eighteen dollars a week. Maria Cole, his second wife, a singer and mother of his children, wrote:

*Nat King
Cole.*

Eddie, Nat and the Rogues eventually joined a revue called "Shuffle Along." It was while playing piano in the revue that Nat, who was then only seventeen years old, met dancer Nadine Robinson, whom he later married. When "Shuffle Along" got ready to shuffle westward, . . . leader Eddie Coles chose to stay behind. Nat Coles chose to go.

He became arranger–musical director of the Broadway road company of "Shuffle Along" shortly following high school graduation in 1936. The show folded in Long Beach, California, in 1937. After "giggling" at various "joints" in Los Angeles for about a year, Coles formed the King Cole Trio (minus the final "s"). Coles was pianist, Oscar Moore, guitarist, and Wesley Prince, string bassist. Originally scheduled to be a quartet when the fourth member, drummer Lee Young, failed to show on opening night at the Swanee Inn, the trio was born.

Nat Cole named King   The King Cole Trio was formed in California in 1938. Rumor has it that the "King" title was given to him when the trio appeared in Hollywood and the manager urged him to wear a gold paper crown. Another speculation is that a patron placed a crown on his head and the title "King" followed.

It was 1940 before the trio became fully accepted. But the jazz community never forgave Cole for moving into the commercial arena. In later years, if he had desired returning to the "purity" of jazz, his new lifestyle would not have permitted it. Albert McCathy and others wrote:

> Cole's success as a popular singer virtually robbed jazz of a talented pianist. . . .
> Prior to that date Cole's vocals had occupied a chorus or so on otherwise instrumental recordings by his piano-guitar-bass trio.

By 1954 John S. Wilson of the *New York Times* wrote:

> Cole has seen fit to make his transition complete so that in place of a pianist who occasionally plays the piano. . . . Cole has developed an alarming ability to lend credence to even the most atrocious Tin Pan Allen products.

His first big hit, in 1943, was his own "Straighten Up and Fly Right," based on one of his father's sermons. With his recording of "The Christmas Song" in 1947, his fame reached phenomenal levels. His recordings were selling a million copies each. Many believe his most sensational recording is Cole's 1948 hit "Nature Boy." According to James Haskins:

> Within a week, it was the number one song in the country, and Nat King Cole became one of the first black male singers to accomplish a nearly complete crossover to the white market. . . . His recordings . . . consistently topped the white and black record charts for many years.

A succession of hits followed: "Lush Life," "Mona Lisa," "Frosty the Snow Man," "Unforgettable," "Sweet Lorraine," "Too Young," "I Love You for Sentimental Reasons," "Chesnuts Roasting on an Open Fire," "It's Only a Paper Moon," "Embraceable You," "Caravan," "When I Fall in Love," "Mood Indigo," and many others. Maria Cole's complete discography in her 1971 biography lists over eight hundred titles released between November 1943 and March 1965.

The King Cole Trio was an official unit in 1939, but attracted wide attention in 1943 with its recording of Cole's *Straighten Up and Fly Right*. Gradually, his audience began to request more vocals. By 1952, he was more of a popular singer than a jazz pianist. The King Cole Trip was a summer 1946 replacement for Bing Crosby on the *Kraft Music Hall* radio show, the same year that the trio appeared in four musical motion pictures. Cole's first European tour was in 1950. In 1955 he made ten guest appearances for CBS-TV and was the subject and featured star of the movie, *The Nat "King" Cole Musical Story,* produced by Universal Pictures. In 1958 he was honored by the Ralph Edwards television show, *This Is Your Life.* Maria Cole, Nat's second wife, collaborated with writer Louie Robinson on the intimate biography *Nat King Cole,* published in 1971, six years following her husband's death.

Not all of Cole's experiences were pleasant ones. When he refused to join the NAACP in speech-making, though he did many benefits for the organization, a press release suggested that he flatly refused to take out a membership in the NAACP. Blacks referred to him as a sort of "Uncle Tom." Cole saw this as a public insult and was infuriated. Only upon insistence from his wife and manager did he take out a membership.

In the all-white neighborhood of Hancock Park in Los Angeles, where his luxurious twenty-room house was located, there was extreme hostility when Cole and his wife moved in. Through the resident's lawyer came the message, "We don't want undesirable people coming here." Only his fame brought any kind of tolerance. A national sponsor could not be found to keep his extremely successful television show on the air in 1956–57. Then he was viciously attacked by six white men while he was performing in an integrated show before a segregated audience in Birmingham, Alabama. Finally, the government's claim that Cole owed taxes amounting to some $150,000 was believed to be a contributing factor to his acute ulcers in 1953, which caused him to collapse during an Easter Sunday concert at Carnegie Hall in New York City.

Cole appeared successfully in several film musicals, including *Breakfast in Hollywood* (1946), *China Gate* (1957), and *St. Louis Blues* (1958). In the latter, Cole starred as W. C. Handy. His final film was *Cat Ballou,* completed prior to his February 15, 1965, death. He died

*Nat King
Cole.*

at St. John's Hospital in Santa Monica, California, on February 15, 1965, from complications following an operation for lung cancer. He was forty-five. More than 500,000 letters and postcards arrived during his hospitalization. Visitors included major personalities from the world of show business. Besides his wife, Nat King Cole left four daughters and a son.

Be it jazz or pop, piano or voice, Cole was a pioneer. According to Eileen Southern, the King Trio was one of the first jazz combos; the trio was "the first instrumental group to have a sponsored radio series," and Cole, along with William "Billie" Eckstine, was one of the first black entertainers to earn international attention "as a singer independent of association with an orchestra." His legendary status, in live performance and on recordings, was the result of sheer talent, hard work, good advice, and strategic planning.

On February 17, 1965, it was announced that Cole was to have received an honorary doctorate from Hobart and William Smith colleges on June 13, 1965, but it was customary not to award honorary degrees posthumously. The same day it was announced that a permanent memorial would be erected at Los Angeles's new music center in honor of Cole. Cole was selected posthumously to receive the Lifetime Achievement Award at the 32nd Grammy Awards Ceremony in 1990, and Capitol Records declared February 1990 as Nat King Cole month.

Cole becomes unforgettable   Cole's songs are almost as familiar today as they were when he was alive. He was a consistent winner of popularity polls conducted by *Down Beat, Metronome, Esquire,* and *Billboard*. His gifted singing daughter Natalie used the electronic innovations of recent years to release a duo adaptation with her father. The remixed version of the original 1961 song "Unforgettable" earned her Grammy Awards for record of the year and album of the year.

Nat King Cole, without a doubt, paved the way for future African American entertainers on the stage, in radio, movies, and television. Both the name and the music have endured.—D. ANTOINETTE HANDY

ANNIE J. **COOPER**

c. 1858–1964

Pan African scholar, feminist

Throughout a lifetime that spanned slavery, the Civil War, Reconstruction, segregation, two world wars, the Great Depression, and an era of civil rights struggle, Annie J. Cooper expressed strong concerns for racial justice and equality for women. On her century-long quest to understand and thereby improve human social interaction, Cooper traveled extensively throughout the world and, at the age of sixty-six, was among the first African American women to earn a doctorate. Through her teaching and writing, Cooper communicated a global, historical, and highly modern view of racism and sexism in Western civilization.

Anna "Annie" Julia Haywood Cooper was born on August 10, 1858, in Raleigh, North Carolina, the daughter of Hannah Stanley (Haywood), a slave, and probably George Washington Haywood, the owner. A precocious child, Cooper went to Saint Augustine's Normal School and Collegiate Institute. There she soon distinguished herself and became a tutor and then a teacher. In 1877 she married George A. C. Cooper, a fellow teacher from Nassau who had entered Saint Augustine's in 1873 to study theology. He died in 1879, just three months after his ordination, and Annie Cooper never remarried.

In 1881 Cooper entered Oberlin College, one of the few institutions accepting blacks and women at the time. After earning her bachelor's degree in 1884 and her master's degree in mathematics in 1887, she accepted a position in Washington, D.C., at the Preparatory High School for Colored Youth, which in 1891 became the M Street High School. Most of her career as an educator would be at this distinguished institution.

During the 1890s, while racist terrorism escalated, Cooper and other black intellectuals mobilized to arouse public action. Although teaching full time, Cooper found time for other commitments. She attended numerous conferences, presenting papers to diverse organizations. Early in the decade she went to Toronto on a summer exchange program for teachers, and in 1896 she visited Nassau. Cooper traveled to London in July of 1900 to attend the first Pan African Conference, where she spoke about racism in America. Her London stay was followed by a tour of Europe.

Cooper was principal of the M Street School from 1902 until 1906. When she disputed the board of education's design to dilute the curriculum of "colored" schools, she was dismissed from her position. She served as chair of languages at Lincoln University in Jefferson City, Missouri, from 1906 to 1910, then returned to the M Street School as a teacher of Latin. Later, she became president of Frelinghuysen University, a unique institution that only briefly became a university before socio-economic conditions and accrediting requirements caused it to close.

During her stint as principal of M Street School, Cooper had impressed a visiting French educator, who served as an important contact when she decided to pursue the doctorate in France. By studying summers at the Guilde Internationale in Paris and then at Columbia University, Cooper was able to finish her course requirements for a Ph.D. She successfully defended her dissertation at the Sorbonne on March 23, 1925, and at age sixty-six she was the fourth known African American woman to earn a doctorate. Remarkably, she managed to find time for research and study despite working full time, raising two foster children while in her forties, and adopting her half brother's five orphaned grandchildren in her late fifties.

A dedicated feminist and black advocate   Cooper's earliest writings, collected in *A Voice from the South* in 1892, mark her as a dedicated feminist and an advocate for African Americans. Her concern for women's rights grew out of her own experiences, when as a student she was not encouraged in her schoolwork. In fact, her announced intention of going to college "was received with . . . incredulity and dismay." Of the colleges that would admit women in those days, only a handful had ever graduated any African American women. In *A Voice from the South,* Cooper challenged the then-prevalent argument that education ruined a woman's chances to marry, arguing that all of humanity would benefit from the education of women:

> The cause of freedom is not the cause of a race or a sect, a party or a class— it is the cause of human kind, the very birthright of humanity. . . . Woman's strongest vindication for speaking [is] that *the world needs to hear her voice.* It would be subversive of every human interest that the cry of one-half of the human family be stifled.

L'Attitude de la France à l'égard de l'esclavage pendant la Révolution (*France's Attitude Regarding Slavery During the Revolution*), Cooper's doctoral thesis and best known work, studies the social and racial complexities of the Americas in a global and historical framework. Nominally a study of French racial attitudes, the dissertation is equally a study of the successful struggle of slaves in Saint Domingue to throw off an oppressive system and to create a new order. And although this work centers on Haiti and France, Cooper shows that it is not limited geographically or historically. Events that took place in antebellum North Carolina, in pre-1843 Bahamas, and in revolutionary Saint Domingue/Haiti were all chapters in the same book of history.

Cooper's *L'Attitude* is among many studies of the establishment of a black state by slaves who revolted in Saint Domingue. Yet Cooper's work possesses the unique characteristic of its point of view. As the work of an African American scholar who was born a slave, the dissertation has insight and sensitivity that elude most histories. Cooper's position is that of direct identification with the oppressed, whom she sees as victims of Western civilizations— civilizations she often describes as "barbarian." One of her most memorable references is this quote, describing white invaders in the new world:

> Huge white bodies, cool-blooded, with fierce blue eyes, reddish flaxen hair; ravenous stomachs, filled with meat and cheese, heated by strong drinks. Brutal drunken pirates and robbers, they dashed to sea in their two-sailed barks, landed anywhere, killed everything; and, having sacrificed in honor of their gods the tithe of all their prisoners, leaving behind the red light of burning, went farther on to begin again.

Cooper believed that social equality is inherent to human nature, but that Western civilization, by stressing force, has destroyed the natural balance of things. "Progress in the democratic sense is an inborn human endowment—a shadow mark of the Creator's image, or if you will an urge-cell of the universal and unmistakable hallmark traceable to the Father of all," she wrote in *The Third Step.* She concluded that equality should not be the equilibrium of force, conceded only when one cannot crush or exploit the other, but the equilibrium that comes when "the big fellow with all the power and all the controls" respects others as being as good as he is.

Civilizing the powerful seems to have been one of Cooper's primary motivations. "Let the Ruler bear in mind that the Right to Rule entails the duty and the inescapable responsibility to Rule Right," she invokes in *The Third Step*. "Let him recognize the differences among men . . . not as obstacles to fulfillment of destiny . . . [but as] the providential contribution to that heterogeneity which offers the final test of our civilization, harmony in variety." Cooper suggests that the task of rebalancing the power will likely fall on those who are not abusing power: the cultivated. "If the cultivated black man cannot endure the white man's barbarity," Cooper observed in *A Voice*, "the cure, it would seem to me, would be to cultivate the white man."

Cooper's intellectual evolution mirrored her social development. From the confined environment of a small, newly emancipated rural community, she grew to become a highly educated and knowledgeable scholar and teacher. From a young woman concerned with sexism and racism, she expanded her horizons to international proportions. Cooper's lifetime pursuit of knowledge and understanding had a humanistic basis. As an educator, she wanted to pave the way for a better, more rational, more "cultivated" world. As she researches, learns, and teaches, she once told a reporter: "I am soundly convinced that every scrap of information I may gain in the way of broadening horizons and deepening human understanding and sympathies, means true culture, and will rebound to the educational values of my work in the school room."

Cooper died at the age of 105, on February 27, 1964. She was interred in the Hargett Street Cemetery in Raleigh next to her husband, whom she had outlived by eighty-five years.—DAVID W. H. PELLOW

BILL **COSBY**

1937–

Comedian, philanthropist

Entertainer Bill Cosby, a popular father image on television, has consistently used the entertainment industry to portray a positive image of blacks. He was the first black actor to star in a nationally broadcasted dramatic television series. He has long had success as a stand-up comedian in nightclubs, and he is a dominant comic on television and in recordings. He has demonstrated his advocacy for education by becoming highly educated himself and by contributing significantly to black academic institutions.

Born in Germantown, Pennsylvania, a predominantly poor black section of North Philadelphia, on July 12, 1937, William Henry Cosby Jr. was the oldest of William Cosby Sr. and Annie "Anna" Perle Cosby's four sons. The Cosby's second son, James, had rheumatic fever and died in 1945 when he was six years old. His job as a welder enabled Cosby Sr. to support his family, but after the family increased the Cosbys moved to a low-income, all-black public housing project, the Richard Allen Homes. Later the senior Cosby joined the U.S. Navy, where he became a mess steward. This took him away from the family for long periods of time. To provide for the family then, Annie Cosby worked as a domestic. She still had time to read to her family selections from the Bible and the works of Mark Twain. Bill Cosby's new role was caretaker of his brothers, Russell and Robert, as he also shined shoes and delivered

Bill Cosby doing what he does best: telling a good story.

groceries to help make ends meet. Still, at times the family's income was supplemented by public assistance.

Cosby attended Mary Channing Wister Elementary School, then Fitz-Simons Junior High School. The talented Cosby had a high IQ and later joined a class for gifted students at Central High School. But his high IQ didn't result in good grades, so he decided to transfer to Germantown High School. He was talented in athletics as well and was captain of the track and football teams. He also played basketball, baseball, and football, and practiced the humor that had surfaced earlier in school. His athletic endeavors and work schedule took their toll on his studies; consequently, Cosby was asked to repeat the tenth grade at Germantown High. By now economic conditions had improved for the family, and the Cosbys moved to Twenty-First Street, where he had his own room for the first time. Still needing money, however, he worked at several menial jobs.

Cosby dropped out of Germantown High in 1956 and worked for a while as a shoe repairman. That same year he joined the U.S. Navy. The lean six-footer worked to keep his weight under one hundred and ninety pounds, ran track, and won track awards on the navy's team. The physical therapy that he learned while in the navy led him to an assignment at Bethesda Naval Hospital, where he enjoyed being able to help those with physical needs. He also had some travel experience to such places as Newfoundland and Guantanamo Bay and still found time to complete his high school equivalency through a correspondence course. When his four-year term was over, he was honorably discharged and in September 1960 enrolled in Temple University on an athletic scholarship, where he majored in physical education. He joined the football team, and his success there led to his induction into the Temple Hall of Fame in 1984. A scout from the Green Bay Packers thought that he might become a professional player. Cosby also excelled in track, including discus and javelin throwing, high-jump, and broad-jump, and earned a letter. Although sports took a considerable amount of his time, he maintained a B average.

To help support himself at Temple, Cosby worked as a bartender in a local basement bar known as the Underground, which paid him five dollars a night plus tips. His humor made him a popular bartender; consequently, when the regular stand-up comedian was absent, Cosby was asked to perform instead. This increased his regular income to twenty-five dollars each performance. Soon he became known around Philadelphia for his comedy, and the Cellar Club next door hired him as a comedian for twelve dollars and fifty cents nightly. Meanwhile, his cousin Del Sheilds, a popular local radio disc jockey who had helped him land the new job, also showed him ways to increase local bookings. Cosby became serious about comedy and prepared himself well for the jokes he would tell. He refused to tell dirty jokes but did add some racial quips. He was funny and had a natural "cool." He also borrowed material from such successful comedians as Dick Gregory, Nipsey Russell, Flip Wilson, and Jonathan Winters.

By 1962 Cosby began to take his talent elsewhere—to New York City on weekends, working at the Gaslight Cafe in Greenwich Village, where in time he earned $175 a week. His positive reviews by newspaper critics further increased his popularity, and he accepted a gig at Chicago's Gate of Horn for $200 a week. Now that he felt he was doing rather well financially, Cosby decided to ignore the advice his mother had always given him—to get an education—and left his athletic scholarship and Temple University in the middle of his sophomore year to go for bigger purses. In early 1963 Cosby, then only twenty-six years old, had bookings at popular night spots across the country and began to use his own material rather than comedy borrowed from others. His bookings picked up to the extent that he hired a manager at the William Morris Agency to aid in his career development.

Cosby worked hard not to be regarded as another Dick Gregory, which some audiences thought he was. He wanted his American identity shown through his material. He developed nonracial routines that were good, true, and real, like the Mark Twain stories his mother had read to him in his childhood. Soon Cosby landed contracts to do albums with Warner Brothers and in 1963 recorded his first live album at the Bitter End Club in Greenwich Village. Other comedy and music albums followed, reaching a total of twenty recordings over several years; he sold millions of copies and became highly successful. In August 1963 he appeared at Mr. Kelly's in Chicago for $500 a week. In September 1963 he appeared at the "hungry i" in San Francisco for $750 a week.

In 1963 as well, Cosby met Camille Hanks on a blind date arranged by mutual friends. At that time she was a student at the University of Maryland and attended his performance at a local club. Two weeks later he asked her to marry him and she said no, but three weeks after that she agreed. Her parents thought the nineteen-year-old was too young, wanted her to complete her studies, worried about Cosby's future as a comedian, and initially opposed the marriage. Despite family obstacles, Cosby and Hanks married on January 25, 1964, in Olney, Maryland.

Comedian's career takes off Beginning in 1965, Cosby's career blossomed and Camille Cosby left school to travel with her husband. Cosby's performance on Johnny Carson's *Tonight Show,* hosted by stand-in Allan Sherman, led to other offers, particularly as costar with Robert Culp in NBC's television series *I Spy.* Cosby broke television's color barrier and became the first black in a nontraditional role and the first black star in a television series that excluded racial themes. The show was also the first since *Amos 'n' Andy* to cast a black in a lead role. *I Spy* aired from 1965 to 1968. In the summer of 1968 he narrated the first of a seven-part series, *Of Black America,* on the *CBS News Hour.* This segment, "Black History: Lost, Stolen or Strayed?" illustrated the negative racial themes depicted in the media and stimulated widespread concern for removing such images. A videotape of the two-part segment was frequently used as a teaching tool in academia. Cosby's television appearances continued with the *Bill Cosby Show,* NBC, 1969–71; and the *Electric Company,* PBS, 1971–76. Cosby's friends at Wister Elementary School, where his education began, became Fat Albert, Dumb Donald, Weird Harold, Mush Mouth, Weasel, and others who were preserved in his TV cartoons. *Fat Albert and The Cosby Kids,* later called *The New Fat Albert Show,* aired on CBS from 1972 to 1984.

As a comedian, Cosby made show business history as a stand-up comic. In 1986 his fifteen shows at Radio City Music Hall grossed $2.8 million, setting a record in the hall's fifty-four-year history.

Continuing with television, Cosby was featured in the *New Bill Cosby Show,* CBS, 1972–73; and *Cos,* ABC, September–October 1976. His next series, *The Cosby Show,* NBC, 1984–92, was a family-based program reflecting elements of his own life. He helped create the show, was a coproducer, served as executive consultant, and composed some of the theme music. So concerned was Cosby with presenting real-life situations and with making a positive impact on his audiences that he hired psychiatrist Alvin Poussaint as consultant and advisor for the show. Cosby played the character Dr. Heathcliff Huxtable, while Phylicia Rashad played his wife, Claire, an attorney. Cosby's son Ennis was the inspiration for the character Theo, the son on the show. Although the entire Huxtable family concentrated on positive images of blacks, some critics claimed that the show was an unrealistic portrayal of black family life.

At its peak the show had as many as eighty million viewers. *The Cosby Show* won three Emmys in 1985, for outstanding comedy series, outstanding writing in a comedy series, and outstanding directing in a comedy series. The show also received a Golden Globe award from Hollywood's Foreign Press Association and four People's Choice awards. Syndicated in 1987, the show earned for Cosby, who was half owner, a handsome sum of $333 million. Its spinoff, *A Different World,* first telecast on September 24, 1987, was aired concurrently with *The Cosby Show* for a while. Again Alvin Poussaint was his script consultant. Set on a fictional black college campus, the show was an advocate for education and some critics claim it helped stimulate an enrollment increase in black colleges. Cosby stimulated curiosity and interest among his viewers by wearing sweatshirts from various colleges; the sweatshirts became his trademark. Cosby's next shows were the short-lived *You Bet Your Life,* 1992–93, and *The Cosby Mysteries,* 1994; beginning 1996 he appeared again with Phylicia Rashad in *Cosby.* In May 1997 he hosted a special, *Children Say the Darndest Things,* a salute to the show's founder Art Linkletter.

In addition to his television shows, Cosby has appeared in a number of films, including *Hickey and Boggs* (1971). He teamed with Sidney Poitier in *Uptown Saturday Night* (1974) and *A Piece of the Action* (1977). Other films include *Let's Do It Again* (1975), *Leonard Part VI* (1987), and *Ghost Dad* (1990). In 1996 he appeared with Robin Williams in the Francis Ford Coppola comedy-drama, *Jack.*

Cosby has become a best-selling author with books that humorously reflect his personal struggles as a parent. His writings include *Fatherhood* (1986), *Bill Cosby's Personal Guide to Power Tennis* (1986), *Time Flies* (1987), *Love and Marriage* (1989), and *Childhood* (1991). Scholastic's Cartwheel Books has begun to publish his series of books for children, targeting readers aged seven to ten. His Little Bill stories use subtlety, humor, and storytelling to discuss a variety of subjects, such as honesty, kindness, courage, family, and friendships.

Education and philanthropy   Bill and Camille Cosby are firm believers in higher education. Bill Cosby never lost sight of his mother's urging to get an education. He studied at the University of Massachusetts at Amherst and received a master's degree in education in 1972 and an Ed.D. in 1977. He said in *Bill Cosby in Words and Pictures,* "I didn't get that degree to have something to fall back on." Instead, he has used it as a teaching tool at home and elsewhere with young people. Later, Camille Cosby received a doctorate from the University of Massachusetts at Amherst. The Cosbys continued to advocate higher education for their children.

The Cosbys' concern for education led them to provide substantial support to black colleges. The Cosbys gave $1.3 million to Fisk University in 1986. In 1987 they contributed $1.3 million to be divided among Central State (Wilberforce, Ohio), Howard University, Florida Agricultural and Mechanical State University, and Shaw University. The next year they gave another $1.5 million to be divided between Meharry and Bethune-Cookman College. Their largest gift was to Spelman College. In 1988 they gave Spelman $20 million to erect the Camille Olivia Hanks Cosby Academic Center, which houses classrooms, offices, the Women's Research and Resources Center, the college's archives, art museum, and other

Bill Cosby.

facilities and programs. The bulding was dedicated in February 1996. The Cosbys continued their philanthropy to higher education in 1994 by giving $100,000 to Morehouse College to establish a scholarship in the name of *Jet* magazine editor Robert E. Johnson Jr. In 1994 as well, the Cosbys supported the work of African American women by assisting the National Council of Negro Women in their campaign to establish the National Center for African American Women in Washington, D.C. The Cosbys gave the organization a building located at 1218 16th Street N.W., valued at $1.8 million. Their interest in art and in education prompted the Cosbys to give Fisk $100,000 in May 1977 for scholarships for art students.

In recognition of his contributions as an entertainer, Bill Cosby has been honored widely. He received four Emmy Awards for outstanding performance by an actor in a leading role in a dramatic series for *I Spy*. He also received Emmys for *The Bill Cosby Special,* 1969, and for outstanding achievement in children's programming for "The Secret" episode of *The New Fat Albert Show,* 1981. Cosby won eight Grammys for his recordings from 1963 through 1976.

A star bearing Cosby's name was added to Hollywood's Walk of Fame in 1979, and in 1983 Harvard University's *Lampoon* gave Cosby its first Lifetime Achievement Award. In 1985 he won the Spingarn Medal from the NAACP. He also won the NAACP Image Award and in 1996 was awarded the College Board Medal, the highest award given by the organization. The award recognizes individuals who demonstrate a commitment to the purposes of the College Board. In 1997 Cosby won his fifteenth People's Choice Award, as favorite male in a new television series, *Cosby*. Again that year Bill and Camille Cosby won an Essence Award for philanthropy. Bill Cosby was inducted into the Academy of Television Arts and Sciences Hall of Fame in 1994. Both Bill and Camille Cosby continue to deplore negative and stereotypical images of blacks on television and work to promote positive images. Bill Cosby has bought the television rights to *The Little Rascals* and vows never to show them because of derogatory characters such as Buckwheat. He has also criticized Martin Lawrence's show *Martin* for its buffoonery.

Among the numerous honorary degrees awarded to Cosby are those from such institutions as Fisk University, Morehouse College, Spelman College, Temple University, and George Washington University. His memberships include the United Negro College Fund, the NAACP, and Operation PUSH (People United to Serve Humanity). He has been president of Rhythm and Blues Hall of Fame and a member of the Sickle Cell Foundation.

The Cosbys have four children: Erika Ranee, Errin Chalene, Ensa Camille, and Evin Harrah. All of his children's names begin with "E," signifying excellence. The nation joined the Cosbys in mourning the death of their fifth child and only son, Ennis William, who was fatally shot early on January 16, 1997, while changing a tire on his car on a freeway near the Santa Monica mountains. A separate issue arose two days later when a woman who claimed to be his daughter out of wedlock tried unsuccessfully to extort $40 million from Cosby. After his son's death, Bill Cosby returned to stand-up comedy. The *Nashville Tennessean* for February 3, 1997, summarized his comments on his return to a stand-up comedy tour just two weeks later, stating that he needed to have release for himself and his audience.

Bill Cosby is a devoted family man who publicly acknowledges his wife's wisdom, beauty, and business acumen. With his quick humor, much of it based on personal experiences, he also remains one of the nation's most highly successful comedians. Cosby is a storyteller whose anecdotes are filled with the cold truth as well as warm remembrances of his life and family. He has a special view of life that appeals to all ages, whether in films, on television, or on the stage.—JESSIE CARNEY SMITH

DOROTHY **DANDRIDGE**
1922–1965
Actress

One of Hollywood's legendary beauties, Dorothy Dandridge was a multitalented woman who set several precedents in the motion picture industry. A child actress who went on to star in such films as Carmen Jones *and* Island in the Sun *and such television series as "Beulah" and "Father of the Bride" (1961–1962), she was the first black woman to be nominated for an Oscar in a lead role and the first to be held in the arms of a white man on the silver screen.*

Dandridge was born on November 9, 1922, to Cyril and Ruby Dandridge. As a child, she performed with her older sister and only sibling, Vivian. Billed as the Wonder Kids, the sisters toured Baptist churches around the country with a two-act show scripted by their mother. In 1934, after moving to Chicago and subsequently Los Angeles, the Wonder Kids changed their stage name to the Dandridge Sisters and added the talents of thirteen-year-old Etta Jones. Together the trio triumphed in an amateur competition on radio station KNX, Los Angeles, defeating twenty-five white contestants.

Two years later the Dandridge Sisters were invited to perform at New York's famed Cotton Club, a nightclub that featured black talent and catered to white audiences. The act was so successful that they were given a spot in the regular program, performing on the same bill as the legendary artists Cab Calloway and W. C. Handy. Another prominent act found regularly in the line-up was the dynamic dance team of Harold and Fayard Nicholas, the Nicholas Brothers.

In 1937 the Dandridge Sisters made their Hollywood debut, with minor roles in the Marx Brothers' classic film *A Day at the Races*. But after several one-night stands and recording dates with Jimmie Lunceford and His Orchestra, the trio dissolved. In 1941 and 1942 Dandridge performed solo in several musical film shorts: *Yes Indeed, Sing for My Supper, Jungle Jig, Easy Street, Cow Cow Boogie,* and *Paper Doll*.

Dandridge married Harold Nicholas in 1942 and settled with him in Los Angeles as he pursued a career in motion pictures. In 1943, Dandridge gave birth to a daughter, Harolyn Suzanne Nicholas. Several years later, Harolyn was diagnosed as severely retarded. Dandridge and Nicholas had the child institutionalized. A double blow of heartache came for Dandridge when divorcing her adulterous husband, Harold. To help ease the pain of losing her daughter and husband, Dandridge pursued a career as a nightclub singer, traveling the globe. In 1951

*Dorothy
Dandridge.*

she appeared with the Desi Arnaz Band at the Macombo, and, in that same year, became the first black to perform in the Empire Room of New York's Waldorf-Astoria Hotel.

Dandridge continued to work in Hollywood films and in 1954 obtained the role that would launch her career, the lead in Otto Preminger's all-black musical extravaganza *Carmen Jones.* The film, which featured Harry Belafonte, as well as Pearl Bailey and Diahann Carroll in supporting roles, was a critical success, winning a Golden Globe Award for the Best Musical of 1954, an Audience Award from the Berlin Film Festival in 1955, and an Oscar nomination for best actress for Dandridge, the first ever received by a black woman. *Carmen Jones* catapulted Dandridge into superstardom quickly. The media was ablaze and on November 1, 1954, Dandridge's photo was on the cover of *Life* magazine dressed as Carmen Jones. She was the first African American woman ever to grace the cover of that magazine. In comparisons to Marilyn Monroe and Elizabeth Taylor, Dandridge was labelled sultry and deemed a bona fide sex symbol.

Along with the enthusiastic publicity that the film *Carmen Jones* brought, rumors grew of Dandridge's liaisons with various Hollywood celebrities. During the filming of *Carmen Jones,* Dandridge was romantically linked to its director, Otto Preminger, and actor Peter Lawford.

Time magazine thought that the success of the film would create more opportunities for blacks in the film industry, but that was not the case. Rather than being offered a wide variety of roles, Dandridge was typecast into the stereotypical roles commonly given to black actresses. As Dandridge explained in *Ebony,* "I consider myself an actress, and I have always worked to be a confident one. I interpret a role to the best of my ability, and more often than not, and more often than I'd like, the role calls for a creature of abandon whose desires are stronger than their sense of morality."

In 1957 Dandridge again broke ground, this time as the first black woman to be held in the arms of a white man in a Hollywood motion picture. *Island in the Sun,* a highly controversial film, not only paired Dandridge and white actor John Justin, it also offered the reverse with the pairing of Harry Belafonte and Joan Fontaine. The trend of interracial romance continued with Dandridge in such features as *The Decks Ran Red* (1958) and *Tamango* (1958). Dandridge paired again with director Otto Preminger in the musical *Porgy and Bess,* which furthered Dandridge's role as a Hollywood beauty. But this role was to be one of her last in a major motion picture.

Unable to find enough quality roles in feature films, Dandridge returned to nightclub performing. During her tour she met Las Vegas restaurateur Jack Denison, whom she married in 1959. Three years later Dandridge divorced him and found herself bankrupt after a series of bad investments. She then tried to resurrect her failing career, but found little opportunity, making only a few television appearances and doing lounge acts in hotels. Alone and discouraged, Dandridge died in her West Hollywood apartment on September 8, 1965, of an overdose of an antidepressant drug. She was forty-two years old.

Dandridge appeared in over twenty films, but her contribution to films and her status as a black icon has been overlooked in conventional texts covering Hollywood history. Acknowledging mainstream Hollywood's oversight, in 1997, author Donald Bogle completed a biography of the tragic life of Dorothy Dandridge. More than thirty years after her death, some of the top black actresses in the entertainment industry are discussing a film based on the life of one of the first black female sex symbols.—FRANCES K. GATEWARD

ANGELA **DAVIS**

1944–
Social activist, educator

A sensitive child of the 1950s who became a militant revolutionary in the 1960s, Angela Davis fights for women's and civil rights and against poverty and racism with a passion that inspires millions.

Davis was born on January 26, 1944, in Birmingham, Alabama, the oldest of four children. Her father, B. Frank, was an automobile mechanic who owned a gas station. He had been a teacher, but gave up the profession because of the meager salary. Davis's mother, Sallye E., was also a teacher and taught Angela to read, write, and calculate before she began the first grade.

In class-conscious Birmingham, Davis experienced the disadvantages and advantages of a segregated school system. She faced old, dilapidated school buildings that lacked facilities and outdated textbooks discarded by white schools. However, blacks could run the schools the way they wanted (except when the superintendent for "colored" schools visited). Davis and her classmates learned about black history—about the lives of Frederick Douglass, Sojourner Truth, Harriet Tubman, Denmark Vesey, and Nat Turner—and learned "traditional" Negro material, such as James Weldon Johnson's "Lift Ev'ry Voice and Sing" (often referred to as the Negro National Anthem). These cultural activities instilled in her a sense of pride. Nevertheless, Davis eventually realized that segregated schools provided few opportunities for the total development and growth of black children.

Angela Davis.

Political activism begins early Davis's mother was politically involved and influenced her daughter considerably. In college Sallye Davis protested against the imprisonment of the Scottsboro boys and participated in the activities of the NAACP, even though the organization was outlawed in Birmingham in the mid-fifties. Davis learned from her mother's activism that she could protest against the system and count on her mother's moral support. Her grandmother, who constantly talked of slavery so that her grandchildren "would not forget about it," also influenced Davis.

During her childhood, Davis spent several summers with her mother, who at that time was studying for a master's at New York University. At the age of fifteen, when she was in her junior year at Parker High School in Birmingham, Davis received a scholarship from the American Friends Service Committee and moved to New York to enter the more academically stimulating Elizabeth Irwin High School, a progressive private school in Greenwich Village. Many teachers at this school had been blacklisted by the public schools because of their political ideology. Her parents had made arrangements for Davis to live in Brooklyn with the family of William Howard Melish, an active Episcopalian minister and winner of the 1956 Stockholm Peace Prize. While in New York, Davis was introduced to socialist ideology and consequently joined Advance, a Marxist-Leninist group.

In 1961 she entered Brandeis University in Waltham, Massachusetts, and developed into an excellent student. She majored in French and spent her junior year at the Sorbonne in Paris. It was here, in conversations with students from Algeria, that Davis became aware of revolutions against French colonialism and struggles for first-class citizenship among oppressed people. Her sensitivity to oppression was further ignited in September, 1963, when four girls Davis knew were killed during the bombing of a church in Birmingham. Davis's philosophy of life also altered considerably as she began to study under the philosopher Herbert Marcuse at Brandeis in 1964. He felt that it was the duty of the individual to resist and rebel against the system—an idea that influenced Davis profoundly.

A magna cum laude graduate of Brandeis with Phi Beta Kappa membership, from 1965 to 1967 Davis studied with the faculty of philosophy at the Johann Wolfgang von Goethe University in Frankfurt, West Germany, and with Oskar Negt and Theodore Adorno. In addition to philosophy, Davis mastered French and German.

Davis's radical activism ignites   After receiving her master's degree in philosophy, Davis began her active involvement with the civil rights movement, assisting in the development of the Black Students Council, developing a program for an experimental college for minorities, and supporting the San Diego Black Conference, an organization dominated by Ron Kerenga's rebellious group "Us."

In 1967 she attended a workshop in Los Angeles sponsored by the Student Nonviolent Coordinating Committee (SNCC), which altered her life radically. There she met Franklin and Kendra Alexander. Alexander was involved with the SNCC, the Black Panthers, and the Communist party, while his sister, Charlene, was the leader of the Che-Lumumba Club, an all-black community cell in Los Angeles.

In 1968 Davis moved to Los Angeles and grew close to the Alexanders, who influenced her considerably. She became deeply involved with radical protests and rallies, although she eventually grew disillusioned with the SNCC and especially Stokely Carmichael, "Us," and the Black Panthers. Davis complained about the male chauvinism in these groups: women did all the work when a protest was organized, only to have the men complain that the women were taking over. After reflecting about the groups who were in tune with her political and social philosophy—her sensitivity for oppressed and repressed people and her distaste for racism and discrimination—she decided to join the Communist party in June, 1968.

In the spring of 1969, Davis joined the faculty of the department of philosophy at the University of California at Los Angeles (UCLA) and developed four courses in philosophy, politics, and literature. In spite of the popularity of her courses, Davis ran into conflict because of her membership in the Communist party. On July 1, 1969, an ex-FBI informer revealed in a letter published in the UCLA *Daily Bruin* that a communist was on the faculty. Eight days later a Los Angeles *Examiner* reporter identified Davis as the person. In spite of the recommendations of the department of philosophy and the chancellor of the university, the

One of the FBI's most wanted, Angela Davis walks into court
to stand trial for murder. In 1972, she was acquitted.

board of regents—under pressure from the governor of California, Ronald Reagan—fired her. Eventually the courts reinstated her since the dismissal violated her constitutional rights.

Although the administration of UCLA continued to monitor and evaluate Davis's courses, students found the instruction excellent and unbiased. The board of regents was determined to terminate her contract, however. At the end of the academic year of 1969–70, the board denied her a new contract because she lacked a doctorate and because of her allegedly inflammatory rhetoric in the community.

The Soledad Prison Incident   Davis outraged the UCLA Board of Regents with her speeches made in the defense of the "Soledad Brothers." George Jackson and W. L. Nolen were two inmates at Soledad Prison in California who organized a Marxist-Fanonist revolutionary cell. In January of 1970 Nolen and two other prisoners got into a fistfight and were killed by shots from the guard tower. When a white guard was found murdered, Jackson and two other prisoners were indicted.

Davis reacted emotionally to the event and threw herself energetically into the cause, organizing, picketing, and making speeches to raise defense funds.

By now Davis symbolized the radical outlaw. Then she was indicted because she owned several guns that were used in a murder. Davis had bought the guns because of threats on her life, but, on August 7, 1970, Jonathan Jackson, George's brother, took the guns to the Marion County Courthouse in San Rafad, where prisoner James McClain was on trial for stabbing an inmate at San Quentin. Jackson pulled out the guns, took hostages, and made a run for a van in the parking lot. Before the van could pull away, Jackson, a judge, and two prisoners were killed. Since the guns found in the van were registered in Davis's name, a federal warrant was issued for her arrest. Rather than accept the warrant, Davis went into hiding. On August 18, 1970, the FBI placed her on the ten-most-wanted fugitive list, charged by the State of California with kidnapping, conspiracy, and murder. The FBI's hunt for Davis became high drama across the world. After a two-month search, the FBI found her in a motel in New York. Extradited to California, she remained in jail without bail until the movement for her release boomed into a world-wide protest. Rallies took place everywhere from Los Angeles to Paris to Sri Lanka. The slogan "Free Angela" appeared on billboards, in newspapers, and on posters worldwide. Protests took place outside her jail cell. On February 23, 1972, a judge released Davis on $102,000 bail.

At the trial, Davis's lawyer argued that since Davis was not at the scene of the murder, there was insufficient evidence to prove she was part of the murder plans. After thirteen hours of deliberation, the jury of eleven whites and one Mexican American acquitted her on all counts. After the acquittal she held a mass benefit in New York to defray her legal expenses. The National Alliance Against Racist and Political Repression grew out of the "Free Angela" movement. She has spoken on behalf of the organization and has led demonstrations on various issues since 1972.

Because of her militant activities, the California state Board of Regents and Governor Reagan voted in 1972 that Davis would never teach at a state-supported university. The American Association of University Professors censured UCLA at the time for lack of due process in its failure to renew Davis's contract. Although the university's department of philosophy requested her services, the board refused. For a year, beginning in 1975, Davis was a lecturer in black studies at Claremont College in Claremont, California; in 1976 she lectured in philosophy and political science at Stanford University; from 1983 to 1985 she lectured in ethnic studies at California College of the Arts and Crafts in Oakland; and in 1984 she lectured in history of consciousness at the University of California at Santa Cruz. Beginning in 1978, she was a lecturer in women's and ethnic studies at San Francisco State University, and in the humanities at San Francisco Art Institute.

Davis received several honorary degrees in 1972, and in 1979 she was awarded the Lenin Peace Prize. She has been a professor of philosophy at Moscow University and of political science at Havana University. In 1980 and again in 1984, the Communist Party, U.S.A., nominated her as its vice presidential candidate. From 1985 Davis has been a member of the executive board of the National Political Caucus of Black Women. She has served on the board of directors for the National Black Women's Health Project since 1986.

Davis has written numerous essays and books on political and judicial reform, the rights of women, sexism, violence against women, and the rights of prisoners and mental health patients. She has also written *Ma Rainey, Bessie Smith and Billie Holiday: Black Women's Music and the Shaping of Social Consciousness*. A documentary on Davis, "Portrait of a Revolutionary," has been produced by one of her students at UCLA. Because she is constantly in demand as a speaker and she publishes extensively in journals and books, she has never finished her dissertation on eighteenth-century German philosopher Immanuel Kant. She remains in the doctoral program in the department of philosophy of Berlin's Humboldt University.

Even though her affiliation with the Communist party still brings her controversy, Davis is in the forefront in the fight against injustice. Her appearance is different but her devout activism remains intact as she implores students to envision a new, stronger movement to combat racism that, according to Davis, "is much more difficult now because [it] is more entrenched and complicated."—JOAN CURL ELLIOTT

BENJAMIN O. **DAVIS SR.**
1877–1970
Military officer, educator, government official

As the first black American general in the U.S. Army, Benjamin Oliver Davis Sr. served as a role model and mentor for black military men and women in World War II. He was not only a leader but also a living lesson in coping with and overcoming adversity, especially the effects of segregation in the armed forces. His rewards came late in his life and career, but he stood erect in victory the same way as in his darkest moments, serving the country he loved.

Davis was born on May 28, 1877, the youngest of the three children of Louis Patrick Henry Davis and Henrietta Stewart Davis of Washington, D.C. Although his father was a house servant, the circumstances of that service were not those of the usual master-servant relationship. Louis Davis worked for General John A. Logan, who later served as the U.S. representative and senator from Illinois. Louis Davis was so well respected by Logan that he became the companion of Logan's son and was rewarded for his service with an appointment as messenger in the Department of the Interior. As a measure of his financial standing, Louis Davis became a homeowner in northwest Washington, then a prestigious neighborhood for blacks in the nation's capitol. The next two generations of the Davis family would be born at the Eleventh Street address.

Benjamin Davis was afforded opportunities not available to most black youths in Washington or elsewhere. He was a graduate of M Street High School, an institution with a sterling reputation. He was an outstanding cadet there and after graduating, Davis attended Howard University and became a member of the black unit of the District's National Guard. Louis Davis realized that his son had great potential and sought to find ways to lead him toward a military career through his connections to General Logan. Despite Logan's reputation and prestige, Davis was denied an appointment to the U.S. Military Academy; not even President William McKinley could overthrow the shackles of racial dis-

Benjamin O. Davis Sr.

crimination that kept West Point "lily white." Louis Davis was bitterly disappointed, but his son took it in stride and enlisted in the army as a means of seeking a military commission by competitive examination. Davis's mother disapproved of this course of action as well, because she wanted her son to enter the ministry. Benjamin O. Davis Jr. wrote of the effects of this decision in his autobiography: "a breach developed between my father and grandfather that lasted almost until my grandfather's death in 1921, when I believe some sort of reconciliation occurred."

In 1898 Davis enlisted as a volunteer soldier during the Spanish-American War and served in the 8th Volunteer Infantry as one of the "black immunes," those supposedly immune to tropical fevers. On June 14, 1899, he reenlisted in the regular army and was assigned to the 9th Calvary at Fort Duchesne, Utah, at a pay rate of twenty-five dollars every two months. He advanced rapidly because he was highly literate. Because of his prior military experience, Davis was already familiar with army regulations and administrative procedures and soon achieved the rank of sergeant-major. By 1901 Davis had achieved his goal of receiving a regular commission by being promoted to the rank of second lieutenant in the 10th Cavalry. He was assigned to Troop M, 9th Cavalry in the Philippines and thus joined an elite group of only four black American officers other than chaplains.

Before being promoted to captain, Davis served at Fort Washakie, Wyoming; at Fort Robinson, Nebraska; in Monrovia, Liberia as a military attache; at Wilberforce University as instructor of military science; at Fort D. A. Russell, Wyoming, and its successor in Douglas, Arizona, where the 9th Cavalry patrolled the U.S.-Mexican border. In 1915 Davis was reassigned to Wilberforce as professor of military science and tactics. For fourteen years as an army officer, Davis served in noncombat positions that ensured that he would not have the opportunity to

Benjamin O. Davis reviews strategic plans with
General George Patton during World War II.

either command white enlisted men or outrank white officers. His son, Benjamin Davis Jr., wrote in his biography:

> his policy remained the paramount consideration . . . [and he was] restricted to "safe" assignments: Junior Reserve Officer Training Corps (ROTC) units at black colleges, black national guard units, military attache to Liberia . . . [despite] his strong preference for duty with troops.

With each successive promotion, Davis became more of a problem for the War Department. Personally, he faced the dilemma of his family's welfare. In 1902 Davis had married Elnora Dickerson. Elnora Davis was trained as a dressmaker and began traveling with her husband to his assigned bases. She returned to Washington only to have their first two children, Olive in 1905 and Benjamin Jr. in 1912. During their fifteen-year marriage, the couple was constantly shunned by white officers' families on American army bases. Overseas duty assignments were always preferable since American blacks were treated more humanely on foreign soil than in their own homeland.

In 1906 Elnora died in Wilberforce, Ohio, after bearing another daughter, Nora. Now a newly promoted lieutenant colonel, Davis had to deal with the ramifications of a new duty assignment and the raising of three children in addition to coping with the loss of his wife. Within a year of her death, Davis was reassigned to the Philippines as supply officer of the 9th Cavalry at Camp Stotsenburg. His parents volunteered to keep the children. During his three-year overseas assignment, Davis began a letter-writing courtship with Sadie Overton, a Wilberforce English teacher who was a member of a prestigious black Mississippi family. Her father was a state representative and a teacher whose children were college educated. In 1919 the couple married in the Philippines.

In 1920 Davis and his new wife returned stateside and she became mother to three children who adored her. Davis was assigned to Tuskegee Institute, as it was known then, as a professor of military science and tactics. Although he would return there for a six-year stint (1931–37), this was a special time because now his family was intact for the first time since Elnora's death.

When the Davises moved to Cleveland, Ohio, in 1924, they became homeowners for the first time as Davis began a new assignment as instructor of the 372nd Infantry of the Ohio National Guard. This was another in a long line of noncombat long-term tours of duty. While commanding this all-black unit, Davis was at least able to travel across the state and supervise annual maneuvers at an Ohio army camp. In 1929 he went to Europe as the official army representative for a group of World War I mothers and widows of slain soldiers buried in European cemeteries. His exemplary service was rewarded with a promotion to colonel in 1930. That same year Davis was reassigned to Wilberforce, but only for a year before being reassigned to Tuskegee and back to Ohio. Every few years he was rotated to avoid being placed over a white company and over white officers.

After forty-two years of stoical and faithful service as a career solider in the army Davis loved, in October 1940 he became the first black American general in the U.S. Army with a promotion to brigadier general. There was controversy over the promotion of an officer due to retire in less than one year. Many army officers complained, calling it a political move designed to appease the large number of black voters in New York and Illinois and the NAACP, an unrelenting advocate for fair treatment of blacks in the military. Until his retirement in June 1941, Davis served as brigade commander at Fort Riley, Kansas, with the 2nd Cavalry Division. Whatever plans Davis and his wife may have made for his golden years were not realized at that time because he was recalled to active duty before the end of the month. Davis was activated as assistant to the Inspector General, a job that entailed such duties as investigating racial incidents and supporting promotions of black soldiers and officers. In conjunction with this position, Davis was also appointed to the Committee on Negro Troop Policies. From 1942 to 1945, he served in Europe as adviser on the use of black troops and to avert and deal with racial problems.

One of Davis's first tactics was to film the all-black 92nd Division in Italy. The resulting product, an unabashedly propagandistic tool, was entitled "Teamwork" and designed to make more palatable the plan to increase the number of black combat troops in Europe. The presence of Winston Churchill congratulating the men was an added public relations coup.

Davis was also adviser to General Dwight D. Eisenhower, then commander of the European Theater and a well-documented balker at efforts to integrate black troops into white units. One of Davis's greatest achievements was his unrelenting insistence on instituting a proposal to retrain black service troops as combat soldiers. This was a critical venture because the bravery, aptitude, and morale of black soldiers had been seriously questioned, especially by some of the more highly visible army commanders. In particular, the 92nd Division had received much negative criticism about combat behavior in the Italian mountains against heavy German opposition. Lieutenant General George S. Patton Jr. was an unabashed segregationist who openly declared blacks to be inferior, especially for armored combat. Quoted in *Black America,* he gave another view: he said of the all-black 761st Tank Battalion, "I would have never asked for you . . . if you weren't good enough."

Davis has always been credited as being a major player in the efforts to change the military's polices of segregation and he was awarded the Distinguished Service Medal for his untiring efforts to combat segregation in the armed forces. As well, he was a role model in illustrating that blacks could effectively serve in positions of authority and leadership. At his July 20, 1948, retirement ceremony, Davis received tributes from President Harry S. Truman and high ranking military officials. Thereafter, he served as a member of the American Battle Monuments Commission, a job that required overseas travel to inspect American cemeteries.

Despite his stellar accomplishments, Davis was often criticized for his rigid and unyielding adherence to the army's way of doing things. In the "Chappie" James biography, Phelps discussed the feelings of some Tuskegee Airmen who had been subjected to violent physical attacks and psychologically demeaning treatment by prejudiced white citizens of Alabama. They wondered how Davis could rationalize his command to remember: "You are in the South. There are certain laws and customs you must abide by. The Army is not to take part in any incident. Those who get involved do so at their own risk and must suffer the consequences." While the airmen could not suppress their anger, Davis and his son had practiced tightly controlled restraint as a matter of course throughout their army and air force careers.

Another reaction to Davis's slavish adherence to the "army way" came earlier in his career as ROTC commanding officer at Wilberforce University. In his autobiography, Benjamin Davis Jr. wrote about the friction between his father and the college administrators over applying army regulations in a civilian setting. Davis was also criticized for his absolute insistence on firm discipline of cadets by the school's commandant, who was not strict enough for a diehard army officer. Davis, however, was highly respected by students and faculty alike and many of his programmatic suggestions and plans were implemented.

Most photographs of Davis show a stern, unsmiling visage, one guaranteed to elicit immediate attention and obedience to orders and instructions. These were reactions that were expected and taken for granted by a career soldier who realized from the beginning that the ordinary friendships and close relations enjoyed by the average citizen would have little, if any, place in the army of the first half of the twentieth century. Before his final retirement in 1948, Davis had the pleasure of seeing his son accomplish what the army had denied him. In 1944 he was privileged to pin the Distinguished Flying Cross on his son at the Ramitelli Air Force Base in Italy. He also vicariously experienced the joy and pleasure in his son's promotion to the rank of brigadier general in the U.S. Air Force by President Dwight D. Eisenhower, whom the senior Davis had advised in the European Theater during World War II. Just as he had been the first black American general in the army, now his son was the first black American general in the air force. He also saw his son become the first black American lieutenant general. Other awards and decorations presented to the senior Davis were: the Bronze Star Medal; the Grade of Commander of the Order of the Star of Africa (Liberia); and the French Croix de Guerre with Palm.

Colonel Davis Sr. died of leukemia on November 26, 1970, at Great Lakes Naval Hospital in North Chicago. His funeral was held at Fort Myers Chapel outside Washington, D.C., and he was buried in Arlington National Cemetery with full military honors. This grandson of a slave who bought his freedom in 1800 strove to end racism in the institution designed to guarantee the safety and well-being of all Americans. Still willing to serve the U.S. Army that he loved, according to *Book of Firsts,* just before he retired Davis said: "I think I have done my share but if the War Department desires me to continue to serve in the national emergency, I will have an open mind."—DOLORES NICHOLSON

SAMMY **DAVIS JR.**
1925–1990
Entertainer, humanitarian

Sammy Davis Jr. was one of the world's greatest entertainers because of his versatility. The June 4, 1990 issue of Jet *described him as "a megastar whose career span showcased him as a dynamic drummer, talented trumpeter, brilliant bassist, sensational singer, dazzling dancer, acclaimed actor, venturesome vibraphonist, master mimic, renowned recording artist, creative cook, consummate comedian, and author of three books . . . a businessman, philanthropist, producer/director, and collector of art, cars and guns." Despite racism, he became popular with white audiences in a career that began in vaudeville.*

Davis was born December 8, 1925, in New York City's Harlem, to Elvera Sanchez Davis, a chorus dancer, and Sammy Davis Sr., a tapdancer who toured with a troupe headed by Will Mastin. Because his parents were at the peak of their careers and constantly traveled, he and his sister Ramona were left with family to be reared, Davis with his paternal grandmother, "Mama Rosa" M. Davis made his stage debut at the age of one.

By the time Davis was three years old, his parents had separated, both professionally and maritally, and his father gained custody of him. At this time, he began to travel and perform with the Mastin troupe and became a full-time professional. He and the troupe continued to perform with a great deal of success until vaudeville began to be replaced by the movies. Mastin then began cutting back on the troupe membership; over a period of time, it went from twelve members to three and became known as The Will Mastin Trio, featuring Sammy Davis, Jr. During his travels with the troupe, he came under the influence and tutelage of Bill "Bojangles" Robinson, the world's greatest tapdancer; later in his career, Davis immortalized Robinson in the song "Mr. Bojangles."

This lifestyle allowed little time for formal schooling and it was not until he was drafted into the United States Army and sent to Fort Francis E. Warren in Cheyenne, Wyoming, that this

Sammy Davis Jr.

was corrected. Davis was befriended by an African American sergeant who gave him remedial reading lessons and the basics of a high school education. It was also during this period that he encountered the violent and brutal racism with which he was to contend throughout his career. While in the army, he was assigned to a Special Services unit and toured various military installations. He produced and performed in shows that were often revisions of his old vaudeville acts. At the end of his tour of duty in the army, he rejoined the Will Mastin Trio.

Appears in clubs and films   After the army, Davis returned to performing and appeared in small places as well as Chicago, New York, and Los Angeles. Just as his touring prior to the war led to his meeting Robinson, after the war it led to contact and work with rising stars like Mickey Rooney, Frank Sinatra, Bob Hope, and Jack Benny. He continued to appear in clubs throughout his life. In 1954 Davis was in a near fatal automobile accident in which he lost an eye. Most importantly, he began to concern himself with his spiritual life and to study Judaism. In spite of the fact that his mother was a Roman Catholic and his father a Baptist, he converted to Judaism. When he returned to performing following his 1954 accident, he rejoined the Trio and appeared at such clubs as Copa City in Miami, the Chez Paree in Chicago, and the Latin Casino in Philadelphia. Davis was a regular on the Las Vegas club circuit and as part owner of the Tropicana Hotel was a regular performer. Often appearing with him were his friends Jerry Lewis, Liza Minelli, and others. He regularly appeared at top nightclubs, supper clubs, and concert halls in the United States. In 1988 he embarked on a national tour with Frank Sinatra, Dean Martin, and Liza Minelli. Davis was known for his showmanship and integrity. At a 1977 performance at Harrod's Tahoe Club, he picked up the tab for the entire club night because he believed his performance had not met his standards.

Davis began his film career with *Rufus Jones for President,* in which he starred in the title role as a little boy who falls asleep in his mother's lap and dreams he is president. This was followed in the same year by *Season's Greetings.* Between 1931 and 1989, he appeared in more than twenty-nine films. He played Fletcher Henderson in *The Benny Goodman Story* (1956); costarred with Eartha Kitt in *Anna Lucasta* (1958); he played Sportin' Life in the screen version of Gershwin's folk opera *Porgy and Bess* (1959), a role for which he is well known; he appeared as himself in *Pepe* (1960); he sang the title song for the soundtrack for *Of Love and Desire* (1963); as the ballad singer in *The Three Penny Opera* (1963), he sang "Mack the Knife"; and in 1965 he played the supporting role in *Nightmare in the Sun.* In 1972 he appeared in *Save the Children,* an all-star music documentary filmed at a benefit show for Jesse Jackson's Operation PUSH (People United to Serve Humanity) in Chicago. His last screen appearance was in 1989 in *Taps,* in which he costarred with Gregory Hines and performed his last dance routine for the camera.

***Sammy on the set of his one man show
"Stop The World I Want to Get Off."***

171

He became a member of a group of Hollywood actors called the "Rat Pack" which included Frank Sinatra, Tony Curtis, Dean Martin, Peter Lawford, and Joey Bishop. They appeared with Davis in such films as *Oceans Eleven* (1960), *Sergeants Three* (1962), *Johnny Cool* (1963), *Robin and the Seven Hoods* (1964), *Salt and Pepper* (1968), and *One More Time* (1970). As a result of these movies, Donald Bogle in *Toms, Coons, Mulattoes, Mammies, and Bucks* wrote that "he alienated black movie patrons because he was too much the coon-pickaninny figure. On the surface the clan pictures were egalitarian affairs; underneath they rotted from white patronizing and hypocrisy." Bogle wrote in *Blacks in American Film and Television* that "Davis was frequently used as a token . . . [and] portrayed . . . mainly as a comic sidekick, with racial jokes sometimes at Davis's expense."

Recording, television, and stage career   Davis began recording songs for Capitol Records in 1946. During his career, he recorded with other labels such as Decca, Reprise, and Warner Brothers. His "The Way You Look Tonight," one of his first cuts, was named *Metronome's* Record of the Year. Other songs recorded by him are "Mr. Bojangles"; "Candy Man," his all-time bestseller; "Hey There"; "The Lady is a Tramp"; "Birth of the Blues"; "Too Close for Comfort"; "Gonna Build a Mountain"; and "Who Can I Turn To." His numerous record albums include *Starring Sammy Davis Jr.,* which contained impersonations of such artists as Dean Martin and Jerry Lewis, Jimmie Durante, Johnny Rae, and Big Crosby; *Sammy Swings; Mood to Be Wooed; I've Got a Right to Swing; As Long As She Needs Me;* and *Sammy Davis and Count Basie: Our Shining Hour.*

Contacts made by Davis during his travels following his stint in the army were instrumental in his initial appearances on television. He was provided a place on Eddie Cantor's *Colgate Comedy Hour* television program. His small troupe then was a summer replacement for an NBC regular. Davis appeared in both variety shows and series on television. These included *The Ed Sullivan Show; All in the Family,* where he was the first celebrity to appear on this program; *Mod Squad; General Electric Theatre; The Cosby Show;* and *Dick Powell Theatre.* He revised Pigmeat Markham's vaudeville routine, "Here Come De Judge," for the *Laugh In* program and hosted *The Tonight Show* several times in place of host Johnny Carson. Davis was so well received that he was able on several occasions to have his own television shows, *The Swinging World of Sammy Davis Jr., Sammy and His Friends,* the short-lived network series *The Sammy Davis Jr. Show,* and *Sammy and Company.*

Davis's major Broadway appearances came after 1954. In 1956 he opened on Broadway in *Mr. Wonderful,* a musical comedy created especially for Davis, about an African American entertainer who used his talent and will to overcome racial odds and become a star. It ran for over 380 performances. In 1965 he had the lead role in Clifford Odet's *The Golden Boy,* the story of an African American boxer struggling to free himself from poverty; it ran for over 560 performances. For his performance, he was nominated for a Tony for best actor in a musical in 1965. He returned to Broadway in 1974 in *Sammy on Broadway,* a revue.

Davis was the author of three popular autobiographies. *Yes I Can, The Story of Sammy Davis Jr.* (1965) was written with Jane and Burt Boyar. It chronicles the trials, especially the racism Davis experienced in the U.S. Army, and triumphs in the first thirty-five years of his life. The second autobiography, *Hollywood in a Suitcase* (1980), details not only his life in show business but also personalities with whom he came in contact during this period of his career. His final book, *Why Me* (1989), was again written in collaboration with Jane and Burt

Boyar. According to *Jet* magazine, "It explores the song-and-dance man's glitzy lifestyle on America's West Coast and its effect on his health, finances, fatherhood role, civil rights stance and alienation from the Black community to name a few" of the answers to the questions posed by the title.

He was one of the largest donors to the United Negro College Fund (now UNCF/The College Fund). He participated in numerous fund raisers for the organization, including serving as chairman of the special events committee for the *Lou Rawls Parade of Stars* yearly fund raisers for the UNCF. In spite of the fact that he was a registered Democrat and a supporter of the Kennedy family, at the 1972 Republican Convention he came under fire when he publicly endorsed Richard Nixon. However, in 1974, he renounced his support. He was a life member of the NAACP and aided or led fund raising drives.

Davis was an avid collector of art, a highly regarded photographer, and a collector of photographs. His collection contained paintings of him by both Pablo Picasso and Charles Wright.

In Davis's entertainment career, he garnered numerous awards and recognitions. He was named the Most Outstanding Personality of 1946 by *Metronome* magazine; in 1969 Davis was awarded the NAACP Spingarn Medal for his outstanding achievements; in 1979 he was awarded *Ebony*'s first Lifetime Achievement Award for his years of joy and goodwill to all peoples; and in 1986 he received an honorary degree from Howard University. In 1974 he won the grand prize at the Cannes Film Festival for his television commercials for Japan's Suntory Whiskey and was honored by the National Academy of TV Arts and Sciences for his unique contributions to television. Additionally, he received honors from various Jewish organizations in recognition of his efforts to bring African Americans and Jewish Americans together. Before he died in Los Angeles on May 16, 1990, Davis was given a tribute that was enormous even by Hollywood standards. The event was televised and featured stars such as Eddie Murphy, Frank Sinatra, Michael Jackson, and Clint Eastwood. The proceeds from the show went to the United Negro College Fund.

The *Nashville Tennessean* called Davis "one of the first black performers to cross into the entertainment mainstream and . . . to be embraced by all audiences of all types." On the day of his passing, all of the lights in the Las Vegas Strip were extinguished for ten minutes, an American institution paying tribute to an American original.—HELEN R. HOUSTON

THE DELANY SISTERS

SADIE **DELANY**

1889–

Educator, humanitarian

BESSIE **DELANY**
1891–1995
Dentist, civil rights activist

Sadie Delany was the first African American domestic science teacher at the high school level in the New York City public schools. Bessie Delany was the second African American woman licensed to practice dentistry in New York City. Sadie, at 108 years old, is the oldest surviving member of one of America's most prominent black families. In 1993 the Delany Sisters became celebrities with the publication of their autobiography, Having Our Say, *which chronicles the first one hundred years of their lives and shares their unique perspectives on American history.*

Sarah Louise "Sadie" Delany, born September 19, 1889, and Annie Elizabeth "Bessie" Delany, born September 3, 1891, were the second and third of the ten children born to Henry Beard Delany and Nanny Logan Delany. Their father studied for the ministry at St. Augustine's College in Raleigh, North Carolina, and he eventually became vice principal of the college and stayed on to raise his family there. Henry Delany also became this nation's first black Episcopal bishop. According to Bessie in *Having Our Say,* "It was religious faith that formed the backbone of the Delany family." The sisters witnessed their parents putting into practice the family motto: "Your job is to help somebody." For instance, the family yearly distributed Thanksgiving baskets to the down-on-their-luck former slaves who lived in the neighborhood of St. Augustine's.

At five and seven years of age, the Delany sisters were introduced to Jim Crow when they were forced to sit at the back of a segregated trolley car. Although their parents tried to shelter them from the brutalities of the southern racial caste system, the girls heard about lynchings from the whisperings of the teachers at school. With family friend W. E. B. Du Bois, they also learned to combat the racist ideology by remaining strong and well educated. All of Henry Delany's children worked their way through college.

Delany sisters become educators   Upon graduating from St. Augustine's, Sadie took a job as supervisor of the domestic science curriculum in the black schools in Wake County, North Carolina, but ended up assuming the duties of the county school superintendent at no extra pay. She proudly recalls driving Booker T. Washington around to show him her schools. Bessie, who also graduated from St. Augustine's, spent two lonely years as a young, single teacher in the mill town of Boardman, North Carolina, before getting another teaching job in Brunswick, Georgia. She came close to being lynched when she rebuffed a drunken white man on a train while on her way to assume her teaching position in Brunswick. As she admits in *Having Our Say,* "I am lucky to be alive. But I would rather die than back down."

The Delany sisters moved to Harlem in their mid-twenties to further their educations. Sadie enrolled in the domestic science program at Pratt Institute in New York, then a two-year college. After graduating from Pratt, she enrolled in Columbia University's Teachers College. In 1920 she graduated from Columbia with a bachelor of science degree. Her first teaching job in New York was at a mostly black elementary school. Continuing her studies, she obtained her master's degree in education from Columbia in 1925. During the Depression she landed a job at an all-white high school by being appointed to the position, skipping the required face-to-face interview (which would reveal her race), and then showing up on the first day of class. Thus she became the first black high school domestic science teacher in New York. Sadie taught in various New York high schools from 1930 to 1960, when she retired.

Bessie, who had taken some science courses at Shaw University in Raleigh, enrolled in Columbia University's dental school in 1919. She was awarded her doctor of dental surgery degree in 1923 and became the second black woman licensed to practice dentistry in New York. In her practice, located in the heart of Harlem, Bessie experienced not only discrimination from whites, who would not patronize a black dentist, but also from some blacks, who would not patronize a woman dentist. But she soon earned the reputation of taking any patient, no matter how sick, and she never turned away anyone who did not have money. When she retired in 1950, her rates were the same as when she started her practice in 1923; two dollars for a cleaning, two dollars for an extraction, five dollars for a silver filling, and ten dollars for a gold filling. As she explained in *Having Our Say,* "I never raised my rates because I was getting by OK. I was always proud of my work, and that was enough for me."

By the mid-1920s Bessie's dental office had become a meeting place for black activists. At her urging, sociologist E. Franklin Frazier; future executive director of the NAACP, Walter White; and noted educator, writer, and friend of the family, W. E. B. Du Bois, demonstrated at the 1925 rerelease of the movie *The Birth of a Nation,* which featured black villains, Ku Klux Klan heroes, and whites in blackface. Also in this year Bessie experienced a harrowing encounter with the Ku Klux Klan. She and a boyfriend were on an outing on Long Island when they ran into twenty white-robed Klansmen stopping and searching the cars of blacks. Bessie credits the powerful engine of her companion's Cadillac for zooming them right around the Klansmen. After this encounter with the Klan, Bessie became a staunch activist for the rights of blacks.

Continuing familial closeness   The Delany siblings all moved to Harlem, and by 1926 they lived together in the same apartment building. Bessie and Sadie proudly maintained in Harlem the wholesome, family-oriented lifestyle that they had in Raleigh. Their favorite pastime was having friends over for dinner, and every Sunday found them at Saint Mark's Episcopal Church. In *Having Our Say* Bessie noted, "We were proud of the Delany name, and because of our self-discipline it came to mean in Harlem what it had meant in North Carolina—that is, it stood for integrity."

Bessie and Sadie's father passed away in 1928 after a brief illness. The sisters then persuaded their mother to move to New York. At the age of fifty-nine Bessie retired from her dental practice to take care of their mother, who was then over ninety years old. As a special surprise for their mother, their brother Hubert—an assistant U.S. attorney in New York—arranged for her to meet Eleanor Roosevelt. In *Having Our Say* Bessie recalled, "It was pretty wonderful to see the former first lady of the United States jump up, so respectful like, to greet Mama, an old colored lady." After the death of two of the Delany brothers in quick succession, Mama Delany herself died at the age of ninety-five. Shortly afterward, in 1957, the sisters moved to Mount Vernon, New York, joining an exodus of middle-class blacks from New York City to the suburbs.

One of Bessie and Sadie's biggest regrets was not going to the March on Washington in 1963 and hearing Martin Luther King's "I Have a Dream" speech. In *Having Our Say* Bessie recalled, "The civil rights movement was a time when we thought: Maybe now it will finally happen. Maybe now our country will finally grow up, come to terms with this race mess. But it seemed like the momentum was lost when the Vietnam War happened. It was like all the energy of the young people, and the focus of the country, got shifted away from civil rights."

Bessie explained that women's rights have always been important to her as well, though in *Having Our Say* she noted that "no matter how much I had to put up with as a woman, the bigger problem was being colored. People looked at me and the first thing they saw was *Negro*, not *woman*. So racial equality, as a cause, won my heart." One of the happiest days of her life occurred back in 1920 when women finally won the right to vote. She and Sadie immediately registered and have not missed a vote since.

Sisters become authors of best-selling autobiography   In 1993 the Delany sisters became celebrities with the publication of their best-selling autobiography, *Having Our Say: The Delany Sisters' First 100 Years*. The book resulted from eighteen months of interviews with Amy Hill Hearth, a free-lance writer who collaborated with them on the project. Hearth wove thousands of anecdotes into a lively, seven-part, largely chronological narrative. Before each part, she also provided a brief overview that placed the narrative in the context of black history. Camille Cosby acquired the film, stage, and television rights to the book, and in 1995 co-produced a stage play of the book entitled *Having Our Say*.

Because of the popularity of the autobiography, the sisters have been featured on a number of television shows, where they have graciously shared their secrets to a long and productive life. These include yoga exercises, eating up to seven vegetables a day, and taking daily vitamin supplements, garlic, and cod liver oil. Reading the newspaper, watching *The MacNeil/Lehrer News Hour*, and praying twice a day are also part of their routine.

In *Having Our Say* Bessie stated, "If you asked me the secret to longevity I would tell you that you have to work at taking care of your health. But a lot of it's attitude. I'm alive out of sheer determination, honey!" Bessie also attributes their longevity to having never married. In *Having Our Say* she noted, "When people ask me how we lived past one hundred, I say, 'Honey, we never had husbands to worry us to death!' . . . And why would I want to give up my freedom and independence to take care of some man? In those days, a man expected you to be in charge of a perfect household, to look after his every need. Honey, I wasn't interested! I wasn't going to be bossed around by some man!" After receiving much fan mail, the Delany sisters followed the success of *Having Our Say* with the publication of a second book, 1994's *The Delany Sisters' Book of Everyday Wisdom*. The American public continues to be enthralled by their spirit.

At the age of 104, the youngest of the Delany sisters, Bessie, died in her sleep. Many people mourned the life of a woman who had seen so much. First Lady Hilary Clinton stated, "I feel so blessed to have known her, she lived honestly and well." Sadie has confronted the loss of her sister with the same strength that has granted her longevity, "I'm not going to give up, I'll just do the best I can without her."—PHIEFER L. BROWNE

DAVID N. **DINKINS**

1927–

Lawyer, public official, educator

Courtly, calm, cautious, deliberate, and always polite are the terms used most often to describe David Dinkins. These characteristics are not generally recognized as selling points in winning elections in New York City's rugged, rough politics. They did, however, help to overcome white New Yorkers' suspicions that David Dinkins lacked leadership qualifications and enabled him to be elected New York's mayor in 1989, the first African American to hold that position of power.

David Norman Dinkins was born on July 10, 1927, in Trenton, New Jersey, the older of the two children of William H. Dinkins and his wife, Sally. His father, initially a barber, became a real estate agent in 1962. His sister, Joyce, lives in a Trenton, New Jersey, suburb. Dinkins was six years old when his parents divorced. He and his sister lived briefly with their mother in Harlem where Sally Dinkins worked as a domestic and later as a manicurist. They grew up mostly in a predominantly middle-class neighborhood in Trenton with their father and stepmother, Lottie Hartgell Dinkins, a high school English teacher, who encouraged them in their studies. Dinkins and his wife have two children, David Jr. and Donna Hoggerd, and two grandchildren, Jamal and Kalila Hoggard.

In school, "Dink," as he was called by his classmates, was ambitious and responsible even as a youngster. He earned money by delivering newspapers and doing odd jobs around the neighborhood. At one time, he sold shopping bags on 125th Street in Harlem. He graduated from a segregated junior high school in Trenton. His leadership qualities surfaced when he was elected president of his high school homeroom class in 1943, winning over his white classmate. No stranger to institutional racism at the time, the predominantly white Trenton High School even barred blacks from the swimming pool. After graduation from high school in 1945, he tried to enlist in the Marine Corps but was rejected because the "Negro quota" was filled.

Dinkins was then drafted into the United States army, but later he transferred to the marines, spending most of his thirteen-month military service at Camp Lejeune, North Carolina. Once, while on military leave and returning from Washington, D.C., he was denied one of two remaining seats on a bus, even though he was in uniform. The memory of that episode still angers him. Later on he brought to his job as mayor of New York a personal knowledge of the ravages of racism and empathy for those who suffer oppression.

David Dinkins.

*David Dinkins speaks at the 1991
Democratic Convention in New York City.*

Honorably discharged from the service in August, 1946, and making use of the G.I. Bill, Dinkins enrolled in Howard University, where he majored in mathematics and graduated magna cum laude in 1950. Awarded a mathematics fellowship to Rutgers University, he grew restless, dropping out after attending only one semester. He then sold insurance for a firm in Red Bank, New Jersey, and became one of its top salesmen. In 1953 he entered Brooklyn Law School. On August 30 of that year, he married his college sweetheart, Joyce Burrows, the daughter of Daniel Burrows, the state assemblyman from Harlem who introduced him to politics. While in law school, he worked nights in his father-in-law's liquor store in Harlem.

After receiving his law degree in 1956, Dinkins joined the firm of Dyett and Phipps, reconstituted the following year as Dyett, Alexander, and Dinkins. He remained there until 1971, when he went into law practice with Basil Paterson, then the vice-chairman of the Democratic National Committee. At the Dyett firm, Dinkins had a modest neighborhood practice involving banking, probate, and real estate matters. Meanwhile, he developed a reputation as a skilled mediator.

Public service career begins

Dinkins eventually complied with the wishes of his wife's father, who introduced him to J. Raymond Jones, nicknamed the "Harlem Fox" and the leader of the Carver Democratic Club. The organization was the training ground for young black business and political leaders. The club was well entrenched within the city's power structure. Dinkins became a cog in a powerful political machine, doing all kinds of footwork such as hanging posters at Harlem subway stops, searching out unregistered voters, and other necessary activities that are part of every campaign. J. Raymond Jones recognized Dinkins's ambition and made Dinkins his protégé. With Jones's support, he started on his career in public service with his election to the New York State Assembly in 1966. After Dinkins's district was redrawn, he chose not to run again at the end of his two-year term. In 1967, he succeeded his mentor as district leader of the Carver Democratic Club, a position that he held for the next two decades.

Dinkins served as president of the New York City Board of Elections from 1972 to 1973, establishing guidelines that encouraged wider voter registration. He was appointed city clerk in 1975, a post he held for ten years. His responsibilities mainly involved signing marriage certificates and processing the financial disclosure forms of public officials. This plum patronage position afforded him the opportunity to establish political ties that would later prove useful. Tuxedo-clad almost every night, he attended several events, shaking hands and stopping to talk to guests. During this time, he headed the Coalition of Black Elected Democrats. Despite his reputation for caution, he took a bold position in 1984, endorsing Jesse Jackson for president when most mainstream black politicians were supporting the former vice president, Walter F. Mondale.

In 1977, when Percy Sutton resigned as Manhattan borough president to become the first African American to run for mayor of New York City, he urged Dinkins to try for the borough presidency. Defeated twice, Dinkins was elected on his third try in 1985. The primary power of a borough president derived from his ex officio seat on the Board of Estimate, New York City's governing body until 1990. The board reviewed the city's budget and major contracts. During his four-year term, Dinkins put together task forces on a range of urban issues and took a strong stance in support of community-based AIDS services. He earned a well-deserved reputation as a friend of the poor and the homeless, and as a voice of reason in a racially tense city. Because he withheld his opinions or votes until he could confer with aides, he was called a procrastinator by political enemies. To the public, however, he appeared deliberate and cool-headed.

In 1989 Dinkins came under increasing pressure from his political friends to challenge Edward I. Koch, who was making a bid for an unprecedented fourth term as mayor. Dinkins commissioned a poll to determine his chances, and bolstered by its findings, announced his candidacy. Drawing heavily on his political stronghold in Harlem, he defeated Koch in the Democratic Party primary election by about 50 to 42 percent. Dinkins's "nice guy" image attracted a multiethnic coalition of African American, Hispanic, and white voters, which, in his public speeches, he called a "gorgeous mosaic." Ninety-one percent of the African Americans and 65 percent of the Hispanics voted for him, along with about 30 percent of the whites, including about 30 percent of the Jewish voters. His dignified reserve, cautious speech, and behind-the-scenes diplomacy were also prime factors in his defeating the popular Republican district attorney, Rudolph Giuliani, in the general election in November 1989. Dinkins became the 106th mayor of New York City.

When Dinkins went into mayoral politics, the perception of him as a healer, coupled with his abilities as a conciliator, enabled him to reduce the racial tensions besieging the city after twelve years of combative, confrontational government under Koch. Having risen to power as a quiet champion of the poor, once in office he faced the formidable task of dealing with racial violence, drugs, and crime in addition to the city's ominous fiscal crisis.

During his tenure as mayor, Dinkins experienced first-hand the difference between a candidate who can promise the sky and an office-holder who cannot deliver all things to all people. His priorities were the construction of more housing for the poor and homeless, better health care—especially for children—and a crackdown on drugs and crime. In the eyes of many politicians, the city he inherited was looking more ungovernable with each passing day. Confronted with a budget deficit leaving few resources for programs that he cherished, Dinkins began to face attacks on his financial handling of the city. His 1991 budget included $800 million in new taxes, representing the largest tax increase in the city's history. In addition to cuts in spending in nearly all social services, he had to cut the city's work force as well. These actions, though praised as fiscally prudent, had political reverberations later on.

Besides the attacks on his financial handling of the city, Dinkins faced further shattering of his "gorgeous mosaic." In 1991 violent protests erupted after a car in the entourage of a Brooklyn Jewish leader struck and killed a black child. Dinkins brokered a fragile peace when he appealed to both sides to be reasonable rather than violent. Also in 1991, when riots erupted in many places after white officers were found not guilty in the Rodney King police brutality case in Los Angeles, Dinkins visited several New York neighborhoods urging calm. His healing powers deactivated a racial time bomb and earned for him a temporary respite from critics.

David Dinkins's sound fiscal management produced a budget surplus in 1992. The mayor added another feather in his cap by having the city become host to the lucrative Democratic National Convention. Nevertheless, as the 1993 election approached, Dinkins faced a steady stream of criticism. Forgotten were his real successes during a recession. He had kept the city's budget balanced, won new taxes in order to hire thousands more police officers, extended library hours, and had seen crime decline. As an incumbent, he did not want to be the first black mayor of a major city to lose his first reelection bid.

In New York City, Democrats normally outnumber Republicans five to one. New York voters, however, had been known to switch sides when the issues were race and liberal ideology. Dinkins won easy renomination in the Democratic primary election. He was defeated in the November general election by the Republican candidate, Rudolph Giuliani, whose prosecutor's image was softened by a media campaign portraying him as a warm family man and a good manager.

Dinkins was many things to many people, but even his political enemies would agree that he was and is always a gentleman. People were impressed by his dignified demeanor, even during chaotic and trying times. He had worked hard at being a good mayor, but New Yorkers did not fasten on Dinkins's strengths.

Since leaving office, Dinkins has enjoyed the affection shown by New Yorkers he encounters every day in his still very public life. When he stops for a red light while behind the wheel of his car, nearby drivers honk their horns and wave enthusiastically. When he walks down the street or enters a restaurant, someone will stop to shake his hand and wish him well.

Maintains high visibility   Dinkins currently teaches at Columbia University, where he is professor in the practice of public affairs at the School of International and Public Affairs and senior fellow of the Barnard-Columbia Center for Urban Policy. He hosts, twice a week, an hour-long interview and call-in radio show, "Dialogue with Dinkins," on WLIB-AM, and continues to advocate help for children and education, a compassionate urban policy, and tolerance.

The former mayor is active as a member of several corporate boards and at least two dozen nonprofit charitable groups and other organizations. He is on the board of the Aaron Diamond Foundation, the Andrew Goodman Foundation, the Association to Benefit Children, the Federation of Protestant Welfare Agencies, Friends of the Nelson Mandela Children's Fund, Goods for Guns, Hope for Infants, the Howard Samuels Foundation, the Lenox Hill Neighborhood Association, the March of Dimes, the New York State International Partnership Program, and the New York Junior Tennis League. He was also a founding member of the Black and Puerto Rican Legislative Caucus of New York State, the Council of Black Elected Democrats of New York State, 100 Black Men, and the Black Americans in Support of Israel Committee. He is an honorary life trustee of the Community Service Society of New York, an honorary trustee of the Friends of Harlem Hospital, and a life member of the NAACP.

The former mayor also works as a consultant to Ronald O. Perelman, the financier who is chairman of the Revlon Corporation. He was the first male member of the National Women's Political Caucus, and at one time the vice president of the United States Conference of Mayors.

Among the many awards he has received are Pioneer of Excellence, World Institute of Black Communications, 1986; the Righteous Man Award, New York Board of Rabbis, 1986; Man of the Year Award, Corrections Guardians Association, 1986; Man of the Year Award, Association of Negro Business and Professional Women's Clubs, 1986; Distinguished Service Award, Federation of Negro Civil Service Organizations, 1986; and Father of the Year Award, Metropolitan Chapter, Jack and Jill of America, 1989.

Affable, neat, and impeccably groomed, about the only hint of extravagance Dinkins displays is his penchant for elegant custom-made pinstripe suits. He loves big band music. An avid tennis player with a strong forehand, he still plays, even after heart surgery in August of 1995. Among his peers and cronies are Basil Paterson, Percy Sutton, and Charles Rangel—all important among New York City's former or current black politicians.

While he is no longer a candidate for elected office, he still makes the rounds, attending receptions, dinners, cocktail parties, benefits, fund raisers, and award ceremonies that are the staple of an elected official's day.—VIVIAN D. HEWITT

M. J. DIVINE (FATHER DIVINE)
1879–1965
Religious leader

In Brooklyn in 1917, a man who called himself the Messenger took on a new name to satisfy the demands of a society that required persons to have a name and surname. He named himself M. J. Divine. His followers knew the initials stood for Major Jealous ("for the Lord, whose name is Jealous, is a jealous god." Exodus, 34: 14); they also believed he was God. For many years this new identity concealed his earlier life, and Father Divine was known only as the leader of a religious cult that attracted wide-spread and often hostile attention in the 1930s. Divine's Peace Mission Movement was a true cult and has been the object of study for several classic analyses, but it is also increasingly studied as a creative religious reaction to the plight of poor urban blacks.

Father Divine was born George Baker Jr. in Rockville, Maryland, in May 1879, the oldest child of George Baker and Nancy Smith Baker. Little is known of George Baker except that he was probably a former slave and worked as a farm laborer when he moved to Rockville and married Nancy Smith. Before emancipation, Smith had two Catholic masters who required attendance at Catholic services. In Rockville Smith joined a black Methodist church controlled by the predominately white denomination. Until she became too overweight to work she continued the domestic work she had begun as a slave. The local newspaper noted her death in 1897 because this five-foot woman weighed 480 pounds.

Nancy Smith had three children before her marriage: Annie (b. 1860); Margaret (Maggie; b. circa 1864); and Delia (b. 1866). The girls eventually took the Baker surname. There was another Baker son, Milford, born in 1880. The census of that year gives some idea of the poverty the family endured. Fourteen people lived in Luther Snowden's Rockville cabin: Snowden's family of four, a young married couple, a bachelor, and the seven Bakers. In spite of their poverty, the Baker children received at least a rudimentary education. George Baker Jr. also acquired the skills of a yard worker and gardener.

In 1899 George Baker Jr. had moved to Baltimore where he sought work as a gardener; he was fortunate enough to find housing in the servants' quarters of a white household. As an underemployed black manual worker, Baker was not attracted by the established black churches but instead entered the world of storefront churches,

Father Divine.

where he developed his powers as a preacher and worked out his own religious ideas. Drawing on Methodist, Catholic, and popular black traditions, he was also profoundly influenced by the movement called New Thought, a forerunner of both the Christian Science of Mary Baker Eddy and the modern New Age movements. In particular, Baker was profoundly influenced by the Unity School of Christianity founded by Charles Fillmore.

In 1902 Baker set out to save souls in the South and then in 1906 went to the West Coast, where he heard William J. Seymour at the Azuza Street revival meetings in Los Angeles that sparked the Pentecostal movement among both blacks and whites. Baker himself experienced speaking in tongues. This experience led to a reshaping of his religious thought, which continued after his return to Baltimore.

In 1907 he met Samuel Morris, who came into a storefront church to preach. When Morris proclaimed, "I am the Father Eternal," the congregation threw him out for blasphemy, but Baker was interested. Morris joined Baker in lodgings at the house of Harriet Anna Snowden, laundress and religious worker. Morris was accepted as Father Jehovia, and Baker assumed the identity of the Messenger, the Son, and obliquely proclaimed Father Jehovia was God during the services held several times a week. Next to appear was Reverend Bishop Saint John the Vine (John A. Hickerson), who also drew on elements of New Thought but explicitly claimed affiliation to Ethiopianism, a black tradition maintaining all blacks in the country were descendants of Ethiopian Jews and that Christ was African.

For some years the three collaborated in building up a following at their Fairmont Avenue residence. The true leader in terms of teaching and organizing was the Messenger, who in the 1910 census gave his name as Anderson K. Baker and changed the year and place

*Father Divine with his followers on their way
to his 500-acre estate called "Heaven."*

of his birth, foreshadowing a more profound change of identity. In 1912 the three broke: Baker denied both Father Jehovia's claim to be God and Bishop John the Vine's claim that everyone is God.

The Messenger establishes a sect   In the next few years, the Messenger traveled about, often in the South, spreading his message and meeting great hostility. He had already established a pattern of worship: preaching, singing, and Holy Communion banquets as lavish as resources allowed. Worshippers sang, danced, and testified in free-form services that often lasted into the night. Perhaps alone among itinerant ministers, Divine did not pass a collection plate at services and consistently rejected money from non-members. The "International Modest Code" may not yet have been formalized but its tenets were upheld: "no smoking; no drinking; no obscenity; no vulgarity; no profanity; no undue mixing of the sexes; no receiving of gifts, presents, tips or bribes." No undue mixing of the sexes also implied the celibacy Divine demanded of his followers.

There was often hostility from black ministers. In 1913 a confrontation in Savannah led to Divine's serving sixty days on the chain gang. The most fully documented case of community reaction occurred in Valdosta, Georgia. After being thrown out of a local church for proclaiming himself God, Divine built up a following among black women who found a liberation from male chauvinism in his teaching. He also alarmed the black men of the community, especially when he ordered the women to stop having sexual relations with their husbands. African American men arranged for his arrest on lunacy charges on February 16, 1914. This only increased his notoriety and the number of his followers. Improvised services held at the jail even attracted some white worshippers. J. R. Mosely, a white peach farmer and religious seeker, was impressed by Divine and obtained the free services of one of the town's leading lawyers to defend him. In spite of the defense, the jury found Divine insane but not in need of incarceration, much to the anger of the black men of the town. At their insistence Divine was rearrested on a charge of vagrancy. The uproar continued for some time until Divine agreed to leave town and not come back in exchange for his release.

Alone among black cults, the mission had the distinction of attracting a significant minority of whites, some of whom were quite affluent. The presence of an interracial membership and a political agenda explains the hostile attention given to the sect in sensation-seeking publications like the Hearst newspapers, and the sustained interest of law enforcement officials ranging from local authorities to the Federal Bureau of Investigation, which maintained extensive files on the movement. For the next few years Divine continued to travel both in the South and in the North, accompanied by a group of disciples ranging in number from six to twelve, mostly women. One woman named Peninnah, older and larger than Divine, joined him, possibly in Macon, Georgia, after he cured her of arthritis. Her origins are completely obscured and the date given for her marriage to Divine—June 6, 1882—has a spiritual rather than a literal meaning. Peninnah became known as Mother Divine and was a very able second-in-command. In 1917 Divine and his followers settled in a Brooklyn apartment, continuing the communal living tradition of the group. Some members worked outside while others maintained the living quarters.

On October 27, 1919, Divine purchased a house in Sayville on Long Island, some seventy miles from New York. He became the first black homeowner in the town. Nine followers accompanied Mother and Father Divine in the move that winter. Divine found work as domestics for many of them, and their willingness to work hard, coupled with absolute honesty, appealed to employers. Initially the growth of Divine's following was slow, and he had time to read extensively in New Thought literature borrowed from the local library. He reflected and developed his theology. Biographer Jill Watts points out that while his sermons rambled and contained neologisms, "they had a consistent and comprehensible core. Indeed, he was as intelligible as any New Thought advocate."

Divine turned to distributing New Thought literature that supported his views. This led to a growth in the number of persons he attracted. He also began to win more white supporters. The combination of self-help ideas and the promise of healing, affluence, and bodily immortality in this world was a heady mixture. By 1930 the number of people living in the house in Sayville and the number of seekers visiting on Sunday began to fray the tolerance of the white neighbors. In April 1930, a young black police informant, Susan Hadley, infiltrated the house where thirty persons were living. She discovered that the rumors about sexual license were completely unjustified and that nothing illegal was taking place. The only thing that baffled her was the affluence of the household, which she could not believe rested on the work of the members. Her report was sensationalized in various Long Island newspapers. One result was to attract even more attention to Divine. William Lanyon, a noted New Thought lecturer, was one of the whites converted, and he spread the message in Europe. Still, after much insistence by the fearful neighboring whites, Divine was finally arrested by the local authorities on May 8, 1931 for creating his interracial denomination.

Bond was set at a thousand dollars, and Peninnah immediately paid it in cash. Trial was set for the fall. All summer Divine tried to control the noise and the crowds, but on November 15, 1931, he deliberately prolonged the service and allowed the noise level to increase. The police arrived after midnight and arrested seventy-eight blacks and fifteen whites. Tensions in Sayville were high, and some residents went so far as to call for lynching. Divine apparently negotiated an agreement with the police that legal charges against him would be dropped in exchange for his departure—a promise that was broken.

Divine was now attracting wide support in New Thought circles, attracting new white followers, mostly middle- and upper-class, and poor, working-class blacks. He began to shift his base of operations from Long Island to New York City. In December 1931 Divine held the first of a series of successful meetings at the Rockville Palace in Harlem, where he moved in March 1932. On Easter Sunday of that year fifteen hundred people appeared for a communion banquet in a space that had seats for only six hundred. The overflow was housed in a neighboring church. Finally on May 24, Divine's Sayville case came to trial, and he was found guilty. On June 5 Divine was sentenced to a year's imprisonment and a fine of five hundred dollars. On June 9, Lewis J. Smith, the judge in the trial, died of a heart attack at the age of fifty-five. This supposed example of divine justice struck fear into many hearts. Divine was soon freed on appeal.

Peace mission grows   Restaurants were the first Peace Mission businesses. Many others soon followed and provided the mission with much of its revenue. The movement grew nationwide, and the Los Angeles missions were especially successful. Since newspapers portrayed Divine as heading a very large movement, he was courted by the communists. He formulated his own political program, the Righteous Government Platform, to further civil rights and religious reform. Ultimately, he had little impact on electoral politics. In spite of the publicity the Peace Mission generated, the number of followers and sympathizers at the peak was probably about forty to fifty thousand in New York with another ten thousand nationwide. Among these were a substantial number of Garveyites, who came in spite of Divine's insistence on racial integration.

After a period of spectacular growth, 1937 was a year of crisis as a string of events, which had begun the year before, reached a climax. John the Revelator (John Wuest Hunt), a wealthy and unstable white disciple, had sexual relations with seventeen-year-old Delight Jewett, whom he had taken across state lines. His trial for violating the Mann act was a national sensation. Sternly reprimanded by Divine, John the Revelator openly confessed at the trial and took the name of the Prodigal Son as he began his prison sentence. One of the persons testifying for the prosecution was Faithful Mary (Viola Wilson), a former tubercular alcoholic from Georgia who had risen to a prominent position as one of the leading angels in the mission. She had accepted money from a contributor in direct violation of Divine's instructions. Breaking in a spectacular fashion with Divine, she was supported by the Hearst papers and the *New York Amsterdam News* in her allegations of sexual misbehavior against Divine. She repeated these stories in a book, *God, He's Just a Natural Man* (New York: Gailliard Press, 1936). In addition, Peninnah fell sick and entered a hospital, apparently to die. This cast doubt on Divine's promises of earthly immortality. Tensions within the movement as a result of these developments reached such a level that on April 20, followers beat up a process server in New York, forcing Divine to go into hiding. And finally, Verinda Brown won a judgment for four thousand dollars against the movement, which Divine refused to pay.

There was a rebound in 1938. A repentant Faithful Mary, who had turned to drink and drugs after her sponsors abandoned her, returned to the fold although not to her former position of power. Peninnah recovered. The judgment in favor of Brown, however, continued to hang over Divine's head. Thus, after the final failure of appeals in 1942, Divine could appear in Harlem only on Sundays since New York law did not allow subpoenas to be served on that day.

The institutional response to these difficulties was a gradual restructuring of the Peace Mission and its eventual incorporation as a church, completed by 1942. Communion banquets were closed to non-members, and relief missions disappeared. The unemployed were no longer allowed to testify, and control of the whole movement was much more centralized. Some political activity continued. Divine managed to collect 250 thousand signatures in support of an anti-lynching bill, but his influence was still slight. With the outbreak of World War II, Divine, the patriotic pacifist, had to guide the mission through the war years.

With the move to Philadelphia, the Peace Mission began a slow decline. Peninnah died in 1943, affecting Divine profoundly. On April 29, 1946, he married a young white Canadian, Sweet Angel (Edna Rose Ritchings), who became the new Mother Divine, or rather, in the movement's view, the same one reincarnated. Divine assigned a black angel to be ever at her side to show that husband and wife remained celibate. In 1953 Mother and Father Divine moved into a large house near Philadelphia. The house, Woodmont, became the center of the movement and a place of pilgrimage. It was a serene setting for an aging and increasingly frail Divine, who was rumored to be suffering from arteriosclerosis and diabetes. He ceased public appearances in 1963 and died on September 10, 1965. His earthly remains are in a "Shrine to Life" at Woodmont. His followers speak always of him in the present tense and set a place for him at Communion banquets. Mother Divine has skillfully continued to lead a movement that is dwindling as its members age and few recruits join.

In folk memory Divine is still maligned. He was caricatured in a 1980 television film on Jim Jones and the People's Temple. *The National Enquirer* reprinted old hostile stories in connection with the Jim and Tammy Bakker scandal in 1987. Divine did lead a cult that radically reshaped members' beliefs and controlled their behavior. Still, for many persons, including some who stayed only for a time, he offered stability and a chance to integrate personality denied by the outside world. Father Divine and his Peace Mission form an interesting chapter in the history of religion and throw much light on relations between the races during his era.—ROBERT L. JOHNS

AARON **DOUGLAS**
1899–1979
Artist, educator

From early in his life Aaron Douglas demonstrated a refusal to accept the limits that his country placed on African Americans in the early part of the twentieth century. Optimistic, adventurous, and self-confident, he was determined to become an artist, committed to receiving the best training possible, and convinced that he should play a role in the changing fortunes and fate of his race. It was this unflinching resolve and dogged faith in his own ability that led Douglas to become the primary illustrator of the Harlem Renaissance and one of the most significant African American artists of the twentieth century.

Douglas was born in Topeka, Kansas, on May 26, 1899. His father, also named Aaron, had worked as a baker in Nashville, Tennessee. His mother was a native of Alabama. Douglas had several brothers and sisters. The Douglas family experienced constant financial struggle through his childhood, but his parents insisted that he pursue an education. Determined to continue his studies after graduating from high school, Douglas went north to the factories in Detroit, Michigan, and Dunkirt, New York, to make money to pay for school. After completing work in several factory jobs, Douglas returned to Topeka late in 1917. His had been a successful adventure, and whetted his appetite for more.

Douglas spent a month in Topeka and then left for Lincoln and the University of Nebraska (UNL). He wrote in his autobiography in the Douglas Collection at Fisk University that he became "the fair-haired boy" of the UNL Art Department when he received first prize for drawing. Douglas's first serious painting was created the first or second year of college, as part of a rigorous course in the drawing of plaster casts. At Lincoln, Douglas deepened his acquaintance with the writings of W. E. B. Du Bois and began to ponder the larger dimensions of the nation's racial situation. By 1921 Douglas had become a constant reader of *Crisis*, then of *Opportunity* magazine. As Douglas wrote in a speech for Fisk University's Negro Culture Workshop:

> The poems and stories, and to a lesser degree the pictures and illustrations were different. The poems and other creative works were *by* Negroes and *about* Negroes. And in the case of one poet, Langston Hughes, they seemed

to have been created in a firm and technique that was in some way consonant or harmonious with the ebb and flow of Negro life.

After four years of hard work, Douglas received his bachelor of fine arts degree from the University of Nebraska in 1922. He worked various jobs to obtain the diploma, including tough physical labor. He came to regard the drudgery as simply one more dimension of his artistic preparation. He wrote in his autobiography, "Fortunately, this experience proved to be the best possible training and orientation for the creation and interpretation of the life that I was later called on to depict." Douglas always sympathized with and even romanticized the role of the laborer, whose experience he had briefly shared.

In 1923 Douglas received a bachelor of arts degree from the University of Kansas. After college, Douglas secured a job as teacher of art at Lincoln High School in Kansas City, Missouri. His teaching experience in Kansas City provided more than a secure income. Douglas experienced an enlightenment of his own on a small scale when he met William L. Dawson, a black musician with whom he developed a lifelong friendship. According to his personal writings, Douglas felt this was more than just a chance meeting of two young ambitious artists of "like mind and purpose." For Douglas, it was an "embryo, or first step" of a Renaissance or revival. Finding someone of common racial and cultural background who lived and worked "in the same milieu" made all the difference. He no longer felt isolated, a feeling he later called "the cross the Black artist had to bear, who was often isolated physically, as well as in time, interest and outlook." This desire to overcome isolation would play a critical role in his decision to go to Harlem.

Douglas's confidante through this period was Alta Sawyer, a bright young teacher who was very unhappily married to someone else. The two fell in love and remained determined someday to be together. Over a period of two years, they wrote wonderful love letters that have provided some of the very best information on Douglas's hopes and dreams. Alta Sawyer was his main support, but he also had friends who encouraged him to submit his works to new avenues. While still in Kansas City, Douglas received letters from a friend in Harlem urging him to enter his work in a competition sponsored by *Survey Graphic* magazine for a special 1925 issue it planned on "Negro life in Harlem." As it turned out, Douglas was profoundly impressed by the spectacular issue of the magazine, which would later be expanded into Alain Locke's *New Negro*. *Survey Graphic* was, Douglas explained in his "Harlem Renaissance" speech, "the most cogent single factor that eventually turned my face to New York," and *The New Negro* "eventually proved to be one of the most extraordinary books of the period and more clearly than any other single publication reflects the nature and extent of this unique movement." Douglas decided to make the move to New York.

Studies with Winold Reiss   Upon Douglas's arrival in Harlem, he almost immediately began to study with Bavarian artist Winold Reiss, who had provided the cover of *Survey Graphic* featuring Roland Hayes. He greatly admired the forthright manner in which Reiss portrayed blacks, and Reiss encouraged him to paint his own people in a way that he felt only a black man could accomplish.

In moving to what had become the largest black city in the United States, Douglas sought to end the isolation from other blacks that had hindered his artistic growth. One can see Douglas's growth and experimentation through his magazine illustrations, where he created some of his most forceful and interesting works and through which his artistic language evolved, immersed in African art in a way no other American artist had to date. His work was made up of murals that included lessons from African American history. As a result, a new passion for African art took hold in many of the Harlem Renaissance artists of the 1920s and 1930s, a passion that would spread across the country.

African American artists previously had no opportunity to truly explore a connection with Africa, but for the first time, during the Harlem Renaissance, several visual artists, led by Douglas, began to incorporate Africanisms in their work. This trend did not just occur in painting and sculpture, but in illustrations as well. Illustrators had the unique ability to bring African imagery to a large and varied audience, and Douglas was the ideal person to carry out this mission.

Becomes Harlem Renaissance artist Within weeks of his arrival in Harlem in 1925, Douglas was recruited by the NAACP's W. E. B. Du Bois, editor of the *Crisis*, and the Urban League's *Opportunity* editor Charles S. Johnson, to create illustrations to accompany articles on lynching, segregation, theatre, and political issues as well as poems and stories. Within this largely literary movement, Douglas was hired to create a visual message for a public that had grown dramatically with the increase of black migration to the North during World War I. Du Bois had complained often in the *Crisis* of a lack of black patronage and a black audience, most notably in his "Criteria of Negro Art" in the October 1926 issue. It was his hope that Douglas could reach a new emerging black public across the United States, starting with Harlem. The *Crisis* had a wide national readership, and any illustrations Douglas made, which frequently appeared on its cover, were seen in libraries, schools, and homes across the country. Douglas tried to reach this new black middle class public with the language of African art as one of his most important tools.

Douglas was unsure of his abilities as an artist when he first started illustrating for the *Crisis*. He stated in his speech, "Harlem Renaissance,"

> These first efforts, as I recall them, cannot by any stretch of the imagination be described as masterful . . . but . . . they seemed to have been so readily accepted at the time. As I remember now, they were gladly received with no questions asked. They seemed to have been in a miraculous way [a] heaven-sent answer to some deeply felt need for this kind of visual imagery. As a result, I became a kind of fair-haired boy and was treated in some ways like a prodigal son. I began to feel like the missing piece that all had been looking for to complete or round out the idea of the Renaissance.

Douglas tried to carry out Du Bois's wishes by creating a new, positive, African-influenced black image for his audience. He was tired of the white man's depictions of blacks and felt his work could touch the black audience in a unique way. He wanted to bring the language of African art to Harlem, and then across the United States. Douglas explained in a 1925 letter to Alta Sawyer, located in the Douglas papers in the Schomburg Collection,

> We are possessed, you know, with the idea that it is necessary to be white, to be beautiful. Nine times out of ten it is just the reverse. It takes lots of training or a tremendous effort to down the idea that thin lips and a straight nose is the apogee of beauty. But once free you can look back with a sigh of relief and wonder how anyone could be so deluded.

The May 1926 issue of the *Crisis* provides an ideal example of Aaron Douglas's signature style. Du Bois published Douglas's "Poster of the Krigwa Players Little Negro Theatre of Harlem" in the issue, not attached to any particular play, but rather as a type of advertisement for Du Bois's theatre project. This illustration is heavily influenced by Egyptian and African imagery. It is in solid black and white, very boldly executed, almost resembling a woodblock print. The poster shows a single figure, sitting in a cross-legged position, with his or her face turned to the side in profile. The figure is very angular, a primarily rectilinear form, with exaggerated thick lips, the appearance of tribal make-up in geometric form, an afro hairstyle, and a large hoop earring dangling from the only visible ear. Stylized plants and flowers, resembling both African motifs and Art Deco patterning, surround the figure, as does a palm tree. The figure's left hand holds an African mask or ancestral head. Above the figure the influence of Egypt is everywhere, with pyramids on the left, a sun form above, and a sphinx on the right. Wave patterns form the bottom one-third of the composition, perhaps representing the Nile. The obvious inspiration is Africa, and no matter the extent to which the work is based on actual African imagery, the viewer can see the connections immediately.

In the spirit of the Harlem Renaissance, Douglas often collaborated with other artists of the movement, especially his good friend, poet Langston Hughes. In his December 21, 1925, letter to Hughes, located at Yale University, Douglas said of their collaboration:

> Your problem, Langston, my problem, no our problem is to conceive, develop, establish an art era. Not white art painted black. . . . Let's bare our arms and plunge them deep through disappointment, into the very depths of the souls of our people and drag forth material crude, rough, neglected. Then let's sing it, dance it, write it, paint it. Let's do the impossible. Let's create something transcendentally material, mystically objective. Earthy. Spiritually earthy. Dynamic.

In addition to his magazine illustrations, Douglas turned to a more radical publication. Late in the summer of 1926, a group of Harlem artists, including Douglas, created the publication *Fire!!* to lash back at the limits on artistic freedom. Only one issue of *Fire!!* ever appeared, yet it was important because it showed the artists' effort to break from the confines of Harlem leadership, both black and white, and express themselves freely and without censorship to a younger, separatist, more militant black audience.

Douglas's book illustrations exhibit his innovative draftsmanship, a skill that impressed both authors and publishers. They are executed in the same style as the magazine illustrations, heavily influenced by Art Deco, Art Nouveau, Synthetic Cubism, and Egyptian art. Some examples of Douglas's work have been lost, since his cover jackets in the 1920s are no longer used on reprinted copies of the books. His more notable illustrations include his work for Alain Locke's *New Negro*, for James Weldon Johnson's *God's Trombones*, and for Paul Morand's *Black Magic*. One of Douglas's most striking images was that of Brutus Jones in *Plays of Negro Life*, which accompanied *The Emperor Jones*. This also appeared in the magazine *Theatre Arts Monthly*. Jones appears with a hard silhouette outline. The surrounding forest is made up of jagged edge. *Forest Fear* is a particularly successful example of the dramatic flat, hard-edge, cut-out Douglas style.

Douglas paints murals   Some of Douglas's most important commissions came with his murals. He executed a number of important works based on African and African American history, including his impressive series in Cravath Hall at Fisk University, created to represent a panorama of the history of black people in the New World, beginning in Africa and culminating with freedom symbolized by Fisk's Jubilee Hall.

Douglas's most famous mural series was executed in 1935, his Marxist-inspired WPA murals now at the Schomburg Center in Harlem. Douglas's large murals chronicled the struggle of the black man and woman from Africa, through slavery, emancipation, and their role as workers in the industrial age. The murals appealed directly to a public suffering from the harsh conditions of unemployment and poverty. They show Douglas's talent as a colorist and storyteller.

Douglas spent 1928 studying at the Barnes Foundation in Merion, Pennsylvania, and 1931 in Paris. But the majority of his career was spent as the founding chairman of the Art Department at Fisk University in Nashville, Tennessee. He loved teaching and hoped he could bring his unique experiences as the premier visual artist of the Harlem Renaissance to his students at Fisk. While at Fisk he studied at Columbia University for four consecutive fall terms and received a master of fine arts degree in 1944. He remained in Nashville from 1937 until his death in 1979.

Douglas was always interested in painting the common man, the common experience, the average worker. The mural commissions for the Countee Cullen Library, executed in 1934 when Douglas was thirty-five years old, marked the most politically vocal point in Douglas's career. Douglas led the illustrators of the Harlem Renaissance in his quest to explore their African heritage. Douglas was unique in his efforts because he was the first black artist in the United States to consistently create racial art, and as an illustrator was able to reach a vast readership through black magazines. He had to confront the problem of trying to reach a public that was still difficult to define and locate, and was geographically isolated. Despite these challenges, Douglas was successful in his efforts to address important issues to a growing black middle class. He was sought after repeatedly by black leaders to illustrate their messages and received regular commissions until his departure from Harlem in 1937. Douglas brought African art in his work to Harlem in a new, accessible, immediate way, and then, through his illustrations, to America. In addition to his murals and other drawings, he designed book plates and did portraits of such black luminaries as Mary McLeod Bethune, Charles S. Johnson, and John W. Work. He was the first African American artist, indeed American artist of any race, to regularly incorporate African imagery into his work. Douglas's message was one of pride in African heritage that found a life beyond the white fascination with what was called "primitivism." It was a message that would find a rebirth in the work of later artists and subsequent movements.

As a teacher, Douglas reminded his students that despite their struggles in contemporary America, they should remain optimistic and hopeful in keeping their eyes on the prize, a credo he maintained throughout his career.

Douglas died of natural causes in his Nashville home on February 2, 1979, when he was seventy-nine years old. His ashes were shipped to New York for burial beside his wife, Alta Douglas. After his death, an art and scholarship fund was established at Fisk University. In 1972 the Aaron Douglas Wing, a large art gallery, was established in his honor in the university library.—AMY KIRSCHKE

CHARLES R. **DREW**

1904–1950

Physician, educator, athlete

Committed to the principle of service to humanity, Charles R. Drew worked long and tedious hours. His tireless efforts catapulted him into international prominence as the pioneer of the preservation of blood plasma and the establishment of blood banks for emergency needs. His system for the safe storage of blood plasma saved thousands of military lives during World War II, and laid the foundation for the blood program of the American Red Cross. It was this contribution to humanity that earned him the title of "Father of Blood Plasma."

Born in Washington, D.C., on June 3, 1904, Charles Richard Drew was the eldest of five children born to Richard T. and Nora Burrell Drew. His father was a carpet-layer; his mother was a graduate of Miner Normal School in Washington and was known for her beauty and graciousness. Drew grew up in a cultured, Christian, and close-knit family. His primary education was completed at Stevens Elementary School in 1918, and Paul Lawrence Dunbar High School in 1922. It is during these years that he developed leadership skills and competitive qualities through his abilities as a good student and a gifted athlete. At the age of eight he began to compete in swimming. He gained swimming experience paddling around in the harbor of Washington's Foggy Bottom, a poor section of the city, and later at the 12th Street YMCA. By age nine he had won a medal for swimming. During his four years at Dunbar he participated in track, football, basketball, and baseball. For his athletic prowess he received the James E. Walker Memorial Trophy for two consecutive years and was acknowledged by his senior classmates as the best athlete, the most popular student, and the one who had done the most for Dunbar.

Immediately following high school, Drew entered Amherst College in Massachusetts on an athletic scholarship. During his freshman year he was the star player on the football team and won a letter in track. He was selected for the renowned All Little Three Elevens as the halfback in 1924 and 1925. Also during his junior year, he won the Thomas W. Ashley Memorial Trophy as the most valuable player on the football team. The years he played on the football team were not unlike Jackie Robinson's experience as the first black major league baseball player for the Brooklyn Dodgers. According to his wife, Lenore Robbins Drew, in the *Reader's Digest,* Drew endured "racial slurs both on and off the field. The insults made him flush the dangerous, dark red color that earned him the nickname 'Big Red.' He controlled his temper though, for he had decided that our people—any people—could make real progress by doing and showing than by any amount of violent demonstration."

As a senior, he was elected captain of the track team, won the National Junior AAU Championship in the 120-yard hurdles, and won honorable mention for All-American eastern halfback in football. For his outstanding athletic ability in five sports, Amherst honored him with the Pentathlon Award. At his graduation in 1926, his crowning moment came when he was awarded the Howard Hill Mossman Trophy, an annual award given to the student who had contributed the most to athletics during his four years at Amherst.

Dr. Charles Drew.

Writing in the November 1973 *Negro History Bulletin,* Anne Bittker speculated that a football injury requiring surgery, which Drew received while playing at Amherst, encouraged him to select medicine as a career. After graduation he had hoped to attend medical school; however, financial debts delayed his plans. In order to pay off some of his debts, he worked two years as director of athletics and instructor of biology at Morgan College in Baltimore, Maryland. Within two years he had transformed the school's football and basketball teams from "insignificant quality to championship caliber," Montague W. Cobb wrote in the *Negro History Bulletin* for June 1950. Although he had gained an extraordinary reputation as a coach, his ultimate goal was a medical career. To realize this dream, he first made application to Howard University Medical School, but was denied admission because of what Anne Bittker called "a technical insufficiency of points."

In 1928, Drew was accepted at Magill Medical College in Montreal, Canada. At Magill he won first prize in the annual neuroanatomy competition; membership in Alpha Omega Alpha, the medical honorary scholastic fraternity; a $1,000 Rosenwald Fellowship; and in his senior year the Williams prize, awarded annually on the basis of a competitive examination to the top five men in the graduating class. Despite stiff competition, he earned the top honors. In athletics he won the Canadian championships in hurdles, high jump and broad jump, scoring in one meet an all-time record of sixty-six points. He also served as captain of the track team in 1931.

In 1933 at the age of twenty-nine, Drew graduated with high honors and received the degrees of M.D. and C.M. (Master of Surgery) from Magill. After graduating, he spent one year as an intern at the Royal Victoria and another as a resident at Montreal general hospitals. After completing his residency, he switched from internal medicine to surgery.

In 1935, Drew accepted a faculty position at Howard University Medical School as instructor in pathology. That year he lost his father. As the eldest son, he now became head of the family. The following year he became a resident in surgery at Freedmen's Hospital, a federally-operated hospital affiliated with Howard. Two years later, in 1938, he was awarded simultaneously a two-year Rockefeller fellowship for graduate work at Columbia University and a residency in surgery at Presbyterian Hospital, both in New York.

Conducts research on blood plasma   At Columbia, while working on his doctorate, Drew became a research assistant to John Scudded and worked with a team on blood chemistry. The major problem they faced was how to increase the time blood could be stored. In his research he dealt with blood chemistry, but he was about to deal with matters of the heart. In April 1939, while on his way to a medical convention in Tuskegee Institute in Alabama, Drew stopped over in Atlanta, Georgia, for a dinner party. There he met Lenore Robbins, twenty-eight, a home economics teacher at Spelman College. Due to his previous professional obligation, he left Atlanta without telling Robbins of his feelings. Three nights later he returned to Atlanta. Not wanting to wait to tell her about his love interest, she remembered in the *Reader's Digest* article, "he roused the matron of our dormitory at one o'clock in the morning and insisted that she wake me. I went down to meet Dr. Drew on the moonlit campus. He proposed and six months later we were married."

After the marriage, Lenore Drew moved to New York. Any hopes of spending long hours with her husband were dashed. Charles Drew had three time-consuming jobs: one as a member of a research team, a second as an assistant research surgeon, and a third completing his doctor of medical science degree. His wife protested that he could not manage an eighteen-hour-a-day work schedule. Realizing that she would see little of her husband, Lenore Drew volunteered as a laboratory assistant. Columbia University awarded Charles a doctorate in medical science in 1940.

Only a year after World War II had started, Drew published his dissertation thesis entitled "Banked Blood: A Study of Blood Preservation," which proposed the storing of plasma rather than whole blood in blood banks. With the help of the research team, he demonstrated that plasma, unlike whole blood, could be stored for months unrefrigerated without spoiling. In addition, patients could receive plasma without matching blood types. Three months after Drew returned to Howard, John Beattie, a former teacher of anatomy and a close friend, suggested Drew as the medical supervisor of the Blood for Britain Project. On a leave of absence from Howard, he returned to New York to serve in this capacity. In February 1941 Drew was appointed director of the American Red Cross Blood Bank located at New York's Presbyterian Hospital. He also became assistant for the National Research Council's blood procurement program. In the latter position he was in charge of blood for use by the army and navy.

As a result of his administrative and organizational skills, the collection and shipping of blood plasma to Great Britain and the national blood bank program were successes. By 1941, Britain had taken over its blood bank operations and the American Red Cross had set up blood donor stations to collect blood plasma for the American war effort. After three months the program was operating smoothly. However, the issue of race led Drew to resign as director of the American Red Cross Blood Bank. The Armed Forces directed the Red Cross to accept only Caucasian blood for transfusion to members of the military forces. In his resignation statement, published in the *New York Times,* Drew said:

> I feel that the ruling of the United States Army and Navy regarding the refusal
> of colored blood donors is an indefensible one from any point of view. There
> is no scientific basis for the separation of the blood of different races except
> on the basis of the individual blood types or groups.

After his resignation, Drew returned to Howard University to become professor of surgery and medical director of Freedmen's Hospital. As he embarked on a third career, teaching, Drew now turned all of his enthusiasm to training well-qualified and skilled surgeons. During Drew's nine-year tenure at Howard, over half the nation's black surgeons who received A.B.S. certification studied directly under him.

Many different groups recognized Drew's research, scholarly articles, and contributions to science. Among the awards he received were the E. S. Jones Award for Research in Medical Science in 1942; the Spingarn Medal of the NAACP for his work on the British and American blood plasma projects in 1944; an honorary degree of D.Sc. from Virginia State College in 1945; and the same degree from Amherst College in 1947. He was elected a Fellow of the International College of Surgeons in 1946; and in the summer of 1949, he was the first black to serve as a surgical consultant to the Surgeon General of the United States Army.

In March 1950, Drew left with three other doctors, John R. Ford, Walter R. Johnson, and Samuel Bullock, to attend the annual John A. Andrew Clinic in Tuskegee, Alabama. Around 7:30 a.m. near Burlington, North Carolina, Drew's car overturned. Shortly after arriving at the hospital, he died from severe chest injuries. There are conflicting reports of the care Drew received. He was taken to the Alamance County Hospital where *Crisis* magazine reported that he received "excellent care, including blood and plasma transfusions, but died about forty-five minutes after the accident." The *New York Times* reported that he was taken to a "segregated hospital that did not have any blood plasma that might have saved his life."

Drew, forty-five years old, left behind his wife, three daughters, and a son. Services were held at the 19th Street Baptist Church in Washington, D.C., a church he had attended since his childhood. On the day of the funeral, it has been reported that flags at some government buildings in Washington and Great Britain were flown at half-mast. Years later, a monument honoring Drew for his work was erected on the road near the site of his death.

Charles Drew was a public servant of the world. His research with blood and blood plasma enriched and saved the lives of many in war and peace. According to Anne Bittker, Drew once said, "There must always be the continuing struggle to make the world bear some fruit in increasing understanding and in the production of human happiness."—PATRICIA A. PEARSON

W. E. B. **DU BOIS**

1868–1963

Writer, scholar, activist, Pan Africanist

If a "Renaissance-man" is one with a stinging wit, an impeccable education, a profound knowledge of human history and culture, a "gentleman's good taste" in art, music, and theater, and a philosopher's vision for a better humanity, then for African Americans that person could easily be William Edward Burghardt Du Bois. Du Bois's career as a first rate scholar-activist through writing and organizing is unprecedented in the modern era.

Du Bois was born three years after the American Civil War on February 23, 1868, in Great Barrington, Massachusetts. His mother was Mary Sylvania Burghardt, a short and attractive brown-skinned woman who worked most of her life as a domestic in Great Barrington. His mulatto father, Alfred Du Bois, was a descendent of French Huguenot ancestry from Haiti and a barber by trade. In Du Bois's recollection, his father was "run off by the clannishness of the Black Burghardts who disliked his father's light-skinned complexion." Perhaps for this reason Alfred Du Bois left his wife and infant son in 1869 before Du Bois was two years old. Du Bois also had an older brother of five years named Adelbert.

The "Burghardt clan" was the family that Du Bois grew up with, and included his mother, older brother, aunts, uncles, and cousins. Though most of the Burghardts were literate, Du Bois (or Willie, as he was affectionately called in his youth), became the first of this poor, working-class black family to graduate from high school in 1884. "Ordinary farmers and laborers," he wrote in *Dusk of Dawn*, the Burghardts were to Du Bois "primarily Dutch and New England in outlook." It was this lineage that determined his life as a black man. Great Barrington, located in western Massachusetts, was not free from prejudice, but he considered it more a "prejudice of income and ancestry than of color."

Du Bois knew much less about his father, although he was able to trace his father's ancestry to a seventeenth-century white French Huguenot farmer residing in the West Indies named Chretien Du Bois. Further down the lineage was Du Bois's grandfather, the short, stern Alexander Du Bois, who was light enough to pass for white but choose a black identity instead.

From Great Barrington to the university

As a young boy Du Bois was obedient, hard working, and diligent at school. He added to his mother's limited income by working odd jobs after school such as mowing lawns, selling newspapers and tea, and writing for the *Springfield Republican*. In 1883, at age fifteen, he wrote for T. Thomas Fortune's *New York Age* (later the *New York Globe*) covering church activity and community fraternal organizations.

He attended Great Barrington High School from 1881 to 1885 and excelled academically with an almost perfect attendance record. He learned the basics of reading, writing, spelling, grammar, and history, normally outdoing his white counterparts. He was the only black student to attend the school and was popular with his white classmates. His high school principal, Frank Hosmer, recognizing the young lad's intelligence, encouraged him to attend college, as did a local white Congregationalist minister named C. C. Painter. As valedictorian of his graduating class in 1885, Du Bois gave a masterful speech about the great abolitionist Wendell Phillips, which received praise in a local newspaper.

W. E. B. Du Bois.

Though Harvard University was his first and only choice for college, its high admission standards, which his high school did not satisfy, delayed his admittance. The local Congregationalist church, with Painter and principal Hosmer in full support, raised money to send the young Du Bois south to Fisk University, a small, black, liberal arts college in Nashville, Tennessee. This turn of events, however, proved to be an invaluable experience for Du Bois. Fisk was his introduction to the land of the South—a region he had only read about and knew through stories, and a region culturally different from his conservative northern background.

Du Bois entered Fisk University in 1885 at age seventeen and was granted sophomore status. At Fisk Du Bois met what seemed to him "a beautiful world of Black folk with various shades and extraordinary color." His southern colleagues brought to him their experiences of mob violence, lynching, and naked Jim Crow segregation that plagued the southern black communities of the post–Civil War South of 1865–1890.

Du Bois was determined that these black students should become the trained, educated elite that would protect and advance the race forward. From a liberal, northern-trained white faculty that included only one black professor, Du Bois learned Greek, mathematics, philosophy, and science. He became concerned with local and national events and edited the school newspaper, the *Fisk Herald*.

One of the more profound experiences Du Bois encountered, however, was teaching summer school in the rural back area of east Tennessee between school terms. For the first time he heard what he later called the "sorrow songs," the old Negro spirituals of the black church. These gripping songs moved Du Bois to tears as they were a testament of how blacks survived through slavery and freedom. The people he met during these summers were humble and poor, yet lively and expressive compared to those in his reserved Massachusetts. Though he taught in dilapidated one-room school houses without chalk, black board, or desks, he was impressed with the number of black students of all ages determined to get an education. Upon graduation from Fisk in 1888, with excellent recommendation from the faculty, Du Bois entered Harvard University but was required to do so at the undergraduate level. He received the Price Greenleaf Award of $300 dollars towards tuition, majored in philosophy under the tutelage of the famed professor William James, and received a second bachelor's degree, the A.B., in 1890. The following year he obtained his master's degree and traveled abroad to the University of Berlin from 1892 to 1894, studying sociology and economics. He almost completed the requirement for a degree from Berlin when time and money ran out. Forced to come back to Harvard, William James steered him away from philosophy into history, considered more practical for earning a living. In 1896, Du Bois won his Ph.D. in history at Harvard under the tutelage of Albert Bushnell Hart and wrote a dissertation on "The Suppression of the African Slave Trade." Du Bois, with a Harvard Ph.D. and having traveled abroad, was prepared for the life of a black intellectual.

Du Bois as scholar-activist   Du Bois was prolific as a scholar, author, editor, writer, and social activist. He combined his scholarship with organized social protest from 1896 to 1963, producing an enormous amount of written work in history and sociology as well as critical pieces about current events. His amazing ability to utilize the unique insights of so many disciplines gave his work depth and beauty. Beginning with his dissertation, published in 1896—the first of the Harvard historical studies project—Du Bois commenced a long career of examining key aspects of the black experience. In his work he showed America's failure to stop the Trans-Atlantic slave trade of Africans because of economic considerations, even though its abolition was a matter of morally and the enforcement of constitutional law.

In 1897 Du Bois became a founding member of the American Negro Academy with one of the greatest black intellectuals of the nineteenth century, Alexander Crummel. In a pamphlet entitled *Conservation of the Races*, Du Bois wrote: "We need our race organizations . . . we must lead our own liberation." The following year, while professor at the University of Pennsylvania, Du Bois produced *The Philadelphia Negro* (1899), which introduced the study of urban sociology to America. It revealed the historic cause and context of conditions in Philadelphia's black seventh ward at the turn of the century. Personally interviewing some 3,000 families, Du Bois showed that good social theory grows out of carefully gathered facts.

In 1900 he attended the Pan African Conference in London, England, called by the Trinidadian barrister Henry Sylvester Williams. Du Bois would add further clarity to Williams's revolutionary concept that all people of African decent, regardless of national origin, are tied to a common destiny in a world dominated by whites, particularly the European powers France and England. Du Bois wanted Ethiopia—then called Abyssinia—Liberia, and Haiti, the only free black republics, to remain independent. He was prophetic about the future of the black world, writing:

The millions of Black men in Africa, America, and the islands of the sea, not to speak of the Brown and Yellow myriads elsewhere, are bound to have great influence upon the world in the future by reason of sheer numbers and physical contact.

While professor of economics and history at Atlanta University 1898–1909, he produced his most popular book, *The Souls of Black Folk* (1903). These fourteen passionately-written essays sought to explain in beautiful, almost poetic prose "the meaning of being Black in America at the turn of the century." The book contained Du Bois's prophesy that:

the problem of the twentieth century is the problem of the color line, the relation of the darker to the lighter races of men in Asia and Africa, in America and the islands of the sea.

His eloquent explanation of the inner turmoil felt by black Americans he called a "double consciousness" of "un-reconciled ideals" of being both black and American. In *Souls* Du Bois critiqued Booker T. Washington of Tuskegee Institute in Alabama, perhaps the most popular and influential black leader from 1896 to 1915.

Washington's willingness to surrender the ballot and accept second–class citizenship for blacks in exchange for white philanthropic support of industrial and manual training met sharp opposition from Du Bois by 1903. Du Bois's liberal arts education and a strong faith in democracy led him to believe that there could be no black advances without the ballot, citizenship, and higher education in the arts and sciences of a trained black talented elite, which he called "the tenth."

His philosophy took organizational shape in the Niagara Movement of 1905–1909, which advocated total integration of blacks into mainstream society with all the rights, privileges, and benefits of other Americans. A direct challenge to the dominance of Booker T. Washington's "Tuskegee machine," the Niagara Movement was seen in some circles as the "anti–Bookerite camp," which was not far off the mark.

During these same years at Atlanta University, beginning in 1898, Du Bois edited the Atlanta University Publications, which were sociological investigations of important areas of black life, such as business, education, and religion. Though he left Atlanta in 1909, he continued to co-edit the proceedings of the annual conferences through 1913.

In addition, Du Bois edited two short-lived periodicals: the *Moon Illustrated Weekly* and *Horizon: A Journal of the Color Line*. The *Moon* lasted from December 1905 through July 1906 and was followed by *Horizon*, which lasted from January 1907 to July 1910 and appeared irregularly. These magazines covered an array of topics, from current events in other parts of the world to race relations, art, politics, education, and even good literature.

Du Bois joins NAACP   In 1909 Du Bois became a member of the NAACP, a multiracial civil rights organization founded by blacks and liberal whites to aid in the black uplift movement. The Atlanta University professor, upon invitation, left Atlanta to join this new group with headquarters in New York. With better funding, organization, and more members, the NAACP was even more of a threat to the conservative politics of Booker T. Washington. In November 1910 Du Bois became director of publications and research and edited the *Crisis* magazine, the NAACP's official organ. Du Bois used the *Crisis* as a private journal to expose his views on nearly every important social issue that confronted the black community, from the presidential election of Woodrow Wilson in 1912 to lynchings and World War I. Thousands of subscribers to the magazine, particularly in the black community, were now kept abreast of local, state, national, and international events that affected their community.

In July 1918 in an article entitled "Close Ranks," Du Bois urged blacks to join the fight against the greater evil of fascism despite blatant American racism at home "while the War lasts." After black soldiers made outstanding contributions to the war effort, Du Bois wrote in "Returning Soldiers" in 1919, "We Return, We Return from Fighting, We Return Fighting!"

In 1920 Du Bois created the *Brownies Book*, an offshoot of the *Crisis,* lasting from January of that year until December of 1921. Designed to reach children, Du Bois wanted black youth to know black history and to appreciate the beauty of their color. Unfortunately, finances aborted many of Du Bois's meaningful and ambitious projects. While engaged in

Du Bois gives one of his many speeches on the plight of African Americans at an NAACP conference.

these projects he wrote *Dark Water: Voices from Within the Veil* (1921), his first of three autobiographies. After candid criticism of NAACP leadership and direction, Du Bois retired under pressure in 1934, having edited the organization's magazine for twenty-four years. He would come back to edit the magazine briefly from 1944 to 1948 at the behest of Walter White.

With Germany's defeat at the end of World War I and the founding of the League of Nations among the European allied powers in 1918, Du Bois revived the concept of Pan Africanism started two decades earlier. His call for African unity was answered and the Pan African Congress convened in Paris in February 1919 (the congress also met in 1921, 1923, and in 1927). Black leaders from the United States, the Caribbean, Africa, and Europe attended this historic event. Du Bois's view was that defeated Germany's colonial territory in southwest Africa should be returned to the Africans who initially owned it. He also advocated the participation of Africans in the European colonial governments in Africa.

Du Bois joined the multi–talented, avowed communist Paul Robeson, who was also an actor, singer, lawyer, and Pan Africanist, in the Council on African Affairs to monitor developments with the colonial situation in Africa in 1939. In 1940 Du Bois created *Phylo*, a periodical established to study race relations during his second tenure as professor at Atlanta University. This same year he wrote his second autobiography *Dusk of Dawn: An Essay Toward an Autobiography of a Race Concept,* which contained most of the information about his ancestry and childhood years.

By the fifth Pan African Congress held in 1945 in Manchester, England, Du Bois was deemed the "Father of Pan Africanism" for his earlier contributions to its theory and organization. At this conference he advised young Africans concerned with the liberation of Africa from European control, such as Ghana's future president, Kwame (Frances) Nkrumah.

In 1946 Du Bois published *The World and Africa,* a sweeping history of Africa's role in world civilization.

In the 1950s Du Bois was leaning more and more towards a socialist conception of the world and became acutely critical of capitalism, a system he felt was incapable of providing food, clothing, and shelter for the masses of working-class people, both black and non-black. Du Bois always believed that there was a connection between world war and who controlled the rich mineral and material resources in Africa. He ran for senator of New York on the Progressive Party ticket and collected a quarter-million votes. He was also chairman of the Peace Information Agency. As a leader in this peace movement, Du Bois was indicted, put on trial, and eventually acquitted for allegedly being a spy for the Russians. This period, known as the McCarthy era, was a time when any citizen with socialist leanings, sympathy for Russian politics, or criticism of the American government was subject to arrest as a foreign agent. Du Bois was used to harassment by the government for his "radical views" most of his adult life.

As a result of the harassment, Du Bois's passport was suspended from 1950 to 1958. After the suspension, he toured Russia and China and became further convinced that the end of world hunger, poverty, disease, and ignorance lay with communism. In 1959, Du Bois celebrated his ninety-first birthday in Peking, China with a speaking engagement. In the *Auto-Biography of W. E. B. Du Bois,* he addressed the nation:

> I speak with no authority of age or rank; I hold no position, I have no wealth.
> One thing alone I own and that is my own soul. Ownership of that I have ever
> while in my own country for near a century I have been nothing but a nigger.

In 1961 he moved to Ghana at the invitation of his younger friend and president of Ghana, Kwame Nkrumah, to work on his long time dream, *Encyclopedia of the Negro*. Never having had funding or time, the giant intellect who for half a century fearlessly defended the race would begin the project at the age of ninety-three. He died around midnight on August 27, 1963, the evening before the March on Washington for Jobs and Freedom.

Du Bois is probably the greatest example of a black intellect in America. It was his vast knowledge and skill at utilizing the specific insights of so many disciplines that made his written work so profound and insightful. The amount of work he produced is so voluminous that his literary executor Herbert Aptheker compares him to Charles Dickens. Henry Louis Gates estimates that his *Annotated Bibliography* of writings in magazines, journals, books, encyclopedias, pamphlets, leaflets, and manifestos balances out to Du Bois writing something scholarly every twelve days of his life for over fifty years. He was indeed a "Renaissance man" in the sense that at the turn of the century, few blacks were trained in history, philosophy, sociology, psychology, literature, and mythology, with the discipline of a scientist and the imagination of the artist. Yet Du Bois wrote twenty books, including three in history and one on sociology; he wrote two novels and a play; he produced studies on religion, business, education, and labor; he organized conferences; he taught at three universities; he wrote hundreds of essays and articles for several newspapers, some of which he submitted weekly; he created periodicals for adults and children; and he was a husband and a father. He remained "cutting edge" for the majority of his adult life and changed as times and circumstances changed. He left his mark through the vision and genius of his writings and certainly will be read for generations to come.—DAVID LEON REED

KATHERINE **DUNHAM**

1909–

Dancer, anthropologist

Taking a bow to a standing ovation for her leadership of Treemonisha, *performed at Southern Illinois University's Carbondale campus in 1972, Katherine Dunham had again lived up to her title as the "Grand Dame of American Dance." And Dunham is still taking bows. She has traveled the world as the guest of kings and rulers, not only performing her brilliant dances but also teaching through them the universal truths that intermingle and bind together the many cultures of the world.*

Her path has carried her far from Glen Ellyn, Illinois, where she was born on June 22, 1909, to Albert Dunham and Fanny June (Taylor) Dunham. Through her ancestral heritage of African, Madagascan, Canadian-French, and American Indian, she was a "small League of Nations—largely black," Terry Harnan observed in her book *African Rhythm—American Dance.*

Dunham opened her first dance school with the help of friends and her Russian dance teacher, Madame Ludmila Speranzeva, during the Great Depression. For the first time, she began to work seriously on choreography. In 1931 Dunham's dancers performed "Negro

Rhapsody" as the first act at the Chicago Beaux Arts Ball and received hearty applause from the audience. However, the good friends who had helped finance the studio were soon out of money, and it was closed. Feeling lonely and perhaps bereft, Dunham married Jordis McCoo, a fellow dancer. In a very short time she realized that she really was unready to forget her dreams and settle down. Fortunately, the marriage demanded very little since she went to school in the daytime and her husband worked nights at the post office. After school she and her friend Ruth Attaway, a drama teacher, looked for an inexpensive place to rent for a studio. They found an old stable with large, open spaces for their classes. It became a gathering place for such personages as Charles Sebree, Charles White, Langston Hughes, Sterling North, Arna Bontemps, Horace Mann, and others. All went well until winter came; lacking fuel to heat the stable properly, they were forced to close.

Katherine Dunham.

Dunham's next school, the Negro Dance Group, was a good stepping-stone, mainly because Madame Speranzeva allowed Dunham the use of her studio for pupils, and she coached Dunham privately in ballet and mime. Through Speranzeva, Dunham was introduced to the Isadora Duncan Dance Company and Fokine. She met Argentina, the famous Spanish dancer, and her partner Escudero. Though the school appeared to flourish, the parents of her black students wanted their daughters to study ballet for the sake of social graces and were concerned that the name of the school meant that they would be taught African dances. Dunham knew that the basic steps of the popular lindy hop, cakewalk, and black bottom had their origins in African tribal dances, but she was also aware that she could not explain this easily to these parents. This whole dilemma worked out for her benefit, however, for through a presentation of Robert Redfield, a professor in ethnology, Dunham decided to study anthropology. Through this door perhaps she could teach blacks not to be satisfied only with imitating others, but rather to develop their own natural talents through hard work and technical training. "I started a thing they called 'dance anthropology'," Dunham explained. "I wanted the study of anthropology and dance put together."

Dunham studies African and West Indian dances   In 1933 Dunham was chosen to hire and train 150 young blacks to present a program for the 1934 Chicago Century of Progress Exposition. Following this honor, in 1935, came a scholarship from the Julius Rosenwald Foundation to help further her studies. In addition to studying the dances of Africa and the West Indies in their native environments, Dunham also studied for approximately three months with Melville Herskovits, head of Northwestern University's African studies, before beginning her travels. This time proved invaluable to her, according to Harnan, and Dunham later called

*Katherine Dunham
in 1946.*

Herskovits "a fantastic guide for getting to the bottom of things, the heart of the matter." At twenty-five years of age she began a career that would take her many times to Europe, Mexico, South America, Africa, Australia, and Japan. This first journey brought her to Jamaica, Martinique, Trinidad, and Haiti.

Upon returning home, Dunham appeared again before the Julius Rosenwald Foundation and spent a memorable evening reporting with music, dancing, pictures, and speech the many experiences of her trip. A short time after this, the Rockefeller Foundation granted her a fellowship for further studies toward her master's degree under the direction of Herskovits. In August of 1936, Dunham graduated from the University of Chicago with a bachelor's degree in anthropology. She later earned a master's degree from the University of Chicago and a Ph.D. from Northwestern University.

One evening in 1938, Dunham, as dance director of the Federal Theatre Project in Chicago, opened a program with *Ballet Fedre*. The next morning's newspapers praised all of the program, according to Harnan, but were wild about the "firey folk ballet with choreography by Katherine Dunham," saying that *L'Ag'Ya* was "danced with enough abandon to make some of the preceding events seem pallid by comparison." Dunham's artistry was beginning to be seen and appreciated. The teachings of Madame Speranzeva with their emphasis on acting and story line as well as the dancing skill, and the work that Dunham had done in Martinique where she had first seen *L'Ag'Ya,* the fighting dance, were very important background influences.

On this same evening came honors for the man who designed the sets and costumes, John Pratt. This 1938 presentation was the first time Pratt and Dunham had worked together as a team, but they later became known throughout the world. Born in Canada, John Pratt was a very tall, handsome white man who was then twenty-four years old. He had designed sets and costumes while studying at the University of Chicago, as well as having his artwork exhibited at a Chicago gallery and university shows. Working together for many months strengthened the ties between Dunham and Pratt. After Dunham received her divorce, she and John Pratt were married in a private ceremony July 10, 1939, in Tecade, Mexico. Happily, in the world of artists in which they moved, color, creed, and nationality mattered little.

"Le Jazz Hot" deemed a phenomenal success   In February 1940 the Katherine Dunham Dance Company opened at the Windsor Theatre, West 48th Street, with Dunham's own *Tropics and Le Jazz Hot*. The show was a phenomenal success. Harnan recalled one critic's words: "Katherine Dunham flared into unsuspecting New York last night like a comet. Unknown before her debut, she is today one of the most talked-about dancers." From this night her name and her dances took her behind the footlights of the world's greatest stages. Her unique technique and stylistic perfection were the forces that propelled her toward that magic moment where the dancer, the dance, and the cultural story become one.

Soon after this success, an offer came for the Dunham Dance Company to take part in an all-Negro musical entitled *Cabin in the Sky*. The salary was three thousand dollars a week, more than any of them had ever dreamed of earning as dancers. Dunham's role was Georgia Brown, and for the first time she had the opportunity not only to dance, but to sing and act as well. The drama had a long and successful run.

Near the end of a most rewarding and successful tour of Mexico and Europe, 1947–1949, Dunham, Pratt, and the members of the troupe welcomed an opportunity to return to Haiti through an invitation from her old friend, Dumarsais Estimé, now president of the island. The warmth and blue water offered a much-needed rest. Before Dunham's first trip to the islands in 1935, she had learned that her brother, Albert, had apparently suffered a mental breakdown. He was under the care of the best doctors available, and it was believed that given time, rest, and treatment, he would recover completely. In May 1949, however, she received the news in Europe that her beloved brother had died. As the year 1949, filled with both joy and sorrow, closed, Dunham received the sad news of her father's death, and also learned that her friend, President Estimé, had been forced to resign and was now exiled from Haiti. Katherine Dunham and John Pratt returned to the United States, and in 1950 she was dancing again for Broadway fans.

In December of 1952 Pratt and Dunham adopted Marie Christine Columbier, a five-year-old French Martinique girl of mixed heritage. For a while she accompanied her new parents on their travels but was eventually sent to school in Switzerland. In the succeeding years, Dunham choreographed several movies and the opera *Aida;* performed all over the United States; toured Europe, Australia, South America, and Asia; and opened a medical clinic in Haiti. In 1959 *A Touch of Innocence,* the story of the first eighteen years of her life, was published.

At the request of President Leopold Sedar Senghor, in 1965 and 1966 Dunham helped train the Senegalese National Ballet and served as technical cultural advisor to Senghor in preparation for the First World Festival of Negro Arts at Dakar, Senegal. Here in Africa, the mother country of all of the dance studies Dunham had made, she felt quite at home. It was in her rented home in Dakar that she finished her frank, captivating, personal narrative *Island Possessed,* about Haiti and its people. In 1969 she and Pratt gave up their house in Dakar to return to the United States. The political unrest was one factor in this decision, but a proposal that Dunham had made in 1965, the East Saint Louis project, was the main impetus for their return.

With this project, Dunham faced one of the biggest challenges of her life. Funding came from several philanthropic organizations who were willing to support the work of Southern Illinois University, but getting to those students she wanted to help was still an unsolved problem in her mind. Through her daughter Marie Christine, now nineteen years old, and Jeanelle Stovall, a vacationing United Nations interpreter, Dunham's door to the students was opened. By December 1967, Dunham had become cultural affairs consultant to the Edwardsville campus of Southern Illinois University. She was also named director of the Performing Arts Training Center and the Dynamic Museum. Her home was located in the East Saint Louis, Illinois, ghetto among the people with whom she expected to work.

The Dynamic Museum was a wonderful teaching aid, for here the objects that the Dunham Dance Company had collected all over the world were displayed, touched, and used. John Pratt was the curator of the museum and his own artistic costumes were on display, along with books, foreign theater posters, programs, records, and films of the dancers at the zenith of their fame. Having started schools of dance, theater, and cultural arts in Chicago, New York, Saint Louis, Haiti, Stockholm, Paris, and Italy, Dunham knew both the rewards and the difficulties that a school can bring; this one offered specific knowledge to students that could not be found elsewhere.

After Dunham retired, she opened the Katherine Dunham Center for the Arts and Humanities, a school and museum, in East Saint Louis. Her husband, John Pratt, died March 3, 1986. Their daughter, Marie Christine, lives in Rome, Italy. An activist in more than just performance art, Dunham helped publicize the plight of Haitian refugees in 1992 with a forty-seven-day fast, protesting U.S. policy that refused admission to the refugees. Dunham, over ninety years old, divides her time between East Saint Louis and Haiti, avoiding the cold winter months that increase the pain of her arthritic condition.

Early in her career Dunham said: "I would feel I'd failed miserably if I were doing dance confined to race, color or creed. I don't think that would be art, which has to do with universal truths." Her life is a testimonial to those universal truths and she surely has not failed. The recipient of numerous accolades, including a Kennedy Center Award for Lifetime Achievement in the Arts, an NAACP Image Award, UNESCO's Gold Medal for Dance, and more than thirty honorary degrees, Dunham has immeasurably enriched humankind through the deeply moving, exquisite message of her dance.—PHYLLIS WOOD

MARIAN WRIGHT **EDELMAN**

1939–
Children's rights crusader

"The children—my own and other people's—became the passion of my personal and professional life. For it is they who are God's presence, promise, and hope for humankind." Marian Wright Edelman, attorney and founding president of the Children's Defense Fund, wrote of her vocation in her 1992 book The Measure of Our Success: A Letter to My Children and Yours. *Edelman has been an advocate for disadvantaged Americans for her entire professional career and is known primarily as a crusader for children's rights.*

Edelman was born the youngest of five children on June 6, 1939, the daughter of Arthur Jerome Wright and Maggie Leola (Bowen) Wright in Bennettsville, South Carolina. Her father was the minister of Shiloh Baptist Church and had been influenced by Booker T. Washington's self-help philosophy. He expected his children to get an education and to serve their community. "The only bad thing about that is that none of us learned how to relax," Edelman recalled in an interview for a lengthy profile that appeared in a 1989 issue of the *New Yorker.* "Working for the community was as much a part of our existence as eating and sleeping and church." Arthur Wright established the Wright Home for the Aged in the segregated town of Bennettsville, and Maggie Wright ran it. Edelman recalls that her father probably never made more than two hundred dollars a month, "but none of us ever felt poor, and compared to the people around us, we weren't." Her father also believed in black role models, and whenever prominent blacks came to town, the Wright children were taken to hear them. Marian was named for Marian Anderson, whom she heard sing as a child. Her father, who had a profound

Marian Wright Edelman.

impact on her development and her priorities, died when Edelman was only fourteen.

After graduating from Marlboro Training High School, Edelman was persuaded by her mother and brother, Harry, to attend Spelman College in Atlanta, Georgia, though her first choice was Fisk University in Nashville, Tennessee. "I hated the idea of going to a staid women's college," she observed, "but it turned out to be the right place for me after all." She entered Spelman in 1956. Because of her outstanding scholarship, she won a Charles Merrill grant for study abroad during her junior year. She spent the first summer at the Sorbonne University studying French civilization but decided to spend the remainder of the academic year at the University of Geneva in Switzerland.

During the second semester, Edelman studied for two months in the Soviet Union under a Lisle Fellowship; because of her interest in Tolstoy, she had always wanted to go to Russia. After her travels in Europe over the course of a year and two summers, she returned to Spelman a different person: "It was a great liberating experience. After a year's freedom as a person, I wasn't prepared to go back to a segregated existence," she recalled. In 1959, the year of sit-ins and the first student protests in the South, she returned to Atlanta for her senior year and became active in the embryonic civil rights movement that was to alter profoundly United States race relations in the South. During her senior year in 1960, she participated in one of the largest sit-ins in Atlanta at City Hall. Fourteen students were arrested, including Edelman. It was during this time that she decided to go to law school instead of pursuing graduate work in Russian studies at Georgetown University, which would have prepared her for a career in foreign service. During this time she also became aware that civil rights lawyers were scarce and sorely needed.

Edelman fights for freedom and equality After graduating as valedictorian of her Spelman class in 1960, she applied to Yale University Law School and entered as a John Hay Whitney Fellow. In 1963, during spring break of her last year in law school, she went to Mississippi and got involved in the voter registration drive, which her friend, Robert Moses, led as a field secretary for the Student Nonviolent Coordinating Committee. She returned to New Haven, graduated from Yale in 1963, and after a year's training in New York went to Jackson, Mississippi, as one of the first two NAACP Legal Defense and Education Fund interns. In the spring of 1964 she opened a law office and continued civil rights work, which consisted largely of getting students out of jail. During this time she was threatened by dogs, thrown into jail, and, before taking the Mississippi bar, refused entry into a state courthouse.

Asked if at that time she despaired about the law as a viable instrument of social change, she replied, "Sure, like every morning. But one keeps plugging, trying to make our institutional processes work." At age twenty-six, she became the first black woman to pass the bar in Mississippi. Her civil rights crusading continued when she headed the NAACP Legal Defense and Education Fund in Mississippi from 1964 to 1968. Edelman wrote about her intense commitment to liberation and struggle after her return from a year abroad in an article that appeared in the Spelman *Messenger:*

> I realize that I am not fighting just for myself and my people in the South, when I fight for freedom and equality. I realize now that I fight for the moral and political health of America as a whole and for her position in the world at large . . . as I push the cause for freedom a step further, by gaining my own. . . .

Marian Wright Edelman
celebrating Children's Day.

I know that I, in my individual struggle for improvement, help the world. I am no longer an isolated being—I belong. Europe helped me to see this.

While in Mississippi, she met Peter Edelman, a Harvard law school graduate and one of Robert Kennedy's legislative assistants, who was working in 1967 on the Senate's Subcommittee on Employment, Manpower, and Poverty. She was going through a transition, realizing that in order to change things in Mississippi, she had to affect federal policy. After receiving a Field Foundation grant to study how to make laws work for the poor, she moved to Washington, D.C., in March 1968 and started the Washington Research Project. This was a difficult time for the nation and the movement. Martin Luther King Jr. had been assassinated in April, and Robert Kennedy was shot two months later. In July Marian Wright married Peter Edelman, one of the Kennedy aides who, after Kennedy's death, received Ford Foundation grants to help in the transition to other careers.

211

In 1971 the Edelmans left Washington and moved to Boston, where Peter became vice president of the University of Massachusetts and Marian became director of the Harvard University Center for Law and Education. She flew to Washington weekly to oversee the activities of the Washington Research Project. By this time their interracial marriage had produced two sons, Joshua and Jonah. Ezra was born in 1974.

Edelman establishes child advocacy group   In 1973 Edelman founded the Children's Defense Fund (CDF), a nonprofit child advocacy organization based in Washington, D.C. Its mission was to provide systematic and long-range assistance to children and to make their needs an important matter of public policy. Her work with the CDF and her passionate devotion to the rights of children have brought her national recognition as "the children's crusader." The Edelmans returned to Washington in 1979, where Peter Edelman obtained a teaching post at the Georgetown University Law Center.

Teen pregnancy, especially in the black community, became a major issue in 1983. "I saw from our own statistics that fifty-five and a half percent of all black babies were born out of wedlock, a great many of them to teen-age girls. It just hit me over the head—that situation insured black child poverty for the next generation." In 1983 CDF launched a major long-term national campaign to prevent teenage pregnancy and provide positive life options for youth. It included a multimedia campaign that consisted of transit advertisements, poster, television, and radio public service announcements, a national prenatal care campaign, and local volunteer Child Watch coalitions in more than seventy local communities in thirty states around the country. CDF was also largely responsible for the Act for Better Child Care, which Senator Alan Cranston, a liberal Democrat from California, introduced in November 1987.

Under Edelman's leadership, CDF has become one of the nation's most active and effective organizations concerned with a wide range of children's and family issues, particularly those that most affect America's poorest citizens: children. CDF's mission is to teach the nation about the needs of children and encourage preventive investments in them before they get sick, drop out of school, suffer too-early pregnancy or family breakdown, or get into trouble. CDF has become an effective voice nationwide in the areas of adolescent pregnancy prevention, child health, education, child care, youth employment, child welfare and mental health, and family support systems. Following the welfare reform bill that passed in 1996, cutting $54 billion from welfare programs over six years and turning most welfare decisions over to local instead of federal government, CDF enacted plans to become more active at the state level. And in June 1996 Edelman organized a march called Stand for Children in Washington, D.C., attended by about 200,000 people, to draw attention to the needs of the nation's youth.

In 1971 *Time* magazine named Edelman one of America's two hundred young leaders. That year she became the first black woman elected to the Yale University Corporation, and for the next five years she was on the board of the Carnegie Council on Children. In 1980 Edelman became the first black and second woman to chair the Board of Trustees of Spelman College, her alma mater. Currently she serves on the boards of the NAACP Legal Defense and Education Fund, Citizens for Constitutional Concerns, Joint Center for Political Studies, United States Committee for UNICEF, Center for Budget and Policy Priorities, Spelman College, and others. She is also a member of the Council on Foreign Relations, and in 1985 she received the prestigious MacArthur Foundation Prize Fellowship. In 1996 the National Black Caucus of State Legislators granted Edelman the Nation Builders Award "for her unwavering support of children."

A 1987 *Time* magazine article called Edelman "one of Washington's most unusual lobbyists" whose "effectiveness depends as much on her adroit use of statistics as on moral persuasion." In the same year Harvard University Press published *Families in Peril: An Agenda for Social Change,* based on Edelman's W. E. B. Du Bois lectures delivered at Harvard in 1986. In this pioneering book Edelman states that "the tide of misery that poverty breeds and that Blacks have borne disproportionately throughout history has now spread to a critical mass of white American families and children."

An extensive writer, Edelman is also author of *Children Out of School in America; School Suspensions: Are They Helping Children?; Portrait of Inequality: Black and White Children in America; The Measure of Our Success: A Letter to My Children and Yours; Guide My Feet: Prayers and Meditations on Loving and Working for Children;* and *Families in Peril: An Agenda for Social Change.*—BEVERLY GUY-SHEFTALL

KENNETH "BABYFACE" **EDMONDS**

1959–
Singer, songwriter, producer

If greatness lies within the ability to bring out the best in others, then Kenneth "Babyface" Edmonds has proven his talents again and again. Producing and writing mega-hits like "Exhale (Shoop, Shoop)," "Take a Bow," "Unbreak My Heart," and "Change the World" for even bigger stars like Whitney Houston, Madonna, Toni Braxton, and Eric Clapton, to name only a few, Babyface Edmonds has rekindled interest in the art form of producing and songwriting. In short, he has written, produced, or contributed to more than 100 pop singles over the last decade. By doing so, he has drawn comparison with one of the great producers and songwriters of our time, Quincy Jones. Yet it was not until years after getting into the music business that his talents were recognized by the public and his peers. After gaining the ear and hearts of the public, Edmonds received an unprecedented twelve Grammy nominations in 1997. The six-time Grammy winner has finally arrived as a singer, songwriter, music producer, and now film producer. His soulful ballads about love, relationships, and now hard-hitting issues like spousal abuse can be heard on cable television stations MTV, VH1, and BET, and thousands of radio stations in the United States.

Marvin and Barbara Edmonds gave birth to their fifth son, Kenneth Brian Edmonds, on April 10, 1959. The Indianapolis, Indiana couple would have a total of six sons. Talent seems to run in the family; his brothers Kevon and Melvin Edmonds are members of the successful vocal trio After 7. When Edmonds was in the eighth grade, his father died of lung cancer. His mother, a process manager for a pharmaceutical plant, raised the family.

Babyface wins two Grammys for his songs "I'll Make Love to You" and "When Can I See You."

Edmonds found solace in music, teaching himself to play guitar while in high school. He counts Stevie Wonder and the Jackson Five as early influences. "I was a pretty shy kid and music gave me a way to express my feelings," recalled Edmonds to the *Los Angeles Times* in 1996. "I began by writing my thoughts in a diary." His family's stoic nature made it hard for him to express his feelings as a child. "We weren't a touchy family, saying, 'I love you,'" recalled Edmonds in a 1995 interview with *People* magazine. "I'm still not a real 'Give me a hug' kind of person."

Edmonds's personality became a mixture of his family's stoicism mingled with his own sensitivity. At a young age he would conduct imaginary relationships with girls he had crushes on, but rarely shared his feelings with the objects of his affection. His infatuations revealed the early seeds of his romantic nature. Later, this same fanciful inclination allowed him to connect with women fans through his music. His handsome, boy-next-door looks do not hurt. "He is the only guy I know who can write about how a woman feels," said Whitney Houston to the *New York Times Magazine* in 1997. "It's strange that a male can do that. But somehow he's able to reach down in the core of his soul and pull it out."

Throughout high school and after graduation, he played guitar in a series of bands. The scene may have been funk, funk, and more funk, but the sound that Edmonds became known for would be love ballads or slow jams.

Babyface got his nickname from guitarist and 1970s funkmaster Bootsy Collins when he played with local funk bands and toured with headlining acts like Manchild and the Crowd Pleasers in the late 1970s. In all honesty, Edmonds did not like the name, but it stuck after he was introduced on stage by former bandmate Dee Bristol of the Deele. Today he still goes by Babyface, but he is known to close friends as Kenny or Face. The band had a series of hits in the 1980s, most notably "I Only Think of You on Two Occasions." The Deele was headed up by Antonio "L.A." Reid, who, like Edmonds, later produced and wrote for other artists like Sheena Easton and Edmonds himself.

Edmonds's solo efforts finally launched him in the music business. The year was 1989, and Edmonds found his sophomore effort, "Tender Lover," reaching double-platinum status. While auditioning people for the title song's video, he met his second wife, Tracey, in 1991. A little over a year later, they decided to marry. Edmonds credits Tracey, a Stanford University graduate, with being level headed and adept at the technical side of the business. The two are proud parents of a young son, Brandon. In 1996, shortly after the birth of his son, Edmonds expressed to *Jet* magazine the joys of fatherhood: "When he wakes up, you wake." Edmonds and Tracey have built play areas for Brandon at their places of work. His 1996 album "The Day" is titled after the day Brandon was born.

Edmonds's own success as an artist has not reduced his desires to produce others. With the backing of Arista Records, Reid and Edmonds launched LaFace Records in 1989, the Atlanta-based label that discovered such R&B acts as the hip hop female trio TLC, soulful diva Toni Braxton, and the southern comfort rappers Outkast.

Seven years later the two no longer collaborated creatively on materials because of personal differences. However, they have remained successful business partners. "We have defined our relationship. He's an executive, so he deals with the ins and outs of the company. I deal with the creative," Edmonds told *People* magazine in 1995. Reid has agreed. "It was a natural evolution that things would change. At the end of the day, he's probably one of the most important songwriters of all time."

With Reid handling the business aspects of LaFace, Edmonds moved west to Beverly Hills, California. The move offered him more creative space and less interference from stargazers—not that he minds signing autographs or talking to fans. He once joked to the *Los Angeles Times* in 1995, "I don't like going places and everyone saying, 'Hey Babyface' . . . But here in L.A., who cares? I mean, why you gonna look at me when Arnold Schwarzenegger just walked by?"

That was twelve Grammy nominations ago, and with Edmonds and Tracey getting a successful foot in the movie industry door, he may become just as recognizable as Arnold. In 1997, their company, Edmonds Entertainment, produced *Soul Food,* starring songstress and actress Vanessa Williams. Tracey describes it as a story of a family struggling to maintain its ties. Edmonds prepared the soundtrack, as he did for the highly acclaimed and successful movies *The Bodyguard, Waiting to Exhale,* and *The Preacher's Wife.*

Success has not spoiled Babyface Edmonds yet, and from the looks of it, it never will. With six Grammys, six BMI Songwriter of the Year Awards, four Billboard Music Awards, and the Soul Train Music Award in 1997 for Entertainer of the Year, he bears the fruits of his success with an easygoing, modest temperament that endears him to fellow artists and music fans.—KENNETTE CROCKETT

JOYCELYN **ELDERS**

1933–

Former U.S. Surgeon General, physician, educator

Joycelyn Elders was named the first woman and first black director of the Arkansas Department of Health in 1987, and in 1993 she became the first woman and the first black U.S. Surgeon General. The honor came under President Bill Clinton's administration. Elders is a crusader for health-care reform and advocates health care for all citizens. Her outspokenness and progressive stand on sex education in schools ultimately led to her dismissal from that federal position late in 1994.

Joycelyn Jones Elders was born Minnie Lee Jones on August 13, 1933, in Schaal, Arkansas, the oldest of eight children born to indigent sharecroppers Curtis and Haller Jones. During her childhood Elders worked with her parents and siblings as a field hand in this tiny farming community. She also experienced poverty and deprivation; her family lived in inadequate housing with no plumbing. She walked miles to school, where the children studied in old, dilapidated buildings with outdated textbooks discarded by white schools. While growing up, she never saw a doctor, let alone thought seriously about becoming one.

Her family was astonished when she decided to go to college, but Elders persevered despite her lack of role models and encouragement. She even persuaded her brothers to do the same, convincing them that their lives could improve. Upon receiving a scholarship at the age of fifteen, Elders entered Philander Smith College in Little Rock, Arkansas, and changed her name to Joycelyn, a name she had found on a wrapper of peppermint candy. At first, when she discovered she enjoyed biology and chemistry, she decided to become a laboratory technician. But after hearing a speech by Edith Irby Jones—the first black to study at the University of Arkansas and the first black woman president of the National Medical Association—Elders became more ambitious. She received her B.S. in 1952, joined the army, and became a physical therapist. After serving from 1953 to 1956, she was admitted to the University of Arkansas School of Medicine; she was the only black woman and one of only three students of color in her class.

After graduating from medical school in 1960, Elders worked as a pediatric intern at the University of Minnesota Hospital and was a resident in pediatrics at the University of Arkansas Medical Center. Because she had a strong interest in research, she began studies for a master's degree in biochemistry at the University of Arkansas Medical Center in 1967, receiving that degree in 1971. She also taught at the medical college for several years, becoming a professor in the department of pediatrics in 1976. By this time, she had done extensive research in

Former Surgeon General Joycelyn Elders speaks before the
House Subcommittee about the nation's health care system.

metabolism, growth hormones, and somatomedia in acute leukemia. Her research made her an expert in the treatment of juvenile patients with insulin-dependent diabetes.

Volatile Health Care Issues Addressed in Arkansas   When then–governor Bill Clinton appointed Elders to head the Department of Health in Arkansas in 1987, it marked the first time a woman or an African American had held that post. One of her main goals in this position was to lower the rate of teenage births in Arkansas, which was second-highest in the nation. She was also concerned about the state's high abortion rate, non-marital birthrate, and pregnancy rate. To address these issues she advocated wide-ranging sex education, and her views created a great deal of controversy. For example, she outraged many conservatives when she encouraged the distribution of condoms in schools.

Elders's outspoken nature also drew criticism. Although pro-choice, she discouraged abortion and instead focused on preventing unwanted pregnancies. She condemned right-to-life proponents for having undue concerns about the fetus and blamed male domination in various areas for the prevailing attitudes toward abortion. In the June 3, 1993, issue of *USA Today* she said: "Abortion foes are part of a celibate, male-dominated church, a male-dominated legislature and a male-dominated medical profession."

When Elders suggested placing health clinics in schools to address issues such as venereal disease and contraception, opponents blasted her idea as little more than how-to sex clinics that led to promiscuity and the breakdown of the family. Liberals applauded her support of a woman's right to an abortion, while some conservatives felt her views threatened the moral fiber of the country. Opponents also viewed Elders as a radical doctor because she advocated the use of marijuana for medicinal purposes.

In addition to her other professional concerns, Elders also supported health-care reform, though she believed that the lack of health insurance was not the only problem. She contended that geography and transportation were also significant factors in the health-care crisis, as few doctors and hospitals were available to citizens in poor and rural areas. Elders recommended addressing the shortage of doctors by training a mix of health care providers for underserved areas and utilizing certified nurse midwives, nurse practitioners, and physician assistants.

Elders confirmed as Surgeon General   President Bill Clinton nominated Elders for the position of U.S. Surgeon General in July 1993. Her nomination was confirmed by the Senate after considerable debate on September 7, and she was sworn in the following day. During the confirmation hearings, Elders explained her philosophy as quoted in *USA Today*:

> The government in the 1990s must be prepared to grapple with some very tough challenges as we focus on health care for all the people—not just the rich and privileged. Our work is not socially valuable and satisfactory until the needs of all the poor and indigent are met. We cannot be content with devising a narrowly satisfactory patch-work solution for this dilemma. We must work for a society in which people of all classes find satisfactory health care delivery a priority.

Controversy surrounded Elders's confirmation hearings. At first, some conservative senators—not realizing that Elders was not only a physician but a leading pediatric endocri-

*Joycelyn Elders administers an influenza shot
to promote Medicare's services to the elderly.*

nologist and noted professor—tried to block her nomination by passing legislation that would require all nominees for Surgeon General to be physicians. Elders also faced intense criticism over her advocacy of condom distribution in schools, and she was accused of a cover-up in Arkansas. Tests on four lots of the condoms purchased by the Arkansas Department of Health found a defective rate more than twelve times higher than the limit set by the Food and Drug Administration. State officials in Arkansas decided to withhold the information about possible defects rather than inform people that the condoms were unreliable. Elders concurred with her staff's decision, and her political opponents used this incident to try to prevent her confirmation.

Elders's confirmation hearings before the Senate were delayed until September 1993 as her nomination came under fire. Senate opponents raised questions about Elders's finances, and anti-abortion groups attacked her outspoken views on abortion and sex education. In addition, her husband was accused of not paying social security taxes for a nurse who attended to his mother, a victim of Alzheimer's disease. Elders, however, was backed by the American Medical Association and C. Everett Koop, the conservative former Surgeon General.

As Surgeon General, Elders spoke just as pointedly as she had before on health-care issues, sometimes igniting political controversy. For example, she came under fire in December 1993 for her comments on drug legalization. In what she later called "personal observations" based on experiences of other countries, she stated that she believed the United States should study the legalization of drugs, as legalized drugs might reduce crime. The White House press secretary announced that President Clinton did not share her views. Elders also continued her strong support of sex education in schools and abortion rights, while privately admitting she opposed abortion. She continued to arouse controversy among conservatives by stating in *USA Weekend* that the Boy Scouts and Girl Scouts should admit homosexuals. She also advocated gun control, calling violence a public health issue. In June 1994, *USA Today* reported that a drumbeat of criticism against Elders was mounting, but Elders responded by reminding the public that President Clinton never asked her to soften her rhetoric.

Fired by President Clinton   After Elders delivered a speech on World AIDS Day at the United Nations in December 1994, a psychologist asked Elders if she would encourage masturbation as a means of discouraging school children from becoming involved in other forms of sexual activity. According to *U.S. News & World Report,* Elders replied: "With regard to masturbation, I think that is something that is part of human sexuality and a part of something that perhaps should be taught." The next day President Clinton demanded and received Elders's resignation, explaining in the *Washington Post* that her "public statements reflecting differences with administration policy and my own convictions have made it necessary for her to tender her resignation." Although her position as Surgeon General demanded a leader who was outspoken, her blunt statements and controversial stands had gone too far. Elders explained in a television interview on *Nightline* that her comments had been misunderstood: "I was saying that we need to address all issues related to sexuality and teach our children what's normal behavior, not teach them masturbation. . . . That's not something you have to teach anybody." While Elders regretted the misunderstanding and the resulting media uproar, she told the *Washington Post,* "I don't regret what I said."

Despite her short tenure as Surgeon General, Elders's strength still shines through as she reflects on her job. "I feel that I increased the awareness of the American people on the problems of our adolescents and some of the things we need to do about drugs, violence, teen pregnancy and smoking," she has said. After she left her post, she returned to Little Rock, Arkansas to teach pediatrics at the University of Arkansas and she wrote a candid autobiography called *Jocelyn Elders, M.D.: From a Sharecropper's Daughter to Surgeon General* (1996, Morrow). Elders still continues a rigorous schedule of speaking engagements.

In addition to her work in state and national health care administration, Elders has been active in a number of professional associations. An author of 147 papers and monographs, Elders served as president of the Southern Society for Pediatric Research and of the scientific society Sigma Xi. Most recently, she became a member of the board of the American Civil Liberties Union. Until Elders moved to Washington, D.C., she lived in Little Rock, Arkansas, with her husband Oliver, a coach at a local high school and later a special assistant in the U.S. Education Department. They have two adult sons, Eric and Kevin.

The *New York Times* proclaimed Elders "a fearless and honest professional with forward–thinking ideas." Throughout her tenure as Surgeon General, Elders brought a serious commitment to the health-care issues of the day. Her unwavering stance reflects her dedication to a new approach to health issues. The principle upon which her medical philosophy is based—the dignity of the individual—carried her to the top health-care position in the federal government. Now that she has returned to her teaching position at the University of Arkansas Medical Center, she aims to continue her outspoken approach to health-care issues.—JOAN C. ELLIOTT

DUKE **ELLINGTON**
1899–1974
Band leader, composer, pianist

To tell the story of Edward Kennedy "Duke" Ellington is to tell the story of jazz; to tell the story of his orchestra is to tell the story of his compositions. The man, the music, the life that he lived, the compositions that he wrote, and the orchestra that he fronted were one and the same. As jazz critic Ralph Gleason wrote in 1966, "the man is the music, the music is the man, and never have the two things been more true than they are for Ellington." Duke Ellington is one of the most important figures in the history and development of American music. Often referred to as the greatest single talent in the history of jazz (for many, the history of music), he was variously referred to as "The Aristocrat of Swing," "The King of Swing," and "The King of Jazz."

Ellington was born April 29, 1899, in Washington, D.C. The youngest of two children, his parents were James Edward "J.E." Ellington and Daisy Kennedy Ellington. The mother, a Washington, D.C., native, was a housewife; the father, a North Carolina native, was a butler, caterer, and finally a blueprint worker in the Navy Yard. His mother was a high school graduate and his father had an eighth grade education. Both were well–spoken, however, and sought only the best for Duke and his sister Ruth. As Ellington recalled in his autobiography, *Music Is My Mistress*, he was "pampered and pampered, and spoiled rotten as a child." He was almost an adult when his sister was born.

Both parents played the piano, the mother "by note" and the father "by ear." Ellington began taking piano lessons at the age of seven, studying with a local piano teacher called Miss Clinkscales. Unofficially he was guided by pianists Oliver "Doc" Perry, Louis Brown, and Louis Thomas. Initially, piano was not his recognized talent. His recognized talents were drawing and painting. His other interest was watching baseball. As he wrote in his autobiography:

> The only way for me to do that was to get a job at the baseball park. . . . I had to walk around . . . yelling, "Peanuts, popcorn, chewing gum, candy, cigars, cigarettes, and score cards!" . . . By the end of the season, I had been promoted to yelling, "Cold drinks, gents! Get 'em ice cold!"

Sophisticated gentleman
Duke Ellington.

Other early employments included dishwashing at a hotel and soda jerking at the Poodle Dog Cafe. As a result of the latter employment, he wrote his first composition, "Soda Fountain Rag," which met with favorable approval. He was enrolled at Armstrong High School, but withdrew just three months short of finishing. Having won a poster contest sponsored by the NAACP in 1917, he was offered a scholarship by the Pratt Institute of Applied Art in Brooklyn, N.Y., but turned it down in order to pursue music full time. Ellington received his diploma in 1971, long after he was the recipient of several honorary doctorates. "I needed this diploma more than anything else," Ellington wrote in his autobiography.

One of his first professional jobs as a musician was playing for a half magic and half fortune–telling act. It featured one individual; Ellington was the backup, with the job of matching the featured artist's moods. Then he became relief pianist for the leading local pianist. According to Ellington in his autobiography:

> I was beginning to catch on around Washington, and I finally built up so much of a reputation that I had to study music seriously to protect it. Doc Perry had really taught me to read, and he showed me a lot of things on the piano. Then when I wanted to study some harmony, I went to Henry Grant.

The nickname "Duke" was given to him prior to enrollment in high school. It was a childhood friend who noted Ellington's special impeccable taste in dress, food, and lifestyle. He carried himself like one of means. He was a natural aristocrat, tall, debonair, urbane, and suave, with a sophisticated manner at all times.

Forms first band   Ellington formed his first band, The Duke's Serenaders, in 1917. The band's first job was at the True Reformers Hall in Washington, D.C. For five dollars a night (total), they played at dance halls and lodges. During the day, Ellington operated a sign and poster business. He also played with other bands, led by a contractor. When the contractor sent Ellington's band out on a job, one that paid one hundred dollars, the contractor instructed Ellington to take ten dollars and bring him the remaining ninety. Discovering this aspect of the business, within a short period, Ellington had assembled several bands himself and was supplying the city with "a band for any occasion."

Ellington also supplied bands for the wealthy in nearby Virginia. His personal earnings increased to ten thousand dollars a year. He married his childhood sweetheart, Edna Thompson, in 1918. By age twenty, Ellington was able to buy a house for his parents and purchase an automobile. His son Mercer, who in later years joined the band as trumpeter and road manager, was born in 1919.

The Duke's Serenaders—a trio made up of Ellington on piano, Otto Hardwick on saxophone, and Sonny Greer on drums—made its first trip to New York City in 1922, working with the clarinetist and leader Wilbur Sweatman. After a short while, they returned to Washington, being not quite ready for the requirements of "the Big Apple." One year later, upon the suggestion of pianist Thomas "Fats" Waller, the trio, along with trumpeter Arthur Whetsol and banjoist Elmer Snowden, returned to New York City. This move brought an end to his marriage.

The five–piece band worked under the name The Washingtonians, originally under the leadership of Elmer Snowden. Ellington assumed the group's leadership in 1924 and expanded the number to nine. By the time the band moved to the Cotton Club in 1927, it had grown to eleven musicians. Nightly radio broadcasts enhanced the band's popularity throughout the country. Joel Dreyfuss of the *Washington Post* for May 25, 1974, wrote:

> The Cotton Club was a perfect place for him to develop his skills as a composer. There were new stage shows frequently and Ellington was required to write fresh music to accompany the shows, dance routines and tableaux. His tenure at the Cotton Club led to important recording contracts and between 1928 and 1931 he made more than one hundred and sixty recordings.

In 1929, the band played its first Broadway musical, *Show Girl*, and made the first of its many films, *Check and Double Check*, in 1930. Other film appearances followed: *Murder at the Vanities, Belle of the Nineties, A Day at the Races, Cabin in the Sky*, and *Reveille with Beverly*.

Ellington began experimenting with extended compositions in 1931, with the writing of *Creole Rhapsody*. He inaugurated a series of annual concerts at Carnegie Hall in New York City in January 1943. On this occasion, the band performed Ellington's monumental work *Black, Brown and Beige*. The annual Carnegie Hall concerts continued until 1955, with Ellington writing a new work for each occasion, including *Liberian Suite, Harlem, Such Sweet Thunder, New World A-Comin'*, and *Deep South Suite*. Written in 1963 for the Century of Negro Progress Exposition in Chicago was his *My People*. Five film scores were also provided by Ellington: *Anatomy of a Murder, Paris Blues, Assault on a Queen, The Asphalt Jungle*, and *Change of Mind*. In 1957 he wrote the score for the television production *A Drum Is a Woman* (CBS). In 1970 he composed the ballet *The River* for Alvin Ailey and the American Ballet Theater.

The band's first trip to Europe took place in 1933, followed by another in 1939. Foreign tours became more frequent: to the Soviet Union, Japan, and Australia, with return visits to Europe. An entire section of *Music Is My Mistress* is devoted to the 1963 State Department Tour, a trip that he referred to in the book as "one of the most unusual and adventurous" the band had ever taken.

Ellington worked twenty–hour days and was referred to as "the busiest man in the business." Ellington wrote in the foreword of the piano version of his *Sacred Concerts*:

> The incomparable Ellington Orchestra . . . was the only musical aggregation in the world playing 52 weeks a year and rarely with a day off. . . . Little wonder that President Nixon appointed the personable Dr. Duke Ellington official goodwill envoy for American music abroad.

Ellington rarely featured himself as a soloist, though he was an extremely capable pianist. Instead, he fed ideas to the band. Wrote musicologist Eileen Southern, "his music represented the collective achievement of his sidemen, with himself at the forefront rather than the sole originator of the creative impulse."

Ellington's bands were unique. As jazz historian Dan Morgenstern indicated:

> The development of Ellington's band followed that of jazz bands in general. His originality expressed itself in what he did with this format and instrumentation, which was to imbue it with an unprecedented richness of timbre, texture and expressiveness. . . . Each member of the ensemble was an individual voice, each had a special gift, each contributed to the totality of what could be called an organism as well as an organization.

Gleason reminded us that:

Duke lived well. He came from a family that lived well. . . . He traveled in the 30s on his tours of the United States not on a bus, but in two railroad cars. That was the way the President traveled.

Duke himself stated:

It's a matter of whether you want to play music or make money. I guess I like to keep a band so that I can write and hear the music the next day. The way to do that is to pay the band and keep it on tap fifty-two weeks a year. . . . [B]y various little twists and turns, we manage to stay in business and make a musical profit. And a musical profit can put you way ahead of a financial loss.

The collection of instrumentalists playing Ellingtonia for close to half a century included Harold Baker, Sidney Bechet, Louis Bellson (the band's first white member), Barney Bigard, Jimmy Blanton, Lawrence Brown, Harry Carney, Wilbur DeParis, Mercer Ellington (Duke's son), Tyree Glenn, Sonny Greer, Jimmy Hamilton, Johnny Hodges, Ray Nance, Russell Procope, Elmer Snowden, Rex Stewart, Billy Strayhorn (Ellington's collaborator, protégé, and alter ego), Clark Terry, Ben Webster, and Cootie Williams.

A scene from the documentary
A Duke Named Ellington.

Three periods of Ellingtonia Posthumously, Dreyfuss, in the *Washington Post* for May 25, 1974, divided Ellingtonia into three periods: the 1920s and '30s, when he established his trademark the large orchestra with virtuoso instrumentalists; the 1940s, when he reached a height of productivity and became a cultural hero; and the period following his appearance at the Newport Jazz Festival in 1956—Ellington's most adventurous. This was the period when he concentrated on extended works, including a satirical suite for the Shakespeare Festival at Stratford, Connecticut; *My People*, which traced the history of blacks in America on the occasion of the 100th Anniversary of the Emancipation Proclamation; and his *Sacred Concerts*. The first of his Sacred Concerts was performed in 1965 at Grace Cathedral Church in San Francisco, California; the second, in 1968 at the Cathedral of St. John the Divine in New York City; and the third, on United Nations Day in 1973 at Westminster Abbey in London.

Ellington wrote in the introduction to the score *Sacred Concerts Complete*:

As I travel place to place by car, bus, train, plane . . . taking rhythm to the dancers, harmony to the romantic, melody to the nostalgic, gratitude to the listener . . . receiving praise, applause and handshakes, and at the same time, doing the thing I like to do, I feel that I am most fortunate because I know that God has blessed my timing. . . . When a man feels that that which he enjoys in his life is only because of the grace of God, he rejoices, and sometimes dances.

Dreyfuss contended that Ellington's greatest contribution was perhaps "forcing the critical world to deal seriously with jazz as an art form." Most Ellington historians would concur with this assessment. Jazz journalist Leonard Feather wrote, "It is . . . Ellington . . . of concert halls, cathedrals and festival sites around the world that deserves his longest life of all."

Ellington was deservedly honored during his lifetime. Recognitions include: the Spingarn Medal (NAACP, 1959); a gold medal from President Lyndon B. Johnson (1966); Grammy Awards (National Academy of Recording Arts and Science, 1968, 1969, 1973); National Association of Negro Musicians Award (1964); appointment to the National Council on the Arts, National Endowment for the Arts (1968); Pied Piper Award (American Society of Composers, Authors and Publishers, 1968); Presidential Medal of Freedom, President Richard M. Nixon (1969); Fellow, American Academy of Arts and Sciences (1971); *Down Beat* Awards (Duke Ellington Band)—First Place (1946, 1948, 1959, 1960, 1962–72); *Esquire* magazine (Duke Ellington Band); and the Gold Award (1945, 1946, 1947). He received honorary doctoral degrees from sixteen institutions, including Wilberforce, Milton, and Rider Colleges and Howard, Fisk, Morgan, Columbia, Wisconsin, St. John's, Washington, Brown, and Yale Universities.

In 1965 the Pulitzer music committee recommended Ellington for a special award. The full Pulitzer committee turned down the recommendation.

Edward Kennedy "Duke" Ellington died at Columbia Presbyterian Medical Center on May 24, 1974. He had cancer of both lungs and a week prior to his death, developed pneumonia. Surviving was his widow Bea "Evie" Ellis, his son Mercer, his sister Ruth, and three grandchildren.

After his death, Western High School in Washington, D.C., was renamed the Duke Ellington School for the Arts. The Calvert Street Bridge, also in the nation's capitol, was named the Duke Ellington Bridge. Streets, schools, art centers, and scholarships throughout the country have been named in his honor. The first of the International Duke Ellington Conferences was held in 1983. Such conferences continue annually. The United States Postal Service issued a twenty-two-cent commemorative stamp on April 29, 1986, honoring Duke Ellington.

On April 26, 1988, the National Museum of American History of the Smithsonian Institution in Washington, D.C., acquired more than two hundred thousand pages of documents reflecting the life and career of Duke Ellington, following more than three years of negotiation with the Ellington estate. The acquisition was made possible by a special $500,000 appropriation from the U.S. Congress. Included were more than three thousand original and orchestral compositions, five hundred studio tapes, scrapbooks of world tours, and more than two thousand photographs, programs, posters, awards, citations, and medals. The American Masters series, focusing on the cultural contributions of prominent American artists, included a two–part documentary on the music and influence of Ellington. *A Duke Named Ellington* was aired on PBS July 18 and 25, 1988. The 1943 Carnegie Hall debut of Duke Ellington and His Orchestra on January 23, 1943, was recreated in July 1989, Maurice Peres conducting, at Carnegie Hall.

Ellington excelled as a composer, pianist, and leader. He stood tall among his contemporaries and remains in that position more than two decades following his death. His instrument was his orchestra; together, they produced the epitome of sophisticated jazz for all others to emulate. Ellington is today a popular subject for conferences, dissertations, and biographies.—D. ANTOINETTE HANDY

MEDGAR W. EVERS

1925–1963

Civil rights activist

Aware of the need to be politically conscious as he lived in Mississippi's Delta area, Medgar Evers devoted

his adult life to civil rights activities. He is known for giving his life to an assassin's bullet, which helped

prompt passage of comprehensive federal civil rights laws.

Medgar Wiley Evers, the leading civil rights leader of Jackson, Mississippi, in the 1960s, was born to James and Jessie Evers in Decatur, Mississippi, on July 2, 1925. He was the third of the Evers's four children, who were raised on their parents' farm. While the father, James, supplemented his income with a part-time sawmill job, Jessie Evers, who was of white, Indian, and African American parentage, served as a domestic worker, cleaning homes for rich whites and ironing for others at home.

Young Medgar's education initially began in a one–room elementary school in Decatur, Mississippi, at six years old, but he later had to join other children to walk twelve miles one way to attend another school in Newton, Mississippi. He was a serious youngster who may have had a mission. Quoted in *Ghosts of Mississippi,* Elizabeth Evers Jordan said, "Medgar was more quietish. I used to see him go way down in himself, like he's in a deep, deep studying. He used to always carve his name on the trees and things: M. W. Evers. See, he had a dream, it was something in him that he wanted."

In 1946 Evers returned to Mississippi from World War II, and enrolled at Alcorn Agricultural and Mechanical (A & M) College, the oldest state-wide college for black students, located in Norman, Mississippi. He wanted to study business administration in order to open his own business. His brother Charles also enrolled at A & M and majored in social sciences. At Alcorn, Charles and Medgar Evers made the football team, on which Medgar was a noted halfback. In order to earn additional money to help their family back in Decatur, Charles operated a taxi service for students of the college and, later, both brothers used their dormitory room to operate a ham sandwich business. Medgar Evers was selected to participate on the college's track team, sang in the choir, and played active roles in the debating and business clubs, sometimes volunteering to work for the local YMCA. Editor of Alcorn's 1951 yearbook, Medgar did so well in college that he was selected to be included in *Who's Who Among Students in American Colleges and Universities*. During this period, he decided to exercise his voting rights, especially since he had done the noble thing of serving his nation in the war. When he and his brother, Charles Evers, attempted to vote, white supremacists threatened their family.

Medgar and Charles Evers were very active in the social life at Alcorn, and in the fall 1950 semester, Medgar began to date a seventeen-year-old freshman by the name of Myrlie Beasley, from Vicksburg, Mississippi, who had graduated second in her high school class. After almost a year of courtship, the couple married on December 24, 1951, and had three children—Darrell Kenyatta, named after Kenyan anti-British colonial rule agitator and first President Jomo Kenyatta; Reena Denise, and James Van Dyke. Medgar Evers wanted his brother Charles to be his best man at the wedding, but that was not possible because the outbreak of the Korean War had prompted the army to call Charles back to his reserve unit.

*Slain civil rights activist
Medgar Evers.*

When Medgar Evers graduated in July 1952, he was employed by Theodore Roosevelt Mason Howard's Magnolia Mutual Life Insurance Company of Mound Bayou, Mississippi, a sleepy town on Mississippi's Highway 61 in the heart of the Delta; he sold insurance policies in the Clarksdale area of Mississippi. Although Myrlie Evers had ambitions to move with her new husband to the North, possibly to Chicago, she had to stay at Mound Bayou, where she also served as a secretary in the insurance office.

Theodore Howard was to influence Medgar Evers in varied ways, especially as the founder of the Regional Council of Negro Leadership in the Delta area, a serious lobby group very much similar to the NAACP, which distributed vehicular bumper stickers reading "Don't Buy Gas Where You Can't Use the Restroom." It was on joining the council and, later, the Mound Bayou branch of the NAACP in 1952 that Evers came into contact with other politically conscious black men and women, including Cleveland, Mississippi businessman Amzie Moore, local NAACP president Aaron Henry—a pharmacist by training—and Thomas Moore, also an insurance agent.

The gravesite of Medgar Evers in Arlington National Cemetery.

As an employee of the insurance company and a member of the council and of the NAACP, Evers used various forms of boycotts to assist in mobilizing his fellow blacks against racism and economic inequality. In 1954 he was appointed salaried field secretary of the then very inactive NAACP in Mississippi. In that position, he fearlessly insisted that the state should enforce the 1954 Supreme Court decision declaring segregation in public education unconstitutional; that insistence and other NAACP activities caused Evers to be marked by white supremacists as being too revolutionary. He became an avowed supporter of Martin Luther King Jr. When the Atlanta native formed the Southern Christian Leadership Conference (SCLC), Evers supported it, even though Evers still worked for the NAACP.

Civil activism leads to death   Like civil rights stalwarts, Evers too was often threatened with death, beaten by white racist thugs, arrested, and jailed. In the early hours of June 11, 1963, he was shot in the back and killed in the driveway of his Jackson, Mississippi home. Evers's death caused blacks to riot in many major cities and meant widowhood for his young wife and fatherlessness for their three children, but it also prompted President John F. Kennedy to seek congressional action for a comprehensive civil rights law. Evers, an army veteran, was buried in Arlington National Cemetery in May 1964. Suspected and later arrested was Byron De La Beckwith Jr., a local postal employee, who was tried twice but acquitted on both occasions.

Myrlie Evers gathered their three children and left for Pomona College in California to complete her first degree. She still pressed on to find her husband's killer and, as a result, Beckwith was arrested a third time, on this occasion in Tennessee, and charged with the murder of Evers. Beckwith's lawyers filed a motion to get the charge dismissed by the U.S. Supreme Court. On October 4, 1993, the court refused to do so, thus clearing the way for the third trial to begin. On February 5, 1994, Beckwith, very frail and wearing a tiny pin of the Confederacy flag on the lapel of his jacket, was found guilty by a jury and sentenced to life in prison by Judge Hilburn, to be eligible for parole in ten years. Over time, life for blacks in Mississippi changed. Charles Evers rose to become the mayor of Fayette, Mississippi, and now runs the WMPR weekly radio talk show.

Medgar Evers's life was cut short but his tireless effort for equality lived on as his wife, Myrlie Evers, became chairman of the board of the NAACP.—A. B. ASSENSOH

LOUIS **FARRAKHAN**

1933–

Leader of the Nation of Islam

Minister Louis Farrakhan—famous and infamous, loved and hated; a prophetic leader to some, an outcast to others—is the head and spirit of the resurrected Nation of Islam or Black Muslims. Farrakhan is a recognized public figure in the United States and in countries throughout the world. This self-styled religious crusader for "freedom, justice and equality," for African Americans and others, has made his mark in history. His frequently provocative nature garners him significant attention, both positive and negative. This history maker has affected the culture of thousands of African Americans. Time magazine has recognized him as one of the twenty-five most influential Americans and has placed him on its cover, as have Newsweek, Emerge, and many other major publications.

Farrakhan's birth was not a welcomed one. Farrakhan's mother, Sarah Mae Manning Clarke, was a Caribbean immigrant and domestic worker from St. Kitts. After separating from her husband, Percival Clarke, Sarah Mae moved in with her new lover, Louis Walcott. Soon she found out she was pregnant with Clarke's child. Despite three attempts to abort the child, on May 11, 1933, in the Bronx, New York City, Sarah Mae gave birth to a son. Her estranged husband, a Jamaican immigrant taxi driver, was not recognized on his son's birth certificate, and Sara Mae named the baby Louis Eugene Walcott, after her lover. Walcott had earlier fathered Farrakhan's older half-brother, Alvan Walcott, in October of 1931. Louis Walcott Sr. and his family subsequently moved to the Roxbury section of Boston, Massachusetts, when young "Gene," as Farrakhan was then known, was approximately four years old.

Farrakhan's youth   Farrakhan grew up in and benefitted from Roxbury's West Indian enclave. Mae worked diligently at various domestic endeavors for whites, but still needed some public assistance to provide for her boys, since the elder Louis Walcott apparently drifted away a year after they arrived in Roxbury. She somehow managed to squirrel away small loose change to pay for young Farrakhan's violin lessons. Farrakhan's public violin performances began at Roxbury's St. Cyrian's Episcopal Church, where he also sang in the choir and served as an acolyte in the early 1940s.

Louis Farrakhan.

His talent was also manifest during his educational career. Eugene Walcott performed well educationally from elementary through high school, and earned a placed in Boston's top-ranked historic Latin School in 1947. Farrakhan was one of a handful of African Americans at Boston Latin, and in 1948 he transferred to Boston's English High School. Farrakhan remained an honor student at English High, and he also discovered the sport of track and field. Farrakhan ranked among the top track performers in the sprints. He also continued his academic study and violin performances. On May 15, 1949, he celebrated his sixteenth birthday with a classical violin performance on the then-popular *Ted Mack Original Amateur Hour* television program. Farrakhan's musical performances were not limited to classical violin presentations, however, since he had discovered Caribbean Calypso and became known as "The Charmer" around Boston's African American nightclubs. Farrakhan's guitar- and ukelele-accompanied songs and gyrations earned him some much-needed money. He was fortunate to escape the snares of questionable liaison seekers and did not fall victim to his marijuana and alcohol indulgences. Instead, Farrakhan, though not giving up future violin and Calypso performances, chose to attend Winston-Salem Teacher's College in North Carolina in September 1950 over New York's Juilliard School of Music.

Farrakhan performed better musically and athletically than he did academically at Winston-Salem Teacher's College, and he found a new interest during his first vacation away from college. Her name was Betsy Ross, a Roman Catholic from Roxbury, whom he married on September 12, 1953, after ending his college education. Soon becoming a husband and father, Farrakhan needed a job providing steady income. He continued his entertainment career as "Calypso Gene," and during a 1955 eight-week Midwest tour of Farrakhan's "Calypso Follies" he encountered a man and a movement that changed his life.

Exposure to the Nation of Islam   Farrakhan had heard about Elijah Muhammad and the Nation of Islam (NOI) from Malcolm X in 1952. This time Farrahkan encountered Elijah Muhammad himself, along with the NOI when he and his wife attended an annual convention gathering at Temple No. 2 on the south side of Chicago, Illinois, in 1956. Gene was moved by Minister Muhammad's message, but highly conscious of his poor grammatical expressions, as the leader had no formal education beyond the third grade. According to *Sepia* in May 1975, Elijah Muhammad had, unbeknownst to Farrakhan, been informed of who he was and where he was sitting. Speaking directly to Farrakhan, Muhammad said: "Brother, don't pay attention to how I speak. Pay attention to what I'm saying. I didn't get the chance to go to the white man's fine schools, because when I tried to go, the doors were closed. But if you take what

I say and place it into the beautiful way of speaking you know, you can help me save our people." Thus, when new members were solicited, Farrakhan and his wife Betsy joined the NOI and became ardent members.

The religious body of the NOI Farrakhan embraced is a curious mixture of orthodox Islamic beliefs, Christianity (needed to attract African American Christians), apocrypha, and invention, mindful that other religious groups such as the Mormons have manufactured their religious practices as well. More specifically, the NOI (formally called the Lost Found Nation of Islam in the Wilderness of North America) has its roots in the Moorish American Science Temple Movement of Noble Drew Ali, founded in 1913 in Newark, New Jersey, and in some of the principles and philosophy of Marcus M. Garvey's Universal Negro Improvement and Conservation Association and African Communities Imperial League, founded in 1914 in Jamaica. The leader of the NOI was Elijah Poole, son of former slave sharecroppers.

Also known by many aliases, Poole was primarily known as the Messenger Elijah Muhammad. Muhammad had migrated to Detroit, Michigan, in 1923 in search of employment. There he met a man who was long identified as Allah incarnate, called variously Master Wali Farrad Muhammad, Wallace Fard, W. D. Fard, and Willie D. Fard, among others. Fard "vanished" in 1934, but left Elijah Muhammad with a religious belief system claiming that the black or colored race was created as the original or chosen people by Allah, and constituted the Tribe of Shabazz. However, the Tribe of Shabazz was placed under the control or hegemony of corrupt "white devils" (created by a mad black scientist named Yacub) for a period of six thousand years. But the Tribe of Shabazz need not worry, since a powerful Mother Plane— "one-half mile by one-half mile"—will ultimately destroy all "white devils" and allow the original people to enjoy their original rule, and live in joy and paradise void of "white devils." All "so-called Negroes wishing to be part of this Heaven on Earth" had to embrace the NOI and its teachings. Elijah Muhammad was recognized as a prophet alongside Moses and Jesus. These are some of the things Malcolm X and fledging Farrakhan taught to all who would listen.

Louis Farrakhan (until this time called Eugene Walcott) became Louis X in 1955 and was appointed a captain in the male police-like cadre known as the Fruit of Islam (FOI); female members of the NOI were organized into a more domestic unit known as the Muslim Girls Training and General Civilization Class. Shortly thereafter, Farrakhan was promoted to minister and set out to develop and expand Temple No. 11, Malcolm X's former temple. Farrakhan emulated Malcolm X and Elijah Muhammad while making his own contributions to the growth, development, and popularization of the NOI. One of his late-1950s contributions was a popular song he recorded, entitled "A White Man's Heaven Is a Black Man's Hell." It was named for one of Elijah Muhammad's written and spoken phrases. "A White Man's Heaven" is nearly ten and one-half minutes long with a Calypso beat, and was played on juke boxes within and outside of the NOI. His next recording was entitled "Look at My Chains." Farrakhan went a step further when he wrote and performed in two plays, *The Trial,* about whites on trial, and *Orgena? or A Negro Spelled Backwards,* a satire about worldly black prostitutes, dope fiends, alcoholics, and other misguided non-members of the Nation. Both his and Malcolm's stars were on the rise, until revelations about their leaders surfaced in 1963.

Trouble in the Nation   News about adulterous behavior by Elijah Muhammad surfaced when two of his former young secretaries revealed they had been impregnated by him in 1955 and 1956 respectively. Additionally, four more former secretaries came forward by 1960

*Farrakhan speaks during the
Million Man March, 1995.*

to indicate he had fathered their children as well. Malcolm X confirmed the revelations after speaking with Wallace Muhammad, Elijah Muhammad's legitimate seventh child, and informed Farrakhan. Dismayed that Farrakhan not share his anguish, Malcolm immediately met with his leader. Much to Malcolm's chagrin, Muhammad confirmed and "biblically justified" his misdeeds. Malcolm was further shaken when allegations surfaced that Farrakhan—his protegee—had sent a report to Elijah Muhammad accusing Malcolm of spreading provocative rumors about Muhammad's liaisons. Things went from bad to worse for Malcolm, as he was silenced for commenting on the assassination of President John F. Kennedy in 1963, and ultimately removed as the NOI's national representative and minister of Temple No. 7 in Harlem. After observing the silence for a time, Malcolm publicly rebuked Elijah Muhammad for his indiscretions in a televised interview with journalist Mike Wallace, and thus became a marked man. Farrakhan played an active role in excoriating Malcolm after he quit the NOI, made the pilgrimage to Mecca in Saudi Arabia, changed his name to El Hajj Malik Shabazz, and formed his own non-racialist organizations.

Farrakhan's verbal attacks on Malcolm X helped create, as he publicly admitted in 1985, the volatile conditions that led up to the February 21, 1965, assassination of Malcolm X. Malcolm was called an "international hobo," and the December 4, 1964 edition of *Muhammad Speaks,* the newspaper established by Malcolm X, included Farrakhan's statement that:

> Only those who wish to be led to hell, or to their doom, will follow Malcolm. The die is set, and Malcolm shall not escape. . . . Such a man as Malcolm is worthy of death, and would have met death if it had not been for Muhammad's confidence in Allah for victory over his enemies.

Eugene Walcott/Minister Louis X was renamed Abdul Farrakhan by Elijah Muhammad in May, 1965, and stepped into Malcolm's former position as minister of Harlem's Temple No. 7. Farrakhan also became Muhammad's NOI national representative, as Malcolm had been in 1967. Perhaps Farrakhan believed he would become the leader of the Nation of Islam if he outlived Elijah Muhammad, but fate was not that kind.

A new Nation of Islam The NOI's membership and wealth rebounded between 1965 and 1975. When Elijah Muhammad died of congestive heart failure on February 26, 1975, he left behind a fortune exceeding $46 million, seventy-six temples throughout the United States, and a membership of between sixty and 100 thousand. Farrakhan's hopes to succeed Muhammad were dashed when it was announced that Wallace D. Muhammad, Elijah's son (who had previously left the Nation and denounced his father), was divinely chosen to be Elijah Muhammad's successor. Approximately four months later, in June of 1975, Wallace moved Farrakhan from Harlem's Temple No. 7 to NOI headquarters in Chicago, Illinois, and named him his special ambassador. Farrakhan's contempt grew as Wallace Muhammad, a student of Islamic orthodoxy, began to demystify and dismantle the beliefs and doctrines of his father's NOI. Wallace claimed his father had manufactured the Black Muslim religion to recruit African Americans, but had ordered it to move out of its "baby phase" and into the "mature phase" of its existence. Wallace also shockingly revealed that "Allah incarnate" W. D. Fard, founder of the NOI, was still alive and serving as the minister of the Oakland, California mosque. Wallace began referring to his followers and those of Negroid ancestry as "Bilalians," in recognition of Muezzin Bilal, a slave so recognized by the prophet Mohammed. Farrakhan was shaken again when Wallace named New York's Mosque No. 7 for the late Malcolm X, and ceased to consider whites as devils. Whites were considered as respectable as Bilalians, as long as they did not display a devil mentality, and were allowed to become members of the vanishing NOI. The NOI was formally dismantled by Wallace on October 18, 1976, and renamed the World Community of Al-Islam in the West. Anyone was allowed to join the World Community and could learn more about it by attending mosque or masjid services and reading the new organization's official newspaper, the *Bilalian News.* A dazed Farrakhan was once again renamed, becoming Minister Abdul Haleem Farrakhan, by Minister Wallace (Warith) Muhammad. This and Wallace's "new orthodoxy" spurred Farrakhan to break with Wallace in September 1977 and, in March 1978, revive Elijah Muhammad's Nation of Islam. Wallace continued his transitions by changing the name of the World Community of Al-Islam in the West to the American Muslim Mission in 1980. Warith Deen Muhammad, as he had come to be known, made a final organizational move when he dissolved the American Muslim Mission in 1985 and further embraced universalistic Islamic orthodoxy.

Farrakhan's resurrected NOI and troublesome times

Farrakhan resurrected the NOI in Chicago, Illinois, in a funeral home he purchased on 79th Street. There he established and began publishing *The Final Call* in 1979, resurrecting a newspaper started by Elijah Muhammad in 1934. He reestablished the whole belief system of Elijah Muhammad's NOI and elevated Elijah Muhammad to the status of a messiah. Interestingly, he upgraded the recognition and involvement of women in the NOI. Moreover, the Nation's organizational frame was re-upholstered, and Farrakhan cleverly placed the "blood" of Elijah Muhammad upon center stage in the form of the thirteen children Muhammad fathered by his six former secretaries; they, along with their mothers, became members of the new Nation. Finally, Farrakhan adroitly purchased Elijah Muhammad's mansion in Chicago's Hyde Park in 1986 for $500 thousand after paying off overdue real estate taxes, and subsequently purchased the majestic former Temple No. 2 in Chicago for $2.3 million in 1988 from Warith Muhammad's financially strapped former organization. Farrakhan's successful actions helped rebuild the membership of his NOI, bringing it to slightly more than twenty thousand members. He and his ministers have also diligently searched for converts during the late 1970s and early 1980s and capitalized upon the publicity that kept the NOI before the public eye.

The NOI's positive press stemmed from its cleaning up many dope-ridden street corners, housing units, and neighborhoods. The negative press, however, outweighed the positive and embroiled the Nation and Farrakhan in an ugly public battle with Judaism. Problems developed shortly after Jesse Jackson (who, like Farrakhan and the NOI, had previous conflicts with Jewish leaders) declared, in November 1983, that he was a presidential candidate for the Democratic Party's nomination. Jackson's publicity was running high as he, along with Farrakhan, had traveled to Syria in 1984 and negotiated the release of African American Robert O. Goodman, a Navy Lieutenant airman whose plane had been shot down while on a bombing mission over Lebanon. Farrakhan involved himself and the NOI in electoral politics for the first time when Jackson declared his candidacy, and later led, on February 9, 1984, a group of his followers to Chicago's City Hall to register to vote. Jewish leaders were quick to question the campaign relationship of Jackson and Farrakhan, and took advantage of a statement printed by African American journalist Milton Coleman in the *Washington Post*. Specifically, Coleman reported in the February 3, 1984 issue that he had heard Jesse Jackson privately refer to Jews as "Hymies" and called New York City "Hymietown" or "Hymieville." Jackson attempted to repudiate the allegation and publicly apologized on February 27, 1984, at Temple Adath Yeshurun in Manchester, New Hampshire. Unfortunately, things got worse when Farrakhan vehemently attacked Milton Coleman for his statement, and the media twisted his diatribe into an outright threat against Coleman and his wife. Jesse's campaign was sorely hurt, and he gently maneuvered publicly away from Farrakhan. Things worsened when Farrakhan referred to Adolph Hitler as a "wickedly great man" in March 1984. Farrakhan was not, as he tried to indicate when he was attacked for this statement, adulating Hitler, but repudiating him while admitting he achieved recognition as a wicked man. Another storm erupted in June 1984, when the *Chicago Sun-Times* reported that Farrakhan called Judaism a "gutter religion," when in fact he was generally indicating that anyone can "practice a dirty religion" if they use religion to hide their misdeeds. Farrakhan would later admit that he made a poor choice of words, but the furor was great enough to motivate the United States

Senate to censure Farrakhan. Many African Americans believed Farrakhan was being unfairly treated, and continued to rally when he gave speeches.

Farrakhan, never one to let pressure put him down, refused to be silenced and sought greater exposure outside the United States during the late 1980s and 1990s. He visited Europe, the Middle East, and Africa. His attention turned to economics when, in 1984, he secured a five million dollar interest-free loan from Libya's Colonel Muammar Quaddafi to fund the manufacturing of personal care products under his People Organized to Work for Economic Rebirth (POWER) organization. Farrakhan had an opportunity to secure more monetary funds during his controversial World Friendship Tour of early 1996, but the U.S. government said he must register as a foreign agent if he accepted foreign monies.

The year prior to his World Friendship Tour, Farrakhan successfully dealt with an alleged assassination plot by Malcolm X's daughter Quibilah Shabazz, and made history once again with the October 16, 1995, Million Man March. He and the many speakers who preceded him inspired those gathered there in their call for respect, dignity, and atonement.

Today, Farrakhan speaks widely. He remains married to his wife Khadijah (Betsy) after forty-four years, nine children, and nearly thirty grandchildren. He and his family still reside in multi-racial Hyde Park, Chicago.

Even though he wants to appeal to mainstream America, he remains a polarizing figure in America with his choice of actions and words. Farrakhan is an enigma and enjoys it.—W. BRAXTER WIGGINS

ELLA **FITZGERALD**

1918–1996
Singer, songwriter

Ella Fitzgerald's voice has been described as sounding more like an instrument than any other voice in this century. In technical terms, she had an impeccable and sophisticated rhythmic sense, flawless intonation, and an extraordinary harmonic sensibility. Henry Pleasants in his book The Great American Popular Singers *described Fitzgerald as "endlessly inventive," saying that "new melodic deviations and embellishments are as varied as they are invariably appropriate." These facts, coupled with her classic simplicity and genuine humility, made Fitzgerald a one-of-a-kind entertainer, a true legend in her own time.*

Fitzgerald was born April 25, 1918, in Newport News, Virginia. Both of her parents were interested in music. Her father filled their house with his guitar playing and singing, and her mother had a beautiful soprano voice. When Fitzgerald's father died shortly after World War I, the rest of the family moved to Yonkers, New York. Mrs. Fitzgerald had a

*Ella
Fitzgerald.*

sister there and hoped to find a better life in the North, close to relatives.

Fitzgerald grew up just across the Hudson River from the Bronx and in the shadow of a Harlem that was then in vogue. Yonkers was a mixed neighborhood, and Fitzgerald had a variety of friends. She studied music in school, sang in the junior high school glee club, and took piano lessons. But the five dollars a month for lessons soon became too much for her mother to afford. Forced to quit, Fitzgerald soon forgot how to read music, a loss she recalled with regret.

In her early teens, Fitzgerald discovered Harlem and its night magic firsthand. She and her girlfriends went there on weekends to hear celebrities sing and to beg for autographs. On one such occasion, she found herself at the Harlem Opera House on Amateur Night. It was 1934; Fitzgerald was sixteen, tall, and awkward. Her friends dared her to enter the talent contest. She accepted the challenge. In her hand-me-down dress and ill-fitting shoes, she entered the spotlight. The audience laughed. She had intended to dance, but her knees were knocking together so rapidly that she chose not to move from the spot where she stood, rooted in fear. She decided to sing instead. The audience ceased laughing as Fitzgerald sang "The Object of My Affection." She had learned the song from a Connie Boswell record, but the voice that emerged was a genuine talent of her own. She won first prize and received three encores.

This was the first of many talent contests she would win. Fitzgerald went on to appear at the Lafayette Theater on Seventh Avenue and 132nd Street. Her repertoire consisted of only three songs: "Believe It, Beloved," "The Object of My Affection," and "July." She sang these songs in every talent contest she entered in Harlem.

In 1935 Fitzgerald entered another competition at the Harlem Opera House. Winning first prize, she landed a week's work singing with Tiny Bradshaw and his band. This engagement landed her an audition at the CBS Radio Network, and they offered her a guest appearance on the Arthur Tracy radio show. Her mother gave permission, as Fitzgerald was still underage, but before anything could come of it, Fitzgerald's mother died. Because she was now an orphan, the contract with CBS was no longer valid. Despite the fact that Fitzgerald went to live with her aunt, the authorities were dissatisfied, and she was forced into the Riverdale orphanage in Yonkers. After her death, accounts of Fitzgerald's childhood have revealed an abusive stepfather who also caused her to face life in an orphanage.

Institutional life bored Fitzgerald, and she often escaped to Harlem to enter amateur contests. Finally she made her way into the Apollo Theater. Nervous as usual, Fitzgerald walked on stage, sang her three songs, and won first prize. Her reward was fifty dollars. Appearing at the Apollo opened another door for her. The night of the amateur contest,

Bardu Ali, who directed Chick Webb's band, had been in the audience. Hearing Fitzgerald sing, he is reported to have said, "This chick sings just like a horn." A few days later, Fitzgerald sang for Webb, unaccompanied: she had perfect pitch. Webb was amazed by her talent and ignored her old clothes and dull appearance. Even though "swing was really a man's thing" and he already had a singer, Webb hired her, and she began her rise to stardom.

In the male-dominated world of jazz and swing, Fitzgerald was a rare asset, one that many men could not seem to evaluate in other than physical terms. Donald Bogle writes in his book *Black Sugar: Eighty Years of America's Black Female Superstars* that if Fitzgerald had been "sexier" she might have developed into a "legendary public heroine." He seems unaware that she did.

Fitzgerald turns professional at 17   At age seventeen Fitzgerald turned professional, singing with Webb's band at the famed Savoy Ballroom. It was not long, however, before her legal status became a problem. To solve this problem, Webb and his wife decided to adopt her, thus becoming her legal guardians. Webb groomed Fitzgerald for success slowly and carefully, telling her to relax, not to rush, and " to go with the beat, always go with the beat," according to Colin. Under his tutelage Fitzgerald blossomed and her confidence grew, but she never ever quite mastered her nervousness before a performance. Proud of his protégée, Webb demanded that band members and other jazz musicians treat Fitzgerald with respect. She responded by always behaving like a lady.

Fitzgerald's first record was *Love and Kisses,* recorded with Chick Webb on June 12, 1935. It has since disappeared without a trace. Possessing a remarkable ear for music and the ability to imitate almost any musical instrument, Fitzgerald began "scat" singing. In October 1936 she recorded "If You Can't Sing It, You'll Have to Swing It" or "Paganini," using this unique style of singing.

Although still a teenager, Fitzgerald's confidence had increased to the point where she began writing songs. On February 18, 1937, Billie Holiday recorded a song composed by Webb with lyrics by Fitzgerald. Titled "You Showed Me the Way," the song stands among Holiday's classic recordings of this period. The lyric is often described as "Tin Pan Alley love song conventions," but reveals Fitzgerald's genuine simplicity.

Continuing to write songs, in the 1940s Fitzgerald wrote the lyrics to Duke Ellington's "In a Mellotone" and to Nat King Cole's "Oh, But I Do." She gained membership in the American Society of Composers, Authors, and Publishers in 1943, becoming the youngest person ever admitted to membership in this organization.

Smash hit is released   While in Boston during the spring of 1938, Fitzgerald was tinkling around on the piano singing the words to a nursery rhyme from her childhood days: "A-Tisket-A-Tasket, a brown and yellow basket." Al Feldman, a pianist and arranger for Webb, helped her, and together they came up with the song—a smash hit that by September of that year sold a million records. Excited by her sudden success, Fitzgerald momentarily lost her head. She married someone whose name she later had trouble recalling. Webb insisted that she have the marriage annulled, and she complied without argument.

Webb's death of spinal tuberculosis in 1939 was a great loss to the jazz world and to Fitzgerald. Webb had been a good guardian and confidant, and Fitzgerald credits him for the positive influence he had on her musical technique. At age twenty-one, Fitzgerald found herself the leader of Chick Webb's band. She kept the band going for three years. During this period, according to one source, she was married to Bernie Kornegay.

In 1942 the Chick Webb Band dissolved. Fitzgerald continued on her own, singing at various night spots. In 1944, Fitzgerald and the Ink Spots had a million-selling hit with "Into Each Life Some Rain Must Fall," and by 1945 they enjoyed another million seller, Duke Ellington's "I'm Beginning to See the Light."

In 1947 Fitzgerald married Ray Brown, a bass player from Pittsburgh. The pair adopted an infant and named him Raymond Brown Jr. When their marriage ended in 1953, Ray Brown Jr. continued to reside with Fitzgerald.

Fitzgerald wins Grammys   Fitzgerald's numerous honors and awards bear witness to her amazing talent. She is the recipient of twelve Grammy awards; the Pied Piper Award presented by ASCAP; the George & Ira Gershwin Award for Outstanding Achievement; the American Music Award (1978); the National Medal of the Arts 1987 (presented at the White House); and innumerable popularity awards from *Down Beat* magazine, *Metronome* magazine, and *Jazz Award Poll.* She was named number one female singer in the sixteenth International Jazz Critics Poll in 1968 and best female jazz vocalist years later, in 1981. Fitzgerald was honored on February 14, 1990, at a benefit concert at New York's Avery Fisher Hall for the American Heart Association.

Among Fitzgerald's greatest recordings are the famous *Gershwin Songbook,* a five-record set released in 1958, and the album *The Best Is Yet to Come,* for which she won her twelfth Grammy award. Renowned jazz impresario Norman Granz has been Fitzgerald's close friend and personal manager since 1954. Buying out her long-term contract from Decca Records, Granz began to record her on Verve Records, his label, in the late 1950s. Since 1972 she recorded exclusively for Pablo, Granz's classic jazz label. Fitzgerald had twenty-five albums to her credit on this label.

Toward the 1980s and early 1990s, Fitzgerald remained in the spotlight regardless of her failing health, which included cataract surgery, triple bypass surgery, and the amputation of both her legs below the knees due to complications from diabetes. It was this illness that would claim this songstress's life at her Beverly Hills home. In 1996, the world over mourned the loss of Fitzgerald, who was known throughout as the "First Lady of Song." Her death was shocking in that her fans attributed her voice to an immortal. Karen Schoemer's tribute in *Newsweek* was the consensus of many who idolized Fitzgerald:

> Her scat was her signature, but her voice possessed a heavenly perfection that could make a poignant ballad or a silly ditty sound equally sublime. She was a master of technique, able to leap octaves, spot tones, reinvent melodies and dance all over complex rhythms. Above all she had class. She never sang an unsophisticated note, and she always left a song better off than she had found it.

After her death, it became apparent that Fitzgerald kept her private life much a secret. She shied away from interviews and personal questions, allowing only her voice and the music do the talking for her. To Fitzgerald, her music was her life, and it was a simple equation that brought much joy to so many.—NAGUEYALTI WARREN

ARETHA FRANKLIN
1942–

Singer

Aretha Franklin was crowned the Queen of Soul in 1967, the year that saw her five singles for Atlantic Records sell over a million copies each. Among the songs to catapult Franklin to fame were "I Never Loved a Man," "Baby, I Love You," and her signature work, "Respect." Her first album for Atlantic, I Never Loved a Man, *also topped the million mark in sales, and she was proclaimed the year's top female vocalist by* Billboard, Cashbox, *and* Record World *magazines. The accolades continued into 1968, when the city of Detroit—her hometown—named February 16 of that year Aretha Franklin Day. The Southern Christian Leadership Conference responded to her rendition of Otis Redding's "Respect" with a special citation, and* Time *magazine honored Franklin with a cover on June 21. Since this explosion into superstardom, her career has had its peaks and valleys, but Franklin has maintained her position as one of the world's greatest musical treasures.*

Aretha Franklin was born the fourth of five children to Clarence La Vaughn Franklin, a noted evangelist preacher and singer, and Barbara (Siggers) Franklin, also an accomplished vocalist. Franklin began life in Memphis, Tennessee, on March 25, 1942. Two years later the family moved to Detroit, Michigan, where Aretha has lived most of her life. She grew up in a substantial and comfortable residence but felt acutely the absence of her mother, who left when Aretha was six and died four years later. Family friend Mahalia Jackson's observation is recorded in Mark Bego's biography of Franklin: "After her mama died, the whole family wanted for love."

The influence of gospel is unmistakable in Franklin's music. Jackson, Clara Ward, and Dinah Washington formed close relationships with Franklin; as famous singers and houseguests of her father's, each exerted a powerful influence on her. The Reverend Franklin also welcomed a number of other musicians into his home, including James Cleveland, Arthur Prysock, B. B. King, Dorothy Donegan, Lou Rawls, and Sam Cooke. Cleveland had a particular influence on the family, tutoring young Aretha on the piano and encouraging the girls in their formation of a gospel group that appeared in local churches for a span of eight months. With the influence of so many talented friends, as well as that of her father, Franklin thrived musically. "I had a piano right off the back porch, and sometimes I'd sing all day, every day, with my sisters and my friends," she recalled. She began playing the piano at age eight or nine but rebelled at formal lessons. A moment of realization came at her aunt's funeral when Franklin heard Clara Ward's emotional singing: "Clara knocked me out!" she said. "From then on I knew what I wanted to do was sing."

Two years later Franklin began traveling with her father's revival, an experience that exposed her to drinking, carousing, all-night partying, and the prejudice of southern whites. At age fourteen, and at that time strictly a gospel singer, she made her first solo recording for Chess Records. A startling set of hymns recorded at her father's church, the record was reissued by Sugar Hill in 1984 with the title *Aretha Gospel*.

Aretha Franklin.

During this time she also joined a gospel quartet directed by Reverend James Cleveland, one of her first mentors; he taught her how to reach notes unknown to her and to imbue her singing with expression. Her range reached five octaves, providing an incredible forty notes at her command. Traveling on gospel caravans from age thirteen to sixteen and singing with the true giants of gospel gave Franklin invaluable experience for later concert tours of her own.

At the age of fifteen Franklin was a talented pianist and a gospel-singing sensation, and was just beginning to get over her childhood disappointments and the loss of her mother, when she became pregnant. She named her son Clarence Franklin, after her father. Bego comments, "What happened to Aretha as a teenager set a pattern of victimization by the men in her life. At the age of fifteen, Aretha Franklin had already earned her right to sing the blues."

Having dropped out of high school to have her baby in 1958, Franklin spent a lot of time at home listening to music and playing the piano. She was fascinated by the blues, especially by the singing of Dinah Washington. Far from an idle time for her, it was at this point that Franklin began planning to leave her family to strike out on her own. With her father supporting her decision, Franklin moved to New York City at age eighteen, hoping to sing secular music and become a successful blues singer like Washington.

Franklin's talent was immediately recognized by John Hammond of Columbia Records, who exclaimed, "This is the best voice I've heard in twenty years!" He signed her to a five-year contract and became her manager. She was also recognized by the media early on, and in July 1962 she was among the headlining acts at the Newport Jazz Festival. Already, she was being compared with Ray Charles and Dinah Washington.

Despite her popularity among jazz critics, Columbia kept Franklin on a nightclub repertoire of pop songs with heavy orchestration, an arrangement that did not suit her and led to artistic and personal frustration. The dreary rounds of engagements in second-rate clubs worsened the situation; Franklin waited out the expiration of her contract while her records maintained modest sales.

After fulfilling her contractual obligation to Columbia, Franklin switched to Atlantic Records, a move well-timed for her popularity and earning power. She was already popular with black consumers, and white consumers were ready for her, having been exposed somewhat to black music through white performers like Elvis Presley. The crossover market made Motown Records and its stars giants in the business, and prompted Atlantic to follow the same path. As a result, Franklin was given the freedom to choose her own material and pursue her own style, allowing her to reach a wide audience without abandoning the qualities that made up her unique appeal to the black consumer. Thus a constantly widening circle of listeners was exposed to her vocal capabilities, characterized by Jim Miller: "[Franklin's] voice, a robust yet crystalline alto, is remarkable for its reliable intonation, expressive vibrato, and great range of pitch dynamics, and expression. She is able to execute changes of register, volume, and timbre with dexterity and fluency, often altering the entire color of her voice in successive verses of a song as the text demands."

A marked discrepancy exists between Franklin's shyness as a person and directness and inhibition as a singer, a quality that a *Time* cover story, among others, emphasized:

> She does not seem to be performing so much as bearing witness to a reality so simple and compelling that she could not possibly fake it. In her selection of songs, whether written by others or by herself, she unfailingly opts for those that frame her own view of life. "If a song's about something

"Queen of Soul" sings at the 1993 Inaugural gala.

I've experienced or that could have happened to me, it's good," she says. "But if it's alien to me, I couldn't lend anything to it. Because that's what soul is about—just living and having to get along."

Four Grammys won early in career   Between 1967 and 1969, Franklin won four Grammy awards: best R&B recording and best female R&B performance, both in 1967, for "Respect"; best female R&B performance in 1968 for "Chain of Fools"; and best female R&B performance in 1969 for "Share Your Love with Me." She produced at least one million-selling song each year from 1967 to 1973.

The 1970s brought six Grammys for Franklin, for "Don't Play That Song for Me," "Bridge Over Troubled Water," "Young, Gifted and Black," "Amazing Grace," "Master of Eyes," and "Ain't Nothing Like the Real Thing."

Throughout her career Franklin has found herself challenged with personal problems. A marriage to Ted White, who also became her manager early in her career, ended in 1969, a situation she found difficult to handle. Her next relationship, with Ken Cunningham, lasted six years and produced many positive changes for her. With Cunningham's encouragement, Franklin was able to lose weight, cut back on alcohol, and focus more closely on her work. He also provided photography for her albums. She ended the relationship in 1977.

Franklin was again married in 1978, to actor Glynn Turman; the marriage ended in 1982, with little explanation. At the time Franklin moved back to Detroit to care for her father, who had been shot by a burglar in 1979. The tragedy deeply affected Franklin, who spent $1,500 a week for nursing care and a total of over $500,000 on his medical support. She gave two benefit performances, in 1979 and 1981, to raise funds for his hospitalization. Her father remained in a coma until his death on July 24, 1984.

Franklin traditionally contributes large sums to charity through benefit concerts. Causes worthwhile to her have included the Relief Center at her father's church, Mother Waddles's Perpetual Mission, the United Negro College Fund, and the NAACP. She also used her voice to raise funds for the Joffrey Ballet in a 1982 performance at Carnegie Hall. The Joffrey in turn honored her with a ballet choreographed to her music. In 1988 she recorded a public-service announcement against driving under the influence of drugs and liquor. Her hit record, "Think," was used in the spot, entitled "Think . . . Don't Drive with Drugs or Drink!"

Franklin earns respect   In 1986 Michigan legislators proclaimed Franklin's voice one of the state's natural resources. In August of 1989, Senator Carl Levin of Michigan presented Franklin with a plaque and a Senate resolution honoring her achievements and her contributions to the fight against drunk driving. Levin said, "For this dedication to her craft, and her community, she earned what all of us covet—R-E-S-P-E-C-T." In 1991 Franklin's home state again honored her, this time with an honorary doctorate of humane letters from Detroit's Wayne State University.

In her more than thirty years in the record business, Aretha Franklin has had a career that other female vocalists can only dream of matching. She is to contemporary pop and soul music what Ella Fitzgerald is to jazz singing. Franklin was the first female performer inducted into the Rock & Roll Hall of Fame and she was given a Grammy for lifetime achievement in 1991. Her vast wealth of creative achievements is staggering, with thirty-five albums and seventeen number-one R&B singles. Franklin's recording career has been narrowed to re-releases of her earlier works and duets with such legendary singers as Frank Sinatra. With a 1992 appearance at the Democratic National Convention, renowned "Queen of Soul" Aretha Franklin remains in the spotlight.—VIRGINIA WILSON WALLACE

JOHN HOPE **FRANKLIN**
1915–
Historian, author, lecturer

On September 29, 1995, John Hope Franklin, a scholar of United States history, received the nation's highest civilian award, the Presidential Medal of Freedom. It is awarded by the president "to those persons whom he deems to have made especially meritorious contributions to the . . . the United States, to world peace, or to cultural or other significant public or private endeavors." President Bill Clinton spoke of Franklin's outstanding contributions, and his citation read in part: "His extraordinary work in the field of American History and his studies of the South have earned John Hope Franklin the respect and admiration of people throughout the world."

John Hope Franklin—named after John Hope, the former president of Atlanta University, who on different occasions, had taught each of Franklin's parents—was born on January 2, 1915, in Rentiesville, Oklahoma, an all–African American town in McIntosh County, to Buck Colbert Franklin and Mollie Parker Franklin. Mollie, a teacher who had earned her certificate at Roger Williams University, and Buck, a lawyer who had attended Roger Williams University and Atlanta Baptist College, had married in 1903. Thereafter they had lived briefly in both Ardmore and Springer, Oklahoma (then Indian Territory). According to *The Vintage Years,* they moved to Rentiesville however, "to be free from the pressures and insults that they had experienced in the larger world," after Buck Franklin's eviction from a Shreveport courtroom by a judge who insisted that "no 'nigger lawyer' could represent clients in his court." In Rentiesville, Buck Franklin farmed, practiced law, edited *The Rentiesville News,* and served as both justice of the peace and postmaster while his wife became an elementary school teacher. Franklin was the youngest of four children. His sisters, Mozella and Anne Harriet were born in 1906 and 1913, respectively. His brother, Buck Colbert Jr., was born in 1907. John Hope Franklin married Aurelia E. Whittington of Goldsboro, North Carolina, a Fisk graduate and librarian, in 1940. To that union was born one son, John Whittington Franklin, on August 24, 1952. In later years, Franklin's family came to include one foster son, Bouna N'diaye of Senegal, West Africa.

The formative years   John Hope Franklin, a precocious child who sat in his mother's elementary school classroom in Rentiesville, learned to read as well as write before the age of five. In 1921, seeking to increase his earnings and improve his family's quality of life, Franklin's

John Hope Franklin.

father left Rentiesville and moved to the city of Tulsa. The rest of the family temporarily remained in Rentiesville. There Franklin attended public school, skipping a grade "to conform to the level of learning that most clearly identified [him] with [his] intellectual peers. . . . Thus, when [he] was nine years old [he] was in the sixth grade."

While separated from Buck Franklin, young Franklin experienced the indignity and virulence of racism. The family had more than its share of unsettling experiences, which included anxiously awaiting word about Buck Franklin's safety following the infamous 1921 Tulsa race riot and the ejection of Mollie Franklin, John Hope, and Anne from a train when Mrs. Franklin refused to move out of the coach designated for whites. By December 1925, however, the family reunited in Tulsa.

The adolescent John Hope completed his secondary education in Tulsa's Booker T. Washington High School. Despite hardships resulting from financial difficulties and racial segregation, Franklin's parents emphasized self-confidence, equality, and racial pride. Consistently, as well, they continued to expose their children to the life of the mind. "I had two highly intelligent parents, [whose] . . . discussions were high level," Franklin once remarked in the *Winston-Salem Journal.* "I had a father who read and wrote every night. I grew up thinking that's what you did every night—you either read or wrote." At the age of sixteen, Franklin graduated valedictorian of his class and won a scholarship to Fisk University.

Franklin continued his education at Fisk, an historically African American university in Nashville, Tennessee, that had been founded in the nineteenth century. Franklin entered in 1931 when virtually all Americans were being adversely affected by the Great Depression. Since the scholarship was insufficient and family funds limited, young Franklin worked in the library and the dining hall to earn money. In his first year of college, Franklin was determined to follow in his father's professional footsteps. He told the *Winston-Salem Journal*: "My father would always take me down to the courthouse and introduce me to the lawyers and judges." He remembered, in *Emerge* magazine, "When I went into the courtroom with him, . . . if it was a jury trial, I'd sit at the table with him. . . . I admired him so."

In Franklin's second year, however, he reached a significant turning point in his life. Theodore S. Currier, a Harvard-trained white professor introduced Franklin to history—its perplexities and problems, its issues and interpretations, its continuity and changes. Franklin later explained Currier's influence in *Currents:* "He raised questions that pushed [our] mind[s] right to the edge." Franklin soon abandoned his pursuit of a career in law and decided to devote himself to historical studies. Franklin graduated from Fisk in 1935, earning his bachelor of arts degree magna cum laude. Although at that time Fisk had no Phi Beta Kappa chapter, Franklin was a founding member of Fisk's chapter, established in 1953.

Receiving financial assistance from Theodore Currier, who borrowed five hundred dollars to help Franklin attend Harvard, Franklin entered the university's graduate program in history during the fall of 1935. Franklin's first choice for his field was British history, but he knew primary research was required and he believed that he would have no opportunity to travel to England. Franklin decided his field of concentration would be United States history and he would subsequently focus on Southern history, then an emerging field. He took courses with professors whose rigorous requirements were met with aplomb by the young Franklin. Franklin earned his master of arts degree in 1936 at the age of twenty-one.

After a year of teaching at Fisk University during the academic year 1936–37, Franklin returned to Harvard for the academic years in 1937–38 and 1938–39 with the support of the Edwin Austin and Julius Rosenwald Fund fellowships. Franklin spent his time completing the requirements for his Ph.D., editing his first journal article on Edward Bellamy (which appeared in *New England Quarterly* of December 1938), and taking his examinations. For Franklin's advanced studies, Arthur Schlesinger Sr. served as his advisor, and Paul H. Buck supervised Franklin's dissertation. Franklin's dissertation research required his return to the South, and he taught while investigating primary sources on free African Americans in antebellum North Carolina. During these years of dissertation research and writing, Franklin was reminded how little Harvard credentials meant in the American South with its own apartheid. Among other experiences of racial discrimination as a young scholar, he was denied permission to sit with white researchers in the North Carolina State Archives and shunted off to a separate, isolated room. Such impediments to research notwithstanding, Franklin wrote an outstanding dissertation of publishable quality and, in 1941, Harvard University awarded him the Doctor of Philosophy degree in history.

Early academic career

Franklin served as a professor of history on the faculties of St. Augustine's College of Raleigh, North Carolina, from 1939 to 1943; North Carolina College for Negroes (now North Carolina Central University) in Durham, North Carolina, from 1943 to 1947; and Howard University of Washington, D.C., from 1947 to 1956. While teaching at historically African American institutions of higher education, mainstream publishers accepted for publication works in which Franklin disclosed history of African Americans that countered myths of inferiority and insignificant achievement. In 1943, Franklin's revised dissertation was published by the University of North Carolina Press as *The Free Negro in North Carolina, 1790–1860*. Four years later Franklin completed and Alfred Knopf released the first edition of *From Slavery to Freedom, A History of Negro Americans*.

Career varies in the post-Brown era

In 1956, the year of the publication of his controversial *Militant South, 1800–1860*, news of Franklin's desegregation of Brooklyn College's history department—his appointment as chair of the fifty-two person department—appeared on the front page of the *New York Times*. Becoming the first African American to head the history department at a major, predominantly white academic institution was discussed at length. During his eight years at Brooklyn College, he published his pathbreaking revisionist study, *Reconstruction After the Civil War* (1961). He served as Pitt Professor of American History and Institutions at Cambridge University in England from 1962 to 1963. Also in 1963, the centennial of Abraham Lincoln's Emancipation Proclamation, Doubleday published John Hope Franklin's monograph, *The Emancipation Proclamation*.

By his own admission in *Race and History*, "There came a time in my own teaching career when I realized that . . . I would never be able to write on all the subjects in which I was deeply interested," and Franklin determined that he should consider moving to an institution in which he could work with graduate students. The University of Chicago provided just such an opportunity and many more. In 1964, he joined the history faculty of the University of Chicago. He immediately began teaching graduate students and undergraduates. Within three years he was chosen to serve as departmental chairperson and headed the department from 1967 to 1970. He was appointed the John Matthews Manly Distinguished Service Professor in 1969. Continuing his research and scholarship throughout his tenure at Chicago from 1964 to 1982, Franklin not only published *A Southern Odyssey: Travelers in the Antebellum North* (1976) and *Racial Equality in America* (1976), a series of lectures given by Franklin for the bicentennial of the nation, but also began editing a series entitled "Negro American Biographies and Autobiographies" for the University of Chicago Press. Particularly rewarding to him during his eighteen years at the University of Chicago was his supervising more than thirty dissertations of students who later published over a dozen books. During his professorship at Chicago, Franklin's influence as a teacher had its most tangible results with respect to the training of young scholars aspiring to academic careers.

It was Franklin's goal, as described in the *Winston-Salem Journal*, to "instill in his students a high standard of scholarship"; as he has publicly contended, "you can't have that without having a high standard of integrity, because the essence of scholarship is truth."

For reasons related to research and publication goals, his health, and the severity of the Chicago climate, in 1980 Franklin took a leave of absence from the University of Chicago and moved to Durham, North Carolina, where he became the Mellon Fellow at the National Humanities Center. In 1982 he retired from the University of Chicago, but retained his title of John Matthews Manley Professor Emeritus. Although courted by a number of academic institutions, Franklin eventually accepted an appointment as the James B. Duke Professor of History at Duke University. In this capacity he was a member of the history department's faculty from 1982 to 1985. Thereafter, he assumed emeritus status with the history department and limited his teaching to service as professor of legal history, an interest of his earlier years. While at Duke University, Franklin published several works: *George Washington Williams: A Biography* (Franklin's personal favorite); *Race and History: Selected Essays, 1938–88* (which he dedicated to his secretary of more than thirty years, Margaret Fitzsimmons); and *The Color Line: Legacy for the Twenty-First Century*. In January 1995, Duke University expressed appreciation to Franklin for his service in a university-wide celebration, chiefly organized by Vice-Provost George Wright. Fellow Fiskite and prize-winning historian David Levering Lewis delivered an eloquent keynote address that not only traced the life and work of John Hope Franklin, but also offered an assessment of his contributions to history, historiography, and social progress. The proceedings were later published by Duke in *John Hope Franklin: The 80th Birthday Celebration*.

Publications and scholarship   Franklin is an exceptional and indefatigable researcher as a well as prolific scholar. Franklin is the author of twelve books. In addition to those already mentioned, his books include *The Emancipation Proclamation* (1961), *Land of the Free* (with John Caughey and Ernest May in 1963), *Illustrated History of Black Americans* (1970), and *Race and History: Selected Essays, 1938–1988* (1990). Franklin is the editor of ten other works and

*John Hope Franklin accepting
the Britannica Award.*

has written more than 125 scholarly articles on United States, Southern, and African American history. Kenneth B. Clark, eminent scholar, friend, and colleague of Franklin for more than forty years, wrote in *Currents* that Franklin "has filled a void in probing and communicating the role of race as an integral part of American History."

Franklin is most widely known for *From Slavery to Freedom,* now in its seventh edition and coauthored with former student Alfred Moss Jr. Since its first edition of 1947, this work has sold over three million copies, has been translated into Chinese, Japanese, German, French, and Portuguese, and has maintained its distinction as the authoritative history of African Americans. In the post—*Brown* v. *Board of Education* era, Franklin's 1956 *Militant South* "was among the earliest works heralding an interpretive shift to a political-cultural paradigm in which economic and political forces are focused through the lens of hegemonic belief systems." Franklin, according to David Levering Lewis, "elevated the South's pandemic violence into the organizing principle of its society." Franklin's 1961 book on Reconstruction, *Reconstruction After the Civil War*, as the distinguished historian William Leuchtenburg reminds us in the *Duke Law Journal*, "did more than any other volume to correct the racist assumptions that, unhappily, once prevailed." Franklin's work in progress, as of 1997, includes three collaborations: one edited biographical work with his son, John Whittington Franklin, on the life of Buck Franklin Sr., John Hope Franklin's father; another with former student Loren Schweninger, "Dissidents on the Plantation: Runaway Slaves"; and with Alfred Moss Jr. an eighth edition of *From Slavery to Freedom*. To this list Franklin has added a fourth project, his autobiography.

Public service, activism, and advocacy   Franklin is forthright in his views, published in *Race and History*, that "historians with no governmental connections should participate in the discussion of public policy issues, . . . raise questions about the operation of a given policy that is defended on the ground that it is in line with historic public policy, . . . [and] challenge the . . . validity of a traditional policy that is followed for the sake of tradition and not necessarily for the sake of the public interest." Accordingly, having once been barred from the University of Oklahoma's graduate school, Franklin, in 1948, was pleased to testify as an expert witness in the case of Lyman Johnson who was seeking admission to the all-white history graduate program of the University of Kentucky. Later, in 1953, John Hope Franklin provided historical research for Thurgood Marshall and the other attorneys fighting racial segregation in the consolidated cases of *Brown* v. *Board of Education*.

Beyond this professional role, however, John Hope Franklin has believed that being an historian has compelled his activism as a citizen. Unabashedly, he has admitted in *Emerge*, "I think knowing one's history leads one to act in a more enlightened fashion. I can [not] imagine how knowing one's history would not urge one to be an activist." So it has been throughout his life that, as he noted in *Race and History*, he believed it "necessary, as a black historian, to have a personal agenda, that involved a type of activism." Franklin deems activism and advocacy appropriate responses to the nation's history, policy, and traditional practices with respect to justice. Having been in England during the 1963 March on Washington, in 1965 Franklin joined the Selma to Montgomery March led by Martin Luther King Jr. "With more than thirty historians who came from all parts of the country to register their objection to racial bigotry in the United States," Franklin wrote in *Race and History* he "marched from the city of St. Jude, Alabama to Montgomery." In 1987, Franklin—with his friends and colleagues Walter Dellinger and William Leuchtenburg—traveled to Washington, D.C., in order to appear before the Senate Committee on the Judiciary and oppose the appointment of Robert Bork to the Supreme Court. With other past presidents of the Organization of American Historians, including Mary Frances Berry, a younger friend and distinguished scholar-activist, Franklin enthusiastically submitted an amicus brief in the racial discrimination case of *Brenda Patterson v. McLean Credit Union*. Franklin later added his voice to other proponents of civil rights, affirmative action, and intellectual excellence who opposed the nomination of Clarence Thomas to the U.S. Supreme Court. John Hope Franklin has written and taught history, but he has also helped to make it.

Recognition, awards, and honors   Franklin remains the only person to have been elected national president of the five major national organizations of scholars: the American

Studies Association (1966–67), the Southern Historical Association (1970–71), the United Chapters of Phi Beta Kappa (1973–76), the Organization of American Historians (1974–75), and the American Historical Association (1978–79). The American Studies Association established in 1986 a John Hope Franklin Publication Prize, and in 1987 Adelphi University inaugurated a John Hope Franklin Distinguished Lecture. Duke University not only chose in 1995 to establish a research center for African and African American studies in honor of Franklin, but has commissioned a portrait of its James B. Duke Emeritus Professor of History to be placed with founders of the university and other distinguished Duke scholars in the university's library.

Franklin has received more than 100 honorary doctoral degrees from colleges and universities in the United States and abroad. In addition to the 1995 Presidential Medal of Freedom, Franklin is the recipient of scores of awards and honors from states, national publications, organizations, and institutions of higher education. Among these are induction into the Oklahoma Hall of Fame (1978), the Jefferson Medal of the Council for the Advancement and Support of Education (1984), Black History Makers Award of the Associated Black Charities (1988), the first Cleanth Brooks Medal of the Fellowship of Southern Writers for Distinguished Achievement in Southern Letters (1989), Encyclopedia Britannica's Gold Medal for the Dissemination of Knowledge (1990), the Bruce Catton Award of the Society of American Historians (1994), the Sidney Hook Award of Phi Beta Kappa (1994), the Distinguished Service Award of the Organization of American Historians (1995), the first W. E. B. Du Bois Lifetime Achievement Award from the Fisk University Alumni Association (1995), and the coveted Spingarn Medal of the NAACP (1995).

John Hope Franklin "has often been called America's greatest black historian. But that term is a misnomer on two counts," according to William Leuchtenburg in the *Duke Law Journal.* "John Hope [Franklin] is one of America's greatest historians, indeed greatest scholars, . . . irrespective of race. And though he has written extensively on the black race, he ought to be thought of as a historian of the South, a historian of America, a historian of the human condition." That is consistent with Franklin's own assessment of himself as historian and scholar, fully committed to learning, truth, and the creation of a better world. He defines himself in *Currents*: "I am a historian of the American people."—GENNA RAE MCNEIL

MARCUS **GARVEY**

1887–1940

Organization founder, Pan Africanist, newspaper publisher, writer

Marcus Garvey founded and led the Universal Negro Improvement Association and African Communities League (usually rendered UNIA), the largest mass movement in African American history. The UNIA flourished from about 1919 to the mid-1920s and existed in almost forty states domestically and over forty countries internationally. Estimates of its membership range from one to eleven million worldwide, making the UNIA also the largest Pan African movement of all time.

Marcus Mosiah Garvey was born on August 17, 1887, in St. Anns Bay, Jamaica, to Marcus and Sarah Garvey. He had one surviving sibling, a sister named Indiana. His father was a stonemason with a love for reading and a library in his home. His parents sometimes engaged in small-scale peasant farming.

It is difficult to surpass the eloquence of Garvey's own account of his beginnings and influences. He said in *The Philosophy and Opinions of Marcus Garvey,*

> My father was a man of brilliant intellect and dashing courage. He was unafraid of consequences. He took human chances in the course of life, as most bold men do, and he failed at the close of his career. He once had a fortune; he died poor. My mother was a sober and conscientious Christian, too soft and good for the time in which she lived. She was the direct opposite of my father.

Garvey received an excellent elementary education, but in lieu of secondary schooling he was apprenticed in his early teens to his godfather's printing business. At the age of sixteen he moved to Jamaica's capital city of Kingston, where he became the country's youngest foreman printer. He became active in politics, public speaking, and journalism.

In 1910 Garvey immigrated to Costa Rica, part of a large exodus of Caribbean workers seeking work in Latin America. He wandered for the next four years around Central and South America and Europe. He observed the plight of African descendants everywhere, agitated on their behalf, and worked at a variety of jobs. In England he worked for the foremost Pan African journal of the day, the *Africa Times and Orient Review*, published by the African Duse Mohamed Ali. In London he also attended law lectures at Birkbeck College of the University of London.

*Marcus Garvey
in regal glory.*

His travels and reading exposed Garvey to the universal suffering of the African race. Africa itself was in the last stages of European imperialist conquest. African Americans had largely lost the civil rights gained during Reconstruction. Disenfranchisement, Jim Crow, and lynching had become their lot. Africans in the Caribbean were mostly excluded from the political process and suffered the myriad discriminations associated with colonial status. Caribbean immigrants in Latin America were treated badly, even wantonly killed. Garvey pondered all of this as he prepared to leave England for home. He feared that a weak and prostrate African race was a standing invitation to reenslavement or even extinction. Towards the end of his European sojourn he had been reduced to penury in England and had come close to being repatriated as a pauper at public expense. But by the summer of 1914 Garvey was able to pay his own way home.

Before leaving he read Booker T. Washington's autobiography, *Up from Slavery.* He admired Washington for his race pride and, above all, for his efforts to pull himself and his race up by their own bootstraps. For Garvey, Washington's book became the final key to unraveling the puzzle of his own life's work. Garvey later recalled in his *Philosophy and Opinions,* in a famous and much quoted passage:

I read "Up from Slavery" by Booker T. Washington, and then my doom—if I may so call it—of being a race leader dawned upon me in London after I had traveled through almost half of Europe.

I asked: "Where is the black man's Government?" "Where is his King and his Kingdom?" "Where is his President, his country, and his ambassador, his army, his navy, his men of big affairs?" I could not find them, and then I declared, "I will help to make them."

My young and ambitious mind led me into flights of great imagination. I saw before me then, even as I do now, a new world of black men, not peons, serfs, dogs and slaves, but a nation of sturdy men making their impression upon civilization and causing a new light to dawn upon the human race.

What Garvey lacked in money and influence he made up for in the intensity of his dream. He felt that the power of organization led to African advancement. And so within five days of arriving home on July 15, 1914, he founded the UNIA. Garvey corresponded with Booker T. Washington and led the UNIA on a round of social, charitable, and educational work throughout Jamaica. The organization's stated goals included the provision of educational facilities, upgrading the status of women, providing for the needy, building African power, and establishing a sense of "confraternity" within the race worldwide.

On March 23, 1916, Marcus Garvey arrived in New York to begin a five-month fund-raising lecture tour to finance his Jamaican operation. He would return to Jamaica to live more than eleven years later. In the interim he would become the best known, most loved, and most hated African in the world.

Soon after his arrival in New York Garvey toured the United States and Canada. Back in Harlem in 1917 he took to the streets, haranguing crowds on a regular basis. As his popularity as a street speaker grew, he hired a hall for weekly indoor meetings. By 1918, Garvey moved the UNIA from Jamaica to Harlem.

The Harlem-based UNIA now took off into a period of explosive growth. Garvey's travels had yielded him valuable contacts and the movement became instantly international.

By 1919 branches had been established or were in the making in Canada, the Caribbean, Central and South America, West Africa, and England.

UNIA consolidates   Garvey moved to consolidate the new organization with great skill. A variety of subsidiaries and related ventures appeared. A Negro Factories Corporation appeared in 1918 and eventually employed over a thousand African Americans in a doll factory, a tailoring establishment, grocery stores, restaurants, a printery, and more. The *Negro World* weekly, soon to become the most widely circulated African newspaper in the world, began publication in 1918. The UNIA's most ambitious economic venture, the Black Star Line Steamship Corporation, launched its first ship in 1919. The line raised over one million dollars and its ships sailed to Haiti, Cuba, Jamaica, Costa Rica, and elsewhere. Its intention was to provide employment for many African seamen, dignified accommodation for African travelers, and a vehicle for Pan African trade and emigration.

The line was sabotaged by opportunists within and forces—including governmental— without, all compounded by the UNIA's lack of business experience and the rapid growth of the company, which almost overwhelmed the organizers. The Black Star Line, nevertheless, caught the imagination of African people around the world like nothing else. There were scenes of great rejoicing wherever the ships appeared. In Costa Rica, African workers stopped work for the day and inundated the Black Star Line ship with flowers and fruit. In Havana, Cuba, people rowed out to the ship in small boats and literally showered it with fruits and flowers. In Aiken, South Carolina, the African community chartered a special train to take them to Charleston to see a Black Star Line vessel.

In 1920 the UNIA held the first of several international conventions—the last being in Toronto, Canada in 1938. Twenty-five thousand people from around the African world filled New York's Madison Square Garden for the opening ceremony. There they elected Garvey president-general of the UNIA.

The conference produced one of African America's major historical documents in the Declaration of Rights of the Negro Peoples of the World. The declaration listed the major grievances of the race and put forward demands to redress them: it declared red, black, and green the colors of the race; it adopted the Universal Ethiopian Anthem as the UNIA's anthem; and it called for African history to be taught in schools attended by African children. The organization was divided into regions for better administration. A commissioner headed each region and organizers systematically traversed their regions, starting new branches, resuscitating faltering ones, adjudicating disputes, and spreading the word of Garveyism everywhere. The work of paid organizers was supplemented by many volunteers, often strangers to the organization, who spread the doctrine of Garveyism with missionary zeal.

Garvey was aided at the helm of the UNIA by a number of talented men and women, many of whom were important figures in their own right. These included John Edward Bruce, one of African America's most famous journalists; T. Thomas Fortune, the "dean" of African American newspapermen, editor of the UNIA's *Negro World*, and for many years a close confidant of Booker T. Washington; William H. Ferris, with a bachelor's degree from Yale and a master's from Harvard, who presided over the UNIA's literary activity; Lady Henrietta Vinton Davis, UNIA international organizer, Shakespearean actress, and former associate of Frederick Douglass; Hubert H. Harrison, Harlem's most popular scholar-activist; Amy Jacques Garvey, one-time personal secretary, *Negro World* associate editor, and Garvey's wife; Archbishop

George Alexander McGuire, sometime chaplain-general of the UNIA and founder of the African Orthodox Church, and many others.

Ideology of UNIA spreads   The spread of the UNIA was due to many factors. The New Negro radicalism of the war and post-war years provided a receptive milieu for Garvey's activities. Garvey's indefatigable energy, his powerful oratory, his moving writing style, and his general charisma drew people to him. Of great importance also was his ideology, for Garvey articulated a well-planned body of ideas that appealed to millions of people.

Garvey was a proponent of African nationalism. This had always been and continues to be an important influence in African American and Pan African life. Garvey succeeded like none of his predecessors of Pan Africanism, however, in channeling these ideas directly into a massive organization.

Race first, self-reliance, and nationhood were the three planks of Garvey's ideological platform. Race first meant that African people should put their self-interest first, as other races did. Garvey cheerfully allowed other groups a similar right, as long as it did not lead to the oppression of anyone else. Race first also meant that African people must see physical beauty in themselves, and African people should critique their own literature. Garvey expressed these ideas in his most famous essay, "African Fundamentalism," republished in the present author's book of the same title:

> The time has come for the Negro to forget and cast behind him his hero worship and adoration of other races, and to start out immediately to create and emulate heroes of his own. We must canonize our own saints, create our own martyrs, and elevate to positions of fame and honor black men and women who have made their distinct contributions to our racial history. . . . We must inspire a literature and promulgate a doctrine of our own without any apologies to the powers that be. The right is ours and God's. Let contrary sentiment and cross opinions go to the winds.

Race first could be seen in practically everything Garvey did, including his desire for an independent African media and his contention, in the tradition of Bishop Henry McNeal Turner, that African people should depict God in their own racial image and likeness.

Self-reliance meant simply that without the psychological benefits of doing for self, an oppressed people ran the risk of perpetual dependency and lack of independence.

Nationhood emphasized the necessity for political self-determination at all levels. Africa assumed special significance as the ancestral home of the race and a place of great natural potential. Garvey attempted in the early 1920s to move his headquarters to Liberia, the only independent country in West Africa. He also planned to facilitate the immigration there of thousands of African American and Caribbean people, imbued with a pioneering spirit and having technical or educational skills to offer.

Opposition towards UNIA   Garvey's phenomenal success brought with it an intense opposition from several disparate directions. Some felt eclipsed by his success; others opposed him on ideological grounds. Imperialist governments resented his radicalizing impact on their African subjects. J. Edgar Hoover, later head of the FBI, considered him a rabble rouser and a fit candidate for deportation. The Communist International was frustrated by Garvey's much greater success with the workers and peasants of the African world. The success of his "race first" idea seemed a reproach to their "class first" theories.

The African American integrationists of the National Association for the Advancement of Colored People (NAACP) and the powerful Jewish element who dominated this association waged all-out war on Garvey and the UNIA. W. E. B. Du Bois was main spokesman for the former. He kept up a constant barrage of criticism, both from the pages of the NAACP's *Crisis* and elsewhere. Garvey's Black Star Line was as much a source of annoyance to Du Bois as were his physical features, which Du Bois described as black and ugly. He described Garvey, in a famous *Crisis* editorial in 1924, as a "lunatic or a traitor."

The Jewish element in the NAACP is epitomized by Julian Mack, NAACP member, founder of the American Jewish Committee, first president of the American Jewish Congress, and president from 1918 to 1921 of the Zionist Organization of America. It was Judge Mack who sentenced Garvey to the maximum jail term, imposed the maximum fine, ordered Garvey to pay the entire costs of the trial, and refused him bail after Garvey's conviction on a trumped-up charge of mail fraud in 1923. Early in the trial he refused to rescue himself, despite his membership in the hostile NAACP, which had recently been waging a "Marcus Garvey Must Go" campaign.

The mail fraud conviction was the major reversal that Garvey's enemies had long worked for. Garvey was accused of defrauding subscribers to Black Star Line stock. After losing his appeal he entered Atlanta Federal Penitentiary on a five-year sentence in 1925. His sentence was commuted by President Calvin Coolidge in 1927 after millions of people signed petitions and otherwise clamored for his release. Commutation was accompanied by deportation.

It was during his trial and imprisonment that the most important of Garvey's books were published. All were compiled and edited by his wife, Amy Jacques Garvey. Amy Garvey published the seminal *Philosophy and Opinions of Marcus Garvey, or Africa for the Africans* in two volumes in 1923 and 1925. These consisted largely of Garvey's speeches and writings. Garvey hoped through these volumes to counter the misrepresentations of his work appearing in the major media. In 1927 Amy Garvey also published two volumes of Garvey's poetry, namely *The Tragedy of White Injustice* and *Selections from the Poetic Meditations of Marcus Garvey*. The title poem of the former compilation was a lengthy epic chronicling the raping, slaughter, and enslavement perpetrated by Europeans against other races. It was republished in Tony Martin's *The Poetical Works of Marcus Garvey*. It was very popular among Garveyites. Garvey's other major book, a secret course of instruction given to his top organizers in 1937, was first published forty-nine years later as *Message to the People: The Course of African Philosophy*, the seventh title in a series called "The New Marcus Garvey Library."

The post–United States years Garvey returned to Jamaica on December 10, 1927, to the largest crowds the island had ever seen. Over the next few years he established two newspapers, *The Blackman* and the *New Jamaican*. In 1929 he held a spectacular Sixth International Convention of the Negro Peoples of the World, which attracted delegates from around the world. In the same year he founded the Peoples Political Party, one of the first modern political parties in the Anglophone Caribbean.

He entered the race for the upcoming 1930 Legislative Council elections and was promptly arrested and jailed by the British authorities, at the start of a country-wide tour. The colonialists thought he committed contempt when he explained that if elected he would work to discourage judicial partiality. From his jail cell he entered the campaign for the Kingston and St. Andrew Corporation Council and won a seat. He was released shortly before the Legislative Council elections and lost. Apart from the disadvantage of a truncated campaign, most of his followers were disenfranchised in the restrictive colonial polity, where mostly white people and a few rich Africans could vote.

It was also at this time that Garvey's two sons, Marcus Jr. and Julius, were born to Amy Jacques, whom Garvey had married in Missouri in 1922.

In the United States, meanwhile, the UNIA split into rival factions. One major faction remained loyal to Garvey and published the *Negro World* up to 1933. Another sought to supplant Garvey with a United States–based leadership. Garvey renamed the loyal faction the Universal Negro Improvement Association and African Communities League of the World. Whether loyal to Garvey or not, the UNIA remained an important presence in several North American cities, especially New York, into the 1950s.

In addition, several important new organizations rose out of the ashes of the UNIA. Most important was the Nation of Islam, whose leader, the Honorable Elijah Muhammad, is thought to have been a UNIA member in Detroit in the 1920s. Carlos Cooks's African Nationalist Pioneer Movement, an important Harlem-based organization in the 1950s and 1960s, was also an outgrowth of the UNIA. In Jamaica the founders of the Rastafarian movement came out of the UNIA and never lost their reverence for Garvey, despite differences of opinion over Haile Selassie of Ethiopia. (Garvey was critical of Selassie during the Italian aggression against Ethiopia in the 1930s. Selassie has always been the most revered figure in the Rastafarian pantheon.)

In 1934 Garvey relocated to London, England. He continued to publish *The Black Man* and toured Canada and the Caribbean. He died in London on June 10, 1940, after suffering a series of strokes. He was fifty-two years old. The period of his greatest glory had begun when he was barely into his thirties.

Garvey's body was returned home in 1964 amidst much pomp and splendor. The newly independent nation of Jamaica made him its first national hero. He remains one of the most popular historical figures around the African world and is frequently celebrated in poetry and song; in the naming of roads, buildings, and schools; on postage stamps and coins; and in the erection of statues bearing his likeness. Prime Minister Kwame Nkrumah of newly independent Ghana in 1957 named his country's merchant marine the Black Star Line. An imposing Black Star Square was constructed in Accra, Ghana. Adulation of Garvey peaked during his centennial year of 1987, when governments, organizations, and individuals around the world honored him in many ways. Congressman Charles Rangel introduced a bill in the U.S. Congress to have Garvey cleared of his mail fraud conviction—the bill apparently died in committee. The London borough of Haringey erected a new library named after Garvey. A statue of Garvey was erected in San Fernando, Trinidad. The University of the West Indies in Jamaica held a major conference to commemorate his work.

Garvey's eminence in history is assured. Perhaps more than any other single individual, he infused a pride in self, a confidence to struggle, and a determination to move his people forward out of the low point of imperialist conquest, disfranchisement, and lynching that threatened to suffocate the African world of the early twentieth century.—TONY MARTIN

HENRY LOUIS **GATES JR.**

1950–

Educator, scholar, literary critic, writer

Literary scholar Henry Louis Gates Jr.'s critical studies have a wide-ranging impact on American oral and literary traditions, and have brought the teaching and analysis of black literature to the forefront in the American academy. In his many studies and popular essays he argues for the inclusion and valuing of differences both in the literary canon and in American society.

Henry Louis Gates was born in Keyser, West Virginia, on September 16, 1950. Gates's father, Henry Louis Sr., was a loader at the town's paper mill. To make ends meet Henry Sr. also worked nights as a janitor at the local telephone company.

The blacks who lived in West Virginia formed close-knit and stable communities. In 1954 integration came smoothly without the hatred and violence that characterized other parts of the country. But this is not to suggest that Gates did not encounter racism. When Henry Jr. was fourteen, he injured his hip playing touch football. To make conversation during the examination, the white doctor attending him asked of his future plans. Gates informed the doctor that he intended to become a physician, at which point the doctor quizzed him, attempting to access his knowledge of science. Gates answered all of the doctor's questions correctly. The doctor then diagnosed Gates's hairline fracture as a psychosomatic illness. "The boy from the hills of Appalachia was an overachiever," he informed Gates's mother. Recalling this experience years later, Gates told the *New York Times*: "Overachiever designated a sort of pathology: the overstraining of your natural capacity." The racism that prevented a correct diagnosis resulted in Gates's sustaining a permanent injury, with his right leg becoming more than two inches shorter than the left. In 1990 Gates's remarks to Maurice Berger for *Art in America* reveal the destructive potential of racism. Gates said, "The most subtle and pernicious form of racism against blacks [is] doubt over our intellectual capacities."

*Henry Louis
Gates Jr.*

The crossroad of childhood

In 1956 Henry Gates Jr. entered the Davis Free School, Piedmont's only elementary school, with a history dating back to 1906. He excelled in school. The 1960s ushered in a decade of growth, change, and expanding awareness for Gates. Gates was in the fifth grade when he became aware of Africa as the class studied current events. Still, the political turmoil of the sixties did not compare to the personal trauma Gates experienced as a result of his mother's illness. In 1962, at the age of forty-six, Pauline Gates was diagnosed with clinical depression and hospitalized. What he describes in his memoir of childhood closely parallels obsessive compulsive behavior. Gates recalled in *Colored People*:

> I had developed all sorts of rituals. I would . . . always walk around the kitchen table only from right to left, never the other way around. I would approach a chair from its left side, not the right. I got into and out of the same side of bed, slept on the same side, and I held the telephone with the same hand to the same ear. But most of all, as if my life depended on it, I crossed my legs right calf over left, and never, ever the other way around. Until one Sunday. For a reason that seemed compelling at the time, probably out of anger or spite, I decided to cross my legs in reverse.

Gates didn't die as he feared for his solitary act of anger, but he believed that his act produced his mother's illness. He feared that she would die. Fortunately for his own sanity, she didn't. Still, his sense of guilt was enormous. To atone for his imagined sin Gates decided to join the church.

Gates's Uncle Harry, a minister in the Methodist Church, persuaded him to go to church camp. In the summers of 1965 and 1966, Gates spent two weeks in Peterkins Episcopal Church camp. This gave him time to reflect on his new religion and grow mentally. The camp provided two uninterrupted weeks where, he said in *Colored People*, he "drank ideas and ate controversy."

In 1968 Gates graduated at the top of his class and as valedictorian delivered a militant commencement address. In the fall he entered Potomac State College of West Virginia University, planning to go from there to medical school. Meeting professor Duke Anthony Whitmore changed the course of his career. Taking English and American literature from the professor opened Gates to new possibilities. Whitmore, glimpsing the spark of genius in Gates, encouraged him to apply to the Ivy League schools. Gates applied and was accepted at Yale.

Graduating summa cum laude from Yale with a B.A. in history in 1973, Gates won a fellowship to England to study at Clare College, Cambridge University, where he received a master of arts degree in 1974. From 1973 until 1975 he worked as a London Bureau staff correspondent for *Time* magazine. Gates returned to the United States in 1975 and became a public relations representative for the American Cyanamid Company. From 1976 until he completed his Ph.D. in English language and literature in 1979, Gates held the position of lecturer at Yale University. On September 1, 1979, Gates married Sharon Lynn Adams. The couple has two daughters.

Gates's essay, "Preface to Blackness: Text and Pretext," in Robert Stepto and Dexter Fishers's *Afro-American Literature: The Reconstruction of Instruction*, marked his entry into the world of academia as an assistant professor of English at Yale University, a position he held until 1984. In 1981 the MacArthur Foundation awarded Henry Louis Gates a grant for $150 thousand. He became widely known for discovering and reissuing an 1859 novel written by a black woman, *Our Nig* (reprinted in 1983), the first novel by an African American published in the United States. Gates's research inspired the growing interest in the black woman's literary tradition.

Gates's Black Periodical Literature Project, initiated in 1980, unearthed numerous nineteenth-century literary works long neglected and forgotten. Soon Gates was promoted to associate professor of English and undergraduate director for the Department of Afro-

American Studies at Yale in 1984. That year his edited work *Black Literature and Literary Theory* was published and a debate erupted over a definition of black literary theory. In the fall of 1985, Gates accepted a full professorship in English and Africana Studies at Cornell University. The 1988 publication of the thirty-one-volume *Schomburg Library of Nineteenth-Century Black Women Writers* is noted for altering the landscape of "American cultural thought, demonstrating that black men and black women have never hesitated to grasp the pen and write their own powerful story of freedom." The collection is dedicated to his mother. In 1988 he became the W. E. B. Du Bois Professor of Literature, becoming the first African American male to hold an endowed chair in the history of the school.

His publication of *The Signifying Monkey: Towards a Theory of Afro-American Literary Criticism* (1989) won the American Book Award. Gates set forth a theory for judging black literature and also accused whites of intellectual racism. In 1990 Gates accepted an endowed chair at Duke University in Durham, North Carolina. Becoming a John Spenser Bassett Professor of English, Gates remained at Duke scarcely an academic year. In 1991, Harvard University recruited him for the W. E. B. Du Bois Professorship in Humanities and as chair for the department of African American studies.

Gates is the recipient of numerous awards, including grants from the National Endowment for the Humanities, 1980–84; Rockefeller Foundation Fellow, 1981; American Book Award, 1989; and the Anisfield-Wolfe Book Award 1989. His edited works include *Black Is the Color of the Cosmos: Charles T. Davis's Essays on Black Literature and Culture, 1942–1981* (1982); Harriet E. Wilson's *Our Nig; or, Sketches From the Life of a Free Black* (1983); *The Slave's Narrative: Texts and Contexts* (1985); *Race, Writing, and Difference* (1986); and *The Classic Slave Narratives* (1987). He also edited *The Norton Anthology of Afro-American Literature* (1990); *Reading Black, Reading Feminist: A Literary Critical Anthology* (1990); *Three Classic African-American Novels* (1990); *Bearing Witness: Selections from 150 years of African-American Autobiography* (1991); and *Future of the Race* (1996). In 1995 Gates was awarded both the Hartland Award and the Lillian Smith Prize for his autobiography, *Colored People*.

Gates is a member of International PEN and the Modern Language Association, and president of the Afro-American Academy. In 1991 he created for the Public Broadcasting System the television series *The Image of the Black in the Western Imagination*. In 1995 Gates delivered the commencement address at Emory University in Atlanta, Georgia, where he was awarded an honorary doctorate.

Henry Louis Gates Jr., a prolific writer and researcher, advanced African American literary and critical theory to a new level of understanding.—NAGUEYALTI WARREN

NIKKI **GIOVANNI**

1943–

Poet, writer, activist, educator

Groundbreaking, prolific, and sometimes controversial poet Nikki Giovanni maintains two guiding forces in her poetry and in her life: a willingness to change and grow, and an emphasis on pride in her black heritage, which she shares with young people and adults alike.

Yolande Cornelia "Nikki" Giovanni Jr. was born in Knoxville, Tennessee, on June 7, 1943, the daughter of Jones "Gus" Giovanni and Yolande (Watson) Giovanni. At age seventeen she entered Fisk University, where she majored in history. After a break in her studies, she received her bachelor of arts degree with honors in 1967. She then did graduate work at the University of Pennsylvania School of Social Work and undertook additional study at the Columbia University School of Fine Arts.

It is customary to discuss Giovanni's development in terms of decades. In the sixties, militancy characterizes her writing; in the seventies, greater introspection and attention to personal relationships; in the eighties and nineties, a more global outlook with a greater concern for humanity in general. However, the various themes reflect changes in emphasis rather than wholesale abandonment of one concern for another. Giovanni's overall approach—seeking and telling the truth and growing in the process—is grounded in her family heritage. Her strong grandmother, Luvenia Terrell Watson, was "terribly intolerant when it came to

Nikki Giovanni accepts the first Sun Shower Award presented by Prince Matchebelli in 1971.

white people." As a result of her outspokenness, Luvenia Watson was smuggled out of Albany, Georgia, under the cover of darkness by her husband, John "Book" Watson, and other family members, who had good reason to believe her life was in danger. Luvenia and John Watson had hoped to reach the North, but settled in Knoxville, Tennessee, "the first reasonable-sized town" on their way. A teacher, John Watson returned to Albany to finish the school term— "Grandfather was like that," Giovanni recalls. He then joined his wife in Knoxville, where they made their home. Of the family surname, she has observed, "It just means that *our* slave masters were Italian instead of English or French."

Giovanni has warned against reading her work—poetry or prose—as strictly autobiographical. Even so, because she assesses life from a personal perspective, her own experiences are essential starting points and often remain central themes for her writing. She states that *Gemini* merely "comes close" to being autobiography—truth being larger than merely what we remember. Nevertheless, Giovanni's summary of the importance of her heritage in *Gemini* is illustrated in her work as a whole:

> Life/personality must be taken as a total entity. All of your life is all of your life, and no one incident stands alone. . . . My family on my grandmother's side are fighters. My family on my father's side are survivors. I'm a revolutionist. It's only logical.

Revolutionary poet attracts national attention

It was as a revolutionary poet in the 1960s that Giovanni first came to national attention. During this period she became known as the "Princess of Black Poetry." The poetry in *Black Feeling, Black Talk* and in *Black*

Judgement captures the spirit of the times. Other poets who became prominent during that period included Don L. Lee (later Haki Madhubuti) and Sonia Sanchez. Like her contemporaries, Giovanni found traditional poetic themes and techniques inadequate for the times.

Giovanni's activism revealed itself not only on paper. As a student at Fisk University in the mid-sixties, she had been a founding member of the university's Student Nonviolent Coordinating Committee chapter. Establishing the chapter was not an easy task, and her commitment is an example of her acting on principles rather than out of conformity.

Giovanni began her college studies at Fisk University in 1960, but she was "released" because she went home for Thanksgiving without asking permission of the dean of women. Giovanni wanted to be with her grandparents, the Watsons, knowing that her grandfather was ill and that her grandmother needed her support. Looking back on the experience, Giovanni points out that she knew what the outcome would be, but if she had not gone to Knoxville, "the only change would have been that Fisk considered me an ideal student, which means little on a life scale." When she returned to college, it was because she felt ready. Grandmother Watson said she would live to see Nikki finish college, and she died about one month after Giovanni graduated.

The significance of family and family-oriented themes deepened for Giovanni with the birth of her son, Thomas Watson, in August 1969. "Don't Have a Baby till You Read This" recounts the experience. Giovanni has noted: "I had a baby at 25 because I *wanted* to have a baby and I could *afford* to have a baby. I did not get married because I didn't *want* to get married and I could *afford* not to get married."

As a mother, Giovanni had even more impetus to provide positive images for black children. Her response included establishing her own publishing company, Niktom, in 1970. At least in part, this endeavor can be read as an extension of the work she began in the sixties—to create literature that speaks directly to black people and that celebrates positive features of black life. In short, the concerns of the revolutionary were rechanneled rather than abandoned.

The titles of many of Giovanni's books of poetry published in the 1970s—*Re-Creation, My House, The Women and the Men, Cotton Candy on a Rainy Day*—have an introspective, thoughtful focus. Paula Giddings finds *The Women and the Men* a "coming of age. For the first time, the woman-child is virtually absent," replaced by an adult. Themes of relationships, of womanhood, and of motherhood are stressed. Again, Giovanni's themes are not easily summarized. The more personal themes are relevant to the wider world in that they suggest the values that should apply in making the world a better place. And Giovanni includes themes other than the personal. In *The Women and the Men,* the final section, "And Some Places," reflects her travel to Africa, which she visited with her friend Ida Lewis in 1971.

Giovanni honors the spoken word   Giovanni's interest in exploring others' ideas is illustrated in the books that transcribe her conversations with James Baldwin and Margaret Walker. Both these dialogues demonstrate mutual respect even in the presence of clear generational differences. Topics are wide-ranging; both volumes include attention to black writing and to relationships between black men and women.

Record albums have served as another effective medium of expression for Giovanni. *Truth Is on Its Way* (1972) helped launch Giovanni's lasting popularity as a speaker and reader of her own poetry. The album consists of Giovanni's reading her poems to background gospel accompaniment.

The conversations and the albums underscore the importance of the spoken word for Giovanni. In a postscript to her conversations with Walker, Giovanni sums up the importance of such an exchange: "I rather like the immediacy of talking . . . the mistakes . . . the insights . . . the risks inherent in hot conversation. Life is all about that balance between risk and inertia . . . that poetic equation."

Giovanni devours myths   The very title *Sacred Cows and Other Edibles,* Giovanni's 1988 collection of short prose pieces, captures the author's continued readiness to take on and devour society's myths, or to "go naked and see what happens." *Sacred Cows* gives attention to sports, supplying special help to women in negotiating the terrain: "If they are in their underwear—it's Basketball; if they have on their pajamas—it's Baseball; if they wear helmets—it's Football." Lighthearted without being trivial, insightful without being ponderous, Giovanni considers the implications of sports as an expression of culture. *Sacred Cows* covers a range of other topics, including selections on writing and on her relationship with her mother. Much of the book is centered on her time as a resident of Cincinnati, where she lived with her parents in 1978 after her father became ill.

Once she has written something, Giovanni moves on. She has acknowledged that she lacks discipline. On that point, William J. Harris observes in *Black Women Writers:* "She has the talent to create good, perhaps important, poetry, if only she has the will to discipline her craft." Finally, however, there can be no disagreement that Giovanni is a productive, talented writer. Her wit and candor as she stays "on the case," whatever the fundamental issues of the times may be, help explain why she remains consistently stimulating and significant. In *Racism,* published in 1996, Giovanni crticizes academia for not doing enough to create more diverse college campuses and end campus racism. But it is also a how-to book for black students to survive and succeed at white colleges.

Giovanni is a fighter. "I was never afraid of losing, that's not what bothers me; I was always afraid that if I didn't fight, what would I be?" Giovanni is also a survivor. Using that same spirit, in 1995, she recovered from cancer treatment that resulted in the partial removal of her lung and ribs.

Giovanni has clearly earned a prominent place in American life and letters. Since she first rose to national attention in the sixties, she has been consistently outspoken and charismatic. Characteristically expressing her ideas with charm and good humor, she allows for opposite points of view as well: "I don't think everyone has to write the way I write nor think the way I think," she was quoted in *Black Women Writers.* "There are plenty of ideas to go around."—ARLENE CLIFT-PELLOW

WHOOPI **GOLDBERG**

1950–

Actor, activist, comedian

From her childhood home in a housing project in New York City, Whoopi Goldberg has emerged as one of

America's best-loved comedians and actors. She has exhibited her wide-ranging talents in films, television

shows, theatrical performances, and recordings, and in the process has won a host of major awards—an Oscar, a Grammy, a Golden Globe award, and the NAACP Image award. Combining her burgeoning career with a deeply felt social conscience, Goldberg has used her vast popularity to combat a number of social ills. Her Comic Relief benefits with Robin Williams and Billy Crystal, for instance, have become annual events that have raised millions of dollars for the homeless. Despite her many career triumphs, though, Goldberg's path to success has not been without obstacles, from poverty and dyslexia to racism and sexism.

Goldberg was born Caryn Johnson in 1950 in New York City, where she and a younger brother, Clyde, lived with their mother, Emma Johnson, in a housing project in the Chelsea section of Manhattan. Goldberg notes that her father abandoned them early on and that her mother had to work a variety of jobs, including as a Head Start teacher and nurse, to take care of them. Of her invented name, Goldberg says:

> It was a joke. First it was Whoopi Cushion. Then it was French, like Whoopi Cushon. My mother said, "Nobody's gonna respect you with a name like that." So I put Goldberg on it. Goldberg's a part of my family somewhere and that's all I can say about it.

Goldberg attended the parish school of Saint Columbian Church on West Twenty-fifth Street, under the Congregation of Notre Dame. She demonstrated a propensity for performing at age eight, when she started acting at the Helena Rubenstein Children's Theatre at the Hudson

Guild, having been influenced early by watching Gracie Allen, Carole Lombard, Claudette Colbert, and other established actresses in old movies on television. By age seventeen she had dropped out of high school, convinced that she was unable to grasp subject matter but unaware that she had dyslexia, which interfered with her performance. In the 1960s she hung out with hippies, but later she asked herself if she was going to keep on doing drugs and kill herself or figure out what to do with her life. She decided on the latter: "I didn't stop altogether at once. It took many, many tries. . . . You fall a lot because it's hard," she revealed.

Goldberg became involved in "hippie politics" and was active in civil rights marches and student protests at Columbia University. She also worked as a counselor at a summer camp on Ethical Culture held in Peekskill, New York. But she soon found her true calling. She had been born a mimic "with a natural, flawless eye and ear for details of character," and her career was set to blossom when she found work on Broadway in the choruses of *Hair, Jesus Christ Superstar,* and *Pippin.* From a

Whoopi Goldberg.

brief marriage to her drug counselor during her drug rehabilitation period in the 1970s, she had one daughter, Alexandrea Martin.

Goldberg moved to the West Coast in 1974 to start over with her daughter and her childhood ambition to act—something she felt confident she could do. Before becoming a star, she held a series of jobs that were somewhat less glamorous than acting, such as styling hair at a mortuary and laying bricks. She was also a licensed beautician and a bank teller. She spent some time on public assistance—an experience she found disconcerting. "The welfare workers used to make these surprise visits because you weren't allowed to have friends," particularly if you gave them food, she recalled. If the welfare worker saw "a friend in the house with a plate of food in front of them, it would be deducted from your money the next month. . . . Getting off welfare, like getting off drugs, was a sweet triumph."

Whoopi Goldberg with her Best Supporting Actress Oscar in 1991.

Frustrated by the dearth of work for black character actors in the straight theater, Goldberg began to create her own varied repertoire and collection of offbeat social types whom she presented as believable individuals. "Although her antic monologues contain elements of improvisational standup comedy," relates *Current Biography,* "the pseudonymous Miss Goldberg is essentially a character actress [or actor, as she sometimes insists] whose original routines are really seriocomic plays, written in her head." She also performed in more conventional theatrical pieces, such as her 1986 role in the one-woman show *Moms,* in which she played the late comedienne Moms Mabley. Goldberg wrote the play with Ellen Sebastian and won a Bay Area Theatre Award for her performance.

Goldberg moves from theater to film and television

Goldberg's theater show caught the eye of film director Mike Nichols, who came on to produce her Broadway show. This show gained her a well-established fan base, which included Steven Spielberg. Spielberg took a gamble with Goldberg by casting her as Celie in the film version of *The Color Purple.* Immediately, Goldberg became an unforgettable face and an instant movie star. For her performance in the film she won a Golden Globe Award, the NAACP Image Award, and an Academy Award nomination.

Following *The Color Purple,* Goldberg continued her work as a comedian, and in 1985 she won a Grammy Award for best comedy album. She wasn't quite as successful with her film career at the time, appearing in a number of movies that were not big hits, including *Jumpin' Jack Flash, Burglar, Fatal Beauty, The Telephone, Homer and Eddie, Clara's Heart,* and *Beverly Hills Brats.* Then, in 1990, with her acting career in a lull, Goldberg appeared in the hugely successful film *Ghost.* That film catapulted her career to a new level and earned Goldberg an Academy Award for best supporting actress. In October of 1990, Goldberg was named winner of the Excellence Award of the sixth annual Women in Film Festival. And when the NAACP held its twenty-third annual Image Awards program in December 1990, she was named Black Entertainer of the Year.

Following *Ghost,* Goldberg solidified her prominence as an actor with roles in several well-received films, including *The Long Walk Home, Soap Dish, The Player,* and *Sister Act,* a surprise hit in the summer of 1992. The sequel to *Sister Act* in 1993 thrust Goldberg into an exclusive club in Hollywood. She earned $8 million to reprise her role, making her the highest-paid actress at that time.

Not limited to the theater and film, Goldberg has also worked on television. She joined Jean Stapleton in 1990 on the short-lived situation comedy *Bagdad Cafe,* in which she played the hot-headed, soft-hearted cafe owner. She also appeared on an irregular basis as a member of the crew of the starship *Enterprise* in *Star Trek: The Next Generation,* and she was nominated for an Emmy for a guest appearance on *Moonlighting.* Goldberg, an adamant proponent against drugs and a staunch supporter for women's rights and various other topics, has become one of the most sought-after black actors. Basking in stardom and notoriety, Goldberg does not want to follow a traditional path for her career or to be labeled a black actress. As she said in *Newsweek,* "People have small minds. . . . I think of myself as an actor. I've said before, I can play a man—or a dog or a chair."

Life in the limelight

With a successful film career going, Goldberg's personal life took on some nasty turns. Her relationship with actor Ted Danson created a well-publicized stir inside Hollywood that resulted in many African American celebrities lambasting Goldberg. A roast at the Friars Club in 1993 involved Danson and Goldberg dressing in blackface and reciting racially inflammatory remarks. Both Danson and Goldberg wrote the material and did not intend for the audience to take the skit seriously. They were wrong. Celebrities such as Dionne Warwick and talk show host Montel Williams walked out and publicly annouced to the press their displeasure. The anger subsided, but at the cost of Goldberg and Danson ending their relationship. Never one to be coy about her opinions, Goldberg angered many minority groups when she did not support Jesse Jackson's boycott of the 1994 Oscar telecast due to poor representation of minorities being nominated. As host of the show and the only African American woman to host it for two years, Goldberg was criticized for her remarks that seemed to belittle the boycott and Jackson's efforts. During the Oscar telecast, Goldberg remarked, "I had something I wanted to say to Jesse right here, but he's not watching, so why bother?" It drew both cheers and jeers. Goldberg shot back in a 1997 *Playboy* magazine interview, "People seem to forget that the mere fact that I'm still here is a huge statement. So is the fact that a lot more people look like me than they did 12 years ago, when I started."

After a decade of wowing audiences in movie theaters, Goldberg returned to the stage in a Broadway revival of *A Funny Thing Happened on the Way to the Forum.*

Whoopi Goldberg's enormous confidence is matched only by her enormous efforts in many charitable causes. Her work for Comic Relief has helped the organization raise millions in the fight against homelessness in America. She also is an outspoken proponent for women's rights and abortion. In 1996, Goldberg donated a $25,000 check to Covenant House, an organization that helps runaway teens. President Bill Clinton personally requested that she host his fiftieth birthday celebration at Radio City Music Hall.

Goldberg, whose main purpose for entertaining is to make people laugh, is a highly gifted performer who clearly achieves her purpose on stage. Her triumphs over dyslexia, drugs, welfare, and divorce are examples of the strength of her own determination and her will to succeed and excel—the mark of an original.—SIMMONA E. SIMMONS

BERRY GORDY

1929–

Songwriter, record producer, entrepreneur

Berry Gordy was the driving force in the creation of Motown Records, starting what was at the time the largest black-owned business in the country and changing the course of popular music. He launched the careers of many recording stars, from Smokey Robinson to Diana Ross. Some of his methods leading to success have led to great bitterness on the part of former associates, but his impact on the 1960s music scene can still be heard today.

Berry Gordy III was born in Detroit, Michigan, on Thanksgiving Day, November 28, 1929, to Berry Gordy II (1888–1978) and Bertha Ida Fuller (1900–75). The Gordys had eight

Berry Gordy.

children: Fuller, Esther, Anna Ruby, Loucye (originally Lucy), George, Gwendolyn, Berry, and Robert. Gordy's grandfather was a successful farmer with over three hundred acres of land in Ocoee County, Georgia. Sadly, he was killed by a lightning bolt on May 31, 1913. Berry Gordy II became administrator of the estate. He married Bertha Ida Fuller, a schoolteacher, in 1918. Astute like his father, Gordy was a successful farmer and also ran a produce and meat business, selling from a wagon on a regular round. Three children had already been born when he moved his family in 1922 to Detroit to cash a check for $2,600; he did not return to the South.

Berry Gordy II faced difficulties in adjusting to the new city environment. Early in the Great Depression, sometime after the birth of Berry Gordy III, he lost a house he was in the process of buying, forcing the family to go on welfare. Berry Gordy II persevered, opening a grocery store, learning how to plaster, and securing a building contractor's permit. He soon began to acquire real estate and eventually opened other businesses, such as a printing shop.

The Gordys were an exceptionally close family. Commenting on this period, Gordy recalled in his autobiography *To Be Loved:*

> We were a close family. We had to be, always bumping into each other just moving from room to room in our new home, where eight kids, four girls and four boys, had to scramble for a place to sleep. Crowding was a way of life. I loved it. I didn't know any better.

Physical crowding and the presence of family, both real and figurative, were marked characteristics of the early years of Motown.

A brief period of piano instruction during childhood was Gordy's only formal music instruction, in addition to a week or so of instruction on the clarinet in high school. By that time his reputation for misbehaving in class was so well-established that his music teacher tossed him out of the only class he wanted to do well in, despite the occasional good behavior he demonstrated. Gordy would remain a musical illiterate. While he could not read or write music, his musical gift was displayed later through his extraordinary ability to shape lyrics and melodies, to catch popular taste, and to provide meticulous attention to all details of performances and recordings.

Gordy family moves to Detroit's east side   When Gordy was six and a half years old, the family moved to the east side where Berry Gordy II had purchased a two-story commercial building located just a block from the infamous Hastings Street, a center for night life, gambling, and prostitution. The family lived in the two apartments on the upper story of the building and ran the Booker T. Washington grocery in the largest of the four storefronts on the ground floor.

Growing up in an achievement-oriented family, Berry Gordy had two outstanding problems. Gordy's inability to perform as well as his siblings in school, along with suffering from enuresis (bedwetting), proved difficult for young Gordy. He turned to hustling on the streets, and at school he took to gambling—an activity that remains a favorite pastime. Attempting to prevent Gordy from spending too much time on the streets, his parents taught him the value of hard work, and Gordy joined his father on weekends on contracting jobs as early as nine or ten years of age. Despite conflicts between father and son, Gordy remained close to his father and credits his father's advice as a major influence on his life achievements.

As a young man Gordy was torn between two ambitions: becoming a songwriter or becoming a boxer. He even dropped out of high school to concentrate on the sport. He eventually fought fifteen professional fights with a record of ten wins, two draws, and three losses. On November 21, 1948, he had the thrill of appearing as a 128-pound boxer on the same ticket as his childhood hero Joe Louis, who gave a six-round exhibition bout.

In August 1950 Gordy gave up fighting and opted for music as a career. After spending the next few months writing songs—Gordy's only successful effort was a one-minute radio commercial for the Gordy Print Shop, which he wrote and performed—he was drafted in September 1951 and sent to Korea, where he escaped front-line combat. While in the army he passed the GED or high school equivalence test.

Soon after his return home Gordy opened a record shop with a friend, Roquel Billy Davis (also known as Tyran Carlo). Gordy used his army severance pay with additional money from the family as capital. The two young men were determined to specialize in selling jazz, unaware that customers were demanding rhythm and blues. By the time they began to change their music selections, it was too late to avoid losing the store. After a stint of selling cookware in homes, Gordy concentrated on songwriting.

Berry Gordy married Thelma Coleman in late 1953. Hazel Joy, their first child, was born in August 1954, Berry IV in 1955, and Terry James in 1956. His father owned an old apartment building and let Gordy and his wife live there rent free. Still, songwriting proved inadequate as a means to support a growing family. With the help of his wife's mother, Gordy eventually found a job on the assembly line at a Lincoln-Mercury plant. The repetitive nature of the assembly line work allowed him to write songs in his head while he was working. With his steady income, Gordy bought a house that paid for itself through the rent from two kitchenette apartments upstairs.

Gordy enters music business   After a couple of years in the factory, Gordy became disenchanted with the prospect of blue-collar work, and quit his factory job in early 1957 to try his luck at songwriting again. His sister Gwen had the photo concession at the Flame Bar, a premier nightclub featuring black talent, which enabled Gordy to make influential contacts. Not yet making much money, Thelma Gordy grew very restless. Thelma and Gordy soon filed for divorce, although the marriage was not dissolved until 1959.

Some of the early songs Gordy worked on began to garner moderate success. His first hit was Etta James's recording of "All I Could Do Was Cry," written with Gwen Gordy and Roquel Billy Davis. Davis also collaborated with Gordy on "Reet Petite," a smash hit

*Berry Gordy holding his award from
the Rock & Roll Hall of Fame.*

sung by Jackie Wilson. In late 1957 Gordy met William "Smokey" Robinson, a member of a group called the Matadors. Gordy worked with Robinson on a song, which was issued by the Miracles, the newly renamed group, on Robinson's nineteenth birthday, February 19, 1958. Over the years, the collaboration between Gordy and Robinson was one of the key elements in the success of Motown.

By the late 1950s, Gordy was moving closer and closer to forming his own recording company. First, Gwen Gordy proposed that her brother join her and Roquel Billy Davis in forming a record company. Gordy turned her down, rationalizing that he would not be happy in a business in which he had partners. He had a keen sense of where the money in recording was, seeking to follow the example of Vee Jay Records, created in 1953 by Vivian Carpenter and Jimmy Braken, a husband and wife team, in Chicago. The largest black-owned business in the country, Vee Jay found success through independents who came to dominate the field of pop music; for example, the Beatles issued their first half dozen records on the label in 1964. Infected with financial difficulties, Vee Jay also played a cautionary role for Gordy, whose company Motown would later supersede Vee Jay, which closed in 1966.

Publishing his music himself was the first step in gaining lucrative financial returns from his songwriting. Gordy created a music publishing company named Jobete after his children, Joy, Berry, and Terry. Gordy also began producing musical materials for singing acts. During this time, Gordy auditioned a singer named Raynoma Liles. Although he didn't like her singing voice, he was attracted to her buoyant personality and skills in arranging and writing sheet music. Their professional relationship developed into a personal one and on June 25, 1959, Kerry Gordy was born to Gordy and Ray Liles, who married about a year later. (The marriage seemed to end with a mail-order Mexican divorce in 1962. It later proved invalid, and final legal separation ensued.) A vital collaborator in the early days of Motown, Raynoma Liles presented her version of the events in her autobiography, *Berry, Me, and Motown.*

Founds Motown   At the end of 1958 Gordy needed money to produce a record. After other sources turned him down, he faced a skeptical family council of Gordys for the first time and asked for a loan from the family investment fund. Eventually, on January 12, 1959, Gordy received a loan for eight hundred dollars at 6 percent interest and found Tamla Records. The first release off this label was a 45 r.p.m. recording of "Come to Me," sung by Marv Johnson, which became a hit. Other records followed with varying success. Then in order to release the song "Bad Girl," written by Smokey Robinson and Gordy, Gordy formed a new company, Motown. This release became a hit.

Another milestone in the summer of 1959 was the move to 2648 West Grand Boulevard, a small house Gordy's company named "Hitsville." Motown eventually took over eight neighborhood houses. In 1988 the original "Hitsville" and its neighboring house expanded and became the Motown Museum. Filling the house with recording studios and offices, Gordy also prepared a space for his immediate family until he could move them to a separate house. Also, he began to assemble a team of very talented people for his company. Through his business acumen, he concluded that he must distribute his music nationwide to fully profit from Motown's activities. His choice of material for his national debut as distributor was Smokey Robinson and the Miracles' song "Way Over There." The song was becoming a big hit when Gordy recut the record, added strings, and thereby killed the sales. Nonetheless, Gordy successfully launched Motown as a national music distributor.

Gordy's impulse to make changes in records until he was satisfied misfired in the case of "Way Over There." However, this intervention contributed to the development of the Motown sound, which was especially prominent in Motown's recordings of the first half of the 1960s and featured elaborate arrangements and often included strings. In the course of production, the elements of black music and performance style were smoothed over, without being abolished. The result of Gordy's concerns was to assure his records tremendous pop sales.

Motown enters the pop field   When Gordy met Mary Wells, he felt he had found the singer who could break Motown out of the restricted rhythm and blues category to the more lucrative field of pop music favored by white audiences. Wells would be extremely popular until 1964 when she disaffirmed her Motown contract. Wells realized that her contract with Motown did not adequately compensate her monetarily, a problem that many artists faced later in their careers with Motown.

To obtain the widest possible market Gordy hired white salesman Barney Ales to distribute his records. Since Ales had to deal mostly with white owners of radio stations all over the country, including the South, he built up a sales department staffed by white salespeople. Only later, when Motown had the power and prestige to insist that people treat any Motown representative with respect, did Gordy demand that Ales hire blacks as salespeople. The preliminary hiring of whites to sell Motown products was one reason underlying the mixed reaction to Motown among blacks. There was pride in Motown as the most successful black business ever, as well as suspicion of a sell-out against the black community due to Gordy's tapping into the white market and his use of whites in key marketing positions. In some quarters, especially in Detroit, Motown's move to Los Angeles in 1970 was never forgiven, and his later sale of the company to MCA in 1988 for $61 million was seen as a betrayal of the black community.

During the early 1960s, Gordy continued to build Motown by introducing new stars to the public like Marvin Gaye, who became both a major Motown artist and a brother-in-law. In 1961 Gordy signed the four Supremes, who soon became a trio consisting of Diana Ross, Mary Wilson, and Florence Ballard; they achieved stardom three years later. Gordy signed the Temptations and a young boy named Steveland Hardaway Judkins, better known as Stevie Wonder. Other groups included Martha Reeves and the Vandellas and the Marvelettes.

By October 1962, as Gordy's marriage to Raynoma Liles was ending, Motown had enough stars to staff an entire tour on its own, and the first Motortown Revue got underway.

By the early to mid-1960s, Gordy had perfected his management style. Many have noted its resemblance to the production line of the automobile factory. His creative staff, the songwriters and producers, competed in weekly meetings to develop new products. While he did hire female executives like Suzanne De Passe in addition to his sisters Esther and Loucye, who occupied key positions, his creative staff was entirely male. Artists were expected to accept Motown's almost complete control over their acts and material. He even hired Maxine Powell away from her own charm school and modeling business to instruct performers in all social graces and tour with his acts from 1964 to 1967. The slogan he originally ran his business by was Create, Make, and Sell, which later became Create, Sell, and Collect. In Berry Gordy's eyes Motown was a factory for producing hits. In *The Motown Album,* Michael Jackson ably characterized the man who brought the Jackson Five to superstardom:

> Berry was my teacher and a great one. He told me exactly what he wanted
> and how he wanted me to help him get it. Berry insisted on perfection and
> attention to detail. I'll never forget his persistence. This was his genius.

In March 1964, Motown was continuing to grow despite the defection of Mary Wells that same year. The Supremes achieved a major breakthrough with "Where Did Our Love Go." Gordy began to open the door to major clubs and showrooms for Motown stars by persuading the television program *Hullabaloo* to allow the Supremes to perform their Motown hit, "You're Nobody 'Til Somebody Loves You." It was in Paris just after the conclusion of the Motortown Revue's first European tour in 1964 that Gordy began an affair with Diana Ross. This relationship eventually resulted in the birth of Gordy's seventh child, a daughter named Rhonda, born in August 1971 after Ross's marriage to Robert Silberstein in late January 1971.

There were also numerous setbacks along the way. Not all of Motown's musicians and acts were satisfied. The defection of the song writing team of Eddie Holland, Lamont Dozier, and Brian Holland, who had produced an enviable string of hits for Motown, was a major blow. Not all spin-off labels proved successful: Melody, country and western; Black Forum, spoken word and activist recordings, whose main success was Martin Luther King Jr.'s "I Have a Dream" speech; and Rare Earth, which had little success after producing three straight hits in 1970 for the white rock group of that name. Yet despite such setbacks, many new groups came along that added new luster to the company, like Gladys Knight and the Pips in 1966 and the Jackson Five in 1969. In 1976 Stevie Wonder received an unprecedented $23 million for renewing his contract with Motown.

Gordy moved to Los Angeles in 1968 and Motown's operations moved there in 1970, although the move did not become official until 1972. This change of location occurred as the company became increasingly involved in other fields like film and television.

Enters film business   Gordy's first major involvement in the movie business was with *Lady Sings the Blues,* starring Diana Ross. His perfectionism and desire for control led to immediate conflict. Gordy insisted on the script being rewritten as shooting was getting underway, and the movie went over budget. Gordy invested more of his money to insure the film's production and in return, the studio gave Gordy control over the film's editing. When it opened in October 1972 the film was a triumph for Diana Ross, who received an Oscar nomination for best actress.

Gordy was less involved with other Motown films like *Bingo Long Traveling All-Stars and Motor Kings, Scott Joplin,* and the megaflop *The Wiz.* He was, however, extremely involved in *Mahogany,* starring Diana Ross, which began production in December 1974 and opened in October 1975. Neither the production nor the year was an easy one. There were problems with Diana Ross, and Gordy fired the director and took over the movie himself. His mother died in late January. In the spring the Jacksons left Motown, except for Jermaine, who had married Gordy's daughter Hazel. (She filed for divorce in 1987 after nearly fourteen years of marriage.) And *Mahogany* was a critical and financial disaster. Gordy would not reenter the movie business again until *The Last Dragon* in 1985.

During the 1970s Motown's success was waning and Gordy wondered if his management style was to blame. By late 1979 Gordy was insolvent; a bank loan, which he repaid within a year, helped him over this crisis. Despite Diana Ross's move to RCA in 1981, there were still stars like Lionel Richie and the Commodores, Smokey Robinson, and, of course, Stevie Wonder, but prospects remained chancy for a company that was small compared to the media giants. In 1983 he nearly sold Motown to MCA, but withdrew at the last moment. He did, however, turn distribution over to MCA.

The financial situation of Motown still remained dismal, and in 1988 Gordy again entered into negotiations with MCA. On June 28, 1988, Motown became a part of MCA's entertainment conglomerate for $61 million dollars. Gordy retained control of Motown's movie and television interests (now Gordy–De Passe Productions) as well as his publishing company Jobete, estimated to be worth approximately $100 million. These properties were organized under the umbrella of the Gordy Company. Berry Gordy was chairman of the board, and his son, Berry Gordy IV, was president. Gordy married once more, to Grace Eaton in 1990; he filed for divorce in 1993. Besides overseeing his company, he has become interested in horse racing as an owner. Gordy also has taken to trading on the futures market.

On January 20, 1988, Gordy was inducted into the Rock 'n' Roll Hall of Fame. His tremendous achievements in the music industry were best summed up in *Billboard*'s listing for the last week of 1968, which cited five of the top ten hits, including Marvin Gaye's number-one hit "I Heard It Through the Grapevine," Stevie Wonder's number-two hit "For Once In My Life," The Supremes' number-three hit "Love Child," plus a duet between Diana Ross with the Temptations on "I'm Gonna Make You Love Me," and finally, the Temptations' number-ten hit, "Cloud Nine." In addition, Motown had held the first three positions on the list for an entire month—a feat that has not been repeated by any company, thus attesting to the fact that Berry Gordy's Motown had created the music all America wanted to hear.—ROBERT L. JOHNS

EARL G. **GRAVES**
1935–
Entrepreneur, publisher, corporate executive

Earl Graves is considered the preeminent authority in America on black business. The locus of that authority is Black Enterprise, *the magazine he founded in 1970 that now has a circulation of nearly 300,000 and revenues of $24 million. He is the magazine's publisher as well as its president and chief executive officer of the parent company, Earl G. Graves Limited. Graves is also co-owner with Earvin "Magic" Johnson of a Washington, D.C.–based Pepsi Cola distributorship, the largest minority-controlled Pepsi franchise in the nation. Johnson serves as chief executive officer. These two business ventures have served as the springboard that has propelled Graves into the ranks of elected board members of prestigious businesses and trustees of well-known foundations. They have also earned him the right to be a leading spokesperson on issues that affect the well-being and economic success of African Americans.*

Earl Gilbert Graves was born on January 9, 1935, in Brooklyn, New York, to Earl Godwin Graves and Winifred Sealy Graves, long-time West Indian residents of the Bedford-Stuyvesant area. Graves's father was a role model and mentor whose economic circumstances curtailed his own dreams and plans for the future. The senior Graves was the only black in his graduating class at Erasmus High School—the second oldest school in America—and his son would be one of only two blacks when he graduated years later. Although he never earned a large salary, Graves's father stressed the value of education, and both parents preached the virtues of cleanliness and thrift. Although he died before the age of fifty, *African-American Business Leaders* noted that the senior Graves had instilled in his children "the twin notions of owning a business and developing a strong economic base for the black community."

Graves took these lessons to heart and, at the age of five, was known as an annual top seller of Christmas cards. After high school graduation, he entered Morgan State University as a scholarship student. He was a high school and college track star and used his athletic skills to help with tuition and fees by working as a New York beach lifeguard during summer months. As a college student, Graves displayed self-discipline and goal-oriented behaviors that led to his later success in the business world. While maintaining his place on the dean's list, he also operated several campus businesses and joined various school organizations.

He graduated in 1958 with a B.A. in economics and, as a member of the ROTC, was commissioned a second lieutenant in the U.S. Army. Before leaving active service, Graves completed the Airborne and Ranger's School and was promoted to the rank of captain as a member of the Green Berets of the 19th Special Forces Group. In 1962 he worked as a narcotics agent with the U.S. Treasury Department and returned to his old neighborhood in Brooklyn. For the next three years, Graves sold and developed real estate and then formed an alliance that would have a tremendous effect on his future.

Earl G. Graves.

The will to succeed In 1966 Graves was hired as an administrative assistant to plan and supervise events on the staff of Senator Robert F. Kennedy. Graves considered Kennedy another mentor who would influence the course of his future. Quoted in *African-American Business Leaders*, he said of the senator:

> The main thing Kennedy did was to continue to foster my attitude that anything could get done once you made up your mind to get on with the work. There was no such thing in Kennedy's mindset as we can't do, it was just a matter of how long it would take us to get it done.

As traumatic as Kennedy's death was in 1968, it also meant that Graves no longer had a job. After a short period of grieving, restlessness, and reflection, Graves focused on the legacies of his father and Kennedy: the constant injunctions to own his own business and to make up his mind to get on with it. In 1968 Graves formed Earl G. Graves Associates, a management consulting firm to advise corporations on urban affairs and economic development. As evidenced by the number of multinational corporations the firm had as clients, Graves was a success, but he had not addressed the second program that his late father had stressed, that of contributing to the economic development of black America. The impetus for formulating a strategy to address this need was Graves's journey to Fayette, Mississippi, to work in the mayoral campaign for Charles Evers, brother of slain NAACP leader Medgar Evers. After Evers was elected as the city's first black mayor in 1969, he used his money and influence to improve the lot of the town's black community. Graves carefully studied Evers's endeavors and then planned a strategy to tap into the Richard Nixon administration's efforts to bring black Americans into the country's economic development programs.

Because there was national focus on black economic development, Graves knew that the time was right to plan, develop, and produce a monthly periodical devoted to news, commentary, and articles for blacks interested in business. After receiving a Ford Foundation grant to study black-owned business in Caribbean countries, he narrowed his focus to developing a business plan and editorial prospectus for the projected magazine. In 1970 Graves borrowed $150,000 from the Manhattan Capital Corporation of Chase Manhattan Bank, which, in turn, bought twenty-five percent of the company as equity.

Graves presented to the prospective lenders a working draft of *Black Enterprise*, a proposed periodical that would foster black economic development, create viable role models for blacks to emulate, and profile successful blacks whose careers had transcended the traditional norms of thought of what black business leaders should be. A major part of the draft was a list of the endorsements of 100,000 black community leaders representative of such organizations as the National Urban League, Organization of Industrial Centers, NAACP, Black Advisory Council of the Small Business Administration, and others of equal importance. Since Graves was not an experienced journalist, L. Patrick "Pat" Patterson later became editor-at-large when Graves decided to become both publisher and editor of *Black Enterprise*.

Black Enterprise *flourishes* *Black Enterprise* began to turn a profit by its tenth issue and at the end of the first year reported $900,000 in advertising revenues. Its ongoing success was due to farsightedness and visionary thinking. Two years after the first issue came off the press, attention was given to researching market possibilities. Under the aegis of other Graves corporations, BCI Marketing, a development firm, and a market research firm, attention was focused on buying patterns of potential readers and subscribers, the differences between black and non-black buying patterns, and the effectiveness of advertising copy. This strategy has enabled *Black Enterprise* to attract general businesses as well as black businesses in luring the black population market, whose purchasing power has been estimated as $100 billion. The promotions arm of Graves's business conglomerate has been the means by which *Black Enterprise* is now included in the magazine offerings on major airlines. Another promotions tactic has been the allocation of each press run to be given to large corporations, irrespective of race.

The Black Press USA highlighted the strategies and procedures employed by Graves's publishing company and its subsidiaries to ensure the success of *Black Enterprise*. As a means of securing integrity, its paid circulation is verified by the Audit Bureau of Circulations, the leading agency in the business. Secondly, it is highly attractive to its readership because of the high quality of materials, advertising, and editorial contributors. The magazine has also reached beyond its original target audience of black business people to encompass large-scale entrepreneurs and the general consumer. Articles now focus on a variety of economic interests ranging from personal investments to solutions for unemployment to science, technology, health, and political issues that involve the business world. Lastly, advertisements are mostly full-page, in color, and identical to those seen in general and specialty magazines purchased by the general population. Each year *Black Enterprise*'s top-selling issue is the one containing the "List of Top Black Businesses," a feature begun in 1972.

The other business interests under the parent publishing company are devoted to ancillary business ventures that support the entire structure. The marketing and research company has developed a Minority Business Information Institute with a census tract data library; and the EGG Dallas Broadcasting Company operates AM and FM stations in Dallas, Texas. The Pepsi Cola franchise owned by Graves and Magic Johnson is headquartered in Forrestville, Maryland, and covers a four-hundred-square-mile territory inclusive of Washington, D.C., and Prince Georges County, Maryland. Some of its key accounts are the White House, the United States Capitol, and Air Force One.

The Graves dynasty Graves provides a nurturing, loving, and supportive home environment for his family. In 1960 Graves married Barbara Kydd of Brooklyn. After teaching school for some years, she became a full partner with her husband and now serves as vice president and general manager of Earl G. Graves Publishing Company. In the Silver Anniversary Commemorative Issue of *Black Enterprise*, Graves praised her in a letter to his grandchildren, saying, "You must know that while I get all the glory, without Gramma there would be no BE. She has been the glue of our business, she is the heart of our family and the love of my life." In an interview in the same issue, Graves further detailed his wife's contributions: "Barbara has been the most important thing to everything we have done."

The three Graves sons are all involved in the family business. The oldest, Earl Jr., is a Yale-trained economist who also earned an M.B.A. from Harvard Business School. Despite being drafted by the Philadelphia 76ers, he chose to join *Black Enterprise* and is now vice president of advertising and marketing. The second son, John, was a Brown University history major who received his law degree from Yale. He was an associate with a prominent New York law firm and now serves as vice president of business ventures and legal affairs for the Earl G. Graves Publishing Company. The youngest son, Michael, was a football player at the University of Pennsylvania, where he majored in communications and sociology. He joined the Pepsi Cola franchise as development manager.

Graves has long been recognized as a civic leader and authority on black business development. He is a member of the board of directors of Rohm and Haas Corporation, New York State Urban Development Corporation, Chrysler Corporation, National Supplier Development Council, and the Magazine Publishers Association. He holds membership in such organizations as the American Museum of Natural History (where he is a trustee), the NAACP, Sigma Pi Phi, Statue of Liberty Ellis Island Centennial Commission, and the Visiting Committee of Harvard University's John F. Kennedy School of Government.

Having once served as National Commissioner of Scouting for the Boy Scouts of America in the early 1960s, Graves has received the organization's highest volunteer service awards: the Silver Beaver (1969), the Silver Buffalo (1988), and the Silver Antelope (1986). He is a member of the executive committee of the Greater New York Council and of the executive board of the National Boy Scouts of America. *Ebony* magazine has continuously listed Graves as one of the 100 Most Influential Blacks and former President Richard M. Nixon recognized him as one of the ten most outstanding minority business leaders in the United States. In the last twenty-five years, Graves has been awarded over twenty-five honorary doctorates from such institutions as Rust College, Hampton Institute (now University), Brown and Lincoln Universities, Morehouse College, Meharry Medical College, and his alma mater, Morgan State University.

Graves has always made public service to educational institutions a priority in his professional life. The depth of that commitment was revealed early in 1996 when he was scheduled to teach two classes at Middle Tennessee State University in Murfreesboro. Despite learning of a family death the day before, he kept the appointment and even made time to talk with students at a luncheon before flying home to Scarsdale, New York.

Always a visionary, Graves nonetheless has been described as having an anachronistic appearance due to his 1950s-style mutton-chop sideburns that offset a receding hairline. But those who dwell on his visage miss his vision for black American businesses. Graves is a true entrepreneur, businessman, and corporate executive whose lifestyle is now commensurate with his stellar achievements. In the Twenty-fifth Anniversary Issue of *Black Enterprise*, Graves engaged in a dialogue with the executive editor, Alfred Edmond Jr., who questioned him about the evolution of the magazine. Graves's ability to keep his professional and personal lives in proper perspective was explained in this way:

> Had we not been involved in so many other causes, we might have been even more profitable and achieved even greater things. But, along the way, other values kicked in. . . . If I had been willing to spend less time with my family, I might have ended up being a couple of million dollars ahead in terms of what this business represents. On the other hand . . . my children and grandchildren . . . would not be with us. So, I think I have achieved the best of both worlds: a solid family and a solid business. I would not trade that.

—DOLORES NICHOLSON

WILLIAM H. GRAY III

1941–

Foundation executive, minister, U.S. congressman

William H. Gray has consistently maintained efforts to improve his community and help African Americans continue to progress spiritually, educationally, politically, socially, and economically. Gray is currently pastor of a five-thousand-member church and administrator of the College Fund/UNCF; he is also a former six-term U.S. congressman whose tenure in the House of Representatives proved beneficial to America and Third World countries.

William Herbert Gray III was born on August 20, 1941, in Baton Rouge, Louisiana. He was the second child born to William H. Gray Jr. and Hazel Yates Gray, who were also the parents of a daughter, Marion. After William's birth, the family moved to St. Augustine where the senior Gray served as president of Florida Normal and Industrial College (now known as Florida Memorial College) from 1941 to 1944. In that year William Jr. became president of Florida Agricultural and Mechanical College (now University) in Tallahassee. Five years later, the family moved to Philadelphia where Gray succeeded his deceased father as pastor of Bright Hope Baptist Church.

The younger Gray attended public elementary and secondary schools in Philadelphia, and in 1959 he graduated from Simon Gratz High School. That year, Gray entered Franklin and Marshall College in Lancaster, Pennsylvania. He majored in history and was urged to consider

*William H. Gray III accepting his position as president
of the United Negro College Fund in 1991.*

a public service career by his political science professor, Sidney Wise. During Gray's senior
year, Wise recommended him for a congressional internship in the office of Pennsylvania
representative Robert Nix. Gray received his B.A. in 1963.

One year after graduating from Franklin and Marshall College, Gray was appointed
assistant pastor of Union Baptist Church in Montclair, New Jersey. In 1966 he became the
church's senior pastor; Martin Luther King Jr. officiated at Gray's installation service. That
same year, Gray received a master's degree in divinity from Drew Theological Seminary in
Madison, New Jersey. He did postgraduate work at the University of Pennsylvania in 1965,
Temple University in 1966, and Mansfield College of Oxford University in 1967 before earning
a master's degree in theology from Princeton Theological Seminary in 1970.

Gray's church and graduate school responsibilities did not deter him from becoming an
activist in the Montclair community. He founded the Union Housing Corporation and other

nonprofit organizations that built apartments for low- and middle-income members of the community. Gray waged a successful battle against housing discrimination in 1970 when he sued a landlord who denied him an apartment because of his race. The New Jersey Superior Court awarded Gray financial damages as a victim of racial discrimination and established a precedent that had national repercussions. Due to these and other deeds on behalf of the Montclair community, he was hailed as a community leader.

Gray remained at Union Baptist until his father's death in 1972. He returned to Philadelphia and assumed the pastorate of Bright Hope Baptist Church, where his grandfather and father pastored before him. Gray remains at the church.

In Philadelphia he continued his community activism, with improving housing conditions as a major goal. As in Montclair, he established nonprofit housing corporations. Gray battled home lending discrimination by helping to create the Philadelphia Mortgage Plan, which enabled individuals in low-income communities redlined by banks to obtain mortgages.

Becomes Philadelphia's Congressman   Due to Gray's intense concern with the community's inadequate housing, high rate of unemployment, and other problems, he challenged the black incumbent for the Second District congressional seat in 1976. Gray's opponent was the same man for whom he had interned during his senior year in college—Robert Nix. He now believed that Nix was unresponsive to the district's needs. Nix defeated Gray in the primary election by approximately three hundred votes. Two years later, Gray ran against Nix again and defeated him in the primary election by capturing 58 percent of the vote to Nix's 40 percent. After his upset victory over Nix, Gray easily defeated his Republican opponent, Roland Atkins, in the general election, where he received 84 percent of the vote to Atkins's 16 percent. Thus he succeeded Nix as Pennsylvania's second elected black congressman. He now had the opportunity to exercise his political talents to advance the social causes he advocated.

During his thirteen-year tenure in Congress, Gray served on many congressional and political committees, including District of Columbia; Foreign Affairs; Budget; Democratic Steering and Policy; Appropriations; Platform; and Drafting for the 1988 Democratic National Convention, and the subcommittees on Transportation, on Foreign Operations, and on Government Operations and Metropolitan Affairs. Gray's most significant congressional contributions were his work as Black Caucus member and later chair of the Budget Committee, member of the Subcommittee on Foreign Operations, chair of the Democratic Caucus, and Democratic Whip.

Gray began his congressional career in 1979, two years before Ronald Reagan was sworn in as president of the United States, and he remained in the House of Representatives three years after Reagan's two terms had ended. Saving social programs from devastation during the Reagan administration was a major objective for Gray. In 1981 and 1982, Gray and other members of the Congressional Black Caucus vehemently opposed the administration's economic plan and created alternative proposals advocating expansion of social programs. In 1983, as a member of the Budget Committee, Gray helped negotiate a budget compromise between the House and the Senate that established an $8.5 billion reserve for recession-relief programs. Two years later, Gray was elected chair of the Budget Committee by acclamation, and he immediately battled the administration's budget for fiscal 1986 that proposed increasing military expenditures by approximately $30 billion at the expense of social programs. William L. Clay, Gray's colleague from Missouri and fellow caucus member, analyzed the outcome:

Gray succeeded in his efforts to retain essential funding for programs designed to rebuild urban America and to meet the human needs of low-income Americans. Striving for a budget of compassion, fairness, and economic justice, Gray's committee provided an increase to offset inflation in thirty-two out of thirty-three low-income programs.

Gray successfully maneuvered fiscal budgets for 1987, 1988, and 1989 through Congress.

Education was another priority of Gray's. He co-sponsored the Black College Act, which provided federal financing to enhance facilities, faculties, and programs in historically black colleges and universities (HBCUs). Gray wrote set-aside provisions that required HBCU participation in the U.S. Agency for International Development (AID) assistance program.

He also wrote set-aside provisions to require participation by minority and women business owners in AID; consequently, they received $300 million in AID contracts in a three-year period. Gray's work as a public servant extends beyond American shores. He emerged as a leading spokesman on African Affairs and an advocate for increased federal aid to Africa. In 1980 as a freshman representative, Gray authored a bill to establish the African Development Foundation to channel federal funding directly to villages in Africa. Gray, who was one of the first members of Congress to warn of famine in Africa, sponsored an emergency relief bill for Ethiopia in 1984. He wrote the House version of the Anti-Apartheid Acts of 1985 and 1986, which implemented economic sanctions against the South African government; Gray helped ensure passage of the acts, despite presidential vetoes. The Anti-Apartheid Acts of 1985 and 1986, along with the Sullivan Principles, contributed to the dismantling of South Africa's apartheid government in 1992.

Gray was able to influence national legislation and policy as well as international affairs because of his political stature. He became one of the most powerful and visible members of Congress. In 1985, the same year Gray became Budget Committee chair, he was elected chair of Congress's Democratic Caucus. In 1989 Gray was elected Majority Whip, the number-three leadership position in the House of Representatives. Gray was then the highest-ranking black American ever to serve in Congress. He was respected by his Republican as well as his Democratic colleagues for his legislative leadership, political acumen, fairness, personal integrity, pragmatism, and ability to build coalitions. Gray was regarded as a charming, charismatic, dignified, cordial, intellectual leader, qualities that made him an extraordinary politican. Political insiders speculated about Gray's future; they predicted he would be Speaker of the House, Secretary of the Treasury, or the 1988 vice presidential nominee. However, they failed to anticipate that Gray would walk away from Congress and politics.

Heads College Fund/UNCF   In June 1991 Gray announced his resignation from Congress effective September of that same year. On September 11, 1991, he became president and chief executive officer of the United Negro College Fund, now known as the College Fund/UNCF. Americans were stunned by Gray's career change, but many, including Columbus Salley in *The Black 100*, praised Gray, saying that his decision showed:

> courage and vision in taking his fame, visibility, and influence—at a time when his political star was rising—to seize the sociology of this particular moment in history to strengthen and expand the role of historically black colleges and universities. Gray's decision came at a critical time, when black America faced

the scandalizing and sobering fact that more college-age black males are in prison, jail, or on probation than in institutions of higher learning!

In assuming leadership of the UNCF Gray followed family tradition a second time. His grandfather was a professor. His father was president of two black colleges. His mother was a dean at Southern University in Baton Rouge, Louisiana. His sister, Marion, is a professor. Prior to promoting education in Congress, Gray taught religion and history during the late 1960s and early 1970s at St. Peter's College, Jersey City State College, Montclair State College, Eastern Baptist Theological Seminary, and Temple University.

Gray told Matthew Scott for *Black Enterprise* that his work at UNCF "is just as important as being a member of the leadership of Congress." He has produced dramatic results in fund raising, administrative reorganization, and initiatives. Approximately one-third of the nearly $1 billion raised in the UNCF's history has been generated since Gray's arrival. Campaign 2000, the organization's most ambitious fund-raising project, has exceeded its $250 million goal by 12 percent. A $50 million gift from media mogul Walter Annenberg helped the campaign raise $86 million in its first year. To increase efficiency, administrative expenses have been reduced while staff was restructured and UNCF headquarters moved to the Fairfax, Virginia, area. The Gray administration has also undertaken the development of a technology center electronically linking its offices and member colleges as well as a research institute to study issues affecting African American students from grade school through graduate school.

In the *Washington Post*, Gray stated the importance of black institutions:

If America is to prosper in the global marketplace and maintain our economic strength, we will have to rely on the skills and productivity of that 21st-century workforce. Thus we need to support the educational institutions that know how to take not just the best and brightest, but also the talented and intelligent, and give them the skills America will need.

Since 1835, these colleges and universities have persevered through difficult and challenging times to prepare leaders for America. Just as the religious and ethnic colleges of early immigrants—Georgetown, Yeshiva, Brigham Young—provided doorways for their rejected community, HBCUs continue to serve all of us. They have a vital role to play. From their halls have come—and will continue to come—the business persons, physicians, scientists, engineers, architects, teachers, public servants and artists we need to be strong in the 21st century.

Gray has received more than fifty honorary degrees from colleges and universities. In 1995 Haitian President Jean-Bertrand Aristide awarded Gray the Medal of Honor for his work as a special advisor to President Bill Clinton in 1994 in developing and implementing policy to restore Haitian democracy.

In taking up the UNCF post, Gray commented that he could spend more time at Bright Hope and with his family. He married Andrea Dash in 1971. They have three sons: William H. IV, Justin, and Andrew. The Grays live in Vienna, Virginia. While Gray is remembered for his service as an influential politician in both state and federal governments, he continues to serve the needs of African Americans through his church and his work as head of the nation's most influential fund-raising organization for black colleges. William H. Gray III remains a man of God, a man of the people, and a man of the future.—LINDA M. CARTER

BRYANT C. GUMBEL

1948–

Broadcast journalist

Bryant Gumbel was the first black to co-host Today, *a popular morning talk show on NBC. Until he left the show in 1997, he remained an influential and a highly visible journalist known the world over and reigned as king of early morning television. Relentless in his preparation, Gumbel consistently demonstrated a hard-driving style that produced among viewers mixed reaction to the articulate and well-read journalist. He has now become a major news star with CBS television.*

The second child of Richard Dunbar Gumbel and Rhea Alice LeCesne Gumbel, Bryant Charles Gumbel was born in New Orleans, Louisiana, on September 29, 1948. He has two younger sisters, Rhonda and Renee, and an older brother, Greg, who is now a well-known sports telecaster. The Gumbels relocated to Chicago when Bryant and Greg were infants. There Richard Gumbel, the son of a New Orleans gambler, who had graduated from New Orleans's Xavier University and worked his way through Georgetown Law School, became a Cook County probate judge during Mayor Richard Dailey's political reign. Both parents were active in Democratic party politics in Chicago.

As Bryant Gumbel grew up in the Hyde Park section of Chicago, a middle-class neighborhood near the University of Chicago, his father remained a central influence in his life and stressed the importance of reading, writing, speaking, and listening. He also introduced his sons to sports, particularly baseball and the art of catching. Gumbel attended Roman Catholic elementary and high schools in Chicago, then in 1966 entered Bates College of Lewiston, Maine, where he played baseball and football. The long-haired young man stood out as one of three blacks in a student body of nine hundred. Although he was not as serious in his studies as he could have been and became a C student, he developed a sense of self-confidence that he has never lost. He decided also that he would devote his time to studies and not become an activist in the civil rights movement of that era. After graduating in 1970 with a B.A. in history, a sports-related injury in college prevented him from being drafted for military service.

For half a year after graduation, Gumbel worked as a sales representative for the Westvaco Corporation, manufacturer of paper bags and folding cartons. Bored, he quit the job and did nothing for a while, yet still maintained an interest in becoming a sports writer. His article about Harvard University's first black athletic director published in *Black Sports* led him to a contract with the magazine; nine

Bryant C. Gumbel.

285

months later he was the magazine's editor and had an annual salary of eleven thousand dollars. This position led to his upward mobility, as he came in contact with many people in a position to drop his name in the right places.

Gumbel's father died in 1972 before Gumbel's career as a journalist began. KNBC-TV in Los Angeles hired Gumbel, at age twenty-three, as weekly sportscaster with a salary of $21,500. Now he felt he had achieved something, and he recorded the word "success" in his appointment book on July 21, 1972, when he auditioned. He became weeknight sportscaster on the 6:00 p.m. news eight months later, then in 1986 became sports director for the station.

It was Gumbel's flair for television journalism and ability to develop appealing stories on a variety of topics that made him attractive. In 1975, after he gave an off-the-cuff commentary on John Wooden, then basketball coach for the University of California, Los Angeles, he was tapped as co-host of the National Football League's pregame show *Grandstand,* televised from New York. Continuing with KNBC in Los Angeles, he kept the New York assignment from 1976 to 1980, commuting on weekends to work for NBC sports as anchor for NFL football, major league baseball, and NCAA basketball. His assignments with NBC Sports expanded beginning in 1976 to include three Super Bowls, one World Series, five Thanksgiving Day Parades, and several golf tournaments.

Signing a three-year, $1.5 million contract with NBC network in 1980, Gumbel was responsible for three sports features each week on the *Today* show. In August of that year he became co-host with Cyndy Garvey on *Games People Play*, and was anchor for NBC's *NFL '80.* By then, *Today*'s rival show, ABC's *Good Morning America*, had climbed above *Today* in ratings.

Co-hosts the Today show

Today's anchor Tom Brokaw left to anchor *NBC Nightly News* and in August 1981 Gumbel was asked to sit in as co-host on the *Today* show with Jane Pauley. On January 4, 1982, the *Today* show was reconstituted; along with the regular members—Jane Pauley, Gene Shalit, and Willard Scott—were newcomers Gumbel and news anchor Chris Wallace. Gumbel, the show's first black co-host, was well-read, performed well, and became a young master of live television interviewing. Critics doubted whether Gumbel, who had very little television news experience, could follow in the footsteps of such journalist greats as John Chancellor, Hugh Downs, and Tom Brokaw. But Gumbel's smooth interview style made him an asset to NBC and the show. After three years of zig-zag ratings for first place in morning television viewing with rivals *CBS Morning News* and *Good Morning America*, in March 1985 *Today* was in first place. That fall Gumbel also hosted a late-afternoon NBC news program each month, and on April 1 of that year he broadcast the show from a private mass at the Vatican. The full cast gathered for an audience with the Pope.

Gumbel's success continued. In 1988 he was key anchor for the Olympic Games held in Seoul, South Korea. Co-host Jane Pauley told Oprah Winfrey of her years on the show with Gumbel that "he has a challenging personality and I enjoy that. . . . [He] made me work harder. He made me be on my toes. We were a darn good team." Deborah Norville was added as news reader from January 1990 to April 1991, a position that discomforted Pauley, who then decided to move off the show. The show's ratings suffered during Norville's presence. Gumbel added that he had not encouraged Norville's appearance in order to give Pauley a jolt, although there was some speculation that he had. His confidential memorandum to his show's producer Marty Ryans in 1989 concerning Willard Scott's birthday recognitions on the

*Bryant Gumbel interviews Richard M.
Nixon on the* Today *show.*

show led to undue negative publicity. The memorandum had been solicited and written six months before it was leaked to the public. Oprah Winfrey cited Gumbel's memo saying that Scott "was holding the show hostage with his assortment of whims with his birthdays and bad taste." Gumbel responded that Ryans "asked me to give him a laundry list of things to respond to. And he said 'I need your input on these,' and I gave it to him." He never knew who leaked the memo, and thought "it was better that I just didn't know and just move on. . . . In retrospect, the only thing that I really regret terribly was a poor choice of words in a lot of instances. I should have been more sensitive to things, but in a business sense, it was simply an attempt to respond to a producer's request." After the memorandum, Gumbel and Scott talked over the phone, cried, and expressed their regrets over the matter. The press gave the affair much publicity, which ended in a reconciliation between Gumbel and Scott. Many still viewed the relationship as strained, a view that Gumbel denied.

In 1992 Gumbel took the *Today* show on a week-long visit to sub-Saharan Africa, later calling this his "proudest achievement." During his career he took the show across the world to Europe, China, and Australia. During the Persian Gulf Conflict, Gumbel covered the war from Saudi Arabia.

Three years before his good friend Arthur Ashe died in 1993, Ashe confided to Gumbel that he had AIDS. Gumbel told Oprah Winfrey that, in keeping the confidence, "The world was not any worse off in not knowing what I knew. This wasn't a case of national security. And so, it was hard and even when Arthur and I had talked on the air, before his death, knowing he had AIDS, it was hard." Gumbel knew that journalists should share their information, but the news had come through their friendship and he was satisfied that he was not derelict in his duty by keeping the secret.

Perhaps the greatest offense Gumbel endured was the denial of an opportunity in October 1995 to join a team to interview his friend, O. J. Simpson, who had been charged with murdering his former wife and her friend. Gumbel told Oprah Winfrey that he was offended because his producers thought he could not be objective and that he was a "subjective risk." "I told the producers that I could not work that day. . . . I was not going to tell people, 'Hey, watch NBC tonight as Tom Brokaw and Katie Couric interview O. J. Simpson'. . . . I wasn't going to be a phoney."

Gumbel resigns from* Today *show   Only one day short of fifteen years as anchor, Gumbel left the *Today* show on January 3, 1997, with its highest ratings dominating ABC rival *Good Morning America*. On hand during his tearful departure, in addition to his NBC colleagues, were poet Maya Angelou, boxing great Muhammad Ali, and the artist formerly known as Prince. Gumbel was succeeded by Matt Lauer, who had joined the team in January 1994 as news anchor. Gumbel's legacy has been called relentless preparation for his work. After his retirement, he played golf, sorted through his offers, then on Thursday, March 13, 1997, Gumbel and CBS News announced Gumbel's new position. Three television networks bidded for his service, and Gumbel accepted an offer from CBS to be a major news star with a weekly magazine, prime-time interview specials, and the opportunity to own and develop syndicated programs with the CBS syndication, Eyemark. The deal could net him over $5 million annually, possibly more if the syndicated programs become big hits. CBS needed to boost its sagging news ratings and Gumbel liked the opportunity for creative ventures. Gumbel also announced his intention to begin an internship program and make other opportunities available for minorities. Gumbel made an unusual prime-time appearance since his retirement as host of the 1997 Emmy awards in September.

Gumbel has been widely recognized for his work. In 1976 he won an Emmy award for an Olympic sports special, another Emmy in 1977, the Los Angeles Press Club's Golden Mike Award in 1978 and 1979, and a New York City Brotherhood Award in 1985. After his trip to Moscow in 1988, Gumbel won the Overseas Press Club's Edward R. Murrow Award for outstanding foreign affairs work. Twice the *Washington Journalism Review*'s Annual Readers Poll named him best morning television news interviewer, 1986 and 1987, and the Associated Press voted him a co-winner as broadcaster of the year. Gumbel received international awards for orchestrating and anchoring the *Today* show's broadcasts from Africa: in 1993 the TransAfrica's International Journalism Award, the U.S. Committee for UNICEF'S Africa's Future Award, and in 1984 the Edward Weintal Prize for diplomatic reporting. In 1993 the Association of Black Journalists named him Journalist of the Year. He also received two Image Awards from the NAACP. He received the Martin Luther King Award from the Congress of Racial Equality and the College Fund/UNCF's highest honor, the Frederick D. Patterson Award. He is a benefactor of the College Fund/UNCF. For more than seven years he has raised over three million dollars for UNCF scholarships through the Bryant Gumbel/Walt Disney World golf tournament. He is active in other philanthropies and has served on the board for United Way and Xavier University.

Gumbel had a tendency to demonstrate a hard-driving style on the *Today* show that brought mixed reactions, ranging from characterization as arrogance to toughness. There were claims from blacks that he did not sound black enough. Yet from early childhood he had been taught to read widely and to speak correctly; it was not a matter of race. He told Joanne Harris in an interview that he hoped that the *Today* show did not "define things as 'black issues.'" He wanted audiences to see a black man in a position of responsibility or intelligence whether the subject was inner-city poverty, food stamps, or welfare programs. "We strive as much as possible when we're having a medical discussion to have a doctor who happens to be black," he continued.

On December 1, 1973, Gumbel married artist June Carlyn Baranco; they became parents of two children, Bradley Christopher and Jillian Beth. Bryant Gumbel brought appeal, skill, and preciseness to television interviewing that drew large audiences and made him a sought-after journalist and an image-builder for those who would enter the field. His comments to Joanne Harris in an interview addressed the art of interviewing that was characteristic of him. Gumbel considered himself a communicator and thought it was his job "to serve as an effective conduit . . . between someone who has information to impart and someone who wants to know what that person has to say." And that is what he does so well.—JESSIE CARNEY SMITH

ALEX **HALEY**
1921–1992
Writer, genealogist

Alex Haley is a writer whose best-known work, Roots: The Saga of an American Family, *recounts the experiences of an African ancestor who was sold into slavery and shipped to America in the mid-seventeenth century.* Roots *sold more than six million copies and inspired a television miniseries that prompted still further interest in black heritage.*

Haley was born in Ithaca, New York, in 1921. His father, Simon Alexander Haley, was a student at the time of Haley's birth, and he later became a professor at various southern institutions. Haley's mother, Bertha George Haley, died when Haley was only ten years old. But Haley enjoyed a sizeable extended family, and the various relatives congregated most summers in Henning, Tennessee, where Haley's grandfather ran a flourishing lumber business.

When he was only fifteen years old, Haley graduated from high school. He studied education for two years, then joined the Coast Guard during World War II. His first position was as a kitchen worker, but before the war ended he was a cook. After the war, Haley remained in the Coast Guard. There he traveled extensively and developed his writing skills by writing letters home and assisting other sailors with their correspondences. In addition, Haley produced nonfiction reports on various matters of interest within the service. Before leaving the Coast Guard in 1959, after a twenty-year stint, he began writing fiction, mostly maritime tales derived from his own observations or the experiences of his fellow sailors.

Upon returning to civilian life, Haley settled in Greenwich Village, a Bohemian quarter of New York City, and determined to support himself as a writer. Journalism initially proved more lucrative than fictional storytelling. Haley proved particularly adept as an interviewer. In 1962, for instance, he executed a compelling *Playboy* interview with the great jazz trumpeter Miles Davis.

Among Haley's other prominent subjects for his *Playboy* interviews was the controversial Malcolm X, a former Black Muslim and separatist who became a proponent of Pan African culture before his assassination in 1965. Haley also collaborated with Malcolm X on the latter's *Autobiography of Malcolm X,* which appeared shortly after the assassination. This volume has come to be regarded as a classic account of black issues and experiences during the post–World War II period and the civil rights era.

Prior to the appearance of *The Autobiography of Malcolm X,* Haley again became interested in the tales his grandmother had shared with relatives during the summers spent in

Alex Haley autographs
copies of Roots.

Henning. His grandmother would tell of Toby, a slave from Africa, and she enhanced her tale with the few African words handed down from generation to generation within the family. Through the assistance of a linguist, Haley derived the meaning of his grandmother's African words. In addition, he conducted archival research that led to the discovery of another African ancestor, one who had worked as a slave in North Carolina.

Throughout much of the ensuing decade Haley immersed himself in genealogical study and history. He uncovered the existence of ship records noting the ancestor of his grandmother's tales, and he traveled to Africa to listen to village historians knowledgeable in the slave trade. In Gambia he managed to relate his grandmother's tales to histories involving the Kinte clan, whose members had been captured and shipped to America, where they were sold as slaves.

Haley ultimately succeeded in fashioning a stirring account of his ancestors, notably Kunta Kinte, and he published that account in 1976 as

*Alex
Haley.*

Roots: The Saga of an American Family. Despite its seemingly uncommercial subject matter, *Roots* soon became a best-seller in the United States. Some historians questioned Haley's rendering of the slave trade, and some critics expressed reservations about the manner in which Haley's account combined facts with fictional elements. But other critics lauded *Roots* as a compelling tale with particular relevence within the fields of American history and, more specifically, Afro-American studies. Book buyers throughout the United States testified to the appeal of *Roots* as both accomplished storytelling and provocative history. The book eventually earned both a special Pulitzer Prize and a citation from the National Book Awards.

In 1977, while sales of *Roots* were still strong, a twelve-hour adaptation appeared on American television. Like the book, the television version proved extremely popular, and it sparked still further interest in the field of black studies. The show has since ranked among television's most widely viewed programs.

The popularity of *Roots* in both literary and televised forms brought Haley immense recognition and success, and for much of the ensuing decade the works continued to be the focus of his professional existence. His related activities included the writing of *Roots: The Next Generation,* a television sequel to the earlier miniseries. In addition, Haley helped establish the Kinte Corporation, which promoted research into black American genealogy.

By the late 1980s Haley had come to realize that *Roots* was overwhelming his other literary projects. He thus withdrew from his Los Angeles home and returned to Tennessee, where he intended to concentrate on a variety of subjects, including a history of Henning, Tennessee, and a biography of C. J. Walker, America's first female, self-made millionaire. He also contributed to the development of *Alex Haley's Queen,* a television miniseries on the life of his grandmother.

While he pursued these enterprises, Haley also appeared regularly as a speaker. He was traveling to an engagement in Seattle, Washington, when he suffered a fatal heart attack on February 10, 1992. At the time of his death Haley was separated from his third wife, television writer Myra Lewis. He was also the father of three children.

Alex Haley's *Queen* appeared on television the year after his death. *Roots,* meanwhile, remains prominent as both a book and as a series available on video.—LES STONE

FANNIE LOU **HAMER**
1917–1977
Civil rights activist

No one in history more powerfully stated the harsh living conditions and brutal racism blacks in Mississippi had to endure than Fannie Lou Hamer. Severe racial hatred and a brutal beating did not stop Hamer from her staunch objective of giving blacks in her community the right to vote and the means of obtaining adequate employment and education. Hamer was a grassroots leader who served her cause, as one writer observed, "selflessly, tirelessly, and fearlessly."

Fannie Lou Townsend Hamer was born on October 6, 1917, in Montgomery County, Mississippi, the twentieth child born to sharecropper parents. Due to extreme poverty, Hamer was deprived of many conveniences and benefits. When her father was finally able to work the family out of abject poverty, an envious white neighbor poisoned the Townsend mules and cows, destroying the family's prospects.

For black sharecroppers, education was secondary to the needs of the plantation. Because of this, Hamer had only six years of school, for at that time, the school period extended from December to March. These four months corresponded to the time black labor was not needed in the fields. Still, because of the lack of adequate clothing during the cold months, only one month of schooling was possible.

In 1942 she married Perry "Pap" Hamer, a tractor driver from another plantation. Because they were unable to have children, they adopted two girls, one of whom died in 1967. Inheriting the impoverished tradition of her sharecropper family, she and her husband continued in the cycle of poverty. But Hamer was a hard worker, and eventually she was promoted from strenuous cotton-picking to the less strenuous but still low-paying job of timekeeper on the plantation.

Civil rights activities attract Hamer   In Mississippi during Jim Crow, African Americans were considered expendable. Because of this, blacks suffered many abuses. Hamer's life was a reflection of that continued abuse, pain, and suffering. L. C. Dorsey in the *Jackson Advocate* describes other dimensions of her suffering:

"No Ameri[ca] "rest while any Am[erican]" is denied his rights...."

Fannie Lou Hamer.

Mrs. Hamer knew about another kind of pain; the pain [of] watching your offspring die from poverty, related illnesses, and of suffering because of a handicap that had she not been poor, could have been corrected.

Hamer's life took a turn in 1962 when she met workers of the Southern Christian Leadership Conference (SCLC) and the Student Nonviolent Coordinating Committee (SNCC), who began mobilizing people to fight for freedom in Mississippi. As a result of this empowering encounter, Hamer became active in Mississippi politics, especially in Ruleville. It all began at a rally led by the Reverend James Bevel of the SCLC and James Forman of SNCC in August 1962. Forman spoke specifically about voter registration, challenging the people to take action to effect change in their political leadership as a route to positive changes in their living conditions.

Fannie Lou Hamer testifies before the Senate Subcommittee on poverty in Mississippi.

When the call came for volunteers to challenge the unjust voting laws, Hamer was among the first recruits; she failed her first two attempts to register but passed her third. She subsequently taught other blacks how to register and pass the literacy test.

Life as a registered voter was not easy, for it became difficult for the Hamer family to get and maintain employment. Hamer then became a field worker in the civil rights movement. Following a civil rights workshop in Charleston, South Carolina, on their return trip to Ruleville on a Trailways bus, Hamer and a group of nineteen stopped at a bus terminal in Winona, Mississippi, to get something to eat. Challenging the "white only" practice, they were attacked by state troopers, arrested, and charged with disorderly conduct. In that Winona jail, Hamer suffered one of the worst beatings of her life. She was taken to a cell with two black male prisoners, who were given a black leather clutch loaded with metal and ordered to beat Hamer or suffer severe consequences for refusing to follow the demands of the white prison guards. Hamer was later returned to her jail cell, where she and the other civil rights workers were released following the intervention of James Bevel and Andrew Young. The incident left Hamer permanently injured.

Hamer gains national attention   Hamer came out of this experience more determined to change the unjust, oppressive, and racist system in Mississippi. In the spring of 1964, the Mississippi Freedom Democratic Party was established after unsuccessful attempts to gain participation in the Mississippi Democratic party. Hamer's work catapulted her to the position of vice chairperson of the Mississippi Freedom Democratic Party (MFDP), under which she campaigned for Congress from the Second Congressional District of Mississippi. Even more importantly, it was as leader of the MFDP that she gained national attention when the group challenged the white Mississippi delegation to the 1964 National Democratic Convention in Atlantic City. The challenge resulted in the nation hearing her story as she testified before the credentials committee. Her story included atrocities such as her loss of employment because of her attempts to register to vote; the beatings such as the Winona, Mississippi, incident; her arrest with a busload of citizens trying to register; and the many other brutalities perpetrated against blacks by whites.

The MFDP delegation did not obtain what it wanted; instead, a so-called compromise was made. The compromise in effect gave two seats to the sixty-eight member delegation. Some saw this as a moral victory. Hamer, along with other MFDP delegates, took exception to this interpretation of the compromise and reportedly said, "We didn't come all this way for no two seats when all of us is tired."

As Hamer's horizons broadened and her involvement deepened, she became global in her interests and was able to see the injustices of the Vietnam War, becoming one of its early critics. Of that war she said, "We are sick and tired of our people having to go to Vietnam and other places to fight for something we don't have here." Consequently, she was able to draw a critical connection between war, racism, and poverty: "We want . . . to end the wrongs such as fighting a war in Vietnam and pouring billions over there, while people in Sunflower County, Mississippi and Harlem and Detroit are starving to death."

Hamer's life was not just about destroying racist and oppressive structures; she also was involved in much community building. She helped to bring to Ruleville the Head Start Program, the most successful of the War on Poverty efforts. In actuality, because she felt that the War on Poverty programs were actually war on the poor—keeping them dependent—she concentrated on building alternative structures that would promote self-reliance. For workers displaced by mechanization, she organized the Freedom Farm Cooperative; two hundred units of low-income housing were built in Ruleville because of Hamer's fund-raising ability. She helped in starting a low-income day care center, and she was involved in bringing to Ruleville a garment factory that provided jobs.

Hamer's motivation was her deep-seated religious conviction. She spoke often of her Christian faith, which undergirded her commitment to the struggle for human dignity for African Americans. She constantly challenged those who professed to be Christian in their actions, saying: "We serve God by serving our fellow [human beings]; kids are suffering from malnutrition. People are going to the fields hungry. If you are a Christian, we are tired of being mistreated."

Hamer's views on a variety of social issues are detailed in her speeches and interviews. She had a special interest in feeding, clothing, and housing the poor. In 1969 she founded Freedom Farm in Sunflower County, Mississippi, and fed fifteen hundred people with the food that was grown. She became involved with the Young World Developers, an organization that built homes for the poor, including impoverished whites. She had an interest in education, and when Shaw University asked her to teach a course in black contemporary history, she agreed. When her class met, "sometimes parents would be there. Sometimes teachers would be there. It was a great experience for me," she said.

Hamer addressed the role and responsibility of black women: "To support whatever is right, and to bring in justice where we've had so much injustice." The special plight and role of the black woman had existed for 350 years, she noted, and she had seen it in her grandmother, a former slave who was 136 years old when she died in 1960. In reference to middle-class black women who a few years earlier had failed to respect the work that she did, Hamer made a statement that was to become widely known and used frequently in other lectures:

> Whether you have a Ph.D., or no D, we're in this bag together. And whether you're from Morehouse or Nohouse, we're still in this bag together. Not to fight to try to liberate ourselves from the men—this is another trick to get us fighting among ourselves—but to work together with the black man, then we will have a better chance to just act as human beings, and to be treated as human beings in our sick society.

For her devotion to the full cause of the civil rights movement and the uplift of black people, many colleges and universities awarded Hamer honorary doctoral degrees. These include Shaw University, Tougaloo College, Columbia College in Chicago, Howard University, and Morehouse College. Though her life had been endangered and threatened many times over, her death actually came on March 15, 1977, from diabetes, heart trouble, and breast cancer.

Hamer was not just a woman of words but a woman of deeds. She dedicated her life not only to challenging unjust political, social, and economic structures, but to creating conditions that helped develop self-reliance and self-determination among African Americans and other poor people of the world. L. C. Dorsey's "Action Memorial" to Hamer not only makes this clear, but makes equally clear the challenge that Hamer left to us:

A proper memorial would be one in which all of us who loved her would
dedicate and rededicate our lives to serving others and helping all of us achieve
a greater measure of freedom, justice and love.

In Hamer's memory, Dorsey's plan called for the organization of registration drives,
voter education programs, and campaigns against hunger, executions, police brutality, ignorance, poverty, and oppression. Addressing these issues will keep Fannie Lou Hamer's life
and contributions to humanity at the forefront.—JACQUELYN GRANT

W. C. **HANDY**
1873–1958
Composer, musician, music publisher, band leader

*William Christopher Handy, the most celebrated black musician of his time, is universally known as
"Father of the Blues." He gave his 1941 autobiography the title* Father of the Blues, *but never claimed to
have originated the musical genre. According to blues historian William Ferris, "Handy became one of
the most prominent figures in the popularization of blues." His twelve-bar blues patterns influenced the
development of popular music in America, making the blues a part of the American vocabulary.*

W. C. Handy was born November 16, 1873, in Florence, Alabama. At age twelve, he
secured work as a water boy in a rock quarry near Muscle Shoals. From this he graduated to
apprenticeships in plastering, shoemaking, and carpentry. But music was always his primary
interest. His father, Charles Bernard Handy, was an African Methodist Episcopal minister, as
was his paternal grandfather. His mother, Elizabeth Brewer Handy, and his father hoped that
young William would follow the tradition. There was no music on either side, except for his
maternal grandfather who was known to play the fiddle for dances before he got religion.
Since there were no instruments in the Florence District School for Negroes, all music was
vocal. Handy wrote:

> We learned all the songs in *Gospel Hymns*. . . . [We] advanced to a point where
> we could sing excerpts from the works of Wagner, Bizet, Verdi and other
> masters—all without instrumental accompaniment.

W. C. Handy recalled in his 1941 autobiography, *Father of the Blues*, that though music
was forbidden in the Handy household, he saved his money and purchased a guitar. Returning
from the store with his purchase, he hastened to show it to his parents. The reaction was not
what W. C. anticipated. Outraged, his father said,

> A guitar! One of the devil's playthings. Take it away. Take it away, I tell you.
> Get it out of your hands. Whatever possessed you to bring a sinful thing like
> that into our Christian home? Take it back where it came from. You hear? Get!

W. C. suggested that the store might not take it back. The father insisted. "For the price
of a thing like that you could get a new Webster's Unabridged Dictionary—something that'll
do you some good." The exchange was made and the father enrolled him in organ lessons,
monitoring his progress. But the lessons were of limited duration.

The appearance of a prominent trumpeter in Florence convinced Handy that music should become his career pursuit and the trumpet should be his instrument for personal expression. He purchased a rotary-valve cornet for one dollar and seventy-five cents. His instructor was Professor Y. A. Wallace, a Fisk University graduate and former Jubilee Singer. Handy credited Wallace with teaching him the fundamental elements of music.

In his early teens, Handy began performing with the local band and minstrel shows. Having joined a quartet, singing first tenor, he and the other members hopped a freight train headed for Chicago and the World's Fair. Upon their arrival, they were informed that the Fair had been delayed until the next year. He returned to Alabama, but sensing that he needed broader exposure, more opportunities, and competition, he left again—this time for good. He took on many jobs—singer, trumpet player, band director, choral director, and educator. At twenty-three, he became bandmaster of Mahara's Colored Minstrels. As an itinerant musician, he directed and played his trumpet in various bands. Seeking work, he made it to St. Louis, Missouri, the inspiration for "St. Louis Blues." In 1898, he married Elizabeth Virginia Price.

Between 1900 and 1902, Handy taught music at Alabama's Agricultural and Mechanical College for Negroes in Huntsville. This career was short lived since he soon resumed his life as a bandmaster and, for a brief period, worked at the Bessemer Iron Works, where the salary was fairly attractive. He eventually settled in Memphis, Tennessee.

Handy became a tenant of the Solvent Savings Bank, where the cashier was Harry H. Pace. Handy wrote in his autobiography that Pace "was a handsome young man of striking personality and definite musical leanings." In 1908, Handy and Pace became collaborators in writing songs, with Pace serving as lyricist. They later founded the Pace and Handy Music Company-Publishers. Pace was president, Handy's brother Charles was vice president, and W. C. was secretary-treasurer.

Writes blues songs   In 1909 one of Handy's bands was hired to work for one of the three mayoral candidates, Edward Crump. For the campaign, Handy wrote the successful "Mr. Crump," with a blues flair. Unable to find a publisher, he prepared one thousand copies for distribution in 1912, at his own expense. With new lyrics and a new title, the song became "Memphis Blues."

Handy's fame as a song writer began to spread. Unfortunately, he sold his rights to "Memphis Blues" for $100,000. "St. Louis Blues," which became one of the most popular tunes in the history of songwriting, was published in 1914. Forty years after publication, the composer was still earning yearly royalties of 25 thousand dollars on "St. Louis Blues." The publisher for both "Memphis Blues" and "St. Louis Blues" was Pace and Handy Music Company-Publishers. Other successful blues compositions by Handy were "Beale Street Blues," "Mississippi Blues," "Joe Turner Blues," "Yellow Dog Blues," "Aunt Hagger's Children's Blues," and "Harlem Blues," to name only a few.

The company moved to New York City in 1918. Two years later, the Pace and Handy partnership was dissolved. Pace moved on to form the first black-owned recording company, Black Swan, and the publishing company continued as a Handy family business. The company published works of other black composers as well as Handy's compositions: more than 150 sacred musical compositions and folk song arrangements, and roughly sixty additional blues compositions.

For many years, Handy collaborated with the New York Urban League in presenting annual concerts of talented young black instrumentalists and singers. He also promoted the music of other black composers as well as his own. Noteworthy was his April 27, 1928, concert at Carnegie Hall. Handy, according to Eileen Southern, "was the first to present the full spectrum of black music from plantation songs to orchestral works." Presented by W. C. Handy's Orchestra and Jubilee Singers, both the presentations and the presenters were outstanding; the program included spirituals, blues, plantation songs, work songs, piano solos, a Negro rhapsody, and jazz. Composers included Will Marion Cook, James P. Johnson, H. T. Burleigh, J. Rosamond Johnson, Nathaniel Dett, and others. The concluding work was "St. Louis Blues," featuring Thomas "Fats" Waller as organ soloist.

An authentic recreation of this historic event took place at Carnegie Hall on March 6, 1981, presented by Carnegie Hall and producer George Wein. Other large-scale concerts that Handy produced were for the Chicago World's Fair (1933–34), ASCAP Silver Jubilee Festival (1939), New York's World Fair (1939–40), and the Golden Gate Exposition in San Francisco (1939–40).

A prolific writer, Handy wrote and edited five publications—*Blues: An Anthology* (also published as *A Treasury of the Blues,* 1926 and 1949); *Negro Authors and Composers of the United States* (1935); *Book of Negro Spirituals* (1938); *Father of the Blues* (autobiography, 1941); and *Unsung Americans Sung* (1944). Of special interest is a series of letters written to his very good friend, composer William Grant Still (1895–1978) and published in *Black Perspective in Music.* Their contact started when Still began arranging for Handy's band in Memphis, Tennessee, in 1915. Still also played cello and oboe in the band. In 1919 Handy sent for Still to join him in New York City to work in the Pace-Handy Music Publishing Company.

Blindness began to set in during World War I. Handy regained some of his lost vision, but in 1943 a fall from a subway platform fractured his skull and caused total blindness. After the death of his first wife, he married his secretary, Irma Louise Logan, in 1954. Handy often remarked that she had been his eyes for many years.

To commemorate his sixty-fifth birthday, there were a series of celebrations: a testimonial dinner at the famous Cotton Club in New York City; the playing of "St. Louis Blues" fifteen times by fifteen different bands at an American Federation of Musicians musical jamboree in Hollywood; and a culminating concert at Carnegie Hall, featuring "name bands" performing the "St. Louis Blues" in a variety of arrangements. In 1940 an All-Handy program was broadcast on NBC.

Handy died March 28, 1958, at age eighty-four. He was survived by his wife, two sons, Wyer Owens and William Christopher Jr., and a daughter, Katherine Handy Lewis. For his funeral, approximately 150,000 people gathered in the streets surrounding Harlem's Abyssinian Baptist Church. The twenty-five thousand people within the edifice heard an African Methodist Episcopal Church minister remind the attendees that Handy "captured the heart throbs of a forlorn and stricken people and set them to music." New York City's mayor Wagner said that Handy's life was "an example for generations to come. Congressman Adam Clayton Powell Jr. extolled, "Gabriel now has an understudy—a side man. And when the last trumpet shall sound I am sure that W. C. Handy will be there to bury this world as a side man."

Trumpeter Charles "Cootie" Williams played Handy's favorite melody, "The Holy City." The Brass Band of Prince Hall Masonic Temple led the funeral procession, alternating Frederic Chopin's "Funeral March" with Handy's immortal "St. Louis Blues." Television cameras rolled and a *Voice of America* broadcaster talked ceaselessly into a portable microphone in French.

In 1958, the year of his death, the movie *St. Louis Blues* was released by Paramount pictures and featured Nat King Cole in the role of William Christopher Handy. A commemorative stamp was issued on May 17, 1969, in Memphis Tennessee.

The occasion of the one hundredth anniversary of Handy's birth was remembered in 1983 in the city of Florence, Alabama, with music and special tours of the restored Handy Home and Museum. The W. C. Handy Festival in Florence, Alabama, is now an annual event. In Memphis, centennial activities took place at Handy Park on Beale Street, where the Handy statue stands. Other ceremonies took place in St. Louis, at Yale University, and at the Library and Museum of Lincoln Center in New York City. Earl "Fatha" Hines cut an album of Handy compositions, and Columbia Records reissued Louis Armstrong's album of Handy tunes originally recorded in 1954.

Fisk University in Nashville, Tennessee, declared November 10, 1978, as W. C. Handy Day, and Handy's younger brother Charles presented some of Handy's sheet music to the university's special collection within the library. Throughout the country, the name William Christopher Handy is kept alive through the dedication of schools, housing projects, streets, theaters, parks, awards, and scholarships bearing his name.

Handy earned his place in history with his composition "St. Louis Blues," which is still one of the world's most popular songs. His style of the blues inspired numerous later composers. His publishing company made available to the world the music of other black composers, and Handy himself played a pioneering role in bringing the blues to the attention of the world.—D. ANTOINETTE HANDY

PATRICIA **HARRIS**
1924–1985
Lawyer, government official

Patricia Roberts Harris made history during her lifetime and achieved many firsts. American history will remember her as the first black woman to serve in a United States president's cabinet, both as secretary of Housing and Urban Development and as secretary of Health, Education, and Welfare; she was also the first black woman to serve her nation as ambassador and to lead an American law school.

Harris was born on May 31, 1924, in Mattoon, Illinois, to Bert and Chiquita Roberts. Early in her life, Patricia's father, a dining car waiter for the Illinois Central Railroad, abandoned the family, leaving her and her brother, Malcolm, to be raised by their mother. In her formative years, Harris became aware of the importance of an education, saying, "We didn't have a lot of money [but] we believed in education and . . . in reading." Since hers was one of the few black families in Mattoon, Illinois, she also came to know about racism when one of her grade school classmates called her a "nigger."

After receiving her secondary education in Chicago, Illinois, Harris entered the School of Liberal Arts at Howard University in 1941, from which she graduated summa cum laude in 1945 with a bachelor's degree. Later she was elected into Phi Beta Kappa. It was during her college days at Howard that Harris gained a social consciousness about the ramifications of segregation in American society. In 1943 she joined other Howard students in one of the first student sit-ins at the Little Palace Cafeteria, which refused to serve blacks.

Patricia Harris.

Harris entered graduate school and worked several years at the Chicago YWCA before becoming executive director of Delta Sigma Theta in 1953. She subsequently married William Beasley Harris, a lawyer who encouraged her to attend law school. In 1957 she enrolled in the George Washington University School of Law, where she excelled. She was a member of the law review and was elected to the Order of the Coif, a national legal honor society, and graduated first in her class of ninety-four students in 1960. After graduation, Harris joined the appeals and research staff of the criminal division of the United States Department of Justice, where she remained until she joined the Howard University Law School faculty on a part-time basis as a lecturer in law in 1961. The rest of her time was spent as associate dean of students at Howard University. Harris's appointment to the law school faculty made her the fifth woman to teach at Howard's law school.

Around 1963 Harris was appointed to Howard's law faculty on a full-time basis, one of two women on the law faculty. In June of 1965, Harris, a Democrat, took leave from her teaching responsibilities to accept an appointment by President Lyndon B. Johnson as ambassador to Luxembourg. She held the position until 1967, and that year she received the Order of Oaken Crown for her distinguished service in Luxembourg.

After retiring as ambassador, Harris returned to Howard's law school as a professor on a full-time basis, serving simultaneously as United States alternate delegate to the Twenty-first and Twenty-second General Assembly of the United Nations and as United States alternate to the Twentieth Plenary Meeting of the Economic Community of Europe.

Harris receives federal appointments   In 1969 Harris, then a professor of law, was appointed dean of the Howard University School of Law, a position from which she resigned within thirty days after being appointed. Although her deanship was short because of a host of issues, ranging from a student uprising and faculty disagreements to a disagreement with the president of Howard University, she was the first black woman to head a law school. She later joined the Washington, D.C., law firm of Fried, Frank, Harris, Shriver, and Kampelman, where she practiced corporate law until President Jimmy Carter appointed her secretary of Housing and Urban Development in 1977. She served in this position for three years. In 1980, Carter

*Patricia Harris as a member of
President Carter's administration.*

appointed Harris secretary of the Department of Health, Education and Welfare, a position in which she served until Carter was defeated in the presidential election of 1980.

In 1982 Harris ran for, but lost, a bid to become the mayor of the District of Columbia. The campaign was tough and bitter. She lost the Democratic primary to Marion S. Barry Jr., receiving 36 percent of the vote. In 1983, twenty-three years after receiving her law degree from George Washington University, she was appointed as a full professor of law in its law school. She held this position until she died of cancer on March 23, 1985, shortly after the death of her husband.

From a very early age Harris never allowed her aspirations or personhood to be controlled by racism or sexism. Rather, her philosophy, one that carried her to extraordinary heights, was to do "what I think I ought to be able to do." That blacks faced barriers of discrimination in America troubled Harris because segregation "limited . . . the experiences that they were permitted to have." Although a lawyer, Harris was "suspicious of those who believe that the protector of minorities is in the courts" and that it took "a combination of action—the enactment of legislation and the courts—to protect the rights of minorities" in America. She believed that social change could be influenced through corporate responsibility, a belief that she practiced as a member of the board of directors of several major corporations, including Chase Manhattan Bank, Scott Paper Company, and IBM, and as a trustee of the Twentieth Century Fund.

Harris is perhaps best known for her response to Senator William Proxmire, who, during her Senate confirmation hearing in 1977 for Secretary of Housing and Urban Development, questioned whether Harris was "sympathetic to the problems of the poor." Harris's response made every major newspaper in the country:

> You do not understand who I am. . . . I am a black woman, the daughter of a Pullman car waiter. I am a black woman who even eight years ago could not buy a house in parts of the District of Columbia. I didn't start out as a member of a prestigious law firm, but as a woman who needed a scholarship to go to school. If you think that I have forgotten that, you are wrong.

Harris articulates her concerns   As a public official, Harris clearly demonstrated a concern for good government, racial harmony, and the elimination of racial and sex discrimination. As secretary of Housing and Urban Development, Harris's words speak for themselves. Speaking on the subject of jobs for minorities and minority youth, Harris stated:

> It should not be new to you that the minority unemployment rate is consistently higher than the unemployment rate for whites, and it generally approaches a factor of two to one. For minority youths, conditions are even worse with unemployment in some areas reaching as high as 30% to 40%. . . . I am concerned that an entire generation may grow up without the opportunity to hold a decent job. We cannot allow that to happen.

In a speech addressing racial discrimination in housing, Harris noted:

> If a Black person looking through newspaper advertisements for an apartment to rent or a house to purchase, were to select four apartments or brokers to visit, the probability of encountering discrimination would be 75 percent in the rental market and 62 percent in the sales market. There is clear probability that discrimination is even more prevalent, especially in view of the fact that the forms it takes have become more extensive and more sophisticated in recent years.

In a speech touching on her visions and the uniqueness of the American people as relates to the world, Harris stated:

> We are a unique nation and a unique people. We are more tied to all the nations and peoples of the world than any other nation in this world. That is why we are more concerned with what happens around the world than any other nation. . . . Because of this, Americans are concerned that the violence, the terrorism, the wars, the threats of war, the poverty, the ignorance, the disease—that all of these things could in time spill over to our own cities and neighborhoods, and threaten our way of life.

Finally, in a speech on the role of women in the future, Harris stated:

I want to hear the Speaker of the House addressed as Madam Speaker and I want to listen as she introduces Madam President to the Congress assembled for the State of the Union. I want Madam President to look down from the podium at the women of the Supreme Court who will be indicative of the significant number of women judges throughout the Federal and State judicial systems.

—J. CLAY SMITH JR.

WILLIAM HENRY **HASTIE**
1904–1976
Jurist, educator, civil rights advocate, governor

Throughout his illustrious career, William H. Hastie was a central figure in social, political, and civil rights struggles of African Americans in the middle part of this century. He was the first black appointed to a federal bench. In 1937 he became U.S. district judge in the Virgin Islands, and in 1949 he became the first black to sit on the U.S. Court of Appeals. He was also the first black governor of the Virgin Islands. He was the architect of the Organic Act that protected the rights of people in the Virgin Islands. As an educator and dean, he prepared African American students for professional careers as lawyers. Hastie aided the NAACP in its fight to eliminate discriminatory salary schemes in the educational system. He also helped prepare lawsuits that set the foundation for the end of racial segregation in public education.

The grandson of slaves and an only child, William Hastie was born in Knoxville, Tennessee, in 1904. His father, William Henry Hastie, studied mathematics at Ohio Wesleyan Academy and pharmacy at Howard University but could not find a position as an actuary or pharmacist because of bigotry. Instead, he took a job in the United States Pension Bureau in Washington, D.C., becoming the first African American clerk appointed to the position. His mother, Roberta Childs, attended Lincoln Normal Institute, Fisk University, and Talladega College and became a teacher in Chattanooga, Tennessee. It was in Chattanooga that she met the senior Hastie. Education was important to the Hasties so the family moved to Washington, D.C., to provide their son with a better education. Hastie attended the renowned Dunbar High School in Washington, D.C., and graduated in 1921 with W. Montague Cobb and Charles Drew. The three entered Amherst that fall and concentrated on sports and scholarship, becoming members of the track team; Hastie became the team's captain. In 1925 he graduated Phi Beta Kappa and magna cum laude, turning down graduate fellowships to study at Oxford University or the University of Paris to become a teacher at the New Jersey Manual Training and Industrial School for Colored Youth, known as the Bordentown Manual Training School. Two years later, in 1927, he entered Harvard's law school where he studied under Felix Frankfurter and earned his law degree in 1930. He returned to study for a doctorate of juridical science in 1933.

When Hastie graduated in the 1930s, out of approximately 150,000 lawyers in the United States fewer than twelve hundred, less than one percent, were black. During this period African American attorneys in many southern communities could not enter a courtroom through the front door. Black lawyers risked their lives practicing law in the South, and they were not admitted to the bar. The bar application inquired about ethnicity, and individuals of African descent were automatically denied admission to the association. It was not until the 1960s that the American Bar Association began to admit non-whites.

After graduation William Hastie joined the prestigious black law firm of Houston and Houston in Washington, D.C. Hastie worked with his old friend Charles Hamilton Houston. Houston was ten years William Hastie's senior, and William admired him. Quoted by Gilbert Ware, he said:

> Indeed . . . I followed his footsteps through college and law school, into the practice of law with him and his father, and into law teaching and, under his inspiration and leadership, into the struggle to correct the appalling racism of American law.

Included in the cases William Hastie represented as an attorney was that of a student, Thomas R. Hocutt, who applied for admission to the University of North Carolina School of Pharmacy. Cecil A. McCoy and Conrad O. Pearson also represented Hocutt. The white bar in attendance during the trial admired the black attorneys' bravery. Hastie's carriage in the courtroom was outstanding. Judge M. W. Barnhill, the jurist in the case, said the Hocutt case was the most brilliantly argued case he had heard in his twenty years as a judge. Faculty from the University of North Carolina talked about how Hastie showed up the attorney general who had been called in to try the case. Hastie was also the attorney in a case regarding equal pay for black teachers in North Carolina. In 1933, according to *Ebony* for September 1994, the NAACP announced that:

William H. Hastie.

> A legal fight on the new salary schedules for Negro teachers in North Carolina will be waged. . . . It is the plan of the association to attack the unequal salary scale on the basis of its being a violation of the constitution. . . . William H. Hastie . . . will go to North Carolina to lay plans for court action.

Begins federal career   William Hastie began his career in the federal government in 1933 as a solicitor for the Department of the Interior. His responsibilities in the department encompassed matters of race. Hastie, quiet and dignified, was also a jurist.

William Hastie contributed to the destruction of Jim Crow in the United States Armed Forces. Appointed by President Franklin D. Roosevelt as a civilian aide to the secretary of war, Henry L. Stimson, Hastie resigned the post in protest over the continued separation of black and white soldiers. Many agreed that his deed, the first of its kind by such a high-ranking black official, increased the pressure to integrate the military.

While a lawyer with the Department of Interior, Hastie wrote the Organic Act of 1936 along with a staff of lawyers and legislators from the Virgin Islands. The legislation facilitated the Virgin Islands' political transition from Danish Colonial Law and gave Virgin Islanders basic American rights.

Prior to the Organic Act, the Supreme Court ruled that the U.S. Constitution did not require a grant of full citizenship rights to people of incorporated territories such as the Virgin Islands. Ware wrote in *William Hastie*, "Congress enjoyed complete command over them." According to Gordon K. Lewis, a mercantile oligarchy who ruled masses of Virgin Islanders, the U.S. Supreme Court decision regarding territories "could be seen, generally, as the ineradicable contradictions between democracy and empire." The mandate Hastie and others created helped to clarify any suspicion about democracy and empire in American territories.

The Organic Act also abolished property and income requirements for voting, and extended the franchise to women and men who were able to read and write English and were citizens of the United States. This clause of the act increased the percentage of Virgin Islanders who were eligible to vote and complimented Hastie's belief that blacks had to vote to share the principal means of control over government. Quoting Hastie, Ware wrote, "Nothing . . . reveals the essence of democracy as does the history of black suffrage: 'Its essence is eternal struggle.' "

In 1936 Harold Ickes, secretary of the interior, submitted Hastie's name to President Franklin D. Roosevelt. Ickes nominated Hastie for a seat on the United States District Court in the Virgin Islands. Ware notes Ickes's description of Hastie:

> He has more than made good [as an assistant solicitor]. . . . He is not only an excellent lawyer but a man of fine character and sensibilities who, in my judgement, is qualified to be judge of any United States District Court anywhere.

Ickes also recommended Hastie to Homer S. Cummings, the attorney general, who opposed the appointment of a "colored continental" to the Virgin Islands. Cummings successfully held up the nomination for months until February 5, 1937, when the president sent the nomination to the Senate.

Hastie's appointment encountered additional opposition in the United States Senate. William H. King, a senator from Utah, opposed the nomination despite promises not to interfere with the appointment. Like Cummings, he contended that native Virgin Islanders did not want a "colored man" in that position. According to Ware, the senator doubted that Hastie could maintain "a judicial point of view" regarding interactions between black islanders and the government. King also questioned Hastie's skills in the courtroom. Millard E. Tidings, senator from Maryland, also resisted Hastie's appointment. He backed down after Ickes sent a black member of his staff to Tidings's black constituents in Maryland. They wrote letters, sent telegrams, and generally protested against his disagreement with Hastie's appointment. William H. Hastie was confirmed on March 19, 1937.

Among those who supported him during the hearings were Thurgood Marshall of the National Bar Association; William L. Houston, president of the Washington D.C. Bar Association; Victor H. Caniel, a native Virgin Islander; and Rufus G. Poole Hasties, a white colleague at the Department of the Interior. His mother and wife gave him moral support during this trying period. Hastie served as a Federal District Judge in the Virgin Islands from 1937 to 1939.

Halfway through his term William Hastie resigned his federal position and became dean of the law school at Howard University. The following year, in 1940, Hastie moved to yet another post. He was appointed civilian aide to the secretary of war. Franklin D. Roosevelt, who was seeking an unheard-of third term, appointed him to the civilian aide post in the army. The jurist began his new position on November 1, 1940. He hesitated before he took the job because, in his own words, cited by Ware:

> I was reluctant not because of any lack of interest or because it was not an important area, but I was rather skeptical as to what [could be done by] a person with no authority of his own whom I was sure the military did not want serving in the Secretary's office.

Thurgood Marshall assisted Hastie in making the decision to take the job. Marshall reminded Hastie that there was no problem as long as the War Department understood that his purpose in becoming a magistrate was to fight against racial discrimination in the armed services. On December 18, 1940, an order went out to the chiefs of staffs and services and the general staff. According to *Ebony* for September, 1994, it said that "matters of policy which pertain to Negroes, or important questions arising thereunder, will be referred to Judge William H. Hastie, civilian aide to the Secretary of War, for comment or concurrence before final action." Hastie noted that the Secretary of War's letter of appointment omitted a commitment to integration within the armed forces. As a result, he immediately announced his intention to fight discrimination in the armed forces.

Judge Hastie resigned the civilian post in January 1943 over the army's hostility and unwillingness to integrate its ranks. Correspondence from Colonel John R. Deane, secretary in the Office of the Chief of Staff, may have helped to spur his resignation. The colonel said in his letter, cited in the *New Yorker* for November 12, 1984:

> The intermingling of the races in messing and housing would not only be a variation from well established policies of the [War] department, but it does not accord with the existing customs of the country as a whole.

Hastie won some battles before he left the Armed Forces. He persuaded the secretary of war to send the army's first black fighter squadron to Liberia, where they could play a larger role in the air war, and he convinced the American Red Cross to accept blood from blacks. The Red Cross, however, continued to label the blood black and white. When asked about his resignation, the jurist said he knew he had a job at Howard University waiting and that, as reported in *Ebony,* he did it "because I wasn't faced with hunger." Many viewed his act as courageous and believed he destroyed his career when he resigned. His letter of resignation, published in *Ebony,* included the following:

> Further retrogression is now so apparent [in the Air Forces] and recent occurrences are so objectionable and inexcusable that I have no alternative but to resign in protest and to give public expression to my views.

On January 31 when his resignation became effective, Hastie wrote several articles condemning the discriminatory policies of the military, especially the Air Force. The articles were published in a pamphlet in 1943 called *On Clipped Wings.* Upon his return to Howard University, Hastie assisted in preparing a successful legal campaign for the NAACP.

Joins black cabinet   Hastie received the Spingarn Medal from the NAACP in 1943 for his outstanding contribution "to the advancement of the Negro status." As a member of

Franklin Roosevelt's "Black Cabinet," which included Robert C. Weaver, Robert Vann, Eugene Kinckle Jones, Mary McLeod Bethune, Lawrence Oxley, Edgar Browne, Frank Horne, and William Trent, he helped to form policies to help blacks progress in many areas, including housing and education. Unlike earlier black presidential cabinets, Hastie's group received paid appointments within the federal government.

In 1946 after a recommendation from an old friend, Harold Ickes, secretary of the interior, Hastie once again became a candidate for a government post. This time he was under consideration to succeed Charles Harwood as the first black governor of the Virgin Islands. At the time Hastie was the vice president of the Washington Committee for the Southern Conference on Human Welfare, the Washington Committee for the Community Planning, and the National Lawyers Guild. He had been chairman of the NAACP's legal committee and an editor of the *National Bar Journal* and the *Lawyers Guild Review*. He had been on the President's Caribbean Advisory Committee since 1942.

Hastie was questioned extensively by a subcommittee of the Senate Committee on Territorial and Insular Affairs, which opened hearings on his nomination. During the hearings, says Ware, he described himself as "a voteless resident of the District of Columbia, and I don't have any party affiliation." He also said, "I think that the American Constitution and laws are one of the great landmarks in world progress and in government, and I shall certainly hope and anticipate that we shall continue to be just that." After the "rather vigorous fight," as Hastie described the dispute over the nomination, he was confirmed by the Senate on May 1, 1946.

His tenure as governor extended for three years. During this period he helped to bring out the black vote for Harry S. Truman. After the election, President Truman asked Hastie what he wanted for his work in the presidential campaign. Hastie asked that Ralph J. Bunche be assistant secretary of state. However, Bunche declined the offer because he did not want to expose his family to Washington's racism and he thought he would be of greater service if he remained in the United Nations. Hastie did not ask a reward for himself. President Truman, nevertheless, nominated Hastie for a seat on the United States Court of Appeals. In October 1949 he became the first black to sit on the bench of a U.S. Circuit Court of Appeals, which had jurisdiction for Pennsylvania, Delaware, New Jersey, and the Virgin Islands. Eventually, he became chief judge of the Circuit Court. He ended many years of public service on June 2, 1971, at the age of sixty-six, when he retired from the bench in Philadelphia. Richard Nixon was president at the time.

William H. Hastie died at Suburban General Hospital in East Norriton at the age of seventy-one. He served twenty-one years on the appellate court, three of them as chief judge. He took the title of Senior Judge when he retired. He was awarded a number of honorary college and university degrees throughout his career, and he served as a trustee to Amherst College and Temple University.

Hastie was married to the former Beryl Lockhart. Their children, William H. Jr. and Karen Williams, are both lawyers. He had one granddaughter.

After he retired, Hastie, in a speech before the sixty-second annual convention of the NAACP, said the trend for blacks to "accept and encourage racial separatism as a desirable and potentially rewarding way of American life" must be halted. He believed this trend "can only lead to greater bitterness and frustration and to an even more inferior status than black Americans now experience." His speech also implied that young black and white Americans had become distrustful of the values of white society and emphasized that many in black society were absorbing and mimicking the destructive values of white society. He reminded the audience that it would not help black America to assume the worst traits of white America, suggesting that separatist goals would only keep the races further apart.

In essence, his speech remained consistent with his life's work: an attempt to bring integration, equality, and justice to all Americans.—MARIO A. CHARLES

CHARLOTTE **HAWKINS BROWN**

1883–1961

Educator, author, civic leader

As the distinguished founder of the Palmer Memorial Institute, Charlotte Hawkins Brown served for more than half a century as one of the pioneering and driving forces in American preparatory education for black youths. Brown was a major contributor to the effort to foster equality of educational opportunity in the South. Her vision for black youth spurred her determination to set high standards of educational excellence for both her faculty and her students.

The granddaughter of slaves, Charlotte Hawkins Brown was born Lottie Hawkins on June 11, 1883, in Henderson, North Carolina. She and her brother Mingo were the children of Caroline Frances Hawkins. Raised in an attractive home on land that was part of a former plantation, Lottie Hawkins came to share the educational and cultural aspirations of her mother and grandmother.

In 1888 Lottie Hawkins moved to Cambridge, Massachusetts, with eighteen other members of her family. Her mother had married a man named Nelson Willis, and together they operated a hand laundry and provided a good home for the family near Harvard University. Lottie Hawkins attended nearby Allston Grammar School.

Lottie Hawkins showed an early talent for leadership and oratory, and at Cambridge English High School she proved to be an exceptional scholar. During the time she met Alice Freeman Palmer, the educator, humanitarian, and second president of Wellesley College. Palmer was impressed by the girl's intelligence and desire for knowledge, and she became an enduring influence in the girl's life.

Convinced that "Lottie" sounded too ordinary to be put on her diploma, Hawkins changed her name to Charlotte Eugenia Hawkins. Inspired by Booker T. Washington to use her northern education to teach black people in the South, she negotiated with her mother to attend a two-year normal school. Palmer voluntarily paid Hawkins's expenses at the State Normal School at Salem, Massachusetts, where she enrolled in the fall of 1900.

At the beginning of her second year at Salem, though, Hawkins met a representative of the American Missionary Association, a group of white advocates from New York who financed and administered schools for blacks in the South. The representative offered Hawkins a job as a teacher at the Bethany Institute in North Carolina. Excited by the opportunity to return to her native state to teach less fortunate members of her own race, she accepted the offer and traveled to North Carolina in 1901.

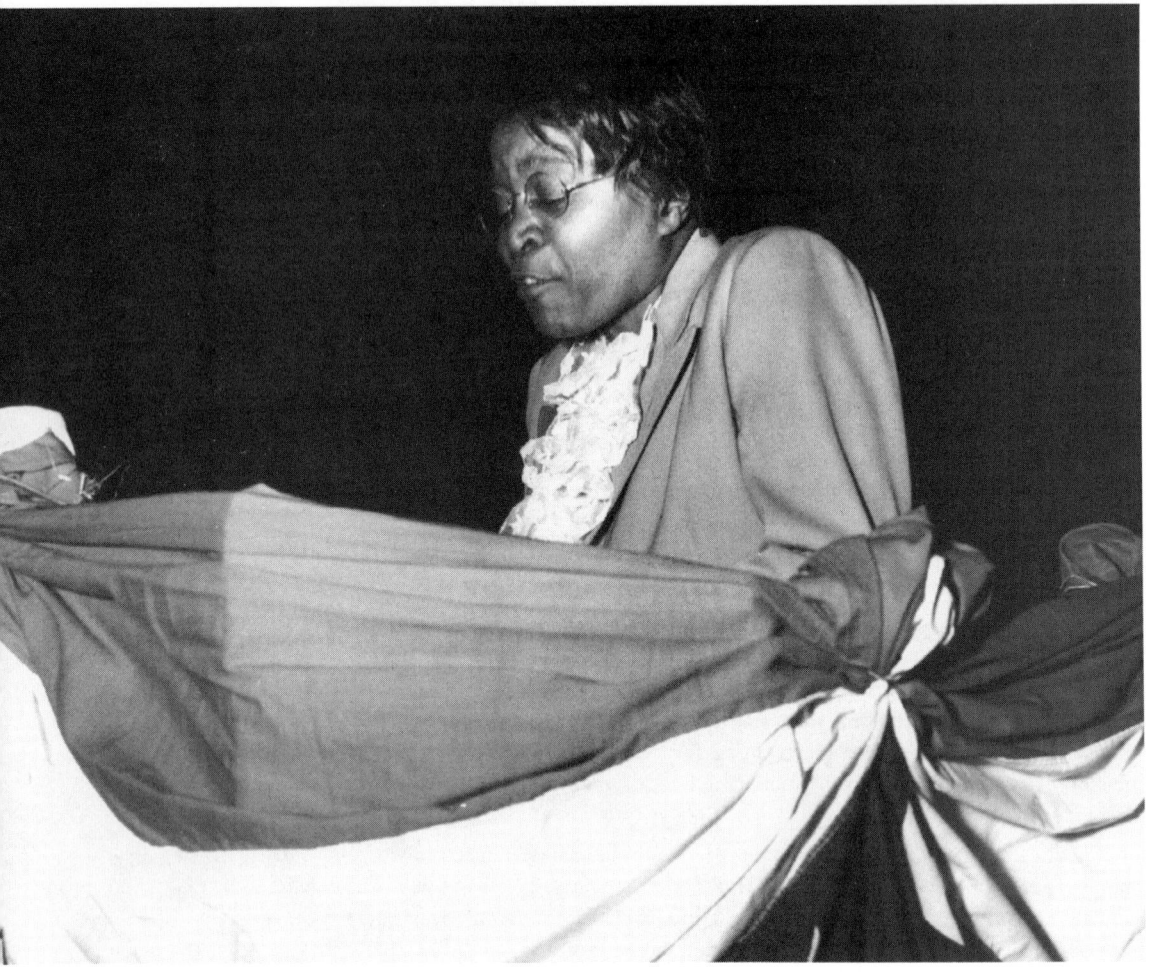

Charlotte Hawkins Brown speaks at
the 1944 Negro Freedom Rally.

On October 12, 1901, Hawkins held her first class for fifty children, who came from miles around. She used most of her salary of thirty dollars per month to buy clothes and supplies for the school children. At the end of the school year the American Missionary Association closed its one- and two-teacher schools—including Bethany—for lack of funds. The group offered her a position elsewhere, but the local community of Sedalia was anxious to have her remain there and teach. She put off her plans to further her education, choosing to stay and build a school for the town.

The Alice Freeman Palmer Memorial Institute

Charlotte Hawkins returned to Cambridge, Massachusetts, in June 1902 and discussed her plan to start a school with Alice Freeman Palmer, who promised to provide financial assistance. Hawkins spent the summer of 1902 in New England, giving recitations and musical recitals to raise money to open her school. When she returned to Sedalia, the people of the community gave fifteen acres of land for the school, and the minister of Bethany Congregational Church donated an old blacksmith shop, which she converted into a school with the money she had raised from northern philanthropists. With meager facilities but great enthusiasm, Hawkins opened her school on October 10, 1902. The school was named the Alice Freeman Palmer Institute in honor of her friend and benefactor. Upon Palmer's death that fall, Hawkins added "Memorial" to the name of the school.

In 1905 Hawkins used the money that she received from a letter-writing campaign to build Memorial Hall, the first new building on the Palmer campus. During the next several years, the school grew steadily. While serving as the school's principal administrator, teacher, and fundraiser, Hawkins furthered her own education. In addition to receiving a diploma from Salem Normal School in 1901, she studied at Harvard University and at Wellesley and Simmons Colleges. On November 23, 1907, the Palmer Memorial Institute was incorporated and a board was appointed. The school purchased additional land and added to their faculty and course offerings. Within a decade the school was known throughout the South.

On June 12, 1911, Hawkins married Edward Sumner Brown. He subsequently taught at Palmer Institute, where he was responsible for the boys' dormitory. After one year, however, he left Sedalia to teach at a school in South Carolina. He and his wife continued to correspond and visit, but their marriage, which had been so happy in the beginning, ended in divorce in 1915.

About this time Charlotte Hawkins Brown took the three daughters of her brother Mingo under her wing after their mother died. In addition, she accepted the responsibility for the four children of her youngest aunt. With these seven children to care for, Hawkins Brown built her own home on the campus, a frame house that she called Canary Cottage. All of these children graduated from Palmer Memorial Institute and went on to well-known institutions of higher education.

In 1919 Hawkins Brown published her first fictional work. *Mammy: An Appeal to the Heart of the South* was an indictment of southern slaveholding families who failed to reward their slaves' loyalty and left them destitute in old age.

By 1922, when the Palmer Memorial Institute graduated its first accredited high school class, Hawkins Brown had built Palmer into one of the nation's leading preparatory schools for black students. After she introduced a junior-college academic program in the mid-1920s, the school began to focus on its secondary and postsecondary components, attracting students from around the country. It also developed a nationally recognized choir, the Sedalia Singers, which was often directed by Hawkins Brown herself.

As the years passed, Hawkins Brown and the Institute became ever more important to the rural Sedalia community. Hawkins Brown encouraged the townspeople to improve their health knowledge, farm methods, political action, and general knowledge, and to seek independent home ownership. Believing that interracial contacts were necessary for the education of black students, she sponsored cultural exchange programs with the North Carolina State College for Women at Greensboro.

Hawkins Brown's national leadership emerges

Hawkins Brown's personal diplomacy and strong resolve were special strengths in advancing the understanding of black

American life among people across the country. In the 1920s, she opposed racial discrimination by bringing lawsuits whenever she was insulted or forced to follow the Jim Crow laws and by speaking about these experiences at large gatherings. In 1921 the YWCA national board appointed Hawkins Brown to its membership, the first such appointment for a black person. She also campaigned openly against lynching, a dangerous position to take in the South at the time. Her leadership on these matters combined a capacity to inspire with practical wisdom.

For her work as an educator, Hawkins Brown was inducted into the North Carolina Board of Education's Hall of Fame in 1926, but her contribution to the state of North Carolina went far beyond her work at the Palmer Memorial Institute. As one of the organizers of the North Carolina State Federation of Negro Women's Clubs in 1909 (and a subsequent stint as president), she worked for the betterment of black women, including establishment of the Efland Home for Wayward Girls. When continuation of this institution became prohibitively expensive, she persuaded the North Carolina General Assembly to establish a new facility, the Dobbs School for Girls. Her influence also spread to other areas of the country through Palmer's graduates, who carried Hawkins Brown's zeal to their home communities.

In 1937 the county opened a public high school at Sedalia and the state withdrew its subsidies from the Palmer Institute, which had been educating the community children through the high school level. Hawkins Brown responded by changing Palmer's curriculum to improve its students' general knowledge and to emphasize the acquisition of good manners and social graces in preparing each student to be a member of American society.

As the reputations of Charlotte Hawkins Brown and the Palmer Memorial Institute grew nationally in the 1940s, Hawkins Brown was in great demand as a lecturer and speaker. With the publication in 1941 of her second book, *The Correct Thing to Do, to Say and to Wear,* she became known as "The First Lady of Social Graces," and she received numerous invitations to lecture on fine manners and decorum.

Hawkins Brown retires from Palmer Memorial Institute   On October 5, 1952, after fifty years of service, Hawkins Brown retired as president of the Palmer Memorial Institute, although she remained on campus as vice chairman of the board of trustees and as director of finances until 1955. Suffering from diabetes, Hawkins Brown died in a hospital in Greensboro, North Carolina, on January 11, 1961. She was buried on the campus of the Palmer Memorial Institute. The grave is marked by a bronze plaque that enumerates both her personal accomplishments and those related to the founding and development of the institute.

The spirit and ideals of Charlotte Hawkins Brown continued after her death to guide those charged with the administration of the Palmer Memorial Institute. The numbers of students who applied to Palmer Memorial Institute diminished, however, while financial difficulties began to beleaguer the school. The school was eventually closed, but in 1983 the Charlotte Hawkins Brown Historical Foundation was incorporated to assist the state of North Carolina in establishing the state's first historic site in honor of a black person and a woman. In 1987 the former campus was designated a state historic site, and the area now features exhibits honoring Hawkins Brown and the Palmer Memorial Institute.

The campus's special status is a fitting tribute to Hawkins Brown. From the inception of the Palmer Memorial Institute in 1902, the history of the institution was inextricably tied to the life of its founder. In developing the school into one of the most important fountains of educational opportunity for blacks in the South, Charlotte Hawkins Brown combined qualities of leadership and appreciation of academic ideals with a profound understanding of national and regional needs, as well as an appreciation of local community aspirations.—MARSHA C. VICK

DOROTHY **HEIGHT**

1912–

Organization leader, social servant

Dorothy Irene Height, president of the National Council of Negro Women since 1957, has helped the council grow significantly and expand its focus to include global issues that affect women. She was also national president of Delta Sigma Theta Sorority for nine years, has served on numerous United States committees concerned with women's issues, won countless service awards, and has traveled extensively for the cause of women's issues worldwide. She spent the majority of her professional life as a staff member of the Young Women's Christian Association's National Board. Through her professional and voluntary responsibilities, Height has fought to improve the status of women and to empower women to speak on their own behalf.

Height was born on March 24, 1912, to James Edward Height and Fannie (Borroughs) Height. The family moved from Richmond, Virginia, to Rankin, Pennsylvania, a small mining town, in 1916. Height attended Rankin High School, and upon graduation she applied to Barnard College in New York City. She was informed by the school, however, that they already had two black students and therefore she would have to wait a term or more. She chose instead to attend New York University, using a one-thousand-dollar scholarship she had won from an Elks Fraternal Society's national oratorical contest. While attending New York University, she lived with her sister and worked at odd jobs to support herself. Height finished her undergraduate course work in three years and in her fourth year worked to receive her master's degree in educational psychology. She completed this course work in 1933.

After completing her formal education, Height took a practice teaching position at Brownsville Community Center in Brooklyn. Also, following the founding of the United Christian Youth

Dorothy Height.

315

Movement in 1935, she became an active member and quickly became one of its leaders. This position enabled her to travel widely throughout the United States and to Europe. In 1937 she represented the organization at the International Church Youth Conference in Oxford, England, as well as serving as a youth delegate at the World Conference of Christian Youth in Amsterdam, Holland. In 1938 Height, acting as a representative of the Harlem Youth Council, became one of ten American youths to help Eleanor Roosevelt plan the 1938 World Youth Congress that met at Vassar College in Poughkeepsie, New York.

In 1938 Height accepted a position with the YWCA after her return from Europe to the United States. She had decided she could use her skills more productively in an organization that was inclusive of the races and international in character. This new job took her from Brooklyn to Harlem, where she became assistant director of the Emma Ransom House, a place of lodging for black women.

Plight of domestic workers addressed   In her new capacity, Height was immediately confronted with the plight of large numbers of black American women in domestic service jobs working under deplorable conditions. She became their advocate, speaking up, for example, in 1938 when she testified before the New York City Council about the despicable practice occurring in Brooklyn and the Bronx daily. Here on the streets, in what she called a "slave market," young black girls would bargain with passing motorists for a day's housework at substandard wages. The battle for fair wages for domestic workers is one that she maintains to this day, urging workers to organize and form unions.

This period of her life set the course for much of her future work. In 1937 Height not only began working with the YWCA but she also met Mary McLeod Bethune, president and founder of the National Council of Negro Women. This meeting was life transforming, as she joined the organization that she was to lead for more than forty years.

In 1939, Height relocated to Washington, D.C., to take a new position as executive secretary of the YWCA Phillis Wheatley Home. At this time she also became a member of Delta Sigma Theta Sorority. She immediately made her presence and ideas known. At an executive committee meeting in June 1940, Height proposed that the Delta Sigma Theta Sorority adopt as a national project a job analysis program that would analyze the reasons black women were excluded from so many of the jobs open to other women, increase the number of positions for black women on jobs already accessible to other women, and improve conditions under which many unskilled workers were forced to work.

During 1944 Height was elected vice president of Delta Sigma Theta, and three years later she became national president. During the nine years she held the position, according to Paula Giddings's history of the organization, "neither the direction nor the substance of the initiatives changed under [her] leadership, but the breadth and interest in them did." She expanded the sorority into one more organization focused on the relationship between black women in America and in Third World countries. When she was invited by the World YWCA to teach for four months at the Delhi School of Social Work in India in 1952, for example, she relayed the similar conditions of women in India and convinced her sorority members to establish a scholarship for two Hindu women.

The creation of international Delta chapters can be directly attributed to Height. Following her participation in the bicentennial celebration of Haiti in Port-au-Prince in 1950, she organized the sorority's first international chapter. Further, the organization established a Haitian relief fund, which after only four years proved invaluable when the island was hit by the destructive Hurricane Hazel. Height also increased the board's international and political consciousness by taking them to meet members of the United Nations' Department of Information and the Political and Economic Committee on the Rights of Women.

Height leads NCNW   After her term as sorority head ended, Height could not remain long outside of club politics. In 1957 she became president of the National Council of Negro Women. The council, created by Bethune, is an umbrella group for local and national women's organizations. Through the organization, Height became an integral part of the leadership of the civil rights movement in the United States and abroad. Beginning in 1948, when Governor

Dorothy Height speaking alongside Benjamin Hooks.   317

Nelson Rockefeller of New York appointed her to the state Social Welfare Board, she has held a variety of official and unofficial positions, representing black American women's issues.

In 1960, in the wake of major changes in the African political scene, the Committee on Correspondence sent Height to study women's organizations in five African countries. As a result of that travel she acted as a consultant to the secretary of state. She also sought both American funding for the African nations and the promotion of a sense of unity between blacks in this country and in African ones.

During the early years of the civil rights movement, Height was known to take a rather moderate stance on matters of integration and civil rights. She did not support the call for black power as a means to attain the rights promised to all citizens of the United States. By 1972, however, she altered her position, stating that:

> White power in the system in which we live is a reality. . . . We have to see that we have been treating the symptoms instead of causes. I think this does call for the more direct approach to the societal conditions.

This change in attitude was evident in her activities in the council and the YWCA. The council was finally coming closer to "bringing all the fingers together in a mighty fist," which was the vision of Bethune at its inception. According to author Jeanne Noble, Height was able to build financial and administrative capabilities that positioned the NCNW to become eligible for large foundation grants, a first in the history of black women's organizations.

The Ford Foundation granted the council $300,000 to begin Operation Woman Power, a project to help women open their own businesses and to provide funds for vocational training. During the same period, the United States Department of Health, Education, and Welfare supplied the means for a job training program for teenagers. The council spent time in areas where community needs were not being met, calling them to the attention of those in power. It went to rural areas and bought seed and food for poor farmers and communities and started food cooperatives.

During the past three decades the council has remained diligent in its role as a catalyst for effecting change in the position of black women. Currently, their focus has been on the revival of black family life, with annual celebrations that they call Black Family Reunions. These events are intended to encourage and renew the concept and admiration of the extended black family. This once-powerful barrier against racism and its attendant ills, such as juvenile delinquency, drug use, and unwanted teen pregnancy, is seen by Height and the NCNW to be the key to restoring the community. The success of these reunions prompted Height to author a cookbook entitled *The Black Family Dinner Quilt Cookbook* (1994).

Under Height's leadership the council publishes *Black Woman's Voice* and runs a Women's Center for Education and Career Advancement for minority women in nontraditional careers, an Information Center for and about black women, and the Bethune Museum and Archives for black women's history. It has offices in West and South Africa, working to improve the conditions of women in Third World countries. Height has spoken extensively on the responsibilities of the United States, United Nations, and local organizations in pursuit of these improvements. The NCNW has collaborated with Fisk University and the National Council for Black Studies to present African American artifacts online. The council has been a recognized force that gave African American women a voice during the twentieth century. The NCNW will end this century with added attention on African American teenage girls, as Height has petitioned them to get involved in positive organizations as an alternative to street gangs. This theme ran throughout the NCNW's forty-seventh convention of 1995.

Height has been honored with many awards. In 1994, President Bill Clinton recognized Height's endeavors by presenting her with the Presidential Medal of Freedom. In response to her honor, Height remarked, "I have spent most of my life working for equality, and it's just incredible to feel that what you've tried to do is recognized by the president of the United States."

Height has been central in the success of three influential women's organizations. As president and executive board member of Delta Sigma Theta, Height left the sorority more efficient and globally focused, with a centralized headquarters. Height's work with the Young Women's Christian Association led to integration and sincere and productive participation in the civil rights movement. The National Council of Negro Women continues to act as an umbrella for 240 local groups and thirty-one national organizations. In different ways each organization has been striving toward the unified goal of equal rights for black women all over the world. Through diligence, excellent managerial skills, good use of contacts, and well-earned authority, Height has left an undeniable mark with each endeavor she has undertaken.—J. L. GRADY, M. EDWARDS, AND A. L. JONES

JIMI **HENDRIX**
1942–1970
Musician, guitarist

A famous photo shows Jimi Hendrix, bandanna tied around his thick wavy hair, leaning back and playing

one of his many amazing guitar riffs. The photo became a poster that, during the height of his popularity

and especially following his untimely death in 1970, hung in the homes of many of his fans. An enigma in

life and death, Hendrix changed the way the electric guitar was played and regarded in the music scene.

A black performer in the late 1960s, his fans were mainly white. Marketed by the record industry to white

audiences as "a rock and roll wild man," he was rejected by many in the black community. Yet before

becoming a front man, Hendrix played rhythm guitar for several popular R&B artists like the Isleys, Little

Richard, and Sam Cooke. When his music found a black listener, he or she was usually a teenager who

was "into" the rock scene, had a fondness for electric guitar, and could relate to Hendrix's escapist lyrics.

Today, Hendrix and his music are viewed through a new lens—one that connects his rock and roll style

to its origin, good old-fashioned blues. His music now has a following among a wide variety of listeners.

It is only fitting that Seattle would be Hendrix's birthplace. It is a place of rain and the perfect setting for one contemplating life and the universe over a cup of coffee, while listening to good rock and roll. Hendrix has said about his music, "I've heard these sounds in my dreams. Most of the time I can't get it on the guitar" (*Rolling Stone,* 1970). Today Seattle is

*Jimi
Hendrix.*

known for its grunge bands. But before grunge, there was a sound created by a young guitarist so new there was not anything to call it or compare it to. The guitarist was Jimi Hendrix.

On November 27, 1942, Johnny Allen Hendrix was born to Al Hendrix and Lucille Jeter. When he was four, his father legally changed his son's name to James Marshall Hendrix. The name change served as an example of the couple's tendency to disagree. The young couple had married only eight months before Jimi's birth, while Al Hendrix was in the service. They only sporadically lived together as a family. Three other children—two sons, Leon and Joseph Allen, and a daughter, Cathy Ira—were born to their union. Following the birth of Cathy, the couple divorced in 1951.

The split separated the children, sending Jimi, Leon, and Joseph to live with their father. Taking care of three young boys proved difficult, so Joseph and Leon often lived with friends or other family members. Jimi remained at home with his father. His mother died on

February 2, 1958. Neither sixteen-year-old Jimi nor his father would attend the funeral. The defining point of young Hendrix's childhood came when his father gave him a ukulele a few months after his mother's death. He was so taken with the tiny instrument that he purchased a five-dollar guitar that same year. The inexpensive acoustic guitar must have sounded pretty good with Hendrix strumming it—good enough to land him in his first group, the Velvetones.

Noticing his son's musical talents, the elder Hendrix bought him an electric guitar. Armed with a better instrument, Hendrix joined another band, the Rocking Kings. Music was so enticing for Hendrix that he dropped out of high school in October of 1961. He played local gigs and basically bummed around getting into scraps with the Seattle police. Sensing that he was getting nowhere fast, he enlisted in the U.S. Army on May 31, 1961. The army gave Hendrix the discipline that he lacked, as well as excitement. He joined the 101st Airborne Division, where he jumped out of airplanes until he broke his ankle. During it all, he still played his guitar. Close friend, army buddy, and bandmate Billy Cox recalled first hearing Hendrix. "I heard this guy playing a guitar with a sound I had never heard before," he told *Guitar Player* in 1995. "It was in its embryonic stage, but I knew that sound was destined to be developed into something great."

After suffering the parachuting injury, Hendrix was discharged from the army on July 2, 1962. He spent the next five years jumping from band to band playing blues and R&B for the Isleys, Jackie Wilson, Sam Cooke, and Little Richard. He even lived with the Isleys for a while. Ernie Isley, who was a youngster at the time, remembered Hendrix's talents. "He could play wonderfully without an amp. He would play in the hallway of our house while we were in the dining room. With his back to us, no amplifier, the sound and the feeling emanating from him was quite something," he told *Rolling Stone* in 1992.

Others heard Hendrix's distinctive guitar and were drawn to him. Finally, in July of 1966, Hendrix began to break through. Linda Keith, girlfriend of Rolling Stones guitarist Keith Richards, caught a Hendrix show in Manhattan and was so impressed that she tried to get the Stones' manager, Andrew Oldham, to sign the group. Oldham was not impressed, but an associate, Chas Chandler, a bass player, became taken with Hendrix's sound. Three months later Hendrix and Chandler headed for London to play its music scene. Chandler's business partner, Mike Jeffrey, also took an interest in promoting Hendrix.

London proved good for Hendrix. Other popular musicians like Mick Jagger, Pete Townsend, and Eric Clapton took an interest in him. Clapton's group Cream's biggest hit, "Sunshine of Your Life," was inspired by Hendrix. He met the band members, Noel Redding and Mitch Mitchell, who joined him in the Jimi Hendrix Experience. The single "Hey Joe," which talks about a man hurt by a woman and his plans to shoot her, was so successful that it got them the chance to record an entire album. In April of 1967, the Jimi Hendrix Experience released their first album, *Are You Experienced?* The album was a huge success, containing such memorable songs as "Purple Haze," "Hey Joe," and "Burning of the Midnight Lamp."

Over the next three years, Hendrix recorded two more albums, *Axis: Bold As Love* and the amazing *Electric Ladyland*. He also recorded his famous version of "The Star Spangled Banner." Hendrix's phenomenal London successes were not lost on America. On June 18, 1967, he and the Experience performed at the Monterey Pop Festival in California. His memorable performance sealed his reputation as a musical genius and built his U.S. popularity. It was in Monterey that Hendrix sent his guitar up in flames and thanked the crowd for their appreciation. Many more successful tours and performances followed, including Woodstock.

Success came so quickly for the group that outside pressures soon led to the group's breakup. Hendrix got his old friend Billy Cox to replace bass player Noel Redding in July of 1969. The new Experience had the same success as the original group; after all, the main talent was still there. And so were Hendrix's bouts with drugs and the police. In December of 1969, he was arrested in Toronto on drug possession, for which he pled guilty. Another foreshadowing of his pending overdose came early in September 1970, in Denmark, just days before his fatal overdose, when he left the stage after performing three songs. Hendrix had taken too many sleeping pills. He returned to London and, not long after, took a lethal combination of alcohol and barbituates in a London hotel. When the ambulance arrived, he was found unconscious, believed to have choked on his own vomit in his sleep. He was taken to St. Mary Abbott's Hospital and officially pronounced dead shortly after midnight, September 28, 1970.

The mystery surrounding Hendrix's death is like that of Jim Morrison of the Doors, with whom Hendrix performed informally. Hendrix's death left many issues unresolved. He had been working on an album at the time. There was also the matter of his estate, which was in shambles due to bad management. It would take his father almost twenty years to gain royalties and access to his son's estate.

It is without question that Hendrix's death made his popularity soar, along with record sales. In 1992, he received a star on the Hollywood Walk of Fame, which his father accepted on his behalf. He was also inducted into the Rock & Roll Hall of Fame that same year. More than twenty years after his death, *Rolling Stone* magazine estimates that he will sell more than three million albums worldwide, as well as rock and roll paraphernalia bearing his likeness and name. Hendrix even joked that "once you're dead, you've got it made." What is clear from Hendrix's short, stunning life is his musical legacy and the way he shaped the sound of the electric guitar.—KENNETTE CROCKETT

LENA **HORNE**
1917–
Entertainer, singer, actress

If one sifts through the many clippings documenting world media coverage of Lena Horne's career, a chronological study of language, especially the adjectives, quite accurately reflects her gradual maturity as a person and performer—from the "sultry, sloe-eyed, alluring, exotic, luscious, dusky beauty," to a "scintillating voice" with "talent, poise, dignified charm," to "character and dignity, giving credit to race, sex, and country," to, ultimately, the "American Dream."

Lena Calhoun Horne was born June 17, 1917, in the Bedford-Stuyvesant section of Brooklyn, New York, to Teddy Horne and Edna (Scottron) Horne. Even though both her parents belonged to black middle-class families, Teddy, a numbers banker, and Edna, a struggling actress, were financially unable to maintain an independent household for themselves and moved in with Teddy's parents on Chauncey Street. The strained marriage of

Lena Horne.

Edna and Teddy Horne ended within four years when Teddy left his wife. Though deprived of a natural father at age three, Lena Horne later benefited from her father's return to play a protective role in her life at a time that was professionally crucial, and the two developed a closeness that was to last until his death.

In the early 1920s, soon after Teddy left his wife and daughter, Edna Scottron Horne also departed, leaving Lena with her paternal grandparents, to pursue her aspirations as an actress with the Lafayette Stock Company in Harlem.

Lena Horne's grandmother, Cora Calhoun Horne, was a domineering woman who had a formidable influence on Horne's early life. Extremely civic-minded, Cora Calhoun Horne was active in the Urban League, the Women's Suffrage Movement, and the NAACP. In addition to starting Lena Horne's formal education at the Brooklyn Ethical School, she also registered the two-year-old Lena as a member of the NAACP.

Around 1924, Lena Horne moved in with her mother, who was struggling as an actress and generally in ill health, and during the next few years they had nomadic experiences living with relatives, acquaintances, and strangers in Philadelphia, Miami, Macon, and Atlanta. She returned to Brooklyn to stay with members and friends of the Horne family. This was the beginning of the several "extreme contrasts, conflicts and constant moving" that Lena Horne reflects on in her essay "Believing in Oneself," which she wrote for *Many Shades of Black*. While her mother was gone again, Lena Horne attended the Brooklyn public schools and the Girls High School until she was fourteen years old. Then her mother returned from a Cuban tour with a Cuban husband, Miguel "Mike" Roderiguez, to claim Lena again. These were difficult times during the Great Depression that followed the stock market crash of 1929. The Cuban immigrant with a strong Spanish accent and an ailing actress, who had never been very successful anyway, had an even more difficult time finding employment. Thus Horne's early teen years were spent in near poverty in the Bronx area of New York City, where the Rodriguezes had moved to avoid the snubs of the very insular black middle-class residents of the Brooklyn area.

Lena Horne, who as a little girl aspired to be a teacher, quit school at age sixteen to work for the famous, for-whites-only Cotton Club in Harlem. This arrangement materialized through the influence of the club's dance choreographer, Elida Webb, who knew Horne's mother. Horne qualified easily, for she was light-skinned, tall, slim, with "good" long hair, young, and beautiful. At the Cotton Club, she worked with some established names of black entertainment, such as Cab Calloway, Ethel Waters, Billie Holiday, Count Basie, and Duke Ellington.

By 1934, much to the distress of the Cotton Club management, Horne came to the attention of Lawrence Schwab, the producer of *Dance with Your Gods,* where she got her feet wet with brief exposure on Broadway. Soon afterward she left the Cotton Club to be a singer with Noble Sissle's Society Orchestra in Philadelphia—a move that helped heighten her image in the public eye. At this point in her life, Horne's career had pivoted on her looks rather than on her talent as a singer.

Teddy Horne, Lena's father, reappeared in her life to give Horne much-needed support. He was now operating the Belmont Hotel in Pittsburgh.

During travels with the Noble Sissle Society Orchestra, Horne once again faced not only the inconveniences of being without a regular home but the crude realities of the Jim Crow existence. These conditions pushed her to a kind of desperation that caused her literally to marry the first person she could. Her first husband was Louis Jones, a friend of her father's, who was nine years her senior.

Horne wore black, which she considered a sophisticated color, when she married Louis Jones in her father's house on Wiley Avenue in Pittsburgh in January 1937. A difficult four-year marriage produced two children—Gail, and two years later, Teddy. Lena Horne's mother opposed her marriage, and their relationship remained strained until her mother's death in 1981.

Career in show business opens   Horne's tour with Noble Sissle's band led to a starring role in the revue *Blackbirds of 1939*—a show of short duration. By the fall of 1940, a twenty-three-year-old Horne left her husband and children to return to New York City to renew her

*Lena Horne bowing to
a standing ovation.*

career. While gone, she wanted to arrange for a suitable place for her children so they could eventually live with her. After an initial struggle, Horne got a career break that she considers the "real" beginning of her show business profession. Charlie Barnett made her the chief vocalist with his all-white band in late 1940. While with this band, she recorded, under the Bluebird label, "You're My Thrill," "Haunted Town," and "Good For Nothing Joe"; the latter soon became a hit. Horne could now provide a comfortable home for her children, but in 1941 when she went to Pittsburgh, Jones permitted her custody of Gail alone. She did not fight for Teddy and settled for sharing him during visits. In New York Horne was now enjoying the stability she had struggled hard to achieve. In 1941, she was the featured singer at the Cafe Society Downtown, earning seventy-five dollars a week. Her fame was rising, and she was dating the world heavyweight champion, Joe Louis.

At Cafe Society in 1941 she met Paul Robeson, the world-famous black American performer, and Walter White, the executive director of the NAACP. Through their friendship and influence Horne began to appreciate the strength of racial solidarity and developed a heightened awareness for the part her grandmother, Cora Calhoun Horne, played in that mission.

Horne had been at the Cafe Society barely a few months when the offer came for her to perform at the Trocadero Club in Hollywood. As someone who had frequently experienced the harshness of the Jim Crow system and had found Hollywood, during her brief stay there for the filming of *The Duke Is Tops,* just as racist, Horne was reluctant. Walter White, however, counseled the young singer to accept the challenge and help break the traditional stereotyping of black Americans in films. In early 1942, Horne moved to Hollywood with her daughter and cousin, Edwina, who had been taking care of Gail.

Horne had been performing less than two months at the Little Troc Club when she came to the attention of Robert Edens of Metro-Goldwyn-Mayer (MGM), who arranged for her to audition for producer Arthur Freed. The audition was successful. She had the timely counsel of her father, who had joined her, and Walter White, who happened to be in Hollywood during this crucial time. In 1942, Horne became the second black American woman to sign a contract with a motion picture company in Hollywood. (The first black woman was Madame Sul-Te-Wan, who was signed by D. W. Griffith in 1915.) The seven-year contract provided for an initial salary of two hundred dollars per week and clearly stipulated that Horne would not be asked to play any stereotypical roles.

Ironically, Horne lost her first chance to play a speaking part in a mixed-cast movie as the wife of Eddie "Rochester" Anderson in *Thank Your Lucky Stars* to Ethel Waters because she was too light, and a darker makeup made her seem to be in blackface. The next speaking role in a mixed film came almost thirty years later in *Meet Me in Las Vegas* in 1956. Her first movie at MGM was *Panama Hattie,* which featured her in a role that was to become MGM's typical presentation in her many other films during the next two years. Her performance was always limited to a guest-spot number that could easily be edited out during showings in southern theaters. She was usually featured elegantly gowned, leaning against a pillar. In contrast, her television appearances in the 1960s and 1970s, which she fiercely controlled, usually portrayed her doing solos sitting on a stool or standing alone on the stage.

In the only all-black film that Horne did for MGM (*Cabin in the Sky,* released in 1943), she played the major role as temptress Georgia Brown. This was the only major screen assignment MGM afforded her. Other films that featured Horne in a guest spot were *As Thousands Cheer, Swing Fever, Broadway Rhythm, Two Girls and a Sailor, Ziegfeld Follies,* and *Till the Crowds Roll By*. Her last film with MGM was *The Duchess of Idaho* in 1950. Several factors contributed to the decline of offers to Horne. Besides the "painful pragmatism" of sales and southern audiences, the managers at MGM felt they had done their duty toward Horne's contract. Besides, the political changes and fear of communism and blacklistings by *Red Channels* publications all contributed negatively toward demands for several other black American performers as well.

Star excels in Stormy Weather   The managers at MGM obviously had no new major roles for Horne after *Cabin* and loaned her to Twentieth Century–Fox, where she did another all-black film, *Stormy Weather*, a musical on the thinly disguised life of Bill "Bojangles" Robinson. The title track of "Stormy Weather" is still her classic number.

It was during the filming of *Stormy Weather* that Horne met Leonard "Lennie" George Hayton, her musical mentor, whom she secretly married in 1947. Lennie Hayton, like Louis Jones (whom Horne had divorced in 1944), was nine years her senior. Hayton had joined MGM in 1941 as composer-conductor. He is most remembered for his music direction in *The Harvey Girls* with Judy Garland and *Singin' in the Rain* with Gene Kelly. In 1949 he won an Oscar for *On the Town* and in 1970 for the film version of *Hello, Dolly*. Lena and Lennie Hayton enjoyed their "easy" marriage for twenty-four years until Lennie died unexpectedly in 1971. Horne admitted after Hayton's death that she grew to love him even though she initially married him for career reasons.

Horne was soon the pinup girl for thousands of black American soldiers during World War II, and she performed on USO tours only when *all* soldiers were admitted to the auditorium.

In earning power, Lena Horne was one of the nation's top black entertainers by the mid-1940s. MGM was paying her $1,000 a week for forty weeks a year. Her nightclub and theater appearances easily added up to $10,000 dollars a week, or $6,500 a week plus a percentage of the gate. She was getting royalties for her several recordings and charging up to $2,500 for radio appearances. Her record high was $60,000 a week in the fall of 1948 at Cibacabano in New York, where she returned in 1951 and grossed $175,000 in twenty weeks. By 1952 she was charging $12,500 weekly, which meant that tickets were generally beyond the reaches of most black audiences.

Horne, now a consummate performer, had overlapping assignments in movies, theater, television, and recording studios in the 1950s and the 1960s. An international star, she was performing the world over. Her first Broadway show, *Jamaica*, premiered in 1957, and she frequented national television shows hosted by Ed Sullivan, Perry Como, Steve Allen, Milton Berle, and Frank Sinatra. She did a few benefits with Harry Belafonte and in September 1969 performed *Monsanto Night Presents Lena Horne* for NBC.

Horne was increasingly active in the civil rights movement during these years. She was present at the March on Washington in August 1963. She supported unions and became an active honorary member of the Delta Sigma Theta Sorority.

Her father, who had been a stabilizing factor since her move to Hollywood, died of emphysema during the summer of 1970, and within months, in September, her son Teddy died of kidney disease. She hardly had time to recover when in April 1971 her husband, Lennie, suddenly died. She lived a relatively quiet life in Santa Barbara during the early 1970s, but by 1974 she was performing on Broadway with Tony Bennett. In 1978 Horne played in the black movie version of the *Wizard of Oz,* directed by her son-in-law, Sidney Lumet. *The Wiz,* the most expensive of all-black cast films ever produced, proved to be a box-office failure. But Horne drew favorable praise for her rousing cameo.

Even though Horne did a farewell tour between June and August 1980, she was not ready to retire and triumphed beautifully on April 30, 1981, in *Lena Horne: The Lady and Her Music,* which has been the longest-running one-woman show on Broadway. Since then she has won many awards, including the Kennedy Center Award for Lifetime Contribution to the Arts. In 1979 Howard University presented her with an honorary doctorate degree. Horne declared:

> I had been offered doctorates earlier and had turned them down because I
> knew I hadn't been to college. But by the time Howard presented the doctorate
> to me, I knew I graduated from the School of Life, and I was ready to accept it.

Her honors continue. "Overcoming barriers of racial prejudice, you have always strived to be the best that you could be" said Rosaline Gorin, president of Radcliffe College Alumnae Association, while giving a medal to honor Horne in 1987. These honors are a superb finale for a career that started in the desperation of poverty.

Lena Horne wrote her autobiography with Richard Schickel in 1965, which Doubleday published. She currently resides in New York City.

Regardless that her film clips were edited out while they played in theaters down South, Horne's glamorous image remained intact and was re-examined in 1993 when *That's Entertainment III* showed rarely seen footage of Horne singing. It became clear that Horne is truly one of the ageless beauties from Hollywood's Golden Age.—ESME E. BHAN

CHARLES HAMILTON **HOUSTON**

1895–1950

Lawyer and educator

Charles Hamilton Houston played a principal role in defining and pacing the legal phase of the African American struggle against racial oppression from the early 1930s until his death in 1950. When the unconstitutionality of racially segregated public schools was argued before the Supreme Court of the United States in 1954 in Brown v. Board of Education of Topeka *and* Bolling v. Sharpe, *"there were some two dozen lawyers on the side of Negroes fighting for their schools," recalled Justice Thurgood Marshall in* Amherst Magazine. *"Only two . . . hadn't been touched by Charlie Houston."*

Houston formulated a philosophy, which scholars now call "Houstonian Jurisprudence," which J. Clay Smith Jr. describes in the *Howard Law Journal.* Houstonian Jurisprudence consisted essentially of use of the law for social change, which he identified as "social engineering," and his fundamental beliefs regarding equality, freedom, and justice as the *sine*

Charles Hamilton Houston.

qua non of an ideal society. Veteran civil rights lawyers agree that Charles Hamilton Houston was the first "Mr. Civil Rights."

Houston was born in the District of Columbia on September 3, 1895, to William LePre Houston (1870–1953), a lawyer, and Mary Ethel Hamilton Houston (1867–1947), a hairdresser and former teacher. As an adult, Charles Houston was a handsome man who stood a little more than six feet tall. He married twice. His first union in 1924 with Margaret Gladys Moran ended in divorce; there were no children. Following his divorce of 1937, Houston married Henrietta Williams. Charles Hamilton Houston Jr., their only son, was born March 20, 1944.

The formative years The Houston family, especially Charles's parents and Clotill Houston, an aunt who was a school teacher, placed great emphasis upon education and excellence. Houston attended the District of Columbia's segregated public schools and in 1911 completed his studies at the M Street college-preparatory high school. Enrolling at Amherst College in 1911, he studied hard, earned high grades, was inducted into Phi Beta Kappa and graduated magna cum laude in 1915. He taught English for two years at Howard University in Washington, D.C., but during World War I joined the army and served as an officer from 1917 to 1919. Following his discharge, he enrolled in Harvard Law School and, from 1919 to June 1923, studied with such eminent professors as Roscoe Pound and future Supreme Court justice Felix Frankfurter. Houston became the first African American editor of the *Harvard Law Review* in 1921, received his LL.B. with honors in 1922, and earned his doctor of juridical science degree in 1923. After additional studies in civil law at the University of Madrid in Spain and travels to northern Africa, Houston returned to Washington, D.C., in the summer of 1924.

In 1924 Houston was admitted to the District of Columbia bar, entered law practice, established with his father the firm Houston and Houston, and accepted a teaching position at Howard University Law School. His practice of law at Houston and Houston on F Street Northwest, in the District, consisted mainly of civil law but included some criminal cases. Both Houstons handled matters of domestic relations, personal injury, negligence, wills, and estates. Within a few years, however, Charles Houston added to the practice civil rights claims. He remained with the firm until his death in 1950, taking one leave of absence to direct a phase of the NAACP's special litigation campaign in New York. Among other partners subsequently named were William Henry Hastie, Joseph Waddy, and William Bryant, each of whom became a distinguished jurist. Juanita Kidd Stout, a secretary at the firm, was encouraged by Houston to pursue her interest in law, and became the first African American woman appointed to the Supreme Court of Pennsylvania.

Houston was an enthusiastic participant in civic activities in Washington, D.C., and a law teacher at Howard University's law school. Houston, with other attorneys in the District including J. Franklin Wilson and Louis R. Mehlinger, founded in 1925 the Washington Bar Association. Houston held membership in both the National Bar Association and the National Lawyers Guild; the American Bar Association was not open to African Americans. In addition to membership in the national and local NAACP, Houston participated in the American Council on Race Relations, served on the District of Columbia's Board of Education, and was an advisor as well as counsel to the Consolidated Parents Group of Washington, D.C. In the evenings, he taught law students at Howard a range of courses from administrative law to jurisprudence. His views regarding the potential of Howard's law school and the service he might render as an educator led Houston to accept a special responsibility after only three years of teaching and practicing law. During 1927 and 1928 Houston conducted a Rockefeller-funded national survey on the status and activities of African American lawyers. His findings revealed a striking shortage of African American attorneys: in particular, few with the formal training and experience in constitutional law to handle effectively civil rights cases in the federal courts. After recuperating from a bout of tuberculosis, Houston directed his attention to this problem.

In 1935 Houston published findings regarding African American attorneys, his views on duties, and a challenge to African American law students and attorneys in the *Journal of Negro Education*.

Howard Law School and "social engineering" Becoming resident vice-dean and later vice-dean of Howard's law school in 1929, Houston, with the approval of Howard's president Mordecai Johnson, implemented a plan to transform the evening law school into a full-time, fully accredited day school. Under Houston's leadership as vice-dean and chief educational administrator, the law school's curriculum took on a new form and emphasis consistent with Houston's view given in his manuscript, "Personal Observations on the Summary of Studies in Legal Education as Applied to the Howard University School of Law," dated May 18, 1929. Houston believed it was the duty of Howard Law School to "equip its students with the direct professional skills most useful to them" and to train them to become "social engineers." By 1932, Howard University Law School was an American Bar Association–accredited institution and a member of the Association of American Law Schools. Under Houston and his immediate successors, a highly trained faculty was assembled, including William H. Hastie, Leon A. Ransom, George E. C. Hayes, James Nabrit, and George Marion Johnson. These law professors, many of whom became Houston's life-long friends and associates in NAACP cases, embraced the school's new mission. Howard University Law School became virtually a laboratory for civil rights, and many Howard graduates became distinguished advocates for African Americans.

During his years at Howard in the late 1920s and early 1930s, Houston developed and began to teach his "social engineering" to Howard law students, among them Thurgood Marshall, Oliver Hill, and William Bryant. An element of Houstonian Jurisprudence, social engineering was grounded in beliefs about law in this society: first, that law could be used to promote and secure fundamental social change for the improvement of society; and second, that law was an instrument available to minority groups unable to achieve citizenship with full rights, opportunities, and privileges.

NAACP special counsel   In 1934, when Houston was approached by the NAACP and the American Fund for Public Service about addressing the legal status of African Americans, Houston applied social engineering to the task. First, he carefully studied both data amassed and a proposal for litigation in a report prepared earlier by Nathan Margold. Houston then presented to the NAACP and representatives of the American Fund for Public Service a long-range plan of protracted struggle to establish gradually anti-*Plessy* precedents through litigation and community involvement. Houston's plan, with modifications, guided attorneys of the NAACP and its Legal Defense Fund through the early 1950s as they sought to invalidate *Plessy* and have racial segregation declared unconstitutional. In 1934, a joint committee of the NAACP and the American Fund for Public Service invited Houston to direct a campaign of litigation against racial discrimination in public education and transportation. He served as part-time NAACP special counsel from October 1934 to June 1935 and full-time special counsel from July 1935 to 1940, working in Washington, D.C., and New York City.

The first African American selected by the NAACP to join its staff as a salaried attorney to direct its legal affairs nationally, Houston handled a variety of legal matters that individuals and branches brought to the national offices of the NAACP. Beyond education cases, the most notable were unconstitutional denials of due process and jury discrimination, such as *Hollins* v. *Oklahoma* (1935) and *Hale* v. *Kentucky* (1938). Primarily, however, Houston designed and led a strategically planned campaign of litigation, education, and community activism, the ultimate goal of which he described in his address before the National Bar Association in 1935 as "complete elimination of segregation" in public education. He explained his rationale:

No segregation operates fairly on a minority group unless it is a dominant minority. . . . These apparent senseless discriminations in education against Negroes have a very definite objective on the part of the ruling whites to curb the young and prepare them to accept an inferior position in American life without protest or struggle.

Throughout the legal campaign, Houston sought to develop a sustaining community interest in the program of civil rights. Houston publicized the campaign against discrimination in education, touring the South to film the inequalities in black public schools compared to white public schools. He encouraged community involvement, developed model procedures, regularly provided advice or collaborated with other African American attorneys throughout the states, argued cases, and contributed to the preparation of many cases in the state and federal courts. In many of these tasks, he was aided by Thurgood Marshall, who began service as assistant special counsel in 1936. By late 1938 when Houston was working out of his Washington, D.C., office, Marshall assumed responsibility for operations in New York City. He succeeded Houston as special counsel upon Houston's resignation in September 1940.

As special counsel, Houston argued several cases attacking discrimination in public education before state and federal courts. Cases in which African Americans sought admission to state-supported law schools in Maryland and Missouri were especially significant as first and second steps in the assault upon *Plessy v. Ferguson*. During 1935 and 1936, Thurgood Marshall, who had himself been denied admission to the University of Maryland's law school, and Houston shared in the preparation and argument of *Murray v. University of Maryland*. On appeal, Maryland's highest court affirmed the Baltimore City Court's ruling that Murray's equal protection rights had been violated and ordered Donald Gaines Murray's admission to the tax-supported law school.

In 1938, Houston and St. Louis attorney Sidney Redmond won the NAACP's first major U.S. Supreme Court victory in the legal campaign *Missouri ex rel Gaines v. Canada* (1938). In *Gaines*, the Supreme Court carefully scrutinized the state's equal protection obligation to applicant Lloyd Gaines in providing separate but equal public education. It held that Missouri neither could meet its Fourteenth Amendment obligation of equal protection through provision of out-of-state scholarships, nor could the state constitutionally exclude an African American from the white state university law school if an equivalent black university did not exist.

Concurrently, Houston and Thurgood Marshall provided legal expertise and assistance to local teachers in Maryland and other southern states as they challenged inequality in the salaries of African American and white teachers. With local and national support, such teachers as William Gibbs of Maryland, Modjeska Simkins of South Carolina, and Melvin Alston of Virginia litigated their claims. When in *Alston v. Board of Education* (1940) the U.S. Supreme Court refused to hear the appeal of the Board of Education, the case established the principle that a difference in teachers' salaries based solely on race constituted a denial of equal protection.

Assault on racial discrimination through private practice   The conditions of employment for African Americans as well as their education had long been a concern of Charles Hamilton Houston. Retaining his affiliation with the NAACP through membership on the National Legal Committee, Houston addressed education through the NAACP and employment through his private practice during the 1940s. Racial discrimination against African

American railroad workers occasioned two other successful oral arguments before the U.S. Supreme Court. As general counsel to the Association of Colored Railway Trainmen and to the International Association of Railway Employees, Houston pursued their claims of unfair labor practices in federal and state courts. On the same day, Houston argued before the U.S. Supreme Court *Steele v. Louisville and Nashville* and a companion case, *Tunstall v. Brotherhood of Locomotive Firemen and Enginemen.* In March 1944, the court handed down its opinions in *Steele* and *Turnstall,* both of which involved issues related to racism and representation. In *Steele,* the justices ruled that a white labor union authorized under the federal Railway Labor Act to serve as the collective bargaining representative for railroad firemen must fairly represent all workers regardless of race, including those African American firemen excluded from the white union's membership. *Steele,* a landmark decision, established the duty of fair representation, and *Tunstall* was decided on the same basis.

Addressing the continuing concerns of African American railroad workers, Houston also served as an attorney for the President's Fair Employment Practice Committee (FEPC) as it planned hearings on racial discrimination in the railway industry. From 1944 to December 1945 Houston served on the FEPC, then dramatically resigned in 1945 when President Harry S. Truman refused to issue an order barring racial discrimination by the Capital Transit Company of Washington, D.C. In his letter to Truman dated December 3, 1945, located in the NAACP Records, Houston chastised Truman for his failure "to enforce democratic practices and to protect minorities" in the nation's capital and observed that such failure "makes [the government's] expressed concern for national minorities abroad somewhat specious."

In his private practice throughout the late 1940s, Houston focused his attention on several aspects of racial discrimination in the nation's capital. Working often into the early morning hours, he sought to balance his obligations in such a way as to give serious attention to both the issues of his own community and national matters related to the NAACP Legal Defense Fund's continuing campaign against racial discrimination in education. He provided, according to Thurgood Marshall, indispensable advice and counsel concerning such education cases as *Sipuel v. Oklahoma State Regents* (1948), *Sweatt v. Painter* (1950), and *McLaurin v. Oklahoma State Regents* (1950).

Houston, as well, advocated civil rights in his *Afro-American* newspaper column, his public addresses, his work as an officer of the National Lawyers Guild, and his activities with Mary Church Terrell and other citizens concerned about enforcement of anti-discrimination public accommodations statutes in Washington, D.C. Through the firm, Houston represented African American residents of the District with civil rights claims pertaining to discrimination in housing and education. Insisting that racism must go, Houston appeared in oral argument before the U.S. Supreme Court on the issue of the constitutionality of racially restrictive covenants on property in Washington, D.C., in *Hurd v. Hodge* (1948), the companion case to *Shelley v. Kraemer* (1948). Especially noteworthy was his preparation of a strong, comprehensive brief against restrictive covenants, which drew on law, policy, and social science. Counsel to the Consolidated Parents Group of the District, Houston filed litigation that laid the foundation for *Bolling v. Sharpe* (1950), the District of Columbia's companion case to *Brown v. Board of Education* (1954).

Charles Houston's involvements in the struggle against racial discrimination left him little time for relaxation with family or his friends, among whom he counted Thurgood Marshall, William Hastie, Spottswood Robinson, Raymond Pace and Sadie Alexander, Walter White, Roy Wilkins, Juanita Jackson Mitchell, Z. Alexander Looby, and Juanita Kidd Stout.

In 1949 a heart condition caused Houston to be hospitalized. On April 22, 1950, acute coronary thrombosis—a relapse from his earlier heart attack—ended Houston's life. Among his survivors were his wife, Henrietta Williams Houston; their son, Charles Jr.; his father, William LePre; and his aunt, Clotill Houston. For Houston's funeral, Howard University's Rankin Chapel was filled to capacity. U.S. Supreme Court Justices came to pay their last respects to the man, whom Justice William O. Douglas in later correspondence to J. Clay Smith called "one of the top ten advocates to appear before [the Supreme] court." Interment in Lincoln Memorial Cemetery of Suitland, Maryland, immediately followed funeral services on April 26, 1950. Houston's high competence and success as an educator, constitutional lawyer, legal strategist, and advisor had an immediate impact on interpretation of the law and opportunities for African Americans as well as far-reaching consequences for the ongoing struggle for freedom of African Americans.

In June 1950, Charles Jr. accepted for his father the NAACP's Spingarn Medal. The Board of Trustees of Howard University voted to name their law school after Houston, and in 1981 Thurgood Marshall participated in a ceremony for the unveiling of a bust in Houston's honor. Numerous African American law students' and lawyers' organizations now bear his name, as do several public schools.—GENNA RAE McNEIL

LANGSTON **HUGHES**
1902–1967
Writer, editor, lecturer

Langston Hughes achieved fame and endurance as a poet during the burgeoning of the arts known as the Harlem Renaissance, but people who label him "a Harlem Renaissance poet" have restricted his fame to one genre and one decade. Far better, if one must label, is to note that Langston Hughes followed Paul Laurence Dunbar as one of the few African American writers of the period who became successful at their art. That credential illuminates a popular and critically acclaimed life-long career in writing in every genre. While our legacy includes many notable authors, only a few can claim to have supported themselves throughout their mature lives by earnings from their writings.

Born James Langston Hughes on February 1, 1902, in Joplin, Missouri, a mining town, the young Langston lived among well-educated African Americans. His parents, Carrie Mercer Langston Hughes and James Nathaniel Hughes, separated before Langston could know and enjoy his father, but his extended family provided him with shelter and clothing plus education, heritage, and culture. James Hughes, certified as a teacher and eligible for a civil service position in the post office, was unhappily underemployed as a stenographer with a mining company in Joplin. He became frustrated with racial barriers in the United States and moved to Mexico. Carrie Hughes, who enjoyed literature and theater, then moved her baby and herself into the home of her mother, Mary Sampson Patterson Leary Langston, who had been born free in North Carolina and had been educated at Oberlin College in Ohio. From her side of the family came distinguished forebears whom Hughes proudly acknowledged in his first autobiography, *The Big Sea*. Mary Patterson's first husband, Sheridan Leary, had died in John Brown's raid at Harpers Ferry. Her second husband, Charles Langston, was an ardent abolitionist, and his brother, John Mercer Langston, earned three degrees from Oberlin College, passed the Ohio bar, and represented a Virginia district in the United States Congress. Hughes had been a second child, but his sibling died in infancy.

Early years The search for employment led his mother and stepfather, Homer Clark, to move several times. Hughes lived sometimes with his grandmother, and sometimes with other surrogate parents, moving often. One of his essays claims that he has slept in "Ten Thousand Beds." Growing up in the Midwest (Lawrence, Kansas; Topeka, Kansas; Lincoln, Illinois; Cleveland, Ohio), young Hughes learned the blues and spirituals. He would subsequently weave these musical elements into his own poetry and fiction.

Langston Hughes.

In high school in Cleveland, Ohio, Hughes was designated "class poet," and there he published his first short stories. He adopted as friends an assortment of ethnic classmates, yet he also suffered racial insult at the hands of other whites. He learned first-hand to distinguish "decent" from "reactionary" white folks, distinctions he would reiterate in *Not Without Laughter* and in his "Here to Yonder" columns in the *Chicago Defender*. Like many other writers, Hughes endured periods of loneliness and isolation. Seeking some consolation and continuity in the midst of the myriad relocations of his youth, he grew to love books. Thus, he cared about writing books and sought to replicate the powerful impact other writers from many cultures had made upon him.

In his writing, Hughes accomplished an important feat. While others wallowed in self-revelation as a balm for their loneliness, Hughes often transformed his own agonies into the sufferings endured by the collective race and sometimes all of humankind. After graduating from Central High School in Cleveland in 1920, he moved to Mexico City to live with his father for one year. His mother fumed about his departure, and his father offered him little warmth. Yet, with his unique gift for writing, Hughes transformed his own agony about sparring parents into the noted poem, "The Negro Speaks of Rivers," published by *Crisis* in 1921.

Although Langston Hughes attempted to fulfil his ambitious father's goal for him, he discovered that the pre-engineering track at Columbia University was not his calling. While in New York, however, he savored the excitement of Harlem at the height of the Renaissance. Some of his fascination and appreciation lingers in his poetry, including "The Weary Blues." Breaking abruptly from his insulted father, Hughes withdrew from Columbia University in 1922 and a year later began his independent travels of the world, travels that gave him a

**Langston Hughes
at home.**

global perspective. He visited several ports in Africa and he worked as a dishwasher in a Paris cabaret. Poems and short stories capture some of his impressions abroad, revealing not only the adventures but also the new ways he was viewing himself and black people. He sent a few of the pieces back home, where they were published, enhancing his growing reputation as a literary writer.

When financial strain quelled his travel impetus, Hughes returned to the United States. He once again attempted various forms of salaried employment or hourly wage work, this time in Washington, D.C., where his mother had moved. Besides blue-collar work, he also served briefly in the office of Carter G. Woodson, but he was not satisfied. Nevertheless, he recorded the experiences of workers into lines for poems and fiction. In 1925 he won first prize in poetry in *Opportunity* magazine. He met Carl Van Vechten, who assisted Hughes in securing a book contract with Alfred A. Knopf. Hughes also enjoyed his "discovery" by Vachel Lindsay as the "busboy poet."

First books are published   Hughes's first volume of poetry, *The Weary Blues,* appeared in 1926. In that year, during the period of "The New Negro," Hughes returned to college. This time, as an older student and an acclaimed poet at the nation's first African American college, Lincoln University, in Pennsylvania, Hughes succeeded. Spending any available weekend soaking up theater and music in nearby New York City, Hughes satisfied academic requirements during the week. His outspoken criticisms addressed the contradiction between the alleged leadership being developed and Lincoln's refusal at that time to hire its own graduates as professors.

A second volume of poetry, *Fine Clothes to the Jew,* followed in 1927. The Harlem Renaissance was in full bloom, and Hughes became one of the celebrated young talents who flourished during this era. Some controversy attended his celebrity, however. Not all blacks relished his use of dialect, his interpretation of blues and jazz, or his vivid and sensitive portrayals of workers. Hughes repeatedly denied that he was vulnerable to harsh criticism, and he proved his durability in his early years by withstanding the harsh comments about the second volume, including his designation not as poet laureate but as the "poet low-rate" of Harlem.

As Hughes completed his degree at Lincoln University in 1929, he also completed his first novel, *Not Without Laughter,* published in 1930. Still receiving financial assistance from Charlotte Mason, the patron he shared with Zora Neale Hurston and Alain Locke, among others, Hughes had also accepted her advice regarding the contents and tone of the novel. He expressed disappointment with the completed novel, but the text remains in print, retaining uplifting representations of the diverse populations within the black community.

In 1930, however, Hughes separated from the control and the financial support of Mason. His integrity meant more to him than any luxuries her wealth could provide for him, thus, as with the break from his father, Hughes abandoned financial security in search of his own goals. When Mason disapproved of him, Hurston and Locke, who remained loyal to her, dropped from Hughes's list of associates.

Upon the advice of Mary McLeod Bethune and sponsored by an award from the Rosenwald Foundation, Hughes began to tour the South with his poetry. Accepting humble venues as well as notable ones, he traveled throughout the South. Highly regarded as a reader, handsome and warm as a person, Hughes gained many readers and many admirers during his tours. He also visited the Scottsboro Boys in Alabama, who were accused of sexually attacking a white woman. Hughes created poetic and dramatic responses to the men's plight and the mixed reactions of the American public in *Scottsboro Limited* (1932).

In 1932, Hughes traveled with a group of African Americans to Russia to assist with a film project that never bore fruit. When the project dissolved, most of the participants returned to the United States, but Hughes set off to explore the Soviet Union. In his own observations of the Soviet Union, Hughes saw many reasons to appreciate communism. Thus, while many other American writers were attracted to socialistic perspectives during the depression years, Hughes expressed admiration not for the detached ideals but for the practices he had observed. He wrote numerous poems to capture those travels, and later, in both his *Chicago Defender* column and in his second autobiography, *I Wonder As I Wander*

(1956), he recorded impressions of his travels. After his journey to the Soviet Union, Hughes completed work on his first volume of short stories, *The Ways of White Folks* (1934). Some of those stories he had begun writing during his travels in the Soviet Union. In 1936, he received a Guggenheim Foundation fellowship and worked with the Karamu House in Cleveland, Ohio, on several plays. His interest in theater continued in New York, where he founded the Harlem Suitcase Theater in 1938. A 1941 Rosenwald Fund fellowship further supported his play writing. However, he also moved into another genre. His interesting family heritage, his remarkable travels, and his participation in African American culture led to his first autobiographical volume, *The Big Sea* (1940).

The mighty pen in World War II   When the United States plunged into World War II, Hughes escaped military service, but he put his pen to work on behalf of political involvement and nationalism. Writing jingles to encourage the purchase of war bonds, and writing weekly columns in the *Chicago Defender,* Hughes encouraged readers to support the Allies. His appeals remained consistent with the "Double-V" campaign upheld by the black press: victory at home and victory abroad. Hughes encouraged black Americans to support the United States in its goals abroad, but he encouraged the government to provide for its own citizens at home the same freedoms being advocated abroad. A fictional voice emerged from these columns, that of Jesse B. Semple, better known as "Simple." While the character initially appeared as a Harlem everyman who needed encouragement to support the racially segregated U.S. armed forces, Simple evolved into a popular and enduring fictional character. The first volume of stories to develop from Simple's appearances in the *Chicago Defender* was published by Simon and Schuster in 1950, *Simple Speaks His Mind*.

Hughes retained his interest in theater, working with Kurt Weill and Elmer Rice to develop a musical adaptation of Rice's play *Street Scene.* The musical opened on Broadway in 1947, where it enjoyed a brief run that proved financially beneficial to Hughes. With the proceeds from that effort, Hughes purchased the home at 20 East 127th Street in Harlem. His "aunt" Toy Harper and "uncle" Emerson Harper moved there, too. That home has been designated a historical location.

Another significant theatrical collaboration involved William Grant Still, the first black composer in the United States to have a symphony performed by a major symphony orchestra, the first to have an opera produced by a major company in America, and the first to conduct a white major symphony orchestra in the Deep South. Hughes and Still collaborated on *Troubled Island,* on the life of Jean Jacques Dessalines of Haiti, which Hughes had transformed from a play to a libretto. Hughes was in Spain reporting on the Spanish Civil War for the *Baltimore Afro-American* when Still was adapting his libretto for an opera. Yet the project finally reached completion, with valuable assistance from Verna Arvey, Still's wife. The opera finally opened in New York in 1949.

During the 1940s, his poetry volumes also continued to appear: *Shakespeare in Harlem* (1942), *Fields of Wonder* (1947), and *One-Way Ticket* (1949). He also engaged in some translation projects, involving both French and Spanish original texts. Hughes's successes as a writer were acknowledged through the awarding of one thousand dollars from the American Academy of Arts and Letters in 1945. With his friend Arna Bontemps, he edited *The Poetry of the Negro* (1949).

The 1950s brought the Cold War and the horrors of Senator Joseph McCarthy's subcommittee on subversive activities. With his published record of socialistic sentiments and his public associations with known Communists, Hughes had undergone several years of attacks and boycotts. Thus, in 1953 he was subpoenaed to testify about his interests in communism. Holding fast to his own dream of sustaining his career as a writer, Hughes salvaged his image as a loyal American citizen. Although he had bravely challenged authority figures earlier in life, in this situation he acted to protect his chosen profession. He retained speaking engagements and his works continued to sell, but he lost the respect of some political activists. Communists bitterly resented the way he abandoned professed members of the party, including W. E. B. Du Bois and Paul Robeson, whom Hughes had lauded in earlier decades. Hughes chose self-preservation and sustained his career as a writer.

A flourishing literary career   To sustain his career as a writer, Hughes often accepted multiple book contracts simultaneously, thereby imposing upon himself an arduous schedule of production. His writing was work, not mere pleasure, whim, or hobby. Correspondence housed in the Beinecke collection at Yale University (New Haven, Connecticut), in the Special Collections of Fisk University (Nashville, Tennessee), in the Schomburg Center for Research in Black Culture (New York City), and in the Charles Nichols edition of *Arna Bontemps–Langston Hughes Letters, 1925–1967* (1980) reveal Hughes's frantic pace of writing, editing, revising, and publishing from the 1950s to the end of his life. He began to offer juvenile histories, including *Famous American Negroes* and *The First Book of Rhythms* in 1954, and *The First Book of Jazz and Famous Negro Music Makers* in 1955. He collaborated with photographer Roy De Cavara on *The Sweet Flypaper of Life* in 1956, and in the same year he wrote *Tambourines to Glory, The First Book of the West Indies,* and his second autobiography, *I Wonder As I Wander.*

His character Jesse B. Semple continued to thrive, appearing frequently in his weekly column in the *Chicago Defender.* A second book, *Simple Takes a Wife* (1953), and a third, *Simple Stakes a Claim* (1957), led to a musical version, *Simply Heavenly,* which ran on Broadway in 1957.

The last ten years of his life were marked by an astonishing proliferation of books: juvenile histories, poetry volumes, anthologies, an adult history of the NAACP (*Fight for Freedom,* 1962), and anthologies Hughes edited. Some of his efforts in drama were collected by Webster Smalley in *Five Plays by Langston Hughes: Tambourines to Glory, Soul Gone Home, Little Ham, Mulatto, Simply Heavenly* (1963).

Hughes was inducted into the National Institute of Arts and Letters in 1961, the year he published his innovative book of poems to be read with jazz accompaniment, *Ask Your Mama: 12 Moods for Jazz.* During the 1950s he also recorded an album of himself reading some of his earlier verse, accompanied by jazz great Charles Mingus.

Strangely, despite a life-long celebrated writing career, Hughes was still viewed with unfamiliar eyes as he shifted his weekly newspaper column from the *Chicago Defender* to the *New York Post.* The 1960s are noted for their radical politics, and while Hughes had never shunned aggressive politics, he was mistaken for a timid accomodationist. Readers' letters revealed ignorance about his consistently positive appreciation of black people and culture and his consistently fair treatment of people of all races and cultures. Resilient even to the end of his life, Hughes withstood accusations that he foolishly joked about racial turmoil. He endured the hostile criticism, but in 1965 he ended his twenty-two-year tenure as a newspaper columnist.

His death on May 22, 1967, came quickly and without fanfare, as he was registered in the New York Polyclinic Hospital as James Hughes (his given first and last names). Memorial services followed many of his own wishes, including the playing of Duke Ellington's "Do Nothing Till You Hear from Me."

Volumes after his death   The works of Langston Hughes have continued to flourish, even after his death. He had prepared *The Panther and the Lash* (1967), a collection of poems, but it was not published until after his death. Collaborations such as *Black Magic* (with Milton Meltzer, 1967) and a revision of the 1949 anthology *The Poetry of the Negro: 1746–1970* (edited by Hughes and Arna Bontemps, 1970) were published, acknowledging his contributions and lamenting his death. Subsequent years have brought numerous collections of verse and essays.

Critical assessments of Langston Hughes have included scores of articles in scholarly journals and presentations at conferences, many of which have been collected into volumes of essays. Also, several book-length studies of Hughes's literary works have been added to the core of information.

The remarkable and unusual travels, work experiences, and literary events in his life have prompted many biographical studies of Hughes, in addition to his own two volumes of autobiography. Milton Meltzer, one of Hughes's collaborators, offered one of the earliest biographies, *Langston Hughes: A Biography* (New York: Thomas Crowell, 1968), but it followed most of Hughes's own autobiographical notes. Over a decade after his death, using correspondence and interviews, more scholarly biographies began to appear. In *Before and Beyond Harlem: Langston Hughes, A Biography* (1983, revised in 1992), Faith Berry reveals many interesting details of his life through the 1940s, and she states that Hughes was a homosexual, thereby opening discussion about a personal life that Hughes had painstakingly kept private. Arnold Rampersad offers a two-volume biography, heavily laden with psychological interpretations, that Hughes sought above all the love of the black people: *The Life of Langston Hughes; Volume I: 1902–1941; I, Too, Sing America* (1986); *The Life of Langston Hughes; Volume II: 1941–1967*; and *I Dream a World* (1988). Besides these adult biographies, laden with notes, many juvenile biographies interpret the life of Langston Hughes. Elizabeth Myers (1970), Charlemae Rollins (1970), and noted author Alice Walker (1974) wrote three of the early juvenile biographies. Audrey Osofsky, in *Free to Dream: The Making of a Poet; Langston Hughes* (1996), offers the most recent.

Hughes never married and never had children. Yet, through his writing and through his generosity as a "dean" of literature, he nurtured scores of writers and left behind an enduring legacy of literature. Over twenty years after his death, on the eighty-ninth anniversary of Hughes's birth in 1991, with great celebration by noted writers such as Maya Angelou and Amiri Baraka (Leroi Jones), his cremated remains were interred beneath the commemoratively designed "I've Known Rivers" tile floor in the Schomburg Center for Research in Black Culture in Harlem. Visitors to this noted research center may see this floor, pay respects to his remains, and remember the man for whom the Langston Hughes Auditorium is named.—DONNA AKIBA SULLIVAN HARPER

ZORA NEALE HURSTON

1891–1960
Folklorist, writer

The list of words accurately describing the thirty-year career of Zora Neale Hurston includes anthropologist,

dramatist, essayist, folklorist, novelist, short story writer, and autobiographer. She is noted as the first black

American to collect and publish African American and African Caribbean folklore. Her study of black

folklore throughout the African diaspora shaped her entire career as an essayist and creative writer; she

wrote numerous articles on various aspects of black culture—its dialect, religious rituals, and folk tales—

and three of her four published novels deal with the common black folk of her native southern Florida.

Hurston was born January 7, 1891, in Notasulga, Alabama, to Reverend John Hurston and Lucy Ann (Potts) Hurston. When Hurston was very young, the family moved to Eatonville, Florida, the first incorporated black town in the United States. In her autobiography, *Dust Tracks on a Road,* Hurston credits the adult "lying sessions" (daily exchanges of folk tales) on Joe Clark's store porch in Eatonville for giving her important insights into the nature of human behavior. While many of the adults who engaged in telling tales, singing songs, and "lying" were unemployed at various times during Hurston's childhood, when Hurston described these sessions in her writings, she studiously avoided protesting economic discrimination against blacks in America. She chose to demonstrate the creativity and vibrance of black life in America rather than depicting the surface poverty and one-dimensional acts of social protest. The poet and critic Arna Bontemps, one of Hurston's contemporaries during the Harlem Renaissance, stated in his review of her autobiography that Hurston "deals very simply with the more serious aspects of Negro life in America—she ignores them."

One of Hurston's earliest published essays, "How It Feels to Be Colored Me," states in no uncertain terms her refusal to spend her life lamenting the social plight of the black American:

> I do not belong to the sobbing school of Negrohood who hold that nature somehow has given them a lowdown dirty deal and whose feelings are all hurt about it. Even in the helter-skelter skirmish that is my life, I have seen that the world is to the strong regardless of a little pigmentation more or less. I do not weep at the world—I am too busy sharpening my oyster knife.

We can attribute this defiant confidence in her capabilities and in America's positive responses to her talents to her early life in Eatonville and her mother's encouragement to "jump at the sun" even if she could not land there. Furthermore, her statement reflects her unwavering belief in the fundamental equality between the races: there were good and bad, strong and weak individuals among both races, and no one group was perfect.

In 1925, after studying for a time at Howard University, Hurston migrated to New York City and immediately became involved with the Harlem Renaissance, the black literary and cultural movement of the 1920s. During that time Harlem was the mecca for creative blacks from all over the United States and the Caribbean. Writers such as Claude McKay arrived from Jamaica, Eric Walrond from Barbados, Wallace Thurman from Salt Lake City, Jean Toomer and Sterling Brown from Washington, D.C., Rudolph Fisher from Rhode Island, and Langston

*Zora Neale
Hurston.*

Hughes from Kansas. Hurston, who befriended and worked along with all of these writers, was the only one to arrive in New York from the rural Southeast—the cradle of black folk life that the Renaissance celebrated. The sociologist Charles S. Johnson, who in 1925 founded *Opportunity: A Journal of Negro Life,* and Alain Locke, who edited the anthology *The New Negro,* each admired and published Hurston's stories. She collaborated with Langston Hughes and a few other poets to publish *Fire!,* a one-issue literary magazine of black culture. Primarily because of the attention her stories attracted, Hurston received a scholarship in 1925 to attend Barnard College.

Folklore study is unique Awarded a bachelor of arts degree from Barnard in 1928, Hurston continued her graduate studies at Columbia University under the direction of anthropologist Franz Boas. It was Boas who encouraged Hurston to return to Eatonville to collect black folklore, which she did with the assistance of a private grant from a New York socialite, Mrs. Osgood Mason. *Mules and Men* is a collection of the folklore Hurston gathered in Florida and Alabama between 1929 and 1931 and includes a revision of an essay on hoodoo (or voodoo) she had written in 1931 for the *Journal of American Folklore. Mules and Men* is unique in that it is the first such collection of folklore published by a black American woman, a woman who is indigenous to the culture from which the stories arise.

The traditional practice among academicians in anthropology is to study cultures that are unfamiliar to the researcher to insure a scientific objectivity. Boas theorized, however, that Hurston's familiarity with her native village, Eatonville, and the rural South in general would prove advantageous to collecting African American lore. The manuscript Hurston produced after her trips proved Boas correct. In his introduction to *Mules and Men,* Boas praised her work as invaluable because it "throws into relief the peculiar amalgamation of African and European tradition which is so important for understanding historically the character of American Negro life." Yet several black reviewers did not share Boas's enthusiasm for the affirmative, sometimes happy, side of black rural life represented in *Mules and Men*. Complaints about the absence of bitterness over racism and economic exploitation in Hurston's works recurred throughout her career.

Tombstone of Zora Neale Hurston.

***Hurston writes* Their Eyes Were Watching God**   Hurston published what critics agree is her best novel in 1937. Written in seven straight weeks in the Caribbean after a love affair ended, *Their Eyes Were Watching God* takes as its theme a black woman's search for an identity beyond that which prevailed in her small rural town. The main character, Janie (Crawford) Killicks Starks Woods, is a coffee-and-cream-colored quadroon. Raised by her maternal grandmother, a former slave, Janie rejects the community's expectations that she aspire to be the dutiful wife of a prosperous black farmer. From the onset of puberty, when Janie awakens under a blossoming pear tree, she yearns for an emotionally fulfilling union with another. This pear tree and Janie's expressed yearning to search beyond the horizon of her hometown symbolize her quest for a natural and unconstrained existence.

The novel insists on Janie's complete freedom to such an extent that she lives a feminist fantasy of expressing her sexual passion without facing its natural consequences of conception. This is a radical idea for the 1930s: that a beautiful black woman like Janie, a widow living happily alone in her house at the end of the novel, realizes her fullest potential, sexually and intellectually, by and for herself.

Notwithstanding Hurston's suppression of the biological truisms of human sexuality, *Their Eyes Were Watching God* is a brilliant study of black folk language, stories, and mannerisms. All of this works symbolically as a measure of the characters' integrity and freedom, which in turn demonstrate a contrast to the image of the carefree "happy darky" that prevailed in the fiction of many American novelists.

Hurston's passion remains folklore Despite her literary descriptions of fulfilling relationships, Hurston's own all-consuming passion was collecting and studying African American and African Caribbean folklore. She pursued this with such intensity that she had difficulties maintaining long-term relationships with men. She was married twice, once in 1927 to Herbert Sheen, a musician, and again in 1939 to Albert Price III, with whom she had worked in connection with the Works Project Administration. These marriages each ended in divorce, primarily because Hurston refused to give up her career as a folklorist to remain at home. According to Hurston's biographers, she was at first passionately in love with both of her husbands, but that love was not enough to replace her passion for studying the folkways of blacks and her desire to succeed as a creative writer. She used any money awarded to her (two Guggenheim Fellowships, 1936 and 1938, granted by Mrs. Osgood Mason) or earned through the sale of her novels to travel throughout the southern United States and the Caribbean.

Hurston's second collection of folklore, *Tell My Horse,* was published in 1938 following two trips to the Caribbean, and her third novel, *Moses, Man of the Mountain,* came out in 1939. *Moses* is a retelling of the biblical legend from an African American point of view, with the Israelites cast as dialect-speaking southern blacks and Moses as a black voodoo doctor. The story blends fiction, folklore, religion, and comedy, and most critics assess it as a minor classic in African American literature.

At her publisher's request, Hurston wrote an autobiography, *Dust Tracks on a Road,* which was published in 1942. Despite inaccuracies that her biographers cite, Hurston does offer a straight linear narration of her life, from her birth and nurtured early childhood among the black folk in Eatonville through her turbulent adolescence and her life as a vagabond after her mother's death and her father's remarriage. She outlines her pursuit of an education at Howard University and Barnard College and summarizes her ethnographic research and the writing of her novels. Hence Hurston does attempt to adhere to the conventional innocence-to-experience plot of autobiography, even though she demonstrates an aversion to specific dates and rigorously avoids mentioning many intimate details of her life, such as her two failed marriages.

The 1950s marked the beginning of the end of Hurston's career; her income from her novels and folklore dropped significantly, forcing her to take on a series of menial jobs in various small towns in southern Florida. Moreover, Hurston published only a few articles and reviews during this time. None of her book-length manuscripts made its way into print. On October 29, 1959, after suffering a stroke, Hurston was forced to enter the Saint Lucie County Welfare Home in Fort Pierce, Florida. Her fiercely independent nature kept her from asking friends and family for shelter. She died in poverty at Saint Lucie on January 28, 1960, and was buried in an unmarked grave in a segregated cemetery. The novelist and poet Alice Walker, who identifies Hurston as her own literary foremother, traveled to the Fort Pierce, Florida, grave site in August 1973 and placed a stone marker on the approximate spot of Hurston's grave. Walker's writings about Hurston precipitated a renewed interest in the folklorist's works: many of her works that had fallen out of print have been republished, notably by the Library of America in a recently published two-volume set. *Their Eyes Were Watching God* has sold more than one million copies since 1990, and Oprah Winfrey and Quincy Jones have purchased the movie rights.—ALICE A. DECK

JESSE L. **JACKSON**

1941–

Human rights activist, minister, organization founder

Jesse L. Jackson has been called one of the most eloquent speakers of our time. His speeches have galvanized people around the world into action, acting as catalysts for boycotts, marches, voter registration drives, and social action organized to combat acts of injustice. His negotiations have brought home hostages from abroad and have forged new paths in employment. From humble beginnings, he has risen to greatness.

Jesse Louis Jackson was born to Helen Burns and Noah Robinson on October 8, 1941 in Greenville, South Carolina. At the time, Burns lived with her mother Matilda; Burns gave birth to Jackson when she was only thirteen as the result of an interlude with Robinson, the grocer's son, from a nearby community. Helen Burns, a gifted singer, had aspirations of attending college on one of her five music scholarships. Instead, she made preparations for a career in cosmetology while raising her son.

In Greenville, like many communities in the South, African Americans with financial stability lived in close proximity to those less well off. Noah Robinson lived a comfortable life as a boxer and as a cotton grader for John J. Ryan and Sons, a white-owned textiles firm. Robinson offered his wife and two legitimate sons, Noah Jr. and George, a comfortable existence, but finances were tight for the Burns family living next door. Matilda Burns, Jackson's grandmother, was said to have marched over to the Robinson household on numerous occasions demanding that Robinson purchase certain necessities for his illegitimate child. She insisted that her grandson have "legitimacy," so Robinson gave him the name of his own father, Jesse Robinson. Louis, Robinson's middle name, was passed on to his son as a further act of legitimization.

Jesse Jackson.

347

During Jackson's early childhood, Robinson and his family moved to another section of town. Before her son's third birthday, Helen Burns married Charles Jackson, a shoe shine attendant at a local barber shop. Young Jackson regarded him as his father and was formally adopted by the World War II veteran when he was a teenager. After serving in the United States Army, Charles Jackson went to work as a janitor. He received a promotion and was transferred to the post office building in Greenville. With more money at his disposal, he moved the family to Fieldcrest Village, a nicer community than the residence of Jackson's youth.

Throughout his youth, the message of community responsibility was reinforced in Jackson's psyche. He has referred to his community and extended family in Greenville as a "triangle of care." He learned the importance of community service from his mother as she voluntarily ordered groceries for an illiterate elderly neighbor. One Christmas season when Helen Jackson was sick and Charles Jackson was unemployed, this same neighbor ordered six bags of groceries for the family so they could have an ample holiday. By the age of nine, Jackson was tending to the needs of less fortunate members of his community by volunteering to read the newspaper to illiterate adults. Jackson also knew the value of hard work. He delivered stove wood with a relative, caddied at Greenville's country club, and waited tables at an airport restaurant. He was so energetic that he earned the nickname "Bo Diddley" from his neighbors.

Greenville was home to Furman University, and Jackson's mother did laundry for the college's fraternity members for twenty cents each item. As a youngster, Jackson and his friends found a way to capitalize on college events by selling soda and peanuts to football spectators. They also offered to watch the cars of these spectators for a fee. After performing a hard day's work, Jackson and his contemporaries would sit on a grassy mound so that they, too, could watch the games. They did not know that the section where they sat was called "the Crow's Nest" by Furman's undergraduate students.

As a child, Jackson longed to attend Furman. Understanding the importance of education, he worked diligently as a student at Sterling High School. While there, he demonstrated extraordinary athletic prowess, playing football, baseball, and basketball. Upon graduating in 1959, he was offered a contract to play baseball with the Chicago White Sox. He declined the offer, but soon after, he received a football scholarship to attend the University of Illinois. Finding the racial climate smothering, Jackson transferred to North Carolina Agricultural and Technical State University in Greensboro.

Assumes leadership role early   Jackson took on leadership positions very early in life, becoming involved in numerous civil rights activities while still an undergraduate. In 1963 he was responsible for leading a ten-month demonstration that included marches, sit-ins, and boycotts at area establishments where African American patrons were unwelcome. Jackson's fellow students recognized his ability to persuade, and consequently elected him president of the North Carolina Intercollegiate Council on Human Rights. He was also elected student body president and joined the Omega Psi Phi Fraternity.

During his senior year of college, Jackson married Jacqueline Lavinia Brown, and upon completing a bachelor's degree in sociology in 1964, he was named field representative for the southeast region of the Congress on Racial Equality (CORE). He held this position for one year before leaving the South for Chicago. In 1965 Jackson studied theology on a Rockefeller

Jesse Jackson during his 1988 presidential campaign.

grant at the Chicago Theological Seminary at the University of Chicago. He participated in activities staged by Chicago's Coordinating Council of Community Organizations, an umbrella group for civic and civil rights organizations. He served as the director of field activities from 1965 to 1966. It was through this position that he became allied with a young minister from Georgia by the name of Martin Luther King Jr.

Jackson left the seminary to join King's Selma, Alabama, campaign against injustice. In 1966 he joined the Southern Christian Leadership Conference (SCLC). He assumed the position of Chicago coordinator for SCLC's Operation Breadbasket from 1966 to 1967. Jackson soon became the director of special projects and economic development of SCLC. Receiving an appointment from King, he assumed the role of national director of Operation Breadbasket from 1967 to 1971. The organization, which was founded in 1957, helped African Americans gain thousands of jobs and business opportunities. Through SCLC, African American small business owners secured contracts with white and black suppliers, producers, and vendors. Recognizing the power of the African American dollar, Jackson, through SCLC, threatened to boycott corporations with lax racial hiring practices.

In 1967 the Atlantic and Pacific (A&P) supermarket chain pledged to hire 770 African American Chicago residents. When the chain became slow to hire blacks, Jackson called a boycott of the chain. Two weeks later, forty supermarkets located in African American communities were the sites of boycotts and pickets. Fourteen weeks into the demonstrations, A&P signed a pact in which they promised to use African American extermination and janitorial services. A&P also vowed to invest funds in local African American banking institutions.

Linked to Martin Luther King Jr.   Through agitation and SCLC's regular Saturday morning rallies, Americans became aware of the course of action to facilitate African American empowerment. Thousands attended these rallies, where Jackson inspired the crowds. Jackson's name became linked with King's and the two became quite close. When trouble called, they responded. This is how they came to travel to Memphis, Tennessee, in 1968.

African American sanitation workers were striking as a result of grievances they filed against the city of Memphis. They formed a union and lobbied for better working conditions, but Memphis mayor Harry Loebe refused to grant them an audience, threatening to fire them if they failed to return to work. Responding to the pleas of community activists, King, Jackson, and others began to lobby for equal rights for the workers. They went under the badge of peace, but violence met the organizers as they stood on the balcony of the Lorraine Motel. There, on April 4, 1968, King was assassinated, leaving twenty-six-year-old Jackson stunned.

On April 5, 1968, an angry Jesse Jackson marched into a city council meeting in Chicago. He wore the blood-splattered sweater that he had worn at King's side at his death the day before. He addressed the members of the City Council and Mayor Richard Daley. After Jackson ended, Daley made a commitment to continue the nonviolent goals and practices that King dutifully upheld.

During his crusades to right racial wrongs, Jackson's spirituality was heightened. Ordained as a Baptist minister on June 30, 1968, he followed in the footsteps of twins Jesse and Jacob Robinson, his paternal grandfather and great uncle. Jesse Robinson (1865–1923) preached joint sermons with his twin brother, during which they referred to each other as "Blessed Buddy." As a guest of D. S. Sample, Jackson delivered his first sermon at Long Branch Baptist Church, his mother's church in Greenville, South Carolina. Jackson's mother, father, and stepfather were present. After ordination, Jackson took the position of associate minister at Fellowship Baptist Church.

Jackson continued to work with Operation Breadbasket, the economic arm of the SCLC. Under his leadership, Operation Breadbasket sponsored the first Black Expo, a convention featuring speakers such as business owners who displayed their products, described their services, and detailed ways to start and maintain businesses.

Jackson was such a vocal activist that all of America began to focus attention on him and his projects. In 1969 he received honorary doctorates from Lincoln University in Pennsylvania and Chicago Theological Seminary. In 1970 he received honorary doctorates from Oberlin College, Howard University, and North Carolina A&T, his alma mater.

Establishes Operation PUSH Turmoil began to rock the foundation of SCLC. In December 1971 Jackson resigned after disputes with Reverend Ralph Abernathy, who became president of SCLC in April after King's death. Despite differences of opinions with the SCLC leadership, Jackson remained optimistic. On December 25, 1971, Jackson founded Operation PUSH (People United to Save Humanity). He recognized that not only were African Americans living in blighted conditions, but people around the world suffered in poverty and oppression.

Jackson's willingness to embrace all people regardless of color stemmed from his own diverse ethnic background. Jackson knew that to embrace and uplift African Americans, he had to simultaneously embrace other groups as well.

Jackson continued to lobby for human rights through Operation PUSH. He gained such popularity that a poll conducted in the early 1970s indicated that he was one of the most recognizable figures in America. That aided him in accomplishing many tasks. By 1986 under his aegis, Operation PUSH was expanded to fourteen metropolitan areas, including New York, Los Angeles, Memphis, and Columbus, Ohio. Forging new paths, he was able to produce national agreements with Burger King and Kentucky Fried Chicken, under which the corporations would provide more jobs for African Americans. He also called for the development and expansion of financial institutions that are owned and operated by African Americans.

By 1972 PUSH came to agreements with General Foods and Schlitz Breweries, which totaled over $150,000. The funds were to be channeled into employing African American labor, purchasing goods and services from African American–owned businesses, and investing in African American banking institutions. Other companies that agreed to build pacts with Jackson and Operation PUSH were 7-Up, Coca-Cola, and Heublein.

Over time, Jackson's activism expanded more into the political arena. In 1972, unhappy with the slate of delegates elected to the Democratic National Convention, Jackson challenged Richard Daley on the grounds that the party reform rules had been violated. Jackson observed that young people, women, and African Americans were underrepresented. The outcome was that members of Jackson's group were granted delegate positions.

Jackson also had dreams of building a bridge between Africa and America. In the same year, Jackson visited Liberia, West Africa, to discuss the possibility of African American dual citizenship.

Education was also an important part of Jackson's scope. He developed a program under Operation PUSH called PUSH for Excellence, or PUSH EXCEL, which was designed in 1976 to help motivate African American students. Through PUSH EXCEL, he lobbied for the rights of each child to receive a free, quality education regardless of where the child lived.

Other organizations that were developed under the umbrella of Operation PUSH are the PUSH Commercial Division and the PUSH Minister's Division. The PUSH Commercial Division aids in developing African American businesses by making private and public sector funds available to entrepreneurs seeking domestic and foreign opportunities. The PUSH Minister's Division is an organization of ministers who understand the need for justice based on equity and righteousness.

During the 1980s the focus of Operation PUSH shifted to monitoring Affirmative Action programs in large corporations. This was an important move for the organization, as the 1980s was a decade marred by attacks on the gains that African Americans had made during the civil rights movement. This demonstrated the flexibility of the organization, and illustrated its ability to adapt to the times.

Seeks the U.S. Presidency   In 1984 Jackson did what few African Americans attempted before him. He placed his bid for the presidency of the United States of America, as had abolitionist and orator Frederick Douglass, who sought the Republican ticket in 1888. A year earlier, in preparation for his campaign, Jackson launched voter registration drives that took him through the southern region of the United States. He was called the first serious black contender for the presidency, as he vied for the Democratic nomination.

During his run, Jackson embodied the hopes of many African Americans, which explains how he captured 80 percent of the African American vote. In the primaries, he ran against Walter Mondale and Geraldine Ferraro, and garnered 21 percent of the total primary and caucus votes. His 3.5 million votes, however, were not enough to win the Democratic nomination.

In 1986 Jackson formed the National Rainbow Coalition to act as the political arm of Operation PUSH. It was devoted to social justice, education, mobilization, and empowerment. One way of seeking empowerment for African Americans was to support progressive politicians on the local level. Again, Jackson championed voter registration, this time registering two million new voters. In his speeches, he reminded them of their duty as Americans, but more specifically, he reminded them of their obligation as African Americans whose ancestors were brutally attacked and murdered as they sought suffrage.

During the 1980s Jackson's activism, moral strength, and eloquent speaking ability aided him in gaining power. He was regarded as a highly spiritual man, and regardless of denominational and religious differences, people did not hesitate to approach him for a word of prayer. In 1987, after visiting the mother of educator, entertainer, and philanthropist Bill Cosby, Jackson was asked to pray at the bedside of a Jewish woman who was in a coma. Without a moment's hesitation, he consented.

Jackson was again a presidential candidate in 1988. The outcome of this bid for the Democratic nomination against Massachusetts governor Michael Dukakis was more favorable for Jackson than in 1984. Advised by Ron Brown, who went on to chair the Democratic National Committee and to be appointed Secretary of Commerce, Jackson collected seven million votes, double the total of his 1984 campaign, while Dukakis collected ten million votes. Jackson's count included 12 percent of the white vote, which was three times the number of white supporters he had in 1984. In fourteen primary elections, he placed first. He placed second in thirty-six others. That year, he served as one of the speakers at the Democratic National Convention in Atlanta. At his side were his wife Jacqueline, his daughters Jacqueline and Santita, and sons Jesse Jr., Yusef, and Jonathan. But Jackson's campaign was mired in controversy due to an allegiance with the Nation of Islam leader Louis Farrakhan and racist remarks made to a *Washington Post* reporter that referred to Jews as "Hymies." Jackson apologized for his comments, but it remained a dark cloud over his second failed presidential bid.

In 1990 Jackson ran for and was elected to the position of shadow senator of the District of Columbia; though some perceived this position to be largely ceremonial, holding no real power, Jackson was not content to rest idly on his laurels. Since attaining this position, Jackson has lobbied for statehood for the District of Columbia. Also in 1990, Jackson's persuasive and articulate speaking ability spurred the release of numerous hostages after the Iraqi invasion of

Kuwait. The hostages held by Iraq's Saddam Hussein were granted their release after Jackson held negotiations with the leader.

In 1991 Jackson visited Hamlet, North Carolina, where twenty-five people perished in a blaze at a chicken-processing plant. The plant, which was owned by Imperial Foods, was in violation of safety codes, thus sparking the deaths and seventy injuries. Addressing the Democratic National Committee in Los Angeles's Biltmore Hotel in 1991, Jackson told of the horrors he had witnessed at the facility. Jackson also spoke of the treatment of Gulf War veterans. He encouraged those in attendance to rally for health care for the veterans, to propose plans for home loans for veterans, and to lobby for education loans for veterans and their children. As usual, his speech met with resounding applause.

Jackson did not seek the presidency again in 1992. Instead, his efforts were directed towards registering Americans to vote. In March, with the sentiment that President George Bush had neglected urban America, Jackson challenged presidential hopefuls Bill Clinton, the governor of Arkansas, and Edmund G. Brown, former governor of California, to take a stand against the violence plaguing American cities. Together, in New Haven, Connecticut, the three men joined hands at Trinity Temple Church to begin a march in honor of the six young men murdered in New Haven in an eighteen-day period. While the prayer service and rally were held in honor of the youths who recently succumbed, marchers paid tribute to all of the children in America slain by senseless acts of violence.

With transportation provided by the Democratic National Committee, Jackson maintained a frantic pace throughout the election year. By mid-October, Jackson had visited twenty-seven states. To each state, Jackson brought a similar message: to take advantage of the constitutional right to vote. With soul-stirring speeches centering around topics like the North American Free Trade Agreement (NAFTA), Jackson captivated audiences in western states. While the speeches began with words, they concluded with action, as Jackson marched with supporters to voting booths set up in Colorado, one of the two states where the general election spans a period of a few weeks.

In 1996 PUSH celebrated its twenty-fifth year of service with a Sterling Anniversary Convention set in Chicago. The theme, "Opening New Doors," was echoed throughout the three-day gathering. Present at the event were Roland Burris, former Illinois Attorney General, Willie Barrow, minister and chairman of the board of Operation PUSH, publisher John H. Johnson, communications mogul Thomas Burrell, and Ingrid Saunders Jones, chair of the Coca-Cola Foundation and vice-president of corporate external affairs for the Coca-Cola Company. It was here that Jackson announced the merger of Operation PUSH and the National Rainbow Coalition to form the Rainbow PUSH Action Network.

While Operation PUSH has maintained a focus on economic development, the National Rainbow Coalition has focused on political action and racial parity. Through the newly merged organizations, Jackson intends to take advantage of potential economic growth in the Pacific Rim. He sees a great imbalance in the number of African American–owned import businesses, so he is dedicated to expanding opportunities for advancement. One way of doing so is by establishing chapters of the Rainbow PUSH Action Network abroad in countries like China, Indonesia, and Japan.

Jackson has sustained his stamina, maintaining a hectic pace while writing a syndicated newspaper column, hosting a round table discussion group airing on cable television, publishing books, and negotiating with countries and corporations alike.

Part of Jackson's ability to persuade the masses stems from his first-hand knowledge of problems that continue to plague a large portion of the underclass. He understands what it is like to be born to a single, teenage mother. He understands what it is like to have discrimination play a major role in one's life. He understands what it is like to be poor. Descended from an illiterate grandmother, he understands what it is like to be a first generation success. For these reasons, he makes compelling arguments and arouses the moral passion in both Americans and supporters abroad.—NICOLE L. BAILEY WILLIAMS

MICHAEL **JACKSON**

1958–

Entertainer, humanitarian

Michael Jackson, considered by many to be the most electrifying entertainer of the twentieth century, is a charismatic performer who composes many of his songs and choreographs most of his dances. His phenomenal album and video sales and personal appearance attendance figures have led to great wealth, and his humanistic interests have earned widespread admiration. Jackson's offstage life remains beset by eccentricities and personal insecurities that began at an early age, when his childhood was taken over almost completely by preparation for his astounding music career.

Michael Jackson was born on August 29, 1958 in Gary, Indiana, to Joseph and Katherine Jackson. Katherine Jackson, an adept musician who plays the clarinet and piano, was a wife and homemaker until she and Joe divorced in 1982. The children were Maureen, Sigmund "Jackie," Tariano "Tito," Jermaine, LaToya, twins Marlon and Brandon (Brandon lived less than twenty-four hours), Michael, Janet, and Stephen Randall "Randy."

Joe Jackson, former drummer and guitarist in a group that specialized in blues, guided the development of his children's talents through the early years and built the foundation for their future triumphs as musicians. Joe Jackson's vision of his sons' potential made him demand that they devote a large portion of their waking moments to music. He installed microphones in the home and held long hours of rehearsals, leaving no time for activities outside of class time and homework. Jackson often resorted to strict discipline and severe beatings, which eventually led young Michael to resist and later become withdrawn. Nevertheless, after three years of training, Joe Jackson allowed the brothers, Jackie, Tito, Jermaine, Marlon, and Michael, to appear in public as "The Jackson Five." Five-year-old Michael was the star soloist and dancer, executing routines patterned after James Brown and Sammy Davis Jr.

The Jackson Five won their first local talent show at Roosevelt High School in Gary and other competitions in rapid succession. Before long, Jackson developed a never-resolved conflict between a love for music and joy of performing and the unrelenting pressure to strive towards perfection that would haunt him throughout adulthood.

Rise of the Jackson Five   The first big break for the Jackson Five came in 1968 when they appeared in an amateur night competition in Harlem's Apollo Theater, the coveted springboard

Michael
Jackson.

for African American artists. Their highly successful concert caught the attention of Suzanne dePasse of Motown, the influential black-owned record company, and its president, Berry Gordy. Motown arranged to move Joe Jackson and his sons to Los Angeles in November 1969, to establish residence in that entertainment center. When the boys joined Motown, they followed in the footsteps of Diana Ross and the Supremes, Stevie Wonder, Gladys Knight and the Pips, and other African American singing stars. Gordy took a personal interest in the young boys and hired a consultant to teach them the social graces of correct dress, proper speech, polite conversation, and gentlemanly table manners.

In 1969 the brothers made their debut Motown album, *Diana Ross Presents the Jackson Five*, which included the hit single, "I Want You Back." Before the end of 1971, they had three more singles that sold over a million copies and were on the top of the pop charts: "ABC,"

*Michael Jackson
on stage.*

"The Love You Save," and "I'll Be There." At age eleven, Michael Jackson's professional career and his public image were making strides, but he was still a lonely boy yearning for the companionship of his contemporaries.

The Jackson Five's national television debut in 1969 was in a Miss Black America beauty extravaganza, but their appearance on the highly rated *Ed Sullivan Show* shortly afterwards extended their audience to the entire country. Jackson and his brothers received invitations from other weekly programs whose fans were both young and old. Johnny Carson chatted with them on the *Tonight Show,* and so did Dick Clark on *American Bandstand.* They were welcomed on Don Cornelius's *Soul Train* and joined Diana Ross and the Supremes on *Hollywood Palace.*

Their rapidly growing popularity was reflected by the emerging interest of the media as their faces graced the covers of *Look, Life, Newsweek, Saturday Evening Post, New York Times Magazine,* and *Rolling Stone.* Motown protected their youthful clients from sensationalism and encouraged a portrayal of Michael Jackson as the lovable baby of the group with a charming personality, skill with the sketching pad, and a love of books. With a meteoric rise in popularity, the Jackson Five concerts drew audiences of as many as 115,000 enthusiastic cheerers. They soon drew tons of fan mail, gifts to their door, and crowds wherever they went. Joe Jackson sought to safeguard his family from the public glare by purchasing a guarded estate in the San Fernando Valley, within reach of Los Angeles and Hollywood.

The brothers' first television special, *Goin' Back to Indiana,* was aired in 1971, with Bill Cosby, Diana Ross, Tommy Smothers, and Bobby Darin as supporting artists. An animated cartoon series with characters based on the Jackson brothers was released soon afterwards. In 1972, while still singing with the Jackson Five, Michael Jackson stepped out alone for the first time, with a solo album, *Got to Be There,* and a single record, "Ben." Three of the songs from *Got to Be There* were listed among the top-ten list of that year. Wanting more control over the direction of their careers and more artistic freedom, the Jackson Five severed ties with Motown and signed with Epic Records in 1974. With a new name, the Jacksons, they gave concerts, recorded together, and starred in a CBS television show during the summer of 1976. Eventually Michael Jackson would sever ties with his brothers and embark on a solo career.

Begins career as solo entertainer   Michael Jackson began his solo career not by singing but by acting. He played the scarecrow in the 1977 movie *The Wiz.* The film was a critical and box office failure, but Jackson's performance did receive some praise. When he reached twenty-one, he cut all business connections with his father, and with a keen eye for business, assumed total responsibility for his career. His first major step was to join composer and producer Quincy Jones in a productive collaboration that pooled their expertise to create musical offerings of superior quality for years to come. Their first dual venture was the album *Off the Wall,* whose sales topped the seven million mark at home and abroad.

In 1982, the Jones and Jackson collaboration produced a phenomenal second album, *Thriller,* which catapulted Jackson to superstar status. *Thriller* sold over 40 million copies and became the highest selling album in history. *Thriller* presented Jackson as a coy sex symbol and demonstrated his talented dancing skills. He electrified the fifty million viewers of the 1983 *Motown 25* television special by singing and dancing to one of the album's songs, "Billie Jean," while wearing a black fedora, one white glove, and pants that ended above his ankles. The moonwalk was born and forever became his trademark, along with his one sequined glove. The distinctive attire was as much a topic of discussion as the melody, the lyrics, and the choreography.

Having established his reputation as an entertainer independent of his brothers, Jackson continued to compose, record, sell albums, and appear before live and television audiences of increasing sizes. However, as his success continued, so did his feelings of isolation. He rarely went out socially. His music and the microphone became his life. His immense wealth afforded him a fairy-tale sanctuary called Neverland, which is known for its child-like attractions that encourage Jackson to relive a childhood lost during his early rise to fame.

The first floor of Neverland reflects his love of art, literature, and music, with paintings, books, and a piano. The second and third floors are furnished for the pleasure of children, with toys, games, miniature trains, and room for slumber parties. Outside is an amusement park with rides, lakes, boats, and gardens to delight the terminally ill children who come to enjoy the beauty through the Make a Wish Foundation. The busy entertainer spends time whenever possible with each child, enjoying the pleasures of childhood he never experienced. Jackson's love of animals is apparent in the zoo that occupies a large portion of his 2,700-acre estate. His personal favorites are monkeys, chimpanzees, and snakes. Bubbles, his pet chimp, and Muscles, the boa constrictor, often travel with him.

Jackson has made numerous philanthropic gifts to educational and humanitarian organizations. Nearly one hundred scholarships have been awarded through the fund, which was set up from his gifts to the United Negro College Fund. He used the $1,500,000 settlement from the Pepsi corporation for burns he suffered making an elaborate commercial for the company to establish the Michael Jackson Burn Center. He embarked upon a fifteen-country tour of Europe, Africa, Asia, and Australia, with proceeds designated for his Heal the World Foundation, a charity for children. Neverland hosted an art auction sponsored by the South African Council of Churches in its fight against apartheid. In 1985, at a time of widespread starvation in Ethiopia and the Sudan, Michael Jackson joined Lionel Ritchie to compose the heart-stirring song, "We Are the World." With the assistance of Quincy Jones, they arranged for famous pop artists to make a recording and video that netted millions of dollars for relief in those African countries.

Fisk University presented an honorary doctorate of humane letters to Jackson, and he has been honored by Tuskegee University, the NAACP, and the Urban League. For his musical contributions, Jackson has earned numerous Grammy awards, with eight conferred in the 1984 ceremonies, including a special Award of Merit.

Aside from his musical ability, Jackson has shown his business acumen by purchasing the Sly Stone catalogue and securing, for the sum of $47.5 million, copyrights to the Beatles' songs. In return, he collects royalties each time a song composed by these artists is used for films, airplay, live performances, commercials, and stage productions.

Jackson and his brothers undertook a "Victory Tour," a symbolic final appearance together with fifty-five shows scattered over a broad section of the U.S., for five months from July to December, 1984. Discouraged by initial misgivings related to business and personal problems and staging difficulties, Jackson was not pleased with his personal performance, but greatly gratified by the audience response.

In answer to questions about the difference in his youthful facial features and his unique appearance, Jackson admitted to rhinoplasty and further cosmetic surgery to add a dimple to his chin, but explained the lightening of his complexion as a skin pigmentation disorder called vitiligo, for which he has sought medical treatment.

There have been special points of happiness in Jackson's life as well as times that undermined his contentment. The high points offstage come from his assistance to children and institutions of higher education, and from the warm reception and honors he received throughout the African continent. A low point in family relations required all of his diplomatic abilities to steer clear of involvement in the suit filed in 1990 by his mother against sister LaToya, seeking to reclaim her 25 percent interest in the family's Encino mansion. The sharpest challenge to his serenity came in 1993 in the form of accusations of child molestation. Jackson was greatly saddened, but strongly supported by family and friends. Facing a costly, time-consuming court battle, he chose a financial settlement instead.

A few months after the settlement, the media announced the secret marriage of Jackson and Lisa Marie Presley, daughter of singer Elvis Presley. The marriage, seen by the public as a possible distraction from the still-fresh court publicity, took place on May 26, 1994, in the Dominican Republic. Jackson's hopes that this would be the start of a life of tranquility were shattered when Lisa Marie filed for divorce in January 1996. In November of the same year, Jackson married Debbie Rowe, his plastic surgeon's nurse, in Sydney, Australia. Debbie Jackson gave birth to their son, Prince Michael Jackson, in Cedars-Sinai Medical Center in Los Angeles on February 12, 1997.

Jackson's influence has been felt internationally because of his talent and ingenuity as an entertainer, and because his interests spread into subjects having to do with children, education, and peace and justice for all people. Rather than adhere to current trends, he creates his own physical presentations that fit his unique personality and the style of his music. He has been called "The King of Pop" because of his enormous record sales and concert sellouts. He helped put music television (MTV) on the map with his heavily choreographed and elaborate videos. Many young stars in the music industry are indebted to Jackson, for he is a true fashion, music, and video pioneer.—DONA L. IRVIN

SHIRLEY ANN **JACKSON**

1946–

Physicist

Shirley Ann Jackson is one of the most distinguished African American scientists of the modern era. She has made important contributions to several areas of theoretical physics; these include the three-body scattering problem, charge density waves in layered compounds, polaronic aspects of electrons in the surface of liquid helium films, and the optical and electronic properties of semiconductor strained layer superlattices. Her research led to her heading one of the most technically challenging organizations, the Nuclear Regulatory Commission, which oversees the safety of all U.S. nuclear power plants.

Born in Washington, D.C., on August 5, 1946, Shirley Ann Jackson was the second daughter of Beatrice and George Jackson. She credits her continuing interest in science to the help provided by her father in the construction of science projects and the strong belief in education held by both parents. In addition, excellent mathematics teachers and an accelerated program in mathematics and science at Roosevelt High School provided Jackson with a strong background that prepared her for the rigors of college. Of even more importance were the healthy environments of the home and secondary schools; they provided the necessary basis for the intellectual sharpness and psychological toughness needed to pursue a career in scientific research.

First black female to earn Ph.D. at MIT   Graduating from Roosevelt High School in 1964 as valedictorian, Jackson entered the Massachusetts Institute of Technology, from which she received a bachelor's degree in physics in 1968. In 1973 she became the first black woman to earn a Ph.D. from MIT; her research was in theoretical elementary particle physics and was directed by James Young, the first full-time tenured black professor in the physics department.

After earning her doctorate, Jackson was a research associate at the Fermi National Accelerator Laboratory in Batavia, Illinois, and a visiting scientist at the European Center for Nuclear Research in Geneva, Switzerland. At both institutions she worked on theories of interacting elementary particles. In 1976, Jackson was at AT&T Bell Laboratories in Murray Hill, New Jersey, where she researched various topics relating to theoretical material sciences.

Heads NRC   In 1995 when President Bill Clinton was looking for someone to make significant changes within the Nuclear Regulatory Commission, he chose Jackson to bring back the credibility that the NRC had lost in the past decade. Allegations surfaced stating that the commission allowed some power plants to remain operational despite their glaring safety violations. As chairwoman of the NRC, Jackson made it clear that her main objective was to insure that all of the 108 nuclear power plants are up to code, and to shut down any that failed to meet her standards. The United States receives over 20 percent of its electrical power from these plants, and Jackson's job has been difficult, since many of these plants are old and no new plants are scheduled to be built.

Jackson has implemented her tough stance toward power plants by shutting down three reactors in Maine and Connecticut, which almost resulted in a power outage in that region. Through Jackson's leadership, the NRC once again proved itself a viable indicator for nuclear power plant safety.

Jackson has received more than ten scholarships, fellowships, and grants, including the Martin Marietta Aircraft Company Scholarship and Fellowship; a Prince Hall Masons Scholarship; a National Science Foundation Traineeship; and the Ford Foundation Advanced Study Fellowship and Individual Grant. She has studied at the International School of Subnuclear Physics in Erice, Sicily, and the Ecole d'Eté de Physique Theorique in Les Houches, France.

Shirley Jackson has received numerous honors, including election as a fellow of the American Physical Society, the CIBA-GEIGY Exceptional Black Scientists poster series, and the Karl Taylor Compton Award of MIT. Her professional society memberships have included the

Shirley Ann Jackson.

American Physical Society, the American Association for the Advancement of Science, Sigma Xi, and the National Society of Black Physicists, of which she was a president.

In 1985, New Jersey Governor Thomas Kean appointed Jackson to the New Jersey Commission on Science and Technology, and she was re-appointed for a five-year term in 1989. She has also served on committees of the National Academy of Sciences, American Association for the Advancement of Science, and the National Science Foundation, promoting science and research and women's roles in these fields. Jackson has been a trustee of MIT, Rutgers University, Lincoln University, and the Barnes Foundation.

Jackson has published more than one hundred scientific articles and abstracts. Her papers have appeared in *Annuals of Physics, Nuovo Cimento, Physical Review, Solid State Communications, Applied Physics Letters,* and *Journal of Applied Physics.*

Jackson's erudite career is one made up of several successes. From a small child with a desire to "know how things work," she has become one of the most important scientific figures of the modern world and a true example of how a childish curiosity, if nourished properly, can encourage one to do the impossible.—RONALD E. MICKENS

MAE C. **JEMISON**
1956–
Astronaut, physician, government official, professor

Mae C. Jemison is the first black woman astronaut to take part in a space shuttle flight. Her accomplishments are varied: she is a physician, scholar, and educator devoted to research and to nurturing children's interest in science and learning. She has blended her skills in chemical engineering, medicine, and health care to become involved in one of the nation's leading experimental projects, passed the rigorous training programs necessary for space research, and emerged as a science mission specialist, which allowed her to experiment with metals and new compounds and to study the effects of gravity on the human body.

One of three children, Jemison was born on October 17, 1956 in Decatur, Alabama, to Charlie Jemison, a maintenance supervisor, and Dorothy Jemison, a schoolteacher. The family moved to Chicago when she was three to take advantage of educational opportunities. The Jemisons had a profound influence on their children's development and encouraged their talents and abilities. When Jemison was four, her uncle, a social worker, helped stimulate her interest in science. She became especially interested in anthropology and archaeology. In school, Jemison spent considerable time in the library reading and learning all she could about extinct animals, theories of evolution, science fiction, and particularly astronomy.

While she was in Morgan Park High School, one of Jemison's classes visited a local university, creating in her a curiosity about the biomedical engineering profession. She reasoned that such a position would require her to study biology, physics, and chemistry. Consistently on the honor roll, she graduated from high school in 1973 and entered Stanford University on a National Achievement Scholarship, later earning a degree in chemical engineering. Her versatility extended to nonscientific activities, including participation in dance and theater productions and representing Stanford in Carifesta

Mae C. Jemison.

'76 in Jamaica; she also enrolled in courses in African American studies and earned a second bachelor's degree in that field. Jemison's views on becoming a well-rounded person were firm then, as she indicated to journalist Maria C. Johnson in the *Greensboro News and Record:*

> Science is very important to me, but I also like to stress that you have to be well-rounded. One's love for science doesn't get rid of all the other areas. I truly feel someone interested in science is interested in understanding what's going on in the world. That means you have to find out about social science, art, and politics.

After graduating from Stanford, Jemison entered Cornell University's medical school in the fall of 1977. Her interest in exploring the world and helping people led her to volunteer during medical school for a summer experience in a Thai refugee camp. She saw people who were malnourished, ill with tuberculosis, and asthmatic, and who suffered from dysentery and other maladies. On a grant from the International Travelers Institute, she engaged in health studies in Kenya in 1979. In that same year she organized the New York City–wide health and law fair for the National Student Medical Association.

After graduating from medical school in 1981, Jemison completed her internship at Los Angeles County/University of Southern California Medical Center in July 1982, and worked as general practitioner with INA/Ross Loos Medical Group in Los Angeles until December of that year. From January 1983 through July 1985 she was the area Peace Corps medical officer for Sierra Leone and Liberia in West Africa. There she was manager of health care for Peace Corps volunteers and United States Embassy personnel as well. In addition to handling medical administrative issues by supervising medical personnel and laboratories, she developed curricula and taught volunteer personnel, wrote manuals for self-care, and developed and implemented guidelines on public health and safety issues for volunteers. In conjunction with the National Institutes of Health and the Center for Disease Control, Jemison developed and participated in research projects on the hepatitis B vaccine, schistosomiasis, and rabies. In 1985 she returned to the United States and joined CIGNA Health Plans, a health maintenance organization in Los Angeles.

Jemison joins space program   Jemison reached a decision early on that she wanted to be an astronaut. Here again she could "blend skills" and at the same time continue to develop her talents and abilities. The idea of space travel fascinated Jemison, who was already adventuresome, inquisitive, and eager to learn. While working as a general practitioner in Los Angeles, she applied to the National Aeronautics and Space Administration (NASA) and enrolled in night courses in engineering at the University of California at Los Angeles. During this period an unfortunate turn of events occurred: the space shuttle *Challenger* exploded after lift-off on January 28, 1986, killing the entire crew, and NASA temporarily suspended its astronaut selection process as it made hundreds of modifications to its space shuttles. Saddened but not deterred, Jemison told *Ebony:* "I thought about it . . . because of the astronauts who were lost, but not in any way keeping me from being interested in it or changing my views." Later, Jemison reapplied, and NASA invited her to join the program. She was one of fifteen candidates chosen from a field of approximately two thousand qualified applicants.

Jemison joined NASA's space program in 1987, completing a one-year training and evaluation program in August 1988, which qualified her as a mission specialist. Her technical

*Mae C. Jemison sits in the commander
seat of the space shuttle.*

assignments included processing space shuttles for launching by checking payloads and
the thermal protection system (tiles), launch countdown, and work in the Shuttle Avionics
Integration Laboratory (SAIL) to verify shuttle computer software.

The United States and Japan developed a joint mission to conduct experiments in
life sciences and materials processing on the space shuttle *Endeavor,* launched in September
of 1992, and Jemison was selected as a mission specialist on the space team. As such, she
experimented with new compounds and metals and studied the effect of gravity on the human
body.

At that time there were 104 astronauts, of whom eighteen were women and five were
black. Jemison was the only black woman. Looked upon as a role model, Jemison said that
"if I'm a role model, what I'd like to be is someone who says, 'No, don't try to . . . be like me
or live your life or grow up to be an astronaut or a physician unless that's what you want to

do.'" She admitted that she never had a role model, and that she is concerned about blacks and the NASA program. She readily acknowledged that blacks and other Americans have benefited from the space program and from advances in communications, medicine, and the environment. "Some might say that the environment is not a Black issue, but I worked in Los Angeles and I saw more Black and Hispanic children with uncontrolled asthma as a result of pollution. Just as many of us get sick from those types of things," she said, "and, in fact, we have more problems with them because many of us don't have the availability of health care."

After the space shuttle *Endeavor* completed its mission, Jemison tackled another uncharted territory for her: teaching. She took a position at Dartmouth College's Environmental Studies Program. Jemison served as director of the Jemison Institute for Advancing Technology in Developing Countries. She also ran the Jemison Group, Inc., which tries to improve health care in West Africa. Jemison has made it her own mission to encourage more African American students to gain an interest in science. To see her plan implemented, she has sponsored many youth space camps in Chicago.

Jemison's distinguished career has brought recognition from many groups. In addition to her many speaking engagements, particularly in colleges and schools, she was honored by *Essence* magazine in 1988 when she received the Essence Science and Technology Award. In 1989 she became Gamma Sigma's Gamma Woman of the Year. The mural *Black Americans in Flight* by Spencer Taylor, unveiled in the Lambert–Saint Louis International Airport, honors Jemison as the first black woman astronaut. She is a member of the American Medical Association and the American Chemical Society, and an honorary member of the Alpha Kappa Alpha Sorority.

For her concern with social needs of the community as well as with NASA's space program, Jemison has been called a national asset.—JESSIE CARNEY SMITH

CHARLES S. **JOHNSON**
1893–1956
Sociologist, college president, civil rights leader

Charles S. Johnson conducted pathbreaking sociological research in the South for over three decades. Based at Fisk University in Nashville from the late 1920s to the mid-1950s, he wrote and supervised many studies whose purpose was always the same: to show in depth how the pervasive system of racial discrimination and the socioeconomic structure in which it was embedded deprived black Americans of their fundamental rights to justice and equality of opportunity. There were many other facets to his distinguished career. In 1920 he wrote the greater part of the most comprehensive report of a race riot ever published to that date. Also at that time, as research director of the National Urban League and founding editor of its journal, Opportunity, *he was a pivotal figure in the support of young black writers and artists.*

Charles Spurgeon Johnson was born on July 24, 1893 in Bristol, Virginia. His father, Charles H. Johnson, son of a slave, was educated by his former master along with the master's own son and was sent to Richmond Institute (now Virginia Union University) for his divinity degree. He and his wife, Winifred Branch Johnson, arrived in Bristol in 1890; the Johnson pastorate there lasted for forty-two years, during which time the Reverend Johnson built a large, imposing church whose spire towered over the town. Bristol had very limited educational opportunities for blacks, so Charles Spurgeon, the oldest of five children, went to Wayland Baptist Academy, affiliated with Virginia Union University. He completed his degree at Virginia Union in three years, with distinction, in 1916. The widespread poverty and racial discrimination in the black community in Bristol and Richmond turned him in the direction of sociology and the University of Chicago.

Though he never completed a doctorate at Chicago, Johnson gained a wealth of research experience that served the rest of his career. His mentor and most important teacher was Robert E. Park, who was a leading member of the so-called Chicago school, with its emphasis on the integration of broad sociological theory and the actual social conditions in an urban-industrial setting.

Park, as president of the Chicago Urban League, arranged Johnson's appointment as research director of the league, but Johnson's studies of the Great Migration and the state of race relations in the industrial North were interrupted by war. Johnson enlisted in 1918 and served in battle in France as a regimental sergeant major. Returning to Chicago in 1919, he found himself in the midst of one of the worst race riots in history. The commission formed in the wake of the riot chose him as associate executive director. Its report, *The Negro in Chicago* (1922), was largely Johnson's work, and established a benchmark for all subsequent studies in its realistic portrayal of the social infrastructure underlying the riot as well as the major problems blacks faced in employment, housing, education, and social services. The report reinforced Johnson's emerging credo: that systematic, disciplined research would arm the advocates for change—he among them—with the essential facts to undergird the combat against racism and the quest for justice. In 1921, the national office of the Urban League appointed him research director.

Serves bridging role in Harlem Renaissance From 1921 until 1929 Johnson conducted many more community studies in the Chicago mode; they were largely factual but the facts themselves constituted an indictment of racial injustice. Moreover, in editing *Opportunity*, he brought to public attention the work of leading social scientists, black and white, who exposed the pseudo-science, misconceptions, and stereotypes that served as a rationale for racial prejudice and discrimination. Finally, in a broader cultural context, Johnson devoted himself to connecting the rising young black writers and artists in Harlem with publishers and sponsors downtown, a bridging role essential to the Harlem Renaissance and making him, as much as Alain Locke, "midwife" to the Renaissance. The bridging role would stand him in good stead for many years afterward in the South as he shuttled so often from Nashville to New York to Chicago in search of funding from a Rosenwald or Rockefeller foundation to further sociological research. Perhaps his attention to cultural matters stemmed from his growing awareness of how slowly progress for blacks was taking place in employment. As friend and associate David Levering Lewis noted, "If the road to the ballot box and jobs was blocked, Johnson saw that the door to Carnegie Hall and the New York publishers was ajar." Langston Hughes, Zora Neale Hurston, Ethel Nance, Arna Bontemps, and many others in this movement have testified to Johnson's importance.

All the same, through the years in New York, Johnson remained attached to his primary goal: to return to the South and undertake the most comprehensive study possible of the racial system of the region as prelude to action against it. In 1929 he left the league to take a position directing social science studies and a department of race relations at Fisk University. He had a threefold purpose in mind: to create at Fisk a social science faculty and a center for research in race relations unique in the country; to construct through that research a full, historically-grounded portrayal of the institutional racism of the region; and to make effective use of these countless studies to help bring about social change in the racial system. In this last dimension, Johnson proposed to work with a coalition of white southern liberals and moderates at both the regional and national levels. For this program of collaboration with whites he has been strongly criticized, in particular by a number of black sociologists in the next generation who have found him too conservative, too autocratic in his control of funding and fellowships, and too deferential to the white liberals and the white establishment in advancing the program of the "Fisk Machine."

In Johnson's own time, W. E. B. Du Bois said he was "if not reactionary, then certainly very cautious," and E. Franklin Frazier was scornful of his dependence on the white philanthropic elite. (Ironically, the three black sociologist founding fathers are joined together in the American Sociological Association's Du Bois-Johnson-Frazier award for distinguished work in race relations.) Johnson, defined as a "conciliatory realist," had little choice but to work with his white associates within the hard confines of segregation in the South. Only after *Brown v. Board of Education* in 1954, the Supreme Court decision striking down racial segregation in the public schools, was there sufficient leverage for the coalition to join with the younger black militant leaders in a full-scale direct strategy against the Southern racial fortress. Johnson had no illusions about all of this. Years before *Brown,* he denounced segregation publicly, resisted it when it affected him personally, and continued to hope for integration— though without loss to the distinctive structure and culture of the black community. In 1942, in the celebrated Durham (North Carolina) Statement, of which he was one of the chief architects, he insisted on unequivocal wording on ending segregation.

For over nearly three decades, Johnson largely succeeded in carrying through what he intended to do on all three dimensions of his program. As a national center for social science research on race relations, Fisk came to rival the only other comparable institution, the University of North Carolina, which was equipped with far greater resources and financial support. A striking proportion of the next generation of black social scientists were trained by Johnson at Fisk. He brought in distinguished scholars from this country and abroad, including Park after his retirement from Chicago.

Establishes race relations program   Johnson directed innumerable research studies of race relations in both Southern and Northern communities. His annual institutes of race relations were a dramatic innovation in the South of that era. National leaders and scholars and local and regional activists came together on an interracial basis on the Fisk campus to plan strategies for change. He forged an unprecedented relationship with other Southern sociologists in the service of research; in 1946 his colleagues elected him president of the Southern Sociological Society.

In the outpouring of books, monographs, and articles produced from the Nashville base, three stand out and retain their value today. *Shadow of the Plantation* (1934), which

Johnson himself called his favorite book, is a study of the nearly feudal tenant farm system in one Alabama cotton county, Macon, in the early 1930s. Some six hundred black families were held in such thrall that, as Johnson noted, "nothing remains but to succumb or to migrate." In the study of this ultimately doomed but still functioning system, Johnson called for decisive federal government intervention to curb the worst inequities. *Shadow* also endures (it was reprinted once again in 1996) because it weaves into the sociological data poignant, moving commentary by the tenants themselves. As one informant summarizes, "We jest can't make it cause they pay us nothing for what we give them and they charge us double price when they sell it back to us."

At the end of the decade Johnson published *Growing Up in the Black Belt* (1941), an analysis of black youth in six Southern counties, including Macon, which showed that while a black boy or girl could grow up within a firmly structured community, he or she could not escape "the shadow of the white world." *Growing Up* has been notable for its rejection of the concept of caste governing Southern race relations. For Johnson, as for Oliver Cox and other sociologists, it was extremely important to show that change, however slow, not permanent subordination as in the presumed model from India, was the central issue. In his view, racial segregation in all its forms would eventually crumble, not from a withering away of caste in the far future, but from active social protest from those subordinated and from vigorous governmental action. Pending such changes, it was equally important to show how deeply entrenched segregation in the South and the whole system of separate and unequal made racial discrimination seem all-pervasive and intractable, indeed resembling something like a caste system. *Patterns of Negro Segregation* (1943), Johnson's comprehensive compendium of the endless ways in which this cruel system played out a half century ago, remains the standard reference volume.

Johnson's other books, unlike the three just described, were more general. They surveyed the state of race relations at various times and usually concluded with a plea for using democratic channels to press for further change. They rarely ventured into deeper theory as seen, for example, in some of the work of Du Bois and E. Franklin Frazier. That was in keeping with his basic ethos: systematic research to be then placed at the service of those leaders, black and white, who would advance the struggle to change public policy and achieve a greater degree of racial equality. One exception occurred, however, early on. In 1930, just as his large-scale study, *The Negro in American Civilization*, appeared, he was appointed to conduct an investigation into forced labor in Liberia for the League of Nations. Liberia, nominally independent but economically dependent on the United States, was imposing a kind of slavery on its own people, an irony not lost on Johnson and others who thought about their African roots. His book, *Bitter Canaan*, published posthumously in 1987, revealed Johnson departing from his usual cool and detached sociological posture to give us at once a history of Liberia, a study forming the basis for reforming the forced labor system, and a moving personal memoir.

The building of the social sciences at Fisk, and the extensive research program in race relations in the South, formed the platform from which Johnson advanced the third goal of the Nashville years: the sidelines activism, or, as Lewis Jones, his outstanding student and later his close friend, described it, his "strategy of indirection" in the endless struggle for civil rights at both the regional and national levels. Regionally, Johnson worked to form organizations to combat racism in the South. Among them were the Southern Regional Council (SRC) and the Southern Conference for Human Welfare (SCHW). SRC sought to be as mainstream as an interracial organization could be in the era of segregation. Johnson was a prime mover in its formation and eventually helped persuade it to move against segregation, but by then it had been overtaken by events and by the nonviolent direct-action strategy of newer civil rights groups. SCHW, much more militant than SRC, helped to unite labor and civil rights groups in a common effort at economic and racial change, but Johnson's hopes for it eventually faded as it was constantly hounded by the Southern establishment. At all events, these organizations, whether deemed radical or liberal, represented the only options in the South before the onset of the more dynamic civil rights coalition of the 1960s.

Nationally, Johnson served on a multitude of commissions and presidential initiatives—for example, Franklin D. Roosevelt's farm tenancy policy, Harry S. Truman's organization of UNESCO, and an educational program for postwar occupied Japan. Beyond such assignments, Johnson worked closely with allies in Washington, D.C., including both well-placed white New Dealers such as Will Alexander and Clark Foreman, and with an informal Black Cabinet made up of black leaders such as Mary McLeod Bethune and Walter White. The objective was to persuade the administration, generally uninterested in civil rights and wary in any case of crossing conservative Southern Democrats, to move ahead on civil rights.

The Washington group had little access—they had only two committed and influential allies at the highest level, Harold Ickes, Secretary of the Interior, and Eleanor Roosevelt—and they often failed in attempts to get an antilynching law or eliminate the poll tax. On occasion, however, the strategy worked. Johnson, Will Alexander, who was perhaps the most important Southern white liberal and in the late 1930s and director of the Farm Security Administration (FSA), and Edwin R. Embree, director of the Julius Rosenwald Fund, wrote a landmark report, *The Collapse of Cotton Tenancy* (1935), on the plight of southern tenant farmers. Skirting the racial issue entirely, they proposed "rehomesteading" or settling tenants on their own property in "huge numbers." Eventually, their proposal became law, the Bankhead-Jones Farm Tenancy Act of 1937. Administered by the FSA, the program did not touch "huge numbers," but in this case, Alexander saw to it that, unlike many New Deal measures, at least there was mostly racial fairness and equity in the distribution of assistance.

In his last ten years, as Fisk's president (1946–56), Johnson devoted more time to the college and less to sociological research or activism. He strengthened the academic program, continued to receive substantial support for Fisk from the foundations, and helped to enhance the reputation of Fisk. Internally, the record was less impressive, due in part to his frequent absences and also to his rather reserved and stiff personality, which resulted in somewhat distant and formal relationships with faculty and staff. His reserve and occasional brusqueness with others had been a hallmark through the years in Nashville, though he could be warm and outgoing with close friends such as Langston Hughes and Aaron Douglas of Renaissance days.

Charles S. Johnson died October 27, 1956, as he was traveling to a meeting of the Fisk board of trustees in New York. He is buried in Nashville's Greenwood Cemetery. Johnson was survived by Marie Antoinette Burgette Johnson, a teacher in music and theater, whom he married before leaving Chicago for New York thirty-five years earlier. He also left four children: Charles II, Robert, Patricia, and Jeh. His son Robert carried on his work in sociology.

As Fisk's first black president with most of his significant sociological work behind him, Johnson continued his lifelong advocacy for change in the racial system. In the role of research-advocacy, which he called his "sidelines activism," he collaborated closely with the small band of Southern white liberals who were in a more open and strategic position than he was to press for change such as national legislation to end lynching or aid the embattled black and white farmers in the South. John Egerton rightly said of him, "Throughout the thirties and forties into the fifties, only a small number of black Southerners (and even fewer whites) were able to stay in the region and fight their way to national recognition in the long campaign for racial equality. Charles S. Johnson was one of them."

Johnson's critics have stated that as a national civil rights leader he had not matched the militancy of a Du Bois or a Frazier. It has been an unfair assessment. Given the far greater racial discrimination and constraints on black counterassertion in the South, he and the Southern white liberals with whom he worked did what they could with what they had in resources and power. Lester Granger, then executive director of the Urban League and an old friend, rendered a more judicious verdict in the *New York Amsterdam News:* "He had all of the normal man's ambition, naturally, but the main purpose of his life's work was always clear; it was to dissipate the ghost of social superstition by letting the light of social facts stream in."—RICHARD ROBBINS

EARVIN "MAGIC" JOHNSON

1959–

Basketball player, entrepreneur

Don't tell Magic Johnson that winning is not everything. From his early days of winning Michigan's Class A high school basketball championship, to capturing an NCAA championship, to leading the Los Angeles Lakers to five NBA championships, winning has been everything to the talented, personable former NBA star guard. Magic joined the Lakers in 1979, back when it was an average team. For the next twelve years, Johnson was the man known for bringing "showtime" to the Great Western Forum. His ready smile and good-natured personality helped to make him one of the most likable players in the league, with twelve all-star game appearances. With awesome skills and a great disposition, he ignited a fire in the game of basketball, raising its popularity to new heights.

Earvin "Magic" Johnson retired from professional basketball in 1991 after announcing to the world that he had contracted HIV, the virus that causes AIDS. His disclosure shocked the sports world and bought the reality of AIDS into an area known for healthy, virile athleticism. Despite his good physical condition, Johnson left the game at the suggestion of his doctors. He did, however, participate as part of the U.S. Olympic Dream Team in 1992, where he helped the team win the gold medal. Johnson has since brought his winning edge to causes such as AIDS awareness and rebuilding inner-city areas.

Johnson was born August 14, 1959, in Lansing, Michigan, the sixth child of Earvin Sr. and Christine Johnson. Johnson Sr. worked for a General Motors plant and held several other part-time jobs to help support his ten children. Christine Johnson held a full-time job

*Earvin "Magic" Johnson announces he has
HIV at a press conference in 1991.*

as a middle school custodian. During those rare moments when rest was to be enjoyed, Earvin Sr. watched basketball on TV with his young son, Earvin Jr. Encouraged by his father's love for the game, Johnson started playing ball at a young age. Junior or "June Bug," as his neighbors called him, was on the court by 7:30 a.m. "I practiced all day. I dribbled to the store with my right hand and back with my left. Then I slept with my basketball," Johnson told *USA Weekend*.

Johnson's hard work began to pay off as early as high school, where he was an all-star player at Everett High School. In one game, he scored thirty-six points, sixteen rebounds, and sixteen assists. After seeing him play, a Lansing sportswriter gave the incredible fifteen-year-old player the nickname "Magic." His mother, a devout Christian, at first thought that the name was blasphemous. In his senior year, Johnson led his school to a 27–1 record and clinched the state title. Johnson truly was magic, averaging 28.8 points and 16.8 rebounds.

Being part of a close-knit family, Johnson wanted to attend a college near home; Michigan State University in East Lansing was his choice. His winning ways flourished with the Spartans. During his freshman year he helped the Spartans win the 1977–78 Big Ten Championship. He led MSU to the NCAA championship the following year, matched in the finals against his future rival, Boston Celtic star-to-be Larry Bird. Johnson was named most valuable player in the NCAA tournament.

Having achieved so much so quickly, Johnson wanted to be challenged on a higher level, so he made himself available for the professional draft during his junior year. At six feet, nine inches, Johnson was the first pick. His height also made him one of the tallest guards in the NBA. Lansing, Michigan, was a far cry from Los Angeles, where Johnson would make his adult home and build a basketball legacy, but L.A. proved no different in terms of his outstanding performances. The young all-star led the Los Angeles Lakers to their first championship since 1972. Johnson brought to the game great passing skills, enthusiasm, and high scoring. Twenty-year-old Johnson replaced the injured Kareem Abdul-Jabbar in game six of the 1980 NBA finals against the Philadelphia 76ers. In an amazing performance, Johnson played center and scored forty-two points, leading the team to a championship. In his twelve seasons with the Lakers, he has scored 17,239 points, earned 6,376 rebounds, and made 9,921 assists. He has five NBA championship rings. His three-time selection as most valuable player in the season and finals further highlight his greatness.

The high-flying life of a professional basketball player can be intense anywhere, but in L.A., the land of movie stars and make-believe, the Los Angeles Lakers are a production unto themselves. Fans of all ages line up just to catch a glimpse of these amazing, larger-than-life players. And Johnson—single, handsome, and athletic—was in high demand on and off the court. The trappings of his celebrity lifestyle had their consequences.

On November 7, 1991, after he bravely announced that he had tested positive for HIV, he revealed his mistakes in the hopes of preventing others from getting the disease. Sharing his sexual revelries was not intended as bragging, but to warn others. "I gotta tell the world because people need to know that you can get it from heterosexual sex. People have to be warned to either stop having dangerous sex or get protection," he told *Esquire* magazine.

There was not only his own life to think about; he had recently married his college sweetheart, Earleatha Kelly, nicknamed Cookie, and the two were expecting a baby. "All I could think about was how was I going to tell Cookie?" recalled Johnson. She stood by him, and she and their son, Earvin III, are HIV-negative. A couple of years later, the two adopted a baby girl, Elisa. Johnson is also the father of a son, Andre, from a previous relationship.

In 1996, Johnson returned to the NBA in better physical shape than ever. Yet, at the close of the season, he retired again. Maybe it was the concerns of some of the league's players about the likelihood of getting AIDS through the spread of blood on the court. When he did cut himself in a pre-season game, the fear in the other players' eyes told him that there would be no more "showtime" for him in the NBA. Johnson never complained; instead, he decided to leave the game on his own terms. Aside from his brief return to the NBA as a player, he served as the Lakers' head coach for their final sixteen games in the 1993–94 season. Coaching, though, was not where his heart was, so he gave it up. He remains part owner of the Lakers' franchise, and during home games he can be found holding court beside the Lakers' bench.

*Earvin "Magic" Johnson using magic
on the basketball court.* 393

Johnson's life, though, is not on the sidelines. A joint venture with Sony to place movie houses in inner-city areas is keeping him busy. After the first opened in the South Central area of Los Angeles, its success prompted Johnson and Sony to repeat their efforts in Atlanta, Chicago, and other cities. "It will help to put money in black people's hands—that's important for me," he told *Esquire*. He has also started his own team, the Magic Johnson All-Stars, which competes with teams around the world and brings Johnson the opportunity to hold basketball clinics for youngsters, in which he schools them about life on the court as well as off. His HIV-positive status is shared along with his pearls of basketball wisdom. "I've never cried over HIV," he said in *Sports Illustrated*. "I'm going to beat it." And with his positive attitude, love for life, and the prayers of thousands of fans, he just may work some magic.—KENNETTE CROCKETT

JAMES WELDON **JOHNSON**
1871–1938
Author, activist, lyricist, educator

James Weldon Johnson achieved greatness in a remarkably varied number of fields. Early in his career, he was a successful high school principal in Florida, a diplomat in Central and South America, and a lyricist on Broadway. He achieved pioneering breakthroughs in law and in publishing, even though he devoted relatively brief time to those fields. Many remember Johnson best for writing the words to "Lift Every Voice and Sing," widely known as the Negro National Anthem.

James Weldon Johnson was born on June 17, 1871, in Jacksonville, Florida. His original middle name was William, but he changed it to Weldon in 1913 because he felt that William, in combination with the other two names, was too commonplace.

His parents were James and Helen Louise (Dillet) Johnson. James Johnson was born free in Richmond, Virginia, in 1830 and, as a boy, went to New York City to work. Largely self taught, he worked as a headwaiter in major hotels during much of his adult life. Later in his career, he became a minister. Helen Dillet Johnson was born in Nassau, Bahamas, in 1842 and came to New York City with her family when she was a girl. In addition to a Bahamian background, her family also had roots in Haiti. A talented singer, she and James Johnson met in New York in 1860. Johnson followed her to Nassau after she had returned there with her family during the American Civil War, and they were married in Nassau in 1864. They were still in Nassau in 1868 when their first child, Marie Louise, was born; she lived less than two years. James Johnson had by then moved his family to Jacksonville, Florida, in search of better economic opportunity. James Weldon Johnson was their second child. The third child, John Rosamond, known as Rosamond, was born in 1873. Rosamond Johnson achieved significant fame in his own right as a musician, and he and James Weldon collaborated on many successful projects.

Johnson's early life   Johnson's mother, identified by Keneth Kinnamon in *African American Writers* as "the first black woman public school teacher in Florida," was a major influence on his education. In addition to providing extensive guidance for her sons at home, she was also one of their teachers at Stanton, the public elementary school for "colored" children. Because there was no high school in Jacksonville for blacks, Johnson attended Atlanta University's preparatory school starting in 1887.

In the summer of 1886, Johnson worked for Thomas Osmond Summers, a white physician. As a result, Johnson came into contact with a wide range of books and experienced the perspectives of a free-thinking intellectual. The young Johnson also traveled with Summers to Washington, D.C., another broadening experience. In *Along This Way*, Johnson wrote that Summers provided his "first worthwhile literary criticism and encouragement."

By the time he received his B.A. from Atlanta University in 1894, Johnson had experienced a variety of other opportunities that expanded

James Weldon Johnson.

his formal study. He attended the 1893 Chicago World's Fair, where he heard presentations by Frederick Douglass and Paul Laurence Dunbar. In the summers prior to his graduation, Johnson was part of a male quartet that toured extensively in New England.

But perhaps his most deeply affecting experiences occurred in the summers of 1891 and 1892 when, as a young teacher, he saw firsthand the living conditions for rural blacks near Hampton, Georgia. In *Along This Way*, he cited the experience as central to his understanding and lifelong commitment:

> I was anxious to learn to know the masses of my people, to know what they thought, what they felt, and the things of which they dreamed; and in trying to find out, I laid the first stones in the foundation of faith in them on which I have stood ever since.

Early career achievements   In the fall of 1894, Johnson became principal of Stanton School in Jacksonville. After only one year in the position, he was able to extend the curriculum to include the secondary school years. He did so without fanfare or difficulty with bureaucracy. The consequences were nonetheless highly significant, since black students would not have to leave Jacksonville to receive a high school education.

Despite his busy schedule as an educator, Johnson founded a newspaper, the *Daily American*, in 1895. Although it lasted only eight months, the paper allowed Johnson to share his insights on race-related issues in editorials. Years later in *Along This Way*, he stated that his editorials stood up well indeed.

Perhaps not surprisingly for a man who said in *Along This Way* that he found "spare time" an anathema, Johnson's wide-ranging vision in the same period led him to another career entry point even as he continued to be the Stanton principal. After studying law with attorney Thomas A. Ledwith, he passed the Florida Bar examination in 1897. In *Along This Way*, Johnson noted, "This was the first time in Duval county, and, for all I could learn, in the state of Florida, that a Negro had sought admission to the bar through open examination in a state court." With childhood friend Judson Douglass Wetmore, Johnson practiced law from 1898 to 1901.

Also at the turn of the century, Johnson was developing another career. His mother had seen to it that both her sons had developed their artistic—especially musical—talents, and with special appreciation for African American culture. In 1900 the brothers collaborated on the writing of "Lift Every Voice and Sing," known widely as "the Negro National Anthem." They wrote the song—Rosamond the music and James Weldon the words—practically overnight for a school choir performance in honor of Lincoln's birthday. The song spread through those who learned it as school children and who in turn taught it to others. In *Along This Way*, Johnson wrote, "Nothing that I have done has paid me back so fully in satisfaction as being the part creator of this song."

Music soon played an even larger role in Johnson's life. He spent the summers of 1899 and 1900 in New York City becoming familiar with musical theater. He helped write song lyrics for his brother and Bob Cole, who was a performer, producer, and composer. Rosamond and Bob Cole were already finding success as a team in the world of New York vaudeville and theater.

Johnson resigned the Stanton School principalship in 1902 and moved to New York to devote himself full time to Broadway work. In *Along This Way*, he noted that the Johnsons' partnership with Cole "lasted seven years, in which time we wrote some two hundred songs that were sung in various musical shows on Broadway and 'on the road.'" The Johnson brothers and Cole wrote such popular songs as "Under the Bamboo Tree," "The Maiden with the Dreamy Eyes," "Mandy," and "Oh, Didn't He Ramble." In *The Book of American Negro Poetry*, Johnson identifies "Ramble" a "jes' grew" song, the melody having been in the public domain; the trio's contribution was to provide printable words to the verses. The team also wrote songs for full-length musicals, including *Humpty Dumpty* and *The Sleeping Beauty and the Beast*.

In 1905 James Weldon accompanied his brother and Bob Cole on their performing tour. Despite their celebrity status, prejudice prevented the three from finding decent lodging in Salt Lake City, an incident that remained so indelibly with Johnson that twenty-three years later he refused to leave the train station there when he led an NAACP delegation to a California meeting; others in the group used the layover time to tour the city.

Johnson had a more pleasant experience later in 1905 when he traveled to Europe. The group's first stop was Paris, which Johnson found exhilarating. They then went to London, where his brother and Bob Cole had a successful six-week engagement at the Palladium. The three also visited Brussels.

From 1903 to 1906, Johnson studied at Columbia University, where he worked with literary scholar Brander Matthews. Matthews knew of Johnson's Broadway achievements, and Johnson described his relationship with Matthews in *Along This Way* as "warm and lasting." Before Johnson became more widely known as a writer, however, he moved into yet another career field.

Enters consular service   Between 1904 and 1912, Johnson held two diplomatic posts. His entree resulted from his work as treasurer of the Colored Republican Club in New York, a task pressed upon him by Charles W. Anderson, described in *Along This Way* as "the recognized colored Republican leader of New York." Anderson encouraged Johnson to apply for a post in the United States Consular Service. Johnson was successful, and he served as United States Consul in Puerto Cabello, Venezuela, from 1904 to 1909. His second post in Corinto, Nicaragua, meant an advancement in grade, but it carried more problems than the Venezuelan post. He found the duties more extensive, and he encountered several incidents of racial prejudice from white Americans visiting the country. He served during a time of revolution in Nicaragua, which concluded with U.S. Marines landing in the country.

From his consular posts, Johnson courted Grace Nail, the daughter of successful Harlem real estate entrepreneur John B. Nail. They were married in New York City in 1910. She traveled back to Nicaragua with him, but stayed only two years before returning to New York as Johnson wished to safeguard her health. Johnson resigned his consular appointment in 1912, when it seemed clear that he would not be allowed to advance to an appointment in the Azores.

In 1914 Johnson returned briefly to journalistic writing, when he became editor of the well-established black newspaper *New York Age*. His work, primarily that of a contributing editor, was well received by the readers. Having taken on the post largely for financial reasons, he moved on once it was clear that the work could not provide full-time support.

Serves the NAACP   Johnson's next major career was as a civil rights activist for the NAACP. Hired as the organization's first field secretary, he sought and received approval to organize branches in the South, by no means a routine endeavor at the time. His travels, starting in Richmond, Virginia, in 1917, laid the groundwork for increasing dramatically the number of Southern chapters by 1919. The NAACP led many protest activities in the post–World War I period, which was marked by lynchings and riots. In 1919, for example, Johnson led a delegation to see President Woodrow Wilson in protest of the courtmartialing and death sentences meted out to black soldiers following a racially based conflict in Houston, Texas.

Johnson twice served as acting secretary of the NAACP before becoming its first non-white executive secretary in 1920. In his first year in this post, Johnson visited Haiti to investigate reports of harsh treatment of that country's citizens following the occupation by the U.S. Marines in 1915. Johnson deemed the imperialistic move by the U.S. government unjustified. He was nonetheless careful in his investigations not to compromise the safety of Haitians who felt they or their families would be in danger if they spoke freely. Warren G. Harding used Johnson's critical assessment of the United States' presence in Haiti in the 1920 presidential campaign.

Johnson led the association's efforts to have the Dyer Anti-Lynching Bill passed by Congress in 1922. The bill passed the House of Representatives, but the Republicans stalled it, keeping the bill from being voted on in the Senate. Nonetheless, Johnson felt that the efforts of the NAACP had been successful in placing the issue in the forefront of Americans' thinking. In working relentlessly for voting rights and in investigating many other discriminatory actions, Johnson worked so vigorously that he was twice overcome with exhaustion, once in 1926 and again in 1929.

In 1927 Johnson was the lecturer in a week-long seminar at the University of North Carolina at Chapel Hill, an unusual opportunity for an African American at that time. After receiving the Julius Rosenwald Fellowship, he took a leave from the NAACP in 1929–30 and concentrated on traveling and writing. He attended a conference in Kyoto, Japan, sponsored by the American Council of the Institute of Pacific Relations. He spent time in Toyko as well, and on the return trip, he visited Hawaii.

In 1925 Johnson received the NAACP's Spingarn Medal, and he also received honorary degrees from Atlanta University, Talladega College, and Howard University.

The writings of Johnson   Even as he pursued his many other careers, Johnson was honing his skills as a writer. Cited in *Along This Way*, his first poem, "Sence [sic] You Went Away," published in the magazine *Century* (1900), was in dialect. The poem was later set to music by Rosamond Johnson, and it was a concert favorite of many soloists, including Paul Robeson. In 1913 the *New York Times* published Johnson's poem "50 Years," which had been commissioned in honor of the fiftieth anniversary of Lincoln's signing of the Emancipation Proclamation.

Johnson began to write *The Autobiography of an Ex-Colored Man* (1912) at Columbia University, and he finished it in Venezuela. The anonymous publication and the word "auto-biography" in the title encouraged readers to consider the work to be factual. In *Dictionary of Literary Biography*, Keneth Kinnamon points out that Johnson's friend Judson Douglass Wetmore was the prototype of "the ex-colored man." Johnson identified himself as the author when the book was reprinted in 1927. He wrote his own autobiography, *Along This Way*, to help distinguish his life from that of the narrator's in *The Autobiography*. In 1917 he published a collection, *Fifty Years and Other Poems*, which included some new but mostly previously published poems.

Johnson published many important works during the 1920s, the main decade of the Harlem Renaissance. Indeed, Johnson's preceding works embraced and illustrated themes and forms given prominence by many of the younger writers.

It was during the 1920s as well that the Johnson brothers compiled and arranged two books, which were published together in 1926 as *The Books of American Negro Spirituals*. In his prefaces to these volumes, James Weldon Johnson paid tribute to the beauty and power of the songs and to their anonymous creators. His poem "O Black and Unknown Bards" (1908) had expressed similar appreciation.

God's Trombones: Seven Negro Sermons in Verse (1927), perhaps Johnson's premier creative achievement, paid tribute to the "old-time Negro preacher." The work grew out of his visits to many churches as part of his NAACP speaking tours. "The Creation" (1920) was the first of the seven sermons Johnson wrote, after hearing an especially dynamic sermon by a minister in Kansas City, Missouri. Johnson completed the other *God's Trombones* selections in late 1926. He deliberately avoided the literary, plantation dialect that he felt had only two stops: pathos and humor. Johnson used colloquial yet not substandard language in an effort to convey the dignity and beauty of the sermons; he did not wish to make fun of the largely uneducated preachers through misuse of words. He also conveyed the rhythm of the sermons without strict rhyme schemes. Aaron Douglas, the muralist whose work became prominent during the Harlem Renaissance, provided the illustrations for the original edition of *God's Trombones.*

During the 1930s, Johnson published several major works of nonfiction. His experiences on Broadway and his ongoing interest in a range of settings and people make *Black Manhattan* (1930) an informative source for learning about the history of New York in the pre–Harlem Renaissance years.

Final years In 1932 Johnson began his appointment as the first Adam K. Spence Professor of Creative Writing at Fisk University, a post he held until his death. In *Along This Way,* Johnson wrote of enjoying the more contemplative life of the university setting as well as enjoying the interaction with students.

On June 26, 1938, James Weldon Johnson died in Wiscassett, Maine, as a result of injuries received in a car–train accident. Although injured seriously, Grace Johnson survived the crash. Johnson's funeral was held at Salem Methodist Church in Harlem on June 30, 1938. The Reverend Frederick Cullen, Countee Cullen's father, officiated. Johnson is buried in Greenwood Cemetery in Brooklyn, New York.

The term "Renaissance man" applies to James Weldon Johnson in its most comprehensive sense. Born less than ten years after the end of the Civil War, he mastered a remarkable number of professions. He was an agnostic who demonstrated in his creative efforts a profound respect for the faith that characterized the majority of African Americans. Although he can clearly be identified as a "race man," he was not limited in his outlook nor was he bitter, despite being a victim of both personal and institutional discrimination on many occasions. He had a well-justified sense of confidence as a talented, intelligent human being. His achievements are outstanding in both quality and range.—ARLENE CLIFT-PELLOW

JOHN H. **JOHNSON**
1918–
Entrepreneur, publisher, insurance company executive

John H. Johnson began life in poverty and worked his way up the economic ladder to become a wealthy businessman of international reputation. Founder of Johnson Publishing Company and such spinoffs as Ebony Fashion Fair and Ebony Cosmetics, he was the first successful black publisher to emerge after World War II. Among his publications is Ebony *magazine, the most widely circulated and most popular black magazine, which continuously works to eradicate old stereotypes and replace them with positive black images. Through Johnson's leadership, Johnson Publishing Company consistently has been ranked among the nation's leading black businesses.*

John H. Johnson was born in a tin-roofed shotgun house in Arkansas City, a mill town in rural Arkansas, on January 19, 1918. His mother, Gertrude Johnson, was married first to Richard Lewis and had a daughter, Beulah. After the marriage failed, she married Leroy

*John H. Johnson with his daughter
at the Ebony headquarters.*

Johnson, John's father. After Johnson's father died in a sawmill accident when he was eight, his mother married James Williams. Johnson himself married Eunice Walker on June 21, 1941. The couple later had two children and adopted a daughter.

Johnson was educated in the Arkansas City Colored School, graduating in June 1932. The city offered no public high school; since the family was poor, Johnson could not follow the traditional black option of attending boarding school in Pine Bluff or Little Rock. When she was certain that the family was financially unable to move to Chicago where Johnson could enter high school, Gertrude Johnson Williams made her son repeat the eighth grade rather than run wild on the streets or continue with menial work. He was advised that he would repeat that grade as many times as necessary until they had enough money for the move. Neighbors thought that arrangement was strange and that the mother was "crazy for making sacrifices for a boy who would never amount to anything anyway," Johnson wrote in his autobiography *Succeeding Against the Odds.*

Although the nation was in the middle of the Great Depression and unemployment in Chicago was high, in July 1933, when he was fifteen, Johnson moved to Chicago with his mother; by agreement, his stepfather stayed in Arkansas. Gertrude soon found a job in the garment industry. By late 1933, Johnson's stepfather joined them. Since his stepfather was unable to find a job, and his mother lost her job at the factory, from 1934 to 1936 the family lived on public assistance.

That September Johnson entered Wendell Phillips, a virtually all-black high school. By accident, he skipped the ninth grade and started school in the tenth with intentions of becoming a journalist. Later on he edited the school newspaper, the *Phillipsite,* and was sales manager of the yearbook, the *Red and Black,* presiding officer of the student council, leader of the student forum and the French Club, and junior and senior class president. He began to frequent the Fifty-eighth Street branch of the Chicago Public Library, and read widely in black history and literature, including works by W. E. B. Du Bois and Booker T. Washington and the poetry of Langston Hughes. He also studied self-improvement books, such as those by Dale Carnegie. Johnson wrote, "Faith, self-confidence, and a positive mental attitude: These three were the basic messages of the self-help books that changed my life." When he began to speak out more in class, he soon awed his classmates.

After Wendell Phillips High School burned down, the students transferred to a newly constructed facility named Jean Baptiste Pointe DuSable. Johnson's classmates at the two schools included singers Nat King Cole and Dorothy Donegan, comedian Redd Foxx, and entrepreneur Dempsey Travis.

Near commencement time, persuaded by his white civics teacher, Mary Herrick, he changed his name from Johnnie to John, picked a middle name out of the air, and from then on was known as John Harold Johnson. He graduated from DuSable in 1936. At the school's commencement on June 11, Johnson was the only student chosen to speak and gave an impressive talk on "Builders of a New World." The *Chicago Defender* printed a notice of his impending speech, giving Johnson his first press coverage. Johnson graduated with "a fistful of honors" and a $200 scholarship to the University of Chicago, he said in his autobiography.

Johnson was asked to speak at a routine Urban League luncheon for outstanding high school students, also held in 1936. Legendary business leader Harry H. Pace, one of Johnson's heroes, president of Supreme Life Insurance Company, and head of the New York–based Pace and Handy Music Company, was the main speaker. After Pace's speech, Johnson complimented him on his remarks and, in turn, Pace complimented Johnson on the good reports he had heard about his high school performance. When Pace learned that Johnson needed a part-time job to help finance his college education, he offered Johnson work in his company. Johnson wrote that the meeting with Pace changed and defined his life.

Eighteen-year-old Johnson reported to Pace's office on September 1, 1936, to begin a part-time job for twenty-five dollars a month while attending the University of Chicago part-time. He benefited from his experiences with the company's executives who, in addition to Pace, included journalist and business manager Truman K. Gibson, attorney Earl B. Dickerson, and physician Midian O. Bousfield. When Johnson drove Pace to the bank each day, he used the time to question Pace about business and success. "Not a week goes by that I don't recall and use some lesson that I learned from him and other Supreme executives," Johnson wrote.

For a few months Johnson was assistant editor of the *Guardian,* the company's monthly newspaper; Pace was the paper's editor. In 1939 Johnson was promoted to editor, which placed the ambitious young man in a strategic position.

Although Johnson intended to study for a law degree, he found Supreme Life Insurance Company so exciting that he dropped out of college to work full time.

Begins publishing venture   The world events of that era set the stage for the beginning of Johnson's publishing venture. A new level of black consciousness arose. Pace gave him the task of reading magazines and newspapers and preparing a digest of events in the black world—an assignment that changed Johnson's life. He was determined to begin a publication to pass on to the public the information he had garnered for Pace.

Johnson set up an office in 1942 in the corner of Earl Dickerson's law library in the Supreme building and began the Negro Digest Publishing Company. He wrote letters to policyholders of Supreme Life, offering charter subscriptions for two dollars each. On Sunday, November 1, 1942, his new publication, *Negro Digest,* was officially published. It was similar in name and format to *Reader's Digest,* but differed in that *Negro Digest* published complete reproductions of articles from the white and black press. Johnson described his reaction in his autobiography: "When I held the first copy of the magazine in my hand, I had a feeling of relief, exhilaration, and fear. I hadn't realized the true potential of the magazine until that moment, and I was overwhelmed by the idea that the life and death of this sixty-eight page baby was in my hands."

Johnson distributed 3,000 copies of the magazine to his prepaid subscribers, but needed to sell the remaining 2,000 to pay his bills. He negotiated with Charles Levy Circulating Company, Chicago's biggest magazine distributor, and was finally able to obtain Levy's financial backing. He also broadened the journal's distribution by pushing it in places neglected by major distributors. These included mom-and-pop outlets, black-owned distributors such as Chicago's National News Company, a drugstore chain in Atlanta, and sites in Philadelphia and Los Angeles. He made a profit on the first issue; otherwise, he said in his autobiography, there would have been no second issue.

Until 1944 he and his full-time secretary were the magazine's only two employees; he disguised this fact by listing the names of relatives on the masthead. As the magazine grew in popularity, Johnson included a regular feature, "If I Were a Negro," and posed the question to major figures like Pearl Buck, Orson Wells, Edward G. Robinson, and Marshall Field. After he persuaded Eleanor Roosevelt to write the column for one issue—the cover story in October 1943—the circulation jumped almost overnight, from 50,000 to 100,000. "We never looked back," wrote Johnson. "I was making so much money that I didn't know what to do with it."

In late 1943, Johnson bought his first building. He also bought a three-story apartment home for himself and his wife, with space for his mother and stepfather. He expanded his staff and hired his mother, who remained on the staff until she died in 1977.

Negro Digest grew, setting new records for black magazines. Johnson said that he "didn't start a business to get rich—I started a business to provide a service and to improve myself economically." Now that the future of *Negro Digest* was assured, Johnson turned his attention to a new venture, the founding of *Ebony* magazine on November 1, 1945, and to publishing the company's first book, *The Best of Negro Humor,* which Johnson edited.

Johnson knew that black people wanted to see themselves in pictures. He also knew that blacks at that time in particular needed to see positive images of their race. According to the November 1995 issue of *Ebony*, published during its fiftieth-year celebration, "*Ebony* became the mirror of the struggle of rights activists . . . to desegregate rail and bus transportation, lunch counters, public schools[,] . . . hotels and motels."

After considering several names for the new journal, Johnson's wife, Eunice Johnson, suggested "Ebony" as the title. "It means fine black African wood," she said in Johnson's autobiography. John Johnson added, "the name means . . . a tree, the hard, heavy, fine black wood that the tree yields, and the ambience and mystique surrounding the tree and the color."

The first run of *Ebony*, 25,000 copies, sold out in a few hours and Johnson immediately printed that number again. The journal quickly moved ahead of *Negro Digest* and became the most widely circulated black journal in America, yet *Negro Digest* subsidized *Ebony*. No advertisements were used at first; to make a profit, however, he had to look for advertisers, and was able to secure contracts from major white companies, such as the makers of Zenith televisions, Swift Packing Company, Armour Foods, Quaker Oats, Elgin Watch, and the makers of Chesterfield and Old Gold cigarettes. By then *Ebony* was in competition with another black magazine, *Our World*. When the latter magazine went into bankruptcy, Johnson bought it for $14,000. He hired one of *Our World*'s staff photographers, Moneta Sleet Jr. Later, still with *Ebony*, Sleet became the first black photographer to win a Pulitzer Prize, for the well-publicized, touching photograph of Coretta Scott King and children at Martin Luther King Jr.'s funeral. In retelling the fifty-year history of *Ebony* in the November 1995 issue, Johnson said:

> We wanted to give Blacks a new sense of somebodiness, a new sense of self-respect. We wanted to tell them who they were and what they could do. We believed then—and we believe now—that Blacks needed positive images to fulfill their potentialities.

Johnson hired other black talent around 1948 and 1949 as writers. They included Era Bell Thompson, Edward T. Clayton, Roi Ottley, and Doris Sanders; by then there were close to one hundred full-time employees and over four thousand independent distributors.

Johnson Publishing Company begins The firm's name, Negro Digest Publishing Company, was changed to Johnson Publishing Company in 1949. Book publishing, suspended after the first book was published in 1945, resumed in 1962. The book division first published such works as Paul Crump's *Burn Killer Burn,* Lerone Bennett's *Before the Mayflower,* Freda DeKnight's *The Ebony Cookbook,* and Doris Saunders's *The Ebony Handbook.* In time, the book division ventured into a variety of publications, including a number of children's books. Johnson raided black newspaper staffs and added to his staff photo editor Basil Phillips; writers Lerone Bennett Jr., Robert E. Johnson, and Simeon Booker; and society editor Geri Major.

Negro Digest was suspended in 1951 and revived in 1961 as a literary quarterly until publication ceased. Spinoffs from Johnson's firm include the annual Ebony Fashion Fair, a traveling fashion extravaganza that home economist Freda DeKnight started in September 1958 as the Ebony Fashion Show. Two thousand people attended the first show, and ten additional shows were held that year. Popular worldwide, the Ebony Fashion Fair showcases beautiful black women and men as models wearing exquisite designer clothing. In succeeding years, other sponsors such as local urban leagues, sororities, and the NAACP were added, and Johnson's wife, Eunice, became the director. The show annually produces thousands of subscribers for *Ebony* and *Jet* and raises millions of dollars for charity.

Between 1945 and 1972 Johnson produced other spinoffs: *Tan Confessions,* started in November 1950 as a true-confessions magazine and later developed into a women's service magazine; *Proper Romance;* and *Jet,* a pocket-sized weekly news magazine launched on November 1, 1951. The first issue of *Jet* sold out quickly and became a collector's item. The firm also published *Beauty Salon; Ebony Jr.,* designed for children between six and twelve; *Ebony Man,* launched in 1985 and focused on grooming, appearance, and prospects for young black men; and *Ebony South Africa,* marking the company's expansion into international publishing.

Fashion Fair Cosmetics, the world's largest black-owned cosmetics company, is a subsidiary. Its forerunner was Johnson's mail-order company called Beauty Star, founded in 1946, which sold wigs, vitamins, clothing, and other products. His company also owns Ebony Cosmetics and Supreme Beauty Products.

Johnson had little contact with Supreme Life Insurance Company from 1943 to 1957. Later on he bought 1,000 shares of its stock, and in 1974 was elected chairman and chief executive officer. He admitted in his autobiography that this gave him "a great sense of personal and corporate satisfaction." He also serves as president of WLOU radio station and has bought and sold three other stations. When he purchased his first station in 1972, WGRT, he became the first black to own a radio station in Chicago.

Later, Johnson entered the television market and was offered two major shows, the Ebony Music Awards and the American Black Achievement Awards (ABAA). When the white coproducers backed out, Johnson bought them out, broadened the format, and began sponsoring the annual ABAA show. His adopted daughter, Linda Johnson Rice, runs a weekly variety show, the *Ebony/Jet* Showcase, which is aired in a number of television stations.

During his legendary career, Johnson has served on many boards, including the Dial Corporation, Zenith Radio Corporation, and Chrysler Corporation; he is a trustee of the Art Institute of Chicago and a director of the Magazine Publishers Association. He is a recipient of the John Russwurm Award, National Newspaper Publishers Association, 1966; Spingarn Medal, NAACP, 1966; Communicator of the Year Award, University of Chicago Alumni Association, 1974; and Columbia Journalism Award, 1974. In 1975 he accompanied the Vice President Nelson Rockefeller on a goodwill tour to nine African countries. He received the National Press Foundation Award in 1986, and that same year *Black Enterprise* gave his firm the Number One Black Business Award. Johnson was inducted into the Black Press Hall of Fame in 1987. Other awards that followed were the Founders Award from the National Conference of Christians and Jews; the Mass Media Award; the Distinguished Service Award from Harvard University Graduate School of Business Administration, 1991; and numerous others. He was inducted into the Chicago Journalism Hall of Fame in 1990. *Black Enterprise* for June 1997 named Johnson one of its five "captains of the industry"; Johnson's company has been on the *BE* 100 list since it was started twenty-five years ago, always finishing near the top.

John H. Johnson never forgot his struggle from poverty to wealth; he demonstrated this when he hired Jesse Jackson. Although the date is not mentioned, in his autobiography Johnson remembered hiring Jackson "when he first came to Chicago, penniless, unemployed, and unknown." For this experience, Jackson refers to him affectionately as "Godfather." The name "Godfather" may be deserved also because of his reputation as a hard taskmaster. Johnson's mission now is to see Johnson Publishing survive and grow. He told *Black Enterprise* in June 1997 that he will seize all new opportunities and will embrace technology to get were he needs to be. "Never say never about new things," he said. Although he has no plans to retire, his daughter, company president Linda Johnson Rice, will play an increasing role in managing the company.—JESSIE CARNEY SMITH

ROBERT L. JOHNSON
1946–
Television executive

The founder, chairman, and chief executive officer of Black Entertainment Television (BET), Robert L. Johnson challenged the unknown for blacks, changing television by establishing the first and only firm that provides basic cable television programming by and about blacks. He took BET to the stock market in 1991, making it the first black-owned firm to go onto the New York Stock Exchange, and holds the controlling share of a major diversified media giant.

Robert Louis Johnson was born on April 8, 1946, in Hickory, Mississippi, a rural town twenty-five miles west of Meridian. The Johnson family moved to the industrial farming town of Freeport, Illinois, with a population of about 30,000. Both parents worked in local factories to provide for their large family. Although he was the ninth of ten children, he said that he was able to grow up "pretty independent." He and his siblings were taught to do all they could to help themselves. Johnson told Beverly Smith in a 1992 interview on the CNN show *Pinnacle*, "I had a lot of brothers and sisters that I could sort of pick on if I had to for whatever information." His idea was to become a fighter pilot in the U.S. Air Force, but he apparently lacked the required twenty-twenty vision; instead, he concentrated on his studies and on going to college. A good student in high school, he graduated with honors in history, then entered the University of Illinois on an academic scholarship and graduated in 1968 with a bachelor's degree in history. Although he did not meet Princeton University's usual admission standards, he was considered a worthy risk and in 1969 was admitted to the university's Woodrow Wilson School of Public and International Affairs. He graduated in 1972, ranked sixth in his class, with a master's degree in public administration.

While at Princeton, Johnson established connections that led to his employment as press secretary for the Corporation for Public Broadcasting. He joined the U.S. Army Reserve during the Vietnam War. Afterwards, he learned his way around Washington and became public affairs officer at the Corporation for Public Broadcasting. Next Johnson was director of communications for the Washington Urban League, a press aide for the District of Columbia's city councilman Sterling Tucker, and press secretary for Walter Fauntroy, the District's nonvoting delegate to Congress. From 1976 to 1979 Johnson was vice president of government relations for the National Cable and Television Association (NCTA).

Creates Black Entertainment Television   Johnson's life then became a self-made success story. He was familiar with the A. C. Nielson ratings that put black viewers at an average of seventy hours a week of television-watching compared to forty-eight hours for whites. Even so, in the late 1970s no networks were committed to programming specifically for blacks nor were blacks shown in television programming in powerful, dominant roles. While he was with NCTA he got the idea for starting a cable network company to promote black characters in broadcast programming. He persuaded his NCTA supervisor to promise him a $15,000 consulting contract, then used the contract to secure a loan of that amount from the National Bank of Washington. He also secured a loan of $320,000 from John C. Malone, head of the Denver-based Tele-Communications Incorporated (TCI), one of the nation's largest builders of cable systems. Malone and TCI also paid him $180,000 for a 20 percent share in the network. In 1980 Johnson created BET from the basement of his home. BET made its debut on cable on January 25, 1980, with a two-hour movie with an all-black cast, *A Visit to the Chief's Son,* and despite the views of skeptics, drew an audience of 3.8 million homes in 350 markets. In the beginning, BET kept costs at a minimum by showing low-cost programs that would still appeal to blacks, such as the film *Lady Sings the Blues.* Free music videos from record companies were aired by 1982, marking the dawning of the music video era. Soon BET added black stars, talk shows with black hosts and guests, and black college sports.

BET struggled with consecutive years of losses. In 1982 Johnson took on a new partner, Taft Broadcasting Company, then in 1984 added Home Box Office, a cable subsidiary for Time Incorporated (now Time Warner). BET expanded on HBO's satellite and offered twenty-four-hour daily telecasting and added 7.6 million subscribers. In spite of phenomenal growth, by 1989 BET was still the least carried of all cable networks.

Johnson's BET faced setbacks. Johnson began another cable venture in 1984, District Cablevision Incorporated, that would wire homes and serve the District of Columbia. TCI owned 75 percent of the new company. Several lawsuits by competitors followed, causing more financial pressure. By 1986, however, the financial burden was eased, but it was not until 1989 that the company paid back its investors.

Traded on New York Stock Exchange   BET went on to become highly successful. Johnson established BET Holdings Incorporated, the parent company of BET, and on October 30, 1991, BET became the first black-owned corporation listed on New York Stock Exchange (NYSE), the world's most prestigious marketplace. Although by then three other black firms had gone public with their stock, none had remained on the public market or had been listed by the NYSE. When first listed, in one day alone BET's $9 million enterprise grew to $475 million. Johnson's personal wealth saw $6.4 million in growth, and since he had controlling stock, his net worth in just eleven years of work was then over $104 million. Although the company lost some ground when investors questioned his subscriber count, BET sold some of its stock, clarified the number of subscribers, and later picked up some of its losses.

Commenting on his financial progress in the *Network Journal,* Johnson stated: "Black people will become powerful in this country when they obtain power through control of economic wealth."

The company took a bold step in 1995 when it moved its 350 employees to a new, plush, $15 million headquarters in Washington's industrial corridor north of the Capi-tol. In April 1995 Johnson added to the BET campus one of the largest facilities of its type on the east coast, a fifty-thousand-square-foot film and video production facility. Tony Chapelle quoted Johnson in the *Network Journal* as saying that he has plans to become "the preeminent provider of information entertainment and direct marketing services to the Black community."

By 1995 BET reached 41.3 million households. By 1996 the cable network, still the core of the company's holdings, had a children's literature hour, public affairs show, a weekly show for teenagers, town hall meetings, and other offerings such as music videos. There is a BET on Jazz channel, known as the Cable Jazz Channel, and ventures in such foreign markets as Africa and England.

Johnson moved ahead in 1996 when BET launched the nation's first black-controlled cable movie premium channel. The new channel, called BET Movies/STARZ!3, offered a lineup of classics that included *To Sir with Love* as well as newer films such as *Pulp Fiction* and Spike Lee's *Clockers*. Johnson told the *Los Angeles Sentinel*, "What we're doing is something that's unique. We're branding movies that appeal to an audience that has demonstrated a tremendous amount of interest in viewing film entertainment." The venture expected to expand pay-TV households in urban markets by developing and exhibiting black-oriented, feature-length films. The venture provides access to the black filmmaking community as well, giving wider attention to the interests of an underserved public.

Johnson's announcement to the sports world and government officials in Washington that, in 1994, he would provide the primary funding for a new, downtown sports arena and other services was never realized.

In 1991 BET acquired controlling interest in *Emerge* magazine, which addresses the interests of young adults. That same year BET began publishing *YSB (Young Sisters and Brothers)*, which appeals to adolescents. BET also established a radio network in 1994 that provides news and music to urban stations throughout the country.

Outside his business ventures, in 1981 Johnson founded the Metropolitan Cable Club, a forum for the exchange of information in the telecommunications industry, and served as its president and later a member of its board. He has served as a board member of the Ad Council, Cable TV Advertising Bureau, Minorities in Cable, the National Cable Television Association (NCTA), the Walter Kaitz Foundation, and the Board of Governors of the National Cable Academy. Among the recognitions he has received are the Presidential Award, NCTA (1982); the NAACP's Image Award (1982); the Capitol Press Club's Pioneer Award (1984); the Business of the Year Award from the Washington, D.C., Chamber of Commerce (1985); the Executive Leadership Council Award (1992); and the Turner Broadcasting Trumpet Award (1993).

Described as intensely ambitious and foresighted, Johnson has also been characterized as gregarious, easygoing, graceful, personal, bright, and an effective communicator. To accomplish all that he does, he usually works fifteen hours a day during his six-day work week. On January 19, 1969, Johnson married Sheila Crump Johnson, now BET's executive vice president for corporate affairs. They have a daughter, Paige, and a son, Brett.

In 1996, when Johnson pledged $100,000 to Howard University to help support the School of Communication, the school responded at its twenty-fifth anniversary gala by awarding Johnson the Messenger Award for Excellence in Communications. Jannette Dates, the school's interim dean, praised Johnson for his success and his support of the school. In the *Washington Informer,* Dates summed up Johnson's success:

He showed America that an African American from a not very privileged background can, with the strength of his intelligence and hard work, take a small beginning and become a tremendous success. He has also succeeded in communicating an array of new images of African Americans that are different from those that were portrayed over the years past.

—JESSIE CARNEY SMITH

QUINCY D. **JONES**

1933–

Music producer, composer, arranger, performer, entrepreneur, humanitarian

A multitalented entertainer par excellence, Quincy D. Jones is one of the most celebrated and acclaimed artists in the world of contemporary music. His fifty-year career was once described by Billboard Magazine as a distinctly American odyssey, embracing music in all its dimensions—as an art, a business, and a catalyst for social change and spiritual renewal. Jones's extraordinarily diverse and successful career includes his roles as a prolific composer, arranger, conductor, instrumentalist, record producer, major record label executive, magazine founder, television and movie producer, humanitarian, and civil rights advocate.

Quincy Delight Jones Jr. was born March 14, 1933, in Chicago, the son of Quincy Delight Jones Sr. and Sarah Jones. A native of South Carolina, Quincy Jones Sr. moved to Chicago seeking a better life, free from the racial bigotry and segregation that were commonplace in the South. Unfortunately, Sarah Jones suffered chronic mental illness and spent most of her life in mental institutions or under a doctor's care. Life in Chicago was tough for the Jones family without her guidance. Sarah and Quincy Jones Sr. were divorced after the birth of their younger son, Lloyd. The senior Jones remarried and moved to Bremerton, Washington, just outside Seattle, with his new wife Elvira and their blended family of her three children and his two sons. Jones's father and stepmother eventually had five children together. After several years in Bremerton, the family moved to Seattle in 1948.

Jones's early years While in Chicago, the Jones family took in as much music as the thriving south-side neighborhood offered. Jones showed interest in the piano playing of the elderly men who provided the entertainment for the infamous house rent parties. When the family moved to Bremerton, all of that changed. In Bremerton, Jones was the only African American student in his class and experienced no problems. Unlike Chicago, where black and white gangs controlled certain areas, Jones's experience in Bremerton was extremely positive.

Seattle was the place where Quincy Jones's love affair with music began to grow. Encouraged and inspired by his father, despite the fact he was not a musician, Jones developed his musical interest primarily through the public schools and the local black churches. Initially

Quincy D. Jones.

he helped organize a choir at one of the local churches and began learning to sing spirituals. He started playing the piano, joined the high school band, and became its student manager. As a band member, Jones experimented with a variety of instruments. He played percussion, French horn, baritone, alto saxophone, clarinet, trombone, tuba, and eventually the trumpet. With his musical talent awakened, Jones became an active member of every musical group at his high school until his graduation. He played with the orchestra and dance band and sang with the chorus. Soon he became increasingly interested in jazz. While still in high school, Jones wrote his first suite, "From the Four Winds." This was a testament to Jones's innate musical genius because he wrote the suite without having studied music composition or advanced theory. The suite was impressive because of its form, orchestration, sophistication, and length. It is said that Lionel Hampton, while performing in Seattle, got the charts for the suite and was so impressed with the composition that he offered Jones an opportunity to join his big band. Hampton's wife Gladys, who handled the band's business affairs, vetoed the offer to have Jones join the band because he was too young and needed to finish high school.

Seattle was, to a large extent, the music capital of the Pacific Northwest, and during the swing era many big-name stars, including great African American musical talents, performed there. Jones attended these performances and proved an apt pupil. He listened, observed, asked questions, and learned a lot from playing with musical giants such as popular local bandleader Bumps Blackwell, Cab Calloway, Billie Holiday, Count Basie, and the phenomenal trumpet player Clark Terry of the Duke Ellington orchestra. Other later musical influences included Lester Young, Dizzy Gillespie, and Charlie Parker.

However, it was another teenager from Albany, Georgia, blind since the age of six, who arrived in Seattle in 1950 to obtain greater musical and personal opportunities, who had the biggest overall influence on Quincy Jones. That teenager was Ray Charles. Charles played the piano, organ, alto saxophone, and clarinet; he was a gifted composer and arranger, and he sang the blues in a unique soulful manner. Charles taught Jones methods for arranging big jazz bands, voicing horns, writing polytones, and even how to read and write in braille. Their special relationship, fostered almost half a century ago, still remains intact.

In 1950, after graduating from high school, Jones won two scholarships to study music at the University of Seattle and Boston's renowned Schillinger's House of Music, which is now known as Berklee College of Music. At Berklee, Jones found a musical home. He immersed himself in classes, sometimes taking as many as ten in one day, and worked in local clubs as a semi-professional musician. On weekends, Jones and other students made forays into New York to hear jazz greats such as Art Tatum, Thelonious Monk, Charlie Parker, Miles Davis, Charles Mingus, and others who embraced the be-bop style.

After Jones reached his eighteenth birthday, Hampton again invited him to join his big band. This time there were no objections. Jones left Berklee with the intention of returning to school after a short stint with the Hampton band, but he never did. Instead, Jones toured with the band as a trumpeter, arranger, and sometime-pianist off and on from 1951 to 1959.

Touring with the Lionel Hampton Big Band   From 1951 to 1953 the Hampton band toured major cities in every state in the United States. The members of that band were so closely connected as friends and musicians that it seemed that they would always be together. The band was the first to use the Fender bass and was known for its high-energy performance. During his tour with the band, Jones realized that he was not likely to become one of the premiere trumpet soloists of jazz; rather, his talent would be directed toward the overall sound of music through composing and arranging. The first of Jones's compositions recorded by the band was "Kingfish," which includes Jones playing a rare trumpet solo. During this same period two of Jones's compositions, "Waitbait" and "Brownie Eyes," were featured on a solo album by fellow band member Clifford Brown.

In September 1953 the Hampton band began an extensive European tour that included nightly concerts, frequent matinees, and considerable travel from one venue to the next. The tour included Oslo, Stockholm, Brussels, and Paris. Among Jones's original compositions recorded during this European tour were "Stockholm Sweetnin'," " 'Scuse These Bloos," "Keeping Up with Jonesy," and "Evening in Paris."

The tour ended with eleven of Hampton's band members resigning upon their return to New York, including Jones.

Jones and the recording studio   Jones's career shifted to the recording studio, where he did jazz and commercial recordings as a freelance arranger. He wrote charts for James Cleveland (known as the king of gospel), Benny Carter, LaVern Baker, Chuck Willis, Dinah Washington, Johnny Mathis, and even Lionel Hampton. He also arranged a series of albums for musicians whom he admired and respected, including Clark Terry, Sonny Stitt, George Washington, and Cannonball Adderley. His work with Dinah Washington, arranging and doing some original songs, was fortuitous because it provided a very important connection between Jones and Mercury Records.

In 1956 Jones received the New Star Arranger award in the *Encyclopedia of Jazz* poll. In that same year he organized and arranged tunes for a big band led by Dizzy Gillespie for a State Department tour of the Middle East and South America. Jones left the tour in order to write and spend time with his family, but shortly after his return to the U.S. he was asked to make a big band album of his own jazz compositions for ABC-Paramount. This was something Jones had been wanting to do for a long time. The now classic *This Is How I Feel about Jazz* contained three of Jones's recordings from his European experience. Though he had more than enough work as an arranger and he was also composing occasionally, Jones was disappointed with the overall quality of music in the 1950s. He was also frustrated because, with his extensive experience of writing and conducting in the demanding New York studios, he was still primarily relegated to supervising the rhythm and horn sections.

When the offer came from Barclay Disques in Paris, Mercury's French distributor, to become its staff arranger and director of musical operations, Jones jumped at the opportunity. At Barclay he tackled a variety of projects, had the necessary resources to complete them successfully, and finally got his chance to write strings. He was learning all he could about the recording business at Barclay while continuing his own music studies with Nadia Boulanger, France's most revered music teacher.

Upon his return to New York, Jones received a dream offer to arrange the score for a new Broadway show, *Free and Easy*, to organize his own big band, and then to "go to Europe with the show . . . and break the show in, in Holland, Belgium and France and then meet Sammy Davis Jr. in London and work the show three weeks there and come back to Broadway and open for two years." Simultaneously with organizing his own band, Jones took advantage of the opportunity to compose and arrange an LP for Count Basie, *One More Time*, that proved to be one of Basie's best recordings ever. During the same period, Irving Green offered Jones a recording contract with his new big band, and this resulted in *The Birth of a Band*, one of the most well-liked big band albums of all times. The European tour of the Broadway show and Jones's own big band, the Free and Easy Musician, got off to a good start in Belgium, Holland, and Paris, but then came the Algerian crisis. Sammy Davis Jr. never joined the show, and it closed. Jones now had responsibility for meeting a weekly payroll of $4,800 with no agent, no manager, and no work. Jones called everybody he knew in Europe just to keep things going. Jones's persistence led to bookings in Sweden and Paris, but the Paris agent disappeared with the guarantees for all the performances. In desperation and in order to get his band and their families back to the United States, Jones hocked the publishing interests on all his copyrights. The entire episode left Jones exhausted, burned out, and broke.

From Mercury to Hollywood   Irving Green, the president of Mercury Records, Inc., was familiar with Jones from his earlier sessions with Dinah Washington and his recent success with the *Birth of a Band* LP. Green offered Jones a position with the company as staff arranger and talent developer. Jones accepted the offer in order to keep his band together for future concerts, pay off debts, and learn more about the commercial side of the industry. Prior to joining Mercury, Jones was able to score the major part of an album for ABC-Paramount featuring his longtime friend Ray Charles.

During his tenure at Mercury, Jones was promoted to vice president, becoming the first African American executive in the recording industry at a major label, won his first Grammy in 1963 for his Count Basie arrangement of Ray Charles's *I Can't Stop Loving You,* and scored the biggest successes in the company's history when he produced Lesley Gore, who won ten gold discs representing 10 million singles sales with LP follow-ups. Jones's successes at Mercury allowed him the flexibility to take other occasional prestige jobs, such as conductor and arranger with Frank Sinatra and Count Basie for their classic *Sinatra at the Sands.*

Jones was a pioneer in breaking down barriers in the music industry. As an avid movie buff, he had one more unrealized professional goal: to score soundtracks for movies. As was true of much of film making in the 1960s, scoring musical soundtracks, like producing, directing, and script writing, remained exclusively white. In 1965 Jones left Mercury and moved to Hollywood in order to have greater access to the film industry. Jones succeeded in landing the job of writing the score for Sidney Lumet's independent film *The Pawnbroker,* the first of his major motion picture scores. Although the movie was critically acclaimed and won an Academy Award nomination for best actor, it was not a box office hit. It was nearly a year before Jones had another job scoring a feature film. That film, *Mirage,* was not a financial success either, despite the normally guaranteed box office success associated with its star, Gregory Peck. Jones finally got a break when he was asked to score *The Slender Thread* and *Walk Don't Run.* Both movies were financially successful, and Jones had made his mark on the movie soundtrack by infusing it with jazz and soul. During this period, Jones had more work than he could handle writing music for films such as *In Cold Blood, In the Heat of the Night,* and *For the Love of Ivy,* and themes for television productions like *Ironside* and *The Bill Cosby Show.* His *Ironside* theme was the first synthesized-based pop theme song. Despite his accomplishments in scoring music for films and television and several Oscar nominations, the awards eluded him. Over time, writing the musical scores became less enjoyable and more of a grind. When A & M Records asked Jones to make an album, his first in four years, he readily agreed. The resulting album, *Walking in Space,* received a Grammy for best performance by a large group in 1969. His follow-up album in 1970 was *Gula Matari,* which also won a Grammy for best instrumental composition and best instrumental arrangement.

For Jones, 1974 was both a high point and low point in his career. His new album release, *Body Heat,* caused a sensation in pop music circles; sales exceeded one million in the United States alone, and Jones received his first gold disc for the album. In the midst of such good fortune, Jones suffered a cerebral stroke caused by a ruptured aneurysm. Surgery was required, and during preparation for surgery a second aneurysm was discovered on the opposite side of the brain. Two surgeries were performed without complications within several weeks of each other. After a convalescent period that kept him out of the studio, doctors pronounced Jones fully recovered by February 1975, six months after his first aneurysm was

discovered.

With his health restored, Jones was extremely busy for the remainder of the 1970s. He produced several albums with the Brothers Johnson and received his first platinum record. He wrote the musical score for *Roots,* which drew the highest viewer ratings in history when it aired on television and provided an opportunity for Americans to hear the ancient African origins of modern music. In Stuart Kallen's *Quincy Jones,* the composer remarked:

> African music had always been regarded as primitive and savage. But when you take time to study it you see that it's as structured and sophisticated as classical music; instruments that are plucked; instruments that are beaten; and instruments that are blown with reeds. And it's music from the soil-powerful. From Gospel, blues, jazz, soul, R&B, rock & roll, all the way to rap, you can trace the roots straight back to Africa.

In 1977, while working on *The Wiz,* Michael Jackson and Jones joined forces to cut a state-of-the-art pop album, *Off the Wall,* which blended disco rhythms, pop tunes, and clever arrangements with Jackson's unique singing. The album sold more than seven million copies.

In the 1980s Jones continued to concentrate on recording and producing other artists. He formed Qwest Records, a fifty/fifty joint venture with Warner Bros. Recordings from this venture featured an eclectic assortment of musical talents, including the Winans, a gospel duo; R&B vocalists Tevin Campbell, Tamia, Keith Washington, and Ernestine Anderson; spoken-word artist D-Knowledge; jazzman Milt Jackson; and veteran entertainer Ray Charles.

He teamed with Michael Jackson again to produce another mega album, *Thriller,* which sold more than forty million copies, making it the best-selling album in recording history. Jones broke into film making as co-producer of the 1985 motion picture *The Color Purple,* which was nominated for eleven Academy Awards. He is also responsible for introducing Whoopi Goldberg and Oprah Winfrey to the movie world. In that same year Jones brought together forty of the world's biggest recording stars to record *We Are the World* to raise money to feed the victims of Ethiopia's drought and resulting famine. To some extent, *We Are the World* symbolized the theme of a musical family and the holistic approach to music that runs through his work.

Jones listens up Jones started off the decade of the 1990s with a bang. His life and career were chronicled in the critically acclaimed Warner Bros. film *Listen Up: The Lives of Quincy Jones.* He continued to produce and win awards, but he was more involved with expanding his business interests and developing a multimedia conglomerate. His landmark album *Back on the Block* was named Album of the Year at the 1990 Grammy Awards. The album was the first fusion of the be-bop and hip hop musical styles and brought legendary artists such as Miles Davis, Dizzy Gillespie, Ella Fitzgerald, and Sarah Vaughan together with rap artists like Ice T, Big Daddy Kane, and Melle Mel. Similarly, his 1993 recording *Miles and Quincy: Live at Montreux* won a Grammy for best large jazz ensemble performance. The album featured Quincy Jones conducting as Miles Davis performed Gil Evans's arrangements of classics from such plays as *Miles Ahead, Porgy and Bess,* and *Sketches of Spain.*

Quincy Jones's devotion to music and a commitment to his murch heralded career success took a toll on his personal life. Each of his three marriages ended in divorice. The break-up of his third and longest marriage, to actress Peggy Lipton, was especially difficult. Jones has five adult children: Jolie, the oldest daughter born during his first marriage to Jer Caldwell; Martina-Lisa and Quincy III, offspring of his second marriage to Ulla, a Swedish woman; and Kidada and Rashida, daughters of Peggy Lipton. Jones also has children with actress Nastassia Kinski.

On the business end of Jones's career, he joined David Salzman, who also worked with Jones to produce the incredibly successful *An American Reunion* concert at the Lincoln Memorial, in forming QDE (Quincy Jones David Salzman Entertainment) in 1993. QDE is a co-venture with Time Warner, Inc., in which Jones and Salzman equally share a 50 percent interest, with Time Warner controlling the remaining interest. Jones serves as co-CEO and chairman of the new company, which has a broad-ranging, multi-media focus including programming for network, cable, and syndicated television; motion pictures; magazine publishing; live entertainment; direct response marketing; and interactive projects for home entertainment and educational applications.

QDE launched *Vibe*, a magazine that was Jones's brainchild. It was conceived as an entertaining chronicle of "contemporary cool," targeted to young urban consumers. The magazine is published as a co-venture with Time Inc. Ventures. Another of QDE's publishing co-ventures is with Time Life's Custom Publishing Division. Together they have issued *African Americans: Voices of Triumph*, a three-volume reference highlighting the scientific, cultural, and social achievements of African Americans.

In the feature film area, QDE has a number of projects in active development and a "first look" agreement with Warner Bros. Pictures. Jones continues his work in television as the creator and executive producer of the popular sitcom *Fresh Prince of Bel-Air* and as executive producer of another sitcom, *In the House*, starring rapper L.L. Cool J. The most recent addition to his television repertoire is Fox Television's *Mad TV*. QDE was also tapped to produce the sixty-eighth annual Academy Awards show on March 25, 1996.

The Quincy Jones and David Salzman collaboration continues in the interactive arena with the formation of *QD7*, a joint venture with multi-media publisher 7th Level, Inc., to develop and publish interactive multi-media titles. The first release was *Q's Jook Joint*, a CD-ROM project chronicling the history of African American music through a retrospective of Jones's broad and diverse career.

Still in an expansion mode, Jones became involved with television broadcasting through a partnership with Tribune Broadcasting; Hall of Fame football player and radio station owner Willie Davis; television producer Don Cornelius; and television talk show host Geraldo Rivera to form Qwest Broadcasting, a minority-controlled broadcasting company. With Jones as the company's chairman and chief executive officer, the group has already purchased stations WATL-TV in Atlanta and WNOL-TV in New Orleans for a reported $167 million. These purchases make Qwest one of the largest minority-owned broadcasting companies in the country.

The combination of Jones's phenomenal creative talent, entrepreneurial instincts, practical business acumen, and his passionate love of music have positioned him as one of the most powerful people in the entertainment industry. The evidence of his unparalleled contributions to the music scene is apparent with the numerous awards and citations bestowed upon him for excellence in his field, including twenty-six Grammy Awards—the most of any living honoree in the history of the award.—PAULETTE COLEMAN

BARBARA JORDAN

1936–1996
Politician, lawyer, educator

What made Barbara so special? "Along with all her superior intelligence and legislative skill she also has

a certain moral authority and a . . . presence, and it all comes together in a way that sort of grabs you,

you may be intimidated by it, and you have to listen when she speaks and you feel you must try and do

what she wants. What Barbara has is not something you learn and develop, it's something that God gave

her and it's something you can't really describe." So said Congressman Charles Wilson in 1975 about

Barbara Charline Jordan, whom he called "the most influential member of Congress." Jordan gained

national recognition as a politician first in the Texas State Senate and then in the United States House

of Representatives, where she had a nationwide television audience as the House Judiciary committee

considered articles of impeachment against President Richard M. Nixon.

Barbara Jordan was born February 21, 1936, in the segregated city of Houston, Texas. After graduating from Phillis Wheatley High School in 1952 she attended Texas Southern University, where she earned a degree in government before enrolling in Boston University's Law School. Once in Boston, Jordan competed with white students in a nonsegregated setting for the first time, and the adjustment was not easy. She felt that she "learned at twenty-one that you just couldn't say a thing is so because it might not be so, and somebody brighter, smarter, and more thoughtful would come out and tell you it wasn't so. . . . I was doing sixteen years of remedial work in thinking." She worked hard to overcome her perceived deficiencies. Her religious life began to change also from a focus on God's prohibitions to one on God's love under the influence of Howard Thurman's sermons. She was one of just two black women in the graduating class of 128. Shortly after graduation in 1959, she passed both the Massachusetts and Texas bar exams.

Although Jordan was offered a job in Massachusetts, she opted to open a private practice in Texas. She was soon involved in the 1960 presidential campaign, working for the Kennedy-Johnson ticket. Her first political success came when she developed a highly organized black-worker program for the forty predominantly black precincts of Harris County and managed to get an 80 percent voter turnout, the most successful get-out-the-vote campaign in Harris County that anyone could recall.

Barbara Jordan.

Jordan became increasingly involved in Texas politics in the early 1960s: she was speaker for the Harris County Democratic Party and ran unsuccessfully for the Texas House of Representatives in 1962 and 1964. Jordan's family pressured her to marry, but she made a decision to commit her life to politics. "I couldn't have it both ways," she said. "I reasoned that this political thing was so total in terms of focus that, if I formed an attachment [like marriage], this total commitment would become less than total."

In 1965, Harris County was reapportioned and Jordan found herself in a newly created Eleventh State Senatorial District. In the new district, she won against a popular liberal by a two-to-one margin. Harris County elected two blacks that year—Jordan to the Senate and Curtis Graves to the House. When she went to Austin, the state capital, Jordan worked hard to fit in, because she was the first black elected to the Texas State Senate since 1883 as well as the first woman ever elected. She took this opportunity to hone her political skills. One aspect of this was to know how things worked; she later said: "If you're going to play the game properly, you'd better know every rule." This meant knowing the unwritten rules as well. In an *Ebony* article, Charles Sanders describes her skills in the game:

> She not only dazzled [members of the Texas delegation] with her intellectual brilliance but also with her knowledge of their kind of rough-and-tumble politics. . . . She never permitted the men of the "club" to feel uncomfortable around her. She could smoke and drink Scotch—just like them. She could tone down her Boston University kind of speech and talk Texas lingo—just like them. She knew as much as they did, or more, about such things as oil depletion allowances and cotton prices and the Dallas money market, but she never, says one member of the "club," made men "feel like we had a smart-aleck, know-it-all woman on our hands."

In her six years in the Texas Senate, she "sponsored most of the state's environmental legislation, authored the first Texas minimum wage law, forced the state to place anti-discrimination clauses in all of its business contracts, and pushed the first package of urban legislation through a rural-minded state government dominated by white males," *Ebony* noted. She served in the Texas Senate until 1972, when she chose to run for the U.S. House of Representatives and won, taking office in January of 1973.

Defense of the Constitution brings national acclaim   When Jordan was elected to Congress, she asked Lyndon Johnson's advice on which committee assignments to request. Johnson advised her to request the Judiciary Committee and made arrangements to assure her assignment. In retrospect, that assignment turned into a major task; the Watergate Scandal put pressure on Congress, prompting the Judiciary Committee to initiate impeachment proceedings against President Richard Nixon. Although she originally argued against public speeches on the subject, Jordan received no support for that position, and her fifteen-minute, nationally televised speech on the duty of elected officials to defend the Constitution catapulted her into the public eye as nothing she had ever done before. Jordan disliked the idea of impeachment but felt that the evidence demanded that an indictment of Nixon be presented to the Senate. In her July 25, 1974, speech in favor of impeachment she used all her skills as a lawyer and as an orator to defend the constitutional issues that she felt were pertinent to her decision, and to persuade others of the rectitude of her position. *Newsweek* called her speech "the most memorable indictment of Richard Nixon to emerge from the House impeachment." She began by saying:

*Barbara Jordan makes an impassioned speech
to the United Auto Workers Union.*

"We the people"—it is a very eloquent beginning. But when the Constitution of the United States was completed on the seventeenth of September in 1787, I was not included in that "We the People." I felt for many years that somehow George Washington and Alexander Hamilton just left me out by mistake. But through the process of amendment, interpretation, and court decision, I have finally been included in "We the people."

Today I am an inquisitor. I believe hyperbole would not be fictional and would not overstate the solemnness that I feel right now. My faith in the Constitution is whole. It is complete. It is total. I am not going to sit here and be an idle spectator in the diminution, the subversion, the destruction of the Constitution.

She then moved through the case against Nixon, concluding:

Has the President committed offenses and planned and directed and acquiesced in a course of conduct which the Constitution will not tolerate? That is the question. We know that. We should now forthwith proceed to answer the question. It is reason and not passion which must guide our decision.

In the first session of her first term, the Omnibus Crime Control and Safe Streets Act came up for renewal. Jordan proposed a civil rights amendment to mandate the use of federal funds in a nondiscriminatory fashion. She also introduced a bill proposing the repeal of the Fair Trade Laws, which had allowed manufacturers to establish retail prices and to enforce them, a price-fixing mechanism that had interfered with free competition.

Her reputation as one of the great orators of the twentieth century was sustained by her keynote address to the 1976 Democratic National Convention. She said that "we cannot improve on the system of government handed down to us by the founders of the Republic, but we can find new ways to implement that system and realize our destiny." She went on to quote Abraham Lincoln, evoking his idea of "a national community in which every last one of us participates; 'As I would not be a *slave,* so I would not be a *master.*' This expresses my idea of democracy. Whatever differs from this, to the extent of the difference, is no democracy."

In 1978 she decided against running for Congress again and, in effect, retired into a teaching position at the Lyndon B. Johnson School of Public Affairs at the University of Texas at Austin. In 1982 she was appointed to the Lyndon B. Johnson Centennial Chair in National Policy. She served as a faculty advisor, a minority recruiter, and a teacher at the University of Texas at Austin.

Jordan said that she left Congress because she "felt more of a responsibility to the country as a whole, as contrasted with the duty of representing the half-million people in the Eighteenth Congressional District. I felt some necessity to address national issues. I thought that my role now was to be one of the voices in the country defining where we were, where we were going, what the policies were that were being pursued, and where the holes in those policies were. I felt I was more in an instructive role than a legislative role."

An academic invitation was the catalyst that led her to the decision to leave political office. She received a letter from Harvard University saying they had voted to give her an honorary doctorate at the next commencement. A month later another letter came from Harvard inviting her to speak at that commencement. Thinking about the speech at Harvard led her to the conclusion that she had to "leave elected politics . . . to free my time in such a way that it could be structured by the country's needs as I perceived them."

Health problems began to seize Jordan, which also may have prompted her retirement from politics. In 1988, Jordan nearly drowned in her backyard pool. This incident led to a diagnosis of mulitple sclerosis. The disease confined her to a wheelchair but never slowed Jordan at the campus of University of Texas. She gained the respect and reverence of her students, who lovingly referred to her as "BJ."

After fifteen years away from the political arena, Jordan was called back to uphold the document she loved so, the Constitution. In 1994, because of widespread concern over illegal immigration, President Bill Clinton created a task force to address this issue, and he appointed Jordan as its chairperson. Jordan believed that illegal immigrants should be entitled to tax-paid benefits only in the case of health emergencies and school lunches. Her committee began to create a national employment registry to monitor immigration. This plan, which Jordan created, received much praise from politicians and the public. Because of her enormous contributions, President Clinton awarded Jordan with the Presidential Medal of Freedom in 1995.

On January 17, 1996, Barbara Jordan, at the age of 59, died of viral pneumonia complicated by her bout with leukemia. She is buried in the Texas State Cemetery, the first and only black woman there. Blessed with an incredible voice and stirring words, she electrified everyone who listened, and people did listen.—JAMES DUCKWORTH

MICHAEL **JORDAN**
1963–
Athlete

Professional basketball hero and superstar Michael Jordan, sometimes called "His Airness," is known worldwide as a phenomenal player who has brought success to the Chicago Bulls and the National Basketball Association. An entertaining, skillful, and hard-driving athlete, Jordan appears to soar through the air as he winds his way through opponents and heads for the basket. His versatility makes him an appealing player who draws crowds wherever he plays. Jordan has brought tremendous attention to the game of basketball as well as to the products that he endorses.

Born in Brooklyn, New York, on February 17, 1963, Michael Jordan is the fourth child born to James Raymond and Delores Peoples Jordan. He has two brothers, James Roland and Larry, and two sisters, Delois and Roslyn. The family lived in Brooklyn for a short time, then returned home to Wilmington, North Carolina, where Michael Jordan was raised. James Jordan was an equipment supervisor for General Electric, then became owner of a retail business, while Delores Jordan was a customer-service supervisor at a bank. Lynn Norment wrote in *Ebony* that Delores and James Jordan "wanted to rear children with strong moral character, confidence, high self-esteem, and who would feel that they would accomplish whatever goals they set." Love was predominant in the Jordan household. Michael Jordan and his siblings followed rules and attended to family chores. At times, however, young Michael was able to persuade his brother Larry to do his chores, sometimes

*Michael
Jordan.*

paying for his service. During the family's regular dinnertime, the Jordan children were encouraged to discuss school and other activities. "Church, like school, was not an option," wrote Norment.

Young Michael Jordan was always unselfish, happy-go-lucky, and competitive; he preferred older playmates. He worked hard to achieve the goals that he set for himself in basketball. Using a backyard court that James Jordan built for sons Michael and Larry, the young men played one-on-one with each other and competed with friends as well. Since Larry was taller, Michael developed a fierce determination to win. The hustle that he developed earned him the nickname "Rabbit."

Jordan played Little League baseball but at first was too small for the varsity basketball team at Wilmington's Laney High School, where he studied. At the beginning of his sophomore year he made the basketball team but was soon cut. That same year he played on the football team for a brief period, and played baseball and ran track. He grew rapidly between his sophomore and junior year, from five feet, eleven inches to six feet, three inches, and became a promising basketball player. He already had the ability to high-jump. At the end of his junior year Jordan played with the summer Five Star Basketball Camp in Pittsburgh, where big-time college prospects trained. Before his senior year began, he had accepted a scholarship offer from the University of North Carolina at Chapel Hill. By then Jordan had grown to six feet, six inches. Meanwhile, his high school coach, Clifton Herring, encouraged him further and drove him to the gymnasium for extra practice during his senior year. The more Jordan practiced, the more proficient he became.

In 1981 Jordan enrolled at UNC to pursue a major in geography; he roomed with Buzz Peterson, a white reserve player who later introduced Jordan to golf. In turn, Jordan taught Peterson to play pool. Jordan was a starter for UNC in his freshman season, scored low, but was brilliant in clutches. He had the inspiration of his parents, who attended his games in Chapel Hill and on the road. In the NCAA finals he scored a corner jumper for coach Dean Smith's Tarheels, giving the team a one-point victory over Georgetown, and giving Smith his first title in his twenty-four-year career at UNC. Jordan and Smith had mutual respect and a special rapport that has lasted over the years. Jordan was voted the Atlantic Coach Conference Rookie of the Year for 1981–82 and, due to his winning shot, was nicknamed "Superman" and "Last Shot." In 1982–83 he was unanimously chosen All-American. Twice the *Sporting News* named him College Player of the Year, in 1982–83 and 1983–84. *Current Biography* quotes the *Sporting News* for 1983 in its description of Jordan, who developed a technique that still characterizes him: "He soars through the air, he rebounds, he scores . . . , he blocks shots, he makes steals. Most important, he makes late plays that win games."

Jordan toured with various all-star teams in the summer of 1983; he was a star in the Pan American Games held in Caracas and helped the U.S. basketball team win the gold medal. The next summer he was a member of the U.S. Olympic team, under Bob Knight's leadership, and won the gold medal at the games held in Los Angeles.

Jordan becomes a Bull   The Chicago Bulls had made no National Basketball Association (NBA) playoffs since 1980–81. It was now 1984 and they needed to pull themselves out of the doldrums. They chose Jordan third in the pro draft of college players. He accepted their seven-figure, five-year contract, dropped out of UNC after three years, and became an instant success as a professional player. While his parents wanted him to get his college degree first,

401

*Michael Jordan's Bulls playing against
the Detroit Pistons in 1988.*

they continued to support him and attended his games. The Bulls saw an 87 percent increase
in attendance, while NBA road attendance soared. In 1984–85 Jordan led the NBA in points
and was named Rookie of the Year and winner of the Seagram Award for the NBA's best
player. He was also a starter for the all-star game that year.

A foot injury in 1985–86 caused Jordan to sit out all but eighteen games. When he
rejoined the team, the Bulls began to win again. Although Jordan scored sixty-three points
in one playoff game, the Bulls were eliminated from post-season play by the Boston Celtics.
Celtics superstar Larry Bird commented that Jordan might really be "God disguised as Michael
Jordan." He won the all-star voting for 1986–87 as well as the slam-dunk championship in the
NBA All-Star weekend in Seattle in February 1987. Again in April 1987, Jordan scored sixty-one
points at Chicago Stadium, but the Bulls lost to the Atlanta Hawks. He then became the second
basketball player behind Wilt Chamberlain to pass the 3,000 mark in a season. He signed a

lucrative contract with Nike to promote its sportswear. The "Air Jordan" athletic shoes became a hot item and led to endorsement contracts with McDonald's, Wilson Sporting Goods, Coca-Cola, Chevrolet, Johnson Products, and Excelsior International, which made "Time Jordan" watches.

With the added talent that Michael Jordan provided, the Bulls continued to develop and in 1991 won the NBA championship over the Los Angeles Lakers. The Bulls were the first team in thirty years to win what was called the "three-peat," or three consecutive NBA championships, defeating the Portland Trail Blazers in 1992 and the Phoenix Suns in 1993. Jordan was named NBA Finals Most Valuable Player in each of the championships. He led the first United States Olympic basketball team of professional players to the 1992 Olympics. The "Dream Team," as the men were called, won the gold medal in the Olympics in 1992 and again in 1996.

Although satisfied with his career performance and the fact that he was still at the top, Jordan announced his retirement from professional basketball on October 6, 1993, and aimed to move on to something else. He emphasized, however, that he would not close the door to basketball permanently. Jordan's retirement came three years before he had planned, but followed the untimely death of his father in the summer of 1993. During an apparent car theft, his father was brutally murdered in North Carolina. In his struggle to deal with the tragedy, Jordan tried his hand at professional baseball with the farm team for the Chicago White Sox. While he was unsuccessful as a player, he stimulated a new interest in baseball and drew crowds wherever he played.

Jordan returned to the Bulls in March 1995. He won his fourth NBA Finals Most Valuable Player Award in June 1996—the only player to hold that record—when he led the Bulls in their victory over the Seattle SuperSonics to win their fourth title in six years. He was overcome with emotion after the win; he grabbed the ball, dropped to the floor, then staggered into the dressing room where he dropped to the floor again and cried. This was on Father's Day, and the memory of his deceased father was painful. Then Jordan left the gym to be alone.

On March 12, 1997, Jordan moved past the total set by former Boston Celtic John Havlicek to become the NBA's sixth all-time leading scorer. In the Bulls' game with the Celtics that night, Jordan had thirty-two points and a career total of 26,399. He continues to break records and dominate the game. Quoted in the *Nashville Tennessean* for April 28, 1997, "M. J. is M. J.," Chicago's Ron Harper told the Associated Press. "We allow him to do his thing. If he wants to take over a game there is nothing Scottie [Pippen] can say or Phil [Jackson] can say to stop it." Jordan said in the same article: "That's my job. That's what I get paid the big bucks for. I want to win. I want to win another championship."

When the NBA held an All-Star Weekend in Cleveland, Ohio, in February 1997, Jordan made all-star history by recording the first triple double, with fourteen points, eleven assists, and eleven rebounds. During halftime, the NBA's fifty greatest players in history were announced; forty-seven legendary players gathered at mid-court to wear jackets with their team's logo. Quoted in *Jet* for February 24, 1997, Jordan, who was one of the fifty honored, told the *Chicago Sun-Times*, "Those early stars are responsible for getting this league off the ground."

As the 1996–97 season drew to a close, the Bulls once again had the best record in the league and seemed poised to capture their fifth championship of the decade. Led by

Jordan, the Bulls breezed through the playoffs until meeting the Utah Jazz in the finals. The Bulls took a two-game lead on the Jazz but then appeared mortal when they dropped two consecutive games. As he had done so many times in the past, however, Jordon stepped up his game, scored thirty-nine points in game six, the last game of the series, and the Bulls won their second consecutive NBA championship, Jordan's fifth of his career. To cap off another remarkable championship run, Jordan was named playoff MVP once again.

Outside the game of basketball, in 1991 and again in 1993 the NBA investigated allegations that Jordan had been involved in gambling activities at card games and on the golf course. The NBA, however, ended its probe without uncovering evidence of wrongdoing. Jordan continued to win games for the Bulls and to gain widespread respect. During his career with the Bulls, team captain Jordan has helped his team obtain seven championships during the 1990s, and two of them have resulted in "three-peats."

During his career Jordan has received numerous awards and recognitions. In addition to the honors previously cited, he was a member of the NBA Eastern Conference All-Star Team each year from 1984 through 1992. He was NBA scoring leader in 1984 and again from 1986 through 1993, and was named NBA Defensive Player of the Year in 1988. In 1991 *Sports Illustrated* named Jordan "Sportsman of the Year."

In 1997, Michael Jordan, Colin Powell, and Tiger Woods were named the most popular Americans in a *Wall Street Journal*/NBC poll.

During his many marketing campaigns for Nike, he was teamed up with cartoon icon Bugs Bunny, and the commericals became an immediate hit. In 1996 Jordan starred in an animated children's film, *Space Jam,* with Bugs Bunny; it was his first movie, and Jordan won praise for his acting and the film was a modest success. In addition to earning about $30 million from his 1996 contract with the Bulls, Jordan makes millions from endorsing such products as athletic wear, beverages, food, and underwear. Jordan's exciting life has been the subject of numerous biographies such as *Jordan: The Man, His Words and His Life, Bull Session: An Up-Close Look at Michael Jordan and Courtside Stories About the Chicago Bulls;* and *For the Love of the Game: Michael Jordan and Me.*

Jordan also gives back to the community. He established the Michael Jordan Foundation and for seven years he has contributed to numerous charities through the foundation. In fall 1996 Jordan and his mother Delores Jordan opened the James Jordan Boys and Girls Club and Family Life Center in Chicago, endowed by $2 million from Jordan and $5 million from the Bulls. The club offers educational, cultural, medical, and child care opportunities, and within its facilities maintains a computer learning center, community health center, and youth and sports leagues.

The six-feet, six-inch-tall Jordan has a slim, athletic build and an effervescent smile that charms his many fans. He is also an avid golfer who demonstrates some skill in that game as well. In 1989 he married Juanita Vanoy, whom he met in 1985. They live in Chicago with their three children, Jeffrey, Marcus, and Jasmine.

Jordan's incredible method of handling a basketball and ability to defy gravity by appearing to float in the air enables him to dazzle crowds wherever he plays. He consistently demonstrates that what has been said about him is true: he transcends professional basketball. Jordan makes every fan of basketball exclaim, "I love this game." A versatile guard who slam-dunks, hits the long shot, and has a successful fade-away shot, Jordan has been regarded by many as the best player in professional basketball's history.—JESSIE CARNEY SMITH

PERCY L. **JULIAN**

1899–1975

Scientist, educator, entrepreneur, inventor

Percy Julian is recognized worldwide as a productive organic chemist, a trailblazer whose discoveries are important in medicine and industry. Julian began his brilliant career as a college chemistry teacher and progressed to research in an industrial laboratory, then to the establishment of his own business. His contributions include creating the synthesis of chemicals that made less expensive pharmaceuticals for patients, in the form of physostigmine and cortisone.

Percy Julian, the oldest of six children by James Julian, a railway mail clerk, and Margaret Julian, a school teacher, was born on April 11, 1899, in Montgomery, Alabama. His father was a strict disciplinarian and a perfectionist, barely tolerant of less than top performance from his children. Young Percy, an excellent student, responded to the encouragement of his father to develop his early interest in science. Since there were no public high schools for black students in Montgomery in the early 1900s, he went from the small elementary school to a mission school that had been established for ex-slave children after the Civil War. When his parents saw the lack of motivation and challenge there, they sent him to the State Normal School for Negroes in his hometown.

After Percy graduated from normal school and was contemplating college, he read about the accomplishments of St. Elmo Brady, the first African American to earn a Ph.D. in chemistry. The young man took this news as inspiration to continue his study of science. Although he had not attended an accredited high school, he applied to colleges

Percy Julian.

that seemed to offer the training he wanted. In 1916, when Julian was seventeen, he was admitted to DePauw University in Greencastle, Indiana, in the probationary status of "sub-freshman." He took high school classes in the Ashbury Academy concurrently with freshman and sophomore courses at DePauw to achieve regular student classification. By the end of the second year, having fulfilled the secondary school admission requirements, Julian was a full-fledged college student. In this period, the Julian family moved to Greencastle, where each of the six children graduated from DePauw and began professional careers.

The reward of Julian's four years of long hours and hard work came in 1920 when he achieved a bachelor of science degree from DePauw. He ranked highest in grade point average of the class of 160 students, was named valedictorian, and was elected to Phi Beta

Kappa. Entering graduate school would be the next step in his ambition to emulate St. Elmo Brady's path to a doctorate in chemistry.

To Julian's disappointment, graduation proved to be the signal for racial restrictions that presented major challenges to his future plans. His record as a student was ample preparation to work as an assistant teacher or research assistant while he was a graduate student, but the racial climate of the 1920s prevented him from following his classmates with similar aspirations and qualifications. Instead of giving him employment at a university reflective of his academic studies, Julian's advisors suggested that he consider teaching at a "Negro" school in the South, where a doctorate was not a requirement. Still nursing a desire for further study and a research position, he accepted an appointment to teach chemistry at Fisk University in Nashville, Tennessee. His department head was Thomas W. Talley, the professor who had encouraged Brady to enter the University of Illinois to work for his doctorate.

Julian taught at Fisk for two years, leaving in 1922 with the Austin graduate fellowship in chemistry to study at Harvard University in Cambridge, Massachusetts. One year later, in 1923, he was awarded a master's degree in organic chemistry. Again he had graduated with the best grades of any other student, but was still unable to find an appropriate teaching or research appointment to subsidize uninterrupted graduate course work. Julian remained at Harvard for three years after the master's degree without adequate support and made small progress toward the doctorate.

With diminishing faith that reliable financial assistance would come to his rescue, in 1926 Julian postponed further study and went to another small school. He taught chemistry to African American students in West Virginia State College's one-person department with almost nonexistent equipment and no staff. With no support services, he taught classes, swept and mopped the floors, did research, and performed every other chore for the classroom and laboratory. It became impossible for him to pursue his research goals with the limited facilities at West Virginia State College. Still seeking advancement, he spent the next two years, from 1927 to 1929, at Howard University in Washington, D.C., lecturing in chemistry and developing that department.

At Howard, Julian revived his intense interest in research that had reached its peak during the first year at Harvard. He had begun by investigating the properties of proteins and the linkage of carbon atoms in plants and animals that results in the production of materials that can cure sickness in human beings. Percy wanted to understand the phenomenon of living cells creating materials with healing qualities, and then duplicate them. His ultimate goal was to produce synthetic materials more easily obtainable at lower costs, which would ease the financial burden of patients.

While Percy was at Howard, he secured a grant from the General Education Board and additional financial assistance from supportive friends to leave for Vienna, Austria, in June 1929, to study with Ernst Spath at the University of Vienna. He lived in Spath's home and developed the deep friendship and supportive relationship between professor and student. Julian increased his knowledge of organic chemistry by studying the natural substances in soybeans that produce physostigmine, useful in the treatment of glaucoma. He joined a number of scientists in many countries who wanted to replace soybeans, an extremely expensive source of physostigmine, with a synthetic material having the same properties. After much perseverance, he finally received his Ph.D. from the University of Vienna in

1931, fifteen years after graduation from high school and his initial commitment to follow St. Elmo Brady.

With doctorate in hand, Julian returned to Howard University in 1931, this time as head of the chemistry department, with two German assistants from the University of Vienna. The following year, 1932, he returned to DePauw to teach and conduct research on physostigmine, assisted by Josef Pikl, one of his assistants from Germany, and two senior students. With his research going strong, Percy briefly paused to wed Ann Johnson, a sociology teacher from Howard University, on December 24, 1935. They had three children. He continued the study of physostigmine and published the first of his monographs in the *Journal of the American Chemical Society,* attracting nationwide attention. Aside from the scientific significance of Julian's research, the article was notable because he was the first African American senior author of an article in a major chemistry journal in the United States. At DePauw, Julian came to a major breakthrough by developing a synthetic chemical similar to natural physostigmine.

Develops treatment for glaucoma   In a dramatic moment in 1935, in the presence of W. M. Blanchard, the school's dean, Julian made the crucial confirmation that the synthetic chemical sample produced in his laboratory, and contained in the test tube he held in his hand, had the identical melting point as the natural physostigmine in Pikl's cylinder. Julian had reached a discovery that had evaded scientists for almost a century. When chemists all over the world read of his success in the *Journal of the American Chemical Society,* congratulations poured in to acknowledge the importance of the synthetic drug in the treatment of glaucoma and other muscle conditions.

Disappointed, but not surprised when DePauw's faculty did not approve Blanchard's proposal to appoint him head of the chemistry department, Julian knew that opportunities for African Americans were still defined by racial attitudes regardless of stature in their field of work. Hoping for better conditions, Julian did not hesitate to accept the position of director of research at Glidden Company in Chicago, starting in 1936. Glidden, makers of paints, varnishes, metals, and industrial chemicals, knew the value of soybeans—specifically for casein, a protein that can be extracted from the beans—to manufacture paints in its large industrial laboratory, but wanted a less expensive synthesis to create the same product.

Julian did not succeed in making synthetic casein, but using a new factory and new equipment he designed himself, he extracted a protein substance similar to casein to be used to coat paper so that it would not absorb ink. This discovery proved to be a financial bonus that made a profit for Glidden of more than $100,000 in its first year. In the absence of synthetic casein, he found other valuable uses for soybean proteins, including Aero-Foam. Many lives were saved in World War II by this fire-fighting foam, which was effective in oil or gasoline fires on ships and planes when water was ineffective.

Julian experimented with another component of soybean oils—sterols—a substance found in human sex hormones, testosterone and progesterone, which regulate male and female sexual development and other human characteristics, including immunity against disease. Despite the difficulty in penetrating the oil to reach the sterols, Julian was successful in producing the hormones chemically instead of by the costlier method of using organs and secretions of cattle. Testosterone and progesterone are used primarily to help women during

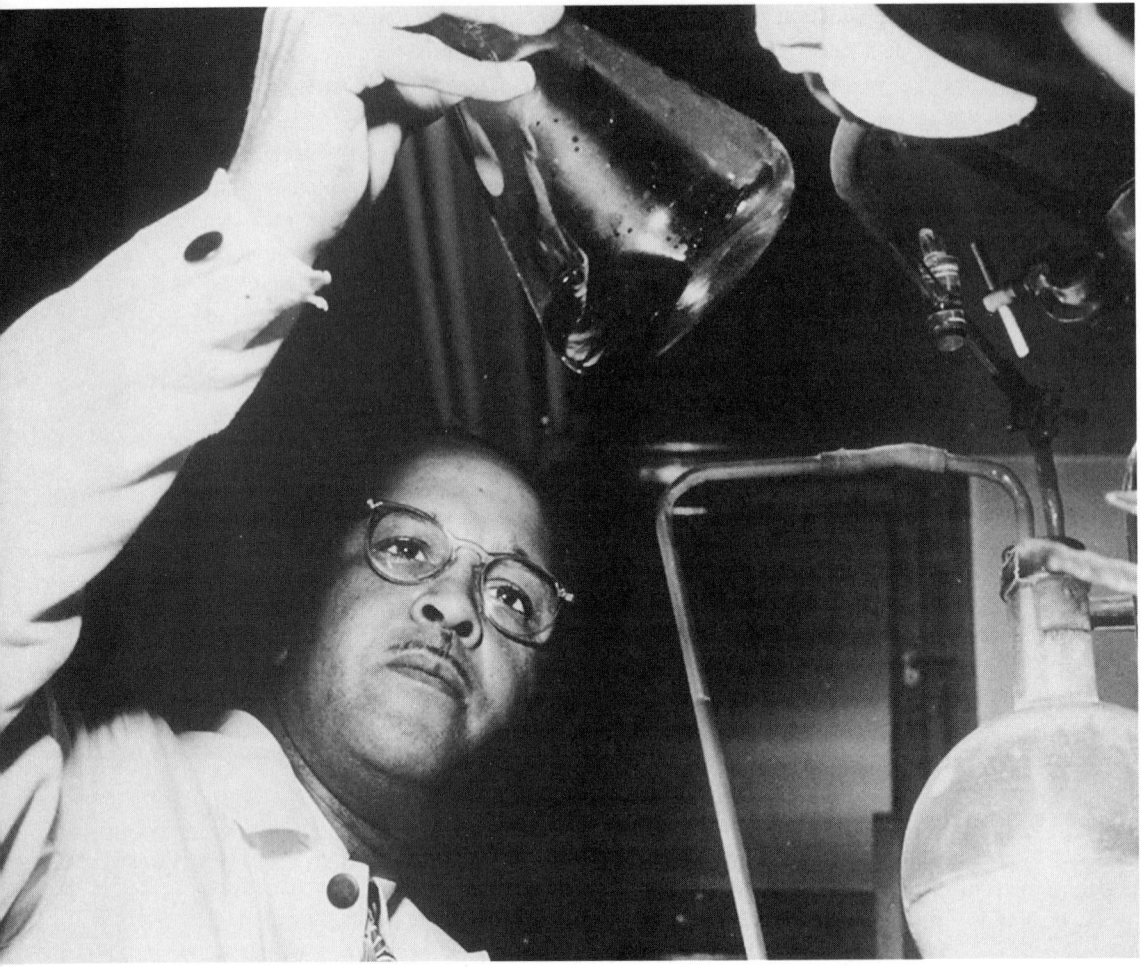

*Percy Julian in
his laboratory.*

pregnancy, increase the virility of young or older men, treat infertility, and in some cases, treat women with breast cancer.

A treatment for arthritis   Perhaps Julian's greatest achievement came in 1949 at Glidden when he created a synthesis of cortisone, a hormone produced in the adrenal gland and useful for the relief of arthritis pain. Because natural cortisone from animal bile is not practical for widespread use due to cost, Julian's synthesis, cortexolone or Compound S, was widely acclaimed by the medical profession. Use of the synthesis is not confined to arthritis, but extends to allergies, asthma, and patients whose immune systems may be overactive. Cortisone has become an inexpensive ointment to relieve itching caused by insect bites, poison oak, or poison ivy.

After seventeen years of making great strides in research, Julian left Glidden in 1953. The next step was to open his own businesses. Julian Laboratories in Franklin Park, Illinois, started in 1954, and Laboratorios Julian de Mexico in Mexico City was established in 1955. He and his partner, organic chemist Russell Marker, learned that they could use the wild yams in Mexico for sterols, and within a short time developed a profitable business. Julian sold the firm in 1961 to Smith, Kline, and French, an American pharmaceutical firm based in Philadelphia.

Education, career success, standing in the international community, or other aspects of good citizenry did not insulate Percy and his family from racist incidents. In 1950, after they bought a home in the all-white suburb of Oak Park, Illinois, and not long after he had been named Chicagoan of the Year, the Julians received threatening telephone calls before they moved in, and it took fear of court action to persuade the water commissioner to turn on the water for the property. Once they settled in the house, a bomb thrown from a speeding car landed inside, but fortunately, no one was injured. In 1951, the Union League Club in Chicago refused entry to Julian at a luncheon for distinguished industrialists and scientists because of its policy against the presence of black people.

In semi-retirement, Julian conducted research but also started two small companies in 1964: the Julian Research Institute and Julian Associates. Although suffering from the effects of cancer of the liver and confined to a wheelchair, he still controlled the businesses and worked as a consultant for Smith, Kline, and French until he no longer had the strength. Julian remained active in his research until his death on April 19, 1975.

Numerous well-deserved honors have been bestowed upon Percy Lavon Julian: the NAACP's 1947 Spingarn Medal; the City of Chicago's 1950 Chicagoan of the Year award; an honorary doctor of science degree from Northwestern University in 1951; and the American Institute of Chemists' 1964 Honor Scroll award and its 1968 Chemical Pioneer award. In 1985, the Illinois state senate passed a resolution in tribute to Julian, the governor issued a proclamation in his honor, and the Oak Park, Illinois Elementary School District No. 97 renamed a junior high school after him. In 1990, Percy Julian and George Washington Carver were elected posthumously to the National Inventors Hall of Fame, culminating a ten-year crusade by the National Patent Lawyers Association, a group of minority lawyers. In 1994, the U.S. Postal Service sold stamps with his picture, honoring Percy's many achievements.

Percy's research had humane as well as commercial value: industrial plants could increase their production output and physicians could hasten the healing process by use of the pharmaceuticals that resulted. Although gratified by each of his successes, his biggest reward was to see the effects of his discoveries in the healing of patients, and to know that he had a part in lessening someone's suffering.

One measure of Julian's success as a research chemist is that he applied for and was granted more than one hundred patents in the span of his career. The patents gave him the exclusive right to manufacture, use, or sell the results of his mental powers—inventions and designs he conceived in his fruitful years as a scientific investigator.

Julian leaves a legacy of dedication and perseverance for African Americans inside the scientific fields. He identified his life's work before he left high school, and learned to cope with setbacks by restructuring his immediate plan of action without abandoning the ultimate end. It was not always easy for the gifted man to put aside his personal disappointments without losing hope for what was ahead, but his experiences paved the way for African American professionals who would come after him.—DONA L. IRVIN

ERNEST EVERETT **JUST**
1883–1941
Biologist, educator, author

Ernest Everett Just was described in Science *as the "best investigator in the field of biology that his people [had] produced." He made lasting contributions to the study of cellular physiology, experimental embryology, and fertilization, and earned international recognition for his research into the embryological resources of marine biology. Among the few scientifically-trained people of color of his era, he served as professor and head of the Howard University Department of Zoology from 1912 to 1941 and taught physiology in the Howard Medical School from 1912 to 1920.*

Ernest Everett Just pioneered by incorporating research into medical instruction, which at Howard and numerous other institutions had traditionally relied on part-time practitioners. He achieved success early in his career and in 1915 won the NAACP's first Spingarn Medal. According to Keith R. Manning in *Black Apollo of Science,* the medal was to be awarded to an individual of "African descent" who had performed "the foremost service to his race." In his examination of marine life reproductive systems, Just went beyond the naturalistic focus of many contemporaries by taking into account external environmental factors and holistic perspectives. As his career progressed, Just attracted the attention of wealthy philanthropists interested in supporting his work, thereby stimulating his impulse to concentrate on laboratory research.

Just was born in Charleston, South Carolina, on August 14, 1883. He was the third of five children born to Mary Matthews Cooper Just and Charles Fraser Just. An older brother and sister died before Ernest Just was a year old; he grew up with younger siblings, Hunter and Inez. Ernest Just was regarded as quite handsome with a broad and prominent forehead and slender frame; he was deeply sensitive, gentle, quiet, scholarly, and dignified. On June 26, 1912, he married Ethel Highwarden, a native of Columbus, Ohio, whom he had met shortly after both had become instructors at Howard. The couple had three children, Margaret, Highwarden, and Maribel. In 1939, Just divorced his wife and married Hedwig Schnetzler, a philosophy doctoral student he had met in Berlin. In 1940, Ernest and Hedwig Just had a daughter, Elisabeth. Just died of cancer on October 27, 1941, at the Washington, D.C., home of his sister Inez, and he was buried in Washington in the Lincoln Cemetery.

Ernest Just grew up in Charleston, South Carolina, where his father and paternal grandfather had served as construction workers in the Charleston harbor, building some of the largest docks in the region. Ernest Just was raised by his mother after his father died when Ernest was only four years old. A devout Christian, Mary Just supported her family by opening a school in Charleston. She also established a farming and industrial cooperative near phosphate fields along the Ashley River, an area eventually designated in her honor as Maryville. Just studied at his mother's school where he enjoyed his earliest formal education, and at age thirteen he enrolled in the academy of South Carolina State College at Orangeburg, a public school for blacks, where he remained from 1896 to 1899.

Early years as student and instructor

With strong encouragement from his mother, Just became an excellent student. He left South Carolina in 1899, working his way to New York on the Clyde Shipping Line. Reading the *Christian Endeavor World*, he learned about the Kimball Union Academy in Meriden, New Hampshire. He enrolled at Kimball in the fall term of 1900, completed the four-year classical program in three years, edited the student newspaper, presided over the debating society, and graduated as the top student in the class of 1903.

Upon graduation Just moved to Hanover, New Hampshire, to study at Dartmouth College where he had been awarded a scholarship. As an undergraduate he continued his outstanding academic career, excelling in Greek and majoring in history and biology under professors Herbert D. Foster and William Patten, respectively. He earned honors in history, biology, and sociology, and "special honors" in zoology; he was awarded a Rufus Choate Scholarship, and graduated *magna cum laude* in 1907 with a B.A. and membership in Phi Beta Kappa.

In the fall semester of 1907, Just was appointed instructor in English and rhetoric at Howard University; he taught first in the Teachers College and the Commercial College, then in the College of Arts and Sciences. Just arrived during the rapidly expanding administration of President Wilbur Patterson Thirkield (1906–1912). Thirkield had strengthened professional education by organizing departments into schools; he also expanded instruction in music, theology, the natural sciences, and engineering.

In this arena of reorganization and growth, Just applied his skills both in and out of the classroom. Well received as a teacher, he also founded the College Dramatic Club, the first such group at Howard, and collaborated with professors Benjamin G. Brawley and Marie Moore-Forrest on a number of dramatic productions that laid the foundation for later professional instruction in drama. Just became a founding member of Omega Psi Phi, a national fraternity of black students; he had succeeded in promoting the value of such organizations to Howard's white administrators.

In 1909, Just altered the course of his academic career, taking on graduate studies in biology at the Marine Biological Laboratory in Woods Hole, Massachusetts. President Thirkield had recognized in Just a keen intellect and induced him to abandon English, develop his scientific abilities, and plan to conduct research in the laboratories then under construction at Howard. Just continued his work during subsequent summers and earned a Ph.D. in zoology from the University of Chicago in 1916. He was influenced and supported greatly throughout his career by Chicago professor Frank R. Lillie, whom he assisted on an investigation of the breeding practices of sea-urchins and marine worms.

Just published his first paper in the *Biological Bulletin* in 1912, and by the time he had completed doctoral studies he had published several more papers and was heavily engaged in teaching. While a professor in the medical school, he taught pharmacy, dental, and medical students in the mornings and zoology students in the College of Arts and Sciences in the afternoons.

Ernest Just.

Success and recognition Just's career took a new turn in 1920 when Lillie introduced him to Julius Rosenwald, the famous philanthropist who had supported the Tuskegee Institute and built hundreds of YMCAs and school buildings for Southern blacks. Rosenwald became concerned that a scientist of Just's stature was being denied access to the much better equipped research staff and facilities in the major public and private universities that were serving whites only. Thus began a series of grants, primarily in support of Just's research, by the Rosenwald Fund (1920–27, 1928–33), the Rockefeller Foundation (1925–30), the General Education Board (1928–33), the Carnegie Foundation (1934–35), and the Oberlaender Trust (1936), and the National Research Council (1920–33). With such strong external support, Just was able to leave the medical school faculty while retaining headship of the department of zoology, and was allowed to spend six months or more each year at Woods Hole. This schedule testified to Just's stature as a scientist, and results were soon evident in the form of scholarly production. From 1912 to 1920, while associated with the medical school, Just had published nine papers. Over the next ten years he wrote thirty-eight papers and a book, *General Cytology*, with Lillie, T. H. Morgan, and others, published by the University of Chicago Press.

Just focused on experimental embryology, investigating parthenogenesis, cell division and mutation, and fertilization. He experimented with the detection of electrochemical reactions in cells, reproducing the histological features of human cancer cells. His work on hydration and dehydration in cellular physiology influenced the treatment of nephritis and edema. According to the *Dictionary of American Negro Biography*, he claimed to be the first scientist to have "increased the number of chromosomes in a mammal." His mentor, colleague, and friend, Lillie, described Just's work as so complicated that it would become a "theme for study for many years to come." *Black Apollo of Science* said that Just had become "the current authority on fertilization," conducting research essential to an understanding of heredity and eugenics.

By the late 1920s Just had begun to synthesize his findings in an effort to define the physics and chemistry of protoplasm and to integrate his basic laboratory research into the study of general biology. He presented the conceptual components of these theories in 1930 as one of only twelve zoologists invited to Padua, Italy, to address the General Session of the Eleventh International Congress of Zoologists. He proposed that by analyzing the physiochemical processes of ectoplasm—studying the interactions between inner cellular substances and the external environment—one could begin to understand evolution and, indeed, life itself. His results subsequently appeared in German in *Naturwissenschaft* and in English in the *American Naturalist*.

According to Just, the direction of his research and the results he produced represented a revolution in thinking about biology. Not surprisingly, his reputation continued to accelerate. He was selected as a member of both the Washington Academy of Science and the New York Academy of Sciences (later in life), and as vice-president of the American Society of Zoologists, and was appointed to the editorial boards of *Biological Bulletin, Cytologia, Journal of Morphology, Physiological Zoology,* and *Protoplasma: Zeitschrift fuer Physikalische*

Philanthropic support allowed Just to abandon the Marine Biological Laboratory at Woods Hole in order to spend much of his leave time in European research laboratories. He was guest researcher and the first American to work at the Kaiser Wilhelm Institut für Biologie, Berlin, regarded by many as the world's leading research laboratory, and the Stazione Zoologica in Naples. In Germany, Just became associated with Harnack Haus, and the great German theologian Adolph von Harnack rekindled the zoologist's interest in theological issues that had lain dormant since his youth, thereby planting ideas later developed in Just's studies of biology and philosophy.

Local discontent and international achievement   Ironically, as his scientific prowess and his reputation grew, his relationship to his home institution, Howard University, deteriorated. Despite the annual leave policy, generous by the standards of most university scientists, he began to view his teaching responsibilities as particularly burdensome. This point of view conflicted with the university, which maintained that the Rosenwald grants had been intended not merely for Just's laboratory work but also for strengthening the department of zoology and further developing a cadre of black scientists at the graduate level. These issues exacerbated Just's relationship with Mordecai W. Johnson, Howard president from 1926 to 1960, casting a pall over the zoologist's closing years at his home institution.

Graduate programs in zoology at Howard had begun in 1929 and during the next four years attracted fifteen students. Eight of these graduated with an M.S., yet from 1933 to 1935 only one student was enrolled. Contemporaries likely compared the enrollment decline in zoology with the gradual increases in other subjects offered in Howard's graduate degree programs during the same period. For Just's part, he claimed that Howard had never met its own responsibilities incurred by the Rosenwald funds, to strengthen the infrastructure— space, staff, students, and equipment—for laboratory research. Just argued that Howard was too impoverished as a university to support the training of graduate biologists and zoologists. A solid undergraduate program, which Just had long supported, was more within the range of Howard's financial resources.

Meanwhile, Just was increasingly attracted to Europe and sought foundation support that would allow him to sever his ties with Howard University. Not only had he been welcomed graciously by the scientific community, he was drawn inexorably to the social, artistic, and cultural life of Germany, Italy, and France. Although he did not succeed in attracting the necessary funds, he remained adamant in his desire for association with European research centers. During a leave of absence of more than two and a half years, he worked at the Laboratoire d'Anatomie et d'Histologie Comparées at the University of Paris and at the Sorbonne's Station Biologique de Roscoff. In 1939, he published *The Biology of the Cell Surface,* a book that synthesized much of his laboratory research with new theoretical perspectives, and *Basic Methods for Experiments in Eggs of Marine Animals,* a handbook for laboratory techniques that further solidified his international stature in marine fertilization.

He set himself apart from most research scientists in his pursuit of interdisciplinary relationships. He described the proper approach to the study of life as neither vitalistic nor mechanistic but rather interactive and holistic, and he sought to connect the biological sciences with social philosophy. He studied the writings of philosophers G. W. F. Hegel, Immanuel Kant, and Ernst Mach, but also explored connections with physicists such as Arthur Stanley Eddington, James Hopwood Jeans, Werner Heisenberg, Max von Laue, Max Planck, and Frederich Schröder.

His discontent with Howard University symbolized, in a sense, his quarrel with American society as a whole. He felt rejected by the major white universities, which denied him access to the facilities commensurate with his interests and abilities. And the infrastructure for scientific research at Howard failed to meet his expanding demands as a research scientist. He decried a racial context that accommodated black scientists as medical practitioners but not as laboratory researchers. European society seemed to offer much richer opportunities to pursue his interests. He sought to create a role for himself not as a black scientist whose parameters of intellectual and social activity would be constricted, but rather as a scientist for the entire human race who could pursue his interests without being restrained by the repressive features of American life. Yet, he made a vital contribution to African America's response to a hostile society by advocating objective, scientific methods over the more subjective humanities as a method for pursuing equality of opportunity.

Final struggles   As the decade of the 1930s drew to a close, Europe became less hospitable and less viable as a place to live. The entire continent was being swept into war. The Nazis overran France and in August 1940, interned Just in a camp, probably at Chateaulin. Fortunately, his wife's family was well-connected politically and succeeded—with the aid of officials from Brown-Boveri, an industrial giant with outlets in Germany and Switzerland—in securing Just's release. Soon thereafter, he and Hedwig Just sailed for America.

Just was also suffering financially since he had chosen to remain in Europe without the benefit of consistent income. He never gave up seeking foundation support for his research overseas, but the philanthropic interests had grown increasingly to favor graduate education for black scientists and physicians over laboratory work in basic fields such as biology and zoology. The best hope for Just became the unattractive option of returning to Howard University.

In 1938, Just had appealed to the University for back pay since 1933, claiming that a 1920 agreement gave him a second semester leave each year without a salary reduction, and he also sought retirement income. He had contracted cancer and was able to secure sick leave at half-pay for the spring semester of 1938 out of "consideration for his long services to the University," according to Rayford W. Logan in *Howard University*. Yet in October 1938, the executive committee at Howard agreed only to sick leave at one-third pay, and the committee rejected his retirement claim, arguing that it would not be fair to Just to retire him on a small amount at age fifty-five. Clearly, Howard had hoped to return him to full-time service in order to strengthen the university's scientific programs. Just was given leave without pay for 1939–40 but reinstated at full pay for 1940–41, the last academic year of his life.

Thus, financial concerns and a debilitating disease marred the closing years of a remarkable life. Possessed of a superior and disciplined intellect, Just was destined for success as a scientific researcher. As the years progressed, he continually pressed for opportunities to pursue his research and to live out his dreams unfettered by the racism of an oppressive American society. He faced the dilemma common to black intellectuals—whether to be known as a black scholar or simply as a scholar—and the ambiguities of his final years indicate a less than satisfactory resolution to this dilemma, despite the national and international stature of his scientific achievements.—JOHN MARK TUCKER

B. B. **KING**

1925–
Musician

B. B. King has been a major figure in the development of the blues tradition. His high tenor voice was called by Henry Pleasants in the Grove Dictionary of American Music *"the finest among blues singers." A forerunner of the change from country to urban blues, his technique of playing the electric guitar as a solo instrument influenced a whole generation of young guitar players, and in addition to his musical talent, King is lauded for his ability to communicate with his audiences. Those who know him best admire him as a man as much as they admire his music.*

B. B. King was born on September 16, 1925 to Albert King and Nora Ella Pully King, in a sharecropper's cabin between Itta Bena and Indianola, Mississippi. Albert King was an orphan who named his son after a brother who had disappeared. A second child died in infancy. Around 1930 Nora Ella King left her husband and moved back to the area her family had come from near Kilmichael, Mississippi. Although King lived from time to time with his mother and her two other husbands, he lived most of the time with his maternal grandmother, Elnora Farr, who sharecropped on a farm near Kilmichael. He was present when his mother died during the summer of 1935 at nearby French Camp. According to Charles Sawyer, she told her son: "If you are always kind to people, your kindness will be repaid, one way or another. And you will be happy in your life." Her admonition made a profound impression on him.

Nora Ella King and her mother were deeply religious Baptists. Archie Fair, brother-in-law of Nora Ella King and pastor of a Holiness church near Kilmichael, also had a profound influence on

B. B. King.

young King. By the time he was eight or nine, King was lead singer in the congregational worship at the Holiness church. His uncle also taught him the basics of playing the guitar. The moral precepts he learned in church remained a foundation of his character, but privately King became a skeptic about some church doctrine. Another major influence on King's moral development was the local schoolmaster, Luther Henson, who valued self-esteem and self-improvement.

Elnora Farr died on January 15, 1940, probably of tuberculosis. She owed her landlord $3.63. King stayed on in his grandmother's cottage and took an acre of land to raise cotton. King's financial plan to save the land did not work, and the bank foreclosed. That fall King moved to Lexington, Mississippi, to live with his father and his father's new family. Two years later he rode his bicycle back to Kilmichael, where a white cash tenant, Flake Cartilage, took him in. King was put up in a shed and ate with the family while he worked for his keep.

Begins musical career   Before his departure from Kilmichael in 1940, King had formed a gospel group with his cousin Birkett Davis and Walter Doris Jr. Birkett Davis had moved to Indianola, Mississippi, and in the spring of 1942 King joined him there with a guitar he had borrowed $2.50 to buy. King went to work for Johnson Barrett, who farmed a thousand acres, as a sharecropper and tractor driver, for which he earned a dollar a day. With Birkett Davis and others, King joined a gospel singing group, the Famous St. John Gospel Singers. King soon discovered that he could earn more money by playing and singing the blues on the street in neighboring towns and cities on Saturday evenings than he could by singing gospel music on Sundays. He married Martha Denton on November 26, 1944. The combination of agricultural work and marriage secured him an exemption from the World War II draft and allowed him to pursue a career in music.

King was eager to leave the farm and quickly left for Memphis with $2.50 to try his luck as a musician. His plan involved getting in touch with another cousin, Bukka (Booker T.) White, an established blues musician. King found that Memphis was full of young guitar players who were just as good or better than him. Bukka White nevertheless took the young man in and found him a job. For ten months King devoted himself to improving his guitar playing under White's mentorship. Unable to adopt White's slide technique of playing the guitar because his hands were too large, King discovered a way of slurring pitch by stretching the strings. King was also a competitor at amateur nights at the Palace Theater. King's musical career came to a halt when he returned to Mississippi, to his wife and a financial debt. He made crops in 1947 and 1948, earning enough to clear his debts and have a small stake. Eventually King left for Memphis again.

His second time in Memphis, King became acquainted with Sonny Boy Williamson II (Rice Miller), who had a fifteen-minute radio program on radio station KWEM in West Memphis. Placing King in his program as a substitute for a conflicting gig, Williamson offered him an opportunity to play a song on the radio. This exposure led to a job offer for King to advertise a tonic called Pepticon, which he represented as "the Pepticon Boy." King was now in a position to send for his wife.

As his popularity grew, radio station WDIA made King a disk jockey on his own show, *Sepia Swing Club*. Originally billed as the "Beale Street Blues Boy," he soon became Blues Boy King, which in turn was shortened to B. B. King. King became the first person at WDIA

to be sponsored by a national advertiser, Lucky Strike cigarettes. King ended his association with WDIA in 1953 when the demands associated with touring became too great.

Early in his career, while King was performing a gig in Twist, Alabama, he named his most famous guitar Lucille. There had been a fight in the club over a woman named Lucille, and a tipped-over space heater caused a fire that claimed two lives. Once King was safely outside, he realized he had left his guitar behind. He reentered the burning building and managed to rescue the instrument. The Blues Foundation, based in Memphis, now offers the Lucille Award to aspiring blues musicians.

In 1949 King recorded four sides for Bullet Records. Although the records were only successful locally, they led to his contract with the RPM label of Modern Records. King remained with this label for ten years. Once again, King reaped only local fame from the six RPM records he recorded in 1949.

King wins wide fame among black audiences The increasing demands and pressures of King's career led him to hire Robert Henry, a Memphis pool hall owner and entrepreneur, as a business manager. In the closing days of 1951, RPM's seventh record of King's music made it on Billboard's rhythm and blues charts, reaching number one and remaining there for fifteen weeks. On the strength of that hit, Universal Artists signed King and booked him at the Howard Theater in Washington, D.C., the Royal Theater in Baltimore, and the Apollo Theater in Harlem. King thus began a national tour that lasted six months. Three years earlier he was earning $22.50 driving a tractor; now he was earning $2,500 a week. King spent his new wealth extravagantly, and continued to do so throughout his career. King is also generous with his friends and loves gambling.

The strain of success became too much for the Kings' childless marriage, which was dissolved in 1952. Over the years King acknowledged fathering eight children with other women, only one of whom grew up in his family. His daughter, Shirley, grew up on the farm near Memphis that King had bought for his father. He gave his name to and accepted financial responsibility for his other children.

In 1953 King broke business relations with Robert Henry, who was unversed in the music business beyond the Mississippi, Tennessee, and Arkansas area, and signed with Maurice Merrit, a Texan. With a steady string of records selling around 100,000 copies and dependable audiences, King found reliable back-up musicians and began touring again. The pace was demanding—in 1956 King played 342 one-night stands; this pace continued into the 1980s. Touring was difficult for black musicians, who faced discriminatory situations such as not being served in eating establishments in the South. The constant touring also increased King's likelihood for vehicle accidents. In 1958, his tour bus was involved in a fiery crash in Texas. In 1961 King was thrown through a windshield with his right arm cut to the bone. After treatment, amazingly, he managed to fill his engagement, using his left hand on his electric guitar. This incident illustrates King's determination to fulfill his engagements, which is a constant of his career. Only in recent years has he slackened the pace of his work. In 1990 he was hospitalized in Las Vegas because of his diabetes, uncharacteristically causing him to miss dates at the New Orleans Jazz and Heritage Festival.

On June 4, 1958, King married for a second time. His wife, Sue Carol Hall, was just eighteen, fifteen years younger than her husband. Their childless marriage ended in 1966 as result of King's hectic touring schedule.

Besides the dissolution of his marriage, King faced other problems in 1966. The IRS put a $78,000 lien on his income, and his bus was stolen. And more important still was King's suspicion that he was at an impasse in his music career. Although King was still touring, still selling records in modest numbers, and still appearing before black audiences, he had been unsuccessful as an opening act for the Rolling Stones, who had insisted on using him because of their veneration for his guitar playing. His slow blues opening numbers had been booed.

At the same time, other black performers were achieving the rewards of crossover stardom. Black rock and roll performers had won recognition since the 1950s; Motown, with its black recording stars, was achieving major successes in popular music. Still, contemporary blues was almost completely confined to black audiences who were growing older. Many young blacks were beginning to perceive King's music as old-fashioned. Today, King's audiences run 90 percent white, a fact King deplores since he feels black youth are neglecting their heritage.

King becomes a national star

In 1965 white artist Bob Butterfield and his mixed-race group released the first amplified blues album to have mass distribution; it was a steady seller rather than a one-time hit and attracted attention to black Chicago blues players. Guitar players in particular began to attract attention, a trend furthered by Charles Keil's book, *Urban Blues* (1967), which included a chapter on B. B. King. Moreover, a small coffeehouse in Cambridge, Massachusetts, achieved renown by booking performers like Butterfield, Muddy Waters, and Howlin' Wolf. Word of this success opened other venues across the country.

For King the breakthrough came a little later in 1968 when he received a standing ovation from a largely white audience at San Francisco's Fillmore West even before he played a single note; this occasion marked the first successful appearance before a white audience. Soon thereafter, "The Thrill Is Gone" became a hit, peaking at number fifteen on the pop charts, King's highest rating ever. Subsequent records and albums would regularly make the charts, but never higher than number twenty-eight.

When King hired new manager Sidney A. Seidenberg, a New York accountant who had been keeping his books, Seidenberg immediately began to upgrade the performer's career by moving King to Associated Booking, renegotiating his contract with ABC Records, and raising his minimum booking fee. (King changed labels in 1978 when MCA absorbed ABC.) Top jazz clubs and rock venues now featured King. Perhaps just as important in building a new long-term audience were his appearances on college and university campuses, where he became extremely popular. Guest host Flip Wilson invited him to Johnny Carson's *Tonight Show,* and other television talk shows soon followed. King's appearance on the *Ed Sullivan Show* on October 8, 1970, serves as a symbolic marker of his complete breakthrough to the mass audience. King's career now was on a stable level. He toured Australia and Europe in 1971, did a world tour in 1972, and was invited by the Russian government to perform in the U.S.S.R. in 1979. King, who has also performed in community theaters and in Las Vegas, primarily attracts middle-aged, middle-class Americans, although his music has touched a much broader audience. In 1973 Tougaloo awarded him an honorary doctorate, as did Yale University in 1977.

King is also active in philanthropy. In addition to his appearances at benefit concerts for such organizations as the NAACP and the National Coalition for the Homeless, he was one of the cofounders of the Foundation for the Advancement of Inmate Rehabilitation and

Recreation in 1971. In 1982 he donated his collection of 20,000 records, which includes 7,000 rare blues 78 r.p.m. records, to the Center for the Study of Southern Culture at the University of Mississippi.

In 1971 King received his first Grammy for best rhythm and blues performer, for "The Thrill Is Gone." He later received Grammys for best ethnic or traditional recording in 1982, 1984, 1986, and 1991. In 1987 he was inducted into the Rock & Roll Hall of Fame. The National Academy of Recording Artists and Songwriters (NARAS) gave King a Lifetime Achievement Award in 1988. In 1990 he was awarded the Presidential Medal of Freedom and a star on Hollywood's Walk of Fame. In that same year he rode on the Mississippi float in the Rose Bowl Parade and in the following year led the Sula Social Aid and Pleasure Club float at the Mardi Gras parade in New Orleans. In 1991 King opened the 350-seat B. B. King's Memphis Blues Club in Memphis, Tennessee.

The NARAS Lifetime Achievement Award has perhaps summed up King's accomplishments, asserting that King is "one of the most original and soulful of all blues guitarists and singers, whose compelling style and devotion to musical truth have inspired so many budding performers, both here and abroad, to celebrate the blues."—ROBERT L. JOHNS

MARTIN LUTHER **KING JR.**

1929–1968

Civil rights leader, minister

At the age of twenty-six, Martin Luther King Jr. took up the leadership role that would fill the rest of his life. He furthered the stubborn determination of black Americans to break down the limits of a racist society. His strategy of nonviolent protest brought passage of far-reaching federal legislation that undermined Southern efforts to enforce segregation through local laws. His vision of a just and equal society where race would be transcended fired the imagination of many Americans.

Michael King Jr. was born on January 15, 1929, in the Atlanta home of his maternal grandfather, Adam Daniel Williams (1863–1931). He was the second child and the first son of Michael King Sr. (1897–1984) and Alberta Christine Williams King (1903–1974). Michael Jr. had an older sister, Willie Christine (b. 1927), and a younger brother, Alfred Daniel Williams (b. 1930). The father and later the son adopted the name Martin Luther, after the religious figure who founded the Lutheran denomination.

Michael King Sr. came to Atlanta in 1918. He had known the hard life of a sharecropper in a poor farming country. His father, James Albert King (1864–1933), was irreligious, an alcoholic, and abused his wife, Delia Linsey King (1873–1924). In the fall of 1926, Michael Sr. married Alberta Williams after a courtship of some eight years. The newlyweds moved into A. D. Williams's home.

When Williams died in 1931, Michael King Sr. followed in his father-in-law's footsteps as pastor of Ebenezer Baptist Church. King too became a very successful minister. The King

*Martin Luther
King Jr.*   423

children grew up in a secure and loving environment. As King Jr. said in "An Autobiography of Religious Development," an essay written for a class at Crozer Seminary when he was twenty-three: "It is quite easy for me to think of a God of love mainly because I grew up in a family where love was central and where lovely relationships were ever present."

King Sr. was inclined to be a severe disciplinarian, but his wife's firm gentleness—which was by no means permissive—generally carried the day. The parents could not, of course, shield the young boy from racism. King Sr. did not endure racism meekly; in showing open impatience with segregation and its effects and in discouraging the development of a sense of class superiority in his children, King Sr. influenced his son profoundly.

King Jr. entered public school when he was five. On May 1, 1936, King joined his father's church, being baptized two days later. His conversion was not dramatic—he simply followed his sister when she went forward. A period of questioning religion began with adolescence and lasted through his early college years. He felt uncomfortable with overly emotional religion, and this discomfort led him to decide against entering the ministry.

Jennie Williams, King Jr.'s grandmother, died of a heart attack on May 18, 1941, during a Woman's Day program at Ebenezer. The death was traumatic for her grandson, especially since it happened while he was watching a parade despite his parents' prohibitions. Distraught, he seems to have attempted suicide by leaping from a second-story window of the family home. He wept on and off for days and had difficulty sleeping.

King studied in the public schools of Atlanta, spent time at the Atlanta Laboratory School until it closed in 1942, and then entered public high school in the tenth grade, skipping a grade. After completing his junior year at Booker T. Washington High School, he entered Morehouse College in the fall of 1944 at the age of fifteen. Since the war had taken away most young men, Morehouse, a men's college, turned to young entrants in desperation.

King attends Morehouse   The five-foot, seven-inch King was a ladies' man and loved to dance. He was an indifferent student who completed Morehouse with a grade point average of 2.48 on a four-point scale. At first King was determined not to become a minister, and he majored in sociology. Under the influence of his junior-year Bible class, however, he renewed his faith. Although he did not return to a literal belief in scripture, King began to envision a career in the ministry. In the fall of his senior year he told his father of his decision. King Jr. preached his trial sermon at Ebenezer with great success. On February 25, 1948, he was ordained and became associate pastor at Ebenezer.

King decided to attend Crozer Theological Seminary in Chester, Pennsylvania, a very liberal school. King rose to the challenges of Crozer, earning the respect of both his professors and classmates. In addition to becoming the valedictorian of his class in 1951, he was also elected student body president, won a prize as outstanding student, and earned a fellowship for graduate study. During this time, King also rebelled against his father's conservatism and now made no secret about drinking beer, smoking, and playing pool. He became enamored of a white woman and went through a difficult time before he could bring himself to break off the affair.

During his last year at Crozer, King began to read the iconoclastic theologian Reinhold Niebuhr. Niebuhr and his challenge to liberal theology—and thus, to King's own ideas at the time—became the most important single influence on King's intellectual development, far

Martin Luther King Jr. addresses students
at the University of California in 1968.

surpassing his later interest in Mahatma Gandhi. After being accepted for doctoral study at Yale University, Boston University, and in Edinburgh, Scotland, he enrolled in graduate school at Boston University in the fall of 1951.

As King pursued his graduate studies, he also sought a wife. Early in 1952 he met Coretta Scott, an aspiring singer. She was the daughter of Obie and Bernice Scott, born in Heiberger, Alabama, on April 27, 1927. Growing up on her father's farm, she learned to work hard before attending Antioch College. King's parents opposed the marriage at first, but King prevailed and the marriage took place in June 1953. Martin and Coretta had four children: Yolanda (b. November 17, 1955), Martin Luther III (b. October 23, 1957), Dexter (b. January 30, 1961), and Bernice Albertine (b. March 28, 1963).

In September 1954 while still working on his dissertation, King became pastor of the Dexter Avenue Baptist Church in Montgomery, Alabama. King completed his Ph.D. dissertation comparing the religious views of Paul Tillich and Henry Nelson Wieman, and was awarded the degree in June 1955. In November 1990, scholars confirmed that significant parts of King's dissertation had been taken from the work of a fellow student, Jack Boozer, and one of the subjects of his dissertation, Paul Tillich.

The Montgomery bus boycott begins   On Thursday, December 1, 1955, Rosa Parks refused to give up her seat on a Birmingham bus, setting off a chain of events that cata-pulted King to world fame. Several groups within Montgomery's black community decided to take action against segregated seating on the city buses. The National Association for the Advancement of Colored People (NAACP), the Women's Political Council, the Baptist Ministers

Conference, and the city's African Methodist Episcopal (AME) Zionist ministers united with the community to organize a bus boycott. After a successful beginning of the boycott on Monday, the Montgomery Improvement Association (MIA) came into being that afternoon, and King accepted the presidency. His oratory at that evening's mass meeting roused the crowd's enthusiasm, and the boycott continued. It took 381 days of struggle to bring the boycott to a successful conclusion.

As MIA leader, King became the focus of white hatred. On the afternoon of January 26, King was arrested for the first time, spending some time in jail. About midnight he was awakened by a hate phone call. As he sat thinking of the dangers to his family, he had his first profound religious experience. As he writes in *Stride Toward Freedom:*

> At that moment I experienced the presence of the Divine as I had never experienced Him before. It seemed as though I could hear the quiet assurance of an inner voice saying: "Stand up for righteousness, stand up for truth; and God will be at your side forever."

On January 30, the King home was bombed. The bombing inspired the MIA to file a federal suit directly attacking the laws establishing bus segregation. In the second half of February the white establishment decided to arrest nearly one hundred blacks for violating Alabama's anti-boycott law. These arrests focused national attention on Montgomery. King was arrested, tried, and convicted on March 22. The following weekend he gave his first speeches in the North.

In April, the U.S. Supreme Court struck down laws requiring bus segregation. Montgomery's mayor refused to yield. After long legal procedures, the Supreme Court's order to end bus segregation was served in Montgomery on Thursday, December 20, 1956. Despite jeopardized jobs, intimidation by the Ku Klux Klan, police harassment, and bombings, the success of the boycott became apparent when King and several allies boarded a public bus in front of King's home on December 21, 1956.

King was in Atlanta when five bombs went off at parsonages and churches in Montgomery in the early morning of January 10, 1957. On this date, a two-day meeting was scheduled to begin in Ebenezer Baptist Church to lay out plans to create an organization to maintain the momentum of the movement for change throughout the South. King returned to Montgomery to inspect the bomb damage, and King was present for only the final hours of the meeting. In a follow-up meeting in New Orleans on February 14, the group adopted the name Southern Christian Leadership Conference (SCLC) and elected King president. King made his first trip abroad to attend the independence ceremonies in Ghana on March 5, 1958. In June, King received the NAACP's Spingarn Medal for his leadership.

King and his organization became increasingly estranged from the NAACP's Roy Wilkins, who feared the effect of another mass black organization on the NAACP's branches in the South and also disapproved of the SCLC's call for direct action. Nonetheless, King pressed forward and the SCLC's plans for a voter registration drive beginning in 1958 went forward. In need of a capable organizer at the Atlanta office, the SCLC's first choice was Bayard Rustin, who was a very effective worker but also vulnerable to smears dealing with his homosexuality. Rustin found a role at SCLC in a less visible position. Ella Baker came to Atlanta to take Rustin's place and shouldered much of the initial burden of organizational work for the SCLC. In spite of her efforts, the 1958 Lincoln Day launch of the voter registration drive failed to attract much attention, and the SCLC seemed on the verge of disappearing.

As King was writing his book on the Montgomery boycott, *Stride Toward Freedom*, he benefited from the very frank criticism of white New York lawyer Stanley D. Levinson, who became one of King's most trusted advisors. Levinson was also a key factor in the FBI's later surveillance of King: there were allegations of a connection between Levinson and the Communist Party that formed one of the legal bases for wiretaps of King's telephone communications. FBI chief J. Edgar Hoover ordered these wiretaps as well as surveillance of King, of King's advisors outside the SCLC, and of their relationships to Communism and homosexuality. The FBI hoped to use the information to discredit King and his organization.

In June 1958, King joined A. Philip Randolph, Roy Wilkins, and National Urban League leader Lester B. Granger in an unsatisfactory meeting with President Dwight D. Eisenhower. In September King was again arrested in Montgomery as he tried to enter a courtroom. King decided to serve his fourteen-day jail sentence for refusing to obey an officer rather than pay the fourteen-dollar fine, but the very racist police commissioner paid the fine to avoid the publicity King would have garnered from staying in jail. After this police incident, while at a book signing, King was critically stabbed by a deranged African American woman.

King spent some time convalescing. In early February 1959 he, his wife, and his biographer, Lawrence D. Reddick, embarked on a busy thirty-day trip to India, sponsored by the Gandhi Memorial Trust. Through much of the year, SCLC floundered in the face of organizational and financial problems, aggravated by the lack of a clear goal beyond voter registration. On November 29, 1959, King announced his resignation from Dexter Avenue Baptist Church to move to Atlanta to take on full-time responsibilities at SCLC.

The sit-ins begin   Student activism provided the spark that gave new life to the civil rights movement. On February 1, 1960, four students from North Carolina Agricultural and Technical College (now University) demanded service at a Woolworth lunch counter in Greensboro and continued to sit after their demands were refused. The sit-ins spread rapidly across the South. The first contact between the students and the SCLC occurred on February 16, 1960, as King delivered a well-received speech at a meeting held in Durham to coordinate more sit-ins. As soon as King returned to Atlanta, he discovered he was under indictment for perjury on his Alabama state tax forms. The ongoing legal procedures would be a matter of great concern to King until an all-white jury returned a verdict of not guilty on May 28, after a three-day trial.

Ella Baker, who realized she could not continue her active leadership role at SCLC much longer, arranged a meeting of student leaders at Shaw University beginning on April 15. King had the votes to establish the student movement as a branch of the SCLC but did not wish to alienate Baker, who aimed at an independent organization. Thus, the Student Nonviolent Coordinating Committee (SNCC) came into existence. Nonetheless, as the sit-ins continued, the adult leaders continued to quarrel; in particular, Roy Wilkins of the NAACP was still very unhappy. Rustin offered to resign from SCLC and King accepted. Ella Baker also left, with bitter feelings on both sides.

On October 2, 1960, King reluctantly joined a renewal of sit-ins at Rich's Department Store in Atlanta. King was arrested and spent his first night ever in jail. A compromise freed all participants except King, who was held as being in violation of the terms of probation for an earlier traffic ticket. Sentenced to a four-month term in prison, he was taken to the state prison at Reidsville, Georgia. Presidential candidate John F. Kennedy called Coretta Scott King to express sympathy, and King was released after eight days in jail. On March 10, 1961, in spite of his private reservations, King spoke in favor of a compromise desegregation plan for Atlanta and won the support of the student organizers, who previously had vociferously labeled the plan a sell-out.

On May 4 the Congress on Racial Equality (CORE) launched the Freedom Rides, inaugurating a new phase in the struggle. On May 14 in Anniston, Alabama, the Freedom Riders encountered violent resistance. After further major trouble in Birmingham, they arrived in Montgomery on May 20 to be beaten by a white mob. At a Montgomery rally on May 21, King called for a large-scale nonviolent campaign against segregation in Alabama. A white mob surrounded the church where the rally took place, and the participants could not leave until about six o'clock the following morning.

King continued a heavy speaking program, bringing in sizable amounts of money to finance SCLC. In August SCLC joined SNCC, the NAACP, the National Urban League, and CORE in establishing the Voter Education Program (VEP). Over the next years considerable friction surfaced between VEP and SCLC over the SCLC's handling of money and its lackluster efforts in some areas. The leading organization of black Baptists also attacked King at this time. Under its leader, Joseph H. Jackson, the National Baptist Convention opposed the sit-ins. In August, Jackson held back an attempt by younger ministers to replace him and denounced King in very strong terms. This dispute eventually led King's supporters to form a rival organization, the Progressive Baptist Convention. At the same time King was involved in a dispute with SNCC over funding. The students felt SCLC owed SNCC part of the funds King's organization raised.

The Albany and Birmingham challenges   In November 1961 SNCC's attempt to establish a voter registration drive in Albany, Georgia, became a major learning experience. King made his first personal effort in December; in August 1962, he gave up the attempt to break down segregation there. The police chief of Albany discerned that the real threat to segregation came from the use of violence, which would provoke federal intervention. He broke the momentum of the protest, and cooperation between SNCC, SCLC, the NAACP, and local blacks broke down in mutual recrimination.

In December the bombing of a Birmingham church drew King's attention to that city. Not only did Fred Shuttleworth's Alabama Christian Movement for Human Rights appear so well-established as to reduce the possibility of friction between various black factions, Birmingham's public safety commissioner, Bull Connor, was an ideal opponent. A staunch segregationist with a hot temper and little judgment, Connor was sure to make hasty mistakes and to resort to violence.

The campaign got off to a shaky start, but Connors, now a lame-duck but clinging to office, helped immensely by unleashing police dogs to attack marchers. In a series of meetings King was able to bring local black leaders to his support—he had belatedly discovered that Shuttleworth was distrusted by many—but problems remained. An intense discussion of strategy with his coworkers ensued. If King did not get himself arrested, he would seem to be making the same kind of retreat that had happened in Albany; if he did, he risked being cut off from the movement at a crucial juncture. After thirty minutes' solitary prayer, King announced his decision to court arrest.

Having been arrested, King passed a difficult first night in solitary confinement, but over the next few days, events began to justify his decision. National support grew and money for bail flowed in—Harry Belafonte, for example, managed to raise $50,000. President Kennedy again made the gesture of telephoning his sympathy to Coretta Scott King.

Before he was released from jail nine days after his arrest, King read an open letter signed by eight white clergymen who denounced demonstrations. King set down a twenty-page response called "Letter from a Birmingham Jail." This document became the most quoted and influential of King's writings. To keep the demonstrations going, James Bevel now recruited schoolchildren who began to march on May 2. Six hundred people went to jail that day. In a few days Connor turned fire hoses as well as dogs on the demonstrators. On May 10, under pressure from the White House, white businesses made some concessions to black demands. Since King found it increasingly difficult to restrain his followers from violence, he accepted the rather weak concessions and declared victory.

In the wake of Birmingham, King now turned his attention to a march on Washington as a way of keeping up pressure for federal civil rights legislation. There were long and difficult negotiations between all parties concerned before the August event came into being.

On August 28, 1963, King won his gamble for a massive nonviolent protest in the nation's capital. Events in the country seemed to be outpacing nonviolence. The peaceful demonstration drew some 200,000 blacks and whites to the steps of the Lincoln Memorial, and King delivered his most famous public address, the "I Have a Dream" speech.

As King kept up a hectic schedule of engagements and speeches, the FBI increased its surveillance. The strain on his family life was so great that he and Coretta King had a telephone quarrel, duly recorded by the FBI. The problems in SCLC continued: staff frictions made it difficult to settle on plans for future direct action. On July 2, 1964, the movement celebrated a victory as President Lyndon B. Johnson signed a new Civil Rights Act. Still, problems were mounting. A white backlash grew in the North and South, and the Ku Klux Klan indulged in increased violence in the South.

FBI director J. Edgar Hoover was determined to discredit King; in November 1964 the FBI sent King a tape of one of his encounters with another woman, along with a note recommending suicide. Rumors of King's infidelities had circulated since the early 1950s but remained principally speculative until Ralph Abernathy's book, with its frank admission of adulteries, brought the matter into the open in 1989.

In October 1964, as a result of extreme fatigue, King had entered a hospital in Atlanta. It was at the hospital that King learned he had received the Nobel Peace Prize for 1964. He was thirty-five years old. Earlier that year, King became the first black American to be named *Time* magazine's "Man of the Year." Journalists and politicians from around the world turned to King for his views on a wide range of issues. However, as King stated in his Nobel acceptance speech, he remained committed to the "twenty-two million Negroes of the United States of America engaged in a creative battle to end the long night of racial injustice."

In the wake of the Civil Rights Act of 1964, SCLC determined to target obstacles to voting, and Selma, Alabama, seemed to be the right place to begin. SCLC dramatized its point on national television on May 7, 1965, when the attempt to march from Selma to Montgomery was brutally stopped by the police. President Johnson then asked Congress for a voting rights bill, which was passed in August. This was also the month that revealed the depth of black frustration outside the South. A civil disturbance in the Watts section of Los Angeles lasted six days and cost thirty-four lives, ushering in a period of several years of endemic urban unrest.

It was not clear how SCLC and King could move from their civil rights work in the South to addressing the economic problems of poverty in the North and elsewhere. In 1966, King undertook a Campaign to End Slums in Chicago. After nine months the campaign ended in failure. King discovered the liberal consensus on race relations stopped short of fundamental economic change. In addition, President Johnson's preoccupation with the war in Vietnam undermined government attention to internal reforms.

King took a stance against American involvement in Vietnam. His position in the Civil Rights Movement was under challenge, and the whole movement fell apart. SNCC began to repudiate him in June 1966 as members adopted the slogan "Black Power," while rejecting white allies and calling for the use of violence. The following year, 1967, became history's worst for urban unrest. In October King announced plans for a new initiative in 1968, the Poor People's Campaign. King wanted to recruit poor men and women from urban and rural areas—of all races and backgrounds—and lead them in a campaign for economic rights.

In an attempt to raise money for the campaign, King accepted an invitation to speak in support of Memphis sanitation workers on March 18, 1968. A mishandled demonstration on March 28 collapsed in disorder. King planned a new, better-organized demonstration and gave a very moving address to an audience of 500 at Memphis Temple on April 3. He spoke of and accepted the possibility of his own death, a recurring theme in his speeches. The following evening, shortly after 5:30 p.m., King was shot and killed on the balcony outside his motel room.

King's assassination led to disturbances in well over one hundred cities and, before the violence subsided on April 11, the death of forty-six people (mostly African Americans), 35,000 injuries, and 20,000 people jailed. On April 9 King's funeral was held in Ebenezer; in addition to the 800 people crammed into the sanctuary, a crowd of 60,000 to 70,000 stood in the streets. He was buried in Southview Cemetery, near his grandmother. On his crypt were carved the words he often used:

Free At Last, Free At Last

Thank God Almighty

I'm Free At Last.

After much rallying, in 1986 Martin Luther King Jr.'s birthday became a national holiday. While alive, King became the symbol of hope for African Americans and for America as a whole that brotherhood and sisterhood could be obtained. The quintessential black leader, King's legacy reminds one of how far America has come, and how far it still has to go.—ROBERT L. JOHNS AND LESLIE NORBACK

JACOB **LAWRENCE**

1917–

Artist, educator

Jacob Lawrence has become recognized by historians as one of the most acclaimed African American artists of the twentieth century. His work is characterized by small-scale tempera and gouache paintings of genre scenes of African Americans and their sociopolitical struggles. His work is often organized through a series, typically accompanied with a simple text that serves as a narrative, based on the artist's careful research. Lawrence has been classified as a social realist whose style is associated with Cubism.

Jacob Lawrence is the eldest of three children born to Jacob and Rosa Lee Lawrence on September 17, 1917, in Atlantic City, New Jersey. Lawrence's father worked as a railroad cook and as a coal miner while his mother was employed as a domestic worker. The family moved to Easton, Pennsylvania, where Lawrence's brother and sister were born. Jacob Lawrence's parents separated when he was seven years old. At that time, Rosa Lee Lawrence and her children moved to Philadelphia, and the Lawrence children were temporarily placed in a foster home. They reunited with their mother in Harlem in the early 1930s after Rosa Lee secured stable employment.

At the age of twelve, Lawrence was enrolled concurrently at Public School 89 and at the Utopia (Settlement) House, which offered after-school classes in arts and crafts. The center was directed by Harlem artist Charles Alston, who immediately recognized Lawrence's artistic abilities. Lawrence's first projects consisted of abstract drawings based on decorative patterns and designs observed in his home, and papier mache masks and cardboard dioramas using crayons and poster paints. Lawrence attended Frederick Douglass Junior High School and Commerce High School through the eleventh grade.

During the Great Depression, Lawrence's mother lost employment and the family was forced to go on welfare. Lawrence dropped out of high school to take odd jobs to support his family. A few years after the economic woes of the country slowly subsided, Lawrence was temporarily employed by the Civilian Conservation Corps, a program sponsored by the New Deal, to plant trees, build dams, and drain swamps in upstate New York.

Between 1932 and 1934, Lawrence studied again with Charles Alston at the Harlem Art Workshop, located at the 135th Street Library in Harlem. Lawrence continued to study under Alston and painter and sculptor Henry Bannarn at 306 West 141st Street, which became known as a central gathering place among Harlem artists. Commonly known as "the 306

*Jacob
Lawrence.*

Group," the gathering attracted artists, musicians, poets, and writers from Harlem, New York, and Europe. Lawrence also met Augusta Savage, a noteworthy sculptor and teacher, who became instrumental in art education in Harlem as the director of community art programs for children and adults. Lawrence attributed his greatest formative influences to Alston, Bannarn, and Savage. During his early years in Harlem, Lawrence also came into contact with such noteworthy individuals as Romare Bearden, Gwendolyn Bennett, Bob Blackburn, Aaron Douglas, W. E. B. Du Bois, Ralph Ellison, Langston Hughes, Ronald Joseph, Gwendolyn Knight (who became the artist's wife), Norman Lewis, Alain Locke, Claude McKay, and Arthur Schomburg.

Lawrence was influenced by Asian wood block prints; the works of Breughel and Goya, who documented African American life in art; and the works of Arthur Dove, Georgio de Chirico, and Charles Sheeler, who represented the growing American Modernist movement and its European counterpart.

Rises to fame   In 1937 Lawrence was awarded a scholarship to the American Artists School in New York City, where he attended classes for two years. He was instructed by Eugene Moreley, Anton Refregier, Philip Reisman, and Sol Wilson. During the evenings, Lawrence frequented Alston's studio as well as the studios of other prominent Harlem artists. The artist had his first public debut in April 1937, at a group exhibition sponsored by the Harlem Artists Guild at the 115th Street Public Library. Lawrence exhibited several paintings at the American Artists School the following month in conjunction with the Harlem Artists Guild. He was represented alongside his mentors, Charles Alston and Henry Bannarn, in both shows.

Savage helped Lawrence secure a Works Project Administration (WPA) Easel Project in 1938, for eighteen months. Lawrence was contracted to complete two paintings every six weeks. During this time he produced his first major works of art and established himself as a leading African American artist. In 1938 the artist initiated the series *The Life of Frederick Douglass,* which was completed in 1939.

Lawrence was given his first one-man show in February of 1938, at the age of twenty, at the YMCA in Harlem. The artist debuted his genre paintings of Harlem, depicting street and interior scenes done in 1936–37. The paintings were small, done with tempera and poster paint on brown wrapping paper. His early style was characterized by the use of flat shapes, frontal or profile views of people displaying overt gestures with mask-like faces, props that punctuate the organization of the figures, and an expressive portrayal of human emotion—attributes that would become his signature as an artist. Around 1937, upon the recommendation of Bearden, Lawrence became interested in using casein tempera (ground pigment, casein-milk protein, and ammonia) on gessoed hardboard panels. This change of medium allowed Lawrence to create a chalky fresco-like appearance in his paintings.

At the YMCA, where Lawrence often played pool, he met "Professor" Charles Siefert, historian of African culture and art. Siefert introduced Lawrence to African and African American resources at the New York Public Library (currently known as the Schomburg Center for Research in Black Culture), which had an enormous influence on the artist. Siefert himself possessed a vast library specializing in African and African American subjects, which he made available to Lawrence. Due to Siefert's inspiration, Lawrence developed a series of forty-one panels in 1937 depicting the Haitian revolutionary Toussaint L'Ouverture.

*Jacob Lawrence at one of his exhibits
at a New York Gallery in 1993.*

Early in his career, Lawrence developed a very disciplined manner of working on his series projects. First, he conceives of a theme and begins to experiment with ideas that lead to sequentially structured compositions. The artist completes a final pencil drawing for each painting in the series. He then paints one color at a time, proceeding from dark to light in each of the individual paintings before continuing with the next color. Works contained within a series are normally accompanied by a text, usually in the form of a narrative description. Due to Lawrence's documentary use of images and captions combined, his work bears a similarity to photojournalism, which has been a popular form of media throughout the twentieth century.

In 1939 the artist had another exhibition at the American Artists School, which was reviewed favorably in *Art News*. That same year, Lawrence's *Toussaint L'Ouverture* series was shown for the first time at the De Porres Interracial Council headquarters, and again at an exhibition cosponsored by the Harmon Fund at the Baltimore Museum later that year. The series was reproduced, in part, in the March 1939 issue of *Survey Graphic* and reviewed favorably by the *Baltimore Sun*. The same year, Lawrence's *Toussaint L'Ouverture* series was again shown at the American Negro Exhibition in Chicago, where Lawrence was honored with a second prize and medal.

In 1940 Lawrence's work was included in several exhibitions including group shows at the Harlem Community Art Center, Columbia University, and the Library of Congress. Beginning that year, Lawrence received a Rosenwald Grant for three consecutive years. This opportunity allowed the artist to move into a studio on 125th Street in New York City. There he began a series of images about black migration in the United States. He developed sixty panel paintings between 1940 and 1941, entitled *The Migration of the Negro*. In this series, the artist depicted the mass exodus of blacks from the rural South to the industrial North in the United States from the early 1900s until the 1940s.

The middle years In 1941 Lawrence married Gwendolyn Knight, whom the artist met as a teenager in Harlem. Knight is originally from the West Indies and is also an artist. She has been a major force behind the artistic achievements of her husband throughout his career. They had no children. After their marriage, the couple lived in New Orleans for one year, during which time Lawrence began his *John Brown* series under the sponsorship of a Rosenwald Grant for a second consecutive year. In December 1941 Lawrence's *Migration* series was represented along with the work of Tanner, Alston, Johnson, Pippin, and Bearden in an exhibition at the Downtown Gallery entitled "American Negro Art: 19th and 20th Centuries." At the age of twenty-four, Lawrence became the first black artist to be sponsored by a prominent New York City art gallery. Concurrent with the exhibition, *Fortune* magazine featured twenty-six color reproductions from the series. The entire series was purchased, half by the Museum of Modern Art and half by the Phillips Collection. The *Migration* series achieved popular success and is touted by scholars as the artist's greatest single artistic achievement.

Lawrence was introduced to many leading contemporary artists, including Davis, Dove, Marin, O'Keeffe, Pippin, Scheeler, Shahn, Tobey, and Weber, through his association with Edith Halpert, owner of the Downtown Gallery. The artist was featured in numerous exhibitions at the Downtown Gallery beginning in 1942 for a period of twenty years.

The artist began his *Harlem* series in 1942, again supported by a Rosenwald Fellowship. Lawrence joined the U.S. Coast Guard in 1943. Both of Lawrence's commanding officers, Captain J. S. Rosenthal and Lieutenant Commander Carltin Skinner, encouraged the artist to continue his painting while fulfilling regular duties as a steward's mate. Rosenthal promoted Lawrence to the position of combat artist. Ultimately, Lawrence became the official Coast Guard painter. During his twenty-six months in the service, Lawrence produced approximately forty-eight paintings in a series entitled *Coast Guard*.

After completing his obligations with the military, Lawrence resumed painting the history of African American people in 1945. He was saluted in 1946 by *New Masses* magazine for his contribution to the arts. Funded by a Guggenheim Fellowship between 1946 and 1947, Lawrence completed a series that documented his memories of World War II. While working on the series the artist was featured in two shows—one at the Phillips Collection and the other at A.C.A. Gallery in New York. The artist was invited by Joseph Albers to teach at Black Mountain College in North Carolina during the summer of 1947. Due to Albers's influence, Lawrence became absorbed in formal considerations based on Bauhaus principles of art and design.

That same year, *Fortune* magazine commissioned the artist to do a series of ten paintings on postwar conditions in the South. In 1948 the artist exhibited the *Migration* series at the Eighth Annual Exhibition of the Art Institute of Chicago and was awarded a silver medal.

Lawrence became psychologically depressed during the late 1940s due to lack of recognition from his colleagues despite his enormous success. Finally, in July 1949, Lawrence committed himself to Hillside Hospital in Queens, New York, to receive treatment for depression. During his stay from 1949 until 1950, the artist completed a series entitled *Hospital,* consisting of eleven panels. Lawrence actively resumed painting after his recovery. He began working on genre scenes of Harlem and a series entitled *Theater,* consisting of twelve panels. Soon thereafter, he began a series depicting the history of war and conflict in America entitled *Struggle—History of the American People* between 1955 and 1956. Thirty panels were completed, although sixty were originally projected.

Lawrence began teaching at Pratt Institute in 1955, where he stayed for fifteen years, while also teaching concurrently at other institutions. He has also taught at the Art Students League, New York City; Brandeis University; the New School for Social Research; Skowhegan School of Painting and Sculpture; California State University at Hayward; and the University of Washington at Seattle.

The mature years   In 1960 Lawrence was given a retrospective by the American Federation of the Arts. He visited Nigeria at the invitation of the American Society of African Culture (AMSAC) and the Mbari Club of Artists and Writers of Ibadan briefly in 1962, and again for eight months in 1964. He gained enormous insight about African aesthetics and design during his early years in Harlem and in Africa, which is evident in his work throughout his career. During his stay in Africa, Lawrence produced a series of paintings entitled *Nigeria*. He initiated a series of paintings based on the theme of civil rights in the South from 1961 to 1969.

In the late 1960s, Lawrence was commissioned by Windmill Books of Simon and Schuster to oversee a book project. He chose the life of Harriet Tubman, which contained seventeen of Lawrence's paintings accompanied with original verse. Some of the imagery in *Harriet and the Promised Land* (1968) was taken directly from Lawrence's *Harriet Tubman* series of 1939. Lawrence also illustrated three other books, including *Aesops Fables* (1970), *Hiroshima* (1983), and *One Way Ticket* (1948). Lawrence completed a number of illustration projects, including three covers for *Time* magazine, a poster for the 1972 Olympics in Munich, a silk screen poster in 1977 for a fund-raising campaign for President Jimmy Carter's inauguration, and several other poster projects.

In 1973 the state of Washington commissioned Lawrence to paint a mural about the life of George Washington Bush, the first black elected to the Washington legislature in 1889, at the State Capital Museum in Olympia. Lawrence was honored with a major retrospective at the Whitney Museum of American Art in 1974 and again at the Seattle Art Museum in 1986. In 1975 the Founders Society of the Detroit Institute of Arts commissioned Lawrence to do an edition of silk screen prints of the *John Brown* series of 1941.

Although Lawrence has used mostly water-based materials throughout his career, during the past several decades he has increased his use of media to include prints, drawings, and murals composed of enamel, as seen in the *Games* mural for the Kingdome Stadium in Seattle (1979), his *Exploration* mural at Howard University (1980), and a second mural for Hampton University, *Origins* (1984). During the 1970s Lawrence created several paintings based on the theme of libraries. In 1982 he was commissioned to produce a series of silk screen prints for Limited Editions Club of New York City, in collaboration with author John Hersey.

In 1994 Lawrence completed a series of paintings based on the theme of the supermarket. The major theme of Lawrence's most recent works during the past two decades has been building, reflecting his love for manual craftsmanship and tools. Lawrence collects antique tools and is an expert on their forms and functions. He uses his intimate knowledge about the subject of tools and hand labor throughout these thematically linked works.

Lawrence has received numerous awards during his career, including election in the Hall of Fame for Great Americans, 1976; the NAACP's third annual Great Black Artist's Award, 1988; the College Art Association's Distinguished Artist Award, 1988; the National Medal of Arts, presented by President George Bush, 1990; the National Art Club Medal of Honor, 1993; and numerous honorary doctorates. He was also commissioner of the National Council for the Arts, 1978–84, and is a member of the American Academy of Arts and Letters and the American Academy of Arts and Sciences.

In addition to the small gouache series paintings that characterize the artist's work, Lawrence has also produced a number of drawings, prints, murals, posters, and illustrations revealing his personal and cultural heritage. He prefers water-based paints and small brushes and usually paints small-scale works on paper or gessoes panels.

Lawrence's work is represented in numerous museums around the country including the Baltimore Museum of Art, the Detroit Institute of Arts, the Museum of Modern Art in New York, and the Toledo Museum of Art.

Lawrence has contributed a legacy of art revealing the expression, challenges, and rewards of black culture and society. He has immortalized his aesthetic philosophy and imagery through his teachings. Jacob Lawrence has been proclaimed the divine translator of the history of the African American experience through art.—BETTY LOU WILLIAMS

SPIKE **LEE**

1957–

Filmmaker, screenwriter, actor, entrepreneur

Spike Lee has been recognized as a key black filmmaker in the American movie business. Since his first film came out in 1986, he has become the nation's most successful and popular black director. Due to his determination to make a success of what he loves to do, his against-the-odds achievements have opened doors for other black filmmakers. Winning acclaim for his accurate depictions of black culture, Lee says his goal is to make films that will capture the black experience by whatever means necessary. According to Current Biography, *he believes that he has a mission "to put the vast richness of black culture on film."*

Shelton Jackson Lee was born March 20, 1957, in Atlanta, Georgia to William Lee, a jazz composer and bassist, and Jacqueline Shelton Lee, an art teacher. His mother, who died in 1977 of cancer, nicknamed him "Spike" when he was a toddler, evidently alluding to his

a new comedy with music
the Director of 'She's Gotta HAVE'

Spike Lee.

toughness. Spike is the oldest of Lee's five children. He has three brothers, David, Cinque, and Chris, and one sister, Joie. The family moved from Atlanta shortly after Spike Lee's birth and lived briefly in Chicago. In 1959 they moved to Brooklyn's predominantly black Fort Greene section. Jacqueline Lee provided a rich cultural upbringing that included attending plays and going to galleries, museums, and, of course, movies. Bill Lee helped expose the family to the music world, occasionally taking them to his performances at the Blue Note and to other Manhattan jazz clubs.

After graduating from John Dewey High School in Brooklyn, Lee majored in mass communications at his father's and grandfather's alma mater, Morehouse College in Atlanta. It was at Morehouse that Spike Lee first took an interest in filmmaking, and upon his graduation in 1979, he was awarded a summer internship with Columbia Pictures in Burbank, California. In the fall, he returned to New York to attend New York University's Institute of Film and Television, Tisch School of the Arts. He was one of the few blacks in the school. Lee's first year at NYU was not without controversy. As his first year project, he submitted a ten-minute film, *The Answer,* that told of a young black screenwriter who was to remake D. W. Griffith's *The Birth of a Nation.* The film was a pointed critique of the racism in Griffith's silent film. The faculty was displeased with his work, saying he had not yet mastered "film grammar." Lee suspected, however, that they were offended by his digs at the legendary director's stereotypical portrayals of black characters. In his second year, he received an assistantship that provided full tuition in exchange for working in the school's equipment room.

Lee received his master's in filmmaking from NYU in 1982, and as his master's film project, he wrote, produced, and directed *Joe's Bed-Stuy Barbershop: We Cut Heads.* His father, Bill Lee, composed the original jazz score, the first of several he would eventually create for his son's films. The film is about a barbershop in Brooklyn's Bedford-Stuyvesant neighborhood that served as a front for a numbers running operation. For the film, Spike Lee received the 1983 Student Academy Award for best director from the Academy of Motion Picture Arts and Sciences. It was also the first student production to be selected for the Lincoln Center's New Directors and New Films series.

Upon graduation, Spike Lee was signed by two major talent agencies, but when nothing materialized from that association, he said he was not surprised. In an interview in the *New York Times,* Lee said it "cemented in my mind what I always thought all along: that I would have to go out and do it alone, not rely on anyone else." Even though his credibility had been enhanced by the honors he received for *Joe's Bed-Stuy Barbershop,* that did not pay the bills. In order to survive, Lee worked at a movie distribution house, cleaning and shipping film. At the same time, he was trying to raise funds to finance a film entitled *Messenger,* a drama about a young New York City bicycle messenger. In the summer of 1984, however, production of the film was called to a halt, due to a dispute between Lee and the Screen Actor's Guild. The guild felt the film was too commercial to qualify for the waiver often granted to low-budget independent films that permitted the use of nonunion actors. Lee felt the refusal to grant him the waiver was a definite case of racism. He was unable to recast the film with union actors and had to terminate the project when he could not get funding to continue. Lee told *Vanity Fair* that he had learned his lesson. "I saw I made the classic mistakes of a young filmmaker, to be overly ambitious, do something beyond my means and capabilities. Going through the fire just made me more hungry, more determined that I couldn't fail again."

Film career launched   With the disappointment of *Messenger* behind him, Lee needed a film that not only would have commercial appeal but could be made for little money. His script for *She's Gotta Have It* (Island Pictures, 1986) seemed to fit the bill. Costing only $175,000 to produce, the film was made in twelve days. It was shot on one location with a limited cast, and was edited in Lee's apartment. The story is a comedy about an attractive African American woman in Brooklyn, Nola Darling, and her romantic encounters with three men. Lee played one of the three suitors, Mars Blackmon. In the film Lee poked fun at the double standard that looks the other way when men boast about the number of sexual relations they had with women, only to condemn a woman who dares to have several men dangling at her fingertips. Lee unapologetically promoted the heroine's promiscuity in his handling of the subject matter. After the film's successful opening at the San Francisco Film Festival, Island Pictures agreed to distribute *She's Gotta Have It,* beating out several other film companies. It was shown at the Cannes Film Festival where it won the Prix de Jeunesse for the best new film by a newcomer. The film was a success in the United States, eventually grossing over $7 million.

Lee's next film, *School Daze* (Columbia, 1988), was a musical based on his four years at Morehouse College. Set on a college campus during homecoming weekend, it looked at the conflict between light-skinned and dark-skinned blacks. Those with light skin were the ones with money, expensive cars, and "good hair." The ones with darker skin were "less cool" and had "bad hair." Lee's aim was to expose what he saw as a caste system existing within the black community. Lee began filming at Morehouse, but was asked to leave after three weeks, as the administration felt the film showed a negative portrayal of black colleges. Filming was completed at Atlanta University. *School Daze* opened to mixed reviews and was a moderate success, ultimately grossing $15 million. Some applauded Lee's sophomoric film effort of reviving the languished genre of movie musical, while others found the mixture of music and interracial strife to be unappealing.

Lee's next film, however, placed him on an elite list of film directors and firmly established Lee's reputation as a controversial *auteur. Do the Right Thing* (Universal, 1989) was the story of simmering racial tensions between Italians and African Americans in Brooklyn's Bedford-Stuyvesant section. Violence erupts when a black man is killed by a white police officer. Some critics said Lee was endorsing violence and that he would be partly responsible if audiences rioted upon seeing the film. Lee responded that he was not advocating violence even though he could understand it. He stated that his intent was not to incite riots but to provoke discussion. The film was a critical success when it screened at the Cannes International Film Festival, and it also received an award for best picture from the Los Angeles Film Critics Association. *Do the Right Thing* received Golden Globe nominations for best picture, best director, best screenplay, and best supporting actor, but failed to win in any category. It was also

Spike Lee on the set of his movie Crooklyn.

nominated for an Academy Award for best original screenplay and for best supporting actor. It failed to receive a nomination for best picture even though the movie was highly acclaimed. According to Lee in *Jet* magazine, "the oversight reflects the discomfort of the motion picture industry with explosive think pieces." Nonetheless, *Do the Right Thing* ended up on many film critics' top ten lists in 1989. The film cost $6.5 million to produce and grossed $28 million.

Music, not race, was prevalent in Lee's 1990 film, *Mo' Better Blues,* starring Denzel Washington. The main character was inspired by Lee's father, Bill Lee, who also wrote the score. It told the story of a jazz trumpeter who is trying to balance his love of music with his love of two women. However, Lee said the film was about relationships in general and not just the relationship between a man and a woman. He also wanted to portray black musicians who are not drug- or alcohol-dependent. *Jungle Fever* (1991), Spike Lee's next film, had another provocative theme, that of interracial sex. A black married architect and an Italian American secretary are attracted to each other because of the sexual mythology that surrounds interracial romance. At the end of their affair, they admit they were "just curious," but not before both are at odds with their families. *Jungle Fever* was multi-themed, hitting on such timely issues as color, class, drugs, romance, and family.

From the onset of his film career Lee made it his mission to direct a film about black revolutionary Malcolm X. Lee quickly researched Malcolm's life to fully equip himself with the idea of taking on a daunting and complex historical figure. In 1991, Norman Jewison had been chosen by Warner Bros. to direct a film on Malcolm X, but when Lee publicly announced that he had a problem with a white man directing the film, Jewison agreed to step down, which gave Lee the chance to get to work on his dream picture. However, several problems arose early on and plagued Lee's production throughout. First, Lee was opposed by a group called the United Front to Preserve the Memory of Malcolm X and the Cultural Revolution. They based their objections on their analysis of the "exploitative" films Lee previously had made. After reworking the script, Lee's next battle was with Warner Bros. over the budget. He requested $40 million to produce a film of epic proportions that would show all phases of Malcolm X's life. Warner offered only $20 million. Lee sold the foreign rights for $8.5 million and kicked in part of his $3 million salary, but Lee still needed more money to make his movie and include a location shoot in Mecca. He set out on a door-to-door crusade among other African American celebrities to get them to invest in the film. Bill Cosby, Oprah Winfrey, and Michael Jordan came to Lee's rescue. While Lee declared himself the only director who could make this film, he collaborated once again with the only actor people thought could play the part of Malcolm X—Denzel Washington. Under Lee's direction, *Malcolm X* was released in 1992, with a running time of three hours and twenty-one minutes. It did not become the event movie Lee and others hoped, but it did receive much praise for its director and star. It also played a major role in elevating the black leader to mythic status, portraying him as a symbol for the extremes of black rage as well as for racial reconciliation.

Next, Lee chose a light family drama that echoed his own experiences growing up in Brooklyn. *Crooklyn* (Universal, 1994), which was written by Lee's sister Joie, was an unusual film, for it dealt with a family that was not dysfunctional, and there was no violence, gangs, or drugs.

In direct contrast to *Crooklyn* was *Clockers* (Universal, 1995), Spike Lee's intimate but violent look at the inner-city drug trade. Adapted from Richard Price's novel, the film was to be directed by Martin Scorsese, and his initial plan was to focus on the story's police murder investigation. However, Scorsese had other commitments, and Lee was asked to take over. Lee shifted the emphasis to the relationship between two brothers. One was honest, and the other was a "clocker," a street-level worker in the drug trade, ready at any hour to provide crack. Lee was more interested in looking at the bonds that connect black men rather than making another "gangsta" movie.

Lee's ninth film, *Girl 6* (Twentieth Century–Fox, 1996), had a cast and crew made up mostly of women. It was the story of a struggling actress who takes a job for a phone-sex line. Her sense of reality begins to deteriorate when the calls begin to matter to her, and she eventually hits rock bottom. Reviews were not good, one saying that this was the worst film Lee had ever made.

Lee's tenth film was an investigation of the Million Man March of 1995. *Get on the Bus* (Columbia, 1996) was about twelve men who were traveling from Los Angeles to Washington,

D.C., to take part in the march. They represented the diversity of African American men, and Lee molded the men's speeches and debates to intensify the differences and tensions between them. Made in eighteen days, *Get on the Bus* cost $2.4 million. Its entire budget came from black male investors, such as Johnnie Cochran, who were inspired by the march's message.

Films stir controversy   Lee's earlier films courted controversy that helped maximize profits, but critics have said that since *Malcolm X,* Lee has been less discerning, and his films have not done as well at the box office. However, his willingness to tackle prickly issues of relevance to the black community has made his films bankable, and has made the industry aware of an untapped market. Despite Lee's several run-ins with the press that have characterized him as somewhat reckless with his words, he stays true to his mission. He told *American Film*, "All I want to do is tell a story. When writing a script I'm not saying, 'Uh-Oh, I'd better leave that out because I might get into trouble.' I don't operate like that." His goal is to prove that an all-black film directed by a black person can be of universal appeal.

Lee has received several honors, among them the Golden Globe and Academy Award nominations for *Do the Right Thing*. In 1990, Morehouse College named Lee as one of seven black men recognized as outstanding role models. He has also been a Morehouse trustee since 1992. At the thirteenth annual American Black Achievement Awards in 1992, he was honored as part of a select group of ten black men and women from a variety of fields. In 1993 the National Association of Black-Owned Broadcasters recognized six superstars, awarding Lee their Pioneer in Entertainment award. In keeping with his interest in encouraging others who want to enter filmmaking, Lee established a minority scholarship at New York University's Tisch School of the Arts in 1989, and he also supports the United Negro College Fund (UNCF). He took part in Jesse Jackson's National Rainbow Coalition Leadership Forum on Violence, a three-day conference held in Washington, D.C., in 1994, which focused on the escalating problem of violence in black America.

Lee is such a huge New York Knicks fan that he is known to plan his film projects around the Knicks' basketball schedule. This passion for the sport helped Lee write *Best Seat in the House: A Basketball Memoir* in 1997, with Ralph Wiley. He has been described by associates as having a fierce determination and unshakable self-confidence. Philip Dusenberry of New York advertising agency BBDO said of Lee in *Business Week,* "You get the impression that Spike is a devil-may-care kind of guy, but he's also a shrewd self-promoter." Other long-time associates told *Ebony* that Lee "is an obsessive workaholic who seems intent on cramming a lifetime of work into a few short years." Lee is unusual in the filmmaking business, for he not only writes, directs, and produces, but he also acts in all his films. Most of his roles are marginal. He does not consider himself an actor, but feels it is better for the box office if he appears in the films.

Lee has made no apology for earning money by endorsements and defends himself against charges of commercialism. He has said the motivation for his business investments comes from Malcolm X's philosophy that blacks need to build their own economic base. Lee was recognized as a marketing phenomenon and multimedia star only four years after his surprise hit, *She's Gotta Have It*. His first enterprise, Forty Acres and a Mule Filmworks, moved from his apartment to a remodeled Brooklyn firehouse in 1987. With tongue in cheek, Lee says the name reflects the arduous struggle he went through to make *She's Gotta Have It*.

In addition to his films, he has written several books aside from his recent basketball book. These include *By Any Means Necessary: The Trials and Tribulations of Making Malcolm X* (1992), *Do the Right Thing: The New Spike Lee Joint* (1989), *Mo' Better Blues* (with Lisa Jones, 1990), *Spike Lee's Gotta Have It: Guerrilla Filmmaking* (1987), *Uplift the Race: The Construction of School Daze* (with Lisa Jones, 1988), and *The X Factor* (1992). He has also produced and directed music videos for Anita Baker, Miles Davis, Michael Jackson, and Branford Marsalis, among others. In 1988 he produced and directed a television commercial for Jesse Jackson's presidential campaign. He also has his own collection of promotional merchandise, such as baseball caps, T-shirts, and posters that are tied to his movies. Beginning with a rapidly expanding mail-order operation, Lee opened his retail store, Spike's Joint, in 1990.

Lee directed commercials for Levi's $20 million campaign for its 501 Jeans, as well as for Nike, Gap, Barney's of New York, Philips Electronics, Quaker Oats, Snapple, and Ben & Jerry's ice cream. Appearing as Mars Blackmon in Nike commercials with Michael Jordan, Lee was criticized for making Nike's expensive "Air Jordans" such a status symbol that many young people were reportedly attacking or stealing from each other to get a pair. According to *Business Week*, Lee dismissed the charges as "thinly veiled racism." He has also appeared in other television commercials, including Taco Bell and Apple Computer.

In late 1996, Lee joined DDB Needham Advertising to form a new ad agency, Spike/DDB. Their agreement called for Lee to direct urban-oriented commercials for a variety of clients. He had previously worked with DDB on an educational spot for the UNCF. Other plans included directing an animated film for ABC/Disney and writing, producing, and directing six episodes of a new comedy series for ABC. Riding on several recent releases dealing with past racial atrocities, Lee's projects include a documentary on four young victims of a 1964 church bombing in Birmingham, Alabama, entitled *4 Little Girls*.

Lee married Tonya Linnette Lewis, an attorney, in October of 1993. The two met in September of 1992 during the Congressional Black Caucus weekend in Washington, D.C. Their daughter, Satchel Lewis Lee, was born in December of 1994. She was named after legendary black baseball star Satchel Paige. In May 1997 their son, Jackson Lee, was born.

Known as one of the most original and innovative filmmakers in the world, Lee tries to look at the different facets of black culture. He is one of a handful of filmmakers who consistently deals with controversial topics and challenges the film medium itself. His films and his means of promotion take away from Lee's greatest achievement, which is opening doors for other African Americans with stories to tell. To some, he is the "Jackie Robinson of Hollywood." He is quick to admit, however, that there are those in the black community among his detractors, and he says he does not presume to act as a spokesman for all thirty-five million African Americans. He will probably continue to court controversy, but with his savvy and salesmanship, Spike Lee will remain a significant influence in the entertainment world.—FLOSSIE E. WISE

ALAIN LEROY **LOCKE**

1886–1954

Philosopher, arts patron, educator

Alain Locke was a major interpreter of black art and culture during the first half of the twentieth century.

He was a brilliant scholar whose activities helped give depth and coherence to the study of black culture,

especially during the period of the 1920s known as the Harlem Renaissance.

Alain Leroy Locke was born on September 13, 1886, in Philadelphia, Pennsylvania, to a distinguished family with a long history in education. His parents, Pliny (1850–1892) and Mary (Hawkins) Locke (1853–1922), were descendants of educated free blacks residing in the North.

Alain's grandfather, Ishmael Locke (1820–1852), who attended Cambridge University in Great Britain, worked as a teacher in New Jersey and Liberia. While in Africa, he married a similarly employed educator. When they returned to the United States, Ishmael found employment as an administrator of schools in Rhode Island. Later he was headmaster at the Institute for Colored Youth in Philadelphia.

Pliny Locke graduated from the Institute for Colored Youth in 1867. He taught mathematics at the school for a couple of years, then traveled to North Carolina after the Civil War to teach freedmen. In the early 1870s, he obtained accounting jobs with the Freedman's Bureau and the Freedman's Bank in Washington, D.C. While in the capital he enrolled at Howard College, earning a law degree in 1874. Afterwards, he returned to Philadelphia where he taught at the Philadelphia School of Pedagogy and worked as a clerk in the U.S. Post Office.

When Pliny Locke died in 1892, his family was among Philadelphia's black elite. His widow, Mary Locke, was determined to keep it that way by continuing the Victorian upbringing of Alain, her only child. A teacher herself, she enrolled Alain in one of the pioneer Ethical Culture schools and started preparing him for a career in medicine. That vocation had to be abandoned when rheumatic fever permanently damaged Alain's heart. Mary Locke responded, however, by encouraging her son in the study of piano, violin, and books.

In 1902, Alain Locke, a brown-complexioned and delicate young man, graduated second in his class from Philadelphia's Central High School. Two years later, he graduated first in his class from the School of Pedagogy. In 1904 he entered Harvard College. Locke was elected Phi Beta Kappa and graduated *magna cum laude* in 1907 with degrees in philosophy and English. From Harvard, he traveled to England as the first black American to be named a Rhodes Scholar. After being denied admission to several Oxford colleges because of his race, Locke was admitted at Hertford College, where he spent the next three years studying philosophy, Greek, Latin, and literature.

Although faced with racial discrimination in England, Locke's warmth, ironic humor, and zest for philosophical debate were not dampened. He found consolation among a small group of Africans residing in London. After completing his studies in England, Locke traveled to Germany to study philosophy at the University of Berlin in 1910. He continued his studies the following year in Paris at the College de France.

Lacking the job opportunities of whites with a similar education, Locke, upon his return to the United States in 1912, spent six months traveling in the South exploring job leads at black colleges. The sojourn had a lasting effect on Locke, who had been sheltered most of his life from the black world. Not only did he gain a firsthand look at the race problem in America, according to Kunitz and Haycroft, he also acquired "an avocational interest in encouraging and interpreting the artistic and cultural expressions of Negro life."

In 1912 Locke obtained an appointment as assistant professor of English and instructor in philosophy and education at Howard University. There, sharing with W. E. B. Du Bois the belief that educated blacks were duty-bound to uplift their race, he became a vocal proponent of the "Talented Tenth." In 1915, responding to Carter G. Woodson's alarming assertion that the Negro was receiving a mis-education, he petitioned Howard's white trustees to establish a course on race relations. But the trustees rejected his proposal, claiming it was incompatible with the institution's "nonracial" mission. Finding the trustees' decision unacceptable, the Howard chapter of the NAACP and the Social Science Club responded by sponsoring a series of lectures by Locke. In the lecture series, entitled "Race Contacts and Inter-Racial Relationships," Locke debunked the premise of white supremacist thought prevalent during that time. The essential message of the lectures was that racial temperaments are not traceable to biological factors, but instead, to "historical and social causes."

Philosophic thought expressed   In 1916, Locke returned to Harvard. There he completed his doctoral dissertation, "The Problem of Classification in the Theory of Value." In this treatise, Locke wrote that values have their origin in specific, culturally determined feelings and attitudes. These feelings and attitudes, he argued, affect logical judgments and yield "facts" or "reality" that are no more than what people interpret them to be. Thus, Locke explained, values are neither objectively true nor false and therefore cannot be set forth as either absolute or universal. Locke reasoned that because of the range and variety of human values, their validity or the appropriateness of the way they are being employed can only be determined by studying them in their own historical, social, and cultural context.

Although Locke revised his philosophic thought as he matured, the main assertions of his dissertation remained unchanged over the span of his life. His views eventually attracted the attention of other philosophical thinkers including Sidney Hook, Horace M. Kallen, and John Dewey. These major philosophers and others quoted Locke or included his writings on value theory in their publications. Noteworthy is Locke's "Values and Imperatives" in *American Philosophy, Today and Tomorrow,* edited by Kallen and Hook (1935), and "Pluralism and Ideological Peace" in *Freedom and Experience,* edited by Sidney Hook and Milton Konvitz (1947).

Locke as art promoter   In 1918 Locke became the first black American to receive a doctorate in philosophy from Harvard University. After that, he returned to Howard to chair the philosophy department and teach.

From Howard's campus, Locke continued to pursue his favorite pastimes: reading literature, viewing art, and attending plays by blacks. In the process of immersing himself in black cultural expressions, he noticed increasing evidence that the older generation of black writers and artists were imitating and even submitting to Anglo-Saxon superiority values. Locke became alarmed because such works, instead of advancing the status of the black race, were helping to maintain its subordinate position.

Seeing that accommodation and protest strategies were also faltering, Locke began to blend his thoughts on value theory with his views on art and race relations. Eventually he decided the most effective way to raise the status of black Americans was through producing literature and art reflecting the true life of black people. In his fussy and often overbearing manner, Locke began to urge his Negro friends to abandon the racial assumptions and images perpetuated by white society. In their place, he encouraged them to use black folk experience as the source material for their creative works.

The depth and breadth of the Negro tradition to which Locke alluded could not be ignored as black migrants from the South and the Caribbean region poured into northern cities following World War I. They brought with them a variety of colorful accents, languages, music, poetry, art, folklore, dance, fiction, and ideologies. The convergence of these expressions fostered a cultural awakening in many cities, including Chicago, Philadelphia, Washington, D.C., and especially New York City's Harlem community. Locke relished these developments and began traveling to Harlem with greater frequency.

Locke was welcomed into the company of black artists and writers who met regularly in Harlem's cafes and nightclubs. Always elegant in attire, he mesmerized his acquaintances with an incomparable display of learning, urbanity, and empathy. At the same time, he began contributing reviews of their work to *Survey Graphic,* the NAACP's *Crisis,* and the Urban League's *Opportunity.* After a few years, he had established himself as the "philosophical midwife" of Harlem's black literary, musical, artistic, and theatrical talent.

Locke carried his enthusiasm for Harlem's cultural awakening back to Howard's campus, where in 1922 he proposed Howard as the center for a national Negro theater. Although his activist bent and caring *hauteur* made him increasingly popular among students, it did not do anything to win him the favor of Stanley Durkee, Howard's white president. Durkee rejected Locke's proposal for a national theater. In 1924 he gladly granted Locke sabbatical leave to do archeological work in the Sudan and Egypt.

With Locke away, the president remained under pressure from students and faculty. Their grievances, however, escalated when Locke returned from Africa. In an attempt to get control of the situation, Durkee fired several faculty members, including the most vocal of them, Alain Locke.

With the freedom afforded by his unexpected departure from academia, Locke became more actively involved with New York's young black artists, writers, and intellectuals, as well as the city's white editors, publishers, and philanthropists. According to David Levering Lewis, he was often seen "walking with his quick step and unfurled umbrella from Hotel Olga along Lenox and Seventh avenues, riding the subway to Downtown meetings and luncheons." In 1925, Locke helped edit a special issue of *Survey* entitled "Harlem: Mecca of the New Negro." The edition received highly favorable reviews. Later that year, he edited *The New Negro* (1925).

The New Negro was a collection of poems, stories, essays, and pictures of African and American Negro art. Contributors to the anthology included W. E. B. Du Bois, Jean Toomer, and many younger artists and writers such as Langston Hughes, Zora Neal Hurston, Claude McKay, Countee Cullen, and Richmond Barthé. In introducing the book, Locke boldly offered this talent as evidence that a "New Negro" had arrived with a "new psychology" and that the "spirit was awake in the masses."

The New Negro was an instant success and caused a vogue among whites for black art and literature. Locke zealously exploited this interest. As spokesperson for the New Negro Movement, he organized many exhibitions of black art, helped found the Harlem Museum of African Art, and, with the support of philanthropists like Mrs. R. Osgood Mason, who wanted to preserve the Negro tradition from the debilitating effects of Western civilization, he obtained the backing that many striving black artists and writers needed in order to produce, exhibit, and publish. Noteworthy among those helped was Locke's protégé, Langston Hughes. Conversant in French, Locke also took to Europe his campaign to inform whites about black art and literature.

In addition to these promotional activities, Locke continued to edit anthologies of black art and literature. Of note, he edited *Four Negro Poets* (1927) and, with help from T. Montgomery Gregory, the first collection of Negro drama, *Plays of Negro Life* (1927). Locke also wrote many articles about black art. In his writings, he disputed the notion that black art was childlike and without technique by documenting the "African influence" on Matisse, Picasso, and other European artists. Also, he explained that black art, in addition to being beautiful, is educationally valuable because it instills an admiration of the black face and form and offers insight into the genius of the black mind.

Although Locke promoted black art to inspire blacks and change white racial attitudes, he chastised black artists who resorted to sensationalism and exhibitionism to make their work marketable. Similarly, he had disdain for artists, writers, and intellectuals who used art as propaganda to protest the injustice of discrimination. On this subject, Locke, in "Art or Propaganda" (1928), as cited by George Hall, wrote that using art for propaganda only "perpetuates the position of group inferiority even in crying out against it." The function and object of art, Locke reminded, is not protest—it is beauty and truth. Thus, he challenged black artists and writers to produce great art and literature as the protest against the attitude that allows discrimination to exist.

Locke as interpreter of cultural expressions

In 1928 Locke returned to the full-time teaching of philosophy at Howard University. From its campus, he continued to write critical essays and began to write a series of annual reviews of black literature in *Opportunity*. In his first annual review, "1928: A Retrospective Review" (1929), cited in Jeffrey Stewart's anthology of Locke's works, he wrote disparagingly of the New Negro's "inflated stock" and predicted the "Negro fad" would soon end. A few months later, October 1929, the stock market crashed, leaving black artists without their wealthy sponsors and causing Harlem's literary and artistic output to decline. In "We Turn to Prose" (1932), cited in Stewart's anthology, Locke praised *The Black Worker* by Sterling Spero and Abram Harris for marking "the beginning of the end of that hitherto endless succession of studies on the Negro *in vacuo*." And in "Black Truth and Black Beauty" (1933), also cited by Stewart, Locke discussed a "score of books that cannot by any stretch be listed as 'literature of the Negro.'"

Some black writers resented Locke's critical tone. According to Stewart, one, Jessie Fauset, responded that "your criticisms . . . point most effectively to the adage that a critic is a self-acknowledged failure as a writer." Indeed, Locke was not an artist or literary writer. Yet, he responded, that was no excuse for him to be an apologist for creative work that lacked excellence and social consciousness. Later, when he stated in "Toward a Critique of Negro Music" (1934), cited by Stewart, that the evolutionary process of development in American black music should eventually produce an American classical music, he was attacked again, this time for being "elitist" and attempting to "concertize" black folk music.

Indeed, Locke's suggestion that black folk music had to advance to something "higher" before it is "vindicated" was a contradiction that he never reconciled to his critics' satisfaction. Nevertheless, Locke attempted to do just that in his famous Bronze Booklet, *The Negro and His Music* (1936), cited by Paul Joseph Bugett. In speaking of formal classical music and Negro idioms, such as the spirituals and jazz, he wrote that eventually they must "be fused in a vital but superior product." What was the "superior" product? According to Locke it was "neither racial, nor national, but universal music."

When the editorship of *Opportunity* changed in 1942, Locke discontinued his retrospective views. He continued to edit and write, especially on race relations and culture. With Bernhard J. Stern, he edited *When Peoples Meet: A Study in Race and Culture Contacts* (1942). The publication included analyses by Ruth Benedict and Margaret Mead. In the same year he edited a special edition for *Survey Graphic* that emphasized the necessity of ending racial privilege in the United States, Africa, and Asia. One of his most noteworthy articles during this period was "The Negro in Three Americas" (1944), which helped focus attention on the diverse African presence in the Western Hemisphere.

In 1946, when Locke resumed his annual reviews in *Phylon,* he used his philosophical insight into underlying issues and trends in black life to plot the future course of the arts and the social sciences. Thus, in "A Critical Retrospect of the Literature of the Negro for 1947" (1948), cited by Stewart, he expressed the hope that the international struggle for the rights of minorities would become the stuff of great literature. In "Wisdom De Profundis" (1950), Locke praised sociologists such as E. Franklin Frazier and historians like John Hope Franklin for focusing attention on the black experience in their respective fields.

Promotes black education   Locke's praise for the sociological and historical work of progressive black social scientists was certainly understandable. After all, for decades he had argued that the black folk experience and African past should be studied and made the primary material from which all categories of art are fashioned. For him, however, the study of black life did more than offer material for art; it also yielded solutions to life's problems. Thus, he urged educational institutions to expose their black students to all aspects of their heritage.

Beginning in the 1930s, after Mordecai W. Johnson had become Howard's first black president, Locke organized a succession of conferences at Howard in an effort to make the university an intellectual clearinghouse on issues concerning race. Simultaneously, he revived Howard's literary magazine, *Stylus,* and expanded the university's library, art gallery, and theater company by supplying them with material that had African and black American folk content. Concurrently, he urged administrators at black colleges to eradicate apathy toward the study of African and black American life by designing curricula that reflect these experiences.

Locke's views on education caught the attention of the American Association of Adult Education (AAAE), a predominantly white national organization. In 1933 the AAAE commissioned him to evaluate adult education centers in Harlem and Atlanta. In 1935, responding in part to the lack of black cultural expressions in such programs, Locke founded the Association of Negro Folk Education (ANFE). Nine highly acclaimed Bronze Booklets were published by the ANFE between 1936 and 1942. According to Logan and Winston, Locke wrote that the booklets were published to bring "within reach of the average reader basic facts and progressive views about Negro life." Booklets written exclusively by Locke include *The Negro and His Music* (1936), *Negro Art: Past and Present* (1937), and *The Negro in Art: A Pictorial Record of the Negro Artist and the Negro Theme in Art* (1940).

It is important to note that Locke's attempts to make black cultural expressions an integral part of education were not made to reinforce racial distinctiveness and separation. Instead, his object was to place learning "upon a broader cultural basis." Such a base, Locke held, would help critical minds to solve racial problems. To that end, Locke led the overhaul of Howard University's liberal arts curriculum during the late 1930s, integrating the major disciplines into a general education program. His innovative leadership was recognized in 1945 when the AAAE elected him as its president.

By the time World War II ended, Locke was one of the best known black scholars in the United States. He continued to promote his ideas by accepting appointments at the University of Wisconsin (1945–1946), the New School for Social Research (1947), and the City College of New York (1948). He also continued to contribute articles on value theory, art, and race to various publications, including *Crisis, Nation,* and the *Journal for the Study of Negro Life.* In addition, Locke remained a persuasive member of many professional organizations, including the American Philosophical Association, the International Institute of African Languages and Culture, and the Association for the Study of Negro Life and History.

In 1951, Locke obtained a grant from the Rockefeller Foundation to write a synthesis of his studies of black culture in America. Hospitalized because of a heart ailment, Locke was not able to work on the manuscript until he recovered. In 1953, he retired from Howard University, receiving the university's honorary degree of doctor of humane letters.

Locke moved to New York City, but his health continued to deteriorate. Having never married, he turned to a colleague, Margaret Just Butcher, for help with the manuscript. The next year, however, sensing he would not live through the summer, he gave his materials and plan for the publication to Butcher, telling her simply that if anything should happen to him, she was to "do the book."

On June 9, 1954, Alain Leroy Locke died in Mount Sinai Hospital at age sixty-seven. His body was cremated at Fresh Pond Crematory, Little Village, Long Island. He bequeathed his extensive African art collection and papers to Howard University. Margaret Butcher carried out Locke's last wish, publishing *The Negro in American Culture* in 1956.

During the first half of the twentieth century, Alain Leroy Locke was a persistent apostle of beauty and truth. Through various fields of art he urged blacks to discover, reflect on, and redefine who they are. In addition, he helped whites to comprehend the unity and equivalence underlying Anglo-Saxon and black cultural expressions. In the process, Locke freed many blacks and whites from the effects of racism and, in so doing, helped raise the status of the black race.—CORTEZ RAINEY

M

JACKIE "MOMS" **MABLEY**
1894–1975
Dancer, singer, comedienne

Stand-up comedienne Jackie "Moms" Mabley played the part of a cantankerous, spicy, raucous old lady with a shabby wardrobe and broad, toothless smile in black nightclubs and vaudeville for half a century. After years of relative obscurity, she enjoyed a surge in popularity in the mid-1960s, buoyed by her recordings and television appearances. Veteran observers of the entertainment industry were pleased, for while her comedy act was typically bulging with insults toward old men, it was her generosity and compassion for all of her fellow performers that had earned her the sobriquet "Moms."

Jackie "Moms" Mabley was born Loretta Mary Aiken in Brevard, North Carolina, in 1894. Accounts of her younger years are sketchy and often contradictory, but a hazy portrait can be drawn. Loretta Aiken was one of twelve children. Jim Aiken, her father, owned several different businesses, including the local grocery store. He was also a volunteer fireman, and he died when the truck in which he was riding exploded. Harriet Smith, a former slave who was Loretta Aiken's great-grandmother, helped inspire young Loretta's religious beliefs.

By the time Loretta Aiken was eleven years old, she had been raped by an older black man. Two years later she was raped again by the white town sheriff. Both rapes resulted in children. With two children to support and a stepfather she could not abide, she prayed to God for deliverance. She left Brevard to escape her hated stepfather, leaving her children in the care of two women, and moved to Cleveland at the age of fourteen. In Cleveland she lived with a minister and his family, and she soon became acquainted with a show business performer named Bonnie Belle Drew. Struck by the teenager's beauty, Drew encouraged Aiken to give show business a try. (Aiken later named her fifth child after Bonnie.)

Aiken felt her prayers had been answered when Drew invited her to Pittsburgh the next day. Later that night, Aiken joined Drew and some other entertainers and performed her first show, dancing, singing, and even trying her hand at some comedy routines. During these early days on the road she met Jack Mabley, also an entertainer, and they became close friends. Looking back on those days, she noted that "he took a lot off me, the least I could do was take his name." Thus, Jackie Mabley was born.

Mabley suffered two cruel blows around this time. The two women who were taking care of her children disappeared with the toddlers. She did not see her children again until

Jackie "Moms" Mabley.

they were adults. Soon thereafter Mabley's mother was hit by a truck and killed on her way home from church on Christmas Day.

Mabley rises on the chitlin' circuit

Mabley's entertainment career continued to grow in modest fashion. She traveled throughout the country to venues that catered to black artists, a series of stops known as the chitlin' circuit. She started at twelve dollars a week. The routine was very difficult, especially in the South, where she did two performances a night—one for blacks and one for whites. One never knew when the racism that was so prevalent in that era might become violent. In an interview with the *Washington Post,* Mabley remarked:

> All those white men had black mistresses, you know what I mean. But in the public they made like they didn't know. And one time, I can't forget this,

we were going in a Jim Crow car and we were travelling from Dallas to San Antone. And the train stops in Paris, Texas, and I look out and see this man tied to a stake. They were gonna burn him. So I pulled down that shade. Ignorance. Just ignorance, I say.

Mabley became pregnant again, and although it is unclear whether she was legally married, she gave birth to her third child. Determined to establish a career in entertainment, though, Mabley returned to show business almost immediately.

During the 1920s Mabley continued to develop her act. Over time she became especially known for her comic talents, though she also danced and sang. She developed the character of the dirty old lady with a penchant for younger men. Mabley typically appeared on stage dressed in baggy dresses, oversized shoes, a hat, and droopy stockings. Her trademarks became her bulging eyes, rubbery face, gravelly voice, and later, her toothless grin. She took to referring to the members of her audience as children, and described her character as a good woman with an eye for shady dealings. Mabley envisioned her character as her granny—the most beautiful woman she ever knew.

On the black vaudeville circuit, Mabley appeared on bills with such diverse talents as Pigmeat Markham, Cootie Williams, Tim "Kingfish" Moore, Bill "Bojangles" Robinson, Dusty "Open the Door, Richard" Fletcher, Peg Leg Bates, and John "Spider Bruce" Mason. In the mid-1920s Mabley was discovered by the dance team of Butterbeans and Suzie. They later brought Mabley to New York, where she made her debut at Connie's Inn. The appearance galvanized her career, and soon she was playing at notable venues such as the Cotton Club

The funeral procession of "Moms" Mabley rides through Harlem. **453**

in Harlem and Club Harlem in Atlantic City, appearing on bills with such luminaries as Louis Armstrong, Cab Calloway, Duke Ellington, and Count Basie.

Moms rules the Apollo   In 1939 Mabley became a regular at the Apollo Theatre in Harlem, playing fifteen-week engagements. Mabley appeared at the Apollo Theatre more often than any other act in the history of the venue. She constantly changed her act to maintain her popularity, and noticed after a time that many white comedians ventured up to the Apollo, notebooks in hand, to see her show. Mabley said that with the exception of Jack Benny and Redd Foxx, every comedian stole her material. She was calm about such thefts, though, because she felt God always gave her more to draw from.

Mabley became a well-known fixture at the Apollo, both in front of and behind the stage. Colleagues commented on her love for card playing, as well as her propensity for cheating. Louis Armstrong, Duke Ellington, and Sophie Tucker noted Mabley's compassion for her coworkers and her willingness to help them in times of need; they named her Moms in honor of this maternal quality, and the nickname stuck.

While Mabley's stints at the Apollo were long, she still had the opportunity to display her talents elsewhere. She played Broadway in such shows as *Fast and Furious, Swinging the Dream,* and *Blackbirds.* She was also a regular on the radio show *Swingtime at the Savoy.* In the 1960s the white audience discovered her. She cut a record album, entitled *Moms Mabley— The Funniest Woman in the World,* for Chess Records, and in 1966 she moved to Mercury Records, where she recorded *Now Hear This* and other recordings. Mabley then appeared on television, debuting on "A Time for Laughter," an all-black comedy special produced by Harry Belafonte in 1967. Mabley's star continued to ascend, and soon she was a guest star on a number of popular television shows, appearing on shows hosted by Ed Sullivan, Merv Griffin, the Smothers Brothers, Mike Douglas, Bill Cosby, and Flip Wilson. "The only difference I found when I started doing TV," Moms said, "was that instead of looking at the audience as my children I looked at the world as my children."

Mabley's fortunes soared as a result of the increased television exposure, and the demand for her talent grew at such top venues as the Copacabana in New York City, the Kennedy Center in Washington, D.C., and Carnegie Hall in New York City. Moms rode her popularity to a starring role in the movie *Amazing Grace.* During the filming she had a heart attack, and a pacemaker was implanted. She recovered and returned to filming.

After more than sixty years in the entertainment business, Mabley died of natural causes on May 23, 1975, in White Plains Hospital. She was presumed to be eighty-one. Mabley was survived by her three daughters—Bonnie, with whom she lived in later years, Christine, and Yvonne—and a son, Charles, as well as five grandchildren.

In 1986 Alice Childress remembered Mabley with *Moms: A Praise for a Black Come-dienne.* The play was based on Mabley's life, with music and lyrics by Childress and her husband, Nathan Woodard. It was first produced by Green Plays at Art Awareness in 1986, then off-Broadway at Hudson Guild Theatre on February 4, 1987. The play honored the talent of Moms Mabley and her influence on American humor.—RICHELLE B. CURL

HAKI **MADHUBUTI**

1942–

Poet, essayist, educator, publisher

In a poem entitled "Gwendolyn Brooks" dedicated to one of his mentors, Haki Madhubuti wrote, "into the sixties / a word was born. . . . Black / & with black came poets / & from the poet's ball points came: / black doubleblack purpleblack." While these lines and others in the poem pay homage to Brooks, ringing numerous changes on the word "black," they also provide a context for the life's work of Haki Madhubuti. In the tradition of the poets of the Black Arts Movement, Madhubuti has conveyed in words the essence of blackness; the promulgation of the cultural values of the black community; and the expression of those spiritual, political, and physical beliefs that lead to the health and survival of the community. The rapid fire changes and riffs throughout the language mark the style of a poet whose works are meant to be performed. In his various roles as poet, essayist, teacher, and businessman, Madhubuti has consistently struggled to solidify his definition of black life, black survival, and commitment to the values that lead to cultural wholeness of the individual and the group. His works can be satirical, celebratory, and politically incisive. He has been guided by a desire to promote change through writing, which he expresses in his book Killing Memory, *saying that "the face of poetry must be fire erupting volcanoes, / hot silk forging new histories, / poetry delivering light greater than barricades of silence, / poetry . . . preparing seers, warriors."*

Haki Madhubuti, born Don L. Lee, spent his first year of life in Little Rock, Arkansas, where he was born in 1942. His parents, Jimmy and Maxine Lee, moved the family to Detroit in 1943. However, his father deserted the family shortly after Lee's sister was born, leaving his mother to rear the two children through a series of domestic jobs. Madhubuti's mother died when he was sixteen, and her death resulted in another move to live with his aunt in Chicago. His own family has had more stability; he has been married since 1974 to Safisha, a professor at Northwestern University. Together they have three children: Lani, Bomani, and Akili. He is also the father of two children, Don and Mari, from two previous unions.

Madhubuti's formal education includes a high school diploma received in 1960 from Dunbar Vocational High School in Chicago. He earned his A.A. degree from Chicago City College and later an M.F.A. from the University of Iowa. During his lifetime, he has received various awards, including the National Endowment Grant for Poetry (1983), the Distinguished Writers Award from Middle Atlantic Writers Association (1984), and the American Book Award (1991). He was named Author of the Year by the Illinois Association of Teachers of English, and was the only poet chosen to represent the United States at the International Valmiki World Poetry Festival in New Delhi, India, in 1985.

Early influences   Madhubuti's development as a man of letters can be traced back to the influence of his mother, who exposed him early to the wonders of exploring the library.

Haki R. Madhubuti.

He notes in *Black Men: Obsolete, Single, and Dangerous?* that once his mother introduced him to the marvels of the Detroit Public Library, he was seldom without a book. From this introductory period, made particularly significant by his reading of Richard Wright's *Black Boy,* until his graduation from high school, he read many black writers, including Chester Himes, Frederick Douglass, and Booker T. Washington. While his initiation into the armed services was marred by the vicious reaction of his commanding officer to his reading Paul Robeson's *Here I Stand,* his stint in the army also became a period of intense self-education in African American literature. He left the army in 1963, having read the poetry of Gwendolyn Brooks and the works of other writers, such as Claude McKay and W. E. B. Du Bois. According to Madhubuti in "A Renewed Spirit," this reading "introduced me to ideas that never were discussed in my formal education."

Following his discharge from the army, he became an apprentice and curator at DuSable Museum of African History (1963–67), another significant step in his development, because he was under the apprenticeship of Margaret Burroughs, long an authority on black history and culture. During this period, he also enrolled in Wilson Junior College (now Kennedy-King College). Meanwhile, he was preparing himself for the disciplined life of a writer by following a rather strict regime consisting of reading a book a day and writing a book review of approximately two hundred words. These activities were conducted while he held various jobs in order to maintain himself economically, including a few in the retail establishments of Chicago (Speigel and Montgomery Ward) as well as a job in the post office.

First poetic expressions   Madhubuti's first volume of poetry appeared in 1966 with the publication of *Think Black,* which signaled the direction of this future prolific poet and essayist. Announcing himself to the world, the speaker in this volume reveals to the reader the year in which he was "born into slavery," thus indicating the political turn that much of the poetry would take. In this volume, which was originally self-published and self-distributed, he defines himself unquestioningly as a black poet. He takes the opportunity to castigate America not only for its enslavement of black people, but also for its forced internment of the Japanese during World War II. One of the most frequently anthologized pieces from the book, "Back Again, Home: Confessions of an ex-executive" speaks to a sense of awareness and rebirth, a call to revolutionize one's thinking. Madhubuti's persona realizes the fallacy of his own enslavement to the materialist dream of upward mobility, an enslavement that has resulted in his loss of self. This message remains a constant in Madhubuti's work. From the earliest, he has challenged those values that are destructive of the individual and the culture and has called for their rejection. The volume also reveals, however, another dimension to

Madhubuti's voice that is softer, much more intimate; a poem such as "A Poem for Black Hearts" fits this category.

In 1967, along with Johari Amini (Jewel Latimore) and Carolyn Rodgers, he launched Third World Press with $400 in the basement of his Chicago apartment. Third World Press has the distinction of being the longest continuously operating African American press in America. Its inauguration is reflective of Madhubuti's role as an institution builder, particularly institutions that perpetuate the word and the world of ideas. It was Madhubuti's belief that institutions should be built within the community to support the values of that community, as well as self-reliance. He has noted that it seemed a bit hypocritical to be in the position of criticizing the institutions of America while remaining dependent upon some of those very institutions to convey his beliefs to the public.

Madhubuti with books his company has published.

As the 1960s ended, Madhubuti published two additional volumes of poetry: *Black Pride* (1968) and *Don't Cry, Scream* (1969). In addition, he started the Institute of Positive Education, a school offering two-to-eight-year-olds an Afrocentric education, and he participated in the first Pan African Festival in Algiers. He was also writer-in-residence at Cornell University.

Expanding the vision   The beginning of the new decade saw the publication of *We Walk the Way of the New World* (1970), a collection of poems that continues and expands upon the themes from his earlier works. While "Back Again, Home" speaks directly to the rebirth on the individual level, the title poem speaks to a rebirth on the collective level. Referring to the black person's sojourn in America as the "dangercourse," the speaker reflects on the changes taking place as the race struggles to truly be part of the nation. The poem suggests that it has been a journey marked by elements of self-hatred, non-acceptance, and enslavement to empty capitalistic values, but that black people emerge as "owners of the New World."

An assessment of Madhubuti's significance must take into account the vision articulated in this poem, for it indicates the driving force behind his roles as poet, essayist, and institution builder: to keep before his audience those values that lead to renewal and survival. Continuing the trend from his previous volumes, this one also contains poems that reveal a more intimate side. These poems are included in the section entitled "Blackwoman Poems."

The decade also saw the publication in 1971 of *Directionscore: Selected and New Poems* as well as *To Gwen with Love,* a book he edited with Frances Ward and Patricia Brown. Of major importance was the publication of *Dynamite Voice: Black Poets of the 1960s,* also in 1971. This volume provided a critical context for the writers of the Black Arts Movement by one of the movement's participants. Published by Broadside Press, the work allowed Madhubuti to articulate his definition of the black literary critic's role. While maintaining that the black critic must not be narrow in focus, Madhubuti clearly indicates that it is the black critic's role to reflect upon his or her black experience, which will enable the critic to develop standards of evaluation related to that experience. In 1972, furthering his role as literary critic, Madhubuti started the *Black Books Bulletin.*

The year 1973 was significant, for Madhubuti decided to change his name from Don L. Lee to Haki Madhubuti, a name that means "justice," "awakening," and "strong" in Swahili. That year he was poet-in-residence at Howard University, and his *Book of Life* was published by Broadside Press. Interestingly, the introduction to the volume reveals a certain disillusionment on the part of the poet. He also uses the opportunity in this volume to encourage his audience to be independent and to understand the connection between the development of the black woman and the black nation to their full potential. In 1973 *From Plane to Planet* also appeared. Published jointly by Broadside Press and the Institute of Positive Education, the book had as its motivation the spiritual building of African minds. Therefore, there are ruminations on such topics as self-hatred, money, power, sex, and drug addiction. The decade ended with the publication of *Enemies: The Clash of Races* (1978) and the launching of the African American Book Center.

The 1980s saw a continuation of Madhubuti's role as poet and an expansion of his role as critic. He wrote *Say That the River Turns: The Impact of Gwendolyn Brooks* (1984) and *Killing Memory, Seeking Ancestors* (1987). Third World Press spearheaded the African American Publishers, Booksellers, and Writers Association in 1989.

In speaking of Africa, Madhubuti notes in the prologue to *Killing Memory* that the "land of sun has a special meaning" for him, although he was "not prepared for the land that gave birth to civilization." A further examination of the prologue indicates it has been Madhubuti's goal to move culturally from "Negro to Black to African," a trip on which he as poet/seer/teacher seeks to guide others. "Seeking Ancestors," a poem written for the First Annual Egyptian Studies Conference in Los Angeles in February 1984, is divided into five parts. The first focuses on the "death traps" in American culture, juxtaposed with a rumination of the first people to use the triangle and cultivate the earth. Storytellers are called to remember those people in order to inspire us to better ourselves ("the monk & trane of us, / the hurston and dubois of us / . . . to recall the tradition & meaning / to rename the bringers of genius"). Throughout Madhubuti's poetical career, he has sought to recall those geniuses to the community by devoting poems not only to Gwendolyn Brooks, but also to Hoyt Fuller, Malcolm X, and the nameless others in the community whose lives are examples of survival under difficult circumstances. His role as the "renamer" the "recaller of tradition" can also be seen in the style of much of his poetry that captures the rhythms of talk, accompanied by performance.

While Madhubuti has continued to write poetry in the 1990s, he has also enhanced his role as essayist. In 1990, he published *Black Men: Obsolete, Single, Dangerous? African American Families in Transition,* a book that addresses those issues that continue to threaten the survival of black men in America, and provides advice on the solution to these issues. In 1991, Madhubuti's Third World Press was successful in adding Gwendolyn Brooks to its list of major authors. Responding to the upheaval caused by the Rodney King case in Los Angeles and to ensuing unrest, Madhubuti edited *Why L.A. Happened: Implications of the '92 Los Angeles Rebellion* in 1993. This was followed by *Claiming Earth: Race, Rage, Rape, Redemption; Blacks Seeking a Culture of Enlightened Empowerment* (1994), a book that the author says concerns the development of one's own resources.

One way of summarizing Madhubuti's significance is to refer to a statement from *Claiming Earth.* In it he notes that there is no separation between "my cultural self and my political, professional, business, familial, and writer selves." In his life and career, he has exemplified the individual's attempt to create a unified self and to live a holistic life; one not broken into fragments of person, poet, teacher, and entrepreneur, but a life in which the self is imbued with the cultural values informed by the black experience.— JOHANNA L. GRIMES-WILLIAMS

ANNIE TURNBO **MALONE**

1869–1957

Beauty culture specialist

Annie Minerva Turnbo Pope Malone, a pioneer in black beauty culture, was acclaimed as the nation's first black millionairess. In the 1920s, at the peak of her career, she was said to be worth $14,000,000; at her death her wealth had dwindled to a mere $100,000. The significance of Malone as an entrepreneur, *philanthropist, and founder of the first center for the study and teaching of beauty culture specifically related to African Americans is often unrecognized by this generation of Americans and rarely mentioned in general black American histories.*

Annie Turnbo Malone was born on a farm in Metropolis, Illinois, on August 9, 1869, the tenth of eleven children of Robert Turnbo and Isabella (Cook) Turnbo. Orphaned at a very young age, she was reared primarily by an older sister in Peoria, Illinois.

Concerned about the styling of her coarse hair, she rejected the hair-straightening techniques of Peoria women who, like many late-nineteenth-century black women, used soap, goose fat, and other heavy oils on their hair. In the late 1890s she began to experiment with chemicals to develop a product that would straighten kinky hair without damaging the hair follicles or burning the scalp like so many hair-straightening products used at the turn of the century. By 1900 Malone had developed successful straighteners, hair growers, tetter reliefs, and special hair oils.

Acknowledged by some sources as the first to develop and patent the pressing iron and comb in 1900, Annie Malone manufactured and sold Wonderful Hair Grower while residing in Lovejoy, Illinois. In 1902 she moved her business to St. Louis, Missouri, where she and three trained assistants sold her products door to door, providing free hair and scalp treatments to attract clients. In that same year, during the World's Fair, Malone opened her first business location. Within a year her products were being widely distributed to black women throughout the Midwest. During this period Malone developed marketing strategies aimed at black consumers nationwide. Advertisements were placed in key black newspapers, press conferences were held, and women were recruited as agents to sell her products. Malone toured the South in an effort to expand her business to the nation's black market. Also at this time, in 1903, she married a Mr. Pope; they soon divorced after he attempted to interfere with her business activities.

Coinciding with Annie Malone's expansion effort was the rise of Madame C. J. Walker. A former washerwoman and one of Malone's first students, Walker was employed as an agent for Poro products (Malone's business) by 1905. Not content to sell Poro products and to work for Annie Malone, Madame Walker began to perfect a hair formula similar to that of Malone's, to develop a complexion cream, and to market the hot iron as the primary straightener of black hair.

Walker is cited in numerous historical sources as the first successful major manu-facturer of black beauty products. However, many sources indicate that Malone's business predated the Walker Company. In 1906 Malone copyrighted the trade name "Poro" in order to safeguard her products and merchandising systems from imitators. (Poro is a West African word for an organization dedicated to disciplining and enhancing the body physically and spiritually.) In the early 1900s Poro products did well against those of many competitors, due in part to Malone's system of exclusive, franchised agent-operators, a system also utilized by Madame Walker.

Poro College aids the black community   In 1902 the Poro business was located in St. Louis, and in 1910 it moved to larger quarters just down the street. Although Annie Malone was an entrepreneur, her special focus was the development of Poro College. In 1917 she built the

Poro College complex in St. Louis, which served as a center for education and employment and became the social hub of the city's black community. It was used by diverse local and national organizations for special functions and as office space. In 1927 during the St. Louis tornado disaster, Poro College served as one of the principal facilities of the Red Cross where storm victims were sheltered, clothed, and fed. The main building and its annex contained classrooms, barbershops, laboratories, an auditorium, a dining room, a cafeteria, an ice cream parlor, a bakery, a theater, and a roof garden. The equipment and furnishings of the Poro plant, which included the Poro College Building, were valued at over one million dollars.

In the early twentieth century, black leaders stressed the need for race improvement and the presentation of a positive self-image. Malone, imbued with the values of the black middle class, felt one's deportment was just as important as education. Poro students were taught how to walk, talk, and eat properly. The college trained women as agents for the Poro System and provided jobs for workers and high school students. By 1926 Poro claimed to have 75,000 agents located throughout the United States, the Caribbean, and other parts of the world. The Poro College employed 175 people. In 1930 the business and college were moved to Chicago. Located at 44th Street on South Parkway, the area was called the Poro Block.

Following a period of major growth in the 1920s, Poro became a vast hair care empire. Shortly after the boom, however, Malone's enterprise suffered from poor decisions made by incompetent and dishonest managers. While Poro was showing its first signs of decline, Malone was also engaged in a power struggle with her husband, Aaron Malone, who was the chief manager and president of Poro until 1927. For almost six years prior to their much-publicized divorce in 1927, they maintained a facade of happiness. Their troubled relationship adversely affected the operation of the business.

Prior to suing Annie Malone for divorce, Aaron Malone actively courted Poro supporters, national black leaders, and key community sources for personal support that would be an effective weapon in wrestling control of Poro from his wife. In the divorce suit, Aaron Malone asserted that Poro enterprises had succeeded because of his business acumen and ability to market the company through an extensive network of contacts developed prior to their marriage. He demanded one-half of the business assets. The black leadership was divided in their support for Annie and Aaron Malone. However, Annie Malone had the backing of powerful black club women like Mary McLeod Bethune, who in 1927 was the national president of the National Association of Colored Women. Since Poro products were marketed primarily to women, many of whom benefitted from Annie Malone's philanthropic efforts, she gained the edge. Annie Malone kept the business from going into receivership, negotiated a settlement of $200,000 with Aaron Malone, and got a divorce. On the surface, she appeared victorious; however, Malone's self-image and the business had suffered.

Following the divorce, Malone's reputation was marred; her resources were further depleted by other legal battles, one of which forced the sale of her St. Louis property. Between 1943 and 1951 Malone was also involved in lawsuits filed against her to claim thousands of dollars in excise taxes, which the federal government required for all luxuries and cosmetics. By 1951 the government had taken control of Poro. Malone's failure to pay real estate taxes led to the sale of most of the Poro property.

Nation's first major black philanthropist   Annie Malone was the nation's first major black philanthropist. Because of her extensive philanthropy, she became known as overgenerous. At one time she reportedly was supporting two full-time students in every black land-grant college in the United States. Numerous black orphanages received $5,000 or more annually. She purchased homes for her brothers and sisters and educated many of her nephews and nieces. Howard University's Medical School Endowment, the St. Louis Colored YWCA, and Tuskegee Institute benefited greatly from Malone's generosity, receiving well over $60,000 during the 1920s. When Poro College opened in 1918, it was said that the Malones had contributed more to charity and Christian associations than any hundred black Americans in the United States.

Malone's philanthropy extended to employees. Her concern for their welfare was demonstrated in lavish gifts. At annual Poro Christmas banquets she gave diamond rings to five-year employees, gold awards to real estate investors, and prizes for punctuality and attendance. As noteworthy as Malone's philanthropy was, it too created financial problems that plagued her from beginning to end.

Throughout her life Malone was intensely concerned about the material and cultural uplift of her race. She held memberships and served offices in a number of organizations, including the National Negro Business League and the Commission on Interracial Cooperation. She served as chairman of the board of directors of the St. Louis Colored Orphans Home, an institution later named after her, and president of the Colored Women's Federated Clubs in St. Louis.

Malone died of a stroke on May 10, 1957, in Chicago's Provident Hospital. Generations will benefit from the contributions Annie Turnbo Malone made during her lifetime as a woman focused on charitable causes and on African American women's beauty.—BETTYE COLLIER-THOMAS

THURGOOD **MARSHALL**
1908–1993
Lawyer, civil rights activist, Supreme Court justice

Thurgood Marshall is a towering presence in the history of the United States and civil rights. As a young attorney working for the NAACP, he spent most of his career forcing the courts and America to look at the U.S. Constitution and realize which rights did not extend to African Americans. His pursuit of this goal led to the ground-breaking Brown v. Board of Education *decision that declared separate but equal educational facilities unconstitutional. The ruling was a triumphant event as it began the deconstruction of segregation in the South. Marshall's brilliant argument of this and several other cases led him to become the first African American justice on the Supreme Court, where his presence was symbolized by his overt libertarian views that placed the individuals and their rights first.*

Thurgood Marshall was born Thoroughgood Marshall on July 2, 1908 to William Canfield and Norma Marshall in Baltimore, Maryland. Marshall was the couple's second son

*Thurgood
Marshall.*

and was named after his great-grandfather, a slave brought over from the Congo. The Marshall family lived a comfortable life with patriarch William having a string of steady jobs as a country club steward and Pullman porter, while mother Norma worked as a teacher in segregated schools in Baltimore.

Thoroughgood Marshall, whose name was shortened to Thurgood beginning his second year of schooling, was not a model student. While in high school, he often got into trouble for fist fights or skipping school. At one time, his high school principal punished Marshall by having him memorize the U.S. Constitution, a lesson he would treasure for the rest of his life. Marshall's mediocrity in high school did not win him any merits, but it did give him a diploma and a dream to go to college.

In September 1925, Marshall entered Lincoln University, an all-black, all-male university in Pennsylvania, with the intent to study dentistry. But Marshall's rowdy behavior from high school carried over into college. Marshall was suspended and almost expelled due to charges of public drunkenness, hazing underclassmen, and initiating a food strike. Marshall's troublesome conduct as an undergraduate later matured in a strength and leadership that would support him during his tenacious days in front of a courtroom. During his senior year at Lincoln University, Marshall became committed to his education and to a woman he met and fell in love with in 1929. Her name was Vivien "Buster" Burey, and she and Marshall married that same year. The newlyweds faced a challenging feat while Marshall struggled to get his degree, but he finally graduated from Lincoln in 1930 with a B.A. *cum laude* in dentistry, but with no desire to use it.

Enters law school   Realizing that he did not possess the temperament to accept a passive occupation such as a dentist, and since his brother was becoming a doctor, Marshall decided on a career in law. He applied to the University of Maryland but was rejected (a rejection that Marshall later challenged in a court case) and attended Howard University, one of the few accredited black law schools, where he would later meet his mentor and colleague, Charles Hamilton Houston. Their first encounter was not a pleasant one: on the first day of class Houston caught Marshall gambling outside the school. But Houston's stern yet inspiring teachings would equip Marshall with the necessary knowledge and training to challenge the decision of *Plessy v. Ferguson,* on which the "separate but equal" practice was based, and which legitimized Jim Crow statues and Maryland's refusal to admit Marshall into its law school. Houston was adamant that his students learn every aspect of *Plessy*'s decision and the 14th Amendment to counter and abolish *Plessy*'s verdict. Houston's inspiration drove deep in Marshall and stayed. Marshall graduated from Howard with honors in 1933.

Marshall assumed from Houston the daunting responsibility of striking down laws that held African Americans, especially children, back from obtaining proper education in poor, dilapidated schools. Through his knowledge of the law, Marshall would partake in a crusade to raise his people from the degradation they faced through current court rulings.

After his graduation from Howard, Marshall moved back to Baltimore to practice law, and Houston went to work as legal counsel for the NAACP. But business was slow and Houston asked Marshall to help him record the conditions of Southern schools so that the NAACP legal counsel could advance their struggle to end segregation. Marshall's findings were a chilling discovery of how terrible conditions were for children in the South. The districts' funding for these schools designated for blacks was a fraction of the money spent on white students. African American children had to learn in classrooms filled to capacity sharing only a few books that were given to them by white schools, and most devastatingly, there were no high schools built for African Americans in some counties. Originally, Houston and Marshall's attempt to gather complaints for a court case against a southern county was met with fear from locals. Therefore, the battle the NAACP started against segregation became a slow and arduous process. Houston and Marshall concluded that going after *Plessy* at this time would be too soon and too massive, and planned instead to "chip away" at it by various cases that dealt with African Americans being rejected from graduate studies in all-white law schools.

First legal victory   In 1935, their first case dealt with an African American named Donald Murray who was rejected by the University of Maryland due to race, but was told that he should attend either Howard or a less accredited law school in Maryland. Murray, an honor student from Amherst, was determined to attend law school in Maryland and therefore became an excellent candidate to set the legal wheels in motion for the NAACP, Houston, and Marshall. In the case, *University of Maryland v. Murray,* Houston argued that if African Americans wanted to practice law in Maryland and could not attend the University of Maryland (the only law school in the state), then there was a need to build one that was equal to the University of Maryland in order to maintain the separate but equal clause of *Plessy*. The judge and others, seeing no need to build a separate law school for "Negroes," ruled in favor of the plaintiff, Murray, and ordered the dean to admit Donald Murray into the University of Maryland law school. It was Houston's and Marshall's first victory, but a limited one since the decision stuck to one school and one state. The two searched for a case that could be appealed to the Supreme Court.

After much agony, in 1938, Houston and Marshall found a second case that would support their cause. Law student Lloyd Lionel Gaines applied to the all-white law school in Missouri, but was rejected. But the Missouri school did offer Gaines a scholarship for him to attend school out of state. Houston, as lead counsel, argued in the case later known as *Gaines v. Missouri* that the university should provide equal facilities to its Negro students, and that the solution of scholarships for these students to go to other states for education was not adequate. "Missouri alone should provide for its own Negroes," argued Houston. The court agreed and ordered the University of Missouri to admit Gaines. It was another victory for the legal team of Houston and Marshall on the path of dismantling *Plessy,* but again, it was a graduate school, and the verdict applied only to one state and one school.

Marshall becomes lead counsel for NAACP   Health problems and a heavy case load forced Houston to step down from the NAACP. He handed his duties to the only man who had the tactics, strategies, and conviction to take on the fight for justice. At the age of thirty, Marshall became head legal counsel for the NAACP. The first case Marshall argued as lead was against the Texas law school, in *Sweatt v. Texas*.

Herman Marion Sweatt applied to the University of Texas law school but was denied admission on the grounds that the state of Texas was in the process of building its own law school for Negroes. The school turned out to be nothing more than a one-room basement hastily set up to avoid prosecution. Sweatt continued his suit with Marshall leading the way. The court case reached the Supreme Court and introduced the first vestiges of what Marshall and the NAACP wanted all along: to end school segregation in all levels of education. The court unanimously granted Sweatt admission to the University of Texas, and abolished any statute that would encourage segregation on the graduate level. Even though the court hesitated to completely reverse the *Plessy* decision, the Sweatt case became a prerequisite to broadening integration to public schools. Encouraged by the decision of *Sweatt v. Texas,* Marshall gathered a group of elite African American lawyers to start taking *Plessy* head on.

Marshall argues the Brown case

Marshall argues the Brown case   The *Brown* case was initiated when the Reverend Oliver Brown tried to enroll his seven-year-old daughter into the Sumner Elementary School in Topeka, Kansas. He was denied. As more and more parents from Clarendon County in South Carolina and Virginia signed petitions, Marshall soon had ample ammunition to argue against school segregation, but a more difficult task lay ahead. In order for the Supreme Court to overturn *Plessy,* Marshall had to prove how segregation was unlawful and harmful to African American children. For this task, Marshall chose Dr. Kenneth Clark, eminent psychologist and researcher, to prove that segregation hurts and impairs African American children. This psychological damage, which brands these children as inferior, prevents them from learning. Marshall accompanied Clark to South Carolina to witness first-hand the chilling effects of young African American children becoming ashamed of who they are. In 1952, Marshall began his arguments for school desegregation, which came before the Supreme Court in 1954. Marshall argued that in order for 'Negro' students to be given equal education, they would have to be exposed to "the same teachers, the same books, the same discussions." Marshall's quest for a "simple justice" involved a heated debate with the great lawyer John W. Davies, who had argued over one hundred cases before the Supreme Court and never lost. Challenged but never unwavering, Marshall's passionate speeches and brilliance in using the law to "give his people the rights denied them after years of enslavement and overturn laws that kept his people still enslaved," convinced the court of the only alternative. In 1954, the court struck down laws and ended over fifty years of school segregation. In its unanimous decision, the court asked the question that Marshall and his team answered:

> Does segregation of children in public schools solely on the basis of race, even though the physical facilities and other "tangible" factors may be equal, deprive the children of the minority group of equal educational opportunities? We believe that it does. . . . In the field of public education the doctrine of "separate but equal" has no place. Separate educational facilities are inherently unequal.

The decision read by chief justice Warren Burger was a resounding drum of victory in Marshall's legal career and for African Americans everywhere.

Marshall continues to engineer social change

Marshall continues to engineer social change   After the Supreme Court's decision in the *Brown* case, attorney Marshall was thrust into the spotlight and given the title of "Mr. Civil Rights." His life hit a sad note when in 1955, his first wife, Vivien, died after a long illness. A year later, he married Cecilla Suyat, a secretary at the NAACP's New York office. His legal battles continued as Marshall fought and won cases before the Supreme Court dealing with white-only primary elections and restrictive covenants. Becoming an experienced lawyer before the highest court, Marshall had the desire of obtaining a judgeship. With his law cases giving him much attention from Democrats who soon took hold of the White House in the sixties, Marshall was given his first appointment by John F. Kennedy in the United States Court of Appeals for the Second Circuit. As circuit judge, Marshall made 112 rulings that were later upheld by the Supreme Court. From 1965 to 1967, Marshall served as Solicitor General under President Lyndon Johnson. When a vacancy in the Supreme Court arose, President Johnson appointed Marshall to fill that vacancy. Johnson received much opposition even from Democrats who tried to block the nomination, but by a vote of 69–11, Marshall was sworn into the highest court. President Johnson said of Marshall's appointment that it was "the right thing to do, the right time to do it, the right man and the right place." In 1967, Thurgood Marshall became the first African American to serve on the Supreme Court.

Justice Marshall upholds his liberal views On the Supreme Court, Marshall is remembered and respected by his peers as a man who did not waver from his liberal views on a bench dominated by conservatives. Marshall adamantly protected freedom of speech and was a staunch opponent of what he labeled cruel and unusual punishment regarding the death penalty. Justice William Rehnquist had once stated that an offender's repeated appeals had cost the state too much money. Marshall interrupted by stating, "It would have been cheaper to shoot him right after he was arrested, wouldn't it?"

With his candid nature, Marshall gained the admiration of supporters and opponents with his opinions on women's rights in regards to abortion, and gender and racial affirmative action programs that were jeopardized. Marshall was an egalitarian judge whose interpretation of the Constitution allowed government to provide certain benefits, such as education and legal services, if people could not afford it. Marshall was a man who represented the poor and weak.

In the 1980s, when the presidency witnessed two Republicans, Marshall saw a clear and present danger to the civil rights of individuals, in particular minorities. He was a constant critic of the Reagan administration, commenting on President Ronald Reagan being "at the bottom" in terms of his commitment to black Americans. As the political climate changed, so did the Supreme Court as more and more conservative judges were appointed. Soon William Brennen retired, leaving Marshall alone to fight for the underdog. But health problems and advancing age forced Marshall to step down from the Supreme Court in 1991. He died two years later at the age of eighty-five.

Thurgood Marshall had a long and illustrious career. The philosophy behind his famous court cases was as plain and simple as the language he used to argue them, "equal means equal." This was apparent to Marshall and his people, but it took Marshall's strength, brilliance, and conviction to convince juries and the Supreme Court to agree. The court cases that Marshall won are regarded as the "quiet frontier" to social justice, but the victories engineered by Marshall could not have been any more triumphant.—MICHELLE BANKS

JAMES H. **MEREDITH**

1933–

Civil rights pioneer, lecturer, entrepreneur

James H. Meredith was a pioneer in the desegregation of higher education in the South. He became known during the civil rights era of the 1960s when he withstood bitter opposition upon integrating the University of Mississippi, becoming its first black graduate. The involvement of the John F. Kennedy administration and the use of the military to ensure Meredith's admittance to the school brought international attention to the case.

Moses "Cap" Meredith named his son J. H. Meredith to prevent whites from calling him simply by his first name. It was not until 1950, when the son enlisted in the Air Force, that he had to bow to regulations and give himself a full name; then he became James Howard Meredith. Meredith was born on June 25, 1933, in Kosciusko, the hill section of Mississippi. He was the seventh of thirteen children born to a farmer. Cap Meredith had children by his first wife, then had James and his younger siblings with his second wife, Roxie Smith, whom he married after being widowed.

Meredith himself was widowed and the father of three sons when he married Judy Alsobrooks, a television reporter from Cincinnati, Ohio; they have a son and a daughter together.

To receive his early education, for eleven years Meredith walked over four miles each way, daily, to Attala County Training School, the elementary and high school for blacks in the area. While white students were bussed to school, no school transportation was provided to the black students. None of his teachers held a college degree. In 1950, Meredith's junior year in high school, the Merediths sent their son away from the inferior, segregated schools in Kosciusko to St. Petersburg, Florida, where he lived with an aunt and uncle and attended Gibbs High School. He graduated the next year, 1951, joined the U.S. Air Force, and spent the next nine years in service as a clerk-typist. Stationed in Kansas, he took extension courses at the University of Kansas before enrolling at Washburn University in Topeka. He also studied in the U.S. Armed Forces Institute from 1954–1960. While stationed in Japan for two years, 1958–60, he enrolled in the University of Maryland's Far Eastern Division.

Before leaving for Japan, Meredith and his wife, Mary June Wiggins Meredith, whom he met on an Air Force post in Indiana and married in 1956, made arrangements to enter Mississippi's all-black Jackson State College (now University) as full-time students in September 1960. James Meredith entered as an advanced junior in history and political science. By December 1961, he had completed all requirements for his degree at Jackson State. He wrote in his autobiography *Three Years in Mississippi* that the Legal Defense Fund, the Justice Department, the Federal Court of Appeals, and other groups advised him not to graduate from Jackson State in order not to be declared ineligible for

James Meredith in 1960.

admission later to the University of Mississippi (Ole Miss). Jackson State had ordered his diploma and a yellow tassel to indicate he was graduating with honors; his name was on the list of graduates. The only way to delay graduation was to refuse to pay a required four dollar and fifty-cent fee, which Meredith did. He continued to enroll in classes well after his class graduated in May of 1962.

Integrates Ole Miss Inspired by the broadcast of President John F. Kennedy's 1961 inaugural address, Meredith, an obscure Air Force veteran, decided he wanted to exercise his democratic rights and apply for admission to the University of Mississippi, although it was off-limits to blacks. Meredith went to see Medgar Evers, Mississippi's NAACP field secretary, who advised him to write to Thurgood Marshall of the Legal Defense and Educational Fund.

*James Meredith
in 1990.* **489**

In his letter to Marshall, reprinted in *Three Years in Mississippi,* Meredith said he wanted to make this move in what he considered the interest of his country, race, family, and himself. "I am familiar with the probable difficulties involved in such a move as I am undertaking and I am fully prepared to pursue it all the way to a degree from the University of Mississippi," he declared.

Meredith applied for admission to Ole Miss's summer term. On May 25, 1961, the school denied his application. After that, Clarence Motley of the Legal Defense Fund filed a class-action suit in the district court; the petition said Meredith had been denied admission solely because of race. While the court ruled in favor of Ole Miss, the U.S. Fifth Circuit Court of Appeals in New Orleans overturned that decision and on June 25, 1962, Meredith's twenty-ninth birthday, the court ruled that Meredith should be admitted to Ole Miss. On September 13, Justice Hugo Black issued an injunction against the university officials, ordering them to admit Meredith according to his application on file, and prohibiting any form of racial discrimination.

Angered by the decision, Mississippi governor Ross R. Barnett defied the federal government on statewide radio and television with the promise that he would interpose the state's authority between the university and the federal judges. Quoted in *Before the Mayflower,* Barnett said, "There is no case in history where the Caucasian race has survived social integration." Barnett would go to jail, if necessary, to prevent integration at the school. After the governor and lieutenant governor had both denied Meredith's admission, President John F. Kennedy responded with an executive order providing assistance in removing unlawful obstruction of justice. Federal marshals escorted Meredith to his dormitory room. The National Guard and army troops were ordered in to quell the violence that erupted on campus and to protect Meredith. Two men died, scores were injured, and over two hundred protesters were arrested. Despite all of this, Meredith graduated in August 1963, the same year federal marshals ended their stay on the campus.

Meredith marches against fear   On June 6, 1966, Meredith, in an attempt to draw attention to black voting rights in the South and to help blacks overcome the fear of violence if they attempted to vote, organized what he called a March Against Fear. The 220-mile march was along Route 51 from Memphis, Tennessee, to Jackson, Mississippi. On the second day of the march, white activist James Aubrey Norvell attempted to assassinate Meredith with gunfire. Martin Luther King Jr., Floyd McKissick, Stokely Carmichael, and other civil rights demonstrators were inspired to continue the march, ending it with a 30,000-person rally at the state capitol. It was during that week that Carmichael launched the Black Power movement.

The assassination attempt didn't stop Meredith. By the latter half of the 1960s, he was in New York obtaining his law degree at Columbia University and found time to become involved in politics. He found resistance when he challenged Adam Clayton Powell Jr. for his seat in Congress. Although the House of Representatives had censured Powell for his political and ethical behavior, he was still popular and widely accepted among his Harlem constituents. Additionally, in 1966, Meredith's autobiography, *Three Years in Mississippi,* was published by Indiana University Press.

Returning to Mississippi in 1971, Meredith again felt the wrath of many blacks for failing to endorse the popular Charles Evers, the black mayor of Fayette and the first black candidate for governor in modern times. Meredith was unsuccessful in his bid for public office five additional times in the 1970s. During this period he made a fairly good living from income earned from speaking engagements. He also formed the Reunification Under God Church and became involved in investment banking, sales, farming, and other activities that were not lucrative.

Meredith took an interest in college teaching, but was unsuccessful in landing a full-time job in Mississippi, including the much-preferred Ole Miss. He did teach a course on blacks and the law at Ole Miss in 1984 and 1985, and later he accepted a position as visiting professor in Afro-American Studies at the University of Cincinnati in Ohio. There he is said to have made undocumented charges of racial discrimination against college and city officials. When his contract was not renewed the next year, Meredith moved to San Diego in search of a position with the Republican party.

In 1989 North Carolina's conservative Republican senator Jesse Helms offered Meredith a $30,000-per-year position as domestic policy advisor, researcher, and writer. They dissolved the relationship later and by 1991 Meredith was in the news again, this time as endorser of former Ku Klux Klan leader David Duke, gubernatorial candidate in Louisiana.

Meredith began to devote more time to writing and research. In 1991 he established Meredith Publishing, located in Jackson, Mississippi, the outlet for his multi-volume set *Mississippi: A Volume of Eleven Books* and other works. Meredith launched another march—the Black Man's March to the Library—thirty years after his first, which aimed to promote reading and the writing of standard English. Quoted in the *Los Angeles Sentinel,* he said: "The language spoken in the black community is not the language used in our education system. . . . Anyone not learning standard English will not excel in our education system." He set out from a Memphis library on June 1, 1996, for a repeat walk along U.S. 51 to reach Jackson on his sixty-third birthday, June 25. Slowed by prostate cancer surgery in April, he had to be driven the last fifty miles.

Recent attention was called to Meredith's historic work at Ole Miss when the film *Ghosts of Mississippi* was released in 1997. The film is a reenactment of the life of Medgar Evers, Meredith's close advisor in the integration of Ole Miss.—JESSIE CARNEY SMITH

KWEISI **MFUME**

1948–

Congressman, civil rights leader, organization official

Kweisi Mfume, as a teenager, was captured by the fast-paced street life in West Baltimore. He refused to allow the negative forces of the inner city to keep him down, however, and broke free from the city's shackles to become a leader in the black community, serving in the United States House of Representatives before becoming head of the NAACP.

Mfume was born Frizzell Gray on October 24, 1948, in Turners Station, Maryland, a small town ten miles south of Baltimore. The oldest of four children, he and his three

*Kweisi Mfume meets
with the press.*

sisters, Darlene, LaWana, and Michele, lived with their mother, Mary Elizabeth William Gray, and Mfume's stepfather, Clifton Gray. Mfume and his family lived in Turners Station until the spring of 1960, when his mother, newly separated from Gray, moved the family to Baltimore. Mfume quickly adapted to his new surroundings. He sold newspapers to supplement the family's income and made new friends. It was during this period that Kweisi Mfume met Rufus Tate, a long-time friend of the family who would help them out with money when they were in a financial bind. The Grays always seemed to be struggling to keep things together and moved from house to house because they were unable to pay rent regularly.

Mfume's interest in politics was first sparked in Baltimore. One evening in the fall of 1962 Mfume slipped out of the house and went down to the Fifth Regiment Armory to see President John F. Kennedy speak to the people of Baltimore. Mfume wrote in *No Free Ride,*

"[I doubt if] there was a soul in the rally who wanted to be there more than [I], or who was as giddy and excited over Kennedy's vision of hope and progress as [I] was."

In 1964 Mary Gray learned she had cancer and had little time to live. Her primary concern was for the care of her children after she was gone. She and the rest of the family decided that the girls would go to live with their grandmother, and that Mfume would move in with his two uncles. When she died in her son's arms one April evening, his life was changed forever. That night Rufus Tate came over to the house, not only to offer his condolences to the family, but also to reveal to the young Mfume that he was his biological father.

At the age of sixteen Mfume was cast into the world of adults. He had to support himself and felt obligated to provide for his sisters as well. He tried to hold down two jobs and go to school, but the task was overwhelming. Mfume felt alone without his mother's guidance and dropped out of school. He had one unsuccessful marriage and relationships with several women, resulting in five children, all boys. The little bit of money that he was making was not enough to support his children and himself.

Mfume began to hang out on the street corner and run numbers to make money. Running numbers paid more than both his jobs and was a lot easier. He began to hang around known hustlers, and as a result his reputation as a hoodlum grew. Mfume was picked up by the police several times. He became engulfed by the street life, making fast money, drinking, gambling, and even carrying a gun. His life was rapidly plummeting in the wrong direction.

There are two major events that Mfume believes turned his life around. Both occurred on the same street corner. The first was a chance encounter with Parren Mitchell, a Maryland congressman. Mitchell challenged Mfume to stop being part of the problem and to start becoming part of the solution. Mfume thought a lot about the encounter; it was not until the second event, however, that Mfume began to change his life.

One night he was standing on the corner shooting dice with his friends when a weird feeling came over him. He had a vision of his mother's face appearing before his eyes. Mfume believed this vision was a revelation from God that indicated it was time to change his life. When the vision ended, he turned and left that corner and the street life for good.

Life turns around   Mfume slowly but surely turned his life around. He earned his graduate equivalence diploma (GED), then enrolled in the Community College of Baltimore. He also worked as a disk jockey at a local radio station owned by James Brown and volunteered to work on some local political campaigns. As a DJ, Mfume created a show called *Ebony Reflections,* on which he discussed issues that were of concern to the black community. Mfume played speeches of Malcolm X and Martin Luther King Jr. and poetry by Nikki Giovanni over jazz tunes.

Ebony Reflections provided Mfume with an arena to voice his political views. It was during this period that Mfume decided to change his name from Frizzell Gray to his present African name to reflect his cultural heritage. Kweisi Mfume means "conquering son of kings." He graduated from the Community College of Baltimore in 1974, then entered Morgan State University. While at Morgan State, Mfume helped the Student Government Association to lobby for a university radio station. The founding of WEAA-FM at Morgan State provided Mfume with the chance to gain experience and expand his creativity.

In 1976 Mfume graduated magna cum laude from Morgan State. He was offered a job at Morgan State as a faculty member, accepted, and served as program director of WEAA while he taught political science and communication courses. As station director and talk show host of WEAA, Mfume continued to voice his displeasure with Baltimore's local government. One caller suggested he run for the Baltimore city council, and that is exactly what Mfume did.

In 1978 he launched his campaign for the fourth district city council seat. Without money, the campaign seemed to be headed nowhere. Still, Mfume's dedication to making a change captured the voters, and his door-to-door campaigning showed people he was willing to fight for what he believed in. Although the election was close, he won. He held the position for seven years.

Mfume continued his education during his tenure on the city council. He attended Johns Hopkins University, where he earned a master's degree in liberal arts in 1989. During his years of service on the city council, he gained a reputation for being an honest politician who would fight tooth and nail for his constituents. Most importantly, he learned how to gain support for his ideas and how to pick and choose his battles.

The departure of Parren Mitchell from the Seventh Congressional District seat opened the door for Mfume to take his views and ideas to the federal level to help more people. He won the congressional seat in 1987 after a tough and slanderous campaign that was marked by attacks against his morality. He was a very active member of the House of Representatives during his five terms. He served on four committees: Banking, Finance and Urban Affairs, Small Business, and the Select Committee on Hunger.

In his first term on Capitol Hill, he served as the treasurer for the Congressional Black Caucus (CBC). Mfume steadily progressed up the ladder in the CBC. Each term he gained a higher position, and in 1993 he became the chairman. At the helm, Mfume and the rest of the CBC had power in numbers to influence legislation in the House of Representatives. Mfume changed the direction of the CBC, choosing to focus on economic empowerment and political networking. The caucus was able to help push some issues through the House, such as tax breaks for the working poor. They also pressured President Bill Clinton to send United States troops to Haiti.

Heads NAACP   Mfume believed his accomplishments as a congressman were few and far between. He stated in a 1996 *U.S News and World Report* article, "It's difficult to bring about the kind of change I want as an individual member of Congress. I could stay and do little or leave and do a lot." On February 20, 1996, Mfume resigned from Congress to become president and chief executive officer for the National Association for the Advancement of Colored People (NAACP). Mfume's first priority was to get the organization out of its seven-figure debt. In Mfume's first year as president, he not only succeeded in erasing its debt, but he also increased its membership. He did this by raising money from a variety of sources including members, foundations, and corporations. Mfume also expanded the scope of the organization to encompass problems facing people on the street corner as well as the larger battles against social, political, and economic injustices. Because he believes that the multidimensional problems facing the black community would benefit from more than one perspective, he has asked other organizations to work with the NAACP to find solutions to these problems.

Mfume is a man who has been at both the bottom and the top of the social order. He has endured pain and suffering in his life with courage and determination to succeed and correct the problems that stood as obstacles in his youth. Mfume's years of public service to the American people reflect his commitment to make the United States the greatest place on earth to live. His life's example offers teenagers and the downtrodden hope to control their own destiny.—DAMIEN BAYARD INGRAM

OSCAR MICHEAUX
c. 1884–1951
Filmmaker, novelist, farmer

A trailblazer for today's independent black filmmakers and a key figure in movie history, Oscar Micheaux was a pioneering filmmaker whose efforts produced forty melodramas, social dramas, gangster movies, and musicals between 1918 and 1948. He was a novelist, publisher, producer, and distributor of his own books and films. He rejected the stereotypical roles for blacks and worked assiduously to create on-screen images that would counter the racist representations of black Americans. Micheaux was the one black filmmaker who survived the competition from Hollywood and even the Great Depression, making the successful transition from silent to talking motion pictures.

Oscar Micheaux was born in January 1883 or 1884 in Metropolis, Illinois, a small town in Masac County near the Ohio River. He was one of eleven children born to Swan and Belle Micheaux. His parents were former slaves who had moved to Illinois from Kentucky when the Civil War ended. His father owned a small farm and his mother, having taught herself to read and write, taught school. An older brother, Lawrence, fought in the Spanish-American War under Teddy Roosevelt in 1898. He later contracted a disease and died in the service.

As a young man Micheaux was curious about the world around him and observed much. He spent a lot of time talking and listening to the black Pullman porters who worked on the Illinois Central railroad that came through his town. He heard stories about Chicago, New Orleans, and Harlem that fired his imagination. He was also told that in big cities he could make more money than he could ever hope to make in Metropolis.

In 1900, Micheaux decided to try his luck in Chicago. He worked in an automobile plant and in a coal mine for $1.25 a day before he arrived. Micheaux's older brother, William, was in Chicago and provided him a place to stay while he looked for work. Micheaux finally got a job pitching hay and moved to Wheaton, Illinois. Here he earned enough money to open his first bank account. In 1902, Micheaux obtained a job as Pullman porter, earning forty dollars a month. He increased his bank account to over $2,000. His travels from coast to coast gave him experience he would later draw upon to create his novels and movies.

Black homesteader in South Dakota   With big dreams, Micheaux left the Pullman Company in 1906. He heard about government land being auctioned off in South Dakota, and decided to try his luck. Near the town of Gregory, South Dakota, he purchased a quarter section of land for $3,000 from Olivet Swanton. In 1909 he purchased another quarter section for $640. He now owned 320 acres of South Dakota farmland. He was the only black homesteader in this section of South Dakota.

Farming proved successful for Micheaux. It seems he planted and harvested simultaneously by rotating the crops so one was ready for harvest at the time he was planting a different crop. Despite his unorthodox methods of farming, Micheaux had cultivated 120 acres of his land by the end of his first year, significantly more than any of his neighbors.

Micheaux's fame as a farmer spread as far east as Chicago, where he often visited. But life on the prairie was lonesome. He urged his friends to homestead in South Dakota but was unable to persuade them to leave the city. On March 19, 1910, Micheaux wrote in the *Chicago Defender:*

> The Negro leads in the consumption of produce, and especially meat, and then his fine clothes—he hasn't the least thought of where the wool grew that he wears and describes himself as being "classy." He can give you a large theory on how the Negro problem should be solved, but it always ends that (in his mind) there is no opportunity for the Negro. . . . I am not trying to offer a solution of the Negro problem, for I don't feel there is any problem further than the future of anything, whether it be a town, a state or race. It depends first on individual achievement, and I am at a loss to see a brilliant future for the young colored man unless he first does something for himself.

In 1909 Micheaux became enamored with a young school teacher from southern Illinois named Orlean McCracken. She was the youngest of two daughters of N. J. McCracken, presiding elder of the African Methodist Episcopal (AME) Church's southern Illinois district. When Micheaux was a young boy, the minister had been pastor of the AME church in Metropolis. After a long-distance courtship, Micheaux proposed marriage to Orlean. They were married in a small church in Chicago by the Reverend W. D. Cook on Thursday, April 20, 1910. Micheaux and his new wife left the same day for their home in Gregory, South Dakota.

From the beginning, the marriage was doomed. His city wife was unhappy in the isolated sod house without family or friends nearby. Farm work was hard and she was accustomed to teaching school; furthermore, his in-laws suspected Micheaux of marrying their daughter as a means of acquiring more land. To make matters worse, in March 1911 their first child was stillborn. Micheaux's in-laws blamed him for not being with his wife when the child was born. Micheaux's absence was due to a farming accident.

Several weeks later his wife left him, going back to Chicago with her father and sister. Micheaux went to Chicago several times to try to win her back but was unsuccessful.

The birth of a writer   Micheaux's days as a homesteader were drawing to a close. The droughts during the summer of 1911 severely damaged his crops, and he was unable to meet his mortgage payments. The *Gregory Times Advocate,* March 20, 1913, included the sale of one of Micheaux's quarter sections for the sum of $1888.27 by the Farmers and Traders Bank. The previous year, in June, the Royal Union Mutual Insurance Company had foreclosed on another section.

Despondent over his failed marriage and disappointed over the loss of his land, Micheaux was prompted to write a book describing his experiences. His book was titled *The Conquest* and was published in 1913 by the Woodruff Press in Lincoln, Nebraska. While the book was marketed as a novel, it actually was the autobiography of Micheaux with fictitious names and places. It details his early life in Metropolis, his job as a Pullman porter, and his experience in homesteading in the Rosebud section of South Dakota. The book presents an accurate account of how life was in this section of the United States from 1904 to 1913.

Months before the book was published, Micheaux was busy marketing it by himself. On April 3, 1913, the *Gregory Times Advocate* contained the following notice: "Oscar Micheaux was in the city Saturday taking orders for his book, *The Conquest*. . . . The editor had the opportunity to read the first chapter of the book, and can heartily recommend it as an interesting story if the first chapter is any criterion."

The book was so successful that Micheaux believed he could earn a living as a writer. By 1915 he had written another book, *The Forged Note,* published by Woodruff Press. To promote his second book, Micheaux went on an extensive tour, traveling to large cities including those in the South such as Atlanta, Memphis, and Birmingham. This novel was promoted as the literary sensation of the decade. In 1916 Micheaux moved to Sioux City, Iowa, and founded his own publishing company, Western Book Supply Company.

Micheaux's third book, *The Homesteader,* was published by his own company in 1917. This novel came to the attention of George P. Johnson, the booking manager of the Lincoln Motion Picture Company in Los Angeles, California. Johnson wanted to purchase the film rights to *The Homesteader*. Micheaux agreed to sell but insisted on two conditions that caused the deal to fall through. First, he wanted to go to Los Angeles and supervise the filming of the story. The second condition was set forth in a letter to George Johnson, written May 13, 1918, and quoted by Sampson: "By your circulars I note that your pictures appear to be limited to 3 reels, whereas I am sure this voluminous work could not be possibly portrayed short of eight reels, for it is a big plot and long story."

The closing of one door meant the opening of another for Micheaux. When the deal fell through with the Lincoln Motion Picture Company, Micheaux went right out and established the Micheaux Film and Book Company in Sioux City, Iowa, with a second office in Chicago. He sold stock in his company to the white farmers and businessmen he had known in South Dakota. The shares ranged in price from $75 to $100.

The Homesteader was produced as an eight-reel film with an all-black cast starring Charles Lucas in the leading role and Evelyn Preer as leading lady. All of the actors were members of the prestigious Lafayette Players of New York City. Many of the scenes were shot on location in Sioux City. According to the *Chicago Defender,* of the opening night in February 1919:

> *The Homesteader,* the greatest of all Race productions . . . is a remarkable picture both as a story and photography; it tells of the troubles of a young man upon the sea of matrimony beginning where he gives up his real sweetheart as a matter of principle, marries another as a matter of accommodation and carries on through the details of a wedded life, made miserable for both parties by the hypocritical father of the girl—a preacher—who takes them both over the jumps, to the end that he is himself bumped off by the girl, who at the same time frees the young man from wedlock.

In 1921 Micheaux established another Chicago office at 119 West 132nd Street. He hired Joseph Lamy, a white man, for foreign distribution. The U.S. distribution office was in Chicago and supervised by his younger brother Swan Micheaux Jr. Micheaux's second film, *Within Our Gates* (1920), was controversial, containing a scene where a black man is lynched by a white mob in the South.

In 1920 there were no ratings for films; however, there was an Illinois State Board of Movie Censors. *Within Our Gates* was first rejected by this board because they feared it would incite a race riot. At a second showing, a number of prominent blacks were invited to the viewing, including representatives from the Associated Negro Press. While opinion was divided, the film was allowed to be shown for the first time in Chicago at the Hammon's Vendome Theater.

The controversy surrounding *Within Our Gates* did not prevent Micheaux from including lynching scenes in other movies. The 1921 release of *The Gunsaulus Mystery* was based on the actual case of Leo Frank, a young Jewish man convicted of killing a young white girl and lynched near Marietta, Georgia, in 1915. Controversy erupted when the film, patterned after the newsreel, showed Frank's body. The Jewish community found it objectionable. The black press responded to their outcry by pointing out that black people found W. D. Griffith's *Birth of a Nation* objectionable, yet it continued to be shown.

In 1924 Micheaux was again censored, this time by the Motion Picture Board of Censors in Virginia. *The Son of Satan* was banned in Virginia because of explicit language, even though it received rave reviews elsewhere. Micheaux released *The Dungeon* and was criticized for his use of fair-skinned characters, although the use of such characters was a rather common practice at the time. D. Ireland Thomas, writing in the *Chicago Defender* for July 8, 1922, suggested that perhaps Micheaux was trying to book his film into white theaters. This was the case, as the black market was limited. Even though he had been able to sell his novels to whites, Micheaux never was able to penetrate the white theater market.

Discovers Paul Robeson   Micheaux had an unorthodox if not altogether bizarre way of identifying talented actors. Sometimes he would be struck by the person's gesture or some other intangible quality. Basically he trusted his intuition. Not only did he discover Lorenzo Turner, who starred in fourteen Micheaux productions, he also cast Paul Robeson in his feature film debut. Robeson made his debut in *Body and Soul* (1925) at the New Douglas and Roosevelt Theaters on November 15, 1925. Robeson went on to become an actor and concert singer of international reputation.

Body and Soul suffered from a confusing plot but still received good reviews. The film dealt with a corrupt preacher who extorts money from gamblers and forces a young member of his church to steal money from her mother, and even includes a suggestion of rape. The subject matter caused the film to be censored in New York for its portrayal of the clergy. This forced Micheaux to edit the film, which, according to Bogle, made the plot all the more confusing. Outsiders suggest that Micheaux's personal experience with his former father-in-law may account for his virulent portrayal of ministers.

In 1926, Micheaux and Alice B. Russell, a stage and screen actor, married and made their home in Montclair, New Jersey. On March 1, 1927, Micheaux's brother, Swan, resigned from the Chicago office and took a job with the Agfa Raiv Corporation in Berlin, Germany.

One biographer speculates that Micheaux forced his brother to resign because Swan had mismanaged the company and almost brought it to bankruptcy. The plot of Micheaux's film *The Wages of Sin* seems to support this theory. The 1927 film portrays a brother who owns a film company and gives his younger brother a position in the company, only to have the younger brother squander the company's money on women and entertainment.

As one might imagine, there were many problems to be faced by independent black filmmakers. Difficulty came when Swan left, forcing Micheaux to close the Chicago office. To save the company, Micheaux and his wife ran the New York office themselves. His wife kept the books, and he did all the film production: scriptwriting, directing, editing, and casting actors. Although he could not pay his actors large salaries, he was still able to get some of the top names of the day. Frequently he drew from his own family members and friends. His wife and her talented sister, actor Julia Theresa Russell, were often cast in lead roles.

Attempting to cut corners in every way he knew, Micheaux cut rehearsal time, used no retakes, and used local citizens as much as possible for extras. But on February 28, 1928, Micheaux was forced to file for bankruptcy in New York U.S. District Court. His assets were listed as $1,400 and his liabilities as $7,827. Financially, Micheaux was down but by no means out.

On the day that the court papers were filed, Micheaux was on the road promoting his two most recent films, *Thirty Years Later* and *The Millionaire*. As a result of his tenacity, in 1929 he reorganized his company, naming it the Micheaux Film Corporation. The officers were Oscar Micheaux, president; Frank Schiffman (white), vice president; and Leo Bracher (white), treasurer. Schiffman, the owner of several theaters in New York that catered to blacks, left after accusing Micheaux of misappropriating funds. It was not long before Micheaux was again running the company practically by himself.

Produces first talking feature film   The first two films released by the newly reorganized company were *The Daughter of the Congo* (1930) and *The Exile* (1931). The former was a silent film with a musical soundtrack; the latter was the first all-talking feature film by a black independent filmmaker. For the two films Micheaux had an all-star cast. They were box office successes, but he was harshly criticized in the black press. Criticizing *The Daughter of the Congo,* Theophilus Lewis wrote:

> The first offense of the new film is its persistent vaunting of intraracial color fetishism. The scene is laid in a not so mythical republic in Africa. Half of the characters wear European clothes and are supposed to be civilized, while the other half are wearing their birthday suits and some feathers and are supposed to be savages. All the ignoble ones are black. Only one of the yellow characters is vicious, while only one of the black characters, the debauched president of the republic, is a person of dignity. . . . Even if the picture possessed no other defects, this artificial association of nobility with lightness and villainy with blackness would be enough to ruin it.

While some of Micheaux's themes were indicative of a lack of black pride, particularly regarding the affirmation of skin color, others appear out of synchronization with the conservative times in which they appeared. These usually were censored by the white establishment. *The Exile* is a case in point. In Pittsburgh, two members of the Censor Board objected to a scene that showed a white man trying to take advantage of a woman and then thrashed by the black man who comes to her rescue. A later scene in the same movie showed a black man making love to what appeared to be a white woman. As it turned out, the actress was multi-racial, which cancelled her claim to whiteness. Micheaux's films offered an interesting and often humorous historical depiction of American cultural values and customs.

The 1938 release of *God's Stepchildren* premiered at the RKO Regent Theater at 116th Street in New York, but after only a two-day run it was stopped. Again the issue was race. This time the Communist League and the National Negro League objected to the portrayal of color snobbery among blacks. Micheaux cut a scene that generated the most protest. As a result of the publicity generated by the controversy, the film did better than expected. Technically *God's Stepchildren* was one of Micheaux's best efforts. It was shot in the home of a friend, which meant the budget was substantially lowered.

The Notorious Eleanor Lee, released in 1940, was the last film to appear under the Micheaux Film Corporation label. Premiering in Harlem, the film opened to floodlights and a carpeted sidewalk. Colonel Hubert Julian, the well-known black aviator, was master of ceremonies. Julian was in formal dress, including top hat, white silk gloves, and a flowing cape. The movie, an exciting gangster story about a prize fighter, became a moderate success at the box office.

World War II forced Micheaux to cease productions because of the scarcity of talented actors and rising costs. During the war, Micheaux returned to his career as a novelist. Again he formed his own publishing company, the Book Supply Company, located in his home at 10 Morningside Avenue, New York City. Over a three-year period he wrote and published *The Wind from Nowhere* (1944); *Case of Mrs. Windgate* (1945); *Story of Dorothy Stanfield* (1946); and *Masquerade* (1947). All were successful, and many were sold by the author on the campuses of historically black colleges and universities.

In 1948 Micheaux unwisely invested a large sum of money to help finance *The Betrayal,* a movie adaptation of his book *The Wind from Nowhere*. Micheaux lost a fortune, which forced him back on the road to sell his books. At sixty-seven, he had crippling arthritis and depended on a wheelchair for mobility. While on a trip in Charlotte, North Carolina, Micheaux suddenly became ill and died in a local hospital a few days later, on Easter Monday, 1951. He was survived by his wife. The couple had no children.

On May 18, 1986, the Directors Guild of America posthumously presented Micheaux with the Golden Jubilee Special Directorial Award for his cinematic achievements. The following year, Micheaux was finally awarded a star on the Hollywood Walk of Fame. Of Micheaux's efforts author and social commentator bell hooks has correctly written that Oscar Micheaux's work was a counter-hegemonic cultural production consciously created to disrupt and challenge stereotypical and racist representations of blacks. Despite criticism from both blacks and whites, Micheaux's films still remain an artistic view of black life in the past.—NAGUEYALTI WARREN

FLORENCE MILLS

1896–1927
Entertainer

Florence Mills was the leading black American musical comedy singer and dancer of the Jazz Age and the Harlem Renaissance. Her starring role in the famous black musical Shuffle Along *gained her fame in the United States and in London. Although her life was short, Mills defined black entertainment in America during the 1920s.*

Mills was born on January 25, 1896 in Washington, D.C., to John Winfree and Nellie (Simons) Winfree. Born in slavery in Amherst County, Virginia, the Winfrees migrated to Washington from Lynchburg because of economic depression in the tobacco industry where both were employed. They settled first in a middle-class neighborhood, where Florence was born, but were soon forced to move to Goat Alley, one of the capital's most poverty-stricken, unhealthy, and crime-ridden black slums. John Winfree worked sporadically as a day laborer and Nellie Winfree took in laundry to keep their family together. Both were illiterate, and even in a city with unusual opportunities for people of color, their prospects and futures were limited.

"Baby Florence," however, demonstrated early her extraordinary gifts for singing and dancing, and as young as age three appeared at local theater amateur hours, where she won prizes. She was even invited to entertain the British ambassador, Lord Poncefote, and his guests. The child received public recognition that no doubt contributed to her developing sense of self-worth, and she became an important source of her family's income, which imbued her with a profound sense of responsibility for those around her.

The high point of Mills's childhood occurred in 1903 when she appeared as an extra attraction in the road company production of Bert Williams and George Walker's *Sons of Ham,* where she sang "Miss Hannah from Savannah." She was taught the song by Aida Overton Walker, the great cakewalk dancer and ragtime singer who had sung it in the original show. Walker was a beautiful, sophisticated, and highly talented star who took time with this ghetto child, thereby becoming Mills's mentor and role model. Walker demonstrated that blacks with ability and determination could find a successful vocation in entertainment.

As a result of her abilities, Mills was hired at about age eight by the traveling white vaudeville team of Bonita and Hearn, entertainers who used her as a singing and dancing "pickaninny" in their

Florence Mills.

routine. Mills may well have felt both gratitude for the opportunity to work on the stage and support her family as well as resentment at the crude exploitation.

At age fourteen, Mills and her sisters Maude and Olivia organized their own traveling song-and-dance act as the Mills Sisters. They played the East Coast black vaudeville houses and received good notices in the black press for their lively performances. Sometimes dressed in male attire, Florence Mills specialized in traditional ballads and the popular tunes of the day.

Just before World War I, Mills found herself in Chicago weary of long hours, low pay, and the difficult traveling conditions blacks faced. She decided to move from vaudeville to cabaret and through Ada "Bricktop" Smith obtained a job at the notorious Panama Cafe on State Street. In the heart of the south side's honky-tonk and red-light district, the Panama was a "black and tan club" well known for sexual liaisons across the color line.

With Bricktop, Cora Green, and occasionally others, Mills formed the Panama Trio, a singing group with the legendary Tony Jackson on piano. This was an exciting time in Chicago: the city was the center of black migration from the rural South, and the white gangsters who controlled the cabarets in the black community fostered the new jazz music and an open social environment. Respectable people, both black and white, however, perceived the Panama as a center of vice, and it was finally closed down.

Mills returned to vaudeville and joined the Tennessee Ten, a traveling black show then on the Keith circuit. A member of the troupe was Ulysses "Slow Kid" Thompson, an acrobatic, tap, and "rubber legs" dancer of considerable skill. Born in Arkansas in 1888, Thompson had spent his life in various circuses, carnivals, medicine, and minstrel shows. He and Mills became romantically involved, were married, and established a devoted relationship that lasted until her death.

The connection with Thompson and the success of the Tennessee Ten brought Mills closer to the center of show business than she had been in cabaret and vaudeville. She was singing at Barron's Club in Harlem when she received an offer that moved her into public notice and the front rank of black entertainers. It was the opportunity to replace Gertrude Sanders as the lead in *Shuffle Along*.

Shuffle Along opened off-Broadway in New York in the spring of 1921. Music and lyrics were by Noble Sissle and Eubie Blake and the book by Flournoy E. Miller and Aubrey Lyles. It was an instantaneous and total hit. Actually, there was nothing new about *Shuffle Along*; similar shows had existed in the black entertainment world for years. What was new was the discovery by white America of the zesty abandon of jazzy music and fast, high-stepping black dancing. Langston Hughes believed *Shuffle Along* even initiated the Harlem Renaissance and inaugurated the decade when "the Negro was in vogue."

Mills presented to national audience   Besides reintroducing blacks into mainstream musical theater and setting the rhythmic beat for the Roaring Twenties, *Shuffle Along* presented Mills to a national audience. Now twenty-six years old, she was a dainty woman, five-feet-four, never weighing much more than one hundred pounds, bronze-colored with beautiful skin texture. She moved deftly and in her strange high voice sang "I'm Simply Full of Jazz" and "I'm Craving for That Kind of Love."

The critics could never quite describe Mills's voice with its curious breaks, soft accents, sudden molten notes, and haunting undertones. Bird-like and flute-like were among the reviewers' frequently used adjectives. It was Mills's dancing, however, and the dancing in all the black shows spawned by *Shuffle Along* during the 1920s, that completely stunned audiences. The jazz rhythms, accelerated pace, skilled precision, intricate steps, and uninhibited movement brought dance rooted in African American folk culture to white audiences who were eager to break loose from restrained convention.

Mills's performances were memorable, too, for her charismatic effectiveness in presentation. Demure and modest personally and in her private life, on stage she was assured, vivacious, and as capable of intimate mutual interaction with her audiences as a black preacher. With her fey and fragile appearance she could be intense as well as melancholy, impudent as well as full of pathos, risqué without being vulgar. Mills's popularity, however, did not mean race and racism were no longer realities; Irving Berlin said if he could find a white woman who could put over a song like Mills, he would be inspired to write a hit a week.

Anticipating the fad for black entertainment and entertainers, Lew Leslie, a white promoter, hired Mills and Kid Thompson to appear nightly after *Shuffle Along* at the Plantation Club, a remodeled night spot over the Winter Garden Theatre. The Plantation's decor included an imitation log cabin, a chandelier in the form of a watermelon slice, and a black mammy cooking waffles. Featuring Mills, the revue itself was a constellation of black talent: Will Vodery's orchestra, Johnny Dunn's cornet, Edith Wilson's double-entendre songs, and visiting performers like Paul Robeson.

The Plantation, as Thompson pointed out, was "the first highclass colored cabaret on Broadway." It drew fashionable white clientele and helped create an accepting atmosphere for things Negro, though old stereotypical images died hard. Florence Mills left *Shuffle Along* to work full time for Leslie, in a mutually beneficial relationship that lasted throughout her career. Also, the Plantation established the format for Mills's and Leslie's future shows: unconnected singing and dancing and musical acts in the vaudeville style with a touch of minstrelsy, and with all black performers.

Leslie soon realized his nightclub production could be turned into a Broadway show. The *Plantation Review* opened at the Forty-eighth Street Theatre on July 22, 1922. Sheldon Brooks presided as master of ceremonies and did a comedy routine; otherwise the bill was the same as the club's. Audiences and reviewers were impressed with the cast's genuineness and enthusiasm and the show's bouyant spontaniety, especially the breathtaking dancing. It was all "strutting and stepping and syncopating," said the *Tribune* on July 18.

The *Plantation Review* was important for Mills, for it was here she was first seen by the New York critics. They liked her energy and vitality, her sinuous dancing, her lack of self-consciousness. She sang Irving Berlin's "Some Sunny Day" and led the Six Dixie Vamps in a "Hawaiian Night in Dixie Land" dance number. There was some criticism of her song "I've Got What It Takes But It Breaks My Heart to Give It Away," not quite the sweet, crooning number that was her specialty. But there was real appreciation for the authenticity of black song and dance, and the realization that Negro portrayals by blackface performers like Al Jolson and Eddie Cantor were only imitations of the real thing.

With *Shuffle Along* and the *Plantation Revue* behind her, Mills emerged as a preeminent black female performer with the potential of breaking into the racially restricted preserves of establishment show business. America was not ready for such a bold move, but the British impresario Sir Charles B. Cochran was looking for ready-made attractions for the London stage. He made arrangements to take the Plantation company to the Pavilion in the spring

Florence Mills does the Charleston dance with a trained seal in 1925.

of 1923. There were immediate problems. British entertainers strenuously objected, citing the competition for jobs but reinforcing that fear with color prejudice. "Nigger Problem Brought to London" ran the headline of one of Hannen Swaffer's articles in the *Daily Graphic*.

The show Cochran devised was a hybrid called *Dover Street to Dixie*. A mild comedy with an all-English cast, "Dover Street" constituted the first half and was totally unrelated to "Dixie," the second half, which was Mills and the Plantation cast in a variation of their standard routines. Prejudice against the visiting black Americans had escalated, and demonstrations were expected in the theater on opening night. Tension intensified because "Dover Street" was a disaster and the audience was restless and bored.

"Dixie" began with a fast number by Vodery's orchestra, a troupe of frantic dancers, and Edith Wilson belting out a song. Then Mills quietly made her entrance and in a small plaintive voice sang "The Sleeping Hills of Tennessee." She electrified the audience. Any threat of opposition vanished, and for the rest of that night and the remainder of the show's run, she received a fervent ovation *before* every song she sang. This was a tribute, Cochran said, that he had never known London to give to any other performer.

Perhaps the most significant consequence of *Dover Street to Dixie* was the serious attention it was paid by British intellectuals. The essence of their response was that Mills's performance and that of her fellow black Americans was art, even high art, and not mere entertainment. One reviewer made the astonishing statement that Mills was "by far the most artistic person London has ever had the good fortune to see." Constant Lambert, musical director of Sadler's Wells Ballet, was deeply inspired by Mills and "Dixie" and began adapting jazz rhythms and techniques to his work, narrowing the separation between popular and "serious" music and infusing the latter with new vitality.

Upon her return to New York, Mills received an unusual invitation—to appear as an added attraction in the *Greenwich Village Follies* annual production opening that autumn at the Winter Garden. With Bert Williams's death the previous year, there were now no blacks in mainstream shows. This was the first time a black woman was offered a part in a major white production. The *Follies* cast responded by threatening to walk out. Even after management smoothed their feelings, the white cast continued to resent Mills's participation.

All-black musical comedy opens
Mills's talent and popularity brought an even more extraordinary opportunity. Florenz Ziegfeld offered her a contract to join the *Ziegfeld Follies*, the country's leading musical revue and the apex of show business success. But Mills turned Ziegfeld down. She decided to stay with Lew Leslie and create a rival show—but with an all-black cast. Bert Williams had broken the color barrier as an individual, she said, but she could best serve the race not by merely following him herself but by providing a venue for an entire company.

Mills wanted to break through Broadway's racial restrictions *and* to create an opportunity for black American entertainers to demonstrate the uniqueness of their culture. Her decision, and what she meant by it, was not lost on the black community. The *Amsterdam News* said:

> Loyalty of Florence Mills to the race as against temptation to become a renowned star of an Anglo-Saxon musical extravaganza has saved for the stage and the race what promises to be one of the most distinctive forms of American entertainment ever created—an All-Colored revue.

The first step toward Mills's goal was *From Dixie to Broadway,* which opened at the Broadhurst Theatre in October 1924. A black musical comedy in the heart of Broadway had been the dream of black entertainers since the turn of the century, and it was now realized. The price for this acceptance was a certain modification of the show's black elements by the whites who controlled the production, but the cast's superactive energy and expressive power broke through and the show was a critical and popular hit.

The cooperative effort between blacks and whites set a pattern for "crossovers" from the black entertainment milieu to the larger, more lucrative, and more influential white world. This resulted in a minimum of traditional "darky" stage imagery. This was an absence some critics missed, but the reviewers could only applaud the vital black American style and exuberant tempo now more free from racist stereotypes.

In *From Dixie to Broadway,* Mills sang "Dixie Dreams," "Mandy, Make Up Your Mind," and the song that became her theme and trademark, "I'm a Little Blackbird Looking for a Bluebird"; behind the song's sentimentality Mills saw a subliminal message: "the struggle of a race" seeking satisfaction. Most critics thought the show's high point was its satirical jazz treatment of Balieffe's "March of the Wooden Soldiers," in which Mills led the male dancers.

Mills clearly dominated *From Dixie to Broadway,* and the reviewers lauded her as "a slender streak of genius" and "an artist in jazz." Writing in the *New York Telegram and Evening Mail* on October 30, 1924, Gilbert W. Gabriel gives a fuller picture of the Florence Mills who captured Broadway, as well as revealing his inability to comprehend the distinctive black American elements in her art:

> This sensational little personality, slim, jaunty, strung on fine and tremulous wires, continues to tease the public's sense of the beautiful and odd. There is an impudent fragility about her, a grace of grotesqueness, a humor of wrists, ankles, pitching hips and perky shoulders that are not to be resisted. Her voice continues to be sometimes sweet and sometimes further from the pitch than Dixie is from Broadway. She is an exotic done in brass.

After the show's road tour, Mills broke another racial barrier. On June 27, 1924, she was the first black woman to headline at "The Taj Mahal of Vaudeville," the Palace Theatre. On Broadway at Forty-seventh Street, the Palace was the country's premier variety theatre, and it was every entertainer's dream to play there. Other blacks had been in Palace programs, but as a headliner Mills received money, billing, the best dressing room, and courtesy from management—real and symbolic achievements for a black American woman.

Mills achieved her great goal of creating a major all-black revue, but she was destined never to return to Broadway. The new show was *Blackbirds,* and it opened at the Alhambra Theatre in Harlem after having been constructed at Plantation Club performances. After successful runs in Harlem and Paris, *Blackbirds of 1926* moved to London's Pavilion Theatre, opening September 26 and lasting for an impressive 276 performances, after which it toured the British provinces.

Blackbirds was an extraordinary hit. Mills sang "Silver Rose" and repeated "I'm a Little Blackbird." She was so popular that she became to London what Josephine Baker was to Paris. The Prince of Wales saw *Blackbirds* more than twenty times and Mills played to him when he was in the theater. She and the cast were taken up by England's ultra-sophisticated "Bright Young People" and joined their outrageous parties in London, Oxford, and Cambridge.

Mills is mentioned in all the diaries of the period and even turns up as a character in Evelyn Waugh's *Brideshead Revisited*. It is likely she had an affair with the King's youngest son, the handsome, wild, and charming Prince George, who later became Duke of Kent. It was not only royalty and decadent aristocrats who were impressed, however; artists and intellectuals caught the infectious freedom and style of the black performers and the energizing tempo of their music and dance. "For the first time," exclaimed critic Arnold Haskell, "I was *seeing* true jazz."

Perhaps because she felt more secure in a less racially prejudiced country or perhaps because the British public and press treated her more seriously than the American public and press did, Mills expressed her race consciousness more strongly in England than at home. At an exclusive dinner party where she was lauded by Sir Charles Cochran as a great artist, she ignored his personal tributes in her response and instead made a moving plea for black freedom. "I am coal black and proud of it," she announced, quoted in *Variety,* at a fashionable soiree where there was some question about black and white seating arrangements.

Mills saw her work as a crusade on behalf of racial justice and understanding. She literally believed that every white person pleased by her performance was a friend won for the race. Her passion led her to drive herself without respite, and it broke her health. She left *Blackbirds* and after an unsuccessful attempt at a rest cure in Germany, sailed for New York. Her condition did not improve, however, and she entered the Hospital for Joint Diseases, where she died following an operation. She was thirty-one years old.

Mills was one of the most popular people in Harlem during the 1920s. On a cold November day in 1927 a congregation of 500,000, a choir of 600, and an orchestra of 200 jammed Mother African Methodist Episcopal Church on 137th Street. More than 150,000 people crowded the Harlem streets to glimpse the famous mourners and participate in a bit of history, but mostly to pay their own silent tributes and say good-bye to a sister they knew was their own. It is reported that a flock of blackbirds flew over the funeral cortege as it slowly made its way up Seventh Avenue toward Woodlawn Cemetery in the Bronx.

The public tributes were lavish. In an unprecedented editorial, the *New York Times* praised "the slim dancer who blazed the way" for others to follow. George Jean Nathan called her "America's foremost feminine player." Theophilus Lewis said Mills "always regarded herself as our envoy to the world at large and she was probably the best one we ever had." One London newspaper commented that if Mills had been a white woman she would have been acknowledged as one of the greatest artists of her time.

Mills made her mark in several ways. *Shuffle Along* introduced jazz song and dance to Broadway musical theater. In *From Dixie to Broadway* she starred in a black revue built around female singing and dancing rather than traditional male blackface comedy. In *Blackbirds* she created a major show composed of vital black American music and movement. She helped minimize the "darky" element in show business while bringing special black qualities to her crossover numbers. Through it all Florence Mills was first and foremost a "race woman" proud of her heritage, uncompromising in her identity, and always using her artistry to build bridges to the white world in the hope of securing greater justice for her people.—RICHARD NEWMAN

TONI **MORRISON**

1931–
Writer, editor, educator

Toni Morrison is considered by many critics to be one of the most significant novelists of the twentieth century. Often compared to literary giants such as William Faulkner and James Joyce, she is noted for her mastery of language—especially her achievements in voice and narrative style and her control of verbal nuance, metaphor, and image. But in spite of formal literary training, Morrison perceives her creativity as emanating from central forces in black American culture and not from the Eurocentric traditions of most authors to whom she is likened. She explains that writing novels gives her a sense of encompassing that ineffable "something" in black culture that, so far, has been best expressed by black musicians. One function of her novels, she points out, is to tell the stories of black people—stories articulated and memorized long before they appeared in print. In finely crafted "meandering" dialogue, her fiction articulates a full spectrum of complex meanings and emotions. Morrison has been given the highest award for any writer, the Nobel Prize for Literature, and became the first black female to do so.

Toni Morrison was born Chloe Anthony Wofford to George and Ramah Wofford in the rust-belt section of Lorraine, Ohio, shortly after the onset of the Great Depression. Morrison's father was a ship welder from Georgia, where racial violence made such an indelible impact on him that throughout his entire life he found it impossible to trust or believe in the humanity of white people. However, her mother, a homemaker, disagreed and approached each new encounter with whites with patience and reason. Although she grew up in an integrated community in which everyone was poor and blacks were not social outcasts, Morrison learned a great deal about racial history from her family. Morrison's most vivid memories of childhood include learning about black folklore, music, myths, and the cultural rituals of her family and community. Her mother sang in the church choir; her grandfather, an artist, once supported his family by means of his violin performances; her grandmother decoded dreams from a book of symbols and played the numbers based on her translations. Storytelling was a major form of family entertainment during her young life.

Not surprisingly, Morrison learned to read at an early age and was the only child in her first-grade class to enter with reading skills. Her mother was a member of a book-of-the-month club and received books on a regular basis. As a teenager, Morrison read widely, from Jane Austen to the great French and Russian novelists to literature of the supernatural. Morrison encountered many stereotypical and even racist portrayals of her people in books by Walt Whitman and Mark Twain, but she would just skip those sections. Morrison graduated from high school with honors and went on to study literature and the classics at Howard University. She also joined the Howard University Players and traveled with the student repertory troupe in the summers, performing in plays across the South. These trips, her first contacts with that region, brought her face to face with the kinds of racist experiences she had heard about in childhood.

Following her graduation from Howard in 1953, Morrison entered Cornell University, where in 1955 she earned a master's degree in English. For the next two years she taught at

Toni Morrison. 489

Texas Southern University and in 1957 she accepted an appointment at Howard and married a Jamaican architect named Harold Morrison. Among her most well-known students at Howard were the acclaimed author Claude Brown and Stokely Carmichael, the famous civil rights activist of the 1960s. The marriage, a strained one, lasted only a few years; by 1964 she was a divorced mother of two young sons, aged three years old and three months old.

In 1965, Morrison began an eighteen-year career in publishing with Random House to help support her and her sons. After moving to New York City in 1968 as senior editor in the trade department, she used her influence to bring the works of several young black writers to publication. Even with the demands of editorship, novel-writing, and single parenthood, Morrison still found time to teach Afro-American literature and creative writing at such schools as the State University of New York at Purchase, Yale University, and Bard College. In 1984 Morrison left publishing to accept a chair in humanities at the State University of New York at Albany, a position she held until 1989, when she accepted a chair at Princeton University.

Morrison begins writing   Morrison first began writing in the late 1950s when she joined a group of ten black writers in Washington, D.C., who met monthly to read each other's works. Once she brought a hurriedly written story about a young black girl who wanted blue eyes. The idea originated from a conversation she had as a child with another black girl who rejected the existence of God after she had prayed unsuccessfully for two years for blue eyes. At the time, Morrison did not think seriously of becoming a writer. Later, living alone with her sons in Syracuse, she turned to writing as a means of coping with loneliness. She developed more fully her idea of the pain of yearning for a dominant, but unrealizable standard of physical beauty, and published *The Bluest Eye* in 1970.

Set in the Midwest, *The Bluest Eye* is the story of nine-year-old Claudia McTeer, her ten-year-old sister, Frieda, and their friend, Pecola Breedlove. Feeling unloved by her family and the black community, Pecola surmises she is flawed by the ugliness of her blackness. Thus convinced, she transforms her need for love into an obsession for a symbol of beauty: blue eyes. She yearns to be like Shirley Temple, whom everyone adores.

Morrison's next novel, *Sula,* focuses on the relationship between two black girls in the 1920s and 1930s, Nel Wright and Sula Peace. Although reviewed in many well-known magazines and newspapers, neither *The Bluest Eye* nor *Sula* was an instant success. In fact, the earlier book was out of print by 1974, when *Sula* appeared. While the handful of predominantly white critics who reviewed *The Bluest Eye* were unanimous in praise of Morrison's vision of black life and the power of her poetic prose, their reactions to the plot were guarded, ambivalent, and sometimes negative. Only two black women, writing for *Black World* and *Freedomways,* openly admired *The Bluest Eye. Sula,* with more notice from black reviewers, fared better than its predecessor. Most reviewers called the second novel "thought-provoking" and a bold attempt to address the black female situation within the black community.

The emergence of her first two novels, however, gained Morrison national recognition as a critic and scholar of literature and African American culture. Between 1971 and 1972 she wrote twenty-eight book reviews and an essay on the women's movement for the *New York Times,* and since then has become a prominent voice in academia and the media. In addition to her fiction, Morrison's publications include a textbook, as well as many essays and articles on American literature, black American writing, and black women. In 1992 Morrison published *Playing in the Dark,* a critical investigation of the way that race has shaped the white "classics" of American literature. She also edited a book of essays on the controversial confirmation hearings of Supreme Court Justice Clarence Thomas.

Widespread recognition as a fiction writer came with Morrison's third novel, *Song of Solomon.* With the guidance of his magically insightful aunt, Pilate, "Milkman" Dead moves from a restless alienation in a northern community to some sense of ancestral grounding in the American South. *Song of Solomon* includes themes of flight, family, and male violence, and embodies black culture's social codes, superstitions, fables, myths, and songs. Featured on the front page of the *New York Times Book Review, Song of Solomon* received considerably more notice than Morrison's first two novels combined. *Song of Solomon* was awarded the National Book Critics Award in 1977. Recently, Oprah Winfrey has included *Song of Solomon* in her book club, where it has generated new interest.

Morrison's next work, *Tar Baby,* is a fusion of fantasy and realism that has roots in the black American folktale of the white farmer who uses a tar baby to trap a troublesome rabbit and is himself outwitted by the clever animal. Most of the novel occurs on the Isle des Chevaliers, an Edenic Caribbean locale invaded by wealthy white Americans. The landscape of *Tar Baby* encompasses the sophistication of Paris, the excitement of New York City, and the certainty of Philadelphia, presenting an overview of the black experience in confrontation with white America. A month after its publication, *Tar Baby* appeared on the *New York Times* best-seller list and remained there for nearly four months.

The idea for Morrison's fifth novel, the Pulitzer Prize–winning *Beloved,* grew from a newspaper clipping about a slave woman, Margaret Garner, who in 1851 escaped from Kentucky to Ohio with her four children. Facing capture and a return to slavery, Garner killed one of her children and unsuccessfully attempted to kill two others. Morrison was struck by the reports of a calm, quiet, and self-possessed Garner while she was in prison. She expressed no remorse for her actions, explaining only that she did not want her children to live in slavery.

In *Beloved,* Sethe, a mother recently escaped from slavery, kills her older daughter to save her from trackers and a return to slavery. Beloved, the daughter, reappears as a ghost and forces her mother to remember the past. In Sethe's search for love and healing, Morrison indicates that her pain is not hers alone to bear: only when Sethe's ties with the community are reestablished does she heal. *Beloved* is about a community confronting its collective past of slavery, suffering, endurance, and strength. A meditation on the legacy of slavery, Morrison describes the book as an effort to rescue the "sixty million and more" to whom she dedicates it from the oblivion to which they had been consigned by history. From Morrison's point of view, no suitable memorial previously existed to remind Americans of those who endured the terrible experience of slavery.

Jazz, Morrison's sixth novel, is set in Harlem in the 1920s, where the rhythm and yearnings of a community in the process of creating itself embody the ineffable power of improvisational jazz. Before the novel opens, Joe Trace, a fifty-year-old cosmetics salesman, shoots and kills his eighteen-year-old lover, Dorcas, in a fit of jealousy. At the funeral home, Joe's wife, Violet, tries to mutilate Dorcas's face with a knife. *Jazz* explores the pasts of these three people, revealing the complexities and suffering of their lives prior to the incident. As the narrative moves back in time to the South of Joe and Violet's childhoods, an anonymous narrator ponders community life in the city and the country, and the nature of family love, romantic love, and desire. Morrison has received widespread praise for the beauty of her articulation of this novel's profound insight into human emotions and history.

Morrison's lyrical body of work caught the attention of the highest critics in literature. In 1993, she was awarded the Nobel Prize for Literature. Morrison is the first black female writer to hold such an honor. In 1996, Morrison was also honored by being named the Jefferson Lecturer in the Humanities by the National Endowment of the Humanities. Although critics have praised Morrison's storytelling—with its illuminating metaphors, graceful syntax, and haunting images—the author says that she writes mainly for her own satisfaction. Writing affords her an opportunity to find coherence in the world, and the discipline it requires helps her to sort out the past—her own as well as the collective past of black people in America. One of her great desires is that her writing continue to develop an element she admires in black music, especially in jazz—the absence of a final chord that keeps listeners on the edge, always wanting something more.—NELLIE Y. McKAY

CAROL E. **MOSELEY-BRAUN**
1947–
Senator, lawyer, radio host

On March 17, 1992, at her campaign headquarters in downtown Chicago, Carol Moseley-Braun lifted her hands, swayed from side to side, and broke into her familiar infectious smile as she moved to the music of "Ain't No Stopping Us Now" and "We Are Family." Having just defeated longtime Democratic Senator Alan Dixon in the Illinois primary, she was on the most important path in her life: the one leading to the United States Senate. Running as a Democrat, Moseley-Braun won the senatorial election the following November. The first black woman in the U.S. Senate, Moseley-Braun, as quoted in Jet *magazine, told her cheering supporters: "We have won a great victory tonight. . . . You have made history. And as much to the point of history-making you are showing the way for our entire country to the future."*

Carol E. Moseley-Braun was born on August 16, 1947, in Chicago, Illinois, the eldest child of Joseph Moseley, a policeman, and Edna A. Davie Moseley, a medical technician. The comfortable, middle-class setting of Moseley-Braun's early life was far from ideal, however, for her father, a frustrated musician, sometimes took out his personal disappointments on Moseley-Braun by beating her. When she was sixteen, Moseley-Braun's parents divorced, her father moved to California, and she and her siblings, along with Edna Moseley, settled in with their maternal grandmother for two years in a black neighborhood nicknamed the Bucket of Blood, a violent and poverty-stricken area.

Moseley-Braun's exposure to the darker aspects of urban life instilled in her a belief in public service. As she indicated in the *Washington Post*, "When you get a chance to see people who are really trapped and don't have options and you've got all these blessings, you've got to be a pretty ungrateful person not to want to do something." The blessings Moseley-Braun referred to included her education at the University of Illinois at Chicago, from which she graduated in 1967, and at the University of Chicago Law School, from which she obtained a

Carol Mosely-Braun during the 1992
Democratic National Convention.

J.D. in 1972. It was at the University of Chicago law school that she met Michael Braun, a white fellow student, whom she married in 1973; he is the father of her only child, Matthew.

Political career begins Moseley-Braun's public life started with her work as an assistant U.S. attorney from 1974–77. Prior to this, she worked at a private firm. The U.S. attorney position was pivotal to her career; as Moseley-Braun noted in the *Chicago Reader*, "It opened up for me the way [federal] government interfaces with local and state government, how policy is made, and what opportunities there are for changing things via the courts." In 1977, running as a Democrat, she won a seat in the Illinois House of Representatives, serving the Hyde Park area near the University of Chicago, a liberal and racially integrated neighborhood.

Moseley-Braun proved to be a bold and effective member of the Illinois legislature. Her performance gained her public notice and the respect of her colleagues, both of which were integral to her future career in Illinois politics. Moseley-Braun was a member of the Illinois House of Representatives until 1988. During these years she championed educational reform and redistricting efforts to create fairer legislative districts. In addition, she worked against investing in South Africa and discrimination by private clubs. She was recognized for her performance on a number of occasions, and received the Best Legislator Award in 1980 and 1982 from the Independent Voters of Illinois. Moseley-Braun also found time to write newspaper articles for the *Hyde Park Herald* and the *South Shore Scene*. In addition, she was a radio talk show host for WXOL in Chicago.

Chicago's first black mayor, Democrat Harold Washington, admired Moseley-Braun's energy. In 1983 he designated her his floor leader in the House, even though she was not the senior legislator. Apparently her relationship with Washington was not without conflict, however. According to the *Washington Post*, he blocked her bid for the lieutenant governorship in 1986.

That year was devastating for Moseley-Braun for other reasons as well. Her mother was seriously ill and had a leg amputated, and one of her brothers died as a result of his drug and alcohol abuse. Her marriage ended as well. When she later ran for the U.S. Senate, however, Michael Braun worked on her campaign.

This low period in Moseley-Braun's life was brief. She successfully campaigned for the office of Recorder of Deeds and in 1988 became the first black elected to an executive office in the history of Cook County government. Managing a staff of three hundred people and a budget of eight million dollars, Moseley-Braun, according to the *Chicago Reader*, "dramatically reorganized" the recorder's office.

Moseley-Braun's personality and appearance have always been counted as pluses in her political career, contributing to her broad appeal. The *National Review*, however, commented that Moseley-Braun was fond of pointing out a sign in the restroom of her Chicago office that read, "I'm 51% sweetheart, 49% bitch. Don't push it." She acknowledges that there have been times when she's had to put away her winning smile and battle in the trenches, and she points to her difficult ascension to the Senate as an example. "In light of the fact that women and minorities are not generally put on the track to access the higher level position in government, or anything else for that matter, the only way that you can move into these circles is to go for it."

Politician becomes activist in U.S. Senate   Moseley-Braun was inspired to run for the U.S. Senate after watching Senator Alan Dixon vote to confirm Clarence Thomas as a Supreme Court justice in 1991. Thomas's confirmation hearings garnered an unusual amount of attention when a former colleague of Thomas's, law professor Anita Hill, accused him of sexual harassment. Moseley-Braun was outraged at Dixon's vote and the treatment that Hill received from the middle-aged white men who made up the confirmation committee. Defining herself in her Senate campaign as an agent of change, Moseley-Braun tapped into an anti-incumbent grassroots sentiment that ultimately carried her to a primary victory over an opponent who had not lost an election in forty-two years.

Moseley-Braun followed up her primary victory with a triumph over her Republican opponent, Richard Williamson. She thus became the first black woman in U.S. history to serve in the Senate. With her Senate seat, Moseley-Braun had become a symbol for her race and for change in general. Among the sea of middle-aged white males on Capitol Hill, there lies a voice for the African Americans. Since taking her seat, Moseley-Braun has been an outspoken and visible member despite the heavy pressure she carries. As Senator Dianne Feinstein noted in the *Washington Post*, Moseley-Braun "has been pulled and tugged and torn. There's a period of testing that goes on—whether it's the first woman, the first black, the first Asian." The daily grind of elected office, combined with the demands of motherhood, have taken their toll as well at times. But the "symbolic senator" has been beleaguered by financial and public relations problems. Her campaign has been consistently investigated for poor bookkeeping regarding donations, and Moseley-Braun was lambasted by fellow Democrats after she secretly

Senator Carol Moseley-Braun campaigning with youngsters.

visited Nigeria's military ruler, General Sani Abacha. Abacha was known for blatant human rights violations and suspected of military assassinations among his people. Moseley-Braun has also been accused of isolating the black community of Chicago by her recent decisions to endorse legislation that would have teens tried as adults and for her support of Mayor Richard Daley over two black opponents who previously endorsed her bid for the Senate. Because of the controversy surrounding her campaign, political analysts have stated that Moseley-Braun's chances for re-election in 1998 look very slim.

Moseley-Braun has also had her triumphs. She has been an outspoken presence on the Senate floor on many issues, and has shown a determination to vote on issues based on her beliefs rather than opinion polls or party dogma. Although regarded as a liberal Democrat in many respects, according to one source, Moseley-Braun "has parted company with her traditional allies by supporting the North American Free Trade Agreement (NAFTA), the General Agreement on Tariffs and Trade (GATT) and the balanced-budget amendment." She also secured a seat on the important Senate Finance Committee, where she makes sure that her voice is heard.

And, noted the *Washington Post*, sometimes Moseley-Braun's "successes are so magnified they take on a folkloric quality—like when she shamed the Senate into killing Jesse Helms's proposal to renew the patent on the United Daughters of the Confederacy's flag insignia. African Americans applauded her as if she were Joe Louis after delivering a knockout punch." This mesmerizing event took place on July 22, 1993. Before a final vote on whether to approve the renewal of the patent, an eloquent and angry Moseley-Braun, speaking on behalf of African Americans everywhere, made her case for voting against Helms:

> The issue is whether or not Americans such as myself who believe in the promise of this country . . . will have to suffer the indignity of being reminded time and time again that at one point in this country's history we were human chattel. We were property. We could be traded, bought, and sold. . . . This vote is about race . . . and the single most painful episode in American history. . . . [The Confederate flag] has no place in our modern time . . . no place in this body . . . no place in our society.

Senator Edward Kennedy later marveled at Moseley-Braun's impassioned words. "That was an extraordinary day," he recalled, "really unique in the time I have been here. She reserves her special kind of force for things she is really moved by." Besides her achievement of becoming the first black female senator, Moseley-Braun is also lauded as the woman who stood up to Jesse Helms.

Moseley-Braun intends to defend her Senate seat in 1998 against all comers. Despite the obstacles her first term has faced, Moseley-Braun has the ability and will to create the magic that surrounded her first campaign. She has proven to be a resilient and eloquent senator, qualities that will no doubt serve her well in the coming years as a proponent for her race.—MARGARET PERRY

ELIJAH **MUHAMMAD**
1897–1975
Muslim leader

Elijah Muhammad was a prominent black nationalist who led the Lost-Found Nation of Islam as its Messenger of Allah from the mid-1930s to the mid-1970s. Muhammad's career is one of controversy and even notoriety, but he steadfastly promoted black heritage at a time—the pre-civil rights era—when such action called for courage and conviction.

Muhammad was born Elijah Poole in 1897 in Sandersville, Georgia. Both his parents had been slaves and subsequently became sharecroppers, although Muhammad's father also served as a Baptist minister. Muhammad had not yet completed his elementary school education when he, too, was compelled to work in the family's fields. When he was only in his mid-teens, Muhammad left home. In 1919 he married Clara Evans, and they soon had two children. In 1923 the family moved to Detroit, Michigan, where Muhammad found work in the city's prosperous automobile industry.

In Detroit, Muhammad made the acquaintance of Wallace D. Fard, founding leader of the Lost-Found Nation of Islam. Muhammad was drawn to Fard's espousal of Islam as the true religion of blacks, and he converted to Fard's Nation of Islam in 1931. Muhammad initially assumed the name Elijah Karriem, but after gaining increasing authority within the Nation of Islam, he changed it, under Fard's direction, to Elijah Muhammad. In addition, he became the church's chief minister.

Muhammad traveled from Detroit to Chicago and founded the Southside Mosque, which eventually became Temple Number Two. Fard, meanwhile, ran afoul of Detroit police,

Elijah Muhammad speaking to his followers with an attentive Muhammad Ali sitting behind him. 497

and in 1933, a year after he spent time in jail, he was banished from the city. He traveled to Chicago, where he was again arrested. And after Muhammad returned to Detroit he was arrested for witholding his children from public schooling.

Despite this regular harrassment from local authorities, Fard managed to shape the Nation of Islam into an effective religion replete with its own educational institution, the University of Islam, and its own paramilitary organization, the Fruit of Islam. But when Fard suddenly disappeared in mid-1934, Muhammad abruptly left Detroit, where various factions were maneuvering for control of the organization, and returned to Chicago. There Muhammad assumed leadership of the Nation of Islam and named himself as prophet of the Islamic deity, Allah.

Under Muhammad's leadership, the Black Muslims developed into a staunchly separatist church. But far from advocating a return to Africa for American blacks, Elijah Muhammad called for the establishment of a black nation within the United States. In addition, he advised blacks to practice self-discipline and self-improvement. He also counseled followers to abstain from alcohol and tobacco, and he advised them to practice sexual fidelity. To help blacks realize greater success within America's white society, Muhammad also offered education and business training to members.

By the end of the 1930s, the Nation of Islam had established temples in black areas of several cities, and Muhammad had gained in influence among the nation's blacks. But after the United States entered World War II, Muhammad again offended law-enforcement officials, who had him imprisoned for urging his Muslim followers to avoid draft registration. Muhammad then managed the church while incarcerated. After the war, he settled again in Chicago in a sumptuous estate that, to some followers, seemed inconsistent with Islamic tenets.

Towards the end of the 1940s, the Black Muslim movement entered a period of increased success when charismatic member Malcolm Little joined from prison and soon became Muhammad's most significant follower as Malcolm X. During the ensuing decade, Malcolm X worked tirelessly on behalf of the Black Muslim cause. Membership grew substantially, temples flourished, and black culture gained significantly, especially in recognition from conventional American media, as a formidable element within white America.

But as Malcolm X realized greater success on behalf of the Nation of Islam, he gained in popularity among some of its members, and this popularity, in turn, ultimately proved threatening to Muhammad. Particularly disturbing were Malcolm X's reservations about Muhammad's materialism and the leader's apparent disregard for some of his own religious tenets, especially those pertaining to sexual conduct. Coupled with Malcolm's discovery that Muhammad had fathered several children out of wedlock and Malcolm X's blunt, seemingly unsympathetic comments regarding President John F. Kennedy's recent assassination, Muhammad was compelled to censor his follower. Malcolm X obeyed Muhammad's order of silence, but after an inspirational trip abroad, he broke from the Nation of Islam and founded his own, pan-black movement. Muhammad thereupon proclaimed Malcolm X a hypocrite.

In early 1965 Malcolm X was assassinated as he prepared to speak in Harlem. Among his three killers were two Black Muslims. Muhammad subsequently became reclusive, and when he did appear in public it was, inevitably, with the protection of Islamic security. He seemed to prefer remaining at Black Muslim offices in Chicago, where he supervised management of the organization's numerous—and varied—business operations. The Nation of Islam remained prominent throughout much of that decade, though, due to the membership of such public figures as Muhammad Ali, boxing's heavyweight champion.

But in the early 1970s the Nation of Islam again received notoriety when a Louisiana-based faction within the church entered into a gunfight with local police. In addition, Muhammad's materialism again seemed a source of contention within the organization. But Muhammad, at least publicly, dismissed internal conflicts as slight, and he contended that the organization was scarcely effected by such dissension or disobedience. He managed, rather, to maintain control of the Lost-Found Nation of Islam despite a range of troubling respiratory ailments and diabetes. He was eventually hospitalized for these health problems, and in 1975 he died in Chicago.

Muhammad's son, Wallace, led the Lost-Found Nation of Islam for a time after his father's death. Later Wallace, who came to be known as Warith Deen Muhammad, embraced a more orthodox interpretation of Islam. Louis Farrakhan, in turn, resurrected Elijah Muhammad's Nation and continues to espouse the faith today.—LES STONE

EDDIE **MURPHY**

1961–

Actor, comedian, producer, recording artist

Eddie Murphy owned the box office in the eighties. Beginning with his startling film debut in 48 Hrs *in 1982, he churned out at least five films that grossed over $100 million during the decade of Reaganomics and insider trading. His films have grossed a combined estimate of $2 billion worldwide. Eddie Murphy's appeal is unrivaled. With his trademark, horse-like laugh, he is known around the world. Murphy's only attribute to his immense success is his commitment to make people feel happy. For almost twenty years, Murphy has done just that.*

Edward Regan Murphy was born on April 3, 1961 in Brooklyn, New York to Charles and Lillian Murphy. Charles, Eddie's father, was a New York City policeman and his mother was a telephone operator. When Murphy was three years old, his parents divorced. A few years later, when Murphy was eight, his father was killed. Mystery surrounds his father's death, but one story insists it was at the hands of a jealous lover. Eddie didn't know his biological father too well and within a year, his mother married Vernon Lynch, a foreman at a Breyer's ice cream factory. The newly formed family moved to the middle-class section of Roosevelt, Long Island, where Eddie spent the rest of his childhood.

During his school years, young Eddie was a television junkie. He religiously watched all that he could, studying the characters he saw and imitating them. Murphy once said that his interactions with family and friends resulted in him talking like cartoon characters Dudley DoRight or Bullwinkle. His cartoon imitations evolved into impersonations of celebrities, which then led the youngster to practice his routine in the house basement. At Roosevelt High School, Murphy took advantage of school talent shows to entertain his classmates. It wasn't

*Eddie
Murphy.*

long before he was voted most popular by his peers. At age fifteen, Murphy was hosting talent shows at local clubs and warming his adult audiences with a barrage of bathroom humor and uncanny impersonations. He was soon cutting classes to make gigs at the local comedy clubs, where his comedic talents caught the eye of Comic Strip club managers Robert Wachs and Richard Tieken, who later became his managers.

During high school, Murphy reportedly told his social studies teacher that he "was going to be bigger than Bob Hope." After graduating high school, Murphy did not relent on making that predication a reality. In an attempt to ground her son in reality, Lillian convinced Murphy to enroll in college, just in case. Murphy enrolled at Nassau Community College. But college couldn't keep this man from chasing a dream.

Murphy's big break comes slowly

Murphy was still making pocket change appearing at local comedy clubs. He realized that his big break had come when he found out that the producers of *Saturday Night Live* were holding auditions in New York and that they were looking in particular for a black comedian. *Saturday Night Live* has long been considered the optimum leaping point for struggling young comedians. It premiered on NBC in 1975 and reinvigorated live television with its risqué comedic sketches. Famed *Saturday Night Live* alumni include Dan Aykroyd, Jane Curtain, the late John Belushi, Bill Murray, and the late Gilda Radner.

Murphy auditioned for one of the producers and was hired as a supporting cast member for the 1980–81 season. His beginnings with *SNL* were humble. Murphy was only given limited time during the show's fall run. After the original players left the show, the public didn't think that *SNL* could ever produce the originality for which it was famous in the 1970s. They were right. The chosen lead players did not win the audiences, and the show was regarded as a flop. All characters except Joe Piscopo were dropped, and Eddie made his move to a Prime Time Player on *Saturday Night Live*. When the following season approached, many thought the show should hang it up. But Murphy's memorable characters made *SNL* not only watchable, but popular again. As Raheem Abdul Mohammad, the adamant film critic; Little Richard Simmons; Buckwheat; Velvet Jones, the pimp/publisher of such books as "I Wanna Be a Ho"; Gumby; convict Tyrone Green, who reads such poems as "C-I-L-L My Landlord"; James Brown; and Mr. Robinson, the urban version of Mr. Rogers, Murphy's comedic genius also caught the eye of Hollywood.

Murphy's blazing film debut

Director Walter Hill was looking for a young black actor to play the hip, streetwise Reggie Hammond in his action picture *48 Hrs*, starring Nick Nolte. After viewing some of Murphy's work on *SNL*, Hill was convinced that he found his Reggie. The film was an immediate critical and box office smash, and pioneered later buddy films such as *Lethal Weapon*. Critics praised Murphy's portrayal of the urbane Reggie Hammond as phenomenal. *Baltimore Sun* film critic Stephen Hunter said of Murphy's performance: "He's not quite the macho-tough black-exploitation stud from an earlier era, like Jim Brown or Fred Williamson, who's all sexual power and coiled, ugly violence. He's too shrewd, too weaselly tough. What he's got—and what the bar scene is contrived to exploit—is a furious sense of *will*."

Critics and audiences were in agreement that Murphy was definitely a star. *48 Hrs* went on to gross nearly $100 million. To prove that Eddie Murphy's appeal was broader and no fluke, his next film, a comedy pairing him with Dan Aykroyd called *Trading Places* (1983), was another box office champ. With back-to-back successes, *Time* magazine in 1984 called Murphy "a force to be reckoned with." When popular action star Sylvester Stallone turned down the lead role of a Detroit cop who travels to Los Angeles to track his partner's killer, Murphy's box office power astounded critics. His third film, which featured his first starring role, *Beverly Hills Cop* broke previous box office records in its opening weekend. The film went on to earn domestic receipts of more than $200 million. It is fourteenth on the list of the 100 top-grossing films of all time. Murphy had the Midas touch, and at the time was given one of the most lucrative contracts by his studio, Paramount. Fittingly, his follow-up to *Beverly Hills Cop* was entitled *The Golden Child* (1986). A sequel to *Beverly Hills Cop* went over well, and his enchanting film *Coming to America* was one of the most successful films of 1988.

Murphy's post-eighties blues   In 1987, controversial filmmaker Spike Lee criticized Murphy for not using his Hollywood clout to create more visibility for other black actors and directors. In his second concert film, *Raw* (1987), the highest-grossing concert film ever, the majority of his jokes were at the expense of gays and women. His box office appeal seemed to have peaked as well. In 1989, Murphy wrote and directed *Harlem Nights*. It was to be a dream project for Murphy as it cast him with two of his idols in the comedy business: Richard Pryor and Redd Foxx. But the film was a disaster. Violence broke out in some theaters showing the film. Critics crucified the movie as a vanity piece. Hal Hinson of the *Washington Post* criticized *Harlem Nights* as "a progressively off-putting exercise in star ego." Stephen Hunter went straight to the jugular: "*Harlem Nights* is a sad and dilapidated movie, a dispiriting filmmaking debut for the most visible and powerful minority star in Hollywood. He owed everybody more and better."

As if the reception for *Harlem Nights* weren't hostile enough, Murphy was met with law suits by theater patrons who were injured in the violence. Murphy's legal battles did not end there. *Washington Post* columnist Art Buchwald reported that the idea for Murphy's film *Coming to America* was plagiarized from a treatment he sent Paramount years ago. The case gained much publicity, and much of the wrongdoing was attributed to Murphy himself. On top of his personal struggles, Murphy still made films, but no one was coming to see them. One by one, *Another 48 Hrs* (1990), *The Distinguished Gentleman* (1992), and *Beverly Hills Cop III* (1994) made not so much as a whimper at the box office. As a change of pace, Murphy wanted to try his hand in horror and created Caribbean vampire Maxmillian in the forgettable *Vampire in Brooklyn* (1994). The failure of *Vampire in Brooklyn* was the catalyst for Hollywood insiders to label that film the last nail in the coffin of Murphy's film career.

Murphy has the last laugh   But the 1990s also saw a maturing Murphy, despite his stalled film career. In 1993, he married model Nicole Mitchell in a ceremony that was called the wedding of the year. With his career at a stalemate, Murphy's cool remained intact, as indicated in this remark about his films from a 1994 *Newsweek* interview: "The reality of the situation is that if my career was on the decline I wouldn't be making movies. They don't give money to blacks in Hollywood because they're swell." In 1995 when Murphy was approached with the idea of remaking Jerry Lewis's *The Nutty Professor* (1963), many in Hollywood speculated

Eddie Murphy claims his Hollywood star
outside Mann's Chinese Theater in 1987.

about the ability of Paramount's "Golden Boy" to successfully remake a comedy classic. Based on his track record, the doubt was thick. With this updated version, Professor Sherman Klump was a brilliant chemist and geneticist who was severely overweight. The summer of 1996, when *Professor* was released, would decide whether Murphy still had his magic to make people happy. Fortunately, he did. *The Nutty Professor* went on to gross over $100 million. Critics praised Murphy's comedic gift for playing eight different characters in the film. Roger Ebert wrote in the *Chicago Sun Times,* "He's back with exuberance and energy, in a movie that's like a thumb to the nose for everyone who said he'd lost it."

Richard Schickel of *Time* magazine raved, "Murphy . . . is something Jerry Lewis never was: a comic actor of astonishing range." Murphy was again embraced by his peers and public with a comedy that showcased a gift that he knew he possessed when he was a skinny kid at Roosevelt High School.

Murphy's other talents   Murphy's talent did not end when the cameras stopped rolling. In 1984, he recorded his first album, *How Could It Be?,* which went gold and featured his most famous hit, "Party All the Time." In 1989, he released his second album, *So Happy.* A third album, *Love's Alright,* came out in 1992 and featured the song "Yeah!" The song included such artists as Paul McCartney, Janet Jackson, and M. C. Hammer, and proceeds from the album went to Yeah!, an organization founded by Murphy. As an entertainment institution unto himself, Murphy created Eddie Murphy Television Enterprises and produced, in 1991, a modest hit for CBS called *The Royal Family,* starring Redd Foxx and Della Reese. The show endured a devastating blow when its leading actor, Foxx, died of a heart attack one month before the show premiered.

Besides the prestige of being granted a multi-million-dollar contract with a major film studio, Murphy's contribution to comedy and humanity has been rewarded on the highest levels. He has received a Golden Globe award and NAACP Image Award for his work in *Trading Places;* Emmy nominations for his work on *SNL;* Grammy Award for best comedy album, *Eddie Murphy: Comedian,* in 1984; People's Choice Award; Star of the Year Award for *Beverly Hills Cop,* in 1985; NAACP Lifetime Achievement Award in 1991; his own star on Hollywood's Walk of Fame; recognition as the first NATO/ShoWest Star of the Decade; and an *Essence* Magazine Spirit Award in 1994. In an April 1996 special issue of *Entertainment Weekly,* Eddie Murphy was called the sixth funniest comedian of all time.

Murphy has three children by his wife Nicole and lives in the beautiful mansion Bubble Hill in Englewood Cliffs, New Jersey. Murphy, in the mid-1980s, was a reigning box office king who never reduced himself to "playing the sidekick, drug addict or Uncle Tom." Murphy can certainly reflect on a career that's still going strong after fifteen years in a fickle business: "I've done something no other black person has done before, my films have been successful the world over. I am not worried about what people say." Murphy has a gift to make us laugh, and most important to audiences everywhere, Murphy stayed true to his gift and shared it with the world.—MICHELLE BANKS

HUEY P. **NEWTON**

1942–1989
Political activist, organization cofounder

Founder of the Black Panther Party, Huey P. Newton was a complex man determined to help African Americans gain their rightful place in the social structure of the United States. He was convinced that the best chances for success in the struggle for equal rights for black Americans depended upon a militaristic, nationalistic approach; this conviction was motivation for his part in bringing about the Black Panther Party for Self-Defense in 1966. The Panthers brought about a decrease in the brutality against African Americans in the Bay Area of California and gave young people a sense of identification with an organization that cared about them and other black citizens.

Huey P. Newton was born in New Orleans, Louisiana on February 17, 1942. His father, Walton, came to Oakland in 1944 with the mass migration of blacks from the South to the West Coast to work in the defense plants of World War II. A year later, his mother, Amelia, followed with their children. Huey, then three, was the youngest of seven children. In his childhood, he was a junior deacon in Bethel Baptist Church, where his father was the minister. Newton graduated from Oakland Technical High School in 1959 with the reading skills of a primary student. Before graduation, Newton had already served a month in juvenile hall for gun possession and was well on his way to a life of dissipation and petty crime that led to alienation from his parents.

Newton knew that he must expand on his education before he could satisfy his growing desire to make a difference in his community. He began to tap his latent mental abilities by reading Plato's *Republic,* and with the help of his brother Melvin, the scholar of the family, Newton read the opus over and over until he could comprehend the meaning of each word. He enrolled in Merritt Community College in Oakland, earned an associate of arts degree, and then spent a semester at San Francisco Law School, not for a law degree, but to learn the intricacies of coping with law enforcement agencies. In his free time he attended meetings of the fledgling Afro-American Association, organized by the young attorney Donald Warden (now Khalid Al-Mansour).

Although he was becoming better prepared academically and more sophisticated politically, Newton continued to run afoul of the law, sometimes using his own legal knowledge in court to avoid prosecution. He could not, however, escape the 1964 penalty of a month in solitary confinement with restricted nourishment in the Alameda County Jail for assault with a deadly weapon. Newton credited this experience in quietness with helping him learn to control his mind for clearer thinking.

Conception and birth of the Black Panther Party

In 1965 Newton and fellow student Bobby Seale joined the Soul Students Advisory Council and the Revolutionary Action Movement at Merritt College in their efforts to bring classes in African American history to the college. They were soon disillusioned when those organizations rejected their proposed demonstration on campus with an open display of firearms. Unshaken from their belief in the power of guns, Newton and Seale set about formulating their vision of a well-armed self-defense group.

Newton and Seale began intense, systematic readings and discussions, concentrating on the examples of the Black Muslim movement and Robert Williams in the United States, Mao Tse-Tung in

Huey P. Newton.

China, Frantz Fanon in the Caribbean and Africa, and Fidel Castro and Che Guevara in Cuba. On October 15, 1966, Newton and Seale opened an office on Fifty-eighth Street in North Oakland, and unveiled a ten-point platform that called for total redressing of the inequities in all areas of African American life in the United States. This was the official birth of the Black Panther Party for Self-Defense. The well-conceived, all-encompassing doctrines of the organization covered employment, economic security, housing, education, dependable police protection without brutality, fair court hearings and release of all African American prisoners, exemption from military service, and a United Nations supervised vote to determine the destiny of black Americans.

Bobby Seale was the first chairman of the new group; Newton, the defense minister; and Eldridge Cleaver, minister of information. The Panthers, in black berets and black leather jackets, soon became a recognizable force and attracted young men seeking their own selfhood and ways to contribute to African American life. Driving cars equipped with cameras and tape recorders, they came to the aid of any African American they saw being interrogated by the police on the streets of Richmond, San Francisco, Berkeley, or Oakland. They were visible advocates for black citizens in need. The Panthers served breakfast to children, provided free medical clinics, escorted seniors to and from their homes, and operated a fully accredited elementary school in a predominantly African American part of Oakland.

The party attracted far-reaching attention from a case that involved a member, Denzil Dowell. Dowell had been fatally shot on April 1, 1967, by Contra Costa County Sheriff Department officers as he supposedly resisted arrest for automobile theft. Unable to accept the verdict of justifiable homicide, party members mounted protests that culminated with the appearance of thirty gun-bearing Panthers, clad in the usual black attire, on the steps of the

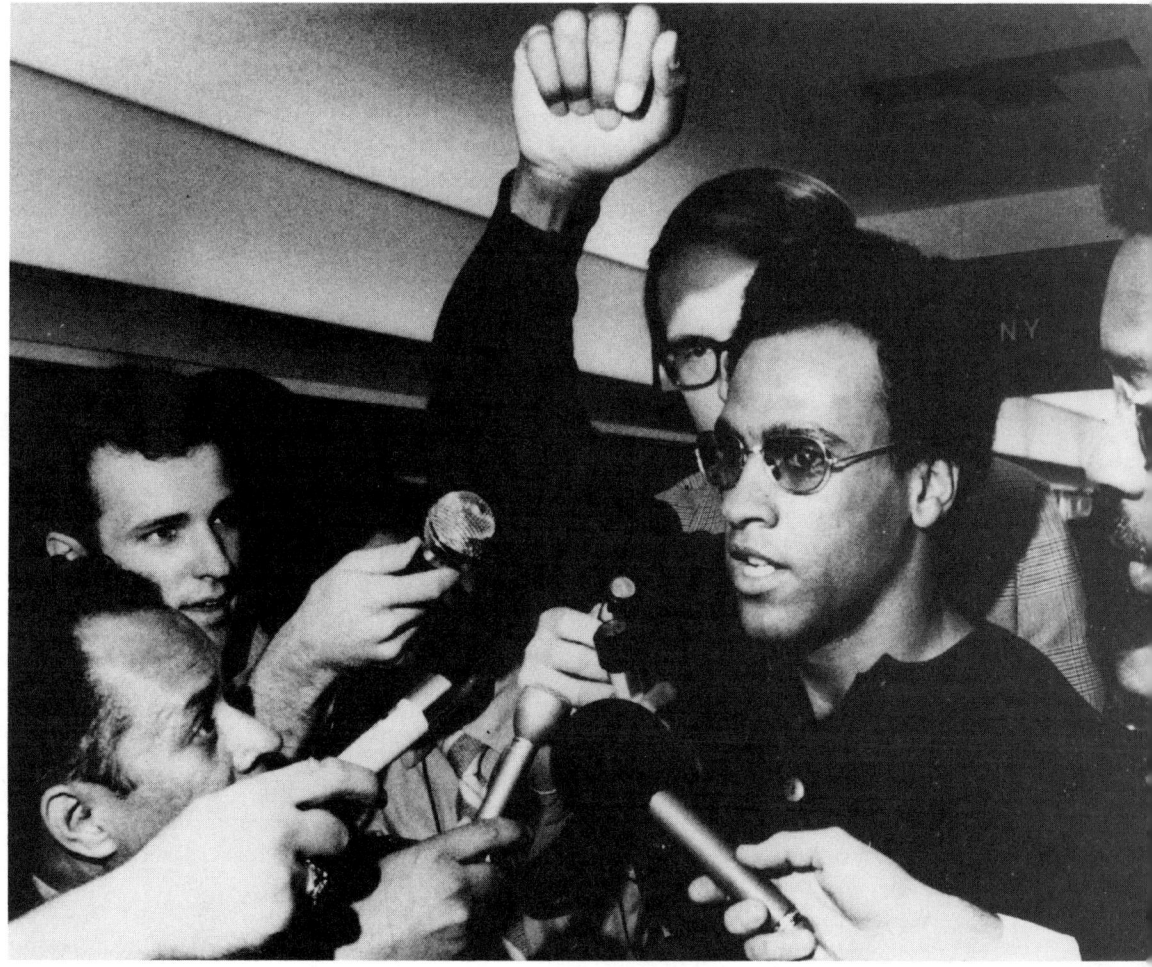

*Huey P. Newton, mobbed by the press, arrives
in Philadelphia for a three-day convention.*

state capitol in Sacramento on May 2, 1967. Law makers were inside debating passage of legislation to restrict use and ownership of firearms.

The twenty-four men and six women in the Panther group stood silently while Seale read, in Newton's absence, the leader's statement of resistance to the proposed law introduced by Representative Donald Mulford, a conservative Republican. That night, armed African Americans with bandoliers appeared on news broadcasts all over the country. The *Mulford Law,* known as the anti-Panther bill, was passed in July of that same year without delay and with few dissenting votes.

Three months later, on October 27, 1967, Newton was the central figure in a case where he was shot in the stomach, and an Oakland police officer, John Frey, was shot to death. Newton pleaded not guilty, but he was convicted of voluntary manslaughter with a sentence of two to fifteen years in prison. Nationwide cries of "Free Huey" led to two retrials

507

on the grounds that the judge did not give proper instructions to the jury. Both trials ended with hung juries and case dismissal.

By the 1970s the Black Panthers were suffering from internal and external pressures. Cleaver, minister of information, and many of his supporters broke with the party. Major damage came from the FBI and CIA's spies within the inner circle and overt outside surveillance. It was suspected that informants from the drug world and from the Communist party were listening in as well. Gun battles with police took a toll on the lives of the membership. Such powerful opposition hastened the end of their effectiveness.

Newton's personal life continued to be a mass of problems stemming from court charges and prison sentences, compounded by drug and alcohol use. He was arrested on a variety of infractions—burglary, illegal possession of firearms, murder, manslaughter, and violation of probation. He fled to Cuba in 1974 to avoid prosecution but returned in 1977.

Newton completed study for a bachelor's degree and a Ph.D. in social philosophy from the Santa Cruz campus of the University of California in 1980. For his dissertation, "War Against the Panthers: A Study of Repression in America," he drew upon his intimate knowledge of the ideals, challenges, frustrations, and successes of the organization he helped conceive.

The end of Huey Newton's life came in the early morning hours on August 22, 1989, after he had been found on a sidewalk in West Oakland, seriously wounded by gunshots to the abdomen and head. He was forty-seven years old. The fatal attack had come not near his home, but in the area where the Black Panthers had concentrated their efforts to improve the lives of its residents. Newton's assailant, Tyrone Robinson, an African American and alleged drug dealer, was reported to have told police that his motive was self-defense and an effort to elevate his status in the Black Guerrilla Family, an organization of black prison inmates. Convicted of first-degree murder, Robinson was sentenced to thirty-two years in prison.

On the day of the funeral, well-wishers and admirers packed the large sanctuary of the church Newton had joined in 1985, Allen Temple Baptist Church in Oakland. In the midst of her grief, Newton's widow Fredrika was aware that Newton had known he might die by violent action, but she took comfort in the value of his work for the people underrepresented in their society. The Reverends J. Alfred Smith Sr. and Jr., the Reverend Cecil Williams, the Reverend Frank Pinkard, Congressman Ronald Dellums, Bobby Seale, David Hilliard, attorney Charles Garry, who pleaded cases for Newton and the Panthers in scores of court appearances, H. Rap Brown, Erika Huggins, Elaine Brown, and Johnny Span paid public tribute to Newton and to the accomplishments of the political party he created.

Initially, the Panthers' support came from disillusioned veterans of the Vietnam war and younger people seeking means to uplift the race. Soon African Americans of all ages welcomed its success in decreasing the widespread police brutality in the Bay Area. While many people distrusted the party's methods, they saw the Panthers' constructive activities, such as its breakfast programs and independent schools, as contributing to racial progress. When Newton died in 1989, thousands expressed sadness over his ignominious end. His death at the hands of drug dealers symbolized the persistent personal and social problems that undermined the very area that this man—known as politically shrewd and capable of motivating large numbers of Americans—tried to help.

Fredrika Newton established the Dr. Huey P. Newton Foundation in 1993 to keep the philosophy and contributions of Newton and the history and activities of the Black Panther Party alive.—DONA L. IRVIN

JESSE **OWENS**

1913–1980
Olympic track star, entrepreneur

Called the "world's fastest human," an Olympic athlete and winner of four gold medals in 1936, Owens became a legend in his own time. He overcame crippling poverty, segregation, and racial discrimination to soar to the heights of his Olympic aspirations. Americans cheered, but when the games were over, Owens was forced to struggle in order to live the American dream.

James Cleveland Owens was born September 12, 1913, in Oakville, Alabama. His father, Henry Owens, was a sharecropper, and Emma Fitzgerald Owens, his mother, took in washing and ironed clothes in order to earn extra money. But the family lived in extreme poverty. Owens was the tenth of eleven children consisting of four girls and seven boys.

As a child, J. C., as he was then called, was chronically ill. Inadequate housing, food, and clothing was injurious to Owens's health. Every winter he suffered from pneumonia and was never treated by a physician as there was no money for medical care. In the segregated town of Oakville, school for black children was a pastime. "We could only go to school when there wasn't anything [else] going on," Owens recalled in William Baker's *Jesse Owens*. Not surprisingly, he faced an academically troubled future.

Owens's mother, naturally optimistic and enthusiastic in her outlook, encouraged Owens to dream. She also prompted her husband to move away from a South that seemed bent on crushing not only her youngest child's dreams but maybe even taking his life.

From J. C. to Jesse The move to Cleveland, Ohio, changed Owens's life. His father found work in the steel mills, as did his three brothers. Owens

Jesse Owens.

509

Jesse Owens runs the 200-meter race at the 1936 Olympics in Berlin.

worked in a shoe repair shop after school and on weekends. For the first time in his life, he attended school regularly. He enrolled at Bolton Elementary School just three blocks from his house. As the now famous story goes, when the teacher asked Owens's name, he replied "J. C.," but she misunderstood his southern accent and thought he said Jesse. He did not possess the courage to correct her.

Owens later attended Fairmount Junior High School. Fairmount was integrated, mostly by immigrants and southern migrants like Owens. Emphasis was not on academics but rather on citizenship, manners, and behavior. This type of education—Americanization, as it were— would have a lasting effect on Owens, although it would not see him through the rigors of college.

Fairmount affected his life in other ways as well, for here he met two important people whose friendship lasted a lifetime. One was a pretty young girl named Minnie Ruth Solomon, whom he later married. The other was a white physical education teacher named Charles Riley. This teacher-turned-coach saw in the young student the talent Owens had once observed in his father. While Owens appreciated the things Coach Riley taught him, he recalled in *The Jesse Owens Story,* "The true beginning of my running really lay with my father. He was an expert on leg exercises because he was the champion runner in our county. . . . I used to watch him . . . for he had legs like no human being I'd ever seen and a way of running that resembled a cat." Owens would also learn to run like a cat, and Riley's training helped perfect the technique. Quoted by William Baker, Riley told Owens to run "like the ground was burning fire."

When Owens entered East Technical High School, Riley continued coaching him. The education that should have taken place at the high school did not. Instead, Owens received vocational training. Owens's homeroom teacher, Ivan Green, took an interest in him as a track and field star, but not as a pupil. Still, Owens was the only child from his large family to graduate from high school.

In 1929, Henry Owens was hit by a car. While he sustained only a broken leg from the accident, he was off work for three months and was required to take a physical examination before returning. The examination revealed that he was blind in one eye. This diagnosis forced him into chronic unemployment at the beginning of the Great Depression. His children dropped out of school in order to work. All hopes were pinned on Jesse Owens.

On August 8, 1932, Owens's first daughter, Gloria Shirley, was born to sixteen-year-old Ruth Solomon, who dropped out of school and found a job working in Wagner's Beauty Shop. According to Owens, he and Ruth secretly married in Erie, Pennsylvania, in the spring of 1935.

On May 20, 1933, Owens took the Interscholastic finals with a long jump measuring twenty-four feet, three and three-quarters inches, breaking the world record by more than three inches. In June 1933, at the National Interscholastic Championship Track Meet at Stagg Field in Chicago, Owens jumped twenty-four feet, five-eighths inches in the long jump, ran the 220 race in 20.7 seconds, and ran the 100-yard dash in 9.4 seconds, which tied the world record. East Technical High School won the meet with fifty-four points, of which Owens contributed thirty. Owens came home to a hero's welcome. The city of Cleveland greeted him with a victory parade. Because of his stellar athletic record, colleges from across the country tried to recruit Owens. Although his academic record was deficient, no one seemed to care as long as he kept running hard and fast.

Jesse Owens prepares to run the 100-yard dash, 1935.

The Buckeye Bullet Despite all his offers from various colleges, Owens felt the need to be close to home. However, Charles Riley wanted Owens to attend the University of Michigan, and the black press informed Owens that Ohio State University was blatantly racist and being sued by the NAACP on behalf of two black students it refused to house. In the end, the need for him to work three jobs to pay his tuition and support his family led him to enroll in his state university.

Owens entered Ohio State University in October. Owens was barred from living on campus because of his race, but lived in a boarding house with other black students on East 11th Avenue, about a quarter-mile from the campus. High Street restaurants refused to serve blacks, and they were only admitted to one movie theater in the slum section of the town, where they were restricted to the back section of the balcony.

Owens rarely discussed the treatment he experienced in Columbus, but his classmates remembered. Charles Beetham, Mel Walker, and William Heintz recalled in Baker's *Jesse Owens* that Columbus was "a cracker town, just like Jackson, Mississippi." One event, however, stuck in Owens's memory. In *Blackthink* he recalled:

> I do remember riding in the Ford that day and not being able to keep down the bitterness that all the Negroes had to be in one car. Not that it wasn't natural in a way. . . . We'd won a lot of races for our team. I myself had set four world's records. . . . We were good enough to compete alongside the white athletes, but often not good enough to take showers with them afterwards or to ride with them on the way to the meets.

The *Chicago Defender* had warned Owens about Ohio and its university. But what made Jesse Owens a hero was not just his athletic ability but his unique way of looking at the world. Baker said that he was always able to see "a flower on the dung heap and cultivate it to his advantage." Owens turned discrimination into an opportunity to study almost without interruption. Perhaps he did not know how to study; nothing in his background had prepared him for college, and by the end of the first quarter he had deficiencies. And by the end of March 1934, he was on academic probation.

Instead of the personal attention Owens needed to succeed academically, his coach arranged for him to address local school and service organizations every Wednesday at noon. The pattern of behavior Owens developed in order to make these public addresses would characterize his entire life. He learned to correct his bad grammar and to cover his limited experience with personal anecdotes, charm, and wit.

In addition to public speaking skills, Owens began to develop a personal magnetism, a charismatic personality. Under Coach Snyder's directions, he altered his running style. The Owens trademark was perfected. It was serious and quiet, without any hint of demonstrative gesturing; it was smooth and graceful, with Owens appearing to glide to victory. Owens's speed earned him the nickname "the Buckeye Bullet."

The road to gold   On May 5, 1935, Owens broke five world records at a meet held at the University of Michigan at Ann Arbor. Many track and field enthusiasts think of that day as the greatest day in track and field history. It was here that, according to Baker, Owens earned the title "the world's fastest human."

Owens returned to campus in the fall as elected captain of the Ohio State Track Squad. He was the first black ever to captain a Big Ten team. There was only one problem facing Owens: his grades had not improved. Working toward a degree in physical education, he had managed to avoid rigorous mathematics and science courses for which he had no preparation; still, he was making little progress toward the degree. Owens, now with his name in record books, had to live up to his reputation.

The 1936 Olympics in Berlin was plagued by a boycott movement dating back to 1933. The Amateur Athletic Union (AAU) delegates voted to withhold American athletes from the Games unless the Nazis altered their treatment of German Jews. The American Olympic Committee disagreed with the conclusion of the AAU, insisting that it was wrong to mix politics and sports. The 1936 Games caused anger and protest not only from American Jews but from others as well. The black press pointed out that Nazi racism affected more than just the Jews.

Blacks in Germany married to German women lived under legal and social discrimination. All the rhetoric surrounding the boycott revealed one irony: racist attitudes and practices in the United States were little different from the fascism of Nazi Germany. On December 8, 1935, the AAU reversed its earlier decision and voted for the American athletes to participate.

Owens had other problems to deal with. In December the AAU informed him that his name had been removed from the list of ten finalists for the Sullivan Memorial Award because of a problem regarding his employment as a page during the summer. The case was later dismissed, but not in time for Owens to be considered for the award, one of the most prestigious awards honoring the year's best amateur athletes. Following this disappointment was another; in the fall quarter, Owens had failed a psychology course. He was now academically ineligible to participate in the winter indoor track season.

On January 21, 1936, Ripley's *Believe It or Not* featured Owens's record-breaking performances of the previous spring. His performance during the spring of 1936 made him a favorite for the Olympics. In the final trials for the Olympic team, Owens finished first in the 100-meter and 200-meter sprints, and in the long jump. There were sixty-six Americans on the 1936 Summer Olympic track and field team. Ten were African American men and two were African American women: hurdler Tidye Pickett and sprinter Louise Stokes. The *Amsterdam News* for July 18, 1936, printed the following comment: "Those who mourn the defeat of Joe Louis at the hands of the determined German, Max Schmeling, can find not only solace, but also genuine pride and appreciation in the results of the Olympic selections."

Olympic glory   The black community, stunned by Louis's defeat, pinned all of its hopes on Jesse Owens as he set sail the morning of July 15, 1936, on the *S.S. Manhattan* bound for Germany. When the Games opened August 1, Owens fought to control his anger; he recalled in *The Jesse Owens Story,* "I'd never had time to be a crusader. But when the hour came for me to compete, I was mad. I was angry because of the insults that Hitler and the other German leaders had hurled at me and my Negro teammates on the Olympic squad. I was angry for all the colored people back home." Owens knew he had to control the negative emotions or they would destroy his chance of winning.

Owens won in the 100-meter sprint, the 200-meter sprint, the long jump, and the 400-meter relay, collecting a total of four gold medals. In the long jump Owens broke his own record, clearing twenty-six feet, five and three-quarter inches. It would be twenty-five years before anyone would break his record. Although the German spectators gave Owens a standing ovation, controversy surrounded Adolph Hitler's reaction to his win. Hitler's legendary snub of Owens by refusing to shake his hand never actually occurred. It is true that on the first day when two Germans won, they were summoned to Hitler's box to shake his hand. As the day grew long and rain began to come, the black high jumper Cornelius Johnson won the gold. Just before the playing of the American national anthem, Hitler and his group of men walked out of the stadium. If anyone was snubbed, it was Johnson and not Owens. Owens did not win his gold medal until the next day, and by then Hitler had been told by the president of the International Olympic Committee that he would have to be impartial in his accolades. The American press, however, exaggerated the story. The *New York Times* headlines read, "Hitler Snubs Jesse." Even though Owens initially denied it, apparently he tired of the constant denial and gave in, so the story continued to circulate. Baker reported in *Jesse Owens* that "the American press shifted the focus of the snub yarn away from Cornelius Johnson onto

Jesse Owens . . . [because] every new medal won by Owens enhanced his appeal as the target of Hitler's supposed insult."

Ticker tape parades, autograph seekers, photographers, and reporters welcomed home the Olympic hero. Then suddenly the band stopped playing, and Owens faced American reality. He told *Ebony* in 1988: "I came back to my native country and couldn't ride in the front of the bus. I had to go to the back door. . . . I wasn't invited up to shake hands with Hitler, but I wasn't invited to the White House to shake hands with the President, either."

Worse, perhaps, than the discrimination Owens faced, were the misleading offers Owens received to pay him fantastic salaries for personal appearances. On the basis of these offers, Owens refused to tour Europe for post-Olympic Games as the AAU insisted that he must. He felt that he was being exploited, receiving no money himself while making money for the AAU. Coach Snyder supported Owens and advised him to return to the United States and cash in on the once-in-a-lifetime offers. The AAU suspended Owens. The best offer he received came from Ohio's premier black college, Wilberforce. They would pay him $2,800 a year to coach the track team. There was one obstacle: Owens would need his college degree.

Owens earned money the best way that he could, hustling his Olympic fame and turning professional. He campaigned for the Republican Party in the presidential election of 1936, and exhibited his speed by running at baseball games, county fairs, and carnivals. In 1937, his second daughter, Marlene, was born. With a growing family and aging parents, Owens felt pressured to earn money and security. He opened a dry cleaning business but went bankrupt. Finally, in 1940, with the birth of his youngest daughter, Beverly, Owens decided to return to Columbus to complete his degree. He enrolled at Ohio State, and paid his tuition by coaching track. After four terms, he gave up. His cumulative grade point average was 1.07. The only degree Owens would obtain from Ohio State was an honorary degree awarded in 1972.

Owens decided to do what he did best besides running and jumping. He loved to talk, and he had a gift for oratory. He capitalized on this strength and went on the lecture circuit talking to young people about sports. He organized the Junior Olympic Games for youths in Chicago in 1956. Eventually he was able to open his own public relations firm and was said to have earned around $100,000 in 1970.

Owens gains the ire of militant blacks   The militancy characterizing the 1960s caught Owens by surprise. The son of an Alabama sharecropper, he was taught to grin and bear insults. His political stance had worked for him. A celebrated speaker, businessman, and Republican, Owens caught the fire of militant blacks for his opposition to the black American Olympic boycott and protest. Burned by charges that he was an "Uncle Tom," Owens fought back, stating his case in a personal memoir, *Blackthink* (1970). In the book Owens assessed black militants and made the mistake of presuming that the reaction by Tommy Smith and John Carlos, who raised their fists in a Black Power salute at Mexico City's 1968 Olympics, did not strike a responsive chord with the majority of black people. In *Jesse Owens,* Baker summarized Owens's position: "It was a view of the world, of success by means of the work ethic, and of the failure that reflects a flawed character." For blacks who had not made it in America, Owens said in *Blackthink* that they needed to "fight harder to make equality work."

While whites lauded the publication of Owens's book, blacks denounced him as insensitive to racism and the deplorable social conditions of most blacks. Owens received   **515** the praise of Republicans, and President Richard M. Nixon made him goodwill ambassador to West Africa. The letters of protest and outrage from angry blacks, however, weighed heavily on Owens's mind.

Owens's reflections led him to write another book, *I Have Changed* (1972), in which he retracted much of what he stated in *Blackthink*. In this book he defended the rights of blacks to protest racism and injustice and admitted that equality had not dawned for most black people who suffered from limited job opportunities, unfair housing, inferior education, poverty, and ill health. With this book, Owens made his peace with the black community, and with himself. He recognized he had much to learn from his daughters' and grandchildren's generations, when he wrote in this book, "I'm still changing."

The last mile In December 1979, Owens, who smoked a pack of cigarettes a day, entered the hospital complaining of fatigue. On December 12, he was diagnosed with lung cancer. On March 21, 1980, he was airlifted to the university hospital in Tucson, Arizona, where he and Ruth had lived since 1971. Owens died on March 31, 1980.

Flags flew at half-mast all over the state of Arizona, and Owens's body lay in the state capitol rotunda in Phoenix. Later his body was flown to Chicago for the funeral held in the Rockefeller Chapel of the University of Chicago. A steel gray casket draped with a white silk flag bearing five Olympic rings held the world's fastest human of 1936. Before he died, Owens, responding to reporters' questions regarding the upcoming Olympics, made a statement characteristic of his life and philosophy. Quoted by Baker, he said: "The road to the Olympics doesn't lead to Moscow. . . . It leads to no city, no country. It goes far beyond Lake Placid or Moscow, ancient Greece or Nazi Germany. The road to the Olympics leads, in the end, to the best within us."

In 1976, forty years after his Olympic feat, Owens was invited to the White House to receive the Presidential Medal of Freedom from Gerald Ford. In 1979 he received the Living Legend Award from Jimmy Carter. In 1990, Owens's widow received a Congressional Gold Medal in his honor. Three campus buildings at Ohio State carry Owens's name, as does the athletic track. In 1982, the Jesse Owens International Indoor Track and Field Meet began in New York. Owens is an appealing hero for all Americans regardless of race or political persuasion because his is the perfect rags to riches story. He had moved from the cotton fields of Alabama to the well-paid, highly visible world of a businessman and international traveler, and was a lovable hero on and off the track.—NAGUEYALTI WARREN

CHARLIE "YARDBIRD" **PARKER**

1920–1955

Musician

Charlie "Yardbird" Parker was one of the greatest jazz figures to appear on the American jazz scene. Raised

and nurtured as a musician in the vibrant musical climate of Kansas City, he soon migrated to New York

City, where he earned the respect of jazz fans and critics alike. Folklore, tales, suppositions, and questions

abound concerning many aspects of his life and career, but his greatness as a musician is never doubted.

Charles Parker Jr. was born in Kansas City, Kansas, on August 29, 1920, the son of Addie and Charles Parker. The family moved to Kansas City, Missouri, when he was eight or nine, and he entered Crispus Attucks grammar school. He went to Lincoln High School in 1933, and came under the tutelage of Alonzo Lewis, the band director. Parker's father was a vaudeville entertainer who became stranded in Kansas City. Parker's father often played piano at home, but he found it difficult to get good jobs, and eventually he drifted away from the home around 1931 and found employment as a railroad chief. His mother worked various jobs as a charwoman, keeping self and family together.

Begins jazz career early   Kansas City was a thriving metropolis during the 1930s, under the dominance of the Pendergast political machine. A rail hub, cattle and wheat market, and entertainment center, Kansas City had a vibrant night life in its many clubs. It was the home base for many jazz orchestras that toured throughout the center of the United States, including the Bennie Moten–Count Basie orchestra, Andy Kirk's Clouds of Joy, and Jay McShann's orchestra. Leading musicians who hailed from Kansas City included Lester Young, Herschel Evans, Ben Webster, and Jo Jones. Many writers proclaimed it the home of the after-hours jam session. It was within this lively musical milieu that young Parker began to develop as a musician.

Alonzo Lewis, Parker's band director, introduced him to the baritone horn, alto horn, and, briefly, the tuba. Eventually his mother bought him his first instrument, an alto saxophone. This brought about a profound change not only in Parker's life, but in the course of black music history. His family lived in a neighborhood near the city's entertainment center and its many jazz venues, and his school friends were mostly young aspiring musicians. In his sophomore year, Parker's mother got another job working the night shift at the Western Union Company main office downtown. This left young Charlie Parker relatively free of supervision in the

*Charlie
Parker.*

evenings, and he began spending most of his time listening to jazz in the clubs, well into the early morning hours. Musically, he developed quickly; he began playing professionally and joined the musician's union in 1934, apparently when he was fourteen. His schooling suffered, however, as he devoted most of his attention to the saxophone and learning jazz.

His most influential friends included pianist Lawrence "88" Keyes and bassist Gene Ramey, both from Lincoln High; Jesse Price, a local professional drummer; and "Old Man" Virgil, a local junk merchant. Virgil often provided Parker with a dose of worldly wisdom and served as an alter-ego, conscience, and partial father figure, as well as the butt of Parker's frequent practical jokes. His sweetheart, Rebecca Ruffing, soon graduated from Lincoln High, and they decided to get married. The Ruffing family moved in with the Parkers, and Charles Parker's son, Leon, was born in 1936.

Charlie Parker performing at the Paris Jazz Festival in 1949.

Fate soon provided an ironic turn to Parker's fortunes. In a road accident after an out-of-town gig in Eldon, Missouri, over the Thanksgiving holiday, the car in which Charles was riding overturned in a ditch coming out of a curve on an icy road. One of Parker's friends was killed and Parker himself was injured but chose to be treated at home. A favorable insurance settlement followed, and Parker was able to buy a new Selmer saxophone, a substantial boost to his musical development. He was treated for pain from the accident later, and drugs were prescribed, perhaps contributing to his later addiction.

Parker's marriage began to sour, and he left home for Chicago in 1938. Seeking to improve his career opportunities, he pawned his saxophone for travel funds. He met saxophonist Goon Gardner, who took him in and helped him with odd jobs. He was also in touch with Buster "Prof" Smith, a Kansas City bandleader who had since moved to New York. Parker headed east, hitching a ride on a band bus bound for New York. Arriving there, he stayed with Smith for a time. Gigs were not easy to obtain, and he took a job dishwashing at the Chicken Shack where pianist Art Tatum provided entertainment. It was here that he heard Tatum's advanced musical ideas, and these were to prove pivotal for Parker. Also at this time, one of his out-of-town gigs took him to Annapolis, where his mother sent word of his father's death, and Parker rushed home for the funeral in Kansas City.

New jazz created   Parker stayed in Kansas City for a time, he and Rebecca divorced, and in 1939 he was hired to work with the newly formed Jay McShann Orchestra. The band toured the region and then headed for a southern tour, finally ending up in New York in 1942. When McShann took the group back to Kansas City, Parker elected to stay in New York. At this point, the new musical style called "bop" evolved in a series of after-hours jam sessions, and Parker was at the center of the new movement. The movement revolved around a nucleus of like-minded musicians seeking new modes of expression: Parker, trumpeter Dizzy Gillespie, pianist Thelonius Monk, and drummer Kenny Clarke, soon joined by others, including drummer Max Roach, trumpeter Miles Davis, and saxophonist John Coltrane.

The first formative sessions took place at two after-hours clubs, Minton's and Monroe's. After a period of experimentation, clashing, and blending of personnel and personalities in free-wheeling "cutting" session challenges, Parker and Gillespie soon solidified their dominance of the field. Their blend of talent and technique gave the new music its trademark "hot" flavor of high-power, high-speed technical display laced with clipped phrases, unexpected turns of melody, rhapsodic improvisatory twists, and humorous scat singing. In short, jazz gave birth to a new child.

Jazz musicians at that time earned their principal livelihood as members of organized bands and in recording sessions. For Parker, these included engagements with Earl Hines's orchestra in 1943, and Billy Eckstine's orchestra in 1944–45, with frequent out-of-town gigs, recording dates, and tours in the South and Midwest. In 1943 he married Geraldine Scott of Washington, D.C. The marriage lasted for five years. After Parker returned to New York for an engagement with Gillespie at the Three Deuces, promoter Billy Shaw arranged a tour that took Parker to California in December 1945.

Several important recording sessions were held in California, as well as engagements at Billy Berg's jazz club and a major concert organized by Norman Granz at Philharmonic Hall in Los Angeles—dubbed "Jazz at the Philharmonic." A major mishap occurred at this point in Parker's career. After a strenuous Dial recording session in July 1946, he had a physical and mental breakdown at his hotel, and was taken into police custody and committed to the Camarillo State Hospital. Drug abuse, his physical condition, fatigue, and stress contributed to his collapse. His friends rallied to his side: Doris Sydnor came from New York, and she and Ross Russell of Dial Records were instrumental in gaining his release into Russell's custody. Parker subsequently left Los Angeles with Doris in 1947 for New York, and they moved in together near the entertainment district. They were married in 1948 in Tijuana.

Parker had become somewhat of a legend in his own time at this point. Billy Shaw presented him with an invitation and engagement at the International Jazz Festival in Paris in 1949, along with a number of the most respected jazz figures of the day: Flip Phillips, Tad Dameron, "Hot Lips" Page, and Sidney Bechet, among others. Later that year Shaw designed and built a new jazz club, opened it the week before Christmas 1949, and named it "Birdland," in honor of Charlie Parker. Parker, of course, played at the opening on December 15 and many times in subsequent years.

Parker's travels next took him on tour in the South, and then to Sweden in late 1950, where he was a great success. He stopped in Paris on the way home, and was urged by jazz writer Charles Delauney to schedule a major concert appearance there. He suffered another physical collapse, however, attributed to severe ulcers, and left Paris quickly without canceling the engagement. He apologized graciously to the Paris concert audience by a radio hookup from New York, where he was interviewed on Leonard Feather's jazz show.

He and his wife, Doris, had since drifted apart, and Chan Richardson and he began living together in 1950. They had dated previously, and she had visited him in California earlier. They lived as common-law man and wife, and this relationship lasted until shortly before his death. Chan had a daughter, Kim, born in 1947, and she and Charles had two other children: a daughter, Pree (b. 1952), and a son, Baird (b. 1953).

Parker's next travels took him on a Jazz at the Philharmonic tour to Germany and Europe in 1951–52. Following recording sessions and short tours, another tour in California was organized in 1954 with the Stan Kenton orchestra. Although the tour was successful, a personal tragedy occurred. While visiting with sculptor Julie MacDonald in Hollywood and sitting for a head sculpture, he heard of the death of his daughter, Pree, of pneumonia. He was deeply affected, blaming himself for being an inattentive parent. He rushed home for the funeral, and took his family for a vacation on Cape Cod.

Several engagements ensued in 1954, including an unfortunate one at Birdland. He was playing with an ensemble that included a strings orchestra and was displeased with the arrangements and performance. He abruptly dismissed the musicians and canceled the performance. This, of course, did not sit well with the musicians or the management. Following the occasion he became very upset, had a serious argument with Chan, and attempted suicide. He was admitted and treated at Bellvue Hospital. Following his release, he was engaged for a Jazz at the Philharmonic Concert on September 25. The concert went well, but he felt stress once again and had himself readmitted to Bellvue Hospital.

Parker becomes a legend Following his release, Parker tried to regain physical and spiritual control, but became openly despondent, speaking to friends of suicide, and at times living as a street person. He was able to play at the "Open Door" jam session early in 1955, hosted by writer Bob Reisner. Arrangements were made for a Birdland gig, followed by a Boston engagement. The group opened well enough, but at the concluding Saturday performance his pianist, Bud Powell, was drunk and unable to perform. This caused a disastrous scene, with Parker canceling the performance.

He then retreated from the scene, seeking to gather his energies. On March 9 he started for Boston, but only got as far as the apartment of a close friend, the well known socialite and supporter of the arts, Baroness Pannonica de Koenigswarter. Charles "Yardbird" Parker died late on Saturday night, March 12, 1955, in her New York apartment. It was several days before the news reached "the streets" of New York City. When it did, rumor accompanied fragmentary truth, and graffiti began appearing in Harlem and Greenwich Village, saying "Bird Lives," emphasizing the aura of mystery surrounding Parker's death. It was some time before full details came to light, and mystery continues to surround several aspects of Parker's life. Certainties remain, such as his love for food, particularly chicken—hence his nickname "Yardbird" (a country name for chicken). He also suffered from a serious case of ulcers, in all probability one of the causes of his death. He had a consuming lust for female companionship, and tales of his sexual prowess are legendary. A heroin addict as well as an alcoholic, he often seemed to his friends to be on a quest to live life to the extremes. He seemed the epitome of the existentialist—believing only in the "now." It is surely a testament to his strong constitution that he was able to accomplish so much in his music while taxing his body so severely.

He left, however, an impressive legacy of recordings and inspiration for musicians and music lovers to contemplate. Virtually all of his recorded works are currently available on cassettes and CDs, and transcriptions of his solos are available from a number of sources, published and archival. Some of his most memorable compositions include "Cherokee," a Kansas City favorite, "Embraceable You," "I Got Rhythm" (particularly the version with the incredible duet solo with Dizzy Gillespie), "Parker's Mood," and "Koko," among many others.

One can paint a picture of stark contrasts in telling Parker's story. In some ways, he led a life of majesty, playing gigs in some of the United States' top jazz venues, including Birdland. He was virtually worshipped by musicians and jazz fans alike for his talent, his improvisatory genius, and his innovative contributions to music, preaching the gospel of a new music with his horn and inspiring numerous young musicians to follow in his tracks. Saxophone students to this day memorize his solos and improvisations.—DARIUS L. THIEME

GORDON **PARKS**

1912–

Photographer, writer, director, composer, musician

Gordon Parks rose from a life of poverty to one of success by following his early teaching and by understanding he could be his own most dangerous enemy. He learned early not to use color or poverty as excuses for poor performance, and that his best weapon against the type of world in which he found himself was his mind. Coupled with this was his drive to succeed.

Gordon Roger Alexander Buchanan Parks was born November 30, 1912, in Fort Scott, Kansas, to Andrew Jackson and Sarah Ross Parks. He described his parents as hard working, always providing, and God-fearing people who were forgiving, compassionate, and active models of love. He was the youngest of fifteen children. He grew up in poverty, attending a segregated elementary school and a high school that was mixed but excluded African American students from social functions, sports participation, and any aspirations beyond the menial. Yet, he said in his autobiography *Voices in the Mirror,* he was "taught how to live honorably and how to die honorably." Parks married Sally Alvis in 1933 and was divorced in 1961; in 1962 he married Elizabeth Campbell and was divorced in 1973; and in August 1973 he married Genevieve Young and was divorced in 1979. He had three children from his first marriage: Gordon Jr., his first born, a film director who died in an airplane crash in 1979 while filming on location in Africa; daughter Toni Parks Parson; and another son, David; and from his second marriage, a daughter, Leslie.

Gordon Parks.

Parks's mother died when he was sixteen, an event that oddly catapulted him into a life of achievements and success. He moved to St. Paul, Minnesota, to live with his sister and her family. He and his sister's husband had differences, and after a brief period, her husband evicted him. Parks was thrust upon his own resources, with little money and no home. For almost a week he spent the night riding the trolley from one end of the line to the other, from St. Paul to Minneapolis. Since he had evinced some musical talent early in life, he eventually gained a job playing the piano nightly in a brothel for tips, a job he held for two years. Then, in 1929, he got a job, as he wrote in *Voices in the Mirror,* in a "Minnesota club as a bus boy in the day, and a general lackey at night." He began to see what success was like, but even more important, he began to read more, using the club library. However, he was forced to seek employment again and to quit high school when the "panic and depression," as he called that time, struck.

Parks returned to playing piano in a brothel where, he said in *Voices in the Mirror,* "the music I fed them was filled with my mood, and it seemed to soothe their souls. Friends began calling me 'Blue,' because of the blues I played." One of the numbers frequently requested was "No Love," which he composed after an argument with his future wife. Later, he decided to go to Chicago, but stayed only a short time and returned to St. Paul. A white band leader, Larry Funk, heard him playing "No Love" and not only played it on national radio but also invited him to join and travel with the band. Parks did, but the band broke up in New York and he was again broke and jobless in 1933.

This time he joined the Civilian Conservation Corps. He left the corps in 1934 and returned to Minneapolis, worked as a waiter, and tried to promote his songwriting. In 1935, he took another job playing the piano and showcased his own tunes. Later, he became a waiter on the North Coast Limited, a transcontinental train, which to him represented the "Minnesota Club on Wheels." It was this job that spawned his interest in photography.

Develops talent for photography   While leafing through magazines on a run, Parks saw pictures of migrant workers taken by photographers who worked for the Farm Security Administration; he wrote in *Voices in the Mirror,* "these stark, tragic images of human beings caught up in the confusion of poverty saddened me." He began to read more on photographers and visit the art museums. When he saw a newsreel of the Japanese bombing of the U.S. gunboat entitled *Panay,* and photographer Norman Alley's work, Parks was "determined to become a photographer." Three days later, he bought his first camera: a seven-dollar and fifty-cent Voightlender Brilliant. Parks commented in *Voices in the Mirror* this "was to become my weapon against poverty and racism." His first pictures gained him respect from the Eastman Kodak Company and a showing in the company's show windows. His subject soon became the tenements and people on Chicago's south side; the pictures were reminiscent of the ones of the migrants seen earlier, and they foreshadowed his later documentary work. He continued to study art and to understand how much could be achieved with the camera.

Having seen pictures in *Vogue,* Parks approached Frank Murphy, the owner of a women's store in St. Paul, Minnesota, regarding photographing fashion and displaying it in the store's windows. These pictures in the window were seen by Marva Louis, the wife of heavyweight boxing champion Joe Louis. She urged him to move to Chicago, where he profited from her encouragement and from contacts at the South Side Community Art Center; he photographed society matrons as well as the South Side. As a result of the latter work, in 1941 he became the first photographer to be a Julius Rosenwald Fellow; for his fellowship, he was apprenticed to Roy Emerson Stryker at the Farm Security Administration in Washington, D.C., for a year. He was appalled at the bigotry and racism and documented this condition with his 1948 "American Gothic" photograph of Ella Watson, a poor, black, government cleaning lady, posed against the American flag with broom and mop in hand. "I didn't think it would be published," he recalled in *Life* in 1997. "It was an indictment of the government."

When the Farm Security Administration was absorbed by the Office of War Information, Parks was assigned to cover the black pilots of the newly formed 332nd Fighter Group and sent to Selfridge Field in Michigan. When he resigned his Washington job in 1944, he moved to New York.

Parks soon applied to *Harper's Bazaar,* which rejected him because of his race. Due to the intervention of Edward Steichen, a photographer, he began receiving casual wear assignments for *Glamour* magazine and six months later received a *Vogue* assignment.

While freelancing for *Vogue,* Parks joined Roy Stryker's photographic team at Standard Oil Company in New Jersey. His work included photographing Standard Oil officials and a documentary series on rural America. At the conclusion of this work, he sought to become a member of the staff of *Life;* he achieved this with his photographic essay on gang life and a young Harlem gang leader, Red Jackson. He joined the staff of *Life* magazine in 1948 and remained until 1972; his more than 300 assignments included fashion, reports on poverty in Harlem and Latin America, the black civil rights movement, Black Panthers, "Crime Across America," "Death of Malcolm X," the Ingrid Bergman–Roberto Rosellini love affair, Broadway shows, personalities, and politics. Phil Kunhardt Jr., then an assistant managing editor, said of Parks in *Smithsonian* magazine, "at first he made his name with fashion, but when he covered the racial strife for us, there was no question that he was a black photographer with enormous connections and access to the black community and its leaders. He tried to show what was really going on there for a big, popular, fundamentally conservative white magazine." As noted in the source, the reasons for this and a testament to Parks is given

Gordon Parks directing his film
The Learning Tree in 1968.

in Malcolm X's autobiography: "Success among whites never made Parks lose touch with black reality."

Book publishing emerges In addition to his photography, Parks wrote and thus embarked on a publishing career. The early efforts were closely related to his work. His first published books were instructional: *Flash Photography* (1947) and *Camera Portraits: Techniques and Principles of Documentary Portraiture* (1948). While still at *Life,* he was encouraged to write about his life in Kansas. Out of this grew his best-selling novel, *The Learning Tree* (1963). The title and the inspiration for the novel grew out of the response of his mother to the question of whether they had to stay in Fort Scott forever. He wrote in *Voices in the Mirror* that she answered, "I don't know, son, . . . but you're to let this place be your learning tree. Trees bear good fruit and bad fruit, and that's the way it is here. Remember that." In 1966, he published the first of three autobiographies, *A Choice of Weapons,* which tells of his struggle to survive after his mother's death. The title "came to him after President John F. Kennedy's assassination," he said. The theme of the book is evident in a *Detroit News* article in which Parks said, "I have a right to be bitter, but I would not let bitterness destroy me. As I tell young black people, you can fight back, but do it in a way to help yourself and not destroy yourself." In 1968, Parks combined poetry and photography for a book entitled *Gordon Parks: A Poet and His Camera.*

He published three more books that combined photographs and poems in the 1970s: *Gordon Parks: Whispers of Intimate Things* (1971), *In Love* (1971), and *Moments Without Proper Names* (1975). In *Afro-American Writers after 1955,* he has said of this book, "The first part . . . says more of what I want to say, what I felt was necessary to say. The back part . . . is the beauty part. It is simply what it is—the beautiful moments." In 1971, he also published *Born Black,* a collection of essays on personalities of the civil rights era such as Malcolm X, Martin Luther King Jr., Huey Newton, and Stokely Carmichael.

The interweaving of his various endeavors is illustrated by his 1978 publication, *Flavio.* In 1961, when he was on assignment from *Life* to document the poverty in Rio de Janeiro by scrutinizing an impoverished family, he met the Da Silvas and their son Flavio, who was twelve years old and dying of bronchial asthma and malnutrition. The photo essay that grew out of the assignment, "Freedom's Fearful Foe: Poverty," appeared in the June 16, 1961, issue of *Life.* Public response was overwhelming: money, offers of adoption, and even this offer from the Children's Asthma Research Institute of Denver: "Without charge we will definitely save him. All you have to do is deliver him to our door." Eventually, Flavio was brought to Denver, treated, and returned home healthy and happy. Parks remained in contact with Flavio. Out of this experience came his award-winning biography of Flavio.

Current Biography noted that, "between 1970 and 1973, Parks was a key figure in the founding and early editorial direction of *Essence* magazine." He produced another installment of his life story with *To Smile in Autumn, A Memoir* (1979), which spans the years 1944 to 1978. *Afro-American Writers* says "it combines passages from his poems, journals, and letters with recollections of wives, children, lovers, and career assignments." In 1981 he published his second novel, *Shannon.*

With the 1990 publication of *Voices in the Mirror: An Autobiography,* Parks again reviewed his life. This recounted his life story from his poor Kansas beginning to his triumphs in both America and abroad. His twelfth book, *Glimpses Toward Infinity,* which combines his poetry, paintings, and photography, was published by Bulfinch Press in 1996.

Film career develops   Parks's creative talents have also led him to a film career. It began as he served as a consultant on several Hollywood films. His first film was a documentary on Flavio. Additionally, he made three other documentaries, including *Diary of a Harlem Family* and *Mean Streets.* He became the first African American to produce, direct, and score a film for a major Hollywood studio, Warner Brothers, with *The Learning Tree* (1968), based on his novel of the same title. Donald Bogle in *Blacks in American Films and Television* divides Parks's films into two general categories: commercial dramas—*Shaft* (1971), *Shaft's Big Score* (1972), and *The Super Cops* (1974), in which he focused on contemporary men of action caught up in urban life—and personal "romances," *The Learning Tree, Leadbelly* (1976), and to some degree, *Solomon Northrup's Odyssey* (1984). Most of his films, excluding *The Super Cops,* present assertive black males facing social and political elements that threaten to rob them of their manhood. In *Voices in the Mirror,* Parks tells of his struggles to get Paramount to distribute and promote *Leadbelly,* the story of the folk and blues singer Huddie Ledbetter and his disappointment with Hollywood. In 1988, his autobiographical film *Gordon Parks: Moments Without Proper Names* was televised on PBS.

Develops talent in music   Parks's many musical compositions include popular and blues tunes from his early career. His films often include his music. He wrote film scores and then adapted the music for their separate release—*Tree Symphony, The Learning Tree,* and "Don't Misunderstand" in *Shaft's Big Score.* He has composed *Concerto for Piano and Orchestra, Piece for Cello and Orchestra, Five Piano Sonatas,* and *Celebrations for Sarah Ross and Andrew Jackson Parks.* He created the music and libretto for the five-act ballet *Martin* (1989), a tribute to Martin Luther King Jr., which premiered in Washington, D.C., and in 1990 was aired on national television on King's birthday. For the television production, he was executive producer, director, and photographer of the documentary that preceded the ballet. His interest in music and his photography were combined when he produced a picture of jazz musicians in the 1996 issue of *Life.*

Wins awards and honors   As a result of his intrepidness and his creative vision, Parks has garnered numerous awards. Included in his recognitions are the Julius Rosenwald Award for Photography (1942); Photographer of the Year from the American Society of Magazine Photographers (1960); Philadelphia Museum of Art Award (1964); Art Directors Club Award (1964); and Notable Book Award from the American Library Association for *A Choice of Weapons* (1966). He also won the Mass Media Award and Award for Outstanding Contributions to Better Human Relations, both from the National Conference of Christians and Jews Brotherhood (1964); Nikon Photographic Award (1967) for promotion of understanding among nations of the world; Emmy Award, best television documentary, for *Diary of a Harlem Family* (1968); Carr Van Anda Award from Ohio University School of Journalism (1970); and the Spingarn Medal from the NAACP (1972). In the Dallas Film Festival he won first place in 1976 for *Leadbelly;* he also won the Christopher Award for best biography, 1978, for *Flavio;* Guild for High Achievement from the National Urban League (1980); NAACP Hall of Fame Award (1984); American Society of Magazine Photographers Award (1985); Governor's Medal of Honor as Kansan of the Year from the State of Kansas (1985); Commonwealth Mass Communications Award (1988); and National Medal of Arts (1988).

Parks has received more than a dozen honorary degrees from universities and fine arts institutes. Other recognitions include the establishment in his honor of the Gordon Parks Media Center of New York City's John F. Kennedy High School and the Learning Tree Schools. Parks was inducted into the Black Filmmakers Hall of Fame in 1973 and received the Frederick Douglass Gold Medal in 1984.

In his autobiography, *Voices in the Mirror,* he says, "I've liked being a stranger to failure since I was a young man, and I still feel that way. I'm still occupied with survival; still very single-minded about keeping my life moving—but not for fame or fortune." Thus, in spite of the racism and the poverty throughout his childhood, he did not bow to convention and managed to excel in various artistic fields. Parks, a Renaissance man, became the first African American photographer to work at *Life* and *Vogue* magazines. In 1989 *The Learning Tree* was one of the twenty-five films placed on the National Film Registry of the Library of Congress.—HELEN R. HOUSTON

ROSA **PARKS**

1913–
Civil rights activist

Rosa Louise McCauley Parks, a long-time advocate of civil rights, is best known for her December 1, 1955, refusal to surrender her seat to a white passenger in a crowded Montgomery, Alabama, bus. Parks's landmark act is described as having "breathed life" into the civil rights movement. Today she is known as the mother of the civil rights movement and continues to talk to children about her struggles of the past and hopes for the future.

Parks was born February 4, 1913, in Tuskegee, Alabama, one of two children of Leona (Edwards) and James McCauley. Her father was a carpenter and her mother taught in rural schools. Her parents separated in 1915, soon after Parks's brother, Sylvester James, was born. After her father went north to live, she had very little contact with him. Her mother returned with her children to Pine Level, Alabama, to live with her parents.

Parks helped with the household chores, not only because her mother was teaching much of the time, but also because her mother and both grandparents were not in good health. In fact, Parks often had to take care of everyone. She especially liked making quilts and cooking. Her mother taught in rural one-room schools and other buildings where classes could be held, and for about three years was Parks's teacher. When Parks was eleven years old, she went to a private school, the Montgomery Industrial School for Girls, and lived with her aunt, Fanny Williamson.

The teachers at the Montgomery Industrial School for Girls were liberal women from the North. In exchange for tuition, Parks cleaned two classrooms. With her duties at school and at home, there was little time for Parks to enjoy childhood. She entered Booker T. Washington High School but dropped out when her mother became seriously ill. Parks learned about the hardships of slavery and about emancipation from stories told by her maternal grandparents. From her family's teaching, her own observations as a child, and her experiences at school, Parks began to view segregation and discrimination as intolerable.

Although Parks's mother hoped she would become a teacher and offered financial support so she could attend Alabama State Teachers College, Parks thought more about nursing as a possible career. In December 1932 she married Raymond Parks, a barber from Montgomery, Alabama. After their marriage, Rosa Parks held a variety of jobs to supplement her husband's income. She sewed at home and worked as a domestic, an insurance salesperson, and an office clerk.

Rosa Parks getting fingerprinted
after her arrest in 1955.

Raymond and Rosa Parks shared a common interest in the problems of inequality and segregation in the South. As a member of the National Committee to Save the Scottsboro Boys, who were charged with raping two white girls, Raymond often brought food to the young men while they were in jail awaiting trial.

In 1943 Parks became a member of the Montgomery Chapter of the NAACP, one of the first women to do so, and she joined the Montgomery Voters League and encouraged blacks to register to vote. In the summer of 1955 Parks attended workshops at the integrated Highlander Folk School in Monteagle, Tennessee, which had been engaged in the civil rights struggle since the 1930s. Whenever she could, Parks avoided the segregated drinking fountains, the "Colored Only" elevators, and other reminders of the low status imposed on blacks in the South.

Parks sparks Montgomery bus boycott   The incident that changed Parks's life occurred on Thursday, December 1, 1955, as she was riding home on the Cleveland Avenue bus from her job at Montgomery Fair, a downtown department store where she worked as an assistant tailor. The first ten seats on the city buses, which were always reserved for whites, soon filled up. Parks was seated next to a man in the front of the section designated for blacks, when a white male got on and looked for a seat. In such situations, the black section was made smaller. The driver, who was white, requested that the four blacks move. The others complied, but Parks refused to surrender her seat, so the driver called the police. Parks had been evicted from a bus twelve years earlier by the same driver, but this time it was different. In a *Black Women Oral History Project* interview, she said, "I didn't consider myself breaking any segregation laws . . . because he was extending what we considered our section of the bus." And in *Black Women* she explained, "I felt just resigned to give what I could to protest against the way I was being treated."

At this time there had already been fruitless meetings with the bus company about the rudeness of the drivers and other issues—including trying to get the bus line extended farther into the black community, since three-quarters of the bus riders were from there. In the previous year three black women, two of them teenagers, had been arrested for defying the seating laws on the Montgomery buses. The community had talked many times about a citywide demonstration, such as boycotting the bus line, but it never developed. The Women's Political Council already had a network of volunteers in place and had preprinted flyers; they needed only a time and place for a meeting.

About six o'clock that evening, Parks was arrested and sent to jail. She was later released on a $100 bond, and her trial was scheduled for December 5. Parks, age forty-two when the bus incident occurred, was seen as a well-mannered, humble woman. Her demeanor was such that even middle-class whites could identify with her and as a result, could not justify segregation. These qualities attracted the NAACP, the Southern Christian Leadership Conference (SCLC), and its president, a little-known minister named Martin Luther King Jr., who rushed to Parks's defense and thus allowed her to become a symbol for the struggle for equality. After consulting with her husband Raymond, Parks agreed to allow her case to become the focus for a struggle against the system of segregation. On December 2, the Women's Political Council distributed more than 52,000 flyers throughout Montgomery calling for a one-day bus boycott on the day of Parks's trial. At a mass meeting of more than 7,000 blacks at the Holt Street Baptist Church, the black community formed the Montgomery Improvement Association and elected King its president. The success of the bus boycott on December 5 led to its continuation. In the second month it was almost 100 percent effective and involved 30,000 black riders. When Parks was tried, she was found guilty and fined ten dollars plus court costs of four dollars. She refused to pay and appealed the case to the Montgomery Circuit Court.

Following her release from jail, Parks went back to work but later lost her job, as did her husband. At home, the couple had to deal with threatening telephone calls. Rosa Parks devoted her time to arranging rides in support of the boycott. Blacks were harassed and intimidated by the authorities in Montgomery, and there was an attempt to break up their carpools. Parks served for a time on the board of directors of the Montgomery Improvement Association, and often was invited elsewhere to speak about the boycott.

On February 1, 1956, in an attempt to have the Alabama segregation laws declared unconstitutional, the Montgomery Improvement Association filed a suit in the United States

District Court in the names of four women and on behalf of all who had suffered indignities on the buses. On June 2 the lower court declared segregated seating on the buses unconstitutional. The Supreme Court upheld the lower court order that Montgomery buses must be integrated, and on December 20, 1956, the order was served on Montgomery officials. After 381 days of boycotting, resulting in extreme financial loss to the bus company, segregation and other discriminatory practices were outlawed on the city buses. Parks's refusal to give up her seat on a bus was the beginning of the civil rights movement of the 1950s and 1960s. Her action marked the beginning of a time of struggle by black Americans and their supporters as they sought to become a respected part of America.

With the notoriety surrounding her name, Parks was unable to find employment in Montgomery. Her husband became ill and could not work, so Parks, her husband, and mother moved to Detroit, Michigan, in 1957 to join Parks's brother. Since Raymond did not have a Michigan barber's license, he worked in a training school for barbers. In 1958 Parks accepted a position at Hampton Institute in Virginia for one year, after which she returned to Detroit and worked as a seamstress. She continued her efforts to improve life for the black community, working with the SCLC in Detroit. In 1965 Parks became a staff assistant in the Detroit office of United States Representative John Conyers; she retired in 1988.

Rosa Parks has been called the mother of the civil rights movement. The *New York Times* reported that Coretta Scott King and former diplomat Andrew Young assured Parks that "she had a permanent place in history." With the publication in 1992 of *Rosa Parks: My Story*, an autobiography written with Jim Haskins, children and readers of all ages can read Parks's first-hand account of her early life and contribution to the civil rights movement. Along with that autobiography, two more books followed. In 1995, Parks collaborated with her longtime friend and attorney Gregory J. Reed to write *Quiet Strength: The Faith, Hope, and Heart of a Woman Who Changed a Nation*. Because she has become a legend in history books, Parks receives thousands of letters from children. She has compiled the best of these letters in the book *Dear Mrs. Parks: Dialogue with Today's Youth*. In her books that recount that fateful day on the bus, Parks revealed the real reason why she did not relinquish her seat. It wasn't her tired aching feet, but her remembrance of her father sitting on the porch with a shotgun as the Ku Klux Klan rode around their house. Parks's feet may have hurt, but Parks felt a pain more deep and reacted.

Parks is the recipient of many awards, including the NAACP's Spingarn Medal, bestowed in 1979. In 1980 Parks was the ninth person, and the first woman, to receive the Martin Luther King Jr. Nonviolent Peace Prize. In 1996, President Bill Clinton awarded Parks the Presidential Medal of Freedom, the highest honor this nation bestows to a citizen. She holds ten honorary degrees. The citation for an honorary degree from Mount Holyoke College in 1981 read in part, "When you led, you had no way of knowing if anyone would follow." In 1984 Parks was the recipient of the Eleanor Roosevelt Women of Courage Award from the Wonder Woman Foundation. In 1986 as part of the celebration for the Statue of Liberty's 100th birthday, Parks was one of eighty people to receive a medal of honor for their contributions to American ethnic diversity.

Parks remains very active. She was one of the few women speakers at the first Million Man March in Washington, and she received a standing ovation. She continues to make speeches across the United States to raise money for the NAACP, and she speaks to young people about the civil rights movement. She remains active in the SCLC, which since 1963 has sponsored the annual Rosa Parks Freedom Award. Her many honors in Detroit have included the naming of Rosa Parks Boulevard, which runs through the black community, and the Rosa Parks Art Center. In 1987 she established the Rosa and Raymond Parks Institute for Self-Development, incorporated as a nonprofit organization in Detroit, to work with young people between the ages of eleven and fifteen. In January 1988 the Museum of African American History in Detroit unveiled a portrait of Parks on her seventy-fifth birthday. On June 30, 1989, the twenty-fifth anniversary of the Civil Rights Act, she attended ceremonies at the White House. The National Committee for the Rosa Parks Shrine is soliciting money for a home on Rosa Parks Boulevard for Parks after her retirement. It will also serve as a library for her personal papers. In 1990, Parks's seventy-seventh birthday was celebrated in Washington, D.C., by 3,000 black leaders, government dignitaries, entertainers, and social leaders.

Rosa Parks, forever modest and humble, never sees herself as a hero. Nonetheless, her defiant act over forty years ago has made a nation view her as a heroic woman who changed the course of American history.—RUTH EDMONDS HILL

BILL **PICKETT**
1870–1932
Wild West show performer, cowboy

Bill Pickett was a major star of rodeos and Wild West shows and the inventor of a unique style of bulldogging in the first years of the twentieth century. For most of his life he was a working cowboy.

Willie M. Pickett was born to Thomas Jefferson Pickett and Mary Virginia Elizabeth Gilbert Pickett on December 5, 1870, in the Jenks-Branch community about thirty miles northwest of Austin, Texas, in Travis County. He was the oldest of thirteen children born to the couple between 1870 and 1890. Thomas Pickett was born a slave in 1854 in Louisiana, as his owners moved from South Carolina to Texas. The racial heritage of both parents was mixed and included Native American ancestry. After slavery, Thomas Pickett moved his family to a small holding near Austin sometime in the early 1870s and began to raise vegetables for market. His oldest son, Bill, went to a rural school through the fifth grade.

About the time Bill Pickett finished his schooling in 1881 at the age of eleven, he learned from observing cattle dogs a method of controlling cattle. Bulldogs had originally been bred to control bulls by biting their sensitive muzzles and holding on. Pickett discovered that he too could subdue cattle by biting; as an adult he leaped from his horse, seized the steer by the horns, and pulled the head back to the point where he could bite the upper lip. The animal would be immobilized and follow as he dropped to the ground, with the animal often landing on top. This technique is forbidden in modern bulldogging—now officially called steer wrestling—which involves much lighter animals weighing between 400 and 750 pounds. Pickett faced steers between 800 to 1,100 pounds. Naturally, he lost teeth and was frequently injured; although he tried to work in spite of damage to his body, he was sidelined on one occasion for nine months. Over the years he estimated that he bulldogged some 5,000 head.

Pickett and several of his brothers worked on ranches around Austin and became skillful cowboys. Pay for cowhands was low, about five dollars a week with board. Thus,

Bill Pickett.

in Austin around 1886, Bill Pickett rode bucking horses on Sunday afternoons to amuse bystanders and picked up some extra cash by passing the hat. He also gave occasional demonstrations of his method of bulldogging, which amazed spectators to whom it was completely new, especially since Pickett was not a large man. At five feet, seven inches, he weighed 145 pounds.

The Picketts moved to Tyler, Texas, around 1888. There, between 1888 and 1890, five Pickett brothers offered their skills at breaking horses.

For some years Pickett worked on various ranches around Tyler. On December 2, 1890, he married Maggie Williams. The Picketts had nine children: Sherman, Nannie, Bessie, Leona, Boss, Willie, Kleora Virginia, Almarie, and Alberdia. The two sons, Sherman and Boss, died in infancy, but all the girls reached adulthood. The family lived in Tyler, where Pickett was a deacon of the Tyler Baptist Church. Pickett took any farm and ranch work available, including cotton picking, and supplemented the family diet by hunting. Sometime in the late 1890s he became blind for eleven months; when the condition cleared up, his eyesight was never troubled again.

Bill and Tom Pickett gave exhibitions of bulldogging at the first Tyler county fair in 1888. It is not clear when Bill Pickett began to tour extensively. Lee Moore, a local rancher, managed his touring, and Pickett made appearances in many Texas towns before making extensive out-of-state engagements beginning in 1900. After the 1902 season, Pickett had a new manager, Dave McClure, who took Pickett to major events like the 1904 Cheyenne Frontier Days celebration. Coverage by a national magazine pushed Pickett and his bulldogging into the spotlight.

Pickett joins 101 shows   Ex-Confederate soldier George W. Miller and his three sons had built up a very large and profitable ranch near Ponca City, Oklahoma, called the 101. To entertain a convention of editors, the Miller brothers staged a wild-west show on their ranch on June 11, 1905. The show attracted some 65,000 persons to the specially built facilities. Pickett's current manager, Guy "Cheyenne Bill" Weadick, a major influence in the development of the modern rodeo, brought to the event his star bulldogger, now billed as "The Dusky Demon."

The 101 Ranch staged another show in 1906. By now the Millers liked the money the shows brought in and were ready to develop a traveling show. In 1907 they signed a contract with Pickett, who maintained his relationship with the 101 for the rest of his life.

The Picketts moved first to accommodations on the ranch, but the family later settled in Ponca City. Pickett lived on the ranch and visited his family when he could. For a traveling cowboy, family life became secondary. From 1907 through 1913 Pickett toured with the 101 show in the United States, with an occasional foray into Mexico. He appears to have been earning about six dollars a week plus board for his efforts in the shows, and during the winters he did regular ranch work. In the winter of 1913 the show went to South America and then to England. All the horses were seized by the British government at the outbreak of World War I, and the troupe had difficulty in booking passage home. At the close of the 1916 season, the Millers ended their shows, which had contributed to the $800,000 profits of the 101 Ranch between 1908 and 1916.

Pickett now did ranch work at the 101 Ranch, with occasional rodeo appearances. In 1920 he moved with his family to Oklahoma City. While his family was happy there, he was not. In 1924 he moved back to the 101. The ranch was now experiencing hard times, so he had no regular salary but asked for money as he needed it. A new 101 show went on the road in 1925 but with little financial success; the shows limped along to an end in 1931.

After a brief illness, Maggie Pickett died in a hospital on March 14, 1929, and was buried near Norman, Oklahoma. Bill Pickett was now left alone since all of his daughters had married and left home. In 1931, the 101 Ranch went into receivership. In March 1932 a horse kicked Pickett in the head. After a fourteen-day coma, he died on April 2, 1932. After a funeral held on the porch of the main residence of the 101 on April 5, he was buried about three miles away on the ranch.

Bill Pickett's skill as a bulldogger can be seen in a film short, *The Bulldogger*, preserved in the Library of Congress. Pickett received posthumous recognition. On December 9, 1971, he was the twentieth person and the first black inducted into to the National Rodeo Cowboy Hall of Fame in Oklahoma City. The North Fort Worth Historical Society unveiled a bronze statue of him in 1987. Millions more people became aware of him when the Postal Service planned to issue a commemorative stamp in March 1994 but discovered that the stamp bore a brother's likeness and had to issue a corrected version. Bill Pickett was a living legend. He was a brave and innovative man who revolutionized the rodeo. A living legacy is his family: Pickett had 215 living direct descendants in 1994.—ROBERT L. JOHNS

SIDNEY POITIER

1927–

Actor, director, producer

Sidney Poitier has served as a model and door-opener for African American actors, such as Denzel Washington, Yaphet Kotto, Morgan Freeman, Laurence Fishburne, and Samuel L. Jackson. Contemporary Biography *called him "the first black man to be given a succession of serious, dignified roles in Hollywood films." According to the* African American Encyclopedia, *he created dignified, educated African American characters and stimulated audiences to question the stereotypical portraits of blacks. He was also "praised and ridiculed for portraying the well spoken and noble but non-threatening African American during a period when African American frustration at racism was major news." As a result of his performance in* Lilies of the Field *(1963), he became the first African American in American film history to win the Oscar for best actor in a starring role.*

Sidney Poitier, the youngest of seven children, was born prematurely—weighing three pounds—in Miami, Florida, on February 20, 1927, to Reginald James and Evelyn Outten Poitier, both uneducated tomato farmers. His parents had come to Miami from Cat Island in the Bahamas to sell their tomatoes. They took him back to the Bahamas when he was three months old. Growing up, he was poor and received a limited education.

*Sidney
Poitier.*

In an attempt to insure a better life for him, Poitier's father sent him to Miami in 1943 to live with his brother Cyril. Because of Poitier's defiance in the face of racism, he soon had to leave Miami to preserve the safety of his brother's family, for he had placed their lives in jeopardy and the Ku Klux Klan was looking for him. Under the cover of night, he left Miami for New York with summer clothes and three dollars. Once in New York, he secured a job as a dishwasher. However, the cold weather was too much for his summer wardrobe; he enlisted in the army saying he was eighteen, not seventeen. He returned to civilian life after one year and eleven days of service.

Stage performance   Upon his discharge from service, Poitier returned to New York and secured another dishwashing job. His interest in acting had been aroused to some extent when he was a youngster in the islands viewing such actors as Tom Mix, Gene Autrey, Wild Bill Elliott, and Roy Rogers. He was further intrigued when he saw an advertisement from the American Negro Theatre in Harlem's *Amsterdam News* calling for actors to audition. He answered the ad. Due to his poor reading ability, accent, and lack of training, he was turned down by the actor, director, and cofounder of the American Negro Theatre, Frederick O'Neal. This rejection served as an impetus for Poitier's development; thus, he began to learn to speak properly, to rid himself of his accent, and to learn to read. Six months later, following these efforts, he re-auditioned and became a student of acting at the American Negro Theatre. In *Blacks in American Films and Television,* Bogle said that he "became part of a group of post–World War II new-style black actors that included Harry Belafonte, Ossie Davis, Ruby Dee, Earle Hyman, and Lloyd Richards."

The theater presented one or two productions a year designed to promote the work of new students. In 1945 the theater performed *Days of Our Youth.* Poitier wanted the part of Liebman, but Harry Belafonte was brought in to play the part in spite of the fact that he was not a student at the theater. This led to a clash between the two men, who would later share a friendship and parallel careers. However, due to the petition of his classmates, he was cast as Belafonte's understudy, and when Broadway director James Light was invited to critique an evening's rehearsal, Belafonte was unable to appear and Poitier had to step in. Following the evening's rehearsal, Light asked Poitier to see him; Light told him he was planning on presenting the play *Lysistrata* with an all-black cast and offered him the part of Polydorus. Poitier made his first Broadway appearance in 1946 in *Lysistrata.*

In the first performance of the play, Poitier was petrified; instead of saying his lines in the natural order, he began with line three, went to line seven, and was never able to recuperate. Even though he was devastated, the audience found the performance hilarious and, according to Poitier in his autobiography *This Life,* some reviewers saw him as "the only saving grace of the evening" and praised his "acute comedic approach to the part of Polydorus." As a result of this performance, he garnered the role of Lester in *Anna Lucasta* (1947) and toured with the play in 1948. In 1959 he appeared as Walter Lee Younger in *A Raisin in the Sun,* directed by Lloyd Richards—a portrayal that has been praised for its emotional power. Other stage performances include *On Striver's Row, You Can't Take It With You, Rain, Freight, The Fisherman, Hidden Horizon,* and *Riders to the Sea.*

Poitier shifts to film   Poitier made his greatest impact in motion pictures; he worked steadily through the 1950s and 1960s. His first film appearances were training films for

Sidney Poitier holds his Best Actor Oscar in 1964.

the army; one of them was *From Whom Cometh My Help* (1949), an Army Signal Corps documentary. He made his first Hollywood appearance in 1950 in *No Way Out;* his character was a dedicated young doctor. Bogle said in *Blacks in American Films and Television,* "By his very presence, by his basic sense of self, he was flipping movie history upside down." In spite of the fact that there had been other black actors demonstrating both action and intelligence and performing serious roles prior to Poitier, they did not become "leading dramatic actor[s] working *consistently* in American films." In 1955 he appeared in *Cry, the Beloved Country,* an adaptation of the novel of the same name by Alan Paton, as the Reverend Msimangu. Part of the film was set in South Africa; Poitier traveled to Africa, where Msimangu was an indentured laborer, to learn about South African society and its inhabitants.

Also in 1950s, Poitier appeared in *Red Ball Express* (1952), *Go, Man, Go* (1954), and *Blackboard Jungle* (1955). The latter film, according to Bogle in *Blacks in American Films and Television,* represents "one of his most exciting roles as a rebellious high school student." He also appeared in *Goodbye, My Lady* (1956), *Band of Angels* (1957), and *Something of Value* (1957). It was with the making of *Edge of the City* (1957) and *The Defiant Ones* (1958) that his career changed and he became established as a star. In *Blacks in American Films and Television,* Bogle says that, in the latter film, he was "sometimes angry, sometimes explosive and almost always likable . . . [and] proved himself one of the screen's most talented dramatic actors."

Bogle suggests in his other book, *Toms, Coons, Mulattoes, Mammies & Bucks,* that there were three reasons for Poitier's rise in the 1950s while other actors failed. First, "for the mass white audience, Sidney Poitier was a black man who had met their standards. . . . For black audiences he was the paragon of black middle-class values and virtues." Second, "in many respects his characters were still the old type that America had always cherished." Third, "Poitier became a star because of his talent. He may have played the old tom dressed up with modern intelligence and reason, but he dignified the figure. Always on display was the actor's sensitivity and strength." Three other movies of the 1950s were *Mark of the Hawk* (1958), *Virgin Island* (1958), and *Porgy and Bess* (1959), his last picture of the decade.

The 1960s found Poitier the subject of controversy. Militants in the African American community did not approve of his roles, which were often seen as white creations and which denied him realistic romantic relationships. Movies of the 1960s include *All the Young Men* (1960); *A Raisin in the Sun* (1961), in the role of Walter Lee Younger, which he had played earlier in his career in the stage production; *Paris Blues* (1961); *Pressure Point* (1962); and the low-budget picture *Lilies of the Field* (1963), for which he received 10 percent of the profits and a Best Actor Oscar. Poitier's win was groundbreaking and promoted the coming of more positive, albeit asexual, roles for African Americans in Hollywood. His consistent filmography included films such as *The Long Ships* (1964), *The Greatest Story Ever Told* (1965), *A Patch of Blue* (1965), and *To Sir With Love* (1967), which insured Poitier's major presence in film. However, his most controversial picture of the period was *Guess Who's Coming to Dinner* (1967), in which Poitier portrayed a man in love with a white woman, on his way to meet her parents, played by Spencer Tracy and Katherine Hepburn. The film was praised for its risqué subject matter, but Poitier's presence took a backseat to the message of the film, which was heavy in liberal theology of love being color blind. Other pictures of the period included *In the Heat of the Night* (1967), *For Love of Ivy* (which was the result of his original idea, 1968), and *The Lost Man* (1969).

In the 1970s Poitier's career seemed to begin to wane. However, he appeared in movies such as *They Call Me Mister Tibbs,* the sequel to *In the Heat of the Night* (1970), and *The Organization* (1971). His movie credits in the 1980s included *Shoot to Kill* (1988) and *Little Nikita* (1988). In the 1990s he appeared in *One Man, One Vote* in the role of the South African President Nelson Mandela. The film tells the story of the negotiations that led to South Africa's first all-race election in 1994. In the fall of 1997, Poitier added grace to a cast featuring Bruce Willis and Richard Gere in an espionage thriller, *The Jackal.*

Becomes producer and director   In *This Life,* Poitier points out his powerlessness in Hollywood. "I was not in control of the film business. I was not even in control of my career in the film business beyond making a decision to play or not to play in a given piece of material. Furthermore, nothing in the material from which I had to choose had anything to do with the kind of family life thousands of . . . guys lived." This realization and a deluge of negative criticism following *To Sir With Love, In the Heat of the Night,* and *Guess Who's Coming to Dinner,* which began a backlash such as the article "Why Do White Folks Love Sidney Poitier So?" by Clifford Mason in the *New York Times,* led him to the crossroads of his career. Poitier needed to take filmmaking to another level—work behind the camera—in order to serve the African American community and provide more positive images in a way that white producers did not; it is behind the camera that images can be altered, decisions made, and audiences impacted. Thus, in *This Life* Poitier reports on his move toward decision-making involvement when he, along with Barbra Streisand, Steve McQueen, and Paul Newman—all members of the Creative Management Associates—formed the First Artists Corporation. Each artist agreed to make at least three films in a six-year period. Each artist would have artistic control. At the same time, Poitier entered into an agreement with Columbia Pictures to produce and star in two films that they would distribute.

Poitier's first major directing job was a picture that he and Harry Belafonte co-produced and costarred in: *Buck and the Preacher* (1972). In 1973 he directed the romance entitled *A Warm December.* His most successful directing and acting in the 1970s was with Bill Cosby in a series of comedies. These included *Uptown Saturday Night* (1974), *Let's Do It Again* (1975), and *A Piece of the Action* (1977). The success of these films bolstered Poitier's confidence in his ability to determine what audiences wanted to see. Thus, the 1980s found him engaged solely in directing such films as *Stir Crazy* (1980), *Hanky Panky* (1982), *Fast Forward* (1985), and *Ghost Dad* (1990).

Television appearances and writing   Poitier has appeared in such made-for-television features as *Separate but Unequal* (1991), portraying Thurgood Marshall, and *Children of the Dust* (1995), as an aging cowboy. He has appeared on numerous television episodes, including *The New Bill Cosby Show* (1972). Additionally, he has participated in television specials such as *The Night of 100 Stars II* (1985), *The Spencer Tracy Legacy: A Tribute to Katherine Hepburn* (1986), and *Bopha!* as the narrator (1987).

Poitier's autobiography *This Life* appeared in 1980. He tells his story with humor, courage, candor, and honesty. He discusses Hollywood and the filmmaking business, and makes observations about child rearing and the conditions of the young. He collaborated with Carol Berman in 1988 to write *The Films of Sidney Poitier.*

Poitier's honors and awards are numerous. Among them are the Georgia Cini Awards from the Venice Film Festival for *Something of Value* (1958). In that same year he received an Academy Award nomination for best actor, Silver Bear Award, Berlin Film Festival, New York Film Critics Award for best actor, and British Academy Award for best foreign actor, all for *The Defiant Ones.* He later received a Tony Award nomination for best actor in a drama (1960) for *A Raisin in the Sun;* an Academy Award for best actor in a drama (1963) and Golden Globe Award nomination for best actor in a drama (1964), both for *Lilies of the Field;* citation from Hollywood Women's Star Press Club (1967); and the San Sebastian Film Festival Award for best actor for *For Love of Ivy* (1968). Poitier was knighted by Queen Elizabeth II in 1968. More recently, Poitier was nominated for an Emmy Award for best actor in a miniseries or special in 1990, and he received the American Film Institute's Lifetime Achievement Award in 1992, the Kennedy Center Award for lifetime achievement in 1995, and the Black History Maker Award from New York's Associated Black Charities in 1997.

Poitier married Juanita Marie Hardy, a dancer, on April 29, 1950, and they were divorced in 1965. On January 23, 1976, he married Joanna Shimkus, an actress. Poitier had six children: Beverly, Pamela, Sherri, and Gina from the first marriage; Anika and Sydney from the second marriage.

In 1995 he received the Kennedy Center Award for lifetime achievement in the performing arts and, according to *Jet* magazine, he was "praised by fellow actor Paul Newman for his pilgrimage of startling grace. . . . 'He has changed the face of film itself.'" Poitier has greatly affected Hollywood both on and off screen. Because of his contributions to the film industry, African Americans are seen on both sides of the camera in roles that are much improved from the earlier stereotypical and lifeless characters presented by Hollywood.— HELEN R. HOUSTON

ALVIN F. **POUSSAINT**

1934–

Psychiatrist, educator, author

It is unusual in America for a physician to have national name recognition. It is even more unusual for a black psychiatrist to have both a name and a face that are recognized by the general public. Dr. Alvin F. Poussaint is a well-known public figure associated with family and children's issues, and an expert on the impact of racism and those whom it affects. Poussaint has spent much of his life at an educational institution where he has consistently kept African Americans, and particularly African American children, at the center of his concerns.

Alvin Francis Poussaint was born in East Harlem in New York City on May 15, 1934, the seventh of eight children of Harriet Johnston Poussaint, a homemaker, and Christopher Poussaint, a printer and typographer. From the time he began school until he finished medical school, Alvin Poussaint was educated at schools in Manhattan. He was raised as a Roman Catholic. Poussaint contracted rheumatic fever at the age of nine, an event that he credits with having changed his life. It gave him months of exposure—three months in a hospital and two months in a convalescent home—to doctors and nurses, influencing him to consider becoming a physician. Physically restricted, Poussaint got lost in the world of books, and when he returned to school he was an avid student. Later, while many of his friends—including a brother with whom he shared a bedroom—became drug addicts, Poussaint aimed himself toward achievement.

While in junior high school, a teacher suggested that Poussaint take a competitive test for admission to one of New York's special public high schools. Poussaint was accepted at the prestigious Stuyvesant High School, a predominantly white public school for gifted students with high academic potential. There he was very active in student life, doing creative writing and editing a literary magazine. He taught himself to play the clarinet, saxophone, and flute. While he was in high school, his mother died of cancer. After Poussaint graduated from Stuyvesant, his father wanted him to go to college locally. Poussaint attended Columbia University, with a four-year New York Regents Scholarship paying his tuition. At Columbia, he continued to excel academically.

At home, however, things were stressful. He told *Child* magazine, "I didn't come home until the [Columbia] libraries closed. That way I had minimal dealings with my [heroin-addicted] brother. But he stayed up late, and it was at night that he did his shooting up. So I was constantly picking him up off the floor, taking the needle out of his arm, dealing with a lot of his craziness, and, on the other hand, trying to help him if I could." Nor was the social scene at Columbia appealing. According to Poussaint in *Contemporary Black Biography*, while in college "social situations were awkward, there being a prevalent feeling among [white students] that blacks shouldn't come to social events. . . . They didn't expect you to show up at the dance."

He graduated from Columbia in 1956 and won a full scholarship to medical school, the only black person in the entering class of eighty-six students. Because his room and board were paid, he was able to move away from home. But then, Poussaint told *Child* magazine, he had to face the "isolation and indignities of being the only black student at the Cornell University Medical College, where [his] mother had given birth to him as a charity patient." Observations about racism and its impact on blacks and whites, which began in high school and continued throughout Poussaint's college and medical school career, eventually fueled his professional interests.

In 1960 Poussaint received his M.D. from Cornell and then trained at the University of California in Los Angeles (UCLA) from 1960 to 1964, first as an intern at the Center for the Health Sciences, and later as a resident and chief resident at the Neuropsychiatric Institute. After UCLA, where he earned an M.S. in 1964, Poussaint turned his attention to the South and the civil rights movement.

As southern field director of the Medical Committee for Human Rights (1964–65) based in Jackson, Mississippi, Poussaint headed a staff of volunteer medical workers and private citizens. They provided medical care to civil rights workers in the South and worked to desegregate health facilities there. Poussaint left Mississippi in 1966 and joined Boston's Tufts University Medical School faculty as director of a psychiatry program in a low-income housing project in Boston, Massachusetts. Since that time, most of Poussaint's career has been centered in the Boston area.

Poussaint was first appointed to the faculty of Harvard Medical School in 1969. He has remained there and, since 1993, has been clinical professor of psychiatry. In addition, he served as the director of student affairs at the school. He has been affiliated with the Massachusetts Mental Health Center in Boston and has been senior associate in psychiatry at the Judge Baker Children's Center in Boston, where he is director of the Media Center.

Writes on black issues in psychiatry and society   Poussaint's professional writings have ranged from clinical studies of bed wetting, low back pain, and epilepsy, to studies of motivation, behavioral science teaching, black suicide, and grief response. In particular, Poussaint has been a pioneer contributor to the discussion of issues surrounding the nurturing of black children. His articles have appeared in publications such as the *Journal of Negro Education, University of Chicago School Review, Psychiatric Opinion, Rehabilitation Record, Journal of Medical Education*, and *American Journal of Psychiatry*. He has written and served as co-author of chapters in books on minority group psychology, the black child's self-image, interracial relations, and black-on-black homicide. He has also contributed to several psychiatry textbooks, professional journals, and other publications.

In an attempt to bridge the gap between professional psychiatry and lay people in the African American community, Poussaint offers a psychiatrist's perspective of how early education can be used to fight racism in an article published in *Ebony* magazine in October of 1970, entitled "Why Blacks Kill Blacks," which was the basis for a book of the same title, published in 1972. Since then he has been a regular contributor to the popular magazine.

Two *Redbook* articles in 1971 and 1972, both written with James P. Comer, marked the starting point for much of Poussaint's most important and popular writing. The first article answered questions that black parents most frequently ask about rearing a black child in a predominantly white society. The second discussed what parents must do to rear their children free from prejudice. Response to the two articles eventually led to the publication of the book *Black Child Care*, written by both Poussaint and Comer. In 1992 Poussaint and Comer revised their book, retitled *Raising Black Children,* maintaining its question-and-answer format and focusing on nurturing black children at various developmental stages. They also collaborated in writing a weekly newspaper column, *Getting Along,* from 1970 to 1985, with United Features Syndicate.

Poussaint's writings center on creating, nurturing, and combating attacks on healthy black self-image. Whether addressing individuals, families, or the black community as a whole, Poussaint focuses on being proactive rather than reactive in the face of racism and stereotypical assumptions that impact on the lives of blacks.

Receives wide professional acclaim

Poussaint is a fellow of the American Psychiatric Association, a fellow of the American Association for the Advancement of Science, a member of the American Academy of Child and Adolescent Psychiatry, and a fellow of the American Orthopsychiatric Association. In 1971 he was a founding member of Operation PUSH (People United to Service Humanity) and served on the board of trustees for more than a dozen years.

Various government agencies have used Poussaint's services as a consultant. These include the Department of Health, Education, and Welfare; the FBI; the State Department; the White House; and several conferences on civil rights and on families and children.

Poussaint has also been an active consultant to media. He was script consultant on the pioneering *Cosby Show,* which made Poussaint's name known in households worldwide. He was also production consultant to the spin-off television show, *A Different World,* for NBC. He has been a consultant to the Congressional Black Caucus and a member of congressional and medical delegations to the People's Republic of China and to Cuba. He was a member of Action for Children's Television, the Boston University School of Social Work, and a Project Interchange seminar for American leaders in public policy held in Israel.

Poussaint has continuously served on the editorial board of publications such as *Black Scholar, Victimology: An International Journal, Journal of African American Male Studies, Young Sisters and Brothers Magazine, HealthQuest: The Publication of Black Wellness,* and *Nurture: The Magazine for Raising Positive Children of Color.* He has been a member of the editorial board of the Council on Interracial Books for Children, *Education Today,* the Urban Family Institute, Memorial for Our Lost Children, Facing History and Ourselves, and *Get Real: Televised Rap Music Forum and Youth Anti-Violence Campaign,* among others.

He belongs to the boards of the National Association of African American Artists and the 21st Century Commission on African American Males; he formerly served on the board of Wesleyan College. Poussaint co-chaired the Jesse Jackson presidential campaign in Massachusetts in 1983–84. Since 1993, he has been national co-director of the Lee Salk Center at KidsPeace.

Poussaint has received numerous awards and honors, including recognition from the Southern Christian Leadership Conference, Cornell University Medical College, Medical Committee for Human Rights, and Northeastern University's Center for the Study of Sports in Society. He has also been recognized with an American Black Achievement Award from Johnson Publishing Company; a Medal of Honor and an Award for Outstanding Service from NAACP chapters, and a media award from the Gay and Lesbian Alliance Against Defamation. He has been recognized by the Jewish Family and Children Services of Kansas City, the Baltimore Health Department, and Morgan State University.

Poussaint has been director for the Media Center at the Judge Baker Children's Center in Boston. Founded in 1994 by Poussaint, the Center produces children's programming and advises the communications industry through message research and advocacy for responsible media. Through the work of the Media Center, the Judge Baker Children's Center has become the first mental health center in the United States to produce a national television pilot, *Willoughby's Wonders,* a program based on contemporary knowledge of psychosocial development in children. This educational show for six- to eight-year-olds features an urban soccer team that explores themes of teamwork, inclusion, and individuality, as well as teaching the social skills of cooperation, empathy, and persistence.

Poussaint's career as a physician, a psychiatrist, an educator, a writer, and an agent of social change has been a successful one. He has increased public awareness of today's mental health challenges. Through his work in and on the media, Poussaint has raised the public's consciousness of the child, particularly the black child, as a television viewer who sees on the screen a representation of life that profoundly affects his or her psychological and social development. Because Poussaint believes that raising a child is everybody's business, his work implores adults to be responsible with children, families, and the media.— MARTIA GRAHAM GOODSON

ADAM CLAYTON **POWELL JR.**

1908–1974

Clergyman, civil rights activist

Adam Clayton Powell Jr. was an outspoken clergyman and civil rights activist who became the first black to be elected to Congress. His flamboyant lifestyle, however, sometimes undermined the significance of his achievements, and his fame, consequently, rests as much on his notoriety as it does on his political accomplishments.

Powell was born in 1908 in New Haven, Connecticut, where his father worked as a Baptist minister. The Powell family eventually settled in New York City, where Powell apparently reveled in life's frivolities. At City College, Powell's unusually light skin color enabled him to avoid racism. Furthermore, it allowed him to indulge in the institution's social activities. Having cultivated his social—as opposed to scholastic—skills, Powell eventually failed to meet the school's academic standards. After leaving City College, he merely turned his attention to Harlem, where the night life was also flourishing. During this period, he supported his active social life by working at various menial jobs.

In the late 1920s Powell decided to resume his academic pursuits by entering Colgate University. There he drew the ire of both white and black students by attempting to join a

Adam Clayton Powell Jr.

fraternity designed exclusively for white membership. After being exposed, Powell decided to join a black fraternity.

While at Colgate, Powell regularly traveled back to New York City to enjoy the night life. On one such excursion, he became enamored with Isabel Washington, a married actress with a young son. Powell's romance with Washington disturbed his parents, and after he graduated from Colgate in 1930, his parents financed his trip abroad—to Europe and the Middle East—only on the condition that he refrain from contacting Washington. Powell, ever independent, refrained from adhering to his parents' stricture.

In 1930, having returned from his journey abroad, Powell began pursuing studies for a career in the clergy. He enrolled at the Union Theological Seminary and began serving as a manager and assistant pastor at his father's church. After a brief period, Powell left the seminary and commenced graduate studies at Columbia University. In 1932 he obtained his graduate degree, and the following year he married Washington. After a few years, Powell began supplying the *New York Post* with pieces analyzing the social, political, and economic causes for the riots that had recently disrupted Harlem life. In these articles Powell tirelessly noted inconsistencies between America's democratic ideals and the actual plight of America's racially disadvantaged.

When Powell's father resigned from the clergy in 1937, Powell assumed his father's position. He quickly developed his pulpit into a platform for social and political change. He worked to establish a committee for promoting black employment, and he endeavored to unite various organizations to better facilitate racial equality. In 1941 Powell successfully contested for a seat on the New York City Council, where he continued to persevere in his efforts to rectify unfair hiring practices.

Powell enters politics   During World War II, Powell established the *People's Voice,* a newspaper for which he produced a column critical of social ills. Powell's following was such that he eventually felt confident to run as a Democratic candidate for the House of Representatives from Harlem. In his campaign, Powell pledged he would work for employment regulation. He won election, and in 1945 he began more than two decades of Congressional service.

By the time of his triumphant political campaign, Powell had become romantically involved with Hazel Scott, a jazz pianist, and he married her in 1945, one year after divorcing his first wife.

In Congress, Powell quickly developed a reputation as an outspoken antagonist of racist activities. Although he lacked sufficient support, Powell endeavored to enact the Powell Amendment, which would outlaw the federal funding of segregated institutions.

In the early 1950s, after years of isolation within the Democratic party, Powell broke rank and announced his support for Republican president Dwight D. Eisenhower. This radical act enabled Powell to obtain a small measure of influence in government. He even obtained appointment as part of a delegation to a conference in Indonesia.

Towards the end of the decade, however, Powell grew increasingly disappointed with the lack of appreciation accorded him from an administration whose civil rights actions were rather slight. The frustrations of supporting a rather indistinguished presidency ultimately led Powell to once again assert his independence. But upon criticizing Eisenhower, Powell suddenly found himself the target of an investigation for tax fraud. This new controversy somewhat undermined Powell's appeal with his Harlem constituency, but he eventually overcame his opponents and won re-election.

In 1960, the year that Powell became divorced from his second wife, he stood trial for three charges of tax fraud. The jury dropped two charges and failed to reach a decision on the third. The government then abandoned its case.

The ensuing period probably constitutes the zenith of Powell's career in government. In 1961 he was appointed chairman of the House Committee on Education and Labor, where he continued to oppose segregation and discrimination; and in 1964 he saw passage of the Civil Rights Act, a version of his earlier Powell Amendment.

But even in Powell's heyday, his conduct was open to criticism. He failed to appear at various House meetings, even those of his own committee. In addition, he fell under suspicion for questionable financial transactions involving his own committee funds. Powell eventually lost his committee chairmanship and found himself excluded, by a three-fourths vote, from Congress. Powell took his case to the Supreme Court, which ruled in his favor. He returned to Congress in 1969 but thereupon failed to distinguish himself.

In 1970 Powell lost a bid for re-election, and in 1971, following a brief period of activity, he withdrew from ministerial practices. By this time Powell was divorced from his third wife, Yvette Diago, who had been implicated in the earlier case regarding financial indiscretions, and was involved with Darlene Expose Hine, who came to be considered his common-law wife. In 1974, only two years after leaving Congress, Powell died of complications following prostate surgery.—LES STONE

COLIN L. **POWELL**
1937–
Military leader

A four-star general in the U.S. Army, Colin L. Powell has been appointed to high positions in both Republican and Democratic administrations. He was the first black national security advisor and the first black chair of the Joint Chiefs of Staff. The mastermind behind the U.S. involvement in the Persian Gulf War, he was involved in Operations Desert Shield and Desert Storm. Later Powell was pursued vigorously by the Republican Party as a vice-presidential candidate in the 1996 presidential elections. He continues to enjoy high visibility, as attested to in the Wall Street Journal/NBC *poll for 1997 that identified him as the most popular American.*

Born on April 5, 1937, in Harlem, Colin Luther Powell is the son of Jamaican immigrants Luther Powell and Maud Ariel McKoy Powell. After immigrating to the area when he was in his early twenties, Luther Powell was a gardener on estates in Connecticut, worked as a building superintendent in Manhattan, then worked himself up to foreman of the shipping department of a garment manufacturer. Maud Powell, a seamstress in the garment district,

548

Colin
Powell.

was a staunch supporter of the International Garment Workers Union. At the time of Colin Powell's birth, his parents lived on Morningside Avenue, then moved to other locations before settling in the Hunts Point section of the South Bronx when Colin Powell was six. While his parents worked, his maternal grandmother, Alice McKoy, took care of Powell and his only sibling, a sister named Marilyn, who was five and a half years older. When he was in college, his family left their decaying neighborhood and moved to their own house in Queens.

While Powell came from a close-knit family and had a secure childhood, he observed the rough life of the streets. His neighborhood was racially mixed, consisting of Jewish, Irish, Polish, Italian, black, and Hispanic families. Most of the black families there had roots in Jamaica, Trinidad, Barbados, or other West Indian islands. Although he was born during the Great Depression, Powell was not consciously affected by it, since his family had what they wanted or needed. Although the Powell family used the British pronunciation of his name, "Cah-lin"—a pronunciation he detested—to his friends and others he was "Col-in."

When Powell was promoted from the third to the fourth grade in Public School 39, he was placed in the bottom form, known as "Fore Up," meaning that he was considered a slow learner. He was not an athlete but enjoyed street games and kite fighting. He studied piano briefly, then flute, but gave up both. When he was fourteen, Powell had his first job at Sickser's, a baby furnishings and toy store.

In high school Powell was a member of the basketball and track teams and for a short time was involved in Boy Scouting. In February 1954, two months before he was seventeen, Powell graduated from an accelerated program at Morris High School. He was accepted at both New York University, a private school, and City College of New York (CCNY), a public college, and chose the latter because of lower costs. To help support himself, he continued to work at various jobs on weekends and vacations, including work with the International Brotherhood of Teamsters, Local 812, and a bottling company. At CCNY he joined the Reserve Officer's Training Corps (ROTC) and after being courted for membership by three military societies, joined the Pershing Rifles, the precision drill team. He found the ROTC appealing and considered the Pershing Rifles an elite, but especially attractive group. He also enjoyed the discipline, structure, camaraderie, and sense of belonging that the Pershing Rifles provided. During his last three years of college the drill hall became his universe, and on weekends he would spend up to seven hours there in practice. He remained a mediocre student through college but pulled up his grades with straight A's in ROTC. Upon graduation from CCNY in 1958 with a B.S. in geology and the honor of Distinguished Military Graduate, Powell was commissioned a second lieutenant in the army.

In his autobiography, *My American Journey,* Powell acknowledged an "unpayable debt" to the New York City public system of education. He said, "I typify the students that CCNY was created to serve, the sons and daughters of the inner-city, the poor, the immigrant." Although he had a C-average, Powell added that he:

> emerged from CCNY prepared to write, think, and communicate effectively and equipped to compete against students from colleges that I could never have dreamed of attending. If the Statue of Liberty opened the gateway to this country, public education opened the door to attainment here. . . . I am, consequently, a champion of public secondary and higher education.

Army career begins   Powell's career in the army began in 1958, with basic training in Fort Benning, Georgia, followed by his first assignment overseas, to the Third Armored Division in West Germany, for a tour of Gelnhausen, located near Frankfort. He was indoctrinated into army life and learned that in the 48th Infantry, the care of the men was the main concern. By the end of the year he was promoted to first lieutenant. After completing a two-year tour ending in late 1960, he was sent to Fort Devens, about thirty miles west of Boston.

Although by 1961 Powell had completed the required three years of service for his ROTC experience, he knew that he was well suited for the military and never considered leaving it. While stationed in Fort Devens, he met Alma Vivian Johnson, a Birmingham native, on a blind date; they developed a lasting friendship that led to marriage on August 25, 1962. In the summer of 1962 Powell was sent to Fort Bragg, North Carolina, for training as a military advisor, then to war in South Vietnam for his first tour of duty in Vietnam. While patrolling the Laos border with an infantry battalion, he stepped into a Punji-stick trap and injured his foot, for which he was awarded a Purple Heart. Later that year he was awarded the Bronze Star as well.

Returning to the states early in 1963, Powell had difficulty locating housing for his family in the Columbus, Georgia, area near Fort Benning, where he had been assigned. They lived in nearby Phoenix City, Alabama, instead. He had a similar experience earlier at Fort Bragg. Powell's encounter with racism included being denied service at a drive-in hamburger joint unless he went to the back window. He refused. At Fort Benning, Powell completed a month-long Pathfinder course for paratroopers. Pathfinders were an elite group. He graduated number one in the class and added the Pathfinder insignia to his Combat Infantryman's badge, airborne wings, and other decorations. Afterwards, Powell was assigned to the Infantry Board at Fort Benning, where he tested new weapons and designed RAM (Reliability, Availability, and Maintainability) standards for the test. He completed the Infantry Officers Advanced Course in May 1965, ranking first among his class of 200. He returned to the Infantry Board after completing a course for instructors and received the traditional oak leaf and a promotion to major.

Powell remained at Fort Benning almost three years, then moved to Fort Leavenworth, Kansas, in spring 1967. He entered the army's Graduate Civil Schooling Program and was ranked among the top infantrymen in his class. From July 1968 to July 1969 Powell was reassigned to Vietnam, to the resurrected World War II Twenty-third Infantry Division known as Americal. He was executive officer of the Third Battalion, First Infantry, Eleventh Infantry Brigade. He was injured again during a helicopter crash landing and received a Soldiers Medal for bravery in helping rescue injured men from the burning wreckage.

Powell entered graduate school at George Washington University in Washington, D.C., and graduated with a master's degree in business administration in 1971. He had earned nearly all A's. After receiving his MBA in 1971, Powell was urged to study for a Ph.D., but he was eager to return to the army. In July 1971 he was assigned to the Pentagon, where he reported to lieutenant general William E. DePuy, who headed the office of the assistant vice chief of staff of the army. He became a White House Fellow for 1972–73, assigned to the Office of Management and Budget (OMB), then headed by Caspar Weinberger. He served briefly under Frank C. Carlucci, then under Fred Malek. He refused an opportunity to remain at OMB another year, and when his year was over Powell returned to the army.

In 1973 Powell was assigned to Camp Casey in South Korea to help obstruct a possible attack by North Korea. When he returned to the states in September 1974, Powell was

Colin Powell visiting U.S.
troops during the Gulf War.

temporarily assigned to the Pentagon until his National War College (NWC) classes, for which he had been selected, began in August 1975. In an accelerated program, he was promoted to full colonel in February 1976, midway through the NWC. He missed the last two months of training because of a new assignment, but graduated with distinction. Powell took command of the Second Brigade of the 101st Airborne Division at Fort Campbell, Kentucky, remaining there until 1977. He said in his autobiography that he wanted to remain at Fort Campbell to become chief of staff of the 101st Airborne. Instead, he was called back to Washington in 1977 where, for two and a half years, he was assigned to the Office of the Secretary of Defense during President Jimmy Carter's administration.

Rises in ranks of general   On June 1, 1979, Powell's formal promotion ceremony to brigadier general was held. President Carter made major shakeups in his cabinet, removing

Joseph Califano as Secretary of Health, Education, and Welfare, and James Schlesinger as Secretary of Energy. He assigned Charles Duncan to take over the Department of Education. Duncan asked Powell to join his transition team, and for a brief period in 1979 Powell became Duncan's executive assistant.

When the 1980 elections were held, Powell felt he could not support Carter as he had done in 1976; he voted for Ronald Reagan instead. Powell wrote in his autobiography that "the Carter administration had been mauled by double-digit inflation and the humiliating spectacle of the Americans held hostage in Iran." In April 1980 Iranian students had seized fifty-three Americans as hostages in the American embassy in Tehran and held them captive for five months. When Ronald Reagan took office, Powell had an opportunity to become undersecretary of the army, but chose to "go back to doing what brigadier generals are supposed to do," as he wrote in his autobiography.

Powell was assigned as assistant division commander for operations and training for the Fourth Infantry Division (Mechanized), Fort Carson, Colorado, remaining there from 1981 to 1983. In August 1983 Powell became deputy commander of Fort Leavenworth, Kansas, and headed an operation called CACDA, or Combined Arms Combat Development Activity. Those who held the position previously found that it served as a launch pad to higher ranks. On June 19, 1983, the last days of his CACDA tour, Powell was promoted to major general. He spent only eleven months in Fort Leavenworth, then returned to Washington as military assistant to Secretary of Defense Casper Weinberger from 1983 to 1986. In 1986, when the U.S. declared that the covert sale of arms to Iran was in this country's interest, Powell wrote to Admiral John Poindexter, head of the National Security Council, that Congress had to be notified about the sale. Poindexter ignored the memorandum. When a scandal arose about the covert sale, however, Powell could prove that he had acted within the law and thus kept his credibility.

On March 26 Powell received a third star that went with his new job as commander of the Fifth Corps in Frankfort, West Germany, where he had been assigned in 1986 to command seventy-five thousand troops. On December 31, 1986, he formally gave up command and on January 2, 1987, was back in Washington as deputy assistant to President George Bush for national security affairs. Powell reorganized the national security staff and also chaired the National Security Commission's policy review group. On September 20, 1988, Powell was the first national security advisor to receive the Secretary's Award, which was given for "distinguished contributions to the development, management, or implementation" of American foreign policy. Powell was promoted to National Security Advisor on November 5, 1987. He remained in the position until 1989, when he was promoted to chairman of the Joint Chiefs of Staff, the top position in the military; he was re-appointed in 1991. While Powell was at Fort Leavenworth, the U.S.-based forces had been organized into two commands: FORSCOM, or U.S. Forces Command, and TRADOC, or Training and Doctrine Command. Now as chair of the Joints Chiefs of Staff, Powell directed what he called in his autobiography "one last command," the command of FORSCOM. He had also reached the highest military rank and was a four-star general. Through his command, Powell successfully oversaw Operation Desert Shield in 1990, where massive numbers of troops and supplies were moved to Saudi Arabia. He also directed the successful Operation Desert Storm, the offensive option developed alongside the defensive stance. General Norman Schwarzkopf directed the integration of communications, operations, and authority of Desert Storm's command network. Six weeks later, President Bush announced from the Oval Office that

Kuwait had been liberated, Iraq's army had been defeated, and the U.S. military objectives had been realized.

Powell's position also involved him in such activities as Operation Safe Harbor, the establishment of camps for Haitian refugees, a plan that Powell rejected. He also had a number of speaking engagements, including the 1992 commencement address at Fisk University in Nashville, Tennessee, which was Alma Powell's alma mater thirty-five years earlier. Quoted in his autobiography, Powell talked about family and diversity: "We must remember that America is a family. There may be differences and disputes in our family. But we must not allow the family to be broken into warring factions. . . . I want you to find strength in your diversity."

Powell retired from the military in September 1993 and devoted himself to writing his autobiography (published in 1995), traveling the lecture circuit, and serving on business, corporate, and academic boards. Powell's retirement was a colorful affair and broadcast nationally from the parade ground at Fort Meyer, Virginia. President Bill Clinton presented him the Presidential Medal of Freedom with Distinction, the nation's highest civilian award.

After his retirement, Powell rejected George Bush's appeal to serve as his running mate in the 1996 presidential elections. Powell was generally regarded as a mobilizer, racial healer, and great leader. His most recent initiative is chairing President Bill Clinton's volunteer program for improving children's lives, called the President's Summit for America's Future. In the April 21, 1997, issue of *Time,* Powell said, "I have arrived at the point in my life where I am trying to use what I have been given by my nation to help the nation." The summit kicked off the program on April 27, 1997, in Philadelphia, where Powell, Clinton, and former presidents George Bush and Jimmy Carter stood together on the steps of Independence Hall. They called for America to unite through volunteer service in what the *Nashville Tennessean* for April 27, 1997, identified as "an effort organizers hope will improve, by the end of 2000, the lives of at least 2 million of America's 15 million poor children."

In an interview for *Meet the Press* held during the President's Summit for America's Future, initiated on April 26, 1997, Powell said that he was comfortable and satisfied in private life; he is convinced that he is making an important contribution as a private citizen. In addition to reiterating that he is not interested in politics, when asked whether it is "fair to say that you will not be a candidate for president in the year 2000," Powell responded, "The assumption is fair."

During his career Powell won eleven medals. In 1972 he received the Legion of Merit. *Time* magazine named him one of the most influential people in America for 1997.

In private life, the Powells are regular worshipers at St. John's Episcopal Church in McLean, Virginia. The Powells have three children—Michael Kevin (b. March 23, 1963), Linda (b. April 16, 1965), and Annemarie (b. May 20, 1969). Colin Powell is calm, mild-mannered, skilled in dealings with civilians and military personnel, and carries himself in a military manner. He gives careful attention to detail. He is neither humble nor a braggart; he is a confident man.

Colin Powell is a significant figure in military history. Although not regarded as a race man, he is an important role model for blacks in mainland America. He achieved greatness because he prepared himself well for the work that he liked best, the military, and executed his assignments with dignity and exactness.—JESSIE CARNEY SMITH

LEONTYNE **PRICE**

1927–

Opera singer

Mary Violet Leontyne Price, the first black lyric soprano to achieve international diva status in her time, emerged as a major artist in the 1950s. She was recognized as an extraordinary talent from her student performances at Juilliard School of Music. When Frederick Cohen, director of Juilliard's opera department, first heard her sing, he proclaimed hers "the voice of the century." Internationally acclaimed by music critics and fans, Price has been crowned "A Prima Donna Assoluta" of the international world of music, "the Stradivarius of singers," and "the prototypical . . . black singer, to whose pinnacle all who have followed aspire." Her preeminent career opened the international operatic stages to younger black singers.

Price—whose name was originally spelled *Leontine*—was born in Laurel, Mississippi, on February 10, 1927. Her brother George was born two years later. They grew up during the Depression and were reared by hard-working, proud, self-reliant, and deeply religious parents—James Anthony and Katherine (Kate) Baker Price.

Marian Anderson influences Price A stimulus for Price's ambitions occurred at the age of nine when she accompanied her mother to hear Marian Anderson at a concert in Jackson, Mississippi: "It accomplished exactly what she wanted it to accomplish," Price recalled in *Ebony*. "I woke up! I was excited! I was thrilled with this woman's manner, her carriage, her pride, her voice." As Price listened to Anderson, her ambition became focused: "When I first heard Marian Anderson, it was a vision of elegance and nobility. . . . I can't tell you how inspired I was to do something even similar to what she was doing. That was what you might call the original kick-off," she is quoted in *Current Biography*.

This strong guidance in Price's early life paid off, for at the age of eleven she was an accomplished pianist, playing for the Sunday school, church services, and at community affairs. Price entered the sixth grade at Oak Park Vocational High School in the fall of 1937, firmly committed to a career in music. She sang first soprano with the prestigious Oak Park Choral Group and was selected to play for all school concerts. On December 17, 1943, she presented her first recital.

After graduating cum laude from Oak Park Vocational High School, Price was awarded a full four-year scholarship at Wilberforce College in Ohio. Initially she sang alto, unaware of the full potential of her vocal range. As Price's visibility increased, her professors realized that there was something special about her abilities and advised her to change her major to voice and to seek expert voice training. When a visiting pianist encouraged Price to sing a song written for a lyric rather than mezzo soprano, she realized for the first time that she had a vocal instrument for a professional career.

Enrolling at Juilliard in the fall of 1948, Price's classmates included an impressive group of promising talent: Andrew Frierson, Martha Flowers, Billie Lynn Daniels, Gloria Davy, and Mary Robbs, many of whom remained Price's lifelong friends. Even more important to

Leontyne Price.

Price was the opportunity to study vocal technique with Florence Page Kimball, a former concert singer, who was her teacher for four years and her lifetime adviser, coach, and friend. Initially, Kimball was not impressed by Price's voice but was encouraged by her seriousness, determination, and charm. After the first year, Kimball's confidence in the young soprano was manifest in inviting noted film composer Max Steiner to hear a concert. His recognition of Price's superb vocal power was immediate. Steiner, looking for someone to cast as Bess in his revival of Gershwin's *Porgy and Bess,* promptly invited Price to star in the role.

Price makes operatic debut   While a student at Juilliard, the excitement that Price experienced when she attended her first operatic performances—Puccini's *Turandot* at the City Center in New York City and Strauss's *Salome* at the Metropolitan—thoroughly convinced her to become an opera singer, in spite of the limited roles for blacks in the standard repertoire. At Juilliard's Opera Workshop, Frederick Cohen immediately recognized Price's extraordinary, powerful talent. Price's first role, that of Aunt Nella in Puccini's *Gianni Schicchi,* was followed by an appearance as Mistress Ford in Verdi's *Falstaff.* After hearing her, composer and critic Virgil Thompson cast her as Saint Cecilia in a revival of his *Four Saints in Three Acts,* a production that ran in New York and Paris in the spring of 1952. That same year she made her triumphant international debut as Bess in Gershwin's *Porgy and Bess.*

Between 1952 and 1954, Price and baritone William Warfield (then her husband) made international headlines. John Rosenfield of the *Saturday Review* declared: "The voice, a bright and focused soprano, has great impact, but even this is only half of it. She brought a lively theatrical imagination to the role . . . and . . . such vivid detail that the first night audience lost its composure when she took her final curtain call." David Hume of the *Washington Post* observed: "Leontyne Price sings the most exciting and thrilling Bess we have heard. . . . But when she is available for other music, she will have a dramatic career. And her acting is as fiery as her singing." European critics hailed her as well.

In 1955, Price's appearance in the role of Flora Tosca on a nationally televised production by NBC-TV Opera Workshop was historic—she was the first black to appear in opera on television—and won for her a succession of leading roles in subsequent NBC productions, such as Mozart's *The Magic Flute* in 1956 and *Don Giovanni* in 1960. Price made her American operatic debut on September 20, 1957, with the San Francisco Opera, as Madame Liodine in *Dialogues of the Carmelites.* In subsequent seasons she starred in such diverse operas as Verdi's *Aida* and *Il Trovatore,* Orff's *The Wise Maiden,* Mozart's *Don Giovanni,* and Massenet's *Thaïs,* performing in major opera houses throughout the United States. Her European reputation was established when conductor Herbert von Karajan cast her as Aida with the Vienna State Opera in 1958, after which Price appeared in a succession of roles at the Vienna Arena, the Salzburg Festival, and London's Covent Garden. When she sang *Aida* at La Scala in 1960, Price emerged as *the* Verdi soprano. One Italian critic exclaimed in *Time:* "our great Verdi would have found her the ideal Aida."

Price sings at the Met   Price was well prepared when she made her historic debut as Leonora in Verdi's *Il Trovatore* at New York's Metropolitan Opera on January 27, 1961. As the fifth black artist to sing a major role at the Met since Marian Anderson made the breakthrough in 1955, Price was triumphant. A review in the *New Yorker* stated: "Her interpretation was virtually without flaws." At the conclusion of the performance, Price received "an unprecedented forty-two minute ovation," according to *Ebony*. In this extraordinary season she had five starring roles.

Price's grace and regal appearance also gained her considerable attention. "Her best features are her almost translucent brown skin, high cheekbones, and expressive eyes set in charcoal shadows," Hugh Lee Lyon declared in his book *Leontyne Price: Highlights of a Prima Donna*. Critics acclaimed her as a statuesque Aida, the most impressive they had seen in years. According to Ross Parmenter of the *New York Times*, "She was Aida of such physical attractiveness that, for once, it was thoroughly understandable that Radames should prefer her to the highborn princess."

Although a veteran of 118 Metropolitan performances between 1961 and 1969, Price reduced her appearances at the Met considerably during the 1970s. She explained in *Divas:*

> I feel that you rest the voice and avoid pressure for considerable periods. You have to reflect too. . . . I think a career, if it is good, should be handled like something really beautiful. . . . I'm beginning to forget what I started out with—the completely natural joy of singing. It's almost coming back, and I'm trying not to lose it.

Price returns to recitals From the late 1970s until her retirement in 1985, Price concentrated on her "first love," recitals, which allowed her to "indulge a long standing predilection both for spirituals and for songs by such contemporary composers as Samuel Barber, John LaMontaine, Ned Rorem, Margaret Bonds, and Dominick Argento," according to *Time*.

Price bade farewell to the opera stage on January 3, 1985, singing *Aida* to a tumultuous ovation. Robert Jacobson sums up her distinguished reign in *Opera News:* "Perhaps *the* opera event of 1985 was the stage farewell of Leontyne Price who bid adieu with *Aida* . . . on the stage of the Metropolitan Opera—a fitting platform for the Mississippi-born soprano, who over the decades had become *the* American prima donna personified."

Among Price's many awards are the Presidential Medal of Freedom and an American Academy of Arts and Sciences fellowship. She was awarded honorary doctorates from Dartmouth College, Howard University, Fordham University, Central State University, and Rust College. Besides being a trustee and member of the Board of Directors of International House and a member of the Advisory Board of the National Cultural Center, Washington, D.C., Price also has served as honorary vice-chairperson of the U.S. National Committee of UNESCO. She received the Spirit of Achievement Award from Albert Einstein College of Medicine and the NAACP's Spingarn Medal, as well as the Order of Merit from the Republic of Italy. During her career she was presented twenty Grammy awards from the National Academy of Recording Arts and Sciences.

Since 1958, Price has recorded almost exclusively for RCA Victor. Her records include Negro spirituals, pop tunes, Christmas carols, hymns, American, French, and German art songs, and complete operas.

Price lives in a spacious federal-era townhouse in New York's Greenwich Village. Relishing her privacy, she enjoys working with her neighborhood block association and gardening. Price continues, however, to accept new challenges; in addition to her recitals, she is working on her autobiography and is actively involved with civic organizations. Of interest to both young readers and adults is the 1990 book *Aida,* told by Price and illustrated by Leo and Diane Dillon, which captures the thrill of the opera as told by a diva.

Price is especially proud of the part she has played in opening the world's stages to younger black singers. She insists in *Opera News:* "to the end of time . . . I will be the vehicle for major exposure for young black artists—sopranos, baritones, the whole thing."—JACQUELYN JACKSON

SAMUEL D. **PROCTOR**
1914–1997
Minister, college president, educator, public servant

Educator, theologian, social activist, and Christian icon Samuel Proctor was a powerful public speaker who quickly won over an audience by making difficult concepts understandable. When he delivered a message he spoke to all age groups and genders. He was able to weave in contemporary thought with the abiding faith that he lived by and believed in. Proctor's career was threefold: heading a church, teaching theology, and performing public service. For most of his life, he did at least two out of three, and in some cases, carried on all three major activities simultaneously.

Samuel Dewitt Proctor was born on July 13, 1914, to Velma Gladys Hughes Proctor and Herbert Proctor. His parents were students together at Norfolk Mission College just as his maternal grandparents had been when they met and married. Proctor and his five siblings grew up in a loving home that had a strong spiritual foundation. His family was active in church life. Aunts and uncles sang in the choirs and played the organ in several churches. Four of his uncles were pastors, and two of the largest churches in Norfolk were founded by his great-grandfather Zechariah Hughes. Proctor recalled in *The Substance of Things Hoped For:*

> Church and family were like a seamless garment cloaked about us. Hymn-singing, praying, and Bible reading and quoting were as close as breathing and nearer than hands and feet. We never sat down to eat anything—a bowl of oatmeal, a piece of buttered spoon bread, a chicken leg—without bowing our heads and mumbling a fast prayer.

Proctor attended Virginia State College on a music scholarship and graduated in 1942 with an A.B. He had been an outstanding student and skipped three grades, putting him in college at the same time as his older sister and brother. Although money was a problem, Proctor's faith and hard work helped him to succeed.

In 1943 he was ordained to the ministry. He was a graduate student at the University of Pennsylvania in 1944–45 and received a B.D. from Crozer Theological Seminary in 1945. During his year at Crozer he was the only black student. During a return visit to Crozer in 1950, he met Martin Luther King Jr., a student there at the time, and established a relationship with him that remained intact over the years. Proctor was the pastor of the Pond Street Church in Providence, Rhode Island, from 1945 to 1959. In 1945–46 he spent four days per week tending to his duties at Pond Church and the other three studying for a doctorate at Yale University in New Haven. He ultimately transferred from Yale to Boston University to be closer to his family and graduated in 1950 with a doctorate in theology. Proctor soon found that as a minister with a great formal education he must not only nurture his congregation's spiritual growth, but also become involved in social activism. Soon after he was called to the Pond Street Church he became a leader in the efforts to pass a Fair Employment Practices Act in the Rhode Island legislature.

From 1949 to 1950 Proctor was dean of the School of Religion and professor of religion and ethics at Virginia Union University, which was founded less than a mile from the plantation where his grandmother grew up as a slave. He continued to teach at the school and lectured widely. By 1953, he was appointed vice president of Virginia Union University. While he was vice president he was invited by the American Baptist Foreign Mission to join a team of clergy to transfer institutions from American control to that of indigenous people. Their job was, in consultation with the Burmese and Indian missions, to put in place the procedures for transition.

Samuel D. Proctor.

Proctor served as president of Virginia Union from 1955 to 1960. In 1960 he moved to North Carolina to become president of the Agricultural and Technical College of North Carolina, as it was known then. He was president of A and T until 1964 but was on leave from 1963 to 1964 while he served as the associate director of the Peace Corps in Nigeria and Washington, D.C. From 1964 until 1965 he was the associate general secretary for the National Council of Churches. From 1965 through 1966 he worked in the Office of Economic Opportunity as special assistant to the director, then director, of the North East Region. The next two years, 1966–68, Proctor served as president of the Institute for Service to Education. Then it was back to academia at the University of Wisconsin as dean of special projects for a year, 1968–69. He moved on to Rutgers University in 1969 and was a professor of education in the graduate school until 1984 when he became professor emeritus. While at Rutgers, he also held the position of senior minister of the Abyssinian Baptist Church from 1972 until 1989. He succeeded Adam Clayton Powell Jr., who kept the Abyssinian Baptist Church in the forefront of the civil rights struggle. Proctor continued the tradition. Under his leadership, the church created the Abyssinian Housing Development Program, which provided over fifty housing units to needy families in Harlem. Proctor also invited the New York Philharmonic to give annual concerts at the church.

Proctor's philosophy   In 1966 the National Board of the Young Men's Christian Association published Samuel Proctor's *The Young Negro in America: 1960–1980,* in which he acknowledged the need for literacy and skill development and showed a keen understanding of the young African Americans of that period. Proctor did not excuse violent behavior but understood the genesis of the frustration that the black youth were experiencing at that time. In a chapter from *The Young Negro in America: 1960–1980,* entitled "Outliving the Stereotype," he stated:

> Negroes, in spite of their long-suffering and reputed docility, have no natural propensity for nonviolence. A sophisticated theory of nonviolence is the result of tireless spiritual discipline such as Gandhi's, and what makes us think that the Negro is more capable of such discipline than the Klansman?

Proctor believed that there was enough room in American society for diversity. In *The Young Negro in America* he insisted that people not be given immutable labels based upon race. He told all Americans that outliving the stereotype did not mean the diminishing of their heritage, changing their music, or becoming white. It meant:

> stepping out of the mire of bad statistics in those matters that affect any and all Americans, mortality rates, crime rates, financial competence, educational attainment, and political participation.

The title of Proctor's most recent book, *Substance of Things Hoped For: A Memoir of African American Faith,* comes from Paul's letter to the Hebrews ("Now faith is the substance of things hoped for, the evidence of things not seen"), and was his belief that religious faith has sustained African Americans and remains the key to survival and improvement.

Proctor has been recognized widely for his work. His awards include: Distinguished Service Award, State University of New York at Plattsburgh (1966); Outstanding Alumnus Award, Boston University; Rutgers Medal for Distinguished Service; and forty-five honorary degrees from colleges and universities.

In addition to the books already mentioned, he wrote *Sermons from the Black Pulpit* (1984), *The Epistle to the Abyssinians and Other Sermons of Inspiration* (1977), and *Preaching about Crisis in the Community* (1988). While speaking to students at Cornell College in Mount Vernon, Iowa, on Wednesday, May 22, 1997, Proctor suffered a heart attack and died the next day in Mercy Medical Center, Cedar Rapids, Iowa, at age seventy-five. Proctor and his wife, Bessie Louise Tate Proctor, had been married for fifty-two years and lived in Somerset, New Jersey. His funeral was held a week later at the church he had pastored, Abyssinian Baptist Church in Harlem. In addition to his wife, he was survived by four sons—Herbert; Timothy D.; Samuel T.; and Steven. His survivors also include five grandchildren, a great-grandson, one sister, Harriet Tyler of Philadelphia, and one brother, Oliver W. Proctor.

Samuel D. Proctor was known as a quiet activist and a charismatic speaker who, even in his retirement years, was one of the most sought-after speakers in America. Proctor believed in the inherent good of humanity and rejected the negative images that appeared in the media as descriptions of the African American community. He chided us to recall success mechanisms that have worked for us in the past and renew the most powerful of them all, faith. He indeed spoke of hope.—AUDREY WILLIAMS

A. PHILIP **RANDOLPH**

1889–1979

Union organizer, labor leader

A. Philip Randolph is one of the most important black labor leaders of his era. Early in life he became a

socialist, and as part of his efforts to further the cause, he edited the Messenger *from 1918 to 1927. Randolph*

then turned his efforts to leading the Brotherhood of Sleeping Car Porters to recognition as a bargaining

agent, in a twelve-year struggle. Using the power and reputation he had acquired in the struggle, Randolph

called for a March on Washington in the summer of 1942 to protest government indifference to black rights

in the war effort. The prospect of this protest resulted in a major advancement for the civil and economic

rights for blacks.

Asa Philip Randolph was born on April 15, 1889, two years before his brother James Jr., in Crescent City, Florida to James William Randolph (1864–1924) and Elizabeth Robinson Randolph (c. 1872–1926). James William Randolph, originally of Montecello, Florida, received some education in a school set up by white Northern Methodist missionaries. He became a tailor and then an AME minister. The elder Randolph served only small and poor churches and always had to work at other jobs in the effort to make ends meet. In 1884 he was appointed to the church in Baldwin, Florida. The following year he married the youngest Robinson daughter, who was one of the best students in his Sunday school class. She was only thirteen, and two years later gave birth to their first son, James William Jr., who died in 1928.

The Randolph family was desperately poor, and there were few books in the house. Randolph Sr. insisted that his sons spend part of every afternoon reading. By example, he instilled pride in their black heritage. Later, as the position of blacks in Jacksonville worsened, he would not let his sons read in the segregated facilities of the public library or use the segregated streetcars.

When Asa Randolph entered Cookman Institute, a Methodist school, in 1903, he blossomed intellectually, displaying great ability in literature, public speaking, and drama. In addition, he became a star baseball player and a fine singer. At his graduation in 1907, Asa was chosen class valedictorian.

Since the family lacked money to send their sons on to any university, their prospects for jobs were limited. Even though they were not good prospects for the ministry, they pretended to undergo the conversion experience and joined the church. For four years Asa

A. Philip Randolph.

Randolph held a series of menial jobs in Jacksonville. He maintained his intellectual interests and gave public readings, sang, and acted in an amateur dramatic group. He also continued to read. Although Randolph did not continue to follow Du Bois's lead in later years, he told Jarvis Anderson that the *Souls of Black Folk* was "the most influential book he ever read." In early 1911 Randolph told his parents that he was going to New York for a few months; he did not confide in them that his goal was to become an actor nor that the move was likely to be permanent.

Randolph arrives in Harlem   Randolph and a Jacksonville friend, who returned to Jacksonville some eight months later, arrived in Harlem in April, 1911. When their money ran out, they sought out the menial jobs available. Randolph's pattern of work in these early years is exemplified by a 1914 stint as a waiter on a boat traveling between New York and Boston. Randolph first used his verbal skills to talk himself into a waiter's job but was nearly fired the first day when it became clear that he did not have the experience he claimed. Placed on probation for the rest of the trip, he was proud to be fired for trying to organize the waiters and kitchen help on the return trip. In these years Randolph worked just long enough to scrape together some money, and he tried, usually with little success, to raise his fellow workers' consciousness of their exploitation.

Toward the end of 1911, Randolph sought contact with educated blacks by frequenting the Epworth League, a young persons' organization at Salem Methodist Church, pastored by Frederick Cullen, foster father of poet Countee Cullen. Randolph had, of course, absolutely no interest in religion. He also participated in the theater club, memorizing much Shakespeare and presumably acquiring the "Harvard" or "Oxford" accent characteristic of him in later life. He also maintained his lifelong habit of dressing impeccably. Randolph abandoned his plans to become an actor in the face of his parents' horrified reaction when he finally broached the subject to them.

Randolph had discovered that City College offered bright young New Yorkers a free education. His enrollment in February 1912 marked a turning point in his life. In addition to the courses he began taking, he now came in contact with the thriving student radicalism of the campus and adopted the belief in socialism that would be a major influence in his life. In addition to his usually short-lived jobs, the longest being a stint of several months as a porter for the Consolidated Gas Company, Randolph organized his own discussion and political action group, the Independent Political Council.

In 1914 Randolph met Lucille Campbell Green (1883–1963); they married in November. Green was one of the first beauty salon operators trained by Madame C. J. Walker when Walker came to New York in 1913. In addition to becoming very successful in her profession, Green became a close friend of Walker and her daughter. Superficially Lucille and Asa Randolph were very different; she was as gregarious as he was reserved and formal. Nonetheless, the marriage was a great success, and Asa Randolph had a reputation of undeviating fidelity. During the last ten years of her life, when Lucille Randolph was confined to a wheelchair, her husband read to her every evening when he was home and sat by her bed at night holding her hand when she was in pain. They had no children.

Randolph becomes an agitator   Toward the end of 1916 Randolph and his close friend, Chandler Owen, joined the Socialist Party. Emulating Hubert H. Harrison (1883–1926), the St. Croix native who had the reputation of being the father of radicalism in Harlem, they became soap-box orators at the corner of Lenox Avenue and 135th street. Randolph became an accomplished orator, holding listeners' attention with his fine baritone voice. In January 1917, Randolph and Owen were invited to edit a monthly magazine for the Headwaiters and Sidewaiters Society of Greater New York. Randolph now adopted as his byline the form of his name under which he became famous, A. Philip Randolph. Randolph and Owen published the *Hotel Messenger* for eight months before being fired.

Randolph and Owen began a new magazine, now simply called the *Messenger,* which appeared in November 1917. It managed to survive until 1928, although it never made money and did miss a few issues. From a high circulation of 26,000 in 1919, it struggled to reach 5,000 in the 1920s. After Owen lost interest in socialism and left for Chicago toward the end of 1923, the overall quality of the magazine declined. Under George Schuyler, who joined Randolph as second member of the staff in 1924 and soon became de facto managing editor, the magazine focused more on black culture than on politics by publishing the early short stories of Langston Hughes and many poems of Georgia Douglass Johnson.

The *Messenger* was at the center of a shifting group of radicals, including W. A. Domingo; Lovett Fort-Whitman; Abram L. Harris, later a Howard University economist; Robert Bagnall, the NAACP's director of branches; William Pickens, NAACP field organizer; Wallace Thurman, fiction writer; and Theophilus Lewis, drama reviewer. During World War I, the magazine took an uncompromising antiwar stance. In August 1918 Randolph and Owen were arrested in Cleveland during an antiwar speaking tour. The judge felt that the youthful-looking "boys" were both too young and, as blacks, not smart enough to have written the incriminating articles in the *Messenger,* so he released them. In late 1919 during the postwar red scare, a report of the Justice Department, as cited by Anderson, characterized the *Messenger* as "by long odds the most able and the most dangerous of all Negro publications."

In addition to their involvement with the *Messenger,* Randolph and Owen were busy in politics. They organized the first socialist club in Harlem in support of socialist Morris Hillquit's campaign for mayor of New York. In losing the election, Hillquit appeared to have drawn twenty-five percent of the vote in Harlem. In 1920, Randolph ran for state comptroller and won 202,361 votes, only a thousand less than socialist presidential candidate Eugene V. Debs. After another losing campaign for secretary of state in the next election, Randolph never ran for office again.

The war years marked the peak of socialist influence in the black community. The educated "Talented Tenth" tended to be socially conservative and seek their advantage through white patronage and the Republican party. The black masses were not attracted by the idea of joint class-based activities with white labor because of the long history of anti-black discrimination in the union movement. While blacks did discover that Randolph and the Socialists were correct in asserting that participation in the war effort would lead to no gains, the widespread postwar disillusionment furthered recruitment by the more spectacular black nationalism of the Marcus Garvey movement.

Randolph and Garvey began their relationship with cautious cooperation, but Randolph later joined other black leaders in opposing Garvey in 1920, especially as rumors of financial irregularity in the finances of Garvey's Black Star Line began to circulate by the end of the year. On September 5, 1922, after Garvey had been indicted for mail fraud, Randolph received a package with a cover letter ostensibly written by a member of the Ku Klux Klan threatening dire consequences to Randolph if he did not come to terms with Garvey's Universal Negro Improvement Association (UNIA). (The circumstances were never elucidated.) In response, the *Messenger* stepped up its attacks on Garvey, although Randolph was not one of the eight prominent blacks who signed a letter of January 25, 1923, to the Attorney General urging the government to act against Garvey and UNIA with vigor. Randolph's associate, Chandler Owen, however, was one of the signers and the probable instigator since the return address on the letter was that of the *Messenger.*

Randolph and the sleeping car porters

By 1925 Randolph had achieved no success in any of the political or trade unions he had founded over the years; all were defunct. Except for continued publication of the struggling *Messenger,* at the age of thirty-six Randolph seemed at a dead end in his career. Then Ashley L. Totten, a Pullman porter, asked Randolph to speak to a group of porters about trade unions and collective bargaining. Some time after Randolph delivered a successful talk, he was asked by Totten and other dissatisfied porters to help them form a union. Randolph published articles on Pullman porter grievances in the July and August issues of the *Messenger,* and then took on the role as their leader. The Brotherhood of Sleeping Car Porters was unveiled at a mass meeting on August 25, 1925.

Porters in New York were initially enthusiastic. In Chicago, headquarters of the Pullman Company and base for the largest number of porters, reaction was more hesitant. Randolph, however, was able to recruit the support of Milton Price Webster. Randolph and Webster differed in most things except for their devotion to building up a union. Randolph again revealed his ability to work with people of differing temperament and opinions. Over the years the two men developed a close working relationship characterized by mutual trust.

In its opposition to the union, the Pullman Company could rely on a network of informants and the support of most of the leaders of the black community. Union activity eventually led to firings. The passage of the Railway Labor Act on May 20, 1926, gave railroad workers the right to organize and slowed the erosion of membership. The struggle between union and company now went to a Board of Mediation. A complete impasse resulted in the mediation board's calling for arbitration in the summer of 1927, but arbitration was not required by the law and the Pullman Company refused to budge. The Brotherhood was not strong enough to support a strike, so a 1928 strike vote was only a tactical weapon in a struggle that the union again lost. The nearly 7,000 members in 1928 declined to 771 in 1932. Randolph worked hard to sustain the organization, even leading the Brotherhood into the AFL (American Federation of Labor) in 1928.

The chance to revitalize the Brotherhood came in the wake of the election of Franklin D. Roosevelt, when new legislation gave increased power to railroad unions, but unfortunately not to the porters' organization. As a common carrier, the Pullman company was not covered by the new legislation, which was amended in 1934. After a new wave of firings by the Pullman Company and another attempt to set up a company union, the Brotherhood of Sleeping Car Porters was finally recognized in the summer of 1935 as the legal bargaining agent for porters, the first black union to achieve this status. Two years of effort followed before the company began bargaining in good faith and finally came to terms on August 25, 1937, the twelfth anniversary of the establishment of the Brotherhood.

From union organization to civil rights   Randolph always connected his union activities to a broader vision of economic and social progress for blacks. In 1935, Howard University sponsored a conference on economic conditions for black Americans. From this meeting grew a new organization, the National Negro Congress, to further "progressive" programs affecting blacks. Randolph became the first president of the organization, whose first meeting was in February 1936. He warned implicitly against overreliance on Communists in the presidential address he wrote but did not deliver in person. By the third convention of the congress in 1940, Communists had indeed come to dominate and Randolph publicly resigned.

Ironically, in 1940 the issue was for the war against Hitler and Fascism. Randolph supported the struggle against Nazism, while the Communists in the wake of the pact between Stalin and Hitler were against war preparations. As the United States built up its ability to carry on a war, blacks continued to suffer discrimination in employment and housing, as well as segregation in the armed forces. Randolph was not happy with the modes of protest used so far, such as public statements and conferences with officials including the president. In December 1940, he decided on more direct action in the form of a march on Washington. As leader of the coalition formed to further the march, Randolph issued a public call in March 1941 for a demonstration on July 1. Alarmed by the prospect of 100,000 blacks converging on Washington, the administration sought to dissuade Randolph. In a meeting with the president on June 18, Randolph maintained his refusal to call the march off. Executive Order 8802 was hammered out and issued on June 25. A Fair Employment Practices Committee was set up to oversee the workings of the order, which forbade discrimination in employment in defense industries and government. To the dissatisfaction of younger and more militant persons who were pushing also for desegregation in the armed forces, Randolph stood by his pledge to the president and called off the march. The March on Washington organization held together long enough to hold a series of mass rallies in different cities during the summer of 1942 before it began to disintegrate in the face of bitter criticisms by some blacks.

A new chance for Randolph to lead the effort to create significant changes for African Americans occurred with the passage of the 1947 Draft Act. Since segregation continued to be the rule in the armed forces, Randolph formed an organization that became known as the League for Nonviolent Civil Disobedience Against Military Segregation; Bayard Rustin, who became one of Randolph's closest collaborators, served as its executive secretary. With Hubert Humphrey leading a floor fight for a strong civil rights plank at the Democratic National Convention, which was also being picketed by blacks led by Randolph, President Harry Truman measured his need for black votes in the upcoming election and issued Executive Order 9981 on July 26, 1948. While the language of the order was ambiguous, Truman issued a clarification saying that it did indeed abolish segregation in the armed forces.

A. Philip Randolph speaks to the National Press Club, August 1963.

In spite of all his efforts in the AFL, Randolph made only slow progress in combating racial prejudice in the labor movement. He did not follow John L. Lewis of the United Mine Workers into the CIO. It was the 1950s before some AFL unions began to allow blacks to join. When the AFL and CIO united in 1955, the new organization adopted a more progressive stance on blacks in unions. Randolph joined Willard Townsend of the CIO as one of the two blacks on the Executive Committee. Although George Meany, who became president of the AFL in 1952, and Randolph would develop deep admiration for each other from the beginning, the relation was forged in bitter confrontation. After a clash with Meany at the AFL convention, Randolph formed the Negro American Labor Council in 1959 to work against discrimination in the union movement. The council could not claim great success as militant blacks pushed for an independent black labor organization on one side while on the other, white racism remained well-entrenched in some unions and locals. Randolph resigned from the council in 1964. Still, on the national level, the AFL-CIO became a strong lobbyist for civil rights legislation in the mid-1960s, and it now continues to sponsor the A. Philip Randolph Institute to monitor black affairs in labor.

Decline in railroad passenger service had made the Brotherhood of Sleeping Car Porters a moribund union, so Randolph's influence depended more and more on his personal prestige. Beginning in the 1950s, Randolph became a respected elder statesman rather than the most visible black figure in the political world of the United States.

Randolph performed one last major service to the civil rights movement. Early in the 1950s, Randolph had worked with Martin Luther King Jr. to support mass demonstrations in Washington, such as the Prayer Pilgrimage, although these demonstrations attracted little attention. In 1962 he consulted with King and then told Bayard Rustin to organize a 100,000-person demonstration on August 23, 1963. At the insistence of Roy Wilkins of the NAACP, Randolph took on the job of national director for the march but also insisted on retaining Rustin as organizer. Again it was Randolph who said no to President John F. Kennedy, who held a meeting to try to get the march called off.

As the years passed, Randolph became increasingly frail. After he was mugged in his Harlem apartment building in the summer of 1968, he was moved to a safer apartment. He became weaker, and developed a heart condition. Randolph died in New York on May 16, 1979, at the age of ninety.

Since Randolph's achievements are written large in history, two honors will stand for many. In 1971, Harvard University conferred an honorary degree on this socialist and activist, and in 1989 his likeness appeared on a postage stamp issued for Black Heritage Month.

In the last major speech of his career, Randolph was the first person to address the 200,000 persons assembled by the March on Washington at the Lincoln Memorial on August 28, 1963. Anderson cites this speech, in which Randolph summarized the goals he pursued throughout his life, civil rights and economic justice:

> But this civil rights revolution is not confined to the Negro, nor is it confined to civil rights, for our white allies know that they cannot be free while we are not, and we know that we have no future in a society in which six million white and black people are unemployed and millions live in poverty.

—ROBERT L. JOHNS

PAUL **ROBESON**

1898–1976

Actor, civil rights activist

Paul Robeson was probably the most prominent black American in the years between the two world wars. His talents in sports and the performing arts, together with his civil rights activism and his equally controversial political beliefs, brought him fame, admiration, and notoriety.

*Paul Robeson
as Othello.*

Robeson was born in 1898 in Princeton, New Jersey. When Robeson was still a child, his mother died in a fire. He was subsequently raised by his father, a former slave who had become a minister. Robeson first drew significant attention while a student at Rutgers College, where he was named to the Phi Beta Kappa honors society and selected as his class's valedictorian. Robeson studied with distinction at Rutgers while playing on four of the school's sports teams, and he became the institution's first athlete to be named to the All-American football squad.

After graduating from Rutgers in 1919, Robeson commenced studies for a law degree at Columbia University. In 1921 he married Eslanda Cardozo Goode, who was also attending Columbia. During this period Robeson also played professional football, but upon finishing his studies at Columbia he pursued a career in law.

Robeson had barely begun working when an incident with a racist coworker compelled him to abandon the law. He turned to the theater, having already performed occasionally in amateur productions. His talents were such that he succeeded in joining the Provincetown Players, whose activities centered on the works of their leading member, playwright Eugene O'Neill. While with the Provincetown group, Robeson won acclaim as the lead in O'Neill's *Emperor Jones,* the story an oppressed black man who briefly becomes, through various adventures and circumstances, the domineering leader of an African tribe. Robeson also garnered attention in another O'Neill production, *All God's Chillun Got Wings,* and that same year, 1924, he made his motion picture debut in *Body and Soul.*

In 1930 Robeson traveled to London to perform the lead in a production of William Shakespeare's tragedy *Othello.* But his performances in this work failed to match the acclaim accorded his earlier efforts, and he soon determined to concentrate on his singing abilities. By this time, the early 1930s, Robeson had already distinguished himself in the musical *Show Boat,* where his rendering of the song "Ol' Man River" was especially prized. In addition, he had appeared in film versions of both *The Emperor Jones* and *Show Boat.*

Despite his immense popularity, Robeson still found himself the victim of racist double standards. Hotels and restaurants denied him entrance, and theaters forced him to use stairs or freight elevators rather than the more convenient facilities available to white workers or customers. As a consequence of these experiences, Robeson grew increasingly involved in leftist causes, including racial and economic equality. His singing performances showed the influence of his growing political involvement, and he began featuring spirituals and songs sympathetic to the working classes and the underprivileged.

Robeson's championing of leftist causes grew more vehement after a stay in the Soviet Union left him convinced that communism and socialism

Paul Robeson.

offered an alternative to racial and economic injustice. He came to believe that the plight of American blacks, with their past linked to slavery, was similar to that of Russian laborers descended from serfs, or peasants. When Robeson returned to the United States he began vigorously calling for an end to inequality. He protested against segregation, for example, and even refused to sing before audiences separated on the basis of color. Furthermore, he courted danger by speaking out against lynching, which was still being practiced with gruesome frequency in the South.

During World War II, the United States and the Soviet Union fought together against the Axis powers; but after the war, the two nations found their wildly different ideologies incompatible, and each nation grew suspicious of the other. In America, anti-communism reached near hysteria when Congress commenced a series of ludicrious investigations. Robeson appeared before one such hearing and justified his continued American citizenship by expressing his conviction that—although he championed the Soviet system—he was entitled to live in America, a country that his ancestors, as slaves, helped create.

As a consequence of his communist sympathies, Robeson eventually experienced an extreme decline in his career as a performer. Managers and promoters refused to book him in theaters or other media, and his earnings dropped by more than ninety percent. Work abroad, meanwhile, was denied him, for the U.S. government had revoked his passport, and he was thus denied the right to travel outside America. By the mid-1950s, Robeson had fallen into obscurity.

In 1958 Robeson regained his passport by virtue of a Supreme Court ruling. But the opportunity to work abroad no longer seemed much of an option, for he no longer enjoyed substantial popularity elsewhere. When he published his autobiography, *Here I Stand,* some publications refused to even acknowledge it, let alone review it, and Robeson's forced obscurity seemed complete.

After retaining his passport, Robeson traveled again to the Soviet Union, but the trip failed to sufficiently inspire him. His health had begun to decline, and he lapsed into depression. On two occasions Robeson tried to take his own life, and on still other occasions he experienced breakdowns that left him addicted to drugs prescribed for his emotional problems. For many years, Robeson managed to survive despite these problems. In 1976, however, he suffered a stroke that proved fatal. In the ensuing years, interest in Robeson has increased dramatically, and his books, recordings, and films are now prized not only as examples of his talent but as exemplifications of his spirit and determination in the face of inequality and injustice.—LES STONE

JACKIE ROOSEVELT **ROBINSON**
1919–1972
Baseball player, activist

Honored internationally as the central figure in baseball's "Noble Experiment," Jack Roosevelt Robinson,

known in the world of baseball as Jackie Robinson, took the first step towards integrating that sport's major league teams when he signed a contract to play with the Brooklyn Dodgers in 1947. This gigantic stride,

which prepared the way for the legendary feats of Willie Mays and Henry Aaron, was an early harbinger for

the significant changes in contract negotiations, compensation, and general status of professional athletes

addressed in the 1994–95 baseball strike. His individual challenge to the accepted policies of organized

sports demonstrated that change was possible through concentrated effort of a player's union.

Jackie Robinson was born in Cairo, Georgia, on January 31, 1919. His parents were Jerry Robinson, a plantation farm worker, and Mallie Robinson, a domestic worker. There were five children in the Robinson family: Edgar, Frank, Mack, Willa Mae, and Jackie. Frank—his youngest brother's greatest fan—and Edgar are no longer alive, but Mack and Willa Mae still live in Pasadena. Mack, Robinson's early role model, a world-class sprinter, made sports history himself by coming in second to Jesse Owens in the 200-yard dash in the 1936 Olympics.

Jerry Robinson left his wife and children, never to return, when Jackie was six months old. When she was thirty and Jackie was thirteen months old, Mallie, a deeply religious woman who believed in the possibility of advancement for herself and her children, set out by railroad to start a new life in Pasadena, California. Mallie washed and ironed clothes for well-to-do people and had to augment her meager earnings with welfare relief. Money was limited, but Jackie never felt deprived of her love and attention.

Despite the absence of some of the more arduous racial conditions of Georgia, Pasadena had similar restrictions—the movie theaters were segregated, African Americans could swim in the municipal pool and attend the YMCA only on designated days, and some eating places were closed to African Americans. From the teachings of his mother, however, Robinson learned the important lessons of self respect and self-confidence that would later serve him on the baseball field.

Carl Anderson, a neighborhood automobile mechanic, pointed Robinson in the right direction of athletics when the young boy engaged in petty misbehavior with his friends. Karl Downs, youthful minister of Robinson's Methodist church, paced the sidelines whenever Robinson was on the playing field and counseled him when his athletic, social, or academic life became burdensome. Encouraged by his mother and his mentors and by the exhilaration of successes in sports, Robinson turned more and more of his energies to the playing fields.

Introduction to sports Robinson's first competitive game took place when his fourth grade soccer team played the sixth graders. After soccer came football, tennis, basketball, the track team, and table tennis. In athletics, Robinson had more freedom to relate to people on equal terms, with less emphasis on race and more on body development, coordination, and performance level. Because of his skill as an exceptional football quarterback, high-hitting baseball player, and remarkable broad jumper, Robinson was accepted as a friend by his white teammates. Still, with added age and broadened experience, Robinson saw that athletic success did not guarantee full freedom in the racially and economically unequal American society. Opposing players often reminded him of his ethnicity by physical contact, arguments, and racial slurs.

Robinson gained honors in football, baseball, basketball, and track at Muir Technical High School and Pasadena Junior College. When he left the junior college in 1939, he declined

*Jackie
Robinson.*

attractive offers from universities nationwide and chose The University of California, Los Angeles (UCLA), just an hour's drive from his mother's home in Pasadena. Robinson's honors at UCLA were impressive: for two years he was the highest scorer in basketball in the Pacific Coast Conference, national champion long jumper, the school's first athlete to letter in four sports, All-American football halfback, and varsity baseball shortstop. He left UCLA in 1941 because of financial pressures, few credits short from a bachelor's degree.

Directly after UCLA, Robinson worked for a few months as an athletic director in the National Youth Administration, in Atascadero, California. Driven by a growing, overwhelming desire to play professional sports, Robinson went to Hawaii in the fall of 1941 to join a semiprofessional, racially integrated football team, the Honolulu Bears. On weekends he was a member of the team, and during the week a construction worker. At the end of the short season, he returned to the United States in December 1941, right after the attack on Pearl Harbor.

Not long afterwards, in 1942, Robinson was drafted into the United States Army and sent to a segregated unit in Fort Riley, Kansas, where under existing policy he could not enter Officer's Candidate School. After protests by heavyweight boxing champion Joe Louis, then stationed at Fort Riley, and other influential persons—including Truman Gibson, an African American advisor to the secretary of war—black men were accepted for officer training. Upon completion of the course of study, Robinson was commissioned as a lieutenant in 1943.

A racially charged incident at Fort Hood, Texas, threatened to discredit Robinson's service record, when in defiance of a bus driver's command to go to the rear of the bus, he refused to leave his seat. Robinson, a lifelong teetotaler and non-smoker, was charged, originally, with public drunkenness, conduct unbecoming an officer, and willful disobedience. With a public outcry by fellow servicemen, the NAACP, and the black press, led by the *Pittsburgh Courier* and the *Chicago Defender,* the court martial resulted in exoneration. However, instead of going to meet with black soldiers in the European Theater of Operations as he desired, Robinson's next assignment was athletic director to new recruits at various camps in the United States. He left the service in November 1944 with an honorable discharge.

For a while Robinson coached a basketball team at what is now Huston-Tillotson College, in Austin, Texas, but the genesis of his professional baseball career came in 1945, when he signed with the Kansas City Monarchs of the Negro American League for $400 a month. In this league, which included such luminaries as Satchel Paige, Josh Gibson, and "Piper" Davis, Robinson was treated with reverence because of his overall playing skills, speed, and batting average that approached .400.

Signs major league contract   Even though playing with the Monarchs had the hardships of long, uncomfortable bus rides from town to town, uncertain away-from-home accommodations, low pay, poor playing fields, and the humiliation of the prevailing discrimination and segregation, this was the perfect springboard for Robinson's debut into the major leagues of baseball. It was the arena where he attracted the attention of Branch Rickey, who opened the door for him.

Before he decided on Robinson, Rickey, a devout Christian and president of the Brooklyn Dodgers, had searched nationwide for the ideal African American man, talented enough to play on major league teams and well enough adjusted within himself to withstand the attacks sure to come in the racially prejudiced setting. Rickey had scouted Robinson with the Monarchs and was impressed enough to meet with him for a personal assessment.

Rickey interrogated Robinson extensively for three hours on August 28, 1945. In a dramatization of hotel, restaurant, and game situations, he glared at Robinson, shouted demeaning words and phrases while observing his reactions. At the end he quoted the biblical passage that advises turning the other cheek. Satisfied that Robinson met the tests of ability, stamina, and tolerance, Rickey exacted a promise of extreme patience and forbearance for three years, then offered him a contract. On October 23, 1945, Rickey made the historic announcement that Jackie Robinson, a black man, would play for the Montreal Royals, the minor league affiliate of the Brooklyn Dodgers. Satchel Paige gave a ringing endorsement of Robinson as the best possible selection for "The Noble Experiment."

In the midst of the fiftieth celebration of Robinson's debut as a Dodger, former players spoke publicly of votes by most National League teams whether to go on strike when the black man took the field. Had it not been for the leadership of Dodgers president Branch Rickey, National League president Ford Frick, commissioner Happy Chandler, and players like Stan Musial, the course of professional baseball might have taken a different turn.

While Robinson was playing with Montreal, he married Rachel Isum, in the winter of 1946. Both were students at UCLA when they first met. Her greatest interest was her future as a registered nurse, and his was a career in professional sports. Because Rachel was not an avid sports fan, nor was she initially overwhelmed by the attention of a college superstar, it took some time for the relationship to develop. They were married six years after the initial introduction.

At the end of one year with the Montreal Royals, the Brooklyn Dodgers brought Robinson up from the minors to open the 1947 season. The team won the league title and Robinson finished with a .297 batting average, a league-leading twenty-nine stolen bases, and the title of Major League Rookie of the Year.

After Robinson had kept silent for the agreed time, he began to speak up when pitchers narrowly missed his head, fans shouted epithets, or obscene mail came to his home. He fought the denial of equal service in eating and sleeping quarters, or wherever he faced discrimination. Finally, the curative effects of time and recognition of Robinson's value to the team caused the majority of players to settle into the spirit of cooperation. With Robinson on the roster, the Dodgers won National League pennants in 1947, 1949, 1952, 1953, 1955, and 1956. In 1955, for the first time, they defeated the New York Yankees in the World Series. This was the only world championship the Dodgers would win in Brooklyn. In 1958, the Brooklyn Dodgers moved to Los Angeles and became the L.A. Dodgers.

When the Dodgers decided to trade Robinson to the Brooklyn Giants after the 1956 World Series, he retired from the game, declining to join his team's arch rivals from the same city. It was a fitting time for the star to leave—with a .311 lifetime batting average, and 197 stolen bases over his career.

Robinson was inducted into baseball's Hall of Fame in 1962 during his first year of eligibility. His induction was a cause for celebration for black people around the world. He chose his wife, Rachel, his mother, Mallie, and his friend, Branch Rickey, to accompany him to the Cooperstown award ceremony. This highest possible recognition of Robinson's skill and service was a symbol of victory to African Americans in the continuing struggle against injustice, and became proof that African Americans are viable contributors to any game.

Robinson's Hall of Fame plaque records the highlights of his brilliant career. With the Brooklyn Dodgers, Robinson led the National League in double plays from 1949 to 1952, he was voted on the All-Star team six times out of his ten year career, he compiled a lifetime batting average of .311 and helped the Brooklyn Dodgers win six National League pennants, and he also led the National League in stolen bases in 1947 and 1949 and was named Most Valuable Player in 1949.

After professional baseball

After baseball, Robinson headed the personnel office of the New York–based restaurant chain Chock Full O' Nuts. He took an active role in the Harlem YMCA and other social and community events, and was a key figure in establishing and nurturing Harlem's African American-owned and-controlled Freedom Bank—now defunct—through its initial period in the mid-1960s. Despite black America's pride in Jackie Robinson's strength as a trail blazer, his exceptional performance on the baseball diamond, and his high visibility in community efforts, he was not free from controversy or from disagreement with other popular African American figures. While Robinson loved Martin Luther King Jr. like a brother and felt the pain of his suffering, he knew that his own temperament was not suited for King's nonviolent demonstrations. He preferred to volunteer time as head of fund-raising drives for churches in Georgia destroyed by arsonists.

Robinson embraced King's dream of equality but used an issue of his syndicated newspaper column that appeared in the 1950s and 60s, mostly in the *New York Post* and the *New York Amsterdam News,* to air his disagreement with the civil rights leader's stand against the war in Vietnam. King telephoned Robinson and explained his motivation for the opposition. After their long talk Robinson had not been persuaded to accept King's stance but understood why King, a champion of nonviolence in the U.S. South, could not condone armed conflict in Asia.

To Robinson, Malcolm X was a talented man with a message of promise for African American youth but hampered by a philosophy based on hatred. In a much publicized war of words the two men feuded over Malcolm's characterization of Ralph Bunche, former undersecretary to the United Nations, as a man muzzled by white people who had put him in that position. Robinson defended Bunche's integrity, and Malcolm criticized successful African Americans who distanced themselves from the struggle for equal rights. Malcolm X's and Robinson's goals were identical, but their approaches took divergent routes.

At one time Robinson resigned from the NAACP, citing its failure to listen to younger, more progressive black people. Nevertheless, he was labelled an "Uncle Tom" by black militants who resented what they interpreted as Robinson's identification with a conservative, affluent white society.

In 1949 the House Un-American Activities Committee subpoenaed Robinson to rebut singer, actor, and political activist Paul Robeson's declaration that African Americans would not support this country in a war with the Soviet Union. In his autobiography, *I Never Had It Made,* published shortly before his death, Robinson defended his 1949 testimony that he would not desert his country based on "a siren song sung in bass." He disavowed the phrasing, which he then saw as an insult to the older, wiser Robeson, a hero to the people for whose causes he had made meaningful sacrifices.

Robinson's political alliances were unlike those of most African Americans who shied away from the Republican party. He campaigned for Democrat Hubert Humphrey in the primary, yet he chose Republican Richard M. Nixon over John F. Kennedy in the 1960 general election. When Robinson compared his observations of the two candidates for president long after the election, he wished he had chosen Kennedy. During the campaign, Nixon was friendly and charming in private meetings, and seemed interested in the civil rights of African Americans. On the other hand, when Robinson met Kennedy, he wondered whether the Democrat's failure to make eye contact as they talked was due to an unspoken prejudice. Robinson's fears disappeared with the news of Kennedy's public objections to the persecution of Martin Luther King. Robinson came to the belated conclusion that Kennedy was the better man.

New York governor Nelson Rockefeller, a Republican, named Robinson Special Assistant for Community Affairs in 1966, with the responsibility of improving the governor's popularity among residents of Harlem. In response to criticism, Robinson defended his membership in the Republican party as a way to make heard the otherwise ignored voice of black opinion.

In protest against baseball's failure to add African Americans in managerial positions and in front office personnel, Robinson declined to participate in the 1969 old timers game. Three years later, he came to Dodger Stadium in Los Angeles for ceremonies to mark the twenty-fifth anniversary of his first major league contract. By that time the effects of heart disease, diabetes, and failing eyesight were apparent. Still a handsome, proud man, dressed in a business suit, his hair was totally white, and his gait was noticeably slower.

Jackie Robinson's last public appearance was on October 15, 1972, at Riverfront Stadium in Cincinnati, when he threw out the first ball in the 1972 World Series. Nine days later, rescuers were unable to revive him from the heart attack that struck when he was fifty-three years old, in his Stamford, Connecticut home, on October 24, 1972. His funeral was held on October 27, 1972, at Riverside Church in New York. The pallbearers were all sports figures: Ralph Branca, Larry Doby, Junior Gilliam, Don Newcombe, Pee Wee Reese, and Bill Russell. A year after his death, Rachel Robinson founded the Jackie Robinson Foundation to provide motivational and financial support to minority students and maintain an archive of material relating to his career. She lives in Connecticut, still a major force in the foundation's success.

Robinson Jr., the oldest of Rachel and Jackie Robinson's children, born in 1946, was killed in an automobile accident in 1971. Sharon, born in 1950, is a midwife, living in Stamford. Her brother, David, two years younger, operates a coffee farm in Tanzania, East Africa.

1997 marks the fiftieth anniversary of Robinson's heroic steps to first base in Brooklyn. Major league baseball has commemorated that occasion with several events, including retiring Robinson's jersey, number 42, from the game of baseball. This historic and unpredecendent step by major league baseball has immortalized Robinson.

On its way to Cypress Hills Cemetery, Robinson's funeral procession passed through Harlem and Bedford-Stuyvesant, where thousands lined the route. They were paying tribute not only to Robinson's athletic abilities, but to Robinson as the symbol of opportunities for African Americans in professional sports without limitations of race. He had withstood the pains and frustrations of the trailblazer while giving record-breaking performances on the field of play, leaving lasting encouragement to players who followed long after he retired.—DONA L. IRVIN

RANDALL **ROBINSON**

1941–
Civil rights activist, lawyer

Randall Robinson is an activist who believes that peoples of color around the world merit support and representation. Additionally, he believes that one person can make a difference. The validity of his beliefs can be seen in the significant roles African Americans play in foreign policy decisions affecting peoples of color, spearheaded and guided by Robinson.

Randall Robinson was born in Richmond, Virginia, on July 6, 1941, to educators Maxie Cleveland, a high school history teacher, and Doris Robinson Griffin, a teacher and homemaker. In the *Black Collegian,* Robinson credits his father with being "a real pillar" for him. He was educated in the public schools of Richmond where he and his brother Max— the first African American network television news anchor—were coached as players on the Armstrong High School basketball team. As a result of his athletic skills, in 1959 he won a basketball scholarship to Norfolk State College (later University) where he was politically active, although he dropped out of college in his junior year. Following this, he was drafted into the army and spent his tour of duty in Georgia. When he returned, he attended Virginia Union University in Richmond, from which he graduated in 1967 with a B.A. in sociology. Upon graduation, he entered Harvard University Law School. He also joined a campus protest against apartheid in South Africa. In 1970 he graduated with a J.D. and won a Ford Foundation fellowship, which allowed him to work in Tanzania.

From 1972 to 1975 Robinson was community development division director of the Roxbury Multi-Service Center in Roxbury, Massachusetts. In 1975 he moved to Washington, D.C., to become staff assistant to William L. Clay, U.S. representative from Missouri, and was responsible for writing policy pronouncements. From 1976 to 1977 he served as staff attorney for the Lawyer's Committee for Civil Rights Under Law Compensatory Project in Washington, D.C. His responsibility was to examine the legal requirements for compensatory education as given in Title 1 of the Elementary and Secondary School Act. During this period he was administrative assistant to Michigan representative Charles Diggs; it was as a staff member for Diggs that he joined a congressional team on its visit to South Africa and witnessed the dehumanizing effect of apartheid.

TransAfrica and its forum   Following his visit to South Africa, Robinson and the Congressional Black Caucus at a Black Leadership Conference recognized the absence of African voices in international policy-making and a general neglect of black countries. An advocacy group was established. Thus, in 1977, TransAfrica came into existence with Randall Robinson as its executive director and founder, a position he still holds. Robinson admits that times have been lean but at no time has he entertained the idea of leaving the organization. The success of the group is reflected in its achievement. As he works for contemporary issues, he also recognizes the need for establishing what he called in the June 7, 1993, issue of *Jet,* "an institution to hand down to the next generation." To this end, in 1993 the TransAfrica headquarters, which is African America's only foreign policy home in the world, was dedicated. The foreign policy library and resource center is named in honor of tennis legend Arthur Ashe, who had worked for black liberation. With its concern for both the present and the future, it is a lobbying agency as well as a center for research and education. TransAfrica holds annual conferences and a series of seminars on foreign policy. It also publishes two quarterlies, *TransAfrica Forum* and *Issue Brief.*

TransAfrica also maintains an educational affiliate known as TransAfrica Forum, which was established in 1981. The forum collects and disseminates information and helps plan U.S. foreign policy affecting black areas throughout the world. Ed Lewis, publisher of *Essence,* serves as its president. Through conferences, publications, and educational programs, it examines political injustices that television news coverage has ignored.

TransAfrica has often used tactics that were used by civil rights activists of the 1960s, including hunger strikes and sit-ins. Utilizing these strategies, Robinson was instrumental in

Randall Robinson inspects work being done on
TransAfrica's new Washington home, May 1993.

bringing the plight of South Africa and Haiti to the attention of the world. This is in keeping with the focus of the organization, which is concerned with both Africa and the Caribbean. It has lobbied, testified, and asked for more overall aid to Africa and to those countries that are working toward democracy, while at the same time asking for a decrease in aid to those countries that have compromised human rights.

Robinson's commitment to the work and guiding principles of TransAfrica is evidenced in his actions and successes. In the mid-1980s, he helped establish and coordinate the Free South Africa Movement, which used the tactic of protesting in front of the South African embassy for over a year. Among the protestors were such famous people as Mary Frances Berry, Walter Fauntroy, Arthur Ashe, Harry Belafonte, Amy Carter, and two of late Senator Robert Kennedy's children. More than 5,000 were arrested. The protestors demanded the release of Nelson Mandela and other political prisoners and a repeal of South Africa's apartheid rules and laws. Robinson's fight led to the Comprehensive Anti-Apartheid Act of 1986, which was passed in spite of President Ronald Reagan's veto.

In the 1990s Robinson entered into a twenty-seven-day hunger strike to protest the United States policy toward Haiti, the return of Haitian refugees, and the admission of Cubans to the United States. This action led to the deposing of military leaders in Haiti and the reinstatement of exiled President Jean-Bertrand Aristide. Robinson and other prominent African Americans protested for democracy in Nigeria outside the Nigerian embassy and protested against unfair American policies in the Caribbean at the office of the U.S. Trade representative in Washington, D.C., by dumping two thousand pounds of bananas on the doorstep.

According to the TransAfrica report for February 29, 1996, in addition to the above, since 1980 the organization has spoken out against human right violations in Liberia, Zaire, Kenya, Malawi, and Ethiopia; spearheaded the struggle to maintain economic sanctions against Rhodesia (now Zimbabwe); facilitated meetings between American policymakers and foreign leaders; and organized meetings between African American leaders and Secretary of State James Baker on apartheid, famine relief, and human rights. According to the TransAfrica mission statement, the goal for the organization under Robinson and deputy director Maryse Mills is to "pursue all opportunities to create an understanding among policymakers and assist in the formulation of constructive U.S. foreign policy as it affects Africa and the Caribbean."

Robinson's awards of recognition and appreciation include the National Association of Black Journalists' Community Services Award; the Africa Future Award presented by the U.S. Committee for UNICEF; the Humanitarian Award from the Congressional Black Caucus and another from the Martin Luther King Jr. Center for Non-Violent Social Change; the Hope Award from the National Rainbow Coalition; the Drum Major for Justice Award from the Southern Christian Leadership Conference; and the Trumpet Award for International Service by the Turner Broadcasting System. He has also been recognized by the Johnson Publishing Company, Omega Psi Phi Fraternity, WJLA Channel 7, Alpha Kappa Alpha Sorority, Jackie Joyner-Kersee Community Foundation, and Howard University Hospital. Honorary degrees have been awarded by such institutions as Columbia College, Delaware State College, Morehouse College, North Carolina Agricultural and Technical State University, Ohio Wesleyan University, the University of the District of Columbia, and the University of Massachusetts, Amherst.

In 1987 Randall Robinson married Hazel Ross Robinson, a foreign policy advisor. From the marriage to his first wife, Brenda Randolph, a librarian, he has two children, Anikie and Jabari.

Robinson has not hesitated to put his life and well-being on the line in his effort to involve African Americans in international affairs. His tactics have created an influencial political tool in TransAfrica and keep before the public the well-being of Africa and the Caribbean.— HELEN R. HOUSTON

CARL T. **ROWAN**

1925–

Journalist, author, public official

Nationally syndicated columnist and radio and television journalist Carl T. Rowan has made a respected career of many firsts. He was one of the first African American officers in the Navy, the first African American journalist for the Minneapolis Tribune, *and the highest-ranking African American ever to serve in the State Department, as ambassador to Finland and U.S. Information Agency director. Rowan has gained much admiration for his deeply moving recounts of life in the South for African Americans in the fifties and as a first-hand witness during the civil rights movement during the sixties. From the seventies to current events, Carl T. Rowan is a distinguished author checking the pulse of American race relations and offering remedies. With his seventh book,* The Coming Race War in America: A Wake-Up Call *(1996), Rowan sharply comments on the polarization of the races as an aftermath of the O. J. Simpson trial.*

Carl T. Rowan was born in 1925 to Thomas David and Johnnie B. Rowan in Ravenscroft, Tennessee, but when he was an infant, the family moved to McMinnville, Tennessee. The Rowan household faced extreme poverty. As a child, Rowan grew up in a house where he and his siblings lived with no electricity, told time only by the trains that ran past their house, and battled constantly with rats. Rowan noted in his autobiography, *Breaking Barriers,* that he was once awakened by a bone chilling shriek from his sister who had been bitten on the ear by a rat. Their poor conditions often led Rowan's mother to criticize her husband for subjecting their children to such squalored conditions. But the family continued to struggle with the patriarch's meager salary from stacking lumber and the mother doing laundry. Like many black youths, Rowan did various menial jobs to support the family, but he found a creative outlet through education.

Particularly important to him were teachers who stressed the values of education and persistence as the way to confront the obstacles facing him as a black youth. One high school teacher in particular, "Miss Bessie," to whom Rowan dedicated a 1980 column, smuggled him books out of the all-white library in McMinnville. Rowan recounted the important message imparted to him by Miss Bessie in *Breaking Barriers*: "If you don't read, you can't write, and if you can't write, you can stop dreaming."

Rowan excelled as a student a McMinnville's all-black Bernard High School, where he graduated as valedictorian of his class. After graduation, Rowan headed for Nashville with only seventy-seven cents to his name but hopes of attending college in order to become an officer

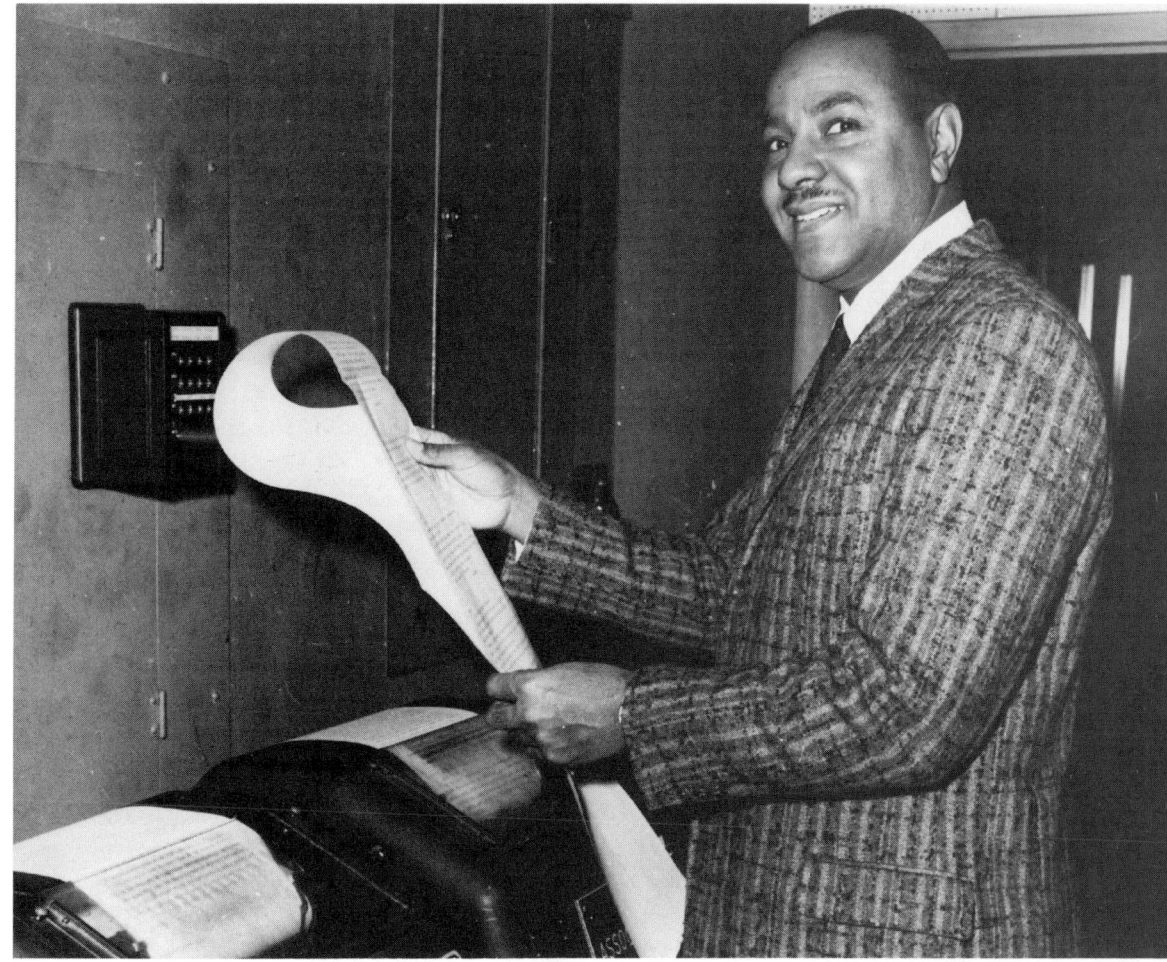

Carl T. Rowan.

in the Navy in case he was drafted. He moved in with his grandparents and worked as an attendant at the hospital where his grandfather was employed, earning thirty dollars a month for his college expenses. He enrolled at all-black Tennessee State University in 1942, and the following year was recommended by a professor for an opportunity to take an examination for a U.S. Navy commission. Rowan passed the examination, and was later assigned to Washburn University in Topeka, Kansas, as one of the first fifteen blacks in Navy history to be admitted to the V-12 officer-training program. Rowan later attended Oberlin College in Ohio as part of the program, and then the Naval Reserve Midshipmen School in Fort Schuyler, the Bronx. He was eventually commissioned an officer and was assigned to sea duty, where he excelled as deputy commander of the communications division.

Rowan's naval duties ended in 1946 and he briefly returned to McMinnville, but his time in the Navy had pointed him towards new goals in his life. "When you are plucked out of a totally Jim Crow environment at age seventeen and thrown into a totally white environment where more is at stake than your personal life, you mature rapidly," he wrote in *Breaking Barriers*.

Rowan returned to Oberlin to complete his college degree, with hopes of eventually becoming a journalist. He found Oberlin's "egalitarianism" a positive experience, and learned much from students who, unlike himself, "came from homes where political, economic, and social issues were discussed daily." Rowan majored in mathematics, and obtained work as a free-lance writer for the Negro newspaper chain, the *Baltimore Afro-American*. When he was accepted into graduate school in journalism at the University of Minnesota, Rowan worked as a northern correspondent for the *Afro-American,* and also wrote for the Twin Cities' two African American papers, the *Minneapolis Spokesman* and the *St. Paul Recorder.*

Began journalism career   Rowan got a big break after graduate school when he was hired at the copy desk of the all-white *Minneapolis Tribune*. Two years later, he became the paper's first African American reporter, and one of the few in the entire United States. Rowan was working as a general-assignment reporter when he remembered the advice of a white Texan he had met in the Navy who told him that if he became a writer, he should "tell all the little things it means to be a Negro in the South, or anyplace where being a Negro makes a difference." Rowan proposed to the *Tribune* management that he take a trip through the deep South and report on the effects of Jim Crow discrimination laws on Negroes. The *Tribune* enthusiastically agreed to Rowan's proposal, and he embarked upon a 6,000-mile journey through thirteen states, writing a series of eighteen articles in 1951 entitled "How Far from Slavery?"

Rowan's articles caused a sensation among *Tribune* readers and brought him wide critical recognition, in addition to earning him the Sidney Hillman Award for the best newspaper reporting of 1952. *Time* magazine praised the articles as "a perceptive, well-written series on segregation and prejudice in the South as only a Negro could know them." Rowan noted in *Breaking Barriers* that his objective was "to tell the American people some truths they do not know, explain some things that they clearly do not understand, and . . . fulfill every journalistic obligation that burdens any reporter of any race." The articles also became the basis for Rowan's first book, *South of Freedom,* published in 1952.

Hodding Carter, white editor of a liberal Mississippi newspaper (father of State Department spokesperson Hodding Carter Jr.), wrote in the *New York Times* that Rowan's book is "a noteworthy contribution to the sad folklore of American interracial relations." Reviewer Harold Fleming in the *New Republic* noted that Rowan's "return to the South was a profound personal experience. And he communicates that experience to the reader with unusual skill."

Rowan returned to the South for a second series of articles entitled "Jim Crow's Last Stand," which reviewed the various court cases comprising the historic 1954 *Brown v. Board of Education of Topeka* Supreme Court decision outlawing racial segregation in public schools. Rowan gained further recognition with "Jim Crow's Last Stand," and in 1954 received the prestigious Sigma Delta Chi Journalism Award for the best general reporting of 1953, in addition to being named by the U.S. Junior Chamber of Commerce as one of America's ten most outstanding men of 1953.

In 1954, Rowan was invited by the U.S. State Department to travel to India and lecture on the role of a free press in a free society. Rowan wrote a series of articles for the *Tribune* on India, which earned him his second consecutive Sigma Delta Chi Award, this time for best foreign correspondence. Rowan's trip was extended to include Southeast Asia, and he wrote another series of articles on the tense political climate in the region, in addition to covering the 1955 Bandung Conference, a gathering of twenty-three underdeveloped nations. For these articles, Rowan won an unprecedented third straight Sigma Delta Chi Award, while his 1956 book, *The Pitiful and the Proud,* which recounted his Asian journeys, was named one of the best books of the year by the American Library Association.

Covered Montgomery bus boycott
Rowan returned to the United States and continued as a reporter for the *Minneapolis Tribune.* In the late 1950s, he covered the burgeoning civil rights movement in the South, including the Montgomery (Alabama) bus boycott in 1955, resulting from Rosa Parks's refusal to relinquish her seat to a white passenger. As the only black reporter covering the story for a national newspaper, Rowan struck a special friendship with the boycott's leaders, including Martin Luther King Jr. When news of an unlikely compromise settlement of the boycott came to Rowan's attention across the Associate Press wire, he notified King, who made quick steps to discredit the story, which was about to appear in a Montgomery newspaper, thus ensuring the continuance of the boycott. Rowan wrote an acclaimed series of articles for the *Tribune,* entitled "Dixie Divided," which explored efforts in the South to resist the Supreme Court's desegregation orders.

In addition to his reporting, Rowan was a member of the Committee of 100, a group of citizens who raised money across the United States for the NAACP Legal Defense Fund. As one of the country's few African American reporters, Rowan was increasingly called upon to comment upon the impact of the civil rights movement, and his articles appeared throughout the country in a number of magazines and newspapers. His 1957 book, *Go South to Sorrow,* which generated both controversy and acclaim, was, as he describes in *Breaking Barriers,* a "lashing out at President Eisenhower, Hodding Carter, and other gradualists who, in my view, were compromising away the freedom of America's black people."

In 1956, Rowan was called away from the South to cover the United Nations, as the world witnessed two events of major international importance: the Suez Canal crisis in which England, France, and Israel attempted to seize the canal from Egypt, and the Hungarian uprising against the Soviet Union. Rowan was especially outraged at the brutal Soviet reprisal against the Hungarians, and reflected in *Breaking Barriers* on its relation to the U.S. civil rights movements: "In the mentalities of our White House, our Congress, our media, there were no 'troublemakers on both sides' in Hungary. The villains were the brutal Soviet rapers of innocent Hungarians who had dared to reach out for freedom. But in America the air was filled with cries, even by Eisenhower and Stevenson, for a 'moderate' approach to ending segregation and a national rejection of 'the extremists on both sides.'"

Joined Kennedy administration
In 1960, Rowan had the opportunity to interview presidential candidates Richard M. Nixon and John F. Kennedy for the *Tribune.* After Kennedy was elected, the new president asked Rowan to become his Deputy Assistant Secretary of State for Public Affairs, responsible for press relations in the State Department. Rowan was involved in the sensitive area of news coverage of increasing U.S. military involvement in Vietnam, and was also trusted to the negotiating team that secured the exchange of pilot

Francis Gary Powers, who was shot down over the Soviet Union in his U2 spy plane. He also accompanied Vice President Lyndon Johnson on a tour throughout Southeast Asia, India, and Europe. In 1963, Kennedy named Rowan U.S. Ambassador to Finland, making him the youngest ambassador in the diplomatic service, and first African American to serve as an envoy.

When Lyndon Johnson became president following Kennedy's assassination, he named Rowan head of the United States Information Agency (USIA), a position that made him the highest-ranking African American in the federal government and the first to ever attend National Security Council meetings. As head of USIA with a staff of 13,000, Rowan was responsible for overseeing a vast government communications network, which included the international Voice of America radio system and the daily communiques to U.S. embassy personnel around the world. Rowan was assigned the task of developing a massive psychological warfare program to assist the Vietnam War effort, and was criticized for drawing away from the other USIA activities. In 1965, Rowan resigned from USIA to take a lucrative offer to write a national column for the Field Newspaper Syndicate, in addition to three weekly commentaries for the Westinghouse Broadcasting Company.

Return to journalism As a columnist and commentator on the national scene, Rowan developed a reputation as an independent and often controversial voice on national political and social issues. He publicly urged Martin Luther King Jr. to remove himself from his increasing anti-war stance, in that it was damaging the thrust of the civil rights movement. He called for the resignation of powerful FBI director J. Edgar Hoover, holding that Hoover's lengthy tenure was leading to serious abuse of power, including unethical and illegal investigations of citizens. When Ronald Reagan became president, Rowan became a passionate critic of the president's policies, noting that the gains made in the civil rights movement for disadvantaged groups were seriously being undermined by cuts in vital social and economic programs.

While Rowan has been throughout the years a frequent spokesman for civil and economic rights for blacks and other disadvantaged groups, he has also been critical of those African Americans he feels should more aggressively address the serious issues that affect them. Neil A. Grauer, in his book *Wits & Sages,* calls Rowan "a vigorous exponent of self-improvement . . . and has little patience for those who won't work at it."

In 1988, Rowan made national headlines when he shot and wounded an intruder in his Washington, D.C., home. A frequent advocate of national gun control laws, Rowan was charged with possession of an unregistered firearm, but the charges were later dropped in court. Many criticized Rowan for his pro-gun control rhetoric and the media used him as the perfect pawn for the argument for and against gun control. Rowan accused former Washington, D.C., mayor Marion Barry—a frequent target of criticism in Rowan's column—of extortion by offering to not pursue the charges against Rowan if the columnist would tone down attacks on the mayor's administration. Rowan came under criticism again for speaking out against Barry, yet responded with a statement: "I have learned over four decades as a journalist that 'City Hall' becomes more and more corrupt as more and more citizens lose the guts to fight."

Rowan has become aware of how important education is in reaching dreams. Rowan has made it possible for African American students to pursue careers in journalism by establishing a million-dollar scholarship fund to high school students in Washington, D.C., called Project of Excellence.

United Press White House correspondent Helen Thomas has called Rowan "one of the most respected and admired journalists on the Washington scene." His journalistic endeavors have enabled Rowan to use mainstream media to expose the truth about being African American in America, and his commentary on the constant state of race relations continues to elevate Rowan as an extremely influential journalist.—MICHAEL E. MUELLER AND MICHELLE BANKS

BAYARD RUSTIN

1910–1987

Pacifist, human rights activist, political strategist

Though often called "Mr. March" for his prime organizational role in one of the most important nonviolent protests in American history—the 1963 March on Washington—Bayard Rustin is still something of an unsung hero in the history of the American civil rights movement. The ongoing specter of homophobia and fear of "red menace" Communism that shadowed his career of over five decades reached a zenith in the middle part of this century and forced him to step behind the scenes at the height of his political power. Still, once his accomplishments are noted, Rustin is easily categorized as one of the most influential political, nonviolent strategists who fought not only for the rights of African Americans, but for the dignity of all oppressed minorities. From his early labor union years to his "senior statesman" lectures at colleges and gay organizations around the country, Rustin held fast to the belief that the rights of African Americans were best secured and maintained in the long run as an integral part of deeper social reforms for everyone.

In the 1930s and 1940s, a youthful, radicalized Bayard Rustin worked with and recruited for the Communist Party, the War Resisters League, and various labor unions. He teamed with Martin Luther King Jr. in the 1950s and was a confidant, advisor, and speech writer until King's tragic death in the spring of 1968. He helped create both the Congress of Racial Equality (CORE) and the Southern Christian Leadership Conference (SCLC). In the 1980s, he urged gays and lesbians to follow his example and embrace their role in furthering social equity for *all* minorities. It was this holistic focus on broader social objectives that spotlights Rustin as unique among twentieth-century social activists. "I reject the idea of working for the Negro as being impractical as well as immoral, if one does that alone," he said in a 1965 interview. To the end of his life, Rustin maintained this world view—the political was ever the personal, and vice versa.

"Fated" activism   Bayard Rustin grew up in a poor section of West Chester, Pennsylvania, one of nine children supported by parents in the catering business. At the age of eleven, he was told that the woman he thought was his sister, Florence Rustin, was actually his mother, and that his "parents," Janifer and Julia Davis Rustin, were actually his grandparents.

Bayard Rustin.

Feeling that the then-teenage Florence was ill-prepared for maternal responsibilities, his grandparents had adopted Bayard soon after his birth. Florence didn't marry Bayard's father, a West Indian man. Julia Davis was a rarity: an African American Quaker who instilled her religious values and a sense of social commitment in young Bayard. It was a combination of hard work, extended familial responsibility, and this commitment to social justice that formed the heart of Rustin's lifelong moral/activist code.

West Chester had been an important stop on the underground railroad, a fact that Rustin, in retrospect, felt fated his future as an activist. As he noted in his 1976 *Strategies for Freedom,* "The anti-slavery sentiment of the inhabitants was revealed in the town's architecture, for beneath its aging, Colonial homes ran hidden passageways which had concealed runaway slaves from (their) southern plantation owners."

The beginning of Rustin's college career coincided with the onset of the Great Depression, so Rustin, gifted as he was, had to drop out. In 1931 he moved in with a relative in Greenwich Village and put himself through classes at New York City College by occasionally singing at local clubs with singers like Josh White and Leadbelly. Strictly enforced segregation in places of public entertainment was still the norm for most of New York, except in those integrated clubs operated by Communist organizers. It was during this time that Rustin, like many black intellectuals of his day, embraced the Communist promise of racial equality and a cure for economic ills. He was soon traveling to colleges and union halls throughout the United States to speak out against segregation and social injustice. With the outbreak of World War II and the subsequent shift by the Communist Party away from domestic reforms, Rustin was asked to stop his anti-segregation work. He quickly resigned.

A most beloved mentor By the mid-1940s, an undaunted Rustin was principal aide to labor leader A. Philip Randolph, an originator of the 1941 March on Washington. One of Rustin's first tasks was to target racial discrimination in the defense industry. It was Randolph who had been instrumental in pressuring Franklin Delano Roosevelt into creating the Fair Employment Practices Commission, and it was Randolph who, according to Rustin in his *Strategies for Freedom,* used "careful daring, (and a) sense of timing and strategy" to get Truman to sign an executive order in 1948 that finally ended racial discrimination in the military.

Randolph was Rustin's most beloved mentor. Shortly after Randolph's death in 1979, Rustin wrote that Randolph had unearthed for him the critical *economic* roots of racism, and had taught him above all "that the struggle for the freedom of black people is intertwined with the struggle to free all mankind."

In 1942, Rustin was hired by radical reformer A. J. Muste, founder of the international pacifist organization Fellowship for Reconciliation (FOR), to spearhead a Department of Race Relations. From this committee emerged the interracial Congress of Racial Equality (CORE), whose philosophy was patterned after the nonviolent direct action as exercised by Indian leader Mohandas Gandhi, and whose focus was on challenging racial discrimination in public accommodation and transportation through nonviolent mass protest. Here, Rustin found the heart of lasting, truly forward-moving success for the civil rights movement. CORE strategies satisfied his progressive agenda, utilized the energy and talents of both blacks and sympathetic whites, and salved his Quaker-bred sensibilities for nonviolence.

Ironically, it was in the years during and immediately following the war that Rustin faced the most grueling mental and physical challenges to these ideologies. His life's work became a roller coaster ride of peaks and valleys. In 1942, he worked in California on behalf of the interned Japanese and, as a conscientious objector in 1943, served three years in the Lewisburg Penitentiary rather than perform hospital duties. On his release in 1946, he resumed his CORE duties and traveled to India as chairman of the Free India Committee and a guest of Ghandi's Congress Party. In 1947, he served twenty-two days on a North Carolina chain gang (just one of dozens of beatings and arrests he was to suffer in his life) for joining one of the first Freedom Rides through the South—dubbed the "Journey of Reconciliation"—designed to test the U.S. Supreme Court prohibition against segregation in interstate travel.

Career-crippling homophobia   In the early 1950s, Rustin fought for self rule in West Africa, assumed a leading role in the Aldermason Peace March in England, and joined the All African People's Conference in Addis Ababa. Yet despite his growing worldwide success, Rustin now also faced the ongoing, career-crippling isolation of homophobia, despite the "all encompassing" rhetoric of the political organizations he worked for. He had long been nonchalant and open about his homosexuality in private, and always discreet professionally. Yet, given the political/sexual hysteria and hypocrisy of the 1950s, he was now considered a potential liability by many of his colleagues.

According to *Contemporary Black Biography* (1993), "when Rustin began to run into trouble with laws against homosexual activity, FOR chairman Muste warned him that any such further actions would cause his dismissal." When he was arrested and sentenced to thirty days in jail on a morals charge in Pasadena, California, in early 1953, a dispirited Rustin was forced to resign from FOR. It was a tragically humbling step behind the scenes that was to shadow his life and career to the end.

In December of 1955, the civil rights struggle in America reached a watershed when Rosa Parks refused to move to the back of the bus in segregated Montgomery, Alabama. The resulting bus boycott received nationwide attention and was viewed by Rustin as an opportunity to rejoin the fight and regain some lost political influence. He traveled to Montgomery, but was soon reproached by several black political leaders who feared that his personal life and past Communist connections would prove a liability to the cause. Led by A. P. Randolph, they convinced him to leave Montgomery.

Rustin had come too far to simply withdraw, however. As he wrote in his diary in 1956, "I had a feeling that no force on earth (could) stop this movement. It has all the elements to touch the hearts of men." Martin Luther King Jr., then head of the Montgomery movement, was quick to recognize Rustin's talents, and thus initiated a lifelong professional liaison. Rustin became ghostwriter, confidant, and tireless promoter of the "cult of personality" that was growing around King. Recognizing the movement's need for a charismatic, younger leader (by now, Rustin was twenty years King's senior), and reluctantly acquiescent to his personal "liabilities," Rustin helped the emerging leader behind the scenes by briefing him for meetings, drafting speeches and press releases, and introducing him to wealthy civil rights supporters.

Marches and morals   With the arrival of desegregation orders from the Supreme Court in December 1956, the Montgomery boycott ended. Strategies for expanding the campaign throughout the South were just beginning though, as was Rustin's role as senior statesman. But once again, the potential for scandal loomed large. In 1960, the powerful black congressman Adam Clayton Powell threatened to expose Rustin's personal and political past, which precipitated Rustin's resignation from the SCLC. He was forced to forfeit his role as official head of the 1963 March on Washington. However, his long association with King nonetheless assured his central role as a behind-the-curtain organizer of one of the most important nonviolent protests in American history, best remembered as the march at which King delivered his riveting "I Have a Dream" speech.

It is important to note the fear that political segregationists wielded at the time. Right down to the eve of the march, Rustin's most stalwart supporters were afraid that conservatives and liberals alike would exploit Rustin's homosexuality and former Communist ties to "taint and dilute" the purpose of the protest—which was, for the first time in history, designed to draw attention to the *economic* roots of racism in America. But seventy-three-year-old Randolph, considered the most politically safe figurehead to lead the march, was by then vesting responsibility for the day-to-day planning and logistics almost completely to Rustin. In the end, thanks largely to King's intervention, Randolph appointed Rustin as his official march deputy and he was back on board.

In a last-ditch effort to derail the march, Senator Strom Thurmond told the press about Rustin's 1953 morals arrest and denounced him on the floor of the Senate as a draft dodger and Communist. The sabotage backfired and the attack served to rally black leaders around Rustin all the more. Throughout, Rustin himself kept a cool head, answering Thurmond's charges with prideful proof that he knew quite a bit more about morals and decency than the cagey senator. "With regard to Senator Thurmond's attack on my morality," he wrote just prior to the march in 1963, "I have no comment. By religious training and fundamental philosophy, I am disinclined to put myself in the position of having to defend my own moral character. Questions in this area should properly be directed to those who have entrusted me with my present responsibilities."

Radicals "of all stripes" needed   By 1964, Rustin had grown disillusioned with nonviolent action as means of change. He turned his focus to the political arena, and from 1965 to 1979, he headed the A. P. Randolph Institute, a liberal think-tank sponsored by the AFL-CIO and designed to address social and economic ills. In 1975, he founded the Organization for Black Americans to Support Israel, a group that continues to this day.

From his "senior statesman" vantage point later in life, Rustin witnessed the violence, factionalism, and frustration that characterized the movement for racial equality well into the 1980s. His allegiance to radical reforms—total restructuring of political, economic, and social

Bayard Rustin, deputy director of the 1963 March on Washington, describes the march's route.

institutions—remained intact, and he continued to stress the importance of strong labor unions, coalition politics, and the vote. To those who advocated racial separatism, he answered that without equality for all, there simply is no equality for the few—no political base or ideology from which to take a stand. "The real radical," he wrote in a speech to black students in 1970, "is that person who has a vision of equality and is willing to do those things that will bring reality closer to that vision. And by equality I do not mean 'separate but equal,' a phrase created by segregationists in order to prevent the attainment of equality. I mean equality based upon an integrated social order."

Toward the end of his life, Rustin often spoke to gay organizations, emphasizing the importance of including gays and lesbians of all colors and backgrounds in the ongoing struggle for racial equality. Integration and "crossover" radicalism were the keys to true progress, he would argue; one group's gain against oppression is a step forward for all. Radicals "of all stripes" were needed.

Another common theme when he spoke to lesbian and gay groups was the importance of coming out. "Although it's going to make problems," the *Alyson Almanac* quotes him as saying, "those problems are not so dangerous as the problems of lying to yourself, to your friends, and missing many opportunities."

Bayard Rustin held fast to his dreams and his truths all his life, and consequently, never missed an opportunity to throw himself into the thick of this century's social struggles for equality.—JEROME SZYMCZAK

ARTHUR ALFONSO **SCHOMBURG**

1874–1938
Bibliophile, library curator, writer

The work of Arthur Alfonso Schomburg, a distinguished black bibliophile, is a tribute to the world of scholarship and is preserved in one of the world's largest repositories of materials for the study of peoples of African descent—the Schomburg Center for Research in Black Culture in Harlem. A self-taught historian with a remarkable memory, he worked to inspire racial pride both through his organizations and through the encouragement of study and research on black themes.

Arthur Alfonso Schomburg was born on January 24, 1874, to Carlos Féderico Schomburg, a German-born merchant, and Mary Joseph, a black midwife and washer woman. On January 28 of that year, young Schomburg was baptized Arturo Alfonso. Although the story of his birth and early childhood is often conflicting and mysterious, Schomburg chose not to clear up many of the mysteries. According to his biographer, Eleanor Des Verney Sinnette, he knew little about his father. He identified his mother as born free in St. Croix, Virgin Islands, in 1837; she was educated at the elementary level and later became a midwife. He had one sister, Dolores María, known as "Lola," who was born in San Juan and was fourteen years older than he. Both maternal grandparents were born free in St. Croix.

Although the only primary schools available to him in San Juan charged tuition, Schomburg may have attended, but did not complete his work at the Instituto de Párvulos, a Jesuit school. Schomburg also claimed to have attended the Institute of Popular Teaching, or Institute of Instruction in San Juan. There are also statements that he was completely self-educated.

During his childhood, Mary Joseph either remained in San Juan and sent Arturo to the Virgin Islands to live with her parents to attend school, or she moved to the Virgin Islands with him. In either case, he had friends in St. Croix and St. Thomas, joined a debating team there, and according to his biographer, Schomburg claims, without documentation, that he attended St. Thomas College.

Schomburg was preoccupied with his own heritage and is said to have become curious about his past through a literary club in Puerto Rico, where history was a favorite topic of discussion. When whites spoke of the accomplishments of their Spanish ancestors, he became curious about his own ancestors and about people of color in Puerto Rico and the Caribbean. Haitian revolutionary Toussaint L'Ouverture was one of his early heroes. He began to read

Arthur A. Schomburg.

widely in areas of his interest, both in Spanish and English, and developed a lifelong interest in Caribbean and Latin American history.

By adolescence, Schomburg was described in his biography as "somewhat self-effacing, soft-spoken . . . of medium height with a *café au lait* complexion, soft curly brown hair, and rather large, limpid, warm brown eyes." While Schomburg was in the Virgin Islands, he became more curious about Puerto Rico's and Cuba's struggle for independence than his own heritage. He knew that he needed to leave the islands to become educated, and he had considered either a career in medicine or a place in the revolution. He may have returned to San Juan to work as a printer to earn money to travel north. Aged seventeen, Schomburg left the Caribbean for New York City, arriving on Friday, April 17, 1891, with letters of introduction to cigarmakers in Manhattan verifying his experience as a typographer. He settled on the lower east side of Manhattan.

To sustain himself while attending night school at Manhattan Central High School, Schomburg held various jobs—elevator operator, bellhop, printer, and porter. He sustained his interest in the Puerto Rican struggle for independence and on April 3, 1892, when he was eighteen years old, he became a founding member and secretary of a political club, Las Dos Antillas (The Two Islands), that assisted in Cuba's and Puerto Rico's independence. His last major involvement in the movement came on August 2, 1898, when a meeting was held in which the revolutionary support groups disbanded. His interest later shifted from the Cuban and Puerto Rican movement to the freedom of people of color everywhere. Later, however, he severed his ties with the Puerto Rican community and from then on lived as a black man, or "a Puerto Rican of African descent," as he became known.

He became active in fraternal organizations, first in freemasonry through El Sol de Cuba Lodge, No. 38, founded by Cuban and Puerto Rican exiles. By 1911 he was elected master; later the organization was renamed the Prince Hall Lodge to honor Prince Hall of Cambridge, Massachusetts, the first black accredited Mason. While serving as master, Schomburg gathered and organized the Masons' documents, papers, books, pamphlets, correspondence, photographs, and other items, and was largely responsible for preserving the black lodge's early history. From 1918 to 1926 he was grand secretary of the Grand Lodge of New York and in 1925 became a Thirty-third Degree Mason.

For a while Schomburg may have considered becoming a lawyer. From 1901 to 1906 he worked with the New York law firm Pryor, Mellis & Harris and, according to his biographer, led others to believe that he was studying toward a degree from the firm by "reading law." After he was denied permission to take the New York State Regents examination to qualify for a "law certificate," he left the clerk-messenger position and became messenger for the Latin American department of Bankers Trust Company in lower Manhattan. He rose in rank to become supervisor of the mailing department before retiring in 1929 on a medical disability.

Schomburg collects black materials Schomburg's interest in black history became apparent in 1911, when he began to collect items rigorously and systematically. He had met John Edward Bruce (Bruce Grit), journalist, lay historian, and bibliophile, and joined the Men's Sunday Club that Bruce founded. The club meetings usually included some discussion of racial issues as well as books, and the members raised funds to purchase items on black history for the club's library. In April of that year, Schomburg and Bruce co-founded the Negro Society for Historical Research, which would greatly influence black book collecting and preservation as well as the study of African American themes. In 1914 Schomburg became a member of the American Negro Academy (ANA), founded in 1897 by Alexander Crummell, where he met such black scholars as W. E. B. Du Bois, Alain Locke, Kelly Miller, and Carter G. Woodson. This affiliation furthered Schomburg's interest in collecting black materials. In 1922 he was elected fifth president of the ANA. Since the ANA was based in Washington, D.C., Schomburg was primarily an absentee president; his friend John W. Cromwell attended the executive committee meetings and provided direct supervision of the organization until he died in 1927. In time, Schomburg became unhappy with the ANA, losing his enthusiasm for the weakening organization, but he held the office until the ANA dissolved in 1929.

Schomburg was in New York when the Harlem Renaissance was at its peak. If he had not known them already, he came in contact with such luminaries as Claude McKay (who became his closest friend), Walter White, and James Weldon Johnson. He had great respect for Marcus Garvey and supported many of Garvey's principles of black development. The Harlem Renaissance period provided fertile ground for Schomburg to promote his interest in black themes and stimulated further his interest in collecting books by black writers. The rigor with which Schomburg collected was manifest in the sizeable collection that he gathered. He sought out materials from booksellers throughout the United States as well as in Europe and Latin America. By 1925 he had acquired 5,000 books, pamphlets, manuscripts, prints, etchings, and other items. When the New York Public Library opened the Division of Negro Literature, History, and Prints at the 135th Street Branch in May that year, he sold his collection for $10,000 to the Carnegie Corporation to be placed in the new library. His collecting practices continued. He sailed for Europe on June 25, 1925, in search of missing pieces of black history to strengthen his collection now at the library.

Schomburg's close relationship with Charles Spurgeon Johnson, who had headed the Department of Research and Investigations for the National Urban League and edited the league's official journal, *Opportunity,* and by 1928 chaired the Social Science Department at Fisk University, led to Schomburg's position in 1929 as curator of the Negro Collection in the university library. During his brief tenure at Fisk, Schomburg established a distinguished collection similar to his own, then left in 1932 to become curator of the Division of Negro Literature, History, and Prints at the New York Public Library (renamed in 1973 the Schomburg Center for Research in Black Culture). Continuing to travel extensively, he spoke at conferences and before other groups to solicit materials for the collection. The same meticulous care was used in developing the collection that he used in building his private library, and he was instrumental in building an impressive collection of rare and current books and materials for the library that he now served. Schomburg sought support for the collection wherever he could, using friends such as Langston Hughes to locate materials during Hughes's travels, and persuading black writers, composers, artists, and others to contribute works. He also built a network of people who led him to materials in this country or abroad, or purchased them in his stead. Schomburg did what he could to persuade the library system to purchase items for the collection, and when the library refused to pay for materials he had ordered improperly, he often paid for the works himself. He also organized two notable exhibitions—one on the achievements of blacks, and a traveling exhibition of African art and handicrafts.

Writes on black themes   Schomburg's interest in the black experience was expressed also in his writings. Although he had little formal training and clearly was not a good writer, influential black intelligentsia respected his potential for enhancing scholarship. Such scholars as W. E. B. Du Bois, Charles Spurgeon Johnson, and Alain Locke edited his works carefully to make them more readable. Schomburg also promoted the study and research on black themes in the nation's black colleges, as seen in his essay "Racial Integrity: A Plea for the Establishment of a Chair of Negro History in Our Schools, Colleges, etc.," published in 1913 in Nancy Cunard's work, *Negro*. His publications also included such works as *A Bibliographical Checklist of American Negro Poetry* (1916) and "Economic Contribution by the Negro to America," published in 1916 as an occasional paper of the American Negro Academy. He also published articles in *Crisis, Opportunity,* the *Messenger, Negro World, Negro Digest,* the *A.M.E. Review, New Century,* and *Survey Graphic.*

Once highly visible through thirty organizations to which he belonged (including the Urban League, the NAACP, and the Negro Writers' Guild), in time Schomburg became disenchanted with many of the black organizations—often because of a dispute—and resigned. He became annoyed with the black intelligentsia as well, sometimes because of trivial matters, sometimes because he felt overlooked, or merely due to dissatisfaction with another person's point of view. In time he removed himself from the limelight.

On June 30, 1895, Schomburg married Elizabeth "Bessie" Hatcher, a fair-skinned beauty from Staunton, Virginia, and they lived in the San Juan Hill section of New York. They had three sons, Maximo Gomez, Arthur Alfonso Jr., and Kingsley Guarionex. After Bessie Schomburg died in 1900, Shomburg married Elizabeth Morrow Taylor on March 17, 1902, a native of Williamsburg, North Carolina. She died early, leaving two young sons, Reginald Stanfield and Nathaniel José. All of Shomburg's children lived with their respective maternal relatives— Bessie's in Virginia and Tennessee, and Elizabeth's in Virginia and New Jersey. About 1914 Schomburg took a third wife, Elizabeth Green, a nurse and friend of Bessie Schomburg's sister, and they had three children—Fernando, Dolores Marie (his only daughter), and Plácido Carlos.

Schomburg, who was of medium build, had remarkable energy and determination, but in 1936 his health began to fail, and his pace was slowed. As late as 1938, Schomburg expected to continue his speaking engagements and attend meetings. He developed a dental infection, however, that required extraction. After that he became ill, failed to respond to treatment, and on June 10, 1938, died at Brooklyn's Madison Park Hospital. After a private funeral held on June 12 at Brooklyn's Siloam Presbyterian Church, Schomburg was buried in Cypress Hills Cemetery in Brooklyn.

Charles Spurgeon Johnson's tribute to Schomburg at a memorial service held on June 8, 1939, serves as a summary of his work. He called the Schomburg Collection a "visible monument to the life's work of Arthur Schomburg. It stands for itself, quietly and solidly for all time, a rich and inexhaustible treasure store for scholars and laymen alike, the materialization of the foresight, industry and scholarship" of Schomburg.—JESSIE CARNEY SMITH

BETTY **SHABAZZ**

1936–1997

Educator, nurse, community activist

Widow of the preeminent civil rights fighter Malcolm X (El Hajj Malik El-Shabazz), Betty Shabazz was the mother of four girls and pregnant with two more when she witnessed the assassination of her husband on February 21, 1965, in the Audubon Ballroom in New York City. A remarkable woman who possessed great strength and determination, Shabazz successfully raised her six daughters while continuing her education (she received a Ph.D. in 1975). She was instrumental in perpetuating the true legacy and memory of Malcolm X, and is an inspiration to the countless young people who want to carry on the struggle against the oppression of black people.

Betty Shabazz was born Betty Sanders in 1936. She was reared in Detroit, Michigan, by foster parents who apparently adopted her, and attended Northern High School. During her childhood and young adulthood she seldom thought about the outside world and her relationship to it. She told *Essence* magazine, "I was not that exposed at the time I met Malcolm, nor did I have a lot of experience in the challenges that women face. Pick a week out of my life. If you understood that week, you understood my life. I went to school from Monday to Friday. On Saturday I was at my parents' store. On Sunday I went to church."

Shabazz attended Tuskegee Institute in Alabama, which was her father's alma mater. She left Tuskegee, though, to go to nursing school in New York City. She disliked Tuskegee because she experienced hostility in Alabama from whites, an issue her parents did not want to deal with; they thought her departure was her own fault.

Shabazz met Malcolm X in her junior year when she was invited by a friend to attend a lecture at Temple Seven in Harlem. The first time Shabazz saw Malcolm X, she was immediately impressed with his clean-cut, no-nonsense, and focused demeanor. At the time, she felt that somehow she knew him: "I felt that somewhere in life I had met this energy before."

Begins work with Malcolm X at Temple Seven   As time passed, the relationship between Shabazz and Malcolm X grew stronger. She began to teach a women's class at Temple Seven, and Malcolm X advised her on what matters to stress. She typed and corrected papers for him as well. Shabazz recalled that "he would actively seek me out, ask me questions. He was different. He was refreshing, but I never suspected that he thought of me in any way other than as a sister who was interested in the Movement. . . . There were too many people in line for his attention."

Shabazz eventually discovered, though, that Malcolm X was very attracted to her. She later recollected, "I knew he loved me for my clear brown skin—it was very smooth. He liked my clear eyes. He liked my gleaming dark hair. I was very thin then, and he liked my Black beauty, my mind. He just liked me." They had an unusual courtship; Shabazz, a Methodist, never "dated" Malcolm X, a Muslim, because at the time single men and women of the Muslim faith did not "fraternize," as they called it. Men and women always went out in groups.

Betty
Shabazz.

Even with such restrictions in place, though, their attraction to one another grew. One night Malcolm X called Shabazz from Detroit, their hometown, and proposed to her. While her parents liked Malcolm X and thought he was a nice young man, they objected to the marriage because he was older and belonged to a different religion. Shabazz defied her parents and eloped. At some point after her marriage, Shabazz converted to Islam.

Shabazz described her seven years of marriage to Malcolm X as hectic, holistic, beautiful, and unforgettable. They fought occasionally on Malcolm's insistance that Shabazz remain at home with the children despite her desire to pursue a career. Nevertheless, their marriage was solid, with Shabazz the rock behind one of the twentieth century's most charismatic leaders. Shabazz never wavered in saying that Malcolm was a good husband and father to their daughters. "I was destined to be with Malcolm," Shabazz declared. "And I think that Malcolm probably needed me more than I needed him—to support his life's mission."

During the brutal murder of her husband, Shabazz, pregnant with twins, quickly threw herself on her four young kids to shield them from the gunfire. After it was over, she rushed to her husband who later died in her arms. Shabazz was unable to sleep for three weeks following her husband's assassination. She traveled to Mecca, where she sought solace and looked for meaning in her shattered life:

> I really don't know where I'd be today if I had not gone to Mecca to make Hajj [a pilgrimmage] shortly after Malcolm was assassinated. . . . Going to Mecca, making Hajj, was very good for me because it made me think of all the people in the world who loved me and were for me, who prayed that I would get my life back together. I stopped focusing on the people who were trying to tear me and my family apart.

After the death of Malcolm X, Shabazz divided her time between her daughters and continuing her education. Shabazz raised her six daughters (Attallah, Qubilah, Illyasah, Gamilah, Malaak, and Malikah) according to their father's principles and ideas. She gave them a well-rounded education and sought to instill in them a sense of ethnic responsibility for themselves, their people, and the broader society. For example, they studied Arabic and French and attended ballet classes in addition to taking black history courses. She also encouraged them to travel so they could learn more about Africa, the West Indies, and the Middle East.

Shabazz received an R.N. degree from the Brooklyn State Hospital School of Nursing, a B.A. in public health education from Jersey City State College, and became a certified school nurse. In 1975 she earned her Ph.D. in school administration and curriculum development from the University of Massachusetts at Amherst. Shabazz became a professor of health administration at Medgar Evers College, Brooklyn, New York, and served as the college's director of institutional advancement and public relations.

Activist became national figure   Even though Shabazz was essentially a private person and considered herself a follower rather than a leader, she became a national figure. She was in constant demand for speaking engagements across the country, and received many honors, tributes, and prestigious awards, including the Congressional Record Award for her community service. A one-time radio talk show host, she also made guest appearances on a number of radio and television shows. In addition, Shabazz worked with Columbia Medical School on the Malcolm X Medical Scholarship Program for African American students.

Shabazz became an inspiration to young people as well as an advocate for their proper development. She challenged parents to be good role models for their children and to provide them with guidelines. A strong believer that parents should take chief responsibility for passing on black cultural traditions to their children, Shabazz contended that parents have a spiritual and moral duty to teach their children to help oppressed people. In a speech before the National Urban League in 1990, Shabazz urged the audience to "sponsor our children . . . call newspapers and TV stations to complain about the way African American children are portrayed. . . . We have to give them pride in their own culture, their roots, but we must make these decisions for children, not let them make too many careless ones on their own."

Shabazz emphasized to parents and educators the importance of teaching young people in such a way that they understand that the twenty-first century will be a century of self-sufficiency. In Shabazz's view, young people need to learn that they have to make things happen for themselves. Like Malcolm X, Shabazz cared deeply about the struggle of people of African descent in the United States:

> We have been in this country so long and have made such a vast contribution, not only with our lives but in terms of development, invention, and contributions. Other ethnic groups have come to America and are automatically treated as citizens with all rights and privileges, and somehow, African descendants still are struggling. Other ethnic groups can receive money for reparations, and yet, with our several hundred years of free labor and the additional years of unfair compensation for our labor, we have not received the rights and privileges of other ethnic groups. . . . However, I don't know of an ethnic group that is more powerful, that has made such contributions, that has been as tolerant, and that still is willing to share and to do and to be. . . . We're a good people.

Shabazz also firmly believed that black women have had an immeasurably positive impact on America. "Given our resources and limited opportunities and options, Black women in America . . . are functioning at a remarkable high level, and compete on any level with women of the world."

As Shabazz continued her activist efforts on behalf of the black community, she maintained her connection to the energy of the universe around her. "And then, too, there's Malcolm's energy and his spirit," she said. "I don't feel sad. I feel fortunate. I feel very blessed spiritually. My soul is at peace. My heart is full of concern and love, and I understand the meaning of my own life and the lives of others. So, no, no, I'm never alone."

Three of Shabazz's daughters have emulated their mother's success. One is in public relations, a second is a writer, and another is an actress. But one daughter, Qubilah, was a source of constant heartache for Shabazz. Despite attending Princeton University, Qubilah could not escape a life poisoned by drug and alcohol abuse. In 1995, she was arrested and charged with conspiracy to assassinate Louis Farrakhan, but the charges were dropped under the condition that Qubilah would seek substance abuse counseling.

The attention that Qubilah's assassination plot gained prompted Shabazz and Farrakhan to a public reconciliation that was to ease the tension between the controversial Nation of Islam leader and Malcolm's family.

In 1997, Qubilah's unstable and often times violent lifestyle affected her twelve-year-old son Malcolm, who was sent to live with Shabazz, his grandmother. Bitter over his troubled life, Malcolm set fire to Shabazz's apartment in Yonkers. Trapped in the blaze, Shabazz was eventually rescued but endured third degree burns over 80 percent of her body. Twenty-two days after the incident, Shabazz died at Jacobi Medical Center in New York. Thousands mourned the loss of a woman who was in the shadow of her prominent husband, but through adversity, bounced back to make her own mark in education and civic duty. Shabazz is buried next to her husband in New York.

On June 3, 1997, Shabazz's grandson, Malcolm, pleaded guilty to manslaughter and arson and was sentenced to eighteen months at a New York juvenile detention facility.— BOBBIE T. POLLARD

CHARLES C. **SPAULDING**

1874–1952

Insurance executive, entrepreneur, civic leader

From the time Charles Clinton Spaulding was recruited by the fledgling North Carolina Mutual Life Insurance Company as company manager until his death in 1952, he was the dominant force who ruled supreme over the largest black business in America at that time. It had assets then of nearly $38 million and insurance in force of over $179 million. Spaulding was always a salaried employee of the company, who never owned company stock and whose final estate was some $200,000. He was a man who believed in both self-help and racial solidarity.

Charles Clinton Spaulding was born on August 1, 1874, in Columbus County, a rural area west of Wilmington and near Whiteville and Clarktown, North Carolina. It was populated by freeborn blacks who first settled there in the early nineteenth century. They were descendants of Wilmington-based plantation slaves. Spaulding's father, Benjamin McIver Spaulding, was an extraordinary man who was a farmer, blacksmith, cabinetmaker, artisan, Reconstruction-era county sheriff, and community leader. Although he had a sterling reputation, he did not place a high priority on education for his ten children, who all worked on the family farm and helped their mother with household chores. Spaulding's mother, Margaret Moore Spaulding, was the sister of Aaron McDuffie Moore, the man who would shape his nephew's young adulthood. Although Spaulding credited his father as being his role model because of the post-Emancipation life he created for himself and the lessons he imparted to his son on the farm, it was his uncle who gave him a home in Durham, North Carolina, in 1894, and urged him to get an education. Moore was a physician who founded a hospital and commanded respect from white civic and business leaders because of his philanthropical and religious activities, and his strong character. He was also very fair-skinned so he could pass for white.

In Durham, at the age of twenty, Spaulding went to Whitted Grade School for two years and earned the equivalent of a high school diploma. He worked as a dishwasher, bellhop, waiter, and cook in the home of a rich white family to support himself while attending school.

After graduation, in 1898 he secured a job as manager of a cooperative grocery store, a venture started by twenty-five black Durhamites, all of whom withdrew their initial investments at the first sign of financial problems. Although Spaulding was left with no stock on the shelves and $300 worth of bills, the failure was not attributed to his management.

During this time, Aaron Moore and a group of six other investors had organized an insurance company, North Carolina Mutual and Provident Association, that was chartered in 1898. This prominent group included John Merrick, a former slave and a barber, real estate speculator, and extension worker for the Grand Order of True Reformers, a leading secret fraternal order and benefit association founded in 1897; and James Shepard, founder of the National Religious Training School of Durham, now North Carolina Central University. The True Reformers, according to Frazier, was the most notable organization set up to create business undertakings and serve as a role model for fledgling black businesses. By 1900 the insurance company was in deep trouble and neither Merrick nor Moore, who had bought out the other original investors, could manage the business due to their professional pursuits. They knew of Spaulding's entrepreneurial talent and offered the position of general manager to Spaulding, who needed a job and so accepted. In 1900 he also married Fannie Jones, a home office clerk who would become the mother of their four children before her death in 1919.

In a two-dollar-a-month rented desk space in the corner of a doctor's office, Spaulding worked as janitor, agent, and general manager. The company was in dire straits because the first policyholder died shortly after being insured for forty dollars on a sixty-five cent premium. The company also faced the problem of not being able to bond workers because of racial discrimination. Since this was a state charter requirement, the owners were forced to establish their own firm, the Southern Fidelity Trust. Ingham and Feldman quoted others' descriptions of Spaulding as a "go-getter [and] natural born salesman." In *Black Leaders,* Weare also described him as an irrepressible optimist with a "quick mind" and "boundless energy." He represented the "New Negro" of that era. He was the complete antithesis of Merrick, who often displayed the requisite behaviors of one whose livelihood depended on the goodwill and largesse of white clients:

> John Merrick would say "Thank you, sir" for every fifty-cents tip that came his way. . . . But not Spaulding. Lean, Cassius-like, he seldom smiled. He sought no tips. All he asked of life was an open field and a fair change. He was strictly business.

Spaulding was a door-to-door salesman who would stand on street corners to sell policies, and more policies needed to be sold because Merrick and Moore had to pay the dead policyholder's beneficiaries forty dollars. Spaulding always displayed the claim receipt to prove that the company had a history of financial stability. As a recruiter, he was successful in amassing a large sales force of teachers and ministers, who always needed to supplement their meager incomes. While this expansion increased premium income, it also increased expenses, so Spaulding was by no means becoming wealthy. The next three years were indeed precarious ones due to sickness and death claims in addition to higher office and travel expenses. Because Merrick and Moore earned independent incomes, they were able to pay claims and expenses out of their pockets. Finally, in 1903, premiums began to exceed claims, and two decisions heralded their growing prosperity. First, Spaulding was put on salary at fifteen dollars a week, and next, the triumvirate decided to expand by aggressively advertising their product.

The rise of North Carolina Mutual   In 1903 Moore and Merrick's decision to hire Spaulding was justified because of his move to publish a company newspaper that would serve the dual purpose of benefitting the black community and advertising their business. The Duke family donated a printing press, and a newspaper called the *North Carolina Mutual* became a reality. Another highly successful venture was the distribution of advertising novelties such as black art calendars. By 1904, Spaulding had significantly upgraded the company by expanding into other states and expanding the range of offerings. Because industrial insurance was more expensive for policyholders and more costly to administer, Spaulding began offering industrial straight life policies.

The company showed its viability as a new office building was constructed on a street separating black and white Durham. By 1906, additional property had been purchased and the building enlarged to house the insurance offices, Moore's medical offices, fraternal order offices, a drugstore, a barbershop, lawyers' offices, the newspaper offices, clothing stores, a tailor shop, and a black bank—the Farmers and Mechanics Bank founded in 1908.

By 1913, Spaulding's leadership had resulted in the bank's reaching the level of "old line legal reserve" status, a definite indication of company stability and respectability. By 1916 the company territory had extended northward to Virginia, Maryland, and the District of Columbia. By 1924 the parent company's umbrella covered a fire insurance company, a savings and loan association, a Raleigh branch bank, a mortgage company, and a finance corporation.

Spaulding's first wife died in 1919 and the following year he married Charlotte Garner of Newark, New Jersey, reportedly the only person able to influence him in any way. Merrick also died in 1920, but the company was both stable and expanding its services and offerings to the black community. Spaulding was elevated to secretary-treasurer of the firm, now named the North Carolina Mutual Life Insurance Company. In 1923 Moore died and Spaulding became president, an office he held until his death twenty-nine years later.

Becomes civic leader   In 1920 Spaulding was the overseer for the construction of North Carolina Mutual's marble-trimmed, six-story home office building. Its impact on Durham was described by Weare in *Black Leaders:*

> By the end of the 1930s the Mutual had taken on a cultural legitimacy that transcended Negro business. . . . The company served as a landmark in the minds of visitors and townspeople, blacks and whites, and in the collective psyche of the community. . . . As long as it stood six stories tall as a black institution in a Southern town of squat warehouses and dimestores, and in the white rather than in the black business district, it commanded attention. . . . It came to represent in the white mind a self-delusory promise of what the black community might be. The black success was made over into a white success, even a sectional success. Durham offered three glittering examples of Southern achievement: Duke University, American Tobacco, and the North Carolina Mutual—three satisfying symbols of the New South.

Spaulding was the living black symbol of the New South largely because his power in the black community was firmly lodged in his ability to get from powerful whites what black Durham needed and to secure patronage from white powerbrokers. He became the determinant of who got what in nearly every arena of black life in Durham. Spaulding's power base was North Carolina Mutual, a black company that white economic sanctions could not affect.

Spaulding utilized his church, the White Rock Baptist Church, as a contact base for insurance agents and, in turn, North Carolina Mutual financed the church and thus had a major say in the hiring and firing of ministers. He controlled Lincoln Hospital, built by Moore, Merrick, and the Duke family, as chairman of the Board of Trustees. One collaborative relationship was between Spaulding and James E. Shepard, former original partner in the insurance company and founder-president of the predecessor of North Carolina Central University. In 1944 Shepard made overtures to the white state legislature to make his school the first publicly supported black liberal arts college in the South, and was supported by Spaulding at legislative hearings.

With Louis Austin, editor of the Durham-based *Carolina Times,* Spaulding averted what could easily have been an adversarial relationship because Austin, like Spaulding, could not be controlled by blacks or whites. A self-avowed town radical, according to Weare in *Black Leaders,* in the community Austin was regarded as "that nigger communist from Massachusetts."

Although they were polar opposites in terms of personality and politics, Spaulding and Austin respected one another and so created a complementary relationship that allowed the two to come together as a solid front to gain benefits for Durham's black citizenry. Each man benefitted from this reciprocity. The alliance, in turn, made Spaulding more acceptable to Durham's black working class.

Spaulding was on the board of trustees of Howard and Shaw universities in Washington, D.C., and Raleigh, N.C., respectively, and the Oxford, North Carolina, Colored Orphanage, and worked tirelessly to save other black institutions from extinction. On a political level, he was appointed to the State Council of Unemployment and Relief at the onset of the Great Depression and had access to Franklin D. Roosevelt's "Black Cabinet," and also served on Herbert Hoover's Federal Relief Committee. In *Black Leaders,* Weare said that, in the 1930s, Spaulding "emerged as a racial statesman." In 1931 Spaulding became the first black elected to the board of the Slater Fund and also functioned as a regional broker for the Rosenwald Fund. His influence was so widespread that he successfully spearheaded a fund-raiser in black Durham to build Duke University's Gothic Chapel. The fact that Duke was totally segregated was not an issue since even the few blacks who donated money, as well as those who abstained, knew that Spaulding's gesture could later be used as a bargaining chip to benefit black Durham. Another power base was his appointment as national chairman of the Urban League's Emergency Advisory Council. This was coordinated by the league and the federal government with a goal of drumming up black support for the National Recovery Administration and other New Deal agencies during Franklin D. Roosevelt's Administration.

Despite his seemingly magic touch, not even Spaulding could work miracles, and his notable failures were in the realm of discrimination in many federal programs because of the multi-tiered layers of racist bureaucracy that were totally immune to his charm, reputation, or political connections. After a series of local and national events that were personally painful and humiliating, Spaulding began to realize the need for a local black political base. On one occasion in the early 1930s, he was assaulted by a white drugstore clerk who was not arrested by the Raleigh police despite Spaulding's stellar reputation in the white community. He became the head of the Durham Committee on Negro Affairs (DCNA), an organization that was still, in the 1980s, a viable political factor in the local black community at large. The foci of the DCNA were economic welfare, civic rights, and electoral politics. Major successes were mostly political. The DCNA, in tandem with Austin's *Carolina Times,* endorsed candidates and voter registration, community education, and political independence. Spaulding's membership on the executive committee of the Atlanta-based Commission on Interracial Cooperation afforded him the opportunity to work and converse with southern white liberals in the first half of the twentieth century.

Spaulding's community affiliations were numerous. He was president of the Farmers and Mechanics Bank, a trustee of the Morrison Training School for Boys of North Carolina, a deacon and trustee of White Rock Baptist Church, a member of the Knights of Pythias and the Masons, treasurer of the National Negro Bankers Association, a founding member and first president of the National Insurance Association in 1921, and vice-president of the United Negro College Fund; he was a member of the National Committee of the Urban League, the Southern Education Foundation, the Chambers of Commerce of New York City and Durham, and the Kappa Alpha Psi Fraternity. In 1926 he received the Harmon Award for creativity in business and industry. He held honorary degrees from Atlanta University, Shaw University, and Tuskegee Institute (now University).

Spaulding died in Durham of heart failure on his seventy-eighth birthday, on August 1, 1952, before the full flowering of the civil rights era. Upon his death, Durham's mayor declared the day of the funeral to be one of respect for his memory and deeds. Over 3,000 crowded into the White Rock Baptist Church auditorium and the overflow spilled out on the lawn and sidewalks. The memorial address was given by Mordecai Johnson, then president of Howard University, and Spaulding was buried afterward in Beechwood Cemetery.

In 1980 Spaulding was posthumously inducted into the National Business Hall of Fame by *Fortune* magazine and Junior Achievement. Spaulding's overwhelming presence was attested by a prominent executive as quoted by Ingham and Feldman in *African-American Business Leaders:*

> There was never nobody behind C. C. Spaulding. [He] was his own man in every way. The only somebody that governed him just a teensey weensey little bit was his wife . . . and when I say teensey weensey, I mean teensey weensey.

Spaulding was a role model for black racial and economic progress nationwide. The great measure of Spaulding's leadership was that his death, like those of Moore and Merrick, only occasioned sadness and a sense of loss, but not an upheaval in the company's ongoing success. His son, Asa, the Kennedys, and Clements created a successful transition, and North Carolina Mutual Life Insurance Company still stands as tribute to a twenty-year-old general manager who made good the beneficiaries' claim at the death of the first policyholder.—DOLORES NICHOLSON

MABEL KEATON **STAUPERS**

1890–1989

Nurse, organization executive

Mabel Doyle Keaton Staupers led the decades-long struggle of black nurses to win full integration into the mainstream of the American nursing profession. During the Great Depression, Staupers assumed the

leadership of the almost moribund National Association of Colored Graduate Nurses (NACGN). Possessed of superb organizing skills and a remarkable talent for political maneuvering, Staupers served as the executive secretary of the NACGN from 1934 to 1949, when she became its president. Staupers is perhaps best known for the major role she played in the desegregation of the Armed Forces Nurse Corps during World War II. She published an illuminating account of this and other battles of black nurses in No Time for Prejudice: A Story of the Integration of Negroes in the United States *(1961). It is impossible to grasp the full significance of the history of black women in the nursing profession without devoting considerable attention to her life and work.*

Staupers was born in Barbados, West Indies, on February 27, 1890. In April 1903 she and her parents, Thomas and Pauline Doyle, migrated to the United States, settling into the Harlem community in New York City. She completed primary and secondary school in the city and in 1914 matriculated at Freedmen's Hospital School of Nursing (now Howard University College of Nursing) in Washington, D.C. Three years later, Staupers graduated with class honors from the nursing program and was married to James Max Keaton of Asheville, North Carolina. The marriage, however, ended in divorce. A second marriage in 1931 to Fritz C. Staupers of New York City proved more resilient, ending only with his death in 1949.

Black women encountered virtually insurmountable obstacles in their pursuit of nursing training. Although the first three schools of nursing opened in America in 1873, few welcomed black students. Mary Eliza Mahoney (1845–1926) became in 1879 the first black professional nurse after completing requirements at the New England Hospital for Women and Children. Most institutions either excluded black women altogether, as was the case in the South, or, as was seen in the North, regulated quotas for admission along racial and ethnic lines. Black communities in both the North and South, often with financial contributions from white philanthropists, assumed the major responsibility of establishing a network of hospitals, clinics, and nursing schools in order to provide black women a means of entering the nursing profession and to provide facilities for black physicians to attend their patients. By 1927 the nation's 1,797 nursing schools had trained 18,623 graduate nurses. In 1925 the number of black graduate nurses stood at 2,784. There were thirty-six schools of nursing available to them.

By the 1920s, graduate nurses practiced their profession in one of three settings: private duty nurses in the homes of patients; hospital staff nurses; and as visiting nurses affiliated with municipal health departments, various public health agencies, or settlement houses. Like the vast majority of both black and white graduate nurses, Staupers began her professional career by accepting private-duty cases. Her private-duty work, however, was short lived. In cooperation with black physicians Louis T. Wright and James Wilson, Staupers helped to organize the Booker T. Washington Sanitarium and became the first executive secretary of the Harlem tuberculosis committee of the New York Tuberculosis and Health Association. The Washington Sanitarium was the first inpatient center in Harlem for black patients with tuberculosis and was one of a few city facilities that permitted black physicians to treat their patients.

Staupers's work with black health care facilities and organizations enlarged her awareness of the discrimination and segregation that blacks encountered in their search for adequate treatment. A 1921 working fellowship at the Henry Phipps Institute for Tuberculosis in Philadelphia enabled her to leave New York. While in Philadelphia, Staupers accepted an assignment at the Jefferson Hospital Medical College. First-hand observations of the ill-treatment and lack of respect for blacks by college administrators and physicians left an indelible impression on the young nurse.

In 1922 the New York Tuberculosis and Health Association invited Staupers to conduct a survey of the health needs of the Harlem community, and she readily accepted. She assessed and found wanting the city's efforts to meet the community's health needs. With consummate thoroughness, Staupers evaluated the services offered for the care of minorities in tuberculosis institutions in the city and state. Her subsequent report led to the establishment of the Harlem Committee of the New York Tuberculosis and Health Association. For twelve years Staupers served as the organization's executive secretary. She worked assiduously to channel aid and resources to minority groups afflicted with tuberculosis. Staupers's work with the Tuberculosis and Health Association left her well-prepared to assume the leadership of the National Association of Colored Graduate Nurses (NACGN).

In 1908 a group of fifty-two black nurses under the urging of Adah Belle Thoms (1870–1943) of New York and Martha Franklin (1870–1968) of Connecticut met to form the NACGN. Franklin served two terms as the NACGN's first president. The objectives of the new organization focused on securing for the black nurse integration into the mainstream of the profession. The integration sought included full membership in the key professional bodies, in particular the American Nurses' Association (ANA), and unfettered access to all schools, hospitals, and advanced study programs, along with equal salaries and fair opportunities for advancement to administrative positions. The organization would promote higher nursing standards and raise the requirements for admission into the black schools of nursing. That there existed a need for such an organization was undeniable. Both the ANA and the National League of Nursing Education had refused to accept individual membership from black nurses residing in seventeen states. Every southern state association barred black women, thereby making the majority of black nurses professional outcasts in a large section of the country. The NACGN pledged to advance the status of black nurses on many fronts. Thoms, who served as acting director of the Lincoln Hospital Nursing School from 1906 through 1923, also served as president of the NACGN from 1916 to 1923. The exclusion of black nurses from the Armed Forces Nurse Corps during World War I had been one of the most trying episodes of Thoms's presidency.

The NACGN achieved mixed results during its early years. The lack of a salaried official seriously hindered its effectiveness. In the mid-1930s the organization's fate improved as grants from the General Education Board of the Rockefeller Foundation and the Julius Rosenwald Fund enabled the NACGN both to employ Staupers and to move into permanent headquarters at Rockefeller Center, where all the major national nursing organizations had offices. Fortuitously, Staupers took the post of executive secretary just as Estelle Masse Riddle (1903–1981), the superintendent of nurses at the Homer G. Phillips Hospital in Saint Louis, Missouri, assumed the presidency of the NACGN. In 1933 Riddle had become the first black nurse to earn a master of arts degree in nursing education. Together Staupers and Riddle fought to win integration and acceptance of black nurses into the mainstream of American nursing.

The fight for integration involved a series of strategies. Staupers decided the first requirement was a stronger, more resilient NACGN replete with programs that addressed the immediate needs of black nurses. Accordingly, she spent the first few years in her new position collecting data, organizing state and local nursing associations, advising and counseling black nurses, and representing them in the larger community. She worked closely with the NACGN's biracial national advisory council that she organized in 1928 to develop greater public interest in, and support for, the association's programs.

Efforts lead to desegregation of nurse corps

The struggle to win professional recognition and integration of black nurses into American nursing acquired new momentum and urgency with the outbreak of World War II. Staupers adroitly seized the opportunity created by the war emergency and the increased demand for nurses to project the plight of the black nurse into the national limelight. By the time of the Japanese attack on Pearl Harbor in December 1941, Staupers had developed a sharp sense of political timing. When the army set a quota of fifty-six black nurses and the navy refused even to consider admitting black nurses into the nurse corps, Staupers swung the NACGN into action. She publicized the quotas. She joined with other black leaders to meet directly with the army generals and high-ranking government officials to protest the imposition of quotas. The pressure did result in some success, although not as much as desired.

In 1943 Staupers received notice that the navy had decided to place the induction of black nurses under consideration. The army raised its quota of black nurses to 160. In an effort to draw even more attention to the unfairness of quotas, Staupers requested a meeting with Eleanor Roosevelt. In November 1944, the First Lady and Staupers met, at which time Staupers described in detail the black nurses' troubled relationship with the armed forces. Eleanor Roosevelt, apparently moved by the discussion, applied her own subtle pressure on Norman T. Kirk, the surgeon general of the United States Army, Secretary of War Henry Stimson, and Navy Rear Admiral W. J. C. Agnew.

Actually, a well-publicized confrontation between Staupers and Kirk best demonstrated Staupers's indomitable courage and political adroitness. In January 1945 Kirk announced the possibility of a draft to remedy a nursing shortage within the armed forces. Staupers immediately challenged him: "If nurses are needed so desperately, why isn't the Army using colored nurses?" Her question exposed the hypocrisy of the call for a draft. Afterwards she encouraged nursing groups, black and white, to write letters and send telegrams protesting the discrimination against black nurses in the Army and Navy Nurse Corps. This groundswell of public support for the removal of quotas that so severely restricted the enrollment of capable and willing black women proved effective.

Buried beneath the avalanche of telegrams and seared by the heat of an inflamed public, Kirk, Agnew, and the War Department declared an end to quotas and exclusion. On January 20, 1945, Kirk stated that nurses would be accepted into the Army Nurse Corps without regard to race. Five days later Admiral Agnew announced that the Navy Nurse Corps was now open to black women, and within a few weeks Phyllis Daley became the first black woman to break the color barrier and receive induction into the corps. The end of discriminatory practices by a key American institution helped to erode entrenched beliefs about the alleged inferiority of black health care professionals and paved the way for the integration of the American Nurses' Association.

The battle to integrate blacks into the Army and Navy Nurse Corps exhausted Staupers. In 1946 she relinquished her position as executive secretary to take a much-needed and well-deserved rest. It was to be of short duration, however, for Staupers considered her work incomplete. She had not accomplished her major objective, the integration of black women into the American Nurses' Association. Beginning in 1934, Staupers and Riddle had appeared before the House of Delegates at the biennial meeting of the ANA. After the 1944 meeting, Staupers expressed optimism that integration would soon be accomplished. Indeed, so convinced was she of this possibility that she advised the black nurses attending the four NACGN regional conferences in 1944 to recommend to the board of directors that it be "ready and willing to vote for complete integration, if and when the American Nurses' Association House of Delegates accept us to full membership."

General integration into the ANA did not come until four years later. In 1948 the ANA's House of Delegates opened the gates to black membership, appointed a black nurse as assistant executive secretary in its national headquarters, and witnessed the election of Estelle Riddle to the board of directors. The decision to grant individual membership to black nurses barred from state associations in Georgia, Louisiana, South Carolina, Texas, Virginia, Arkansas, Alabama, and the District of Columbia was followed by the adoption of a resolution to establish biracial committees in districts and state associations to implement educational programs and promote development of harmonious intergroup relations.

With the removal of the overtly discriminatory barriers to membership in the ANA, Staupers and the leadership of the NACGN persuaded the members that the organization was now obsolete. The ANA agreed to take over the functions of the NACGN. Furthermore, it agreed to continue to award the Mary Mahoney Medal to the individual contributing the most to intergroup relations within a given period, regardless of race. Thus, during the NACGN's 1949 convention, the members voted the organization out of existence. The following year, Staupers, then president of the NACGN, presided over its formal dissolution.

Staupers wins Spingarn Medal   Staupers received many accolades for her leadership. The crowning acknowledgement of her role in and contribution to the quest of black nurses for civil rights and human dignity came from an unexpected source. The Spingarn Committee of the NAACP chose her to receive the Spingarn Medal for 1951. Channing H. Tobias, director of the Phelps-Stokes Fund, confided to Staupers, "I know the committee was especially appreciative of the fact that you were willing to sacrifice organization to ideals when you advocated and succeeded in realizing the full integration of Negro nurses into the organized ranks of the nursing profession in this country."

Staupers deserved all of the praise, awards, and recognition heaped upon her in the aftermath of the dissolution of the NACGN. For more than fifteen years she and Estelle Masse Riddle had labored to develop cooperative relations with leading white women and black male heads of organizations. More significantly, they had cultivated and sustained mutually beneficial ties with the leaders of the NAACP, the National Medical Association, the National Urban League, and the National Council of Negro Women. Staupers, furthermore, manipulated the press extremely well by releasing statements at the most strategic moments. Her public remarks unfailingly emphasized the cause for which she was fighting. In so doing, she constantly reminded the country of the plight of black nurses, of the racism and sexism that robbed them of the opportunities to develop their full professional potential. Small of frame, energetic, and fast-talking, Staupers knew when to accept a half-loaf of advancement and when to press on for total victory. It is unlikely that the eventually complete integration of black women into American nursing on all levels could have been accomplished without Mabel Keaton Staupers at the helm of the NACGN. Mabel Staupers died on November 29, 1989. She was ninety-nine years old.—DARLENE CLARK HINE

MARY CHURCH **TERRELL**

1863–1954
Writer, lecturer, educator

During Mary Church Terrell's long and notable life, it seemed that there was little she didn't attempt in order to improve the social, economic, and political conditions of black Americans. Her excellent education and her travels abroad helped equip her for a career that began with teaching and continued with leadership positions in the Colored Women's League and the National Association of Colored Women. Terrell worked vigorously for women's suffrage and women's rights, particularly black women's rights.

Mary Eliza Church Terrell, born in Memphis, Tennessee, on September 23, 1863, was the eldest child of Louisa (Ayers) Church and Robert Reed Church, both former slaves. Terrell's early schooling was in Memphis, but schools for black children there were so inadequate that her parents decided to send her to the Antioch College Model School in Yellow Springs, Ohio, when she was about six years old. She was often the only black child among her classmates. She boarded with a kind black family, the Hunsters, and when she was older, divided her summers between homes. After two years at the Model School, Mary attended public school in Yellow Springs, then began eighth grade at the public high school in Oberlin, Ohio, graduating in 1879.

At Oberlin College, Terrell was one of several black students. One of the few integrated institutions of higher learning in the United States, it had first opened its doors to blacks in 1835. Most women at Oberlin chose the two-year ladies' curriculum, but Terrell decided to pursue the "gentleman's course"—four years of classical studies. She performed well in classes and was active in many campus activities, including Bible studies, the church choir, literary societies, and various recreational activities such as dancing. She graduated in 1884, and in 1929 she was named among the 100 most successful students to graduate from Oberlin.

Teaching career launched   When she accepted a job in Ohio at Wilberforce College in 1885, her father was livid and refused to speak to her for almost a year—he had strictly forbidden her to pursue any career. Although pained by the estrangement, Terrell nevertheless pursued her goal, teaching five different courses and acting as the college secretary. They did eventually reconcile, however, and he later relinquished all efforts to keep her from a professional career.

Following Wilberforce, Terrell accepted a position in the Latin department of the Colored High School in Washington, D.C. There she worked under the direction of Robert Heberton Terrell, who had graduated with honors from Harvard College in 1884. While she was working in the District of Columbia she completed the requirements for a master of arts degree from Oberlin, which she received in 1888. She spent two years—from 1888 to 1890—traveling and studying in France, Germany, Switzerland, Italy, and England, relishing the cultural opportunities that were open to her in Europe because of the freedom from racial tensions.

After she returned to the United States, she was soon convinced that she should marry Terrell, who had finished his law degree at Howard University while she was gone. She was momentarily tempted away from the wedding with an offer to work as the registrar at Oberlin College, a position of responsibility that she believed no other black person had ever held at any predominantly white institution of higher education. However, she decided to marry Terrell as scheduled in October 1891. Her father gave her an elaborate ceremony in Memphis that received favorable coverage in both white- and black-owned newspapers.

Because married women were legally barred from working as teachers, Terrell dedicated herself to managing her household. During the early years of her marriage, she was depressed by three miscarriages that she attributed to poor medical facilities for blacks and finally traveled to New York to be with her mother when she gave birth to a healthy baby girl, Phyllis (named after Phillis Wheatley, the black poet), in 1898. Later, in 1905, the Terrells adopted her brother Thomas's daughter, who had been named after her aunt, Terrell Church.

The primary event that drove Terrell back into the political and professional arena was the 1892 lynching of her lifelong friend from Memphis, Tom Moss, who was murdered by whites jealous of the success of his grocery store. Never had such blatant injustice struck Terrell so personally. She and Frederick Douglass were able to make an appointment with President Benjamin Harrison to urge him to speak out forcibly about such racial violence. Although the president gave them a sympathetic hearing, he made no public statement.

Club leader becomes orator   In the same year, 1892, Terrell assumed the leadership of a new group formed in the District of Columbia, the Colored Women's League. Three years later black women in Boston under the leadership of Josephine St. Pierre Ruffin formed the Federation of Afro-American Women. Margaret Murray Washington, the wife of Booker T. Washington, was elected president of the Boston organization. In 1896 the two groups, along with other black women's organizations, merged to become the National Association of Colored Women (NACW), and elected Terrell as the first president. Thus began one of the endeavors for which Terrell would become most well known—the fight for equal rights for women, especially black women. She was later elected to a second and a third term and then named honorary president for life. One of the women's early endeavors was to establish kindergartens and daycare for black working mothers—an effort that continues to this day. They also were concerned with equal rights for blacks, work opportunities for black women, female suffrage, and the criminal justice system. During her many years of work with the association, Terrell came into contact with most of the black women leaders, such as Mary McLeod Bethune and Nannie Helen Burroughs.

In 1898 she delivered a speech before the National American Women's Suffrage Association entitled "The Progress of Colored Women" and in 1900 gave a thirty-minute presentation before the same group entitled "Justice of Women Suffrage." In 1904 she spoke at the Berlin International Congress of Women, at which she was the only representative of the darker races of the world; she impressed audiences with her ability to speak French and German. In 1919 she addressed the delegates of the International League for Peace and Freedom, meeting in Zurich, and in 1937 she represented black American women at the World Fellowship of Faiths held in London. Meeting with women's groups both at home and abroad, Terrell had the opportunity to become acquainted with many of the leaders of suffrage organizations, including Susan B. Anthony, Alice Paul, Carrie Chapman Catt, and Jane Addams. In the years leading up to the passage of the Nineteenth Amendment, Terrell and her daughter marched with suffrage groups, picketed in front of the White House, and pointed out to some of their white counterparts the inconsistency of their lukewarm stance about suffrage for black women.

In addition to Terrell's ongoing work with both black and white women's organizations, she was recruited in the 1890s by the Slayton Lyceum Bureau (also called the Eastern Lyceum) to be a professional lecturer. She composed a number of speeches on subjects such as black women's progress since Emancipation, racial injustice, lynching, female suffrage, economics, crime, and various aspects of black history and culture. While preparing and practicing her addresses, Terrell became interested in publishing articles on a wide variety of social issues. Early in her career she wrote under the pen name Euphemia Kirk, but soon abandoned it and used her own name. Copies of many of her publications are among the Mary Church Terrell papers in the Manuscript Division of the Library of Congress.

In 1895 Terrell was appointed to the District of Columbia School Board, served until 1901, was reappointed in 1906, and served five more years until 1911. One of the first black women in the country to serve in such a capacity, she worked for equal treatment of black students and faculty members in Washington's segregated school system. She was also the first black woman to be elected to the presidency of the Bethel Literary and Historical Association in Washington, D.C., serving the 1892–93 term, and was one of the early members of the Association for the Study of Negro (later Afro-American) Life and History, which was organized in 1915.

Terrell vacillated in her feelings toward the Booker T. Washington philosophy of accommodation and industrial education, but after visiting Tuskegee Institute she decided that Washington was doing great work; thereafter she generally supported his strategies and programs. However, several years later, when the NAACP was organized in 1901, Terrell became a charter member of that organization at the invitation of W. E. B. Du Bois, Washington's intellectual rival, and cooperated with Du Bois's more militant political tactics.

In 1911 Terrell helped organize a birthday centenary celebration in memory of abolitionist Harriet Beecher Stowe, author of *Uncle Tom's Cabin*. A few years later, after the United States entered World War I, Terrell worked at the War Risk Insurance Bureau, where she soon became involved in a protest about the treatment of black women. Soon after the armistice, Terrell worked for a short time with the War Camp Community Service as the director of work among black women and girls. In 1920 she was asked by the Republican National Committee to be the supervisor of the work among black women in the east. Terrell continued to work with the Republican party, campaigning in 1929 for Ruth Hannah McCormick, who ran unsuccessfully for United States senator from Illinois. In 1932 Terrell served as an advisor to the Republican National Committee during the Hoover campaign. She remained a Republican until 1952, when she decided to vote for Democratic presidential candidate Adlai Stevenson.

Famous autobiographical work published   In 1940, the culmination of Terrell's writing career involved the publication of her autobiography, *A Colored Woman in a White World,* with a preface by H. G. Wells. In this work she traced her life from early childhood days, emphasizing her experiences growing up and living in white-dominated America. In 1949, Terrell was elected chair of the Coordinating Committee for the Enforcement of District of Columbia Anti-Discrimination Laws. These laws, forbidding discrimination in the district's public accommodations, had been passed in 1872 and 1873 and never repealed. Segregated public facilities had become the norm in the nation's capital, and blacks who attempted to integrate were fined or jailed. The coordinating committee, under Terrell's direction, decided to test the laws both in practice and in court. Terrell joined a small demonstration in the city targeting Thompson's Restaurant, which refused to serve the group. The group sued, and the case went all the way to the Supreme Court, where Terrell had the opportunity to testify on behalf of the cause of equal accommodations. The committee won the case in 1953, and the desegregation of the capital was set in motion.

One of Terrell's last major crusades was in behalf of Rosa Ingram, a black sharecropper from Georgia, who was sentenced to death along with her two sons for killing a white man who had assaulted them. Terrell agreed to head the National Committee to Free the Ingram Family. She led a delegation to the United Nations where she spoke in the Ingram's behalf and then traveled to Georgia in an unsuccessful attempt to win a pardon from the state governor. After a decade-long campaign, the Ingrams were finally freed in 1959.

Mary Church Terrell was an internationally known speaker and lecturer, a widely published writer, a member of numerous boards and associations, a founding member of a church in Washington, D.C., an active member of the Republican party, and a charter member of the NAACP. Terrell led and won the fight to desegregate Washington, D.C., a struggle that was finally resolved in 1953.

Terrell died on July 24, 1954, a scant two months after the Supreme Court's *Brown v. Board of Education* decision sounded the death knell of segregation in the United States. Her funeral was held at the Lincoln Temple Congregational Church, where she had been a member for many years. She was buried in Lincoln Memorial Cemetery.

Terrell had been honored many times during her long life for her accomplishments and had received honorary doctorates from Howard University, Wilberforce and Oberlin colleges, and numerous citations and plaques from the organizations she had worked with or supported. A Washington, D.C., school was named in her honor, and many black women's clubs are named in her memory.—DEBRA NEWMAN HAM

WILLIAM MONROE **TROTTER**

1872–1934

Journalist, entrepreneur, civil rights activist

An elite militant integrationist and one of America's most important black spokesmen of the early twentieth

century, William Monroe Trotter was a diligent race man who has been called the precursor of the civil rights movement of the 1960s. Most of his significant work was done before he was forty years old. He was

active in a number of local groups, most of which were forums for militant race activities. A journalist as

well, Trotter was a founder of The Guardian, *an organ dedicated to equal rights for black Americans.*

William Monroe Trotter was born on April 7, 1872 near Chillocothe, Ohio, to James Monroe Trotter and Virginia Isaacs Trotter. His parents moved to Boston when he was seven months old. Of the Trotter's three children—the other two were Maude (b. 1874) and Bessie (b. 1883)—Monroe was the only son and the favored child. He grew up in suburban Hyde Park, which until the 1890s was predominantly white.

His father, a demanding patriarch, was a race man as well and may have steered his son to become a career protest leader. By age five, Monroe Trotter, as he was known throughout life, knew that race work would be an important part of his future. Although surrounded by whites in the community and at work, James Trotter was highly race-conscious. He had been a lieutenant in the Civil War and recorder of deeds (1897–98) for the federal government. In Boston he worked in musical promotions, as an agent for the local telephone company, and had a real estate business. He had an interest in politics as well. In 1878 his noted work *Music and Some Highly Musical People* was published; it was a tribute to black musicians and became a classic. Monroe Trotter was a good student and led his class academically both in Hyde Park Grammar School and Hyde Park High School. He was the only black in his high school class and was elected president of his senior class. Influenced by his mother, he had considered becoming a minister, received some training by the pastor of the white First Baptist Church of Hyde Park, but respected his father's strong dislike for his religious tendency and gave up the idea. In James Trotter's view, as a black minister his son would not fight the world's race problems but serve a segregated congregation instead.

Trotter worked as a shipping clerk in Boston after graduating from high school. He entered Harvard University in 1891. James Trotter's death in February 1892 brought an interlude of sorrow to Monroe Trotter and also put him in the role as head of the household. At Harvard, however, he won scholarships for the next three years and worked during summer months to supplement his income. He was active in the church, played tennis, and rode his bicycle around Cambridge and Boston. Although he steered clear of frivolous college activities, he did belong to the Wendell Phillips Club, the YMCA, and the Prohibition Club. He was an organizer and president of the Total Abstinence League for undergraduates. He was a serious student who studied hard and took extra courses as well. He ranked third in his freshman class and never lower than eighth in his college career. During his junior year Trotter became the first black in the university's history elected to Phi Beta Kappa. He graduated in June 1894 with an A.B. degree magna cum laude.

Already one of Boston's young luminaries in the black society—now more so with his Harvard degree—Trotter was a member of the Boston Bachelors as well as the Omar Khayyam Circle. The latter was an exclusive literary group for blacks that met at the home of Maria Baldwin, schoolteacher in Cambridge.

Neither his Harvard degree, academic record, nor exclusive background could combat the evils of racial discrimination that he soon knew. Trotter preferred a business career in real estate but in the interim worked as a clerk for an industrial fair. Until he opened his own business in 1899 as insurance agent and mortgage negotiator for mostly white clients, he worked variously as a shipping clerk for a Boston bookseller, indexing clerk for the

Boston Book Company, statistical clerk for a genealogist, and as employee for Holbrook and Company, a Boston real estate firm.

On June 27, 1899, Trotter married the petite, vivacious, blue-eyed blond African American Geraldine Louise Pindell, known as "Deenie," of Boston, who had a family background of racial militancy. They had known each other since childhood and dated while Trotter was at Harvard. They had no children and never wanted any.

By now Trotter dabbled in politics. He worked for the Republican and municipal candidates and was alternate delegate from his ward at several political conventions. He volunteered as assistant registrar of voters in Boston. Conditions for blacks in the South had worsened and the attitude of southern whites toward blacks was spreading north. Although race leader and educator Booker T. Washington rose to prominence, his policies and public statements were too moderate and conciliatory for some blacks. By the turn of the century, Trotter decided that it was time for him to address matters of race in another style.

Feuds with Booker T. Washington   The Boston Literary and Historical Society that Trotter and other black elites organized in March 1901, with Archibald Grimké—a Trotterite at the time—as president, provided a forum for them to discuss race matters. Trotter was also one of three blacks who founded a weekly newspaper in Boston, *The Guardian.* The others were William H. Scott, a minister and leader of the Massachusetts Radical Protective Association of which Trotter was a member, and George W. Forbes, an outspoken man who in the 1890s worked on another Boston newspaper. *The Guardian,* which Trotter financed, was first published on November 9, 1901, and appeared every Saturday. It was not designed to turn a profit but to address the needs and aspirations of black America and was the mouthpiece through which the anti-Washingtonites spoke. It was, at the time, the only channel for publicizing national black agitation.

While Trotter and Washington were from vastly different backgrounds—Trotter was born free while Washington was born a slave—and disagreed on racial policy—Trotter was a militant while Washington was an accommodationist—they both agreed that education for blacks was essential. Trotter argued for the long-range implications of education, that education was needed to prove the intellectual ability of the race, and that blacks should have access to the highest form of education. Washington, however, stressed the immediate advantages of education and believed in industrial training as a route to a good job. Washington saw Trotter as corrupt; Trotter saw Washington as one who sought power, wanted to be a political leader, and could not tolerate criticism of his approach to black progress.

Trotter's camp, who called themselves "radicals," were talented, elitist, and generally better educated than Washington's followers, who were called "Bookerites." There were prominent blacks on both sides. At that time, however, race men W. E. B. Du Bois and Kelly Miller had not chosen between the two groups; Reverdy Ransom, a minister, was anti-Washington. On the other hand, *New York Age* editor T. Thomas Fortune, Boston lawyer and later assistant district attorney in Boston, and James Carroll Napier, Nashville businessman and later register of the U.S. treasury, were Bookerites. Agitation between the camps continued and came to a head on July 30, 1903. Washington spoke to a crowd at Columbus Avenue African Methodist Episcopal Church, sponsored by the local branch of the National Negro Business League. As Trotter stood on a chair and presented a list of race questions to Washington, the police escorted him and his sister, Maude Trotter, from the church and arrested them;

their mother bailed them out. Charges against Maude Trotter were later dropped; Monroe Trotter was tried, convicted, and fined twenty-five dollars; he also served a thirty-day jail sentence. While Trotter was imprisoned, his friends and his wife, Deenie Trotter, continued *The Guardian.* The church incident came to be known as "The Boston Riot." The Trotter and Washington camps became even more hostile and Forbes left the paper, only to be replaced by Du Bois.

Trotter continued to affiliate with change groups. After the riot he founded the Boston Suffrage League in 1903. In April 1904 the league sponsored a protest meeting at Faneuil Hall and planned a convention in New England that fall. In Providence that October, blacks from Massachusetts, Connecticut, and Rhode Island formed the New England Suffrage League and elected Trotter president. In addition to suffrage activities, the group endorsed anti-lynching legislation, federal aid to southern schools, integrated seating on interstate carriers, and other issues.

Niagara movement and the NAACP The Washington camp enjoyed the success of the Afro-American Council and the National Negro Business League; both organizations contributed to Washington's power. Trotter knew that there was a need for radical mobilization among his own camp. He and his followers then organized the National Negro Suffrage League in 1904 and elected a Richmond lawyer, James H. Hayes, president. Meanwhile, in 1905 Du Bois invited twenty-nine blacks from all over the country—all anti-Bookerites—to a small hotel in Fort Erie, on the Canadian side of Niagara Falls, to a conference in support of freedom and growth of the black race. They formed the Niagara Movement with Du Bois serving as general secretary and Trotter head of the Press and Public Opinion Committee. Du Bois and Trotter drafted a "Declaration of Principles," a radical document that the members endorsed. Although he had supported women's suffrage early in 1906, when Du Bois organized a women's auxiliary to the movement, Trotter initially opposed the group, but later relented. Deenie Trotter then joined. The Trotters' affiliation lasted only until 1907 when they both resigned from the movement. The movement faced other problems, however, and in 1909 merged with the National Association for the Advancement of Colored People (NAACP). Trotter attended the founding conference in New York, and had limited contact with the organization for a few years, then severed his relationship, having become estranged from the local leadership and at odds with the two early NAACP leaders, Oswald Garrison Villard and Du Bois. He was also unable to accept the fact that whites provided both leadership and financial support to the organization.

In the meantime, Trotter was a founder of the National Equal Rights League (NERL) in 1908 and worked through the organization for a number of years to agitate for black rights. Those who could not accept the NAACP had as an alternative the NERL.

By 1912 Trotter and Du Bois supported Woodrow Wilson for president but found him less supportive of blacks than they envisioned. Among other actions, Wilson rejected black advisors, supported segregationist policies in federal office buildings, and kept blacks out of key civil service positions. In protest, Trotter led a delegation to the White House to meet with Wilson and he and the president engaged in a heated argument for forty-five minutes, until Wilson ordered the group to leave. The incident received public notice through such newspapers as the *New York Times,* the *Boston Evening Transcript,* and the black *New York*

Age. In the *Age,* James Weldon Johnson praised Trotter for taking a stance but condemned the way he did it.

Protests racial film   D. W. Griffith's viciously racist film, *The Birth of a Nation,* was shown at the White House in February 1915 by arrangement of Thomas Dixon, who wrote the book on which the film was based. Although President Wilson praised the film, Trotter vehemently protested it, especially when it was to be shown at Boston's Tremont Theatre. Trotter and ten others were arrested for attempting to ban the Boston showing, which Trotter called a rebel play. Though banned in Chicago, St. Louis, all of Ohio, and areas in Massachusetts, the film still ran in various theaters in Boston for six and a half months. When attempts were made to return the film to Boston in spring 1921, Trotter again gathered his forces, including the Knights of Columbus and the NAACP, and was instrumental in having the censorship law affecting moving pictures passed in Massachusetts. This time he was successful in banning the film.

While in 1901 Trotter owned, through inheritance, property all over Boston, by 1908 he had run into financial difficulty. Advertisers in his paper owed him money that he was unable to collect. He put a second mortgage on his Dorchester home where he and Deenie Trotter had lived, and the next year sold his last two houses. He worked long hours and took no vacation. Deenie did all she could to handle the bookkeeping, subscriptions, and other newspaper matters. When the influenza epidemic ravaged the nation in fall 1918, she succumbed to it on October 8, when she was barely forty-six. Trotter concentrated on *The Guardian* after that and for several years continued to publish her photograph in the paper. Still, without his wife, the paper lost its former intellectual caliber and literary touch. His sister, Maude Trotter Steward, took over for him when he was out of town.

He turned back to the Republicans and supported their presidential candidate, Warren G. Harding. On race matters, Trotter clung to his old ideas, concentrated his efforts in the Boston area, and in time was left in the dust of the new black leaders and their activities. He continued to work with the NERL but apparently did not fully embrace the increasingly powerful NAACP. He and the NERL rejected Marcus Garvey and his work. He deplored Garvey's references to African heritage and use of the term "Negro." Instead, Trotter always used "Colored American," "Colored people," or "Afro-American." After 1919 he refused to use "Negro" in *The Guardian*'s editorials. Trotter also remained outside the cultural activities of blacks that occurred as the Harlem Renaissance.

In his last years Trotter continued his attempt to collect from his advertisers. He even resorted to dances, picnics, and other benefits to raise money for *The Guardian.* A few of his friends did contribute to the paper.

In 1934, financial difficulty forced Trotter to share an apartment with benefactor Mary Gibson and her son. His health was also deteriorating. In the early morning of his sixty-second birthday, unable to sleep, he went to the roof of the building where his family believed he lost his balance and fell to his death; some sources claim his death on April 7, 1934, was an apparent suicide.

Although at times Trotter's historical significance has been obscured, he was an important figure in the first third of this century, consistently using protest to remove barriers to racial integration.—JESSIE CARNEY SMITH

ROSINA **TUCKER**

1881–1987

Labor organizer, social and civil rights activist, educator

As founder and secretary-treasurer of the International Ladies' Auxiliary and a major force in the establishment of its parent organization, the Brotherhood of Sleeping Car Porters, Rosina Tucker helped to improve the economic fortunes of large numbers of black people in the United States and Canada. She organized porters' wives in activities to support the auxiliary and the union, and their efforts helped ensure that porters received adequate pay, decent working conditions, and new benefits. The brotherhood also focused on battling racism and, with Tucker's assistance, organized civil rights marches in 1941 and 1963.

Rosina Budd Harvey Corrothers Tucker, one of nine children, was born on November 4, 1881, in northwest Washington, D.C. Her parents, Lee Roy and Henrietta Harvey, had been slaves in Virginia before they relocated to Washington after their emancipation.

Although raised as a slave, Lee Roy Harvey taught himself to read and write. As a freeman he worked as a shoemaker and surrounded himself with the books he loved, developing a particular affection for history books. Harvey was protective of his children and prevented them from working as service employees or as house servants.

Tucker had pleasant memories of her early childhood, which was marked by musical training and her father's teachings. In 1897, while still in her junior year of high school, Tucker visited an aunt in Yonkers, New York, and met James D. Corrothers, a guest minister. A graduate of Northwestern University, Corrothers became known as a poet and writer of short stories, and his sketches on black humor and folklore garnered special attention.

Rosina Harvey and James Corrothers married on December 2, 1899. The couple had one son, Henry Harvey Corrothers, who later became a fine athlete and a physical education instructor at Wilberforce University. Rosina and James Corrothers also raised a son from his previous marriage.

After marrying, the couple first lived in New York City and then in Michigan. James Corrothers continued to practice his ministry and to write and publish poetry. Tucker occupied herself by teaching music to some thirty students. The family moved to Washington, D.C., in 1904, when James Corrothers took a position with the National Baptist Convention. Tucker, meanwhile, became the organist for Liberty Baptist Church in the Foggy Bottom section of the District. Two years later James Corrothers became pastor of the First Baptist Church in Lexington, Virginia. During their years in Lexington, First Baptist worship services were often spiced with James's storytelling and poetry reading and Tucker's classical piano pieces. At this time she composed "The Rio Grande Waltz."

After James Corrothers died in 1917, Tucker returned to Washington, D.C., where she worked as a file clerk with the federal government and became involved in civic activities. There she met Berthea J. Tucker, known as B. J., who worked as a Pullman car porter. They married on Thanksgiving eve in 1918 and moved into a two-story brick house near Gallaudet College. She lived at the house for the rest of her life.

Porter's union established   In the 1920s the Pullman Company had a virtual monopoly on railroad sleeping-car facilities throughout the United States. The company was a major employer of black men, and those who had jobs as Pullman porters were held in considerable esteem in the black community. Porters, whose responsibilities included working the sleeping coaches, making beds, and shining shoes, collected hefty tips. "To be a Pullman porter in those days meant respect, prestige, social status and prominence," recalled Tucker in an interview. Nonetheless, porters were poorly paid, and charges for any damage to Pullman equipment were deducted from their small salaries. They were required to work long hours without overtime pay, sometimes working up to 400 hours a month with "dead-heading" and "doubling out" responsibilities. In the absence of a union to protect the men's rights, the company took full advantage of its black labor force.

In 1909 the porters formulated their grievances and made their first efforts to organize. While the attempt was unsuccessful, the Pullman Company made small gestures to address some of the men's concerns. Driven by the continued abuse of the black Pullman workers, Ashley Totten, a militant New York porter, made a bold move in 1925. He engaged A. Philip Randolph, a radical journalist and social theoretician who was later prominent in the civil rights movement, to organize a porters' union. On August 25 of that year, the Brotherhood of Sleeping Car Porters was launched and Randolph began his long tenure as president. The union also established the Women's Economic Council, an organization through which women could work for the rights of the brotherhood. To protect the workers who could be fired for their connection with the union and their criticisms of the Pullman Company, Randolph handled all aspects of the first meeting himself. The next day some 200 porters came to his office, the brotherhood's headquarters, to join the union.

Randolph and Totten tried to establish a meeting with porters and their wives in Washington, D.C., but many porters were reluctant to join for fear of losing their jobs. B. J. joined the union immediately—in time he became a member of the executive board—and he and Tucker subsequently took up the union's cause in the District.

The long hours demanded of porters left them little time for union activities. As a result, their wives tackled much of the union's work themselves, even holding secret meetings so that the men's employment would not be threatened. When Tucker met with Randolph and Totten, they did so in secrecy so that informers would be unable to report on the sessions to the company. To organize unions in the South, Tucker visited the homes of some 300 porters who lived in the Washington area, distributed literature, discussed the organization with prospective members and their wives, and collected dues.

International Ladies' Auxiliary formed   The next step for Tucker was to organize the local Ladies' Auxiliary. From the very beginning, the women raised a great deal of money by hosting parties, dances, dinners, and other activities. Tucker called upon her church and social service background to help families experiencing illnesses and other difficulties, including loss of employment.

In time the Pullman Company learned about Tucker's work on behalf of the fledgling union. They fired her husband in retribution, an action that aroused her anger. She marched into the company's offices and demanded to see her husband's supervisor. She strolled triumphantly out of his office several minutes later. B. J. Tucker was rehired.

The 1937 agreement between the porters and the Pullman Company marked the first formal agreement between a union of black workers and a major American corporation. The next year Tucker attended the union's national convention in Chicago and chaired the Constitution and Rules Committee. Immediately after the brotherhood's convention, the International Ladies' Auxiliary was established.

Over the years, the Brotherhood of Sleeping Car Porters and the Ladies' Auxiliary became more powerful. Through its official presence in the House of Labor, a speaking platform for the workers, the union was able to focus on the evils of racism, the need for civil rights legislation, the protection of minority voting rights, and the preservation of dignity on the job. The auxiliary remained a consistent part of the effort.

Some sources report that, although the brotherhood is generally given credit for the work, Tucker helped the group organize its first March on Washington, scheduled to occur in 1941. The march was called off when A. Philip Randolph convinced President Franklin D. Roosevelt to issue Executive Order 8802, which addressed fair employment practices and discrimination in government offices and defense plants. In 1963, again with Tucker's assistance, Randolph and the brotherhood organized another March on Washington. As the years passed, however, technological advances and declining demand for rail passenger service undermined the union. In 1978 the Brotherhood of Sleeping Car Porters merged with the Brotherhood of Railway and Airline Clerks.

In 1981 an award-winning documentary, *Miles of Smiles, Years of Struggle,* was released. The film recounted the story of the work of the porter's union and the auxiliary, as well as Tucker's pivotal role in their creation. The documentary even included footage of Tucker singing "Marching Together," which she wrote in 1939 in honor of the Pullman porters.

Unfaltering devotion to social and civil rights   Tucker's interest in civil rights never wavered. Over the years Tucker testified before Senate and House committees on education, day care, labor, and voting rights for the District. She lobbied Congress for legislation on labor and education and helped organize unions for laundry workers and domestics. When she was 102 years old, she testified before a Senate Labor and Human Resources subcommittee on aging. In 1986, when she was 104 years old, Tucker was still giving lectures across the country. She also completed a book-length manuscript about her life entitled *Life As I Have Lived It.*

Rosina Tucker was honored on many occasions for her union work and her civil rights leadership. Organizations recognizing her achievements included the Leadership Conference on Civil Rights, the National Coalition of 100 Black Women, the Coalition of Labor Union Women, and the District of Columbia Hall of Fame.

Even in her latter years Tucker remained an iron-willed, robust, and witty personality, and a woman who appreciated the life she led and her part in improving the status of black people. As she indicated in her autobiography, "today is my day as it is your day. Although I live far removed from the time I was born I do not feel that my heart should dwell in the past. It is in the future. Each day for over a century added to another has culminated in growth that has led to my present experience and has made the person I am today and will be tomorrow. . . . While I live let not my life be in vain. And when I depart may there be remembrance of me and my life as I have lived it." Rosina Tucker died on March 3, 1987, at the age of 105.—JESSIE CARNEY SMITH

MELVIN **VAN PEEBLES**

1932–

Film director, writer, actor, composer, stock market trader

Melvin Van Peebles broke barriers and stereotypes with his films, books, and music, creating works with a radical, political, or, as he was quoted in Variety, *"sociological edge," raising awareness of racial prejudice and societal problems among all groups. He is considered a Renaissance man and contemporary jack-of-all-trades who is never at a loss when faced with the need to learn or to create another direction. His film* Sweetback *earned him recognition as the "godfather of independent black film." He is also called "the grandfather of rap" for his musical compositions with talk-singing.*

Melvin Van Peebles was born on August 21, 1932, in Chicago to Marion Van Peebles and Edwina Griffin. Marion Van Peebles was a hard worker from Georgia who taught himself to read. Becoming a small businessman in Chicago, he was able to send son Melvin away to college after he graduated from Thornton Township High School in 1949. Van Peebles graduated with a degree in literature from Ohio Wesleyan in Delaware, Ohio. A partial scholarship with the ROTC led, thirteen days after graduation, to three and a half years as an officer in the air force. The young lieutenant returned to civilian life, discovering his expertise as radar operator, bombardier, and navigator on a jet bomber powerless in gaining work with civilian airlines who still refused to hire minorities. Van Peebles met his wife Maria in California and moved to Mexico. Their first son, Mario, was born in 1957. Growing tired after a few months of the confinement of painting portraits for a living, the family returned to settle in San Francisco where Van Peebles found a new challenge while driving cable cars. Heeding the inquiries of patrons eager to learn more about the cable cars, he wrote *The Big Heart,* a sentimental pictorial book on cable cars, in 1957. In that same year, Van Peebles also decided to expand in another direction, films. His first feature movie turned into three eleven-minute shorts, a borrow-the-camera, listen-to-the-friend, learn-on-the-way project. Hollywood rejected the films, while Van Peebles rejected their offer of an elevator or dancing job.

Having been a celestial navigator and having studied radar, physics, and astronomy in the service, Van Peebles decided to expand those interests by working toward a Ph.D. in astronomy in Amsterdam. He moved his family by way of a ship from New York to Amsterdam. In Amsterdam, he studied with the Dutch National Theatre and toured as an actor in Brendan Behan's play *The Hostage.* A letter from Cinémathèque, telling him he should be making films and inviting him to Paris, interrupted his new life. He accepted the invitation and the red

Melvin Van Peebles.

carpet treatment but was not offered a job, so once again he taught himself a new language to continue his writing.

The family had increased to include a daughter, Megan, before the Van Peebles moved to Amsterdam. Their second son, Melvin, was born in Paris. Van Peebles wrote in French and English, directed films, and gained awards that brought him recognition in the United States and a return to this country.

Not speaking French inititally, nor having any friends in Paris, Van Peebles did whatever he could in Paris to earn a living. His inquisitiveness gained him work as a crime reporter, and finally he became editor of *Fara Kiri*, France's version of *Mad* magazine. Having learned that a French writer could have a film director's card, he wrote five novels in French. His first book, *Un Ours pour le F.B.I.* (1964), *A Bear for the F.B.I.* (translated in 1968), tells about racial problems in the life of a middle-class American black. Seeking American writers, an American literary agent found Van Peebles and asked him to write a black book with rage. In response, he wrote *Un American en enfer* (1965), *The True American* (1976), about George Abraham Carver, a black prisoner accidentally killed by falling rocks. In hell, Carver and other blacks are treated well, causing greater hell to the white residents there. The agent wouldn't publish it due to its subject matter; however, the book was finally published in the United States in 1976. He wrote a collection of short stories, *Le Chinois du XIV* (1966) and two short novels, *La Fete a Harlem* (1967) and *La Permission* (1967). Now qualified for a French director's card, Van Peebles received financial assistance from the French Ministry and a private citizen, which allowed him to make his first feature film, *La Permission* or *The Story of a Three-Day Pass,* a bittersweet story of a black soldier's harassment from his army buddies for his affair with a French woman, which eventually took him back to the United States.

Becomes film director   Van Peebles brought *The Story of a Three-Day Pass* to the 1967 San Francisco Film Festival as the delegate of France. The film won Critic's Choice award for best film, finally opening the door in the United States for a black film director. Van Peebles was receiving wide press and was touted as a filmmaker with an edge. Based on the success of *The Story of a Three-Day Pass*, Columbia hired Van Peebles to direct and write the score for *Watermelon Man* (1970), a humorous tale of a bigoted white insurance agent who wakes one morning to find that he's black. Van Peebles became the second African American to direct a film for a major Hollywood studio. The film received mediocre reviews and made little money.

Preferring the freedom from studio control for making his own choices of material and messages, Van Peebles found his own financing for his next film, *Sweet Sweetback's Baadasssss Song* (1971, Yeah, Inc.). *Sweetback* paved the way for blaxploitation films with super stud-type heroes portraying action and violence against the establishment, allowing black urban audiences to fantasize about power and retribution. Van Peebles wrote the script and music, and produced, directed, and starred in *Sweet Sweetback's Baadasssss Song,* which he made in three weeks with nonunion help. Because of its inflammatory content, the film recieved no publicity or airplay. To counter his lack of advertising, Van Peebles resorted to drastic measures, which eventually paid off. He passed out leaflets on street corners, promoting the film as "Rated X by an All-White Jury," and he dedicated it to "All the Brothers and Sisters who have had enough of The Man." Audiences advertised it by word of mouth, and their attendance placed the film on *Variety*'s list of moneymakers. Zimmerman notes in *Newsweek* that the "episode in the nightclub, as Sweetback, dressed in drag, makes love to a black woman amid the chuckling applause of a predominantly white audience, is one of the most effective metaphors of black degradation ever filmed . . . one man, telling it like he sees it, his dream of liberation unadulterated by studio pressures or commercial considerations." The plot involves Sweetback, a pimp, who chooses to avenge the beating of a youth by two white policemen. He turns revolutionary, stomps the policemen unconscious, and runs, eventually, to his freedom in Mexico. It showed the audience a black who fought the Man and won. Eventually *Sweetback* took in $10,000,000, becoming one of the highest-grossing independent films of its day.

After the success and controversy over *Sweetback,* Van Peebles went into an idle stage in filmmaking, but his attention and achievements went toward other areas such as music and the theater.

Brer Soul, Van Peebles's first album, uses minimalist music and monotone talk-singing to tell stories of black street life. On September 26, 1968, A&M released the album featuring metered musical monologues by DJ King Stitt, U Roy, and the Last Poets. In addition, Gil Scott-Heron came along to further develop what is referred to as rap. In *Billboard* Van Peebles explained the inspiration for the album:

> When I was growing up in the streets of Chicago, a brer was a bro, a homeboy. The idea of doing a record employing the Brer Soul character arose back in 1967, when I returned to this country after living for several years in Holland and France. From abroad I knew the ferment of the civil rights movement, but I was struck when I got back here that almost none of the black popular or protest music mirrored the black experience *per se.*

The words are accompanied with funky jazz music. "In each song, I wanted to describe a part of life rarely seen," says Van Peebles. This desire to reproduce less visible parts of life, ghetto or street life, characterizes Van Peebles's focus in his creative efforts. He later directed and supervised the editing of *Funky Beat* (Artista Records), a music video by rap group Whodini, and composed the music and lyrics for *The Apple Stretching*. *Ghetto Gothic* (1995), his ninth album, portrays the now mellowed Van Peebles.

Three Broadway plays show Van Peebles's creativity, ingenuity, and expertise. He wrote the books, music, and lyrics and produced and directed *Ain't Supposed to Die a Natural Death* (1971), which portrays street life, including frank and controversial discussions of lesbians and prostitution, and adapts the recordings from *Brer Soul*. Black celebrities increased attendance and the life of the play, which performed 325 times. *Don't Play Us Cheap* (1972) is a comedy about Harlem life, which he adapted for film in 1973, using his own company, Yeah, Inc. Together, the plays garnered eleven Tony nominations and a featured cover story in the *New York Times Magazine Section.* In 1973 Van Peebles toured the United States with his one-man show *Out There by Your Lonesome.* Van Peebles's third Broadway play, *Waltz of the Stork,* came out in 1982. He and son Mario both acted in the play. He also did off-Broadway plays *Champeen* (1979) and *Kickin' the Science* (1992).

Turning to television, Van Peebles wrote two scripts that were produced as films for NBC. *Just an Old Sweet Song* came out in 1976. This film was a mild-tempered family drama which countered Van Peebles's earlier film work. He then wrote the teleplay *Sophisticated Gents,* filmed in 1979, about nine boyhood friends that are members of a black athletic team, who reunite after twenty-five years to honor their old coach and to discuss how their lives have been affected by their race. It was a topic not comfortably shown on the small tube, but Van Peebles was mild in inserting his anti-bourgois ideas into this acclaimed drama.

To even counter his radical, folk-hero stance from the early 1970s, Van Peebles took a 180 degree turn in his career. In 1985, Van Peebles worked on the American Stock Exchange for three years, becoming their only African American trader. His experiences in option trading led to a series of weekly television commentaries in New York and to writing a how-to book, *Bold Money: A New Way to Play the Options Market* (1986), which tells about trading in easy-to-understand language. This was followed by *Bold Money: How to Get Rich in the Options Market* (1987).

Father and son work together   During the late 1980s and early 1990s, Van Peebles made a return to film making with the help of his son, Mario Van Peebles, who is also a noted filmmaker and actor. Mario made his screen debut in *Sweet Sweetback's Baadasssss Song*. The two worked together in a small film, *Identity Crisis (1990)*, a comedy about a gay French couturier popping in and out of a black rapper's body. The elder Van Peebles produced and directed the film. In 1993 Van Peebles acted in the film *Posse*, an all-black Western written by Mario Van Peebles. Later they collaborated on *Panther*. Portraying the earlier rage of *Sweetback,* the film retold the political activities of the 1960s and early 1970s. Van Peebles wrote, produced, acted in, and coedited *Panther,* directed by son Mario. Quoted by Karen G. Bates in *Essence*, Van Peebles points out that "Nothing has changed! The gravity then is parallel with the gravity of our situation now." Mario Van Peebles adds:

> One of the biggest things Dad brought to this film was the whole parallel between the then and now of drugs and alcohol being brought into the Black community. These same communities that were insisting on power to the people have been flooded with alcohol and drugs; they've been medicated. And the gangs have inherited the bravado of what might have been Panther life—but without the ideology to understand what their actions are.

Van Peebles recently appeared in the television remake of *Stephen King's The Shining* (1997) on ABC.

Van Peebles is a member of the Directors Guild of America and the French Directors Guild. He was awarded first prize from the Belgium Festival for *Don't Play Us Cheap*. Hofstra University awarded him an honorary doctorate in humane letters in December 1994.

Van Peebles is a rebel who follows his own rules and does what he pleases. His oft-repeated saying, "The golden rule is that he who has the gold makes the rules," has dictated Van Peebles's preference for financing his own work, allowing him to produce that which is most important, right, and necessary to him. As a film folk hero, he has led the way for independent African American cinema. "Grandfather of rap" and "godfather of modern Black Cinema," Van Peebles continues to write, publish, direct, act, and do the unexpected.— CLAIRE A. TAFT

MADAME C. J. **WALKER**
1867–1919
Entrepreneur, philanthropist

Among the early entrepreneurs of the twentieth century, no one is more intriguing than the black beauty culture genius Madame C. J. Walker—not only because of her development of the "hot" comb but because of her remarkable business acumen. A black woman with one dollar and fifty cents in her pocket in 1904, Walker was one of the first black women in the United States to become a millionaire through her own efforts. Walker burst on the scene in 1904 and changed the way business people marketed their products. She also revolutionized the methods for treating black hair.

Sarah Breedlove McWilliams Walker, later known as Madame C. J. Walker, was born in 1867 in Louisiana. Born to Owen and Minerva Breedlove, indigent former slaves, Walker lived in a dilapidated shack with her parents on the Burney family plantation in Delta, Louisiana, on the Mississippi River. Her parents worked as sharecroppers on the plantation until their deaths. As a child and an adult, Walker toiled in the cotton fields with other black laborers.

During the Reconstruction era, 1865–1898, Walker could not have lived in a more hostile environment. Although blacks had moved from being slaves to being sharecroppers, nothing on the plantation had changed. Walker experienced extreme poverty in all aspects of her daily life. The windowless shack in which she lived had one door, no water, no toilet, and a dirt floor. She and other family members slept on the ground.

After her parents died during her childhood, Walker moved to Mississippi with her married sister Louvenia, at which time she experienced domestic violence and abuse. Insensitive and tyrannical, her brother-in-law showered only cruelty on seven-year-old Sarah. She eventually moved away and married Moses McWilliams at the age of fourteen. In 1885, she had a daughter, Lelia. Two years later when Sarah McWilliams was twenty years old, it is said that her husband was killed by a lynch mob.

Her difficulties continued to mount as she became a single parent with a two-year-old child to rear. Vicksburg, Mississippi, was not an ideal place for blacks. Since they had the best chance for employment and education in urban areas, Walker moved to St. Louis, Missouri, where she had relatives, found work as a cook and a laundress, and supported her daughter with her meager earnings. Although she was unable to read and write at the time, she sent her daughter, Lelia Walker, not only to school but to Knoxville College, a private black college located in Knoxville, Tennessee. As an uneducated black, Walker was proud of this accomplishment.

Sarah Walker Finds Her System   Poverty continued to haunt Walker. At the same time she began to experience baldness due to the stressful wrap and twist method then used to straighten the hair of blacks. With intimate knowledge of hair loss, agony, and the inconvenience of black hair care, Walker set out to address the problems black women faced with their hair. Using patent medicines of the day and her own secret ingredients (supposedly sulfur), she stopped her own hair loss. She was amazed how quickly her hair grew back. Her friends, using the products, were intrigued by her efforts and became enthusiastic customers. According to A'Lelia Bundles in *Ms.* magazine, Walker said her formula came to her in a dream after she had prayed to God to save her hair:

> He answered my prayer, for one night I had a dream, and in that dream a big black man appeared to me and told me what to mix up for my hair. Some of the remedy was grown in Africa, but I sent for it, mixed it, put it on my scalp, and in a few weeks my hair was coming in faster than it had ever fallen out. I tried it on my friends; it helped them. I made up my mind to begin to sell it.

Black people needed methods for handling hair since many didn't have running water and supplies and equipment did not exist for them. Bringing water from outdoors and placing the body in awkward positions to shampoo the hair, Walker and other black women found taking care of their hair was one more arduous task to deal with. Walker went on to develop the hot comb and her Wonderful Hair Grower. Faced with the prospect of domestic and laundry work for life, she took her chance with destiny and became a successful businesswoman.

Walker Establishes a Hair Preparations Company   Walker soon moved to Denver, Colorado, to live with her sister-in-law and her four nieces. With one dollar and fifty cents, she began a hair preparations company. She gradually moved away from working as a domestic to manufacturing hair products. Encouraged by the success of her formula on the hair of other black women, she, her daughter, her sister-in-law, and her nieces began to fill jars with the hair preparations in the attic of their home. Six months after her arrival in Denver, she married C. J. Walker, a newspaper man with knowledge of advertising and mail order procedures, which she used successfully.

Although the business gradually became successful, she experienced incompatible differences with her husband, who failed to share the dream for the company she envisioned. Following the dissolution of her marriage, she continued to use the initials of his name. At the time whites called all black women by their first names no matter who they were, so black women frequently kept their first names a secret, if possible. Hence, she is referred to as Madame C. J. Walker rather than Sarah Breedlove Walker.

Like most inventors, no one is totally original, for the inventor responds to a situation, improves upon it, and draws from the environment around him or her. Walker was not the first to organize a hair preparations company; Annie N. Turnbo Malone with her Poro Company and "Wonderful Hair Grower" preceded her in 1900. Walker was first an agent for Malone and later her rival in the beauty empire business. Walker was also not the first to heat a comb to straighten hair, since the French Jews pressed hair in the early eighteenth century. Nor was she the first to send products through the mail, for many white companies had used this strategy with much success. However, she was the first woman to organize supplies for black hair preparations, develop a steel comb with teeth spaced to comb the strands, place the comb on a hot stove, send the products through the mail, organize door-to-door agents, and develop her own beauty school. From a combination of these ideas she nursed her company and it grew.

In spite of her early struggles as a single parent, her daughter, Lelia Walker, became her chief asset in the business. Working side by side with her mother, she assisted in the product manufacturing, helped with business decisions, trained the students in the Walker method, and traveled around the country to sell the products. In 1906, Walker placed her daughter in charge of the mail-order operation while she continued to introduce the products

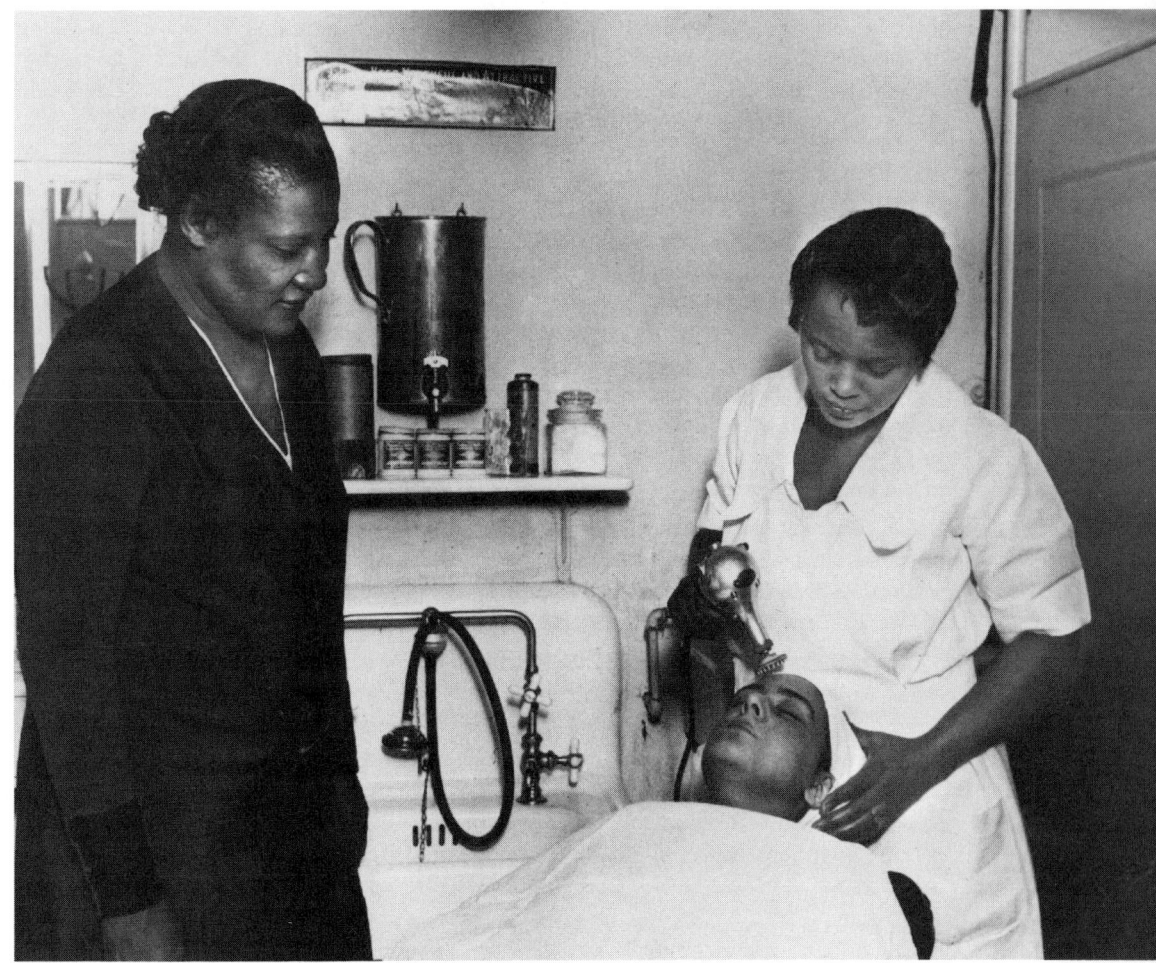

Lelia Walker, Madame C. J. Walker's daughter, supervises a facial in one of Madame Walker's many beauty parlors during the 1930s.

in different parts of the South and East. By 1908 mother and daughter moved to Pittsburgh, Pennsylvania, and set up a beauty school, Lelia College, to train cosmetologists in the Walker method. Lelia Walker handled the manufacture of the hair products as well as the beauty school, while Madame Walker continued to sell the products personally to black women around the country. Through her personal endeavors and travels she contacted thousands of women who became Walker agents. During one of her stops in 1910 she decided that Indianapolis, centrally located in mid-America, would be an ideal location for the company's headquarters; Lelia Walker moved part of the business operations to New York in 1913 and set up another Lelia College.

Walker Becomes a Millionaire

Although she began her company with door-to-door selling techniques, Walker eventually sold on a national level. She established a chain of beauty parlors throughout the United States, the Caribbean, and South America, and she built her own factories and laboratories. By 1910 Walker had five thousand black agents selling her products on a commission basis. These agents averaged over one thousand dollars a day, seven days a week. In addition, they removed themselves from the tyranny of domestic work.

Walker's career as an entrepreneur continued as an odyssey of personal discovery. She continued to expand her distribution by recruiting and retaining her sales force of black women, who used, demonstrated, and sold the products. Her agents taught other women to set up beauty shops in their homes and to learn techniques of bookkeeping. By 1919, 25,000 women called themselves Walker agents.

Many in the black community accused Walker of trying to remake black women into an imitation of white European women. Even the church became an opposing force. Walker believed that she could make contact with large groups of black women if she approached churches. The churches, in many instances, rejected her. Black clergymen claimed that if God meant for blacks to have straight hair, he would have endowed them with it. Notwithstanding, black women turned to these products in an effort to eliminate the stigma assigned to the hair of the lower socioeconomic caste.

Illiteracy was another negative force which Walker overcame; unable to read and write, she surrounded herself with educators and lawyers to assist in her business transactions. Indeed, for a while she wrote her name in an illegible script on checks and bank documents. As she gradually became financially able, she employed tutors to teach her to read and write.

After she became wealthy, Walker built a palatial mansion on the Hudson River in Irvington, New York. She named the mansion Villa Lewaro, after her daughter Lelia Walker Robinson, now married, using the first syllables from the first, middle, and last names. Madame Walker and A'Lelia Walker Robinson (Lelia added an *A'* to her name) invited leaders of the black community to socials, soirées, and dinners at the mansion. She bequeathed the mansion to her daughter, A'Lelia, at her death, with the idea that the NAACP would inherit it from A'Lelia. Due to the depression the NAACP could not support the mansion, which it sold for the proceeds.

Walker Becomes Benefactor

Even at the height of her success, Walker was unable to forget the black experience that had shaped her life. She contributed to philanthropic causes and black educational institutions. She donated five thousand dollars to Mary McLeod

Bethune's school in Florida, Daytona Normal and Industrial Institute for Negro Girls; she left five thousand dollars to Lucy Laney's Haines Institute in Augusta, Georgia; she sponsored a teacher at Charlotte Hawkins Brown's Palmer Memorial Institute, a black preparatory school in Sedalia, North Carolina; and she gave five hundred dollars to redeem and restore Frederick Douglass's home, Cedar Hill, in southeastern Washington, D.C.—a project sponsored by the National Association of Colored Women's Clubs.

Although Walker placed emphasis on education, she also promoted the idea of black economic self-help, recounted Bundles. If women could develop a business, Walker reasoned, they could manage their lives:

> The girls and women of our race must not be afraid to take hold of business endeavors. I started in business eight years ago with one dollar and fifty cents. [Now I am] giving employment to more than a thousand women. . . . I have made it possible for many colored women to abandon the washtub for a more pleasant and profitable occupation.

Walker, faced with prejudice throughout her life, remembered her roots, became a social activist, and supported causes which fought racism. She provided funds for Monroe Trotter's National Equal Rights League and supported the NAACP's anti-lynching drive. In 1917 she accompanied other black leaders from Harlem to the White House to confront President Woodrow Wilson concerning federal anti-lynching legislation. Wilson pretended he was too busy to see the black coalition, but at the Walker agents' convention in 1917, the women sent a telegram encouraging President Wilson to give support to the federal anti-lynching legislation. These women also voiced their concern over the killing of black people in a riot in East St. Louis, Illinois.

Gender bias in the workplace was a force Walker experienced all of her life. Limited to working as a laundress and maid, she dared to take a chance and developed her company. Even after she became a success she still faced the male chauvinism of black men. At the National Negro Business League in 1912, Booker T. Washington and other men at the convention did not intend to let her speak. As Washington praised a black male banker for his bank's operations, Walker proceeded to the podium and stated emphatically:

> I am a woman who came from the cotton fields of the South. I was promoted from there to the washtub. Then I was promoted to the cook kitchen, and from there I PROMOTED MYSELF into the business of manufacturing hair goods and preparations. . . . I have built my own factory on my own ground.

At the 1913 convention Walker was a presenter on the program.

Walker's company was not just her expression of her own possibilities, but became an ethnic statement giving credence to the ingenuity of black people. Walker proved to the world that a black could overcome obstacles and succeed with a creative idea. Her dramatic commercial success was intriguing to her people. News articles invariably stressed her wealth and material acquisitions, as they have always done when discussing a folk-derived entrepreneur who has made it big. Admittedly, Walker's earnings and investments were enough to attract anyone's notice. By 1914 her gross from company earnings were over a million dollars.

Walker died on May 25, 1919. Funeral services were conducted in the Villa Lewaro by the pastor of her church, the Mother Zion African Methodist Episcopal Zion Church of New York, and she was buried in Woodlawn Cemetery in the Bronx.

In the 1980s, a New York developer wanted to demolish the Villa Lewaro and build condominiums. But neighbors and a city ordinance protecting the older trees on the land (a 200-year-old Chinese ginkgo and a 300-year-old American beechnut) prevented the development. The trees are on the National Registar of Historic Places and the Villa Lewaro has new owners occupying its lavish hallways. They have renovated its interior to preserve the legacy of a brillant businesswoman and devoted humanitarian.—JOAN CURL ELLIOTT

DENZEL **WASHINGTON**
1954–
Actor, humanitarian

Denzel Washington is a leading actor with a reputation for selecting quality roles, especially those that compliment African Americans. He earned his place in Hollywood through superb performances, and when he won an Academy Award for best supporting actor in the film Glory, *he became the fifth African American to win an Academy Award.*

Denzel Washington was born on December 28, 1954, in Mount Vernon, New York, to Denzel Washington, a Pentecostal minister, and Lennis Washington, a beautician, owner of several beauty shops and a former gospel singer. He has an older sister, Lorice, and a younger brother, David. He grew up in an integrated neighborhood that bordered the Bronx where he associated with West Indians, Italians, and blacks, and learned much from the different cultures. He was brought up in a very disciplined home; his father was strict in the rearing of his children and allowed no smoking, no use of alcohol, and no swearing. Denzel Washington's mother was very influential in his life and grounded her children with solid values and exposed them to various activities such as the Boys Club and YMCA camps.

Washington's parents divorced when he was fourteen years old, an action that devastated the young man and led to behavioral problems. He rejected religion and became unruly, just the opposite of what he had been. To help curb his behavior, his mother sent him to Oakland Academy, a private preparatory school in New Windsor, located in upstate New York, where most of the students were rich and white. The school challenged him in sports. Although he became active and achieved excellence in baseball, track, football, and basketball, academically he was still an underachiever. He also played piano in a local black band called the Last Express.

Washington entered Fordham University in 1972 to begin work on a college degree in pre-medicine. To pay his expenses, he acquired several loans and ran an after-school baby-sitting service at a Greek Orthodox church in Upper Manhattan. He dropped out of school one semester because of poor grades and worked at the post office and later as a trash collector for the sanitation department, but later returned to Fordham. During a summer job at a camp, he made a recitation on stage that apparently set the direction of his career. He was lauded for his performance because it appeared to be so natural. He enrolled in a theatre workshop and wrote poetry as well. His career plans changed; he dropped his earlier choice of pre-medicine as a major and embraced journalism. While at Fordham he starred in two university

Denzel Washington holds his Oscar for best supporting actor for the movie Glory.

drama productions, a student production of *The Emperor Jones* and *Othello*. In 1977, he had a professional offer to act in *Wilma*, the story of track star Wilma Rudolph, a made-for-television movie. Meanwhile, Washington completed his college degree with a double major in drama and journalism.

Becomes professional actor   With his new goal in place, the study of acting became Washington's focus. He completed one year of a three-year study of professional acting at the American Conservatory Theater in San Francisco, having won admission as one of forty-five applicants. He won key roles in *Man and Superman* and *Moonchildren*. As the class size was reduced after a tough competition, Washington retained a place in the school. He was a quick learner and as school progressed, Washington, who now believed he had learned the techniques necessary for good acting, missed class often. He left the conservatory and moved to Los Angeles to try his hand at professional acting.

Unsuccessful in Los Angeles, Washington moved back to his mother's house in Mount Vernon. While attending an off-Broadway play, he ran into Pauletta Pearson, whom he met briefly when the two played in *Wilma*. Their relationship grew; Pearson moved into the Washington home and later they married. It was his wife who gave him the encouragement that he needed during the frustrating years of the 1970s.

Washington landed a role in a social comedy, *Carbon Copy* (1981), which flopped at the box office and kept him from getting other parts for a while. Believing that he would not fulfill his dream of becoming an actor, he accepted a job at an urban recreation center where he was to teach sports and acting to children. One week before he was to report to work, he auditioned for and landed the role of Malcolm X in *When the Chickens Come Home to Roost*, which played at the Henry Street Settlement Arts for Living Center. Washington studied hard for the role and learned to imitate Malcolm X. He also dyed his hair red so that he would look more like Malcolm X. He appeared in the Negro Theatre Ensemble's production of *A Soldier's Play*, which offered Washington the chance to play another prominent role. For his performance in that play, critics acclaimed his brilliant acting and honored him in 1982 with the Obie Award and the Outer Circle's Critic Award. These two performances caused a career upturn in the 1980s.

He appeared in several African American productions, including *The Might Gents* and *Ceremonies in Dark Old Men*. Returning to Shakespeare, he acted in *Coriolanus* as Aedilus, through the Black and Red Ensemble production for the Shakespeare-in-the-Park program.

Washington did other work for television, appearing in *License to Kill* and *Flesh & Blood*. He declined a number of movie offers that would have required him to play stereotypical roles such as a pimp or druggie. He accepted an offer to play a doctor in the television program *St. Elsewhere* and believed that the role would cast him as a positive role model for young blacks. He played the role of Phillip Chandler, a Yale-educated doctor in the television series, which was set in the struggling St. Eligius Hospital in Boston. He was in the show for its full run from 1982 to 1986, but took breaks to appear in movies; for example, in 1984 he starred in the movie, *A Soldier's Story*. He appeared in *Power* (1986), which set out to expose the problems of the media. In 1987 he acted in the powerful, moving story portraying martyred South African activist Steve Biko in *Cry Freedom*. This film received mixed criticism; some critics felt that too little emphasis was on Biko and too much focus was on the white newspaper editor Donald Woods. Using the same preparation techniques he utilized in *When*

Denzel
Washington.

Chickens Come Home to Roost, he immersed himself in tapes and speeches about Steve Biko. Physically, he changed his appearance to somewhat resemble Biko, removing caps from his teeth and putting on several pounds. Washington's excellent performance in *Cry Freedom* earned him the nomination in 1987 for an Academy Award as Best Supporting Actor and the NAACP's Image Award for best supporting actor.

Other movies he appeared in in the 1980s include *For Queen and Country* (1988), *The Mighty Quinn* (1989), and *Glory,* the story of African American soldiers trained to fight in the Civil War, the Fifty-fourth Massachusetts Volunteer Infantry unit formed in 1863 by white colonel Robert Gould Shaw of Boston. Masses of the American people felt that African Americans could not fight in the Civil War. However, the courage and strength of these men under Shaw's supervision enabled them to fight an heroic battle ending in the July 18, 1863, attack on Battery Wagner, a key fortification of Charleston, South Carolina. Denzel Washington played the part of Trip, a former slave, who had become angry, tough, and bitter from his slave experiences. As in previous movies, Washington immersed himself in the Civil War experience in preparation for the movie, reading about the war and experiences encountered by slaves through slave narratives. Quoted in his biography, *Denzel Washington,* he said, "It was difficult to break myself down and become a primitive man; that was the challenge of this part." This role brought a second Academy Award nomination in 1990 for Best Supporting Actor, and this time Washington won the coveted and prestigious Oscar.

Although Washington consistently received moving and stirring roles to play, he rejected an offer to play in the film *Platoon,* because he wanted to play the part of a Native American rather than a black. Washington claims both ethnic groups in his background.

Spike Lee, African American film director, tailored and fashioned the role of Bleek Gilliam, the jazz musician, for Washington in *Mo Better Blues* (1990). Presumably, this story is about African American jazz trumpeter Miles Davis, yet it shows African Americans as human beings who have good times, fall in love, and face many obstacles. The critics were mixed in their reviews but Washington's performance was outstanding. Utilizing his familiar training techniques for a role, Washington engaged himself in the character of Miles Davis by learning to play a trumpet and staying in the company of this legendary musician.

Washington moved on to *Ricochet* (1991), then to *Mississippi Masala* in 1992. For the latter film he won the NAACP's Best Actor Award.

Also in 1992, Washington and Lee teamed together as actor and director for the powerful movie, *Malcolm X*. His extraordinary performance in this stirring movie earned him the Academy Award's nomination for best actor, the NAACP Image Award for best actor, and the Berlin Film Festival's Award. The film was named the best picture for 1992 at the festival, a plus for Spike Lee and Denzel Washington.

Movie scripts continued to come to Washington. He appeared in *Much Ado About Nothing* (a film version of Shakespeare's comedy), *The Pelican Brief* (the story of a newspaper reporter's investigation of the assassinations of two Supreme Court justices), and the highly acclaimed *Philadelphia* (the story of a lawyer who learns about life and love from his AIDS-stricken client), all in 1993. His films for 1995 were *Crimson Tide,* an action film in which he was a young, Harvard and U.S. Naval Academy trained executive officer aboard a beleaguered nuclear submarine further beset by mutiny, and *Devil in a Blue Dress,* in which he plays a private detective who, after wrestling with racism, reconfirms his American dream. His next venture was a military drama, *Courage Under Fire,* the story of a lieutenant colonel, played by Washington, and his command in the Persian Gulf. The officer gave an order to fire during the night on what he thought was the enemy; later the officer found out that the unit fired on was one of his own.

In 1996, Washington filmed the light-hearted movie, *The Preacher's Wife*—an adaptation of an old movie classic, *The Bishop's Wife*. Washington and singer Whitney Houston starred in this delightful and entertaining movie about a church couple who get some help from a friendly ghost. Beyond these latest films, there is some speculation that Spike Lee will ask Washington to play the role of Jackie Robinson, who broke the color barrier in professional baseball in the 1950s. Washington may also be paired with Susan Sarandon in the film version of Christopher Darden's book *In Contempt,* where Darden and Marcia Clark prosecute the O. J. Simpson murder case.

Very handsome, suave, with a well-chiseled visage, tall, and brown skinned, Denzel Washington is very often considered the next Sidney Poitier. He works with the Boys and Girls Club and does commercials for the national organization. He has given generously—one million dollars—to the Children's Fund of South Africa and $2.5 million dollars to his church, the Church of God in Los Angeles.

Denzel and Pauletta Pearson Washington are the parents of four children, John David, Katta, Malcolm, and Olivia. They live in a Beverly Hills home built by black architect Paul Williams. Washington believes in religion and family. Quoted in his biography, he said: "I always try to have my family with me when I am out in public" and wants to show that "black people can have families," thus helping to remove negative stereotypes of the one-parent black family. During a family visit to Africa in summer of 1995, the Washingtons renewed their marriage vows, in a ceremony performed by archbishop Desmond Tutu. Although Washington receives many accolades, he works to remain unaffected by them.

In his acting career, Washington's trademark for success in portraying a character is to learn as much about the individual as possible, including his social, historical, and political environments as well as physical traits. With this kind of dedication and zeal to be true to the character, Washington has established himself as a leading actor in the movie world.— BARBARA WILLIAMS JENKINS AND JESSIE CARNEY SMITH

MAXINE **WATERS**
1938–
Politician

Throughout her political career in the California State Assembly and the United States House of Represen-

tatives, Maxine Waters has been known as a feisty, articulate, and passionate crusader for her constituents.

Growing up poor, Waters learned as a child to work hard and strive for success in all of her endeavors.

These lessons have served her well in adulthood, as one observer noted in Essence: *"If Maxine Waters*

maneuvers as easily among the makers and shapers of public policy on Capitol Hill as she does among

the welfare mothers, blue-collar workers and street toughs in Watts [suburb of Los Angeles], it's because she

knows, firsthand, what it's like at both ends of the spectrum."

Maxine Moore Waters was born in St. Louis, Missouri, on August 15, 1938, to Remus Moore and Velma Lee Carr Moore, who divorced when Maxine was two years old. The fifth of thirteen children (Maxine's mother remarried), Waters grew up determined to make her mark in the world. A conscientious student, she also participated in extracurricular activities such as music, track, and swimming. At thirteen, she secured her first job as a busgirl at a segregated restaurant.

After graduating from high school in 1956, Waters married her childhood sweetheart, Edward Waters. They had two children, Edward and Karen, and secured factory jobs for themselves. In 1961 the couple decided to move to Los Angeles, where Maxine found work in a garment factory and at a telephone company. After suffering a miscarriage in the mid-1960s, though, she had to quit her telephone operator job.

In the aftermath of the 1965 Watts riots, Waters took a job as an assistant teacher in the newly created Head Start program. This nationwide project was sponsored by the federal government and was designed to give children from poor families a more advantageous start in school and life. She soon became the voice for frustrated parents whose children attended the Head Start program. She encouraged parents to make federal budget requests, to contact legislators and agencies for increased funding, and to lobby for Head Start program components tailored for their community.

In 1968, while working at Head Start, Waters decided to attend college. Three and a half years later, in 1972, she graduated from California State University at Los Angeles with a

*Maxine
Waters.*

degree in sociology. That year she also divorced Edward Waters. In the meantime, Waters's Head Start work led her to become involved with local elections. She became chief deputy to city council member David Cunningham from 1973 to 1976, and campaigned for several other California politicians.

Heads to the California State Assembly

Sidney Williams, a Mercedes-Benz salesman in Los Angeles and a former Cleveland Browns football player, wooed Maxine Waters for five years before they wed in 1977. He supported her successful candidacy for the California State Assembly in 1976, a legislative body that Waters subsequently served for the next fourteen years. During this time she kept a small apartment in Sacramento, where she stayed during the week, returning home on weekends to attend functions and to meet with constituents.

During her tenure in the state assembly, Maxine Waters became the chairperson of the Ways and Means Subcommittee of State Administration. She was the first woman to serve on the Joint Legislative Budget Committee, the Judiciary Committee, the Elections Reapportionment and Constitutional Amendments Committee, the Natural Resources Committee, the Joint Committee of Legislative Ethics, and the California Commission on the Status of Women.

Waters also served notice that she was not afraid to confront the male-dominated system in the assembly. She made her presence known on often controversial issues with her knowledge and self-confidence, and introduced legislation that reflected her views. Waters sponsored legislation, for example, that prohibited policemen from conducting strip searches and body-cavity searches of persons arrested for misdemeanors. Her membership on the Joint Committee on Public Pension Fund Investments also led to groundbreaking legislation. After eight years of furious lobbying and six different submissions of the bill, she finally secured the passage of a landmark law that required California to divest state pension funds from firms doing business in South Africa, which still operated at the time under laws of apartheid. She also worked tirelessly to get other United States companies to divest in South Africa.

As she became known as the conscience of the California legislature, Waters also evolved into a powerhouse in the state Democratic party. In 1981 she proved influential in garnering the speakership position for Willie Brown Jr. A close friend and ally in the assembly. Brown, in turn, supported her successful bid to become the majority whip. She thus became the first woman in the state to be elected chair of the Democratic Caucus, ranked number four on the leadership team.

One of Maxine Waters's primary concerns was women's rights. To involve more women in Los Angeles in this issue, she, along with Ethel Bradley (wife of Los Angeles's Mayor Bradley) and publisher Ruth Washington, formed the Black Women's Forum. This

Maxine Waters, Democrat from California, and House Minority Whip David Bonior of Michigan discuss a negative Republican political campaign, 1985.

organization sponsors lectures and strives to motivate women to develop their own lists of important concerns. On a national level, Waters joined with a number of other prominent black women in founding the National Political Congress of Black Women in 1984. The *Washington Informer* noted the primary mission of this nonpartisan, nonprofit organization: "to promote and encourage the participation of Black women in the political process to gain the social, educational and economic empowerment needed to enhance the quality of life for Black women, their families and community."

Waters's commitment to job training for her constituents has been demonstrated through her efforts to build the Maxine Waters Employment Preparation Center, an extension of the Watts Skills Center, founded in 1966. At the center, approximately 2200 students and young adults receive training lasting from three to six months in a range of vocational occupations. Waters also created Project Build, a program to provide much-needed information regarding child care, health, and day care, as well as educational and job-training services, to families in six Los Angeles housing projects. In addition, Waters has sponsored legislation in areas of child abuse prevention, work laws, and environmental protection.

Waters becomes U.S. Representative   After fourteen years in the California State Assembly, Waters ran for the seat vacated by retiring congressman Augustus Hawkins in the Twenty-ninth Congressional District of California. Although her opponent in the June 1990 primary was endorsed by the Democratic political machine, Waters soundly defeated him, garnering eighty-eight percent of the vote. She also won the general election handily with eighty percent of the votes cast.

Prior to taking on her new responsibilities, Waters commented on the significance of the election of black women to national office: "The women of this country, the Black women, . . . have wanted very much to increase their numbers. So I think our voices are going to be extremely important, not only to articulate the aspirations of Black women, but to add our voices to the voices of Black men."

In 1992, running in the much larger Thirty-fifth Congressional District, Waters accrued eighty-three percent of the votes cast to win reelection for a second term. Ranked as one of the most liberal members of Congress, she served on the Banking, Finance and Urban Affairs Committee, the Small Business Committee, and the Veterans' Affairs Committee. She also joined several organizations, including the Congressional Black Caucus and the Congressional Caucus for Women's Issues. But while her congressional responsibilities were significant, Waters still actively involved herself in California politics, where her constituency is predominately African American and Latino American. Her congressional district includes South Central Los Angeles, Inglewood, Hawthorne, and Gardena.

Waters' district office burned in the Los Angeles riots that broke out in 1992 after the Rodney King verdict. Waters subsequently invited herself to a meeting at the White House, where President George Bush and top advisors were consulting about how to aid the city. Since the primary people involved were Congressman Waters's constituents, she felt obligated to offer concrete suggestions to improve the quality of life, not just in Los Angeles, but in urban communities across the nation. Representative Waters, through personal lobbying, helped raise $3 million in Labor Department funds for a South-Central Los Angeles relief organization. She was instrumental in ensuring that peace prevailed in the urban Los Angeles area after a second trial of the four policemen in the Rodney King case was held (two of the officers were given thirty-month sentences).

Waters has also been a key figure in shedding investigative light into allegations that the CIA was behind the distribution of drugs to blacks in the inner cities. Her obligation to this speculation has raised some eyebrows among her peers, but Waters has vowed to see it through until each angle has been examined.

Waters, always known as a fiery woman, drew headlines as she and fellow Representative Peter King engaged in a shouting match during the House Banking Committee's Whitewater hearings. The bitter shouting match ended with Waters telling King to "shut up" and a division of the House supporting Waters bravado and others claiming that she hit a "new low."

In recent years Waters has lent her support to diverse corporate and private organizations, including the National Women's Political Caucus, the Elizabeth Jackson Carter

Foundation of Spelman College, the National Minority AIDS Project, and the National Council of Negro Women. She was one of the founders of the TransAfrica Foundation, serves on the board of *Essence* magazine, and is a board member of the Overseas Education Fund of the League of Women Voters, which provides Third World women with financial support. In 1997, she was appointed the new president of the Congressional Black Caucus, an appointment that was heralded as good news by former president Kweisi Mfume.

Maxine Waters remains deeply committed to the concerns of the American people. The issues of urban poverty and despair continue to consume her waking moments, and she concedes that her passion to improve the situation has ruffled feathers. "Most people say I'm too pushy, I'm too aggressive, I'm too assertive, I'm too confrontational. That I ask for too much. I've never been considered patient, or even conciliatory in most instances." Waters remains unapologetic for her demeanor, however, citing the importance of her work and the needs of the people she represents.—JACQUELINE BRICE-FINCH

FAYE **WATTLETON**

1943–
Reproductive rights activist, author

Faye Wattleton has been one of the most influential black American women in the area of reproductive rights. As president of the Planned Parenthood Federation of America from 1978 to 1992, she transformed a declining service-oriented organization into a high-profile, aggressive proponent of women's right to reproductive choice. As one admirer remarked, "Her political savvy and her remarkable ability to communicate difficult issues have made her a giant in the ongoing battle to preserve America's fundamental liberties."

The only child of George Edward and Ozie (Garrett) Wattleton, Alyce Faye Wattleton was born on July 8, 1943, in St. Louis, Missouri. George Wattleton, who died in 1970, was a factory worker. Ozie Wattleton—one of Faye Wattleton's role models, along with Martin Luther King Jr., and John F. Kennedy—was a seamstress and minister of the Church of God, who did not believe in birth control or abortion. Living one's politics was important in the Wattleton family. Her father, for example, refused to buy gas from a service station that failed to provide bathroom facilities for blacks.

Faye Wattleton's family was poor but stressed the importance of helping those who were even less fortunate. At the age of sixteen she entered Ohio State University Nursing School, and in 1964 she became the first person in her family to receive a college degree. Her first postgraduate job was as a maternity nursing instructor for the Miami Valley Hospital School of Nursing in Dayton, Ohio. It was during her two years there that she was first exposed "to the medical and emotional complications of women who had life-threatening illegal abortions," wrote Constance M. Green in *Black Enterprise*. In 1966 Wattleton moved to New York to study at Columbia University on a government stipend; a year later she received an M.S. in maternal and infant health care, with certification as a nurse-midwife. While a student at Columbia, she was an intern at Harlem Hospital, where the importance of access to safe abortion became

*Faye
Wattleton.*

clear to her. As she recalled: "One of the cases I remember in Harlem was a really beautiful 17-year-old girl. She and her mother had decided to induce an abortion by inserting a Lysol douche into her uterus. It killed her."

Wattleton heads Planned Parenthood   In 1967 Wattleton moved to Dayton, Ohio, to work as consultant and assistant director of Public Health Nursing Services in the City of Dayton Public Health Department. She was asked to join the local Planned Parenthood board and a year and a half later, at the age of twenty-seven, was asked to serve as its executive director. Under her leadership, the number of clients tripled, and the budget increased from less than four hundred thousand dollars to almost one million dollars.

In 1973 Wattleton married Franklin Gordon, a social worker raised in Roxbury, Massachusetts. Two years later she not only gave birth to her daughter, Felicia, but also became chairwoman of the national executive director's Council of Planned Parenthood Federation of America (PPFA). In fact, Wattleton was in labor when she won the election to the position. Three years later, in 1978, she was appointed president of PPFA.

As the first black person, first woman, and youngest individual to head the organization, Wattleton shocked many people with her appointment. According to one local director, "Nobody believed our board would settle on 'a little nurse from Dayton' with no national experience for the highest-paid job [seventy thousand dollars a year] in the largest voluntary health agency in the country." How, then, did the board decide to appoint a woman, particularly a black woman, as president? In Wattleton's opinion, there were at least three factors involved: her demonstrated compassion for human suffering, the organization's realization that its primary reason for existence was women's issues, and her competence.

Even Wattleton, however, could not have imagined just how tough her job would be. The Hyde Amendment, passed in 1977 and "aimed to prohibit the use of any federal funding for abortion, unless the life of the mother was endangered," was one of the early indicators that anti-abortion or Right to Life groups were having a significant influence on the political process. During that same year, Planned Parenthood of Miami Valley came under attack from a local Baptist group and Right to Life chapter and also was subjected to a federal inquiry into its use of government financing. In addition, Planned Parenthood clinics in Minnesota, Virginia, Nebraska, Vermont, and Ohio were burned or bombed. Thus the anti-choice stage had been set. One of the ongoing efforts of the Reagan administration was an attempt to repeal the United States family planning program, Title I of the Public Health Service Act. As family planning services and their funding were being threatened, Wattleton worked to bring PPFA into public view. She appeared on radio and television talk shows, including *Donahue,* to rally support around her cause. In fact, Phil Donahue called Wattleton "a talk show host's dream guest" because she got to the point and was always well-informed.

President Reagan attempted to enact a "squeal rule," which would have required federally funded clinics to receive parental consent before distributing diaphragms, intra-uterine devices, or birth control pills to minors. Wattleton, however, argued that the mandatory notification of parents would merely lead to an increase in teen pregnancies. A "gag rule," which would have prevented abortion counseling by federally funded family-planning agencies, was also vigorously fought by Wattleton.

Because PPFA served men and women in the developing countries of Africa, Asia, and Latin America, the Reagan administration's "Mexico City" policy particularly disturbed

Wattleton. In essence, the policy was an attempt to restrict United States family-planning aid to foreign organizations that referred, performed, or advocated abortion. However, according to Wattleton and the majority of Americans who participated in the 1988 Harris poll, the United States should provide family-planning funds to developing nations—even those nations where abortion was a legal option.

"By engaging in political activism, Ms. Wattleton has brought Planned Parenthood full circle," observed Nancy Rubin in *Savvy Woman*. Wattleton's spirited ways caused her peers to compare her with pioneer public health nurse Margaret Sanger, who opened the nation's first birth control clinic in 1916. Because of early efforts, such as those of Sanger and her associates, the distribution of information about birth control became widely accepted by the medical establishment.

Almost seventy years later, Wattleton had to struggle to keep family planning on the national agenda. By this time, Planned Parenthood had lost much of its attraction among middle and upper class women. Most of the organization's clients were poor or of the working class and thus were particularly vulnerable to reductions in federal funding, such as Medicaid. The Hyde Amendment, for example, cut off Medicaid abortion funding, which meant that hundreds of thousands of poor women could no longer have their abortions paid for by Medicaid. As Epstein notes, Wattleton argued that poor people, like the rich, should have access to the full range of health care services:

> The women who came to my hospitals under less than dignified circumstances were not affluent. That girl in Harlem who died was not affluent. . . . *That's* when I became aware of the political significance of these people. If they really cared about equity and fairness in life they would say that as long as abortion is legal in this country, poor people should have the same access as the rich.

Equal access was not the only issue raised concerning reproductive choice and freedom. Wattleton attempted to locate the reproductive issue in a wider context of federal neglect. In her view, the Reagan-Bush administration tried to dismantle programs designed to confront not only the issue of inadequate health care but also homelessness and poor education. Thus, one had to look at the circumstances under which so many women chose to end their pregnancies—many of which were unintended.

One of the major setbacks for PPFA as well as other advocates of reproductive choice was the Supreme Court's ruling in the *Webster v. Reproductive Health Services*. The case challenged certain aspects of *Roe v. Wade*. the 1973 Supreme Court decision that legalized abortion. On July 3, 1989, the Supreme Court gave states the right to limit access to abortion. Although this event may have signaled defeat to even the most resolute leader, noted Marianne Szegedy-Maszak, Wattleton confidently asserted after hearing the decision, "My commitment and my determination is in no way diminished. I am furious as can be."

Public advocacy drive initiated   Planned Parenthood is dedicated to working for a society where unintended pregnancies would be reduced, and sex education and information about contraceptives are very important elements of this commitment. Under Wattleton's leadership the agency "expanded its public advocacy drive through newspaper and television advertisements geared toward educating teens, parents, and public officials on the financial and human costs of runaway teen pregnancy," Green reported. Wattleton also co-authored a book entitled *How to Talk to Your Child about Sex.* which sold more than thirty thousand copies. It angered her, however, that by 1989 "no major network [would] accept contraceptive advertising [and] only seventeen states and the District of Columbia require[d] sex education in their school systems," wrote Marcia Ann Gillespie in *Ms.* In Wattleton's view, children need to be taught about sexuality before they become adolescents. Wattleton attributes the increase of teen pregnancies to children's contradictory exposure to sex: children are bombarded with sexual messages and exploitation by a society that is, for the most part, sexually illiterate.

Wattleton's demanding role as president of PPFA unfortunately took its toll on her personal life. Although she commuted from New York to Dayton on weekends to be with her husband and daughter, her marriage to Franklin Gordon crumbled in 1981. In retrospect, Wattleton said that her demanding schedule "probably accelerated" the demise of an already shaky marriage. In spite of her personal problems, however, her calm and rational outward demeanor were not shaken. In fact, cool composure and articulation have become her trademarks, and these qualities have allowed her to disarm enemies and inspire supporters.

In January 1992, Wattleton announced her resignation as president of PPFA, saying that she would begin hosting a Chicago talk show dealing with a variety of women's issues. Of her resignation, Planned Parenthood board chairman Kenneth Edelin said, "There was a gasp all the way from Texas."

Wattleton's awards and accomplishments are impressive, coming from such organizations as the World Institute of Black Communication, the American Nursing Association, the Better World Society, and the American Public Health Association.

Retirement meant a lengthy rest for Wattleton after her battles on the issue of abortion. Her spare time also gave her moments to reflect on her career and life which she compiled in a best-selling autobiography in 1995 entitled *Life on the Line.* Four years after her combative days with Planned Parenthood, Wattleton founded a think tank organization, the Center for Gender Equality in New York, at which scholars address issues of gender equality that women will face in the twenty-first century.

Wattleton's accomplishments with Planned Parenthood has helped make abortion one of the most heavily debated issues of our time. And throughout her fourteen years of service, Wattleton has made it clear that any woman, rich or poor, should have that option allowed to her. Wattleton, despite her calm composure, has no clear answers to how the gender and abortion war can end, nor does she think it will be easily won. But she will continue the struggle.—C. CUNNINGHAM AND A. L. JONES

ROBERT C. **WEAVER**
1907–1997
Government official, scholar

Robert Weaver spent a lifetime dedicated to public service, illustrated prominently by his appointment in 1966 as Secretary of Housing and Urban Development by President Lyndon B. Johnson. He became the first African American in the nation's history to serve as a Cabinet officer. He began federal service in 1933 in the Interior Department, continued his career in the federal government, then extended his career into

academia. He made important contributions as a scholar, lecturer, college president, and board member

of public and private organizations. He earned respect as one of the country's foremost experts in the fields

of labor, housing, and race relations, and was an influential advisor to Presidents Franklin D. Roosevelt

and Lyndon B. Johnson, working in the spirit of the New Deal liberalism.

Robert Clifton Weaver was born in Washington, D.C., on December 29, 1907, the son of Mortimer Grover, a postal clerk, and Florence Freeman Weaver. His grandfather, Robert Mortimer Freeman, was a member of the first graduating class of Harvard's dental school and the first African American to earn a degree in dentistry. Weaver was also a nephew of the black composer and musician—Harry Burleigh. Robert Weaver had a brother, Mortimer, who became an assistant professor at Howard University but died suddenly at the age of twenty-three. Robert Weaver credits his mother with inspiring her children to seek intellectual achievement.

Weaver grew up as one of seven African American families in a Washington suburb. Even before he graduated in 1925 from Dunbar High School in Washington, D.C., Weaver demonstrated his skill and hard work. By his junior year, he was a paid electrician, operating his own electrical business. Weaver continued on to Harvard University, where he majored in economics and received his B.S. cum laude in 1929, M.S. in 1931, and Ph.D. in 1934.

Weaver worked in Franklin D. Roosevelt's administration under the New Deal. He served in the Department of the Interior in several official capacities from 1934 to 1938, first as an aide to Secretary Harold Ickes. This was the first of many positions he filled as advisor on black affairs to an agency head. He was a very influential member of Roosevelt's "Black Cabinet," a group of blacks working in Roosevelt's administration called together in August 1936 by Mary McLeod Bethune, who enjoyed a friendship with Eleanor Roosevelt and who was one of the few blacks to have access to the President. The group organized two national conferences on black problems. The first, held in January 1937, produced a report that had little influence on administration policy. Still, the group's pressure secured important advancements for blacks in housing and employment.

The most dramatic effect of Weaver's influence in the Roosevelt administration is said to have occurred just days before the 1940 presidential election. Roosevelt's press secretary jostled a black policeman to the ground after a major campaign speech by Roosevelt in New York's Madison Square Garden. White house aides contacted Weaver at midnight about how to repair the damage this incident might cause among black voters. Weaver suggested that more than a speech was necessary and transmitted some recommendations. Within forty-eight hours, the nation had its first black general, Benjamin O. Davis Sr., a black assistant to the Selective Service Director, Campbell Johnson, and a black civilian aide to the Secretary of War, William H. Hastie.

Weaver continued to hold government positions after leaving his initial post in the Interior Department. From 1938 to 1940 he served as special assistant to the head of the National Housing Authority, Nathan Strauss. In 1940 he was assistant to Sidney Hillman at the National Defense Advisory Commission. During World War II, he served on the War Production Board and the Negro Manpower Commission, promoting the cause of integration in industry and greater participation by black workers in the war effort.

Robert C. Weaver.

665

Weaver turns to service at state and local level   By 1944, Weaver felt that the implementation of antidiscrimination measures was going too slowly. He left the national government to serve the city of Chicago as executive director of the Mayor's Committee on Race Relations. When he left Chicago, he plunged into a variety of sometimes overlapping positions in teaching and service as a government and organization official. From 1945 to 1948 he was director of community services for the American Council on Race Relations.

In 1946, Weaver was called to service for the United Nations Relief and Rehabilitation Administration, working in several official capacities in the Ukraine, including acting as deputy chief of mission. Returning to Chicago, he entered academic life as a visiting lecturer at Northwestern University, Evanston, Illinois, in 1947–48. He also served on the board of the Metropolitan Housing Council and as an officer of the American Council on Race Relations. From 1949 to 1955 Weaver was director of the opportunity fellowships program of the John Hay Whitney Foundation. He also served on the national selection committee of the Fulbright fellowship program, the fellowship selection committee of the Julius Rosenwald Fund, consultant to the Ford Foundation, and as chair of the faculty selection committee of the United Negro College Fund.

Further involvements in academia continued. Weaver taught summer school at Columbia University Teachers College (1947 and 1949) and New School for Social Research (1949), as well as serving as visiting professor at New York University School of Education from 1948 to 1951. After leaving his cabinet post, he was president of Bernard M. Baruch College in 1969–1970, a branch of New York University that was projected for an urban renewal area of the city, and from 1971 until he retired in 1978, he was Distinguished Professor of Urban Affairs at Hunter College. He was also an invited lecturer at many other schools.

Weaver continued his active involvement in politics when the Democrats returned to power in New York in 1955. In 1960, Weaver became vice-chair of the New York City Housing and Development Board. Newly elected Mayor Robert F. Wagner wanted Weaver to follow Hulan Jack as Manhattan Borough president after Jack's conviction on conflict of interest charges, but President-elect John F. Kennedy intervened to name Weaver director of the Federal Housing and Home Finance Agency. Weaver achieved a great success in coordinating the activities of five subordinate agencies. Kennedy tried to make the agency a cabinet department in 1961, but Congress tried to block his attempt because of his obvious plan to name Weaver to head the new department. President Lyndon B. Johnson succeeded in having the Department of Housing and Urban Development created four years later.

Weaver becomes Housing Secretary   On January 13, 1966, President Lyndon B. Johnson appointed Weaver Secretary of the newly created Department of Housing and Urban Development; he was sworn in five days later. A strong believer in the positive social values of urban development, and to set an example, he lived in an apartment development in Capital Park, an urban redevelopment area in Washington, D.C., during his tenure as Secretary of HUD. Among his major responsibilities were the coordinating activities and functions within the Federal Housing Authority, Small Business Administration, Government National Mortgage Administration, and the Model Cities Program. Weaver helped expand the federal government's role to affect all areas of urban development, such as finding long-range solutions to the nation's urban problems. Weaver left government service when Richard Nixon became president in 1968. He then served in academic positions until his formal retirement from Hunter College in 1978. After leaving government service, he continued to serve on many boards, some in the field of business, like the boards of the Metropolitan Life Insurance Company and the Bowery Savings Bank, and others in the fields of education and public service, such as the visiting commission of the Harvard University School of Design, the New York City Conciliation and Appeals Board (for rent control), the board of Mount Sinai Hospital and Medical School, and the executive committee of the board of the NAACP Legal Defense Fund. He also served as chairman of the board for the NAACP in 1960–61. Civic concerns led him to serve as president of the National Committee Against Discrimination in Housing (1973–87). His distinguished position in American life was recognized by his election to the American Academy of Arts and Sciences in 1985.

Weaver was also a productive scholar. He authored four books: *Negro Labor: A National Problem* (1945); *The Negro Ghetto* (1948); *The Urban Complex* (1965); and *Dilemmas of Urban America* (1965). He also has 185 articles to his credit. Weaver stated in *Contemporary Biography*: "When I can't relax . . . then I feel real frustrated and start writing." With his scholarly work as with his public service duties, Weaver focused on the role and function of government at several levels and the interrelationships among these levels. His views were wide ranging and unabashedly liberal, calling for an expanded role for the federal government in urban development, integration of the federal service at all levels, and the expansion of opportunity in housing and employment for the urban poor of all races. He singled out segregation in housing as the root cause of mass segregation and consequent discrimination in many other areas.

Among his innovative ideas in the field of urban renewal and housing was the concept of government intervention through financial offsets, easing of loan requirements, government loan guarantees, and tax incentives to broaden the base of home ownership through direct federal participation as well as encouraging private investment and development. Always a forward thinking problem solver, Weaver called for planners to anticipate needs far into the future. His critiques frequently postulated solutions for problems he anticipated resulting from analytical projections. An example of his methodology was his suggestion that city planners note the current lack of land for public use in the nation's major cities and seek to acquire marginal lands for public use many years over the horizon of current city planning. Another innovative concept called for balanced urban planning, allowing for a sharing of functions and inputs between government, industry, and private and public organizations. He also pointed to the need for a balance in the sharing of expertise, funds, and responsibilities between federal, state, and city institutions, acknowledging the danger of divided loyalties, trusts, and suspicions that frequently cause difficulties in such partnership attempts.

Frequently in Weaver's writing, the fruits of experience flavored his research. This was the case with his extensive federal experience in Franklin D. Roosevelt's administration, working to increase participation by African Americans in the nation's work force, particularly during World War II, in wartime industry, in the military, and in the federal service itself. Such experience resulted in many publications studying this very broad topic, including his book *Negro Labor: A National Problem.*

Weaver was a member of Omega Psi Phi fraternity. He has received over thirty honorary doctorates. Among his numerous other recognitions and awards were the Spingarn Medal of the NAACP, 1962; Russwurm Award, 1963; Albert Einstein Commemorative Award, 1968; Merrick Moore Spaulding Achievement Award, 1968; Award for Public Service, U.S. General Accounting Office, 1975; New York City Urban League's Frederick Douglass Award,

1977; election to the Hall of Fame of the National Association of Home Builders, 1982; the M. Justin Herman Award, National Association of Housing and Redevelopment Officials, 1986; and the Equal Opportunity Day Award, National Urban League, 1987.

Weaver grew into a five-feet, ten-inch, 195-pound man, who was a chain smoker. He disliked exercise, but liked playing cards with friends and working in his home workshop. He married Ella V. Haith on July 18, 1935; she died in 1991. They had one adopted son, Robert C. Weaver Jr., who died in the 1960s.

On July 17, 1997, Robert C. Weaver died of lung cancer at his home in Manhattan. He was eighty-nine years old. His country and the world mourned the loss of the man many regarded as the first man who put urban renewal as a priority in Washington, D.C.

Weaver's life was reflective of a personal commitment to serve the public. Active over a period of many years in governmental, academic, and civic pursuits, and showing concern in his writing for the betterment of his fellow citizens, he advocated respect for differences and a sharing of responsibilities for improving the quality of life for all Americans.— DARIUS L. THIEME

IDA B. **WELLS BARNETT**
1862–1931
Journalist, social activist

Characterized by the print media as courageous, determined, forceful, fearless, fiery, and militant, Ida Bell Wells Barnett came of age during the post-Reconstruction period and spent her adult life fighting to redress the inequities brought about by Jim Crow laws and attitudes. Her fight against the racial injustices endured by her race have earned her the highest respect in the years since her struggles. She may have alienated herself from her colleagues during her crusades, but Ida B. Wells Barnett's strength could not be ignored and is never forgotton.

Ida B. Wells was born a slave on July 16, 1862, in Holly Springs, Mississippi, to James Wells and Elizabeth (Bell) Wells. Her mother was the child of a slave mother and an Indian father. The oldest in a family of four boys and four girls, she attended Rust College, a freedmen's high school and industrial school formerly called Shaw University.

The yellow fever epidemic of 1878, which ravaged Memphis, Tennessee, and northern Mississippi, claimed the lives of her parents and her youngest brother. At the age of sixteen she assumed responsibility for her siblings and taught for a short time in the rural district of Holly Springs. In the 1880s, Wells engaged her brothers and sisters in apprenticeships and, with her two younger sisters, moved to Memphis to be close to her father's sister and to obtain a higher-paying teaching position.

Legal suit filed against railroad   A train ride from Memphis to Woodstock was the beginning of Wells's lifelong public campaign against the inequities and injustices faced by

Ida B. Wells Barnett.

blacks throughout the South. In May 1884 she purchased a first-class ticket on a local Memphis-to-Woodstock line operated by the Chesapeake, Ohio, and Southwestern Railroad Company. Taking a seat in the ladies' coach, she was asked by the conductor to move to the forward car, a smoker. Wells refused, got off the train, returned to Memphis, and subsequently filed suit against the railroad company for refusing to provide her the first-class accommodations for which she had paid.

In December 1884 the Memphis circuit court ruled in favor of Wells, levied the maximum fine of three hundred dollars against the railroad company, and awarded her personal damages of five hundred dollars. Headlines in the Christmas edition of the Memphis *Daily Appeal* read, "A Darky Damsel Obtains a Verdict for Damages Against the Chesapeake and Ohio Railroad—What It Cost to Put a Colored Teacher in a Smoking Car—Verdict for $500." Wells's success against the railroad company was short-lived. The railroad appealed the case to the Tennessee Supreme Court, which on April 5, 1887, reversed the lower court's decision on the grounds that the railroad had satisfied the statutory requirements to provide "like accommodations." Six days after the court's decision, Wells noted in *Crusader for Justice:*

> I felt so disappointed because I had hoped [for] such great things from my suit for my people generally. I [had] firmly believed all along that the law was on our side and would, when we appealed to it, give us justice. I feel shorn of that belief and utterly discouraged, and just now, if it were possible, I would gather my race in my arms and fly away with them.

Wells taught in the Memphis city schools from 1884 to 1891, attending summer sessions at Fisk University in Nashville to sharpen her skills. She met weekly with other teachers at the Memphis Vance Street Christian Church to play music, give recitals, read essays, and engage in debates. These literary meetings closed with the reading of the *Evening Star,* an internal journal of current events that Wells went on to edit. While serving in this capacity, she became known throughout the community and in 1887 wrote for the *Living Way,* a religious weekly. She also began writing regularly for the black press throughout the country. At the 1889 meeting of the Colored Press Association, later called the Afro-American Press Association, she was elected secretary. During this same year, the "Princess of the Press" was invited to become editor of and partner in the *Free Speech and Headlight,* a militant journal owned by the Reverend Taylor Nightingale, pastor of the Beale Street Baptist Church, and J. L. Fleming.

Wells called a fearless journalist   Wells gained a reputation for fearlessness because of the scathing and militant opinions she openly expressed in print. In 1891 Wells openly sanctioned retaliatory violence by blacks in Georgetown, Kentucky, who avenged the lynching of a black man by setting fire to the town. Because Wells wrote an editorial critical of the Memphis Board of Education and its unequal distribution of resources allocated to the segregated black schools, the board dismissed her from its employment in 1891. Disheartened but not discouraged, Wells devoted all her energy to the paper, shortening its name to *Free Speech* and working diligently to expand its circulation, which she increased by thirty-eight percent.

In 1892, events in Memphis changed the course of Wells's life. Thomas Moss, Calvin McDowell, and William Stewart, all friends of hers, opened the People's Grocery Store in a black section of Memphis. The black entrepreneurs successfully competed with white merchant W. H. Barrett, who operated a grocery store across the street. Barrett retaliated against the new competition with violence, and after several episodes, the Shelby County grand jury indicted the owners of People's for maintaining a nuisance. On Saturday, March 5, after dark, when nine deputy sheriffs dressed in civilian attire converged upon the grocery store owners, the deputies were taken for a mob and fired upon by a group of blacks determined to protect the owners. Three deputies were wounded; McDowell, Stewart, Moss, and scores of other accused rioters were arrested.

Judge Dubose of the Shelby County criminal court illegally disarmed the Tennessee Rifles, a black state militia company that guarded the jail for three nights in an attempt to protect the prisoners. On Wednesday, March 9, 1892, nine white men abducted Moss, McDowell, and Stewart from the jail, carried them one mile north, and barbarously shot them to death. *Crusader for Justice* contains Wells's reaction:

> The city of Memphis had demonstrated that neither character nor standing avails the Negro if he dares to protect himself against the white man or become his rival. There is nothing we can do now about the lynching, as we are out-numbered and without arms. The white mob could help itself to ammunition without pay, but the order was rigidly enforced against the selling of guns to Negroes. There is therefore only one thing left that we can do; save our money and leave a town which will neither protect our lives and property, nor give us a fair trial in the courts, but take us out and murder us in cold blood when accused by a white person.

The black community encouraged all who could to leave Bluff City, and those who stayed to refrain from patronizing the City Railroad Company. Prodded by angry editorials in the *Free Speech* and calls of "On to Oklahoma," 2,000 blacks left Memphis and put the streetcar company in dire financial straits. Throughout the following weeks and into the spring, Wells's editorials "demanded that the murderers of Moss, McDowell, and Stewart be brought to justice."

In May 1892, Wells wrote an editorial in the *Free Speech* provoked by the lynching of eight more blacks. Her fiery pen punctured the ego of white men of the South, calling into question the hackneyed excuses used by whites for executing blacks without due process of the law by inferring that white women of the South were sexually attracted to black men. In response, terroristic statements poured forth from the local papers, the *Free Speech* presses and offices were destroyed on May 27, 1892, and Wells was warned not to return to Memphis.

Fiery journalist exiled from the South   Exiled from the South, Wells persevered in her struggle against racial injustice and the lynching of blacks as a columnist for the *New York Age,* a paper owned and edited by T. Thomas Fortune and Jerome B. Patterson. On June 7, 1892, the *New York Age* published a detailed analysis of lynching, refuting the myth that the white men in Memphis intended to shield white women against rape and providing a history of black lynchings since 1863.

Discontented with narrating the story in the black press, Wells began lecturing through-out the Northeast. This lecture circuit brought her international attention, and in 1893 Catherine Impey, the British editor of the *Anti-Caste,* invited her to speak in England. Wells left the United States on April 5, 1893, and lectured throughout England, Scotland, and Wales, with the tour ending in May 1893.

Founding of black women's clubs   While abroad, Wells learned of the enterprising endeavors of the women of England through their civic groups. Upon her return home she strongly advised her sisters to become more involved in the matters of their communities, cities, and the nation through organized civic groups. According to Gerder Lerner, on the eve of Wells's departure for England, she spoke at a fund-raising rally attended by a group of prominent New York women who organized this event in her support. This meeting had a profound effect on the black women's club movement:

> This 1892 meeting, which brought together Mrs. Josephine St. Pierre Ruffin of Boston, Victoria Earle Matthews of New York and Dr. Susan McKinney of Brooklyn, inspired the formation of the first two black women's clubs. The New York and Brooklyn women formed the Women's Loyal Union and somewhat later, Mrs. St. Pierre Ruffin organized the Woman's Era Club of Boston.

Josephine St. Pierre Ruffin in 1895 had actively promoted a national organization, the First National Conference of Colored Women. In that same year, the National Federation of Afro-American Women was founded with Mary Margaret Washington as president.

Wells moved to Chicago in 1893 and began working for the *Chicago Conservator,* the first black American paper in the city, founded and edited by Ferdinand L. Barnett, a black lawyer. She continued her interest in women's clubs and organized Chicago's first civic club for black women, which was later named in her honor. In February 1894 she returned to England. During her six-month stay, a Chicago daily paper, the *Inter-Ocean,* edited by William Penn Nixon, published her articles in a column entitled "Ida B. Wells Abroad." While there, she spoke widely on the increasing occurrences and savageness of lynchings in the South and of the negligence of regional authorities. Wells was the impetus behind the Britons' formation of an anti-lynching committee for the purpose of investigating and publicizing the persecution of blacks in America's South.

"Crusader for Justice" continues the struggle   On June 27, 1895, Wells married Ferdinand L. Barnett. Barnett shared his wife's interests, and together they championed the black cause for equal rights. They had four children: Charles Aked, Herman Kohlsaat, Ida B. Wells, and Alfreda.

Domesticity did not distract Wells Barnett from her crusade, however. She continued to write articles and took an interest in local and national affairs. In 1909 Wells Barnett was one of two black women—Mary Church Terrell was the other—who signed the "Call" for a conference on the Negro, which came in response to three days of racial violence in Springfield, Illinois, in August 1908. On May 31, 1909, the conference convened in New York City and led to the formation of the National Association for the Advancement of Colored People (NAACP). At the close of the conference, Wells Barnett was placed on the NAACP's executive committee and was a strong advocate of the NAACP's having its own publication to express the views of the organization. Thus, *Crisis* was founded in 1910.

Wells Barnett continued to fight injustice and discrimination in Chicago and throughout the United States. The Springfield riots had motivated her, with students in her Sunday School class at Grace Presbyterian Church, to establish an organization called the Negro Fellowship League. Just before the NAACP was chartered in May 1910, the Negro Fellowship League established a settlement house in Chicago. In 1913 Judge Harry Olson of the municipal court appointed Wells Barnett adult probation officer, a job she held until 1916. She worked out of the Fellowship League's social center and contributed her monthly salary of $150 to the center's budget.

Wells Barnett believed in the power of the ballot box and encouraged black men to register and exercise their right to vote. She worked in the women's suffrage movement and on January 30, 1913, founded the Alpha Suffrage Club of Chicago, the first black suffrage organization. Wells Barnett marched in suffrage parades and led her club members in the parade of June 16, when suffragists marched to the Republican National Convention and demanded a plank in the Republican platform to give women the right to vote.

In December 1920, Wells Barnett was hospitalized and underwent surgery. After her recovery a year later she again became active in the civic and political affairs of Chicago and was one of the founders of the Cook County League of Women's Clubs. When the National Association of Colored Women met in Chicago in 1924, Wells Barnett ran for president of the organization but was defeated by Mary McLeod Bethune. Six years later, in 1930, Wells Barnett entered Chicago's political arena as an independent candidate for state senator. Running against Warren B. Douglas and Adelbert H. Roberts, she was defeated handily.

On March 21, 1931, she became ill and was rushed to Daily Hospital on Monday, March 23, suffering from uremic poisoning. Two days later, at the age of sixty-nine, the ever-vocal "crusader for justice" died. She was buried in Chicago's Oakwood Cemetery. In 1941 the Chicago Housing Authority opened the Ida B. Wells Housing Project, and in 1950 the City of Chicago named her one of twenty-five outstanding women in the city's history. Barnett was able to record her extordinary life and her autobiography, *Crusade for Justice,* was published posthumously in 1970. On July 16, 1987, the 125th anniversary year of her birth and ninety-five years since she had been forced from the "Bluff City," the Memphis Community Relations Commission, through the Tennessee Historical Commission, dedicated a historical marker at the former site of the *Free Speech* newspaper offices.

For the 1990 Black History Month observance, the United States Postal Service issued a stamp honoring this civil rights activist. Also in 1990, the first full-length biography of Wells Barnett, *Ida B. Wells Barnett,* by Mildred Thompson, was published in the sixteen-volume series entitled *Black Women in the United States History: From Colonial Times to the Present.*— LINDA T. WYNN

CORNEL **WEST**

1953–

Philosopher, scholar, educator

Henry Louis Gates, in Emerge *magazine, has called Cornel West "our black Jeremiah." West is a new breed of black scholar, erudite but also accessible, an intellectual but equally an activist who seeks to define black intellectual responsibility. In* The Ethical Dimensions of Marxist Thought, *West challenges black scholars with questions regarding political action and commitment. He asks:*

How do we put the fundamental issues of employment, health and child care, housing, ecology, and education on the agenda of the powers that be in a world disproportionately shaped by transnational corporations and nation-state elites in a global multipolar capitalist order? How do we keep a focus on these issues while we fight racism, patriarchy, homophobia, and ecological abuse? What effective forms of progressive politics can emerge in this new moment of history?

Such challenging questions mark West as a philosopher and prophet grounded in present-day realities; structured by the black experience, his vision of what ought to be is fueled by, in his own words in the reference above, "the Christian ethic of love-informed service to others."

Cornel West was born in Tulsa, Oklahoma, on June 2, 1953. He was the youngest son in a family of two daughters, Cynthia and Cheryl, and an older brother, Clifton III. His father, Clifton L. West Jr. was a civilian Air Force administrator. His mother, Irene Bias West, taught elementary school and later became a school principal. West's grandfather, Clifton L. West Sr., was pastor of Tulsa Metropolitan Baptist Church.

West grounds his childhood experience in the social and political milieu of post-World War II America. No one, West insists, has escaped the effects of European modernity, for at one point Europe dominated and controlled more than two-thirds of the world's people. He calls the world he grew up in, and which led to the formation of his character, the "American century," a term borrowed from Henry Luce. In *The Ethical Dimensions of Marxist Thought,* West defined it as "a period of unprecedented economic boom in the United States, the creation of a large middle class . . . and a mass culture primarily based on African American cultural products."

Born into this world, West saw his father and mother earn a living while demonstrating to him the ideals of dignity, integrity, and humility. During the late 1950s, the family moved to Sacramento, California. West's grounding in Christian theology took place during this period of his life. According to *The Ethical Dimensions of Marxist Thought,* the Christian narratives, symbols, rituals, and concrete moral examples provided him with "existential and ethical equipment to confront the crises, terrors, and horrors of life." West came to understand an aspect of Christianity that moved him from passivity to activism.

Political action   West's first important political action took place when he marched with his family in a civil rights demonstration in Sacramento in 1963. He was ten years old. This would later influence him when as a high school student and class president, he and his best friend, Glenn Jordan, organized a strike of students demanding courses in black studies. The strike was city-wide and brought positive results.

In 1970, West entered Harvard College in Cambridge, Massachusetts. He understood clearly who he was and why he was there. Of his college experience, he recalled in his book:

> I became part of the first generation of young black people to attend pres-
> tigious lily-white institutions of higher learning in significant numbers. . . .
> Owing to my family, church, and the black social movements of the 1960s, I
> arrived at Harvard unashamed of my African, Christian, and militant decolo-
> nized outlooks.

At Harvard, West became involved in social activities which actually were social actions. He participated in a breakfast program for low-income children in the Jamaica Plains area of Boston and made weekly visits to the Norfolk State Prison. As a member of the Black Student Organization in 1972, he participated in the protest against Harvard's interest in the Gulf Oil Corporation. The demonstration resulted in the takeover of Massachusetts Hall, including president Derek Bok's office.

West studied government under Martin Kilson, one of the few black professors at Harvard during the early 1970s. According to Kilson, in the *New York Times Magazine,* West was "the most intellectually aggressive and highly cerebral student [he had] taught in . . . 30 years at Harvard." Kilson arrived at Harvard in 1959. West credits Harvard for broadening his world view.

West majored in philosophy and then changed to the Near Eastern languages and literature department, where he studied the Hebrew and Aramaic languages. Focusing on history and social thought, West doubled up on his courses in order to graduate a year early. He received his bachelor of arts degree magna cum laude in 1973.

Wanting to further his studies in philosophy, West applied to and was accepted by the philosophy department at Princeton University. In 1975, West earned a master of arts degree from Princeton and continued to study for his Ph.D., which he earned in 1980. After completing his course work for his doctorate, West became an assistant professor of philosophy and religion in 1977 at Union Theological Seminary in New York, where he remained until 1984, when he accepted a position at Yale University.

West believed that his move to Yale Divinity School gave him the opportunity to reflect on the crisis in American philosophy and social thought. While West valued and cultivated the life of the mind, he by no means became disconnected from the world of active demonstration and protest. In fact, when he arrived at Yale, the campus was embroiled in two issues: one, the movement for a union of clerical employees, and the other, objection to Yale's investments in South African companies.

Critical thought and focused action   West was no arm-chair revolutionary (1960s term for intellectuals). He took to the streets with the mass of protesters, and when he was arrested and jailed, he said, as noted in his book, "My arrest and jail . . . served as a fine example for my wonderful son, Clifton, quickly approaching adolescence"—an example his son followed as a progressive student body president of his predominately black middle school in Atlanta. West was married twice, with each ending in divorce. Clifton is the son of his first marriage and lives in Atlanta.

In the spring of 1987, West was angered by the Yale administration, which denied his request for a leave of absence and insisted that he teach a full load, two courses at Yale. West had made prior arrangements to teach three courses at the University of Paris in the spring of 1987, anticipating his leave from Yale. When his leave was denied, West commuted every five to seven days between New Haven and Paris from February to April. While teaching abroad, he was amazed at the lack of knowledge regarding American philosophy and African American intellectual thought in particular.

West returned to the United States with a fiancee, Elleni Gebre Amlak, an Ethiopian, and a new job. He left Yale and returned to Union. After only a year at Union, he again went to Princeton where he was professor of religion and director of the Afro-American Studies Program.

The crisis of leadership   In returning to Princeton West wanted to form a critical mass of black scholars, with Toni Morrison at the center, in order to address the problems plaguing Americans approaching the century's end. West's vision of the coming millennium is one of social chaos and self-destruction unless Americans seize the moment, and, as noted in his book, galvanize "demoralized progressives and liberals across racial, class, regional, age, and gender lines."

Writing and publishing since the 1970s, West had many important books in print when in 1993 Beacon Press published his first best seller, *Race Matters*. In this book, perhaps more accessible to the general reading public than his more philosophical works, West scrutinizes race and cultural diversity and pronounces the political body terminally ill. Healing, however, is within our capabilities. West's prescription for society's ills is love.

In 1994 Henry Louis Gates, the W. E. B. Du Bois Professor and director of Afro-American Studies at Harvard, recruited West to come to Harvard. West and his wife now reside in Massachusetts.

West is a member of the editorial collective for *Boundary 2: An International Journal of Literature and Culture*. He also writes a column for *Tikkun,* a Jewish journal.

He has written the following books: *Black Theology and Marxist Thought* (1979); *Prophesy Deliverance! An Afro-American Revolutionary Christianity* (1982); *Prophetic Fragments* (1988); *The American Evasion of Philosophy: A Genealogy of Pragmatism* (1989); *The Ethical Dimensions of Marxist Thought* (1991); *Beyond Eurocentrism and Multiculturalism* (1993); and *Race Matters* (1993). He is coeditor of *Theology in the Americas* (1982); *Post-Analytic Philosophy* (1985); and *Out There: Marginalization of Contemporary Cultures* (1990). West and Bell Hooks together have written *Breaking Bread: Insurgent Black Intellectual Life* (1991), and he and Henry Louis Gates have edited *The Future of the Race* (1996).

In 1982, West joined the Democratic Socialists of America. He has served on the national political committee for seven years and became its honorary chairperson. A popular scholar in great demand as a speaker, Cornel West is an important black intellectual known for his challenging and provocative views on social and political issues.—NAGUEYALTI WARREN

WALTER **WHITE**

1893–1955

Civil rights worker, organization executive, writer

When Walter White became leader of the NAACP, the organization's priorities had been set. His contribution

was to move those priorities forward. During his lifetime and in large part due to his efforts, lynching ceased

to be a common event. His courage, energy, and hard work did much to bring the problem of race relations

in the United States to the center of the political stage. It was at White's urging that President Harry Truman

set up a Civil Rights Committee whose report, "To Secure These Rights," was reflected in civil rights planks in the 1948 platform of the Democratic National Convention and set a political agenda for liberals. When the Supreme Court dismantled school segregation in Brown v. Board of Education *shortly before White's death, he could look with pride at a long legal campaign led by the NAACP.*

Walter Francis White was born on July 1, 1893, in Atlanta, Georgia, to George White and Madeline Harrison White. Walter White, the fourth child, had an older brother, George Jr., the oldest child, and five sisters, Alice (Glenn), Olive (Westmoreland), Ruby, Helen, and Madeline, the youngest child. George White Sr. came from Augusta, Georgia, and attended Atlanta University's high school. His parents' deaths came close together and put an end to his schooling after completion of his freshman year at the university. Madeline Harrison came from Lagrange, Georgia, and completed her schooling in Atlanta. She then returned to Lagrange to teach. Her future husband secured a job with the postal service, and saved enough money on his small salary to buy a lot on Houston Street and build a small five-room house. When the Whites finally built a larger eight-room house on the lot, the first house was moved to the back of the lot and rented out.

Walter White begins his autobiography, *A Man Called White,* with the statement: "I am a Negro. My skin is white, my eyes are blue, my hair is blond. The traits of my race are nowhere visible upon me." All members of the White family were light-skinned. Walter White's maternal grandfather was a Dr. E. Harrison, white. Geneologist and author Caroline Bond Day gives his mother's heritage as one-sixteenth black, one-sixteenth Indian, and seven-eighths white, and Day estimates that his father was one-fourth black and three-quarters white. When George White Sr. was struck down by an automobile in 1931, he was taken unconscious to the white side of the hospital—only when a brown-skinned son-in-law made inquiries about him was George White taken to the much inferior black side, where he died seventeen days later.

In addition to skin color, the family's education, home ownership, and aspirations set it apart from the black masses. Its religious affiliation was also not widely shared—they were members of the First Congregational Church, which was just a half block away from the family home. The pastor of the church during White's youth and young manhood was famed black minister Henry Hugh Proctor (1868–1933), a Fisk classmate of W. E. B. Du Bois and holder of a B.D. degree from Yale University. After the Atlanta riots, Proctor led his church into extensive social work, constructing the first gymnasium open to the community as well as the first church-sponsored home for black girls, the Avery Home for Working Girls.

George White Sr. saw to the family's religious training in a nearly Puritan tradition, with long family prayer sessions on Sunday. White's childhood was generally happy. As he grew older, he sought a job as a bell-hop in a leading downtown hotel. In his first hotel job he inadvertently passed as white.

In his autobiography Walter White ascribes his firm identification as an African American to his experiences in the September 1906 Atlanta race riot. White and his father witnessed episodes of violence on Saturday, September 7, the first day of the riots, as they made his father's rounds to collect the mail. The following evening, the neighborhood prepared for the visitation of the mob. Walter White heard the son of their grocer yell, "That's where that nigger mail carrier lives! Let's burn it down! It's too nice for a nigger to live in!" Very quietly, George White said then, "Son, don't shoot until the first man puts his foot on the lawn and

Walter White urges the adoption of a civil rights program in 1948.

then—don't you miss." Fortunately, shots rang out from a house further down the street and the mob turned aside.

White attended high school at Atlanta University—there were no public high schools for blacks. He then attended the college, receiving his degree in 1916. We know little of his experiences at university other than that he was a member of the debating society, played football—"not too good football," he says in his autobiography, possibly since he was only five feet seven inches tall—and was president of his graduating class. In the summer of 1915, he gave up hotel work to sell insurance for the Standard Life Insurance Company, headed by Harry Pace, who later set up a music publishing company and then founded Black Swan records. Since Atlanta had been pretty thoroughly canvassed by this time, White devoted much of his effort to selling in rural areas. This gave him valuable first-hand experience of the conditions of rural blacks. During the following school year, White worked part-time for the insurance company and then accepted a job as a clerk upon graduation.

In 1916, the Atlanta school board decided to cut out the seventh grade in black schools to save money to be used for white schools just as it had previously cut out the eighth in 1914. White grasped eagerly at the suggestion that blacks form a local branch of the NAACP to spearhead a protest; when the branch was formed, Pace was president and White, secretary. Their protests to the school board set in motion a series of actions that eventually led to the establishment of Atlanta's first high school for blacks in 1920.

James Weldon Johnson was invited to address the first public mass meeting of the NAACP. White was called upon to deliver an unplanned speech and gave a fiery address. A friend said much later, "When human rights are involved . . . Walter is never at a loss for a word. Or even several paragraphs." Johnson had dinner with the Whites before he left Atlanta and closely questioned Walter. Johnson later wrote Walter White to offer him a job as assistant secretary in the NAACP's New York office. White hesitated. The organization was in a shaky condition, and he would take a reduction in income. Physician Louis T. Wright (a future chair of the NAACP board and White's personal physician in New York in later years) and White's father urged him to accept the offer. In his autobiography, White quotes his father as saying:

> Your mother and I have given you . . . the best education we could afford, and a good Christian home training. . . . Now it is your duty to pass on what you have been given by helping others less fortunate to get a chance in life. I don't want to see you go away. I'll miss you. But remember always, God will be using your heart and brains to do His will.

White joins national NAACP office staff   White took up his duties in New York on January 31, 1918. Originally, he was to perform clerical and office duties, but on February 12, he and James Weldon Johnson read of a terrible lynching in Estill Springs, Tennessee. White volunteered to go to the scene and, passing as white, make an investigation. This investigation in Tennessee was the first of many occasions that he risked his life. In the summer of 1919, as White investigated a disturbance in which as many as two hundred blacks may have been killed, he was identified and barely escaped lynching in Phillips County, Alabama. After some years, White's fame became too great for him to continue his undercover investigations. The dangers he ran as a result of his efforts to combat racism were principally but not solely from whites. White had some close calls also when blacks identified him as white in tense racial situations. He narrowly escaped a bullet in the aftermath of the 1919 Chicago riots.

White undertook a very active pattern of work for the NAACP. In the ten years following 1918, he made personal inquiries into forty-one lynchings and eight race riots. In Tulsa of 1921 he was even drafted as a temporary deputy sheriff on the basis of his appearance. White worked assiduously in publicizing his findings. Under the tutelage of James Weldon Johnson, he developed great skills as a lobbyist. There was always much travel and many speaking engagements. White covered twenty-six thousand miles and spoke eighty-six times. In February 1927, White spoke seventeen times and had several conferences in a twelve-day span.

In addition to his work for the NAACP, White's horizons also expanded as he developed wider intellectual interests. Here again his mentor was James Weldon Johnson, who became a close friend. On February 15, 1922, White married Leah Gladys Powell, a fellow

member of the NAACP staff; the marriage produced two children, Jane (b. 1923) and Walter Carl Darrow (b. 1927).

In 1922, White made negative comments about a novel on blacks by a white author in a review for *Smart Set*. The magazine's editor, H. L. Mencken, challenged him to do better. Mary White Ovington lent her Massachusetts cottage to the Whites during the summer of 1922, and during twelve days of intense work, White produced the draft of *The Fire in the Flint*. The novel was about the return of a Southern born doctor to his hometown where he is eventually forced to confront racism head on. Within the novel, the doctor is burned at the stake because of a false claim that he had raped a white woman, his sister is raped, and his brother murdered by whites. The sensational nature of the material led to the novel's garnering extensive reviews and good sales for a first novel when it was published in 1924 by Knopf. White's second novel, *Flight*, published in 1927, attracted less attention. This novel ended with the heroine's decision to rejoin the black community after passing as white. White thought his third novel would be a three-generation work based on his own family. In June 1927, using the money from a Guggenheim Fellowship Grant, White took his family to France for a year to work on the book. Away from the United States, White's attention was drawn to the racial situation in his native country and he devoted much of his time to an analysis of the causes of lynching. The book which resulted, *Rope and Faggot*, was published in 1929. White eventually wrote about forty five thousand words of the family novel, some two-thirds of the whole.

White becomes "new negro"   Alain Locke chose White as one of the contributors to *The New Negro* (1925), one of the Harlem Renaissance's defining works. White's role in the Renaissance went far beyond writing. In his prominent position he was active as a link between people and as a promoter of works. Black writers and white sympathizers met at parties. Carl Van Vechten contacted White after reading *The Fire in the Flint*. He and White became friends, and White introduced him to other Harlem writers and artists. Other aspects of White's efforts on the behalf of artists and writers are amply represented in the NAACP files. For example, the poet Claude McKay used White as one of his main contacts in Harlem over the years, and White assiduously promoted his favorite black poet, Countee Cullen. In music, White's activities succeeded in attracting a larger audience to one of Paul Robeson's early recitals, helping to launch his career.

White's absence in 1927–28 during the time he held the Guggenheim indirectly led to his advancement at the NAACP. James Weldon Johnson began to overwork himself, and in the spring of 1929, he took a leave of absence from the NAACP. During Johnson's absence, White was very effective as one of the three acting secretaries. White helped the NAACP to win an important victory in 1930—the defeat of Herbert Hoover's nomination of John J. Parker of North Carolina to a seat on the U.S. Supreme Court. As White explains in his autobiography, Parker had declared in 1920, "The participation of the Negro in politics is a source of evil and danger to both races and is not desired by the wise men in either race or by the Republican Party of North Carolina."

Parker's nomination was defeated by one vote in the Senate. The unprecedented protest campaign organized by the NAACP, especially by black voters in Northern and border states, was credited for the defeat. The political power of the NAACP was enhanced by the role of blacks in the defeat of several of Parker supporters in subsequent elections.

Afraid, Johnson resigned on December 17, 1930, and White became executive secretary in his place, a position he held until his death. By now the NAACP had institutionalized the goals which were central to White's activities for the rest of his life. It investigated and publicized lynchings, it attacked racial injustice in the courts, and it lobbied against segregation in the legislatures.

The NAACP was now faced with the problems of severely declining revenues. It was heavily dependent on memberships for funding, and the Depression following the stock market crash of October 1929 sharply cut black earning power and also philanthropic contributions. By 1934 the organization was on the verge of financial collapse.

White becomes executive secretary of the NAACP   White was named executive secretary of the NAACP at the same board meeting that made Joel E. Spingarn president. The relation between the two men shaped the administrative history of the organization between 1930 and 1935. White had consulted Spingarn, who was then an editor at Harcourt and Brace, about his first novel in 1922. Spingarn continued to offer advice and encouragement to White over the years, but they did not address each other on a first name basis until 1932. Spingarn took the lead in formulating the NAACP's financial policies, especially from 1930 to 1933. Although White appears to have been a meticulous record keeper, Spingarn took up a large role in financial affairs and retrenchment. The financial measures brought about a rift between White and the other salaried executives; all attacked White in a signed memorandum presented to the board in December 1931, charging him with presenting false information to the board. The financial crisis had reached such a point in mid-1933 that Roy Wilkins, then assistant secretary, was placed on half salary and Robert W. Bagnall, director of branches since 1919, was fired and his position abolished.

The financial crisis had a major effect on the relations between White and W. E. B. Du Bois, the editor of the NAACP's publication, *Crisis*, which were not good to begin with. In 1929, the magazine began to lose money. Du Bois struggled to retain his editorial autonomy as the board formed a committee to supervise the magazine. Significantly, all signers of the December 1931 memorandum to the board attacking White withdrew their signatures except Du Bois. It is not clear what the reasons were for the intense dislike the two men took to each other beginning sometime in the 1920s. Du Bois and White, however, were both proud men with a considerable measure of vanity. Since Spingarn wished to retain Du Bois as editor of the *Crisis*, these struggles were patched up in 1933.

Du Bois then stepped up his ultimately futile efforts to change the goals of the NAACP. In January 1934 he endorsed voluntary self-segregation in an editorial in *Crisis*. In February, Du Bois refused to publish White's heated reply affirming absolute opposition to segregation in any form, even though White had incorporated some softening changes suggested by Spingarn. On April 9 the board rejected separate statements on segregation proposed by Du Bois (two members supported him) and by Spingarn. The board then adopted a position condemning segregation without resolving the question of whether black churches and schools were to be considered forms of forced segregation. For this and other reasons, Du Bois severed all connection with the NAACP by July and White took over management of *Crisis*, appointing Roy Wilkins, then assistant secretary, editor.

Another attempt by White to change the goals of the NAACP by a group of young intellectuals also came to nought. One of the leaders, Abram Harris of Howard University, was elected to the board in 1934. Harris led a board committee to draft a plan for a reorganization intended, among other things, to change the way the board operated and to address the economic problems of working-class blacks. Harris and his supporters won only a partial victory on board changes, and the economic plan entailed costs the organization could not support. Harris was chagrined to learn that the proposed economic plan was almost the same as the program of the Urban League.

One result of the internal struggles was the resignation of Joel E. Spingarn as chairman of the board in 1935—he remained president of the association until his death in 1939, when his brother followed him in the now largely ceremonial position. His replacement was Louis T. Wright, a distinguished black surgeon and White's personal physician. (Wright once saved White's life by carrying him seven blocks to the hospital and operating on him for appendicitis.) This change shifted power into White's hand; for approximately the next fifteen years, he was essentially in sole control of the NAACP. In 1937 he received the organization's Spingarn Medal.

White continues the battle One of White's major achievements dates from 1935. He was instrumental in securing a foundation grant which enabled the NAACP to hire Charles Hamilton Houston, a noted black lawyer. Although the legal department retained a degree of independence from White's control, Houston led a brilliant team, including such persons as William H. Hastie and Thurgood Marshall, which undertook a legal campaign to dismantle legal segregation culminating in *Brown v. Board of Education* in 1954, shortly before White's death.

White's life involved much hard work, with great attention to detail, travel, and writing. In later years he seems to have been the almost indispensable black representative on advisory committees, being involved in such matters as the formation of the United Nations in 1945 and serving as a delegate to the General Assembly of the United Nations in Paris in 1948. He wrote articles for major magazines like *Saturday Evening Post* and *Reader's Digest*. He wrote a regular column for the *Chicago Defender* and a syndicated column for the *New York Herald-Tribune*. When he was called on to investigate the condition of black troops during World War II in 1943 to 1945, he became a war correspondent for the *New York Post* and produced another book, *A Rising Wind*. His final book, *How Far the Promised Land*, was published in 1955 after his death.

In the late 1940s about five percent of blacks eighteen or older were members of the NAACP, a formidable pressure group. This gave White considerable leverage as a lobbyist; all politicians may not have loved him but he was feared where he was not liked. A gregarious man, he was on a first name basis with many members of Congress and with at least five of the nine Supreme Court justices. As a lobbyist he was forthright in expressing his opinion and notorious for his refusal to compromise his principles. This is proven by his refusal to accept a compromise offered by President Roosevelt on an anti-lynching bill, as well as by his vigorous opposition to the establishment of a segregated flight training program at Tuskegee during World War II, just as he had opposed segregated training camps for black officers in World War I. Roy Wilkins sums up his impression of White's temperament by saying, "he was brash, outgoing, effusive, a great salesman, propagandist, and maker of friends."

White published his autobiography, *A Man Called White,* in 1948. A very interesting and well-written work, it reflects the institutional and representational side of Walter White and concentrates on race relations in the first half of the twentieth century.

In an acrimonious meeting on his return to the NAACP in 1950, the board retained White as executive secretary but gave Roy Wilkins the responsibility for day-to-day operations and made Wilkins report directly to the board. With lessened power, White continued to formulate broad policy and serve as spokesperson for the NAACP.

White died of a heart attack on March 21, 1955. After a large funeral at St. Martin's Episcopal Church in Harlem, his remains were cremated at Ferncliff Cemetery, Hartsdale, New York. He was survived by his widow and two children.

For at least a quarter of a century, Walter White and the NAACP claimed the attention of white Americans as the voice of black Americans. White must receive great credit for making black concerns visible to the majority community and helping to build a liberal consensus on race relations. In addition to leading the NAACP to important legal victories, White initiated great changes in public attitudes, opening the way to the further gains of the civil rights era. It was just over eight months after his death that Rosa Parks refused to give up her seat on a Birmingham bus.—ROBERT L. JOHNS

L. DOUGLAS **WILDER**
1931–
Lawyer, governor, politician, radio host

When Beulah and Robert Wilder named the ninth of their ten children after the poet Paul Laurence Dunbar and the abolitionist, author, and statesman Frederick Douglass, they could not have known that one day he would join his famous namesakes on the roll of pioneering African American leaders. Born January 17, 1931, in Richmond, Virginia, Lawrence Douglas Wilder became the nation's first elected African American governor when he overcame his white Republican opponent J. Marshall Coleman in a hard-fought race. During his 1989 gubernatorial campaign, Wilder said in his biography by Margaret Edds, Claiming the Dream, *of the two miles that separated his family's home from Richmond's Capitol Hill, "It's a short distance to walk, but it's a mighty, mighty mountain to climb."*

Wilder grew up in a segregated Richmond neighborhood, Church Hill, in a house his parents built in 1923. Nevertheless, he describes the years he spent living in the two-story frame house with his parents, six sisters, and one brother as poor but happy.

His father, Robert Judson Wilder Sr., born to former slaves twenty one years after the Civil War's end, supported his wife and children by working as a salesman for Southern Aid Insurance, the nation's oldest black-owned insurance company. From Robert Wilder, Wilder learned industry, discipline, and frugality, the last in particular being a trait he has used to his advantage when campaigning for political office.

Although Wilder's strict but loving father provided him with guidance and a positive role model, his mother, Beulah Olive Richards Wilder, whom Donald Baker characterizes in *Wilder: Hold Fast to Dreams* as a "tee-totaling Christian woman," played the most significant

L Douglas Wilder.

role in shaping the character and self-confidence of her son. According to Edds, Beulah Wilder often told Wilder he was "a special little boy." In the same source, Wilder's sister, Agnes Nicholson, describes her mother and brother as "the best of friends" who enjoyed spending time together working crossword puzzles, reading, and talking.

Some of the credit for Wilder's successful career as a lawyer, state senator, lieutenant governor, and governor must also be given to his hardworking Church Hill neighbors and to the unique experiences this poor but tight-knit African American community offered the bright, ambitious young boy. In addition to performing numerous chores around the family home, Wilder worked as a newspaper salesman for the *Richmond Planet* (a weekly black newspaper later called the *Richmond Afro-American*), shined shoes, shot pool, sang in the choir of Richmond's First African Baptist Church, and attended George Mason Elementary School. At Billy's Barber Shop in Church Hill, a place Wilder would later call "my stadium," Wilder began to hone his oratorical skills. Edds tells of one of the barbershop's regular customers, Arthur Burke, who remembered another patron telling young Douglas Wilder: "You should be a lawyer. You argue too much and you tell the biggest lies in the world."

At the age of twelve, Wilder skipped the eighth grade and entered Richmond's segregated Armstrong High School. Although Wilder was a good enough student to be elected to the National Honor Society, he had not distinguished himself sufficiently to earn a college scholarship. For financial reasons and because his parents would not grant permission for their seventeen-year-old son to enter the navy, Wilder enrolled at Virginia Union University, a black liberal arts college founded soon after the Civil War and located in Richmond, as a chemistry major with the intention of becoming a dental surgeon. His mother gave him twenty five of the one hundred dollars he needed for a semester's tuition; the rest he earned as a waiter at Richmond hotels and country clubs, jobs he continued to hold in order to pay his way through college.

An indifferent student who perhaps devoted too much time to his social life, Wilder graduated in August 1951 after repeating a calculus course in order to raise his grade point average to meet the graduation requirements. But in spite of his lack of direction as a college student, Wilder considers his years at Virginia Union to have been instrumental to his achieving political success. At the dedication of Virginia Union University's $7.5 million L. Douglas Wilder Library and Learning Resource Center on February 14, 1997, he was quoted in the *Richmond Times Dispatch* as saying that "But for Virginia Union, I could never have been governor of any place or anything. . . . I could never have really believed in myself."

Though he had yet to settle on a profession, in August 1952, a year after receiving his college diploma, Wilder embarked on a new phase of life. He was drafted into the army and sent to Korea in August 1952. While stationed in Korea, Wilder began to display leadership qualities and to speak out openly against racism. Private Wilder, aghast at his fellow African American soldiers' complaints that they were being passed over for deserved promotions, arranged for them to meet with the battalion commander, Major Earl C. Acuff. Wilder's political skills were evident at this meeting and African American soldiers began receiving promotions; Wilder himself became a corporal.

While in Korea, Wilder helped to capture nineteen North Korean prisoners on April 18, 1953. Three months later, he returned to the United States and received a permanent promotion to field sergeant, a rank Major Acuff had temporarily bestowed on him in Korea. Wilder was discharged from the U.S. Army in December 1953. He also won a Bronze Star for his role in capturing the Korean soldiers but kept the honor a secret until he began his 1969 campaign for the Virginia State legislature.

Enters the law profession   After his stint in the army, Wilder returned to his parents' Church Hill home still uncertain about his future. He spent six months working sporadically as a waiter, until eventually becoming a mail carrier. His next position, a technician in the state's medical examiner's office, allowed him to make use of his chemistry degree. In 1956 he finally realized he wanted to be a lawyer and entered Howard University's Law School. The state of Virginia strongly discouraged blacks from attending the University of Virginia's School of Law, although a black student had been admitted there in 1950. Rather than integrate its law school, the state preferred to give black law students scholarships to go elsewhere.

While at Howard, Wilder met undergraduate Eunice Montgomery, an economics major from Philadelphia. The couple wed on October 11, 1958. Their first child, Lynn Diana, was born May 19, 1959, the same month both Wilder and his wife received their degrees. Soon Wilder went to work as a law clerk for William A. Smith, a Newport News, Virginia, lawyer who specialized in personal injury cases, and commuted to Richmond on weekends to visit his wife, who worked in a Richmond bank, and their infant daughter. Soon after passing the Virginia Bar Examination, Wilder set up a law office close to his parents' home. Soon Wilder won his first case and his legal practice began to thrive. By 1962, Wilder was clearly beginning to realize the American dream. That year the Wilders bought their first house and had their second baby, Lawrence Douglas Jr., born February 17; he is now an attorney with his father's firm. Their third child, Loren Deane, was born November 5, 1963.

Political aspirations and success   As Wilder's reputation as a trial lawyer grew, so too did his ambition. In 1969, he made a successful bid for the Virginia State Senate, the first African American elected to this office in Virginia. During his sixteen years as a state senator, Wilder proved himself a force to be reckoned with. Less than a month into his first term as senator, Wilder introduced a bill to repeal the state's official song, "Carry Me Back to Old Virginni," which includes the line "that's where this old darkie's heart am long to go," an act that upset many of his colleagues, who voted against the bill. Twenty seven years later, the Virginia senate finally decided that Wilder had a point and retired the song. As Edds observes:

> Throughout the 1970s Wilder pursued a liberal, civil rights-oriented legislative agenda. He pushed for fair housing laws and a holiday honoring Martin Luther King Jr. He backed proposals to strip the sales tax from food and

L. Douglas Wilder
speaks in 1989.

nonprescription drugs. . . . He opposed the death penalty and fought tough crime legislation including bills creating a sentence of life in prison without parole and prescribing a separate offense for the use of a gun in committing a felony.

In the midst of his political triumphs, Wilder's marriage failed. Eunice Wilder filed for divorce in 1975. Wilder continued to support the children, who lived with their mother.

Aside from these personal difficulties, Wilder continued to enjoy political success throughout the 1970s and 1980s, although many of his critics claim that he sacrificed the concerns of African Americans for the sake of his own aspirations. While his reasons for becoming more moderate on subjects such as the death penalty, underage abortions, and parole remain open to debate, by the time he became the state's lieutenant governor, Wilder's platform was most assuredly that of a moderate Democrat, not that of a liberal. By his own admission, Wilder has never been a black activist or a civil rights leader, though he often used his political clout to fight discrimination and to promote the careers of African American political allies. Describing his relationship with Jesse Jackson, to whom he is sometimes unfavorably compared, Baker quotes Wilder as saying, "Jesse Jackson understands me and I understand him. He runs to strike the conscience of the country; I am running to be elected." When Wilder announced his decision to run for the governor's seat in 1989, Jackson supported his candidacy and praised him for his courage.

First black elected governor   During his four-year term as governor of the state of Virginia that began in 1990, Wilder placed his name on the list of contenders for the 1992 Democratic presidential nomination. He eventually withdrew from the race, stating that the campaign was keeping him from devoting his full attention to his gubernatorial duties. While in office, among other programs, he trimmed the state's budget and removed the $2.2 billion deficit and stressed the need for civil rights legislation. After completing his term as governor— Virginia does not allow its governors to serve consecutive terms—he remained a major figure in Virginia politics, in part because of what has become known as the Robb-Wilder feud. In 1994 Wilder declared himself an independent candidate for the U.S. Senate seat held by Charles Robb. Also vying for this seat were Republican Oliver North and Marshall Coleman, who, like Wilder, was running as an independent candidate. Democratic solidarity led Wilder to set aside his considerable differences with Robb. He withdrew from the race and openly supported Robb. Since 1995 Wilder has hosted *The Doug Wilder Show*. In *Jet* magazine, Wilder called the show "My way of continuing in public service."

Each time Wilder has thrown his hat into the political ring and declared himself a candidate for office, his campaigns have served as instruments for measuring the depth of the effects race and racism have on American politics. On the one hand, Wilder seems to be a man of contradictions: an African American willing to play the race card while simultaneously denying that he is doing so, and a team player who sometimes prefers to wear a maverick's stripes rather than conform to others' game plans. On the other hand, he is a consummate politician, wise in the ways of the political arena dominated by white people in the South and in the United States—a man who knows that his personal political victories herald a brighter future for all African Americans.—CANDIS LAPRADE

AUGUST **WILSON**

1945–
Playwright, poet

Prolific playwright August Wilson is a modern-day griot who has eloquently and consistently chronicled black American life. His critically acclaimed dramas, Ma Rainey's Black Bottom, Fences, Joe Turner's Come and Gone, The Piano Lesson, Two Trains Running, *and* Seven Guitars, *have been performed at regional theaters across the United States as well as on Broadway; they have also been published. Thanks to*

Wilson's focus on identity, culture, and history, his plays take audiences and readers on a journey through black American life. Wilson, who ranks as a prominent theatrical voice, was the first black American to have two plays running simultaneously on Broadway and is one of seven American playwrights to win two Pulitzer Prizes.

The man the world knows as August Wilson was born Frederick August Kittel on April 27, 1945, in Pittsburgh, Pennsylvania. Earlier, his maternal grandmother exhibited great strength and determination when she walked from North Carolina to Pennsylvania in search of a better life. Wilson's mother, Daisy, inherited her mother's strength and determination, qualities she needed to raise six children in a two-room apartment behind a grocery store in Pittsburgh's Hill District, a poor neighborhood inhabited by blacks, Italians, and Jews. Daisy supported her family on income earned as a cleaning lady. Her husband, Frederick Kittel, a German immigrant and baker, seldom spent time with his family. Decades later, in the 1970s, August, Daisy and Frederick's fourth child and eldest son, adopted his mother's maiden name, Wilson, and dropped his paternal surname.

During Wilson's teen years, his mother married David Bedford, and the family moved from the Hill to a predominantly white suburban neighborhood in the late 1950s. The Bedfords, moving to Hazelwood in search of a better life, encountered racial hostility. Bricks were thrown through a window at their new address. When Wilson transferred to Gladstone High School, he was subjected to additional racial incidents. His white schoolmates frequently left notes on his desk advising "Nigger go home." Yet an even greater insult to Wilson was the inability of a teacher to fathom that a black student could create a well-written term paper. After reading Wilson's paper centered on Napoleon, the instructor accused him of plagiarism. The racial animosity exhibited at Gladstone led Wilson, at age fifteen, to drop out of school.

Although Wilson's formal education ended abruptly, he continued to learn through disciplined self-study at the Carnegie Library. Wilson, who learned to read at age four and who began perusing black writers at age twelve, spent the remainder of his teen years educating himself. Reading works from the public library by Ralph Ellison, Richard Wright, Langston Hughes, Arna Bontemps, and other black writers, *Contemporary Black Biography* noted that Wilson was caught up in the power of words.

His fascination with this power of words generated tension at home. During his teens, Wilson became determined that he would become a writer and worked a series of odd jobs. His mother, who wanted Wilson to pursue a career as an attorney, did not approve and forced him to leave the family residence. He enlisted in the United States Army in 1963 only to be discharged in 1964.

Begins writing career   On April 1, 1965, a few weeks shy of his twentieth birthday, Wilson invested in his writing career; he purchased his first typewriter. During the fall of 1965, Wilson moved to a rooming house in his native city. Reflecting on that period in his youth, Wilson described himself in the preface to *Three Plays* as "a twenty-year-old poet wrestling with the world and his place in it, having discovered the joy and terror of remaking the world in his own image through the act of writing." He supported himself by working a series of low-paying jobs—as dishwasher, short-order cook, porter, stock boy, gardener, and mail room clerk—for approximately the next twelve or thirteen years; during his leisure time,

August Wilson stands beside one of his playbills.

Wilson frequently sat in a restaurant and created poems on paper bags. Although he did not gain fame as a poet, his initial writing efforts were poetic, and his poems were published in the late 1960s and early 1970s in several periodicals such as *Negro Digest* (which later became *Black World*) as well as *Black Lines* and in at least one anthology published in the early 1970s, *The Poetry of Black Americans: Anthology of the Twentieth Century,* edited by Arnold Adoff. Among the poems published during this period were "For Malcolm X and Others," "Morning Song," "Muhammad Ali," "Theme One: The Variations," and "Bessie."

Hearing the blues singer Bessie Smith led to an awakening in Wilson. He wrote in the preface to *Three Plays:*

One night in the fall of 1965 I put a typewritten yellow-labeled record titled 'Nobody in Town Can Bake a Sweet Jellyroll Like Mine,' by someone named

Bessie Smith on the turntable of my 78 rpm phonograph, and the universe stuttered and everything fell to a new place.

Although the business of poetry is to enlarge the sayable, I cannot describe or even relate what I felt. Suffice it to say it was a birth, a baptism, a resurrection, and a redemption all rolled up in one. It was the beginning of my consciousness that I was a representative of a culture and the carrier of some very valuable antecedents. With my discovery of Bessie Smith and the blues I had been given a world that contained my image, a world at once rich and varied, marked and marking, brutal and beautiful, and at crucial odds with the larger world that contained it and preyed and pressed it from every conceivable angle.

After listening to Smith's voice, Wilson assumed the responsibility passed on from his black American ancestors en masse; hearing the blues motivated, challenged, and empowered the young poet to document black American culture and history in his writings. He continued in the preface to *Three Plays:*

I had to look at black life with an anthropological eye, use language, character, and image to reveal its cultural flashpoints and in the process tell a story that further illuminated them. This is what the blues did. Why couldn't I? I was, after all, a bluesman. Never mind I couldn't play a guitar or carry a tune in a bucket. I was cut out of the same cloth and I was on the same field of manners and endeavor—to articulate the cultural response of black Americans to the world in which they found themselves.

During the remainder of the 1960s, Wilson continued to write and was instrumental in founding two organizations that promoted black American writing: the Center Avenue Poets Theatre Workshop, formed in 1965, and Black Horizons (BH), formed in 1968. Wilson cofounded BH with his friend, Rob Penny, a playwright and teacher, in efforts to politicize black Americans and to increase their race consciousness. Wilson's earliest plays were written for BH including *Recycle,* written in 1973 and produced at a Pittsburgh community theater; *The Homecoming,* about blues singer and guitarist Blind Lemon Jefferson, written in 1976 but not produced until 1989; and *The Coldest Day of the Year,* a drama focusing on relationships between black American men and women that was written in 1977 but not produced until 1989.

In 1969 Wilson married Brenda Burton, a member of the Nation of Islam, and one year later, their daughter, Sakina, was born. The Wilsons divorced in 1972.

In 1978 Wilson traveled to St. Paul, Minnesota, to visit his friend Claude Purdy, who had worked in theater while in Pittsburgh before becoming the director of St. Paul's Penumbra Theatre. Wilson decided to move to St. Paul and was employed as a scriptwriter for the Science Museum of Minnesota. On the Museum's behalf, Wilson wrote several brief scripts including *An Evening with Margaret Mead, How Coyote Got His Special Power, Used It to Help the People,* and *Eskimo Song Duel;* years later Sandra G. Shannon quoted Wilson in *The Dramatic Vision of August Wilson* who commented on his association with the museum: "Well, it was a good experience. If nothing else, it was the first time that I was getting paid for writing. Someone was actually paying me—it was good money as I recall—to sit down and write these things."

In his spare time, Wilson continued to create plays. According to *Contemporary Black Biography,* in 1979 "in ten days of writing while sitting in a fish-and-chips restaurant," he wrote *Jitney!*, a drama about Pittsburgh's black jitney drivers set in 1971. *Jitney!* was accepted by the Minneapolis Playwrights Center (MPC) in 1980; the theater group named Wilson an associate playwright of the MPC, and awarded him a $200 per month fellowship. In 1982 *Jitney!* was produced at Pittsburgh's Allegheny Repertory Theatre. *Jitney!* was followed by Wilson's *Fullerton Street,* written in 1980 and set in the 1940s. His next play, *Black Bart and the Sacred Hills,* is a musical satire written in 1977, produced in 1981, and is based on a series of poems about a legendary outlaw of the Wild West. Wilson quit his job as the museum's scriptwriter in order to devote more time to creating his own plays. He was encouraged in this endeavor by his second wife, Judy Oliver, a white social worker he married in 1981.

Debuts on Broadway   In 1980 Rob Penny encouraged Wilson to apply to the National Playwrights Conference (NPC) at the O'Neill Theatre Center in Connecticut where each summer fifteen playwrights are selected to participate from the approximately 1500 who apply. The O'Neill rejected five Wilson scripts before accepting *Ma Rainey's Black Bottom* (*MRBB*) for a workshop in 1982, the same year Wilson wrote the play. The NPC's director, Lloyd Richards, who is also director of the Yale Repertory Theatre and dean of the Yale School of Drama, staged a production of *MRBB* at the Yale Repertory Theatre in April, 1984. *MRBB* marks the beginning of Wilson's association with Richards. Wilson stated in the preface to *Three Plays* that Richards is "my guide, my mentor, and my provocateur" and added that "from the O'Neill to Yale to Broadway, each step, in each guise, his hand has been firmly on the tiller as we charted the waters from draft to draft and brought the plays safely to shore without compromise." *MRBB* is the first of six Wilson plays that Richards, at Yale and on Broadway, has directed.

MRBB opened, after a brief stint at the University of Pennsylvania's Annenberg Center, on October 11, 1984, at Broadway's Cort Theater. Set in Chicago in 1927, *MRBB* "examines the relationship between black artists and the world of mass communications in the early twentieth century." According to *Masterpieces of African-American Literature,* "this relationship mirrors the position of black people in the society at large—a society dominated by white racism." *MRBB,* which brought Wilson national attention, was a popular and critical success. After 275 performances, it closed in June 1985 with several Tony nominations and the New York Drama Critics Circle Award.

MRBB is the first play of a ten-drama cycle; according to *The Norton Anthology of African American Literature,* Wilson, "in efforts to tell a history that has never been told" announced his plan to create a play for each decade of the twentieth century, each focusing on a major black American issue. Although Wilson's pre-*MRBB* plays are set in various decades, the cycle begins with *MRBB.* Thus *MRBB* is his 1920s play while his next drama, *Fences,* is Wilson's 1950s drama.

Wins first Pulitzer   *Fences,* written in 1983, was staged at the O'Neill in 1983, produced at the Yale Repertory Theatre in April 1985, and opened on Broadway at the 46th Street Theatre on March 26, 1987. Discussed in the *Oxford Companion to African American Literature,* *Fences* focuses on the "struggles of a 1950s working-class family to find economic security. A garbageman, ex-con, and former Negro Baseball League player, Troy Maxson . . . is unable to believe that his son will be allowed to benefit from the football scholarship he is being offered." *Fences* was a commercial and critical success. It grossed eleven million dollars in one year, breaking the record for nonmusical plays. *Fences* solidified Wilson's reputation as a major playwright. The *Chicago Tribune* named Wilson as Artist of the Year. *Fences* won the New York Drama Critics Circle Award for Best Play, four Tony Awards (Best Play: Wilson; Best Director: Richards; Best Actor: James Earl Jones; and Best Featured Actress: Mary Alice), and the Pulitzer Prize for Drama.

While *Fences* was still on Broadway, Wilson's *Joe Turner's Come and Gone* (*JTCAG*) opened at the Ethel Barrymore Theatre, earning Wilson the honor of being the first black American with two concurrent plays on Broadway. Written in 1984 and prior to its Broadway debut, *JTCAG* was staged at the O'Neill, produced at the Yale Repertory Theatre in 1986, and at Washington's Arena Stage in 1988. Wilson, who cites artist Romare Bearden as a major influence on his work because he views Bearden's paintings as expressive and varied as the blues, was inspired by Bearden's "Millhand Lunch Bucket" as he created *JTCAG*. The play, set in 1911 Pittsburgh, focuses on slavery's lingering effects, blacks fleeing from the agrarian South to Northern urban areas, and black Americans' search for identity. *JTCAG*, Wilson's drama of the second decade, received Tony nominations, the New York Drama Critics Circle Award, and the Drama Desk Award.

Romare Bearden's painting *The Piano Lesson* inspired Wilson to create a play with the same title. *The Piano Lesson* (*TPL*), written in 1986, was staged at the O'Neill in 1987, produced at the Yale Repertory Theatre in 1988, and opened April 16, 1990, at Broadway's Walter Kerr Theatre. Set in 1937 Pittsburgh, *TPL* examines family conflict over a heirloom built by a slave ancestor. According to the *Encyclopedia of African-American Culture*, "This play perhaps best expresses Wilson's view of black history as something to be neither sold nor denied, but employed to create an ongoing, nurturing, cultural identity." *TPL*, Wilson's drama of the 1930s, won the New York Drama Critics Circle Award, the Tony for Best Play, the Drama Desk Award, the American Theatre Critics Outstanding Play Award, and the Pulitzer Prize for Drama, making Wilson one of seven American playwrights to win two Pulitzers.

Wilson's next play, *Two Trains Running* (*TTR*) was written in 1989, produced at the Yale Repertory Theatre in 1990, and opened on Broadway at the Walter Kerr Theatre in 1992. *TTR*, Wilson's drama of the 1960s, is centered on a group of friends in Pittsburgh who are caught up in the chaos generated by the Vietnam War and racial unrest. Nominated for a Tony, *TTR* received the New York Drama Critics Award and American Theatre Critics Association Award.

Wilson's most recent play and his drama of the 1940s, *Seven Guitars* (*SG*), set in Pittsburgh, opened at the Walter Kerr Theatre on Broadway on March 28, 1996. *SG* focuses on Floyd "Schoolboy" Barton's friends who gather after his death and the sense of hope for black American empowerment and self-reliance. It received the New York Drama Critics Circle Award for Best New Play.

Additional honors have been bestowed upon Wilson. He is the recipient of Bush, McKnight, Rockefeller, and Guggenheim Foundation fellowships in playwrighting. An alumnus of New Dramatists, Wilson was elected to the American Academy of Arts and Sciences and inducted into the American Academy of Arts and Letters.

Wilson lives in Seattle, Washington, with his third wife, Constanza Romero. Romero is a costume designer, and her credits include *Seven Guitars*.

August Wilson, former poet turned preeminent playwright, eloquently and diligently provides a panoramic vision of his people to regional theaters, Broadway, and the world as he remains steadfast in his quest to dramatically document twentieth century black American life, decade by decade.—LINDA M. CARTER

OPRAH **WINFREY**

1954–

Talk show host, actress, producer, entrepreneur

Oprah Winfrey has become the most powerful woman in television. When Oprah talks, America not only listens—it acts, too. Her influence has stretched from the publishing industry (her television book club has placed novels on best-seller lists overnight) to the meat industry (her "Mad Cow" show plummeted meat sales). She is the pulse of America. Her talk show is the most widely watched program of the genre. Winfrey's swift rise from local Chicago talk show host to one-woman conglomerate is an extraordinary story of personal achievement.

Oprah Gail Winfrey was born on January 29, 1954, in Kosciusko, Mississippi, a small town seventy miles north of Jackson. Her parents, Vernita Lee and Vernon Winfrey, never married. Vernon Winfrey was twenty years old and in the service when his daughter was born. He had been on furlough from Fort Rucker in Alabama in 1953 and had returned to his military duties when his leave ended. He had no knowledge of his fatherhood until Vernita Lee mailed a card to him announcing the baby's arrival and scrawled across it a request for clothing for the infant. Lee had intended to name her daughter "Orpah" after the Biblical woman in the Book of Ruth, but someone, perhaps the midwife who attended the delivery, the clerk at the courthouse, or even Vernita Lee herself, misspelled the name by transposing the *p* and the *r*.

There was little work for a young black woman in Kosciusko who had no specific skills and no advanced training in any area of employment. Lee had heard that jobs were more plentiful in Milwaukee and that the pay was better. Shortly after Oprah's birth, she moved to Milwaukee, Wisconsin, leaving the baby in the care of Vernon Winfrey's mother. She hoped to find a job as a domestic worker at wages of fifty dollars a week.

Grandmother Winfrey was a woman of strong, disciplined character, closely attached to her church. Much of Oprah Winfrey's early life was spent at church, which provided her with her first opportunities to display her talents. Winfrey was three years old when she made her first speaking appearance in an Easter program. She was a precocious child who grew comfortable speaking around adults.

Eventually, Winfrey left her grandmother's farm in Mississippi and joined her mother in Milwaukee. The less-than-spacious living quarters her mother had were a disappointment for young Winfrey. Her mother had only a room in another woman's house and had to work many hours, which meant she had little time or energy to devote to her daughter. As she became

Oprah
Winfrey.

more and more aware of city life, Winfrey became increasingly rebellious and resentful of the lack of material comforts and simple diversions that marked her life with her mother. As she had proven to be too much for her grandmother to control, so too was she more than her mother could handle.

It was Vernon Winfrey's turn now. He had moved to Nashville, Tennessee, upon completing his military commitment, married, and established a home with his wife. The couple welcomed Oprah Winfrey during the summer of 1962, just after she had finished first grade. They were pleased to have Vernon Winfrey's daughter with them.

The church was still a major influence in her life. Vernon Winfrey was active in the Progressive Baptist church and brought his daughter with him for Sunday church services, youth activities, holiday programs, and church–sponsored community activities. Oprah Winfrey was a dependable performer in religious pageants, choral presentations, and the activities of the various organizations within the church.

Finally it was summer again, and Vernita Lee wanted to see her daughter. Despite misgivings, Vernon Winfrey and his wife agreed. Months later, their fears of a summertime visit proved well-founded: when summer ended and Vernon went to retrieve his daughter, he found both her and her mother reluctant to resume the arrangement of the previous year.

Vernita Lee had persuaded Oprah Winfrey that life "at home" could now be much more pleasant than it had been earlier. She was soon to marry a Milwaukee man with whom she had maintained a relationship for several years. The new family would include the man's two children, a son and a daughter. It was for the Winfreys quite a blow to return Oprah Winfrey to an environment they knew did not offer the support and discipline she needed and deserved, but they felt a certain respect for Lee's wishes. The return to Milwaukee represented a downturn in Oprah Winfrey's fortunes, and the negative aspects of her life became more intolerable to her as she grew older.

Winfrey suffers in silence   Winfrey developed a painful concern relating to skin color and standards of physical attractiveness. She felt cast off, and her pain was all the more intense because it seemed to her that her mother was as guilty of her mistreatment as anyone else.

It was also during this period, beginning as early as her ninth year, that Winfrey was subjected to frequent sexual abuse, initially by a cousin, then by a family friend, and finally by a favorite uncle. She found the attacks confusing and frightening but suffered them in silence because she did not know what else to do and because she thought she was somehow to blame.

In spite of her miserable home life, Winfrey remained a good student. Gene Abrams, one of her teachers at the inner-city Lincoln Middle School, recognized her exceptional abilities and took an active interest in her. He helped her get a scholarship to a prestigious suburban school in the affluent Fox Point area. Winfrey encountered few scholastic difficulties there, but her emotional problems were proliferating and her behavior was reflecting the chaos she was experiencing. Out of her fertile mind, Winfrey was hatching and staging one preposterous scheme after another. On several occasions she destroyed family belongings and pretended that their apartment had been burglarized in order to get herself a more fashionable pair of glasses. Twice she ran away from home. Winfrey's mother was constantly bewildered by her increasingly frequent escapades and again had to acknowledge her inability to deal with her rebellious daughter. At fourteen Winfrey became pregnant but miscarried. Lee was unsure what to do with her daughter. The resolve was a choice to a bitter and confused Winfrey: go to a school for wayward girls or go live with your father. During the summer of 1968 Oprah Winfrey returned to her father and his wife in Nashville.

Life takes a new course   It was a vastly different Oprah Winfrey who returned to Nashville after five years in Milwaukee. Early adolescence is a period of rapid growth and change for any individual, but the circumstances under which Winfrey had lived had brought great negative influences into her life, which forced her to grow up exceptionally quickly. Adjustment between father and daughter was not easy, but Vernon Winfrey prevailed. He set high standards of conduct and achievement for his daughter and saw that she met them. She enrolled in Nashville's East High School and was soon involved in numerous school activities, especially those having to do with public speaking and dramatics.

By the time Winfrey entered her senior year of 1970–71, she knew that her future lay in the performing arts. She was chosen to attend the 1970 White House Conference on Youth in Washington. She went to Los Angeles to speak at a church and toured Hollywood while she was there. A local radio station, WVOL, managed and operated by blacks, hired Winfrey to read the news. She was soon ready to enter college and hoped to attend an institution far removed from Nashville, perhaps in New England. Once again, Vernon Winfrey made a decision that countered his daughter's preferences, and she attended Tennessee State University in Nashville.

Winfrey continued her work as a news announcer at WVOL and was soon hired away by WLAC, a major radio station. It was not long before she moved to WLAC-TV (later WTVF) as a reporter-anchor, becoming that station's first black anchor. Although she was earning a five-figure salary while she was in college, her father had not softened his strict requirements of her in terms of conduct or scholarship, and with each succeeding year she was finding his restraints on her social life harder and harder to accept. She began to look beyond Nashville and found a new position at WJZ-TV in Baltimore, Maryland, in 1976. She was only a few months short of her college graduation when she left Nashville and Tennessee State University without having received her bachelor's degree.

Winfrey's tenure in Baltimore began less auspiciously than she would have liked. She became the object of an intensive makeover effort on the part of her station management, which sought to develop an entirely new persona. The attempt was not completely successful. She had little formal training in journalism or mass communication, and her reporting often failed to achieve the desired degree of objectivity. Indeed, she resisted the necessity to be objective, preferring to approach a story from the inside and react to it in a subjective manner. She had never before accustomed herself to a self-disciplined point of view and seemed unable or unwilling to do so now.

Winfrey finds her niche   Winfrey was well-protected by the contract she had with the station, and management was forced to find a better use of her talents. She was assigned to co-host a local morning show called "People Are Talking." Neither she nor her employers recognized the fact immediately, but Winfrey had found her niche. Her engaging personality and her amazing ability to communicate with a diverse audience were indisputable assets in

Oprah Winfrey speaks at an awards ceremony in Philadelphia, 1997.

her new assignment. Sherry Burns, who was producer of the show, said of her, "Oprah is a wonderful, wonderful person. Who she is on-camera is exactly what she is off-camera. . . . She's a totally approachable, real, warm person." The very traits of emotionalism and subjectivity that had hampered her efforts as a reporter helped make her an effective and stimulating interviewer. Winfrey had to stand out in a field dominated by white men in suits. This black, overweight woman did stand out by being herself.

As the popularity of her show began to grow, as well as her satisfaction with and enjoyment of the program, Oprah Winfrey began sending tapes of her broadcasts to other markets around the country. She sensed that she was ready for big-time broadcasting. The woman who had been co-producer of "People Are Talking" left Baltimore in 1984 for a new position on "A.M. Chicago," a morning talk show broadcast by the ABC-TV Chicago affiliate, WLS-TV. The station manager had observed Winfrey on some of the tapes his new producer had screened for him and quickly decided to hire her for "A.M. Chicago," which would compete with the "Phil Donahue Show," the well-established favorite in the local and national market. With Winfrey's coming, "A.M. Chicago" took off and quickly outdistanced Donahue in the ratings. In early 1985 Phil Donahue moved his show to New York and left Chicago to Winfrey.

Winfrey exercises acting talent   In high school and college Winfrey had pursued an interest in dramatics and had attracted favorable attention as an actress, so she found the idea of portraying Sofia in the 1985 Quincy Jones/Steven Spielberg film production of Alice Walker's novel *The Color Purple* appealing. She took leave from her show and went south to create her role. The film opened to favorable reviews, box office success, and much controversial discussion, but most film critics praised Winfrey's performance, and it earned her an Academy Award nomination. Close on the heels of *The Color Purple,* she appeared in 1986 in a motion picture based on Richard Wright's novel *Native Son.* Hers was not a major role, and the film, which was neither a critical success nor a popular one, was not widely distributed.

Winfrey's "A.M. Chicago" having become such a sensation, WLS-TV decided to allot it a full hour instead of its former thirty minutes and changed its title to "The Oprah Winfrey Show." By late 1986 the show was in syndication. It was reported that the deal grossed $125,000,000 and that its star would receive more than $30,000,000 in 1987–88. A five-year contract secured her position as a television host through the 1990–91 season.

Winfrey forms Harpo   Winfrey soon became one of the best-known and highly paid figures of the 1980s. As the show expanded, Winfrey's contracts reflected her desire to not only host the show but control its content and eventually own it. With her lucrative deals, she was able to build her own production studio, Harpo, Oprah spelled backwards. The company plans to bring to the screen productions that convey important social and spiritual messages that might not be deemed commercially promising by others, and has already brought television audiences a movie version of Gloria Naylor's *The Women of Brewster Place.* Plans call for productions of Toni Morrison's Pulitzer Prize-winning novel *Beloved,* Mark Mathabane's autobiographical *Kaffir Boy,* and Zora Neale Hurston's much-admired *Their Eyes Were Watching God.* Harpo's creation makes Winfrey the third female (predecessors Lucille Ball and Mary Pickford) and only black female to own her own studio. Another first for Winfrey is that she is well on her way to becoming the first black billionare.

In 1988 Winfrey was invited to deliver the main address at commencement exercises at Tennessee State University. At that ceremony the university awarded her a diploma in recognition of her accomplishments, although she left the institution without having completed degree requirements. For her part, Winfrey established a scholarship fund at her alma mater that will furnish payment of expenses for ten students enrolled in the university each year. Characteristically, she reserves the right to choose the students who receive these annual awards, then maintains a personal relationship with each recipient and requires that each student maintain a "B" average.

Eight years into her nationwide run, Winfrey found herself at a crossroads with her show. Talks shows were being lambasted by congressmen for glorifying sleazy topics such as pornography and prostitution. The genre was labeled "trash t.v." Winfrey's show was guilty of the charge by having exploitative guests previously, and Winfrey wanted to set her show apart from the sensational pack. She refocused her show to deal with human interest stories, and self-help tips, content her audience could use in their daily lives. The top-rated show took a slight dip in its ratings, but "The Oprah Winfrey Show" still outnumbers the rest in viewers.

Besides the shows that dealt with deep family secrets, what also became a focal point for "The Oprah Winfrey Show" was Oprah herself. Her constant battle with the bulge became a centerpiece for her show and career. In 1988, Winfrey shockingly displayed her new figure (she went on a liquid diet) with the help of 60 pounds of animal fat in a cart on her show. Within three years, Winfrey was back to her size fourteen and admitting her defeat. But thanks to a combination of chef, dietitian, and personal trainer, Winfrey has lost close to eighty pounds. Winfrey's war on weight was victorious after all.

Winfrey's success in television has netted her many accolades. She has won six daytime Emmy awards; her show was honored by the British Academy as best foreign television program in 1994; and she has been inducted into the T.V. Hall of Fame.

Winfrey is an extremely wealthy woman who shares her wealth with many charities. She has donated millions to educational institutions such as Tennessee State University, Morehouse College, and the Harold Washington Library. She also is a regular contributor to the United Negro College Fund. Winfrey's traumatic sexual abuse during childhood has made her a passionate spokeswoman for children's rights and safety. She speaks to numerous youth groups and urges her them to strive for higher standards. She seeks to raise the level of confidence and self-esteem of her female listeners of all ages and speaks of helping women to win self-empowerment.

Additionally, she served as a mentor to girls from a Chicago housing project and also was an advocate for children, appearing before Congress in 1991 to urge passage of proposed protective legislation—the National Child Protection Act—which would create a national registry of convicted child abusers. The registry would allow day-care center staff to conduct background checks on potential employees—no idle need, since in the six states which already use such registers, 6,200 convicted criminals were discovered seeking work in child care in a given year. Winfrey also hopes that legislators eventually will put into place nationwide mandatory sentencing for child abusers, with no plea bargaining nor parole permitted.

Finally, she also anticipates establishing a center that would offer counseling and support to women who need assistance. Says Winfrey, "I want to be able to spread the message that you are responsible for your life and to set up a format to teach people how to do that." It is difficult to envision a more able teacher of that lesson than Oprah Winfrey.

It is uncertain just how much longer "The Oprah Winfrey Show" will remain on the air. There will definitely be a void in daytime television when it leaves. But one thing is sure: whatever Winfrey's next endeavor may be, America will be waiting.—LOIS L. DUNN AND MICHELLE BANKS

TIGER **WOODS**
1975–
Athlete

Golf sensation Tiger Woods won the prestigious sixty-first Masters golf tournament in Augusta, Georgia, on Sunday, April 13, 1997, and at age twenty-one became the youngest winner and the first black to claim a major professional golf championship. His lead was the greatest winning margin since 1862. Already a champion, Woods had won three consecutive U.S. Golf Association junior title championships, three consecutive U.S. Amateur championships, the 1996 Invitational, the Walt Disney World/Oldsmobile Classic, the 1997 Mercedes Championship, and a host of other competitions.

Eldrick "Tiger" Woods was born in a Long Beach, California, hospital on December 20, 1975. His father, Earl Woods, a mixture of African American, Chinese, and Cherokee Indian, was at one time a catcher for Kansas State University and the first black to play baseball in the Big Seven Conference, now the Big Eight. He was also a Green Beret who did two tours of duty for the army in Vietnam. His son was nicknamed Tiger in memory of Earl Woods's Vietnamese combat friend, Nguyen Phong. Tiger Woods's mother, Kultida "Tida" Punsawad Woods, met Earl Woods while she was a secretary in the U.S. Army office in Bangkok. They married in 1969. A Buddhist from Thailand, her parents separated when she was five; she then grew up in a boarding school. Earl and Tida Woods, who lacked security in their childhood, feel a special need to be totally committed to their son Tiger and shower him with love.

After the war, Earl and Tida Woods moved to Brooklyn where Earl was stationed at Fort Hamilton. He first played golf when he was forty-two, at an army base in Fort Dix, New Jersey, and has been hooked on golf ever since. After Earl Woods retired from military service in 1974 with the rank of colonel, he and his wife moved to Orange County, California, where Woods worked for the McDonnell Douglas rocket program. Before young Tiger could walk, his father took him to the garage of their Cypress, California, home, strapped him in a high chair, then practiced his golf shots. Tiger Woods hit his first golf ball at age two. When he won a Pitch, Putt and Drive competition against ten- and eleven-year-olds at age three, news quickly spread about his golf swing. A sportscaster from Los Angeles wrote a feature story on the young golfer. After the producers of the *Mike Douglas Show* saw the story, they put young Tiger Woods on the air where he played with Bob Hope. The T.V. show, *That's Incredible*, followed by putting him on with Fran Tarkenton. Quoted in the book *Tiger Woods*, he said, "When I get big I'm going to beat Jack Nicklaus and Tom Watson." After *That's Incredible* was aired, his schoolmates in kindergarten, where he was the only black, began to ask for his autograph, and Woods, who could not yet write in script, responded by printing his name.

Wins amateur championships   During his early life, Woods "hung out" with his father at golf tournaments, where he mixed and played with golfers from five to thirty years older than he. At an early age Woods's good hand-eye coordination was noticed and by the time he was five or six, he is said to have demonstrated remarkable precision in golf. He did well in other sports, but preferred golf. Although at times his parents tried to restrain him from playing so much of the game, it was Woods himself who wanted to play regularly and to enter every tournament he could find. His parents stressed schoolwork and said that should be his primary concern.

Woods, whose career is managed by the International Management Group (IMG), shot five under par at Presidio Hills to win the Junior World Championship in the ten-and-under

Tiger Woods.

division when he was eight years old. By age ten, he had won two Junior World ten-and-under championships in San Diego. In August 1989, when he was thirteen and about to enter the eighth grade, he played his first national tournament, the 21st Insurance Golf Classic at the Texarkana Country Club. Although he lost the match, he drew heavy applause from the audience. In the summer of 1989 he won his fourth Optimist Junior World title and by age fourteen he won the title for a record fifth time.

On July 28, 1991, Woods won his first national title, the U.S. Junior Amateur Championship. He was fifteen years old, the youngest winner in the Junior Amateur in golf, and the third black to win a USGA title. He won the title again in 1992 at the championship in Milton, Massachusetts. When he won his third consecutive amateur championship in 1993 at the Waverly Golf Course and Country Club in Portland, Oregon, he became the first person ever to win the title three times consecutively.

After finishing middle school in Anaheim, California, Woods entered Western High School. At Western, Woods was an honor student as well as an athlete, and won the Dial Award as the top high school male athlete in the country. During his high school years, he won a number of other championships, including the CIF-SCGA High School Invitational Championship, the Southern California Junior Championship, the Ping Phoenix Junior, the Los Angeles City Junior, the Optimist International Junior World (for the sixth time), and others.

He had become interested in Stanford University after watching ice skater Debi Thomas perform in the Olympics and wanted to study there for a degree in accounting. His interest in the University of Nevada—Las Vegas, known for athletics, was so intense that he became physically ill as he tried to make a choice between the two schools. He preferred Stanford for its academics and announced his decision on November 10, 1993, at the Western High School gymnasium. In Spring 1994, his final semester of high school, Woods had a hectic schedule: a host of golf tournaments from Orlando to New York to Chicago. On December 30, 1993, his eighteenth birthday, Tiger Woods and his father plotted a game plan to prepare the young golfer for the U.S. Amateur Championship at the Sawgrass-TPC in Florida, with a view toward the majors. To the surprise of no one, he won the Amateur in 1994, the first of three consecutive U.S. Amateur championships. His win in August 1994, which he pulled off with a dramatic comeback, made him the youngest player ever to win the Amateur. This victory was a benchmark for Tiger Woods; he appeared for the first time before a national audience on television.

His hometown, Cypress, gave Tiger Woods the key to the city before he left for Palo Alto. He entered Stanford in 1994, where he became a member of Stanford's NCAA defending championship team. He won both the 1996 NCAA, shooting 69–67–69–80, and the U.S. Amateur that year, to become one of only two golfers to win both titles in the same year. After his freshman year, he returned to Cypress with a summer schedule that included playing in his first U.S. Open and his first British Open. He returned to play in the Western Open and made his debut in the Scottish Open. Woods's success and popularity caused speculation that he would leave college and turn professional. In Tim Rosaforte's biography of Woods, Woods denied the rumors, stating that he would not turn pro until graduation in 1998 "unless something exciting happens." Sometime later Woods said on *The Tonight Show with Jay Leno* that a viable offer that outweighed both Stanford and amateur golf would persuade him to turn pro. About this time, IMG was househunting for Woods in Orlando. On August 28, 1996, Woods turned professional, leaving Stanford after two years of study.

Woods's climb up the professional ladder was quick. He had already played in nine professional tournaments (as an amateur) by the time he turned pro. In fact, his appearance in the Los Angeles Open in March 1992 made him the youngest person ever to play in a Professional Golf Association event. By the time he won the 1997 Mercedes Championships in Carlsbad, California (his third professional win), he had earned his first million dollars faster than any other golfer in history.

After turning professional, Woods immediately won two PGA Tour events in seven attempts—the first in Las Vegas and the second at Disney World. For the 1997 Mercedes Championship, Woods won $216,000 as first-place prize, pushing him past the $1 million mark. Since turning pro, he has made endorsements totaling $100 million. In November 1996, he signed a deal with Titelist that would pay him more than $20 million over a five-year period. He also signed a $40 million endorsement deal with Nike. In May 1997 Woods added to his wealth again when he signed a five-year contract for a reported $40 million to become a spokesman for American Express. Of this amount, some sources report that American Express donated $1 million to Woods's foundation to benefit junior golf for minorities. American Express executive Kenneth Chenault told the *New York Times* for May 20, 1997, "In Tiger Woods, we have a representative who has captured the imagination of many different kinds of people." He added that "discipline, hard work, and preparation" characterize Woods, and those "are the pillars of our business."

Tiger and the race issue   Tida Woods believes her son is "the Universal Child." She told *Sports Illustrated* for December 23, 1996, "Tiger has Thai, African, Chinese, American Indian and European blood. He can hold everyone together."

While Tiger Woods has a multiracial background, he acknowledges that, in the United States, even the smallest amount of black blood in his background means that he is black. He told Oprah Winfrey that he came up with the name Cablinasian to describe his mixed heritage. In school he was asked to identify his racial background; he said in the interview that he checked African American and Asian. "Those are the two I was raised under and the only two I know," he added. Being a golf prodigy has not shielded Tiger or his family from racism. As a three-year-old, he and his father were forbidden to play on some golf courses, including the Navy Gold Course in Cypress. Bigotry was demonstrated in the integrated neighborhood where the Woods lived. Their home was pelted with limes and BB gunfire. On his first day of kindergarten, when he was five years old, a gang of older children tied him to a tree, threw rocks at him, and called him "monkey" and "nigger."

Wins the Masters   When he was nineteen years old, in April 1995, Tiger Woods first competed in the Masters Tournament, at Augusta, Georgia. Although he didn't win the tournament, he made history by becoming the first black amateur to compete in the Masters. He made history again on April 13, 1997, when he overpowered the course and the field with a record four-round score of eighteen-under par 270 and a twelve stroke margin of victory. With the win, he became the youngest man and the first man of color to win the Masters tournament. When he won the Masters, he and his father shared a long, emotional embrace that was one of the most revealing moments in golf history and came to be known as "The Hug." Quoted in the *New York Times* for April 30, 1997, President Clinton called the image that was shown around the country "the best shot of the day." Woods then slipped on his green jacket, a Masters tradition, and accepted his prize of $486,000, completing his rite of passage into the most elite level of championship golf.

Quoted in *USA Today* for April 14, 1997, Woods praised black pioneers Charlie Sifford, Lee Elder, and Ted Rhodes, saying that "these are the guys who paved the way. . . . Coming up eighteen, I said a little prayer of thanks to those guys. Those guys are the ones who did it." Quoted in the same source, Elder said he was proud. "We have a black champion. That's going to have major significance. It will open the door for more blacks to become members here. It will get more minority kids involved in golf." Quoted in the *New York Times* for April 14, 1997, the seventy-four-year-old Charlie Sifford, still active in senior PGA Tour matches, called Woods's win "a wonderful thing for golf—never mind the racial thing. . . . This is the kid who's doing what I wanted to do, but never had the chance to do." Golf legend Jack Nicklaus, who first played with Woods in 1996, was not surprised at the victory.

Woods's performance and appearance at the Masters led to record-breaking audiences on the course and on television. The overnight television ratings set a record for Saturday viewing. Woods had raised golf's level as a sport and increased its lure. His success continued when he won the 1997 GTE Byron Nelson Classic played in Irving, Texas, in May, and the Motorola Western Open in June, his fourth title of the year. With the win, Woods regained his ranking as the number one golfer in the world, a distinction he held, then lost, earlier in 1997. At twenty-one years of age, Tiger is the youngest golfer ever to achieve this ranking.

In 1992 Woods was named *Golf World*'s Man of the Year. He was honored at the Fred Haskins Award dinner which cited America's outstanding college golfer of 1996. In December 1996 *Sports Illustrated* named Woods Sportsman of the Year. He has appeared on the cover of numerous magazines such as *Jet* (April 26, 1997) and *Sports Illustrated* again (April 21, 1997). Also in April, *Time* magazine named Woods one of "The Most Influential People in America." Results of the latest *Wall Street Journal*/NBC popularity poll, cited in *Jet* magazine for May 19, 1997, show that Americans gave Woods a seventy-six percent positive rating, placing him higher than even Michael Jordan.

Tiger Woods draws a crowd and creates excitement on the golf course. Many who come to see him previously displayed no interest in the sport, and many of his followers are young children and minority groups. Because of Woods's influence in the sport, he has the power to confront the prejudice that has dominated golf for hundreds of years. This may well be what inspired Woods and his father to establish a Tiger Woods Foundation to provide golf scholarships for inner city youngsters across the country, set up golf clinics and coaches, and provide the youngsters access to golf courses. Woods plans to complete his Stanford degree by enrolling in correspondence courses. He told Oprah Winfrey that he is a firm believer in education and wants to return because of the value of education instilled in him by his parents.

Quoted in *Training a Tiger*, Woods remembers the strength, support, and guidance that he received from his parents from the beginning. "Their teachings assist me in almost every decision I make. They are my foundation." Tiger Woods is an artist who transcends golf and continues to overwhelm audiences and other golfers with his winning record and magical golfing technique. He has a will to win, and he does.—JESSIE CARNEY SMITH

CARTER G. **WOODSON**
1875–1950
Historian, writer, publisher

Carter Godwin Woodson, called "The Father of Black History," co-founded the Association for the Study

of Negro Life and History in 1915. He began issuing the quarterly Journal of Negro History *in 1916,*

established Associated Publishers in 1921, started Negro History Week in 1926, and instituted the Negro

History Bulletin *in 1937. Woodson was a man with a mission. He sacrificed all of his time, talent, and*

money to demonstrate to the world that African American history and culture offered an engrossing study

for all who cared to pursue it.

Carter G. Woodson, the son of former slaves named Ann Eliza and James Henry Woodson, was born in 1875, just ten years after the close of the Civil War in New Canton, Virginia. The South was still reeling from its loss in that fray and resisting the improved legal status of its former slaves. Woodson was born at a time when Social Darwinism proclaimed that of all the races of the world, blacks were the least capable of intellectual prowess. Even in schools and colleges for the emancipated slaves, African American students were so hampered by racist philosophies that they were taught to admire European culture and civilization and despise their own African past.

Freed slaves like Woodson's parents had to find some way to provide for their own needs. The Woodson family earned a living as sharecroppers. Woodson was one of nine children, two of whom died in infancy. He worked long hours as a sharecropper along with his family. Because of the rigors of farming, the local school was only open four months out of the year. Woodson and his siblings attended as often as possible. Woodson had an intense hunger for more education. His father often asked him to read aloud, particularly old newspapers. In this way, young Woodson learned about various places and events around the world.

Due to slavery, African American heritage and history had fallen prey to whites who wanted to use the African past and slavery as a justification for racial subjugation. Woodson grew up among relatives who recounted histories of their enslavement and participation in the Civil War. Because of his family's involvement in the black church, he witnessed the role that this important institution played in the development of the post-bellum community. Later, Woodson even debated about entering the ministry. His writing in his 1926 *History of the Negro Church* is interspersed with Biblical phrases and hymns reflecting his lifelong commitment to Christianity.

When the family moved from Virginia, it gave Woodson even more opportunity to learn about black history. His family traveled to West Virginia where Woodson worked in the mines. While working there, he often had the opportunity to visit a black-owned establishment where the laborers would gather around. The owner, Oliver Jones, was a black Civil War veteran who had a keen interest in the history of blacks in America. Jones owned a few books about black life, and the miners who frequented his shop subscribed to newspapers owned by blacks. Woodson used his leisure time to read the history texts and regularly read to the group of

Carter G. Woodson.

black laborers from a wide variety of newspapers. He also listened to their accounts about their lives in the antebellum days.

After his family settled into a new home in Huntington, West Virginia, Woodson soon had enough money to enroll in school full time. He attended Frederick Douglass High School in Huntington, just a few months before his twentieth birthday. An exceptional student, Woodson graduated in less than two years. He continued his education from 1896 to 1898 at an integrated institution in Kentucky, named Berea College. Returning to West Virginia, Woodson was hired as a teacher in Fayette County where he performed all of the duties necessitated by a one-room school house, including lighting the stove in the morning and cleaning up in the evening. He was subsequently called back to his alma mater, Douglass High School, where he became principal. He returned to Berea College for more training and eventually to the University of Chicago after a Kentucky law closed Berea's doors to blacks. With the aid of the courses he took in Chicago, he finally earned his B.A. from Berea in 1903.

Woodson applied for a teaching position in the Philippines and was hired by the United States Bureau of Insular Affairs as a General Superintendent of Education. He traveled by train to California, then by ship to Hong Kong and finally arrived in Manila. Initially Woodson was not able to communicate effectively with his students in a school in San Isidro. To improve his skills he studied French by taking University of Chicago correspondence courses and was soon fluent in French. Woodson taught English, health, and agriculture in the Philippines until 1907 when physical problems prompted him to return to the United States.

After recovering, Woodson decided to travel to other parts of Asia, Europe, and North Africa. He studied for a semester at the Sorbonne in Paris. While improving his French-speaking skills, he visited numerous libraries and museums, and learned even more about the peoples and cultures of the world. Woodson also learned the rudiments of locating primary source materials for research and methods of integrating these into his writing.

Woodson decided to return to the University of Chicago to work on a graduate degree. University officials did not accept all of his courses from Berea so Woodson had to take some undergraduate courses. Undaunted, he worked on another bachelor's degree and his master's simultaneously. History was his major and his thesis discussed French diplomatic relations with Germany in the eighteenth century. Woodson received a second B.A. in 1907 and a master's degree in history, romance languages, and literature in 1908 from the University of Chicago. Woodson soon applied to Harvard University and was accepted. He completed his coursework by 1909.

Woodson was financially strapped and planned to return to the Philippines, but a combination of physical infirmities and a change in his financial status altered his decision. Upon receiving a scholarship to pursue his dissertation research, Woodson sought a teaching position in Washington, D.C., where he would use the vast resources of the Library of Congress to prepare his dissertation about the secession of Virginia. Although he taught at several district schools, his longest tenure (1911–17) was at the M Street High School where he taught French, Spanish, English, and American history.

While at M Street, Woodson passed his doctoral examinations, completed a dissertation on "The Disruption in Virginia," and was awarded his doctorate in history by Harvard University in 1912. Woodson's graduation from Harvard was an arduous journey fraught with difficulties and prejudice, but Woodson remained undaunted by the obstacles he faced. The other Woodson children became teachers, doctors, businessmen, and professionals in other fields, but only Woodson would command prominence as a black intellectual. He was the first person of slave ancestry—and the second black—in United States history to receive a doctor of philosophy degree, preceded only by the eminent scholar W. E. B. Du Bois.

Woodson unsuccessfully enlisted the support of his Harvard professors to procure a publisher for his dissertation. Still resolute in his desire to become a published historian, Woodson submitted another book, *The Education of the Negro Prior to 1861*, to G. P. Putnam's Sons, and it was published in 1915. Black suffragist and civil rights advocate Mary Church Terrell reviewed the book in the *Journal of Negro History*, noting that she found it hard to imagine any phase of black history "more thrilling than an account of the desperate and prolonged struggle . . . for the mental and spiritual enlightenment of the slave." Terrell, expressing nothing but admiration for Woodson's first book, commented upon its thorough documentation and called it a "work of profound historical research."

Helps establish black history association   After having his first book published, Woodson did not really seem to find his life's work until he, along with several other men, founded the Association for the Study of Negro Life and History (ASNLH) in 1915. Woodson spent almost every hour of each day in an effort to see that all persons, black and white, rich and poor, would have the opportunity to learn about African American history. Finding little time for family or friends, Woodson never married nor had any children. The association and its work became his obsession.

Woodson's experiences with whites proved to him that they doubted whether blacks had any history worth recording. And his interactions with other blacks prompted Woodson to conclude that his people were so afflicted by the specter of racial inferiority and of their perception of the humiliation of slavery that they did not seek to know more about their past. Woodson decided that he would use his historical training to demonstrate to the world that blacks had an interesting and admirable history.

In 1916, Woodson started the *Journal of Negro History*, a periodical for scholars to disseminate their knowledge of black history and culture. The first volume included an article by Woodson entitled "The Negroes of Cincinnati Prior to the Civil War," and an article by Tuskegee sociologist and fellow ASNLH founder Monroe N. Work called "The Passing Tradition of African Civilization." Other articles were written by Mary Church Terrell, teacher and writer Jessie R. Fauset, and historian Walter Dyson. Years later, black theologian Benjamin E. Mays commented upon the journal's contribution in the first sixty-five years of its existence. In "I Knew Carter G. Woodson," Mays stated that the journal had documented black life so well that "no term paper, no thesis, no monograph, and no book dealing with the Negro can be written" without consulting its pages.

With the incorporation of the ASNLH and the launching of the journal, Woodson had found his niche. Even though the association had a small office and a secretary, Woodson still needed to earn extra income to keep both projects operational. He became the principal of the Armstrong Manual Training School in the District of Columbia from 1918 to 1919 but left that position to work at Howard University, where he served three positions as dean of the School of Liberal Arts, head of the graduate faculty, and professor of history. Although Woodson worked full time, he did not stop his tireless research and writing. In 1918 the Association published Woodson's study, *A Century of Negro Migration*.

As a professor at Howard, Woodson had five graduate students. Four out of the five did not complete the program. The one student who did, Arnett J. Lindsay, had nothing but praise for Woodson. Lindsay later wrote that Woodson warned his five students that they had to maintain at least a B average in order to remain in the program, stressed the seriousness of graduate study, and urged the students to develop a broad concept of history, considering the contributions of blacks to American history as "constructive parts of a whole, not as solitary fragments." Lindsay said that Woodson "added romance and spice to our study of American history." Woodson instructed Lindsay to spend at least six hours each day at the Library of Congress in order to write his thesis and complete his program. Lindsay met his deadline and submitted his thesis, "The Diplomatic Relations between the United States and Great Britain Bearing on the Return of Fugitive Slaves, 1776–1828," in May of 1920. Woodson published it in the October 1929 issue of the *Journal of Negro History*.

Disputes with Howard University president J. Stanley Durkee shortened Woodson's stay at the university to one year. In 1920 Woodson became dean at West Virginia Collegiate Institute until 1922. After his second stint as a dean, Woodson was able to work full time as the director of the Association for the Study of Negro Life and History. In addition to issuing a variety of publications, Woodson regularly spoke at churches, schools, civic associations, and scholarly meetings, including the association's annual conferences. Woodson was also a frequent researcher at the Library of Congress, where he was pleased to discover the reading rooms were not segregated.

Because of the library's open access to researchers regardless of race, Woodson donated a five-thousand-item collection of black historical artifacts to the Manuscript Division. He sent the collection in several installments. The 1929 *Report of the Librarian of Congress* noted that the first group of documents received dated from 1804 to 1927 and included letters, bills of sale of slaves, certificates of freedom and manumission, diaries, and manuscript books. The report noted that "an item of special interest is a bill of sale, dated April 19, 1809, of a slave conveyed by Thomas Jefferson to James Madison." Association members held annual meetings to present research papers on various subjects relating to black history and culture. Woodson published information about the proceedings of the conferences and some complete papers in the *Journal of Negro History*. Woodson was also interested in the black nationalist movement led by Marcus Garvey and by the early 1920s regularly wrote articles for Garvey's newspaper, the *Negro World*. Woodson also developed several other important means of popularizing black history materials, including the establishment of the Associated Publishers in 1921. This press published a number of volumes by Woodson and other scholars relating to black history and culture. Woodson published his study *The History of the Negro Church* in 1921, *The Negro in Our History* in 1922, and *The Mind of the Negro As Reflected in Letters Written During the Crisis, 1800–1860* in 1926.

Woodson's most popular work, however, is the *Mis-Education of the Negro*. Originally issued by Associated Publishers in 1933, this book condemned any educational institution for blacks that failed to make the education relevant to the needs of the students. Woodson argued that education which venerates European and white American culture, while condemning Africa and belittling the contributions of blacks to the development of American life, undermines the whole purpose of academic training and produces a sense of inferiority among the students.

Begins Negro History Week   Because Woodson wanted black history to reach young people, teachers, and laymen, he created one week each year when churches, schools, and other organizations would hold a special commemoration of African people and events of historical significance. Negro History Week began in February 1926 between the birthdays of Washington, Lincoln, and Frederick Douglass. The association published history kits with materials to be used for exhibits, lectures, skits, and curriculum development.

Although Woodson's scholarly works and articles addressed the needs of scholars, Woodson felt that the association needed a periodical aimed at the needs of elementary and secondary school teachers. To reach this audience, Woodson began publishing the *Negro History Bulletin* in 1937. He believed that children who learned about the accomplishments of their African American forebears would become productive, emotionally balanced adults.

Because of Woodson's indefatigable efforts, his ideas slowly caught on and by the Bicentennial Year (1976), Negro History Week became Black History Month with a celebration of the achievements of African Americans extended to encompass the entire month of February. The name of Woodson's organization was changed to the Association for the Study of Afro-American Life and History.

The fact that the nation now commemorates Black History Month proves that Woodson's mission was successful and his sacrifices beneficial. Today, African American history programs are celebrated not just in February but throughout the year because of the work of pioneers such as Woodson.

Woodson died in Washington, D.C., on April 3, 1950. Many of his collegues agreed that Woodson, "through his scholarly writings, is responsible more than any other single person for familiarizing the American public with the contribution of the Negro to world history."— DEBRA NEWMAN HAM

RICHARD **WRIGHT**
1908–1960
Writer

Richard Wright was one of the most important writers of the twentieth century. During his remarkable literary career as a novelist, dramatist, essayist, autobiographer, and poet, Wright documented the experiences of African Americans in a hostile and racist society. Among his notable early works are Native Son, *a novel portraying Chicago's black ghetto, and the largely autobiographical* Black Boy.

Born on September 4, 1908, in a sharecropper's cabin on a plantation in Roxie, near Natchez, Mississippi, Wright was the first-born son of Nathan Wright, a sharecropper, and Ella Wilson Wright, a schoolteacher. Two years later, the Wrights had another child, Leon Alan Wright.

Life for the Wrights during the first two decades of the twentieth century was extremely difficult. The experiences of poverty and racism in the racially segregated South greatly influenced Wright's literary works. Poverty forced Ella Wright and her two sons to move in 1911 from the farm to Natchez, Mississippi, to live with her family. Nathan Wright eventually abandoned farming to become an itinerant worker. He later joined his family in Natchez where he found work in a sawmill. In his efforts to improve the family's economic status, Wright moved his family by steamboat to Memphis, Tennessee, in 1913.

The move to Memphis proved a new experience for Richard Wright and his brother. Their mother worked as a cook to support the family, and his father drifted into the atmosphere of Beale Street, with its bars, blues singers, and available women. Richard and Leon Wright learned to prefer street life to staying home alone.

By 1914 Wright's father had deserted his family for another woman, which resulted in further financial hardship. With Richard's mother working only at low-paying, menial jobs, Wright and his brother were frequently left without food. In his autobiography, *Black Boy* (1945), Wright records his incidents of privation:

> Hunger had always been more or less at my elbow when I played, but now I began to wake up at night to find hunger standing at my bedside, staring at me gauntly. The hunger I had known before this had been no grim, hostile stranger, it had been a normal hunger that had made me beg constantly for bread, and when I ate a crust or two I was satisfied. But this new hunger baffled me, scared me, made me angry and insistent.

Because of their destitute condition, Wright's mother often sent Richard to his father's job or home to beg for money. Wright wrote in *Black Boy*: "As the days slid past the image of father became associated with my pangs of hunger, and whenever I felt hunger I thought of him with a deep biological bitterness." Because of this, Wright remained estranged from his father into his adulthood.

When Wright's mother became ill in 1915, her sons were sent temporarily to the Settlement House, a Methodist orphanage. Around the summer of 1916, when his mother recovered from her illness, she moved the family first to Jackson, Mississippi, then to Elaine, Arkansas, to live with her sister and her husband, Silas Hopkins. Wright became very fond of his uncle and spent a considerable amount of time with him. His first encounter with racial violence occurred, however, when a group of white men murdered his uncle in order to seize his valuable property. Fearful for their own lives, the Wrights and his aunt fled to West Helena, Arkansas. Wright was about nine years old when this incident occurred.

Following this event the family moved several more times over the years, disrupting the children's education. In addition, their mother's illnesses made regular attendance at school nearly impossible. Nonetheless, Wright showed an early interest in writing and, in ninth grade, saw his first story, "The Voodoo of Hell's Half Acre," published in the *Southern Register,* a black newspaper in Jackson, Mississippi.

Richard Wright.

Writing career begins to flourish   By November 1925, Wright returned to Memphis, where he found work as a dishwasher and delivery boy for the Merry Optical Company. Wright's mother and brother joined him in Memphis. Wright continued his passion for learning by reading magazines and the literary works of H. L. Mencken, Fedor Dostoevski, Sinclair Lewis, Sherwood Anderson, and Theodore Dreiser. To gain access to such works, he forged a note to present to the librarian at the "whites only" public library. Wright was strongly influenced by the works of Mencken, whose writings awakened him to the possibility of social protest.

Wright and his family left Memphis for Chicago in 1927 in search of better economic opportunities. Chicago, for Wright, was an interesting and stimulating city that was not as racially oppressive as the South, although this urban center had other problems associated with a large metropolitan city. After a series of menial jobs as dishwasher, porter, insurance salesman, and substitute postal clerk, the Depression forced him into unemployment and relief.

In 1931 Wright published the short story "Superstition" in *Abbott's Monthly Magazine,* a black periodical. During the 1930s he became acquainted with Communist activities in the African American community. He was particularly interested in the views of Communist organizers and orators who were affiliated with the League of Struggle for Negro Rights. By 1932 Wright began attending meetings of the mixed-race Chicago John Reed Club—a communist literary organization whose purpose was to use art to achieve revolutionary results. Wright's talents won him easy acceptance in the left-wing literary circle of the John Reed Club. Wright began to read and study the publications of the International League for Revolutionary Writers, *New Masses* and *International Literature.*

Elected executive secretary of the Chicago John Reed Club, which was predominantly white, Wright organized a lecture series that allowed him to interact with a variety of intellectuals. He published several revolutionary poems in magazines such as *Left Front, The Anvil, International Literature,* and *New Masses.* By 1934, the party decided to disband the John Reed Club and ceased publication of *Left Front,* leading to Wright's disillusionment with his place as an artist in the party.

In 1935 Wright was hired by the Federal Writer's Project (FWP), which was a division of the Works Progress Administration, to assist with the research on the history of Illinois and the Negro in Chicago. Wright continued to publish poetry in small journals, and he began submitting manuscripts for his first novel, *Cesspool,* to publishers. Over the next few years it was rejected repeatedly. Finally, in 1963, it was posthumously published as *Lawd Today* by Walker and Company. Wright traveled to New York in 1935 to attend the American Writer's Congress, where he spoke on "The Isolation of the Negro Writer." He also published a poem about lynching in *Partisan Review* during the same year, and he wrote an article for *New Masses* in 1935 entitled "Joe Louis Uncovers Dynamite." By 1936 Wright published "Transcontinental," a six-page radical poem that was published in *International Literature.*

Wright transferred to the Federal Theatre Project, where he served in the capacity of adviser and press agent for the Negro Federal Theatre of Chicago. He also became involved in the dramatic productions of this group and finished two one-act plays based on a portion of his unpublished novel. Wright joined the new South Side Writers' Group and took an active role in this organization, which included members such as Arna Bontemps, Frank Marshall Davis, Theodore Ward, Fenton Johnson, Horace Cayton, and Margaret Walker.

By 1936 Wright took a major role in organizing the Communist party-sponsored National Negro Congress, and reported on it for *New Masses*. His short story "Big Boy Leaves Home" appeared in the FWP anthology *The New Caravan* (1936), where it attracted mainstream critical attention.

In 1937 Wright turned down a permanent position with the Postal Service and moved to New York City to pursue his writing career. After residing briefly in Greenwich Village he moved to Harlem, where he became the Harlem editor of the *Daily Worker*. He also helped launch the magazine *New Challenge*, which he said in *Black Boy* was "designed to present black life in relationship to the struggle against war and Fascism." Wright published "The Ethics of Living Jim Crow" in *American Stuff: WPA Writers' Anthology* (1937).

Wright's influential essay "Blueprint for Negro Writing" appeared in the first and only issue of *New Challenge*, in 1937, which presented a Marxist criticism of earlier black literature. During this time he developed a friendship with the young and upcoming writer Ralph Ellison and he wrote a second novel manuscript, "Tarbaby's Dawn," which was regularly rejected by publishers. Yet, his short story, "Fire and Cloud" (1938) won first prize of $500 in *Story Magazine*'s writers's contest. After being hired by the New York Federal Writers' Project, Wright had the opportunity to write the Harlem section for *New York Panorama* and "The Harlems" section for *The New York City Guide* (1938).

Wright hired a literary agent, Paul Reynolds Jr., in 1938 who assisted him with the publication of *Uncle Tom's Children: Four Novellas* with Harper and Brothers. *Uncle Tom's Children* was published in March to wide acclaim. As a result Wright was awarded a Guggenheim Fellowship of $2,500 in March of 1939. This award allowed him to continue his writing and resign from the Federal Writers' Project.

Wright met Ellen Poplar, daughter of Polish Jewish immigrants and a Communist party organizer, in Brooklyn and they developed a friendship. Wright considered marrying Poplar but instead he began dating Dhima Rose Meadman, a dance teacher of Russian-Jewish ancestry. He married Medman in August 1939 at the Episcopal Church with Ralph Ellison as his best man. It was not a successful match. By 1941 Wright began divorce proceedings because he had very little in common with his wife. Shortly after his divorce, he married Ellen Poplar on March 12, 1941. From this marriage they had two daughters. Julia Wright was born April 14, 1942, and Rachel Wright was born on January 17, 1949.

Wright's story "Bright and Morning Star" (1938) appeared in *New Masses* and was included in two books of *Best American Short Stories*. He soon joined the *New Masses* editorial board and began work on a new novel. About this time he wrote Margaret Walker (Alexander), also an African American writer, to send him newspaper clippings relating to the Robert Nixon case in Chicago. By October, he finished the first draft of his novel relating to the case, which he called *Native Son*. By June he had completed the second draft of *Native Son*.

Native Son, published by Harper and Brothers Publishers in March 1940, became the Book-of-the-Month Club main selection. Less than six weeks after its publication, *Native Son* had sold a quarter of a million hardcover copies and it was on the best-seller list for twelve to fifteen weeks. Moreover, every major newspaper and periodical in the country reviewed *Native Son*. According to some critics, *Native Son* was a powerful, intense, and stirring novel. Other critics took displeasure with the work. In Birmingham, Alabama, for example, *Native Son* was banned from the public libraries. In New York Wright gave a talk at Columbia University on March 12, 1940, on "How Bigger Was Born."

Wright continued his travels and accompanied sociologist Horace Cayton to Chicago to write an article about the South Side of Chicago. The article was never published but Wright and Cayton began a long friendship. Wright traveled to Mexico with his family in 1940. During this time his wife's demands and his work put a strain on their marriage. He left Mexico alone in June and traveled throughout the South. There he visited his father, who was poor and working as a farm laborer. Although Wright tried to reconcile his differences with him, they still remained distant. Wright also traveled to Chapel Hill, North Carolina, to begin talks with Paul Green about the stage adaptation of *Native Son*. He later became unhappy with Green's work. Consequently, Wright and John Houseman revised it with Orson Welles as director. His play, *Native Son,* opened on June 15, 1940, at the St. James Theater and ran until March 24, 1941.

When he left the South, Wright traveled to Chicago to conduct research for a new book on African American life. His story "Almos' a Man" appeared in the *O. Henry Award Prize Stories of 1940.* Wright was elected vice-president of the League of American Writers and he was the guest of honor along with Langston Hughes at a reception to launch the magazine *New Anvil.*

The period of the 1940s was an extremely busy and critical time for Wright. He was involved in many activities including travel abroad, debates, lecturing, and writing. His writings continued his previous themes of racism, oppression, poverty, migration, bondage, and nationalism. *Uncle Tom's Children* was reissued with two additional essays: "Bright and Morning Star" and "The Ethics of Living Jim Crow." In September 1940, Wright was elected a vice-president of American Peace Mobilization, a Communist sponsored group that opposed America's involvement in the World War II effort. He criticized President Franklin Roosevelt's racial policies in a June 27 speech to the NAACP, although the Communist party pressure forced him to lessen his critique. Wright expressed opposition to the war first by signing an antiwar appeal by the League of American Writers, and second by publishing "Not My People's War." Both items appeared in *New Masses* in 1941. However, following the Japanese attack on Pearl Harbor, Wright signed a petition, which appeared in *New Masses*, supporting America's entry into the war. Wright avoided the draft because he was his family's sole support. However, he tried unsuccessfully to secure a special commission in the psychological warfare or propaganda services of the army.

In January 1941 the NAACP awarded Wright the Spingarn Medal; in his acceptance speech, Wright criticized the Roosevelt administration's racial policies.

Wright's creativity also led him to become involved in music. His "Note on Jim Crow Blues" prefaced blues singer Josh White's *Southern Exposure* album. Paul Robeson, accompanied by the Count Basie orchestra, recorded Wright's blues song, "King Joe" (1941). Wright's work *Twelve Million Black Voices: A Folk History of the Negro in the United States* was published in October 1941. This was a sociological study of African American history and their migration patterns from the rural South to the urban North. Wright's focus changed as he became interested in psychoanalysis as a result of his reading Fredic Wertham's *Dark Legend.* He continued to publish articles in magazines including "The Man Who Lived Underground" in *Accent* (1942) and "What You Don't Know Won't Hurt You" in *Harper's Magazine.*

Wright traveled to Fisk University in April 1943 with Horace Cayton and delivered a talk on his experiences with racism. Because of the strong audience reaction that he received, he began to write the novel, *American Hunger*, in December 1943. The Book-of-the-Month Club informed Harper that it only wanted the first section of *American Hunger*, which described Wright's southern experiences. Wright agreed to this demand and titled the new volume *Black Boy*. The second section was published posthumously in 1977 (as *American Hunger*). Harper published *Black Boy: A Record of Childhood and Youth* in March 1945 to favorable reviews. This novel remained on the best-seller list from April 29 until June 6. *Black Boy* was denounced as obscene in the U.S. Senate by Democrat Theodore Bilbo of Mississippi. Wright took issue with Bilbo's position and countered his attack on *Black Boy* by taking part in several radio programs including the nationally influential "Town Meeting," where he argued the question, "Are We Solving America's Race Problem?" Quoted in *Conversations with Richard Wright*, he rhetorically responded by stating that

> It is here in America that the Negro has given the greatest demonstration of his capacity to attain to the highest levels of civilization and America, albeit grudgingly, has shown a willingness to accord him an opportunity. If America were not solving the race problems, then neither a Paul Robeson nor a Marion Anderson could have emerged to win the plaudits of a civilized world. Nor could the genius of George Carver have been dedicated to the advancement of science and the enrichment of his country.

In 1942 he parted ways with the Communists because of his disillusionment with the party. Wright aired his split with the Communist party in his essay, "I Tried to Be a Communist" which appeared in the *Atlantic Monthly* (1944), causing *New Masses* and *Daily Worker* to denounce and disown Wright. During this period the Federal Bureau of Investigation began to interview Wright's friends and associates. Wright continued some leftist activities, developing friendships with C. L. R. James, a Trinidad historian and Trotskyite, and his wife Constance Webb.

Continuing his amazing level of productivity, Wright completed "Melody Limited" in 1944, a story about a group of black singers during Reconstruction. Introduced to existentialist literature and philosophy during the late 1930s by Dorothy Norman, a *New York Post* editorial writer and editor of *Twice a Year*, Wright began to study the subject. The Wrights moved to Greenwich Village in 1945. In order to circumvent racial discrimination they used their lawyer as the middle man to purchase a house. He wrote the introduction to *Black Metropolis* (1946), a sociological study by Horace Cayton and St. Clair Drake. As young writers emerged, Wright befriended many, including James Baldwin, with whom he assisted in winning the Eugene F. Saxton Foundation Fellowship in 1945.

In 1946 Wright, Fredrick Wertham, and others founded the Lafargue Clinic, a free psychiatric clinic in Harlem. When Wright met Jean-Paul Sartre in New York, Sartre extended an invitation to him to visit France. Wright requested a passport but he met opposition from the government. He traveled to Washington for an interview and enlisted the aid of Dorothy Norman, Gertrude Stein, and French cultural attache, Claude Levi-Strauss, who sent him an official invitation from the French government. The strategy worked and the passport was issued. On May 1, Wright left New York for Paris, where Gertrude Stein welcomed him. He assisted Leopold Sedar Senghor, Aime Cesaire, Alioune Diop, and others in the Negritude movement by establishing the magazine *Presence Africaine*. He left Paris in December of 1946 and returned to New York.

*Richard Wright
at home.*

Becomes an expatriate   During his time in France, Wright decided to move his family to Europe permanently. They arrived in Paris in August 1947 and the French translation of *Native Son* came out in the fall. Wright deepened his interest in existentialism by reading Edmund Husserl and Martin Heidegger and hanging out with Jean-Paul Sarte and Simone de Beauvoir. Camus's *The Stranger* strongly impressed Wright, and he begun working on an existentialist novel, which became *The Outsider.* The translation of *Black Boy* by Gallimard won the French Critics Award in 1948. He visited Italy to support the Italian translation of *Native Son.* He continued his travels to London by way of Belgium, where he saw a performance of *Native Son.*

Wright joined Sartre and Camus in the leadership of the Rassemblement Dèmocratique Rèvolutionnaire (RDR), an organization of intellectuals who criticized both the United States and the USSR. At the RDR's writers' congress, held in Paris on December 12, 1948, Wright delivered a long speech which was translated by de Beauvior. Wright and Sartre later became distant as Sartre moved toward Communism.

On March 30, 1951, the film version of *Native Son* opened in Buenos Aires, where it was titled *Sangre Negra*. Wright himself portrayed the main character, Bigger; his acting in this version was considered awkward by American critics, yet praised by the Milan (Italy) press. In February 1952, Wright traveled to England, where he completed a full version of *The Outsider*. It published by Harper and Brothers in March. Despite initially selling well the novel's momentum did not last because of mixed critical reviews.

Wright continued his quest to write and publish. His next book required him to collect materials on Africa. Wright traveled during the summer of 1953 to the British colony of the Gold Coast (which became Ghana following its independence in 1957). During the trip he met with pro-independence leaders, as well as with ethnic group rulers. His travels throughout the continent allowed him to visit slave-trade fortresses and dungeons. On September 22, 1954, Wright's book about Africa, *Black Power: A Record of Reactions in a Land of Pathos*, appeared to mixed reviews in America but enthusiasm in France. In 1995 Banner Books published the paperback *Savage Holiday*, Wright's novel about a white psychopathic murderer.

Wright returned to Paris in December 1956, where he started working on a novel set in Mississippi. In February 1957, *Pagan Spain* appeared although it failed to sell well, despite favorable reviews. In the spring of 1957, Wright worked on a new novel, and he took his wife on a visit to Italy. In July 1957, Wright traveled to West Germany to interview African American servicemen about their experiences. Doubleday published a collection of Wright's lectures entitled *White Man, Listen!* in 1957, which was based on interviews by African American servicemen and their experiences.

In 1958, Wright finished *The Long Dream*, his novel about Mississippi, and he began to work on its sequel, "Island of Hallucination," which was set in France. When *The Long Dream* was published by Doubleday in October 1958, it received poor and even hostile reviews. Wright contemplated moving to England during this time; however, his mother became seriously ill, and on January 14, 1959, she died. By February 1959, Wright sent his agent at Doubleday, Paul Reynolds, the manuscript for "Island of Hallucinations" on which Wright's new editor, Timothy Seldes, asked for substantial revisions. This work was a sequel to *The Long Dream*. In the spring of 1959, his play "Daddy Goodness" opened in Paris.

Wright's "Big Black Good Man" was included in *Best American Stories of 1958*. The stage adaptation of *The Long Dream* opened on Broadway February 17, 1960, to poor reviews and closed within a week. The French translation of *The Long Dream* did better that its English version, but it did not sell well enough to satisfy Wright. He began a new novel, "A Father's Law," during the summer of 1960, but when he returned to Paris in September, he became ill. Wright was afflicted with amoebic dysentery. On November 8, 1960, Wright delivered a lecture on black artists and intellectuals at the American Church, during which he accused the American government of being the source of disunity and infighting between these two groups. On November 26, 1960, he received Langston Hughes at his home, but later in the day he checked into the Eugene Gibez Clinic for diagnostic examinations. Two days later, at 11 p.m. on November 28, Wright died. The cause of death was listed as heart attack. On the third of December, Wright was cremated along with a copy of *Black Boy*. His ashes remain at the Père Lachaise cemetery.

Richard Wright was one of America's prized literary giants of the twentieth century. His books and articles have been translated into numerous languages throughout he world. He exposed oppression and racial discrimination to the world, and his autobiographical works revealed his experiences as an African American male growing up in the Jim Crow South. His works are classic pieces that are used in classrooms throughout the United States.—VIVIAN NJERI FISHER

MALCOLM X

1925–1965

Political and religious leader

Malcolm X is known for his religious and political activism and for his controversial advocacy of black unity. The intensity of his conviction and the eloquence with which he articulated his beliefs remain inspirational, as does the courage with which he conducted himself despite hostility from various racial factions.

Malcolm X was born Malcolm Little on May 19, 1925, in Omaha, Nebraska. His father, Baptist minister Earl Little, was a staunch supporter of Marcus Garvey, a black separatist who led a back-to-Africa movement in the 1920s. As a result of Earl Little's activism, his family ran afoul of the Ku Klux Klan organization, which eventually ran the Little family out of Omaha.

During the next few years the Little family moved regularly. When Earl Little died, Malcolm X's mother, Louise Little, relied on welfare assistance to maintain her family. The strain eventually proved too much for her, and she was admitted to a mental institution, whereupon Malcolm and his siblings were consigned to various foster homes. Despite these hardships, Malcolm maintained high marks as a student. But when his achievements and aspirations were diminished by a teacher's racist comments, Malcolm withdrew from school and took to working menial jobs.

Malcolm, then living with a sister in Boston, began consorting with gamblers and criminals, including drug dealers. Soon he was operating his own prostitution ring and selling narcotics, to which he ultimately became addicted. He then began committing robberies to obtain the funds necessary for supporting his drug habit. His criminal activities, in turn, marked him for observation by the Boston police. In 1946, after an arrest for robbery, he was convicted and sentenced to ten years in prison. He was only twenty years old.

While in prison, Malcolm initially maintained a dangerous profile. He used drugs and alienated and antagonized other inmates. He did, however, make the acquaintance of a convicted burglar, Bimbi, who regularly patronized the prison library. Malcolm also developed an interest in reading, and he soon began studying political science, black history, and philosophy. In the course of his readings Malcolm discovered the existence of the Black Muslims and the Lost-Found Nation of Islam. This religion, which considered leader Elijah Muhammad as a messenger of the Muslim god, Allah, advocated black separatism. Malcolm was powerfully effected by Elijah Muhammad's message, and he converted to the Black Muslim faith. It was at this time that he assumed the name Malcolm X.

Malcolm X.

Malcolm X speaks at a Black Muslim rally, 1963.

Before leaving prison in 1952, Malcolm X exchanged letters with Elijah Muhammad, and after completing his prison term, Malcolm traveled to the Muslim leader's impressive home in Chicago. There Malcolm studied under Elijah Muhammad and became an active member of the Black Muslims. He worked as an assistant minister in Detroit, then served as a minister in Harlem, where he quickly drew attention as a forceful advocate of the Black Muslim faith and its separatist cause. Malcolm rose in prominence as he protested against America's white society and lampooned notions of civil rights and equality as ultimately ineffective within a culture that was, he believed, inevitably and irrevocably racist. The Black Muslims, he declared, constituted a viable alternative—indeed, a source of pride and independence—for blacks.

As a consequence of Malcolm's tireless support, Black Muslim membership increased substantially from the mid-1950s to the mid-1960s. Malcolm's work initially endeared him to Elijah Muhammad, who named him national minister in 1963. But as Malcolm X assumed increasing importance within the Black Muslims, he began expressing himself with regard to some of Muhammad's less admirable aspects. Malcolm questioned the necessity of Muhammad's substantial possessions, including expensive clothes, costly automobiles, and an imposing estate in Chicago. He also decried Muhammad's sexual indiscretions, which directly contradicted Black Muslim tenets regarding sexual conduct.

Elijah Muhammad, meanwhile, became uncomfortable with Malcolm X's fame and his increasing influence with other Black Muslims. When Malcolm made controversial comments regarding the assassination of President John Kennedy, Muhammad siezed the opportunity to impose three months of censorship on his prominent follower. Malcolm yielded to Muhammad's imposition of public silence but continued to grow dissatisfied with the Black Muslims. In return, factions within the Black Muslims continued conspiring to undercut Malcolm's authority.

Rather than remain in the United States during this time, Malcolm X traveled to Mecca, the Muslim holy land. Once there Malcolm underwent an extraordinary change. He abandoned black separatism as advocated by the Black Muslims and instead promoted the notion that all blacks, not just Black Muslims, were capable of contributing to the establishment of a formidable black society. To promote his new beliefs, Malcolm X—who began referring to himself as El-Hajj Malik El-Shabazz—founded the Organization of Afro-American Unity. Through this organization, Malcolm X endeavored to unite blacks throughout the entire world.

After Malcolm X left the Black Muslims, he came to be perceived as a substantial threat to the organization's success. Fearful that members would leave to join Malcolm's group, Black Muslim members took lethal measures to undermine Malcolm's activities. Despite increasingly violent actions, including the firebombing of his home, Malcolm maintained an exhausting schedule of speaking and organizing. On February 21, 1965, he drew more than four hundred people to a Harlem ballroom. As he stepped to the podium, three spectators stood and blasted him dead with shotguns and pistols. The killers, who were overcome by the spectators, included two members of the Black Muslims.

Although Malcolm X has been dead more than thirty years, his ideas and actions continue to inspire and influence lives. His *Autobiography of Malcolm X,* written with Alex Haley, is still read, as are his posthumous volumes of speeches and commentaries. In addition, filmmaker Spike Lee's epic *Malcolm X,* which was released in 1992, has served to spark still further interest.—LES STONE

ANDREW **YOUNG**

1932–

Clergyman, civil rights activist, politician

In 1976 Young was called America's most powerful black, having become the first black man since

Reconstruction elected to Congress from the South (Barbara Jordan was the first black woman in 1972).

A public servant in numerous ways, Young has ministered to the spiritual needs of black Americans, and

served as Martin Luther King Jr.'s trusted aid, as ambassador to the United Nations, and twice as mayor of

Atlanta. He helped create a new South with his unwavering commitment to freedom and justice for all.

Andrew Jackson Young Jr., popularly known as Andy Young, was born March 12, 1932, in New Orleans, Louisiana. His father was a dentist, trained at Howard University, and his mother, Daisy Fuller Young, was a teacher. She taught young Andy to read and write before he entered school. Young began the third grade at Valena C. Jones Public School. He and his younger brother Walter were taught to fight if anyone called them a "nigger." They were the only black family in a middle-class, predominantly white neighborhood.

Young graduated from Gilbert Academy, a private high school, when he was fifteen, and in the fall of 1947 he enrolled at Dillard University in New Orleans. The next fall he transferred to Howard University in Washington, D.C. Majoring in biology, Young prepared to follow in his father's footsteps and become a dentist. He pledged his father's fraternity, Alpha Phi Alpha. David Dinkins, a marine veteran a year older than Young, was the pledgemaster (Dinkins would later become mayor of New York City). Young made the swim team and ran track. All seemed to be going as planned until his senior year. Young was greatly influenced by Howard's first black president, Mordecai Wyatt Johnson, who preached Mahatma Gandhi's idea of passive resistance. He also became acquainted with a young minister on his way to Africa to become a missionary, John Heinrich. Young recalled in his autobiography, *A Way Out of No Way,* that the young white man was willing to travel to Africa in order to help others. "No one at the schools I had attended ever suggested that I try to help black folk. Howard University's emphasis, and the mission of most black colleges in those days, was to better yourself and advance the race through your own achievements."

Young received his bachelor of science degree in biology from Howard University in 1951, but the nineteen year old would not be attending dental school. He had decided to enter the ministry. Young traveled to Connecticut where he enrolled in the Hartford Theological Seminary. After studying the teachings of Mahatma Gandhi, Young was convinced that he could change the injustice in America without violence. In 1955 he graduated with a bachelor of divinity degree and was ordained a minister in the United Church of Christ.

Young spent the summer following his first year in seminary in Alabama. He had planned to go to New York to work at a settlement house, so that he could run with the Pioneer Track Club of Harlem. Instead, he was asked to take an internship at a small Congregational church in Marion as temporary pastor until a permanent minister could be found.

Young arrived in town on a Saturday afternoon. He went to the home of Norman and Idella Childs, members of the church who welcomed him and provided his meals. Their youngest daughter, Jean, was a college student at Manchester College in Indiana. When Young arrived, Jean Childs was still away at school. Before meeting her, Young discovered that she was a serious student of the Bible and also a good swimmer.

One in a million, chance of a lifetime   Young, who had been upset about not being able to run with the track club, suddenly began to wonder if God had plans for him that were better than his own. When he met Jean Childs he knew the answer. Describing his future wife, Young said in his autobiography, "I had known many beautiful women, but with Jean, the beauty was not external. It was her spirit, her dedication, and her purpose to serve others which made her the 'one in a million, chance of a lifetime.'" They married on June 7, 1954.

Writing in his autobiography, Young said, "Jean and I . . . have always felt that our union was made in heaven. We both decided that God's plan for us was greater and better than we could make for ourselves."

Andrew Young.

Wanting to do missionary work in Africa, Young asked permission to establish a mission in rural Angola upon his graduation from Hartford Seminary in 1955. His request was denied because the church would not send single people. Jean Childs Young had applied from Indiana and Young from Connecticut. By the time it was clear they were a couple, the Youngs had returned South where he became pastor of a small church in Georgia from 1955 to 1957.

In the South, the Youngs hoped to work for the liberation of black people. Jean Young and Coretta Scott King had grown up in the same town; this led to Young's introduction to Martin Luther King Jr. In 1957, however, almost as soon as they began to make headway in the South, the sign came for them to move again. Young was offered a job as associate director of the department of youth works for the National Council of Churches of Christ in America, an opportunity too good to refuse. The couple moved to New York City and Young took over the Council's athletic and media programs. Jean Young enrolled in graduate school.

Young felt that his sojourn in the North prepared him to return to the South. He recalls being deeply moved by the student effort at the Nashville sit-in, which he watched on television from his living room in Queens, New York, during the summer of 1960. Young says in his autobiography that as he and his wife watched they "could literally feel God calling [them] back to the South." At the time Jean Young was pregnant with their third child and completing a master's degree in education at Queens College. The decision to leave a secure position and return to the South with a young and growing family was not easy.

In 1961, however, the United Church of Christ started a voter education program in the South. Young was selected as the Field Foundation's new supervisor to work with Septima Clark's citizenship schools. By the fall of that year, the family had moved back to Georgia and purchased a small home in southwest Atlanta. Young worked with Clark and Dorothy Cotton touring the South, recruiting workers and voters. One of their first recruits was Fannie Lou Hamer. It was at this point that Young joined the Southern Christian Leadership Conference (SCLC).

In the valley of the shadow of death   Young marched in the front line of Martin Luther King Jr.'s protests and demonstrations, directed the massive campaign against segregation in Birmingham, and was in charge of the May 3, 1963, demonstration when police commissioner "Bull" Connor unleashed attack dogs and high pressure fire hoses to stop the peaceful marchers. On the night of Medgar Evers's assassination on June 12, 1963, Young and two other civil rights workers drove into Mississippi to rescue Fannie Lou Hamer and two others from jail. The South was becoming increasingly dangerous. Young recalled that he and other workers talked about death as inevitable, but they believed they would be fortunate if they were able to die for their cause. Over the next five years Young became an expert in nonviolent resistance tactics. Young moved from focusing on racism only to a position that attacked the problems of poverty. Plans for the Poor People's Campaign, set for the summer of 1968, claimed much of his time and attention. In 1964, Young helped draft the Civil Rights Act and the Voting Rights Act of 1965.

When Martin Luther King Jr. was assassinated in April 1968, Young heard the shots and mistook them for fire crackers or a car backfiring until he saw his leader and friend fall. Then he knew what he had felt all along was true. He wrote in his autobiography, "God had changed the world through the shedding of innocent blood." He thought,

> It often takes the courageous death of an innocent human being doing the right thing in the right place, at the right time, to mobilize the "coalition of conscience" that changes the world and takes human history to higher levels. Death is an inevitable part of life to be embraced rather than feared.

Following King's death, Ralph David Abernathy took over the leadership of SCLC and Young became his executive vice president. Together they planned the Poor People's Campaign, which climaxed in a second March on Washington to pressure Congress to enact anti-poverty legislation. By 1969, SCLC had lost much of the support that surged forth following King's death. Young outlined its new course, stressing voter registration and political action.

Running for political office   Young resigned from SCLC in 1970 to run for the United States House of Representatives. He organized a biracial campaign but lost to the conservative

Republican Fetcher Thompson, who told voters that if Young won it would lead to the end of western civilization. Two years later Young ran again. This time the Fifth District, which had been predominantly white in the previous election, had been reapportioned to reflect the changing demography. Still, the district was 62 percent white. Young won with 53 percent of the vote. He was the first black from Georgia to serve in the U.S. House since the Reconstruction period. He returned to Congress in 1974 with 72 percent of the votes and again in 1976 with an 80 percent victory.

During his freshman year in Congress, Young established himself as a hard-working representative sensitive to the needs of his constituents. He served on the House Banking and Currency Committee and also made frequent weekend visits to his district. He believed he needed to keep in touch with the people who sent him to Washington. Young was always an advocate for the poor. He voted to increase the minimum wage and to extend it to domestic workers, to broaden the food stamp program, to establish federal day care programs, to expand the Medicaid program to include coverage for abortions, and to create federally funded public service jobs for the unemployed. Young also voted for the creation of a consumer protection agency and introduced a bill outlining a comprehensive national health care plan.

Young met Jimmy Carter when Carter was running for governor of Georgia. Carter was impressed with Young and actively sought his support. Young, on the other hand, had his doubts about Carter but was aware of Carter's great empathy for black people and the nation's poor. While Young wanted a more liberal Democrat, he supported Carter. What made Carter less than perfect were his comments about whites having the right to resist "black intrusion" and "alien groups" and the need to preserve "ethnic purity" of their neighborhoods. To Carter's credit, when Young pointed to the "loaded and Hitlerian connotations" of Carter's statement, Carter issued an apology.

Young gave the seconding speech for Carter's nomination at the Democratic Convention in New York City in July 1976. Then he went to work to garner the black vote for Carter. In the end, he was the only person to whom Jimmy Carter felt he owed a political debt. Young had mobilized a massive door-to-door voter registration in the inner cities. When Carter became president, he nominated Young as ambassador to the United Nations. Young was unanimously confirmed on January 25, 1977.

Working for human rights   Young saw the world from the perspective of his experience. His friendship with students from all over the world at Hartford Seminary and from his association in the World Council of Churches rendered the world not an alien place but one where people faced the same problems of human survival and development. When Young became U.S. Ambassador to the United Nations, he was surprised to find himself labeled a radical by the New York media simply because he was the most outspoken proponent for human rights in the Carter administration.

Both Young and his wife had a long-standing interest in Angola. People were shocked when one ambassador said that the presence of Cuban troops brought a certain stability and order to Angola. Until Young's tenure, the U.N. ambassador had acted as a spokesperson for the State Department. Clearly Young had no intention of doing likewise. He told *New York Times* reporter Joseph Lelyveld:

There is a sense in which the United States Ambassador speaks to the United States, as well as for the United States. I have always seen my role as a thermostat, rather than a thermometer. I have always had people advise me on what to say, but never on what not to say.

While his statements on apartheid in South Africa and his attacks on human rights violations and racism in the United States often angered conservative Americans who called for his resignation, Young kept President Carter's support. Carter understood that possibly for the first time since Ralph Bunche, an American official was credible in the Third World.

All were not pleased when Young left Congress for the U.N. According to the *New York Times Magazine,* veteran civil rights colleague Hosea Williams called Young's appointment a "political kidnapping [engineered] by Atlanta's white power structure to retake political control of Atlanta." Members of the Congressional Black Caucus also expressed disappointment. They felt he would have been more useful in Congress. Quoted in the same source, from the beginning Young made it clear that he would not be " 'the White House nigger' in the Carter Administration." He never was.

When it became a choice between what was correct and what was morally right, Young always chose the latter. As U.N. ambassador this choice led to his undoing. In August 1979, Young met with Zehdi Labib Terzi, the U.N. observer for the Palestine Liberation Organization (PLO). The State Department expressly forbade official contact with the PLO. When news of the meeting became public, Young was forced to resign. He expressed no regrets.

After leaving the U.N., Young, his wife, and youngest child and only son, Andrew III (Bo), returned to Atlanta. Andrea, the oldest daughter, graduated from Georgetown Law School and came to Atlanta to study for the Georgia Bar. Paula Jean entered Duke University, and Lisa was completing her final year in the School of Engineering at Howard University. Young recalled in his autobiography, "Our family hardly missed a step due to my resignation."

Called to serve again   On returning to Atlanta, Young established his own consulting firm, Young Ideas, with the intention of living life as a private citizen. In 1981, Coretta Scott King and other black Atlantans urged Young to run for mayor. Maynard Jackson, two-term mayor of Atlanta, could not run for a third term. During Jackson's tenure as mayor the city had moved toward racial polarization. State and federal aid was drying up, whites were fleeing to the suburbs, and nationwide white backlash sent Ronald Reagan to the White House. In Young's opinion, Jackson had been a good mayor. In fact, he had made so many necessary changes, Young stated in his autobiography, "that there was the same backlash emerging locally that helped elect Reagan nationally." Thinking that he could mend some of the strained relationships, Young agreed to run.

Some critics doubted Young's ability to do the job as mayor. They thought he was a weak administrator. Young soon silenced the critics. By 1984, there was so much new business in Atlanta it experienced a major growth spurt. The crime rate dropped dramatically and the city became the first choice of executives looking to locate a business. In 1985, Young won reelection with a wide margin of victory.

In his second term as mayor, Young got the idea from Horace Sibley and Billy Payne, successful Atlanta attorneys, for Atlanta to host the 1996 Olympics. He recalls that most of his staff laughed at the idea. Young bought the idea at once and was off and running with it. With Billy Payne in charge, Young believed the Olympics would come to Atlanta. Although competing with fourteen other cities hoping to host the 1996 Olympics, in 1990 Atlanta was the site chosen. Young credits the many people who were involved who sacrificed time and money to develop the idea. Others credit Young, his vision of Atlanta as an international city, and his friends on the International Olympic Committee from the seventy-three nations and countries where he had visited as U.N ambassador.

In 1990, Young decided to run for governor of Georgia. Apparently he felt compelled to run but at the same time was tired of politics, for he had said if he did not win, he would be "free" to pursue other things. Young's record as mayor—Atlanta's economic boom, the Olympics—made him a viable candidate. However, the conundrum of race entered the picture, and excuses were made. Since the crime rate had risen again, Young was blamed. Black voters were again apathetic, and some were angered by Young's effort to win white votes, taking black votes for granted. Many blacks especially resented Young's campaign in Marietta in the "redneck bar" that played racist songs on its jukebox. In the end, low black voter turnout and Young's failure to win the white vote caused him to lose the primary election to lieutenant governor Zell Miller.

When Young lost the Democratic primary for governor, he saw it as a major setback but said in his autobiography, "I have never been so totally dominated by politics that I could not readily adjust to alternatives." Little did he know that the next phase of his life would be the most trying, and most extreme test of his faith.

On July 26, 1991, following a three-week business trip he and his wife took to Zimbabwe, and a weekend in the Bahamas with their children, sons-in-law, and grandchildren, Young and his wife returned to Atlanta. After they returned, Jean Young became ill and was rushed to Crawford Long's emergency room. Shortly thereafter Young was told that his wife of thirty-seven years had cancer of the colon that had metastasized to her liver.

The week that Young's wife came home from surgery, his son, Bo—in his first week as a freshman at Howard University—was stopped by police a block from campus and beaten in full view of witnesses, for no apparent reason. An investigation later cleared the Washington, D.C., police from any wrongdoing. Although these were trying times for Young, he never lost faith. Jean Childs Young died September 16, 1994.

A deeply spiritual person, Young believes that at each stage of his life, God has provided for all of his needs. Young was co-chair for the Atlanta Olympics Committee, and is chairman of the Metro Atlanta Chamber of Commerce and vice chairman of Law Companies Group, a consulting firm. In April 1996, Young married Carolyn McClain, a longtime family friend, in Cape Town, South Africa.

Young received the Pax-Christ Award from St. John's University in 1970, the Spingarn Medal from the NAACP in 1978, and the Presidential Medal of Freedom from President Jimmy Carter in 1980. Andrew Young, a veteran of the civil rights movement, a politician with integrity, and a spiritual leader, has earned his place in American history as an elder statesman.—NAGUEYALTI WARREN

COLEMAN **YOUNG**

1918–

Politician, former mayor of Detroit

Coleman Young ranks among the nation's most prominent black leaders. The outspoken Young presided as

mayor of Detroit, Michigan, for twenty years, and during that economically turbulent period he persevered

in his efforts to stabilize the city's infra-structure and maintain reasonable standards of service.

Coleman Young was born in 1918 in Tuscaloosa, Alabama. He was raised in nearby Huntsville, and his family was sometimes targeted for harassment by the Ku Klux Klan there. Young's family eventually moved north to Detroit, and in the late 1920s his father established a dry-cleaning business. Although Young was a superior student, he was unable to obtain the financial assistance necessary to afford a college education. After his request for financial aid was rejected by the University of Michigan, Young apprenticed as an electrician in a Ford Motor Company program. But again, despite superior achievement, his subsequent job application was rejected. A white applicant was accepted instead.

After failing to secure an electrician's position, Young managed to find work at Ford on the assembly line. He quickly became active in both union and civil rights causes, but he just as quickly angered company personnel, whose thugs maneuvered him into a violent altercation that prompted termination of his employment. Young thereupon obtained a post office job in which he maintained his union and civil rights activism. He eventually became known in Detroit for his advocacy of equal pay and equal treatment for black workers in the city's automobile industry.

Young was drafted into military service during World War II, and he flew as a bombardier-navigator with the Army Air Corps' Tuskegee Airmen. While in the service Young continued to protest against racial inequality. On one occasion, he was imprisoned after participating in a protest against segregation at an officers' club. But his efforts proved successful, for the army ultimately allowed for the club's integration.

After the war, Young returned to Detroit and resumed his union activism. In addition, he established the National Negro Labor Council, which called for equal rights in labor. As a result of this latter endeavor, Young came under suspicion from the House Un-American Activities Committee, who questioned Young for possible communist sympathies. Young refused the committee's requests for disclosure of the Labor Council's membership, and he eventually abandoned the organization rather than cooperate with the Congressional investigators.

In the late 1950s Young became increasingly active within the Democratic party. In 1960 he won election to the Michigan Constitutional Convention, and in 1964 he successfully contested for a seat in the Michigan senate. At the state capital, Young soon drew attention for his staunch advocacy of fair business practices and integration measures. He thus developed a sizeable following among Detroit's increasingly black population.

In 1974 Young ran for election as mayor of Detroit. His opponent, John Nichols, was the city's police commissioner. Young successfully exploited the weaknesses of his white opponent's position by characterizing the city's largely white police as unfair and unnecessarily violent. If elected, Young assured voters, he would take measures to maintain discipline within the city's police force. Furthermore, he would work to promote racial harmony in the city. Young's platform powerfully appealed to the city's black voters, whose support enabled him to narrowly triumph in the mayoral election.

Once in office, Young altered the Detroit police force by favoring promotion of black officers, and he alienated some white officers by introducing a requirement that all

Coleman Young speaks with officials from Detroit, Michigan, and Windsor, Ontario, 1993.

law enforcement personnel must live within the city. He also sought to promote increased interaction between the police and the public by adding small stations in various locations.

While Young worked to reshape Detroit's police force, he also tried to stabilize the city's wavering economic structure. He attempted to lure city businesses—through generous tax incentives and other enticements—into remaining a part of the city, and he used similar incentives to lure other businesses into the city. Such monumental efforts, unfortunately, were not entirely successful, and the city's economic stability faltered as city businesses regularly departed to developing areas.

During fellow Democrat Jimmy Carter's presidency, Young managed to find federal support for his projects. But during the Republican administrations of Ronald Reagan and George Bush, Young saw aid dwindle considerably. Furthermore, Young's own administration came under a series of investigations for possible violations such as abuse of city contracts and misappropriation of police funds. But Young was never found guilty of any criminal acts.

Despite diminished support from the capital, Young managed to bring about some major changes in Detroit. He developed the city's scenic waterfront to exploit its appeal to tourists, and he enhanced transportation services and options to improve movement within the city. These endeavors improved the city's appeal to outsiders and even led to Detroit's increasing use as a convention location. Of course, problems remained in Detroit. Crime fluctuated, but it continued to influence perceptions of the city as dangerous. In turn, the population declined as portions moved to areas perceived as safer.

Young, however, continued to work for improvement and change. His autocratic manner and his blunt demeanor endeared him to a substantial number of Detroit voters, and he ultimately presided as Detroit's mayor for five terms. During the course of his tenure, he became the nation's highest paid mayor. But in 1994, after twenty years in office, Young finally left politics. Almost immediately, he assumed a post as professor of urban affairs at Wayne State University.—LES STONE

WHITNEY MOORE YOUNG JR.
1921–1971
Social worker, civil rights leader

Whitney M. Young Jr., a social worker by profession, served as the head of the National Urban League during the most turbulent years in civil rights history. Young propelled the conservative organization into the forefront of the civil rights movement through his aggressive programs for equal opportunities in education, employment, and housing for black Americans. He also sought a "domestic Marshall Plan" to remedy the economic and educational problems that plagued African Americans.

Born at Lincoln Institute, a private high school for blacks, in Lincoln Ridge, Kentucky, on July 31, 1921, Whitney M. Young Jr. was destined to become a household name in American civil rights history. His father, Whitney M. Young Sr., was the first black principal of the small private high school for blacks in a rural central Kentucky community. His mother, Laura Ray Young, was the first black postmaster in Kentucky and the second one in the United States. Whitney Young and his siblings, Arnita and Eleanor, obtained their college degrees from Kentucky State College (now University) and each became prominent in their fields of study.

His sister, Arnita Young Boswell, founded the National Hook-Up of Black Women, which provides projects to aid African American youth. She also became a professor at the University of Chicago. Eleanor, his younger sister, became an educator like their father. She was the first black administrator at the University of Louisville, and remained there for twenty-five years.

Whitney Young married Campbellsville, Kentucky, native Margaret Buckner, whom he met while in college. They had two daughters, Marcia Elaine, who now resides in New

York City where she is on the faculty at Columbia University, and Lauren Lee (Cantarella), now head of the Hunt Alternative Fund in Denver. His widow, who also resides in Denver, is the author of several children's books on civil rights and history.

Young grew up during the Jim Crow era but remained in a sheltered and isolated black environment for most of his formative years. When his father was principal of Lincoln Institute from 1936 to 1966, the family resided on the school campus. Lincoln Institute had both white and black teachers on the faculty, which served to provide examples of racial understanding and cooperation for Lincoln students and the Young children. The senior Young was a Baptist and his wife was a Methodist, so the family and the students at the Institute attended a nondenominational church.

The senior Young taught his son, who was called "Junior," the importance of ambition, high moral and religious standards, and racial tolerance. The father also emphasized education and convinced the youngster that he could accomplish anything. Young Sr. always presented a calm, controlled manner, never displaying a temper or raising his voice to his children. Laura Young, Whitney Jr.'s mother, served as a strong role model for young Whitney through her benevolent acts. Laura Young was known for helping orphans and caring for the elderly and sick. It was not unusual for her to feed vagabonds who were traveling by train or to take clothing and packages of food to persons in the rural areas near the campus or to house orphans at Lincoln so they could acquire an education. She would also send small amounts of money inside cards to ill persons and others. From his mother Whitney Jr. learned the skills in human relations, compassion, and caring—skills that would serve him throughout his professional career.

After completing his high school curriculum with valedictory honors, Young Jr. enrolled in Kentucky State College in Frankfort. On campus he gained the reputation for being an efficient organizer and was affectionately called "Hitler" by classmates. After graduating from college in 1941, Young planned to become a doctor because of the freedom the profession offered him politically and economically. He felt that doctors, unlike other black professionals, could speak their minds and not fear the white politicians.

To earn money for medical school, he initially coached and taught school at Rosenwald High School in Madisonville, Kentucky, for a year. However, his plans changed after he enlisted in the army in May 1943. Still hoping to become a doctor after service, he signed up for the Army Specialized Training Program and was sent to the Massachusetts Institute of Technology for a short period before receiving an assignment with an engineer combat unit in Virginia. As an educated black man, he was promoted to first sergeant after only two weeks in the field. Most of his responsibility involved administrative duties, but he soon became the liaison between the white officers and the black recruits. The white officers used Young as a negotiator with the troops, who often challenged their officers' authority once they were in Europe. His army experiences revealed many differences between him and the other black recruits, and perhaps for the first time he understood the exact state of most of black America, economically, morally, and culturally. This experience changed Young's career goals, and he decided to move into the field of race relations.

Becomes activist While on a five-day military leave, Whitney and Margaret Young were married on January 2, 1944. After military service, Young applied for admission to the University of Kentucky for graduate study. Since Kentucky law did not allow blacks to attend

*Whitney
Young.* 713

the university's graduate programs, both Young and his wife pursued master's degrees at the University of Minnesota. As a graduate student, he joined the Congress of Racial Equality and protested in student demonstrations and sit-ins in Minneapolis. These protests resulted in the integration of restaurants and lunch counters near the school.

While he pursed his master's degree, Young's first field placement was with the Hennepin County Welfare Board in Minneapolis, in an area with a large underprivileged black clientele. He requested that he also receive some white clients so that he could see both sides of the problems. Young was assigned to work in the Minneapolis Urban League for his second year field placement. He received his degree in social work in 1947, while Margaret received an educational psychology degree. Young then began his career as the industrial relations secretary of the St. Paul Urban League. Young was appointed to head the Omaha Urban League office in 1950. His work with the Omaha black community showed his acceptance of different tactics for accomplishing social change in America. In Omaha, other groups, including the DePorres Club, were engaged in boycotts, picket lines, and other types of direct action against racial injustice. Although these activities were too radical for the Urban League to support, Young formed close relationships with these groups. He also worked with these groups and city officials to settle disputes.

Kentuckian Rufus E. Clement, who was president of Atlanta University, went to Omaha in 1953 to invite Young to head his School of Social Work. The civil rights movement was gaining momentum in the South and Young wanted to be involved to a greater extent, so he agreed to head the School of Social Work at Atlanta University. Under Young's direction, the school became one of the top social work schools in the South. Young expanded the school's curriculum, provided additional training and professional development opportunities for his faculty, doubled the school's budget, and increased the number of full-time faculty.

In the Atlanta community, Young continued to be involved in the civil rights movement by serving as co-chair of the Atlanta Council on Human Relations. In this leadership role, he led the fight for the integration of the public libraries in Atlanta. He was also one of the founders of the Atlanta's Committee for Cooperative Action (ACCA), which was comprised of both professional and business persons who worked for civil rights initiatives. *A Second Look: The Negro Citizen in Atlanta* is the major publication produced by the ACCA and was co-authored by Young. *A Second Look,* published in 1958, documented the inequities in health services, education, and social services in Atlanta at the time.

Leads National Urban League   In 1960 Young interrupted his tenure at Atlanta University to continue his studies through a Rockefeller grant at Harvard. The next year, he became the executive director of the National Urban League, one of the two oldest black civil rights organizations. Young, who was adept at human relations, focused his energies on corporate America to win support for black causes and black employment in their organizations. It was not unusual for him to receive promises of thousands of jobs for blacks as well as financial support for Urban League programs from white corporate leaders after meeting with them. He was an outstanding salesperson for the Urban League. Young implemented several new programs, which included the National Skills Bank, On-the-Job Training with the Department of Labor, the Secretarial Training Project, and the Broadcast Skills Bank. During the ten years that Young headed the Urban League, his efforts brought financial stability while increasing the budget from $270,000 to $3 million, expanding the number of branches from sixty-two to ninety-eight, and increasing the staff from 300 to more than 1,200 persons.

In 1964 Young published *To Be Equal,* which included a full discussion of the plea for a domestic Marshall Plan, intended to increase educational and economic opportunities for African Americans. President Lyndon Johnson incorporated parts of Young's plan in his War on Poverty program.

Although the Urban League was traditionally a conservative organization, under Young's administration it began to take on a more activist stance within the civil rights movement. The league remained one of the most conservative groups working for civil rights, but Young's aggressive leadership expanded its programs and increased funding. Young, a skilled negotiator, served black interests on a national and international scale. He interacted with the presidential administrations of John F. Kennedy, Lyndon B. Johnson, and Richard M. Nixon; corporate moguls; and local black groups in meeting the needs of blacks. He was one of the sponsors of the March on Washington for Jobs and Freedom in 1963, and he organized the Community Action Assembly to fight poverty in black neighborhoods in 1964. In 1968 Young introduced the "New Trust" program of the Urban League. The program's goals were to attack the problems of the ghettos, including poor housing, inadequate health care, and limited educational opportunities.

Some blacks criticized him for his moderation. Nevertheless, understanding the aversion that some whites felt toward the militant black movement, he took advantage of his own polite demeanor. To the white leadership, Young represented a more respectable and acceptable black leader for them to negotiate with, and they did not view him as a threat. Young, who had a highly developed gift for understanding and relating to people in all backgrounds, effectively served as an outspoken leader for the league, providing a somewhat more aggressive approach than leaders in the past.

As a black leader he was less visible than the majority of black leaders in the civil rights movement era who offered a different idealogy and approach. Young emphasized the racial uplift perspective as a member of the black middle class. His family upbringing had included many black role models who had stressed that it was the responsibility of the more fortunate and more educated blacks to help others who were from less economically sound backgrounds. In a National Urban League press release issued July 11, 1966, Young stated that:

> What we will continue to do . . . is expand and develop positive programs of action which bring jobs to the unemployed, housing to the dispossessed, education to the deprived, and necessary voter education to the disenfranchised. In the final analysis, these are the things . . . which bring power to both black and white citizens, and dignity and pride to all.

Young possessed excellent writing skills and wrote a weekly syndicated newspaper column and published many articles and addresses in professional journals. In 1969, Young published his second book, *Beyond Racism: Building an Open Society.* This book was awarded the Christopher Book Award in 1970.

He was also involved in many community groups and projects. He became a member of Alpha Phi Alpha Fraternity while in college and continued to be a active member of this black service fraternity throughout his life. Other involvements included the NAACP, Greater Atlanta Council on Human Relations, and the Atlanta Committee for Cooperative Action.

During his career, he served in many professional capacities, including vice president and president of the National Association of Social Workers; member of the Advisory Board of the New York School of Social Work; consultant to the U.S. Public Health Organization; and president of the National Conference on Social Welfare. Young served on seven presidential commissions during the eight years of the Kennedy and Johnson administrations. More concerned about helping his people than about personal economic gain, Young turned down offers of corporate and cabinet positions.

Young also received numerous honors, which include the Florina Lasker Award in 1959 for outstanding achievement in the field of social work. The University of Minnesota named Young the recipient of the 1960 Outstanding Alumni Award. In 1961 North Carolina Agricultural and Technical College, as it was then known, gave Young an honorary doctorate. And in 1969 Young was awarded the nation's highest civilian honor, the Medal of Freedom.

While swimming in Lagos, Nigeria, Young had a heart attack and died March 10, 1971. A memorial service was held in New York, attended by such dignitaries as Roy Wilkins, Vernon Jordan Jr., James L. Buckley, Edward Kennedy, Nelson Rockefeller, John Lindsay, and John Mitchell. The service was followed by a procession down Broadway and through Harlem, where thousands of mourners lined the streets to pay their last respects to the controversial leader. Young's body was later flown to Louisville, Kentucky, for a second memorial service followed by a funeral procession of three hundred cars. The cortege passed the Lincoln Institute campus, then continued through the Frankfort campus of Kentucky State University before ending in Lexington. Conflict between President Nixon and Margaret Young, Whitney's widow, caused some hesitation in allowing Nixon to give Young's eulogy. However, Margaret Young finally agreed to permit Nixon to speak. Young's body was buried beside his mother in the Greenwood Cemetery, Lexington, Kentucky. Three months later, against the wishes of Young's sisters and father, his wife Margaret moved his remains to Ferncliff Cemetery in Hartsdale, New York.

Whitney M. Young Jr. became nationally known for his work as the head of the National Urban League. Throughout the United States many facilities bear his name as a lasting tribute to his work. In his home state of Kentucky, an elementary school in Louisville is named for him, as well as two educational programs. The Whitney M. Young Jr. College of Leadership Studies at Kentucky State University, his alma mater, is an honors program that strives to develop leadership abilities in its students through a comprehensive liberal studies curriculum. The other program, administered by Young's sister Eleanor Young Love through the Lincoln Institute, provides educational enrichment programs and funds college scholarships for talented underprivileged high school students. The state of Kentucky has recognized the Lincoln Institute birth site of Whitney M. Young Jr. with a historic marker.

Young's philosophy could easily be summed up by the pin on his lapel, which bore the algebraic symbol for equal. Quoted in *Kentucky's Black Heritage*, he once said, "We must learn to live together as brothers or we will all surely die together as fools."—KAREN COTTON McDANIEL

Photo Credits

Front cover photo courtesy of **AP/Wide World Photos.** Back cover photo courtesy of **Reuters/Corbis-Bettmann Archive.** Courtesy of **AP/Wide World Photos:** 2, 3, 11, 14, 21, 24, 29, 31, 33, 37, 44, 45, 47, 55, 59, 63, 65, 73, 75, 78, 84, 87, 89, 92. 95, 99, 104, 116, 118, 120, 125, 128, 135, 138, 141, 144, 146, 150, 154, 158, 160, 162, 165, 166, 170, 171, 177, 182, 183, 193, 200, 203, 204, 209, 211, 214, 217, 219, 225, 228, 229, 232, 242, 243, 246, 249, 263, 266, 267, 272, 277, 281, 287, 292, 293, 296, 303, 304, 307, 320, 325, 335, 342, 347, 355, 356, 361, 362, 364, 373, 380, 389, 395, 397, 402, 417, 419, 432, 434, 452, 453, 456, 457, 468, 469, 472, 489, 493, 495, 500, 503, 506, 507, 510, 523, 525, 529, 545, 548, 551, 555, 559, 566, 568, 569, 572, 578, 581, 586, 589, 592, 621, 633, 636, 637, 640, 645, 658, 664, 666 669, 674, 677, 681, 691, 700, 701, 704, 710, 713; **Archive Photos:** 70, 178, 238, 254, 285, 440, 664; **Jerry Bauer:** 260; **The Bettmann Archive/Newsphotos, Inc.:** 234, 315, 317; **Corbis-Bettmann:** 101, 132, 197, 222, 481, 497, 562, 627, 686, 696; **Georgia Curry:** 343; **Fisk University:** i; **Hurok Attractions:** 27; **Nikki Giovanni:** i; **The Granger Collection Ltd.:** 412; **The Library of Congress:** 405, 408, 423, 425, 463 569; **UPI/Corbis-Bettmann:** 19, 67, 130, 323, 329, 349, 438, 484, 512, 518, 519, 533, 538, 596, 649; **The Library of Congress/Carl Van Vechten:** 50, 569.

Contributors

A. B. Assensoh
Michelle Banks
Esme E. Bhan
Jacqueline Brice-Finch
Cynthia Stokes Brown
Phiefer L. Browne
Linda M. Carter
Mario A. Charles
Arlene Clift-Pellow
Paulette Coleman
Bettye Collier-Thomas
Grace E. Collins
James Craddock
Kennette Crockett
C. Cunningham
Richelle B. Curl
Alice A. Deck
Alan Duckworth
James Duckworth
Lois L. Dunn
M. Edwards
Joan Curl Elliott
Vivian Njeri Fisher
Frances K. Gateward
Martia Graham Goodson
J. L. Grady
Jacquelyn Grant
Johannal Grimes-Williams

Arthur C. Gunn
Beverly Guy-Sheftall
Debra Newman Ham
D. Antoinette Handy
Donna Akiba Sullivan Harper
Jeffrey Hermann
Vivian D. Hewitt
Ruth Edmonds Hill
Darlene Clark Hine
Helen R. Houston
Damien Bayard Ingram
Dona L. Irvin
Jacquelyn Jackson
Barbara Williams Jenkins
Robert L. Johns
A. L. Jones
Casper Le Roy Jordan
Amy Kirschke
Candis Laprade
Theresa A. Leininger
Tony Martin
Karen Cotton McDaniel
Nellie Y. McKay
Genna Rae McNeil
Ronald E. Mickens
Michael E. Muller
Richard Newman
Dolores Nicholson

Leslie Norback
Patricia A. Pearson
David W. H. Pellow
Margaret Perry
Bobbie T. Pollard
Cortez Rainey
David Leon Reed
Richard Robbins
Simmona E. Simmons
J. Clay Smith Jr.
Jessie Carney Smith
Elaine M. Smith
Les Stone
Jerome Szymczak
Claire A. Taft
Darius L. Thieme
John Mark Tucker
Patricia Turner
Marsha C. Vicks
Virginia Wilson Wallace
Nagueyalti Warren
Flossie E. Wise
W. Braxter Wiggins
Audrey Williams
Betty Lou Williams
Nicole L. Bailey Williams
Phyllis Wood
Linda T. Wynn

Index

Baker, George Jr. *See* Divine, M. J.
Baker, Harold *225*
Baker, Jean Claude *42*
Baker, Josephine *39–42, 486*
Baker, Nancy Smith *182*
Baldwin, James *139, 264, 695*
Ballard, Florence *274*
Banks, Ernest *43–6*
Banks, Ernie *See* Banks, Ernest
Bannarn, Henry *431, 433*
Baptist World Alliance *110*
Baraka, Amiri (Leroi Jones) *340*
Barnett, Charlie *326*
Barnett, Ferdinand L. *652*
Barnett, Ida B. Wells *See* Wells
  Barnett, Ida Bell
Barnett, Ross R. *470*
Barrett, W. H. *650–1*
Barrow, Willie *353*
Barry, Marion S. *304, 584*
Bart, Ben *94*
Baseball Hall of Fame *4, 46, 574*
Basie, William "Count" *46–9, 172,
  392, 694*
Bates, Peg Leg *453*
Baxter, Vivian *28–9*
Bearden, Romare *49–54, 433, 672*
Bechet, Sidney *225, 521*
Beckwith, Byron De La Jr. *229–30*
Belafonte, Harold George Jr. *16,
  35, 54–60, 159, 327, 429, 454,
  537, 579*
Belafonte, Harry *See* Belafonte,
  Harold George Jr.
Bell, Cool Papa *43*
Bellson, Louis *225*
Beloved (book) *491, 678*
Bennett, Lerone Jr. *60–2, 383*
Berbick, Trevor *21*
Berlin, Irving *483*
Bernadotte, Folke *107*
Berry, Faith *340*
Berry, Mary Frances *62–6, 250,
  579*
BET *See* Black Entertainment
  Television
Bethune, Albertus *68*
Bethune-Cookman College *69*
Bethune, Mary McLeod *66–72,
  191, 310, 316, 337, 461, 644,
  653*
Bevel, James *296, 297, 429*
Beverly Hills Cop (film) *502*
Big Brothers/Big Sisters *4*
Bigard, Baney *225*
Biko, Steve *632–3*
Bird, Larry *372, 402*
Birth of a Nation (film) *478, 616*

Bishop Saint John the Vine *See*
  Hickerson, John A.
Black Academy of Arts and Letters
  62
Black Arts Movement *455, 458*
*Black Boy: A Record of Childhood
  and Youth* (book) *690–1, 695,
  696*
Black Cabinet *See* Federal Council
  on Negro Affairs
Black Enterprise 276, 278–80
Black Entertainment Television
  (BET) *385–8*
Black Expo *350*
Black Filmmakers Hall of Fame
  527
Black history *36, 60–6, 152,
  190–1, 198–9, 200–1, 248–51,
  318, 591–4, 685–90*
Black History Month *690*
Black Horizons *670*
Black, Hugo *470*
Black Muslims *138–9, 231–7,
  496–9, 506, 595–9, 699,
  701–2*
Black Panthers *115, 117–18, 122,
  139, 140, 142, 161, 505–8*
Black Periodical Literature Project
  261
Black power movement *115–19,
  470*
Black Press Hall of Fame *384*
Black Profiles in Courage (book)
  12
Black Star Line Steamship
  Corporation *256, 258, 564*
Black Students Council *161*
Black Swan *300*
Black Women's Forum *636–7*
Blackbirds of 1926 (revue) *486,
  487*
Blackmon, Mars *439, 443*
Blackwell, Bumps *390*
Blake, Eubie *482*
Blakely, Henry Lowington II *87*
Blanton, Jimmy *225*
Blood plasma *192, 195*
Blue Devils (band) *47–8*
Blues Boy King *See* King, B. B.
Boas, Franz *343*
Boghetti, Giuseppe *24*
Bogle, Donald *172*
Bok Award *25*
Bond, Horace Julian *72–6*
Bond, Horace Mann *72–4*
Bond, Julian *See* Bond, Horace
  Julian
Bonita and Hearn *481–2*

Bontemps, Arna W. *77–82, 338,
  668, 692*
Bontemps, Paul Bismark *77*
Booker, Simeon *383*
Boozer, Jack *425*
Borg, Bjorn *34*
Bork, Robert *250*
Boswell, Arnita Young *711*
Boulanger, Nadia *391*
Bousfield, Midian O. *381*
Boxing Hall of Fame *23*
Boy Scouts of America *4, 84, 220,
  279*
Bradley, Ethel *636*
Bradshaw, Tiny *238*
Brady, St. Elmo *405, 406*
Braken, Jimmy *272–3*
Branca, Ralph *576*
Brantly, Clint *93*
Brawley, Benjamin G. *411*
Braxton, Toni *215*
Brer Soul (album) *623*
Bridges, Todd *140, 142*
Bristol, Dee *215*
Bronze Booklets *447–8*
Bronze Star *83, 169, 550, 665*
Brooke, Edward William Jr. *82*
Brooke, Edward William III *82–6*
Brooke, Helen Seldon *82*
Brooklyn Dodgers *573–4*
Brooks, Gwendolyn Elizabeth
  86–90, 459
Brooks, Walter Henderson *110*
Brotherhood of Sleeping Car
  Porters *564–5, 617, 618–19*
Brown, Charlotte Hawkins *See*
  Hawkins Brown, Charlotte
Brown, Claude *490*
Brown, Clifford *390*
Brown, Edmund G. *353*
Brown, James *90–8, 354, 473*
Brown, Jim *142*
Brown, Joe *90–2*
Brown, Lawrence *225*
Brown, Oliver *466*
Brown, Ronald Harmon *98–102,
  352*
Brown, Sterling *341*
*Brown v. Board of Education of
  Topeka 130, 132, 133–4, 250,
  328, 333, 367, 582, 657, 662*
Brown, Willie Jr. *636*
Browne, Edgar *310*
Bruce, John Edward *256, 593*
Bryant, William *330, 331*
Buchwald, Art *502*
Bunche, Ralph J. *83, 102–8, 131,
  310, 575, 707*
Bunche, Ruth Ethel Harris *105–6*

Teenage pregnancy *212, 218–19, 220, 642–3*
Television Hall of Fame *679*
Temptations, The (musical group) *274*
Terrell, Mary Eliza Church *333, 609–12, 652, 688*
Terry, Clark *225, 390*
Terry, Johnny *93*
Their Eyes Were Watching God (book) *343*
Think Black (book) *456*
Third World Press *457*
Thirkield, Wilbur Patterson *411*
Thomas, Clarence *250, 491, 494*
Thomas, Millard *56*
Thompson, Era Bell *383*
Thompson, Louise *79*
Thompson, Ulysses "Slow Kid" *482, 483*
Thoms, Adah Belle *605*
Thriller (music album) *357–8, 393*
Thurman, Howard *37, 395*
Thurman, Wallace *78, 341, 563*
Thurmond, Strom *588*
Till, Emmett *88*
Tillich, Paul *425*
TLC *215*
Toccoa Band *93*
Today (television show) *285, 286, 288–9*
Tonight Show with Johnny Carson (television show) *58, 152, 172, 357, 421*
Tony Award *57, 172, 623, 672*
Toomer, Jean *80, 341*
Toscanini, Arturo *25*
Totten, Ashley L. *564, 618*
Toure, Sekou *118*
Townsend, Willard *566*
Tracy, Arthur *238*
Tracy, Spencer *539*
TransAfrica *577–9*
TransAfrica Forum *35, 578*
Travis, Dempsey *381*
Trent, William *310*
Trotter, James *613*
Trotter, Maude *614, 616*
Trotter, William Monroe *612–16, 629*
Truman, Harry S. *168, 310, 333, 565, 586, 656*
Tubman, Harriet *122*
Tucker, B. J. *618*
Tucker, Rosina *617*
Tucker, Sophie *454*
Ture, Kwame *See* Carmichael, Stokeley
Turner, Lorenzo *478*

Tuskegee Airmen *168, 709*
Tuskegee Institute *167*
"Tuskegee Machine" *199*
Tutu, Desmond *635*
Twain, Mark *152*

U

UCLA *See* University of California at Los Angeles
UNIA *See* Universal Negro Improvement Association
UNICEF *See* United Nations International Children's Education Fund
United Daughters of the Confederacy *496*
United Nations *102–8, 303, 662, 706–7*
United Nations International Children's Education Fund (UNICEF) *59–60, 207, 212*
United Negro College Fund (UNCF) *37, 129, 154, 173, 280, 283–4, 289*
United States Army *113–15, 164–9, 177, 195, 309*
United States Coast Guard *435*
United States Commerce Department *101–2*
United States Commission on Civil Rights *62, 65–6*
United States Health, Education, and Welfare Department *302, 304*
United States Housing and Urban Development Department *302, 303–4, 305, 643, 646*
United States Information Agency *584*
United States Interior Department *307–8*
United States Marines *177*
United States Navy *151*
United States Open tennis tournament *34*
United States State Department *106*
Unity Democratic Club *126*
Unity School of Christianity *183*
Universal Negro Improvement and Conservation Association and African Communities League (UNIA) *233, 253, 564*
University of California at Los Angeles (UCLA) *11, 15, 34, 105, 161, 163*
Up from Slavery (book) *255*

Urban League *84, 100, 189, 365, 366, 381, 711–16*

V

Van Peebles, Mario *620, 623–4*
Van Peebles, Melvin *620–4*
Van Vechten, Carl *79, 336, 660*
Vann, Robert *310*
Vaughan, Sarah *393*
Vee Jay Records *272–3*
Vehanen, Kosti *25*
VEP *See* Voter Education Program
Vibe (magazine) *394*
Vietnam War *18, 20, 23, 75, 96, 114, 117, 139, 430, 508, 550, 575, 584, 680*
Villard, Oswald Garrison *615*
Vodery, Will *483*
Voter Education Program *136, 428*

W

Waddy, Joseph *330*
Walcott, Louis Eugene *See* Farrakhan, Louis
Walker, Aida Overton *481*
Walker, Alice *340, 344–5, 678*
Walker, Lelia *627–8*
Walker, Madame C. J. *460, 562, 625–30*
Walker, Margaret *264, 692, 693*
Walker, Minnie *92*
Walker, Sarah Breedlove McWilliams *See* Walker, Madame C. J.
Wallace, Mike *234*
Waller, Thomas "Fats" *47, 223, 301*
Walrond, Eric *341*
Ward, Clara *241*
Ward, Joe *77*
Ward, Theodore *692*
Warden, Donald *See* Al-Mansour, Khalid
Warfield, William *556*
Waring, Julius Waties *135*
Warsoff, Louis *126*
Warwick, Dionne *269*
Washington, Booker T. *174, 199, 255, 381, 456, 611, 614, 629*
Washington, Denzel *440, 441, 535, 630–5*
Washington, Dinah *241, 243, 391*
Washington, Harold *494*
Washington, Keith *393*
Washington, Margaret Murray *69, 610*
Washington, Mary Margaret *652*

Occupational Index

Activism
Stokely Carmichael (Kwame Ture)
Eldridge Cleaver
Angela Davis
Medgar W. Evers
Marcus Garvey
Fannie Lou Hamer
Dorothy Height
Jesse L. Jackson
Martin Luther King Jr.
James H. Meredith
Huey P. Newton
Rosa Parks
Adam Clayton Powell Jr.
A. Philip Randolph
Randall Robinson
Bayard Rustin
Betty Shabazz
Mary Church Terrell
Rosina Tucker
Faye Wattleton
Walter White
Malcolm X
Whitney Moore Young Jr.

Art
Romare Bearden
Elizabeth Catlett
Aaron Douglas
Jacob Lawrence

Business
Earl G. Graves
John H. Johnson
Robert L. Johnson
Annie Turnbo Malone
Charles C. Spaulding
Madame C. J. Walker

Dance/Choreography
Alvin Ailey
Katherine Dunham

Diplomacy
Ralph J. Bunche

Education
Nannie Helen Burroughs
Septima Clark
Sadie Delaney
Charlotte Hawkins Brown

Entertainment
Bill Cosby
Dorothy Dandridge
Sammy Davis, Jr.
Whoopi Goldberg
Spike Lee
Jackie "Moms" Mabley
Oscar Micheaux
Florence Mills
Eddie Murphy
Bill Pickett
Sidney Poitier
Paul Robeson
Melvin Van Peebles
Denzel Washington
Oprah Winfrey

History
Lerone Bennett Jr.
Mary Frances Berry
Annie J. Cooper
W. E. B. Du Bois
John Hope Franklin
Arthur Alfonso Schomburg
Carter G. Woodson

Journalism
Robert Sengstacke Abbott
Bryant C. Gumbel
Gordon Parks
Carl T. Rowan
William Monroe Trotter
Ida B. Wells Barnett

Law
Johnnie Cochran
William Henry Hastie
Charles Hamilton Houston
Thurgood Marshall

Literature
Maya Angelou
Arna W. Bontemps
Gwendolyn Brooks
Henry Louis Gates Jr.
Nikki Giovanni
Alex Haley
Langston Hughes
Zora Neale Hurston
Alain Leroy Locke
Haki Madhubuti
Toni Morrison
Cornel West
August Wilson
Richard Wright

Medicine/Dentistry
Bessie Delany
Charles R. Drew
Joycelyn Elders
Alvin F. Poussaint
Mabel Keaton Staupers

Military
Sherian Grace Cadoria
Benjamin O. Davis Sr.
Colin L. Powell

Music
Marian Anderson
Josephine Baker
Count Basie
Harry Belafonte
James Brown
Nat "King" Cole
Kenneth "Babyface" Edmonds

Duke Ellington
Ella Fitzgerald
Aretha Franklin
Berry Gordy
W. C. Handy
Jimi Hendrix
Lena Horne
Michael Jackson
James Weldon Johnson
Quincy D. Jones
B. B. King
Charlie "Yardbird" Parker
Leontyne Price

Politics

Mary McLeod Bethune
Julian Bond
Edward W. Brooke
Ron Brown
Shirley Chisholm
David N. Dinkins
Joycelyn Elders
William H. Gray III

Barbara Jordan
Kweisi Mfume
Carol E. Moseley-Braun
Maxine Waters
L. Douglas Wilder
Andrew Young
Coleman Young

Psychology

Kenneth B. Clark
Alvin Poussaint

Public Policy

Marian Wright Edelman
Patricia Harris
Charles S. Johnson
Robert C. Weaver

Religion

M. J. Divine (Father Divine)
Louis Farrakhan

Elijah Muhammad
Samuel D. Proctor

Science

Shirley Ann Jackson
Mae C. Jemison
Percy L. Julian
Ernest Everett Just

Sports

Hank Aaron
Kareen Abdul-Jabbar
Muhammad Ali
Arthur Ashe
Ernie Banks
Earvin "Magic" Johnson
Michael Jordan
Jesse Owens
Jackie Roosevelt Robinson
Tiger Woods